S0-AEC-482

WITHDRAWN
University of
Illinois Library
at Urbana-Champaign

The person charging this material is responsible for its return on or before the
Latest Date stamped below.

**Theft, mutilation, and underlining of books
are reasons for disciplinary action and may
result in dismissal from the University.**

UNIVERSITY OF ILLINOIS LIBRARY AT URBANA-CHAMPAIGN

APR 2 1972

S... Mr 30 72

JUL 2 0 1975

AUG 1 1 1975

APR 2 9 1982

MAY 0 8 1982

DEC 0 6 1983

NOV 0 8 1983

L161— O-1096

NATURAL RESOURCES IN LATIN AMERICAN DEVELOPMENT

NATURAL RESOURCES IN LATIN AMERICAN DEVELOPMENT

By

Joseph Grunwald and Philip Musgrove

Published for Resources for the Future, Inc.

by The Johns Hopkins Press,
    Baltimore and London

RESOURCES FOR THE FUTURE, INC.
1755 Massachusetts Avenue, N.W., Washington, D.C. 20036

Board of Directors:
Erwin D. Canham, *Chairman*, Robert O. Anderson, Harrison Brown, Edward J. Cleary, Joseph L. Fisher, Luther H. Foster, F. Kenneth Hare, Charles J. Hitch, Charles F. Luce, Frank Pace, Jr., William S. Paley, Emanuel R. Piore, Stanley H. Ruttenberg, Lauren K. Soth, P. F. Watzek, Gilbert F. White.

Honorary Directors: Horace M. Albright, Reuben G. Gustavson, Hugh L. Keenley-side, Edward S. Mason, Leslie A. Miller, Laurance S. Rockefeller, John W. Vanderwilt.

President: Joseph L. Fisher
Vice President: Michael F. Brewer
Secretary-Treasurer: John E. Herbert

Resources for the Future is a nonprofit corporation for research and education in the development, conservation, and use of natural resources and the improvement of the quality of the environment. It was established in 1952 with the co-operation of the Ford Foundation. Part of the work of Resources for the Future is carried out by its resident staff; part is supported by grants to universities and other nonprofit organizations. Unless otherwise stated, interpretations and conclusions in RFF publications are those of the authors; the organization takes responsibility for the selection of significant subjects for study, the competence of the researchers, and their freedom of inquiry.

Joseph Grunwald is Senior Fellow at The Brookings Institution. Philip Musgrove was Research Associate at Brookings during preparation and writing of the manuscript.

RFF staff editors: Henry Jarrett, Vera W. Dodds, Nora E. Roots, Tadd Fisher.

Copyright © 1970 by The Johns Hopkins Press
All rights reserved
Manufactured in the United States of America

The Johns Hopkins Press, Baltimore, Maryland 21218
The Johns Hopkins Press Ltd., London

Library of Congress Catalog Card Number 77-108381

Standard Book Number 8018-1145-7

330.98
G92n
cop. 2

FOREWORD

The role of resources and resource-based industries in economic development, while not well understood, frequently is the subject of strong opinion. This is particularly true in Latin America where throughout the centuries of that area's history since the age of discovery, the production and export of minerals, food, and, more recently, petroleum have been the principal means of livelihood. Despite periods of advance and prosperity in some countries, Latin Americans have tended to feel bypassed by the mainstream of progress and more recently have accounted for their lagging development in terms of their dependence on resource exports.

No single study can hope to solve all of the riddles of the relationship between resources and growth. Development is a complicated process and there probably is no one true path. However, for any discussion of the matter it is useful to have a background of facts organized in such a way that the data can be employed to test some of the ideas in dispute.

This study by Joseph Grunwald and Philip Musgrove is an ambitious effort to present some of the details of the economic importance of resource industries in Latin America. Data on the resource base, production, consumption, and trade are assembled for the principal resource commodity exports of the area. The figures are presented in a context which describes the organization of these agricultural and mineral-based industries and the nature of the markets. Although some longer historical perspective is provided, a large part of the data pertains to the years since 1925 — a period long enough to permit the tracing of recent history and some speculation about the future.

When examined closely, the resource industries are shown to have been important contributors to the Latin American economies, and they are expected to continue this role, although some shift to emphasis on intraregional and internal markets is expected as local economies expand. Wise use of the proceeds of resource-based exports, the restructuring of institutions, and the fostering of other sources of growth are all essential to rapid development, but, as the study suggests, disregarding the resource industries is not helpful to any of the other steps.

The present volume is one of a number of studies on resources and development in Latin America which RFF is undertaking. Two already have appeared under the joint sponsorship of RFF and the Instituto Latinoamericano de Planificación Económica y Social (ILPES): *The Water Resources of Chile*, by Nathaniel Wollman, and *Natural Resource Information for Economic Development*, by Orris Herfindahl. Other works include an evaluation of the experience of the Alliance for Progress and a forthcoming study of American investment in resource industries, primarily in Latin America, which examines the experience in a number of cases. Studies dealing with urban infrastructure in the region, with the determinants of agricultural productivity in a sample of Chilean farms, and with the Latin American experience in tropical land settlement are well advanced.

The origin of this book dates back to 1962 when RFF became interested in natural resource development in Latin America. In that year a grant was made to Yale University for a project dealing with "resources planning for the economic development of Latin America" to be undertaken by Joseph Grunwald, then visiting professor there. It was felt that one of the major gaps in Latin American efforts at economic development was the inadequacy of an informational base for natural resources policy. While the project was not designed to yield studies in depth of either individual resources or specific countries, one of its important purposes was to provide assistance to Latin American institutions for the launching of resources studies.

To this end, Joseph Grunwald helped organize a seminar at the Economic Commission for Latin America (ECLA) and the then newly created Latin American Institute for Economic and Social Planning (ILPES) in Santiago, Chile, in November 1962. This meeting laid the groundwork for the collaboration between RFF and ILPES, and for the joint sponsorship of several studies. In 1963 Grunwald prepared a summary of preliminary research findings for ECLA for presentation at its conference in Mar del Plata. Also in that year he contributed a paper, discussing major issues and problems in the relation between natural resources and Latin America's development, to an RFF symposium on Natural Resources and International Development; the re-

sulting book was published in 1964. After Grunwald transferred from Yale University to The Brookings Institution,
he recruited Philip Musgrove in mid-1964 to share with him
the responsibilities of preparing the present book. We be-
lieve that it will prove to be especially useful in providing a
basic set of facts on the main resource industries of Latin
America and that the data and analyses can provide a

framework for more enlightened discussion of their role in
development. It should also prove useful in university
classes and seminars, and as a reference for research and
planning staffs in both government and business.

September, 1969   Joseph L. Fisher

ACKNOWLEDGMENTS

As happens in much collaborative research, the lines of specific responsibility of each author cannot be clearly drawn. While Musgrove wrote the major portion of the book, Grunwald was responsible for its general guidance and the preparation of chapters 2, 14, and 15.

The first research on this project was undertaken at the Economic Growth Center of Yale University by Grunwald with the assistance of his research associate J. M. Davis. Musgrove was able to build upon these draft materials for an early version of the present book. Helpful comments from staff members of Resources for the Future provided the main basis for a redrafting of the manuscript. New research was incorporated, new chapters were added, and several chapters were given major emphasis as case studies. Later, the text and most of the tables were updated in accordance with information available as of early 1969.

A book which tries to cover as much ground as does the present volume cannot be undertaken without the collaboration of many persons. It is impossible to mention all debts, but some must be singled out to indicate the extent of the assistance received.

Harvey S. Perloff, the former director of regional and urban studies at RFF, inspired the conception of the project. Particularly during the early stages of the work we have benefited from his great insight on the general subject matter. Joseph Fisher, president of RFF, gave us helpful criticism, constant encouragement and support.

Sterling Brubaker was our principal contact at RFF during the final preparation of the manuscript. He gave much of his time in counsel and administrative support, and helped in the revising and preliminary editing of chapter 2. Others at RFF who have read all or parts of the study include David Brooks, Francis Christy, Marion Clawson, Pierre Crosson, Orris Herfindahl, Hans Landsberg, and Sam Schurr.

We are also indebted to many outside readers who have given us the benefit of their criticism. Among them are Dwight S. Brothers, Harvard University; Raymond F. Mikesell, University of Oregon; David Pollock, ECLA; Thomas F. Carroll, Maxwell I. Klayman, and Alfred Thieme

of the Inter-American Development Bank, all of whom have read and commented on Part One. Raymond Mikesell has also given us his observations on two commodity chapters.

Special thanks are due to specialists of the U.S. Department of Agriculture, the U.S. Bureau of Mines, the International Wheat Council, the International Tin Council, the International Sugar Council, the Pan American Coffee Bureau, and the Food and Agriculture Organization of the United Nations, who have been of great assistance in the gathering of basic information. Some also have reviewed specific commodity chapters. At the USDA, Leslie C. Hurt commented on coffee, cocoa, and sugar, Howard L. Hall on wheat, Richard B. Schroeter on bananas, Q. Martin Morgan on beef, and James E. Thigpen on cotton. John Zivnuska, of the University of California at Berkeley, commented on the forestry chapter. Gerald Manners, of University College at London University, and Simon D. Strauss, of the American Smelting and Refining Company, reviewed the iron and steel and the lead and zinc chapters, respectively. The copper chapter was much improved by information received from Eduardo Figueroa, former Minister of Finance and Economics of Chile; Henry Gardiner, Vice President of Anaconda Copper Company; Ramón Eyzaguirre, of Chile's Copper Department and the Ministry of Mines of Zambia; and Eric N. Baklanoff of Louisiana State University. The petroleum chapter benefited from a reading by M. A. Adelman, of the Massachusetts Institute of Technology, and the wheat chapter by L. W. Binkhorst, of the International Wheat Council in London, and also from suggestions by our colleague at Brookings, Peter T. Knight.

At later stages in the preparation of the book, Catita Levin and George Montalván, both of Brookings, provided invaluable assistance — Miss Levin in the management and coordination of the various processes involved in producing a final typescript, and Mr. Montalván in the final revision of statistical materials.

We owe a special debt to The Brookings Institution for cooperating in granting leaves of absence to us on various occasions and providing its facilities during those times and during nights and weekends when much of the book was written. H. Field Haviland, the former director of the Foreign Policy Studies Program, and Kermit Gordon, president of Brookings, were remarkably understanding.

Henry Jarrett, RFF director of publications, made helpful suggestions for the revisions of the introduction and chapters 1 and 2. Special mention must be given to Vera W. Dodds who, with the assistance of Rachel Johnson, was responsible for the complete editing and preparation of the manuscript for the printer. Given the size of the manuscript this was no mean job. Mrs. Dodds not only improved the style and layout of the book but also helped to uncover errors and inconsistencies. Needless to say, neither she nor any of the persons mentioned can be held responsible for any remaining errors. These, and the analyses and interpretations in the book, are the exclusive responsibility of the authors.

September, 1969

Joseph Grunwald
Philip Musgrove

CONTENTS

PART TWO – THE COMMODITIES

LIST OF TABLES

Chapter 16, Cotton

Chapter 17, Forest Products

Chapter 18, Fishery Products

INTRODUCTION

The object of this study is to assess the contribution of the natural resource sector to the economic development of Latin America.[1] Historically, this is by far the most important sector of the regional economy; in fact, the economic history of Latin America from colonial times to the present is largely a reflection of the region's natural resources and of the uses made of them. Throughout four centuries the bulk of the population has been engaged in the primary sector, earning its living by farming, mining, forestry, or fishing. The share so employed was probably 90 percent or more until the nineteenth century, and even today primary activities absorb half the working population. The importance of the natural resource sector is still more evident in the region's links with the rest of the world. Ever since the conquest it has been an exporter of primary goods: foodstuffs, fibers, forest derivatives, metals and other minerals. Raw materials were essentially the only exports until well into the twentieth century, and only in the last decade has the share fallen below 95 percent of total regional exports. The same pattern appears in every country of Latin America, even in those which are considerably industrialized and in which primary activities employ only a small fraction of the labor force. The export sector was the chief source of

dynamism and economic growth in every country until the Depression of the 1930s, and in the smaller and less developed economies of the region it still holds that position. In the course of four and a half centuries, a variety of products have at different times dominated the region's trade. Changes in the location and nature of economic activity as one product was displaced by another have been substantial in most countries without, however, affecting the position of the natural resource sector as the principal source of employment, income, and trade.

Choice of Approach

The nature and importance of the natural resource sector of an economy may be evaluated by direct study of the resources themselves: that is, of the land forms, climate, distribution of rainfall and water, qualities of the soil, and extent and type of mineralization.[2] This approach emphasizes the potential contribution of resources and the limits on their exploitation. It is useful when the development of previously undiscovered or unexploited resources is in question, and it assists in the continuing development of

---

[1] Latin America is defined as the twenty independent countries that were formerly dependencies of Spain, Portugal, or France: Argentina, Bolivia, Brazil, Chile, Colombia, Costa Rica, Cuba, the Dominican Republic, Ecuador, El Salvador, Guatemala, Haiti, Honduras, Mexico, Nicaragua, Panama, Paraguay, Peru, Uruguay, and Venezuela. This definition includes all of Central America and the South American continent except for the Guianas and Belize, and takes in all the members of two regional trading groups, the Central American Common Market and the Latin American Free Trade Area. The exclusion of the Guianas and of the remaining countries or dependencies of the Caribbean is somewhat arbitrary, since the economies of these territories are in many respects similar to those of Central America, Cuba, and Hispaniola (Haiti and the Dominican Republic). However, the excluded areas are generally not considered to be politically part of Latin America, and their economies are oriented toward the United Kingdom and France (through preferential trading arrangements or other ties), whereas the economies included are generally oriented toward the United States. Where the excluded territories are important producers of a commodity, they will be referred to collectively as Caribbean America. Whenever the term "the region" is used without further identification, the reference is to Latin America as here defined.

[2] Brief surveys of Latin America's natural resources are included in a number of general studies of the region. See for example, P. E. James, *Latin America*, 3rd ed. (Odyssey Press, 1959); or J. P. Cole, *Latin America: An Economic and Social Geography* (Butterworths, 1965). More detailed surveys have been prepared by international agencies concerned with Latin America, such as ECLA, *Los Recursos Naturales en America Latina: Su Conocimiento Actual e Investigaciones Necesarias en Este Campo* (Santiago: UN, 1963) consisting of five volumes: I, *Los Recursos Minerales*; II, *El Agua*; III, *Los Recursos Forestales*; IV, *Los Recursos Pesqueros*; V, *Los Suelos*. See also ECLA, *Los Recursos Hidráulicos de America Latina*, vol. I, *Chile* (Mexico: UN, 1960), and vol. II, *Venezuela* (New York: UN, 1962), and *Los Recursos Hidráulicos de Argentina*, doc. E/CN.12/625, 1963, and *Los Recursos Hidráulicos de Bolivia*, doc. E/CN.12/688, 1963. Also CIDA, *Inventory of Information Basic to the Planning of Agricultural Development in Latin America* (Pan American Union, 1963), especially the Regional Report and the Selected Bibliography. Studies are also available for individual countries, such as CORFO, *Geografía Económica de Chile* (Santiago: Editorial Universitaria, 1965). Studies dealing with individual commodities are cited in the appropriate chapters in Part Two.

Organization names, abbreviated here and elsewhere in this study, are listed in full at the end of the book.

known resources. As the background to a complete evaluation of the primary sector, it provides a basis for speculation about the future and offers a partial explanation of the past. The study of natural resources does not, however, indicate the economic role or significance of the primary sector in the past or present. A resource has economic significance only through its "usefulness," which depends upon the demand for the specific products which may be produced from it. And the value of a natural resource in a given region can be appraised only relative to the existing state of technology. Changes in the demands for resource products and the costs of supplying them alter the economic importance of natural resources, making some redundant and others more useful. The more a resource has been used to produce a particular commodity, the more is known about its suitability for that use. This limitation is particularly important for minerals but is of some significance in agriculture as well.

It is difficult to determine the value of natural resources as they exist in nature. First, the discovery, development, and exploitation of resources always require investment of labor and capital. Second, in most cases some processing is required before the resource can be transported from the place where it occurs to another location. It is usually at this stage when the value of a resource can be measured; it is the combined value of all the inputs that have contributed to making the basic resource usable in some form.

For these reasons, relatively little attention will be given in this study to natural resources themselves: the emphasis will instead be on the commodities produced from them.[3] This approach has the advantage of including a somewhat wider range of economic activity, since attention will be directed to the resource-using industries, some of which draw on several different resource products and comprise several stages beyond the production of raw material. In this way the links between the primary or resource sector and other sectors of the Latin American economy may be noted. The number of primary commodities is so large that it is impossible to treat each one separately, even if closely related products are classed together. Where the entire primary sector is concerned, any analysis must be in highly aggregated terms. This approach is followed in Part One of this study, to present the evolution and current economic role of the resource sector and to analyze some of the major issues and problems related to resource exploitation in Latin America. It does not, however, permit a detailed examination of the interaction of economic and political forces affecting particular products or of the differences and similarities among products or among countries. Part Two of the study is therefore devoted to studies of individual commodities or groups of related products. These commodities are all of considerable interest in themselves to one or more countries, and together they exemplify many of the economic and political characteristics of the Latin American resource sector.

Selection of Resource Products

Primary commodities may be classified into four main groups: minerals, agricultural products, forest products, and fishery products. The group of minerals may be further divided into three classes — metals, fuels, and other nonmetallic minerals — and agricultural products may be similarly but less precisely divided into animal products, tropical crops, and temperate crops. With the exception of nonmetallic nonfuel minerals, each of these categories is represented among the products chosen for study. Several other criteria were considered in selecting products, such as:

richness of resources by comparison with the rest of the world;
effect on the pattern of settlement or land use, or other features of economic history;
contribution to dynamism or economic growth;
earning of foreign exchange;
provision of income or government revenue;
provision of employment;
attraction of direct foreign investment;
political significance;
consumption by domestic industry; and
direct personal domestic consumption.

The first eight of these criteria coincide to a considerable extent. In accordance with these tests and also because less data were available, those products were excluded that are produced or used in extremely small amounts, or are produced chiefly for direct domestic consumption, or are distributed throughout the region and are generally available for local use. These criteria eliminate from consideration many agricultural products such as fruits, vegetables and tubers, and some livestock products, as well as the various minor metals and a variety of nonmetallic minerals such as gems, sand, clay, and dimension stone.[4]

Altogether, sixteen products or product groups were selected for study: copper, iron and steel, lead, zinc, tin, petroleum, coal, coffee, cocoa, sugar, bananas, wheat, beef, cotton, forest products, and fishery products. This list includes at least the first or second ranking export of every Latin American country, and nearly all the important exports of the region as a whole. Several commodities — iron and steel, petroleum, coal, cotton, wheat, and beef — are also significant imports into one or more countries. The two largest industrial inputs — iron and cotton — are included, as are the sources of virtually all the region's inanimate energy and several major elements in the Latin American diet. Three products — tin, coffee, and wheat — have for several years been traded under some form of international commodity agreement, and similar arrange-

---

[3] The distinction between resources in the general sense and specific products is relatively insignificant for minerals, since the resource is usually identified as the product that can be extracted. Geography, water, and climate influence the accessibility of a particular resource and thus partly determine its value, but their effects are usually subordinate to the characteristics of the mineral deposit itself. The situation is quite different in agriculture, where the products created are distinct from the resources that enter into their production.

[4] Five metals of which Latin America has significant resources or production and which are of particular importance in steelmaking — manganese, chromium, molybdenum, nickel and tungsten — are discussed briefly in Part Two, chapter 5 (Iron and Steel).

ments have recently been reached for sugar and brought under consideration for cocoa. This set of commodities embraces a wide variation in the extent and type of government participation or control, and a still wider range of participation by foreign private capital. Together, these products are intended to represent the natural resource sector except for subsistence agriculture and most of commercial agriculture for the domestic market. Thus, except for coal, which is included because of its importance in steelmaking and for comparison with petroleum, the list is concentrated on export commodities.

The group of products studied is limited in other ways. In the case of forest products and of fisheries products it has been convenient to treat together a variety of commodities of common origin. In the livestock sector the same procedure would have been more lengthy and complex, so attention is limited to one product, beef. The exclusion of other commodities of animal origin chiefly affects cattle hides and wool which, until late in the nineteenth century, were more important exports than beef; both products, in fact, are still major exports from Uruguay and are of some importance to Argentina and Paraguay. Otherwise the limitation is less serious, since beef is by far the principal meat consumed in Latin America and other animals are raised only for domestic consumption. Among cereal crops only wheat is discussed, although maize is produced and consumed in larger amounts and is a significant export from Argentina. In both cases the selection was determined by the need to give particular attention to Argentina and Uruguay, neither of which produces significant quantities of most of the other commodities included. Similarly, among fibers cotton is the only crop studied. In contrast, five metals and four tropical crops are included, partly in order to select products of importance to the largest number of countries and partly to permit comparisons among commodities in the same class. No major tropical agricultural product has been excluded and aluminum is the only major metal not represented. Bauxite (aluminum ore) is now exported from Haiti and the Dominican Republic, and aluminum smelters have recently been built in Mexico and Venezuela. Only in Brazil has there been an aluminum industry for as much as a decade, however, and the metal is not yet so important to the region or to any one country as the five metals included in this study.[5] Among nonmetallic minerals the most significant omission is that of sulfur, which is a major commodity only in Mexico; that country is however represented by several other products.

A number of products which at one time were extremely important to one or more countries and may have greatly affected the region's economic history are today of little or no significance. These are excluded altogether or treated briefly in Part One. Gold and silver, nitrates, natural rubber, and guano are among the products in this category. The precious metals were the products most sought by the Spanish and Portuguese in much of the New World, and

greatly influenced the pattern of settlement and the relative wealth of different areas during the colonial period. Silver is still the second or third largest export of Bolivia, but elsewhere the precious metals are now of slight importance compared to the industrial metals. Natural nitrates were Chile's principal export in the late nineteenth and early twentieth centuries, but now rank behind copper and iron ore. The market for the natural product was sharply reduced when synthetic production of nitrates was achieved during World War I. For two decades around 1900, Brazil's Amazon basin was the source of 90 percent of the rubber required by the world's rapidly growing automobile industry. The boom collapsed when lower cost estate production began in Indonesia. Rubber continues to be grown in Brazil and in some other countries of the region, but it is now a minor item of trade. The development of a synthetic substitute for the natural product may have prevented a resurgence of the industry in Latin America but did not cause its initial decline. In the mid-nineteenth century guano collected from offshore islands was the chief export of Peru. The boom was ended by the rapid depletion of the deposits; today the fish which were once indirectly responsible for the guano production are themselves the country's largest export item.

Finally, no attempt has been made to include products that are not now produced in appreciable quantities but that may become economically or politically important in the foreseeable future — for example, nuclear fuels or the minor metals now finding application in more industrially advanced countries. In evaluating the importance of the resource sector in past development this omission is of no consequence, but it should be remembered that the relative importance of different primary products has changed greatly in the past and that such changes can occur within a decade or two. The products that are currently most significant may not have the same position in the future.

The Scope of the Study

As indicated above, this study is divided into two parts, the second of which is devoted to the individual commodities or product groups. Lead and zinc are treated together, and each of the other products is the subject of a single chapter. For most products, attention is given to the world market and to the position of Latin American countries as suppliers or consumers in that market, at the raw material stage. At subsequent phases of processing the emphasis is usually confined to the region. Because the products were chosen to exemplify particular issues and problems or the situation of particular countries, the scope and treatment vary somewhat among chapters. Four commodities, one from each of the main product classes — copper, petroleum, coffee, and wheat — are discussed at considerable length, with some attention being given to issues or characteristics common to other products in that class. Iron and steel and beef also receive more extended treatment than the remaining commodities. These chapters also serve as case studies to illuminate some of the issues treated in chapter 2.

To the extent possible, basic statistical information is presented on a uniform basis for all products. For produc-

---

[5]The exclusion of aluminum is primarily a consequence of the omission of Jamaica and the Guianas from the definition of Latin America. Jamaica is now the world's foremost bauxite exporter, and both Guyana (formerly British Guiana) and Surinam (Dutch Guiana) export large amounts.

tion and prices, data are given for the period from the late 1920s to 1967, with more detailed attention to the years 1950-67. This shorter interval is also used for information on exports; for earlier years, exports were approximately equal to output for many commodities and countries, and financial data are difficult to obtain on a consistent basis. Consumption, being generally more stable than production or trade, is discussed for only four periods: the late 1930s, the early 1950s, the early 1960s, and with few exceptions the years 1965-67. The discussion in the text covers all of 1967 and part of 1968, the exact terminal date varying slightly among products. A few of the statistical series end in 1966 or 1965, and the discussion of long-term price stability is confined to the forty-year interval 1925-64.

Part One consists of a historical and analytic survey of the entire primary sector, together with a summary of the statistical material of Part Two. Chapter 1 surveys the role of the resource sector in the past and its importance in shaping the Latin American economy of the present. The period from the late 1920s to the early 1960s is described in considerably more detail than the colonial period and the first century of independence. Attention is given to trends within the primary sector as a whole and to its relation to the other sectors of the regional economy.

Chapter 2 presents a discussion of the principal economic and political issues associated with natural resource exploitation in Latin America, illustrated with references to the products treated in Part Two. The issues of interest in the natural resource sector can be divided, for convenience, into those concerned with demand and those related to supply. This separation focuses attention on the mechanisms and problems of achieving balance in commodity markets and particularly on the determination of prices; it may also allow one to conclude that the difficulties, for a given product or country, arise primarily from one side or the other. There are, however, two limitations to this mode of analysis which must repeatedly be taken into account. First, the existence of substitute sources of materials for many products means that supply conditions not only affect prices and trade patterns but may produce major changes in demand functions. Second, the same institutions, mechanisms, or political factors frequently influence both supply and demand, and their aims and effects must be considered jointly.

On the side of demand, five principal matters deserve attention: the low level of internal demand and the consequent dependence of the resource sector on foreign trade; short-run instability of demand and its effects on output, prices and proceeds; the long-run expansion of demand, with respect to both quantity and relative price changes; barriers to trade in resource products and their processed derivatives; and the various national or international remedies for these problems, now in operation or contemplated. All these points are of political concern within developing countries and greatly influence their economic

and political relations with the industrially developed nations.

On the side of supply are general questions concerning the ownership, management, and use of natural resources, and the scope, aims, and instruments of public policy toward this sector. Of particular interest for some products are the problems of rigidity or inelasticity and of asymmetry of supply response to changes in prices or other conditions. These "structural" problems, as they are commonly described, derive from a great many features of the whole underdeveloped economy, its resource sector, and the particular industries and products considered.

Basically, there are two classes of issues which embrace both supply and demand, with rather more importance for supply. These are concerned, first, with the treatment of foreign capital and, second, with the domestic exploitation of natural resources under government protection or control. In some instances these questions overlap; in nearly all cases they are matters of considerable economic importance, and the first has often been the chief political issue in the primary sector. The question of foreign exploitation of resources may also be a major element of relations with the industrially advanced countries, particularly the United States. Each of these issues has arisen for at least one country and product; several of them affect nearly the entire resource sector in almost every nation of Latin America.

In chapters 1 and 2 the statistical series are carried through to the latest year appropriate to their content — in most cases 1965 and, for exports, 1966. Finally, five key tables in chapter 3 summarize the statistics on the sixteen commodities of Part Two, first for the region as a whole and then, in an appendix, for each of the twenty countries. This arrangement permits comparisons to be made among countries as well as among products and over time. The information on production, consumption, trade, and prices is also elaborated into various indices for easier analysis. A brief evaluation of the natural resource base is also given, and the size and structure of several of the resource-using industries are described. Chapter 3 also contains extensive notes concerning the methods used to compile the statistical data.

The reader wishing an introduction to the primary sector of the region as a whole should consult Part One, relying on Part Two chiefly for more detailed illustrations of particular issues or events. While there are some cross-references among the commodity chapters, any of them may be read in isolation or together with Part One for information about a particular product. The reader interested in an individual country should consult the appendix to chapter 3, Part One, to learn which of the commodities included here are of importance to that country, and then read the relevant chapters of Part Two. Chapters 1 and 2 of Part One may also be seen as an introduction to other studies of products which are not treated here, and chapter 3 may be useful for statistical comparisons.

PART ONE
THE REGION

Historical Survey

Major Issues and Problems

Statistical Summary

Appendix

Chapter 1

HISTORICAL SURVEY

Latin American economic history may be divided roughly into three convenient intervals for examination: the colonial era, from the early sixteenth century to the close of the wars of independence in the 1820s; the first century of independence, from the 1830s into the 1920s; and the years from the late 1920s to the present. In this chapter each period will be briefly surveyed, with emphasis on the role of the natural resource sector in economic expansion and in the evolution of economic structure. This historical survey, together with the information in the commodity chapters of Part Two, will then be used as a basis for summaries of the past contribution and present situation of the resource sector and of the experience of different products and countries.

The Colonial Era

The conquest of Latin America was achieved by a very small number of people, intent largely on the search for natural riches. They established permanent settlements only where they found, or hoped to find, precious metals or other valuable goods for export to Europe; and they turned to subsistence farming only when no such riches were found. Initially, it was possible for expeditions with no fixed base to obtain large amounts of gold and silver from the Indians; certain products of the forest such as cocoa and dyewood (brazil wood) could similarly be collected without creating permanent centers of production. The wealth obtainable in this way was exhausted early in the sixteenth century, however, and thereafter economic activity was concentrated in a few primary producing centers containing the bulk of the European population.

The earliest such centers, first in Hispaniola and then in Cuba and Puerto Rico, were based on gold mines. Silver soon became more important, and Mexico and Peru (including Bolivia) were established as the chief sources of wealth. Throughout Spanish America the search for precious metals was the principal motive for exploration and settlement, and the distribution of population reflected the success of that search in different areas. The mining centers also developed some trade in agricultural products such as

cocoa, tobacco, cotton, and various forest derivatives, but only one primary center was established in the sixteenth century solely on an agricultural basis: that was the sugar colony of northeastern Brazil. During the seventeenth century sugar cultivation for export spread to most of the islands of the Caribbean, making important producing centers of areas which had been bypassed or abandoned in the earlier search for precious metals.[1] Other agricultural colonies, such as the grain and livestock economies of the River Plate region, did not become significant until the eighteenth century or later.

The primary producing centers were the dynamic points of the colonial economy and the only sources of expansion and development in the non-subsistence sector. Their influence was exercised in three principal ways. First, they required relatively large amounts of labor. This demand could not be met by European immigration. The Spanish and Portuguese who came to the New World could obtain land for themselves and constituted a demand for labor rather than a supply of it. Immigration from other countries was discouraged by the colonial powers and would not in any case have been attractive to Europeans, given the conditions of work in the mines and plantations. Initially the labor required was supplied by the native population, which was resettled when necessary. Outright slavery was common in the mining centers, with a milder form of servitude for agricultural labor. The *encomienda* system, under which a settler acquired the rights to a certain amount of native labor along with his land and was in turn expected to provide various forms of protection and help, has left its mark in much of Latin America to the present time. In the tropical parts of Brazil and in the Caribbean islands Indian slavery quickly destroyed much of the native labor force, and hardier slaves were imported from Africa for the sugar plantations and other enterprises. Even where labor was legally free there was essentially no payment of wages and the bulk of the population lived at or near the subsistence level.

[1] For a summary account of this period, see H. Herring, *A History of Latin America*, 2nd ed., (Knopf, 1962), especially pp. 197-203.

Second, the primary centers constituted virtually the only market for the output of other sectors, and were thus responsible for the diversification and development of the economy. Their chief input was undoubtedly food produced in the immediately surrounding area, but they also required draft animals, tools, clothing, fuel, some machinery, buildings, and other supplies and equipment. In some cases these demands gave rise to specialization in the production of certain inputs in areas quite distant from the export center. The mines of Upper Peru, for example, relied on the northwestern provinces of Argentina for textiles and foodstuffs and on the littoral provinces for mules and horses.[2] Similarly, the sugar economy of northeastern Brazil led to the creation of a livestock economy in the interior, cattle being raised for meat for local consumption and hides for export. The value of production in these activities, and the population the activites supported, must have been much less than in the export sector,[3] but they furthered the settlement of areas lacking the resources to become primary centers themselves. The raw material centers also provided employment for those engaged in shipping goods to the ports and from there to Europe.

Finally, these centers provided the income to pay for the region's imports and thereby supported the shippers and merchants of imported goods. Imports included some items of capital equipment, such as slaves, machinery for sugar milling, and some inputs to the mining industry, but very little of the income earned by exports was invested outside the export sector. The bulk of imports consisted of consumer goods, particularly luxury items.

In summary, the entire monetary economy of colonial Latin America depended on the production for export of a few primary commodities. The territorial expansion and income growth of this economy were closely tied to the development of the export sector, which was the only link among the other sectors such as agriculture, manufacturing, and trade. These linkages and effects were considerably distorted, however, by the mercantilist policies pursued by Spain and, with less vigor, by Portugal. These policies took three main forms: restrictions on manufacturing in the colonies; outright prohibition of, or prohibitive tariffs on, imports into the colonies from third countries; and restriction of trade to certain favored ports in Spain and in the New World. In the case of Portugal, mercantilism was greatly weakened by a series of treaties in the seventeenth century which gave England preferential access to the Brazilian market, and by the monopoly position of the Dutch in the sugar trade. In the 1760s and 1770s the laws were considerably relaxed, allowing more ports to share in trade with Spain and among the colonies.

Despite the restrictions imposed, manufacturing expanded appreciably during the colonial era. Most items of everyday consumption were made in the colonies. The range of articles produced included textiles of all but the

finest grades, processed foodstuffs, leather goods and metal manufactures. By 1800 Latin America possessed a more extensive and efficient industrial sector than did Spain. The value added in manufacturing was still small compared with the value of agricultural or mineral output, but manufacturing had probably surpassed commerce as a source of income and employment. This development was due in large measure to the mercantilist regulations on trade. The high tariffs on imports from third countries protected producers in the colonies from competition with more advanced nations, especially England. As silver from the New World flowed into Spain, that country experienced a severe inflation and its industry deteriorated: as the price of Spanish manufactures rose and their quality fell, the protection to local industry increased.[4]

The effects of mercantilism on the expansion and development of the Latin American economy were therefore varied. Manufacturing industries were inadvertently promoted. The integration of the economy both by sector and by area was retarded, however, by the restraints on trade which isolated the various primary centers and raised the cost of transportation between each one and its hinterland. Certain centers were favored, but the creation of new ones and the diversification of the region's exports were limited by discrimination both among external trading partners and among ports and colonies in the New World. Thus, both the range of products exported and the total growth of exports were less under mercantilism than they would have been under a system of relatively free trade. For this reason, among others, the experience of mercantilism contributed powerfully to the dominance of laissez faire in the economic philosophy of Latin America in the century following independence.

As population increased and the precious metals declined in importance, agriculture overtook mining as the chief extractive activity. Manufacturing expanded, and the domestic use of natural resources increased. None of these developments, however, changed the position of the natural resource sector as the dynamic part of the economy and the point to which all the other monetary sectors were linked. Despite the important change between the conquest and the wars of independence, Latin America at the end of the colonial period remained fundamentally an export economy or, rather, a group of export economies each oriented to Spain or Portugal and exchanging, under restrictive conditions, a small number of resource products for a relatively wide range of consumption and luxury goods.

The First Century of Independence

The revolutions which separated Latin America from Spain and the achievement of independence in Brazil produced three closely related changes in the regional economy. The last traces of the mercantilist system were swept away, and all the former colonies were opened to trade with all other countries. With the end of the Crown's domination, political and economic power in the new countries passed firmly into the hands of the primary producers, the landowning and mining class which

---

[2] A. Ferrer, *The Argentine Economy* (University of California Press, 1967), p. 21.

[3] It is estimated that the output of the Brazilian livestock industry can hardly have exceeded 5 percent of the value of the sugar production on which it depended. C. Furtado, *The Economic Growth of Brazil* (University of California Press, 1963), pp. 62-71.

[4] Herring, *A History of Latin America*, pp. 193-204.

accounted for nearly all the region's exports and imports. This class benefitted from free trade by acquiring wider markets for its output of raw materials and also by being able to satisfy its consumption requirements and its smaller need for capital goods through imports. Thus the changes occasioned by independence did nothing to lessen the dynamic importance of the resource sector and the dependence of other sectors upon it; if anything, the Latin American economies became even more tied to their export sectors. The new states, like the colonial administrations, derived most of their revenue from this sector.

During the nineteenth century the creation of new primary centers and the shifts among products and producing areas continued. At first this process was simply an extension of the changes that had occurred in colonial times, and the volume of trade grew slowly and remained small. From about the middle of the century onward, however, the growth of the export sector and the changes within it underwent a considerable transformation. This period, which lasted at least until the First World War, is generally described as one of integration into world markets.[5]

As the countries of Europe, particularly England, developed manufacturing industries and began to specialize in producing manufactures for export, they came to require large imports of foodstuffs and industrial raw materials. The accompanying rise in income greatly expanded the market for a number of goods, such as sugar, coffee, and cocoa, which had previously been high-priced luxuries.

As demand increased, costs were reduced for many primary products through shifts in the location of production or through technical advances. Sugar prices, which had dropped sharply with the end of the Brazilian monopoly in the seventeenth century, fell further. The price of cotton fell drastically as production expanded in the southern United States. Early in the twentieth century the price of cocoa dropped by two-thirds, and developments in large-scale mining brought down the costs of nonferrous metals. Products that had not previously figured in trade became prominent: meat and grains from the River Plate countries, bananas from Central America, natural nitrates from Chile. The present dependence of certain countries on particular products — Brazil on coffee, Central America on coffee and bananas, Cuba on sugar, Argentina on meat and grain — was formed in the second half of the nineteenth century.

It is estimated that between 1700 and 1820 the volume of total world trade increased about threefold, or at less than 1 percent yearly. Between 1820 and 1870 trade expanded fivefold, and fivefold again between 1870 and the First World War, or at a rate of over 3 percent annually.[6] The industrial revolution produced a much more specialized world economy, into which Latin America was drawn as a supplier of large amounts of foodstuffs and raw materials. During the nineteenth century nearly all the expansion took place in agricultural products. The industrial metals and petroleum did not become important exports until the 1920s or later, and the precious metals had lost most of their significance by the late eighteenth century.

These developments had two further consequences of importance to the Latin American economies. They prompted a large-scale European migration to the New World, to incorporate into the world economy areas rich in natural resources but thinly populated and with very little capital. The labor shortage which had plagued the primary producing centers throughout the colonial period, leading first to Indian slavery and then to the use of Negro labor, was ended by the flow of immigrants, particularly to Argentina and Brazil.[7] At the same time large amounts of capital were invested by Europeans, particularly by England, in North America and Latin America. Some of this investment was directly in the resource sector, but most of it was in railroads and other infrastructure or in industries processing resources for export. Direct investment and foreign control of resource production did not become prominent until the development of oil and metals for export in the twentieth century. But there were exceptions: the nitrate deposits of Peru and Bolivia, which Chile exploited with substantial financial support from England and Germany in the 1870s, and sugar in Cuba and bananas in Central America.

The great expansion and increased economic importance of the resource sector also figured in the economic and political struggles within and among the various Latin American countries. In Argentina the littoral provinces and particularly Buenos Aires increased their dominance, and the interior provinces, which had been the economic centers in the sixteenth and seventeenth centuries, stagnated.[8] With the development of the coffee economy, the center of power in Brazil was established in the center-south and that area became the locus not only of the export sector but of the industrial sector which grew up after the mid-nineteenth century. The War of the Pacific, 1879-83, in which Chile defeated Peru and Bolivia and took territory from both, was fought largely for control of the nitrate beds in the coastal desert. Nitrates, which might have become important exports for Peru or Bolivia, were the dynamic element in the Chilean economy from the 1800s until World War I and furnished the bulk of foreign exchange and government revenue throughout that period. The Chaco War of 1932-35 between Paraguay and Bolivia was more complex in origin, but derived partly from the expectation of finding oil in the disputed area of the Gran Chaco.

---

[5]The phrase is applied by Ferrer to the period 1860-1930 in Argentina, and by D. Baerresen et al., *Latin American Trade Patterns* (Brookings Institution, 1965), to the interval 1820-1914. A. Pinto, *Chile: Un Caso de Desarrollo Frustrado* (Santiago: Editorial Universitaria, 1959), speaks of independence "opening the doors" of the Chilean economy. The region's economic growth in the nineteenth century is generally characterized by ECLA as "externally oriented development."

[6]Ferrer, *The Argentine Economy*, chap. IX. Estimates on trade, capital flows, and migration are presented on pp. 81-84.

[7]See Furtado, *The Economic Growth of Brazil*, chaps. 21-24, for a discussion of "the manpower problem" in Brazil in the early nineteenth century.

[8]This struggle is the major element in nineteenth century Argentine history. See Ferrer, *The Argentine Economy*; and for a discussion of the political factors and events, see Herring, *A History of Latin America*, pp. 617-59.

During the first century of independence some further industrial growth took place in Latin America, but for the region as a whole this sector remained quite small. Much of the expansion of industry took place, in effect, within the export sector and represented only the processing of primary commodities for export. In part, as in sugar milling, there was no increase in the degree of processing and the industry could grow only as rapidly as the production of its raw material. In other cases the value added in industry expanded more rapidly than primary output through the incorporation of further stages of processing: the shift from hides to meat in the cattle industry is the most striking example.

The production of manufactured goods for domestic consumption also increased, particularly in the larger countries. The cotton textile industry was established in Mexico in the 1830s and in Brazil in the 1840s and became the largest manufacturing activity; other consumer goods industries followed. The level and rate of growth of primary exports per capita reached a peak for many products and countries in the decade immediately preceding the First World War. This was also a period of rapid expansion in Latin American manufacturing. In 1900-1904 Argentina was already a significant industrial country, with 20 percent of the labor force and 8 percent of the capital in that sector.[9] During the war total industrial output grew more slowly, but the interruption of imports from Europe stimulated the creation of new industries and a diversification of the manufacturing sector. By 1929, manufacturing accounted for 6 percent or more of gross domestic product[10] in five Latin American countries, and in Chile and Argentina industrial output had reached 30 percent and 38 percent of the levels attained in 1960 (see table A-1). In no country, however, was there much development of heavy or

the United States a major industrial power in the late nineteenth century.[11]

Latin America possessed the resources not only for a much wider range of industry but for a number of the capital goods industries required to sustain the consumer goods sector; and during fairly long periods the export sector provided a growth in income seemingly adequate to support a more intensive industrial expansion. That this development did not occur is due to a number of factors, such as the geographic and economic barriers to the movement of goods; the very low income of much of the population and the physical and economic isolation of the subsistence sector; the traditional organization and high degree of self-sufficiency of the commercial primary producing centers; and so on. One factor is given particular attention here because of the contrast between the first century of independence and the interval since the Depression of the 1930s: that is the absence, in the earlier period, of any substantial or coherent governmental support for industry. In marked contrast to the United States, almost no protective tariffs were enacted in the region in the nineteenth century. One passed in Brazil in 1844 resulted in the formation of the cotton textile industry; but the motive in that case was to aid cotton growers by providing a domestic market for that part of their output which could no longer be exported against United States competition.[12] Chile raised a number of tariffs in 1904 and subsequent years to protect the consumer goods industries created in the preceding two decades. That tariffs or other measures could have been much more widely used to stimulate industry is suggested by the response of the manufacturing sector to the protection afforded by an interruption of imports in wartime — as in Chile during the War of the Pacific, and in several countries, notably Argentina, during World War I.

TABLE A-1. Growth of Manufacturing Industry Before 1930: Selected Latin American Countries

Country	Index of Industrial Production (Base: 1960 = 100)			Share of Manufacturing in Gross Domestic Product		
	1900	1914	1929	1900	1914	1929
Argentina	5.9	13.1	29.5	18.1	19.8	22.8
Brazil		4	12			11.7
Chile		23	38		9.8	7.9
Colombia			8.7			6.2
Mexico	7	7	15	13.4		14.2

Source: ECLA, *The Process of Industrialization in Latin America, Statistical Annex,* doc. E/CN/12/716/Add.2, pp. 1, 2.

Note: Gaps in series indicate that data are not available, not comparable or not applicable, or that the amount is negligibly small.

complex industries. Metalworking was on a very small scale, and little or no steel was produced until after 1900; production of capital goods was negligible. In particular, there was no development of the machine tool industries, which made

There were some intervals of state intervention to promote economic development, as in Brazil in the mid-nineteenth century, during which considerable public in-

[9]ECLA, *Análisis y Proyecciones del Desarrollo Económico: V, El Desarrollo Económico de la Argentina* (Mexico City: UN, 1959), part I, pp. 32, 37.

[10]Gross domestic product (GDP) is equal to gross national product (GNP) plus or minus net payments abroad.

[11]See H. E. Krooss, *American Economic Development,* 2nd ed. (Prentice-Hall, 1966), pp. 352-54, for a discussion of the growth and importance of these industries.

[12]S. J. Stein, "The Brazilian Cotton Textile Industry, 1850-1950," in *Economic Growth: Brazil, India, Japan,* ed. S. Kuznels et al. (Duke University Press, 1955).

vestment in infrastructure took place, but generally laissez faire was unchallenged. The governments of the period lacked the theoretical and administrative basis for almost any sort of economic policy. Furthermore, intervention was incompatible with the gold or gold-exchange standard to which the Latin American countries tried to adhere throughout the nineteenth and early twentieth centuries.[13] Depressions in the advanced countries of Europe and North America caused frequent lapses from this standard in Latin America during this period, but the crisis was never long enough for much new industry to be created. The announced intention of returning to fiscal good behavior as soon as possible would in itself have discouraged investments needing more than a few years to be profitable. The adherence to orthodoxy in turn resulted from the economic and political dominance of the export sector. The primary producers who were the most powerful class in every country benefitted from free trade for both their exports and their imports and would have borne much of the cost of a policy of protection for local industry. They were also often linked financially or otherwise to foreign countries — especially England — which had a strong interest in continued freedom of access to the regional market. A similar situation would have prevailed in the United States had the southern states, overwhelmingly agricultural and the chief source of exports, dominated the manufacturing and commercial interests of the north. Instead, the United States embarked almost from its inception on a policy of industrialization, while comparable efforts were not made in Latin America for more than another century.[14] Thus the resource sector remained the dynamic element of the economy much longer in Latin America than in North America or Europe.

In many instances, such as the silver mines of Bolivia and the sugar economy of northeastern Brazil in the late sixteenth and early seventeenth centuries, development based on the production of raw materials for export was capable of providing a satisfactory growth in per capita income. And during the second half of the nineteenth century the Brazilian economy grew at a comparatively high rate.[15] Nevertheless, as with the rest of the region, the history of Brazil reflects difficulties resulting from reliance on the resource sector for economic growth: from the last quarter of the eighteenth century to the middle of the nineteenth century Brazil experienced stagnation or even decline in per capita income. In certain regions, such as the cattle and sugar areas of the northeast, income per head appears to

have fallen steadily for decades in consequence of the decline of export values. In mining areas such as Bolivia virtually all activity outside the subsistence sector ceased when exports dwindled.

In general, the level of productivity in the primary export sector, whether agricultural or mineral, is much higher than in subsistence agriculture. As there was virtually no other source of income and employment — or only a small industrial and commercial sector incapable of absorbing much labor — throughout the colonial period and the first century of independence, growth could occur only by an increase in the primary export sector. Any contraction in the export sector forced labor into subsistence production or into such largely subsistence activities as low-density cattle raising. Acceleration or continuation of growth most frequently depended on the development of new resource products, often through the incorporation of new territory and the decline or abandonment of older producing centers. The integration of Latin America into world markets under a regime of almost completely free trade greatly increased the number and quantities of such products which could be exported, without much diminishing the system's reliance on primary exports for its economic progress.

Depression and World War

The phase of economic development through integration into world markets for raw materials came to an abrupt end with the Great Depression of the 1930s. Between 1930 and 1945 Latin America experienced a crisis which resulted in fundamental changes in the region's economic structure and initiated a new stage in its economic history. Parallel changes occurred in economic philosophy and in the policies of governments. The Great Depression was not the first external shock to which the Latin American economy was subjected. Even during the colonial era, particular areas experienced economic dislocation and a decline or reversal of growth through the exhaustion of a resource, a decline in demand for a product, or competition from other producing areas. As the region became integrated into the world economy in the nineteenth century, its raw materials exports became increasingly subject to fluctuations in the pace of industrial activity and the level or rate of growth of income in the more advanced nations. The great crisis of the twentieth century differed from these previous disturbances, however, in three significant respects: in scope, in structure, and in the reactions it evoked.

The trade crisis of the 1930s was unquestionably the most severe in Latin America's history. Demand for all kinds of raw materials fell drastically, bringing down the price or quantity, or both, of almost every one of the region's export products. Ten of the commodities included in this study suffered an average decline in real price of about 60 percent between the peak year of the late 1920s and the low point of the Depression.[16] Since incomes fell

[13] For a fuller discussion of the obstacles to state intervention in the economy, see ECLA, *Inflation and Growth in Latin America* (doc. 1 E/CN.12/563), vol. I, chap. 1, "A Summary of the Region's Experience, 1929 to 1959" (New York: UN); also published in ECLA, *Economic Bulletin for Latin America*, VII, no. 1, (February 1962).

[14] This discussion is based on Joseph Grunwald, "Some Reflections on Latin American Industrialization Policy" (Paper presented at the Conference on Key Problems of Economic Policy in Latin America, University of Chicago, 9 November 1966).

[15] It is estimated that between the 1840s and the 1890s the economy of Brazil grew at an annual rate of about 3.5 percent, or at 1.5 percent in per capita terms. See Furtado, *The Economic Growth of Brazil*, pp. 155-65 (for an analysis of income in the sugar economy, see pp. 43-66).

[16] The commodities are copper, Venezuelan crude oil, Brazilian coffee, free market sugar, Brazilian cotton, lead, zinc, tin, Brazilian iron ore, and Ecuadorean cocoa. The first five of these, if weighted by their shares of total Latin American exports in 1956-59, show an average decline of 45 percent between 1927 and 1933.

farther and sooner in the export sector than in the rest of the economy, demand for imports remained high at first, and the immediate effect of the crisis was a massive external disequilibrium. Before balance was restored at a much lower level of trade, the continuation of imports had largely exhausted gold reserves and forced the Latin American countries to end convertibility of their currencies.[17] The sharpest contraction anywhere in the world took place in Chile, which suffered a decline of 85 percent in the value of its total trade (imports plus exports) between 1929 and 1932. The contraction exceeded 65 percent for seven other Latin American countries.[18]

The crisis was also severe in four other respects. First, it came at a time when demand for certain products was already weakening or when prices were being maintained only by accumulation of surplus stocks. This situation was most serious for coffee, but it affected petroleum and a few other products as well. Second, the Depression lasted much longer than its predecessors in the nineteenth century which, however violent, could be partially offset by changes in reserves and inventories. The duration of this crisis forced the Latin American economies to adjust as fully as possible to a much reduced level of trade and to defend themselves against the deflationary effects of the fall in export incomes. Third, the effects were spread more widely over the population and among sectors than at any previous time. The economic growth of the region had enlarged the class which depended on the export sector either for income from the supply of inputs and consumer goods or for foreign exchange with which to buy imported goods such as light manufactures. Finally, Latin American raw material exports never completely recovered the rate of growth or the purchasing power of imports, in per capita terms, that they had enjoyed in the years preceding World War I. The rate of growth the region could achieve through reliance on exports of primary commodities was reduced by a number of factors: changes in the relative prices of resource products and manufactures, restrictive trade measures adopted by the industrially advanced countries, decline in the rate of growth of demand for certain products, and the opening of new producing areas. Some of these developments were largely independent of the crisis, but others resulted directly or indirectly from measures taken to cope with the Depression.

With respect to structure, the crisis of the 1930s differed from previous depressions particularly in the years immediately following the recovery of incomes and the resumption of trade. Normally, an increase in income in the developed countries had been reflected in a rise in imports of raw materials; the additional income earned by exporting countries such as those of Latin America allowed them to increase imports of manufactures to restore equilibrium

at higher levels of income and trade. The Great Depression was immediately followed, however, by the Second World War. Demand for raw materials, especially metals and petroleum, rose sharply, and although most prices were controlled during the war there was a substantial recovery of export value. The income generated by exports could not find an outlet in imports because Europe was cut off from Latin America by the war, the United States had greatly reduced output of consumer goods, and shipping was extremely scarce. Only high priority goods such as fuel and capital equipment could be imported, and even those were limited largely to the needs of the export sector and the infrastructure that served it. Shortages of fuel were so severe that several million tons of coffee and grains were burned in Brazil and Argentina, respectively.[19] Thus, only one side of the reduced trade balance of the 1930s was restored, and the Latin American countries were in effect forced to enjoy a trade surplus and to accumulate sizable reserves. At the same time they were under great pressure to develop domestic supplies of all kinds of goods, from raw materials to capital equipment. Where exports were blocked by the scarcity of shipping, there was also a stimulus to further processing and domestic use of traditional resource products. The effect of this situation was twofold: it extended by five years or more the period of import scarcity and thus helped consolidate the adjustments originally made to deal with a shortage rather than a surplus of foreign exchange; and it provided an interval of rapidly growing income in which a new economic structure could become established. It thereby precluded an abandonment of the measures taken to cope with the initial crisis and allowed them to evolve toward a definite policy for the region's future growth.

The crisis of 1930-45 produced a variety of responses in Latin America. At a time when demand for all raw materials was depressed, there was little reason to expect that new primary exports could be established; such an adjustment has in any case usually taken a decade or more with incomes remaining low in the interval. (The high demand for metals during World War II and the consequent depletion of resources in the advanced countries did lead to an increase in the share of minerals in total Latin American exports, but the change was slight and did not initiate a new period of export growth.) In the short run, the only changes possible were shifts among traditional resource products in response to changes in relative prices. In Brazil, for example, there was a considerable transfer of capital from coffee to cotton, as the price of coffee fell drastically and remained low while cotton prices were maintained through controls in the United States.[20]

International efforts were also made to control the markets for particular commodities, by reducing production and exports, liquidating excess stocks, and raising or maintaining prices. Six international agreements, covering

---

[17] Brazil held gold reserves of £31 million in September 1929; by December 1930 they had entirely disappeared. Furtado, *The Economic Growth of Brazil*, p. 203.

[18] League of Nations, *World Trade Review, 1932* (Geneva: 1933); the comparison covers eighty-three countries. A more detailed discussion of the effects of the Depression is given in the League's *World Economic Report* for 1932-33. Of the thirty-nine countries surveyed, Chile is again the country which suffered most.

[19] ECLA, *Inflation and Growth* . . . , vol. I, chap. 1, p. 17.

[20] Furtado, *The Economic Growth of Brazil*, pp. 216-17. For a discussion of the measures taken in the United States, see J.W.F. Rowe, *Primary Commodities in International Trade* (London: Cambridge University Press, 1965), p. 132.

tin, sugar, tea, wheat, rubber and copper, were signed between February 1931 and January 1936; and a second agreement was reached for sugar in 1937.[21]

All these measures were ended by the outbreak of World War II, although agreements for tin, sugar, and wheat were re-established in the first postwar decade. The agreements concerning tin and sugar were of particular importance to Latin America: the former was quite successful, and protected the relatively high-cost industry of Bolivia, on which the national economy depended, from the severe competition and continued low prices which would otherwise have ensued. The sugar scheme was less successful, because of increased production by non-members, but it reduced the impact of the Depression on Cuba, the largest free market exporter. The short-lived copper agreement was of some benefit to Chile and Peru, but its effect was fairly slight. None of these schemes could do more than maintain prices and thereby protect exporters' incomes; in the absence of a resumption of growth in demand they could not restore dynamism to the export sectors of the producer countries.

The crisis produced two other important reactions in Latin America: compensatory policies to maintain incomes in the export sector or in the economy as a whole; and efforts to substitute domestic production for imports. These two reactions were ultimately related, since maintenance of the domestic market was necessary if import substitution was to succeed in creating new sources of income and employment; initially, however, they were pursued independently. Neither was entirely novel. The early history of industrialization through import substitution has been briefly described. Similarly, previous crises had produced, deliberately or inadvertently, mechanisms for protecting incomes through public expenditures or shifting part of the losses from the export sector to others through devaluation. The major compensatory scheme, that of accumulation and destruction of coffee stocks in Brazil, was in effect a continuation of the various "valorization" programs effected in 1907 and 1923, with emphasis shifted from price maintenance to the liquidation of excess supplies and capacity. A high rate of planting during the 1920s had created a productive capacity double the amount of exports by 1929. When demand declined, new planting stopped; but the price of coffee would have had to fall very far to discourage harvesting, so that capacity and supplies remained far in excess of demand. The government responded by buying up and destroying between 4 and 5 million tons of coffee, about one-third of production during the 1930s. Between the late 1930s and the end of World War II some 550 million trees were also destroyed, and 30 percent of the land in coffee was taken out of production. These measures finally restored some balance in the coffee market, but they were not followed by other producing countries, with the result that Brazil lost a large share of the market. Other crops, with a more rapid supply response, experienced a sharp decline in prices and incomes between 1929 and 1933 but recovered substantially in the next several years as in-

comes rose again in the importing countries: coffee prices, in contrast, remained very low until late 1940 when they were raised by the imposition of export quotas for the United States market. Despite the slight effect on prices, these measures greatly cushioned the impact of the Depression on Brazil, so that monetary income fell by only about 25 percent and began to rise again in 1933, and the contraction entailed very little unemployment or reversion to the subsistence sector.[22] Compensatory policies, including public works expenditures and credit expansion in particular, were also followed in Argentina, Chile, Colombia, and Mexico.[23] These measures were part of the departure from orthodox financial policy which began with the abandonment of the gold-exchange standard. They were most important in the larger and more urbanized countries of Latin America, where there was already a sizable industrial sector to protect and where a large-scale transfer of labor to subsistence farming was least feasible.

The larger countries were also most involved in the second reaction, that of replacing imports by further domestic industrialization. This effect was a rather inadvertent consequence of measures taken in the first years of the crisis to cope with the acute shortage of foreign exchange. Tariffs and import quotas were established over a wide range of goods, with little concern for effective rates of protection or the structure of tariffs which resulted. Governments assumed control of dealings in foreign exchange, often through multiple exchange rates, import licensing, and a welter of quotas, taxes and other restrictions. These measures afforded a high degree of protection to many manufacturing industries which expanded or were established to meet the needs of the domestic market. Although raw materials remained virtually the only source of foreign exchange, the industrial sector gradually emerged as a new source of dynamism in the economy, providing the fastest growth in income and employment.[24]

This process did not occur smoothly or uniformly throughout Latin America. The possibility of import substitution depended, in each country, on the resources and skills available and on the size of the market for manufactures. Since many items of consumption were already produced domestically, substitution meant producing goods exhibiting some economies of scale or requiring labor and management skills and other inputs not readily available. Furthermore, the almost random distribution of tariffs undoubtedly gave too much protection to some industries and not enough to others, creating an inefficient and poorly integrated industrial structure. During the 1950s the tariff

[21] For an account of these commodity control schemes and an evaluation of their effects, see Rowe, *Primary Commodities . . . ,* pp. 136-55.

[22] See Furtado, *The Economic Growth of Brazil,* pp. 175-201, for a discussion of the coffee price maintenance policy and its effects before 1930, and pp. 208-13 for a discussion of the compensatory effects of coffee policy during the Depression. The Brazilian valorization scheme is also described by Rowe, *Primary Commodities . . . ,* pp. 133-36.

[23] ECLA, *Inflation and Growth . . . ,* vol. I, chap. 1, pp. 6-7.

[24] An excellent history of industrial growth is provided by ECLA, *The Process of Industrial Development in Latin America* (New York: UN, 1966), especially pp. 5-55 and 155-226. See also S. Macario, "Protectionism and Industrialization in Latin America," in ECLA, *Economic Bulletin for Latin America,* IX, no. 1 (1964).

structures of many countries were simplified and exchange controls were relaxed or unified. More recently, interest has developed in the effective rates of protection enjoyed by different industries and different stages of processing within industries, and the effects of this protection on the rate and type of industrial growth and on the structure of imports.[25]

While substitution of consumer goods proceeded rapidly in several countries, this process in turn required much larger amounts of raw materials, intermediate goods, and other inputs such as fuel and electricity. The Latin American countries that had succeeded in the first stage of domestic manufacturing found that they must either earn enough foreign exchange to import the needed primary and intermediate goods, or carry import substitution back toward the production of raw materials. Despite the initial lack of a definite purpose or policy to that effect, the crisis of 1930-45 resulted in a great impetus to manufacturing industry and the transfer of dynamism in the economy to that sector. As a policy of industrialization through import substitution evolved, governments began to intervene directly to establish or support manufacturing. Institutions such as the Corporación de Fomento de la Producción in Chile and the Nacional Financiera in Mexico were created to direct public funds toward certain industries; in other cases, particularly in raw material production and a few basic industries, state monopolies were established.[26] All these developments gave rise to a philosophy of economic growth based on industrialization. Again, as with the changes of attitude in the late eighteenth and early nineteenth centuries, a new economic ideology evolving directly from Latin America's economic experience was designed to liberate the region from the restrictions previously imposed on its economic growth. Import substitution was seen as the chief instrument of this liberation, and the primary sector was correspondingly neglected in public policy.[27]

---

[25]While the nominal tariff is the import duty imposed upon a product, the "effective" rate is the tariff on the value added in the production of the commodity within the country and will therefore depend upon the import duties imposed on raw materials and other inputs used in the production. Thus, the higher the tariff rate on inputs, *ceteris paribus*, the lower the effective protection on the final product.

See the papers prepared by Bela Balassa et al. for the conference on tariff structures of underdeveloped countries at the International Bank for Reconstruction and Development, Washington, April 1967; Argentina, Chile, and Mexico are among the countries studied. Earlier studies of Latin American tariffs and import controls concentrated on average nominal rates of duty for different classes of products. See ECLA, *Customs Duties and Other Import Charges and Restrictions in Latin American Countries: Average Levels of Incidence*, doc. E/CN.12/554 (Caracas: 13 February 1961), with annexes I-XI for Argentina, Bolivia, Brazil, Colombia, Chile, Ecuador, Mexico, Paraguay, Peru, Uruguay, and Venezuela.

[26]For a list of these institutions with their dates of founding, methods of operation, and fields of activity, see ECLA, *The Process of Industrial Development in Latin America*, pp. 170-82.

[27]The change from an externally oriented model of development to one in which domestic industrialization through import substitution became the dynamic element is summarized, with an extensive study of the Brazilian case, in "The Growth and Decline of Import Substitution in Brazil," ECLA, *Economic Bulletin for Latin America*, IX, no. 1 (1964). See especially pp. 1-11, 49-59.

Development Since the Crisis

The changes in economic conditions, attitudes, and policies brought on by the crisis of 1930-45 have continued to determine the economic history of Latin America to the present. The last four decades have been a period of rapid and often difficult change for the economies of the region, and this period can be expected to extend for another decade or more before developments now in progress result in a new phase of Latin America's economic history. Furthermore, it is only for this recent period that many kinds of statistical information are available. It is not therefore surprising that the region's economic experience since the late 1920s is the subject of a vast and detailed literature.[28] For the purpose of this study, only three subjects will be considered:

a) changes in the structure of the regional economy, in employment and output by sector;
b) the scope of import substitution and its effects on industrial growth, the shift of dynamism from the export sector to the industrial sector, and the composition of imports; and
c) the growth and composition of exports.

Changes in Structure

The Latin American economy has undergone a considerable transformation since the 1920s. Particularly in the more developed countries of the region there has emerged a partial, or non-integrated, industrial economy, comparable in some respects to the advanced economies of Europe, North America, or Oceania.[29] As recently as 1925 more than 60 percent of the Latin American labor force was engaged in agriculture. Although the total number of people in that sector has continued to increase, the absorption of employment in other sectors has been so much more rapid that the share in agriculture has fallen to less than 47 percent (see table A-2). The manufacturing sector as a whole employs almost exactly the same share of the population as in 1925, but within that sector there has been a large-scale transfer of labor from artisan activities to factory employment. Since the latter is about eight times as productive as the former — and the disproportion has increased in recent years — total productivity and output in manufacturing have increased rapidly.

In the late 1930s agriculture accounted for over 30 percent of gross domestic product in Latin America and manu-

---

[28]See, in addition to the sources cited in the previous section, ECLA, *The Economic Development of Latin America in the Postwar Period* (New York: UN, 1964), and ECLA's annual *Economic Survey of Latin America*. There is no complete list of books and articles, but see J.R. Wish, *Economic Development in Latin America: An Annotated Bibliography* (Praeger, 1965). More detailed bibliographies exist for certain subjects: see for example T. F. Carroll, *Land Tenure and Land Reform in Latin America: A Selective Annotated Bibliography*, 2nd, rev. version (Inter-American Development Bank, December 1965).

[29]Ferrer, in *The Argentine Economy*, describes the economy of Argentina since 1930 in these terms. For a summary of changes in economic structure, with comparisons to the historical experience and present situation of more advanced countries, see Grunwald, "Some Reflections . . . ," sect. IV.

TABLE A–2. Latin America: Percentage Distribution of Labor Force by Economic Sector, 1925-1965

Sector	1925	1930	1935	1940	1945	1950[a]	1955[a]	1960[a]	1965[a]
Agriculture	62.4	60.0	59.5	58.0	55.9	53.5	50.4	47.7	46.1
Mining					1.2	1.1	1.1	1.0	1.0
Manufacturing	13.7	13.6	13.4	13.7	14.1	14.4	14.2	14.2	13.8
Factory	3.5	4.2	4.7	5.6	6.6	6.9	7.0	7.4	7.5
Artisan	10.2	9.4	8.7	8.1	7.5	7.5	7.2	6.8	6.3
Construction					2.9	3.7	4.5	4.8	3.9
Basic services[b]					3.7	4.2	4.7	5.2	5.2
Trade and finance					7.6	7.8	8.4	9.1	9.5
Government					3.0	3.3	3.5	3.7	3.8
Other services[c]					11.6	12.0	13.2	14.3	16.7

Sources: 1925-45 – ECLA, *The Process of Industrialization in Latin America, Statistical Annex*, doc. E/CN.12/716/Add.2, pp. 13, 17. 1945 – ECLA, *The Economic Development of Latin America in the Postwar Period*, p. 30. 1950-60 – ECLA, *Economic Survey of Latin America, 1964*, p. 42. 1965 – ECLA, *Economic Survey of Latin America, 1966*, p. 31.

Note: Gaps in series indicate that data are not available, not comparable or not applicable, or that the amount is negligibly small.

[a]Excludes Cuba.
[b]Electricity, gas, water, transport and communications.
[c]Includes overt and disguised unemployment.

facturing for only 15 percent; by 1965 the shares were 22 and 23 percent, respectively (see table A-3). The rapid increase of productivity in manufacturing and the transfer of labor out of agriculture have meant that increased open unemployment has been prevented only through absorption of labor in the service sector, especially in services outside of trade, finance, government, and the basic services such as transport and communication. Productivity in the "other services" is about equal to the average for the whole economy, but has been declining as more and more labor is drawn into them; employment in this sector is often the urban equivalent of rural underemployment.

In every country there are enormous differences in productivity among sectors and even among industries or activities within one sector. Labor productivity is generally highest in mining (including petroleum) which is highly capital intensive and employs only 1 percent of the regional labor force and not more than 5 percent in any one country. Manufacturing productivity is also much above the average, especially in the factory sector. Agricultural productivity is less than half the average, as it includes much subsistence farming; but even commercial agriculture shows a relatively low level of output per man. Much of Latin America's income growth in the last four decades can probably be attributed to the transfer of labor from low to high productivity occupations; but this process is limited by the fact that the more productive sectors cannot absorb much labor unless productivity and income rise in the other sectors, and progress there has been generally slow.

The rapidity and thoroughness of this transformation have varied greatly among countries; averages for Latin America as a whole give only an approximate view of what has occurred in individual economies. In the countries that already had a sizable industrial sector in the late 1920s, such as Argentina and Chile, most of the shift among sectors took place between 1930 and 1950. In those countries that industrialized later, the transfer was concentrated in the 1950s, and in the poorer countries of the region it has only recently acquired significance. Thus in Central America, for example, agriculture continues to absorb more than half the increase in the labor force, while the share is as low as 6 percent in Argentina, Chile, and Uruguay, and the bulk of new employment is provided by the service sector. Changes among economic sectors have been at least as rapid for some Latin American countries as that experienced in the past by the more advanced nations. Argentina's increase in the share of gross product contributed by manufacturing rose by 12 percentage points between 1935 and 1950; a comparable change in the same length period appears to have occurred only in Germany, between about

TABLE A–3. Latin America: Percentage Distribution of Gross Domestic Product by Economic Sector, 1936-40 to 1965

Sector	1936-40	1941-44	1945-49	1950[a]	1955[a]	1960[a]	1965[a]
Agriculture	31.1	29.7	25.5	24.6	23.8	21.7	21.8
Mining	3.8	3.7	4.3	4.0	4.5	4.9	4.9
Manufacturing	15.2	16.7	18.0	18.7	19.7	21.7	22.7
Construction	2.7	2.7	3.5	3.4	3.4	3.3	3.2
Basic services[b]	6.5	6.9	7.4	7.0	7.4	7.4	7.6
Trade and finance	18.0	17.6	18.9	17.3	17.7	18.0	17.8
Government	6.6	6.8	7.1	8.6	7.8	7.1	6.5
Other services	16.1	16.0	15.2	16.4	15.7	15.9	15.5

Sources: 1936-40 to 1945-59 – ECLA, *The Economic Development of Latin America in the Postwar Period*, p. 27. 1950-65 – ECLA, *Economic Survey of Latin America, 1965*, p. 20.

[a]Excludes Cuba.
[b]Transport and communications only, 1936-40 to 1945-49; thereafter includes electricity, gas and water as well.

1890 and 1905.[30] In the transfer of labor out of agriculture, Uruguay appears to have undergone as rapid a change as any of the presently advanced countries.

By comparison with the countries of North America and Europe, however, the transformation of the Latin American economy is still far from complete. When judged by the relative importance of its industrial sector, the region is in the position of the United Kingdom, Germany, and France some eighty years ago or the United States fifty years ago. Even where, as in Argentina, the manufacturing sector is now relatively as large as in all but a few of the advanced nations, the agricultural sector remains quite large. The fact that agricultural employment continues to increase in Latin America, while it is declining in North America and in most European countries, is enough to indicate that the region's economy has not yet entered the phase of growth characteristic of the more developed countries.

The transformation of the economy carries two notable implications for the natural resource sector. In the first place, a great many more raw materials are required than formerly. An economy dependent exclusively on primary exports uses directly only foodstuffs, some fuel, and certain materials for construction: and the range of goods produced can be much narrower if the bulk of output is exported to buy imports of other materials. An economy developing through industrialization requires much more fuel, and metals and agricultural raw materials as well. If the capacity to import is limited, then as many as possible of these materials must be produced within the economy.

In the second place — again, particularly if imports are limited — the success of the structural transformation depends very much on the ability of the resource sector to maintain or increase output while releasing labor to other sectors. For example, agricultural productivity must rise if labor is to be shifted to other activities without leading to imports of food which reduce the imports needed by the industrial sector. More generally, a rise in productivity is often needed to enlarge the national market so that domestic industry can operate at reasonable levels of cost. As the resources sector is integrated into the economy in a new pattern, its flexibility and supply response continue to influence the growth of other sectors; if some of these are potentially more dynamic than the primary sector, any restraint on their growth slows the development of the entire economy.

In the years since 1930 the most dynamic sector of the Latin American economy has been that of manufacturing industry. Before the 1930s manufacturing industry in Latin America expanded only slightly more rapidly than total product, or — since the latter included a large subsistence sector — at approximately the pace set by the growth of exports and of the monetary economy which depended on them. Between 1929 and 1960, however, the combined industrial sector of the five major Latin American countries (Argentina, Brazil, Chile, Colombia and Mexico) grew twice as rapidly, in percentage terms, as total gross domestic product in those countries, and more than ten times as rapidly as their total imports (see table A-4). These two

TABLE A-4. Import Substitution in Manufactures in Selected Latin American Countries, 1929, 1950, and 1960
(Millions of U.S. dollars at factor cost in 1960 prices)

Concept	Year	Argentina	Brazil	Chile	Colombia	Mexico	Total Five Countries
Total gross domestic product	1929	8,031	7,106	2,428	1,661	4,045	23,271
	1950	13,564	14,773	3,346	3,526	9,688	44,897
	1960	18,086	25,807	4,418	5,499	17,521	71,331
Industrial product	1929	1,836	833	192	99	573	3,533
	1950	4,023	2,965	595	500	1,990	10,073
	1960	5,804	7,145	828	936	4,036	18,749
Imports of manufactures	1929	1,327	708	542	267	418	3,262
	1950[a]	933	1,052	384	361	887	3,708
	1960	1,033	1,225	480	497	1,344	4,579
Total supply of manufactures	1929	3,163	1,541	734	366	991	6,795
	1950	4,956	4,017	979	861	2,877	13,781
	1960	6,837	8,370	1,308	1,433	5,380	23,328
Increase in industrial product	1929-50	2,187	2,132	403	401	1,417	6,540
	1950-60	1,781	4,180	233	436	2,046	8,676
	1929-60	3,968	6,312	636	837	3,463	15,216
Elasticity of growth of industrial product[b] with respect to:							
Total gross domestic product	1929-50	1.73	2.37	5.55	3.60	1.77	2.02
	1950-60	1.33	1.87	1.22	1.55	1.26	1.46
	1929-60	1.73	2.88	4.04	3.65	1.80	2.09
Total imports	1929-50	(c)	4.57	(c)	14.47	2.18	13.36
	1950-60	4.00	7.37	1.39	2.48	2.08	3.74
	1929-60	(c)	9.03	(c)	11.60	2.82	10.50

[30]S. Kuznets, "Quantitative Aspects of the Economic Growth of Nations: II. Industrial Distribution of National Product and Labor Force," *Economic Development and Cultural Change*, supp. to vol. V (July 1957).

TABLE A–4 – Continued

Concept	Year	Argentina	Brazil	Chile	Colombia	Mexico	Total Five Countries
I. Import Substitution Relative to Gross Domestic Product							
Import coefficient of manufactures	1929	16.5	9.9	22.3	16.1	10.3	14.0
Anticipated imports of manufactures[d]	1950	2,238	1,463	746	568	998	6,286[e]
	1960	2,984	2,581	985	885	1,805	9,986[e]
Difference between actual and anticipated imports	1950	1,305	411	362	207	111	2,578[e]
	1960	1,951	1,356	505	388	461	5,407[e]
Share of industrial growth due to substitution[f] (%)	1929-50	60	19	90	52	8	39
	1950-60[g]	36	23	61	41	17	33
1929 base	1929-60	49	21	79	46	13	36
1950 base	1950-60[h]	13	15	11	15	13	15
Share of anticipated imports replaced by domestic production[j] (%)	1929-50	58	28	49	36	11	41
	1950-60	11	1	10	8	0	7
1929 base	1929-60	63	47	51	44	25	54
1950 base	1950-60	17	34	5	12	16	20
II. Import Substitution Relative to Total Supply of Manufactures							
Import coefficient	1929	41.9	44.9	73.9	73.0	42.2	(48.1)
Anticipated imports of manufactures[k]	1950	2,079	1,843	723	629	1,210	6,605
	1960	2,862	3,842	964	1,046	2,263	11,210
Difference between actual and anticipated imports	1950	1,146	791	339	268	323	2,897
	1960	1,829	2,617	484	549	919	6,631
Share of industrial growth due to import substitution[f] (%)	1929-50	53	36	83	70	23	44
	1950-60	38	44	62	64	29	43
1929 base	1929-60	46	41	74	68	26	44
1950 base	1950-60	14	23	15	24	15	19
Share of anticipated imports replaced by domestic production[j] (%)	1929-50	55	43	47	43	27	44
	1950-60	10	10	9	11	6	9
1929 base	1929-60	64	68	50	53	40	59
1950 base	1950-60	20	44	6	17	19	27

Sources: 1929 and 1960 – ECLA, *The Process of Industrialization in Latin America, Statistical Annex*, p. 8. 1950, gross domestic product and industrial product – ibid., p. 26. 1950, imports of manufactures – from data in ECLA, *Statistical Bulletin for Latin America*, I, no. 1 (March 1964), p. 119 (imports in millions of 1955 dollars). For methodology, see fn. 33, p. 18.

[a] Total imports in 1960 dollars estimated from 1950 and 1960 imports in 1955 dollars and 1960 imports in 1960 dollars; i.e., ratio of price indices for 1955 and 1960 assumed to be the same for 1950 imports as for 1960 imports. Share of manufactures in total imports estimated from corresponding data for 1929 and 1960, assuming linear change over the 31-year period.

[b] Ratio of percentage increase in industrial product to percentage increase in gross domestic product (or value of imports) during period indicated.

[c] Negative growth (decline) of total import value.

[d] 1929 import coefficient of manufactures applied to gross domestic product in 1950 and in 1960.

[e] Calculated from average 1929 coefficient (14%); does not equal sum of figures for five countries.

[f] Difference between actual and anticipated imports (import saving) as a share of growth of industrial product.

[g] Difference between import saving in 1929-60 and import saving in 1929-50 as a share of growth of industrial product, 1950-60.

[h] Import saving in 1950-60 as a share of growth of industrial product in the same period.

[j] Import saving as a share of anticipated imports.

[k] 1929 ratio of imports to total supply applied to total supply in 1950 and in 1960.

indices describe the transfer of dynamism from the export sector to the manufacturing sector and the emergence of an economy able to grow much more rapidly, for some decades, than the value of its exports increased. The shift was especially pronounced between 1929 and 1950, when there was little or no growth of exports in most countries.[31]

During the 1950s Latin American exports and imports increased appreciably, chiefly as a result of rapidly growing incomes in the advanced importing countries. The ratio of growth of industry to growth of imports, again for the major countries of the region, fell from 13 for the years 1929-50 to less than 4 in the next decade, and the ratio of industrial to total growth also declined.

The Process of Import Substitution

The replacement of imports by domestic production resulting from the crisis of the 1930s became a major stimulus to industry and thereby to total economic growth. The strategic importance of import substitution and its effects on the various sectors of the Latin American economy cannot be determined without an examination of the particular goods produced in each country and the contribution of each to the country's further development. In theory, production of any good formerly imported releases foreign ex-

change to import other items, so that it may not matter for which products substitution occurs. However, the differences of scale, complexity, and linkages among industries; the existence of multiple exchange rates and complicated tariff structures; and the wide variations in factor costs and productivities in the Latin American economies undoubtedly made substitution of certain products more valuable to economic growth than others. Further discussion of substitution in the production and processing of particular resource commodities is presented in Part Two.[32]

If it is assumed that in the absence of import substitution, imports of manufactures would have increased at the same rate as gross domestic product in Latin American countries, then the amount of substitution or import saving may be defined as the difference between anticipated and actual imports. When this amount is compared to the increase in industrial production during the same period, it appears that the substitution of imports of manufactures accounted for some 36 percent of total industrial growth in the principal Latin American countries between 1929 and 1960 (see table A-4, section I).[33] With some exceptions, the importance of substitution by this measure is inversely proportional to the growth of imports, as is to be expected: thus it is only 13 percent in Mexico, where imports more than tripled in three decades, and 79 percent in Chile,

---

[31] These calculations are based on estimates of gross domestic product, industrial product, and imports of manufactures for 1929 and 1960, in 1960 dollars. Similar estimates are not available for other years, so the comparison must be made between individual years rather than averages for longer periods; however, 1929 and 1960 are believed to be reasonably representative of the period just before the Depression and the period three decades later. The estimates for 1950 are somewhat less reliable because of assumptions about price changes in the interval 1950-60 and about changes in the share of manufactures in total imports over the period 1929-60 (see fn. a, table A-4). The latter assumption is particularly questionable, imports of manufactures in 1950 probably being understated and the transfer of dynamism to industry between 1929 and 1950 being exaggerated somewhat. The errors in these estimates are not enough, however, to invalidate the conclusion that this transfer was appreciably more rapid before 1950 than in the ensuing decade.

[32] See tables 5-8 (Steel), 8-7 (Crude Oil and Refined Products), 9-7 (Coal and Coke), and 17-9 (Wood Pulp and Pulp Products) and the attendant discussion in these chapters; and for data on a number of industries, see "The Growth and Decline of Import Substitution in Brazil," pp. 27-49.

[33] Let M_i be imports of manufactures in year i,

X_i, industrial product

$S_i = M_i + X_i$, total supply of manufactures, assuming no exports, and

P_i, gross domestic product.

Then the measures of import substitution between year 1 and year 2 used in table A-4 are as follows:

	Section I gross domestic product	*Section II* total supply
Share of increased production due to import substitution	$\dfrac{M_1 P_2/P_1 - M_2}{X_2 - X_1}$	$\dfrac{M_1 S_2/S_1 - M_2}{X_2 - X_1}$
Share of anticipated imports replaced by import substitution	$\dfrac{M_1 P_2/P_1 - M_2}{M_1 P_2/P_1}$	$\dfrac{M_1 S_2/S_1 - M_2}{M_1 S_2/S_1}$

The numerator is the difference between anticipated imports in year 2 and the actual imports in that year.

The calculations of import substitution in the interval 1950-60, using 1929 rather than 1950 as a base, are as follows, for section I (year 1, 2, and 3 represent 1929, 1950, and 1960):

$$\frac{(M_1 P_3/P_1 - M_3) - (M_1 P_2/P_1 - M_2)}{X_3 - X_2} \quad \text{and} \quad \frac{(M_1 P_3/P_1 - M_3) - (M_1 P_2/P_1 - M_2)}{M_1 P_3/P_1}$$

The results are quite different when 1950 is the base and the formulas presented earlier are used.

The formulas based on total supply (section II) are also used in calculations for individual commodities in Part Two of this book, but imports and production are given in physical units rather than in value.

where imports of manufactures in 1960 were still below the 1929 level. The same relation is observed for four of the five countries if the two periods 1929-50 and 1950-60 are considered separately, and import saving in the latter is defined by the 1929 rather than the 1950 ratio of imports to gross product. When a separate calculation for 1950-60 is made using 1950 as a base, the contribution of import substitution to industrial growth appears to be much less, reflecting the fact that imports in 1950 were generally much below the amount anticipated from growth in gross product during 1929-50.

It also seems that import substitution has been more important to industrial output in countries which already possessed a sizable industrial sector in 1929 than to those which industrialized later. This relation follows from the higher incomes and consequently greater propensities to import manufactures of Argentina and Chile than of Brazil and Mexico, as indicated by their respective import coefficients in 1929. In the latter countries the low initial level of consumption of manufactures meant that more of the output of new industries represented additions to supply rather than just a shift among sources.

The amount of import saving may also be compared to anticipated imports at the end of a period, to show what share of those imports has been replaced by domestic output. Except in Mexico, this share ranges from 44 to 63 percent for the period 1929-60, being somewhat lower in every country for the interval 1929-50 and generally very low in 1950-60. A separate calculation for the latter period, using 1950 as a base, shows appreciably more substitution but, with the exception of Mexico, the share is still much below that observed before 1950.

Taken together, these measures indicate that until 1950 import substitution accounted for a relatively large share of industrial growth in the principal Latin American countries and was successful in replacing about 40 percent of the imports that might otherwise have been anticipated. In the next decade substitution was less significant; only a small further amount of imports was replaced and a larger share of the output of manufactures went to increase supplies. Both measures can also be calculated on the assumption that in the absence of substitution, imports would form a constant share of supplies of manufactures (see Section II of table A-4). These supplies grew more rapidly than gross domestic product in Brazil, Colombia, and Mexico, so the share of increased industrial output attributed to substitution is higher by this measure, doubling in Brazil and Mexico. In Argentina and Chile industrial supply grew less rapidly than gross product, despite the great emphasis given to substitution of manufactures. The share of anticipated imports replaced is appreciably higher in Brazil and Mexico when supply rather than gross product is the base; in the other three countries there is little difference.

The measures thus far discussed take no account of import substitution in sectors other than manufacturing and do not distinguish among different classes of manufactured goods. Some information on these aspects of the process may be gained by considering the composition of imports. Data on the distribution of imports by type are available for Latin America as a whole only for the postwar period,

and show little change. It is evident, however, from data for eight major countries over the entire period 1928 to 1962 that there has occurred a profound and relatively permanent transformation of the structure of the region's imports (see table A-5). More recent information shows a sharp reduction in capital goods imports in Argentina and Brazil and relative stability of the import structure in five other countries. Data are not available for the region as a whole.

The most pronounced change is the decline in the share of consumer goods; in several countries where these formerly were about half of total imports the share is now in the vicinity of 10 percent and there are no imports at all for many classes of goods. This decline has to a large degree been balanced by a relative increase in imports of capital goods, especially industrial machinery and equipment. In several countries goods of this type now account for at least 30 percent of all imports, and they are important even to countries such as Cuba, Peru, and Venezuela, which still have rather little industry. This shift from consumption goods to capital equipment is a principal consequence of what may be regarded as the first phase of import substitution, when emphasis is given to the relatively simple consumer goods industries. In a second phase substitution proceeds to the manufacture of equipment required by these industries, and in a third phase to the production of the raw materials and intermediate goods used as inputs to the consumer and capital goods industries. These phases cannot be clearly distinguished when they occur at different times for different products and industries, so they show up in the composition of imports in only a few cases. For example, although capital goods industries are now fairly large in Argentina, Brazil, and Mexico especially, only in Brazil has the share of machinery and equipment in total imports fallen steadily and significantly. The third phase may also have begun by 1965 in Argentina, Peru, Mexico, and Chile. In Venezuela this share also fell, primarily because imports of equipment for the oil industry were unusually high in 1948-49 and 1957-58.

If consumer and capital goods are considered together to represent all manufactured goods, it appears that the share of manufactures in total imports has declined slightly in most countries. There is somewhat less uniformity in the experience of the various groups of nonmanufactures. In five countries — Brazil, Chile, Colombia, Peru, and Venezuela — there has been a marked decline in imports of metals. Steel industries were established after World War II in all these countries, but the initial decline preceded domestic steel production and appears rather to reflect wartime and postwar steel shortages. The existence of domestic industries has undoubtedly kept the share low in recent years, however. Import substitution in metals is limited in Argentina by a shortage of resources and the need to import iron ore for the steel industry, and in Mexico by heavy use of imported ferrous scrap.

For Latin America as a whole petroleum imports rose sharply during the 1950s, chiefly as a result of increases in Argentina and Brazil. The subsequent decline partly reflects import substitution through the establishment of refineries in some countries which shifted from imports of products to lower valued crude oil.

TABLE A–5. Latin America and Selected Countries: Percentage Distribution of Imports by Type

Country	Year	Import Coefficient[a]	Consumer Goods	Raw Materials and Intermediate Products			Capital Goods[c]
				Fuels	Nonmetallic[b]	Metallic	
Argentina	1928	17.8	50	14		17	19
	1938	12.1	38	5	16	15	26
	1948-49	11.2	13	11	39	9	28
	1957-58	5.8	13	20	32	15	20
	1962	7.1	8	8	25	11	47
	1965	10.3	8	11	36	20	24
Brazil	1928	11.3	46	19		17	18
	1938	6.2	21	8	22	16	33
	1948-49	6.6	16	11	28	6	39
	1957-58	5.8	8	18	30	6	38
	1962	4.5	7	16	34	7	36
	1965	5.1	8	20	36	9	27
Chile	1928	31.2	42	21		17	19
	1938	14.9	30	10	16	23	25
	1948-49	11.5	12	9	38	5	36
	1957-58	9.5	17	8	36	3	36
	1962	11.3	17	6	35	3	40
	1965	12.3	16	5	40	4	34
Colombia	1928	18.0	56	11		15	18
	1938	11.0	32	2	25	17	24
	1948-49	10.6	20	4	33	4	39
	1957-58	8.2	13	3	46	5	33
	1962	8.8	13	2	39	7	38
	1964	17.2	12	1	36	8	41
Cuba	1928		64	19		9	8
	1938		54	30		8	8
	1948-49		52	7	25	5	11
	1957-58		38	10	27	5	20
	1962		24	11		38	28
Mexico	1928	14.2	45	20		15	20
	1938	7.0	30	3	30	15	22
	1948-49	8.5	17	4	33	10	35
	1957-58	7.8	14	6	36	11	33
	1962	6.8	14	3	35	15	44
	1965	11.7	10	2		47	41
Peru	1928		47	18		17	19
	1938		27	30		15	29
	1948-49	9.6	22	2	37	5	34
	1957-58	16.1	27	3	30	5	36
	1962	13.6	22	3	30	5	41
	1965	27.3	21	3	40	6	30
Venezuela	1928		43	13		23	21
	1938	22.1	39	11		19	31
	1948-49	37.8	30	1	21	5	43
	1957-58	40.5	24	1	23	6	46
	1962	21.4	39	1	28	6	25
	1965	15.8	38	1	27	6	28
Total Latin America	1948-49	10.2[d]	22.0	7.4	30.1	6.8	31.9
	1957-58	9.9[d]	18.7	10.0	27.2	7.3	31.5
	1962	8.7[d,e]	18.8	7.1	30.5	7.5	34.8

Sources: ECLA: *Inflation and Growth*, vol. II, pp. 264-65; *The Economic Development of Latin America in the Postwar Period*, p. 20; *Statistical Bulletin for Latin America*, III, no. 1 (February 1966), pp. 89-90, 101-18; *Economic Bulletin for Latin America, Statistical Supplement*, V (November 1960), pp. 70-78; *The Process of Industrialization in Latin America, Statistical Annex*, p. 5; *Economic Survey of Latin America, 1965*, pp. 30, 74-75; *Statistical Bulletin for Latin America*, IV, no. 2 (September 1967), pp. 171-79; and *Economic Survey of Latin America, 1966*, pp. 23, 189.

Notes: Figures for 1928 and 1938 refer to imports from Europe and the United States only, at 1948 prices. Figures for 1948-49 and 1955-57 are based on 1955 prices for Argentina, Brazil, Chile, Colombia, Mexico, and Venezuela. All other postwar data are based on current values of imports, in dollars.

Gaps in series indicate that data are not available, not comparable, or not applicable, or that the amount is negligibly small.

[a]Imports of goods and services as a percentage of gross domestic product at market prices. 1929 figure is used for 1928; unweighted averages used for 1948-49 and 1957-58.

[b]Includes construction materials, which in 1958 and 1962 includes some metallic materials.

[c]Machinery and equipment for agriculture, industry, transport, and communications; excludes construction materials.

[d]Excludes Cuba.

[e]1961 figure; 1962 not available for Uruguay.

In summary, the process of import substitution which Latin America has experienced in the last few decades has resulted in a relative reduction of imports of manufactures, particularly of consumer goods, and a shift toward imports of raw materials, especially non-metallic materials and fuels. In order to sustain this process it has been necessary to devote increasing attention to import substitution of primary materials and the development of domestic resources. Thus although the natural resource sector has given way to manufacturing as the most dynamic sector of the economy it has gained in importance as a source of inputs to industry and of domestic consumption. In addition it has retained its role as the chief – virtually the only – source of foreign exchange. The internal transformation of the Latin American economy since the 1920s is reflected in the composition of the region's imports but not in the composition of exports.

The Export Sector

The sixteen primary commodities studied here accounted for about 63 percent of total Latin American exports in the 1930s. The share rose to two-thirds in the late 1940s and to slightly over 70 percent in the early 1960s. If a small number of other resource products, chiefly temperate foodstuffs and agricultural raw materials, is included, the share shows a very slight decline from a level of about 80 percent (see table A-6). Over three decades the same few products have dominated the region's exports, their total weight in trade being nearly constant despite a large shift from agricultural to mineral commodities and sharp changes in the importance of some individual products. Among the mineral products there has also been a great increase in the degree of processing before export.

If individual countries and products are considered more shifts appear, but there is still surprisingly little change. In at least five countries where two or more commodities accounted for 60 percent or greater of total exports in 1937-38, the same products provided almost exactly the same share of exports in 1965-66 (see table A-7). In several other countries the leading commodities of the 1930s have lost ground by some 10 to 20 percentage points, but still account for the bulk of exports. Significant shifts have occurred in only seven countries. If the comparison is restricted to the years 1937-38 to 1955-56 this number drops to three or four, since much of the change has been due to the development of cotton for export in Central America within the last decade. A decline in the shares of traditional exports does not necessarily indicate diversification, since the degree of dependence on one or two commodities may be greater now than three decades ago. Finally, the new exports developed during this period are virtually all primary commodities also: cotton in several countries, bananas in Ecuador, fishmeal in Peru. The concentration of exports on a few resource products continues to be characteristic of all the economies of the region, even those whose internal structure has undergone the greatest changes and which are now considerably industrialized. At least for some countries, the degree of concentration has been increased by public policies which discriminate against the

TABLE A–6. Exports of Selected Commodities as Percentage Shares of Total Latin American Exports, 1934-38, 1946-51, and 1963-64

Commodity or Product Group	1934-38	1946-51	1963-64[a]
Temperate foodstuffs	17.2	10.8	8.2
Wheat and wheat flour	5.1	4.2	1.7
Maize	6.3	2.0	2.0
Meat[b]	5.4	4.0	4.0
Butter	0.1	0.2	0.1
Cattle	0.3	0.4	0.4[c]
Tropical foodstuffs	21.3	30.0	21.2
Coffee	12.8	17.4	15.0
Cocoa	1.2	1.6	0.8
Sugar	6.1	10.2	3.3
Bananas	1.2[d]	0.8[e]	2.1
Agricultural raw materials	12.6	11.8	7.6
Cotton	4.5	4.7	4.3
Wool	4.3	3.7	2.0
Hides	3.5	3.2	0.5[f]
Oils and oilseeds	0.3[g]	0.2[g]	0.8
Forest products	1.0	2.3	1.0
Timber and manufactures	0.3	1.2	0.8
Quebracho	0.7	1.1	0.2
Fishery products	0.0[h]	0.1[h]	2.4
Petroleum	18.2	17.3	26.4
Crude	15.5	14.9	16.3
Refined	2.7	2.4	10.1
Iron and steel	0.0	0.2	2.9
Ore	0.0	0.1	2.8
Metal	0.0	0.1	0.1
Copper	4.7	3.4	4.9
Ore	0.3	0.3	0.2
Metal	4.4	3.1	4.7
Lead	1.5	1.3	0.7
Ore	0.3	0.2	0.3
Metal	1.2	1.1	0.4
Zinc	1.0	0.6	0.6
Ore	0.8	0.4	0.4
Metal	0.2	0.2	0.2
Tin, predominantly ore	1.6	1.0	0.5
Nitrates	1.4[d]	0.8[j]	0.3
Total, Selected Products	80.5	79.6	76.7
Agriculture, forest and fishery	52.1	55.0	40.4
Mineral	28.4	24.6	36.3
Crude or concentrated	19.9	17.7	20.8
Refined or smelted[k]	8.5	6.9	15.5
Total, 16 Resource Products[m]	63.2	66.9	70.4

Sources: 1934-38 and 1946-51 – ECLA, *Inter Latin American Trade: Current Problems* doc. E/CN.12/423 (UN: 1957), pp. 90-92. 1963-64 – ECLA, *Economic Survey of Latin America, 1965*, p. 68. Supplementary information from ECLA, *Economic Survey of Latin America, 1951-52*, p. 138, and *1953*, p. 51; and from chaps. 5, 8, 14, and 15 of this volume. Data from different sources may not agree.

[a] Excludes Cuba; the share for sugar is most affected.
[b] Beef, mutton, pork, poultry, and offal, in all forms.
[c] Estimate.
[d] Estimated from data for 1937-38.
[e] 1947-51 average.
[f] Untanned hides only.
[g] Oilseeds only, including some edible oils.
[h] Canned and processed products only.
[j] Average for 1947 and 1950.
[k] Includes all wrought metal, some of which is classified as manufactures in the Standard International Trade Classification (SITC) category 6.
[m] Wheat, beef, all tropical foodstuffs listed, cotton, timber, fishery products, petroleum, and all metals listed.

expansion or diversification of traditional exports. Exchange rates and licensing procedures have been used in Brazil, for example, to divert supplies of several products, such as cocoa, cotton, sugar, and beef, from the export to the domestic market: these policies not only concentrated exports on coffee but appreciably slowed the total growth

TABLE A-7. Exports of Leading Primary Commodities in 1937-38 as Percentage Shares of Total Exports of Latin American Countries, 1937-38 to 1965-66

Country	Product	Unweighted Average Share (%) of Exports in				
		1937-38	1946-47	1955-56	1963-64	1965-66
Argentina	Wheat and corn	37	24	26	23	31
	Meat	19	15	24	24	10
	Wool	9	8	13	10	8
	Hides	7	8	6	5	4
	Oilseeds	13	19	3	3	2
	Total	84	78	72	65	69
Bolivia	Tin	65	71[a]	56	71	68
	Silver	8	6[a]	6	6	4
Brazil	Coffee	44	36	64	53	44
	Cotton	19	15	8	8	6
Chile	Copper	54	56	64	54	72
	Nitrates	21	15	12[b]	6[b]	4[b]
Colombia	Coffee	63	77	81	70	64
	Petroleum	25	14	11	15	15
Costa Rica	Coffee	51	47	48	45	40
	Bananas	27	28	40	25	23
	Cocoa	10	7	6	4	2
Cuba	Sugar	78	81	79	86[c]	
	Tobacco	9	7	7	4[c]	
Dom. Rep.	Sugar	61	57	41	55	53
	Cocoa	14	12	16	9	7
	Coffee	9	6	26	14	16
	Tobacco	2	10	4	7	6
	Total	85	84	87	85	82
Ecuador	Cocoa	32	23	16	18	10
	Coffee	15	7	23	20	19
	Petroleum	18	3	(c)	(c)	1
El Salvador	Coffee	94	83	82	50	49
Guatemala	Coffee	67	59	69	73	46
	Bananas	26	23	14	10	2
Haiti	Coffee	52[d]	36[e]	69	43[f]	52
	Sisal	8[d]	28[e]	15	10[f]	6
	Sugar	10[d]	9[e]	6	8[f]	9
Honduras	Bananas	68	46	56	37	47
	Silver	17	12	4	4	3
Mexico	Nonferrous metals	40	18	20	8	7
	Silver	17	7	3[d]	2	3
	Petroleum	14	3	6	4	3
	Cotton and henequen	5	12[e]	32[g]	21	18
	Total	76	40	61	35	31
Nicaragua	Coffee	49	40[a]	39	19	17
	Bananas	17	2[a]	(d)	2	1
Panama	Bananas	73	66	73	42	50
	Cocoa	16	11	2	1	
Paraguay	Cotton	32	16[a]	15	8	6
	Quebracho and maté	22	17[a]	17	8	9
	Hides	10	10[a]	5	3	4
	Meat	6	14[a]	10	28	30
	Total	65	57[a]	47	47	49

TABLE A–7 – Continued

Country	Product	Unweighted Average Share (%) of Exports in				
		1937-38	1946-47	1955-56	1963-64	1965-66
Peru	Petroleum	35	10	9	1	1
	Cotton	22	28	27	15	12
	Copper	17	6[a]	11	16	22
	Sugar	9	30	12	11	6
	Total	83	71	59	43	41
Uruguay	Wool	45	39	59	45	46
	Meat	19	19[a]	7	31	28
Venezuela	Petroleum	91	94	95	93	93
	Coffee	6	3	2	1	1

Sources: IMF, *International Financial Statistics*, II, no. 1 (January 1949) and supp. to 1966/67 issues, XI, no. 1 (January 1968) and XXI, no. 10 (October 1968). ECLA, *Economic Survey of Latin America*, 1963, p. 274 (Cuba). Universidad de Chile, Instituto de Economía, *La Economía de Chile en el Período 1950-1963,* p. 176. Banco Central de Chile, *Balanza de Pagos de Chile,* 1963 and 1964. Mexico, Nacional Financiera, *La Economía Mexicana en Cifras,* 1965, p. 210. UN, *Yearbook of International Trade Statistics, 1966.*

[a]1946 only.
[b]Includes iodine.
[c]1962-63.
[d]1937 only.

[e]1948.
[f]1963 only.
[g]Includes henequen for 1956 only.

of exports and thus accentuated the process of import substitution.[34] Policy obstacles to the export of other commodities in other countries are discussed in several chapters of Part Two.

The absence of any fundamental change in the region's export structure also largely reflects the nature of Latin America's industrialization. Almost the whole of the region's industrial output consists of goods which were formerly imported or for which there would be an import demand in the absence of domestic production. There has been very little development of manufacturing for export.

The share of manufacturing output exported can be computed accurately only from an input-output table which is sufficiently disaggregated, and such information is not available for any Latin American country for recent years. A rough measure can be constructed by comparing exports of manufactures to total value added in manufacturing. The inclusion of unwrought metals in manufactures would make this share about 30 percent in Chile and in Peru, and the inclusion of processed foodstuffs would make it between 5 and 10 percent in Argentina. When these products are excluded, the share is 2 percent or less in every country except Mexico, where manufactures are a large share of total exports (see table A-8). Exports of manufactures form a still smaller share of the total value of manufactured output, probably 1 percent or less in all countries except Argentina, Chile, and Mexico. By comparison, the measure shown here is about 12 percent for the United States, 33 percent for Japan, and 61 percent for the United Kingdom where virtually all exports consist of manufactures and exports are one-fifth as large as gross domestic product.

In the first instance this type of industrialization was simply a reaction to the trade crisis of the 1930s, and depended on the existence of a sizable market for manufactures. The continued dominance of import substitution in industrial growth is a consequence of at least three other factors. First, it is much easier to produce for a protected market than to compete with more advanced countries in a relatively free export market. Requirements of cost and quality can be less stringent and investors are more likely to respond to opportunities. Second, when a developing country does become competitive in world markets for certain goods, the advanced countries which must be its principal market may erect tariffs or other barriers to protect their own industries. This possibility arises especially for labor-intensive manufactures, in which the exporting country may have an advantage because of low labor costs, but which represent potentially sizable unemployment in importing countries. Even when nominal tariffs are low, the effective tariff, or the degree of protection afforded to the value added in manufacturing, can be quite high.

Finally, import substitution can provide relatively rapid industrial growth and thereby promote satisfactory expansion of the whole economy over several decades. Where shortages of foreign exchange have held imports below the level of demand, import substitution can also release and benefit from a sort of multiplier effect, as it meets a previously frustrated demand in addition to the former effective demand.

Given the relative ease and advantages of import substitution and the difficulties of alternative means of industrialization, it is hardly surprising that Latin America's industry has been directed almost exclusively to the domestic market. Most developing countries have followed the same strategy. For a small country, however, import substitution cannot be carried very far because of economies of scale in basic industries. Even in large countries the process eventually slows down. Latin America appears to have reached a

[34] See N. H. Leff, "Export Stagnation and Autarkic Development in Brazil, 1947-1962," *Quarterly Journal of Economics,* 81, no. 2 (May 1967).

TABLE A-8. Exports of Manufactures as Percentage Shares of Total Exports and of Value Added in Manufacturing, Selected Latin American Countries, 1963

Country	Share (%) of GDP Represented by		Exports of Manufactures as Share (%) of	
	Value Added in Manufacturing (1)	Total Exports (2)	Total Exports (3)	Value Added in Manufacturing (4)
Argentina	30.4	11.0	5.20	1.9
Brazil	24.4	5.8	2.82	0.7
Chile	19.3	13.0	2.93	2.0
Colombia	17.7	7.9	3.28	1.5
Cuba	29.0[a]	15.7	1.21	0.7
Ecuador	16.1	15.7	0.92	0.9
Mexico	21.3	6.3	13.40	4.0
Peru	18.4	22.2	0.90	1.1
Venezuela	12.9[b]	28.0[c]	0.47[c]	1.0

Sources: UN, *Statistical Yearbook, 1965*, pp. 542-45; *Yearbook of International Trade Statistics, 1963* through *1966*. ECLA, *Economic Survey of Latin America, 1965*, pp. 24-25. IMF, *International Financial Statistics*, supplement to 1966/67 issues.

Notes:
(1) Value added in manufacturing as a share of gross domestic product.
(2) Exports as a share of gross domestic product.
(3) Sum of exports in SITC categories 5 (chemicals), 6 (manufactures classified by material), 7 (machinery and transport equipment) and 8 (other manufactures), less exports of unwrought metal, metallic oxides and uncut gems from SITC category 6, as a share of total exports.
(4) (3) $\times$ (2)/(1): exports of manufactures, as defined in (3), as a share of total value added in manufacturing.

[a] Excludes value added in sugar processing.
[b] Data for 1965.
[c] Data for 1966.

stage at which further import substitution within national boundaries is difficult and does not promise continued satisfactory growth.[35] Thus the type of economic development which the region has experienced in the last few decades may be coming to an end.

Neither the nature of the next phase of Latin America's economic history nor the means by which it will be reached can be predicted with any certainty, but it seems clear that the principal change must be the development of manufactures for export, or the integration of the industrial and export sectors to a much greater degree than at present. This is most likely to occur through the economic integration of the region, particularly through the intended evolution of the present Latin American Free Trade Area (LAFTA) into a common market, perhaps including the Central American Common Market. A development of this sort would have three implications of importance to the natural resource sector.

First, the degree of domestic processing of raw materials would increase more rapidly as the industrial sector recovered its dynamism. If exports of primary commodities continued to grow quite slowly, the share of output processed within the region would also rise more quickly. Second, manufactures would constitute an increasing and possibly large share of exports. If manufactured goods were exported only within the region, as is essentially the case

now, primary products would continue to dominate exports for a considerable period. The share of exports represented by manufactures would increase much more, however, if the reduction of costs associated with integration permitted exports of industrial goods to the advanced countries or if the advanced nations were to grant trade preferences to the manufactured exports of less developed countries. Finally, the distribution of production of resource products would change if there were free trade within Latin America. Integration should eventually result in considerably more trade in raw materials and intermediate goods, with greater concentration of production in each. Efficiencies and costs vary greatly among Latin American countries in both the primary and secondary sectors, so that integration under competitive conditions would require a substantial redistribution of productive capacity in both sectors.

In one sense, the next few decades of the region's economic development will almost certainly continue the strategy and experience the individual countries have followed since the 1930s: import substitution, this time on a regional scale, will still be a major element of industrial growth. However, the structure of exports, which has changed little in four centuries, may be considerably transformed by an increase in the share of manufactures. The composition of imports is, initially, at least, less likely to undergo substantial change. The resource sector may ultimately yield to industry its predominant role in earning foreign exchange. The result would be an economy in which the primary sector finally had ceased to be a sector apart from the rest and had become fully integrated with the rest of the Latin American economy.

[35] The issues raised by this situation will be discussed at greater length in chap. 2. For a summary view of the problem and references to recent literature on the subject, see Grunwald, "Some Reflections . . . ," sect. V.

Chapter 2

MAJOR ISSUES AND PROBLEMS

In the course of Latin American development, the resource sector more than any other has given rise to economic, political, and social controversy. The issues that have emerged have taken an important place in Latin American policy making for several decades, preoccupying the intellectual community, as well as statesmen.[1] While this concern reflects the importance of natural resources in the development of every country in the region, its ramifications go far beyond the relations of resources to economic growth.

Deep-seated political factors enter the debate. Nationalism of various kinds and non-economic welfare goals mingle in an often confused pattern with the objective of economic growth. The non-economic aspects of the issues remain poorly articulated, if they are expressed at all, while economic aims are enunciated conspicuously. For the pure economic-theorist who is interested only in economic efficiency, it is relatively easy to separate facts from fancy; for the scholar who is interested in understanding development processes, it is very difficult to recognize the true rationale of policy statements and actions that may be expressed in economic terms but often have different objectives. In the latter case policies cannot be evaluated by their apparent aims.

The purpose of this chapter is modest. The issues as viewed by Latin Americans will be stated and discussed. They will be examined also in the light of the information accumulated in the commodity chapters of this book, but there will be no formal testing of hypotheses against empirical data. The evidence presented in this study is not sufficiently complete nor are the issues formulated in precise enough terms to lend themselves to rigorous socioeconomic-political analysis.

[1]The issues and problems discussed in this chapter are based in varying degrees on the commodity analysis of Part Two. Particular attention has been given in chaps. 4, 8, 10, and 14 of Part Two (Copper, Petroleum, Coffee, and Wheat) to illuminate the points made here. For instance, the extensive section on Argentina in the Wheat chapter illustrates many of the issues and problems of resource development which are treated in general terms in the present chapter.

Natural Resources and Economic Growth: The Image

The issues that have arisen basically derive from the widely held Latin American view, discussed in the previous chapter, that exclusive focus on the exploitation of natural resources will not achieve desired development objectives and that industrialization is the engine of modern economic growth. The concentration on primary production, it has been claimed, creates an economic and social structure which, if not antagonistic, at least is not conducive to industrialization. Several factors underlie this assertion: they concern the type of infrastructure that has emerged from a concentration on primary production, weak linkages with other sectors of the economy, the great dependence of foreign exchange receipts and government revenues on natural resource products, the instability of their earnings, an alleged long-term deterioration of raw material prices compared with those of manufactured goods, and the relatively significant role of foreign interests; all these factors have combined to deprive Latin American economies of dynamism in economic growth.

Because natural resources have been developed to a large extent for the purpose of exports, the infrastructure also has been outward oriented. Railroads and highways were built to connect the mine or plantation with the sea, and ports were constructed for raw material exports. Energy development and even basic "social overhead capital" such as schools and hospitals have been geared to the mine and plantation. Such an infrastructure, it is argued, is not adapted for economic development through industrialization. The development of industry requires not only a transportation and communications network which connects the centers within the country but also a more general increase and balance in "overhead capital" in order to maximize the mobility of the factors of production.

The economic linkages of natural resource exploitation in general are very weak. One of the characteristics of mining operations and plantations is that they are often located in geographically isolated regions. Therefore, the labor force employed in the mines is generally separated from the commercial centers of the economy and the mining and sometimes the estate communities tend to be self-contained units. Their requirements of supplies from the domestic economy (the "backward linkages") have been relatively small until recently, and on the other side, the resource products — with some exceptions — have not yet been important as inputs for domestic production ("forward linkages").

Furthermore, because of the high productivity existing in the export resource sector, the proportion of the total labor force employed there is usually small (see chapter 1, table A-2). Venezuela and Chile, for instance, are among the region's most resource-oriented economies; petroleum accounts for about one-quarter of Venezuela's gross domestic product and almost 90 percent of its total exports, and copper about one-twentieth of Chile's gross domestic product and two-thirds of its total exports. Yet the petroleum sector in Venezuela and copper in Chile employ less than 1 percent of all production workers in each of these countries. Although wage levels in the export resource sector are much higher than in the rest of the economy, wage payments to petroleum production workers are estimated to constitute less than 5 percent of Venezuela's total wage bill and copper wages about 2 percent of Chile's production labor income.[2] Hence, mining payrolls are not likely to produce a great impact on the economy.

Meanwhile, subsistence agriculture has accounted for not only by far the major part of agricultural employment, but also for a substantial proportion of the total labor force. Thus, extreme poverty and economic stagnation have existed side by side with relatively well-to-do, modern export sectors.

A large part of the nonwage income in the resource sector has flowed out of Latin America and therefore has not contributed to the national income of countries in the region. This is particularly true of mineral development which, because of its large capital requirements in capital-poor economies, has attracted a considerable amount of foreign investment. Remittances of profits and amortization charges and the procurement of equipment and supplies abroad have left the host country with only part of the export proceeds. Even in countries where natural resources have been exploited by domestic private capital on a large scale, profits often have found their way into foreign bank accounts rather than into internal domestic investment because of lack of confidence in the national economy.

These factors — that only part of the export proceeds accrues to the country, the special infrastructure, the small labor force, and the weak economic linkages — have caused the spillover effects of natural resource exploitation for exports to be comparatively small.

The resource-based economy is said to be uncongenial to growth also because of its low supply elasticity (i.e., the response of the quantity supplied in relation to price change). The special infrastructure and poor linkages mentioned previously lower the flexibility of industrial production, while the distribution of income and property and the structure of ownership fostered by this type of economy also make the supply elasticity within the resource sectors small. The vast subsistence sector in agriculture hardly responds to price stimuli while the concentration of large landholdings in the hands of a few is also not conducive to flexibility in output. But land reform is a long-run process and it cannot be expected to raise the elasticity of supply quickly.

It has also been argued that in mining, foreign ownership has added to the inelasticity of supply of certain raw materials in individual countries. Since the interests of foreign companies operating in Latin America generally are not confined to the host country but extend to their home countries and perhaps other countries as well, their production decisions are motivated by much wider considerations than the concerns of the host countries. A foreign enterprise will not increase output to maximize the profits of its subsidiary in a given country if this should contravene the company's international interests. In view of the large capital requirements for expansion of mining capacity, nationalism and the resulting unfavorable "investment climate" also have contributed to supply inelasticity.

The poor viability of a resource-based economy is further accentuated by the problems of demand. Until very recently natural resources, except for some temperate zone and subsistence farm products, have been exploited nearly exclusively for export and production has depended primarily on foreign demand. Two aspects of this dependency have been distinguished by Latin American analysts: a short-run instability of demand which induces fluctuations in prices, output, and earnings; and a long-run weakening of demand relative to the demand for processed goods. Short-run fluctuations are said to be due mainly to vagaries in foreign purchases and are magnified because of an inelasticity in foreign demand alleged to characterize many of the region's traditional products.

A source of the instability in the value of primary goods production and exports has been the exogenous shocks that have hit the Latin American economy from time to time. There were three major ones in recent history: the world depression of the 1930s, the greatest single dislocation, when raw material exports collapsed; the Second World War, which meant the loss of European markets; and the early 1950s, which marked the recovery of Europe and the Korean War. The effect of the first shock was so profound that, with the major exception of Venezuela, the per capita purchasing power of exports has not recovered its predepression levels in Latin America since 1929 (see table A-9). Each shock has required an adjustment process, but because of the nature of raw material production there is often a substantial time lag and the process cannot be smooth.

This can be seen clearly for some of the tropical crops, particularly coffee. It takes about eight to ten years for a coffee tree to come into full production. Investments in new plantings stimulated by one shock, may come to fruition to coincide with a new event which pulls in the opposite direction. Although this inelasticity of supply is

[2] For data on Chile, see: Instituto de Economía de la Universidad de Chile, *Desarrollo Económico de Chile 1940-1956* (Santiago, 1956); and *La Economía de Chile en el Período 1950-1963* (Santiago, 1963). For Venezuela, see: Jorge Salazar, "Primary Export Activities as Leading Sectors in Economic Growth: the Venezuelan Case" (Ph.D. diss., University of California, Berkeley, 1967).

TABLE A–9. Latin America and Selected Countries: Indices of Per Capita Purchasing Power of Exports, 1928-1966
(1958=100)

Year	Argentina	Brazil	Chile	Colombia	Mexico[a]	Venezuela	Latin America
1928/29	340	172	243	127	183	27	132
1932	192	90	44	92	55	29	67
1940	127	74	106	87	78	32	67
1950	144	156	105	132	124	86	117
1960	99	119	103	109	99	102	104
1965/66	123	129	115	100	112	100	113[b]

Sources: ECLA, *Inflation and Growth* (1961), tables II-9, II-10, II-11 (adjusted to 1958 as base year). UN, *Statistical Bulletin for Latin America*, III, no. 1 (1966), tables 3, 30. UN, *Statistical Bulletin for Latin America*, V, no. 1 (1968), tables 7, 27.

Note: Data from 1928/29 to 1950 are adjusted by the terms of trade (relation of export prices to import prices). Data for 1960 and 1965/66 are based on quantum figures for exports, because terms of trade data were not available.

[a]Includes net earnings from tourist trade.
[b]1965 only.

not important for some agricultural crops, it affects the production of most primary goods where it takes time to expand capacity. Thus, overproduction alternates with supply shortages and sharp swings in prices appear inevitable.

The long-run aspect of the demand for raw materials is that the rate of growth of their exports appears to be limited. Discussion focuses on the question of whether the long-run position of the developing countries deteriorates (or would deteriorate) relative to the developed countries because of a concentration on raw material exports. Latin American thinking, particularly as molded by the writings of Raul Prebisch, the former head of the United Nations Economic Commission for Latin America, has played a major role in fomenting this controversy.[3] The debate covers a wide range of factors but in essence it can be reduced to two major theses: the possible expansion in the volume of raw material exports from the developing to the industrial countries is limited and the terms of trade of the developing countries tend to decline in the long run.

There are various forces that are alleged to underlie this situation:

a) The income elasticity of import demand for raw materials among the industrial countries (i.e., their response in the quantity of imports demanded to changes in import prices) is low relative to the income elasticity of import demand for processed goods among the developing countries.
b) Increases in productivity in the production of raw materials do not accrue in full measure to the less developed

exporting countries but are passed on through a fall in relative prices to the industrial importers.
c) Technical progress in developed countries causes:
  i) specific raw materials to be increasingly replaced by ubiquitous materials as synthetics come into greater use;
  ii) the value of raw material inputs to become a smaller share of the value of manufacturing output as industrial development progresses and research and development become a greater part of the value of the product.
d) The industrial countries protect their raw material producers through import restrictions of various types.

In this way an image has been created in Latin American countries that the contribution of natural resources to modern economic development is limited at best over the long run and may even be negative if too much of the economy is geared to the exploitation of natural resources for exports. This image is colored by the importance of foreign interests in this sector both as owners of production and distribution facilities, and because of the sector's dependence on foreign demand.

Some Empirical Notes

As with all generalizations, the issues which Latin American economists claim to be intimately connected with natural resource exploitation do not equally involve all commodities or all countries in the region. A review of the individual commodity chapters in Part Two reveals a mixed situation: the experiences of some countries with some commodities seem to support the contentions made; others do not. Not only do the problems differ among the various products studied, but often also among countries for the same product.

The main issues of natural resource development have been conceived by Latin Americans principally in terms of foreign demand problems. The available evidence assembled here and elsewhere suggests that, with a few notable exceptions in tropical agriculture, supply problems have been more important in holding back the natural resource sector's contribution toward economic development. Particularly in the case of temperate zone foods, output has

[3]Raul Prebisch: "Commercial Policy in the Underdeveloped Countries," *American Economic Review*, XLIX, no. 2 (May 1959); "The Economic Development of Latin America and Its Principal Problems," *Economic Bulletin for Latin America*, II, no. 1 (February 1962); (this is a reprint of his article on this subject written in 1949); *Toward a Dynamic Development Policy for Latin America* (UN, April 14, 1963). The most recent related works Prebisch wrote as Secretary-General of the United Nations Conference on Trade and Development (UNCTAD) are: *Towards a New Trade Policy for Development* (UN, 1964) and *Towards a Global Strategy of Development* (UN, 1968).

hardly been able to keep up with population growth, much less with the rising demands of an urbanizing society (see table A-10). As a consequence, in some countries export surpluses have dwindled and in others the need for increasing food imports has burdened the economy. Chile, for example, which was once self-sufficient in temperate zone food products and even exported them occasionally, has had to devote over one-quarter of its scarce foreign exchange earnings to the purchase of needed food supplies from abroad in recent years.

Linkages

With the exception of coal, all of the natural resource products studied in this volume contribute to national economic development in general through foreign exchange earnings and tax revenues. However, the specific linkages with the rest of the economy vary from one commodity to another. For some products the linkages with industrialization have been very strong indeed.

The use of local raw materials in domestic industrial production became important first in the case of cotton. The production of textiles based upon domestic resources dates back well into the nineteenth century. With the exception of coal and wood, the industrial use of other natural resource products is of more recent origin. Forestry long has been an important source of energy and has also supplied the construction and furniture industries, but its most important role has only come recently with the emergence of the pulp and paper industry in several Latin American countries. Petroleum and iron ore have become probably the region's most important raw materials contributing directly to Latin American industrialization. The development of fisheries has expanded enormously during the past decade but their use for domestic animal feed and fertilizer production is still in its infancy.

A large share of temperate zone agricultural output has always been processed domestically. The Argentine meat packing industry is the outstanding example. In addition to export trade, temperate zone agriculture has been linked closely with national consumption.

The direct economic linkages of most other natural resource products are very weak. Only a small proportion of tropical agricultural products are consumed or processed in the region. Brazil tends to be an exception: the major part of banana and sugar production is consumed locally, about one-half of the cocoa output is ground locally, and, more recently, some coffee is processed domestically for export as "instant" coffee. The bulk of mining output is shipped abroad (see chapter 3, table B-1). As pointed out in the following chapter, processing is not strictly related to domestic consumption. For instance, while about one-third of the region's output of copper is refined domestically, only one-tenth is directly used as input for domestic industry.

Latin American agriculture and mining have only recently begun to utilize supplies and equipment produced within the region, so the "backward linkages," too, are still small. With the emergence of regional fertilizer, tractor, and other industries, natural resource development will increasingly draw on local products.[4] Government policy has already encouraged the national steel industries in Chile and Venezuela to supply copper and oil companies with milling equipment and steel pipes respectively.

Indirect linkages, however, have often been very substantial. The most important of these is the great contribution of the natural resource sector to government revenues. Taxes, foreign exchange differentials,[5] and other levies on primary goods production and exports have constituted a sizable share of public incomes. In nearly all countries they supply most of the foreign exchange for the public treasury.

Short-Run Fluctuations

This study does not attempt to test the assertions regarding the short-run instability of exports and the long-term deterioration of foreign demand. The price and quantity data collected in this volume and discussed in chapter 3 do indicate sharp year-to-year fluctuations. Of the sixteen commodities reviewed in table B-2, only five showed average year-to-year deviations of less than 10 percent (oil, coal, bananas, wheat, and fishmeal) and for only two (oil and coal) were the average deviations from the long-run average less than 10 percent. The majority of the prices studied showed average deviations of 20 percent.[6] Year-to-year fluctuations are also substantial in the volume of production and exports of Latin America's primary commodities.

Nevertheless, a recent study by Alasdair MacBean appears to show that export earnings of underdeveloped countries are not subject to significantly greater instability than those of developed countries, and that "export fluctuation has not been an important obstacle to their [developing countries'] economic development."[7]

---

[4]Detailed projections have been made for several industries. See Programa de Estudios Conjuntos sobre Integración Económica Latinoamericana (ECIEL – Program of Joint Studies on Latin American Economic Integration), in *Industrialization in a Latin American Common Market*, ed. Martin Carnoy (Brookings Institution, forthcoming).

[5]Difference between the rate of exchange received by the exporter and the rate at which the government (Central Bank) sells the foreign exchange earnings from exports. This mechanism played a strong role in Argentine export agriculture under Perón, in Chilean copper before the "New Deal" law of 1955, and in Brazilian coffee policy. In various forms this disguised tax has been applied in most Latin American countries at one time or another.

[6]The only other important Latin American export commodity, wool, which is not analyzed in this volume, showed an average price fluctuation from the 1950-59 average of 21 percent. See Joseph Grunwald, "Resource Aspects of Latin American Development" in *Natural Resources and International Development*, ed. Marion Clawson (Johns Hopkins Press for Resources for the Future, 1964), p. 328.

[7]Alasdair I. MacBean, *Export Instability and Economic Development* (Harvard University Press, 1967), p. 127. MacBean investigated a number of less developed countries, including some in Latin America. He finds that variations in export quantities have been particularly severe but have tended to be offset by price fluctuations. An examination of the commodities studied in this book appears to corroborate MacBean's finding that variations in export volume have been an important source of export instability, but also

MacBean's conclusions have been disputed on statistical and analytical grounds.[8] It is possible that Latin American export instability is greater than that found by MacBean in his analysis of a wider array of countries. What is more important is that MacBean's cross-section analysis does not take into consideration that a given instability may have a widely different impact on individual economies. The fluctuations in raw material prices or in export proceeds received may seriously affect certain developing countries, while similar fluctuations in industrial goods exports may not be felt significantly in developed nations.

Because a substantial portion of public income is based on taxes and other levies on primary goods, government operations are also affected by export fluctuations. Export instability is reflected in the variation of public revenues. The average annual variation of government revenues deriving from exports over the 1948-58 period was 26 percent in Colombia, 25 percent in Chile, 13 percent in El Salvador, 18 percent in Mexico, and 26 percent in Venezuela.[9] This instability increases the difficulties in planning public expenditures.

Terms of Trade

This is not the place to enter the much more complex argument about the long-run tendency of the terms of trade to move against primary products. Prebisch's theory has been explored and criticized in a number of works on trade and growth. Theoretical deficiencies have been exposed.[10] Adequate research is still lacking on this matter. Some specific studies have supported, but more have found that the

empirical evidence does not confirm, the Prebisch thesis. The data presented in chapter 3, table B-2, do not indicate a long-term decline in real prices of raw materials but perhaps the time period available for study (1925 to the mid-1960s) is still too short for this type of analysis. The data do show a decline in real primary goods prices from the peak of the early 1950s to the mid-1960s.

Nevertheless, there are indications that Latin America has not fared as well as other areas in respect to its external sector. United Nations studies show that the long-term expansion of raw materials exports has been considerably slower than the exports of manufactured products and that Latin American exports have grown even less than world primary goods exports. Thus, while the volume of world manufacturing exports rose by 103 percent between 1928 and the 1955-57 average, the volume of exports of primary products increased only 32 percent and Latin American exports only 28 percent during the same period (excluding Venezuela, Latin American exports decreased by 1 percent). Between 1955 and 1962 the value of world exports of manufactures jumped by 74 percent compared with a 30 percent rise in the value of primary goods exports and a 17 percent increase in Latin American exports (only 10 percent excluding Venezuela).[11]

A more recent study shows that since 1950 the terms of trade of Latin America have declined more than for any other area in the world.[12] Although using 1950 as a base year may be misleading for terms-of-trade measurements because it was a year of particularly favorable raw material prices, the point made here is not that the purchasing power of a Latin American unit of exports diminished, but that it decreased relative to the experience of other regions. This situation is also borne out by the fact that exports per capita of Latin America declined somewhat during this period, contrary to the trend in the rest of the world. Whatever the long-range trend, changes in the terms of trade are important for Latin American countries. For example, Vanek shows that a 10 percent decline in Colombia's terms of trade reduces that economy's growth by one-third of 1 percent.[13]

shows that export earnings still show considerable fluctuations for most Latin American countries. In nine out of eleven commodities (copper, iron ore, lead, zinc, tin, oil, coffee, cocoa, sugar, wheat, and beef) for which some pertinent statistics are available, variation of export earnings for the period 1950-64 was greater than or about equal to price variability, and in only two were price changes significantly offset by quantity changes in the opposite direction (lead and cocoa).

Price instability is more conspicuous than variation in export quantities of natural resource products. Prices are quoted very frequently, often on a daily basis; information about quantities is gathered over long periods and therefore is not publicized as often.

[8] See, for example, the review by A. Maizels in *American Economic Review*, LVIII, no. 3 (June 1968), pp. 575-80. Using MacBean's data, Maizels finds that in about half of the sample of developing countries "a close connection does, in fact, exist between fluctuations in exports and in GNP" (p. 577).

[9] ECLA, *Inflation and Growth* (Santiago, Chile, 1961, mimeo.), chap. IV, table 12.

To a great extent this factor is responsible for the chronic budget deficits because there is considerable rigidity downward in current public expenditures. Although there is no problem in raising outlays, governments in Latin America usually do not find it politically feasible to reduce operating expenses or social security contributions even when they are confronted with declining revenues due to a drop in foreign trade.

[10] A major examination of the theory is by M. June Flanders, "Prebisch on Protectionism: An Evaluation," *The Economic Journal*, 74 (June 1964), pp. 305-26. The most recent discussion is in Harry G. Johnson, *Economic Policies Toward Less Developed Countries* (Brookings Institution, 1967), particularly pp. 25-29 and pp. 249-50.

[11] UN, *World Economic Survey, 1958* (1959). ECLA, *Inflation and Growth*, table II-8. Inter-American Economic and Social Council, *Study of the Prospects and Some Problems Facing Latin America in Expanding its Exports of Manufactures* (Pan American Union, 26 March 1965), tables 2.5 and 2.6. UN, *Monthly Bulletin of Statistics* (March 1961 and 1964). It should be noted that the fact that the earlier data refer to quantities and the later figures to values does not affect the point made in the text.

[12] See Poul Host-Madsen, "Balance of Payments Problems, Finance and Development," *The Fund-Bank Review*, IV, no. 2 (June 1967).

[13] Jaroslav Vanek, "The Role of Foreign Resources in the Next Decade of Economic Development of Colombia" (paper presented at a conference on The Next Decade of Latin American Economic Development, held at Cornell University, April 20-22, 1966).

A one-cent decline in the price of copper, to give a related although not a terms-of-trade example, signifies a $7 million reduction in the public revenue of the Chilean government or about 1 percent of that country's total tax receipts. (*La Economía de Chile en el Período 1950-1963.*)

The Problem of Access

Latin America competes with both developed and underdeveloped countries in the production of primary goods. The industrial countries are the region's competitors primarily in temperate zone agriculture and, to a lesser extent, in minerals. Other developing countries compete with Latin America in tropical products and minerals, including petroleum. The region therefore faces two types of trade restrictions in the developed countries: those which protect their own producers of primary goods, and those which discriminate against Latin American producers in favor of other less developed countries.

Although trade barriers have come down enormously in many economically advanced countries since the Great Depression of the 1930s, the reductions of tariffs and other restrictions applying to raw materials and food products have been considerably less than on manufactures. Furthermore, the formation of trading blocs, particularly the European Economic Community (EEC), has tended to discriminate against Latin America. For instance, of the thirty-eight African nations, eighteen are at present associated with the EEC. An additional twelve are now part of the British trading system and would also become associated if Britain joins the EEC. Thus, while a sizable part of the underdeveloped world has access to the lucrative EEC market, Latin America is at a disadvantage. Despite the Kennedy Round tariff reductions, the EEC external tariffs and other restrictions for the region's traditional products are still significant.[14]

Temperate zone agricultural products face one of the most difficult situations. Tariffs severely discriminate against Latin American beef in the EEC, while direct and indirect subsidies affect regional exports in other countries and the U.S. market is restricted because of sanitary regulations and quotas. Non-tariff barriers are the greatest obstacles to the wheat export trade of the River Plate countries.

The production of beef and wheat and other temperate zone products is caught up in worldwide efforts at import substitution and agricultural diversification in the importing countries. Protection has become a natural concomitant of these objectives which encompass both developed and underdeveloped countries (including many in Latin America). Only rapidly rising per capita consumption levels in many importing nations have been able to offset what would otherwise have been an adverse long-term trend. For obvious reasons, import substitution efforts do not affect tropical exports very much, except in the case of sugar where protection of domestic beet sugar production has been high in most importing countries.

A mixture of trade barriers affecting other Latin American products includes: tariffs and excise taxes on bananas and coffee in the EEC; still existing subsidies in the United States with respect to cotton exports (they were sharply reduced in 1965); the Cotton Textile Agreement; quotas in the United States and elsewhere regarding petroleum; and stockpile disposal policies in the United States affecting tin and other products.

Trade restrictions applied by the Communist countries are probably even higher than those applied by the West,[15] but it is doubtful whether they have affected Latin American trade as much as the barriers of the non-communist world. It also should be noted that the levels of protection in the less developed countries themselves have been higher than in the advanced countries, but thus far they have had a negligible impact on Latin America because the limited purchasing power in the poorer countries has not made them significant markets for the region's exports.

The Role of Foreign Capital

Foreign capital is a far bigger issue in Latin America than is warranted by its significance for the region's economic development. Foreign capital plays a considerable role in copper (and by-products such as molybdenum), iron ore, lead, zinc and, of course, petroleum. The production of some less important mine products, not examined in this volume, to a large extent is also controlled by foreign firms: examples are nitrates (and a by-product, iodine) and aluminum. However, for some of the less important minerals, such as coal, there is almost no foreign ownership.

The foreign presence varies from country to country. Until the recent "Mexicanization" and "Chileanization" laws,[16] over 90 percent of copper production and the major part of lead and zinc output in Latin America was controlled by foreign companies. Although petroleum pro-

[14] For a discussion of postwar restrictions on Latin American and other underdeveloped regions' exports, see Johnson, *Economic Policies Toward Less Developed Countries*, especially p. 158 and other parts of chap. V. For crude estimates of the effects of developed country trade barriers on Latin American trade, see Joseph Grunwald, Miguel Wionczek, and Martin Carnoy, "Latin American Economic Integration and the United States" (Brookings Institution, 1970, multilith), chap. V.

Latin America apparently gained little from the results of the Kennedy Round of tariff reductions, concluded in Geneva in 1967 after many years of negotiations. The EEC countries did not grant most-favored-nation treatment for any concessions in tropical products. (Presumably the EEC wished to preserve the preferential trading arrangements with the associated overseas territories.) Few of the other tariff reductions agreed upon in Geneva benefit important Latin American exports. "After the tariff reductions negotiated in the Kennedy Round have been implemented, the group of commodities left with the greatest degree of protection in the developed countries' markets will be the labour-intensive processed goods and manufactured products in which the less developed countries have an undoubted comparative advantage and which are consequently of greatest current or potential export interest to them." (David Wall, "Latin America in an Atlantic Free Trade Area," *Bank of London and South America Review*, 2, no. 16 [April 1968], p. 186.)

A study by Bela Balassa on "The Effects of the Kennedy Round on the Exports of Processed Goods from Developing Areas" indicates "the continuation of the tendency for tariffs on goods which are traded chiefly among industrial countries to be reduced more than tariffs on imports from developing areas." (UNCTAD, *Trends and Problems in World Trade and Development*, TD/69, New Delhi, February 1, 1968, p. 4.)

[15] See Frederic L. Pryor, "Trade Barriers of Capitalist and Communist Nations Against Foodstuffs Exported by Tropical Underdeveloped Nations," in *Review of Economics and Statistics*, (November 1966).

[16] The "Mexicanization" law requires majority Mexican ownership of firms in certain industries; the "Chileanization" law refers to Chilean control over copper production and is discussed more fully in chap. 4. See also chap. 6.

duction is also dominated by a few integrated international concerns, in several countries, among which are Brazil, Chile, Mexico, and now Peru, foreign ownership has been completely shut out.

The degree of foreign interest also differs between mining and processing. In iron, for instance, it is concentrated in mining operations, while processing is mainly in local hands; in copper, lead, and zinc, foreign firms are important in smelting but, with the exception of copper, their role is less in mining.

The influence of foreign capital is generally less in agriculture than in mining. There are, of course, some conspicuous cases in which foreign control has been very strong: bananas in Central America and beef in the River Plate countries, to give the most important examples. In the case of bananas, a large part of production and all of the shipping and exporting are in foreign hands. In the case of beef, foreign interests have concentrated on packing and exports rather than on basic production. The degree of foreign ownership has declined markedly in the postwar period. Foreign interests have almost disappeared in the production of sugar, where once they were important in Cuba and other Caribbean countries. Now foreign firms are active primarily in sugar mills and refineries. However, the official U.S. sugar policy, which exerts a powerful influence on Latin American production, is in part determined by the distribution of U.S. capital in that region. Little foreign capital can be found in forestry and almost none in cocoa and coffee. In wheat only the exports are controlled by international firms, although British companies once were active in flour milling. Japanese capital has made some appearance in cotton and fishing (foreign interests are particularly strong in Peruvian fishing), but these commodities are dominated by local firms.

The Role of the State

The image of the weakness of a raw-material–oriented economy in fostering economic growth has led Latin American governments to try to make economic growth less dependent on natural resources. The resulting governmental policies, many of which were originally triggered by the Great Depression, have had several and often conflicting objectives. The first one has been an attempt to diversify the economy. This has taken the form of encouraging import substitution often through haphazard rather than co-ordinated measures. Nonetheless, Latin American countries remained acutely aware of their continuing dependence on primary goods production to provide the necessary financial resources for industrialization. But until recently no special government support was given to raw material production and exports. On the contrary, in attempting to obtain from the natural resource sector the necessary funds for industrialization, public infrastructure programs for economic development, and general government operations, traditional exports have been taxed substantially. Such taxation has been heavier and politically more palatable when foreign countries have been involved.

High tariffs, foreign exchange restrictions, and other controls which were designed to stimulate industrialization and protect the balance of payments have had negative effects on raw material production and exports. So have government efforts to transfer incomes from exporters to the industrial sector through multiple exchange rate systems and other devices. These measures have changed relative prices to producers and have discouraged not only exports, but also imports of essential equipment and supplies.

Thus, public policies which may have been originally provoked by problems of demand have contributed to the emergence of supply difficulties. With a few exceptions (notably coffee) Latin American countries have often found themselves in the position of being unable to provide desired quantities of primary goods to their foreign customers. For many of Latin America's traditional commodities the regional share in world production and exports has declined.

Instability of Public Policy. The prejudice against dependency on natural resources on the one hand, and the awareness of their importance in the economic development process on the other, have given rise to great ambivalence in government policy. "Stop-and-go" measures regarding primary goods production and exports have characterized the postwar period in many Latin American countries and policies to stimulate natural resource development have alternated with those that have discouraged it. Policy for copper in Chile, oil in Venezuela, and wheat in Argentina and Uruguay are pertinent examples (see the respective commodity chapters in Part Two). This ambivalence in the public posture has dampened the expansion of raw material and food production in the long run.

Uncertainty concerning government policy has played a key role in deterring private investment, especially in agriculture. Continual policy changes have made it impossible for landowners to know what to expect and long-term business planning is made extremely difficult. Therefore, private investors frequently have not responded to favorable policies because they did not feel secure about their stability. Agriculturalists in Argentina and Chile are cases in point.

This situation often has led to a vicious circle. The apparently weak responsiveness of primary goods production and investment to favorable prices and government stimuli reconfirms the image policy makers have that the natural resources sectors cannot be relied upon in the process of economic growth. Public neglect of these sectors has followed, or in their frustration governments have proposed changes much more extreme than are warranted by economic considerations alone. For instance, to increase the elasticity of agricultural supply, massive land redistribution schemes have been thought necessary in order to make agriculture more receptive to the introduction of new techniques and more responsive to price incentives. However, this objective could also be attained with greater stability of positive public policies regarding research and experimentation, extension services, credits and education.[17] Further-

---

[17] On the other hand, it must be recognized that the true aims of land reform usually have been much farther reaching than the explicit economic goals and have included in most cases, at least implicitly, objectives involving fundamental changes in a nation's social and political structure.

more, the extended public discussion of recent land reform measures before they have become law has been much more detrimental to private agricultural investment than their actual enactment. Even if unfavorable to the potential investor, a well-defined law will make improved planning possible and thus may facilitate increased economic activity.

It can be argued that stability in government policy and an atmosphere of internal certainty about public actions in an export-oriented economy requires external stability. Governments would feel surer about their policies if they in turn are reassured of the steadiness of foreign markets. If this is so, then commodity agreements and other stabilization schemes which would give some external reassurance might have positive net effects on economic development despite inefficiencies from a narrow economic point of view.

Agricultural Policies. Although government influence in agriculture has risen substantially, the role of government has been characterized more by neglect than anything else. Generally, no national land policy governed the passage of the usable public domain into private hands. There is hardly any government ownership in agriculture. No special effort was made to stimulate immigration or to encourage the immigrant to stay on the land and work it efficiently (see chapter 14). Tariff and exchange policies often have been detrimental to agriculture because they have made it more difficult to obtain the needed inputs with which to intensify cultivation and expand production. The absence of price support policies and export subsidies until recently has retarded development.

Rather than controlling production directly, governments have regulated prices and exercised other controls which have impaired output of specific products (see particularly chapters 10, 14, and 15). As a consequence of the Great Depression, wheat was one of the first products to become subject to price control. Public policy regarding this commodity has been caught between the desire to keep domestic bread prices down and the effort to keep producer incomes and export prices up. A similar situation has existed in government policies regarding beef.

There has been a strong but sometimes haphazard state role with respect to coffee. The Brazilian government has bought up and destroyed coffee output from time to time and maintains large inventories; on two occasions it has also encouraged the destruction of coffee trees. Recently Brazil instituted a program of discouraging replanting coffee trees and of uprooting old trees in order to reduce stockholding costs, improve the nation's competitive position in mild coffees, and stimulate agricultural diversification. While the program seems to have had success in uprooting the trees and holding back output, production has not declined so far because of intensified cultivation and a consequent increase in yields. Unlike coffee, there has been little public control in cocoa.

Other government activities in the agricultural sector have included the regulation of the contracts between farmers and mills, e.g., in sugar, and provision of the physi-

cal infrastructure needed in forestry or in the production of bananas in Ecuador.

Tax policy has been an important influence on resource development. Except for the revenue taxes on sugar consumption, in agriculture taxes have concentrated mainly on exports of such commodities as coffee, cotton (in contrast to the United States where subsidies were provided for cotton exports), beef, wheat, wool, hides, etc. Only to a minor extent have these taxes been intended to limit exports in order to increase the domestic supply of a particular commodity. The major objective has been revenues. Fortunately, the tax has not usually been high, but export taxes in principle do restrain production and shipments abroad[18] and encourage speculation, especially when tax rates are changed as often as they have been in Latin America.

Minerals Policies. Direct government control over mineral resources is significant in Latin America, but there are substantial differences among countries. It is most pronounced in petroleum; every country in the region except Ecuador has a national oil company, and in Brazil, Chile, and Mexico the government holds the monopoly of oil production. Argentina and Bolivia only recently admitted the operation of private (mostly foreign) companies after many years of complete nationalization of petroleum, but the new Bolivian military government expropriated the foreign oil company at the end of 1969. Government ownership of refineries also is common, but only in two oil-producing countries, Chile and Mexico, does the government have a refining monopoly. In other cases investment in new plants and expansion of existing ones are reserved for state companies. Most of the public enterprises in petroleum production and refining have great autonomy and freedom of management.

The degree of public ownership of other minerals is much less than in petroleum. However, government participation is relatively high in tin, iron ore, and copper and in the processing of the latter two metals. There are national steel industries in almost every steel producing country in the region. In most states it has been the government that started the first steel plant. The major exception is Mexico, where private capital built the first mill. (A few small mills existed also in Brazil before the construction of the large publicly owned Volta Redonda works.) In several countries iron ore resources are held in reserve for national exploitation just as petroleum lands are no longer given as concessions to private companies in Venezuela. Until recently, government ownership of copper has been confined to some smelting and refining in Chile, but with the new Chilean copper law the state will also have a controlling interest in the production.

In the mineral sector, taxes concentrate primarily on the profits of the producers which mostly are foreign com-

[18]This holds true generally when production is within the range of decreasing returns. For the complexity of this subject see R. Goode, G. E. Lent, and P. O. Ojha, "Role of Export Taxes in Developing Countries," *International Monetary Fund Staff Papers*, (November 1966).

panies. Taxes have not generally affected short-run output significantly, but on occasion they have restrained investment. An example is the case of Chile before the 1955 copper law; there taxes applied in conjunction with exchange control amounted to an export tax.[19] The Chilean 1955 "New Deal" law was designed to stimulate increases in output through tax incentives, but the effect wore off after certain output levels were reached at the end of the 1950s.

Conclusions. In general, the resource development policies of Latin American governments have concentrated on the demand side of the problem whenever export products have been involved. Attention has focused on undertakings to stabilize prices and to gain increased access to markets in developed countries. Latin American countries have urged regulation of the market in order to stabilize prices and they have sought improved access by opposing interferences with international trade.

Price stabilization has been a main objective of proposals for international commodity agreements. Usually they have involved maximum and minimum prices, frequently supported by export quotas and sometimes buffer stocks. The difficulties inherent in stabilization measures are reflected in the fact that only very few international commodity agreements have been put into effect. While this may be a result of conflict between exporters and importers and the limitations of the number of commodities which lend themselves to this kind of manipulation, it also suggests that exporting and importing countries do not consider the costs of operating such schemes worth the expected benefits. Only four formal commodity agreements involving Latin American countries have been instituted since World War II — for wheat, sugar, tin, and coffee.[20] Of these, the sugar agreement was suspended from 1961 to 1968 and the tin scheme lost control on several occasions. The latter now functions partially because of U.S. stockpile releases. Although the coffee agreement is of too recent origin to have proved itself as an effective long-run stabilization mechanism, and Brazil has had to bear the brunt of the adjustments under the agreement as it had to do before the scheme was instituted, in the short run exporters have benefitted significantly. The wheat agreements appear to be working well, yet it has been the national policies of the two major exporters, the United States and Canada, rather than the international arrangements which have brought a measure of stability for this product in the postwar period.

In reviewing the role of Latin American governments in the development of the region's natural resources in the past, however, the paucity of efforts on the supply side is notable. Research assistance and the provision of tech-

nology and specialized knowledge have been nearly absent. In the mineral sector this function has been performed to a large extent by foreign companies. Only very recently have governments become concerned with modernization of agricultural operations and improvement of production techniques. The deficiency in the training of specialized personnel, the lack of adequate research, agricultural experimentation, and extension have been among the most important elements holding back agricultural development in Latin America. In the absence of the required technical basis, even a very favorable price policy on the part of the government cannot bring a significant response from producers. Thus, the change of relative prices in favor of agriculture in post-Perón Argentina had little effect on farm and livestock production because of the lack of technology which could be adopted by Argentine agriculturalists and the scarcity of needed inputs which could be obtained only from abroad.

While the foregoing describes the policies of the recent past, the current role of Latin American governments in the natural resource sector is mixed and the situation is more fluid. The one-time prejudice of Latin American policy makers against resource development has given way to a more rational approach in recent years. It has come to be recognized that the confrontation of primary goods production versus industrialization was false and that sound economic growth requires complementary efforts in both directions. The new programs of developing the copper industry in Chile, livestock in Argentina and other countries, and the improvement of cotton production in Colombia and Central America are cases in point.

Perspective and Policy Implications

Preoccupied with attempts at industrialization, Latin American countries only recently have recognized the implications that industrialization has for resource development. The slowness was due in part to the past pattern of Latin American industrialization, which consisted primarily of the substitution of domestic production for consumer goods imports. This made relatively small direct demands on the region's resources. With a few exceptions, material inputs were imported. As intermediate and capital goods become a greater share of Latin America's industrial output, the domestic use of her own resources increases. This has occurred in recent years. Minerals from the region have been employed in substantial quantities: oil, for the rapidly rising energy requirements, and metal resources for industrial raw materials, especially iron ore for steel production.

Aside from industrial uses, the conjunction of several trends increases the demand for resources in Latin America. The high rate of population growth, the highest of any comparable region in the world, the accelerating urbanization process, and the increased income which accompanies industrialization and urbanization, all intensify the strain on agriculture in particular. This speeds the shift from subsistence to commercial agriculture. But agricultural production in nearly all countries has failed to keep in step with the mounting domestic requirements and supply deficiencies in agriculture have become a major problem in Latin

---

[19]Moreover, exchange controls imposed upon copper producers in Chile prior to 1955 induced a shift toward labor-saving operations (see the discussion in chap. 4).

[20]Informal arrangements have been made at one time or another for several products of which copper and petroleum are the most important cases. An agreement on cocoa has been in the making for a long time.

American economic development (see table A-10). Urbanization also signifies a growing use of construction materials, particularly lumber and non-metallic minerals which can be supplied by the resources of the region.

Natural resource development must also provide the means for export expansion. Latin American industrialization has not yet advanced far enough to become independent of foreign supplies of machinery, equipment, replacement parts, and such material inputs as special chemicals and fuels. Accelerated industrialization will therefore require increased imports of the needed materials for domestic production. While import-substituting industrialization has made the region less dependent upon consumer goods imports, dependence on imported materials and equipment to keep the local industrial plant in operation has increased, and imports have therefore become more important than ever before.

Meanwhile, Latin American industrial products are not yet able to compete effectively in the world market. Unless the region receives special treatment in developed country markets, which seems unlikely, manufactured exports cannot be relied upon in the foreseeable future to earn the foreign exchange needed for economic development. Nor can Latin America look to foreign aid to fill the "import gap"; if the recent mood of the United States Congress is any guide, foreign assistance is not likely to increase significantly.

Primary goods exports remain as the only major source for meeting the region's import requirements. Despite the basic transformation of the internal economic structure due to industrialization, about 90 percent of Latin American exports still consists of the output of mines, land, and fisheries. Yet these exports have not been sufficient to pay for the imports required for industrial expansion. It is becoming increasingly obvious that if industrialization continues to be Latin America's main economic focus, increased exports of natural resource products must play the major supporting role in the development process.

While the need for an expansion of primary goods exports in order to finance economic growth continues stronger than ever, there are considerable obstacles in the way of this objective. Some are based on problems of demand, some on problems of supply.

Demand

Despite recent and partially successful worldwide attempts to lower tariff barriers, some onerous trade restrictions remain and will continue to affect Latin American export expansion possibilities. All indications point in the direction of a continuation of national import substitution and the diversification of agricultural production within countries all over the world.

This is abetted by international and national aid-giving agencies which continue to support local efforts in developing countries to increase the domestic production of temperate zone foods, particularly of grains and meat. In developed nations domestic beet sugar production is also fostered on a large scale. It is clear that these efforts are

TABLE A–10. Latin America: Indices of Agricultural Per Capita Production, Exports, Imports, and Supply, Selected Yearly Averages, Prewar-1965
(1953-57 = 100)

	Prewar[a]	1948-52	1953-57	1958-62	1963-65
(1) Agricultural production	109	83	100	105	104
Tropical crops[b]	130	100	100	113	93
Temperate crops[c]	100	94	100	99	103
(2) Agricultural exports					
Tropical crops[b]	138	108	100	92	83
Temperate crops[d]	316	111	100	132	169
(3) Agricultural imports					
Tropical crops[b]	98	92	100	87	83
Temperate crops[c]	80	108	100	103	121
(1) Domestic supply					
Tropical crops[b]	127	76	100	166	118
Temperate crops[c]	89	95	100	100	102

Sources: FAO, *Production Yearbook, 1966*. FAO, *The State of Food and Agriculture* (1965 and 1967). UN, *Yearbook of International Trade Statistics, 1955* and *1958*. UN, *Statistical Bulletin for Latin America*, III, no. 1 (February 1966). FAO, *Trade Yearbook, 1955* to *1964*. USDA, Economic Research Service, *Indices of Agricultural Production for the 20 Latin American Countries*, Rev. 1954-1965 (1967).

Methodological Notes: Indices were calculated on the basis of the following weights:
(1) Weights for agricultural production and domestic supply – sugar = 100, bananas = 30, coffee = 550, cocoa = 425, wheat = 100, maize = 60, rice = 131 (paddy rice converted at 65%), milk = 80, beef and veal = 260.
(2) Export unit values – sugar = 139, bananas = 140, coffee = 1698, cocoa = 1146, wheat = 100, maize = 83, beef and veal = 962. (1953-57 average Latin American export unit values expressed as a percentage of wheat value.)
(3) Import unit values – sugar = 117, bananas = 80, coffee = 1597, cocoa = 1097, wheat = 100, maize = 89, rice = 255, milk = 566, beef and veal = 812. (1953-57 average U.S. export unit values expressed as a percentage of wheat value. Sugar based on world market price 1953-57. Coffee and cocoa based on 1953-57 average Brazilian export unit value. Bananas based on 1953-57 average Latin American export unit value.)

[a]1935-39 average for coffee, cocoa, and sugar; 1934-38 average for bananas, wheat, beef and veal, rice, milk, and maize.
[b]Centrifugal sugar, bananas, coffee, cocoa.
[c]Wheat, maize, rice, milk, beef and veal.
[d]Wheat, maize, beef and veal.

geared to substitute current or potential imports of commodities in some of which Latin America has a comparative advantage.

The market for Latin American food products and minerals in less developed countries cannot be expected to grow rapidly over the next decade or so. Moreover, the food surplus disposal programs of the United States and of other developed countries are supplying part of the most vital needs of the underdeveloped world at subsidized prices; Latin America could not possibly compete with these assistance programs even if it could substantially increase production.

Developed nations will probably keep certain trade barriers also against non-competing goods. Some of these are revenue tariffs, as, for instance, on coffee in some countries; others are import restrictions which affect all but preferred suppliers. The European Economic Community most likely will continue to give preferences to its associated territories in filling its requirements of tropical commodities, thereby discriminating against Latin American and other possible producers. A similar situation may develop in regard to the Japanese market. Several Latin American countries have counted on a vast expansion of that lucrative market in making their development plans. These hopes may be disappointed because cultivation of some of the region's commodities is being introduced into the Far East — bananas in Taiwan, the Philippines, and Borneo, for example — that would have better access to the Japanese market than distant Latin American supplies.

Another restraint on foreign demand is the substitution of synthetic and natural materials in importing countries for products in which Latin America has a comparative advantage. It is difficult to determine whether the net result of all substitutions has been significantly detrimental to Latin America in the past. On a product-by-product basis there have been many adverse effects. Synthetic fibers have been substituted for wool, cotton, and other natural fibers; nitrogenous fertilizers and synthetic rubber compete with nitrates and natural rubber; but all these are made from petroleum, and so are the plastics which substitute for certain metals. Latin America is hurt by the substitution of aluminum for copper, and of steel, glass, chrome and other finishes for tin. On the other hand, Latin America has clearly benefited from the greatest of all substitutions, that of oil for coal all over the world.

Substitution may become a more serious problem for the region in the future as will be discussed in the relevant commodity chapters of Part Two. It should be noted, however, that substitution often is not an autonomous problem of demand, but frequently derives from difficulties in increasing supply sufficiently and rapidly enough to meet the current requirements of importing countries. When such shortages arise, user countries are induced to look for substitutes to meet their needs. Generally, even after supply has finally increased in response to increased demand, the substitutions made for the product during the period of shortage will not be abandoned, so that part of the market may be irretrievably lost. In this, as in other cases, demand and supply problems are closely interrelated.

In efforts to raise and stabilize demand, Latin American countries will unquestionably continue to press the developed world for concessions. These demands range from guarantees of minimum export prices, quantities, and earnings, to special arrangements for increased access. International commodity agreements, financial compensation arrangements, and tariff preferences[21] are the principal instruments for these objectives.

Commodity agreements can succeed only if the developed importing countries are a party to the agreement or there are only a few exporters and no close substitutes, but even then the benefits to the region are not clear. The chief difficulty in stabilization schemes has been in forecasting long-run equilibrium prices. Therefore international agreements need to be renegotiated periodically or must have such a high built-in flexibility that it in effect would thwart their basic aim.

Commodity arrangements can maximize short-run export incomes of developing countries when demand and supply elasticities tend to be low. If the long-run elasticities are higher than in the short run, the immediate gains may be at the expense of future revenues. But developing countries tend to discount such possibilities because of the implicit expectation that industrialization will bring them greater viability and other earning opportunities in the long run.

Although efforts are still being made to reach international covenants — much progress has been made toward an agreement for cocoa — formal commodity treaties seem to have lost their original appeal. Attention has shifted to informal accords, such as those for copper and petroleum, among some producing and exporting countries. These resemble cartel arrangements except that they are controlled by governments rather than companies. They have had little effect on markets thus far, in part because the largest producers, such as the United States, do not participate. The aims of these associations are to increase the income accruing to the exporting countries through efforts, not always successful, to control output, maintain prices and, in the case of the Organization of Petroleum Exporting Countries (OPEC), raise the government share in export earnings.

Increasing attention has gone to the stabilization of a nation's total export income rather than to the price or earnings of particular commodities. The central idea is to compensate a country for losses incurred due to fluctuations of earnings, or more precisely shortfalls of earnings from a certain "norm," over a period of time. These arrangements seem to avoid the difficulties of organizing international commodity agreements and attack the problem

---

[21] The concept of preferences usually involves the formal commitment of the developed countries to eliminate or reduce their trade barriers to the imports of the underdeveloped countries without expecting any reciprocity and without any corresponding reduction to other developed nations. The case for preferences is based upon the "infant industry" argument, but in fact is generalized to an "infant economy" concept. For a fuller discussion of preferences, see Johnson, *Economic Policies Toward Less Developed Countries*, and, in relation to Latin America, Grunwald et al., "Latin American Economic Integration . . . ."

of variation in export proceeds directly. Only very limited compensatory finance systems have been put into operation so far, including a borrowing scheme introduced by the International Monetary Fund in 1963. Compensation schemes, because they involve an explicit or implicit transfer of real resources from the developed to the less developed countries, depend more on the willingness of the developed countries to channel their aid-giving operations in these directions than on formal international arrangements.[22]

As pointed out earlier, regardless of the strict economic merits of commodity agreements and other stabilization schemes – and these indeed have been questioned on grounds of economic efficiency – such arrangements can create a climate of security for given developing countries which may be conducive for an expansion in investment and economic growth. Governments may gain greater self-confidence in instituting and persevering in positive economic policies. In this manner, stabilization schemes can promote business confidence and a favorable investment climate and thus economic growth, even though they may not result in the most efficient allocation of world resources.

However, the emphasis recently given to obtaining preferential tariff treatment in the developed countries for products of Latin America and other developing areas will undoubtedly continue. Increased access for Latin American commodities will probably take precedence over stability objectives in future regional policies. Latin America, as well as other less developed areas, has a good case in demanding the elimination of remaining trade barriers in developed countries. Latin America has tended to concentrate on obtaining special treatment for manufactured commodities only.[23] Such tactics could be a mistake. They are founded upon the assumption that the region's industries are "infants" which require protection vis-à-vis those of developed countries, and that a substantial export expansion can be based upon manufactured goods. While the chances are good that this will occur in intraregional trade if the economic integration of the region accelerates, it is doubtful whether it can take place in Latin American trade with the developed countries in the near future. Latin American industrialization has been based almost exclusively on the substitution of imports. Oriented to the domestic markets, it is generally inefficient and high cost when compared with the industrially advanced countries. The rationalization of Latin American industrialization will have to rely to a great extent on regional integration before much progress toward extra-regional manufacturing exports can be made. Latin

America's natural resources will continue to provide the bulk of the region's foreign exchange in the foreseeable future and rapid economic growth will require an acceleration of primary goods exports. Any measures, such as developed country preferences, which would increase access should therefore also include raw materials and food products.

Regarding the long-term trend of demand, there is little question that Latin America has tended to overemphasize improvement of the terms of trade as if it were an economic "cure-all." Improvement in the terms of trade increases the purchasing power of exports, but the use to which increased import capacity is put is often more important for economic growth than its magnitude.[24] The main issue is whether export expansion will be sufficiently high and whether its proceeds can be oriented to support vigorous economic growth. The adequacy of exports depends on the rate of growth to which Latin American countries aspire. In the past, economic development was closely tied to exports. Given the present economic structure, growth will not be much faster than the growth of exports.[25]

In recent decades, exports of developing countries to the industrial countries generally have increased less than the national incomes of the latter. Bela Balassa projected for 1975 a rise in raw material exports of the developing countries in about the same proportion or less than the growth in the gross national product of the industrial countries, depending upon the assumptions.[26] Balassa estimates the developed economies to grow at an annual rate of about 4 percent under the best assumptions. Such a growth rate of exports would not be considered satisfactory in Latin America, particularly in the face of a population growth of about 2.8 percent.

There are, of course, measures that Latin American countries could take themselves to enhance their export possibilities. Apart from cost reducing changes, the modernization of marketing techniques is a very promising field. Much can be done to make Latin American products more attractive to foreign consumers through packaging and

---

[22]A recent UNCTAD study argues for an overall primary commodity strategy. Its recommendations range from commodity agreements of various types adjusted to the characteristics of each particular product, to the promotion of consumption of developing country products in developed nations and the fostering of trade with the Communist countries. UNCTAD, *The Development of an International Commodity Policy*, TD/8/Supp. 1 (Geneva, November 1967).

[23]See, for instance, the Proceedings of the meeting of the Inter-American Economic and Social Council (IA-ECOSOC) of the Organization of American States in Viña del Mar, Chile, July 1967.

[24]Moreover, Latin American countries cannot always take full advantage of better relative prices for raw materials because of lack of technology and other supply inelasticities which hinder the expansion of output.

[25]The correlation between growth in primary goods exports and growth in national income for most Latin American countries is much higher for smaller countries than for larger ones. See, for instance, IA-ECOSOC, *The Future of Latin American Development and the Alliance for Progress* (OAS, April 1966). But it can be assumed that before the massive import-substituting industrialization began, the correlation was also high for the large countries. During the period of import substitution economic growth has proceeded faster than export growth. The real problem is that this kind of industrialization cannot continue indefinitely to provide the engine for growth – unless the internal economy is large and diversified enough – and thus exports eventually become the limiting factor again. Cf. Joseph Grunwald, "Invisible Hands in Inflation and Growth," in *Inflation and Growth in Latin America*, eds. W. Baer and I. Kerstenetsky (Economic Growth Center, Yale University, 1964).

[26]*Trade Prospects for Developing Countries*, Economic Growth Center, Yale University (Homewood, Ill.: R. D. Irwin, 1964).

styling, as, for example, if Latin American food exports were appropriately packaged for display in supermarkets. The boxing of bananas raised their demand while at the same time cutting wastage. Efforts in this respect should be in both directions: to adapt the merchandising of Latin American export commodities to conform to developed country tastes and to influence preference patterns in developed countries in favor of products from the region.

Demand problems are not confined to the external sector. A substantial component of the output of some primary goods depends upon domestic demand. That component is expected to increase in the process of economic development and income growth. Any significant expansion in the domestic use of the region's natural resources will be closely linked to the magnitude, type, and speed of industrialization. These factors will affect not only the quantities of the material inputs needed to feed the factories, but also the degree of urbanization and the rise in personal incomes which will result in a greater demand for food, raw materials and, of course, industrial products.[27]

Here, too, there is a link between demand and supply problems. Insofar as industrial growth is limited by the size of the market, smaller countries will be at a disadvantage compared to the larger ones and individual nations will provide a smaller impetus to industrialization than a combination of nations. The economic integration of Latin American countries has, therefore, been one of the objectives in the effort to accelerate economic development. Through widening the markets beyond the boundaries of individual nations, it is hoped that Latin American industrialization will be able to take advantage of the lower costs of large-scale production and the benefits of increased competition. Failure to move toward regional integration would signify weakening of the growth of industry and incomes in general, and would therefore restrain the potential demand for domestic raw materials and food.

Greater attention to the production, distribution, and marketing of some foods could enhance demand for domestic products. Consumption of fish, for instance, is low in Latin America compared with other regions that have similar access to maritime resources. Likewise, consumption of meat other than beef — particularly of poultry, mutton, and pork — is not as high as elsewhere. These characteristics of Latin American tastes can, of course, be changed in the future, but such changes will in part depend upon greater efficiency in production, better distribution, and lower prices. For example, the region's production of edible fish has concentrated on luxury items such as tuna and shrimp, which are too expensive for the average Latin American. Poultry production also is high cost, lacking the modern techniques employed in the United States and elsewhere. Faulty distribution and high prices have discouraged the development of tastes and changes in this direction will

depend on how successfully supply conditions can be improved.

Supply

Although some of the demand problems are quite serious and will affect production and export possibilities of Latin American commodities, difficulties in the efficient expansion of supply of many products will also be important for the region's economic development. Supply problems have been severe in the case of most minerals and temperate zone agriculture. There are few difficulties in increasing the supply of tropical commodities in the long run, but a lack of flexibility in changing their output levels, especially of coffee, has meant that shortages have alternated with surpluses with a profound effect on income.

After many decades of neglect, Latin American governments have begun to take a more active role in developing the region's resources. The Great Depression oriented government policies towards problems of demand. In the postwar period, however, it became apparent that, with some exceptions, the real impediments to resource development outside of tropical agriculture are now related to supply bottlenecks. Public policy in the region will have to be increasingly geared toward lowering costs of production and distribution and raising the elasticity of supply. While the demand outlook for the region's commodities must be taken into account, public attention to demand should not distract policy makers from the need to accelerate output growth and introduce greater flexibility in production.

Some production problems in the natural resource sector will be relatively easy to eliminate. Others cannot be corrected in the near future either because they are rooted in the structure and attitudes of society and take time to change or because the results of new efforts will make themselves felt only in the long run. The nature of major types of supply problems will be discussed briefly.

Nationalism and the Role of Foreign Capital. In mineral production, economic nationalism has retarded exploration and the expansion of production facilities. Therefore, output is considerably smaller than is warranted by the resource base, despite the fact that production techniques are generally modern in most countries and productivity is comparatively high.

The negative impact of nationalism has varied from product to product and country to country, depending not only on the attitudes of Latin American governments, but also on the reactions of foreign investors and their governments and the competence of national public enterprises. Bolivian tin output declined disastrously after the 1952 nationalization and has begun to recover only in recent years. By contrast, oil production by national companies in Mexico and Chile has fared relatively well. Frequent changes in attitudes, and the ensuing actions and reactions between Latin Americans and foreigners have resulted in intermittent co-operation alternating with hostility toward foreign capital. This "stop-and-go" effect has hampered mineral production and exploration.

In the past foreign capital played a decisive role not only in the economic but also in the political life of many Latin

---

[27]The size of the total effective demand will also depend upon the distribution of personal incomes. In some countries of the region a substantial improvement of the income distribution may require fundamental structural changes such as land reform. Obstacles to such reforms would therefore also constitute impediments to industrialization and the expansion of effective demand for natural resource products.

American nations. Paradoxically enough, during that period its contribution to Latin American economic growth was relatively limited. Taxes and other government charges on foreign enterprise in the natural resource sector were light, a major part of foreign exchange earnings was retained abroad, and the other economic linkages were weak. Foreign firms bought most of their supplies and equipment from abroad, the domestic labor force employed was relatively small, and the local elaboration of the output of the mines was not yet important. Furthermore, foreign firms did little to train local personnel for managerial, supervisory, and technical positions. Most of the technicians and management were imported.

Today greater benefits can be expected from outside investments. The complaints against foreign capital which were voiced in the past have less applicability now. The failure to transfer technology or to train managerial and technical personnel, the propensity to engage in corruption of officials or to intervene directly in national politics — all of these forms of conduct which have occured with lamentable frequency in the past — are far less characteristic of foreign firms today.

Foreign capital is now taxed much more heavily, more foreign exchange is returned to the country, the backward and forward economic linkages are becoming more significant, and the transfer of knowledge is now an important contribution of foreign investment. Corruption, while still existing in some areas of the region, has diminished and the involvement of major foreign firms has all but disappeared.

Yet the conspicuous cases from the past linger on in Latin American memory. The image of what happened long ago has become the symbol of foreign capital of today: economic exploitation and domination, political intervention, and perversion of Latin American values. Current nationalism has in part embraced this image and thus has acted to restrict foreign investment, often to the disadvantage of national economic development.

There is, however, another basis for Latin American suspicions: that the policies of foreign governments vis-à-vis the region are influenced by their nationals operating businesses in Latin American countries. Thus, the United States has used its aid and trade policies to further the business interests of its nationals, as when aid was withheld from Peru during the government dispute with a U.S. oil company in the early 1960s.[28] Also, international strategic considerations affect foreign governments' treatment of some of the region's important export commodities. Copper was considered a strategic material during wartime. The United States therefore controlled the copper price, maintaining it at a low level, while the Chilean government, the region's most important exporter of this metal, wanted to receive the higher world market prices. The fact that U.S. companies produced most of Chile's copper had in theory little to do with this conflict, but in practice it helped to enforce U.S. policy and thus contributed to the hostility against foreign capital. U.S. commodity stockpiling policies have affected prices and provoked external difficulties.

Economic nationalism has manifested itself in forms that have given rise to international problems. For instance, nations on the west coast of South America have claimed an extended national sovereignty by pushing the limits of the coastal waters 200 miles out to sea. While these actions have expanded the region's fishing opportunities, they have also produced international confrontations.

Nationalism exerts strong pressure to reduce foreign control, particularly in the natural resources sector. Since mineral resources, land, and fisheries tend to be regarded as a public utility, foreign operations in this sector have become increasingly restricted and subject to control by the host government.

It is difficult to evaluate the impact of nationalism on a country's development. In addition to the problems in measuring the economic costs and benefits and the even greater difficulties in weighing the short against the long run, it is nearly futile to compare economic costs with the non-economic objectives implicit in nationalist policies. It is possible, and in many cases probable, that the non-economic benefits of nationalism may outweigh any economic costs. Every nation-state wishes to maintain control over its own affairs even if this signifies some costs in terms of economic growth. If foreign firms play a large role in a country's economy, then foreigners may exert a strong influence over its economic future, thus diminishing the "political welfare" of the nation, although its economic welfare may be maximized. While the general problem of nationalism should be examined from this broad point of view, it is beyond the scope of this study, whose primary concern is with the quantitative characteristics of the natural resource economy.

The ownership and operation of national resource industries is a particularly sensitive area, because the economic and political power vested in them is very great.[29] Most Latin American governments realize that mineral investment and output would undoubtedly increase were they to encourage foreign companies to operate freely in the exploitation and distribution of metals and petroleum by granting more favorable tax treatment and foregoing restrictions on the repatriation of capital and profits. The national economy would, therefore, also gain despite the repatriation of profits. The difference in national economic welfare between a laissez faire situation and the conditions that actually exist can be viewed as the price the community pays for greater control over its own affairs.

Control of external investments may have an economic rationale. Foreign firms either are not covered by or can elude many economic measures instituted by the govern-

---

[28] This conflict arose before the crisis based upon the expropriation of the U.S. oil company late in 1968.

[29] An intensive analysis of the pressures applied by foreign-controlled companies on the trade policies of nations dependent on natural resource exports is contained in John E. Tilton, "The Choice of Trading Partners: An Analysis of International Trade in Aluminum, Bauxite, Copper, Lead, Manganese, Tin, and Zinc," *Yale Economic Essays*, 6, no. 2 (Fall 1966), pp. 419-74.

The relationship between foreign investor and the host country is examined thoroughly in a series of case studies by Raymond Mikesell et al., in *Foreign Investment in the Petroleum and Mineral Industries: Case Studies on Investor-Host Country Relations* (Johns Hopkins Press for Resources for the Future), in press.

ment of the host country. For example, foreign enterprises have access to credit from their home office and, therefore, may not be affected by credit restrictions which the host country may impose in order to fight inflation. Aside from the question of "unfair" advantage of the foreign firm vis-à-vis the domestic enterprise, the dominance of foreign business can thwart the effectiveness of the national policies of the host country.

There may be also some long-run economic basis in restricting foreign investments. It may tend to mobilize local effort to explore and increase investment and production, particularly if the country is convinced of the necessity of domestic resource development. While at first national efforts, public and private, may be more wasteful and less efficient than foreign operations, this may be the price for a learning process which will pay off in the long run.

More doubtful is the argument, often made in Latin America, that minerals are irreplaceable assets which should be reserved for national economic development instead of being exported to foreign consumers. This argument is not valid because earnings from exports of resources can also contribute to economic development. One must compare the contribution of export earnings with the contribution of future domestic use of national raw materials. Presently known reserves may be only a small share of the country's total deposits. Conserving resources assumes that reserves now known cannot be increased, which is often false. Resource development now will tend to spur exploration and keep the country abreast of technology.[30]

From the standpoint of national economic welfare, the proper question is whether current gains are larger or smaller than the discounted future gains. In other words, the comparison must be between the current contribution which the resource can make to national economic development and the possible contribution of future resource use. A comparison of national benefits with the benefits accruing to the foreigners is not pertinent in economic considerations.[31]

The Chilean case with respect to nitrates is relevant. It has been claimed that during the period before the 1920s, when Chile supplied about 90 percent of the world's fertilizers, approximately $8 billion in nitrates was taken out of the country by the foreign companies that mined this raw material. A comparatively small proportion of the export proceeds remained in the country. One question is whether foreign enterprise was remiss in not investing earn-

ings in Chile: the country then was a strict minority society — most of the population lived at subsistence levels outside the market economy — and if there were no investment opportunities, would domestically owned nitrate companies have done better? Or more realistically, since capital for such large mining operations could not have been raised locally, would it have been better for Chile's welfare not to have exploited its nitrate resources at all rather than allow foreign capital to do it? A complete answer must be based upon noneconomic considerations, because in economic terms the mining payroll and any other expenditures of the foreign firms constituted a definite addition to the country's welfare in the absence of other opportunities. And holding the resource in reserve until national exploitation would have become feasible would clearly have signified an irretrievable loss, because of the subsequent massive substitution of natural nitrates by synthetic materials.

Agriculture is significantly different from mineral exploitation; since agricultural resources are replenishable, the underutilization of land unequivocally signifies an irreplaceable loss of potential output. Thus, the problem of foreign ownership and exploitation of land cannot be put in terms of present benefits to be derived from foreign ownership versus future benefits from domestic ownership. Failure to use the land now entails the irretrievable loss of whatever return the nation gets from the foreigner's investment. It can be argued, of course, that no agricultural production on a given land area may be preferable to foreign exploitation which would create a land use structure inimical to the long-run economic interests of the nation.

As in the case of minerals, what should be weighed are the returns to the country over a given time period from alternative uses of land, whether exploited by foreigners or nationals. While the distribution of gains between foreigners and nationals is not relevant as an economic question, land, perhaps even more so than minerals, is highly sensitive to noneconomic considerations and economic objectives are easily subordinated to sociopolitical desiderata.

There is little doubt that nationalism will continue to be an important factor in Latin American economic life and will have a particularly strong impact in the natural resource sector. Nationalist views are not confined to any special economic or political group but are found in most countries of the region and from one extreme of the political spectrum to the other.

At the same time, the expansion of the natural resource base has become an integral part of the economic development programs of many Latin American countries, and governments have recognized that such expansion presently needs the co-operation of foreign capital. Therefore, an accommodation with foreign capital has become necessary. Foreign investors, too, have learned to make compromises and have entered into arrangements which they never would have accepted only a few years ago. One case in point is the Chilean accommodation with the United States copper companies. In a 1968 arrangement, the Chilean government gained control of a substantial part of the country's copper production and the U.S. companies received certain guarantees for their operations in return for a com-

---

[30]In the case of minerals, the definition of reserves becomes more inclusive over time and accounts for much of reserve growth.

[31]As pointed out earlier, the use made of the foreign exchange earnings that are returned to the country by the foreign companies is quite as important as the magnitude. A government may waste large export incomes in expenditures that contribute little to economic growth, or it may direct relatively small earnings exclusively to economic development purposes which would have a large impact on economic welfare. The efficient channeling of export earnings requires a fair amount of government planning and control. Therefore, consideration must also be given to institutional arrangements such as the degree of planning of public investment and the general efficiency of public administration.

mitment of substantial investments to expand output. The most recent negotiations resulted in an agreement between the Chilean government and the Anaconda Mining Company in mid-1969, which provided that the U.S. holdings will be sold to Chile under certain terms during a seven-year period.

It is clear that foreign ownership of natural resource industries in Latin America will become more circumscribed. Joint companies or partnerships between domestic and foreign capital have found rising acceptance by host governments and foreign investors. But foreign investment might be viewed as a revolving fund that would supplement temporarily, over periods of varying lengths depending on the kind of investment, the scarce technical and financial resources of local enterprise. According to this view, the foreign investor should always be ready to transfer majority interest in the firm to local investors and seek other investment opportunities in those activities where technological contributions continue to be of fundamental importance.[32] But if foreign investors do not share this view, it may become more difficult to reconcile two needs of Latin American countries: to raise investment from the outside in capital-starved economies, and to identify more closely any productive operations within their borders with the nation as a whole.

Agriculture. The problems of expanding output in agriculture appear more severe than in the mineral sector. No serious long-run supply problem has arisen with tropical export crops (except for disease and quality control), most of the difficulties having been concentrated in the supply of temperate zone foods where the expansion of domestic demand has been of greatest importance. Nationalism plays a minor role, but basic changes in the structure of production will be necessary before significant progress in agriculture is possible. This sector has been the weakest link in the chain of Latin American economic development, and in many countries agricultural production has lagged seriously behind population growth in the post World War II period.

In the past, by far the major part of the increase in agricultural output derived from extension of cultivation rather than from improvement in yields. In some countries, such as Argentina, Chile, and Uruguay, the best lands have been used for at least half a century and there is now very little free land available that would lend itself for efficient farm or livestock production. Latin America still has vast, almost untouched "hinterlands," primarily jungle and tropical forests. However, given the current state of technology, these abundant lands appear to be of doubtful immediate value for agriculture. For instance, it appears that the enormous Amazon basin has a thin layer of soil which would be destroyed if the jungle were cleared.[33] Thus even if the

enormous obstacle of access could be resolved and an adequate road network and other infrastructure could be rapidly created, a great deal of technical progress would still be required before these lands could be utilized for agricultural production at reasonable costs.

Furthermore, reliance on the extension of cultivation may only postpone the needed reorganization of agriculture without which significant long-run gains will be difficult. The focus of agricultural development in the future must be on raising the productivity of the already cultivated regions. Yields of many products have not improved markedly in decades. It is becoming clear that acceleration of agricultural development will depend on how intensively existing technology is utilized, how fast new production methods are introduced and new infrastructure is created, how much and how cheaply fertilizers, machinery, equipment, and other inputs are made available (through credits and other mechanisms), how effectively land reforms can be carried out and, perhaps above all, how quickly and well people can be educated and trained for agricultural pursuits. There are, of course, other changes that need to be made in order to inject dynamism into agriculture. Not the least among these is improvement of the distribution system for food products.

The shift of emphasis from extensive to intensive production carries with it significant implications. Because the application of technology is one of the basic ingredients of this new focus, technical knowledge and managerial and administrative competence become of paramount importance. Much of the existing technical knowledge is suited to conditions prevailing in the advanced industrial countries of North America and Europe and cannot be applied directly in Latin America. Therefore there is a need for trained professionals who can make the necessary adaptations. One of the region's first requirements is the training of such high-level manpower.

After the adaptation of existing techniques and the elaboration of new knowledge for application to local conditions, the chief problem becomes the absorption and use of this know-how by the farmers. Often the introduction of new techniques will not require a great amount of additional and expensive capital. A significant acceleration of agricultural output can be attained through changes in farming habits and the application of new labor-intensive methods.

The difference in ownership patterns between mining and agriculture provides an interesting contrast in connection with the transfer of technical knowledge. In the large mining operations the techniques used have been imported and usually the most modern known methods are employed. The number of persons engaged in mining enterprises is relatively small so that training can be effected

---

[32]*Multinational Investment in the Economic Development and Integration of Latin America* (Round Table Conference of the Ninth Annual Meeting of the Board of Governors of the Inter-American Development Bank, Bogota, Colombia, April 1968), p.8.

[33]A detailed technical experiment was recently undertaken on an area under high tropical rain forest in Ghana. It indicated a rapid loss of nutrients that follows the cutting and burning of the forest cover and the subsequent cultivation of the soil by various methods.

See P. H. Nye and D. J. Greenland, "Changes in the Soil After Clearing Tropical Forest," in *Plant and Soil*, XXI, no. 1 (August 1964), The Hague, pp. 101–12. The most recent pertinent research in Latin America is contained in papers presented in a symposium on "Utilization of Humid Lands" held in Rio de Janeiro in June 1966 under the auspices of the Brazilian Research Council (Conselho Nacional de Pesquisas). The Council has also undertaken other studies on this subject.

without too much of a problem. A majority of the high-echelon staff at the mines are now nationals and the passage of ownership from foreigners to nationals need not cause serious disruptions in output and efficiency because of lack of technical knowledge.

Agricultural production, on the other hand, is more widely dispersed and involves a vastly greater number of people even where the ownership of land is highly concentrated. Well over one-third of Latin America's labor force is still absorbed in agricultural pursuits, compared with less than one percent in mineral production. Production methods are tradition based and the land tenure structure adds to the rigidities in agriculture. Training for modernization cannot concentrate on a few persons but signifies a profound change in the way of life of a major segment of the population. This explains the apparent paradox in agriculture: productivity and output could be increased through the introduction of relatively simple techniques, but the problems of transfer of knowledge are especially difficult in this sector.

The major rationale for land reform is to facilitate the acceptance of modern production methods. Changes in the land tenure structure hasten the training of farmers and the adoption of new techniques. The recent land reform in Chile, for instance, provides for a close co-operative working arrangement of the new settlers with government technicians for a period of three years before they are given title to expropriated land. Land reform does not make much sense without the possibility of absorbing new technology. A premature land reform may be worse than none. The effects of land reform are likely to extend beyond the farms directly involved as the landowners not affected by the reform will be motivated to modernize their production.[34]

Of course, much improvement in agricultural productivity will depend on the extent to which new material inputs can be made available. Agricultural inputs have been relatively expensive in Latin America. The region's industrialization effort has led to formidable tariff and other trade barriers. In effect this has constituted an indirect tax on agriculture because imported materials came to be high priced. This, combined with the detrimental inflation in many countries, has made investment in agriculture very expensive.

Therefore, the cost of agricultural inputs must be reduced if growth is to be accelerated over the long run. Much progress has already been made in this direction. Import restrictions on capital and intermediate goods for agriculture have been lowered in several countries of the region, and in some nations, such as Argentina, tax credits are given for investments in this sector. The larger countries have undertaken the production of tractors and other agricul-

tural machinery and equipment. This has permitted the mechanization of a substantial part of Argentine agriculture.

However, even in a country like Argentina it may be more important in the near future to seek efficient use of present inputs than to introduce new inputs, such as fertilizers, which are still high priced. Argentine wheat varieties do not respond well to fertilizer application and, as is mentioned in chapter 14, the returns under current conditions would not warrant expensive fertilizer inputs.

This situation may change in the future if Latin America can produce fertilizer at low cost. Given the distribution of the petroleum resources, not every country can become an efficient fertilizer producer. Moreover, this industry is efficient only at a scale of output that is generally greater than the market requirements of the smaller countries. Therefore, regional production must be combined with elimination of trade barriers among Latin American countries if agricultural inputs are to be made available at low prices. The economic integration of the region therefore is an important element in the process of Latin American agricultural development.[35]

The chief role of Latin American governments in agriculture must be the development of know-how, the adaptation of techniques developed elsewhere to the conditions prevailing in the country, and the application of such new production methods. These tasks involve research, experimentation, training, education, and institutional arrangements. In addition, however, tax and fiscal policies should be adjusted so as to insure adequate farm prices and low relative prices of agricultural inputs, whether imported or domestically produced.

Concerning agricultural tax policy, governments may find it difficult to institute basic reforms in the near future. Export taxes imposed by withholding a proportion of the proceeds per unit sold are relatively easy to administer. They have also been used as a device to capture for the public purse a part of the windfalls accruing to traditional exports after a strong devaluation, which has been a frequent occurrence in Latin American countries experiencing rapid inflation.

Faced with enormous needs for public revenues, generally poor tax administration (especially insofar as income and land taxes are concerned), and the ease of administering retention taxes, governments have pursued the path of administrative expediency, thereby penalizing efficient producers through export taxes. It would be more efficient from an economic point of view to concentrate on land taxes whose incidence would vary in accordance with the imputed productivity of land, but this must await the general improvement of the administrative machinery of Latin American countries.

Distribution. Not all supply problems of natural resources are rooted in production. There are formidable distribution bottlenecks which limit the degree to which the region's resources can reach the local consumer. Deficient distribution facilities and inefficient packaging and market-

---

[34] Wolf Ladejinsky, the world-renowned land reform expert who is credited with designing the reforms of Japan and Taiwan, suggested that the rapid growth of Mexican commercial agriculture was stimulated by the Mexican land reform. Among other things the reform restricted the land holdings, and therefore the landlord exerted greater efforts to maximize his economic returns on his remaining lands. (Seminar, Inter-American Development Bank, June 15, 1966.)

[35] For detailed demand and cost projections of the fertilizer industry, see ECIEL, "Nitrogenous Fertilizers," in *Industrialization in a Latin American Common Market.*

ing methods have constituted severe restraints on the supply of several agricultural commodities. They have also affected exports of fish, fruit, and some temperate zone products, but have had particularly detrimental effects on the domestic supply of these goods. An unduly large share of the value of food products is absorbed by intermediaries and some production does not reach consumers at almost any price. Technological advances to expand production can be useless in the face of gross inefficiencies in distribution. Policy must seek to link natural resources more closely to the consumer through improving transportation, storage, processing, and distribution facilities, and by regulating the operations of middlemen.

Improvements in marketing may result in lower prices to consumers or an increase in producer revenues, or both. If it raises farm incomes it will constitute an incentive for greater production. Advances in this direction will help to increase the domestic utilization of the region's resources while at the same time reducing the gap between agricultural and nonagricultural incomes.

Another obstacle to bringing Latin American resources directly to consumers is the deficiency in domestic processing facilities. This is particularly important for the products of the mines. For instance, there are no processing facilities for refining tin in Bolivia, and direct domestic consumption of copper has been limited by the inadequacy of fabricating plants. In forestry, too, the small number of efficiently sized sawmills in the region has hampered domestic wood consumption. However, progress can be anticipated. Recent international arrangements provide for establishment of tin processing plants in Bolivia, and Chile's agreement with the U.S. copper companies includes a substantial expansion of refining capacity in the country.

Comparative Advantage. The supply of Latin American natural resources is basically a reflection of the region's cost of production and distribution. At present, Latin America in relation to the rest of the world appears to be a low-cost producer only of copper, iron, sugar, bananas, wheat, and beef among the commodities studied in Part Two. It is competitive with respect to fish and forest products, tin and other minerals, and some tropical products. In oil, although it is a high-cost producer the region can compete because of the structure of the industry and the market. It has lost part of its comparative advantage in a few tropical commodities.

The statistical examination of the following chapter shows that Latin America's share of world production and exports has declined for several products since the 1930s. As has been pointed out, this development may be due in part to demand factors, such as discrimination against the region, and in part to ill-advised Latin American policies; however, to a large extent it does mirror a loss in Latin America's competitive position. The emergence of effective competitors in certain primary products signifies that the region's costs have increased relative to costs in other parts of the world.

Any cost advantage other less-developed areas may have today over Latin America will probably not quickly disappear. There are indications that land and labor costs in the production of some agricultural commodities will be lower in places like Africa, one of the region's chief competitors, than in Latin America. While both in Latin America and Africa the possibilities of bringing new lands under cultivation are becoming increasingly limited, in Africa there still appears to be an extensive margin.

The labor cost differential between Africa and Latin America is not only a matter of differences in direct wages but also in non-wage labor costs. Particularly since the last World War, Latin American labor has been able to increase its economic power significantly. Unions have become an important factor in economic life, especially in the industrial and mining countries of the region. Labor has learned to defend its position through strikes and other economic and political means despite (or because of) rampant inflation in some countries. Social legislation has been far more advanced in Latin America than in Africa and encompasses also the agricultural sector. Social security payments figure heavily in production costs and in many Latin American countries they represent an expense about equal to direct wage costs. Furthermore, political instability and real and imaginary social unrest have negatively affected investment decisions and thus have contributed indirectly to the cost burden in Latin America.

In the newly emerging countries, such as those in Africa, labor's economic, social, and political consciousness is of much more recent origin. With the attainment of political independence, the economic climate in African countries is changing and labor costs are bound to increase. Whether these changes will redress the balance of comparative advantage in some products between Africa and Latin America in the near future is a moot question. Much will depend not only on the changes in Africa but also on economic policies and political developments in Latin America.

Regional Integration. The speed and magnitude of the future development of the region's natural resources will in large measure depend upon the degree to which Latin American countries succeed in liberalizing trade among themselves. This is not the place to argue the case for integration, but it is plain that an easy flow of goods among the countries of the region will stimulate specialization and the establishment of large-scale industries which could not operate sufficiently within the confines of national markets only.[36] The absence of such industries, combined with the impediments of high tariff walls and other trade barriers, accounts for the relatively small regional utilization of Latin American mine output.

Intraregional trade in agricultural commodities already is comparatively high. Of the nearly $1 billion of agricultural imports by the nine countries which comprised the Latin American Free Trade Association in 1964[37] about 43 per-

[36] For a discussion and references regarding this topic see Grunwald et al., "Latin American Economic Integration . . . ," particularly chap. II.

[37] Since then Venezuela and Bolivia have joined LAFTA, so that there are now eleven member countries (Argentina, Bolivia, Brazil, Colombia, Chile, Ecuador, Mexico, Paraguay, Peru, Uruguay, and Venezuela).

cent originated among themselves. However, the absolute volume of trade is not high because of agricultural import substitution and diversification efforts.

The greatest benefit that agricultural development would derive from regional integration is the emergence of industries that produce the inputs for agricultural production. Efficient fertilizer and tractor industries depend on the reduction of intraregional trade barriers, which will permit low-cost production. Inexpensive inputs, in turn, will encourage the expansion of agricultural output at low prices through the adoption of modern techniques and intensive production methods. Although domestic inputs currently are more expensive, in a Latin American common market the production of nitrogenous fertilizers and tractors would be competitive with imports from the United States.[38]

Thus, the expansion of the industrial sector in Latin America will provide a strong stimulus for agricultural and mineral development. Industrialization can provide the inputs for agriculture and utilize the output of the mines and wells, and the products of agriculture. It will be efficient if production can be large enough to take advantage of economies of scale, and trade restriction within the vast regional market can be reduced. Latin American economic integration should, therefore, be a high priority item in policies for the development of the region's natural resources.

Conclusion

The basic changes required to promote the development of natural resources, particularly in agriculture, have a long gestation period. Policies and reforms must be introduced now in order to get results ten years hence. Natural resource development and industrialization must go hand in hand. While they compete for scarce human resources such as managerial and administrative talent, they do not conflict but rather reinforce one another.

Above all, public policies must have some stability. The farmer and private businessman are already confronted with the uncertainties of world markets. Fluctuating government policies make private production plans much more complicated by introducing additional uncertainty into economic planning. In the past, instability has been an important factor in discouraging private investment decisions. Latin

American governments will, therefore, have to recognize their responsibility for formulating long-term policies which provide a stable investment climate.

The new industrialization, unlike the earlier national import-substituting production, will need to be geared to exports as well as to the home market. Industries based upon the processing of Latin America's natural resources are obviously good candidates.[39]

During earlier stages of Latin American development dependence on a few raw materials may have stood in the way of industrialization and introduced rigidities in economic growth. Now and in the foreseeable future, the expansion of the supply of natural resources will be irretrievably enmeshed with industrialization. Resource development is essential to give Latin American economies greater viability through raising foreign exchange earnings, providing the inputs for manufacturing, and absorbing part of the output of industrialization.

While the development of its resources is a Latin American responsibility, achievements will be limited by the degree of co-operation of the developed countries. Direct aid to the region is not as important as removing obstacles to an expansion of imports from Latin America. The tendency toward increasing protectionism in the United States and elsewhere can stifle the region's new efforts to increase raw material output. Latin American attention will not shift from demand to supply problems of primary goods exports if greater efficiency in production results only in the raising of new import barriers in the United States and other developed countries. Massive investments in the development of Latin American natural resources can be expected only if the protectionist trend in the United States is reversed and the developed countries, too, reallocate their efforts in more efficient directions, so that there will be no serious problems of access to their markets.

[38] See ECIEL, "Nitrogenous Fertilizers" and "Tractors," in *Industrialization in a Latin American Common Market*.

[39] A good example of government efforts to establish export-oriented industries is the resource-based industrial complex which was started in the Guayana region in the eastern part of Venezuela. Iron ore, oil and natural gas, cheap hydroelectric power, and easy access to ocean transport constitute the backbone for this undertaking. The output will consist of raw materials such as iron ore, and processed goods such as petrochemicals, steel, and aluminum, which would serve as inputs for agriculture and industry. (For details see Alexander Ganz, "Regional Planning as a Key to the Present Stage of Economic Development in Latin America: The Case of the Guayana Region," Harvard-MIT Guayana Project, 1962; and the reports of the Corporación Venezolana de Guayana in Caracas, Venezuela.)

Chapter 3

STATISTICAL SUMMARY

An important aim of this study is to assemble and present statistical information on the sixteen commodities chosen to represent the natural resource sector in Latin America. This chapter summarizes that information, which is drawn primarily from the individual commodity chapters of Part Two but which includes some additional calculations and extensions of data. Attention here is given to five major subjects:

1) production, consumption, and trade, including the degree of domestic processing and of participation in world markets for each product;
2) the prices of primary commodities, including differences among sources and markets and the degree of stability over time;
3) the volume and value of exports, including rank among exports and share of foreign exchange earnings;
4) the present resource base, including the amount and quality of resources, costs, relation to output, and comparison to other parts of the world;
5) the size and structure of the resource-using industries, including production, trade, and use at each of several stages of processing.

The data are presented for all of Latin America in five tables; in all cases except the second (prices of raw materials) there are separate tables giving the same information for each of the twenty republics. These supplementary tables form an appendix to this chapter. In discussing each subject reference will be made to the relative importance of different nations and the conditions peculiar to each, but the emphasis will fall on the region as a whole.

Within the first three subjects, attention will be directed to the principal trends and changes of the last few decades, and to the factors responsible for those developments. In the next two cases, only the situation in recent years can be described, as data are lacking or difficult to interpret for earlier periods. Various measures are introduced to analyze the position of the resource industries in the early or middle 1960s. With some exceptions, 1967 is the final year for which data are presented. No effort is made to project output, consumption, or prices for the future. Instead, reference is made at the end of this chapter (footnote 6) to

projections published in recent years for the mid-1970s, and these sources are also used in the discussion of individual resource products. Given the differences in bases and assumptions for different commodities, the considerable range in the available projections, and the fact that estimates only a few years old are already in need of revision for some products, no attempt has been made to assemble the numerical estimates or to adjust them to a common basis. In Part Two, where emphasis is placed on factors likely to be significant over the next five or ten years, projections are used chiefly for illustration. No new estimates have been made for this study, which with a few exceptions covers the period ending in the middle 1960s.

Production, Consumption, and Trade

In the four periods selected for reference in this chapter — the late 1930s, the years around 1950, the early 1960s, and the mid-1960s — Latin America has accounted for between 10 and 22 percent of the world's production of copper, lead, zinc, tin, petroleum, and forest products. The only products for which the share is consistently below 10 percent are iron ore, coal, and wheat. The share rises to between 20 and 30 percent for cocoa, sugar, and beef, and to about the same level for bananas. Only in the case of coffee does the region produce more than half the total world output. These shares correspond approximately to the region's relative wealth in natural resources for each commodity, which is discussed at greater length below (see table B-4 and accompanying text). In only one case, coffee, is there a pronounced steady decline in the share, resulting from a transfer of production to Africa in consequence of that region's relatively good resources and its privileged position in certain European markets, and of the efforts of Brazil over a considerable period to maintain prices by restricting output. Now that coffee is traded under an international agreement with export quotas, this trend has been moderated. Three products show a consistent increase, appreciable in the case of cotton and rather dramatic for iron ore and fishmeal. All three experienced an export boom in Latin America during the 1950s: cotton in Central America, iron ore in Brazil, Venezuela, and Peru, and fishmeal in Peru.

The region's share of world exports follows the share of world output at a somewhat higher level, except for a few products where much of world production is for domestic use and a relatively small share enters world trade. Until 1964, this was most notably the case with wheat, Latin America's portion of world exports falling from 24 to only 5 percent while the share of production was nearly constant. This resulted from the efforts of many countries in Latin America and elsewhere to achieve self-sufficiency in wheat, and from the emergence of the United States as the world's foremost wheat supplier. In 1964-66 Latin America supplied 11 percent of world wheat exports. A comparable trend toward self-supply has had the opposite effect in the case of sugar, until the early 1960s more than doubling the region's share of exports. In Cuba, which has been by far the largest exporter, this resulted from preferential access to the U.S. market, large-scale U.S. investment in the sugar industry, and the existence of ample land and labor for expansion. As other suppliers withdrew, Cuba increased its dominance of the market. Other Latin American producers with equal or lower costs, such as Brazil, Mexico, Colombia, and Peru greatly increased their exports of sugar over this period. Petroleum is the only other product for which the share of exports has behaved quite differently from the share of output, falling from more than half to only one-fourth in consequence of the development of the Middle East. Venezuela is still the largest single exporter of oil in the world, but it now ranks well behind the principal Middle Eastern producers as a group.

Several of the trends already noted are also evident in the share of Latin American production that is exported: for example, the rise of cotton and fish products. For iron ore, the share rose appreciably in the 1950s, following a somewhat greater decline between the 1930s and 1950 when the region first began to produce steel in quantity. For most commodities at all times, at least 50 percent of output has been exported, the ratio being nearer 90 percent in some cases, especially during the 1930s. In general, a larger share of metals produced is exported than of other products, reflecting Latin America's slight degree of industrialization and consequently its low demand for metals compared with the region's resources.

The shares of output consumed domestically, especially low for metals, are extremely high only for wheat and beef. With the partial exception of lead, the ratio of consumption to production has increased steadily for all nonferrous metals as industrialization has advanced. A similar and even more striking development occurs for iron if, instead of iron ore consumption, the measure used is steel production as a percentage of steel consumption. Even with a fairly rapid rise in domestic use, Latin America continues to account for less than 10 percent of world consumption of every commodity except coffee, beef, forest products, and sugar. The high share for coffee results from its availability and relatively low price in all producing countries, especially Brazil; the regional figures for beef reflect the high per capita consumption of Argentina and Uruguay. The large share of consumption in fishery products reflects

chiefly losses in processing. Where a trend is discernible it is usually upward, rather consistently so for copper, steel, tin, cocoa, and sugar. Most of the relative increase in each case occurred before the 1950s; in several instances an increase up to that time was followed by a slight decline — lead and wheat are examples. The share for petroleum also rose and then fell, largely because of the shift from coal to oil, which has occurred in Europe in recent years and which has greatly raised that region's share of world petroleum consumption. The steady decline unique for coal is not related to this development but merely reflects the continued replacement of coal by oil in Latin America's energy economy.

The share of production refined domestically applies only to the metals, petroleum, cocoa, forest products, and fishery products. The meaning of this ratio varies somewhat among products and must be interpreted with care. Since commodities may be processed either for domestic use or for export, this measure may reflect not only changes in consumption but changes in the degree of processing of exports (or imports), responding to a variety of technical, economic, and geographic changes over time. Thus the experiences even of relatively similar products such as the nonferrous metals may be quite different.

There is a steady decline in the share of lead ore output smelted domestically, reflecting principally a shift of production from Mexico (where the share is about 90 percent) to Peru and the various minor producers (where the share is lower because of higher grade, low total production, or difficulties in transporting ore to smelters within the country). Zinc shows a modest increase in recent years, a trend which has continued with the installation of a new smelter in Mexico. The share has also risen for tin, but in this case much of the increased smelting took place not in Bolivia, the chief producer, but in Brazil and Mexico, which are also producers but are more significant as consumers. Much of the ore smelted in Brazil was imported from Malaya. Copper, unlike the other metals, is measured at the refining rather than the smelting stage. Smelting nearly always takes place near the mine because of the low grade of the ore, whereas refining may be performed in either the producing or the consuming country. The share of copper refined in Latin America rose from the 1930s to the early 1950s·as the region consumed an increasing share of its output, and then declined greatly while the latter share remained constant. The decline was due partly to reduction of refining in Chile during the 1950s, but the chief cause was the opening of a large mine with a smelter but no refinery in Peru in 1960. Smelting of iron ore nearly always takes place at a steel mill; the prereduction of iron ore for export is acquiring some importance and there is almost no trade in pig iron — that is, metal which has been smelted but not otherwise processed. Thus the share of iron ore smelted has varied inversely with the share of output exported.

As shown in table B-1, the share of crude oil output refined in Latin America has doubled since the 1930s, with most of the rise occurring after 1950. The share of production exported as crude has declined, while imports of crude from outside the region have risen relative to regional out-

TABLE B-1. LATIN AMERICA: Evolution of Production, Exports, and Consumption of Natural Resource Commodities, Late 1930s, Early 1950s, and Early and Mid 1960s
(Thousands of cubic meters of petroleum and forest products, and thousands of metric tons of all other products)

Commodity	Period	Production	Exports	Consumption	Share of Production (%)			Share of World Total (%)		
					Exported	Consumed	Refined	Production	Exports	Consumption
Copper	1935-39	416	377	9	91	2	51	22	25	0.5
	1950-51	494	444	54	90	11	69	19	32	2.1
	1962-64	854	809	93	95	11	39	19	30	1.9
	1965-66	896	805	144	90	16	47	17	29	2.9
Iron ore	1935-39	1,959	1,810	1,668	92	(14)	17	1	3	
	1952-53	9,394	6,354	4,763	68	(41)	26	3	9	2.1
	1962-64	42,898	35,057	10,222	82	(68)	18	8	21	2.6
	1965-66	61,284	47,100	11,144	77	(78)	14	10	23	2.7
Lead	1935-39	295	272	26	92	8	84	18	26	1.6
	1950-51	365	305	92	84	25	79	22	37	5.8
	1962-64	396	304	103	77	26	76	16	24	3.9
	1965-66	404	279	89	69	22	74	15	16	3.6
Zinc	1935-39	183	165	14	90	7	19	11	19	0.9
	1950-51	339	302	41	89	12	19	15	23	2.2
	1962-64	479	453	88	95	18	26	13	19	2.6
	1965-66	547	490	115	90	34	28	12	17	1.6
Tin	1935-39	28	26	3	89	10	3	16	17	1.8
	1950-51	33	32	4	97	12	6	20	19	2.8
	1962-64	25	23	6	92	23	23	18	14	3.6
	1965-66	27	25	6	91	22	16	17	15	3.7
Petroleum	1935-39	43,578	30,424	13,153	65	30	29	14	53	4.4
	1950-51	117,608	92,290	35,974	78	31	36	18	41	6.2
	1962-64	245,523	181,362	88,400	74	36	52	16	26	5.6
	1965-66	261,941	198,496	106,942	76	41	58	14	29	5.2
Coal	1935-39	4,087		9,704		(40)				0.7
	1952-53	7,397		10,011		(64)				0.5
	1961-63	9,665		10,535		(73)	31			
	1965	10,780		12,277		(88)	41			
Coffee	1935-39	2,027	1,436		71			87	86	
	1950-52	1,842	1,532	420	83	23		83	82	20
	1962-64	2,794	1,924	710	69	25		70	69	19
	1965-66	2,875	1,785	878	62	30		68	65	23
Cocoa	1935-39	215	201	32	97	15		29	26	4.8
	1950-52	265	178	59	67	22	30	34	22	6.1
	1961-63	270	194	76	72	28	48	23	25	7.1
	1964-66	289	205	117	71	41	51	20	25	7.5
Sugar	1935-39	5,475	3,509	1,948	64	36		21	29	8.3
	1951-53	10,949	6,387	4,283	58	39		30	43	12
	1961-63	13,869	7,768	7,886	56	57		26	65	15
	1964-66	15,778	7,207	7,984	46	50		25	22	12
Bananas	1934-38		1,631						65	
	1953-57	5,802	2,142	4,220	37	73		29	69	21
	1962-64		2,875						65	
	1965-66		3,324						67	
Wheat	1934-38	8,042	3,445	6,940	43	86		5	24	2.6
	1951-53	8,123	2,332	9,453	29	86		4	7	6.3
	1961-63	10,184	2,328	11,235	23	91		4	5	5.8
	1964-66	13,791	6,282	12,659	46	92		5	11	5.9
Beef	1934-38	3,286	507	2,780	15	85		23	39	19
	1951-53	4,294	165	4,141	4	96		27	21	26
	1961-63	5,706	502	5,215	9	91		22	39	20
	1964-66	5,707	639	5,096	11	89		20	44	18
Cotton	1935-39	661	336	220	51	33		6	11	3.3
	1950-52	915	430	482	47	53		12	17	6.5
	1961-63	1,536	921	680	60	44		14	26	6.4
	1964-66	1,646	1,035	758	63	46		14	26	8.5
Forest products	1951-53	177,637	3,149	179,212	2	(99)	14	13		13
	1961-63	234,979	3,038	238,744	1	(98)	14	12		13
	1964-66	262,430	3,558	265,695	1	(98)	15	13		14
Fishery products	1938	283	6.4	334	2	(85)		1		1.6
	1951-53	689	57	715	8	(96)	16	3	2	2.9
	1961-63	7,931	1,266	6,777	16	85	80	17	26	15
	1964-66	10,391	1,757	8,644	17	83	89	20	28	17

NOTE: These sources and notes apply to table B-1 and appendix tables B-1-1 through B-1-20.

Production refers to:
    metal content for nonferrous metals
    gross weight for iron ore
    total timber removals, including fuelwood, for forest products
    total liveweight catch of fish, molluscs, and crustaceans
    volume of output for petroleum
    gross weight for all other commodities

Exports refer to gross exports to all destinations, not to net exports (exports less imports) or to gross exports to destinations outside Latin America

Consumption refers to actual consumption where data are available and to apparent consumption (production plus imports less exports) for all all other commodities. Data refer to:
    consumption in manufacturing for nonferrous metals
    consumption of crude steel, in ingot equivalent weight, for iron and steel
    consumption of refined products for petroleum
    consumption of coal and imported coke, in hard coal equivalent weight, for coal
    consumption of cocoa beans only, 1935-39 and 1951-53; of cocoa beans and imported products in bean equivalent weight, for 1961-63 and
        1964-66, where data are available
    actual food consumption of fish plus losses in industrial processing (reduction) of fish to meal and oil

Share of Production Consumed is consumption as a percentage of production. Where consumption exceeds production, the ratio is reversed and appears in parentheses. For iron ore, the ratio shown is production of crude steel (not ore) as a percentage of consumption of crude steel.

Share of Production Refined refers to:
    refining for copper
    smelting for iron ore, lead, zinc, and tin
    refining for crude oil
    conversion to metallurgical coke for coal
    grinding for cocoa beans
    industrial (nonfuel) use for forest products
    reduction to meal and oil for fishery products for Peru and Chile only, 1951-53 (data for 1955-56), 1961-63 (data for 1959-61); for 1964-66
        data are available for Argentina, Chile, Ecuador, Mexico, Peru, and Venezuela.

Data do not always refer to the same years for different commodities or for different countries and a single commodity. Production is for 1935-39 for all commodities, exports for 1934-38 for all agricultural products and consumption for 1936-38 for most products. Nearly all data for the 1950s and 1960s are for the years shown: some refer to 1950-52, 1952-53, or 1962-64. Because data are not available for a fully consistent presentation, figures for apparent consumption and total for Latin America are in many cases approximate. (Consumption does not equal production less exports where imports occurred.)

Gaps in Statistical Series: See p. 65.

Sources and notes for individual products
    Copper: tables 4-4, 4-5, 4-6, and 4-11
    Iron and Steel: tables 5-2, 5-4, 5-6, and 5-7
    Lead and Zinc: tables 6-2A, 6-2B, 6-3, 6-4A, 6-4B, 6-6A, and 6-6B
    Tin: tables 7-2, 7-3, and 7-4
    Petroleum: tables 8-2, 8-3, 8-7, 8-9, and 8-13
    Coal: tables 9-2, 9-4, and 9-7
    Coffee: tables 10-5, 10-6, and 10-11
    Cocoa: tables 11-1, 11-2, and 11-5
    Sugar: tables 12-3, 12-4, and 12-8
    Bananas: tables 13-1, 13-2, and 13-6
    Wheat: tables 14-2, 14-4, and 14-6
    Beef: tables 15-4, 15-8, 15-10, and 15-12
    Cotton: tables 16-2, 16-4, and 16-6
    Forest Products: tables 17-3, 17-4, and 17-10
    Fishery Products: tables 18-1, 18-2, and 18-7

Information not included in these tables is taken from the sources cited for them.

put. A sharp expansion of such imports by Argentina, Brazil, and Uruguay took place as those countries built their own refineries and sought the cheapest sources of crude oil for them; thus crude from the Middle East and the Communist countries displaced imports of refined products from Venezuela. It is important to note that this measure treats shipment of oil from Venezuela to the Netherlands West Indies for refining and subsequent export, as exports of crude rather than products. If the fraction of Latin American oil refined within the region is redefined to include processing in the Netherlands West Indies, the ratio instead of rising from 29 to 58 percent falls from over 90 percent in the 1930s to less than 75 percent at present.

The share of domestic processing of cocoa has increased partly in consequence of the rising fraction of output consumed, and also because a sizable export trade in cocoa products has developed, especially in Brazil. This change occurred during and just after World War II as a means of providing additional employment and of using beans that could not be exported immediately because of shipping shortages. The figures for forest products show the share of timber cut which was used for some industrial purpose rather than as fuel. The amount of fuelwood consumed in Latin America has been roughly constant for some decades despite the region's population growth, while fuelwood's share of total energy provision has declined steadily, giving way especially to petroleum. The figures for fish show approximately the amount of the total catch processed into oil and meal, changes in the index being more reliable than the level for any one period because of weight losses in processing. The sharp increase in recent years, like the changes in shares of world production and exports, reflects the development of fishmeal exports in Peru and to a lesser degree in Chile.

A much more detailed examination of the resource-using industries and the various stages of processing can be made for recent than for earlier years (see table B-5 and accompanying discussion). The indices presented here are only a rough measure of the extent to which Latin America's natural resource commodities are processed within the region, whether for export or for domestic use. It should also be remembered that this measure and the others given here vary greatly from one country to another. Data for individual countries are somewhat less complete than for the region as a whole, since information is usually better for major than for minor producers, but they should be consulted to obtain an idea of the amounts and shares of production, consumption, and trade of the twenty Latin American nations and the importance of each in the world economy of primary commodities. (See tables B-1-1 to B-1-20 of the appendix to this chapter.)

Prices

The prices of many raw materials, including most of those studied here, have followed approximately this path over the last four decades: a peak sometime during the 1920s; a sharp decline in the early 1930s, with a partial recovery later in the decade or at the outbreak of World War II; stability under governmental control during the war; a postwar rise leading to a new peak between 1950 and 1955; a subsequent decline, and a recovery or even a new peak in the period 1962-65. Within this pattern, however, there is considerable variety, and the factors determining the prices of different products are quite diverse. The speed of recovery during the 1930s varied greatly, being generally rapid for metals and extremely slow for products such as coffee and cocoa which continued in excess supply as the result of heavy planting in the previous decade. The postwar recovery of prices was equally varied, with a new price peak reached as early as 1946 for sugar and not until 1954-56 for coffee, cocoa, and copper.

Price behavior is somewhat more regular if the commodities are divided into groups with common properties. The simplest such distinction is that between metals, especially the major nonferrous metals, and most agricultural products. Demand for the former reflects to a large extent the rate of investment and growth of industrial economies and is particularly sensitive to cyclical changes and to wars. Autonomous changes in supply are rare. Demand for agricultural products, especially foodstuffs, is related more to levels of income and personal consumption and is relatively stable, being rather unresponsive to price changes as well. Supply, on the other hand, can vary greatly in response to weather conditions, alternative opportunities for farmers, the actions of governments, and other factors. In the case of tree crops, supply often reflects the prices prevailing several years earlier: adjustments are slow and increases in particular can be very large. Sizable and rapid changes in demand have occurred for agricultural goods, most notably in the closing of the European market at the start of World War II and its recovery in the late 1940s. Year-to-year variations in price in normal times, however, usually reflect changes in output or availability rather than in demand. The prices of nonferrous metals were held down during the war by government controls, while the prices of a few agricultural goods such as coffee were raised. Metals prices reached a peak during the Korean War, when the only agricultural prices much affected were those of industrial inputs such as rubber. The price peaks for commodities such as coffee, cocoa, and sugar reflected increases in demand unrelated to the war, or marked reductions of supply. More recently, metals prices have responded to the industrial boom since 1964 and to the war in Vietnam, while the price increases of sugar in 1963 or of coffee since 1964 were due to entirely different factors operating on the side of supply.

The prices of individual raw materials and the conditions which determine them are discussed in the commodity chapters of Part Two, where some sixty series are presented covering all or part of the period 1925-67. Of these, twenty-three have been selected for presentation in index form (see table B-2). Each series has been converted where necessary to U.S. currency, and then deflated by the U.S. wholesale price index based on 1957-59. The resulting indices were adjusted to a new base year, 1956, when the prices of most products were close to their average values for the years 1949-64. Where prices are not regularly reported or where posted prices are not used for many transactions, unit values of exports or imports are employed. An index constructed in this manner is only a

TABLE B-2. LATIN AMERICA: Indices of Deflated Prices of Selected Primary Commodities, 1925-1964
(Base 1956 = 1000: All prices deflated by the U.S. wholesale price index, base 1957-59 = 100)

	1	2	3	4	5	6	7	8
Commodity	Copper	Iron Ore	Lead	Zinc	Tin	Crude Oil	Crude Oil	Coal
Market	LME	U.S.A.	LME	LME	LME	U.S.A.		
Producing or Exporting Country		Brazil				Venezuela	Venezuela	U.S.A.
1925	555	1546	907	1101	975	921		778
1926	537	1927	814	1061	1125	925		905
1927	541	1090	665	930	1173	969		850
1928	612	996	573	815	912	707		777
1929	735	792	641	814	830	705		813
1930	587	592	549	598	621	794		885
1931	454		438	496	627	719		1004
1932	326		346	468	582	556		1060
1933	399	833	406	644	996	541		982
1934	389		398	588	1179	612		1016
1935	373		472	553	1104	591		926
1936	452	605	586	588	1005	603		918
1937	596	376	723	818	1107	608		883
1938	484	781	513	557	938	646		948
1939	469	711	485	538	1037	628		983
1940	577	793	692	848	1000	682		964
1941	547	617	622	761	960	664		974
1942	484	538	551	674	896	660		964
1943	463		526	644	856	716		963
1944	460		523	641	927	745		1003
1945	451		514	703	911	715		913
1946	492		865	921	854	677		1008
1947	677	445	1246	1218	922	775		645
1948	643	431	1294	1285	1082	1050		974
1949	614	571	1345	1356	1158	1112		1004
1950	604	565	1015	1355	1051	1037		936
1951	668	656	1388	1755	1363	914		907
1952	814	1155	1186	1549	1251	941	927	940
1953	797	1101	820	792	960	1033	1024	907
1954	788	931	861	831	947	1054	1036	876
1955	1103	993	938	963	971	1032	1032	920
1956	1000	1000	1000	1000	1000	1000	1000	1000
1957	647	1081	806	821	932	1028	1084	1012
1958	578	1067	602	651	895	1017	1024	969
1959	694	860	584	806	954	922	898	934
1960	717	820	588	866	966	912	865	902
1961	671	822	531	762	1081	926	872	913
1962	683	820	463	659	1088	915	849	911
1963	683	822	524	752	1109	916	835	904
1964	1023	759	832	1153	1511	910	809	917
Entire Period Average	626	873	721	858	996	822		928
(1) Average deviation from the average	15.7	22.7	26.3	26.2	12.5	18.8		8.5
(2) Average year-to-year variation	13.2	14.1[a]	17.5	16.5	10.8	6.4		0.6
Postwar Period[b] Average	755	876	843	1004	1077	979	943	935
(1) Average deviation from the average	16.4	17.0	52.2	26.8	11.8	6.1	8.9	3.4
(2) Average year-to-year variation	14.3	9.9	18.7	18.8	10.0	3.9	4.5	3.4

TABLE B–2 – Continued

	9	10	11	12	13	14	15	16
Commodity	Coffee	Coffee	Cocoa	Cocoa	Sugar	Sugar	Bananas	Bananas
Market	New York	New York	New York	U.S.A.		New York	U.S.A.	U.S.A.
Producing or Exporting Country	Brazil	Colombia	Ghana	Ecuador	Cuba			
1925	709	642	593	1094	1194	1211	625	
1926	668	676	740	1049	1241	1248	668	
1927	586	624	1065	1230	1469	1423	700	
1928	725	670	851	996	1231	1252	679	
1929	702	569	704	895	939	1140	690	
1930	462	495	603	932	742	1122	760	
1931	365	531	459	711	783	1318	869	
1932	498	434	435	731	606	1300	919	
1933	422	380	429	640	668	1409	924	
1934	452	454	447	635	613	1154	813	
1935	336	318	402	511	555	1165	762	
1936	348	324	542	573	550	1283	725	
1937	389	331	627	636	662	1151	665	
1938	300	333	426	538	643	1080	745	
1939	294	357	400	643	937	1119	791	
1940	277	251	418	681	714	1025	852	
1941	395	408	560	552	844	1117	780	
1942	411	383	581	623	1377	1094	715	
1943	393	366	555	582	1316	1046	718	
1944	390	363	551	610	1307	1038	759	
1945	389	357	542	643	1499	1023	779	
1946	468	413	618	831	1773	1097	752	
1947	538	482	1515	1416	1712	1208	665	
1948	510	481	1592	1485	1330	996	627	906
1949	650	583	912	1059	1377	1099	755	1046
1950	963	798	1303	1292	1586	1079	693	1064
1951	928	790	1294	1253	1621	990	744	954
1952	951	789	1327	1269	1226	1052	772	995
1953	1034	839	1411	1241	1017	1072	938	1014
1954	1403	1120	2193	2005	970	1036	951	1041
1955	1014	901	1414	1335	961	1009	990	1024
1956	1000	1000	1000	1000	1000	1000	1000	1000
1957	952	840	1089	1140	1441	996	932	1034
1958	798	678	1555	1491	964	987	925	939
1959	609	585	1282	1251	816	980	929	833
1960	602	580	994	970	862	988	897	819
1961	594	567	794	703	802	992	933	789
1962	560	527	736	816	816	1013		778
1963	563	513	889	901	2337	1288		725
1964	769	631	821	936	1612	1085		697
Entire Period Average	610	560	867	948	1103	1117	796	
(1) Average deviation from the average	33.7	29.0	40.2	23.7	30.8	8.4	16.0	
(2) Average year-to-year variation	14.7	12.7	22.6	18.4	18.9	7.0	6.0	
Postwar Period[b] Average	837	734	1188	1166	1213	1042	881	922
(1) Average deviation from the average	23.1	20.5	23.9	19.4	27.9	5.1	9.8	11.5
(2) Average year-to-year variation	14.9	22.8	22.9	20.9	24.0	19.0	4.9	5.2

TABLE B–2 – Continued

	17	18	19	20	21	22	23	24	25
Commodity Market	Wheat Canada	Beef Smithfield	Beef Cattle Buenos Aires	Cotton Liverpool	Cotton Liverpool	Fishmeal Buffalo	Fishmeal	Indices, Major Export Commodities	
Producing or Exporting Country		Argentina		Brazil	Peru		Peru	5[c]	17[d]
1925									
1926									
1927				1325					
1928				1243					
1929				1057					
1930				766					
1931				600					
1932				771					
1933				392					
1934		884		1079		753			
1935		798		980		774			
1936		791		1019		898			
1937		868		688		754			
1938			628	715		842			
1939				944		908			
1940			548			1062			
1941			565			1136			
1942			632			1063			
1943			593			1016			
1944			605			1009			
1945			600			1052			
1946			578	1275		1365			
1947			577	1147		1219			
1948			561	1229		1399			
1949	1323	744	680	1263		1303		981	
1950	1260	785	694	2172		1090	892	1133	1026
1951	1313	776	777	1840	1131	1026	842	1055	1052
1952	1292	1001	1070	1714	752	1036	880	1025	1009
1953	1130	1136	1309	1182	776	1042	874	1025	998
1954	1049	1212	1333	1282	829	1080	885	1146	1104
1955	1032	1311		1114	868	1082	988	1027	1036
1956	1000	1000	1000[e]	1000	1000	1000	1000	1000	1000
1957	932	1042		924	751	1001	950	1026	967
1958	942	1096			539	1073	965	892	871
1959	945	1205	521		658	784	990	793	806
1960	922	1225	552	881	656	743	669	797	803
1961	986	1140	535	876	624	906	571	789	790
1962	995	1192	475	829	570	927	829	772	780
1963	1030	1114	551	836	641	968	796	970	872
1964	1012	1404		831	655	1088	938	960	910
Entire Period									
Average		(f)	685[g]	1066		1013			
(1) Average deviation from the average			24.4	25.0		12.2			
(2) Average year-to-year variation			11.8[h]	16.8[j]		8.9			
Postwar Period[b]									
Average	1073	1086	772[g]	1196	746	1009	871	962	935
(1) Average deviation from the average	11.1	29.6	32.9	27.4	16.3	9.1	13.1	10.0	10.2
(2) Average year-to-year variation	4.1	11.7	15.2[h]	15.9[k]	10.1	7.7	9.5	7.1	4.9

TABLE B–2 – Continued

Price Series Used: Description and Sources

No.	Commodity	Years	Description of Product	Market	Nature of Price	Unit	Source Table
1	Copper	1925-64	electrolytic wirebars	LME	spot	cents/pound	4-7
2	Iron ore	1925-55	all grades lump ore	U.S.	unit value imports (Brazil)	dollars/long ton	5-3
		1956-64	hematite, 68.5% iron	Victória, Brazil	contracts for export	dollars/long ton	
3	Lead	1925-64	pigs or bars	LME	spot	cents/pound	6-5
4	Zinc	1925-64	slab	LME	spot	cents/pound	6-5
5	Tin	1925-64	metal	LME	spot	cents/pound	7-5
6	Crude oil	1925-64	all grades, dutiable	U.S.	unit value imports (Venezuela)	dollars/barrel	8-5
7	Crude oil	1952-64	all grades	Venezuela	unit value exports	dollars/barrel	8-5
8	Coal	1925-64	bituminous and lignite	U.S.	unit value exports	dollars/short ton	9-5
9	Coffee	1925-64	Santos No. 4 (Brazil)	New York	spot	cents/pound	10-6
10	Coffee	1925-64	Manizales (Colombia)	New York	spot	cents/pound	10-6
11	Cocoa	1925-64	Ghana (proxy for Brazil)	New York	spot	cents/pound	11-3
12	Cocoa	1925-47	flavor grade	U.S.	unit value imports (Ecuador)	cents/pound	11-3
		1948-64	flavor grade	Ecuador	unit value exports	cents/pound	
13	Sugar	1925-60	raw	Cuba	spot, FAS	cents/pound	12-7
		1961-64	raw	Caribbean	spot, FAS	cents/pound	
14	Sugar	1925-64	raw, duty paid	New York	spot	cents/pound	12-7
15	Bananas	1925-64	all edible types	U.S.	unit value imports	dollars/stem	13-3
16	Bananas	1948-64	first class green stems, importer to wholesaler	U.S.	spot	cents/pound	13-3
17	Wheat	1949-64	No. 1 Manitoba Northern	in store, Fort William/ Port Arthur	open market export quotation	dollars/bushel	14-11,12
18	Beef	1934-37	Argentine chilled hind- and forequarters	Birmingham, Leeds, London, Manchester	spot	pence/pound	15-14
		1949-64	Argentine chilled hindquarters	Smithfield	spot	pence/pound	15-14
19	Beef cattle	1938, 1940-54 & 1959-63	fat steers for export	Buenos Aires		cents/kilogram	15-14
20	Cotton	1927-39 & 1946-64	São Paulo type No. 5, 1 1/32 inch (Brazil)	Liverpool	spot	cents/pound	16-3
21	Cotton	1951-64	Pima No. 1, 1 9/16 inch (Peru)	Liverpool	spot	cents/pound	16-3
22	Fishmeal	1934-64	bagged, 60% protein	Buffalo	spot, FOB	dollars/short ton	18-7
23	Fishmeal	1950-64	Anchoveta, 60% protein	Peru	unit value exports	dollars/short ton	18-7

Note: Gaps in series represent years for which data were either not available or not comparable. See p. 65.
(1) Average absolute value of the difference between the current year's price and the average price, as a percentage of the average price.
(2) Average absolute value of the difference in price between successive years, as a percentage of the average price.

[a]Assuming monotonic price movements in 1930-33, 1933-36, and 1942-47.

[b]1949 to 1964, except for crude oil (7: 1952-64), bananas (16: 1948-64), cotton (21: 1951-64) and fishmeal (23: 1950-64). Bananas (15) ends in 1961; cotton (21) is missing the years 1958-59.

[c]Index composed of the prices of the following five commodities, weighted according to their unweighted average shares of Latin American total exports in the years 1956-59; copper (1), 0.0664; crude oil (6), 0.4321; coffee (9), 0.3052; sugar (13), 0.1282; and cotton (20), 0.0681. These five products accounted for 64.6% of total Latin American exports on the average, 1956-59; the entire set of 16 natural resource products accounted for approximately 70% of total exports.

[d]Index composed of the prices of 17 commodities (bananas, sugar, coffee, cocoa, cotton, beef, wheat, maize, wool, linseed oil, quebracho, copper, lead, zinc, tin, natural nitrates, and crude oil) weighted according to shares of total Latin American exports in 1959-61. Original (undeflated) index from ECLA, *Economic Survey of Latin America, 1964*, p. 225.

[e]Estimate: data are not available for the years 1955-58.

[f]Calculations made only for postwar period; prewar data cover too few years and/or are insufficiently comparable or reliable.

[g]Average excludes 1956.

[h]Assuming monotonic decrease in price, 1938 to 1940 and 1954 to 1959.

[j]Average for two periods 1927-39 and 1946-64 considered separately; average for entire period 1927-64, assuming a monotonic increase in price from 1939 to 1946, is 14.9.

[k]Assuming monotonic decrease in price, 1957 to 1960.

rough measure of real or relative price, intended to take account of the general decline in prices during the Depression and the sharp inflation following World War II. Several of the series (particularly for the earlier years) do not refer to a perfectly defined product, so that variations reflect changes in quality as well as in price. Furthermore, the wholesale index used to deflate the commodity prices includes some of those same commodities, sometimes at different prices or stages of processing. The indices presented are therefore not simply the prices of certain well-defined products expressed in terms of the prices of other equally well-defined goods. Especially, it should be noted, these indices do not represent the terms of trade between Latin America and the United States or the capacity to import obtained by exporting these commodities. The exclusion of European prices further weakens these indices as measures of the purchasing power of exports, at least for years when European and United States wholesale prices did not move together.

Within these limitations, the series show the price behavior of most of the major Latin American export products. The data do not indicate any definite trend other than the long cycle already described; they do not show a long-term decline in real prices for primary commodities. In the 1950s there was a considerable deterioration of primary prices, many of which were below their long-term average levels in the late 1950s and early 1960s. However, this is the longest decline to appear in the series, and it was at least temporarily ended or reversed for many products by the mid-1960s under the influence of such factors as rapid industrial growth, wartime demand, and the implementation of commodity control schemes. Much of the recent attention given to commodity prices and the efforts to control those of several products derive from the experience of the decade following the Korean War, when real prices for primary materials unquestionably did decline, sometimes by large amounts, and when this decline was one of the factors responsible for a steady slowing down of economic growth in Latin America.

Two measures have been calculated to indicate the stability of these prices, over approximately the period 1949-64 in all cases and over the longer period 1925-64 when data were available. The first measure is the average deviation of the current year's price from the average price, as a percentage of that average price: it indicates how far away, on the average, the price has been from the mean for the period. This measure gives no indication of the frequency of price changes; it does not distinguish, for example, between a price that is uniform in each of two periods with a single change between them, and a price that fluctuates between the two limits. The second measure is the average variation in price from one year to the next, again as a percentage of the average price for the period. The average price is employed so that an ascending series will not yield a larger variation than a descending series with the same absolute annual changes. This measure indicates the rapidity of price change, being higher for a quickly fluctuating series than for one which moves more slowly between the same limits. A high average deviation together with a low average annual variation indicates ap-

proximately monotonic behavior over a wide range; a high annual variation with a low deviation indicates rapid change within narrow limits; and so on.

By either measure, certain prices are quite stable: coal, crude oil, bananas, wheat, and fishmeal. Sugar in the protected U.S. market is relatively stable except in 1963. The unstable prices are somewhat more difficult to determine consistently. Over the longer period Ghanaian cocoa (used to represent Brazilian cocoa) and Cuban sugar are extremely unstable, followed, according to the measure used, by Brazilian and Colombian coffee, Brazilian cotton, lead, and zinc in varying order. Over the shorter interval since 1949, these products continue to be the least stable in price variation but are joined by Argentine beef and cattle if stability is measured by deviation from the average price. The remaining metals — copper, tin, and iron ore — and Peruvian cotton fall in the middle of the range at all times.

Series are presented for two distinct grades of each of three products: coffee, cocoa, and cotton. The higher quality commodity has the more stable price in every comparison except that between Brazilian and Colombian coffee in annual variation since 1949, which circumstance reflects the disruption of normal coffee price margins in the years following the peak of 1954. The differences in price stability between grades, however, appear to be significant only for cocoa, 1925-64, and cotton, 1951-64. The first case partly reflects the shift in tastes as cocoa became an article of mass consumption, which greatly narrowed the differential between prices for base and flavor grades of cocoa.

A similar comparison, with slightly more significant results, can be made for three products where series are given for two different markets or definitions: Venezuelan crude oil, sugar, and fishmeal. In each case prices are more stable in the United States than in the exporting country, the difference being especially marked for sugar. The United States is a major producer of all these products, and in the cases of petroleum and sugar domestic output is protected and controlled, with imports admitted to balance demand at desired price levels. Quotas have been in effect for oil since 1957 and for sugar since 1934. Other restrictions or tariffs, combined at times with direct controls on prices or output or with purchases and releases from government stockpiles, have influenced the prices of nonferrous metals, beef, wheat, and cotton as well. In these cases where the United States is a major exporter, maintaining a higher price for its domestic market, or where its influence has affected prices in all markets for a product, no attempt has been made to draw up series for the different markets.

The differences in price stability by the measures that are used here would be extremely small, for example, between the London Metal Exchange and the U.S. metal markets in New York and St. Louis. Similarly, prices have not been collected for goods such as tropical agricultural products in the major European markets, since these either follow prices in the United States or are largely closed to Latin American exporters through arrangements between European countries and their former dependencies. International agreements involving export controls or buffer stocks affect, or have in the past affected, the prices of copper, tin, coffee, sugar, and wheat. The effect in raising prices can sometimes be seen dramatically as for tin in the late 1930s or coffee since 1963. However, with the possible exceptions of tin and wheat these agreements do not appear to have made prices appreciably more stable over a period of a decade or more. There is no distinction in price stability between minerals and agricultural products, or between those commodities produced chiefly by large expatriate firms in Latin America and those produced by individual farmers. Except for Argentine cattle and beef, it is not possible to compare prices at different stages of processing, and that one comparison is uncertain because of inadequate data on cattle prices. A number of other factors influence the prices of individual commodities without affecting these indices consistently.

The price series for single products have been combined into two indices of major export commodities, and the same measures of stability applied to them. One contains only the five largest export products – copper, crude oil, coffee, sugar, and cotton – weighted according to shares of Latin American exports in 1956-59, when these goods accounted for 65 percent of the total. This index exaggerates price instability, since total exports of each product are valued at the least stable price: all sugar, for example, is assumed to be sold in the free or residual market, although much of it was in fact sold at the more stable U.S. price. The second index contains seventeen products, including some such as maize, wool, and nitrates that are not studied here, and several different prices are used when distinct grades or markets exist for a product. The two indices yield almost identical values of about 10 percent for the average deviation from the average price in 1950-64, but differ appreciably in the average annual variation: 7.1 percent for the shorter list against 4.9 percent for the longer. The difference is partly due to the use of more stable prices for the five major products in the longer list. It may also be that the prices of the minor commodities are more stable, or move on the average in the opposite direction, than the prices of copper, oil, coffee, sugar, and cotton. For Latin America as a whole, diversification of products and markets appears to result in slightly greater price stability from year to year, without reducing the range of price variation. The variables of greater interest to the exporting countries, however, are the rate and stability of growth of their export proceeds. The prices discussed here are only one component of export value, and even the unit value of exports may behave quite differently because of differences in the degree of processing or destination of the commodities sold.

Volume and Value of Exports

The volume of Latin America's exports of primary products has already been discussed with respect to regional production and total world exports. It remains to consider in somewhat more detail the volume and value of exports over the interval 1950-66 selected for analysis.

Total regional exports increased during this period from somewhat less than $7,000 million to more than $11,000 million. There was a very sharp increase in 1951, to $8,000 million, a level not reached again until 1954. Thereafter

growth was slow, with a decline in 1958 and a slow recovery, until a level of $9,000 million was approached in 1961. The fifteen export commodities studied here accounted for 70 percent of the total in 1950 and again in 1964. In the intervening years the share rose slowly and rather steadily to a peak of 81 percent in 1955-57 and then declined to 75 percent in 1961. This cyclical pattern was interrupted in 1962, when the shares due to copper, iron ore, petroleum, cotton, and fishery products in particular were unusually high and the total share reached 86 percent (see table B-3).

Only a few other trends can be noted in this period for the region as a whole. There was a considerable shift from agricultural to mineral products. Temperate foodstuffs, cotton, and forest products show no trend, so the change is from tropical foodstuffs to metals and petroleum. This transfer occurred despite the relatively high prices for metals in the early 1950s; metals did reach a peak of 8.8 percent of total exports in 1952 but surpassed this level from 1960 onward as the result of a rapid growth in iron ore exports from several countries and increased copper exports from Peru. In some individual countries, particularly in Mexico and Peru, changes in the structure of exports were much larger than for the whole region (see tables B-3-1 to B-3-20 of the appendix to this chapter). Great increases in the importance of copper and fishmeal in Peru and of coffee and cotton in Mexico appear only slightly or not at all in the regional totals. Only three products show a definite increase in the share of regional exports in this period: iron ore, petroleum, and fish and fishmeal. Only two exhibit an equally marked decline: lead and coffee. The same five commodities – petroleum, coffee, sugar, cotton, and copper – occupied the first five ranks among exports in all years. Less important products have changed rank sharply.

The commodities differ greatly in stability of export value during this period. The same measure of average annual variation that was applied to prices gives values ranging from 6 percent for petroleum and 8 percent for coffee to 30 percent for copper and 43 percent for wheat. There is no consistent distinction between agricultural and mineral products nor between products of which Latin America is a major supplier and those for which its exports are relatively small.

The same calculation can be made separately for the quantity of exports (metal content of nonferrous metals and gross weight of other products) and for the unit value. A comparison of unit values with the corresponding price series reveals no consistent differences in stability. If the comparison is made between unit values and quantities, it is possible in some cases to conclude that one factor is primarily responsible for variations in total export value. Unit value appears to be dominant for copper, lead, and zinc; not only is the instability greater than for quantity, but the percentage change in unit value exceeds that in volume in most years. Similarly, quantity variations predominate for petroleum and wheat. No such identification is possible for the remaining products. For coffee and sugar, and perhaps for cocoa to a lesser extent, this is because Latin America is such a major supplier that the volume of its exports is the principal determinant of prices and the two factors cannot

TABLE B-3. LATIN AMERICA: Exports of Selected Primary Commodities, 1950-1966
(Thousands of metric tons or cubic meters and millions of U.S. dollars)

Commodity	1950	1951	1952	1953	1954	1955	1956	1957	1958	1959	1960	1961	1962	1963	1964	1965	1966
Copper	439	449	448	420	471	538	590	607	579	647	746	787	796	801	830	775	835
Value	204	238	327	253	309	439	457	313	253	340	429	422	433	440	497	624	851
Share total exports (%)	3	3	4.5	3.3	3.9	5.4	5.4	3.5	3.0	3.9	4.9	4.7	4.6	4.4	4.7	5.9	7.6
Rank among exports	5	5	5	5	5	5	5	5	5	5	4	5	5	5	4	4	3
Iron ore	3,670	4,885	5,487	7,220	11,058	13,658	18,735	26,338	24,795	29,119	35,179	32,749	33,208	33,430	38,534	46,850	47,350
Value	7	25	51	49	67	83	132	191	178	202	282	227	231	228	272	372	376
Share total exports (%)	0.1	0.3	0.7	0.6	0.8	1	1.5	2.2	2.1	2.3	3.2	2.5	2.8	2.3	2.3	3.4	3.4
Lead	337	273	363	348	337	312	310	321	336	276	280	335	352	273	288	276	281
Value	91	111	112	86	87	91	94	94	66	61	62	66	49	50	63	77	70
Share total exports (%)	1.3	1.4	1.5	1.1	1.1	1.1	1.1	1.1	0.8	0.7	0.7	0.7	0.5	0.5	0.6	0.7	0.6
Zinc	306	299	376	350	345	427	407	401	391	388	414	498	417	442	501	474	513
Value	42	69	77	35	37	50	66	65	36	41	51	53	53	52	75	79	78
Share total exports (%)	0.6	0.9	1.1	0.4	0.5	0.6	0.7	0.7	0.4	0.5	0.6	0.6	0.6	0.5	0.7	0.8	0.7
Tin	31	33	32	35	29	28	27	28	18	24	19	20	22	23	24	24	26
Value	64	93	85	73	60	57	59	57	36	53	43	50	54	57	81	93	93
Share total exports (%)	0.9	1.2	1.2	0.9	0.7	0.7	0.7	0.6	0.4	0.6	0.6	0.6	0.6	0.6	0.7	0.8	0.8
Petroleum	86,268	98,311	106,753	104,510	112,270	124,490	143,690	153,330	147,726	152,535	157,542	162,660	175,854	180,119	188,406	200,600	196,391
Value	1,327	1,549	1,619	1,594	1,861	2,092	2,303	2,494	2,404	2,474	2,526	2,527	2,739	2,800	2,678	2,702	2,647
Share total exports (%)	19.2	19.4	22.6	20.5	22.8	25.4	26.4	28.2	28.3	28.7	28.4	27.4	32.5	27.8	22.6	25.9	23.9
Rank among exports	2	2	2	2	2	1	1	1	1	1	1	1	1	1	1	1	1
Coffee	1,449	1,558	1,588	1,716	1,335	1,555	1,699	1,553	1,564	1,881	1,823	1,819	1,896	2,055	1,820	1,665	1,905
Value	1,418	1,705	1,774	2,005	1,990	1,801	1,953	1,791	1,550	1,540	1,443	1,381	1,386	1,424	1,634	1,531	1,579
Share total exports (%)	21	21.4	24.8	25.8	24.4	21.9	22.4	20.3	18.3	17.9	16.3	15	16.5	14.3	13.9	14.7	14.3
Rank among exports	1	1	1	1	1	2	2	2	2	2	2	2	2	2	2	2	2
Cocoa	225	178	145	215	225	220	233	226	222	219	274	225	178	202	179	207	230
Value	130	125	98	131	231	164	131	150	190	158	159	110	91	112	92	74	109
Share total exports (%)	1.9	1.6	1.4	1.7	2.8	2	1.5	1.7	2.2	1.8	1.8	1.2	1.1	1.1	0.8	0.7	1
Sugar	6,026	6,321	5,980	6,862	5,441	6,562	6,689	7,218	7,759	6,979	8,799	9,497	7,604	6,175	6,306	7,956	7,360
Value	638	789	672	628	544	614	625	854	759	634	745	830	692	856	911	795	775
Share total exports (%)	9.4	9.9	9.4	8.1	6.7	7.5	7.2	9.7	9	7.3	8.4	9.3	8.2	8.6	8.6	7.2	7
Rank among exports	3	3	3	3	3	3	3	3	3	3	3	3	3	3	3	3	4

TABLE B-3 – Continued

Commodity	1950	1951	1952	1953	1954	1955	1956	1957	1958	1959	1960	1961	1962	1963	1964	1965	1966
Bananas				2,045	2,039	2,037	2,150	1,560	2,358	2,438	2,607	2,559	2,444	2,589	2,619	2,685	3,165
Value	136	146	157	179	182	196	210	217	204	204	203	199	208	232	211	249	287
Share total exports (%)	2	1.8	2.2	2.3	2.2	2.4	2.4	2.5	2.4	2.4	2.3	2.2	2.5	2.3	1.8	2.3	2.5
Wheat	2,748	2,552	280	2,605	3,280	4,080	2,928	2,778	2,378	2,440	2,470	1,056	2,830	1,882	3,720	6,742	5,184
Value	153	209	31	251	235	284	183	168	143	139	143	66	173	120	242	377	287
Share total exports (%)	2.3	2.6	0.4	3.2	2.9	3.4	2.1	1.9	1.7	1.6	1.6	0.7	2.1	1.2	2.2	3.6	2.6
Beef	385	307	217	143	256	306	514	561	588	533	458	473	593	778	697	643	711
Value	149	223	181	209	211	224	278	302	357	341	284	294	306	418	458	466	507
Share total exports (%)	2.2	2.8	2.5	2.7	2.6	2.8	3.2	3.4	4.2	4	3.2	3.3	3.3	4.2	4.3	4.4	4.5
Cotton	425	435	396	562	729	661	759	521	584	738	618	755	1,006	971	904	1,024	1,050
Value	333	473	329	349	502	480	488	332	343	376	355	423	551	540	499	511	488
Share total exports (%)	5.4	6.6	5	4.9	6.6	6.2	6	4.1	4.4	4.4	4	4.7	6.6	5.4	4.2	4.9	4.4
Rank among exports	4	4	4	4	4	4	4	4	4	4	5	4	4	4	5	5	5
Forest products	1,156	1,247	884	1,015	1,052	1,300	1,027	1,308	1,205	1,042	1,066	1,182	1,024	995	864	1,425	1,566
Value	67	91	68	83	104	173	66	105	90	81	72	89	76	72	92	101	124
Share total exports (%)	1	1.1	0.9	1.1	1.3	2.1	0.8	1.2	1.1	0.9	0.8	1	0.8	0.7	0.9	1	1.1
Fish and fishmeal	42	49	57	55	70	89	105	142	204	422	671	974	1,391	1,380	1,794	1,755	1,722
Value	8	8	11	29	33	38	48	60	75	107	113	175	223	227	268	286	334
Share total exports (%)	0.1	0.1	0.2	0.4	0.4	0.5	0.6	0.7	0.9	1.2	1.3	1.9	2.7	2.3	2.2	2.7	3
Total Latin America (15 commodities):																	
Value	4,766	5,854	5,590	5,951	6,452	6,786	7,092	7,193	6,683	6,750	6,910	6,912	7,266	7,628	8,074	8,332	8,604
Share total exports (%)	70.3	73.9	78.4	76.9	79.5	82.7	81.7	81.7	79.3	78.2	78	76.1	85.9	76.2	71.1	79.3	77
Mineral products only (metals and petroleum):																	
Value	1,734	2,085	2,269	2,088	2,420	2,812	3,111	3,214	2,972	3,170	3,393	3,345	3,559	3,627	3,666	3,941	4,114
Share total exports (%)	25	26	31.6	26.7	29.6	33.9	35.5	36.2	35.1	36.7	38.3	36.4	42.1	36.1	31.8	37.5	37
Agricultural products only (incl. forest and fish products):																	
Value	3,032	3,769	3,321	3,862	4,032	3,974	3,981	3,979	3,711	3,580	3,518	3,567	3,708	4,001	4,408	4,390	4,490
Share total exports (%)	45.3	47.9	46.8	50.2	49.9	48.8	46.2	45.5	44.2	41.5	39.7	39.7	43.8	40.1	39.3	41.8	40

Sources: Tables 4–11, 5–4, 6–6A and 6–6B, 7–8, 8–9, 10–11, 11–5, 12–8, 13–5, 14–7, 15–10, 16–6, 17–10, and 18–7.

NOTE: These sources and notes apply to table B-3 and appendix tables B-3-1 through B-3-20. In these appendix tables some commodities are not included for the countries and years indicated: Argentina, 1950-1966, sugar and copper; Cuba, 1950-1960, cocoa; Guatemala, 1950-1966, fishery products; Haiti, 1950-1966, copper; Honduras, 1950-1957, fishery products; Nicaragua, 1950-1966, copper; Venezuela, 1950-1957, fishery products. In every case the commodity is less than 0.05% of the country's total exports, or the value is unknown but believed to be extremely small. These exports are included in the totals in table B-3, Latin America, wherever value data are available; therefore, the regional total for a commodity may slightly exceed the sum of exports of that commodity from all exporting countries in tables B-3-1 through B-3-20.

Units: Nonferrous metals–metric tons metal content; iron ore–metric tons metal content; petroleum–cubic meters; forest products, crude and products; forest products–metric tons estimated total weight; all other products–metric tons total weight.

be separated. In the other cases value and volume are less closely related and neither is dominant.

The distribution of the region's exports by destination has changed greatly during this century and appreciably even since 1950. This information is not given in table B-3, because the data for individual countries show only the principal countries of destination, and aggregation would be difficult, but the main developments may be readily summarized. The two world wars have had the greatest influence on Latin America's trade by shifting it to the United States as European markets were reduced or cut off. In each postwar period there has been a gradual return to the prewar distribution. Thus in 1910 the United States took just over one-third of Latin America's total exports and Western Europe somewhat more than 40 percent, the United Kingdom, Germany, and France being the major importers. By 1917, with the German market closed, the European share was only about 30 percent and the United States was taking more than half. The postwar redistribution toward Europe was accentuated by the Depression, when U.S. trade fell more than that of Europe, and by 1933 the former was absorbing only 29 percent of Latin America's exports. By 1941 that share had climbed to 54 percent; it fell to less than 40 in the late 1940s but reached 51 percent during the Korean War. Since then U.S. participation has declined fairly steadily, to about one-third at present. The share of exports going to Western Europe, also now one-third of the total, has increased slightly but the principal growth is in trade to other destinations, including the Communist countries and Japan.[1] Intraregional trade has increased for some products but is still a small share of the total in all cases.

Exports of the primary commodities studied here may be assumed to have followed roughly the same pattern since they constitute so large a share of total exports. Moreover, during wartime the U.S. demand for metals and fuel increased sharply, so that those commodities probably showed even greater changes in trade distribution. The shift of agricultural exports to the United States was in part due to additional wartime demand but reflected to an even greater degree the closing of alternative markets. The recovery of the European economies is the principal cause of each postwar redistribution in trade, and affects both mineral and agricultural goods. The extent to which this recovery of demand is reflected in the shares of Latin American exports absorbed depends largely on the situation in other exporting countries, especially in Africa and Oceania.

In the years since 1950 the influence of certain other factors may be noted. The U.S. market is now approximately saturated — that is, demand responds only slightly to changes in either income or price — for certain products such as coffee and bananas. In the lower income countries of Europe and especially in new markets such as Japan, demand for these commodities has grown very rapidly with increased income and changes in consumer tastes. In the cases of lead, zinc, petroleum, and to a lesser degree sugar, quotas have at least temporarily restricted the growth of U.S. imports. In still other cases, notably iron ore, products were originally developed for export to the United States, but once the demand of that market was met further growth in exports depended on sales to other destinations.

The Present Resource Base

The products chosen for this study are, almost without exception, commodities in the production of which Latin America possesses a comparative or absolute advantage relative to other parts of the world: most are exported in sizable amounts to competitive markets. This fact, however, gives very little indication of the quantity or quality of the region's natural resources. For example, it cannot always be assumed that markets are in equilibrium, with the level of output determined by equality of marginal costs with prices; severe imbalance for a particular product may persist for years, as a result of slow supply response in the case of tree crops or of more extraordinary factors for other products. Even in the absence of such factors, production reflects the level of taxes and other aspects of government policy, and not only of costs. For various reasons, therefore, it is advisable to examine the natural resource base itself and evaluate production and prices accordingly. Ideally, such an examination should result in a supply function for each commodity, showing the amounts that could be produced in a given period of time, with current knowledge and techniques, at different levels of price. However, the information available is inadequate; in only a few cases could a reasonable approximation be constructed.[2] For purposes of projecting supply and demand in the short run, it is generally assumed either that output is independent of price, or that output will equal demand so long as the price remains within a fairly wide range. It is therefore necessary to use simpler and more readily accessible data, referring principally to the quantity of resources, and then to supplement this information with such data as may be available on quality and other factors bearing on cost. Since the resources involved are quite distinct for minerals and agricultural products, different measures must be used for the two classes of commodities. In each case, considerable care is required in the interpretation of the data presented.

For minerals, the principal measure is the quantity of reserves, in metal content in the case of metals and total recoverable volume in the case of fuels (see table B-4). The definition of reserves varies somewhat among minerals, but in general it refers to the amount of material known with relative certainty to exist in specified deposits, which could be profitably extracted at current prices (or "normal" prices if the current price reflects disequilibrium) using present techniques.[3] Reserves may be distinguished ac-

---

[1] See D. Baerresen et al., *Latin American Trade Patterns* (Brookings Institution, 1965), pp. 20, 76, for a summary of total Latin American trade by destination between 1910 and 1963; data on Mexico and the countries of South America are given for the period 1938-63 on pp. 81-101.

[2] See, for example, the estimates of tin production in 1970 at three different price levels, in W. Robertson, *The World Tin Position* (London: International Tin Council, 1964), pp. 74, 159, 164.

[3] For a discussion of the concept of reserves and the various terms employed, see Hans H. Landsberg et al., *Resources in America's Future*, (Johns Hopkins Press for Resources for the Future,

TABLE B–4. LATIN AMERICA: Natural Resource Base, circa 1960
  (Size of reserves or resources in use, and shares of world totals)

I. Minerals Product and Classification	Year	Unit	Size of Resource in L.A.	Share of World Total (%)	Lifetime (years) in L.A. at 1962-64 Rate of Production	Ratio to World Lifetime
Copper: metal content of reserves	1965	mill. m.t.	55	28.4	64	1.5
Iron Ore: iron content of	1962	mill. m.t.				
explored reserves			2,972	10.2	69	1.3
potential resources			9,157	21.7	213	2.7
total resources			12,129	17.1	282	2.1
Lead: metal content of measured and indicated reserves	1963	thous. m.t.	6,500	13.0	16	0.8
Zinc: metal content of measured and indicated reserves	1962	thous. m.t.	10,000	12.0	21	0.9
Tin: metal content of measured, indicated, and inferred reserves	1965	thous. m.t.	776	15.5	31	0.9
Petroleum: proved reserves of crude oil	1965	thous. m^3	3,968,000	7.4	16	0.5
Coal: proven, probable, and possible reserves of	1963	mill. m.t.				
all grades of coal			94,238	2.0	9,400	6.0
bituminous coal			57,346		5,700[a]	
coking coal			3,780		380[a]	

II. Agriculture: Crops Product and Classification	Year	Area Planted (thous. ha.)	Share of World Total (%)	Share of Cultivated Area in L.A. (%)	Share of Total Land Area in L.A. (%)	Yield (kg/ha)	Ratio to World Average
Coffee: total	1960-65	7,267	69	7.18	0.35	437	1.1
Mild Arabicas		2,734	86	2.80	0.14	370	
Brazils		4,523	91	4.40	0.22	502	
Cocoa: all types	1954-64	740	22	0.75	0.037	370	1.1
Sugar (area harvested)	1958-60						
total		2,787	25.3	2.85	0.14	5,045	1.17
cane		2,769	52.5	2.84	0.14	5,300	1.00
beet		18	0.3	0.018	0.0009	3,000	0.91
Bananas: all types	1963-64	700		0.71	0.035	22,000	
Wheat: all types	1962-64	8,082	3.9	8.25	0.40	1,507	1.08
Cotton: all lengths of fiber	1964-65	4,556	13.8	4.65	0.23	344	1.02

III. Miscellaneous Products		Pasture Area				Stock (thous. head)	Share of World Total (%)
Beef Cattle	1950-61 to 1964	393,103	15.3		19.8	206,505	19.3
		Total Area		Growing Stock (mill. m^3)		Removals (m^3/ha)	Ratio to World Average
Forest: all types	1960-62	899,000	23.7	143,629	44[b]	0.2	0.4

Sources: Tables 4–3 and 4–4; 5–1 and 5–2; 6–1, 6–2A, and 6–2B; 7–1 and 7–2; 8–1; 9–1 and 9–2; 10–3, 10–4, and 10–9; 11–2 and 11–4; 12–1 and 12–2; 13–4; 14–1 and 14–3; 15–1 and 15–2; 16–1; and 17–1. FAO, *Production Yearbook*, various years, and *World Forest Inventory, 1963*. CIDA, *Inventory of Information Basic to the Planning of Agricultural Development in Latin America: Regional Report, 1963-65.*

NOTE: These sources and notes apply to table B–4 and appendix tables B–4–1 through B–4–20. (For explanation of gaps in statistical series, see p. 65.)

[a]Assuming 1962-64 level of production to consist entirely of bituminous (or of coking) coal.
[b]Includes the eastern region of Ecuador, for a total area of the country in excess of 44 million hectares. Statistics for crops are based on only the settled part of the country, with an area of some 27 million hectares.

cording to the degree of certainty of information, which reflects the extent of exploration, as: measured, indicated, and inferred, or proven, probable, and possible. As is evident from table B-4, reserves are more strictly defined for some products than for others; comparisons among different minerals are therefore hazardous. In no case do reserves account for more than a small fraction of the mineral believed to be ultimately recoverable from the earth's crust; they reflect, rather, present and anticipated demand for a product and the extent to which resources have been identified to satisfy that demand.

The amount of reserves may be combined with a current or anticipated level of output to yield another measure, the lifetime of reserves at a constant rate of production. This figure varies considerably among products, chiefly because of differences in the ease and cost of exploration. Where exploration is costly relative to production, as for oil, the lifetime is generally low. It is much higher where large amounts of the mineral can be easily found, as for coal and iron ore. For two or more metals occurring in roughly similar types of deposits with comparable ease of exploration, a comparison of these lifetimes gives a rough indication of relative scarcity in relation to demand. A comparison of lifetimes for the same mineral in different producing areas indicates the relative rates at which reserves are being used up.

Reserves may further be distinguished by quality: coking properties of coal, for example, different densities of petroleum, and different grades of ore for metals. Information of this sort partly indicates the suitability of the material for different uses and is partly related to the cost of production, the latter particularly where metallic grade is concerned. In most cases it has not been possible to obtain much data on quality. Iron ore resources in Latin America can be approximately classified by grade and the average grade of resources of other metals is known. Similarly, the gravity or density of petroleum is known, and coal resources can be distinguished according to type and suitability for making metallurgical grade coke.[4] In the case of iron ore, potential resources, too low in grade to be counted as reserves, are included.

Latin America appears to enjoy a favorable position with respect to all five metals studied, having 10 percent or more of world reserves and a rate of production such that the region's resources are being used up, in the worst case, only slightly more rapidly than those of the rest of the world. The area's wealth is most striking in copper and iron ore.

The grade of iron ore mined is high by world standards; for copper the grade is high in comparison with copper in the United States and lower than the grade of the major African deposits, but the Latin American deposits are so large and uniform that costs of production there are perhaps the lowest in the world. It should be noted that the very high lifetime for copper reserves will fall considerably

as production is expanded in Chile and Peru in the next few years. Iron ore output may also be expected to increase, but Latin America has been so little explored for iron ore that large increases in reserves are also possible. The situation is less satisfactory for the remaining metals, especially for lead. Its declining importance as an export commodity is traceable in part to the relative scarcity, or rapid depletion, of reserves, which in turn is partly due to exhaustion of the lead in mixed lead-zinc-copper or lead-zinc ores and a consequent shift to production of the other metals. The estimates for tin should be treated with special caution, because of the disruption of the Bolivian mining industry following nationalization in 1952. The mines were operated at a deficit until 1965, and very little exploration was done. There are also large amounts of low-grade ore residues which may shortly become economical to treat for their tin content.

Petroleum is also relatively abundant in Latin America, although both the share of world reserves and the relative lifetime of reserves are appreciably lower than for the metals. This situation results primarily from the postwar oil boom in the Middle East, where enormous deposits, easily explored and tapped by a small number of wells, have resulted in a very high output per well and consequently in the world's lowest production costs. These factors alone made exploration for petroleum less attractive in Venezuela, which dominates reserves and production in Latin America, and they were reinforced by a government policy of maintaining prices and holding back output. Thus additions to reserves have not kept up with production in Venezuela and the lifetime of reserves has fallen. The low average for Latin America as a whole also reflects the greater scarcity of oil in such countries as Colombia, Mexico, and Peru.

The region's coal resources are small in volume, of poor quality, and costly to mine. For the rest of the world, bituminous coal accounts for the great bulk of reserves, and a fairly large share can be used to make coke; in Latin America coking coal is scarce, and about one-third of reserves consists of subbituminous coal and lignite. The extremely high lifetimes recorded, therefore, do not indicate an abundance of coal. They show instead the low level of production and indirectly point out the region's heavy dependence on petroleum for fuel. Much of the coal used in Latin America is imported, which further restricts domestic production; however, the share imported has declined greatly in recent decades.

With the partial exceptions of iron ore and petroleum, all these minerals are highly concentrated in one or a few countries (see appendix tables B-4-1 through B-4-20). Production is generally much more widely distributed than reserves, although the two are roughly proportionate. This concentration of resources is partly real; metals in particular occur in a relatively small number of large deposits which are unevenly distributed and which overshadow the more numerous smaller deposits. In part, however, the appearance of concentration simply reflects the fact that information on reserves is often not available for a small producer. The regional total may include an allowance for such countries without showing the amount estimated for

---

1963), pp. 424-25. The special case of petroleum is treated at length in Wallace F. Lovejoy and Paul T. Homan, *Methods of Estimating Reserves of Crude Oil, Natural Gas, and Natural Gas Liquids* (Resources for the Future, 1965).

[4] See Part Two, tables 5-5 and 9-1, which indicate quantities of iron ore and coal, respectively, at different grades or qualities.

each; thus production is sometimes shown for a country for which no reserves are reported. This situation does not apply to petroleum, for which reserve data are available for all countries on the same basis and are revised annually.

For agricultural crops, two measures of the resource base are employed: the area planted (or harvested) and the average yield obtained. Ideally, these measures should be combined into a function showing the yield which could be obtained most economically (at lowest unit cost) from each relatively homogeneous area suitable for production of the crop, including land not presently planted. However, the data for such a function are not available; thus the information presented includes no assumptions about the amount or location of land best suited for each crop or the yields that would result if production were achieved at the lowest possible cost.

The six crops studied here take up some 24 percent of the total cultivated area of Latin America, amounting to only 1.2 percent of the total land area. The remaining cropland is used almost entirely for foodstuffs, with maize and other staples accounting for much of the total. In comparison to the rest of the world, Latin America holds a dominant position only in coffee and in sugarcane. The region's natural resources for cocoa are excellent, but production has largely shifted to Africa in consequence of lower labor costs and a greater availability of land. Latin America dominates world trade in bananas, but probably has a small share of the total land in production; estimates for other areas are not available.

The region's yields equal or exceed the world average for every product except sugar beets, despite the fact that Latin America produces the costlier grades of coffee and cocoa and that several producing countries have rather poor conditions for wheat. Data are not available for bananas, but it is reasonable to assume that Latin American yields are much higher than those elsewhere. Comparisons of yields do not give an accurate indication of relative costs or of resource quality, however. Average sugarcane yields are no higher for Latin America as a whole than for other areas, but in some countries they are extremely high. Elsewhere the availability of land or labor or substantial investments in transportation and processing partially offset lower yields. The high average yield for total sugar production reflects the dominance of cane, whereas other producers grow far more sugar beets. Cotton yields in the United States, the world's major producer, are raised by a combination of price supports and restrictions on area planted; in comparison with other producers Latin America has extremely high yields.

Pastures for cattle occupy almost 20 percent of total land area in Latin America, four times as much as all crops together. The region has some 15 percent of the world's pasture area but supports 19 percent of the cattle stock; the density of cattle per hectare is thus 25 percent above the world average. This disparity results from the extremely low carrying capacity of pastures in most of Africa and Asia. In comparison with the United States or Western Europe, Latin America's livestock production is still extensive in nature and artificial or improved pastures account for only a small share of the total grazing area.

The region currently produces 20 percent or more of the world's beef and veal; the yield of meat per hectare of pasture is between one-third and one-half higher than the world average. The higher cattle density in Latin America than elsewhere means that the production per head of cattle in stock is only slightly above the world average. Data are not available for a comparison of carcass weights, or meat production per animal slaughtered; thus it cannot be determined how much of these differences is due to lower weight per animal in Latin America and how much to a lower slaughtering rate as a percentage of the total stock. Some intercountry comparisons are given in chapter 15. With respect to natural resources alone, the region appears to be quite well suited to beef production. Its importance in the world beef economy would be still greater were it not for the protection afforded domestic producers in Europe and the United States. The obstacles to exports which have beset Argentina and Uruguay in recent years do not reflect a scarcity or deterioration of the resource base, but result from difficulties in packing and shipping and market organization and to some extent from government policies toward agriculture.

Forest resources are particularly difficult to describe by indices such as those used for other agricultural products. Three measures are used here, growing stock being given in addition to area and yield. Data on total timber stock are not available for many other producing areas, so that inter-regional comparisons of forest volume and density are impossible. All figures refer to all types of forest together, no distinction being fully available in the data as to species, use, or other characteristics.

In gross terms, Latin America is extremely rich in forest resources: 44 percent of the region's total area, amounting to 24 percent of all the world's forests, is covered by trees. Furthermore, the rate of cutting is less than half the world average and amounts to only one-eighth of 1 percent of the growing stock annually, a rate easily offset by the normal growth of the forest. These measures need a great deal of qualification, however. In the first place, cutting is concentrated in a very small part of the region's forests, so that removals there outstrip growth and the area forested is being reduced, in some places quite rapidly. Second, there are still large areas in Latin America where land is cleared by cutting and burning for shifting agriculture and the forest cover is destroyed with little use being made of the timber. Third, artificial forests or plantations are still relatively small and are concentrated in only a few areas in Chile and Brazil. It will probably be several decades before the bulk of production can be obtained from stable forests with high enough yields to support rapid cutting. Finally, the bulk of the region's forests are mixtures of scores or even hundreds of species of hardwoods about whose properties and uses very little is known. These forests, including most of the Amazon basin, cannot be economically exploited unless a number of species can be produced together; their relative inaccessibility makes it too costly to cut only the scattered trees of one or a few types. Thus while Latin America is extremely well supplied with forests, probably no other resource currently used in appreciable amounts is so underdeveloped.

Fishery products are omitted from table B-4 because of the difficulties of measuring marine resources in physical terms and the further problem of relating production to cost. The best single measure is the maximum sustainable yield, or the largest catch which can be maintained without depleting the stock of fish. This level is approximately 7 to 9 million tons in the anchovy fishery of Peru and perhaps 50,000 to 100,000 tons for the major inshore shrimp species in Central America and northern South America. Little is known, however, about the yield obtainable from grounds and species that have not yet been extensively exploited. The total Latin American catch of over 10 million tons, while less than the total obtainable catch by some unknown but presumably not very large amount, is a rough measure of the region's wealth in marine resources. All the region's fishing effort is concentrated on the immediately adjacent waters, which are in large measure closed to vessels based elsewhere; thus although the bulk of fishing occurs in international waters, the resources may be identified with Latin America. Physical capacity is somewhat easier to measure in vessels and processing plants than directly in fish, but because output at later stages is limited by the catch actually obtained, part of the measured capacity may be redundant and not translatable into production. In qualitative terms, Latin America is extremely well supplied, with major fishing grounds along both coasts of Mexico and Central America, on the west coast of South America, and to a lesser extent on the northern and eastern coasts of the continent. Some of these grounds, however, are already fished to the limit for particular species, and the potential for expansion is either slight or believed to be large but still unknown.

In summary, it may be said that Latin America's resources are excellent, relative to the rest of the world and to the region's own needs, for copper and iron ore, coffee, sugar, bananas, and cotton. They are somewhat less satisfactory in amount, but otherwise entirely adequate, for lead, zinc, tin, and petroleum; and probably adequate but not very well used for wheat. Resources for cocoa are good but not competitive in costs except for a limited area in Brazil. The resources for beef, forest products, and fish are all potentially large, varying from relatively well-developed to quite underdeveloped and even badly exploited. Only in coal is the region unequivocally poor, and even that judgment does not hold for two or three countries. The extent of resource adequacy and quality varies greatly among countries: a few countries such as Brazil, Mexico, and Peru possess good resources for the production of as many as eight commodities; other countries are notable for only one or two (see appendix tables B-4-1 through B-4-20).

The Resource-Using Industries

Natural resource commodities differ considerably in the extent of processing they undergo and consequently in the size and complexity of the industries to which they are inputs. A few, such as bananas, ordinarily are not processed at all beyond packing for shipment. Others pass through more stages or are converted into a variety of products, but the economy based on them can be adequately described by reference to only one or two of these phases or products. Frequently, complete and comparable data cannot even be obtained for the other degrees of processing. Thus production, trade, and consumption of coffee are reported in terms of unroasted (green) beans; the operations of roasting and grinding necessary before use are almost invariably performed at the point of consumption and may be ignored. The only significant processing is in the production of soluble coffee, nearly all of which until quite recently took place in importing countries. Similarly, but with rather less accuracy, sugar can be described by reference only to raw (unrefined) centrifugal sugar, omitting for most purposes noncentrifugal sugar, molasses, alcohol, and other products of the sugar economy. Wheat, beef, and cotton are best described at two stages: whole grain and flour, live cattle and meat, raw cotton and yarn. Cotton textiles are not included in this summary, as the region's trade in textiles is small and there are considerable difficulties of definition and measurement. Only cocoa, among the agricultural products studied here, can be treated in great detail, and then only for trade. Minerals and forest products, however, generally undergo a great deal of processing, the different products being successive stages in a series — as for the metals — or alternative end products — as for petroleum and wood.

If information is assembled on production, trade, and consumption at each of the various stages of processing, the result is a sort of cross-section of the resource-using industry. This presentation is of little value for such products as coffee and sugar but gives a good indication of the size and structure of the industry in the case of products undergoing greater elaboration (see table B-5). No attempt is made in this summary to indicate the size distribution of processing units, which is not known for some products and is difficult to compare between commodities. A similar presentation for each individual country allows one to compare degrees of self-sufficiency at different levels of processing and the relation between raw material production and industrial use (see appendix tables B-5-1 through B-5-20). The data are relatively complete and accurate, but it has been necessary to make estimates in some cases and to define consumption somewhat arbitrarily for the intermediate stages of certain products. Data are generally more readily available for trade than for production or use; in particular, figures frequently could not be obtained on the production or consumption of metal semimanufactures or of the various cocoa products.[5]

[5] Each row in table B-5, except those marked "Total," refers to a commodity at a given stage of processing: consumption equals imports plus production less exports. This is the only information given for such commodities as coffee, sugar, bananas, wheat, beef, and cotton. For the remaining commodities, the "Totals" and the relations of the figures in each column require somewhat more explanation. The total for exports or imports is simply the sum of trade at all levels of processing, with all figures adjusted to a common basis. Thus, for example, total exports of iron and steel include only the estimated iron content, not the gross weight, of iron ore exported from Latin America, so that the total of 21 million tons is much less than iron ore exports of 33 million tons.

The total for production, however, refers only to the first stage

TABLE B–5. LATIN AMERICA: Imports, Production, Exports, and Consumption of Natural Resource Commodities in Different Stages of Processing, circa 1963-1967

Commodity and Product Description	Year	Unit	Imports	Production	Exports	Intra-regional Trade	Actual or Apparent Consumption
Copper	1966	metric					
content of ore		tons		923,658	81,886		
unrefined metal				833,909	366,929		
refined metal			} 87,072	445,823	355,599 }	16,897	
semimanufactures					34,093 }		
other forms			3,577		2,626	1,412	
total			92,915	923,658	841,859	18,309	144,154
Iron and Steel	1963	metric					
ore, gross weight		tons	759,000	41,171,000	33,429,000	757,000	8,501,000
pig iron and ferroalloys			247,000	5,183,000	155,000	8,000	5,275,000
crude steel			130,000	6,908,000	134,000	1,000	6,904,000
semimanufactures			2,022,000	4,906,000	330,000	117,000	6,894,000
total iron content			3,056,000	25,647,000	21,147,000	883,000	8,596,000
total rolled steel, ingot equivalent			2,918,000	7,703,000	603,000		10,185,000
Lead	1965	metric					
content of ore		tons		414,679	110,033		
metal			6,166	294,065	227,964 }	5,548	
semimanufactures			1,036				
total			13,655	414,679	337,997	5,548	81,696
Zinc	1965	metric					
content of ore		tons		579,412	526,448		
metal			42,141	181,939	89,705 }	16,418	
semimanufactures			1,873				
total			54,570	579,412	616,153	16,418	151,907
Tin	1963	long					
content of ore		tons	2,084	24,967	20,574	26	
tin metal			2,701	5,568		14	5,821
tinplate, gross weight			321,600	283,665			605,365
tin content of tinplate			2,500	2,218			4,718
total contained tin			5,200	5,568		14	8,320
Petroleum	1964	thous.					
crude oil		cubic	24,641	253,875	99,469	12,598	
refined products		meters	10,347	189,076	93,879	10,564	102,901
gasoline			1,510	35,842	8,327		27,150
kerosene			642	15,202	7,067		6,028
distillate fuel oils			2,571	35,958	15,213		17,299
residual fuel oil			3,007	99,213	59,533		33,916
lubricants			652	1,684	725		1,566
Coal	1965	thous.					
coal, all grades		metric	2,088	10,926			13,014
hard coke: actual		tons	1,015	2,904			3,919
coal equivalent			1,497	4,370			5,867
soft coke				331			
Coffee	1965/66	thous.					
unroasted beans		m.t.	51	2,875	1,785	50.5	878
Cocoa	1966	metric					
beans		tons	32,315	320,100	200,253	32,315[a]	155,358[b]
butter			439		21,658	439[a]	
powder			1,223		1,781	1,223[a]	
chocolate and products			1,023		8,205	1,023[a]	119,469[c]
Sugar	1967	metric					
centrifugal, raw value		tons	235,833	13,279,000	7,972,100	235,833	8,413,108
Bananas	1966	thous.					
edible, fresh		m.t.	251		3,506	251	
Wheat	1964-66	thous.					
grain		metric	4,345	13,346	1,969		15,722
flour		tons	644	7,565	35		8,174
Beef and Veal	1966	thous.					
live cattle		head	227		804	227	
meat		m.t.	32	5,869	694	32	5,207

TABLE B-5 – Continued

Commodity and Product Description	Year	Unit	Imports	Production	Exports	Intra-regional Trade	Actual or Apparent Consumption
Cotton	1964	thous.					
raw cotton (fiber)		metric	174	1,635	1,254	174	555
cotton yarn		tons	12	414	3	12	423
Forest Products	1964-66	(d)					
fuelwood		(*)		199,992		(e)	199,992
industrial wood		(*)	4,435	24,240	402		28,273
roundwood		(*)	338		427		
sawnwood		(†)	1,219	12,668	1,709		12,178
sheet materials		(†)	29	419	13		435
fiberboard		(‡)	7	156			163
wood pulp		(‡)	571	418	30		959
pulp products		(‡)	874	2,391	58		3,207

Fishery Products, 1964 (thousands of metric tons)

Disposition of Catch	Liveweight	Type	Net Weight			
			Production[f]	Imports[f]	Exports[f]	Apparent Consumption
Total Catch[g]	11,158.3	All uses	2,250.9	92.6	1,787.0	921.6
Marketed fresh	676.4	total (fish & shellfish) }	43.4 }	2.9 }	22.6	348.5
frozen	150.1	fish				28.2
		shellfish	44.8		43.8	1.0
cured	115.8	total (fish & shellfish)	80.6	24.1	0.4	104.3
canned	211.3	fish	90.6	1.6	15.8	76.4
		shellfish	7.7	0.4	4.1	4.0
reduced	9,980.1	white fishmeal	18.9			18.9
		oily fishmeal	1,732.0	59.4	1,574.6	216.8
		fish oil	232.0	4.1	125.4	110.7
(offal for reduction)	(52.8)					
miscellaneous	24.6	molluscs	0.9	0.1	0.3	0.7

Sources: Tables 4–12; 5–10; 6–8; 7–9; 8–13; 10–4, 10–5, and 10–11; 11–6; 12–3, 12–4, and 12–8; 13–1 and 13–2; 14–8; 15–2, 15–9, 15–10, 15–12, and 15–13; 16–9; 17–11; and 18–8.

NOTE: These sources and notes apply to table B–5 and appendix tables B–5–1 through B–5–20. (For explanation of gaps in statistical series, see p. 65.)

[a]All imports assumed to originate in the region.
[b]Grindings; tonnage of beans ground to yield cocoa products.
[c]Total cocoa consumption, in terms of beans.
[d]Thousands of: cubic meters roundwood equivalent (*); cubic meters actual volume (†); metric tons (‡).
[e]Not calculated; destination of exports not shown for forest products (see table 17–10).
[f]Processed commodities only, net product weight; excludes fish marketed fresh.
[g]Eight major fishing countries: Argentina, Brazil, Chile, Colombia, Ecuador, Mexico, Peru, and Venezuela.

of processing indicated; thus the 25 million tons shown for iron and steel is the iron content of iron ore production in Latin America, not the output of pig iron, steel, or later products. This figure represents the total amount of iron (or copper or oil or cocoa) that came out of the ground in the region. Summation of the production figures at different stages would involve double counting, the extent of which would vary with the number of stages and with the amount of imports at stages other than the last one shown.

Finally, the total for consumption represents the quantity of the commodity produced within the region that is not exported at any stage and is therefore consumed domestically, plus the sum of imports at all stages of processing. This is equivalent to production at the first stage plus net trade at all stages. Theoretically, this figure should equal consumption at the final stage of processing, since all data are adjusted to a common basis. But in fact the two are not usually equal, because the adjustment is imperfect – metal semi-manufactures, for example, are assumed to be 100 percent of the metal indicated with no allowance for alloys – and because losses at each stage of processing are not accounted for. Also, production data are frequently not available for the last stage of processing, so that the comparison cannot be made.

Fishery products are treated somewhat differently from all other commodities, a distinction being made between (gross) liveweight and (net) edible or product weight. The disposition of the catch by channel of utilization is shown in liveweight, while so far as possible production, trade, and apparent consumption are shown in net terms. Apparent consumption equals production plus net imports in net weight but not in liveweight.

For some products there is a well-defined stage at which the raw material is greatly purified or transformed: smelting of metals, refining of petroleum, grinding of cocoa, slaughtering of cattle, spinning of cotton into yarn. The significance of processing at this stage differs considerably among products, however. Copper ores, for example, are generally of such low grade that they cannot be economically shipped far even after concentrating. Thus the bulk of metal is smelted where it is produced and smelting is usually an adjunct of mining. Smelting of iron ore, on the other hand, nearly always takes place at a steel mill and therefore reflects the existence of a steel producing and fabricating industry. An intermediate situation prevails for the other three metals. Two or more decades ago petroleum was usually refined in producing areas and most trade was in products. More recently, as markets expanded and became concentrated enough to be served by refineries at the point of consumption, refinery capacity migrated toward consuming areas. Thus the presence of a refinery may indicate processing for a domestic market or for export, depending on such factors as the date of installation and the volume of domestic oil output. The processing of cocoa, at least in Brazil, has migrated in the other direction. Where once nearly all trade was in beans there is now a sizable traffic in products and a domestic industry oriented toward exports. These factors must be considered in interpreting the industrial structure described in table B-5.

Several further observations may be made from the data presented. For nearly every product there now exists in Latin America a considerable processing industry, usually adequate for the domestic market and often exporting at stages beyond the raw material as well. The only significant exceptions appear to be coffee, sugar, and bananas. Fishery products are unique in that the bulk of exports consists of highly processed commodities, with domestic use concentrated on less processed goods. Net imports of processed goods are still necessary only for iron and steel, tin metal and tinplate, semimanufactures of lead and zinc, and wheat flour, and the amounts involved are generally small. Even where one stage is largely absent, the succeeding stages may be well developed. Thus, although the region exports the bulk of its tin output as concentrates and imports much metal, the manufacture of tinplate is advanced in several countries and imports go largely to countries without steel industries. Latin America likewise produces most of its metallurgical coke, importing coal where necessary.

Consumption within the region is often only half of production or even less. The ratio varies considerably, however, according to the level of processing at which it is measured. For example, Latin America uses only about 20 percent of its iron ore but is a net importer of steel. The region refines over 60 percent of its crude oil but consumes only 55 percent of the refinery output and only one-third of the residual fuel oil. Even where total exports are large relative to production, the amount of intraregional trade is generally small. Only for wheat, petroleum, and beef cattle does intraregional trade appear to surpass 10 percent of exports. Imports of raw materials from outside the region are sizable only for petroleum, coal, and wheat. As the level of processing rises for other products, however, so does the re-

liance on suppliers outside the region, such trade being most important for steel, metal semimanufactures, wood pulp, and newsprint.

Unfortunately, these data are not available in similar detail and comparability for earlier years, so it is impossible to present the evolution of the resource-using industries over time. Only rough measures taking all stages of processing together can be constructed, as in table B-1 discussed above. The information assembled here can, however, be used to interpret the indices of domestic processing and use for recent years and thereby to give some idea of the industrial structure of the Latin American resource sector in earlier periods.

Finally it should be noted, as with the other information summarized in this chapter, that conditions vary considerably from one country to another within the region. Certain stages of processing are missing altogether for some products in some countries, or are extremely small. The present distribution of the processing industry reflects both demand and supply and is therefore rather different from the distribution of the natural resources alone. This difference shows up only slightly and for a few products in the regional totals, but is more striking in comparisons among particular countries (compare appendix tables B-4-1 to B-4-20 with tables B-5-1 to B-5-20).

The Outlook for Natural Resources

Each of the commodity chapters of Part Two ends with a brief consideration of probable future developments. These discussions are based in part on published estimates of future supply and demand. Projections over one or a few years are regularly made by a variety of organizations — international bodies, organs of national governments, associations of producers or consumers, and publications serving these groups. Such estimates typically deal with only one commodity, and their assumptions and methods differ enough to prevent assembling or comparing them on a common basis. In addition to longer-term projections for a few single products, there are available two principal sources of estimates for the year 1975, covering a number of commodities with uniform bases and procedures.[6]

With few exceptions — tin and cocoa are examples —

[6]For agricultural products (except fish), the most recent and complete source is FAO, Committee on Commodity Problems, *Agricultural Commodities — Projections for 1975 and 1985*, vol. I (Rome, 1966). This publication supersedes the volume of *Projections for 1970*, published in 1964. Bela Balassa, *Trade Prospects for Developing Countries* (Homewood, Ill.: Richard D. Irwin, 1964), a publication of the Yale Growth Center, gives estimates for 1970 and 1975; it includes agricultural commodities as well as metals and fuels. The chief difference is that Balassa estimates demand only in the "industrial countries" of North America, Western Europe, and Japan, and then projects the distribution of imports by those areas from the less developed countries and also from Oceania and the Communist countries; the FAO study projects demand and supply for each area separately to arrive at an import requirement or exportable surplus, but does not estimate distribution of the resulting trade. Projections for crude petroleum to 1975 and forest products to 1975 are cited in chaps. 8, and 17, respectively. Other estimates and sources of statistical information relevant to future output and consumption are indicated for several other commodities.

prices are assumed constant at the level of the base years or a "normal" level for the commodity and do not influence the estimates of either demand or supply. In the case of metals and petroleum it is assumed that the amount demanded will be supplied, at normal prices; if there is any imbalance it will occur in mine or field capacity rather than in actual output. For agricultural products, balance between requirements and output is not assumed, except approximately in the case of cotton where both supply and demand are more responsive to price than for many foodstuffs. No projections of supply were made for bananas, forest products or fishery products; in the former case balance in the export sector can be assumed, but perhaps at the cost of price stability. Productive capacity, rather than output, is estimated for coffee, cocoa, sugar, and beef, with capacity and demand (or consumption) not assumed to be in balance.

In addition to stability in price, the projections assume constancy in a number of other factors, such as trade rela-

tions and the major uses of raw materials. The pressures for changes in these factors, the prospects of their realization, and their probable effects were considered in the last chapter, but no effort is made to estimate the degree to which such changes would influence output, trade, use, or prices by 1975. It does not now seem likely that new international commodity agreements or the granting of trade preferences by the advanced nations to the less developed countries will be realized extensively, if at all, before that time, or that such arrangements could immediately have an appreciable effect on trade in primary commodities. The distribution of exports, and perhaps prices, would presumably be changed more than total supply or demand or the distribution of either among countries. All these factors are mentioned rather as reminders that projections, however scrupulously prepared, often misread the future; and that no set of numbers is an adequate substitute for understanding the conditions unique to each product and their probable future effects.

NOTE ON STATISTICAL COVERAGE

Limitations of the Data

In all cases the data present certain difficulties and limitations; information is not always available for the same intervals; the periods chosen for comparison may not be representative; the original numbers include many estimates and omissions. As a consequence, and because of rounding, component figures seldom add to totals. There are also more subtle problems of measurement and comparison, particularly for the amount, quality, and cost of natural resources. Comparisons among countries within Latin America or between that region and other areas are sometimes hazardous; comparisons between products are frequently impossible. The world markets for all of these products are known to be imperfect to some degree, and national markets show still more distortion. Thus the actual location of production and flows of trade give only a rough measure of comparative or absolute advantage. Political factors complicate the situation further. Some of these obstacles have been noted in the previous chapters; all are described at greater length in Part Two where particular commodities are discussed. They do not vitiate the analysis, but they do necessitate careful attention to definitions and to a number of factors that give meaning to the numbers presented.

For the purposes of this chapter, statistics on production, exports (or imports), and consumption have been given for each product in each of four periods, and these numbers have then been combined into several ratios show-

ing the distribution between trade and domestic use, the degree of processing within Latin America, and the region's place in the world economy of each product. The periods chosen for reference — the late 1930s, the years around 1950, the early 1960s, and the mid-1960s — are probably not fully representative of the entire interval covered in this study, and there are numerous deficiencies in the data. Especially for the 1930s, the statistics do not refer to precisely the same years for each product or even for the different kinds of information about a single product; thus the resulting ratios are only approximate and production may not be entirely accounted for by consumption and trade. The first three periods do, however, avoid the markedly unrepresentative years of the early Depression and of World War II, and are about equally spaced in time. It is also possible to use a great deal of statistical material compiled for the years following 1934 but excluding the late 1920s and early 1930s. The beginning and end of the interval for which detailed data on Latin American exports are given — 1950 to 1966 — are also covered.

Gaps in Statistical Series

Blank spaces in the tables indicate that data are not available, not comparable, or not applicable, or that the amount is negligibly small. Data are reported to the nearest whole unit or the nearest tenth of a unit, except for prices, which are sometimes reported to the nearest hundredth of a unit. An amount is negligible if it is less than 5 percent of the unit employed in a particular table: if the unit is thousands of metric tons, any amount less than 50 tons is disregarded; and similarly for 50 kilograms when the unit is tons, 0.05 percent when percentages are reported, $50,000 when data are in millions of dollars, etc.

Geographic Definitions

It is extremely difficult to compile statistical information on a consistent and satisfactory geographic basis when the data must be drawn from a variety of sources and span four decades. Latin America is consistently defined for all commodities, periods and types of information, but the definitions of other major regions of the world vary over time and among commodities. Even where the data permit consistent classification, geographic, political, and economic criteria do not necessarily coincide, and for convenience a region may be defined in a way that makes little geographic sense.

To the extent possible, in the tables in Part Two the world is divided into the following major regions: some clarifications or modifications are noted for particular commodities.

Latin America: the twenty independent republics of Argentina, Bolivia, Brazil, Chile, Colombia, Costa Rica, Cuba, the Dominican Republic, Ecuador, El Salvador, Guatemala, Haiti, Honduras, Mexico, Nicaragua, Panama, Paraguay, Peru, Uruguay, and Venezuela. This definition includes all the states on the mainland of Central and South America except Belize (British Honduras), Guyana (formerly British Guiana), Surinam (Dutch Guiana) and French Guiana, as well as Cuba and the two republics on the island of Hispaniola. It embraces the five member nations of the Central American Common Market (CACM) and the eleven members of the Latin American Free Trade Association (LAFTA).

North America: Canada, Greenland, and the United States, including Alaska and Hawaii but excluding Puerto Rico and the Virgin Islands. In the case of sugar, the latter two are shown as part of the offshore internal market of the United States (see table 12-6).

Caribbean America: All countries and possessions in or bordering the Caribbean and not included in Latin America or North America. The most important of these are Belize, Guyana, Surinam, French Guiana, Jamaica, Barbados, and Puerto Rico. This region is referred to only for sugar (chapter 12) and bananas (chapter 13) of which the territories concerned are significant producers. In all other cases Caribbean America is included in the world total but is not separately distinguished. These three regions together comprise the western hemisphere.

Western Europe: the six member nations of the European Economic Community (EEC) – France, West Germany, Italy, the Netherlands, Belgium, and Luxembourg – the eight members of the European Free Trade Association (EFTA) – the United Kingdom, Portugal, Austria, Den-

mark, Norway, Sweden, Finland, and Switzerland – together with Ireland, Spain, Iceland, Greece, and Yugoslavia. Prior to World War II, all of Germany is included in Western Europe. Yugoslavia is included with Western Europe rather than among the Communist Countries as a matter of statistical convenience, since that is the practice followed in many sources. The small states of Lichtenstein, Andorra, Monaco, etc., and such islands as the Canaries, the Azores, the Balearic Islands, Malta, and Crete are included in this region.

Africa: all states and territories of the African continent (except for the Republic of South Africa) plus the islands of Zanzibar, the Malagasy Republic, Fernando Poo, and São Tomé. In the case of petroleum (chapter 8), the oil-producing states of North Africa – Egypt, Algeria, Libya, and Tunisia – are distinguished as a group from the rest of the continent.

Asia: all states and territories of the Asian continent (except mainland China, Mongolia, North Korea, and North Vietnam) plus Japan, Taiwan, the Philippines, Indonesia, Ceylon, and the islands presently or formerly part of Malaysia. Asia thus defined extends to the Mediterranean and the Sinai peninsula and includes Turkey, Syria, Lebanon, and Israel. In the case of petroleum the oil-producing states of the Middle East – Iran, Iraq, Syria, Kuwait, Saudi Arabia, and the other states of the Arabian peninsula – are distinguished as a group.

Oceania: Australia, New Zealand, and the Republic of South Africa.

Communist Countries: the Soviet Union (including Latvia, Lithuania, and Estonia), China, Mongolia, North Korea, North Vietnam, and the seven countries identified as Eastern Europe – Albania, Bulgaria, Czechoslovakia, East Germany, Hungary, Poland, and Rumania.

This classification is not followed uniformly in the available sources, and it is not always feasible to adjust the data to obtain the desired regional totals. Thus, Yugoslavia is sometimes included in Eastern rather than in Western Europe, the Republic of South Africa is sometimes included with Africa rather than with Oceania, and a number of small states for which data may not be available are included in world totals with no distinction as to region.

In a few cases Western and Eastern Europe can be distinguished with difficulty or not at all: the combined region, which excludes the Soviet Union, is then referred to simply as Europe. Similarly, China, Mongolia, North Korea, and North Vietnam are sometimes included in Asia when it is impossible to distinguish the Communist countries as a group.

No attempt is made systematically to classify countries as developed or underdeveloped, but a rough distinction may be made by grouping North America, Western Europe, Oceania, and Japan together as developed countries, and Latin America, Caribbean America, Africa, and Asia except for Japan together as less developed. The distinction is not made for the Communist countries. In the cases of coffee (chapter 10), cocoa (chapter 11), and bananas (chapter 13), countries are classified as producers or as importers; the classification differs somewhat among commodities and corresponds only very approximately to distinctions on geographic or economic criteria. Other groupings such as the Organization for Economic Cooperation and Development (OECD) or major currency areas are not distinguished.

Finally, it should be noted that only a few countries may be listed under a regional total and that the choice of countries varies from table to table according to the commodity and the type of information presented. The countries shown are those with the greatest resources, production, trade, or use of the commodity. Only in the case of Latin America are data presented for all countries in a region; elsewhere the regional total alone is frequently given.

Appendix to Chapter 3

STATISTICAL SUMMARY BY COUNTRY

STATISTICAL SUMMARY
BY COUNTRY

As has been indicated in chapter 3, much of the statistical information assembled in this study can be presented for individual countries as well as for Latin America as a whole. Data disaggregated in this way serve two somewhat distinct purposes: they offer a more detailed view of the structure and geographic distribution of each resource industry, and they permit one to examine the resource sector of each country separately. Of the five tables discussed for the entire region, four are disaggregated here:

B-1 Evolution of production, consumption and trade;
B-3 Volume and value of exports;
B-4 Natural resources base;
B-5 The structure of the resource industries.

Prices (table B-2) are not reported for each country, since the same price often holds for several producers; or where differences exist, only the prices of one or a few specified grades or types of a product are reported. The list could have been expanded by more extensive use of unit values of exports or imports, but this was thought unlikely to add much information. It should however be noted that for several agricultural commodities two or more price series are given, each identified with a particular exporting country. The major exports of Brazil — coffee, cocoa, cotton, and iron ore — are all represented, for example.

The definitions, measures used, sources, and notes for the tables of this appendix are the same as for the tables for all of Latin America, presented in chapter 3. It should be noted, however, that information is considerably less complete for individual countries, particularly as regards the natural resource base. In general, the data are more thorough and more reliable for the large and relatively well-developed countries than for the smaller producers. Comparisons among countries can be made with reasonable confidence.

With only two exceptions, Mexico and Peru, the twenty nations of Latin America may be divided into a small group of mineral producers (Bolivia, Chile, and Venezuela) and a larger group of agricultural producers. But this distinction, which is quite striking in the statistics, should be qualified in several ways. First, it is sharpest in the case of exports,

that is, if only those products are considered in which a country has a sufficient advantage to engage in trade. When all natural resources are taken into account the emphasis on one group of products is less. Second, partly as a consequence of this, a country's internal economic structure need not reflect what it exports. Argentina and Brazil, both major "agricultural" countries, have large and complex industrial sectors drawing on a variety of domestic mineral resources. Argentina has a much smaller share of its labor force in agriculture than do such "mineral" countries as Bolivia and Venezuela. The predominant class of exports appears to bear no relation to the level of development or income reached or to the present degree of industrialization. Third, these identifications have changed greatly for at least some countries in the course of their economic history. Bolivia and Chile have always been mineral exporters, but Venezuela was once an agricultural trader exclusively and Brazil's chief export was gold before coffee assumed its present dominance. The changes in export structure which have recently occurred in Mexico and Peru, the countries with the most diversified primary export sectors, suggest that shifts of this sort are continuing.

From the analysis of natural resources in economic development (chapter 1) it appears that until the 1930s the role of the resource sector was essentially the same in all Latin American countries. In recent decades, as industrialization through import substitution has proceeded, that role has changed much more for some countries than for others. It does not appear, however, that these distinctions, or differences in prior economic growth among countries, are related to the particular resource products exported or to the markets in which they are sold. No single characteristic of the primary sector can be identified as a major influence on the rate or type of economic development or as the cause of the differences among Latin American economies today. In conclusion it may, however, be useful to indicate three factors which appear to have exerted considerable influence over time and whose existence or effects may sometimes be noticed in the tables in this appendix.

These three factors are the richness of the country's natural resource base, the diversity of resources it includes, and the size of the national market, particularly for processed and manufactured goods. The first is obviously important, as the principal determinant of a country's export history and the opportunities for investment and employment offered.

The second factor, diversity, is often thought of primarily as protection against short-term fluctuations in exports and the damaging effects of these variations on the entire economy. The statistical evidence suggests that diversification has less effect on fluctuations and that such fluctuations are less serious than is usually supposed.[1] There remain nonetheless two ways in which diversity of natural resources may be, and appears to have been, extremely valuable. The first is in providing new export commodities when traditional products cease to expand or decline in value. Latin American economic history records a great number of booms based on different primary commodities; the more products a country can produce, the more such booms it can enjoy and the more rapidly its exports can be expected to grow over the long term. This point is of some importance since periods of stagnation in a country have usually intervened between the decline of one export product and the emergence of another. Since the 1930s the value of a diversified resource base has changed somewhat, at least for the larger countries of the region. As they have begun to industrialize they have come to require a much

greater variety of raw materials than formerly; and as more of these products can be supplied domestically, less must be spent to import them. So long as exports are relatively high and growing rapidly the absence of a particular resource may not be important. Once export values become the limiting factor in economic growth, the possession and development of domestic resources, provided they are not too costly, can increase the rate of growth by freeing export revenues for other purposes. This is the reason for the great amount of import substitution in raw materials — not only in manufactures — which has been achieved or attempted in Latin America in recent decades. In the cases of iron and steel, petroleum, coal, wheat, and forest products it has been striking.

Finally, it appears that the success of industrialization through import substitution depends to a considerable degree on the third factor, the size of the domestic market. This observation is commonplace in the literature on Latin American economic development; it is now widely realized that small national markets set limits to the degree of industrial development possible without excessive costs, and thereby furnish a major argument in favor of regional economic integration. Market size is not a property of the resource sector, although the past rate of immigration and the current level of income, both of which contribute to market size, result in large part from the history of that sector. Thus the present ability of an economy to use its resources for internal development depends on the richness of those resources and the way they have been used in the past.

---

[1]This point and several others concerning primary exports and their relation to economic stability and growth are treated at greater length in chap. 2.

TABLE B-1-1. ARGENTINA: Evolution of Production, Exports, and Consumption of Natural Resource Commodities, Late 1930s, Early 1950s, and Early and Mid 1960s
(Thousands of cubic meters of petroleum and forest products, and thousands of metric tons of all other products)

Commodity	Period	Production	Exports	Consumption	Share of Production (%)			Share of World Total (%)		
					Exported	Consumed	Refined	Production	Exports	Consumption
Copper	1950-51			4						
	1962-64			16	100	(2.5)				
	1965-66			21	60	(2.7)				
Iron ore	1935-39			703		(1.7)				
	1952-53	70		755		(27)	100			
	1962-64	115		1,951		(21)	100			0.7
	1965-66	136		2,260		(58)	100			0.5
Lead	1935-39	15	16		100		65	0.9	1.5	
	1950-51	21		34		(62)	100	1.2		2.2
	1962-64	27		25		93	88	1.1		0.9
	1965-66	31		29		94	87	1.1		1.0
Zinc	1935-39	8.9		6.5		73		0.5		
	1950-51	14	2.8	10	20	72	62	0.6		0.5
	1962-64	28	18	20	65	71	71	0.8	0.8	0.6
	1965-66	28	2.7	22	9.6	79	82	0.7		0.5
Tin	1935-39	1.3	0.8	1.1	62	85	68	0.8	0.6	0.7
	1950-51			1.3		(19)	80			0.9
	1962-64			1.2		(14)				0.7
	1965-66			1.7		(17)				1.0
Petroleum	1935-39	2,601	11	4,200		(62)	100	0.9		1.5
	1950-51	3,802		9,335		(41)	100	0.6		1.6
	1962-64	15,675	804	18,600	5.1	(84)	97	1.0		1.2
	1965-66	16,373	1,068	18,550	6.7	(88)	100	0.9		0.9
Coal	1935-39			3,223						
	1952-53	96		1,643		(5.8)				
	1961-63	302		1,090		(36)				
	1965	374		1,148		(33)	100			
Coffee	1935-39			24						1.3
	1950-52			27						1.5
	1962-64			30						1.0
	1965-66			33						1.2
Cocoa	1935-39			5.0						0.8
	1950-52			6.1						0.8
	1961-63			7.0						0.6
	1964-66			15						0.9
Sugar	1935-39	476	8.2	427	1.7	90		1.8		1.8
	1951-53	667		627		94		2.1		1.9
	1961-63	820	186	792	23	97		2.7	3.8	1.6
	1964-66	1,112	53	888	4.8	80		1.8	2.7	1.4
Bananas	1934-38			160						
	1953-57			169						0.8
	1962-64			169						
	1965-66			177						
Wheat	1935-39	6,036	3,445	2,811	57	47		3.6	20	1.8
	1951-53	5,313	2,332	3,299	44	62		2.4	9.2	2.2
	1961-63	6,347	2,328	3,198	37	50		2.5	5.1	1.6
	1964-66	8,730	6,196	3,225	71	37		3.2	11	1.5
Beef	1934-38	1,653	409	1,244	25	75		11	56	8.6
	1951-53	1,817	107	1,710	5.9	94		10	26	10
	1961-63	2,376	397	1,979	17	83		9.3	30	7.7
	1964-66	2,134	483	1,651	23	77		7.5	33	5.8
Cotton	1935-39	63	30	28	48	44		0.9	1.0	
	1950-52	118	28	109	24	92		1.6	1.0	1.5
	1961-63	115	39	106	34	92		1.1	1.1	1.0
	1964-66	115	25	116	22	(99)		1.0	0.6	1.3
Forest products	1951-53	13,152		14,438		(91)	17	1.0		1.1
	1961-63	12,835		14,645		(88)	16	0.9		0.8
	1964-66	11,692		16,298		(72)	19	0.9		0.8
Fishery products	1938	55	3.1	62	5.6	(89)				
	1951-53	78	1.7	77	2.2	99				
	1961-63	104	3.6	103	3.5	99				
	1964-66	188	6.8		3.6		33			

For notes and sources, see chapter 3, table B-1.

TABLE B–1–2. BOLIVIA: Evolution of Production, Exports, and Consumption of Natural Resource Commodities, Late 1930s, Early 1950s, and Early and Mid 1960s
(Thousands of cubic meters of petroleum and forest products, and thousands of metric tons of all other products)

Commodity	Period	Production	Exports	Consumption	Share of Production (%)			Share of World Total (%)		
					Exported	Consumed	Refined	Production	Exports	Consumption
Copper	1935-39	3.2	2.2		69					
	1950-51	4.8	5.3		100					
	1962-64	3.4	3.7		100					
	1965-66	5.2	5.2		100					
Iron ore	1952-53			11						
	1962-64			33						
	1965-66			55						
Lead	1935-39	14	12		87			1.4	1.2	
	1950-51	31	31		100			1.8	2.7	
	1962-64	19	19		100			0.8	1.6	
	1965-66	18	18		100			0.6	1.4	
Zinc	1935-39	10	10		100			0.6	1.1	
	1950-51	25	25		100			1.1	1.3	
	1962-64	6.0	6.0		100	1.3				
	1965-66	14	14		100					
Tin	1935-39	26	26		100			15	16	
	1950-51	32	32		100		1.3	20	19	
	1962-64	23	23		100		12	16	14	
	1965-66	24	25				9.2	17	15	
Petroleum	1935-39	26		60		(43)	85			
	1950-51	91	11	165	12	(55)	89			
	1962-64	498	81	423	16	85	89			
	1965-66	761	185	525	24	69	43			
Coal	1935-39			31						
	1952-53			9						
Coffee	1935-39	4.0	0.1		2.5					
	1950-52	1.8	1.0		56					
	1962-64	3.0	1.0	2.6	33	87				
	1965-66	3.1	1.1	2.8	34	90				
Cocoa	1935-39	2.5		2		80				
	1950-52	3.0		3.0		100	100			
	1961-63	2.1		2.1		100	100			
	1964-66	2.3		2.7		(85)				
Sugar	1935-39	1.0		23		(4.4)				
	1951-53	3.0		48		(6.3)				
	1961-63	56		68		(82)				
	1964-66	94		89		94				
Wheat	1934-38	23	35	65		(35)				
	1951-53			74						
	1961-63			148						
	1964-66			192						
Cotton	1935-39									
	1950-52			3.3						
	1961-63			2.2						
	1964-66			3.4						
Forest products	1951-53	7,533		7,547		100	1.8	0.5		0.5
	1961-63	4,322		4,337		100	2.0			
	1964-66	4,795		4,824		(99)	2.4			
Fishery products	1938		0.7	2.0		(35)				
	1951-53		0.9	1.8		(50)				
	1961-63		1.1	1.3		(85)				
	1964-66		1.4	1.6		(87)				

For notes and sources, see chapter 3, table B-1.

TABLE B-1-3. BRAZIL: Evolution of Production, Exports, and Consumption of Natural Resource Commodities, Late 1930s, Early 1950s, and Early and Mid 1960s
(Thousands of cubic meters of petroleum and forest products, and thousands of metric tons of all other products)

Commodity	Period	Production	Exports	Consumption	Share of Production (%)			Share of World Total (%)		
					Exported	Consumed	Refined	Production	Exports	Consumption
Copper	1950-51			19						0.7
	1962-64	2.4		33		(7.4)				0.7
	1965-66	2.2		51		(4.3)				1.1
Iron ore	1935-39	225	188	417	84	(18)	69			0.5
	1952-53	3,386	1,587	1,393	47	(68)	37	1.1	2.7	
	1962-64	11,334	8,309	3,454	73	(82)	30	2.1	4.7	0.7
	1965-66	20,712	12,821	3,357	62	99	21	3.3	5.1	0.8
Lead	1935-39				100					
	1950-51	3.8		19		(20)	95			1.2
	1962-64	17		18		(92)	100	0.7		0.7
	1965-66	23		12		52	57	0.8		0.9
Zinc	1935-39			2.6						
	1950-51			11						0.6
	1962-64			41						1.2
	1965-66			36						1.1
Tin	1935-39			0.7						0.5
	1950-51			1.6		(13)	100			1.1
	1962-64	1.0		2.1		(48)	100	0.7		1.3
	1965-66	2.0		2.1		(95)	100	1.0		1.2
Petroleum	1935-39			1,290						
	1950-51	82		5,565		(1.5)	100			1.0
	1962-64	5,428		19,050		(28)	97			1.2
	1965-66	6,169		19,958		(31)	100			1.0
Coal	1935-39	820		2,407		(34)				
	1952-53	1,994		2,859		(70)	25			
	1961-63	2,489		2,427		(98)	44			
	1965	3,383		4,628		(73)	42			
Coffee	1935-39	1,362	1,304		96			59	78	
	1950-52	1,076	940	240	87	22		48	52	11
	1962-64	1,590	1,017	420	64	26		40	36	11
	1965-66	1,599	916	497	57	31		38	27	13
Cocoa	1935-39	124	114	3.0	92	2.4	8.1	17	16	0.5
	1950-52	154	104	6.3	67	4.1	15	21	13	0.8
	1961-63	116	96	16	83	14	41	10	12	1.5
	1964-66	137	115	25	84	18	44	10	8.0	1.6
Sugar	1935-39	759	47	649	6.2	86		2.9		2.8
	1951-53	1,798	103	1,592	6.7	89		7.9	0.7	4.8
	1961-63	3,210	570	2,732	18	85		11	2.7	5.3
	1964-66	3,960	698	2,861	18	72		6.2	3.6	4.4
Bananas	1934-38		198						7.9	
	1953-57	2,945	200	2,745	6.8	93		15	6.4	14
	1962-64		216						4.9	
	1965-66		211						4.2	
Wheat	1934-38	135		1,149		(12)				0.6
	1951-53	628		1,966		(32)				1.3
	1961-63	539		2,434		(22)				1.2
	1964-66	614		2,505		(24)				1.2
Beef	1934-38	826	43	783	5.2	95		5.7	6.0	5.4
	1951-53	1,170	6.1	1,169	0.5	100		6.5	1.5	6.5
	1961-63	1,368	24	1,344	1.8	98		5.3	1.8	5.3
	1964-66	1,455	31	1,424	2.1	98		5.1	2.1	5.0
Cotton	1935-39	424	194	114	46	27		6.2	6.3	1.7
	1950-52	399	114	177	29	44		5.3	4.5	2.4
	1961-63	502	214	280	43	56		4.8	6.0	2.8
	1964-66	494	215	276	44	54		4.3	5.7	3.1
Forest products	1951-53	104,630	1,890	103,432	1.8	99	11	7.6		7.5
	1961-63	130,510	1,924	129,478	1.5	99	11	6.8		6.8
	1964-66	152,077	2,229	148,920	1.5	98	12	3.2		7.2
Fishery products	1938	103		120		(86)		0.5		0.6
	1951-53	165	0.7	202	0.4	(81)		0.7		0.8
	1961-63	355	1.9	384	0.5	(92)		0.8		0.8
	1964-66	331	2.4	351	0.7	(94)		0.6		0.6

For notes and sources, see chapter 3, table B-1.

TABLE B–1–4. CHILE: Evolution of Production, Exports, and Consumption of Natural Resource Commodities, Late 1930s, Early 1950s, and Early and Mid 1960s
(Thousands of cubic meters of petroleum and forest products, and thousands of metric tons of all other products)

Commodity	Period	Production	Exports	Consumption	Share of Production (%)			Share of World Total (%)		
					Exported	Consumed	Refined	Production	Exports	Consumption
Copper	1935-39	327	300		92		68	17	20	
	1950-51	373	337	22	90	5.9	73	14	24	0.8
	1962-64	604	590	15	98	2.5	43	13	21	
	1965-66	635	557		88		51	12	19	
Iron ore	1935-39	1,311	1,262	121	96	(12)		0.7	2.4	
	1950-51	2,572	2,135	295	83	(76)	17	0.8	4.1	
	1962-64	8,774	7,824	693	89	(73)	7.8	1.6	4.4	
	1965-66	12,186	10,912	619	90	(85)	5.1	1.9	5.1	
Lead	1935-39									
	1950-51	5.6								
	1962-64	1.2	1.7		100					
	1965-66	0.8			88					
Zinc	1950-51									
	1962-64	0.7								
	1965-66	1.6								
Tin	1935-39									
	1950-51									
	1962-64			0.6						
	1965-66			0.6						
Petroleum	1935-39			700						
	1950-51	111	107	1,340	96	(8.3)				
	1962-64	2,045		3,330		(61)	100			
	1965-66	2,027		3,719		(55)	100			
Coal	1935-39	1,931		1,609		83				
	1952-53	2,393		2,575		(93)	15			
	1961-63	1,781		1,970		(91)	19			
	1965	1,727		2,858		(60)	18			
Coffee	1935-39			3.4						
	1950-52			4.9						
	1962-64			5.1						
	1965-66			8.2						
Cocoa	1935-39			1.0						
	1950-52			0.9						
	1961-63			1.3						
	1964-66			3.0						
Sugar	1935-39			123						0.5
	1951-53			198						0.6
	1961-63	71		285		(25)				0.5
	1964-66	129		317		(41)				0.5
Bananas	1934-38			13						0.5
	1953-57			18						0.6
	1962-64			39						0.9
	1965-66			35						0.7
Wheat	1934-38	859	23	844	2.7	98		0.5		0.5
	1951-53	976		1,056		(93)				0.7
	1961-63	1,221		1,319		(93)				0.6
	1964-66	1,224		1,535		(80)				0.7
Beef	1934-38	107		108		(99)		0.7		0.7
	1951-53	114		114		100		0.6		0.6
	1961-63	143		150		(95)		0.6		0.6
	1964-66	133		145		(92)				0.5
Cotton	1935-39			2.5						
	1950-52			17						
	1961-63			24						
	1964-66			28						
Forest products	1951-53	5,707	243	5,511	4.3	97	43			
	1961-63	6,417	290	6,188	4.5	96	50			
	1964-66	6,973	284	6,764	4.1	97	53			
Fishery products	1938	32	0.2	32	0.6	100				
	1951-53	107	5.7	101	5.3	94	39			
	1961-63	610	82	528	13	87	43	1.3	1.7	1.2
	1964-66	1,084	157	927	14	86	86	2.0	2.5	

For notes and sources, see chapter 3, table B-1.

TABLE B–1–5. COLOMBIA: Evolution of Production, Exports, and Consumption of Natural Resource Commodities, Late 1930s, Early 1950s, and Early and Mid 1960s

(Thousands of cubic meters of petroleum and forest products, and thousands of metric tons of all other products)

Commodity	Period	Production	Exports	Consumption	Share of Production (%)			Share of World Total (%)		
					Exported	Consumed	Refined	Production	Exports	Consumption
Copper	1961			4.5						
	1966			7.0						
Iron ore	1935-39			88						
	1952-53			227		(4.4)				
	1962-64	694		483		(41)	100			
	1965-66	684		375		(61)	100			
Zinc	1962			1.8		(23)	45			
	1966		0.8	2.6		(31)				
Petroleum	1935-39	3,255	2,328	461	72	14	13	1.1	4.0	
	1950-51	5,761	4,811	1,282	84	22	85	0.9	1.9	
	1962-64	9,268	5,163	4,300	56	46	54	0.6	0.7	
	1965-66	11,621	7,079	5,186	61	45	53	1.0	0.9	
Coal	1935-39	340		331		97				
	1952-53	1,261		1,098		87				
	1961-63	3,000		2,950		98	19			
	1965	3,100		3,100		100	24			
Coffee	1935-39	263	252		96			11	15	
	1950-52	353	286	37	81	10		16	15	1.8
	1962-64	459	382	60	83	13		11	14	1.6
	1965-66	449	336	66	75	15		11	10	1.7
Cocoa	1935-39	11		12		(92)	100	1.4		1.8
	1950-52	15		18		(83)	100	2.0		2.4
	1961-63	16		23		(69)	100	1.4		2.1
	1964-66	17		33		(50)	100	1.3		2.3
Sugar	1935-39	44		46		(96)				
	1951-53	195	29	178	15	91		0.9		0.5
	1961-63	378	51	344	13	91		1.2		0.7
	1964-66	483	82	397	17	82		0.8		0.6
Bananas	1934-38		162						6.5	
	1953-57		199						6.4	
	1962-64		174						4.0	
	1965-66		298						6.0	
Wheat	1934-38	113		123		(96)				
	1951-53	134		186		(72)				
	1961-63	155		259		(60)				
	1964-66	116		336		(35)				
Beef	1934-38									
	1951-53	283		283		100		1.6		1.6
	1961-63	355		355		100		1.4		1.4
	1964-66	408		408		100		1.4		1.4
Cotton	1935-39	5.4		8.5		(64)				
	1950-52	8.0		27		(30)				
	1961-63	78	21	51	27	65		0.8	0.6	0.5
	1964-66	66	9.9	61	15	92		0.6	0.2	0.7
Forest products	1951-53	22,291		22,291		100	10	1.6		1.6
	1961-63	25,330	157	25,525	0.6	(99)	12	1.3		1.3
	1964-66	25,045	198	26,166	0.8	(96)	11	1.1		1.7
Fishery products	1938	10	0.1	12	1.0	(83)				
	1951-53	16	0.2	18	1.3	(89)				
	1961-63	49	1.1	51	2.2	(96)				
	1964-66	54	0.8	54	1.5	100				

For notes and sources, see chapter 3, table B-1.

TABLE B-1-6. COSTA RICA: Evolution of Production, Exports, and Consumption of Natural Resource Commodities, Late 1930s, Early 1950s, and Early and Mid 1960s
(Thousands of cubic meters of petroleum and forest products, and thousands of metric tons of all other products)

Commodity	Period	Production	Exports	Consumption	Share of Production (%)			Share of World Total (%)		
					Exported	Consumed	Refined	Production	Exports	Consumption
Petroleum	1935-39									
	1950-51			121						
	1962-64			256						
	1965-66			226						
Coffee	1935-39	24	20		80			1.0	1.2	
	1950-52	21	19	3.4	90	16		0.9	1.0	
	1962-64	65	53	7.8	82	12		1.6	1.9	
	1965-66	67	51	9.9	76	15		1.6	1.5	
Cocoa	1935-39	6.8	6.0		88			0.9	0.9	
	1950-52	3.5	3.2		91			0.5		
	1961-63	12	11		91			1.0	1.0	
	1964-66	9.4	8.1		86			0.7	0.7	
Sugar	1935-39	8.0	0.4	8.0	5.0	100				
	1951-53	28	2.4	20	7.1	71				
	1961-63	82	29	42	35	51				
	1964-66	112	50	67	45	60				
Bananas	1934-38		96						3.8	
	1953-57		320						10	
	1962-64		282						6.5	
	1965-66		338						6.9	
Wheat	1934-38			11						
	1951-53			31						
	1961-63			51						
	1964-66			60						
Cotton	1935-39									
	1950-52			1.7						
	1961-63	2.0		3.0		(67)				
	1964-66	3.3		2.3		70				
Forest products	1951-53	923		934		(99)	44			
	1961-63	1,859	13	1,880	1.9	(99)	25			
	1964-66	2,073	13	2,122	0.6	(98)	24			
Fishery products	1938	1.0	1.5	0.3	150	30				
	1951-53	1.0	1.0	0.9	100	90				
	1961-63	2.4	0.9	2.6	38	(92)				
	1964-66	2.8	1.1	3.0	41	(93)				

For notes and sources, see chapter 3, table B-1.

TABLE B-1-7. CUBA: Evolution of Production, Exports, and Consumption of Natural Resource Commodities, Late 1930s, Early 1950s, and Early and Mid 1960s
(Thousands of cubic meters of petroleum and forest products, and thousands of metric tons of all other products)

Commodity	Period	Production	Exports	Consumption	Share of Production (%)			Share of World Total (%)		
					Exported	Consumed	Refined	Production	Exports	Consumption
Copper	1935-39	11	14					0.6	0.9	
	1950-51	20	22					0.8	1.4	
	1962-64	5.8	6.4			48				
	1965-66	6.0								
Iron ore	1935-39	300	254	71	85			0.5	0.5	
	1952-53	144	154	169						
	1962-64	5.0		217						
	1965-66									
Petroleum	1935-39			780						
	1950-51	23		2,330		(1.0)	100			
	1962-64	23		5,050			100			
	1965-66	68		4,867		(1.4)	100			
Coal	1935-39			414						
	1952-53			84						
	1961-63			87						
	1965			60						
Coffee	1935-39	33	2		6.3			1.4		
	1950-52	31		33		(94)		1.4		1.6
	1962-64	34	4.7	29	14	(84)		0.8		0.8
	1965-66	27		33		(82)		0.7		0.9
Cocoa	1935-39	3.2					100			
	1950-52	2.8		2.1	3.9	75	82			
	1961-63	2.5		2.5		100	100			
	1964-66	1.8		2.2		(82)	100			
Sugar	1935-39	2,887	2,678	159	93	5.5		11	23	0.7
	1951-53	6,048	5,322	284	88	4.6		27	36	0.9
	1961-63	5,134	5,022	402	98	7.8		17	23	0.8
	1964-66	5,180	4,642	554	90	11		9	24	0.9
Bananas	1934-38		121						4.8	
	1953-57	55		55						
	1962-64									
	1965-66									
Wheat	1934-38			121						
	1951-53			206						
	1961-63			361						
	1964-66			545						
Beef	1934-38	122		122		100		0.8		0.8
	1951-53	173		173		100		1.0		1.0
	1961-63	151		151		100		0.6		0.6
	1964-66	185		185		100		0.7		0.7
Cotton	1935-39			2.0						
	1950-52			17						
	1961-63	4.0		17		(24)				
	1964-66	1.0		25		(4)				
Forest products	1951-53	1,028		1,291		(80)	26			
	1961-63	2,034		2,741		(74)	29			
	1964-66	2,296		2,859		(80)	31			
Fishery products	1938	10	0.7	22	7.0	(46)				
	1951-53	9.9	1.1	30	11	(33)				
	1961-63	34	0.6	54	1.8	(63)				
	1964-66	40	0.9	66	2.3	(61)				

For notes and sources, see chapter 3, table B-1.

TABLE B-1-8. DOMINICAN REPUBLIC: Evolution of Production, Exports, and Consumption of Natural Resource Commodities, Late 1930s, Early 1950s, and Early and Mid 1960s
(Thousands of cubic meters of petroleum and forest products, and thousands of metric tons of all other products)

Commodity	Period	Production	Exports	Consumption	Share of Production (%)			Share of World Total (%)		
					Exported	Consumed	Refined	Production	Exports	Consumption
Iron ore	1952-53	55	55	40	100					
	1962-64	47		53						
	1965-66									
Petroleum	1935-39			54						
	1950-51									
	1962-64			571						
	1965-66			524						
Coal	1935-39			3						
	1952-53									
	1962-63									
	1964-66									
Coffee	1935-39	24	13		54			1.0	0.8	
	1950-52	27	19	6.3	70	23		1.2	0.9	
	1962-64	35	30	9.0	86	26		0.9	1.1	
	1965-66	34	24	9.9	71	29		0.8	8.6	
Cocoa	1935-39	23	24				2.6	3.2	3.4	
	1950-52	32	24	4.5	75	14	22	4.3	3.2	0.6
	1961-63	37	25	4.0	68	11	51	3.1	2.4	
	1964-66	32	29	4.0	90	12	18	2.5	2.3	
Sugar	1935-39	354	418	16		4.5		1.4	3.5	
	1951-53	590	535	51	92	9		2.6	3.6	
	1961-63	860	770	103	90	12		2.8	3.6	
	1964-66	700	585	113	83	16		1.1	3.0	
Bananas	1934-38		2							
	1953-57		43						1.4	
	1962-64		119						2.7	
	1965-66		127						2.6	
Wheat	1934-38			7						
	1951-53			24						
	1961-63			50						
	1964-66			55						
Cotton	1935-39									
	1950-52			2.5						
	1961-63			4.0						
	1964-66			6.7						
Forest products	1951-53	1,564	8.3	1,574	0.5	(99)	10			
	1961-63	1,955	10	1,978	0.5	(99)	15			
	1964-66	2,111	5	2,042		97	17			
Fishery products	1938	0.3		2.2		(14)				
	1951-53	0.6		6.9		(8.7)				
	1961-63	2.2		11		(20)				
	1964-66	4.2		16		(26)				

For notes and sources, see chapter 3, table B-1.

TABLE B–1–9. ECUADOR: Evolution of Production, Exports, and Consumption of Natural Resource Commodities, Late 1930s, Early 1950s, and Early and Mid 1960s

(Thousands of cubic meters of petroleum and forest products, and thousands of metric tons of all other products)

Commodity	Period	Production	Exports	Consumption	Share of Production (%)			Share of World Total (%)		
					Exported	Consumed	Refined	Production	Exports	Consumption
Petroleum	1935-39	331		61		18	16			
	1950-51	425	183	289	43	68	61			
	1962-64	415	38	834	9.2	(50)	100			
	1965-66	445	73	894	16	(50)	100			
Coffee	1935-39	14	14		100			0.6	0.8	
	1950-52	23	19	2.1	83	9.1		1.0	1.0	
	1962-64	49	29	11	59	22		1.2	1.1	
	1965-66	70	45	23	64	33		1.7	1.3	
Cocoa	1935-39	18	20				11	2.4	2.9	
	1950-52	23	25	3.5		15	12	3.1	3.4	0.5
	1961-63	35	33	5.7	95	14	16	3.0	3.3	0.5
	1964-66	40	33	6.8	83	17	18	2.6	2.7	0.6
Sugar	1935-39	22	0.2	26	0.9	(85)				
	1951-53	59	3.3	56	5.6	95				
	1961-63	139	52	96	38	69				
	1964-66	180	56	106	31	59				
Bananas	1934-38		48						1.9	
	1953-57		578						18	
	1962-64		1,280						28	
	1965-66		1,233						25	
Wheat	1934-38			32						
	1951-53	25		65		(38)				
	1961-63	74		114		(65)				
	1964-66	62		119		(52)				
Cotton	1935-39	2.6	0.3		12					
	1950-52	2.5		4.8		(63)				
	1961-63	3.0		4.2		(71)				
	1964-66	4.7		6.7		(70)				
Forest products	1951-53	871	60	828	6.9	95	28			
	1961-63	2,473	18	2,505	0.7	(99)	32			
	1964-66	2,397	76	2,905	3.2	(82)	41			
Fishery products	1938	1.8		1.8		100				
	1951-53	9.2		11		(84)				
	1961-63	44	8.6	36	20	82				
	1964-66	49	9.1	40	19	82	10			

For notes and sources, see chapter 3, table B–1.

TABLE B–1–10. EL SALVADOR: Evolution of Production, Exports, and Consumption of Natural Resource Commodities, Late 1930s, Early 1950s, and Early and Mid 1960s
(Thousands of cubic meters of petroleum and forest products, and thousands of metric tons of all other products)

Commodity	Period	Production	Exports	Consumption	Share of Production (%)			Share of World Total (%)		
					Exported	Consumed	Refined	Production	Exports	Consumption
Petroleum	1935-39			27						
	1950-51			83						
	1962-64			329						
	1965-66			382						
Coffee	1935-39	65	61		92			2.7	3.6	
	1950-52	65	65	6.0	100	9.2		2.9	3.5	
	1962-64	105	96	6.9	91	6.6		2.6	3.4	
	1965-66	116	98	17	84	14		2.8	2.9	
Sugar	1935-39	14	2.6	11	19	79				
	1951-53	29	1.7	24	5.9	84				
	1961-63	58	18	42	31	72				
	1964-66	94	29	60	31	64				
Wheat	1934-38			10						
	1951-53			21						
	1961-63			40						
	1964-66			49						
Cotton	1935-39	1		1.0		100				
	1950-52	8	3.4	3.6	43	45				
	1961-63	67	52	6.5	87	9.7		0.6	1.4	
	1964-66	66	59	11	89	17		0.6	1.6	
Forest products	1951-53	2,500		2,523		(99)				
	1961-63	2,960		3,101		(96)	3.7			
	1964-66	2,764		2,725		99				
Fishery products	1938			0.1						
	1951-53			0.8						
	1961-63	6	4.2	2.9	70	48				
	1964-66	9	3.9	6.5	43	72				

For notes and sources, see chapter 3, table B–1.

TABLE B-1-11. GUATEMALA: Evolution of Production, Exports, and Consumption of Natural Resource Commodities, Late 1930s, Early 1950s, and Early and Mid 1960s
(Thousands of cubic meters of petroleum and forest products, and thousands of metric tons of all other products)

Commodity	Period	Production	Exports	Consumption	Share of Production (%)			Share of World Total (%)		
					Exported	Consumed	Refined	Production	Exports	Consumption
Lead	1950-51	3.2	1.7		53		7.2			
	1962-64	6.6	1.1		17		2.0			
	1965-66	1.9	0.9		47		7.9			
Zinc	1950-51	3.4	5.1		100					
	1962-64	0.7	1.2		100					
	1965-66	0.9	1.1		100					
Petroleum	1935-39			84						
	1950-51			291						
	1962-64			710						
	1965-66			703						
Coffee	1935-39	55	55		101			2.4	3.3	
	1950-52	59	55	9.0	93	15		2.6	3.0	
	1962-64	106	100	13	94	12		2.6	3.4	
	1965-66	112	101	13	91	12		2.6	3.0	
Cocoa	1935-39									
	1950-52	0.7			46		96			
	1961-63	0.6			67		67			
	1964-66	0.5			83					
Sugar	1935-39	16	1.7	14	11	88				
	1951-53	30		35		(86)				
	1961-63	111		79		71				
	1964-66	153		105		69				
Bananas	1934-38		167						6.7	
	1953-57		176						5.6	
	1962-64		107						2.4	
	1965-66		68						1.4	
Wheat	1934-38	10		23		(43)				
	1951-53	13		36		(36)				
	1961-63	24		52		(46)				
	1964-66	32		54		(59)				
Cotton	1935-39									
	1950-52	1.5		4.5		(44)				
	1961-63	42	31	7	74	15			0.9	
	1964-66	80	71	8.3	89	10		0.7	1.7	
Forest products	1951-53	6,778	14	6,781		100	2.8			
	1961-63	6,350	35	6,349	0.6	100	13			
	1964-66	7,000	23	7,107		(98)	12			
Fishery products	1938	0.4		0.4		100				
	1951-53	0.7		0.7		100				
	1961-63	1.0	0.2	1.5	20	(67)				
	1964-66	2.6	0.9	2.6	35	100				

For notes and sources, see chapter 3, table B-1.

TABLE B–1–12. HAITI: Evolution of Production, Exports, and Consumption of Natural Resource Commodities, Late 1930s, Early 1950s, and Early and Mid 1960s
(Thousands of cubic meters of petroleum and forest products, and thousands of metric tons of all other products)

Commodity	Period	Production	Exports	Consumption	Share of Production (%)			Share of World Total (%)		
					Exported	Consumed	Refined	Production	Exports	Consumption
Petroleum	1935-39			20						
	1950-51									
	1962-64			122						
	1965-66									
Coffee	1935-39	26	26		100			1.1	1.6	
	1950-52	37	27	9.0	73	24		1.7	1.3	
	1962-64	40	26	9.9	65	25		1.0	0.9	
	1965-66	31	22	9.7	72	31		0.8	0.7	
Cocoa	1935-39	1.5	1.5		100					
	1950-52	1.9	2.1							
	1961-63	2.1	0.8		38					
	1964-66	2.7			12					
Sugar	1935-39	40	35	4.0	88	10				
	1951-53	51	32	25	55	44				
	1961-63	70	40	35	57	49				
	1964-66	65	26	39	39	60				
Bananas	1934-38		11							
Wheat	1934-38			13						
	1951-53			39						
	1961-63			47						
	1964-66			55						
Cotton	1935-39	4.8	5.5							
	1950-52	1.5	0.7	5.0	47	(40)				
	1961-63	1.0		5.0		(19)				
	1964-66	1.0		5.5		(18)				
Forest products	1951-53	8,286		8,296		100		0.6		0.6
	1961-63	8,225		8,235		100	2.8			
	1964-66	9,592		9,599		100	7.0			
Fishery products	1938	1.5		4.0		(38)				
	1951-53	2.1		9.9		(21)				

For notes and sources, see chapter 3, table B–1.

TABLE B-1-13. HONDURAS: Evolution of Production, Exports, and Consumption of Natural Resource Commodities, Late 1930s, Early 1950s, and Early and Mid 1960s
(Thousands of cubic meters of petroleum and forest products, and thousands of metric tons of all other products)

Commodity	Period	Production	Exports	Consumption	Share of Production (%)			Share of World Total (%)		
					Exported	Consumed	Refined	Production	Exports	Consumption
Lead	1950-51									
	1962-64	5.4	5.5		100					
	1965-66	10.7	9.4		88					
Zinc	1950-51									
	1962-64	7.0	7.0		100					
	1965-66	11.8	10.4		88					
Petroleum	1935-39			130						
	1950-51			176						
	1962-64			266						
	1965-66									
Coffee	1935-39	1.1	1.6					0.6		
	1950-52	14	7.7	2.5	55	18		0.7	0.6	
	1962-64	28	18	4.5	64	16		0.7	0.6	
	1965-66	28	24	5.8	87	21		0.7	0.7	
Cocoa	1935-39									
	1950-52									
	1961-63									
	1964-66									
Sugar	1935-39			5.4						
	1951-53	6.7		13		(52)				
	1961-63	25		28		(90)				
	1964-66	34		36		(94)				
Bananas	1934-38		280						11	
	1953-57		344						11	
	1962-64		357						8.2	
	1965-66		641						13	
Wheat	1934-38	0.6		7.0		(8.6)				
	1951-53	0.7		13		(5.4)				
	1961-63	1.0		24		(4.2)				
	1964-66	1.0		27		(3.7)				
Cotton	1935-39									
	1950-52		0.6	1.9						
	1961-63	5.7	2.9	3.1	51	54				
	1964-66	10	10	4.2	100	42				
Forest products	1951-53	2,623	246	2,390	9.4	91	21			
	1961-63	3,285	386	2,963	12	90	24			
	1964-66	3,540	518	3,196	15	90	26			
Fishery products	1938			0.6						
	1951-53	2.6		2.9						
	1961-63	1.0	0.3	1.1	30	(90)				
	1964-66	1.6	0.8	1.2	50	75				

For notes and sources, see chapter 3, table B-1.

TABLE B-1-14. MEXICO: Evolution of Production, Exports, and Consumption of Natural Resource Commodities, Late 1930s, Early 1950s, and Early and Mid 1960s
(Thousands of cubic meters of petroleum and forest products, and thousands of metric tons of all other products)

Commodity	Period	Production	Exports	Consumption	Share of Production (%)			Share of World Total (%)		
					Exported	Consumed	Refined	Production	Exports	Consumption
Copper	1935-39	40	35		88			2.1	2.3	
	1950-51	62	56	8.3	90	13	35	2.4	4.1	
	1962-64	52	31	28	60	54	60	1.1	1.2	0.6
	1965-66	56	19	42	34	75	97	1.1	0.9	0.9
Iron ore	1935-39	123	106	268	86	(51)				
	1952-53	535	177	908	33	(59)	88			
	1962-64	2,111	57	2,103	2.7	(96)	70			
	1965-66	2,456	5	2,693		(97)	74			0.6
Lead	1935-39	234	218		97		98	14	21	
	1950-51	232	201	8.9	87	3.8	97	14	20	0.6
	1962-64	184	116	55	63	30	98	7.3	9.2	2.1
	1965-66	170	100	67	59	39	99	6.1	8.3	2.7
Zinc	1935-39	149	147		99		23	8.9	17	
	1950-51	202	182	11	90	5.5	28	9.0	12	0.6
	1962-64	246	207	28	84	11	24	6.6	11	0.8
	1965-66	233	142	79	61	34	29	5.3	9	0.5
Tin	1935-39					50	5			
	1950-51			0.5		(80)	100			
	1962-64	0.9		1.3		(74)	100	0.6		0.8
	1965-66	1.0		1.2		(83)	100	0.7		0.7
Petroleum	1935-39	6,665	1,233	3,061	19	46	98	2.2	2.1	1.3
	1950-51	11,906	2,772	8,495	23	71	74	1.9		1.5
	1962-64	18,141	2,879	17,900	16	99	100	1.2		1.1
	1965-66	19,283	2,878	20,033	15	(96)	100	1.0		1.0
Coal	1935-39	899		1,256		(71)	78			
	1952-53	1,375		1,433		(96)	49			
	1961-63	1,929		1,910		99	59			
	1965	2,006		2,142		(93)	59			
Coffee	1935-39	56	37		65			2.4	2.0	
	1950-52	70	50	12	71	17		3.1	2.8	0.6
	1962-64	144	88	60	61	42		3.6	3.2	1.6
	1965-66	172	86	70	50	41		4.1	2.6	2.1
Cocoa	1935-39	1		2.0		(55)	100			
	1950-52	8	2.3	6.4	29	80	91	1.1		0.9
	1961-63	24	12	14	50	57	55	2.1	1.2	1.3
	1964-66	31	7.2	13	24	42	44	2.4	0.6	0.8
Sugar	1935-39	327	0.9	278		85		1.3		1.2
	1951-53	778	34	710	4.4	91		3.4		2.2
	1961-63	1,592	448	1,239	28	78		5.2	2.1	2.4
	1964-66	2,097	511	1,561	24	74		3.3	2.6	2.4
Bananas	1934-38		278						11	
	1953-57	228	38	190	17	83		1.1	1.2	0.9
	1962-64		11							
	1965-66		13							
Wheat	1934-38	389		400		(97)				
	1951-53	618		909		(68)				0.6
	1961-63	1,534		1,354		88		0.6		0.7
	1964-66	1,872		1,961		(95)		0.7		0.7
Beef	1934-38	223		223		100		1.5		1.5
	1951-53	354	7.9	346	2.2	98		2.0	1.9	1.9
	1961-63	457	29	428	6.3	94		1.8	2.2	1.7
	1964-66	545	27	518	4.9	95		1.9	1.8	1.8
Cotton	1935-39	69	23	53	33	77		1.0	0.8	0.8
	1950-52	263	187	64	71	24		3.5	7.3	0.9
	1961-63	470	371	104	79	22		4.5	10	1.0
	1964-66	540	404	140	76	26		4.8	10	1.6
Forest products	1951-53	3,683	482	3,688	13	100	76			
	1961-63	4,829	108	5,273	2.2	(91)	65			
	1964-66	4,776	50	5,494	1.0	(78)	70			
Fishery products	1938	17		18		108				
	1951-53	67	16	53	24	79			0.6	
	1961-63	229	47	182	21	79		0.5	1.0	
	1964-66	267	39	228	15	85	13	0.7	0.8	

For notes and sources, see chapter 3, table B-1.

TABLE B-1-15. NICARAGUA: Evolution of Production, Exports, and Consumption of Natural Resource Commodities, Late 1930s, Early 1950s, and Early and Mid 1960s
(Thousands of cubic meters of petroleum and forest products, and thousands of metric tons of all other products)

Commodity	Period	Production	Exports	Consumption	Share of Production (%)			Share of World Total (%)		
					Exported	Consumed	Refined	Production	Exports	Consumption
Copper	1962-64	8.0	8.7							
	1965-66	10	42							
Petroleum	1935-39			36						
	1950-51									
	1962-64			308						
	1965-66			318						
Coffee	1935-39	16	15		95			0.7	0.9	
	1950-52	20	18	2.7	90	14		0.9	0.9	
	1962-64	27	25	2.7	93	10		0.7	0.9	
	1965-66	28	28	4.3	100	15		0.7	0.8	
Cocoa	1935-39									
	1950-52	0.6			22					
	1961-63									
	1964-66									
Sugar	1935-39	8.0	3.3	4.0	41	50				
	1951-53	30	8.4	21	28	71				
	1961-63	81	36	45	45	55				
	1964-66	90	37	55	41	61				
Bananas	1934-38		49						2.0	
	1953-57		7.2							
	1962-64		24							
	1965-66		20							
Wheat	1934-38			6.0						
	1951-53			15						
	1961-63			29						
	1964-66			30						
Cotton	1935-39	0.8	0.7		88					
	1950-52	8.0	4.4	2.4	55	30				
	1961-63	72	54	3.3	93	4.6		0.7	1.5	
	1964-66	120	112	4.5	93	3.7		1.1	2.9	
Forest products	1951-53	1,096		1,099		100	20			
	1961-63	2,275		2,288		100	18			
	1964-66	2,275		2,305		98	17			

For notes and sources, see chapter 3, table B-1.

TABLE B-1-16. PANAMA: Evolution of Production, Exports, and Consumption of Natural Resource Commodities, Late 1930s, Early 1950s, and Early and Mid 1960s
(Thousands of cubic meters of petroleum and forest products, and thousands of metric tons of all other products)

Commodity	Period	Production	Exports	Consumption	Share of Production (%)			Share of World Total (%)		
					Exported	Consumed	Refined	Production	Exports	Consumption
Petroleum	1935-39									
	1950-51			211						
	1962-64		98	935						
	1965-66		145	1,414						
Coffee	1935-39	1.0								
	1950-52	2.9								
	1962-64	4.5	1.2	3.0	27	67				
	1965-66	4.8	2.1	3.7	43	77				
Cocoa	1935-39	4.7	4.7		100			0.6		
	1950-52	1.4	2.1							
	1961-63	1.5	1.1		73					
	1964-66	1.0	0.9		90					
Sugar	1935-39	4.0		5.0		(80)				
	1951-53	18	3.9	14	22	79				
	1961-63	30	6.4	25	21	81				
	1964-66	25	18	20	72	80				
Bananas	1934-38		217						8.7	
	1953-57		238						7.6	
	1962-64		272						6.2	
	1965-66		361						7.6	
Wheat	1934-38			11						
	1951-53			21						
	1961-63			33						
	1964-66			35						
Forest products	1951-53	1,747	22	1,745	1.3	100	3.0			
	1961-63	1,828	3.9	1,894		(97)	6.5			
	1964-66	1,640	5.2	1,766		(93)	8.6			
Fishery products	1938	0.7	0.1	1.5	14	(47)				
	1951-53	1.0	1.3	0.8		80				
	1961-63	13	5.4	9.6	42	74				
	1964-66	46	12	36	26	78				

For notes and sources, see chapter 3, table B-1.

TABLE B–1–17.   PARAGUAY: Evolution of Production, Exports, and Consumption of Natural Resource Commodities, Late 1930s, Early
1950s, and Early and Mid 1960s
(Thousands of cubic meters of petroleum and forest products, and thousands of metric tons of all other products)

Commodity	Period	Production	Exports	Consumption	Share of Production (%)			Share of World Total (%)		
					Exported	Consumed	Refined	Production	Exports	Consumption
Petroleum	1935-39									
	1950-51			30						
	1962-64			161						
	1965-66			181						
Sugar	1935-39	6.0		11		(55)				
	1951-53	20		24		(81)				
	1961-63	35	4.2	34	12	97				
	1964-66	42	5.7	36	13	87				
Wheat	1934-38	1.0		32		3.2				
	1951-53	2.3		44		5.2				
	1961-63	8.7		88		(10)				
	1964-66	7.0		57		(12)				
Beef	1934-38	76		76				0.5		0.5
	1951-53	82	2.2	80	2.7	97			0.5	
	1961-63	85	16	69	19	71			1.2	
	1964-66	115	20	95	17	83			1.4	
Cotton	1935-39	4.4	9.2							
	1950-52	14	12	3.2	86	23				
	1961-63	12	6.8	4.5	57	38				
	1964-66	12	9.3	4.8	77	40				
Forest products	1951-53	1,732	191	1,546	11	89	24			
	1961-63	1,720	179	1,548	10	90	23			
	1964-66	2,123	346	2,102	16	99	28			
Fishery products	1938	0.3		0.3		100				
	1951-53	0.4		0.4		100				
	1961-63									
	1964-66									

For notes and sources, see chapter 3, table B–1.

TABLE B-1-18. PERU: Evolution of Production, Exports, and Consumption of Natural Resource Commodities, Late 1930s, Early 1950s, and Early and Mid 1960s
(Thousands of cubic meters of petroleum and forest products, and thousands of metric tons of all other products)

Commodity	Period	Production	Exports	Consumption	Share of Production (%)			Share of World Total (%)		
					Exported	Consumed	Refined	Production	Exports	Consumption
Copper	1935-39	34	36		100			1.8	2.4	
	1950-51	31	24		78		52	1.2	1.7	
	1962-64	173	171	1.5	99	0.9	21	3.8	6.7	
	1965-66	178	178	6.9	100	3.9	22	3.5	6.9	
Iron ore	1952-53	150	445	140					0.5	
	1962-64	6,232	5,368	269	86	(27)	0.5	1.2	3.5	
	1965-66	7,463	6,341	267	85	(33)	0.5	1.2	4.4	
Lead	1935-39	41	34		82		42	2.5	3.3	
	1950-51	72	71		99		53	4.2	8.8	
	1962-64	142	163	3.9		2.7	56	5.7	7.1	
	1965-66	149	151	7.3		4.8	59	5.4	6.3	
Zinc	1935-39	14	7.3		52			0.8	0.8	
	1950-51	95	88		93		1.2	4.3	8.8	
	1962-64	192	214	2.1		1.1	26	5.2	7.3	
	1965-66	256	275	7.0		2.7	24	3.1	7.9	
Petroleum	1935-39	2,591	1,454	436	56	16	37	0.9	2.5	0.5
	1950-51	2,475	1,142	1,484	46	60	88			
	1962-64	3,483	590	3,985	17	(89)	92			
	1965-66	3,714	380	4,663	10	(80)	94			
Coal	1935-39	91		117		(78)	6.3			
	1950-51	253		183		(72)	2.8			
	1962-64	154		163		(95)	36			
	1965	129		141		(92)	30			
Coffee	1935-39	2.7	3.0							
	1950-52	5.7	1.9	4.5	33	79				
	1962-64	47	40	11	85	23		1.2	1.5	
	1965-66	51	34	14	67	27		1.2	1.1	
Cocoa	1935-39	2.0		2.0		100	100			
	1950-52	4.5		5.0		(90)	96			0.7
	1961-63	5.0		5.5		(91)	100			0.5
	1964-66	2.3		5.0		(46)	100			
Sugar	1935-39	398	300	79	75	20		1.6	2.6	
	1951-53	512	325	173	63	34		2.3	2.2	0.5
	1961-63	789	499	280	63	36		2.6	2.3	0.5
	1964-66	784	416	347	53	44		1.2	2.2	0.5
Wheat	1934-38	89		204		(43)				
	1951-53	163		347		(47)				
	1961-63	152		581		(26)				
	1964-66	153		636		(24)				
Beef	1934-38									
	1951-53	64		71		(90)				
	1961-63	68		71		(96)				
	1964-66	79		95		(83)				
Cotton	1935-39	83	75	7.0	90	8.4		1.2	2.4	
	1950-52	91	71	13	78	14		1.2	2.8	
	1961-63	143	125	19	87	13		1.4	3.5	
	1964-66	128	112	21	88	16		1.1	2.9	
Forest products	1951-53	2,686	29	2,790	1.1	(96)	12			
	1961-63	2,973	3	3,318		(90)	17			
	1964-66	2,887	8	3,282		(88)	15			
Fishery products	1938	23		25		(92)				
	1951-53	152	28	125	18	82	46	0.6	1.1	0.5
	1961-63	6,381	1,104	5,278	17	83	95	14	22	12
	1964-66	8,411	1,525	6,886	18	82	98	15	24	

For notes and sources, see chapter 3, table B-1.

TABLE B-1-19. URUGUAY: Evolution of Production, Exports, and Consumption of Natural Resource Commodities, Late 1930s, Early
1950s, and Early and Mid 1960s
(Thousands of cubic meters of petroleum and forest products, and thousands of metric tons of all other products)

Commodity	Period	Production	Exports	Consumption	Share of Production (%)			Share of World Total (%)		
					Exported	Consumed	Refined	Production	Exports	Consumption
Petroleum	1935-39			397						
	1950-51			1,120						
	1962-64			1,820						
	1965-66			1,935						
Coal	1935-39			295						
	1952-53			102						
	1961-63			50						
	1965			36						
Coffee	1935-39			2.4						
	1950-52			3.0						
	1962-64			2.2						
	1965-66			2.2						
Cocoa	1935-39			1.0						
	1950-52			0.8						
	1961-63			0.8						
	1964-66			1.3						
Sugar	1935-39	2		56		(3.6)				
	1951-53	15		78		(19)				
	1961-63	46		105		(44)				
	1964-66	55		120		(46)				
Bananas	1934-38			10						
	1953-57			17						
	1962-64			31						
	1965-66			26						
Wheat	1934-38	361	81	281	23	78				
	1951-53	574	148	438	25	76			0.6	
	1961-63	353	14	383	4	(92)				
	1964-66	533	173	609	32	(88)				
Beef	1934-38	279	54	225	19	81		1.9	7.4	1.5
	1951-53	308	63	245	20	80		1.7	15	1.4
	1961-63	285	64	221	22	78		1.1	4.9	0.9
	1964-66	316	92	224	29	71		1.1	6.3	0.8
Cotton	1935-39									
	1950-52			7.9						
	1961-63			7.1						
	1964-66			8.9						
Forest products	1951-53	637		743		(86)	14			
	1961-63	1,265		1,567		(81)	17			
	1964-66	1,265		1,557		(81)	15			
Fishery products	1938	3.6		3.6		100				
	1951-53	3.5		3.5		100				
	1961-63	6.0	0.9	5.5	15	92				
	1964-66	14	0.7	14	5.0	100				

For notes and sources, see chapter 3, table B-1.

TABLE B-1-20. VENEZUELA: Evolution of Production, Exports, and Consumption of Natural Resource Commodities, Late 1930s, Early
1950s, and Early and Mid 1960s
(Thousands of cubic meters of petroleum and forest products, and thousands of metric tons of all other products)

Commodity	Period	Production	Exports	Consumption	Share of Production (%)			Share of World Total (%)		
					Exported	Consumed	Refined	Production	Exports	Consumption
Copper	1961			5.8						
	1966			7.2						
Iron Ore	1952-53	2,131	1,942	586	91			0.7	2.7	
	1962-64	13,579	13,499	572	99	(60)	3.0	2.5	8.6	
	1965-66	17,630	17,022	964	97	(60)	3.2	2.8	8.3	
Lead	1962			2.2						
	1965			2.2						
Zinc	1962			0.8						
	1965			5.2						
Petroleum	1935-39	28,109	25,345	1,356	91	4.8	5.2	9.2	44	
	1950-51	92,936	84,136	3,657	91	3.9	14	14	37	0.6
	1962-64	190,548	175,060	9,450	92	5.0	32	13	24	0.6
	1965-66	201,457	186,692	10,113	93	5.0	36	16	28	0.5
Coal	1935-39	6		17		(35)				
	1952-53	27		28		(96)				
	1961-63	33		128		(26)				
	1965	30		317		(9.5)				
Coffee	1935-39	59	44		74			2.5	2.7	
	1950-52	39	22	15	56	38		1.8	1.0	0.7
	1962-64	51	21	30	41	59		1.3	0.6	0.8
	1965-66	58	18	38	31	66		1.4	0.5	1.0
Cocoa	1935-39	17	16	1.0	97	6.1	6.1	2.3	2.4	
	1950-52	15	15	1.1	100	7.3	20	2.0	2.0	
	1961-63	14	11	2.3	80	17	18	1.2	1.1	
	1964-66	22	12	3.2	54	15	15	1.6	1.0	
Sugar	1935-39	18		18		100				
	1951-53	66		110		(60)				
	1961-63	273		250		92		0.5		0.5
	1964-66	350		319		91		0.6		0.5
Bananas	1934-38		2.0							
	1953-57		3.0							
	1962-64		7.5							
	1965-66		17							
Wheat	1934-38	6.0		32		(19)				
	1951-53	5.0		158		(3.2)				
	1961-63	0.7		336						
	1964-66	1.0		575						
Beef	1934-38	44		44		100				
	1951-53	66		66		100				
	1961-63	141		141		100		0.6		0.6
	1964-66	163		163		100		0.6		0.6
Cotton	1935-39	2.6		2.0		77				
	1950-52	2.7		9.1		(29)				
	1961-63	18		17		94				
	1964-66	14		26		(52)				
Forest products	1951-53	3,745		3,874		(97)	6.5			
	1961-63	4,990		5,531		(90)	6.8			
	1964-66	5,282		5,640		(94)	9.2			
Fishery products	1938	22	0.7	24	3.2	(92)				
	1951-53	67	1.1	69	1.6	(97)				
	1961-63	92	5.7	102	6.2	(90)				
	1964-66	116	5.2	113	4.4	98	5.0			

For notes and sources, see chapter 3, table B-1.

TABLE B–3–1. ARGENTINA: Exports of Selected Primary Commodities, 1950-1966
(Thousands of metric tons or cubic meters and millions of U.S. dollars)

Commodity	1950	1951	1952	1953	1954	1955	1956	1957
Wheat		2,740.0	2,430.0	42.0	2,520.0	2,920.0	3,590.0	2,520.0	2,640.0
Value		152.0	200.6	5.9	243.6	205.3	245.9	154.9	158.9
Share total exports (%)		12.9	17.2	0.9	21.6	20.0	26.4	16.4	16.3
Rank among exports		2	1		1	1	1	2	2
Beef		236.0	210.0	154.0	171.0	179.0	281.0	444.0	468.0
Value		79.0	154.5	121.8	154.7	155.6	205.6	241.0	256.6
Share total exports (%)		6.7	13.2	17.7	13.7	15.1	22.1	25.6	25.9
Rank among exports		4	3	1	3	2	2	1	1
Cotton		46.3	36.2	23.4	61.5	27.5	1.8	0.5	10.5
Value		9.2	12.1	7.1	14.2	6.8			
Share total exports (%)		0.8	1.0	1.0	1.3	0.7			
Fishery products		2.0	2.2	1.7	1.2	1.2	0.8	2.1	6.1
Value						0.3	0.2	0.3	0.7
Share total exports (%)									0.1
Total value		240.2	367.2	198.8	142.1	368.0	460.7	396.2	416.2
Share all exports (%)		20.4	31.4	19.6	36.6	35.8	48.5	42.0	42.3

Commodity	1958	1959	1960	1961	1962	1963	1964	1965	1966
Zinc			13.4	25.5	9.9	26.9	16.1		
Value			1.4	2.1	0.8	2.1	1.9	0.1	
Share total exports (%)			0.2	0.2	0.1	0.2	0.1		
Petroleum			2.0	250.0	981.0	900.0	530.0	896.1	1,229.7
Value			0.1	1.1	13.1	11.1	5.9	9.1	13.9
Share total exports (%)			0.1	0.1	1.1	0.8	0.4	0.6	0.9
Wheat	2,113.0	2,390.0	2,470.0	1,056.0	2,830.0	1,840.0	3,710.0	6,661.0	5,055.0
Value	126.1	135.3	142.7	65.6	173.4	116.4	242.3	372.7	279.6
Share total exports (%)	12.7	13.4	13.2	6.8	14.3	8.5	17.2	25.0	17.5
Rank among exports	2	2	3	5	2	4	2	1	2
Beef	474.0	410.0	337.0	343.0	456.0	623.0	476.0	469.5	560.2
Value	295.4	259.3	219.3	217.4	228.5	334.1	328.7	324.5	393.0
Share total exports (%)	26.4	29.8	20.4	22.6	18.8	24.5	23.3	21.7	24.6
Rank among exports	1	1	1	1	1	1	1	1	1
Cotton	2.5	9.5	8.6	22.9	53.1	40.6	6.8	3.9	12.5
Value	0.3	0.3	3.9	11.2	24.0	19.5	2.8	1.4	4.1
Share total exports (%)			0.3	1.2	2.0	1.4	0.2	0.1	0.3
Fishery products	8.4	6.4	1.1	1.0	2.5	7.4	3.4	7.6	9.3
Value	1.3	0.8	0.2	0.2	0.4	1.2	0.6	1.4	1.5
Share total exports (%)	0.1	0.1				0.1		0.1	0.1
Total value	428.1	395.7	367.0	398.4	440.2	484.4	582.1	709.2	692.1
Share all exports (%)	39.1	43.3	34.2	30.9	36.3	35.5	41.2	47.5	43.4

For notes and sources, see chapter 3, table B–3.

TABLE B-3-2. BOLIVIA: Exports of Selected Primary Commodities, 1950-1966
(Thousands of metric tons or cubic meters and millions of U.S. dollars)

Commodity	1950	1951	1952	1953	1954	1955	1956	1957
Copper	5.2	5.3	5.2	4.9	4.0	3.9	4.9	4.3
Value		2.2	2.7	3.0	2.4	2.7	4.0	2.6
Share total exports (%)		1.4	1.9	2.7	2.6	2.7	3.7	2.7
Lead	31.2	31.0	30.0	24.5	17.2	19.1	21.5	26.1
Value	9.2	11.8	11.0	7.1	5.6	6.3	7.6	8.5
Share total exports (%)	9.8	7.8	7.8	6.3	6.1	6.3	7.1	8.9
Rank among exports	2	3	4	3	3	3	3	2
Zinc	19.6	30.5	35.6	24.0	20.3	21.3	17.1	19.7
Value	5.3	12.2	13.2	5.6	4.7	5.7	5.0	5.4
Share total exports (%)	5.6	8.1	9.4	5.0	5.1	5.7	4.7	5.7
Rank among exports	3	2	3	4	4	4	5	4
Tin	31.2	33.1	32.0	34.8	28.8	27.9	26.8	27.8
Value	63.6	93.3	84.7	72.6	60.1	57.3	59.2	57.4
Share total exports (%)	67.5	62.0	60.1	64.5	65.4	57.4	55.5	60.3
Rank among exports	1	1	1	1	1	1	1	1
Petroleum	9.0	13.0	10.0	11.0	9.0	76.0	86.0	163.0
Value					0.3	2.3	2.9	4.6
Share total exports (%)					0.3	2.3	2.7	4.8
Total value	78.1	59.3	58.9	88.3	73.1	74.3	78.7	78.5
Share all exports (%)	82.9	79.3	79.2	78.5	79.5	74.4	73.7	84.4

Commodity	1958	1959	1960	1961	1962	1963	1964	1965	1966
Copper	3.2	2.5	2.5	2.3	2.7	3.3	5.2	4.7	5.7
Value	1.5	1.3	1.4	1.2	1.4	1.9	3.2	3.5	6.2
Share total exports (%)	2.4	1.7	2.1	1.6	1.9	2.3	2.8	2.7	4.2
Lead	22.8	22.0	21.2	20.2	18.4	19.9	17.2	15.9	19.4
Value	5.9	5.0	4.8	4.1	3.5	4.3	4.9	5.3	6.4
Share total exports (%)	9.3	6.6	7.3	5.6	4.7	5.3	4.4	4.1	4.3
Rank among exports	2	2	2	2	3	3	3	3	3
Zinc	14.2	3.4	4.0	5.3	3.6	4.6	9.8	13.7	16.7
Value	3.2	0.9	1.2	1.3	0.9	1.2	3.1	4.2	5.0
Share total exports (%)	5.1	1.2	1.8	1.8	1.2	1.5	2.8	3.2	3.4
Rank among exports	4	5	5	5	5	4	4	4	4
Tin	17.7	23.8	19.4	20.4	21.5	22.6	24.0	23.8	25.8
Value	36.2	52.8	42.6	50.3	54.0	57.3	81.0	93.0	93.3
Share total exports (%)	57.3	69.2	64.4	68.5	72.1	70.7	64.4	72.1	63.2
Rank among exports	1	1	1	1	1	1	1	1	1
Petroleum	191.0	151.0	180.0	129.0	73.0	119.0	50.0	42.9	326.9
Value	5.1	3.1	3.5	2.4	1.5	1.8	2.0		
Share total exports (%)	8.0	4.1	5.1	3.3	2.0	2.2	1.8		
Total value	51.9	63.1	53.5	59.3	61.3	66.5	94.2	106.0	110.9
Share all exports (%)	82.1	82.8	80.7	80.8	81.9	80.2	76.2	82.1	75.1

For notes and sources, see chapter 3, table B-3.

TABLE B–3–3. BRAZIL: Exports of Selected Primary Commodities, 1950-1966
(Thousands of metric tons or cubic meters and millions of U.S. dollars)

Commodity	1950	1951	1952	1953	1954	1955	1956	1957
Iron ore	890.0	1,330.0	1,605.0	1,568.0	1,678.0	2,565.0	2,745.0	3,550.0
Value	6.6	12.6	26.3	8.8	8.0	18.4	27.1	29.1
Share total exports (%)	0.5	0.7	1.9	0.6	0.5	1.3	1.8	2.1
Rank among exports			4			5	4	5
Coffee	890.1	981.5	949.2	933.7	655.0	821.7	1,008.3	859.2
Value	849.8	1,039.4	1,026.3	1,090.2	948.1	843.9	1,029.8	845.5
Share total exports (%)	63.1	59.2	72.8	70.8	60.7	59.3	69.5	60.7
Rank among exports	1	1	1	1	1	1	1	1
Cocoa	141.7	102.7	67.5	135.3	135.5	139.8	147.9	134.3
Value	78.0	69.0	41.0	75.0	135.0	91.0	67.0	70.0
Share total exports (%)	5.8	3.9	2.9	4.9	8.6	6.4	4.5	5.0
Rank among exports	3	3	2	3	3	3	3	2
Bananas	126.0	165.0	190.0	178.7	218.0	210.7	188.0	218.5
Value				9.2	11.3	10.3	12.4	13.3
Share total exports (%)				0.6	0.7	0.7	0.8	1.0
Sugar	24.0	18.4	44.5	246.5	150.5	581.0	23.4	409.0
Value	3.4	3.5	5.1	22.4	12.4	46.9	1.6	45.9
Share total exports (%)	0.2	0.2	0.4	1.5	0.8	3.3	0.1	3.3
Rank among exports					4	4		3
Beef	23.0	8.0	4.0	3.0	1.0	5.0	12.0	30.0
Value	9.5	5.8	2.4	2.3	2.4	6.0	7.8	14.0
Share total exports (%)	0.7	0.3	0.2	0.2	0.2	0.4	0.5	1.0
Cotton	128.8	143.8	28.1	139.5	309.5	175.7	142.9	66.2
Value	105.0	207.0	34.0	102.0	223.0	131.0	86.0	44.0
Share total exports (%)	7.8	11.8	12.4	6.6	14.5	9.2	5.8	3.2
Rank among exports	2	2	3	2	2	2	4	4
Forest products	503	691	399	538	498	692	413	810
Value	35.1	58.2	38.2	55.7	67.8	127.1	33.6	69.8
Share total exports (%)	2.6	3.3	2.7	3.6	4.3	8.9	2.3	5.0
Fishery products							0.2	0.3
Value							0.1	0.4
Share total exports (%)								
Total value	1,087.4	1,395.5	1,173.3	1,365.6	1,408.0	1,274.6	1,265.4	1,132.0
Share all exports (%)	80.7	79.4	93.3	88.8	90.3	89.5	85.4	81.3

TABLE B–3–3 – Continued

Commodity	1958	1959	1960	1961	1962	1963	1964	1965	1966
Iron ore	2,831.0	3,988.0	5,240.0	6,282.0	7,380.0	8,268.0	9,280.0	12,731.0	12,910.0
Value	20.9	21.4	46.7	48.8	53.0	62.2	53.7	103.0	100.0
Share total exports (%)	1.7	1.7	3.7	3.5	4.4	4.4	3.8	6.5	5.7
Rank among exports	5	5	4	4	3	4	3	2	3
Coffee	773.6	1,063.4	1,009.1	1,018.2	982.6	1,170.9	896.9	809.9	1,021.8
Value	688.1	774.0	712.7	710.4	642.6	747.0	759.7	707.4	764.0
Share total exports (%)	55.4	60.4	56.2	50.6	52.9	53.1	53.1	44.3	43.8
Rank among exports	1	1	1	1	1	1	1	1	1
Cocoa	135.9	126.6	169.8	120.0	78.4	88.9	91.9	113.1	140.9
Value	89.4	59.4	69.2	45.9	24.2	35.0	34.8	27.7	50.7
Share total exports (%)	7.2	4.6	5.5	3.3	2.0	2.5	2.4	1.7	2.9
Rank among exports	2	2	2	5	5	5	5	7	6
Bananas	271.4	213.1	241.9	245.9	216.3	206.9	225.5	215.8	205.1
Value	10.9	4.3	4.6	3.8	3.2	2.9	5.8	6.3	6.3
Share total exports (%)	0.8	0.3	0.4	0.3	0.2	0.2	0.4	0.4	0.4
Sugar	775.8	605.9	854.8	744.9	478.6	486.7	268.2	818.4	1,007.4
Value	57.4	33.4	52.6	65.6	39.5	72.9	33.1	56.7	80.5
Share total exports (%)	4.6	2.6	4.1	4.7	3.3	5.2	2.3	3.6	4.6
Rank among exports	3	4	3	3	4	3	6	5	4
Beef	43.0	54.0	15.0	29.0	23.0	19.0	27.0	43.0	32.0
Value	25.2	41.2	14.9	22.9	15.1	11.3	20.8	46.5	30.2
Share total exports (%)	2.0	3.2	1.2	1.6	1.2	0.8	1.5	2.9	1.7
Cotton	40.2	77.6	95.4	205.7	215.9	221.8	217.0	195.7	235.9
Value	25.0	35.5	45.6	109.7	112.2	114.2	108.3	95.7	111.0
Share total exports (%)	2.0	2.8	3.6	7.8	9.2	8.1	7.6	6.0	6.4
Rank among exports	4	3	5	2	2	2	2	3	2
Forest products	648	490	561	615	506	498	644	658	757
Value	55.7	42.0	46.7	52.0	43.2	42.2	54.5	62.4	78.6
Share total exports (%)	4.5	3.3	3.7	3.7	3.6	3.0	3.8	3.9	4.5
Fishery products	0.4	0.6	1.2	1.8	2.7	1.8	1.8	2.5	3.0
Value	0.5	0.7	1.8	3.1	4.0	3.5	2.9	5.1	5.4
Share total exports (%)		0.1	0.1	0.2	0.3	0.2	0.2	0.3	0.3
Total Value	973.1	1,011.9	994.8	1,062.2	937.0	1,091.2	1,073.5	1,110.8	1,226.7
Share all exports (%)	78.2	79.0	78.5	75.7	77.1	77.5	75.1	69.6	70.3

For notes and sources, see chapter 3, table B–3.

TABLE B-3-4. CHILE: Exports of Selected Primary Commodities, 1950-1966
(Thousands of metric tons or cubic meters and millions of U.S. dollars)

Commodity	1950	1951	1952	1953	1954	1955	1956	1957
Copper	331.2	342.0	380.5	310.1	366.5	411.6	464.3	482.1
Value	160.0	178.0	255.0	184.0	222.0	327.0	334.0	240.0
Share total exports (%)	56.9	48.1	56.3	45.0	55.8	69.3	61.6	52.8
Rank among exports	1	1	1	1	1	1	1	1
Iron ore	2,596.0	2,687.0	1,828.0	2,442.0	1,720.0	1,237.0	2,071.0	3,074.0
Value	6.7	8.0	8.1	12.8	7.9	6.1	12.5	21.2
Share total exports (%)	2.4	2.2	1.8	3.1	2.0	1.2	2.3	4.7
Rank among exports	3	3	3	3	3	3	3	3
Lead		0.5	8.1	6.6	1.1	5.6	3.5	4.7
Value			0.2	0.1		0.1	0.1	0.1
Share total exports (%)								
Petroleum	75.0	138.0	128.0	179.0	175.0			
Value		2.2	2.7	3.8	3.2			
Share total exports (%)		0.6	0.6	0.9	0.8			
Forest products	119	81	64	94	129	126	66	52
Value	8.5	9.1	8.0	9.4	15.3	16.9	8.4	5.4
Share total exports (%)	3.0	2.5	1.8	2.3	3.0	3.6	1.5	1.2
Fishery products	1.3	2.9	8.4	0.9	2.0	10.4	5.8	5.9
Value	0.4	0.5	0.8	0.3	0.5	1.7	0.8	1.4
Share total exports (%)	0.1	0.1	0.2	0.1	0.1	0.3	0.4	0.7
Total value	175.6	200.2	274.6	210.4	248.9	351.8	355.8	268.1
Share all exports (%)	62.4	53.5	60.7	51.4	62.5	74.4	65.9	59.5

Commodity	1958	1959	1960	1961	1962	1963	1964	1965	1966
Copper	457.1	537.7	519.3	546.4	567.8	591.8	608.9	520.5	592.9
Value	194.0	279.0	302.0	297.0	313.0	326.0	362.0	480.5	641.1
Share total exports (%)	50.3	56.4	61.9	58.7	58.8	60.4	58.0	63.8	58.7
Rank among exports	1	1	1	1	1	1	1	1	1
Iron ore	3,638.0	4,261.0	5,191.0	6,206.0	7,246.0	7,092.0	9,134.0	10,729.0	11,095.0
Value	23.9	29.1	35.2	44.4	56.2	57.2	69.6	78.3	78.0
Share total exports (%)	6.2	5.9	7.2	8.8	10.6	10.6	11.1	11.4	8.9
Rank among exports	3	3	3	2	2	2	2	2	2
Lead	5.0	0.6	2.6	2.9	2.2	2.9	1.6	0.7	
Value				0.3	0.2	0.3	0.3		
Share total exports (%)				0.1		0.1	0.1		
Forest products	90	139	65	112	80	74	56	99	74
Value	9.2	11.1	5.2	11.5	8.7	7.5	9.2	8.6	11.2
Share total exports (%)	2.4	2.2	1.1	2.3	1.6	1.4	1.5	1.3	1.3
Fishery products	11.8	18.4	30.3	51.1	91.7	103.3	168.5	90.8	212.1
Value	2.0	2.8	3.5	6.0	12.2	13.1	21.4	14.6	34.3
Share total exports (%)	0.5	0.6	0.7	1.2	2.3	2.4	3.5	2.1	3.9
Total value	229.1	322.0	345.9	83.9	392.3	404.1	462.8	582.0	764.6
Share all exports (%)	59.4	65.1	70.9	71.1	74.3	74.9	74.2	78.6	72.8

For notes and sources, see chapter 3, table B-3.

TABLE B-3-5. COLOMBIA: Exports of Selected Primary Commodities, 1950-1966
(Thousands of metric tons or cubic meters and millions of U.S. dollars)

Commodity	1950	1951	1952	1953	1954	1955	1956	1957
Petroleum	4,495.0	5,126.0	4,953.0	5,099.0	4,872.0	4,287.0	4,780.0	4,799.0
Value	64.8	73.5	71.5	76.3	75.8	61.5	69.9	72.4
Share total exports (%)	16.4	15.9	15.1	12.8	11.5	10.6	11.7	14.2
Rank among exports	2	2	2	2	2	2	2	2
Coffee	268.3	287.6	301.9	397.9	344.1	352.0	304.2	289.4
Value	307.9	359.8	379.9	492.2	550.2	484.1	474.6	390.1
Share total exports (%)	77.9	76.9	80.3	82.6	83.7	84.1	79.1	76.3
Rank among exports	1	1	1	1	1	1	1	1
Sugar		53.9	3.6			29.9	58.4	2.7
Value		7.2	0.5			2.4	4.9	0.1
Share total exports (%)		1.6	0.1			0.4	0.8	
Bananas	143.8	154.5	152.6	196.2	195.7	209.6	215.9	184.1
Value	6.1	8.0	6.2	8.4	9.4	16.9	28.1	26.2
Share total exports (%)	1.5	1.7	1.3	1.4	1.4	2.9	4.7	5.1
Rank among exports	3	3	3	3	3	3	3	3
Cotton								
Value								3.0
Share total exports (%)								
Forest products						54	75	29
Value						0.7	0.6	1.3
Share total exports (%)						0.1	0.1	0.3
Fishery products		0.1	0.3	0.1	0.2		0.1	0.2
Value					0.1	0.2		0.4
Share total exports (%)								0.1
Total value	377.8	448.5	458.1	576.9	635.5	565.8	578.1	493.5
Share all exports (%)	95.8	96.0	96.8	96.8	96.7	98.3	96.4	96.0

Commodity	1958	1959	1960	1961	1962	1963	1964	1965	1966
Petroleum	4,550.0	5,173.0	5,633.0	4,799.0	4,496.0	4,389.0	5,603.0	7,404.0	6,753.0
Value	65.4	73.3	80.4	68.2	60.5	76.6	75.0	58.8	47.3
Share total exports (%)	14.2	15.5	17.3	15.6	13.2	17.3	13.7	15.9	12.6
Rank among exports	2	2	2	2	2	2	2	2	2
Coffee	326.4	384.8	356.3	339.0	393.7	368.0	384.7	338.1	333.9
Value	354.8	363.3	333.5	307.9	331.8	303.0	394.2	343.6	328.0
Share total exports (%)	77.0	76.7	71.5	70.8	74.1	67.9	71.9	63.8	64.4
Rank among exports	1	1	1	1	1	1	1	1	1
Sugar				46.0	65.7	42.5	30.6	101.3	113.9
Value				5.2	7.4	5.5	3.3	7.6	8.3
Share total exports (%)				1.2	1.6	1.2	0.6	1.4	1.6
Bananas	174.1	203.3	190.7	205.6	147.1	203.0	172.0	253.4	341.9
Value	15.5	13.9	13.7	14.0	10.6	13.3	12.4	18.6	22.3
Share total exports (%)	3.4	2.9	2.9	3.2	2.3	3.0	2.3	3.5	4.4
Rank among exports	3	3	3	4	3	3	3	3	3
Cotton			23.6	17.1	26.4	17.1	11.7	16.1	4.5
Value		12.7	12.6	10.1	15.6	9.4	6.0	8.0	2.2
Share total exports (%)		2.7	2.0	2.3	3.4	2.1	1.1	1.5	1.0
Forest products	63	69	73	79	107	126	119	112	121
Value	1.3	1.4	1.4	2.3	2.3	3.3	4.3	3.3	3.2
Share total exports (%)	0.3	0.3	0.3	0.5	0.5	0.7	0.8	0.6	0.6
Fishery products	0.4	0.9	1.3	1.0	1.2	1.0	0.6	0.9	0.9
Value	0.5	1.3	1.7	1.4	1.5	1.4	0.6	0.9	0.9
Share total exports (%)	0.1	0.3	0.4	0.3	0.3	0.3	0.2	0.3	0.2
Total value	437.5	465.9	443.3	409.0	429.7	412.5	496.3	441.0	412.0
Share all exports (%)	95.0	98.4	95.2	94.2	95.4	92.3	90.4	92.1	83.2

For notes and sources, see chapter 3, table B-3.

TABLE B-3-6. COSTA RICA: Exports of Selected Primary Commodities, 1950-1966
(Thousands of metric tons or cubic meters and millions of U.S. dollars)

Commodity	1950	1951	1952	1953	1954	1955	1956	1957
Coffee	18.7	18.6	20.0	27.9	21.9	27.8	23.6	28.1
Value	18.1	19.6	24.3	34.8	35.1	37.4	33.8	39.1
Share total exports (%)	32.6	30.8	33.1	43.4	41.4	46.2	50.1	46.9
Rank among exports	2	2	2	2	2	1	1	1
Cocoa	3.1	3.2	4.2	6.8	9.4	9.7	6.2	7.4
Value	2.0	1.9	4.2	4.0	8.3	5.9	2.9	4.1
Share total exports (%)	3.6	3.1	5.7	5.0	9.8	7.3	4.3	4.9
Rank among exports	3	3	3	3	3	3	3	3
Sugar				7.2	5.6	7.0		1.0
Value				0.6	0.5	0.6		0.1
Share total exports (%)				0.8	0.5	0.7		0.1
Rank among exports								
Bananas				355.9	355.3	329.4	232.4	309.9
Value	31.5	34.3	38.3	35.8	35.8	33.2	25.7	32.3
Share total exports (%)	65.7	54.3	52.0	44.6	42.3	41.0	38.2	38.7
Rank among exports	1	1	1	1	1	2	2	2
Forest products						8	10	7
Value						0.2	0.9	0.2
Share total exports (%)						0.2	1.4	0.2
Fishery products	0.2	1.7		0.3	0.4	0.6	0.2	0.1
Value	0.1	0.1		0.1	0.2	0.3	0.2	0.1
Share total exports (%)	0.1	0.2		0.1	0.2	0.3	0.3	0.1
Total value	51.7	55.9	66.8	75.3	79.9	77.6	63.5	75.9
Share all exports (%)	93.0	88.1	91.2	94.0	94.3	95.5	94.4	91.2

Commodity	1958	1959	1960	1961	1962	1963	1964	1965	1966
Coffee	46.3	42.7	45.9	50.1	54.1	55.7	50.4	47.6	54.0
Value	49.9	40.4	44.7	43.3	47.2	45.8	47.1	46.4	52.6
Share total exports (%)	54.3	52.7	52.1	51.4	55.4	48.2	42.1	41.7	38.8
Rank among exports	1	1	1	1	1	1	1	1	1
Cocoa	7.7	11.5	11.8	10.2	11.9	9.5	9.2	6.8	7.7
Value	6.0	7.5	5.9	4.9	4.8	4.3	4.2	2.4	3.3
Share total exports (%)	6.5	9.7	6.9	5.8	5.6	4.6	3.7	2.1	2.4
Rank among exports	3	3	3	3	3	4	4	4	4
Sugar	1.3	7.3	20.4	30.2	23.8	34.1	36.8	45.9	67.5
Value	0.1	0.6	1.8	3.3	3.0	5.3	5.5	4.7	8.7
Share total exports (%)	0.2	0.9	2.0	3.8	3.7	5.5	4.7	4.2	6.4
Rank among exports			4	4	4	3	3	3	3
Bananas	301.6	213.2	272.7	229.4	291.9	261.1	292.9	316.3	359.4
Value	26.5	19.1	20.3	20.9	26.9	24.9	28.3	28.3	29.1
Share total exports (%)	28.8	24.9	23.6	24.8	29.0	27.2	24.9	25.3	21.5
Rank among exports	2	2	2	2	2	2	2	2	2
Forest products	5	4	3	6	13	9	8	14	16
Value	0.2	0.2	0.2	0.2	1.0	0.9	1.2	1.9	2.1
Share total exports (%)	0.2	0.3	0.2	0.2	1.1	1.0	1.2	1.6	1.5
Fishery products	0.5	0.6	0.5	1.1	0.8	0.9	1.2	1.2	1.0
Value	0.5	0.6	0.6	1.3	0.9	0.9	1.5	1.2	1.2
Share total exports (%)	0.6	0.8	0.7	1.5	1.1	0.9	1.3	1.1	0.9
Total value	83.2	68.4	73.5	73.9	83.8	82.1	87.8	84.9	97.0
Share all exports (%)	90.7	89.3	85.7	87.8	90.2	86.5	77.3	76.0	71.5

For notes and sources, see chapter 3, table B-3.

TABLE B-3-7. CUBA: Exports of Selected Primary Commodities, 1950-1966
(Thousands of metric tons or cubic meters and millions of U.S. dollars)

Commodity	1950	1951	1952	1953	1954	1955	1956	1957
Copper	22.5	21.7	19.7	17.8	17.5	20.8	18.2	18.0
Value	7.3	8.5	7.8	8.8	8.3	12.5	12.3	8.5
Share total exports (%)	1.1	1.0	1.1	1.3	1.5	2.0	1.8	1.0
Iron ore	29.0	9.0	98.0	209.0	76.0	121.0	135.0	105.0
Value	0.1	0.1	0.9	1.9	0.3	0.3	0.9	0.3
Share total exports (%)			0.1	0.2	0.1	0.1	0.1	
Coffee						4.5	20.3	11.4
Value						4.2	21.7	12.5
Share total exports (%)						0.7	3.1	1.5
Sugar	5,260.8	5,441.6	5,516.3	4,226.1	4,664.1	5,394.2	5,274.9	5,274.9
Value	555.0	666.0	565.0	518.0	446.0	473.0	524.0	654.0
Share total exports (%)	83.1	82.6	81.4	76.7	79.2	77.4	75.4	77.4
Rank among exports	1	1	1	1	1	1	1	1
Fishery products	1.3	0.9	1.1	1.4	1.6	1.8	2.3	3.0
Value	1.6	1.1	1.4	1.7	2.0	3.1	3.8	4.6
Share total exports (%)	0.2	0.1	0.2	0.2	0.3	0.3	0.4	0.5
Total value	564.0	675.7	575.1	530.4	456.6	493.1	562.7	679.9
Share all exports (%)	84.4	83.7	82.8	78.4	81.1	80.5	80.8	80.4

Commodity	1958	1959	1960	1961	1962	1963	1964	1965	1966
Copper	14.3	9.9	13.1	5.5	6.0	6.6	6.6		
Value	5.9	4.5	3.7		2.2	2.3	5.2	6.6	4.5
Share total exports (%)	0.8	0.7	0.6		0.4	0.4	0.7	1.0	
Iron ore	5.0	4.0	3.0						
Value									
Share total exports (%)									
Coffee	7.2	3.1	5.4	5.1	8.3	0.6			
Value	7.1	2.5	4.5	4.1	6.7	0.5			
Share total exports (%)	0.9	0.4	0.7	0.6	1.3	0.1			
Sugar	5,631.6	4,951.9	5,634.5	6,413.6	5,130.9	3,520.5	4,176.1	5,315.6	4,434.6
Value	588.0	488.0	491.0	532.3	431.9	471.8	626.7	546.1	480.0
Share total exports (%)	75.8	76.9	79.4	85.0	83.0	86.8	88.0	86.1	
Rank among exports	1	1	1	1	1	1	1	1	1
Fishery products	4.3	3.0	1.3	0.2	1.1	0.5	0.4	1.4	1.0
Value	4.6	4.2	3.6	0.7	1.6	1.5	1.2	2.9	3.7
Share total exports (%)	0.6	0.6	0.6	0.1	0.3	0.3	0.2	0.4	
Total value	605.6	499.2	502.8	537.1	442.4	476.1	633.1	555.6	488.2
Share all exports (%)	78.1	78.6	81.3	85.7	85.0	87.7	88.8	87.5	

For notes and sources, see chapter 3, table B-3.

TABLE B–3–8. DOMINICAN REPUBLIC: Exports of Selected Primary Commodities, 1950-1966
(Thousands of metric tons or cubic meters and millions of U.S. dollars)

Commodity	1950	1951	1952	1953	1954	1955	1956	1957
Iron ore			19.0	92.0	95.0	101.0	163.0	150.0
Value			0.2	1.4	1.3	1.3	2.4	2.3
Share total exports (%)			0.2	1.3	1.1	1.1	2.0	1.6
Coffee	13.4	17.4	26.5	22.4	24.0	24.5	26.4	21.7
Value	12.7	17.6	26.4	24.6	31.5	28.4	31.8	25.1
Share total exports (%)	14.6	14.8	22.9	23.4	26.3	24.7	26.2	17.0
Rank among exports	3	3	2	2	3	2	2	2
Cocoa	30.1	28.7	28.3	32.8	29.0	30.7	26.3	32.1
Value	17.3	21.2	19.8	20.7	32.3	23.8	14.3	19.0
Share total exports (%)	20.0	17.8	17.1	19.7	27.0	20.8	11.8	12.9
Rank among exports	2	2	3	3	2	3	3	3
Sugar	430.8	496.4	567.2	570.0	532.4	601.2	717.4	794.8
Value	44.0	66.6	57.4	46.2	40.1	41.9	52.9	88.5
Share total exports (%)	50.6	56.1	49.7	43.8	33.5	36.5	43.5	60.0
Rank among exports	1	1	1	1	1	1	1	1
Bananas	41.9	44.1	40.7	38.4	45.8	43.0	41.0	52.0
Value	1.0	1.3	1.4	1.8	2.2	2.1	2.2	2.9
Share total exports (%)	1.1	1.1	1.2	1.7	1.8	1.8	1.8	2.0
Beef	4.0	2.0	1.0	2.0	2.0	1.0		
Value	1.8	1.0	0.7	1.5	1.2	0.6	0.3	0.3
Share total exports (%)	2.0	0.8	0.6	1.4	1.0	0.5	0.2	0.2
Forest products	7	3	1		5	5	7	7
Value	0.5	0.5	0.3		0.3	0.5	0.6	0.7
Share total exports (%)	0.5	0.4	0.2		0.2	0.4	0.5	0.5
Total value	77.3	108.2	106.2	96.2	108.9	98.6	104.5	138.8
Share all exports (%)	89.0	91.1	91.8	91.3	91.0	85.9	86.0	94.2

Commodity	1958	1959	1960	1961	1962	1963	1964	1965	1966
Iron ore	21.0	51.0	101.0						
Value	0.3	0.6	0.6						
Share total exports (%)	0.2	0.5	0.3						
Coffee	25.8	21.7	28.9	20.1	29.2	27.4	34.4	22.5	25.1
Value	23.7	17.5	22.5	14.4	19.8	18.5	30.2	21.1	21.0
Share total exports (%)	18.5	13.5	12.9	10.1	11.5	10.6	16.8	16.8	15.3
Rank among exports	3	3	2	3	2	2	2	2	2
Cocoa	32.0	30.4	37.1	30.2	30.5	34.5	36.9	23.8	26.9
Value	28.6	22.4	20.9	14.7	13.5	16.8	16.2	7.3	11.2
Share total exports (%)	22.3	17.2	12.0	10.3	7.8	9.7	9.1	5.6	8.2
Rank among exports	2	2	3	2	3	3	3	3	3
Sugar	690.8	694.2	1,099.1	793.4	854.8	671.2	661.5	522.3	571.9
Value	56.6	49.3	85.3	68.2	96.9	100.0	92.7	63.6	76.3
Share total exports (%)	44.1	37.8	48.9	47.7	56.2	57.4	51.5	50.7	55.8
Rank among exports	1	1	1	1	1	1	1	1	1
Bananas	86.0	101.0	180.4	162.6	168.4	119.6	68.7	48.6	11.4
Value	5.0	6.1	11.3	11.3	11.5	8.6	5.2	3.4	1.0
Share total exports (%)	3.9	4.7	6.5	7.9	6.7	4.9	2.9	2.7	0.6
Beef	2.0	2.0	3.0	2.0	2.0				
Value	1.3	1.7	1.8	1.3	0.2				
Share total exports (%)	1.0	1.3	1.0	0.9	0.1				
Forest products	5	6	11	6	3		5	4	
Value	0.4	0.6	0.6	0.5	0.2	0.2	0.3	0.2	0.1
Share total exports (%)	0.3	0.5	0.3	0.4	0.1	0.1	0.2	0.2	0.1
Total value	115.9	98.2	143.0	110.4	142.1	144.1	144.5	95.6	109.6
Share all exports (%)	90.3	75.5	81.9	77.1	82.4	82.6	80.7	76.0	80.0

For notes and sources, see chapter 3, table B–3.

TABLE B-3-9. ECUADOR: Exports of Selected Primary Commodities, 1950-1966
(Thousands of metric tons or cubic meters and millions of U.S. dollars)

Commodity	1950	1951	1952	1953	1954	1955	1956	1957
Petroleum	166.0	199.0	139.0	207.0	213.0	228.0	180.0	192.0
Value		1.5	1.0	1.6	1.5	1.6	1.1	1.4
Share total exports (%)		2.2	1.0	1.7	1.2	1.4	0.9	1.0
Coffee	20.1	16.4	20.4	18.9	21.0	23.1	24.5	28.2
Value	18.9	15.8	20.4	18.9	27.3	22.8	29.0	28.9
Share total exports (%)	25.5	22.4	20.0	20.1	21.9	20.0	25.1	21.8
Rank among exports	1	3	2	2	3	2	2	2
Cocoa	26.8	24.1	23.3	22.5	29.7	24.4	29.2	26.9
Value	18.4	17.8	17.0	15.6	34.1	18.7	17.4	18.6
Share total exports (%)	24.8	25.2	16.7	16.9	27.4	16.4	15.1	14.0
Rank among exports	2	2	3	3	2	3	3	3
Sugar				9.8				10.5
Value								
Share total exports (%)								
Bananas	314.0	234.0	423.5	404.6	480.9	610.0	592.6	794.0
Value	17.2	25.0	43.6	41.2	50.9	62.3	59.8	69.0
Share total exports (%)	23.2	35.5	43.0	44.6	40.8	54.8	51.7	52.0
Rank among exports	3	1	1	1	1	1	1	1
Forest products	16	26	20	20	19	18	18	11
Value	0.7	1.2	1.0	1.1	0.9	1.0	1.1	1.9
Share total exports (%)	0.9	1.7	1.0	1.1	0.7	0.9	0.9	1.5
Fishery products								2.7
Value								1.4
Share total exports (%)								1.1
Total value	55.2	61.3	83.0	78.4	114.7	106.4	108.4	121.2
Share all exports (%)	74.6	87.1	81.6	84.8	92.1	93.7	93.9	91.6

Commodity	1958	1959	1960	1961	1962	1963	1964	1965	1966
Petroleum	115.0	45.0				30.0	84.0	85.6	61.1
Value	0.7	0.3			0.2	0.3	0.7	0.6	1.4
Share total exports (%)	0.5	0.2			0.1	0.2	0.4	0.3	0.8
Coffee	30.2	23.8	31.3	22.9	33.1	29.9	25.0	45.8	43.7
Value	26.3	17.6	21.9	14.3	20.9	18.3	21.7	37.2	32.2
Share total exports (%)	19.7	12.4	15.18	11.3	14.7	12.3	14.7	20.9	17.4
Rank among exports	2	3	2	3	2	3	2	2	2
Cocoa	22.2	28.2	35.6	32.4	31.6	35.5	28.7	39.3	32.2
Value	20.4	21.8	21.4	15.6	15.9	19.8	16.2	19.1	17.2
Share total exports (%)	15.3	15.4	14.8	12.3	11.1	13.3	10.0	10.7	9.3
Rank among exports	3	2	3	2	3	2	3	3	3
Sugar	21.6	33.2	14.2	47.4	63.9	45.4	51.5	54.7	62.9
Value		2.1	0.9	2.3	6.0	5.6	7.1	7.3	6.5
Share total exports (%)		1.5	0.6	1.8	4.2	3.8	4.4	4.1	3.5
Bananas	715.8	885.6	895.1	842.3	897.8	1,014.3	1,086.8	822.8	1,005.0
Value	72.9	89.7	88.9	80.9	88.5	85.2	88.1	95.5	106.0
Share total exports (%)	54.6	63.4	61.5	63.7	62.0	52.3	54.4	53.8	57.4
Rank among exports	1	1	1	1	1	1	1	1	1
Forest products	9	35	5	4	9	8	25	27	29
Value	1.5	1.5	1.3	1.1	1.2	1.6	1.8	1.9	2.3
Share total exports (%)	1.1	1.1	0.9	0.9	0.9	1.1	1.2	1.1	1.2
Fishery products	3.8	7.5	5.5	8.2	9.8	7.7	7.7	10.3	9.2
Value	2.1	2.4	2.1	3.5	4.8	4.7	3.6	4.4	4.2
Share total exports (%)	1.5	1.7	1.4	2.8	3.4	3.2	2.4	2.5	2.3
Total value	123.9	135.4	136.5	117.7	137.5	135.5	134.3	166.0	169.8
Share all exports (%)	93.0	95.6	94.5	92.9	96.5	91.1	91.0	93.4	91.9

For notes and sources, see chapter 3, table B-3.

TABLE B-3-10. EL SALVADOR: Exports of Selected Primary Commodities, 1950-1966
(Thousands of metric tons or cubic meters and millions of U.S. dollars)

Commodity	1950	1951	1952	1953	1954	1955	1956	1957
Coffee	66.4	63.6	65.9	69.0	59.7	71.1	67.9	76.2
Value	61.8	77.9	77.6	76.6	92.0	91.5	87.4	109.8
Share total exports (%)	90.4	92.1	88.9	86.3	87.6	85.6	77.5	79.3
Rank among exports	1	1	1	1	1	1	1	1
Sugar		2.9	1.5	0.8	1.8	2.2	1.4	7.6
Value		0.8	0.2	0.2	0.2	0.4	0.3	0.8
Share total exports (%)		0.9	0.3	0.2	0.4	0.3	0.2	0.6
Cotton	3.9	3.4	6.5	8.6	8.4	12.4	27.9	25.2
Value	2.6	4.1	5.3	6.4	6.5	9.1	17.6	15.8
Share total exports (%)	3.8	4.8	6.0	7.2	6.2	8.5	15.6	11.4
Rank among exports	2	2	2	2	2	2	2	2
Fishery products								0.1
Value								
Share total exports (%)								
Total value	65.4	82.8	83.1	83.2	98.7	101.0	105.3	126.4
Share all exports (%)	94.2	97.8	95.2	93.7	94.2	94.4	93.3	91.3

Commodity	1958	1959	1960	1961	1962	1963	1964	1965	1966
Coffee	83.9	80.7	70.7	85.8	88.7	95.1	105.3	99.3	97.2
Value	78.5	71.3	72.6	70.2	74.2	74.5	90.8	96.1	89.0
Share total exports (%)	67.6	62.9	62.1	59.0	54.5	48.5	51.0	50.9	46.7
Rank among exports	1	1	1	1	1	1	1	1	1
Sugar	7.1	6.8	10.9	12.5	20.7	20.4	19.4	23.0	44.2
Value	1.4	1.0	1.4	1.2	2.0	2.1	2.8	1.5	6.6
Share total exports (%)	1.2	1.9	1.2	1.1	1.5	1.8	1.6	4.1	3.4
Cotton	29.2	44.0	27.2	35.5	54.3	64.0	65.5	73.1	44.4
Value	18.1	23.2	15.8	21.3	32.3	37.6	37.1	37.8	23.8
Share total exports (%)	15.6	20.5	13.5	17.9	23.7	24.5	20.8	21.2	12.9
Rank among exports	2	2	2	2	2	2	2	2	2
Fishery products	0.3	0.7	5.4	4.3	4.2	4.1	4.3	3.1	4.4
Value	0.3	0.8	4.9	5.8	5.7	4.6	4.4	3.1	4.8
Share total exports (%)	0.2	0.7	4.2	4.7	4.2	3.0	2.4	1.7	2.5
Total value	98.0	96.3	94.7	98.5	114.2	118.8	135.1	138.5	124.2
Share all exports (%)	84.6	85.1	81.0	82.7	83.9	77.8	75.8	77.9	65.5

For notes and sources, see chapter 3, table B-3.

TABLE B–3–11. GUATEMALA: Exports of Selected Primary Commodities, 1950-1966
(Thousands of metric tons or cubic meters and millions of U.S. dollars)

Commodity	1950	1951	1952	1953	1954	1955	1956	1957
Lead	0.5	2.9	4.5	6.1	2.4	2.7	6.3	8.2
Value	0.5	0.4	0.5	0.6	0.4	0.5	1.0	2.0
Share total exports (%)	0.6	0.4	0.5	0.6	0.3	0.5	0.8	1.7
Zinc	4.3	5.9	8.9	5.9	3.4	7.6	10.4	8.5
Value		0.8	1.0	0.2	0.1	1.0	1.5	1.3
Share total exports (%)		0.9	1.0	0.2	0.1	0.9	1.2	1.1
Coffee	55.1	50.9	60.4	69.5	53.1	58.9	61.6	62.3
Value	52.8	58.5	71.6	68.2	74.2	75.5	89.2	82.3
Share total exports (%)	66.9	69.4	75.6	69.3	70.7	61.2	76.9	76.8
Rank among exports	1	1	1	1	1	1	1	1
Cocoa	0.4	0.2	0.3	0.3	0.3	0.3	0.5	0.2
Value		0.1	0.2	0.2	0.2	0.2	0.2	0.2
Share total exports (%)		0.1	0.2	0.2	0.2	0.2	0.2	0.1
Bananas			125.0	228.0	194.0	114.0	216.0	129.7
Value	18.9	14.2	11.9	23.1	20.3	17.0	15.0	14.5
Share total exports (%)	24.0	16.8	12.6	23.2	19.4	15.9	12.2	12.5
Rank among exports	2	2	2	2	2	2	2	2
Cotton					4.9	6.2	7.8	6.7
Value					3.7	4.5	5.0	4.2
Share total exports (%)					3.5	4.2	4.1	3.6
Rank among exports					3	3	3	3
Forest products	2	10	6	13	10	28	22	13
Value			1.1	0.8	0.5	0.5	0.4	2.0
Share total exports (%)			1.2	0.8	0.5	0.5	0.3	1.7
Total value	72.2	74.0	86.3	93.1	99.4	99.2	112.3	106.5
Share all exports (%)	91.5	87.6	91.1	94.3	94.7	83.4	95.7	97.5

Commodity	1958	1959	1960	1961	1962	1963	1964	1965	1966
Lead	4.6	0.1	1.6	8.9	1.9	0.3			0.9
Value	0.6		0.2	1.1	1.1				
Share total exports (%)	0.6		0.2	1.0	0.9				
Zinc	5.9		5.5	12.6	2.3	1.3		0.9	1.2
Value	0.7		0.2	0.9	3.7	0.5			
Share total exports (%)	0.7		0.2	0.8	3.1	0.3			
Coffee	72.3	83.1	79.8	75.3	93.1	100.0	86.8	90.6	111.8
Value	83.7	74.4	70.8	64.0	74.0	76.2	71.2	86.1	100.1
Share total exports (%)	77.9	62.3	60.7	56.7	62.9	50.7	43.0	49.0	44.4
Rank among exports	1	1	1	1	1	1	1	1	1
Cocoa	0.6	0.6	0.4	0.5	0.3	0.3	0.2	0.5	0.5
Value	0.4	0.4	0.2	0.2	0.1	0.2	0.1	0.2	0.2
Share total exports (%)	0.4	0.4	0.2	0.2	0.1	0.1	0.1	0.1	0.1
Bananas	115.8	138.7	189.0	157.2	83.5	132.3	111.3	58.0	77.4
Value	13.1	14.7	17.3	13.9	9.5	10.9	9.6	4.4	5.8
Share total exports (%)	12.2	13.7	14.8	12.3	8.1	4.1	6.1	2.5	3.1
Rank among exports	2	2	2	2	3	3	3	3	3
Cotton	9.6	9.7	11.5	18.1	27.0	47.4	62.0	63.8	82.0
Value	5.5	4.1	5.8	10.5	15.5	26.2	23.2	33.9	43.7
Share total exports (%)	5.1	3.8	5.0	9.3	12.7	17.1	14.7	18.1	19.1
Rank among exports	3	3	3	3	2	2	2	2	2
Forest products	13	5	12	12	16	12	8	13	16
Value		0.9	1.1	1.6	1.2	0.9	0.9	1.2	1.9
Share total exports (%)		0.8	0.9	1.5	1.0	0.6	0.6	0.6	0.8
Total value	104.0	90.8	95.6	92.2	105.1	114.9	105.0	125.8	151.7
Share all exports (%)	96.9	81.0	82.0	81.8	88.8	72.9	64.5	70.3	67.5

For notes and sources, see chapter 3, table B–3.

TABLE B-3-12. HAITI: Exports of Selected Primary Commodities, 1950-1966
(Thousands of metric tons or cubic meters and millions of U.S. dollars)

Commodity	1950	1951	1952	1953	1954	1955	1956	1957
Coffee	23.4	25.0	32.5	22.3	31.0	21.3	27.5	18.9
Value	20.6	26.1	34.1	25.1	43.0	23.9	27.2	21.0
Share total exports (%)	53.5	51.2	65.6	65.6	78.8	66.5	64.9	61.2
Rank among exports	1	1	1	1	1	1	1	1
Cocoa	2.1	2.0	2.3	2.0	2.2	1.5	1.2	1.6
Value		1.3	1.2	1.2	2.0	1.2	0.6	0.7
Share total exports (%)		2.5	2.2	3.0	3.6	3.3	1.3	2.1
Sugar		35.5	30.3	28.8	15.1	21.2	27.9	24.3
Value	3.1	4.9	3.6	2.6	1.4	1.8	2.5	3.1
Share total exports (%)	7.9	9.5	7.0	6.9	2.5	4.8	6.0	9.2
Rank among exports	3	3	3	3	3	3	3	3
Cotton		0.5	0.9	1.2	0.8	1.3	0.4	0.4
Value	0.6	0.6	0.8	0.6	0.9	0.2	0.1	0.2
Share total exports (%)	1.2	1.1	2.2	1.2	2.4	0.6	0.4	0.4
Total value	24.3	32.9	39.7	29.5	47.3	27.2	30.4	25.0
Share all exports (%)	62.6	64.3	77.0	76.7	87.3	75.2	72.6	72.9

Commodity	1958	1959	1960	1961	1962	1963	1964	1965	1966
Coffee	32.8	21.9	23.7	20.9	30.8	23.4	22.8	23.9	21.0
Value	29.1	15.3	17.3	13.5	20.6	16.2	19.4	19.8	17.3
Share total exports (%)	73.9	54.6	53.9	41.8	48.9	39.2	48.0	53.3	50.5
Rank among exports	1	1	1	1	1	1	1	1	1
Cocoa	1.9	2.0	2.1	0.9	0.6	1.2	0.5	0.1	0.4
Value	1.3	1.3							
Share total exports (%)	3.4	4.5							
Sugar	6.5	6.2	30.1	39.7	34.6	35.9	22.6	20.2	33.6
Value	1.0	1.0	3.8	5.2	3.6	4.8	2.5	2.4	3.1
Share total exports (%)	2.6	3.4	11.5	16.1	8.5	11.6	6.2	6.7	9.2
Rank among exports	3	3	3	2	2	2	3	3	2
Cotton	0.3								
Value	0.4								
Share total exports (%)	1.3								
Total value	31.8	17.6	21.1	18.7	24.2	21.0	21.9	22.2	20.4
Share all exports (%)	81.2	62.5	65.4	65.4	57.4	50.8	54.2	60.0	59.7

For notes and sources, see chapter 3, table B-3.

TABLE B–3–13. HONDURAS: Exports of Selected Primary Commodities, 1950-1966
(Thousands of metric tons or cubic meters and millions of U.S. dollars)

Commodity	1950	1951	1952	1953	1954	1955	1956	1957
Lead	0.4	0.3	0.5	1.0	1.5	2.5	2.7	2.7
Value	0.1		0.3		0.4	0.2	0.8	1.8
Share total exports (%)	0.2		0.5		0.6	0.4	1.1	2.8
Zinc	0.1	0.1	0.3	0.6	0.7	1.3	2.1	2.4
Value			0.2				0.2	1.0
Share total exports (%)			0.4		0.2		0.2	1.5
Coffee	6.8	8.2	8.3	11.2	9.2	8.9	11.7	10.4
Value	3.2	8.3	8.7	11.2	14.0	8.5	13.3	12.0
Share total exports (%)	5.8	12.6	13.9	16.5	25.7	16.5	18.3	18.5
Rank among exports	2	2	2	2	2	2	2	2
Bananas				395.4	293.0	207.4	392.9	337.3
Value	40.8	43.7	40.6	41.1	28.3	27.4	43.9	33.7
Share total exports (%)	73.8	66.2	64.7	60.4	51.7	51.5	59.8	45.9
Rank among exports	1	1	1	1	1	1	1	1
Cotton	0.1	0.8	0.8	1.1	0.6	0.9	3.4	4.1
Value	0.2	0.1	0.2	0.1	0.1	0.1	4.5	2.5
Share total exports (%)	0.2	0.2	0.2	0.2	0.2	0.2	6.1	3.9
Forest products	41	54	73	67	79	99	85	110
Value	2.1	5.4	4.1	3.6	3.3	5.4	4.8	9.2
Share total exports (%)	3.8	8.2	6.5	5.3	6.0	10.5	6.6	14.2
Rank among exports	4	3	3	4	3	3	3	3
Total value	46.3	57.4	54.1	57.7	52.0	41.6	67.5	60.2
Share all exports (%)	83.8	87.2	86.2	82.4	84.4	79.1	92.1	86.8

Commodity	1958	1959	1960	1961	1962	1963	1964	1965	1966
Lead	3.3	3.3	4.5	5.0	4.5	6.2	5.8	10.5	8.3
Value	1.0	1.0	1.0	0.9	1.2	1.6	1.3	2.4	2.0
Share total exports (%)	1.4	1.4	1.5	1.2	1.5	1.9	1.4	1.9	1.4
Zinc	1.3	1.3	4.3	6.2	6.4	7.5	7.0	11.0	9.7
Value	0.3	0.3	0.6	0.9	2.8	1.2	0.8	1.4	1.4
Share total exports (%)	0.5	0.5	0.9	1.2	3.5	1.5	0.9	1.1	1.0
Coffee	11.4	15.3	15.5	12.6	16.0	20.1	18.5	24.9	22.6
Value	10.9	11.7	11.8	9.0	11.5	14.2	17.0	22.1	19.9
Share total exports (%)	15.6	17.1	18.7	12.4	14.5	16.8	17.9	17.4	13.8
Rank among exports	2	2	2	2	2	2	2	2	2
Bananas	398.2	356.9	360.2	425.7	378.6	343.4	349.4	572.3	710.6
Value	37.7	32.1	28.2	33.3	34.2	32.4	34.2	53.7	69.7
Share total exports (%)	58.0	47.4	44.6	45.6	43.3	38.8	36.1	42.1	48.8
Rank among exports	1	1	1	1	1	1	1	1	1
Cotton	4.4	4.0	1.2	0.8	3.6	4.4	6.9	11.2	11.2
Value	2.6	2.6	0.7	0.3	2.1	2.5	3.8	6.2	5.8
Share total exports (%)	3.7	3.8	1.0	0.5	2.9	3.2	4.6	4.9	4.0
Forest products	111	148	156	128	113	122	184	174	180
Value	6.6	8.3	8.2	7.6	7.2	8.5	10.8	10.3	10.7
Share total exports (%)	9.5	12.0	13.1	10.3	8.8	10.2	11.5	8.1	7.5
Rank among exports	3	3	3	3	3	3	3	3	3
Fish and fishmeal	0.4	0.2	0.2	0.1	0.2	0.5	0.3	0.7	1.3
Value	0.6	0.2	0.2	0.1	0.2	0.4	0.3	0.6	0.9
Share total exports (%)	0.8	0.3	0.3	0.2	0.2	0.5	0.3	0.3	0.5
Total value	59.7	56.2	50.7	52.1	59.2	61.8	64.4	96.7	110.4
Share all exports (%)	89.5	82.5	80.1	71.4	74.7	72.9	68.1	75.8	77.0

For notes and sources, see chapter 3, table B–3.

TABLE B-3-14. MEXICO: Exports of Selected Primary Commodities, 1950-1966
(Thousands of metric tons or cubic meters and millions of U.S. dollars)

Commodity	1950	1951	1952	1953	1954	1955	1956	1957
Copper	57.7	53.4	59.4	62.6	55.1	59.3	55.9	49.8
Value	26.9	33.9	44.1	42.1	55.5	67.8	73.3	37.2
Share total exports (%)	5.0	5.3	6.6	7.1	8.8	8.6	8.8	5.1
Rank among exports	5	6	4	4	4	3	3	6
Iron ore	192.0	175.0	114.0	243.0	145.0	186.0	135.0	239.0
Value	0.6	0.6	0.5	1.2	0.6	0.6	0.4	0.8
Share total exports (%)	0.1	0.1	0.1	0.2	0.1	0.1		0.1
Lead	244.7	157.0	234.8	208.1	208.5	177.7	153.0	162.0
Value	68.7	75.3	76.0	58.5	56.0	57.7	53.1	52.0
Share total exports (%)	12.9	11.7	11.4	9.8	8.9	7.3	6.4	7.1
Rank among exports	2	2	2	3	3	4	4	3
Zinc	203.2	161.0	218.0	221.9	208.0	250.2	233.0	224.3
Value	25.4	40.6	48.5	22.2	22.6	28.4	43.4	41.6
Share total exports (%)	4.8	6.3	7.3	3.7	3.6	3.6	5.2	5.7
Rank among exports	6	4	5	6	6	6	6	5
Petroleum	2,785.0	2,759.0	1,483.0	876.0	2,024.0	1,786.0	1,338.0	642.0
Value	32.0	34.8	32.5	26.9	35.6	51.4	53.6	41.8
Share total exports (%)	6.0	5.4	4.9	4.5	5.7	6.5	6.4	5.7
Rank among exports	4	5	6	5	5	5	5	4
Coffee	46.0	51.9	52.2	76.0	66.7	82.0	75.6	81.9
Value	38.6	46.9	47.0	91.2	108.9	106.3	111.1	113.7
Share total exports (%)	7.2	7.3	7.0	15.3	17.3	13.6	13.4	15.5
Rank among exports	3	3	3	2	2	2	2	2
Cocoa	3.4	1.6	1.9	0.7	3.6	5.3	2.2	7.3
Value	0.9	1.0	1.3	0.5	2.0	2.9	0.9	2.6
Share total exports (%)	0.2	0.1	0.2	0.1	0.3	0.4	0.1	0.4
Sugar			9.4	58.5	72.9	79.8	34.1	93.9
Value	3.0	5.9	6.5	7.8	9.2	10.5	5.5	11.0
Share total exports (%)	0.6	0.9	0.9	1.3	1.5	1.3	0.7	1.5
Rank among exports								7
Bananas				51.0	56.0	29.0	16.0	36.0
Value	1.8	1.4	1.0	1.0	0.8	0.5	0.4	0.9
Share total exports (%)	0.3	0.2	0.2	0.2	0.1	0.1		0.1
Beef	34.0	6.0	6.0	12.0	4.0	9.0	5.0	8.0
Value	3.6	14.4	14.8	4.9	4.1	2.6	1.7	2.2
Share total exports (%)	0.7	2.2	2.2	0.8	0.6	0.3	0.2	0.3
Cotton	164.0	178.0	228.7	234.5	259.4	325.4	421.9	283.9
Value	138.9	151.7	185.9	152.2	182.0	230.1	260.3	170.5
Share total exports (%)	26.1	23.6	27.8	25.6	28.9	29.4	31.2	23.2
Rank among exports	1	1	1	1	1	1	1	1
Forest products	235	156	172	87	83	76	73	70
Value	8.7	4.9	6.7	4.4	3.2	5.7	3.4	4.4
Share total exports (%)	1.6	0.8	1.0	0.7	0.5	0.7	0.4	0.6
Fishery products	132.1	90.8	79.0	22.6	21.8	26.7	32.3	29.8
Value	0.4	0.3	0.3	16.7	15.2	17.6	23.5	25.7
Share total exports (%)	0.1			2.8	2.4	2.2	2.8	3.5
Total value	349.5	411.7	457.1	433.5	429.6	582.1	539.3	493.8
Share all exports (%)	65.6	65.1	69.6	72.2	78.0	74.1	75.6	68.8

TABLE B–3–14 – Continued

Commodity	1958	1959	1960	1961	1962	1963	1964	1965	1966
Copper	48.8	46.3	41.7	29.0	39.0	29.3	24.9	18.6	17.0
Value	29.9	29.9	25.8	19.1	24.5	22.6	20.2	11.4	13.0
Share total exports (%)	4.1	4.0	3.4	2.0	2.6	2.3	1.9	1.0	1.1
Rank among exports	4	4	6	7	7	7	7	7	7
Iron ore	224.0	116.0	156.0	123.0	147.0	2.0	22.0	9.9	0.1
Value	0.7	0.4	0.5	0.4	1.1		0.2	0.1	
Share total exports (%)	0.1	0.1	0.1		0.1				
Lead	166.0	136.0	134.0	157.0	125.0	125.0	98.0	98.2	102.6
Value	35.2	34.0	33.6	37.2	26.3	27.5	23.3	26.0	27.7
Share total exports (%)	4.8	4.5	4.4	4.5	2.8	2.8	2.2	2.3	2.3
Rank among exports	3	3	4	4	6	6	6	6	6
Zinc	195.5	226.8	229.8	240.8	213.4	214.5	193.0	180.7	203.7
Value	20.0	25.0	29.6	27.4	28.3	29.9	42.6	37.7	37.1
Share total exports (%)	2.7	3.3	3.9	3.3	3.0	3.0	4.0	3.3	3.0
Rank among exports	6	5	5	6	5	5	4	5	5
Petroleum	108.0	18.0	1,200.0	2,439.0	2,924.0	2,977.0	2,736.0	2,857.7	2,897.3
Value	23.9	22.4	13.3	33.0	39.0	38.0	39.0	48.1	42.3
Share total exports (%)	3.2	3.0	1.7	4.0	4.2	3.9	3.7	4.2	3.4
Rank among exports	5	6	7	5	4	4	5	4	4
Coffee	78.7	74.4	83.0	89.0	87.4	71.9	106.3	79.6	92.2
Value	82.7	65.4	71.6	70.4	47.2	49.3	101.8	75.7	82.3
Share total exports (%)	11.2	8.3	9.4	8.7	5.1	5.0	9.7	6.3	6.8
Rank among exports	2	2	2	2	2	3	2	2	
Cocoa	5.7	5.6	3.3	5.7	12.2	18.2	3.5	9.4	8.7
Value	2.4	2.9	1.7	2.5	4.5	7.1	1.5	3.4	4.1
Share total exports (%)	0.3	0.4	0.2	0.3	0.5	0.7	0.1	0.3	0.3
Sugar	187.4	130.8	462.4	586.1	364.9	392.5	491.3	541.3	500.0
Value	19.6	18.8	52.9	68.7	43.6	59.6	64.1	58.9	57.1
Share total exports (%)	2.7	2.5	6.9	8.3	4.7	6.1	6.1	5.1	4.6
Rank among exports	7	7	3	3	3	2	3	3	3
Bananas	26.0	33.0	10.0	18.0	7.0	10.0	17.0	14.0	12.0
Value	0.7	0.8	0.3	0.7	0.4	0.6	0.7	0.6	0.5
Share total exports (%)	0.1	0.1		0.1		0.1	0.1	0.1	
Beef	30.0	22.0	19.0	26.0	28.0	34.0	23.0	26.0	33.0
Value	12.1	10.7	10.4	16.5	23.0	28.6	19.6	18.3	28.9
Share total exports (%)	1.6	1.4	1.4	2.0	2.5	2.9	1.9	1.5	2.3
Cotton	341.0	405.9	316.3	305.2	425.2	370.1	322.0	409.0	429.5
Value	190.4	199.0	158.0	160.0	218.5	195.8	170.2	162.1	153.6
Share total exports (%)	25.9	26.4	20.7	19.3	23.5	19.9	16.2	14.1	12.4
Rank among exports	1	1	1	1	1	1	1	1	1
Forest products	45	54	28	29	35	31	19	16	9
Value	5.0	10.5	1.9	5.6	3.8	1.9	1.9	1.8	1.6
Share total exports (%)	0.7	1.4	0.2	0.7	0.4	0.2	0.2	0.2	0.1
Fishery products	35.5	39.4	42.5	46.3	46.1	47.3	41.2	36.2	39.1
Value	35.8	43.2	38.8	46.5	56.2	64.2	51.3	50.1	58.3
Share total exports (%)	4.9	5.7	5.1	5.6	6.0	6.5	4.9	4.4	4.7
Total value	410.8	384.8	476.7	578.7	467.6	473.5	476.7	494.2	506.5
Share all exports (%)	62.3	61.1	57.4	58.8	55.4	53.4	51.0	44.4	41.0

For notes and sources, see chapter 3, table B–3.

TABLE B-3-15. NICARAGUA: Exports of Selected Primary Commodities, 1950-1966
(Thousands of metric tons or cubic meters and millions of U.S. dollars)

Commodity	1950	1951	1952	1953	1954	1955	1956	1957
Coffee	21.0	16.1	18.2	18.8	17.1	22.8	16.7	22.0
Value	17.3	18.5	20.7	21.3	25.1	27.9	23.2	28.5
Share total exports (%)	65.4	50.1	48.9	46.7	46.0	38.7	40.1	44.5
Rank among exports	1	1	1	1	1	2	2	1
Cocoa	0.1	0.2	0.1	0.1		0.2	0.2	0.1
Value	0.1	0.1	0.1	0.1				
Share total exports (%)	0.2	0.3	0.2	0.1	0.1			
Sugar		8.3	7.7	9.2	10.7	8.8	3.9	9.0
Value			0.1	0.1	0.2	0.1	0.1	0.2
Share total exports (%)			0.3	0.2	0.3	0.2		0.3
Bananas		12.0	10.0	9.0	12.0	9.0	4.0	2.0
Value			0.1	0.1	0.1	0.1		
Share total exports (%)			0.2	0.1	0.1	0.1	0.1	
Cotton		3.3	4.4	9.5	12.8	23.2	44.0	36.3	36.0
Value		1.8	5.5	6.8	8.4	16.8	31.0	23.6	21.8
Share total exports (%)		6.9	14.8	16.2	18.4	30.7	43.1	40.8	33.0
Rank among exports									
Total value		19.2	73.3	27.8	30.1	42.1	59.0	46.9	50.5
Share all exports (%)		72.5	65.4	65.8	65.7	77.1	82.1	81.0	78.8

Commodity	1958	1959	1960	1961	1962	1963	1964	1965	1966
Coffee	22.9	16.4	21.7	21.0	20.3	28.0	25.8	30.5	25.3
Value	24.2	13.9	19.2	17.6	15.4	17.5	24.3	28.3	23.7
Share total exports (%)	37.9	21.3	26.3	29.1	18.7	17.5	20.7	18.3	15.8
Rank among exports	2	2	1	2	2	2	2	2	2
Cocoa	0.1	0.2	0.3	0.2	0.2	0.3	0.3	0.3	0.2
Value									
Share total exports (%)									
Sugar	15.4	24.4	34.9	28.0	40.2	44.1	48.9	45.7	17.2
Value	0.2	0.3	0.5	0.4	0.4	0.6	0.6	0.6	0.2
Share total exports (%)	0.4	0.5	0.7	0.7	0.5	0.6	0.5		
Bananas	2.0	2.0	4.0	2.0	11.3	19.0	27.1	8.0	14.0
Value				0.1	0.1	1.3	2.1	7.8	11.8
Share total exports (%)				0.1	0.9	1.4	1.8	5.5	8.6
Cotton	42.7	61.7	27.4	32.5	55.7	73.1	93.5	125.1	111.4
Value	24.9	29.4	14.7	18.3	31.3	39.8	51.5	66.1	56.8
Share total exports (%)	39.0	45.1	20.3	30.2	38.0	39.9	43.5	46.1	41.3
Rank among exports	1	1	2	1	1	1	1	1	1
Total value	49.3	43.5	34.4	36.4	47.2	59.2	78.5	102.8	92.5
Share all exports (%)	77.3	66.9	47.5	60.1	58.1	58.2	65.0	69.9	65.7

For notes and sources, see chapter 3, table B-3.

TABLE B-3-16. PANAMA: Exports of Selected Primary Commodities, 1950-1966
(Thousands of metric tons or cubic meters and millions of U.S. dollars)

Commodity	1950	1951	1952	1953	1954	1955	1956	1957
Cocoa	1.9	1.3	3.1	1.9	2.6	1.2	1.5	1.3
Value	1.0	0.7	1.1	1.0	1.8	1.0	0.6	0.9
Share total exports (%)	4.1	2.6	4.5	4.0	5.8	2.8	1.9	2.6
Rank among exports	2	3	3	3	3	3	3	3
Sugar		5.0	3.1	3.7	3.5			3.3
Value			0.4	0.3	0.4			0.4
Share total exports (%)			1.5	1.0	1.2			1.2
Bananas				188.0	188.0	275.0	251.0	290.0
Value	16.3	16.3	13.0	16.3	22.1	26.2	22.3	24.4
Share total exports (%)	69.7	64.5	55.6	64.0	72.0	73.6	72.6	68.9
Rank among exports	1	1	1	1	1	1	1	1
Forest products	7	12	10	13	10	12	13	11
Value	0.5		0.5	0.8	0.5	0.7		0.3
Share total exports (%)	2.0		2.3	3.2	1.8	1.9		0.9
Fishery products	0.1	0.6	1.1	2.2	1.6	1.9	2.8	4.1
Value	0.2	0.7	1.4	2.1	2.3	2.7	4.4	6.2
Share total exports (%)	0.8	2.8	5.8	8.3	7.4	7.6	14.4	17.6
Rank among exports	3	2	2	2	2	2	2	2
Total value	18.0	17.7	16.4	20.5	27.1	30.6	27.3	32.2
Share all exports (%)	76.6	69.9	69.7	80.5	88.2	85.9	88.9	91.2

Commodity	1958	1959	1960	1961	1962	1963	1964	1965	1966
Petroleum					19.1	148.9	125.2	138.7	152.7
Value					13.9	23.6	24.9	23.7	25.9
Share total exports (%)					29.0	40.0	35.0	30.4	29.3
Rank among exports					2	2	2	2	2
Coffee	0.5	1.0	1.3	0.3	1.6	0.5	1.5	1.4	2.7
Value	0.5	0.8	1.1	0.3	1.4	0.4	1.5	1.1	2.1
Share total exports (%)	1.5	2.3	4.0	1.0	2.9	0.7	2.1	1.4	2.4
Cocoa	1.7	1.4	1.4	1.2	1.1	0.9	0.8	0.6	0.4
Value	1.1	1.2	0.8	0.5	0.5	0.5	0.4	0.2	0.2
Share total exports (%)	3.4	3.4	2.8	1.1	1.0	0.8	0.5	0.3	
Rank among exports	3	3	3	4	5	5	5	5	5
Sugar	5.5	4.0	2.8	5.2	3.6	10.4	22.9	19.1	11.7
Value	0.6	0.6	0.3	0.8	0.5	1.6	2.6	2.1	1.6
Share total exports (%)	2.0	1.7	1.2	2.6	1.2	2.6	3.7	2.7	1.7
Rank among exports	4	5	5	3	4	4	4	4	4
Bananas	267.0	291.0	263.0	271.0	251.0	298.0	267.0	377.4	431.7
Value	21.9	23.5	18.2	20.1	20.1	25.1	30.8	30.6	34.8
Share total exports (%)	66.6	67.8	66.0	66.4	42.1	42.4	43.4	38.6	38.9
Rank among exports	1	1	1	1	1	1	1	1	1
Forest products	3	1	5	1	3	2	3	3	3
Value	0.1	0.1	0.2	0.2	0.4	0.3	0.3	0.3	0.1
Share total exports (%)	0.4	0.3	0.9	0.7	0.8	0.5	0.4	0.3	0.1
Fishery products	4.2	5.7	3.8	5.6	5.5	5.0	7.7	10.6	17.9
Value	5.8	5.3	5.0	6.1	8.1	6.3	7.1	8.7	10.9
Share total exports (%)	17.3	15.3	14.3	20.1	17.0	10.6	11.3	11.0	12.3
Rank among exports	2	2	2	2	3	3	3	3	3
Total value	30.0	31.5	25.6	28.0	44.9	57.8	67.6	66.7	75.6
Share all exports (%)	91.2	90.8	89.2	92.5	94.0	97.6	95.1	84.7	84.7

For notes and sources, see chapter 3, table B-3.

TABLE B–3–17. PARAGUAY: Exports of Selected Primary Commodities, 1950-1966
(Thousands of metric tons or cubic meters and millions of U.S. dollars)

Commodity	1950	1951	1952	1953	1954	1955	1956	1957
Beef	9.3	4.2	0.2		3.1	3.1	6.5	7.4
Value	4.0	3.0	0.6	1.5	2.1	2.3	4.6	3.7
Share total exports (%)	12.0	8.0	1.9	5.0	6.2	6.6	12.5	11.3
Rank among exports	2	3	6	4	4	3	3	3
Cotton	20.0	6.9	15.0	14.4	11.4	9.0	9.8	8.1
Value	6.7	7.3	10.1	10.0	6.9	5.5	5.6	4.5
Share total exports (%)	20.2	19.4	32.4	32.4	20.2	15.7	15.3	13.7
Rank among exports	2	2	1	1	2	2	2	2
Forest products	220	208	133	166	177	180	250	190
Value	9.1	10.3	6.8	6.5	11.1	13.0	11.8	9.4
Share total exports (%)	27.4	27.4	21.6	21.3	32.8	37.2	32.3	28.5
Rank among exports	1	1	2	2	1	1	1	1
Total value	19.8	20.6	17.5	18.0	20.1	20.8	22.0	17.6
Share all exports (%)	59.9	54.7	55.8	58.6	59.5	59.5	60.0	53.3

Commodity	1958	1959	1960	1961	1962	1963	1964	1965	1966
Beef	10.5	12.2	11.7	15.1	13.7	18.1	23.0	19.9	16.4
Value	8.2	9.6	7.1	8.6	7.5	10.5	14.8	17.8	13.8
Share total exports (%)	24.0	30.8	26.4	28.2	22.3	26.2	29.6	35.1	28.2
Rank among exports	2	1	1	1	1	1	1	1	1
Cotton	7.8	5.6	0.8	5.0	7.0	8.5	9.2	9.9	5.0
Value	3.7	2.1	0.3	1.6	2.5	3.2	4.2	4.7	2.0
Share total exports (%)	10.9	6.6	1.1	5.2	7.4	8.0	8.4	8.2	4.0
Rank among exports	3	4	7	4	4	4	3	3	3
Forest products	213	94	158	194	157	125	258	298	352
Value	9.7	4.1	5.0	6.5	6.7	4.7	7.2	8.8	10.5
Share total exports (%)	28.5	13.0	18.6	21.0	19.9	11.8	14.4	15.6	21.4
Rank among exports	1	2	2	2	2	2	2	2	2
Total value	21.6	15.8	12.4	16.7	16.7	18.4	26.2	31.3	26.3
Share all exports (%)	63.3	50.6	46.0	54.3	49.3	45.8	52.5	58.9	53.6

For notes and sources, see chapter 3, table B–3.

TABLE B-3-18. PERU: Exports of Selected Primary Commodities, 1950-1966
(Thousands of metric tons or cubic meters and millions of U.S. dollars)

Commodity	1950	1951	1952	1953	1954	1955	1956	1957
Copper	22.6	26.1	23.0	24.2	28.3	42.3	46.8	52.8
Value	10.1	15.1	16.9	14.8	20.4	29.3	33.6	24.5
Share total exports (%)	5.3	6.1	7.2	6.8	8.3	10.9	10.9	7.7
Rank among exports	6	6	5	4	4	3	2	4
Iron ore				890.0	1,927.0	1,697.0	2,674.0	3,677.0
Value				5.4	13.1	7.8	14.0	23.3
Share total exports (%)				2.5	5.4	2.9	4.8	7.2
Rank among exports				8	6	8	8	5
Lead	60.1	82.0	89.3	105.0	106.4	106.7	120.5	119.3
Value	12.2	23.3	23.7	19.2	24.1	26.2	31.3	29.3
Share total exports (%)	6.5	9.5	10.2	10.3	9.7	9.8	10.1	9.2
Rank among exports	4	3	3	3	3	4	4	3
Zinc	74.6	101.1	112.8	97.7	112.4	146.3	143.5	146.1
Value	10.8	15.5	13.8	6.7	9.5	14.5	15.5	15.7
Share total exports (%)	5.7	6.2	5.9	3.1	3.9	5.4	5.0	4.9
Rank among exports	5	5	6	6	8	6	7	7
Petroleum	1,138.0	1,146.0	1,012.0	924.0	810.0	831.0	932.0	796.0
Value	13.0	21.6	17.1	12.0	17.0	23.5	26.5	15.6
Share total exports (%)	6.9	8.7	7.3	5.5	6.9	8.8	8.6	4.9
Rank among exports	3	4	4	5	5	5	5	8
Coffee	0.8	2.2	2.7	4.7	4.6	6.8	7.1	11.1
Value	0.8	2.3	2.8	5.3	7.2	8.0	8.9	12.9
Share total exports (%)	0.4	0.9	1.2	2.4	2.9	3.0	2.9	4.0
Sugar	276.8	258.8	304.8	410.9	422.2	482.9	428.3	496.3
Value	29.6	34.2	32.8	29.6	33.6	36.9	32.8	49.6
Share total exports (%)	15.6	13.8	14.0	13.5	13.7	13.8	10.7	15.5
Rank among exports	2	2	2	2	2	2	3	2
Cotton	72.3	61.8	82.7	88.5	83.2	84.0	108.0	80.2
Value	67.9	84.6	78.5	55.4	66.1	68.2	85.7	68.1
Share total exports (%)	36.0	34.5	33.9	29.8	36.5	25.4	27.8	21.3
Rank among exports	1	1	1	1	1	1	1	1
Forest products	5	11	8	2	11	15	10	7
Value	1.6	1.1	1.0		1.1	1.2	0.8	0.4
Share total exports (%)	0.9	0.4	0.4		0.4	0.4	0.3	0.1
Fishery products	21.6	23.5	29.9	31.6	46.4	52.6	66.4	103.8
Value	0.6	6.0	7.7	7.5	12.1	12.7	15.7	19.7
Share total exports (%)	0.3	2.4	3.3	3.4	4.9	4.7	5.1	6.2
Rank among exports	8	7	7	7	7	7	6	6
Total value	146.6	203.7	194.3	155.9	189.8	228.3	264.8	239.0
Share all exports (%)	77.6	82.5	83.4	77.3	78.9	85.1	96.8	81.0

TABLE B-3-18 – Continued

Commodity	1958	1959	1960	1961	1962	1963	1964	1965	1966
Copper	55.6	50.6	167.4	199.0	173.0	163.4	177.8	179.8	176.1
Value	21.1	24.8	96.4	104.7	92.3	87.3	106.4	121.3	186.2
Share total exports (%)	7.5	8.1	22.4	21.2	17.2	16.2	16.0	18.2	24.4
Rank among exports	4	4	1	1	3	3	2	2	2
Iron ore	2,510.0	3,320.0	5,171.0	5,573.0	5,149.0	5,749.0	5,205.0	6,374.9	6,307.4
Value	15.6	19.2	33.3	37.0	32.7	36.4	31.9	47.0	53.4
Share total exports (%)	5.5	6.1	7.7	7.4	6.0	6.7	4.7	7.0	7.0
Rank among exports	7	6	5	5	5	5	7	4	4
Lead	136.5	114.7	117.7	142.2	200.6	120.5	166.5	151.0	150.0
Value	23.3	21.0	22.0	22.3	16.4	16.4	33.0	37.9	34.3
Share total exports (%)	8.7	6.8	5.0	4.5	3.0	3.0	5.0	5.7	4.5
Rank among exports	3	5	6	7	8	8	6	5	6
Zinc	137.3	156.3	156.6	207.6	181.3	186.8	274.6	267.7	282.1
Value	11.6	14.9	18.4	20.1	16.7	16.8	26.9	35.8	34.0
Share total exports (%)	4.1	4.8	4.3	4.1	3.1	3.1	4.0	5.4	4.4
Rank among exports	9	9	8	8	7	7	8	7	7
Petroleum	493.0	781.0	898.0	759.0	676.0	587.0	507.0	425.2	334.9
Value	15.9	17.8	17.8	14.5	13.2	9.8	6.6	9.3	7.4
Share total exports (%)	5.7	5.7	4.1	2.9	2.5	1.8	1.0	1.4	1.0
Rank among exports	6	7	9	9	9	9	9	9	9
Coffee	16.5	19.9	26.4	34.0	37.4	40.1	41.7	32.8	35.2
Value	15.1	15.5	18.5	22.8	24.2	25.6	37.6	28.9	29.4
Share total exports (%)	5.4	5.0	4.3	4.6	4.5	4.7	5.6	4.3	3.7
Rank among exports	8	8	7	6	6	6	5	8	8
Sugar	410.7	498.8	513.7	552.4	462.7	480.6	428.4	387.1	433.5
Value	34.0	35.9	47.5	63.9	53.8	64.9	64.0	36.8	46.3
Share total exports (%)	12.1	11.5	11.0	12.9	10.1	12.0	9.6	5.5	6.1
Rank among exports	2	3	4	4	4	4	4	6	5
Cotton	106.2	113.7	98.7	112.5	138.1	123.9	109.7	115.7	113.9
Value	72.1	69.0	74.6	79.8	97.1	91.4	91.5	95.2	84.9
Share total exports (%)	26.8	22.3	17.0	16.2	18.1	16.9	13.7	14.3	11.1
Rank among exports	1	1	2	2	2	2	3	3	3
Forest products	3	2	4	2	4	3	6	7	9
Value	0.3	0.3	0.3	0.2	0.3	0.3			1.4
Share total exports (%)	0.1	0.1	0.1		0.1	0.1			0.2
Fishery products	146.5	352.6	592.1	865.0	1,232.9	1,212.9	1,574.7	1,581.6	1,420.1
Value	20.6	44.4	52.1	71.5	121.6	122.0	166.8	186.3	205.0
Share total exports (%)	7.3	14.2	12.1	14.5	22.6	22.6	25.1	27.9	26.8
Rank among exports	5	2	3	3	1	1	1	1	1
Total value	229.6	262.8	376.9	436.8	468.3	470.9	564.7	598.5	682.3
Share all exports (%)	83.2	84.6	88.0	88.3	87.2	87.1	84.7	89.7	89.0

For notes and sources, see chapter 3, table B-3.

TABLE B-3-19. URUGUAY: Exports of Selected Primary Commodities, 1950-1966
(Thousands of metric tons or cubic meters and millions of U.S. dollars)

Commodity	1950	1951	1952	1953	1954	1955	1956	1957
Wheat	8	122	238	85	360	490	408	138
Value	0.7	8.2	25.4	7.7	29.6	37.9	27.7	9.4
Share total exports (%)	0.3	3.5	12.2	2.9	11.9	20.7	13.2	7.3
Rank among exports			4		3	2	2	4
Beef	80	76	52	57	57	13	41	47
Value	43.2	44.6	40.6	44.2	45.3	7.2	22.2	27.5
Share total exports (%)	17.0	18.9	19.5	16.4	18.3	3.9	10.5	21.5
Rank among exports	2	2	2	2	2	4	3	2
Total value	43.9	52.8	66.0	51.9	74.9	45.1	49.9	36.9
Share all exports (%)	17.3	22.4	31.7	1.9	30.2	24.6	23.7	28.8

Commodity	1958	1959	1960	1961	1962	1963	1964	1965	1966
Wheat	265	50				42	49	81	129
Value	17.2	3.2				3.1		4.5	7.4
Share total exports (%)	12.4	3.3				1.9		2.3	3.9
Rank among exports	2								
Beef	43	10	60	52	65	77	132	85	69
Value	14.6	18.5	30.8	27.4	31.4	33.4	74.3	58.7	41.5
Share total exports (%)	10.5	18.9	23.8	15.7	20.4	20.2	41.5	30.9	22.6
Rank among exports	3	2	2	2	2	2	2	2	2
Total value	31.8	21.7	30.8	27.4	31.4	36.5	74.3	63.2	48.9
Share all exports (%)	22.9	22.2	23.8	15.7	20.4	22.1	41.5	33.2	26.5

For notes and sources, see chapter 3, table B-3.

TABLE B-3-20. VENEZUELA: Exports of Selected Primary Commodities, 1950-1966
(Thousands of metric tons or cubic meters and millions of U.S. dollars)

Commodity	1950	1951	1952	1953	1954	1955	1956	1957
Iron ore		639.0	1,191.0	1,973.0	5,449.0	7,791.0	10,905.0	15,577.0
Value		4.0	14.7	17.1	36.1	48.6	73.9	114.3
Share total exports (%)		0.3	1.0	1.1	2.0	2.4	3.2	4.5
Rank among exports		4	3	3	2	2	2	2
Petroleum	78,570.0	89,702.0	99,668.0	98,083.0	105,968.0	118,883.0	137,293.0	147,473.0
Value	1,216.9	1,414.9	1,493.9	1,473.1	1,727.2	1,951.8	2,151.5	2,357.9
Share total exports (%)	97.0	96.7	95.5	94.5	94.6	96.4	94.2	92.5
Rank among exports	1	1	1	1	1	1	1	1
Coffee	18.6	18.5	29.9	44.0	44.0	29.8	23.2	27.6
Value	16.6	19.1	34.1	45.1	33.5	35.3	33.3	38.4
Share total exports (%)	1.3	1.3	2.2	2.9	1.8	1.7	1.5	1.5
Rank among exports	2	2	2	2	3	3	3	3
Cocoa	15.6	14.3	15.1	17.1	16.3	16.1	18.6	14.9
Value	12.0	11.6	12.0	13.3	15.4	11.1	12.1	10.8
Share total exports (%)	1.0	0.8	0.8	0.9	0.8	0.5	0.5	0.4
Rank among exports	3	3	4	4	4	4	4	4
Total value	1,245.5	1,449.6	1,554.7	1,548.6	1,812.2	2,046.8	2,270.8	2,521.4
Share all exports (%)	99.3	99.1	99.5	99.4	99.2	99.5	99.4	98.9

Commodity	1958	1959	1960	1961	1962	1963	1964	1965	1966
Iron ore	15,572.0	17,379.0	19,320.0	14,565.0	13,286.0	12,319.0	14,893.0	17,006.0	17,037.0
Value	116.6	130.5	165.5	96.6	87.6	72.0	116.7	134.9	140.9
Share total exports (%)	4.7	5.1	6.3	3.4	3.1	2.5	4.1	5.0	5.3
Rank among exports	2	2	2	2	2	2	2	2	2
Petroleum	141,759.0	145,768.0	151,117.0	155,296.0	169,661.0	173,270.0	182,248.0	188,748.0	184,635.0
Value	2,292.6	2,357.0	2,411.0	2,408.1	2,607.8	2,639.2	2,525.0	2,552.0	2,508.4
Share total exports (%)	91.7	92.3	92.0	92.6	93.2	93.1	93.1	93.0	92.4
Rank among exports	1	1	1	1	1	1	1	1	1
Coffee	35.1	28.4	24.5	24.3	19.1	23.4	19.6	17.9	18.2
Value	39.5	24.6	20.9	18.9	14.3	17.1	17.7	17.4	17.1
Share total exports (%)	1.6	1.0	0.8	0.7	0.5	0.6	0.6	0.6	0.6
Rank among exports	3	3	3	3	3	3	3	3	3
Cocoa	13.5	10.4	12.0	9.8	10.9	12.5	12.1	12.3	11.8
Value	12.5	8.8	9.2	7.8	9.7	9.6	7.2	7.4	7.0
Share total exports (%)	0.5	0.3	0.4	0.4	0.4	0.5	0.3	0.3	0.3
Rank among exports	4	4	4	4	4	4	4	4	4
Fishery products	0.3	0.4	0.5	3.0	8.4	6.0	5.8	7.6	2.2
Value	0.1	0.2	0.3	1.8	5.2	3.6	3.1	5.0	2.0
Share total exports (%)				0.1	0.2	0.1	0.1	0.2	0.1
Total value	2,461.2	2,520.9	2,607.3	2,532.0	2,720.2	2,739.5	2,666.9	2,716.7	2,675.4
Share all exports (%)	98.8	98.7	29.5	97.0	97.2	96.6	98.1	99.1	98.7

For notes and sources, see chapter 3, table B-3.

TABLE B-4-1. ARGENTINA: Natural Resource Base, circa 1960
(Size of reserves or resources in use, and shares of world totals)

I. Minerals

Product and Classification	Year	Unit	Size of Resource	Share of World Total (%)	Lifetime (years) at 1962-64 Rate of Production	Ratio to World Lifetime
Copper: metal content of reserves	1965	mill. m.t.				
Iron ore: iron content of	1962	mill. m.t.				
explored reserves			48	0.2	417	7.7
potential resources			36	0.1	312	3.9
total resources			84	0.1	730	5.5
Petroleum: proved reserves of crude oil	1965	thous. m^3	318,000	0.6	19.9	0.61
Coal: proven, probable and possible reserves of all grades of coal	1963	mill. m.t.	400		1,460	0.94

II. Agriculture: Crops

Product and Classification	Year	Area Planted (thous. ha.)	Share of World Total (%)	Share of Cultivated Area (%)	Share of Total Land Area (%)	Yield (kg/ha)	Ratio to World Average
Sugar (area harvested)	1958-60						
total			2.8				
cane		304	5.8	0.9	0.11	3,100	0.6
beet							
Wheat: all types	1962-64	4,763	2.3	14.2	1.53	1,684	1.20
Cotton: all lengths of fiber	1964/65	553	1.7	1.7	0.18	260	0.77

III. Miscellaneous Products

		Pasture Area				Stock (thous. head)	Share of World Total (%)
Beef Cattle	1960-64	124,353	4.8		44.8	40,500	3.8

		Total Area		Growing Stock (mill. m^3)		Removals (m^3/ha)	Ratio to World Average
Forest: all types	1960-62	60,000	1.6	3,195	22	0.2	0.4

For notes and sources, see chapter 3, table B-4.

TABLE B-4-2. BOLIVIA: Natural Resource Base, circa 1960
(Size of reserves or resources in use, and shares of world totals)

I. Minerals

Product and Classification	Year	Unit	Size of Resource	Share of World Total (%)	Lifetime (years) in L.A. at 1962-64 Rate of Production	Ratio to World Lifetime
Tin: metal content of measured, indicated and inferred reserves	1965	thous. m.t.	750	15.0	33	0.94
Petroleum: proved reserves of crude oil	1965	thous. m^3	63,600	0.1	125	3.8

II. Agriculture: Crops

Product and Classification	Year	Area Planted (thous. ha.)	Share of World Total (%)	Share of Cultivated Area (%)	Share of Total Land Area (%)	Yield (kg/ha)	Ratio to World Average
Coffee: total	1960-65		0.1				
mild Arabicas							
Brazils		13	0.3	0.43	0.012	502	1.3
Cocoa: all types	1964	4-8	0.2	0.20	0.0005		
Sugar (area harvested)	1958-60						
total							
cane		5	0.1	0.16	0.0005	3,000	0.6
beet							
Wheat: all types	1962-64	21		0.68	0.019		

III. Miscellaneous Products

		Pasture Area				Stock (thous. head)	Share of World Total (%)
Beef Cattle	1956-62	11,300	0.4		10.3	2,000	0.2

		Total Area		Growing Stock (mill. m^3)		Removals (m^3/ha)	Ratio to World Average
Forest: all types	1960-62			6,960			

For notes and sources, see chapter 3, table B-4.

TABLE B-4-3. BRAZIL: Natural Resource Base, circa 1960
(Size of reserves or resources in use, and shares of world totals)

I. Minerals

Product and Classification	Year	Unit	Size of Resource	Share of World Total (%)	Lifetime (years) at 1962-64 Rate of Production	Ratio to World Lifetime
Copper: metal content of reserves	1965	mill. m.t.	500	0.3	50	1.2
Iron ore: iron content of	1962	mill. m.t.				
explored reserves			1,797	6.2	158	2.9
potential resources			8,488	20.1	749	9.5
total resources			10,285	14.5	907	6.8
Petroleum: proved reserves of crude oil	1965	thous. m^3	143,000	0.3	27.0	0.83
Coal: proven, probable and possible reserves of	1963	mill. m.t.				
all grades of coal			2,136		1,300	0.84
bituminous coal			2,136		1,300	
coking coal			500		300	

II. Agriculture: Crops

Product and Classification	Year	Area Planted (thous. ha.)	Share of World Total (%)	Share of Cultivated Area (%)	Share of Total Land Area (%)	Yield (kg/ha)	Ratio to World Average
Coffee: total	1960-65		41.4				
mild Arabicas							
Brazils		4,510	90.5	24	0.53	502	1.3
Cocoa: all types	1963	470	13.8	2.5	0.055	230	0.7
Sugar (area harvested)	1958-60						
total			7.2				
cane		800	15.2	4.3	0.094	3,800	0.7
beet							
Bananas: all types	1963-64	231		1.22	0.027	27,000	
Wheat: all types	1962-64	757	0.4	4.0	0.089	755	0.54
Cotton: all lengths of fiber	1964/65	2,327	7.0	12.3	0.27	193	0.57

III. Miscellaneous Products

Product	Year	Pasture Area	Share of World Total		Share of Total Land Area	Stock (thous. head)	Share of World Total (%)
Beef Cattle	1950-64	107,633	4.2		12.6	79,918	7.5

Product	Year	Total Area	Share of World Total	Growing Stock (mill. m^3)		Removals (m^3/ha)	Ratio to World Average
Forest: all types	1960-62	335,100	8.8	79,150	40	0.3	0.6

For notes and sources, see chapter 3, table B-4.

TABLE B-4-4. CHILE: Natural Resource Base, circa 1960
(Size of reserves or resources in use, and shares of world totals)

I. Minerals Product and Classification	Year	Unit	Size of Resource	Share of World Total (%)	Lifetime (years) at 1962-64 Rate of Production	Ratio to World Lifetime
Copper: metal content of reserves	1965	mill. m.t.	42,000	21.8	69	1.6
Iron ore: iron content of	1962	mill. m.t.				
explored reserves			120	0.4	14	0.26
potential resources			167	0.4	19	0.24
total resources			287	0.4	33	0.25
Petroleum: proved reserves of crude oil	1965	thous. m^3	35,800	0.1	16.4	0.5
Coal: proven, probable and possible reserves of	1963	mill. m.t.				
all grades of coal			1,110		640	0.41
bituminous coal			110		63	
coking coal			80		46	

II. Agriculture: Crops Product and Classification	Year	Area Planted (thous. ha.)	Share of World Total (%)	Share of Cultivated Area (%)	Share of Total Land Area (%)	Yield (kg/ha)	Ratio to World Average
Sugar (area harvested)	1958-60						
total			0.1				
cane							
beet		9	0.2	0.16	0.012	4,100	1.2
Wheat: all types	1962-64	847	0.4	15.4	1.14	1,511	1.08

III. Miscellaneous Products		Pasture Area				Stock (thous. head)	Share of World Total (%)
Beef Cattle	1955-64	10,331	0.4		13.9	2,900	0.3
		Total Area		Growing Stock (mill. m^3)		Removals (m^3/ha)	Ratio to World Average
Forest: all types	1960-62	16,108	0.4	3,820	22	0.3	0.6

For notes and sources, see chapter 3, table B-4.

TABLE B-4-5. COLOMBIA: Natural Resources Base, circa 1960
(Size of reserves or resources in use, and shares of world totals)

I. Minerals

Product and Classification	Year	Unit	Size of Resource	Share of World Total (%)	Lifetime (years) at 1962-64 Rate of Production	Ratio to World Lifetime
Iron ore: iron content of	1962	mill. m.t.				
explored reserves			24	0.1	35	0.64
potential resources			24	0.1	35	0.45
total resources			48	0.1	69	0.52
Petroleum: proved reserves of crude oil	1965	thous. m^3	190,800	0.4	19.2	59
Coal: proven, probable and possible reserves of	1963	mill. m.t.				
all grades of coal			40,000	0.9	13,000	8.4
bituminous coal			40,000		13,000	
coking coal			500		160	

II. Agriculture: Crops

Product and Classification	Year	Area Planted (thous. ha.)	Share of World Total (%)	Share of Cultivated Area (%)	Share of Total Land Area (%)	Yield (kg/ha)	Ratio to World Average
Coffee: total	1960-65		7.8				
mild Arabicas		810	25.4	16	0.71	567	1.4
Brazils							
Cocoa: all types	1956-57	51	1.5	1.05	0.045	300	0.9
Sugar (area harvested)	1958-60						
total			0.4				
cane		39	0.7	0.79	0.034	7,500	1.4
beet							
Bananas: all types	1963-64	50		1.02	0.027	27,000	
Wheat: all types	1962-64	133	0.1	2.7	0.12	1,123	0.81
Cotton: all lengths of fiber	1964/65	150	0.5	3.07	0.13	440	1.80

III. Miscellaneous Products

	Year	Pasture Area				Stock (thous. head)	Share of World Total (%)
Beef Cattle	1960-64	14,606	0.6		12.8	15,800	1.5

	Year	Total Area		Growing Stock (mill. m^3)		Removals (m^3/ha)	Ratio to World Average
Forest: all types	1960-62	69,400	1.8	11,800	64	0.4	6.8

For notes and sources, see chapter 3, table B-4.

TABLE B-4-6. COSTA RICA: Natural Resource Base, circa 1960
(Size of reserves or resources in use, and shares of world totals)

I. Minerals (see note)
II. Agriculture: Crops

Product and Classification	Year	Area Planted (thous. ha.)	Share of World Total (%)	Share of Cultivated Area (%)	Share of Total Land Area (%)	Yield (kg/ha)	Ratio to World Average
Coffee: total	1960-65		1.0				
mild Arabicas		83	3.2	14	1.67	990	2.5
Brazils							
Cocoa: all types	1960	20	0.6	7.09	0.39	535-670	1.7-2.1
Bananas: all types	1963-64	16		5.65	0.31	27,000	
Wheat: all types	1962-64						
Cotton: all lengths of fiber	1964/65	5		1.82	0.10	607	1.80

III. Miscellaneous Products

	Year	Pasture Area				Stock (thous. head)	Share of World Total (%)
Beef Cattle	1955-64	722			14.2	1,117	0.1

	Year	Total Area		Growing Stock (mill. m^3)		Removals (m^3/ha)	Ratio to World Average
Forest: all types	1960-62	2,981	0.1	660	61	0.6	1.2

Note: Minerals are negligible. For other notes and sources, see chapter 3, table B-4.

TABLE B-4-7. CUBA: Natural Resource Base, circa 1960
(Size of reserves or resources in use, and shares of world totals)

I. Minerals Product and Classification	Year	Unit	Size of Resource	Share of World Total (%)	Lifetime (years) at 1962-64 Rate of Production	Ratio to World Lifetime
Petroleum: proved reserves of crude oil	1965	thous. m^3	80		1.9	0.06

II. Agriculture: Crops Product and Classification	Year	Area Planted (thous. ha.)	Share of World Total (%)	Share of Cultivated Area (%)	Share of Total Land Area (%)	Yield (kg/ha)	Ratio to World Average
Coffee: total mild Arabicas Brazils	1960-65	 132	1.3 4.2	1.5	1.09	329	0.8
Cocoa: all types	1963-64	4	0.1	0.044	0.033		
Sugar (area harvested) total cane beet	1958-60	 1,090	 9.9 21	12	9.00	5.5	1.0

III. Miscellaneous Products		Pasture Area				Stock (thous. head)	Share of World Total (%)
Beef Cattle	1962					4,523	0.4

		Total Area		Growing Stock (mill. m^3)		Removals (m^3/ha)	Ratio to World Average
Forest: all types	1960-62	2,530	0.1		22	0.6	1.2

For notes and sources, see chapter 3, table B-4.

TABLE B-4-8. DOMINICAN REPUBLIC: Natural Resource Base, circa 1960
(Size of reserves or resources in use, and shares of world totals)

I. Minerals (see note) II. Agriculture: Crops Product and Classification	Year	Area Planted (thous. ha.)	Share of World Total (%)	Share of Cultivated Area (%)	Share of Total Land Area (%)	Yield (kg/ha)	Ratio to World Average
Coffee: total mild Arabicas Brazils	1960-65	 135	0.8 2.7	20	2.76	413	1.0
Cocoa: all types	1960	76	2.2	11	1.56	434-526	1.4-1.6
Sugar (area harvested) total cane beet	1958-60	 149	 1.4 2.8	22	3.06	6,500	1.2
Bananas: all types	1963-64	24		3.5	0.49	19,000	

III. Miscellaneous Products		Pasture Area				Stock (thous. head)	Share of World Total (%)
Beef Cattle	1950-63	879			18.0	850	0.1

		Total Area		Growing Stock (mill. m^3)		Removals (m^3/ha)	Ratio to World Average
Forest: all types	1960-62	2,225	0.1		45	0.9	1.8

Note: Minerals are negligible. For other notes and sources, see chapter 3, table B-4.

TABLE B–4–9. ECUADOR: Natural Resource Base, circa 1960
(Size of reserves or resources in use, and shares of world totals)

I. Minerals Product and Classification	Year	Unit	Size of Resource	Share of World Total (%)	Lifetime (years) at 1962-64 Rate of Production	Ratio to World Lifetime
Petroleum: proved reserves of crude oil	1965	thous. m³	3,980		8.9	0.27
Coal: proven, probable and possible reserves of all grades of coal	1963	mill. m.t.	25			

II. Agriculture: Crops Product and Classification	Year	Area Planted (thous. ha.)	Share of World Total (%)	Share of Cultivated Area (%)	Share of Total Land Area (%)	Yield (kg/ha)	Ratio to World Average
Coffee: total	1960-65		1.5				
mild Arabicas		150	5.0	7	0.56	343	0.9
Brazils							
Cocoa: all types	1963-64	163	4.8	7.6	0.60	210	0.65
Sugar (area harvested)	1958-60						
total			0.2				
cane		17	0.3	0.8	0.063	5,400	1.0
beet							
Bananas: all types	1963-64	169		7.9	0.63	20,000	
Wheat: all types	1962-64	76		3.5	0.28	960	0.69
Cotton: all lengths of fiber	1964/65	22	0.1	1.1	0.081	275	0.81

III. Miscellaneous Products	Year	Pasture Area				Stock (thous. head)	Share of World Total (%)
Beef Cattle	1954-64	1,775	0.1		6.5	1,710	0.2

	Year	Total Area		Growing Stock (mill. m³)		Removals (m³/ha)	Ratio to World Average
Forest: all types	1960-62	34,711	0.9	2,460	78	0.07	0.14

For notes and sources, see chapter 3, table B–4.

TABLE B–4–10. EL SALVADOR: Natural Resource Base, circa 1960
(Size of reserves or resources in use, and shares of world totals)

I. Minerals (see note) II. Agriculture: Crops Product and Classification	Year	Area Planted (thous. ha.)	Share of World Total (%)	Share of Cultivated Area (%)	Share of Total Land Area (%)	Yield (kg/ha)	Ratio to World Average
Coffee: total	1960-65		1.4				
mild Arabicas		147	4.5	22	7.10	773	2.0
Brazils							
Sugar (area harvested)	1958-60						
total			0.1				
cane		7	0.1	1.3	0.35	6,700	1.3
beet							
Cotton: all lengths of fiber	1964/65	111	0.3	20	0.92	718	2.12

III. Miscellaneous Products	Year	Pasture Area				Stock (thous. head)	Share of World Total (%)
Beef Cattle	1961-64	605			29.8	920	0.1

	Year	Total Area		Growing Stock (mill. m³)		Removals (m³/ha)	Ratio to World Average
Forest: all types	1960-62	226			11	13.0	26.0

Note: Minerals are negligible. For other notes and sources, see chapter 3, table B–4.

TABLE B-4-11. GUATEMALA: Natural Resource Base, circa 1960
(Size of reserves or resources in use, and shares of world totals)

I. Minerals (see note) II. Agriculture: Crops Product and Classification	Year	Area Planted (thous. ha.)	Share of World Total (%)	Share of Cultivated Area (%)	Share of Total Land Area (%)	Yield (kg/ha)	Ratio to World Average
Coffee: total mild Arabicas Brazils	1960-65	187	1.8 5.7	12	1.72	574	1.5
Cocoa: all types	1963-64	2		0.1	0.018		
Bananas: all types	1963-64	16		1.1	0.15	9,000	
Wheat: all types	1962-64	34		2.3	0.31	600	0.4
Cotton: all lengths of fiber	1964/65	100	0.3	6.8	0.92	718	2.12

III. Miscellaneous Products		Pasture Area				Stock (thous. head)	Share of World Total (%)
Beef Cattle	1958-64	575			5.3	1,500	0.1

		Total Area		Growing Stock (mill. m^3)		Removals (m^3/ha)	Ratio to World Average
Forest: all types	1960-62	4,100	0.1	820	38	1.2	2.4

Note: Minerals are negligible. For other notes and sources, see chapter 3, table B-4.

TABLE B-4-12. HAITI: Natural Resource Base, circa 1960
(Size of reserves or resources in use, and shares of world totals)

I. Minerals (see note) II. Agriculture: Crops Product and Classification	Year	Area Planted (thous. ha.)	Share of World Total (%)	Share of Cultivated Area (%)	Share of Total Land Area (%)	Yield (kg/ha)	Ratio to World Average
Coffee: total mild Arabicas Brazils	1960-65	182	1.8 5.7	15	6.57	231	0.6
Cocoa: all types	1964	8	0.2	0.7	0.29	250-300	0.8−0.9

III. Miscellaneous Products		Pasture Area				Stock (thous. head)	Share of World Total (%)
Beef Cattle	1950	500			18.0		

		Total Area		Growing Stock (mill. m^3)		Removals (m^3/ha)	Ratio to World Average
Forest: all types	1960-62	700		118	26	11.8	23.6

Note: Minerals are negligible. For other notes and sources, see chapter 3, table B-4.

TABLE B-4-13. HONDURAS: Natural Resource Base, circa 1960
(Size of reserves or resources in use, and shares of world totals)

I. Minerals (see note) II. Agriculture: Crops Product and Classification	Year	Area Planted (thous. ha.)	Share of World Total (%)	Share of Cultivated Area (%)	Share of Total Land Area (%)	Yield (kg/ha)	Ratio to World Average
Coffee: total mild Arabicas Brazils	1960-65	106	1.1 3.6	12	1.03	210	0.5
Cocoa: all types	1961-62	0.2		0.02	0.002		
Bananas: all types	1963-64	68		6.9	0.61	29,000	
Wheat: all types	1962-64	2		0.2	0.018	500	0.4
Cotton: all lengths of fiber	1964/65	14		1.4	0.12	778	2.3

III. Miscellaneous Products		Pasture Area				Stock (thous. head)	Share of World Total (%)
Beef Cattle	1955-64	2,000	0.1		17.8	1,641	0.2

		Total Area		Growing Stock (mill. m^3)		Removals (m^3/ha)	Ratio to World Average
Forest: all types	1960-62	5,975	0.2	1,035	53	0.5	1.0

Note: Minerals are negligible. For other notes and sources, see chapter 3, table B-4.

TABLE B-4-14. MEXICO: Natural Resource Base, circa 1960
(Size of reserves or resources in use, and shares of world totals)

I. Minerals Product and Classification	Year	Unit	Size of Resource	Share of World Total (%)	Lifetime (years) at 1962-64 Rate of Production	Ratio to World Lifetime
Copper: metal content of reserves	1965	mill. m.t.	800	0.4	15	0.36
Iron ore: iron content of	1962	mill. m.t.				
explored reserves			60	0.2	28	0.52
potential resources			90	0.2	43	0.54
total resources			150	0.2	71	0.53
Lead: metal content of measured and indicated reserves	1963	thous. m.t.	3,500	7.0	19	0.95
Zinc: metal content of measured and indicated reserves	1962	thous. m.t.	4,000	4.7	16	0.71
Tin: metal content of measured, indicated and inferred reserves	1965	thous. m.t.	28	0.6	30	0.86
Petroleum: proved reserves of crude oil	1965	thous. m^3	445,200	0.8	24.2	0.74
Coal: proven, probable and possible reserves of	1963	mill. m.t.				
all grades of coal			15,117	0.3	7,450	4.8
bituminous coal			15,000		7,400	
coking coal			2,600		1,280	

II. Agriculture: Crops Product and Classification	Year	Area Planted (thous. ha.)	Share of World Total (%)	Share of Cultivated Area (%)	Share of Total Land Area (%)	Yield (kg/ha)	Ratio to World Average
Coffee: total	1960-65		2.8				
mild Arabicas		285	9.0	1.4	0.14	501	1.3
Brazils							
Cocoa: all types	1963-64	68	2.0	0.4	0.035	412-441	1.3-1.4
Sugar (area harvested)	1958-60						
total			2.3				
cane		254	4.8	1.3	0.13	5,400	1.0
beet							
Bananas: all types	1963-64	28		0.1	0.014	13,000	
Wheat: all types	1962-64	862	0.4	4.2	0.41	2,219	1.58
Cotton: all lengths of fiber	1964/65	784	2.4	4.1	0.40	662	1.96

III. Miscellaneous Products		Pasture Area				Stock (thous. head)	Share of World Total (%)
Beef Cattle	1950-64	75,156	2.9		38.1	21,638	2.0

		Total Area		Growing Stock (mill. m^3)		Removals (m^3/ha)	Ratio to World Average
Forest: all types	1960-62	39,747	1.0	4,900	20	0.3	0.6

For notes and sources, see chapter 3, table B-4.

TABLE B-4-15. NICARAGUA: Natural Resource Base, circa 1960
(Size of reserves or resources in use, and shares of world totals)

I. Minerals (see note) II. Agriculture: Crops Product and Classification	Year	Area Planted (thous. ha.)	Share of World Total (%)	Share of Cultivated Area (%)	Share of Total Land Area (%)	Yield (kg/ha)	Ratio to World Average
Coffee: total	1960-65		0.9				
mild Arabicas		110	2.8	10	0.61	280	0.7
Brazils							
Cocoa: all types	1963-64	1		0.1	0.007		
Cotton: all lengths of fiber	1964/65	134	0.4	15	0.91	920	2.72

III. Miscellaneous Products		Pasture Area				Stock (thous. head)	Share of World Total (%)
Beef Cattle	1959-64	475			3.2	1,510	0.1

		Total Area		Growing Stock (mill. m³)		Removals (m³/ha)	Ratio to World Average
Forest: all types	1960-62	6,450	0.2	1,020	47	0.4	0.8

Note: Minerals are negligible. For other notes and sources, see chapter 3, table B-4.

TABLE B-4-16. PANAMA: Natural Resource Base, circa 1960
(Size of reserves or resources in use, and shares of world totals)

I. Minerals (see note) II. Agriculture: Crops Product and Classification	Year	Area Planted (thous. ha.)	Share of World Total (%)	Share of Cultivated Area (%)	Share of Total Land Area (%)	Yield (kg/ha)	Ratio to World Average
Coffee: total	1960-65		0.2				
mild Arabicas		27	0.7	7	0.31	209	0.5
Brazils							
Cocoa: all types	1955	4	0.1	1.0	0.054	450	1.4
Bananas: all types	1963-64	28		9	0.38	17,000	

III. Miscellaneous Products		Pasture Area				Stock (thous. head)	Share of World Total (%)
Beef Cattle	1961	818			10.8		

		Total Area		Growing Stock (mill. m³)		Removals (m³/ha)	Ratio to World Average
Forest: all types	1960-62	4,500	0.1	1,000	60	0.3	0.6

Note: Minerals are negligible. For other notes and sources, see chapter 3, table B-4.

TABLE B-4-17. PARAGUAY: Natural Resource Base, circa 1960
(Size of reserves or resources in use, and shares of world totals)

I. Minerals (see note) II. Agriculture: Crops Product and Classification	Year	Area Planted (thous. ha.)	Share of World Total (%)	Share of Cultivated Area (%)	Share of Total Land Area (%)	Yield (kg/ha)	Ratio to World Average
Coffee: total	1960-65		0.1				
mild Arabicas		10	0.3	1.9	0.025	240	0.6
Brazils							
Sugar (area harvested)	1958-60						
total			0.1				
cane		14	0.3	2.6	0.034	2,400	0.5
beet							
Wheat: all types	1962-64	10		1.9	0.025	1,000	0.7
Cotton: all lengths of fiber	1964/65	71	0.2	13	0.17	200	0.59

III. Miscellaneous Products		Pasture Area				Stock (thous. head)	Share of World Total (%)
Beef Cattle	1954-61	690			1.7	3,690	0.3

		Total Area		Growing Stock (mill. m³)		Removals (m³/ha)	Ratio to World Average
Forest: all types	1960-62	20,906	0.6	1,940	54	0.08	0.16

Note: Minerals are negligible. For other notes and sources, see chapter 3, table B-4.

TABLE B-4-18. PERU: Natural Resource Base, circa 1960
(Size of reserves or resources in use, and shares of world totals)

I. Minerals Product and Classification	Year	Unit	Size of Resource	Share of World Total (%)	Lifetime (years) at 1962-64 Rate of Production	Ratio to World Lifetime
Copper: metal content of reserves	1965	mill. m.t.	11,000	5.9	67	1.60
Iron ore: iron content of	1962	mill. m.t.				
explored reserves			301	1.0	48	0.88
potential resources			31	0.1	5	0.06
total resources			332	0.5	53	0.40
Lead: metal content of measured and indicated reserves	1963	thous. m.t.	3,000	6.0	21	1.1
Zinc: metal content of measured and indicated reserves	1962	thous. m.t.	6,000	7.1	31	1.4
Petroleum: proved reserves of crude oil	1965	thous. m^3	67,600	0.1	18.4	0.56
Coal: proven, probable and possible reserves of	1963	mill. m.t.				
all grades of coal			6,000	0.1	40,800	26.3
bituminous coal			100		680	
coking coal			100		680	

II. Agriculture: Crops Product and Classification	Year	Area Planted (thous. ha.)	Share of World Total (%)	Share of Cultivated Area (%)	Share of Total Land Area (%)	Yield (kg/ha)	Ratio to World Average
Coffee: total	1960-65		0.9				
mild Arabicas		123	3.0	6	0.077	439	1.1
Brazils							
Cocoa: all types	1964	15	0.4	0.9	0.012	280-333	0.9-1.0
Sugar (area harvested)	1958-60						
total			0.4				
cane		42	0.8	2.4	0.034	9,800	1.9
beet							
Cotton: all lengths of fiber	1964/65	260	0.8	4.1	0.057	513	1.52

III. Miscellaneous Products	Year	Pasture Area	Share of World Total		Share of Total Land Area	Stock (thous. head)	Share of World Total (%)
Beef Cattle	1961-64	9,522	0.4		7.4	3,466	0.3
		Total Area		Growing Stock (mill. m^3)		Removals (m^3/ha)	Ratio to World Average
Forest: all types	1960-62	56,300	1.7	11,100	51	0.03	0.06

For notes and sources, see chapter 3, table B-4.

TABLE B-4-19. URUGUAY: Natural Resource Base, circa 1960
(Size of reserves or resources in use, and shares of world totals)

I. Minerals (see note) II. Agriculture: Crops Product and Classification	Year	Area Planted (thous. ha.)	Share of World Total (%)	Share of Cultivated Area (%)	Share of Total Land Area (%)	Yield (kg/ha)	Ratio to World Average
Sugar (area harvested)	1958-60						
total		11	0.1	0.43	0.059	2,900	0.7
cane		2		0.08	0.011	4,000	0.8
beet		9	0.2	0.35	0.048	1,700	0.5
Wheat: all types	1962-64	427	0.2	16.7	2.129	1,042	0.75

III. Miscellaneous Products	Year	Pasture Area	Share of World Total		Share of Total Land Area	Stock (thous. head)	Share of World Total (%)
Beef Cattle	1961-64	14,457	0.6		77.3	8,719	0.8
		Total Area		Growing Stock (mill. m^3)		Removals (m^3/ha)	Ratio to World Average
Forest: all types	1960-62	593		98	3.2	2.1	4.2

Note: Minerals are negligible. For other notes and sources, see chapter 3, table B-4.

TABLE B-4-20. VENEZUELA: Natural Resource Base, circa 1960
(Size of reserves or resources in use, and shares of world totals)

I. Minerals Product and Classification	Year	Unit	Size of Resource	Share of World Total (%)	Lifetime (years) at 1962-64 Rate of Production	Ratio to World Lifetime
Iron ore: iron content of	1962	mill. m.t.				
explored reserves			623	2.1	46	0.84
potential resources			316	0.7	23	0.29
total resources			939	1.3	69	0.52
Petroleum: proved reserves of crude oil	1965	thous. m^3	2,700,000	5.0	13.7	0.42
Coal: proven, probable and possible reserves of all grades of coal	1963	mill. m.t.	350		9,700	6.3

II. Agriculture: Crops Product and Classification	Year	Area Planted (thous. ha.)	Share of World Total (%)	Share of Cultivated Area (%)	Share of Total Land Area (%)	Yield (kg/ha)	Ratio to World Average
Coffee: total	1960-65		2.9	11			
mild Arabicas		257	9.9		0.35	162	0.4
Brazils							
Cocoa: all types	1954-64	78	2.3	2.7	0.086	194-205	0.6
Sugar (area harvested)	1958-60						
total			0.4				
cane		45	0.9	1.5	0.049	3,800	0.7
beet							
Bananas: all types	1963-64	68		2.3	0.075	21,000	
Wheat: all types	1962-64	1		0.03	0.001	1,000	0.7
Cotton: all lengths of fiber	1964/65	45		1.5	0.049	316	0.94

III. Miscellaneous Products		Pasture Area				Stock (thous. head)	Share of World Total (%)
Beef Cattle	1961-63	16,706	0.7		18.6	10,000	0.9
		Total Area		Growing Stock (mill. m^3)		Removals (m3/ha)	Ratio to World Average
Forest: all types	1960-62	47,970	1.3	5,630	53	0.1	0.2

For notes and sources, see chapter 3, table B-4.

TABLE B–5–1. ARGENTINA: Imports, Production, Exports, and Consumption of Natural Resource Commodities in Different Stages of Processing, circa 1963-1967

Commodity and Product Description	Year	Unit	Imports	Production	Exports	Actual or Apparent Consumption
Copper	1966	metric				
content of ore		tons		337	267	
unrefined metal						
refined metal			} 18,499			
semimanufactures					14	
other forms						
total			18,499	337	281	18,485
Iron and Steel	1963	metric				
ore, gross weight		tons	757,000	94,000		851,000
pig iron and ferroalloys			9,734	424,000	2	433,732
crude steel			82,449	913,000	70	995,379
semimanufactures			405,389	759,000	114,564	1,049,825
total iron content			952,000	45,000	115,000	1,286,000
total rolled steel, ingot equivalent			547,000	1,263,000	152,000	1,658,000
Lead	1965	metric				
content of ore		tons		42,536	153	
metal				32,236	11	
semimanufactures						
total			3,000	42,536	164	35,225
Zinc	1965	metric				
content of ore		tons		59,172	2,671	
metal				29,679	148	
semimanufactures						
total			2,566	59,172	2,819	32,097
Tin	1963	long				
content of ore		tons		498	227	
tin metal			1,189			1,189
tinplate, gross weight			92,920			92,920
tin content of tin plate			733			733
total contained tin			1,922			1,922
Petroleum	1964	thous.				
crude oil		cubic	1,699	15,959	18	
refined products		meters	1,648	17,291	512	20,217
gasoline			39	3,676	26	3,890
kerosene			20	1,458		1,478
distillate fuel oils			1,246	2,844		4,106
residual fuel oil			58	6,399	482	7,438
lubricants			95	149		242
Coal	1965	thous.				
coal, all grades		m.t.	657	374		1,031
hard coke: actual			82	461		543
coal equivalent			117	659		776
soft coke				0		
Coffee	1965/66	thous.				
unroasted beans		m.t.	32.9			32.9

TABLE B–5–1 – Continued

Commodity and Product Description	Year	Unit	Imports	Production	Exports	Actual or Apparent Consumption
Cocoa	1966	metric tons				
beans			11,351			11,000
butter						
powder			394			
chocolate and products					19	
Sugar	1967	metric tons				
centrifugal, raw value				731,975	65,105	829,233
Bananas	1966	thous. m.t.				
edible, fresh			173	130		303
Wheat	1964-66	thous. m.t.				
grain				7,636	1,873	5,463
flour				2,248		
Beef and Veal	1966	thous. head				
live cattle			2		119	
meat		m.t.		2,387	634	1,753
Cotton	1964	thous. m.t.				
raw cotton (fiber)			13.8	138	23.6	112
cotton yarn			0.1	86.6		88.5
Forest Products	1964-66	(d)				
fuelwood		(*)		8,864		8,864
industrial wood		(*)	3,515	2,194		5,709
roundwood		(*)	270			
sawnwood		(†)	724	847		1,671
sheet materials		(†)		31		31
fiberboard		(‡)		18		18
wood pulp		(‡)	262	83		345
pulp products		(‡)	210	450		660

Fishery Products, 1964 *(thousands of metric tons)*

Disposition of Catch	Liveweight	Type	Net Weight			
			Production	Imports	Exports	Apparent Consumption
Total Catch	158.3	All uses	54.5	4.8	3.4	66.6
marketed fresh	52.5	fish fillets	16.6	} 1.6	} 0.8	26.3
frozen	45.3	fish	7.6			8.4
		crustaceans	0.3			0.3
cured	6.4	fish	2.7	1.5		4.2
canned	23.8	fish	13.6	0.2	0.1	13.7
		molluscs	0.5			0.5
reduced	30.3	white fishmeal	10.6			} 11.5
		oily fishmeal	1.2	1.5	1.8	
		fish oil	1.5		0.7	0.8
offal for reduction	(31.4)					
miscellaneous		molluscs	0.9			0.9

For notes and sources, see chapter 3, table B–5.

TABLE B-5-2. BOLIVIA: Imports, Production, Exports, and Consumption of Natural Resource Commodities in Different Stages of Processing, circa 1963-1967

Commodity and Product Description	Year	Unit	Imports	Production	Exports	Actual or Apparent Consumption
Copper	1966	metric tons				
content of ore				5,827	5,702	
unrefined metal						
refined metal			} 367			
semimanufactures						
other forms						
total			367	5,827	5,702	367
Iron and Steel	1963	metric tons				
ore, gross weight						
pig iron and ferroalloys						
crude steel						
semimanufactures						
total iron content			29,000			29,000
total rolled steel, ingot equivalent			33,000			33,000
Lead	1965	metric tons				
content of ore				16,313	15,873	
metal				936	1,664	
semimanufactures						
total			19	16,313	17,537	19
Zinc	1965	metric tons				
content of ore				13,607	13,688	
metal						
semimanufactures						
total			25	13,607	13,688	25
Tin	1963	long tons				
content of ore				22,246	20,290	
tin metal				2,462	2,448	
tinplate, gross weight			49			49
tin content of tinplate			1			1
total contained tin			1	2,462	2,448	1
Petroleum	1964	thous. cubic meters				
crude oil				508	49	
refined products			25	470		457
gasoline			17	179		181
kerosene				74		71
distillate fuel oils				71		71
residual fuel oil				126		107
lubricants			3			3
Cocoa	1966	metric tons				
beans				2,500		2,500
butter						
powder						
chocolate and products						
Sugar	1967	metric tons				
centrifugal, raw value				101,905	8,861	93,511
Bananas	1966	thous. m.t.				
edible, fresh					1	
Wheat	1964-66	thous. m.t.				
grain			27	73		
flour			125			
Beef and Veal	1966	thous.				
live cattle		head	12			
meat		m.t.		25		25
Cotton	1964	thous. m.t.				
raw cotton (fiber)			1.5			3
cotton yarn				1.6		1.6
Forest Products	1964-66	(d)				
fuelwood		(*)		4,450		4,450
industrial wood		(*)		325		325
roundwood		(*)	0.3			
sawnwood		(†)		43		43
sheet materials		(†)		1.3		1.3
fiberboard		(‡)				
wood pulp		(‡)				
pulp products		(‡)	3.5	0.8		4.3

For notes and sources, see chapter 3, table B-5.

TABLE B–5–3. BRAZIL: Imports, Production, Exports, and Consumption of Natural Resource Commodities in Different Stages of Processing, circa 1963-1967

Commodity and Product Description	Year	Unit	Imports	Production	Exports	Actual or Apparent Consumption
Copper	1966	metric tons				
content of ore				2,150		
unrefined metal				3,000		
refined metal			43,203	3,000		
semimanufactures			494			
other forms			3,400			
total			47,907	2,150		50,907
Iron and Steel	1963	metric tons				
ore, gross weight				11,219,000	8,268,000	2,951,000
pig iron and ferroalloys			2,411	2,761,000	47,267	2,716,144
crude steel				2,812,000	166	2,811,834
semimanufactures			397,746	2,204,000	6,475	2,595,271
total iron content			400,000	7,629,000	5,676,000	3,203,000
total rolled steel, ingot equivalent			751,000	3,088,000	1,000	3,838,000
Lead	1965	metric tons				
content of ore				22,500	12,925	
metal			2,171	9,665		
semimanufactures						
total			2,207	22,500	12,925	11,872
Zinc	1965	metric tons				
content of ore				5,250	522	
metal			31,574	75		
semimanufactures			443			
total			38,400	5,250	522	38,475
Tin	1963	long tons				
content of ore			2,084	1,153		
tin metal			1	2,051		2,052
tinplate, gross weight			63,317	158,492		221,809
tin content of tinplate			504	1,218		1,722
total contained tin			505	2,051		2,556
Petroleum	1964	thous. cubic meters				
crude oil			12,686	5,296		
refined products			1,500	18,071	185	19,386
gasoline			405	5,809		6,215
kerosene			317	728		1,044
distillate fuel oils				3,802	145	3,657
residual fuel oil				6,247	39	6,208
lubricants			303	1		304
Coal	1965	thous. m.t.				
coal, all grades			1,047	3,383		4,430
hard coke: actual			125	909		1,034
coal equivalent			198	1,436		1,634
soft coke				219		
Coffee	1965/66	thous. m.t.				
unroasted beans				1,598.7	915.9	682.8

TABLE B–5–3 – Continued

Commodity and Product Description	Year	Unit	Imports	Production	Exports	Actual or Apparent Consumption
Cocoa	1966	metric				
beans		tons		171,000	112,498	61,000
butter					21,016	
powder					1,665	
chocolate and products					5,744	
Sugar	1967	metric				
centrifugal, raw value		tons		4,275,057	1,000,747	2,899,235
Bananas	1966	thous.				
edible, fresh		m.t.		4,626	204	4,422
Wheat	1964-66	thous.				
grain		m.t.	2,240	247		2,487
flour			18	1,599		1,617
Beef and Veal	1966	thous.				
live cattle		head	4		3	
meat		m.t.		1,432	43	1,389
Cotton	1964	thous.				
raw cotton (fiber)		m.t.		450	226.4	266
cotton yarn				110.1	0.9	109
Forest Products	1964-66	(d)				
fuelwood		(*)		119,000		119,000
industrial wood		(*)	5.6	9,610	11	9,604.6
roundwood		(*)	3		37	
sawnwood		(†)		5,802	1,157	4,645
sheet materials		(†)		215	8	207
fiberboard		(‡)		69		69
wood pulp		(‡)	23	653	15	661
pulp products		(‡)	68	665		733

Fishery Products, 1964 *(thousands of metric tons)*

Disposition of Catch	Liveweight	Type	Net Weight			
			Production	Imports	Exports	Apparent Consumption
Total Catch	330.8	All uses	90.7	26.3	1.8	230.6
marketed fresh	230.8					115.4
frozen	15.7	fish	11.5	} 1.0	} 0.1	12.5
		shellfish	2.6		1.7	0.9
cured	54.0	fish	46.8	20.7		67.5
		shellfish	5.7			5.7
canned	24.3	fish	22.6	0.1		22.7
		shellfish	0.1			0.1
reduced	6.0	oily fishmeal	0.9	3.6		4.5
		fish oil	0.3	0.9		1.2
		other	0.2			0.2

For notes and sources, see chapter 3, table B–5.

TABLE B–5–4. CHILE: Imports, Production, Exports, and Consumption of Natural Resource Commodities in Different Stages of Processing, circa 1963-1967

Commodity and Product Description	Year	Unit	Imports	Production	Exports	Actual or Apparent Consumption
Copper	1966	metric tons				
content of ore				663,670	29,253	
unrefined metal				624,595	239,212	
refined metal				356,889	323,329	
semimanufactures			551		29,278	
other forms					1,113	
total			551	663,670	622,185	2,618
Iron and Steel	1963	metric tons				
ore, gross weight				8,507,000	7,092,000	1,415,000
pig iron and ferroalloys			272	435,000	11,081	424,191
crude steel			4,779	489,000		493,779
semimanufactures			14,851	376,000	30,088	360,763
total iron content			20,000	5,481,000	4,580,000	484,000
total rolled steel, ingot equivalent			106,000	622,000	41,000	687,000
Lead	1965	metric tons				
content of ore				783	707	
metal			1,784			
semimanufactures			86			
total			1,870	783	707	1,870
Zinc	1965	metric tons				
content of ore				1,383	153	
metal			6,495			
semimanufactures			265			
total			6,760	1,383	153	6,760
Tin	1963	long tons				
content of ore			612			612
tin metal			582		29,371	29,953
tinplate, gross weight			5		250	255
tin content of tinplate			617			617
total contained tin						
Petroleum	1964	thous. cubic meters				
crude oil			497	2,176		
refined products			947	2,758		3,705
gasoline			21	1,031		1,051
kerosene			56	304		359
distillate fuel oils			334	487		821
residual fuel oil			478	647		1,126
lubricants			43			43
Coal	1965	thous. m.t.				
coal, all grades			317	1,904		2,221
hard coke: actual			550	213		763
coal equivalent			814	315		1,129
soft coke				81		
Coffee	1965/66	thous. m.t.				
unroasted beans			8.2			8.2

TABLE B–5–4 – Continued

Commodity and Product Description	Year	Unit	Imports	Production	Exports	Actual or Apparent Consumption
Cocoa	1966	metric				
beans		tons	2,732			2,700
butter			254			
powder			3			
chocolate and products			58			
Sugar	1967	metric				
centrifugal, raw value		tons	187,848	124,151		328,335
Bananas	1966	thous.				
edible, fresh		m.t.	49			49
Wheat	1964-66	thous.				
grain		m.t.	271	1,224		1,495
flour			40	730		770
Beef and Veal	1966	thous.				
live cattle		head	70			
meat		m.t.	14	135		149
Cotton	1964	thous.				
raw cotton (fiber)		m.t.	32.5			28
cotton yarn			0.3	25.3		25.6
Forest Products	1964-66	(d)				
fuelwood		(*)		2,694		2,694
industrial wood		(*)	5.3	1,344		1,349.3
roundwood		(*)	6.6			
sawnwood		(†)	1.6	1,006	45	1,052.6
sheet materials		(†)		8.3		8.3
fiberboard		(‡)	0.4	13		13.4
wood pulp		(‡)	7	220	15	212
pulp products		(‡)	8.6	196	57	147.6

Fishery Products, 1964 *(thousands of metric tons)*

Disposition of Catch	Liveweight	Type	Net Weight Production	Imports	Exports	Apparent Consumption
Total Catch	1,161.3	All uses	203.2		162.5	86.5
marketed fresh	91.6					45.8
frozen	16.5	fish fillets	0.6		0.6	
		crustaceans	1.7		1.5	0.2
cured	1.4	fish	1.0		0.1	0.9
canned	38.7	fish	6.5			6.5
		crustaceans	0.2		} 0.2	} 1.5
		molluscs	1.5			
reduced	1,013.1	white fishmeal	8.3			8.3
		oily fishmeal	165.8		146.4	19.4
		fish oil	17.6		13.7	3.9

For notes and sources, see chapter 3, table B–5.

TABLE B-5-5. COLOMBIA: Imports, Production, Exports, and Consumption of Natural Resource Commodities in Different Stages of Processing, circa 1963-1967

Commodity and Product Description	Year	Unit	Imports	Production	Exports	Actual or Apparent Consumption
Copper	1966	metric tons				
content of ore						
unrefined metal						
refined metal			6,114			
semimanufactures			869			
other forms			47			
total			7,030			7,030
Iron and Steel	1963	metric tons				
ore, gross weight				695,000		695,000
pig iron and ferroalloys			9,025	203,000	33	211,992
crude steel			1,152	222,000		223,152
semimanufactures			169,314		9	
total iron content			179,000	334,000	0	392,000
total rolled steel, ingot equivalent			232,000	249,000		481,000
Lead	1965	metric tons				
content of ore				730	756	
metal			471		229	
semimanufactures			36			
total			1,148	730	985	919
Zinc	1965	metric tons				
content of ore				400		
metal						
semimanufactures						
total			2,585	400		2,585
Tin	1963	long tons				
content of ore						
tin metal			250			
tinplate, gross weight			32,522			
tin content of tinplate			227			
total contained tin			477			
Petroleum	1964	thous. cubic meters				
crude oil				9,953	4,883	
refined products			109	5,128	720	4,516
gasoline			54	1,884		1,939
kerosene				316		316
distillate fuel oils				658		658
residual fuel oil				1,390	719	671
lubricants			18	59	2	75
Coal	1965	thous. m.t.				
coal, all grades				3,100		3,100
hard coke: actual				470		470
coal equivalent				743		743
soft coke						
Coffee	1965/66	thous. m.t.				
unroasted beans				448.6	336	66

TABLE B-5-5 – Continued

Commodity and Product Description	Year	Unit	Imports	Production	Exports	Actual or Apparent Consumption
Cocoa	1966	metric tons				
beans			15,664	17,000		32,700
butter						
powder						
chocolate and products						
Sugar	1967	metric tons				
centrifugal, raw value				596,575	200,367	393,390
Bananas	1966	thous. m.t.				
edible, fresh					341	
Wheat	1964-66	thous. m.t.				
grain			195	116		311
flour			26	207		233
Beef and Veal	1966	thous. head				
live cattle					46	
meat		m.t.		415		415
Cotton	1964	thous. m.t.				
raw cotton (fiber)			2.0	66	10.6	63
cotton yarn				5.6	0.2	5.4
Forest Products	1964-66	(d)				
fuelwood		(*)		22,100		22,100
industrial wood		(*)	2	2,940	75	2,867
roundwood		(*)	1.6		75	
sawnwood		(†)	0.8	950	65	885.8
sheet materials		(†)		39		39
fiberboard		(‡)	0.3	12		12.3
wood pulp		(‡)	51	22		73
pulp products		(‡)	56	133		189

Fishery Products, 1964 *(thousands of metric tons)*

Disposition of Catch	Liveweight	Type	Net Weight			
			Production	Imports	Exports	Apparent Consumption
Total Catch	53.6	All uses	12.6		0.6	33.0
marketed fresh	41.9					21.0
frozen	3.0	fish	3.0			3.0
		shellfish	0.7		0.6	0.1
cured	7.7	fish	7.7			7.7
canned	1.0	fish	1.2			1.2

For notes and sources, see chapter 3, table B-5.

TABLE B-5-6. COSTA RICA: Imports, Production, Exports, and Consumption of Natural Resource Commodities in Different Stages of Processing, circa 1963-1967

Commodity and Product Description	Year	Unit	Imports	Production	Exports	Actual or Apparent Consumption
Copper	1966	metric tons				
content of ore						
unrefined metal						
refined metal						
semimanufactures			284			
other forms			26			
total			310			310
Iron and Steel	1963	metric tons				
ore, gross weight						
pig iron and ferroalloys			4			4
crude steel			6,664			6,664
semimanufactures			29,437			29,437
total iron content			36,105			
total rolled steel, ingot equivalent					10	36,095
Lead	1965	metric tons				
content of ore						
metal						
semimanufactures						
total			131		69	62
Zinc	1965	metric tons				
content of ore						
metal						
semimanufactures						
total			925		3	922
Petroleum	1964	thous. cubic meters				
crude oil						
refined products			280			280
gasoline			86			86
kerosene			16			16
distillate fuel oils			130			130
residual fuel oil			24			24
lubricants			12			12
Coffee	1965/66	thous. m.t.				
unroasted beans				67.2	50.8	9.9
Cocoa	1966	metric tons				
beans				7,000	7,743	1,374
butter					118	
powder					113	
chocolate and products					251	
Sugar	1967	metric tons				
centrifugal, raw value				145,000	62,500	66,250
Bananas	1966	thous. m.t.				
edible, fresh					358	
Wheat	1964-66	thous. m.t.				
grain			5			5
flour			60	4		
Beef and Veal	1966	thous. head				
live cattle					10	
meat		m.t.			7	
Cotton	1964	thous. m.t.				
raw cotton (fiber)				24	2.4	1
cotton yarn			0.3	1.1	0.5	1.4
Forest Products	1964-66	(d)				
fuelwood		(*)		1,608		1,608
industrial wood		(*)	12	501	3	510
roundwood		(*)				
sawnwood		(†)	3.9	311		314.9
sheet materials		(†)	0.3	9.1		9.4
fiberboard		(‡)				
wood pulp		(‡)				
pulp products		(‡)	41			41

For notes and sources, see chapter 3, table B-5.

TABLE B-5-7. CUBA: Imports, Production, Exports, and Consumption of Natural Resource Commodities in Different Stages of Processing, circa 1963-1967

Commodity and Product Description	Year	Unit	Imports	Production	Exports	Actual or Apparent Consumption
Copper	1966	metric tons		6,000	3,518	
content of ore						
unrefined metal						
refined metal			} 4,700			
semimanufactures						
other forms						
total			4,700	6,000	3,518	4,700
Iron and Steel	1963	metric tons				
ore, gross weight				650		650
pig iron and ferroalloys			20,600			
crude steel						
semimanufactures			103,800			
total iron content			124,400	300		124,700
total rolled steel, ingot equivalent						167,000
Lead	1965	metric tons				
content of ore						
metal						
semimanufactures						
total			700			700
Zinc	1965	metric tons				
content of ore						
metal						
semimanufactures						
total			200			200
Tin	1963	long tons				
content of ore						
tin metal			100			100
tinplate, gross weight			40,000			40,000
tin content of tinplate			320			320
total contained tin			420			420
Petroleum	1964	thous. cubic meters				
crude oil			4,005	42		
refined products			1,267	4,047		5,313
gasoline			185	938		1,123
kerosene				191		191
distillate fuel oils			228	731		959
residual fuel oil			796	1,892		2,688
lubricants			56			56
Coffee	1965/66	thous. m.t.				
unroasted beans				33.6	4.5	33.3
Cocoa	1966	metric tons				
beans				1,900		1,900
butter					10	
powder						
chocolate and products						
Sugar	1967	metric tons				
centrifugal, raw value				6,236,000	5,682,872	629,498
Wheat	1964-66	thous. m.t.				
grain			244			
flour			301	210		
Beef and Veal	1966	thous. head				
live cattle			2			
meat		m.t.		195		195
Cotton	1964	thous. m.t.				
raw cotton (fiber)			18.4	4		18
cotton yarn			2.0	12.5		14.5
Forest Products	1964-66	(d)				
fuelwood		(*)		1,533		1,533
industrial wood		(*)		795		795
roundwood		(*)	1.9			
sawnwood		(†)	197	131		328
sheet materials		(†)	10			
fiberboard		(‡)		16		16
wood pulp		(‡)	39			39
pulp products		(‡)	45	103		148

For notes and sources, see chapter 3, table B-5.

TABLE B–5–8. DOMINICAN REPUBLIC: Imports, Production, Exports, and Consumption of Natural Resource Commodities in Different Stages of Processing, circa 1963-1967

Commodity and Product Description	Year	Unit	Imports	Production	Exports	Actual or Apparent Consumption
Copper	1966	metric tons				
content of ore						
unrefined metal						
refined metal						
semimanufactures						
other forms						
total			717			717
Iron and Steel	1963	metric tons				
ore, gross weight						
pig iron and ferroalloys					641	
crude steel						
semimanufactures			59,824			59,824
total iron content			59,800		600	59,200
total rolled steel, ingot equivalent			57,000			57,000
Petroleum	1964	thous. cubic meters				
crude oil						
refined products			647			647
gasoline			212			212
kerosene			27			27
distillate fuel oils			76			76
residual fuel oil			288			288
lubricants			8			8
Coffee	1965/66	thous. m.t.				
unroasted beans				33.6	23.8	9.9
Cocoa	1966	metric tons				
beans				30,500	25,943	1,200
butter					73	
powder						
chocolate and products					927	
Sugar	1967	metric tons				
centrifugal, raw value				819,000	642,202	120,000
Wheat	1964-66	thous. m.t.				
grain			45			45
flour			10	18		28
Beef and Veal	1966	thous. head				
live cattle						
meat		m.t.		20		20
Cotton	1964	thous. m.t.				
raw cotton (fiber)						
cotton yarn			0.3	0.5		0.8
Forest Products	1964-66	(d)				
fuelwood		(*)		1,783		1,783
industrial wood		(*)		158	3	155
roundwood		(*)				
sawnwood		(†)		85		85
sheet materials		(†)				
fiberboard		(‡)				
wood pulp		(‡)				
pulp products		(‡)	17	2.2		19.2

For notes and sources, see chapter 3, table B–5.

TABLE B–5–9. ECUADOR: Imports, Production, Exports, and Consumption of Natural Resource Commodities in Different Stages of Processing, circa 1963-1967

Commodity and Product Description	Year	Unit	Imports	Production	Exports	Actual or Apparent Consumption
Copper	1966	metric tons				
content of ore				223		
unrefined metal						
refined metal						
semimanufactures						
other forms					2	
total			657	223	2	655
Iron and Steel	1963	metric tons				
ore, gross weight						
pig iron and ferroalloys				22	283	
crude steel						
semimanufactures			47,305			
total iron content			47,300		300	47,300
total rolled steel, ingot equivalent			65,000			65,000
Lead	1965	metric tons				
content of ore				114	707	
metal						
semimanufactures			275			
total			351	114	707	35
Zinc	1965	metric tons				
content of ore				236	562	
metal						
semimanufactures			78			
total			78	236	562	78
Petroleum	1964	thous. cubic meters				
crude oil			429	445	84	
refined products			41	774		815
gasoline			14	324		338
kerosene			11	76		87
distillate fuel oils				137		137
residual fuel oil				206		206
lubricants			9			9
Coffee	1965/66	thous. m.t.				
unroasted beans				70.3	44.8	23.3
Cocoa	1966	metric tons				
beans				36,000	32,208	8,000
butter						
powder						
chocolate and products						
Sugar	1967	metric tons				
centrifugal, raw value				293,700	68,843	115,000
Bananas	1966	thous. m.t.				
edible, fresh					1,265	
Wheat	1964-66	thous. m.t.				
grain			56	66	2	
flour						
Cotton	1964	thous. m.t.				
raw cotton (fiber)			1.3	3		6
cotton yarn			0.2	4.4		6.2
Forest Products	1964-66	(d)				
fuelwood		(*)		1,487		1,487
industrial wood		(*)		965	5	960
roundwood		(*)			4	
sawnwood		(†)		432	34	398
sheet materials		(†)	0.3	9		9.3
fiberboard		(‡)				
wood pulp		(‡)				
pulp products		(‡)	47	4		51

Fishery Products, 1964 *(thousands of metric tons)*

Disposition of Catch	Liveweight	Type	Net Weight			
			Production	Imports	Exports	Apparent Consumption
Total Catch	47.1	All uses	11.9	0.7	7.7	17.0
marketed fresh	24.1					12.1
frozen	8.6	fish	3.4	} 0.2	} 3.3	0.3
		crustaceans	2.5		2.5	
cured	0.4	fish	0.1			0.1
canned	9.5	herring	0.8	} 0.2	} 1.9	} 2.5
		tuna	3.4			
reduced	4.5	oily fishmeal	1.7	0.3		2.0
offal for reduction	(4.6)					

For notes and sources, see chapter 3, table B–5.

TABLE B–5–10. EL SALVADOR: Imports, Production, Exports, and Consumption of Natural Resource Commodities in Different Stages of Processing, circa 1963-1967

Commodity and Product Description	Year	Unit	Imports	Production	Exports	Actual or Apparent Consumption
Copper	1966	metric tons				
content of ore						
unrefined metal						
refined metal			} 1,737			
semimanufactures			4		86	
other forms					86	
total			1,741		86	1,655
Iron and Steel	1963	metric tons				
ore, gross weight				480	19	461
pig iron and ferroalloys				342	} 556	32,490
crude steel				32,204		
semimanufactures				33,026		32,470
total iron content						
total rolled steel, ingot equivalent						
Lead	1965	metric tons				
content of ore			47			
metal			227			
semimanufactures			274			274
total						
Zinc	1965	metric tons				
content of ore						
metal						
semimanufactures			57			57
total						
Petroleum	1964	thous. cubic meters				
crude oil			529			
refined products			75	576	242	416
gasoline			25	163	89	100
kerosene			27	38	22	44
distillate fuel oils			10	135	59	87
residual fuel oil				178	73	105
lubricants			4			
Coffee	1965/66	thous. m.t.				
unroasted beans				116.1	98.3	16.7
Cocoa	1966	metric tons				
beans			393			400
butter			11			
powder			41			
chocolate and products			284		43	
Sugar	1967	metric tons				
centrifugal, raw value				125,200	33,687	65,000
Wheat	1964-66	thous. m.t.				
grain			46		1	45
flour			4	36		40
Beef and Veal	1966	thous. head				
live cattle		m.t.	1		19	
meat				26		26
Cotton	1964	thous. m.t.				
raw cotton (fiber)				80	55.6	9
cotton yarn			0.3	3.7	1.0	4
Forest Products	1964-66	(d)				
fuelwood		(*)		2,555		2,555
industrial wood		(*)	5	55		60
roundwood		(*)	0.7			
sawnwood		(†)	74	6		80
sheet materials		(†)	4			4
fiberboard		(‡)	0.3			0.3
wood pulp		(‡)				
pulp products		(‡)	26			26

For notes and sources, see chapter 3, table B–5.

TABLE B–5–11. GUATEMALA: Imports, Production, Exports, and Consumption of Natural Resource Commodities in Different Stages of Processing, circa 1963-1967

Commodity and Product Description	Year	Unit	Imports	Production	Exports	Actual or Apparent Consumption
Copper	1966	metric tons				
content of ore						
unrefined metal						
refined metal			21			
semimanufactures			105			
other forms			8			
total			134			134
Iron and Steel	1963	metric tons				
ore, gross weight						
pig iron and ferroalloys				6,000		
crude steel			27,400			27,400
semimanufactures						
total iron content						
total rolled steel, ingot equivalent			27,400	3,000		27,400
Lead	1965	metric tons				
content of ore				923	30	
metal				114	76	
semimanufactures						
total			109	923	106	147
Zinc	1965	metric tons				
content of ore				867	867	
metal						
semimanufactures						
total			154	867	867	154
Petroleum	1964	thous. cubic meters				
crude oil			230			
refined products			760	186		946
gasoline			124	71		195
kerosene			56	12		68
distillate fuel oils			327	40		366
residual fuel oil			203	35		239
lubricants			11			11
Coffee	1965/66	thous. m.t.				
unroasted beans				111.6	101.2	13.2
Cocoa	1966	metric tons				
beans			4	500	474	300
butter						
powder						
chocolate and products						
Sugar	1967	metric tons				
centrifugal, raw value				170,858	55,920	107,370
Bananas	1966	thous. m.t.				
edible, fresh					77	
Wheat	1964-66	thous. m.t.				
grain			53	33		86
flour			2	59		61
Beef and Veal	1966	thous. head / m.t.				
live cattle		head	38			
meat		m.t.		33		33
Cotton	1964	thous. m.t.				
raw cotton (fiber)				72	65.5	7
cotton yarn			0.3	4.6		4.9
Forest Products	1964-66	(d)				
fuelwood		(*)		3,850		3,850
industrial wood		(*)	1	400		398
roundwood		(*)			5.8	
sawnwood		(†)	2.4	164	14	155.4
sheet materials		(†)	0.9	5	0.8	5.4
fiberboard		(‡)				
wood pulp		(‡)	5.5			5.5
pulp products		(‡)	20	6.5		26.5

For notes and sources, see chapter 3, table B–5.

TABLE B–5–12. HAITI: Imports, Production, Exports, and Consumption of Natural Resource Commodities in Different Stages of Processing, circa 1963-1967

Commodity and Product Description	Year	Unit	Imports	Production	Exports	Actual or Apparent Consumption
Copper	1966	metric tons				
content of ore				2,780	3,960	
unrefined metal						
refined metal						
semimanufactures			23			
other forms					127	
total			23	2,780	4,087	23
Iron and Steel	1963	metric tons				
ore, gross weight			1			
pig iron and ferroalloys			14			
crude steel			18			
semimanufactures			6,510			
total iron content			6,500			6,500
total rolled steel, ingot equivalent						
Petroleum	1964	thous. cubic meters				
crude oil						
refined products			132			132
gasoline			38			38
kerosene			2			2
distillate fuel oils			58			58
residual fuel oil			31			31
lubricants			3			3
Coffee	1965/66	thous. m.t.				
unroasted beans				31.2	22.5	9.7
Cocoa	1966	metric tons				
beans				3,000	443	2,557
butter						
powder						
chocolate and products					1,129	
Sugar	1967	metric tons				
centrifugal, raw value				65,000	25,881	41,000
Bananas	1966	thous. m.t.				
edible, fresh					1	
Wheat	1964-66	thous. m.t.				
grain			53			53
flour			3	35		
Cotton	1964	thous. m.t.				
raw cotton (fiber)						1
cotton yarn			0.4	2.3		2.7
Forest Products	1964-66	(d)				
fuelwood		(*)		9,850		9,850
industrial wood		(*)	26	130		156
roundwood		(*)				
sawnwood		(†)	1.8	14		15.8
sheet materials		(†)				
fiberboard		(‡)				
wood pulp		(‡)				
pulp products		(‡)	1.5			1.5

For notes and sources, see chapter 3, table B–5.

TABLE B–5–13. HONDURAS: Imports, Production, Exports, and Consumption of Natural Resource Commodities in Different Stages of Processing, circa 1963-1967

Commodity and Product Description	Year	Unit	Imports	Production	Exports	Actual or Apparent Consumption
Copper	1966	metric tons				
content of ore						
unrefined metal						
refined metal			} 34			
semimanufactures						
other forms			46			
total			80			80
Iron and Steel	1963	metric tons				
ore, gross weight						
pig iron and ferroalloys			8	329		321
crude steel			965			965
semimanufactures			12,957			
total iron content			13,930		329	13,930
total rolled steel, ingot equivalent						
Lead	1965	metric tons				
content of ore				9,654	10,506	
metal						
semimanufactures						
total			57	9,654	10,506	57
Zinc	1965	metric tons				
content of ore				11,126	10,991	
metal						
semimanufactures						
total			26	11,126	10,991	26
Petroleum	1964	thous. cubic meters				
crude oil						
refined products			253			253
gasoline			65			65
kerosene			19			19
distillate fuel oils			101			101
residual fuel oil			60			60
lubricants			4			4
Coffee	1965/66	thous. m.t.				
unroasted beans				27.7	23.8	5.8
Cocoa	1966	metric tons				
beans			6	200	46	148
butter						
powder			106			
chocolate and products						
Sugar	1967	metric tons				
centrifugal, raw value				44,453	9,933	36,288
Bananas	1966	thous. m.t.				
edible, fresh					710	
Wheat	1964-66	thous. m.t.				
grain			23	1		24
flour			4	18		22
Beef and Veal	1966	thous. head				
live cattle					32	
meat		m.t.		18		18
Cotton	1964	thous. m.t.				
raw cotton (fiber)				11	10.2	
cotton yarn			0.2	0.5		0.7
Forest Products	1964-66	(d)				
fuelwood		(*)		1,200		1,200
industrial wood		(*)		68	30	38
roundwood		(*)			20	
sawnwood		(†)	1.6	565	342	224.6
sheet materials		(†)	0.9			0.9
fiberboard		(‡)	0.1			0.1
wood pulp		(‡)				
pulp products		(‡)	23			23

For notes and sources, see chapter 3, table B–5.

TABLE B-5-14.   MEXICO: Imports, Production, Exports, and Consumption of Natural Resource Commodities in Different Stages of Processing, circa 1963-1967

Commodity and Product Description	Year	Unit	Imports	Production	Exports	Actual or Apparent Consumption
Copper	1966	metric tons				
content of ore				56,513	5,742	
unrefined metal				55,238	7,278	
refined metal				47,960	250	
semimanufactures					4,801	
other forms					1,298	
total			72	56,513	19,369	41,683
Iron and Steel	1963	metric tons				
ore, gross weight			2,103	2,328,137	1,112	2,329,128
pig iron and ferroalloys			162,259	1,028,770	4,741	1,186,288
crude steel			1	2,028,265	259	2,028,007
semimanufactures			95,178	1,379,794	172,153	1,302,819
total iron content			259,000	1,397,000	178,000	2,051,000
total rolled steel, ingot equivalent			224,000	2,046,000	224,000	2,046,000
Lead	1965	metric tons				
content of ore				166,780	2,818	
metal				164,307	140,530	
semimanufactures						
total			27	166,780	143,348	23,804
Zinc	1965	metric tons				
content of ore				232,875	285,003	
metal				89,744	33,841	
semimanufactures						
total			60	232,875	318,844	55,963
Tin	1963	long tons				
content of ore				1,055		
tin metal			197	1,055		1,252
tinplate, gross weight				95,802		95,802
tin content of tinplate				750		750
total contained tin			197	1,055		1,252
Petroleum	1964	thous. cubic meters				
crude oil			92	18,377	569	
refined products			1,515	20,189	2,167	19,319
gasoline			54	5,884		5,571
kerosene			53	2,093		2,006
distillate fuel oils			100	3,294		3,105
residual fuel oil			395	5,871	1,063	3,795
lubricants			23	201		235
Coal	1965	thous. m.t.				
coal, all grades			56	2,006		2,062
hard coke: actual			56	824		880
coal equivalent			80	1,178		1,258
soft coke						
Coffee	1965/66	thous. m.t.				
unroasted beans				172.0	85.9	69.8

TABLE B–5–14 – Continued

Commodity and Product Description	Year	Unit	Imports	Production	Exports	Actual or Apparent Consumption
Cocoa	1966	metric				
beans		tons		24,000	8,442	14,000
butter					199	
powder					3	
chocolate and products					92	
Sugar	1967	metric				
centrifugal, raw value		tons		2,410,705	571,583	1,649,884
Bananas	1966	thous.				
edible, fresh		m.t.			12	
Wheat	1964-66	thous.				
grain		m.t.	4	2,216		
flour			13	1,210		1,223
Beef and Veal	1966	thous.				
live cattle		head	17		590	
meat		m.t.		572	62	510
Cotton	1964	thous.				
raw cotton (fiber)		m.t.		517	348.6	130
cotton yarn				109.0	3.0	102
Forest Products	1964-66	(d)				
fuelwood		(*)		8,227		8,227
industrial wood		(*)	559	2,803		3,362
roundwood		(*)	32		0.2	
sawnwood		(†)	44	1,471	12	1,503
sheet materials		(†)	3.9	63	4.2	62.7
fiberboard		(‡)	3.4	18		21.4
wood pulp		(‡)	66	241		307
pulp products		(‡)	127	576	0.6	702.4

Fishery Products, 1964 *(thousands of metric tons)*

| Disposition of Catch | Liveweight | Type | Net Weight | | | |
			Production	Imports	Exports	Apparent Consumption
Total Catch	249.2	All uses	62.9	37.2	41.8	114.9
marketed fresh	103.3					51.7
frozen	43.7	crustaceans	33.0		33.2	
		fish		0.1	4.6	
cured	11.6	fish	3.3	0.7		4.0
canned	37.4	sardine	10.5	fish } 0.1	} 0.5	} 17.1
		tuna	7.0			
				(crustaceans and		
		abalone	2.9	molluscs 0.1)	2.9	0.1
reduced	28.6	oily fishmeal	5.7	34.7		40.4
		fish oil	0.5	1.5	0.4	1.6
(offal for reduction)	(0.7)					
miscellaneous	24.6	molluscs			0.2	

For notes and sources, see chapter 3, table B–5.

TABLE B-5-15. NICARAGUA: Imports, Production, Exports, and Consumption of Natural Resource Commodities in Different Stages of Processing, circa 1963-1967

Commodity and Product Description	Year	Unit	Imports	Production	Exports	Actual or Apparent Consumption
Copper	1966	metric				
content of ore		tons		9,764	9,764	
unrefined metal						
refined metal						
semimanufactures			133			
other forms			30			
total			163	9,764	9,764	163
Iron and Steel	1963	metric				
ore, gross weight		tons				
pig iron and ferroalloys			13,366		46	13,320
crude steel			1,502		284	1,218
semimanufactures			18,578			
total iron content			33,386		330	33,102
total rolled steel, ingot equivalent						
Lead	1965	metric				
content of ore		tons				
metal						
semimanufactures						
total			142			142
Zinc	1965	metric				
content of ore		tons				
metal						
semimanufactures						
total			1,753		53	1,700
Petroleum	1964	thous.				
crude oil		cubic	319			
refined products		meters	48	289		337
gasoline			17	96		113
kerosene			15	26		41
distillate fuel oils			10	64		74
residual fuel oil				93		93
lubricants			6			6
Coffee	1965/66	thous.				
unroasted beans		m.t.		28.4	27.9	4.3
Cocoa	1966	metric				
beans		tons	40	500	225	315
butter						
powder			61			
chocolate and products						
Sugar	1967	metric				
centrifugal, raw value		tons		108,182	48,009	57,607
Bananas	1966	thous.				
edible, fresh		m.t.			14	
Wheat	1964-66	thous.				
grain		m.t.				
flour			5			5
Beef and Veal	1966	thous.				
live cattle		head			3	
meat		m.t.				
Cotton	1964	thous.				
raw cotton (fiber)		m.t.		124	1,238	3
cotton yarn				1.0		1.0
Forest Products	1964-66	(d)				
fuelwood		(*)		1,383		1,383
industrial wood		(*)	2	204		206
roundwood		(*)	0.6			
sawnwood		(†)		130		130
sheet materials		(†)		9		9
fiberboard		(‡)				
wood pulp		(‡)				
pulp products		(‡)	10			10

For notes and sources, see chapter 3, table B-5.

TABLE B–5–16. PANAMA: Imports, Production, Exports, and Consumption of Natural Resource Commodities in Different Stages of Processing, circa 1963-1967

Commodity and Product Description	Year	Unit	Imports	Production	Exports	Actual or Apparent Consumption
Copper	1966	metric tons				
content of ore						
unrefined metal						
refined metal						
semimanufactures			207			
other forms			16			
total			223			223
Iron and Steel	1963	metric tons				
ore, gross weight						
pig iron and ferroalloys			610		1,000	390
crude steel			2,588		2	2,586
semimanufactures			24,918	6,350	50	31,218
total iron content			28,100		1,100	27,400
total rolled steel, ingot equivalent			35,000			35,000
Lead	1965	metric tons				
content of ore						
metal						
semimanufactures						
total			214			214
Petroleum	1964	thous. cubic meters				
crude oil			2,374			
refined products			73	2,389	1,670	792
gasoline			6	325	223	109
kerosene			1	152	40	114
distillate fuel oils			23	719	660	83
residual fuel oil			36	1,068	747	356
lubricants			5			5
Coffee	1965/66	thous. m.t.				
unroasted beans				4.8	2.1	3.7
Cocoa	1966	metric tons				
beans				700	436	264
butter						
powder			118			
chocolate and products			311			
Sugar	1967	metric tons				
centrifugal, raw value				63,000	29,999	34,000
Bananas	1966	thous. m.t.				
edible, fresh					386	
Wheat	1964-66	thous. m.t.				
grain						
flour			6			6
Beef and Veal	1966	thous. head				
live cattle					5	
meat		m.t.		31	1	30
Forest Products	1964-66	(d)				
fuelwood		(*)		1,735		1,735
industrial wood		(*)		133	3.3	129.7
roundwood		(*)	1.9		2.3	
sawnwood		(†)	6.5	41	1.2	46.3
sheet materials		(†)	0.1	3		3.1
fiberboard		(‡)				
wood pulp		(‡)	0.4			0.4
pulp products		(‡)	41	1	0.3	41.7

For notes and sources, see chapter 3, table B–5.

TABLE B-5-17. PARAGUAY: Imports, Production, Exports, and Consumption of Natural Resource Commodities in Different Stages of Processing, circa 1963-1967

Commodity and Product Description	Year	Unit	Imports	Production	Exports	Actual or Apparent Consumption
Copper	1966	metric tons				
content of ore						
unrefined metal						
refined metal						
semimanufactures			199			
other forms						
total			199			199
Iron and Steel	1963	metric tons				
ore, gross weight						
pig iron and ferroalloys						
crude steel						
semimanufactures			11,186			11,186
total iron content			15,000			15,000
total rolled steel, ingot equivalent			11,200			11,200
Lead	1965	metric tons				
content of ore						
metal						
semimanufactures						
total			96			96
Petroleum	1964	thous. cubic				
crude oil						
refined products		meters	167			167
gasoline			56			56
kerosene			22			22
distillate fuel oils			15			15
residual fuel oil			69			69
lubricants			3			3
Sugar	1967	metric tons				
centrifugal, raw value				38,970	9	36,554
Bananas	1966	thous. m.t.				
edible, fresh					2	
Wheat	1964-66	thous. m.t.				
grain			45	8		53
flour			4	67		67
Beef and Veal	1966	thous. head				
live cattle						
meat		m.t.		115	30	85
Cotton	1964	thous. m.t.				
raw cotton (fiber)				14	10	3
cotton yarn			0.2	2.1		2.3
Forest Products	1964-66	(d)				
fuelwood		(*)		1,713		1,713
industrial wood		(*)		612	268	344
roundwood		(*)			285	
sawnwood		(†)		80	42	38
sheet materials		(†)		1.5		1.5
fiberboard		(‡)				
wood pulp		(‡)				
pulp products		(‡)	3.6	1		4.6

For notes and sources, see chapter 3, table B-5.

TABLE B-5-18. PERU: Imports, Production, Exports, and Consumption of Natural Resource Commodities in Different Stages of Processing, circa 1963-1967

Commodity and Product Description	Year	Unit	Imports	Production	Exports	Actual or Apparent Consumption
Copper	1966	metric				
content of ore		tons		176,394	23,680	
unrefined metal				151,076	120,439	
refined metal			} 960	37,974	32,020	
semimanufactures						
other forms				653		
total			960	176,394	176,139	6,914
Iron and Steel	1963	metric				
ore, gross weight		tons	69	6,574,000	5,748,663	
pig iron and ferroalloys			807	29,000		29,807
crude steel				73,000		73,000
semimanufactures			141,502		36	
total iron content			142,000	3,944,000	3,449,000	214,466
total rolled steel, ingot equivalent			193,000	78,000		271,000
Lead	1965	metric				
content of ore		tons		154,346	65,558	
metal				86,807	85,454	
semimanufactures						
total			47	154,346	151,012	1,400
Zinc	1965	metric				
content of ore		tons		254,496	211,991	
metal				62,441	55,716	
semimanufactures						
total			234	254,496	267,707	6,959
Tin	1963	long				
content of ore		tons		15	57	
tin metal			61			61
tinplate, gross weight			15,000			15,000
tin content of tinplate			106			106
total contained tin			167			167
Petroleum	1964	thous.				
crude oil		cubic	87	3,676	429	
refined products		meters	808	3,575	78	4,493
gasoline			82	950		1,228
kerosene				614		613
distillate fuel oils				946	70	880
residual fuel oil			547	801	6	
lubricants			31	13	2	41
Coal	1965	thous.				
coal, all grades		m.t.	1	129		130
hard coke: actual			8	27		35
coal equivalent			11	39		50
soft coke						

TABLE B–5–18 – Continued

Commodity and Product Description	Year	Unit	Imports	Production	Exports	Actual or Apparent Consumption
Coffee	1965/66	thous.				
unroasted beans		m.t.		51.2	34.1	14.3
Cocoa	1966	metric				
beans		tons	1,584	2,400		4,000
butter			174			
powder			500			
chocolate and products			370			
Sugar	1967	metric				
centrifugal, raw value		tons		731,171	431,472	345,262
Wheat	1964-66	thous.				
grain		m.t.	470	103		
flour			12	396		
Beef and Veal	1966	thous.				
live cattle		head				
meat		m.t.	18	81		99
Cotton	1964	thous.				
raw cotton (fiber)		m.t.		136	106	20
cotton yarn			1.0	15.4		16.4
Forest Products	1964-66	(d)				
fuelwood		(*)		2,500		2,500
industrial wood		(*)		431		430
roundwood		(*)	2.2		1	
sawnwood		(†)	83	224		307
sheet materials		(†)	4.7	6.7		11.4
fiberboard		(‡)	2			2
wood pulp		(‡)	18			18
pulp products		(‡)	41	67		108

Fishery Products, 1964 *(thousands of metric tons)*

Disposition of Catch	Liveweight	Type	Net Weight			
			Production	Imports	Exports	Apparent Consumption
Total Catch	9,047.4	All uses	1,798.1	0.6	1,565.6	284.9
marketed fresh	92.5					46.3
frozen	17.3	fish	17.3		13.2	4.1
cured	11.1	fish	5.6	0.1	0.3	5.8
canned	32.0	tuna	9.0	} 0.4	15.1	
		other fish	0.7			
		crustaceans and molluscs		0.1		0.1
reduced	8,894.5	oily fishmeal	1,553.4		1,426.4	127.0
		fish oil	212.1	0.1	110.6	101.6
miscellaneous		crustaceans and molluscs		0.1	0.1	

For notes and sources, see chapter 3, table B–5.

TABLE B–5–19. URUGUAY: Imports, Production, Exports, and Consumption of Natural Resource Commodities in Different Stages of Processing, circa 1963-1967

Commodity and Product Description	Year	Unit	Imports	Production	Exports	Actual or Apparent Consumption
Copper	1966	metric tons				
content of ore						
unrefined metal						
refined metal			} 628			
semimanufactures						
other forms						
total			628			628
Iron and Steel	1963	metric tons				
ore, gross weight				1,031		1,031
pig iron and ferroalloys			} 23,084			} 29,584
crude steel				6,500		
semimanufactures			31,516	21,970	636	52,850
total iron content			54,600	500	600	60,500
total rolled steel, ingot equivalent			53,000	29,000		
Lead	1965	metric tons				
content of ore						
metal						
semimanufactures						
total			1,072			1,072
Zinc	1965	metric tons				
content of ore						
metal						
semimanufactures						
total			747			747
Tin	1963	long tons				
content of ore						
tin metal			75			75
tinplate, gross weight			7,000			7,000
tin content of tinplate			45			45
total contained tin			120			120
Petroleum	1964	thous. cubic meters				
crude oil			1,694			
refined products			52	1,774		1,825
gasoline			10	377		387
kerosene				257		257
distillate fuel oils			4	370		374
residual fuel oil			22	694		716
lubricants			15			15
Coffee	1965/66	thous. m.t.				
unroasted beans			2.2			2.2
Cocoa	1966	metric tons				
beans			541			
butter						
powder						
chocolate and products						
Sugar	1967	metric tons				
centrifugal, raw value			47,236	70,000		125,000
Bananas	1966	thous. m.t.				
edible, fresh			24			24
Wheat	1964-66	thous. m.t.				
grain			1	532	53	
flour				301		
Beef and Veal	1966	thous.				
live cattle		head	7		7	
meat		m.t.		237	73	164
Cotton	1964	thous. m.t.				
raw cotton (fiber)			7.6			8
cotton yarn			0.2	3.8		4
Forest Products	1964-66	(d)				
fuelwood		(*)		1,050		1,050
industrial wood		(*)	298	85		383
roundwood		(*)	16			
sawnwood		(†)	76	72		148
sheet materials		(†)	2.6	4.5		7.1
fiberboard		(‡)				
wood pulp		(‡)	19	3.8		22.8
pulp products		(‡)	26	36		62

For notes and sources, see chapter 3, table B–5.

TABLE B–5–20. VENEZUELA: Imports, Production, Exports, and Consumption of Natural Resource Commodities in Different Stages of Processing, circa 1963-1967

Commodity and Product Description	Year	Unit	Imports	Production	Exports	Actual or Apparent Consumption
Copper	1966	metric tons				
content of ore						
unrefined metal						
refined metal			63			
semimanufactures			7,891			
other forms						
total			7,954		726	7,228
Iron and Steel	1963	metric tons				
ore, gross weight				11,757,000	12,319,000	
pig iron and ferroalloys			27,726	302,000	89,733	239,993
crude steel			6,608	364,000	133,605	237,003
semimanufactures			390,904	159,000	5,277	544,627
total iron content			425,000	6,813,000	7,145,000	623,000
total rolled steel, ingot equivalent			433,000	328,000	185,000	576,000
Lead	1965	metric tons				
content of ore						
metal			1,693			
semimanufactures			498			
total			2,191			2,191
Zinc	1965	metric tons				
content of ore						
metal			4,072			
semimanufactures			1,087			
total			5,159			5,159
Tin	1963	long tons				
content of ore			191			
tin metal			50,651			50,651
tinplate, gross weight			413			
tin content of tinplate			604			
total contained tin						
Petroleum	1964	thous. cubic meters				
crude oil				197,602	136,750	
refined products			42	63,548	50,152	9,026
gasoline				7,584	2,876	2,817
kerosene				4,156	2,500	676
distillate fuel oils				12,356	8,134	1,139
residual fuel oil				37,199	35,621	3,354
lubricants			11	734	663	85
Coal	1965	thous. m.t.				
coal, all grades			10	30		40
hard coke: actual			194			194
coal equivalent			277			277
soft coke						
Coffee	1965/66	thous. m.t.				
unroasted beans				57.7	18.1	38.3

TABLE B–5–20 – Continued

Commodity and Product Description	Year	Unit	Imports	Production	Exports	Actual or Apparent Consumption
Cocoa	1966	metric				
beans		tons		22,900	11,795	11,000
butter					242	
powder						
chocolate and products						
Sugar	1967	metric				
centrifugal, raw value		tons		413,430	39,995	330,251
Bananas	1966	thous.				
edible, fresh		m.t.			21	
Wheat	1964-66	thous.				
grain		m.t.	568	1		569
flour			6	302		308
Beef and Veal	1966	thous.				
live cattle		head				
meat		m.t.	5	169		174
Cotton	1964	thous.				
raw cotton (fiber)		m.t.	6.5	14		17
cotton yarn			0.3	15		15.3
Forest Products	1964-66	(d)				
fuelwood		(*)		3,478		3,478
industrial wood		(*)	4	487		491
roundwood		(*)	3.7			
sawnwood		(†)	1.7	294		295.7
sheet materials		(†)	0.8	13.7		14.5
fiberboard		(‡)	0.8	10		10.8
wood pulp		(‡)	80.3			80.3
pulp products		(‡)	82	149		231

Fishery Products, 1964 *(thousands of metric tons)*

| Disposition of Catch | Liveweight | Type | Net Weight | | | |
			Production	Imports	Exports	Apparent Consumption
Total Catch	110.6	All uses	42.8	20.5	5.5	89.0
marketed fresh	39.7					29.9
frozen		shrimp	4.0		4.3	
cured	23.2	fish	7.7	1.1		8.8
canned	44.6	herring and sardine	25.3 fish	0.8		26.1
		crustaceans and molluscs	2.5	0.2	1.2	1.5
reduced	3.1	oily fishmeal	3.3	19.3		22.6
		fish oil		0.1		0.1
(offal for reduction)	(16.1)					

For notes and sources, see chapter 3, table B–5.

PART TWO
THE COMMODITIES

Copper

Iron and Steel

Lead and Zinc

Tin

Petroleum

Coal

Coffee

Cocoa

Sugar

Bananas

Wheat

Beef

Cotton

Forest Products

Fishery Products

Chapter 4

COPPER

Latin America furnishes about one-fifth of the world's supply of copper and a considerably larger share of the metal entering world trade. Exports of copper provide some 5 percent of the region's foreign exchange, a share surpassed only by the exports of petroleum, coffee, sugar, and (in most years) cotton. Copper is mined in ten Latin American countries, but in only three – Chile, Mexico, and Peru – are there sizable industries. Exports of copper are now quite important to Peru, but only in Chile is the copper industry a major element in the economy, accounting for some 60 percent of exports, 13 percent of government revenues, and 4 percent of the gross national product. This economic weight alone would make the operations of the copper industry of great political interest. In addition, the world industry is dominated by a small number of very large North American and European enterprises, whose interests have often seemed opposed to those of the countries in which they operate. Finally, in Chile the issues and problems specific to the copper industry have become enmeshed with a number of distinct issues. The result of these factors has been to make copper a political concern of the greatest importance in Chile for at least the last quarter-century. Elsewhere in Latin America the role of copper carries less weight politically, even where it is economically significant.

In the world economy copper is the third most-used metal, having been second until it was displaced by aluminum in the fifties; production is now nearly 5 million tons per year. Copper also has considerable political weight on the world scale, because of its strategic importance to industrial countries and because much of it is produced in underdeveloped nations where political and economic influences can subject supplies to large fluctuations. In this study, the world copper industry will be described in general terms, with particular attention given to those factors relevant to Latin America, especially to Chile. The industry is understood to include the processing of copper from the mine to its consumption in the form of refined metal for fabrication. The production, trade, and use of copper manufactures will not be discussed, nor will the consumption of copper in various nonmetallic forms.[1]

The World Copper Industry

Resources

Present world reserves of copper are estimated as some 200 million metric tons. The richest single area is in western South America, from central Peru to central Chile; reserves there are about 53 million tons, or 28 percent of the total. Somewhat smaller resources – 41 million tons – are found in the copper belt of south central Africa, through the Congo and Zambia. The United States and the Soviet Union each have about 30 million tons; 8 million are found in Canada and 10 million in Poland. These areas together account for 90 percent of the world total. There are also small reserves in other countries in Latin America and in Africa. The remainder is distributed in several countries of Western Europe, Asia, and Oceania, with not more than 4 million tons in any one nation (see table 4-3). In the United States and South America the great bulk of copper is found in disseminated porphyry deposits, which are close to uniform in grade at levels of about 1 or 2 percent. In the African copper belt the metal is found in sedimentary deposits averaging some 6 percent in the Congo and 3 to 4 percent in Zambia. Copper is also produced from thousands of vein deposits at high grade all over the world, but the amount of metal so obtained is quite small. These low levels reflect the rarity of copper in the earth's crust, and the fact that as the grade of ore is lowered, the tonnage of metal available increases very rapidly. Little is known about the

[1] The statistical material in this chapter is taken chiefly from the *Minerals Yearbook* of the U.S. Bureau of Mines, the *Yearbook of the American Bureau of Metal Statistics*, and *Metal Statistics* (Metall Gesellschaft, Frankfurt, Germany). Other publications serving the metal-mining industries have also been used, particularly *Engineering and Mining Journal*, *Mining Magazine*, and *Metal Bulletin*. Information on Chile is drawn from a number of publications prepared by the Instituto de Economía of the Universidad de Chile; these and other sources used are noted in the text. Copper statistics are variously reported in short or metric tons; all data here have been converted to metric tons, referring in almost all cases to actual copper content.

Note: Copper tables 4-1 and 4-2 appear on pp. 157 and 164; 4-3 to 4-14 appear on pp. 175–86.

amount and distribution of potential resources, but it has been estimated that there are 400 to 500 million tons of copper in material of at least 1 percent grade, and double that amount above a minimum grade of 0.5 percent.[2]

Production and Consumption

Copper was first produced in quantity in Europe, but the resources of that region are too small to support a high level of output. Early in the nineteenth century Europe began to draw for supplies on Chile, where mining had begun 200 years before. During the 1800s Chilean production expanded very rapidly from a few hundred tons to some 18,000 tons per year. For several decades Chile was the world's leading producer, and in 1876 it accounted for 62 percent of the world total. Increasing demand for copper also resulted in development of the industry in the United States. Output rose from 14,000 tons in 1870 to 300,000 tons at the turn of the century; and in 1880 the United States, surpassing Chile, became the world's largest producer, a position it has held ever since. From 1900 to 1920 the United States dominated world production to the same extent that Chile had done in the 1870s, supplying three-fifths of all copper mined and exporting some 200,000 tons per year, mostly to Europe.[3]

The production and use of copper increased at a steadily rising rate until sometime in the middle or late nineteenth century. Since then the rate of growth, measured over periods of a decade or more and excluding certain years of extremely high or low output, has been declining steadily. From the 1880s to the decade before World War I, production increased at an average rate of over 5 percent annually; the rate dropped to about 3.6 percent over the next twenty years, to less than 3 percent in the 1920s and 1930s, and to only 2 percent from the late 1930s to the mid-1950s.[4] Over the short run there has been much more fluctuation in production of copper, and for a decade or more after World War II a higher rate of growth prevailed.

In the last four decades world copper production has risen from some 1.5 million tons to nearly 5 million tons (see table 4-4). During this period Western Europe has produced 100,000 tons per year or less. Production in the United States has increased only slightly; all the country's high-grade ore had been exploited by 1920 and there have been few new discoveries of copper since then. As a result, the United States' share of world output has declined from 60 percent to about one-fourth, and production elsewhere

has expanded greatly. The largest percentage increase has occurred in the Communist countries of Europe which, particularly since World War II, have developed a large industry supplying about 90 percent of their requirements. Latin America remained the second largest producing area until 1951, when it was surpassed by Africa. The most rapid growth in Latin American production occurred before 1930; in the late 1920s the region's mine output rose by more than half, and the share of the world total to 25 percent. In the next decade the increase was much slower, while output in Africa grew very rapidly as the result of the development of the Rhodesian copper belt. Even during the Depression, while production was falling in the Congo the output of new, low-cost mines in Rhodesia (now Zambia) increased sharply. In several recent years Zambia produced more copper than Chile and was second only to the United States. Production in Canada and in Asia and Oceania has also increased substantially. Copper is now produced on a large scale in six or seven countries, and world output is more evenly distributed than at any previous time. Of a total of some 4.8 million tons in the early 1960s, North America produced one-third, Africa 22 percent, Latin America 19 percent, and the Communist countries of Europe 17 percent.

Copper sulfide ores, like those of other nonferrous metals, are generally concentrated to a grade of 30 percent or more, at or near the mine. The concentrates can then be shipped elsewhere for processing into metal, but they will not usually bear the cost of transport for long distances. As a result, there is now very little international trade in ores and concentrates, and the bulk of copper metal is produced in the country where it is mined rather than in the country where it is consumed; shipment of high-grade ore or concentrates was formerly more common. When the ores are oxides of copper, the metal is recovered by leaching with acid, followed by precipitation. The copper in the acid salt is replaced by iron, usually from steel scrap. Sulfide ores require smelting to convert the sulfides to oxides and then carry off the oxygen with carbon from the fuel used as a reducing agent: the processing is similar to that for reducing the ores of many other metals.

Most of the world's copper now comes from sulfide ores and is smelted, usually in the producing country. The output of a smelter is called blister copper; it contains 99 percent or more of copper, with metallic impurities such as gold, silver, lead, and zinc. When pure enough, blister copper can be used directly, particularly for the manufacture of certain alloys and chemicals. Its purity can be raised, for some applications, by an extension of the smelting process known as fire-refining. Relatively little metal is used as blister or fire-refined copper, however, since for most purposes — including the electrical applications which absorb much of the copper used in the world — a purity of 99.9 percent or higher is required. This is achieved by electrolytic refining, from which the metallic impurities may be recovered as by-products. Blister and refined copper are so close in copper content that there is no difference in transport costs for the two grades; neither does there appear to be any significant difference in the economies of scale of the smelting and refining processes. Thus, blister copper can

[2]H. H. Landsberg, L. L. Fischman, and J. L. Fisher, *Resources in America's Future* (Johns Hopkins Press for Resources for the Future, 1963), pp. 452-57. The principal source for these estimates is the President's Materials Policy Commission, *Resources for Freedom* (U.S. Government Printing Office, 1952), vol. II, pp. 144-45.

[3]The early history of copper in Chile is described briefly in CORFO, *Geografía Económica de Chile* (Santiago, 1965), pp. 584-85, and M. Vera Valenzuela, *La Política Económica del Cobre en Chile* (Santiago: Universidad de Chile, 1961), p. 30. For the United States, see N. Potter and F. T. Christy, *Trends in Natural Resource Commodities* (Johns Hopkins Press for Resources for the Future, 1962), pp. 378, 454-56.

[4]O. C. Herfindahl, *Copper Costs and Prices: 1870-1957* (Johns Hopkins Press for Resources for the Future, 1959), p. 225.

be refined either where it is produced or where it is consumed; the decision turns on such factors as the costs of labor and electricity, which are major elements of the cost of refining. This situation contrasts somewhat with that of most other primary commodities, where there is a natural location more or less economically determined for each stage of processing. Copper recovered from oxide ores, however, is generally refined where it is produced; only small amounts of precipitated but unrefined metal enter world trade.[5]

World production of refined copper considerably exceeds mine output of new copper, because about one-sixth of demand is met from scrap. The contribution of scrap to refinery production varies greatly among countries and in many cases primary and secondary production are not distinguished; consequently it is impossible to describe the importance of secondary recovery accurately. Generally, scrap is unimportant in areas where consumption is low, such as Africa and Latin America, and is used in large amounts in the United States and in some European countries. In the United States old copper scrap now furnishes between 10 and 15 percent of consumption. The share for all scrap is appreciably higher, as it includes prompt industrial scrap from fabricators.

As is shown in table 4-5, in close to four decades world production of refined copper has risen from some 1.3 million tons to 6.3 million; this increase has been more rapid than the rise in mine output, and reflects the increasing importance of secondary recovery and the decline of applications for unrefined copper. There has also been a considerable redistribution of production: the western hemisphere accounted for 60 percent of the total in the early 1930s, and now provides only 40 percent. This shift is due in part to the changes in mine production during the period as output rose in Africa, in Asia and Oceania, and in the Communist countries, while the United States share declined. It is also due to changes in the share of mine output refined in different producing areas. In this respect the most striking feature is the fact that output of refined copper in Latin America has not increased since the 1930s. In the same period refinery output rose almost fivefold in Africa, much more rapidly than the increase in mine production.

Until the early 1950s, refinery production was about half of mine production in Latin America and about one-third in Africa (both ratios adjusted by the ratio of refinery to mine output for the world as a whole); in the next decade these ratios were reversed (see table 4-1). The initially higher ratio for Latin America reflects the fact that much of the region's production then came from oxide

[5] For these reasons, world smelter production is not described in this study. Instead, refining is taken to be the important stage of processing, and refinery output is compared with mine production. Comparisons of mine and smelter output are difficult because the former is often estimated from the latter, which is easier to measure. Such trade in concentrates as does occur generally comes from mines where copper is a by-product of other metals (as in Bolivia), where the grade is high enough that high-grade concentrates can be easily produced (as in some of the smaller mines of Chile), or where reserves and output are too small to justify construction of a smelter (as in Haiti and Nicaragua).

TABLE 4-1. World Distribution of Copper Refining, Averages for 1930-34, 1950-54, and 1960-64

Exporters and Importers	Ratio of Refinery Production to Mine Production[a]		
	1930-34	1950-54	1960-64
Exporters (Canada, Africa, and Latin America)	0.45	0.47	0.48
Latin America	0.47	0.51	0.33
Africa	0.37	0.34	0.51
Importers (Western Europe, Asia, and Oceania)	1.87	2.73	2.32
Western Europe	2.92	7.61	6.90
United States	1.47	1.27	1.31
Communist Countries (Eastern Europe)	0.61	1.00	1.09

Sources: Tables 4-4 and 4-5.

[a]Ratio of refinery production to mine production, divided by same ratio for world totals. In exporting and importing groups, regions are weighted by mine production, not by production of refined copper.

ores, whereas nearly all African production was and is from sulfide ores. As production shifted to sulfides in Latin America, smelter capacity was increased but refinery capacity was not. The reasons for this are discussed later. Apparently no net shift of refining from exporting to importing areas occurred, however; the ratio of refinery to mine production has remained nearly constant for Canada, Africa, and Latin America taken together. The principal change in importing regions is a great increase in copper refining in Western Europe; this increase has been approximately offset by decreases in the importance of the United States, Asia, and Oceania as refiners of imported copper. The redistribution among importing regions took place in the 1930s and 1940s; the shift among exporters has occurred in the postwar period.

In general, "consumption" of copper means the production of semifabricated shapes, or the passage of copper through a mill. Since there is a considerable trade in semifabricated copper and in manufactures containing copper or copper alloys, consumption as measured corresponds to the treatment of copper at a certain stage and not to its use in final form. Because the discrepancy is great for countries that import most of their copper in manufactured or semimanufactured form, consumption is also calculated to include net trade in semimanufactures in Latin America; the same degree of detail is not applied to other regions, however. Similar definitions and adjustments are used for the other major metals.

Except in the United States, most information refers only to the consumption of new copper; thus world total consumption is closer to mine output than to production of refined copper. On this basis, the world now uses some 5 million tons of copper annually, compared with 2 million just before World War II and 2.6 million tons around 1950. During the 1920s the United States accounted for almost half the total; the share fell to 30 percent in the next decade and then rose above 50 percent during the war. Consumption dropped from the wartime peak of 1.6 million tons to only 1 million in 1949 and then recovered quite slowly. By the early 1960s copper consumption in the United States had increased to some 1.4 million tons, but the share had once more declined to 30 percent. Consumption has increased much more rapidly since World War II in Western Europe, the Communist countries, and Japan. In these countries reconstruction and the postwar boom created a rapidly growing demand for copper, and aluminum was not substituted to so great an extent as in the United States. Western Europe is now the largest consuming region, with about 2 million tons or 40 percent of the total. Growth has been more rapid in the Communist countries, and most rapid of all in Japan (see table 4-6).

Latin America consumes some 100,000 tons of unwrought copper — about 11 percent of regional production and 2 percent of total world use. If trade in semimanufactures is included, the region's consumption rises to nearly 150,000 tons. Consumption in Africa is some 40,000 tons, three-fourths of which is accounted for by South Africa; the exporting countries of the continent consume almost no copper. Fabricating facilities are now planned for Zambia; intially half the output will be exported.[6] Another 150,000 tons are used in Oceania and in Asian countries other than Japan. Estimates of total consumption of refined copper, including secondary material, are available only for recent years. In 1962-64 total use was about 5,350,000 tons. The distribution of consumption by this measure does not differ greatly from that for primary copper, despite differences between countries in the importance of scrap. Facilities for processing scrap are generally located in those countries that have large copper fabricating industries, and these are the same countries that dominate the consumption of most industrial materials: the United States, the United Kingdom, the Common Market countries, the Soviet Union, and Japan.

Market Structure and International Trade

World trade in copper has gone through three fairly distinct phases in the last century and a half, or since the development on a large scale of the resources of the western hemisphere. At first the only sizable flow of copper was from Chile to Europe; this trade reached its peak, as a share of world supplies, in the 1860s and 1870s. It was surpassed in the next few decades by exports of copper from the United States, most of which also went to Europe. For roughly a century, then, Europe was the only significant importing region, and most of its supplies came from the western hemisphere.

The transition to the second phase began in the 1920s and a new trade pattern became evident during the Depression and continued in force until the early 1950s. Three major factors combined to bring about the transition. First, consumption outran production in the United States. Net exports were highest between 1910 and 1920; as the use of copper rose in the next decade, exports fell, and at the start of the war the United States became a net importer. Second, production increased greatly in Latin America, first during the 1920s and again during World War II: these expansions made up for declining North American

exports and then provided the copper for U.S. consumption. Third, in the 1930s African production rose as the mines of the Rhodesian copper belt came into operation. The result of these changes was a considerable separation of the eastern and western hemispheres. The United States became the principal market for copper from Canada, Chile, Mexico, and Peru, while Europe took nearly all the metal produced in Africa, the United Kingdom refining and distributing copper from Rhodesia, and Belgium that from the Congo. There was very little trade from the producing and exporting countries in either hemisphere to consumers in the other; the only sizable transatlantic trade consisted of copper shipped from Latin America to the United States for refining and re-export to Europe.

The third and present phase began about a decade after World War II. As demand in the United States declined and then grew only slowly, that market required a smaller share of Latin America's exports. At the same time Europe's needs expanded more rapidly than output in Africa and Europe together. As a result, Europe became once again the chief direct outlet for Latin American copper. The region's exports of refined copper were shifted almost entirely to Europe, while the bulk of unrefined metal sent to the United States continued to be shipped to Europe after refining. Japan also became a major consumer, and the Communist countries have required net imports of 100,000 tons or so. The shift in trade has affected Latin America primarily and has occurred despite a rather slow growth of production there.

Total world trade in copper, excluding trade within the Communist countries, was some 2.5 million tons at the start of the sixties. Copper was the seventh most valuable primary commodity traded; the total value of exports was some $1,550 million, just under 3 percent of the value of all primary products together.[7] More than half of the copper exported was taken by Western Europe: some 425,000 tons by the United Kingdom and 900,000 tons by other countries. The United States imported 250,000 tons, the Communist countries about 100,000 tons, and Japan and India 50,000 tons each. Another 200,000 tons, approximately, was taken by importing countries in Latin America and Africa. The five principal exporters — Zambia, Chile, the Congo, Canada, and Peru — furnished over 1.7 million tons of copper; Zambia alone exported somewhat more and Chile somewhat less than half a million tons.

The bulk of copper traded, some 70 percent, is refined metal. Most of the smaller consuming countries have no refineries; and even in Western Europe more than half of the copper imported is refined. Europe is also the largest market for unrefined metal, taking about 400,000 tons per year. The ratio of refined to blister copper is about three in the United Kingdom and two in the rest of Europe. The United States imports blister copper almost exclusively — some 250,000 tons annually, all from the

---

[6] *Engineering and Mining Journal*, February 1968, p. 186.

[7] The figures given are averages for the years 1959-61, compiled from the FAO *Trade Yearbook*. See J. W. F. Rowe, *Primary Commodities in International Trade* (London: Cambridge University Press, 1965), pp. 5, 31, 115.

Western Hemisphere. This pattern of trade by degree of processing reflects primarily the distribution of refining capacity in exporting countries, and particularly the present low ratio of refinery to mine production in Latin America.

In general, world trade in copper reflects the distribution of consumption and resources, and changes in the pattern have followed changes in the conditions of demand or supply. However, the pattern of trade is also determined by the structure of the world copper industry, by the size and organization of the principal mining and processing firms, and by the ties among them and between them and their customers. These factors are particularly important in determining the location of refineries and the sizable trade in copper that is refined in neither the producing nor the consuming country. Shipments of copper do not always move by the cheapest route from mine to consumer; a number of non-price factors, including political and financial links, must be taken into account.[8] It may be useful to describe the copper industry outside the Communist countries briefly and then to indicate how its structure affects world trade.

The industry is even more concentrated than the iron and steel or petroleum industries. There are a few state enterprises, none of which is a major producer or exporter. Many small private mining companies exist, but their output is small and most have no processing facilities. The industry is dominated by a few very large firms controlled by U.S., British, Canadian, and, formerly, Belgian capital. These companies control a larger share of smelting and refining than of mine capacity, and they also own fabricating companies to process part of their output. Three firms — Anaconda, Kennecott, and Phelps Dodge — account for three-fourths of mine output and 90 percent of smelter capacity in the United States. Until 1968, Anaconda and Kennecott together produced 90 percent of Chile's output through four subsidiary companies. Anaconda also controls the largest mine and owns part of the only refinery in Mexico. Four U.S. firms supply most of the copper produced in Peru and control all the smelting and refining capacity. They also have refineries in that country to process blister copper from Latin America. The industry in Canada is controlled by domestic capital, the principal firms being Noranda and International Nickel. A single Belgian firm, the Union Minière du Haut-Katanga, owned all the mines and facilities in the Congo until its expropriation in January 1967, and still owns a refinery in Belgium. Two companies, Anglo-American and Roan Selection Trust, operate in Zambia; the former is British and the latter is controlled by a U.S. firm with a British minority interest.

This industrial structure together with two other factors — the political and historical ties between Zambia and the United Kingdom, and the high degree of integration of the Canadian and U.S. economies — account for much of world trade in copper. Zambian copper moves principally to the United Kingdom; the one U.S. firm in Zambia, American Metal Climax, has no fabricating capacity and so imports no metal from its African subsidiary. Copper from the Congo goes to Belgium for refining and a large amount is then re-exported to France. Canadian copper is exported mostly to the United States and the United Kingdom. Copper from Chile moves principally to Europe, either directly or after refining in the United States. Since West Germany and Italy have no financial ties to a producing country, they import much Latin American metal through the United States. Japan, in a similar position, obtains much of its copper from Chile and Peru. If all copper were refined where it is mined, there would be a much larger flow from Latin America to Europe and the United States would be a much less important trader. Thus it is U.S. dominance of the Latin American industry which introduces the chief deviation from direct trade between producers and consumers.

The considerable concentration of the world copper industry gives the larger producers some power to force up prices or offset a decline in demand by restricting supplies. The entry of new companies or the development of new producing areas usually limits such control to a brief period; more recently the development of substitute materials has also weakened producers with respect to consumers. Between the late nineteenth century and the Depression of the 1930s there were several episodes of collusion among producers, usually consisting of or dominated by U.S. enterprises. Sometimes they affected only the domestic market, as between 1870 and 1873 and 1919-22; more often the member firms were exporters, either from the United States or from Latin America, and their control of the market raised prices in all importing areas, as in 1888-90, 1899-1901 and 1929-30. The Union Minière du Haut-Katanga joined the agreement of 1926, known as Copper Exporters Incorporated, which forced the price up sharply in 1929, until first a buyers' strike and then the collapse of demand brought the dissolution of the pool. The next formal agreement, in 1936-39, included producers in Chile, Peru, Rhodesia, and the Congo; quotas were set for exports, but the control was not tight enough to affect prices very much. This agreement was one of several commodity control schemes established in the later years of the Depression. Unlike the agreements for sugar and tin, it was not re-established after World War II.[9] No further restriction on production occurred until 1958, when prices fell sharply following a boom in 1955-56. Producers in Africa reduced their output by 10 percent and in 1961-62 supported the price by purchases on the London Metal Exchange. Producers in Chile, at the urging of the Chilean government, also reduced their production; companies in the United States did not. These measures brought about a rapid recovery of prices and ensured stability from 1959 to 1963.

If the control of prices by producers has become less frequent or less extreme in the last several decades, the

[8]The following analysis is based chiefly on J. E. Tilton, "The Choice of Trading Partners: An Analysis of International Trade in Aluminum, Bauxite, Copper, Lead, Manganese, Tin and Zinc" (Ph.D. dissertation, Yale University, 1960), pp. 125-30. The data are for the years 1960-62, and there have been no great changes in the copper market since then. Major changes are under way in Chile.

[9]Rowe, *Primary Commodities in International Trade*, pp. 154-55. For a survey of the various periods of output control by producers prior to the Depression, see Herfindahl, *Copper Costs and Prices*, pp. 70-200.

influence of governments has become more pronounced. In recent years the government of Chile has intervened in the market by setting prices for copper exports. Over the long run the United States government has exercised far greater control, partly through tariffs, partly through direct price and production controls or stimuli, and partly through the operation of a strategic stockpile of copper. The United States was isolated from the world market by a high tariff during the early years of the industry. No protection was needed from 1900 to the 1920s, when the United States was the leading producer and exporter. A tariff of 4 cents per pound was imposed in 1932, when the price fell to 5 cents, and the domestic industry was thereby partly insulated from the Depression. Another tariff was levied in the late 1940s, and one of 1.7 cents per pound between July 1958 and February 1966. In wartime, tariffs have regularly been suspended and various direct controls applied to the industry. During World War II the price was fixed at 12 cents per pound, with premium prices paid for production in excess of quotas by domestic producers. The United States government also agreed to buy nearly all the copper produced by Anaconda and Kennecott in Chile, but no bonuses were paid.[10] Similar controls were imposed during the Korean War. The price was fixed at 24.5 cents per pound in July 1950; in May 1951 the United States agreed to buy copper from Chile at 27.5 cents, leaving the three-cent difference as revenue for the Chilean government. A scheme of allocation of copper was adopted at the International Materials Conference in 1951, but the accord had no lasting effect, as it was abrogated by Chile within a year.[11] Chile's efforts to obtain a price of 35 cents resulted in a sizable accumulation of stocks in that country as the Korean War demand declined. In 1954-55 some 90,000 tons of these stocks were absorbed by the U.S. stockpile, which since 1964 has been used to relieve a shortage of copper.

In some instances intervention, whether by producing enterprises or by governments of consuming countries, has served only to reduce fluctuations in the price of copper. In other cases, by restricting output or absorbing stocks during periods of surplus, it has clearly maintained prices to the advantage of exporting countries. There is nonetheless a strong belief in Latin America that the United States government and enterprises have, on the average, controlled the market to the detriment of producing countries. When in the past, prices were driven high by collusion, the profits went entirely to producers and not to host governments. Now that countries such as Chile could recapture a large share of those profits, producers are unable or unwilling to force prices up or to take full advantage of periods of scarcity. They may even, as in recent years, deliberately hold prices down when copper is in short supply; and the losses from price control at such times are believed to outweigh the gains from supported prices and reduced volume when copper is in surplus.

Although copper is used throughout any industrial economy, demand is concentrated in a few industries, usually in those sectors that are particularly sensitive to the rate of investment; in the United States, for example, construction and the manufacture of producer durables absorb about 60 percent of all the copper consumed.[12] As a result, world demand is strongly related to the rate of growth of the industrial economies, not simply to their level of income, and is subject to considerable fluctuation. This is generally the case with metals, particularly the nonferrous metals, but not with fuels and most agricultural products. Copper is also required in very large amounts in wartime; U.S. consumption during World War II was half again as much as in the immediate postwar years. Finally, demand for copper has come to depend in part on the possibility and cost of substituting aluminum for it. The rapid growth in consumption of aluminum has occurred in large measure as the result of substitution for copper in many non-electrical applications and even in some cases for conducting electricity, as in long-distance transmission cables. This substitution has proceeded much further in the United States than elsewhere. In Europe and Japan copper consumption has increased rapidly in the last two decades, despite some inroads by aluminum; and in other consuming areas, such as Latin America, aluminum is only now becoming a metal of major importance.

The supply of copper is also subject to fluctuation. In the short run, the industry usually operates at close to full capacity and production cannot be much increased; supplies can be reduced, however, by strikes or other difficulties. Such stoppages are important chiefly for two reasons: since the bulk of copper is produced from a small number of large mines, a reduction at any one of them materially affects total supplies; and strikes are sometimes not simply economic disputes but involve major political issues in producing countries. These political factors also affect the amount and distribution of production in the long run. Among major consuming countries, only the United States and the Soviet Union are approximately self-sufficient in copper. Much of the rest of the world's supply comes from four less developed countries – Chile, Peru, Zambia, and the Congo – where political considerations have influenced output or may cause uncertainty about future production. In recent years extreme political instability has occurred in only one instance, in the Congo in 1960-64, when output was reduced. Political changes in Zambia, especially the attempt to replace foreign personnel, have somewhat reduced efficiency; and shortages of coal from Rhodesia have held back production and led to development of domestic coal mines. There has been only one important case of expropriation of foreign capital in the industry, that of the Union Minière in the Congo; such action has also repeatedly been advocated in Chile. Most often, political disputes have influenced future production by causing producers to delay or reduce investment. Such difficulties in one country may be offset by more favorable terms and increased investment elsewhere; thus on balance there has been little protracted effect on the entire world industry except for brief periods.

[10]USBM, *Minerals Yearbook, 1941*, pp. 93-97, 108-10.

[11]See Rowe, *Primary Commodities in International Trade*, p. 103, and M. Vera Valenzuela, *La Política Económica del Cobre en Chile* (Santiago: Universidad de Chile, 1961), pp. 59-60.

[12]Landsberg et al., *Resources in America's Future*, p. 918.

Political factors influence supplies of many primary commodities, and in this respect copper is in no worse a position than other products such as petroleum; indeed, there have been fewer serious disputes in the case of copper. Only in Chile is copper a paramount, long-standing political issue.

Prices

It is estimated that in the mid-1950s slightly over half of the copper produced outside the Communist countries was usually sold at the price set by the major producers for delivery in the United States. This includes nearly all the copper produced in that country and smaller amounts from Canada, Chile, and several other producers. The remaining output was divided among the London Metal Exchange price, the price set by U.S. producers for export to Europe, and a variety of prices quoted by custom smelters, merchants, and other commodity exchanges.[13] These prices generally move together, differences between them being due to tariffs, shipping costs, and price variations associated with different grades of copper; intervention in one market can drive prices very far apart, however.

In the last four decades, the price of copper has been relatively stable for long periods, more so than the prices of many primary commodities (see table 4-7). Very high prices have prevailed in only a few years — in 1929, in 1955-56, and in 1964-68. Only during the 1930s was there a decrease from a previously stable level; and there have been three principal increases. The price rose from about 12 cents, where it was fixed during World War II and where it had been in the late 1920s, to about 20 cents at the war's end; from 20 to about 25 cents in the early 1950s; and to about 31 cents at the end of that decade. The real price of copper, as deflated by wholesale prices in the United States, appears to have declined gently in the years 1870-1918, to have dropped sharply during and just after World War I, and since then to have risen very slowly. This estimate is derived by excluding those years in which wartime demand, collusion by producers, or the Depression caused prices to deviate considerably from long-run costs in the industry. The entire period since the outbreak of World War II has been "abnormal" in this respect, but it is possible to estimate "normal" prices approximately, as in the range of 25 to 30 cents per pound in the late 1950s and about 30 cents in the early 1960s, or slightly less than the level at which producers held them in 1959-63. The great drop in real price during World War I is the result of the development of non-selective mining methods. These were first applied to underground copper mines, and then made possible the exploitation of the very large, low-grade surface deposits from which most of the world's copper comes today. In the last half century real prices have risen by about 0.2 percent annually, and are still much below the level prevailing before 1914.[14] Within this pattern of stability there have

been many years in which the price was artificially maintained slightly above the equilibrium level, and there have been a few short, violent fluctuations. The most recent of these began in 1964 and has not yet ended.

Recent Events

By the end of 1963, the efforts of the major producers to support prices had created a tight supply situation in copper: while production could be increased to full capacity, inventories were so low that a rise in final consumption would create a much larger increase in demand. Such an increase occurred in late 1963 and early 1964; consumption of primary copper outside the Communist countries rose by 200,000 tons in 1963 and then by 400,000 tons, or nearly 10 percent, in 1964. The increase in consumption, which was largely a result of rapid economic growth in North America and Europe, was reinforced in 1965 by the growing U.S. need for copper brought about by the war in Vietnam. Military requirements were estimated at 300,000 tons per year, or nearly 20 percent of U.S. consumption in 1964.[15] The price of copper as set by producers in the United States rose 7 cents per pound and would have gone much higher but for strenuous efforts to make enough metal available at that level. The price on free markets rose by as much as 60 cents per pound, leading to a sharp separation of markets and a great disparity in prices.

The scope and significance of the shortage cannot be assessed exactly, because some prices have been held artificially low and others have therefore been driven very high. The U.S. producer price was raised from 31 to 32 cents per pound, delivered, then to 34 and to 36 by mid-1965. A further rise to 38 cents was initially prevented only by government intervention and the release of a large amount of metal from the strategic stockpile. In January 1967 the price rose to 38 cents. In the hope of weathering a short upheaval, the major U.S. and African producers also fixed a price for delivery in Europe: this, initially 29.5 cents per pound, was raised by degrees to 42 cents before being abandoned in April 1966. From November 1964 onward this producer price could not always be maintained for all metal, since the Chilean government set a price on exports from that country. The price was usually followed by other producers, but sometimes only after several months' delay. The Chilean export price was raised to 42 cents in early 1966, then to 62 cents and to a peak of 70 cents during the year. These actions made the London Metal Exchange (LME) a marginal market on which prices rose to 60 cents per pound and reached 80 to 95 cents in early 1966. Merchants' prices in the United States followed the LME price, although on a much smaller volume of metal. African producers first raised their prices and then abandoned a producer price and began selling at LME quotations, thus reducing the price on the Exchange. It is estimated that 75 to 80 percent of copper was sold at producer prices during 1964. Some countries, such as the United

---

[13] *Metal Bulletin* (London) 25 February 1955, p. 18; cited by Herfindahl, *Copper Costs and Prices*, p. 186.

[14] Herfindahl, *Copper Costs and Prices*, pp. 201-14. Both the average deviation from the average LME price and the average annual year-to-year variation in that price are close to 15 percent over the entire period since 1925 and over the postwar interval. See table B-2, chap. 3.

[15] T. O'Hanlon, "The Perilous Prosperity of Anaconda," *Fortune*, May 1966. Most of the other material in this section is taken from the monthly market reviews of *Engineering and Mining Journal* for 1965-68.

States, obtained nearly all their requirements without paying premiums; some European importers, such as Germany, had to pay high prices for 40 percent of their copper; and countries such as India and the Latin American importers were forced to pay LME prices for all their supplies.

The price boom shows two distinct peaks, the first in November 1964 and the second in February and March of 1966. (In early 1965, when prices were 50 cents per pound or less, it was widely expected that the boom would end within a few months.) The variation in prices within the general increase has resulted mostly from factors affecting supplies — some to increase, others to reduce the availability of copper. There were major strikes in the United States and Australia in 1964 and in Chile in 1965. At the same time as the latter, the declaration of independence by Rhodesia raised fears that Zambian production, which is exported through Rhodesia and depends on fuel imported from that country, might be cut off in the event of a clash between Rhodesia and the United Kingdom. Thus far there has been no significant interruption of supplies. The United States government released 85,000 tons of copper from its stockpile in 1964, the bulk of it directly to government agencies; then sold 100,000 tons in 1965 and a further 200,000 tons in 1966.[16] Exports of copper were embargoed, and producers were required to set aside a large share of their output for defense needs. In order to hold down the price of imports — or to ensure that imports could be obtained when prices were much higher in Europe — the United States also negotiated an agreement to provide Chile with a $10 million loan for its development program in return for a continued flow of copper at 36 cents per pound. Chile, however, taxed the U.S. firms shipping this copper on the basis of the 42-cent price then in effect. Thus the United States government has intervened most actively to hold down domestic prices and therefore has done the most to drive prices apart. The Chilean government has been the leader in raising producer prices to take advantage of the shortage, so that recently the two governments have been opposed, with other governments and the producers themselves in the middle. The high prices of the last few years have brought out some extra copper production and have accelerated many expansion projects, but little new capacity could be available before 1969, and some of that now planned will not be ready until 1971. In July 1967, strikes closed nearly all copper mines, smelters, and refineries in the United States, and the bulk of capacity remained closed until March 1968. This shutdown necessitated very large net imports and prolonged the shortage and high prices for at least a year. Despite the tight supply situation, the government did not immediately exert pressure to end the strike, in effect countering its policy of 1964-67 except for the continued restraints on domestic civilian use. Chile's influence in the market is related to major developments in that country — the election of a new government in September 1964 and the adoption, over bitter and prolonged political opposition, of a plan to develop the copper industry which will profoundly change the country's relations with pro-

ducers and which may make Chile the largest copper supplier by the early 1970s.

The Copper Industry of Latin America

Development and Structure

The first metals sought and produced in Latin America were gold and silver, and these were the principal mineral exports during the colonial period. Except on a very small scale, the mining of other metals did not begin until the nineteenth century. Copper was first developed in Chile in the early decades of that century. A large industry was developed in Cuba at about the same time; for some years the El Cobre deposit near Santiago de Cuba was the world's third largest copper mine. That mine was closed in 1918, and in this century Cuban production has seldom exceeded 20,000 tons. For several decades Mexico and Peru have also been large suppliers, but until recently neither has approached the output of Chile. Smaller amounts of copper have been produced for many years in Bolivia and in Argentina.

Since the decline of the industry in Cuba and the opening of the large mines of Chile early in this century, there have been few changes in the pattern of copper production within Latin America and only one reversal of position among the larger producers. In the 1940s two mines were developed in Ecuador, at Macuchi and at Zaruma, to supply copper to the United States. Both operations were closed in 1950, when depletion of the gold and silver in the ore made it uneconomical to extract the copper. Altogether about 20,000 tons of metal were obtained. Since 1953 the mine at Zaruma has been worked on a small scale with government assistance. Copper mining was begun in Brazil in the mid-1950s and some 2,000 tons are now produced.[17] More recently, Haiti and Nicaragua have become copper producers. Copper was discovered in Haiti in 1956-58 in the Terre Neuve district, and mining began in 1960. In Nicaragua, production began in 1959 at Suina, Zelaya. Since the mines are small and neither country has much copper-using industry, all the copper is exported as concentrates or other nonmetallic forms. These various increases in production are small compared to the change in Peru, where in 1960 the Toquepala deposit in the extreme south was brought into production. Peru surpassed Mexico to become the region's second-ranking producer, as output rose from 50,000 to about 180,000 tons per year. Production in Mexico increased from about 40,000 tons in the 1930s and 1940s to 60,000 tons in the years following World War II, and has since declined slightly.

Except for the recent great increase in Peru, the change in Latin American copper production has depended almost entirely on Chile. In the late 1920s, output in Chile rose very rapidly from 200,000 to 300,000 tons; in 1932, when the U.S. tariff was imposed and the demand for copper was least, production was cut back to only 100,000 tons. The pre-Depression level was recovered by the late 1930s, and

---

[16] Figures for stockpile releases are given in short tons, since that is how they were always reported, rather than in metric tons.

[17] For a brief summary of the copper industry in each Latin American country, see USBM, *Minerals Yearbook, 1964*, vol. IV.

production rose to nearly half a million tons during the war. During the next decade output varied between 350,000 and 450,000 tons with no net increase. The growth of production was resumed, very unevenly, in the late 1950s; at present output in Chile is close to 700,000 tons, or 70 percent of the Latin American total. During these four decades the region has usually supplied about one-fifth of the world's copper, the share being higher in the late 1930s and at the end of World War II.

Latin America accounts for a larger share of world copper reserves than of production: some 55 million tons, or nearly 30 percent of the world total. This estimate includes 42 million tons in Chile, corresponding mostly to measured reserves of ore. If indicated and inferred material is included, the total rises to more than 90 million tons (see tables 4-3 and 4-8). Similar estimates are not available for most other countries, so comparisons can be made only on the basis of current measured reserves. Chile's copper resources are concentrated in the western flank of the Andes and in the high desert plateaus of six northern and central provinces. The largest reserves are in O'Higgins, with roughly half as much in Antofagasta and Atacama; these are the provinces in which the three largest mines are located. Very little copper is found south of O'Higgins, but there are substantial amounts in three central provinces where the principal medium-sized mines are. Peru has most of the region's remaining reserves, some 11 million tons in all. Copper is widely distributed in the Peruvian Andes for almost the entire length of the country. Until recently, the principal reserves were those in the vicinity of Cerro de Pasco. The largest deposit now is at Toquepala, the only mine comparable in size to the great Chilean mines; but other deposits now under study or development, such as those at Michiquillay, Cuajones, and Cerro Verde, are expected to be equally large. In the last few years several properties have been prepared for mining, and when these are developed Peru's reserves and production will increase considerably. Besides the principal mines in the copper zone of Chile and Peru, there are hundreds of smaller deposits worked by individuals or small companies. These generally produce higher-grade ore and have no facilities for treating it; they sell ore or concentrates to the large mining concerns or, in Chile, to a government agency.

The principal copper belt passes through western Bolivia, on the edge of the tin-bearing zone. Most of the metal is found in ores of tin, lead, zinc, and other metals, and reserves are unknown. Three mines contribute the bulk of the copper produced: Corocoro and Chacarilla in the north, and Tasna in the south. The copper zone appears to extend north into Ecuador, where mineralization occurs in Pichincha and Cotopaxi provinces along the west flank of the central Andean chain. No reserves have been proved except in the mines worked during the 1940s. To the east, the Chilean copper belt appears to extend into Argentina, but very little copper has ever been found on the eastern side of the Andes. The area around San Juan, Mendoza, shows some indications of copper, and discoveries have also been reported near the coast, southwest of Comodoro Rivadavia.[18] More recently, a number of orebodies have been located in the Central Andes near the Chilean border.

Small deposits have been found in Magdalena and Guajira departments in Colombia, but no copper is produced there, nor in Venezuela, Paraguay, or Uruguay. Outside the Andean copper zone, the only deposits in South America are in the highlands of Brazil. Until now production has come from small deposits in Andrades, Rio Grande do Sul, but most of the country's known resources are in two orebodies near Caraíba, Bahia, and another at Camaqua, near São Paulo. Copper is also found in Ceará, Rio Grande do Norte, Minas Gerais and Mato Grosso. Mexico has reserves estimated at 800,000 tons of metal, also mostly of low grade. The largest mine is at Cananea, Sonora; other sizable mines are located in the states of Chihuahua, San Luis Potosí, and Zacatecas, and there are many small workings throughout the north central part of the country. Little is known about the present copper resources of Cuba; at most they are believed to amount to 750,000 tons, principally in Pinar del Río with smaller amounts in Las Villas province. The reserves of eastern Cuba are depleted. Haiti has very small reserves – about 50,000 tons – and those of Nicaragua are probably comparable.

The copper industry in Latin America is based on several hundred mines, of which perhaps ten supply 90 percent or more of the total. The number of concentrating plants is much smaller, for while each large mine includes a concentrator, smaller operators generally sell their ore to a larger company or to a plant established to treat the output of all the mines in an area. The high-grade ore from some small mines is concentrated by hand. Altogether there are perhaps fifty concentrating plants in the region, of which about thirty-five are in Chile. At the next stage, there are about fifteen smelters, including several that are quite small and one or two that operate intermittently. Four of these have capacities of 100,000 tons per year or more, and another of nearly as much. Finally, the region has eight copper refineries, five in Chile and one each in Mexico, Peru, and Brazil. Six produce electrolytic copper, and two only fire refined metal, total capacity being slightly greater for electrolytic refining. Of the region's mine production of copper, virtually all is concentrated, only a small amount of ore being rich enough for direct smelting. Slightly more than 90 percent of the ore is smelted within the region; the remainder is exported as concentrates or used to produce copper chemicals. About 45 percent of mine production, or almost 55 percent of the metallic copper produced, is refined in Latin America, most of the rest being exported as blister copper.

The copper industry of Latin America is dominated by foreign enterprises, particularly by those of the United States. The degree of domination is about the same as for lead and zinc – considerably greater, that is, than for oil, iron and steel, or tin. Generally the importance of foreign capital increases with the degree of processing, as domestic enterprises are active mostly in mining, but this tendency is offset to some extent by government participation in the later stages in Chile. Foreign capital controls the bulk of

[18] *Engineering and Mining Journal*, December 1964, p. 156, and January 1968, p. 104.

production in the three major producers and in Haiti and Nicaragua (see table 4-9). French and Japanese firms operate in Bolivia, Chile, and Peru, and there is some British and Canadian capital in the industry. The major share is produced by such U.S. companies as Anaconda, Kennecott, Cerro de Pasco, Phelps Dodge, Newmont Mining, and the American Smelting and Refining Company. Two of these firms constitute the Gran Minería in Chile, one accounts for the bulk of production in Mexico, and four control most of Peru's output. Domestic private firms are active in six countries, but in only two do they control the industry, and only in Brazil do they own the principal smelting and refining plants. National governments participate in the industry in six countries, through a state mining corporation in Bolivia and presumably in Cuba, by various forms of association with private capital in Ecuador and Mexico, and directly, on a very small scale, in Peru. In Chile the government mineral enterprise is of considerable importance at each stage of processing; it gathers and concentrates the production of many small mines, and accounts for 10 percent of the smelting and 20 percent of the refinery capacity of the country. The state is now also a partner in two of the largest mining companies. Foreign firms also operate fabricating plants throughout Latin America, or participate in them together with domestic capital, but their dominance is less than in earlier stages of the industry. In the copper importing countries particularly, many local firms are active.

Copper in the Latin American Economy

Copper contributes to the economy of Latin America primarily as an export commodity. The copper mining industry was developed for export in every country except Brazil and Argentina, and the bulk of production is exported from every other producing country except Mexico. Total exports are now some 800,000 tons per year and account for 5 percent of the region's foreign exchange earnings. Several features of copper exports in the last decade and a half may be briefly described; no further account will be given of trade before 1950.

Total exports of copper almost doubled in the period 1950-64. Volume has increased fairly steadily, except for sizable reductions in 1953 and 1958 (see table 4-10). Exports were nearly constant in 1961-63 when supplies were controlled by producers' agreements. Before 1960 Chile ac-

counted for about three-fourths of the total; the share dropped slightly when production was expanded in Peru, and has since almost recovered while Peruvian exports have remained constant. Mexico's exports declined slightly in the late 1950s and then more sharply in the 1960s, as consumption cut into supplies. The total value of copper shipped from these three countries rose from $200 million in 1950 to nearly $500 million in 1964; the increase was considerably more rapid in the early 1950s than in recent years. The value of exports fluctuates more than the volume, since output is cut back in years of low prices and increased as much as possible in times of scarcity. Earnings from copper exports rose by 60 percent during the Korean War (when volume increased only 10 percent) and dropped by 40 percent between 1956 and 1956 (while volume held nearly constant and prices fell markedly). From 1960 through part of 1964 prices were stable and earnings increased in line with physical exports. Mexico has become less dependent on copper, and Peru appreciably more dependent; copper has also increased somewhat as a share of total exports in Chile. For the three countries together, copper provides between 20 and 25 percent of all foreign exchange: over 60 percent in Chile, about 20 percent in Peru, and 2 or 3 percent in Mexico.

Copper exports from Latin America have changed in both type and destination during this period. Between 1960 and 1967, due to large exports of blister copper from Peru and a decline in the output of fire-refined metal in Chile, practically all the growth in exports took the form of increased trade in unrefined metal. Exports of refined copper did not increase at all; exports of concentrates and other nonmetallic forms doubled, but are still a small share of the total. The average degree of processing of Latin American copper has declined considerably, lowering the average value of exports and contributing slightly to the recent slow growth of earnings.

In the early 1950s, almost 70 percent of the region's copper exports went to the United States in the form of metal; the bulk of this was refined, but a substantial portion was blister copper (see table 4-2). In these years, the United States exported to Europe more refined copper than it imported from Latin America in the form of blister; thus all the region's exports of unrefined metal went directly or indirectly to Europe, the larger share being refined in the United States, which also imported for consumption a sub-

TABLE 4-2. Latin American Copper in the United States and Western Europe, 1950-52 and 1961-63
(Thousands of metric tons)

Average		Latin American Exports to United States	Europe	U.S. Exports to Europe	Total Direct and Indirect Latin American Exports to Europe	
1950-52:	Refined	223.2	50.6	122.0	Amount	191.9
	Unrefined	87.4	19.3	0.0	Share of total exports (%)	42.0
	Total	310.6	69.9	122.0	Share of consumption (%)	21.0
1961-63:	Refined	4.5	232.7	234.2	Amount	617.9
	Unrefined	296.5	151.0	0.0	Share of total exports (%)	78.1
	Total	301.0	383.7	234.2	Share of consumption (%)	32.6

Sources: Tables 4-6 and 4-10. USBM, *Minerals Yearbook, 1950* to *1952* and *1961* to *1963*.

Note: Totals refer to total refined plus unrefined bulk metal only, excluding trade in all other forms.

stantial amount of refined copper. Immediately after the Korean War, Latin America began exporting large amounts of copper directly to Europe, and by the early 1960s Europe had become a more important customer than the United States. Furthermore, the remaining U.S. imports are almost entirely in the form of blister copper, while Europe takes predominantly refined metal and somewhat less unrefined copper. The United States continues to refine much Latin American copper for re-export to Europe, but now imports only a small volume of refined metal for domestic use. The share of exports from Latin America which ultimately reaches Europe as blister or refined copper has increased from 40 to 80 percent. Latin America now supplies about one-third of Europe's primary copper requirements, compared with one-fifth in the early 1950s.

On a smaller scale copper is also important as an element of domestic consumption in Latin America. Approximately 110,000 tons, or one-eighth of the region's total mine production, was consumed annually in the form of refined copper during the middle 1960s. This is roughly the amount of copper used by the metal fabricating industries of the region. The amount of copper in final use, including trade in alloys and semimanufactures, was some 140,000 tons. Brazil accounts for one-third of this total, and Mexico and Argentina for about 40,000 and 20,000 tons, respectively. Together with Chile and Peru, these are the only countries with sizable metal fabricating industries, and are thus the only consumers of refined copper in appreciable amounts. The other Latin American countries obtain their copper almost entirely in semifabricated form. Venezuela is the largest consumer in this group, taking nearly 8,000 tons annually; Colombia is the next largest, followed by Cuba (see table 4-11). Until recently, the share of imported copper supplied by the neighboring producer countries was quite low. In 1961 intraregional trade in copper was only about 5,000 tons, or some 6 percent of imports and 0.6 percent of exports; since then, because of a large flow from Chile to Argentina and Brazil, it has become more than seven times as large. In all years the bulk of such trade is in refined copper. There is no trade in unrefined metal or in ores and concentrates; and while much of the exports of semifabricated copper go to other countries in the region, the amount is small compared with total imports in that form.

Imports of copper are largest in Brazil, where production is low and constant while consumption is increasing rapidly; domestic mines provide only 3,000 tons out of the 50,000 tons now required, with the remainder imported at a cost of $30 million or more. Except for petroleum, copper has been the country's costliest mineral import for many years, and it therefore receives priority in a ten-year plan to discover and develop domestic mineral resources.[19] Some $3 million were to be spent in the first four years in mapping and evaluating copper deposits in five states, with the greatest effort in Bahia; development of one mine there and one

in São Paulo is expected to raise output by some 5,000 tons.[20] A similar effort is under way in the provinces of Mendoza and Neuquén, Argentina, where 50,000 square kilometers have been mapped. An area the same size is being studied in Sonora, Mexico, in the search for minerals of which copper is the most important; several new deposits have been located. Mexico is currently a net exporter, but its reserves are small and mostly of very low grade, so that rising consumption could result in reduced exports or even imports in the near future. Finally, the copper zone in Ecuador is also to be investigated, in the hope of finding new deposits near the mines worked in the 1940s.[21] These projects, particularly in Brazil and Argentina, indicate the burden of imports into certain countries even though the region as a whole is extremely well endowed with copper.

Latin America's copper resources are rather highly concentrated, and their exploitation has depended on large enterprises with adequate technical and financial strength. For this reason, and because copper has only recently become a significant element of domestic consumption, no country has yet built up a sizable mining industry behind tariffs or other forms of protection. Import substitution in copper has been limited to fabricating. This situation will change to the extent that Brazil increases mine output, but the amounts involved will be small compared to total production in the region. Thus regional integration of the Latin American copper industry will not involve the elimination of much high-cost production or the creation of larger enterprises to enjoy economies of scale.

Although these considerations are extremely important for a number of manufacturing industries and for some industries, such as steel, that are closely related to natural resource commodities, they are negligible for copper at all stages up to refined bulk metal. From there onward, in the fabrication of copper and its alloys and their use in manufacturing, there is considerable scope for integration through increased trade and reductions in costs. At present Latin America is a net exporter of refined copper, shipping about 30 percent of mine output to other regions in this form. However, the importing countries of the region obtain much of their bulk copper from other suppliers, such as the United States; thus a sizable amount of trade could be diverted to go directly from producing to consuming countries in Latin America. In view of the structure of the international industry described above, such a change in trade patterns will probably depend on the creation of more refining capacity in the region. As the share of exports of blister copper declines, the present indirect trade may be eliminated. There is still more room for such substitution in trade in semimanufactures, since many coun-

---

[19] Brazil, Ministério das Minas e Energia, Departamento Nacional da Produção Mineral, *Plano Mestre Decenal para Avaliação de Recursos Minerais do Brasil, 1965-1974* (Rio de Janeiro, February 1965).

[20] *Engineering and Mining Journal*, June 1966, p. 713. The mines are to be developed with Japanese technical assistance.

[21] See *Engineering and Mining Journal*, October 1963, p. 144, November 1965, p. 156, and August 1967, pp. 104-5, 148, for information on Argentina and Mexico. The Ecuadorean plan is described in Junta Nacional de Planificación y Coordinación Económica, *Plan General de Desarrollo Económico y Social, III/3, La Minería y el Petróleo* (Quito, 1963). See also United Nations Development Program, *Report on the Activities of UNDP in 1967*, doc. DP/L.67/Add. 3, 12 April 1968, pp. 66-68.

tries import all their copper in that form, mostly from outside the region. Only Chile exports semifabricated copper, and low capacity and high costs limit the amount of trade. Expansion and improvement of the fabricating industry in Chile, and perhaps in other countries with large metalworking industries — Argentina, Brazil, and Mexico, for example — could result in much greater intraregional trade.

Copper and Political Issues

Except in Chile, copper is not a subject of major political importance in Latin America. In producing countries the issues and problems associated with copper are those of nonferrous metal mining generally; in importing countries the desire for self-sufficiency has not led to much import substitution or to the emergence of significant questions of policy. In both Mexico and Peru, however, important questions did arise in the 1950s and 1960s, and it may be useful to discuss these two situations briefly before considering at greater length the case of Chile.

The "problems" in Mexico and Peru exhibit a sort of symmetry. In the former country, the object of government policy was to reduce the control of foreign enterprise with the minimum economic effect — the least disturbance to investment and output. In the latter, the intent was to raise output and especially exports as much as possible without creating excessive dependence on one product or on the foreign enterprises which would produce it. Both efforts appear to have succeeded in their aims thus far, but either or both could in the future give rise to the difficulties the governments sought to avoid.

By the 1950s, nonferrous metals were virtually the only Mexican exports still dominated by foreign enterprise: agriculture was controlled by domestic capital, mostly private, and petroleum had been nationalized in 1938. Thus it became a goal of government policy to "Mexicanize" the nonferrous mining and processing industry, especially the part devoted to exports, by transferring majority control to nationals. At the same time, it was recognized that output had been stagnant for some time, partly because the country's resources are rather poor and even more because of a great many taxes on production and exports. Expropriation or other extreme measures would probably have driven off foreign investment or aid for the industry and might have created difficulties even for domestic supply. It was decided, therefore, to limit new mining concessions to companies that are at least 51 percent owned by Mexicans, and to induce existing firms to sell a controlling interest by granting them tax reductions in return. The first law to this effect was passed in 1961; in 1963 the entire mining tax code was revised to allow any company to solicit a tax reduction of between 50 and 75 percent, with a 50 percent decrease being automatic upon Mexicanization. The major copper producer, which is the largest company in the industry, was given twenty years in which to sell 51 percent of its stock. The conversion to domestic ownership has been more rapid in the lead and zinc industry, where there are more and smaller firms and where a larger share of output is exported.[22]

The existence of very large deposits of copper in southern Peru has been known for decades, but not until 1960 was the first one brought into production. For some years the ownership of claims to the area was in dispute; in 1948 this dispute was settled, and the American Smelting and Refining Company gained full title to the deposits at Toquepala and Quellaveco. The Cerro de Pasco and Newmont Mining Companies owned the nearby Cuajones deposit; together these orebodies hold some 10 million tons of copper. At that time Peru was producing about 30,000 tons annually, mostly for export, and welcomed an increase in production which would not bring about too heavy dependence on a single export. In 1951, therefore, the government introduced a new mining code and greatly reduced production and export taxes. In 1952 ASARCO finished exploring its properties and entered negotiations with the other companies for a joint enterprise; the Southern Peru Copper Company was formed in 1954, under an agreement with the government on the basis of the new mining code. Development of the Toquepala deposit began the next year on receipt of a loan of $100 million, half the estimated total cost of the project, from the Export-Import Bank of the United States. In 1960 the smelter at Ilo began operations, boosting Peru's copper production to 180,000 tons and raising the share of copper in total exports to more than 15 percent. The process of opening up the resources of southern Peru took more than a decade, but initially it proceeded smoothly with no political difficulties. Peru obtained the desired increase in exports; the companies obtained guarantees against unnegotiated changes in the mining law. Several features combined to make the agreements possible and to reduce political opposition: exports were diversified rather than concentrated on an already dominant product; the number of producing companies was increased; and the United States government, by participating through the Bank, gave the companies some protection against loss and thereby reduced the need for guarantees and concessions by the Peruvian government.

By 1967, however, a combination of economic and political factors made a further expansion of exports highly desirable and at the same time difficult. The fishmeal industry, which provided most of the growth in Peru's exports from 1961 onward, suffered a recession which contributed to the import restrictions and devaluation of September 1967. Copper is the commodity best suited for a large expansion of output because of the continued high demand, which had been intensified by the strike in the United States, and the existence of several large deposits ready for development. The two most likely to be exploited first, Cuajones and Michiquillay, could add some 285,000 tons and over $200 million to Peru's exports. At the time of writing this study, the government's readiness to encourage the required investment had lessened; the tax exemptions granted for the development of Toquepala are now, by Congressional authorization, to be revoked, and the contract negotiated for Cuajones in 1955 is also to be replaced by the ordinary provisions of the country's mining legislation. The success of the Toquepala venture may not there-

---

[22] See *Engineering and Mining Journal*, August 1961, July and October 1963; *Mining World*, March 1963; USBM, *Minerals Yearbook, 1963*, vol. IV.

fore soon be repeated. In this respect, the Peruvian experience resembles that of Chile, which is also marked by successful agreements and later political and economic difficulties.[23]

Copper in Chile

History and Structure

The economy of Chile has depended for several centuries on the export of minerals; gold, silver, copper, iron ore, and nitrates have been important in turn, and several other products have been exported in lesser amounts. Copper has been the country's principal export in two distinct periods. The first of these has been mentioned briefly; it extended from some time in the eighteenth century, or about a hundred years after copper mining began in Chile, into the 1890s. By the period 1800-1820, Chile's production had increased to 9 percent of the world total. The share continued to increase rapidly in the next several decades, to a peak of 44 percent in the 1860s. In the middle of the nineteenth century, when copper production began on a large scale in the United States, and as lower-cost mines came into operation, prices fell sharply. Chilean output was reduced to half the level of the 1870s only two decades later, and the country's share of total world production declined to 6 percent.[24] In this period all production came from small mines working veins of relatively rich ore. A few foreign companies were active in Chile, but 90 percent or more of production was controlled by Chilean nationals. Investments were not large enough to require external financing, and essentially the entire value of exports remained in Chile. Copper was first shipped as concentrates, but after the 1830s a substantial part was smelted in Chile.

For a few decades after the first copper boom, natural nitrates were Chile's principal exports; the country controlled most of the world's supply of these salts and enjoyed high prices and revenues from them. This monopoly was broken at the time of World War I by the development of synthetic nitrates, and the Chilean industry contracted to a low level of output. At the same time, methods of mining large, low-grade copper deposits were developed. Introduced into Chile between 1900 and 1920, these initiated a second period of dependence on copper exports. The large Chilean orebodies are enormous, containing 100 million tons or more of ore of highly uniform grade, between 1 and 2 percent. Their development required investments much larger than those that had previously attracted local capital. Chilean investors were unable or unwilling to finance these projects; as a result, foreign enterprises came to dominate the industry. This is perhaps the chief feature distinguishing the present period of copper mining from that of the nineteenth century.

The first large mine developed was El Teniente, in central Chile, where the high-grade ore had been exhausted by 1897. The property was bought by foreigners in 1904 and in 1915 was sold to the Kennecott Copper Company. Operations began on a small scale in 1906 and regular production in 1912. Chuquicamata, the second large orebody, changed ownership several times before passing to the Anaconda Company in 1923. At one time it was owned, but not worked, by a British trading firm. Anaconda formed a company in 1916 to exploit the third large mine at Potrerillos. Production began at Chuquicamata in 1915 and at Potrerillos in 1926. By 1913, El Teniente alone produced 20 percent of Chile's copper; by 1920 it and Chuquicamata accounted for more than 80 percent of the total. The decline in copper prices brought about by the introduction of the new mining methods made many small mines unprofitable, and production from the Chilean-owned sector declined by almost half between 1911 and 1928. Thus, by the 1920s U.S. enterprises dominated the Chilean copper industry. Measured by the share of total output, this dominance continued to increase until the late 1940s, at which time the major producers accounted for over 95 percent of production. Since then there has been a resurgence of the smaller mines, which now supply over 10 percent of Chile's copper.

The structure of the Chilean copper industry has not changed greatly since the large enterprises were established. The three large mines constitute the Gran Minería. El Teniente was owned until 1966 by the Braden Copper Company, a subsidiary of Kennecott. Chuquicamata was owned until 1969 by the Chile Exploration Company, an Anaconda subsidiary. These are respectively the largest underground mine and the largest open pit copper mine, in copper content, in the world. Anaconda also owns the Andes Copper Mining Company, which works the deposit at El Salvador; this orebody came into production in 1959, after exhaustion of the nearby Potrerillos deposit. All these companies have smelters to treat the ore from their mines, and ship only metal. The first two also have refineries; fire refining only is done at El Teniente, and electrolytic facilities operate to treat oxide ore at Chuquicamata. The entire output of the Gran Minería is exported as metal, except for several thousand tons sold to Chilean fabricators; part of this is exported as semimanufactures. Some 17,000 people are employed in this sector.

Mines producing between 100 and 2,600 tons of ore per day are classified in the Mediana Minería. One mine of 3,500 tons per day is included in this group, as are several concentrating plants and other facilities operated by the state. Two enterprises have their own smelters, and one also produces fire-refined copper. One medium-sized company is a subsidiary of Anaconda; the rest are variously owned by Chilean, French, Canadian, and U.S. capital. The ten largest of these mines produce about 60 percent of the copper outside the Gran Minería. This sector employs some 10,000 people. All smaller mines are counted in the Pequeña Minería; there are about 2,000 such properties in all, employing between 4,600 and 6,200 people. These mines are worked intermittently, according to market conditions; many depend on the value of gold or silver in the ore and

[23]See Engineering and Mining Journal, February 1968, p. 185; and Washington Post, 12 May 1968.

[24]C. W. Reynolds, "Development Problems of an Export Economy: The Case of Chile and Copper," in M. Mamalakis and C. W. Reynolds, Essays on the Chilean Economy (Yale University, Economic Growth Center, 1965), p. 212. See also sources noted in fn. 3 of this chapter. Reynolds' study is the principal source for the discussion of Chilean copper policy, below.

cannot profitably mine copper lacking in precious metals. They sell ore or hand-sorted concentrates to the medium-sized mines or to government agencies. It was estimated that in the early 1960s none of these mines could work ore below 3 percent in grade, or at a price below 30 cents per pound; the limits for the Mediana Minería are about 1.8 percent, or 28 cents. Limits of 1.5 percent and 20 cents were estimated for the largest mines, but these are too strict with respect to grade: production at Chuquicamata now comes from ore of between 1.0 and 1.3 percent.[25]

The government does not directly own or operate copper mines, but its role in the industry is nonetheless considerable. Several agencies are involved. The Casas Compradores de Minerales, or mining banks, buy ore from the smallest mines, providing credit and some degree of stability in prices to keep marginal mines working. Taxes are much lower than for larger operations, and there are also some direct subsidies in the sales of machinery and equipment, provision of low-interest loans, and so on. Technical advice is also available. The small mines are viewed as a means of exploration, particularly for orebodies which might be developed into mines of the Mediana class, and the subsidy is justified on this basis as well as for the volume and stability of employment it provides. The ores and concentrates bought this way are usually delivered to the Empresa Nacional de Minería (ENAMI), the state mining company. ENAMI operates a number of concentrating plants located to serve several mines in an area. (There are about fifty privately owned plants in the Mediana group, to which operators of small mines can sell their ore.) ENAMI also operates two smelters, one at Paipote, built in 1951, and one at Las Ventanas, built in 1964. The Las Ventanas plant includes an electrolytic refinery, built in 1966. These facilities were established to process concentrates from the small and medium mines, to raise the value of exports, and to supply metal to domestic fabricators. The refinery will treat blister copper from the two state-owned smelters and from the smelter at El Teniente. Finally, there is a separate agency for dealing with the companies of the Gran Minería. Until 1966 this was the Departamento del Cobre; now it is the Corporación del Cobre, which is a semi-autonomous branch of the Mining Ministry. The Copper Corporation is empowered to collect and publish information; to regulate production, exports and prices, setting export prices if unsatisfied with those in force; to participate in or create mixed enterprises in association with the foreign companies; and to oversee labor and social conditions in the industry and arbitrate disputes.[26]

The history of copper in Chile since the 1920s has been briefly described above; it will suffice here to point out several features which have contributed especially to the formation of government attitudes and policies toward the industry, and to the place of copper exports in Chile's economy over the last few decades. First, Chile was very hard hit by the Depression.[27] Copper production in 1932 was less than one-third the level of 1929, and prices fell from about 14 cents to only 5 cents; thus the value of exports declined drastically. Production was curtailed even more in the United States, but a high tariff kept out Chilean copper and so shifted part of the burden to Chile; the effects on national income and on the balance of trade were much less severe in the United States. Second, there is a widespread belief in Chile that the country has consistently been discriminated against in efforts by producers or by the United States government to control the market. This is especially the case where prices are concerned: losses of several hundred million dollars are attributed to price control during World War II and the Korean War.[28] This experience has helped make the control of prices by the government an important element of Chilean copper policy. Tariffs, output restrictions, and other types of intervention are also believed to have worked to Chile's disadvantage. Third, since World War II Chile has lost ground to other producers, as production has increased relatively slowly. At the same time the share of copper refined in Chile has declined markedly, and the United States has become more important as a refining center for Chilean copper exported to Europe. These changes in part reflect changes in demand and cost in the world copper industry, and Chilean policy toward the Gran Minería has been designed to compensate for them. To a considerable degree, however, the changes result from Chile's policies and its dealings with the major foreign producers. The history of these policies deserves examination for its relation to international trends and events and its significance for the development of the Chilean economy.

Issues and Policies

The operations of the copper industry in Chile raise a number of issues. Several of these are of minor importance or for other reasons present no political problems. In the small mining sector, for example, it has not been difficult to devise a program of state participation and assistance, the aims and instruments of which have already been described. Similarly, the provision of copper for domestic use is easy to achieve; and such matters as the compensation and working conditions of miners have been dealt with by legislation that does not directly involve major issues. There remain two fundamental questions which together include most of the specific matters that have claimed the attention of successive governments. First, how much revenue in the form of foreign exchange will the production of copper bring Chile? Second, how much control should the state have over certain of the industry's operations and decisions, notably those concerning refining and marketing? Control may be sought simply to increase revenue, but it may also be desired for reasons of economic stability or independence or for motives of national pride. Other as-

---

[25] These estimates are from CORFO, *Geografía Económica de Chile*, pp. 585-89.

[26] These provisions are contained in Law 16,425, published in *Diario Oficial de la República de Chile*, 25 January 1966.

[27] See the discussion in chap. 1, under the heading "Depression and World War."

[28] M. Vera Valenzuela, *La Política Económica* . . . , pp. 50 ff., estimates the total loss, or reduction in export value, due to price control, as some $500 million.

pects of the industry's operations, such as mine production, labor relations, and the employment and training of Chilean nationals, have not generally been at issue.

The question of control or participation, as distinct from that of earnings, was not directly taken up by any Chilean government before 1964. State intervention was limited to occasionally fixing prices for exports. Even this sort of control was first adopted to counter price controls imposed by the United States government, and has been effective only in conditions of severe market imbalance. Most government actions have been directed toward increasing the revenue remaining in Chile from copper mining, and particularly to increasing the share taken by the government.

Of the total value of copper produced by the Gran Minería, part is used to import goods required for current production or investment, and part is repatriated profits for investment or distribution in the United States. The remainder, or the value returned to Chile, includes: payments for labor and other inputs in Chile, purchases of Chilean capital goods, duties on imports, various indirect taxes and charges, and direct taxes on income or profits. The share of profits returned to Chile depends on capital purchases in that country and on direct taxation. The latter is most easily varied by the government and was the principal instrument of Chilean copper policy between the 1920s and the 1969 agreement affecting Anaconda.[29]

In the first years of operation the Gran Minería was quite isolated from the Chilean economy, forming an enclave whose only link with the host country was the purchase of labor. There were no restrictions on the repatriation of profits and almost no purchases on capital account in Chile. The first income tax, amounting to less than 1 percent of the value of production, was levied in 1922. Over the next three decades the rate of direct taxation was repeatedly increased. A levy of 6 percent of profits was established in 1924; this was raised to 12 percent in 1925 and to 18 percent in 1934; in 1939-40 the rate was increased to 33 percent by a further 6 percent rise in the basic tax and a new impost of 9 percent. In 1942, after copper prices were fixed in the United States, an extraordinary tax of 50 percent was levied on all income derived from sales of copper at prices higher than those fixed by Law 7,160. The basic rate under this provision was raised to 60 percent in 1953, by Law 11,137. In 1951 the price of copper was again fixed by the United States government, at 24.5 cents per pound. As this action was violently denounced in Chile, the United States agreed to the European price of 27.5 cents for Chilean copper, the 3-cent difference being retained by the Chilean government. This arrangement was ended in 1952 with the passage of Law 10,255, which authorized the Central Bank of Chile to buy copper from the companies at 24.5 cents and sell it at whatever price could be obtained. The surtax could therefore be much more than 3 cents per pound; for a time, when Chilean copper sold for 35.5 cents, it was 11 cents. When the Korean War ended, copper prices fell sharply and revenues from the surtax declined. As the Chilean government tried to continue selling copper at 35 cents, a substantial stockpile was built up; it was later liquidated by purchases for the U.S. stockpile.

In addition to these direct taxes and a variety of lesser taxes and duties, the government used exchange controls to increase its revenues. By Laws 5,107 and 5,185 of 1932, an exchange rate of 19.37 pesos per dollar was set for purchases of Chilean currency to meet the "legal costs of production," the amount of which could be fixed by the government. In the next two decades various rates were established for the costs of wage increases and for investment purchases made in Chile; the existence of several rates and the difficulty of identifying all the costs to which they applied make it impossible to ascertain exactly the impact of this provision. It is clear, however, that as inflation reduced the value of the peso, the law amounted primarily to a tax on labor, since labor was the major component of the costs of production included; and that by the 1950s the revenues produced by this tax were comparable to those obtained by direct taxation, being some $35 million in 1951, when direct taxes were $47.1 million and import duties $6.7 million.[30]

The result of exchange controls and increases in direct levies was to raise the returned value of copper sales to 94 percent of total value by 1953; taxes amounted to more than half this amount, and labor costs, including the burden of the exchange restrictions, were only one-fifth of the total. Some 86 percent of the companies' profits were taken in taxation, leaving them only a 2 percent return on assets. The total tax rate on copper mining did not exceed 50 percent in any other important producing country, and in several it was 30 percent or less. Taxation and exchange restrictions had in effect converted Chile from a very low-cost producer to one of the highest in the world.[31] In consequence, the companies in Chile made only the investments necessary to maintain their output, and invested instead in properties in the United States. Between 1948 and 1952 Anaconda had spent $125 million at Chuquicamata, for as the oxide ore in the upper part of the orebody was depleted it became necessary to build a smelter to treat the increasing amount of sulfide ore. The company did not, however, add electrolytic capacity to refine the resulting blister copper, and by 1954 its investment program had ended. In that year and the next there was a net disinvestment of more than $50 million in the Gran Minería, and the effect of this on Chile was accentuated by the price decline of 1953-54. The policy of steadily increasing the share of value returned through taxes, without regard to its effect on investment and output, appeared to be leading to a crisis.

In these circumstances, a major change was effected in Chilean copper policy. By the Law 11,828 of 1955 (the

---

[29] This summary is taken from Reynolds, ". . . Chile and Copper." See also M. Vera Valenzuela, *La Política Económica . . . ,* especially pp. 55-86 and 205-7.

[30] R. Goode, *Taxes and Exchange Rates Applicable to Mining: Four Latin American Case Studies* (IMF, 1954, mimeo.).

[31] For a good summary discussion of Chilean copper policy after World War II, see E. N. Baklanoff, "International Taxation and Mineral Development: The Political Economy of Chile's La Gran Minería del Cobre," *Proceedings of the 58th National Tax Conference* (New Orleans, 8-12 November 1965).

Nuevo Trato al Cobre, or "New Deal"), the discriminatory exchange control was abolished and the variety of taxes was replaced by a single direct tax on profits. A rate of 75 percent was established at a base level of production for each company, declining to 50 percent at twice that level and rising to 80 percent if output fell below 80 percent of the base volume. In effect, a 25 percent surtax, declining linearly with output, was added to a basic 50 percent profits tax; the surtax declined more rapidly after production exceeded 150 percent of the base rate.[32] New companies formed under this law would pay only the flat 50 percent tax. At the companies' urging, the amortization rate for new investments under the law was set by decree at 20 percent. This high allowance, together with the declining tax rate, constituted a sizable investment credit, in contrast to the previous policy. The companies were also given full control over their sales again. Anaconda responded by investing $118 million to open the mine at El Salvador and replace output from Potrerillos, and $60 million to expand Chuquicamata; Kennecott invested $25 million at El Teniente. Total Chilean production rose by 100,000 tons or nearly one-fourth between 1955 and 1960, and the country recovered its position as the world's second largest producer. Anaconda's expansion resulted in a 55 percent tax rate; Kennecott paid about 72 percent. Purchases from Chilean suppliers also increased with the abolition of the discriminatory exchange rate, further raising the value returned to Chile.

By 1960, however, the impact of the tax reduction was largely spent. The companies had plans for a major expansion, but they were unwilling to proceed solely on the basis of the Nuevo Trato. Kennecott proposed an investment of $200 million to raise output at El Teniente from 180,000 to 280,000 tons, and Anaconda was considering the expenditure of $128 million for an electrolytic refinery to treat blister output from El Salvador and Chuquicamata. Finally the Cerro Corporation, which is a major producer in Peru but had no mines in Chile, planned to invest $90 million to develop a medium-sized mine at Río Blanco. The companies opened discussions of these projects with the Alessandri government in 1960, but during 1961 the negotiations broke down completely. The producers either postponed their investments or spent their money elsewhere. Efforts by the administration to pass a new copper law in 1963 were unsuccessful, and there were no further initiatives until after the election of the Frei government in 1964.

Several issues were involved in the negotiations of 1960-61. The government was determined not to perpetuate the 20 percent amortization provision which had yielded the companies, especially Anaconda, relatively high profits in the previous five years. The producers yielded on this point when the government declared its intention to limit any tax guarantees to the amortization period. The companies' principal demand was for a twenty-year exten-

sion of the tax rates of the 1955 law, with a guarantee against any increases. In the negotiations, agreement was reached that such guarantees would be granted for specific investment projects, but that the rate of taxation for the entire mining sector could be raised and that the higher rate would apply to future investments. However, there was sufficient political opposition to any guarantee to prevent the administration from introducing a law containing these provisions, which might have been regarded as a "sellout" to the Congress. Chile was at this time undergoing a political crisis which the government was unable to surmount, and this situation more than any specific issue prevented the conclusion of an agreement.

There were nonetheless two questions on which no agreement was possible between the government and the companies. The first was the expansion of electrolytic refinery capacity in Chile. The share of mine output refined had dropped considerably during the decade as a result of the shift to sulfide ores at Chuquicamata and a reduction in fire refining at El Teniente. Anaconda agreed to build a new refinery — this was in fact its principal investment project — but Kennecott refused. The company then had a near monopoly of sales of fire-refined copper in Europe, and had also recently built an electrolytic plant in the United States. The second issue was still less tractable: both companies refused to agree to any intervention by the Departamento del Cobre in setting prices or marketing copper, as it had done from 1952 to 1955. The government could not accept the implied dependence on the producers' decisions, and the negotiations ended in stalemate. The government thereupon returned to the pre-1955 policy, and although the Nuevo Trato remained in effect, additional surtaxes of 5 and 8 percent were passed in 1961. One of these was intended as an extraordinary contribution to reconstruction after the earthquake of 1960, but it was not repealed after the damage was repaired. Early in 1963 the government sought to open negotiations again, and later that year introduced in Congress proposals for a twenty-year moratorium on new copper taxes, but withdrew before widespread opposition. Thus the opportunity for investment was lost, and with it a great deal of much needed foreign exchange. The loss to Chile of postponing the industry's expansion for five years is estimated at some $760 million.[33]

The Christian Democratic Administration, which came to power in the presidential election of 1964, was opposed to the copper companies' plans and demands of 1960-61. However, the new government was under the same pressure as its predecessor to devise a solution permitting an expansion of production, so it immediately sought negotiations with the producers; exploratory discussions were begun even before the election. The companies, eager to invest in Chile rather than in higher-cost areas, had meanwhile modified their plans and had retreated considerably from their opposition to state participation or

[32]The base rate of production was set at 136,842 tons for El Teniente, 154,065 tons for Chuquicamata, and 42,446 tons for Potrerillos-El Salvador. These figures correspond to average annual output circa 1950.

[33]Baklanoff, "International Taxation and Mineral Development . . . ," p. 341. A price of 30 cents per pound is assumed, for an increased output of 380,000 tons and a share of value returned of two-thirds.

control. The impasse was finally broken by the offer of Kennecott to sell the government 51 percent of the Braden Company, for some $80 million. Anaconda responded by offering to form a new joint company, with 25 percent state participation, to develop the deposit of La Exótica, near Chuquicamata. A similar agreement for 25 percent state ownership was reached with Cerro for the development of the Río Blanco deposit.

The adoption of association with the foreign companies, or "Chileanization" of the industry, as the major element of government policy resolved or reduced several previously intractable problems. The confrontation between the government and Kennecott over refining and marketing would end with state acquisition of a majority interest in Braden; the likelihood of expropriation was much reduced, and the difficulties over guarantees of loans or investments thereby lessened; and direct state participation in profits made taxation somewhat less important.

On this basis an agreement was reached in December 1964 that the companies would continue to operate under the modified law of 1955 while the government undertook to pass legislation to guarantee loans obtained by the companies, authorize state participation in joint enterprises, and appropriate the necessary funds. Since the Christian Democrats did not then control either house of Congress by themselves or in coalition, no progress was possible until after the Congressional elections in March 1965. The House, in which the party of President Frei acquired a majority, passed the legislation at the end of June. The Senate, which has the power to block House action by a two-thirds vote, did not assent to the new Law until October: since only one-third of the upper house was elected in March, the Christian Democrats were unable to acquire one-third of the seats. Law 16,425 was finally signed into law in January 1966. Decrees authorizing investment in the new joint company, Compañía Minera Andina, at Río Blanco and by Anaconda at Chuquicamata and El Salvador were signed in December of that year; the decree creating the joint Sociedad Minera El Teniente was signed in March 1967. The new Compañía Minera Exótica was created later in 1967,[34] and development began in September of that year.

The delay of a year in passing the new law resulted from the intense opposition of all other political parties in Chile, which not only were opposed to one or more elements of the Christian Democratic program, but also did not wish to see that party obtain the credit for solving one of the major national problems and thereby greatly increasing its strength. The Socialist-Communist coalition which opposed Frei in 1964 favored expropriation of the Gran Minería and opposed any accommodation which made that event less likely. The parties of the Right were not particularly concerned with the copper legislation, but opposed it in order to force concessions on the other principal items of the administration's program, tax and land reform. These had the strong support of the United States through the Alli-

ance for Progress, so that interference by, or accommodation to, the United States was involved in both major aspects of government policy. As the administration could not afford to wait for the next Congressional elections to proceed, some compromises were made both in the copper law and in the reform program in order to gain the votes necessary for Senate passage of the former. During 1965 and early 1966 there were also considerable labor difficulties, partly political in origin.

The copper law of 1966 follows the Nuevo Trato of 1955 with respect to taxation, except that the minimum rate is now 52.5 percent and the penalty for cutting output below the base level is 85 percent. Special tax reductions or exemptions from import duties can also be granted for new investments to reduce costs, raise output by 30 percent or more, or increase the level of processing. Foreign investments have no privileges or immunities such as are granted to domestic capital, but the foreign investors are guaranteed that there will be no discrimination in exchange rates. The powers of the Corporación del Cobre created by the law have already been described. If investment proceeds as planned, Chile will by about 1971 have a capacity of nearly twice its mid-1960 output, and should once again be the world's leading producer. As part of the agreement with the companies, refinery capacity is to be increased so far as possible in step with mine output, gradually raising the share of production refined electrolytically to more than 50 percent.

For nearly four years after the passage of the law the companies, particularly Anaconda, were able to make and retain very large profits from the high price of copper which has persisted much longer than expected. Chilean tax revenues were in consequence lower than they would have been under the terms prevailing before 1966.

For these reasons the new policy did not greatly reduce the political opposition to association with the U.S. companies. The Frei government, facing national elections in 1970, therefore renewed pressure on Anaconda in May 1969 to accept majority state control. The company was obliged to enter into renegotiation of the twenty-year contract concluded only four years earlier. The objective of the Chilean government was not only to gain majority control but also to benefit from the continued unusually high copper price. Anaconda, whose Chilean operation constituted only one-third of its total sales but gave the company most of its profits, either offered or was compelled to provide the option to sell its entire holdings at Chuquicamata after 1972. Until then, the Chilean government will control 51 percent of the mine and receive 51 percent of the profits. In effect the company agreed to eventual expropriation with compensation, with payment out of the government's share of the profits. In addition, the government also insisted on an overprice arrangement on Anaconda's 49 percent share of the operation; the base price was 40 cents per pound, with the major amount of any excess to be retained by the government on a sliding scale (the Chilean government will receive 70 percent of the overprice above 60 cents per pound). Anaconda agreed to this arrangement on condition that Kennecott would also accept it. After protracted negotiations, Kennecott agreed to the overprice regime.

[34]USBM, *Mineral Trade Notes*, May 1967, p. 8; *El Mercurio*, Santiago, 5 March 1967. See also *Engineering and Mining Journal*, February 1968, p. 184.

The scale of planned investment and output is not altered by the 1969 agreement. There remains the possibility, however, that an immediate takeover of Anaconda and perhaps also of Kennecott will be demanded, or that there will be conflict over the payment for Anaconda's properties, if the political opposition to the Chileanization policy does not abate. The government has usually pressed for the same terms from both companies, and differences in the latters' offers have been a major cause of the extension of state control in recent years.

Copper and Economic Development

From the 1920s until 1955 the object of Chilean copper policy was to increase the share of the value of copper production retained in Chile, and this was pursued chiefly by raising the share taken by the government in direct taxes. The copper laws of 1955 and 1966 modify this policy in two ways: by endeavoring to increase the volume of production and thus the total value rather than the fraction retained in taxes; and by enabling the government to participate directly in the profits of the industry. Whether this policy is regarded as successful or not depends on the test applied; four criteria are discussed below.

First, Chile has unquestionably succeeded in integrating the industry into the national economy and reducing its isolated character. The share of value returned to Chile has risen from about 40 percent in the 1920s to about 80 percent in recent years (and over 90 percent in 1952-54), and from only about $30 million to more than $200 million (see table 4-12). The fraction of copper sold for local fabrication (to domestic firms with state participation or assistance), whether for consumption or for export, rose from nothing to several percent, and the share of investment expenditures made in Chile has also increased as the economy has become able to supply more of the goods and services required by the Gran Minería. Other government policies, such as the development of import-substituting industries, especially capital goods industries based on domestic steel production, have greatly contributed to this result. An index of "returned value terms of trade" shows an increase of 57 percent in the period 1925-58, while the index of copper terms of trade, including changes in the price but not in the share retained, shows an increase of only 6 percent.[35] A large measure of political control has also been achieved without a severe clash with the companies or the United States government. Particularly in times of market disturbances, it is now the Chilean government which sets the price of the country's copper.

Second, Chile's policy has generally discouraged investment in the Gran Minería. This is most evident in the years just before 1955, and again in 1959-63. It has been suggested that Chilean development policy since the 1930s has been highly discriminatory among parts of the economy; some, such as the mining sector, were intended primarily to provide funds to be invested in favored sectors, particularly

in manufacturing industry.[36] For a time this redirection of investment lowers the average productivity of the economy, but it is meant ultimately to provide a more stable and diversified structure with more nearly equal productivity in all sectors. Similar policies, in which revenues from the exploitation of natural resources are funnelled toward other activities, have been adopted in several other Latin American countries. The cases of oil in Venezuela and the whole range of traditional exports in Brazil are noteworthy.[37] Three principal features of this policy and its results in Chile should be noted.

In the first place, the discrimination has not been enough to prevent a rather high rate of investment in copper over the period since the establishment of the Gran Minería. By the late 1950s the three companies had invested some $540 million in their operations. About 52 percent of net profits in the period 1930-59 were reinvested, the share being 60 percent for Anaconda and less for Kennecott. Reinvestment of profits was particularly high during the period of rapid amortization provided by the law of 1955. Net investment was negative only in the early 1930s, in 1938, 1940, 1946, 1949, and 1954-55 (see tables 4-12 and 4-13). When the companies began to disinvest appreciable amounts in the mid-1950s, the government changed its policy. Thus the industry was never decapitalized, as the tin industry of Bolivia was, and output was readily expanded after 1955.

In the second place, the value returned to Chile was affected less than mine production, since part of the resources obtained from the copper industry was invested in industries producing inputs for the mining sector. Substitution of imports of capital and intermediate goods could partly offset the slow growth of output and thus reduce the sharp difference between externally and internally oriented development. This substitution process must end, however, when the cost of domestic inputs becomes too high for the producing companies to accept, or when no further replacement of imports is possible and the value not returned to Chile consists solely of profits. Like import-substituting industrialization in general, it is a solution whose potential is eventually exhausted in economic if not in technical terms.

In the third place, Chile has nonetheless lost ground by discouraging investment in its most productive sector. The country has followed a policy much like that Venezuela has adopted for oil exports, of maintaining prices and raising the value returned at some expense in increased production; but whereas Venezuela faces competition from much lower-cost producers, Chile does not. Although Chile is a relatively low-cost source of copper, its share of world production has fallen from over 20 percent at the end of World War II to only 13 percent (see table 4-4). Since the high share reflected wartime difficulties of supply from other producers, some decline was probably inevitable. If, however, Chile's production could have been held at only 17

[35] Reynolds, ". . . Chile and Copper," pp. 282-83. The comparison for more recent years would show less discrepancy, as prices have risen from 1958 levels while the share of value retained has not changed appreciably.

[36] This is the conclusion reached by Mamalakis in the first section of *Essays on the Chilean Economy.*

[37] The supply problems to which such policies can lead are mentioned in chap. 2. For discussions of the Venezuelan and Brazilian examples, see chaps. 8 and 10.

percent, and the share of value returned not raised beyond the 58 percent prevailing in 1943-46, the total value returned to the country in the early 1960s would have been just as high as that actually reached. In short, the increase in the share of value retained over the last two decades has not been enough to compensate for the relative decline in output. Furthermore, most of the investment that did take place in this interval was concentrated at the mine and the smelter, particularly in developing the mine at El Salvador and in converting operations from oxide to sulfide ores at Chuquicamata. Refinery capacity was not expanded, so that the average degree of processing and unit value of exports declined, further offsetting the increased share of value returned. Since refining need not take place in the producing country but may be located according to power and labor costs, markets, and other factors, the companies' decisions on electrolytic capacity in Chile are quite sensitive to the tax and other treatment accorded by the government. It is noteworthy that the Chilean government, which could not come to terms with Anaconda in 1960-61, has spent part of its proceeds from copper on a new refinery. As part of the new comprehensive agreement, refinery output will now be greatly expanded. It appears, therefore, that until now the producers have been willing to invest only the amounts required to extract their ore and convert it to metal, preferring not to make any investments in Chile which could be made elsewhere without economic penalties. These remarks refer only to electrolytic copper; the sharp decline in fire-refined metal, from 40 percent of output in 1950 to less than 15 percent by 1963, bears no relation to a reluctance to invest or to the policies of the Chilean government but reflects only the disappearance of a market for metal of that grade (see table 4-14).

Third, the use of direct taxation and exchange controls, while offering the greatest scope for increased participation in copper revenues, has been partly self-defeating. The inflation of dollar labor costs by exchange restrictions led the companies to invest heavily in capital equipment to hold down employment, particularly of miners and other relatively unskilled workers. The labor costs per pound of copper for the Braden Company rose from 3.7 cents in 1945 to 8.4 cents in 1952 and then to 12.5 cents in 1954; with the abolition of the fixed exchange rate, the cost fell back to 4.1 cents. Between 1930 and 1959 the company reduced its work force 17 percent, while raising output 115 percent. Technical progress allowed operations to become slightly more labor-intensive at El Teniente; at the Anaconda mines they became much more capital-intensive; at all three the work force is much smaller than at mines of comparable size in Africa. Thus part of the increased government revenue was offset by reduced labor costs. The reliance on direct, or profit, taxes also made the total value returned to Chile only about as stable as the total value of production, and government revenues less stable. The 1955 law reduced the previous instability somewhat by relating the tax rate to the volume of output over a certain range.

Fourth, the Chilean economy has grown quite slowly over the last several decades, much less rapidly than the revenues obtained from copper: from the 1920s to 1960, for example, gross domestic product increased at about 2.7

percent annually in constant terms, while the value returned from copper grew by more than 5 percent per year. The relative stagnation of Chile's economy over so long a period, combined during some periods with quite rapid inflation, has been the subject of much study and debate.[38] The issues raised cannot be satisfactorily dealt with in this study, so it must suffice to note certain ways in which the copper industry is related to the national economy and its difficulties. On the one hand, the production of primary commodities for export has often been isolated from other sectors, providing them little in the way of demand for goods and services or of resources for investment, and thereby leaving them stagnant while the export sector develops.[39] Before the last two or three decades this was the case with copper in Chile. There are still some structural problems associated with the copper industry, such as heavy dependence on a single export, great differences in wages, and highly capital-intensive production coexisting with substantial unemployment and underemployment. These factors are in part the result of Chilean policy, but in any case they no longer appear to be significant obstacles to growth. Nor does it seem that the returns from the industry are wasted on imports of consumer goods by the recipients of that income; labor obtains only a small share of the value retained, and the protection of domestic consumer industries insures a low rate of leakage through imports.

On the other hand, the industry provides the government with about half the total value returned as revenues available for investment. Where similar large revenues have been available to governments elsewhere in Latin America, investment and growth have sometimes proceeded rapidly, as in Brazil during the 1950s. It appears that this did not occur in Chile, primarily because the government diverted an increasing share of its copper revenues to current expenses rather than to development (increases in education, social security, and other services provided by the state). Although taxes on other sectors are relatively high by Latin American standards, their revenues did not increase rapidly enough to meet these requirements, and so they were to some extent replaced by copper taxes. In this respect copper revenues may have repeated the pattern of nitrate taxes in the years 1880-1920; these were intended for development but were eventually absorbed for current government expenditures. In order to limit the extent of such diversion of resources, it is common practice to allocate a share of revenues for investment in economic development; such a fund was set up for CORFO, the state development agency, at its creation in 1939, and a portion of taxes under the new law is similarly delegated to CORFO for investments in the fishing industry and in the provinces where most copper mining occurs.

The success of development efforts does not, of course, depend solely on Chilean copper policy, but on the combi-

[38] The basic data are presented and analyzed in Universidad de Chile, Instituto de Economía, *La Economía de Chile en el Período 1950-1963* (Santiago, 1963), especially vol. I, part II. See also the discussion in A. O. Hirshman, *Journeys Toward Progress* (Twentieth Century Fund, 1961), pp. 95-123.

[39] The several "structural" factors involved in this relation are described in chap. 2.

nation of policies toward all sectors of the economy and on the private propensities to invest in each one. In this regard, two features of the Chilean economy deserve mention: the small size of the national market, and the backward condition of agriculture both economically and socially. These now constitute the major impediments to the country's growth, and both are independent of the mining sector.

Outlook

Recent developments in the copper industry, particularly the adoption of the new Chilean policy, have invalidated projections of supply and demand made in the early 1960s; this is especially the case for the distribution of trade expected in the 1970s. No attempt will be made here to present revised projections, except for anticipated mine capacity where estimates can be based on information about companies' expansion projects now underway or planned.[40]

Total world mine capacity outside the Communist countries was projected in 1965 as some 5.45 million tons in 1970, an increase of almost 25 percent over the 1964 level. More recent projections suggest that capacity may be some 6.2 to 6.3 million tons by 1972, when the Chilean expansion program is completed. The greatest expansion is planned for Chile, raising total Latin American capacity by nearly half. Large increases are also expected in Australia and the Philippines. Capacity will grow rather slowly in Europe, Canada, and Africa, and somewhat more rapidly in the United States. These changes will leave the major producing areas — the United States, Africa, Latin America, and Canada — with the same share of total capacity, but Latin America's share will increase at the expense of the others. As to prices, it seems that any net changes in the quality of resources and the techniques of copper production have not been great enough to make the real cost of copper in the next decade different from what it has been in the last ten or twenty years.

The fulfillment of these projections will depend very much on events in Latin America. Mine capacity is expected to increase more, both in tonnage and proportionally, in Chile than anywhere else; and no other country except the United States will have so large an effect on supplies in the next several years. The Chilean copper program has already been described; its implications may be briefly noted. Chile is expected to regain its position as the world's second largest producer and to raise its share of world output to one-fifth. Part of the increased production will come from the existing mines of the Gran Minería, particularly from a large expansion at El Teniente; part from the development of La Exótica, a large orebody close to Chuquicamata; and part from a vigorous expansion of the Mediana Minería.

The future course of refinery output is somewhat less certain. Ultimately, the bulk of Chilean production may be refined in the country, eliminating exports of blister copper and the present indirect trade with Europe via U.S. refineries. The new copper law envisions a more modest increase in the share refined, to half or slightly more in the early 1970s. This trend may, of course, be interrupted as mine or smelter capacity is brought into operation first.

Chile will be able to export annually between 850,000 and 950,000 tons of copper, of which about 800,000 to 900,000 tons will be unwrought metal. The value of exports, assuming prices in the United States of at least 35 cents per pound, will then be at least $850 million per year. So long as there is a shortage of copper, Chile will be able to obtain a much higher average value; and if the shortage persists until the new capacity is ready, there might be little change in the value of exports while prices decline. In the immediate future, the share of value retained by Chile will probably remain near 75 percent, giving the country net revenues from copper of at least $640 million yearly. The exact operation of the new copper law, and the use to be made of the revenues, remain to be seen. It is not possible to predict from Chile's past experience what the effect will be on economic growth.

Nothing of comparable importance is expected to take place in the next few years in the rest of the Latin American copper industry. In Peru, mine capacity will actually decrease slightly as lower-grade ore is worked at the Toquepala deposit. The slight decline in output will probably be only temporary, however, since, as noted above, Peru has large reserves which could be developed during the 1970s; production was in fact planned to begin at Cuajone in 1972 and at Michiquillay and Cerro Verde some years later. The timing and effect of these projects will, however, depend very much on the attitude of the government.

Production will probably be expanded in Mexico, in order to maintain exports, and expansion of refinery capacity or building of a new copper refinery is contemplated.[41] Production should begin during the 1970s at one or more of the deposits recently discovered in Sonora. The major producing companies do not mine copper elsewhere in Latin America, and there are no estimates available of future production. No significant increases of capacity are likely to occur before 1972, because exploration and development of resources, other than those small mines now producing, have only recently begun. In the somewhat longer run, Brazil may possibly become able to meet its own copper requirements of about 50,000 tons per year, but is unlikely ever to produce on the same scale as Chile or Peru. No estimates are available of future domestic copper consumption in Latin America; it is expected to continue to absorb 10 percent or less of production, as mine output expands, and only a small share of world consumption.

In conclusion, it should be noted that these estimates and projections, especially concerning prices, do not take

[40]The principal sources of this information are C. P. Timmer, *The Free World Copper Outlook, 1965-1970* (W. R. Grace and Co., 8 November 1965, mimeo), and *Engineering and Mining Journal*, February 1968, pp. 84-89. No estimates are available of copper production and use in the Communist countries, it being assumed that for the next several years these countries will continue to import somewhat more than 100,000 tons annually, but that by the middle or late 1970s this trade might stop or be reversed.

[41] Comité Coordinador de las Actividades de los Consejeros Comerciales en el Exterior, *Mexico's Main Export Products* (Mexico: Banco Nacional de Comercio Exterior, 1964), p. 149. See also *Nacional Financiera en el Desarrollo Económico de México, 1934-1964* (Mexico: Nacional Financiera, 1964), p. 65.

account of possible future actions by producing companies or governments to influence the market. For the reasons described earlier, any such intervention is likely to be limited, with appreciable effect only in periods of severe imbalance. There are no long-term trends suggesting the need for international action either to reduce or increase supplies.[42] And it is not possible for companies or governments to act decisively alone without upsetting their relationship and possibly damaging the interests of both. Thus, although various studies have been made of the possible effects of a producers' cartel, or an agreement including both producers and consumers, or a buffer stock, none of these is likely to be implemented.[43] Nevertheless, there remains considerable interest among producer governments in some loose form of co-operation to increase price stability, or set prices at times of disequilibrium, or co-ordinate reductions in output so as to share the burden. This interest has been stimulated by the recent price boom and by the sharply opposed motives and actions of the governments of Chile and the United States. The importance of the latter country as a producer limits the possibilities for market control by the underdeveloped copper exporters, as does the predominance of U.S. and British capital in the industry, but there is believed to be some room for joint action by the principal exporting countries, if only to offset the direct and indirect effects of decisions made in the developed countries. Chile and Zambia opened discussions on these matters, and then in June 1967 held a conference in Zambia attended also by representatives of Peru and the Congo[44] — the same four countries that formed the export control scheme of 1936-39.

These meetings resulted in the creation of the Inter-Governmental Council of Copper Exporting Countries (CIPEC), which may be expected to operate rather like the Organization of Petroleum Exporting Countries in co-ordinating the price, tax, and sales policies of the member governments. It is still too early to tell whether the countries will adopt common policies and what effect these will have; presumably any concerted actions will for some years be more important in times of severe disequilibrium than in normal market conditions. At present Zambia, with perhaps the highest costs of the four major producers, is most interested in a price control scheme; Peru and Chile, with lower costs and planned or potential large increases in capacity, are opposed to joint interference with prices, and their position has prevailed.[45] The governments are in agreement, however, on the desirability of eliminating barriers to trade in copper semimanufactures and of greater fabrication in producing countries.

[42] See the UNCTAD *Commodity Survey*, 1966 (Part I), doc. TD/B/C.1/23, 28 November 1966, pp. 85-86.

[43] See, for example, H. Castro de Patiño, *Las Fluctuaciones del Mercado del Cobre* (Santiago: Universidad de Chile, Instituto de Economía, 1965).

[44] *El Mercurio*, Santiago, Chile, 4 June 1967. Chile made no specific proposals at the meeting, but opposed a suggestion by Zambia to create a buffer stock of copper.

[45] See *Engineering and Mining Journal*, July 1967, pp. 104, 106.

CHAPTER 4 TABLES

TABLE 4–3. World Copper Reserves, circa 1964
(Millions of metric tons copper content)

Country or Region	Reserves[a]	Share of Total (%)[b]	Ratio of Reserves to Production (years)[c]
Latin America	55[d]	28.4	64
Chile	42	21.8	69
Peru	11	5.9	67
Mexico	0.8	0.4	15
Brazil	0.5[e]	0.3	50
United States	30	15.4	26
Canada	8	3.9	18
Western Europe	8[d]	4.2	81
Yugoslavia	2.5	1.3	41
Turkey	0.5[f]	0.3	17
Finland	0.3[f]	0.2	11
Sweden	0.1[f]	0.1	7
Cyprus	0.5[f]	0.3	25
Spain	4.1	2.1	205
Africa	42[d]	21.8	42
Zambia	23	11.9	37
Congo	18	9.5	65
South Africa[g]	0.9[f]	0.5	19
Asia and Oceania	3.2[d]	1.8	9
Australia	1.1	0.6	11
Philippines	1.0	0.5	21
Japan	1.1[f]	0.6	10
India	0.1	0.1	10
Other	4.5	2.2	
Communist Countries	45[d]	23.4	62
Soviet Union	32	16.6	47
Poland	10	5.4	710
China	2.7	1.5	91
World Total	192	100.0	42

Sources: USBM, *Mineral Facts and Problems, 1965*, p. 283; *1960*, p. 250. ABMS, *Yearbook, 1964*, p. 30. *Mining Annual Review*, June 1964, p. 224.

[a] Includes all material of same grades as that currently produced.
[b] Reserves of country as percentage of world total reserves.
[c] Ratio of reserves to average mine production, 1962-64; life of reserves, in years, at constant rate of production.
[d] Sum of countries listed.
[e] Reserves estimated in 1964 as 50.05 million tons of ore with average grade of 1% copper.
[f] Minimum estimate: reserves reported by proprietors of one or more large mines.
[g] Republic of South Africa, Southwest Africa, and the Transvaal.

TABLE 4-4. World Mine Production of Copper, 1925-1967
   (Thousands of metric tons)

Country or Region	Avg. 1925-29	Avg. 1930-34	Avg. 1935-39	Avg. 1940-44	Avg. 1945-49	1950	1951	1952
Latin America	379.5	287.9	415.6	564.2	523.6	481.5	505.9	520.7
Bolivia	7.0	2.4	3.2	6.6	6.0	4.7	4.9	4.7[a]
Chile	248.7	194.6	326.4	463.2	415.8	363.5	381.5	409.5
Ecuador				2.7	1.6	0.5		
Mexico	62.6	47.9	40.4	45.8	61.8	61.8	67.5	58.6
Peru	47.3	33.3	34.4	36.4	25.0	30.3	32.4	30.5
Cuba	13.8	9.7	11.2	8.2	13.6	20.6	19.6	17.4
United States	825.6	357.2	567.6	926.2	709.8	832.2	852.8	847.8
Canada	74.3	137.2	233.2	275.0	209.4	240.2	245.4	234.6
Western Europe	100.8	90.6	106.4	84.2	57.4	58.3	57.5	66.5
Communist Countries[b]	31.2	67.8	129.2	175.4	202.4	276.7	304.2	346.2
Soviet Union	18.1	34.9	89.0	148.4[c]	167.6	218.2	254.5	295.5
Africa	120.7	178.9	322.4	429.2	394.4	519.1	558.0	585.9
Congo		98.1	120.4	160.2	150.8	176.3	192.4	206.2
Zambia		69.9	186.6	246.0	211.4	298.1	320.0	330.2
Asia and Oceania	86.6	96.7	150.0	147.0[d]	78.2	117.6	128.7	151.4
World Total	1,623	1,230	1,916	2,608[d]	2,178	2,526	2,653	2,753
Latin American Share (%)	23.2	23.3	21.7	22.0	24.0	19.1	19.1	18.9

Country or Region	1953	1954	1955	1956	1957	1958	1959	1960
Latin America	478.9	475.9	554.0	611.2	621.1	597.6	665.4	796.9
Bolivia[a]	4.5	3.7	3.5	4.5	3.9	2.9	2.2	2.3
Brazil			0.8	1.3	1.2	1.4	1.4	1.1
Chile	363.9	364.4	434.4	490.8	485.3	463.2	546.0	533.3
Haiti								0.9
Nicaragua								4.9
Mexico	60.3	54.9	54.8	55.0	60.7	65.1	57.4	60.5
Peru	35.5	37.7	43.5	46.3	57.3	53.7	50.8	182.1
Cuba	15.5	15.2	17.8	14.6	13.9	12.7	9.0	11.9
United States	862.3	764.6	922.2	1,013.0	993.4	900.2	763.6	993.2
Canada	230.2	275.2	296.3	322.6	326.5	313.7	359.3	399.3
Western Europe	59.2	61.8	63.6	65.5	73.3	74.3	78.4	77.7
Communist Countries[b]	353.6	366.5	402.0	467.5	491.3	532.8	567.5	580.8
Soviet Union	304.1	319.3	335.7	390.8	405.8	420.9	440.9	460.9
Africa	636.5	679.5	660.8	726.8	761.0	735.4	932.0	975.8
Congo	210.6	224.3	235.6	250.5	242.7	238.0	282.6	302.6
Zambia	373.5	398.8	359.4	404.9	436.6	400.9	544.4	577.6
Asia and Oceania	166.8	186.5	189.4	224.1	245.7	264.9	296.4	315.4
World Total	2,788	2,810	3,088	3,427	3,506	3,406	3,649	4,139
Latin American Share (%)	17.2	16.9	17.9	17.8	17.7	17.5	18.2	19.3

Country or Region	1961	1962	1963	1964	1965	1966	1967
Latin America	815.0	824.7	863.7	889.3	868.5	923.2	922.1
Bolivia[a]	2.1	2.4	3.0	4.7	4.7	5.8	
Brazil	1.7	1.6	1.5	2.0	2.2	2.2	3.0
Chile	548.6	587.3	604.2	633.4	605.9	663.7	663.9
Haiti	3.5	6.1	6.0	5.6	4.0	2.8	2.4
Nicaragua	6.3	7.3	7.3	9.3	10.2	9.8	9.3
Mexico	49.4	47.2	55.1	52.1	55.2	56.5	56.0
Peru	198.5	167.1	180.1	176.4	180.3	176.4	181.1
Cuba	5.0[b]	5.5[b]	6.5	5.8	6.0	6.0	6.4
United States	1,054.1	1,112.7	1,100.6	1,131.1	1,226.3	1,296.5	865.5
Canada	399.1	423.1	410.6	441.7	460.7	460.7	546.7
Western Europe	89.9	96.3	80.4	81.9	77.1	73.1	79.9
Communist Countries[b]	608.2	648.7	717.5	769.2	830.0	881.7	911.7
Soviet Union	476.0	500.0	598.8	648.6	698.5	748.4	798.3
Africa	970.5	955.8	983.2	1,041.3	1,122.2	1,139.7	1,128.3
Congo	295.8	293.6	271.6	276.6	288.6	315.7	320.5
Zambia	575.9	563.5	588.1	632.4	695.8	623.5	662.3
Asia and Oceania	299.2	332.9	459.3	445.2	435.3	481.7	470.8
World Total	4,236	4,394	4,616	4,800	5,015	5,251	4,931
Latin American Share (%)	19.2	18.7	18.7	18.5	17.3	17.6	18.7

Sources: 1925-64 – ABMS, *Yearbook*. 1940-67 – USBM, *Minerals Yearbook*.

[a]COMIBOL production plus exports by small and medium mines.
[b]Estimate.
[c]Estimated from smelter production.
[d]U.S. Bureau of Mines estimate; data not available on production during World War II.

TABLE 4–5. World Production of Refined Copper, 1930-1967
(Thousands of metric tons)

Country or Region	Avg. 1930-34	Avg. 1935-39	Avg. 1940-44	Avg. 1945-49	1950	1951	1952
Latin America[a]	159.8	220.9	365.8	408.8	332.8	347.8	354.2
Chile					296.0	310.0	318.7
Peru					20.7	22.8	20.5
Mexico					16.1	15.0	15.0
Canada	86.2	188.9	238.8	189.7	216.1	222.7	178.1
United States	628.5	888.0	1,313.4	1,121.5	1,344.2	1,245.3	1,207.8
Western Europe	330.0	520.2	429.8	331.7	528.7	556.7	563.4
Belgium	80.7	112.4	27.6	98.5	137.2	142.2	146.7
Germany	178.3	277.8	189.5	54.1	198.3	205.3	187.8
United Kingdom	71.0	30.0	212.8	179.1	193.2	209.2	228.9
Africa	52.9	86.8	133.8	146.0	188.7	224.5	234.7
Congo			81.6	72.8	96.6	106.9	109.5
Zambia			42.1	60.3	78.9	104.8	113.3
Asia and Oceania	92.3	105.5	129.7	79.4	102.6	120.9	137.5
Japan	72.7	79.1	102.2	45.7	84.7	90.9	94.4
Communist Countries	48.2	108.1	161.4	223.7	315.3	364.7	409.4
World Total	1,274	2,175	2,831	2,524	3,172	3,211	3,227
Latin American Refined Production as Share of:							
World Refinery Production (%)	11.0	10.1	12.8	13.6	10.5	10.8	11.0
L.A. Mine Production (%)	55.5	53.1	64.3	64.6	69.1	68.7	68.8

Country or Region	1953	1954	1955	1956	1957	1958	1959	1960
Latin America	257.1	229.1	281.7	291.0	276.9	343.9	316.3	283.7
Chile	216.7	190.8	240.7	240.5	221.2	287.8	259.7	225.6
Peru	23.4	25.3	26.0	17.9	28.1	28.4	27.3	29.9
Mexico	17.0	13.0	15.0	32.6	27.6	27.7	29.3	28.2
Canada	215.0	229.2	263.5	298.0	293.5	298.7	331.5	378.3
United States	1,366.1	1,286.3	1,436.1	1,545.7	1,534.1	1,450.2	1,223.3	1,642.6
Western Europe	550.1	610.5	646.1	628.7	604.3	609.8	644.8	722.9
Belgium	150.3	153.6	155.3	155.3	146.4	145.3	167.5	194.9
Germany	211.7	234.3	260.0	253.5	253.4	268.2	281.9	309.1
United Kingdom	188.1	222.6	230.8	219.7	204.5	196.3	195.4	218.9
Africa	276.0	303.1	305.2	371.2	399.0	388.6	542.8	560.3
Congo	107.8	111.7	110.0	126.0	131.3	126.5	156.0	144.7
Zambia	155.0	176.4	179.9	229.7	250.8	245.4	370.8	402.6
Asia and Oceania	131.8	164.7	171.7	177.4	205.9	204.6	277.5	355.9
Japan	91.1	106.5	113.3	126.2	142.2	124.0	194.0	248.1
Communist Countries	442.0	466.0	524.0	569.4	624.7	664.3	704.0	799.9
World Total	3,391	3,464	3,815	4,081	4,140	4,092	4,307	4,999
Latin American Refined Production as Share of:								
World Refinery Production (%)	7.6	6.6	7.4	7.1	6.7	8.4	7.3	5.7
L.A. Mine Production (%)	53.7	48.2	50.8	47.6	44.6	57.5	47.5	35.6

Country or Region	1961	1962	1963	1964	1965	1966	1967
Latin America	286.7	328.7	349.5	366.1	383.4	450.1	486.0
Chile	226.2	263.7	258.9	278.1	288.9	356.9	397.5
Peru	33.8	34.4	36.9	37.8	40.5	38.0	35.0
Mexico	26.7	30.6	53.7	50.2	54.0	55.2	54.4
Canada	368.7	347.0	344.8	370.1	393.8	393.6	453.6
United States	1,661.8	1,725.0	1,722.2	1,820.8	1,956.8	1,997.7	1,397.1
Western Europe	745.2	741.9	774.7	855.7	903.2	867.3	879.4
Belgium	202.8	202.0	271.4	286.1	309.4	303.4	317.9
Germany	304.3	308.2	302.8	336.3	357.4	375.4	382.4
United Kingdom	238.1	231.7	200.5	231.3	236.4	188.5	179.1
Africa	598.3	593.6	602.7	668.3	693.1	775.3	879.7
Congo	150.9	134.4	130.6	140.2	139.5	152.6	154.2
Zambia	418.9	433.5	438.9	496.9	521.2	586.5	616.8
Asia and Oceania	382.0	399.2	426.8	470.2	532.4	589.5	684.3
Japan	277.0	270.4	295.2	341.7	365.7	404.9	470.0
Communist Countries	840.9	873.9	929.0	968.8	1,032.1	1,099.6	1,171.5
World Total	5,139	5,267	5,415	5,783	6,200	6,493	6,260
Latin American Refined Production as Share of:							
World Refinery Production (%)	5.6	6.2	6.4	6.3	6.2	6.9	7.7
L.A. Mine Production (%)	35.2	39.8	38.0	39.8	44.1	48.7	52.7

Source: 1930-67 – *Metal Statistics* (Frankfurt).

[a]Chile only, 1930-45.

TABLE 4–6. World Consumption of Copper,[a] Averages, 1936-38, 1949-51, and 1962-64
(Thousands of metric tons)

Country or Region	1936-38	1949-51	1962-64
Latin America[b]	9	54	93
Argentina[c]	(d)	4	16
Brazil	(d)	19	33
Chile[c]	(d)	22[e]	15[f]
Mexico[c]	(d)	8	28
United States[g]	668	1,140	1,446
Canada[h]	55	103	158
Western Europe	870	883	1,941
United Kingdom	273	333	572
Germany[j]	251	207	515
France[k]	114	117	261
Italy	81	53	192
Africa[c]	4	19	37
Asia and Oceania	201	100	449
Japan	101	68	304
Communist Countries	216	276	818
Soviet Union	150	226	577
World Total	2,016	2,606	4,917
Latin American Consumption as Share of:			
World Copper Consumption (%)	0.5	2.1	1.9
L.A. Mine Production (%)	2.2	11.0	10.9

Source: ABMS, *Yearbook, 1940* to *1964.*

[a]Estimated consumption of new copper by fabricators: production plus net imports. The data do not permit a uniform method of computation; consumption as calculated can be compared only roughly with mine production. Secondary copper included where shown.

[b]Data available only for countries listed; estimated consumption by all other countries in the region is included in the total.

[c]Figures may not accurately represent consumption because of reshipment to other countries in refined or semifabricated form; discrepancies likely to be largest in Latin America. Net imports represent shipments into these countries by members of the Copper Institute.

[d]Not separately estimated.

[e]Includes decline of stocks during early part of Korean War; amount shown exceeds actual consumption.

[f]1962-63 average only; Latin American total is adjusted accordingly. 1964 figure includes reduction of stocks and greatly exceeds domestic consumption.

[g]Includes copper resulting from secondary intake but not secondary material (old scrap) treated on toll.

[h]Copper used in production of mill products.

[j]Includes a large share of scrap.

[k]Includes variations in stocks.

TABLE 4–7. Copper Prices, Annual Averages, 1925-1967
(U.S. cents per pound)

Year	New York[a]	London[b]	Year	New York[a]	London[b]	Chilean Exports[c]
1925	14.04	13.35	1947	20.96	23.48	
1926	13.80	12.57	1948	22.04	24.12	
1927	12.92	12.08	1949	19.20	21.90	
1928	14.57	13.84	1950	21.24	22.38	19.7
1929	18.11	16.35	1951	24.20[f]	27.58	26.2
1930	12.98	11.85	1952	24.20[f]	32.68	31.9
1931	8.12	7.74	1953	28.80	31.55	34.9
1932	5.56	4.96	1954	29.69	31.26	30.2
1933	7.03	6.15	1955	37.49	43.89	35.2
1934	8.43	6.81	1956	41.82	41.07	42.0
1935	8.65	6.97	1957	29.58	27.36	30.9
1936	9.47	8.53	1958	25.76	24.79	26.8
1937	13.17	12.02	1959	31.18	29.80	30.9
1938	10.00	8.89	1960	32.05	30.81	32.6
1939	10.97	8.45[d]	1961	29.92	28.73	30.2
1940	11.30	10.60[e]	1962	30.60	29.33	30.0
1941	11.80[f]	11.16[e]	1963	30.60	29.25	30.3
1942	11.78[f]	11.17[e]	1964	31.96	43.88	32.2
1943	11.78[f]	11.17[e]	1965	35.02	58.72	37.5
1944	11.78[f]	11.17[e]	1966	36.17	69.04	47.6
1945	11.78[f]	11.16[e]	1967	38.23	51.19	48.5
1946	13.82	13.89				

Sources: U.S. and London prices from *Engineering and Mining Journal*; annual averages summarized in ABMS, *Yearbook*. London price reported in pounds sterling per long ton, converted at annual average pound/dollar exchange rate. Chilean price from Chile, Dirección de Estadística, *Comercio Exterior*, for 1950-64; and USBM, *Minerals Yearbook, 1967*, for 1965-67.

[a]Price ex refinery, Atlantic seaboard, for electrolytic copper. Price of delivered copper is 0.4 cents per pound higher, on the average, in recent years.

[b]LME spot price, electrolytic wirebars, ex warehouse.

[c]Average value of Chilean exports to all destinations of electrolytic copper. This is not the price set by producers or by the Chilean government, and does not equal average value of all Chilean exports of copper, including blister and fire-refined metal.

[d]Average of eight months.

[e]No dealings on LME; price of copper fixed at £62 per long ton during World War II.

[f]Price fixed by U.S. government.

TABLE 4-8. Copper Reserves in Chile, 1963
(Millions of metric tons of copper content)

Province and Principal Mines[a]	Measured	Indicated	Inferred	Total	Average Grade (%)[b]
Tarapacá		3	5	8	2.5
Antofagasta (Mantos Blancos)	6	10	11	27	2.0
Chuquicamata				9.6-16.0	1.6
Atacama	6	4	2	12	3.0
El Salvador				3.4-6.0	1.7
Coquimbo	4	2	2	8	2.5
Anconcagua (Disputada)	5	3	4	12	2.8
Santiago (La Africana, Río Blanco)	3	2	4	9	3.0
O'Higgins	12		4	16	2.0
El Teniente				6.0-6.7	2.0
Total Chile[c]	36	24	32	92	2.3

Sources: CORFO, *Geografía Económica de Chile* (Santiago, 1965), pp. 606-7. M. Vera Valenzuela, *La Política Económica del Cobre en Chile* (Santiago: Universidad de Chile, 1961), pp. 44-48. USBM, *Minerals Yearbook, 1963*, vol. IV.

[a]Total reserves are shown for the three mines of the Gran Minería; data not available on measured, indicated, and inferred reserves. Smaller figures are from M. Vera Valenzuela, larger from *Minerals Yearbook*. Mines listed in parentheses, for which no reserves are shown, belong to the Mediana Minería.

[b]Average percent copper content of all material included in reserves. No data are available for tonnage or grade of potential resources.

[c]Sum of provinces listed; does not include reserves of known copper deposits in other provinces such as Valparaíso, Aisén, and Magallanes. Total amount of such reserves is quite small.

TABLE 4-9. Participation in the Copper Industry of Latin America, 1962-1964
(Percent ownership of production)

Country	Type and Nationality of Enterprise	Percentage of		
		Mining	Smelting	Refining
Argentina	Local private	100		
Bolivia[a]	State (COMIBOL)	57		
	Foreign private (Japan)	43		
Brazil	Local private	100	100	100
Chile[b]	Foreign private (United States)	88[c]	83	74
	(Other)[d]		7	5
	Local private			
	State (ENAMI)		10	21
Cuba	State	100		
Ecuador[e]	State/local private	100		
Haiti	Foreign private (United States)	100		
Mexico[f]	Foreign private (United States)		56	25
	Local private		13	
	State/local private[g]		31	75
Nicaragua	Foreign private (Canada/United States)	100		
Peru	Foreign private (United States)	83[h]	100	100
	(Other)	4[j]		
	Local private	13[k]		
	State[m]			

Sources: Metal Bulletin (London, May 1965). USBM, *Minerals Yearbook, 1963*, vol. IV.

[a]Shares of 1963 mine production.

[b]Shares of capacity in 1965, including Las Ventanas smelter and refinery capacity completed in 1966.

[c]Approximate average share of the Gran Minería in total mine production, early 1960s.

[d]French, Japanese, and Canadian.

[e]Cía. Industrial Minera Asociada, S.A.: 35% municipally owned, 35% private, 30% donated by national government to private individuals. Production from Portovelo, Zaruma, El Oro province; formerly by a U.S. enterprise.

[f]Shares of capacity in 1965, for smelter production. Share of U.S. enterprises in mining approximately 87%, if Mexicanized companies are included as still U.S. owned; 72% if Mexican ownership is taken into account. Greene Cananea (U.S. owned) accounted for 56% of 1963 output.

[g]Mexican government through Nacional Financiera, in association with Mazapil Copper Company.

[h]Share of 1963 mine production accounted for by Northern Peru Mining, Cerro de Pasco, and Southern Peru Copper companies from their own mines (63% for Cerro de Pasco in 1963).

[j]Minimal estimate based on 1963 production from Cía. Minera Condestable (Japan), Cie. des Mines de Huarón (France) and Lampa Mining Co. (United Kingdom).

[k]Maximal estimate based on 1963 production, assuming 37% of Cerro de Pasco's smelter production and all other mine output to have come from local private companies.

[m]Banco Minero del Peru owns and operates a mine at Huachocolpa.

TABLE 4-10. Latin American Exports of Copper, by Destination and Type, 1950-1966
(Thousands of metric tons and millions of U.S. dollars)

	1950	1951	1952	1953	1954	1955	1956	1957	1958	1959	1960	1961	1962	1963	1964	1965	1966
Chile																	
Refined	257.6	249.8	280.6	165.3	195.0	210.2	213.7	216.7	155.9	220.1	213.1	216.9	240.2	245.5	213.4	219.0	323.3
United States	202.7	199.7	240.1	158.5	94.3	60.4	38.5	7.8	0.3	15.1	1.8	2.0	0.8	1.7	10.2		
Western Europe	36.1	37.7	34.6	4.5	98.8	144.4	172.1	207.6	155.6	204.6	211.3	211.9	212.7	205.8	168.0		
Latin America[a]	18.2	10.3	4.1	2.2	1.0	2.5[b]	3.0[b]	0.7[b]		0.1[b]		1.4	22.7	36.3	34.1		
Argentina	5.8	3.4			1.0							0.4	4.0	7.0	12.1		
Brazil	12.3	6.8										1.0	18.7	29.3	21.7		
Unrefined	64.2	58.6	72.1	128.8	156.2	175.4	209.4	234.4	249.8	256.5	272.5	302.0	294.3	295.0	309.7	274.2	239.2
United States	48.0	40.0	51.1	115.8	118.8	128.0	171.7	185.8	179.5	182.2	183.1	208.0	207.5	209.5	218.4		
Western Europe	14.2	18.5	21.0	13.0	30.2	47.4	37.6	46.5	70.3	74.4	89.4	94.8	86.8	85.5	91.3		
Other metallic copper	7.6	31.2	24.8	13.5	13.2	23.3	14.8	3.5	24.6	6.1	6.1	4.6	5.1	7.5	50.1	65.3	29.9
Nonmetallic copper	1.8	2.4	3.0	2.5	2.1	2.8	22.9	29.5	26.9	28.0	27.6	22.9	28.2	43.7	35.7	27.4	30.4
Total copper exports	331.2	342.0	380.5	310.1	366.5	411.6	464.3	482.1	457.1	537.7	519.3	546.4	567.8	591.8	608.9	520.5	592.9
Value of copper exports	160	178	255	184	222	327	334	240	194	279	302	297	313	326	362	481	641
Share of total exports (%)	56.9	48.1	56.3	45.0	55.8	69.3	61.6	52.8	50.3	56.4	61.9	58.7	58.8	60.4	58.0	63.8	58.7
Mexico																	
Refined	5.3	5.6	9.7	7.9	14.0	16.0	10.1	8.9	8.2	13.2	6.3	3.4	5.0	2.8	0.6	0.8	0.3
United States	3.2	0.2	5.7	7.9	6.6	11.1	5.0	6.3	3.7	8.8	2.3		0.7	1.1	0.6		
Western Europe	1.8	5.4	4.0		7.1	4.6	5.0	1.7	4.1	2.2	3.4	2.6	4.3	1.7			
Latin America[c]						0.2[d]		0.8[d]	0.4[d]	0.2[d]	0.1	0.5					
Unrefined[e]	47.0	39.8	42.0	42.8	28.2	29.6	36.0	35.1	35.0	29.0	28.6	21.1	24.4	22.4	15.9	11.5	12.1
United States	47.0	37.8	34.1	40.6	27.8	28.2	35.5	34.1	34.4	20.3	18.2	18.4	22.2	20.6	12.7		
Western Europe			4.3	1.7	0.2	1.4	0.5	0.5	0.6	8.6	10.4	2.7	2.2	1.6	2.8		
Other metallic copper						3.5		0.3	0.6	0.7	0.5	0.9	2.6	2.0	1.2	1.0	1.2
Nonmetallic copper	5.4[f]	8.0[f]	7.7[f]	11.9[f]	12.9[f]	10.2[f]	9.8[f]	5.5[f]	5.0[f]	3.4	6.3[f]	3.6	7.0	2.1	7.2	5.8	4.5
Total copper exports	57.7	53.4	59.4	62.6	55.1	59.3	55.9	49.8	48.8	46.3	41.7[f]	29.0	39.0	29.3	24.9	18.6	17.0
Value of copper exports	26.9	33.9	44.1	42.1	55.5	67.8	73.3	37.2	29.9	29.9	25.8	19.1	24.5	22.6	20.2	11.4	13.0
Share of total exports (%)	5.0	5.4	6.6	7.1	8.8	8.6	8.8	5.1	4.1	4.0	3.4	2.0	2.6	2.3	1.9	1.0	1.1
Peru																	
Refined	19.3	23.5	21.3	21.6	24.7	27.0	18.4	24.0	28.7	27.4	24.6	31.6	36.8	30.1	30.8	38.0	31.5
United States	15.8	0.8	1.5	14.7	12.3	16.5	15.6	12.7	10.5	13.3		0.1		7.1	7.0		
Western Europe	0.5	12.1	19.6	6.3	8.1	8.9	2.8	11.3	15.6	10.1		21.4	26.9	16.9	1.8		
Argentina		9.9	0.1	0.7	3.1	1.5			0.9	0.1		2.2	8.8	6.9	0.8		
Brazil												1.0	1.2	0.1	1.0		
Unrefined	2.4	1.8			1.2	3.8	12.7	11.9	10.8	6.4	122.0	149.4	119.2	114.7	117.0	117.3	120.4
United States	2.4	1.8			1.2	3.2	12.7	11.6	10.8	6.4		72.0	64.1	67.3	70.0		
Western Europe						0.6		0.2				77.4	54.7	47.3	47.0		
Total other metallic copper				0.4	0.4	0.9	0.9	0.3		0.1		0.3	0.1		1.6		0.5
Total nonmetallic copper	0.9	0.8	1.7	2.2	2.0	10.6	14.8	16.6	16.1	16.7	20.8	17.7	16.9	18.6	2.7	24.6	23.7
Total copper exports	22.6	26.1	23.0	24.2	28.3	42.3	46.8	52.8	55.6	50.6	167.4	199.0	173.0	163.4	177.8	179.8	176.1
Value of copper exports	10.1	15.1	16.9	14.8	20.4	29.3	33.6	24.5	21.1	24.8	96.4	104.7	92.3	87.3	106.4	121.3	186.2
Share of total exports (%)	5.3	6.1	7.2	6.8	8.3	10.9	10.9	7.7	7.5	8.1	22.4	21.2	17.2	16.2	16.0	18.2	24.4

Argentina																	
Total copper exports[g]											0.6	0.6	0.5	0.1	0.4	0.3	0.3
Bolivia																	
Total copper exports[h]	5.2	5.3	5.2	4.9	4.0	3.9	4.9	4.3	3.2	2.5	2.5	2.3	2.7	3.3	5.2	4.7	5.7
Value of copper exports	(f)	2.2	2.7	3	2.4	2.7	4	2.6	1.5	1.3	1.4	1.3	1.4	1.9	3.2	3.5	6.2
Share of total exports (%)		1.4	1.9	2.7	2.6	2.7	3.7	2.7	2.4	1.7	2.1	1.6	1.9	2.3	2.8	2.7	4.2
Cuba																	
Total copper exports[j]	22.5	21.7	19.7	17.8	17.5	20.8	18.2	18.0	14.3	9.9	13.1	5.5	8.7	16.4	22.4		
Value of copper exports	7.3	8.5	7.8	8.8	8.3	12.5	12.3	8.5	5.9	4.5	3.7		2.2	2.3	5.2	6.6	4.5
Share of total exports (%)	1.1	1.0	1.1	1.3	1.5	2.0	1.8	1.0	0.8	0.7	0.6		0.6	0.6	0.8	1.0	
Haiti																	
Total copper exports[g,k]											1.0	3.8	6.7	8.9	15.0	10.3	
Nicaragua																	
Total copper exports[g,k]											5.4	6.9	8.0	12.7	34.1	40.8	43.3
Latin America																	
Refined	282.2	278.9	311.6	194.8	233.7	253.2	242.2	249.6	192.8	260.7	244.0	251.9	282.0	278.4	244.8	257.8	355.1
United States	221.7	200.7	247.3	181.1	113.2	88.0	59.1	26.8	14.5	37.2	4.1	2.1	1.5	9.9	17.8		
Western Europe	38.4	55.2	58.2	10.8	114.0	157.9	179.9	220.6	175.3	216.9	214.7	235.9	239.6	222.7	168.0		
Latin America	18.2	10.3	4.1	2.2	1.0	4.2	3.0	1.5	1.3	0.4	0.1	4.1	35.8	44.9	35.9		
Unrefined	113.6	100.2	114.1	171.6	185.6	208.8	258.1	281.4	295.6	291.9	423.1	472.5	437.9	432.1	442.6	403.0	371.7
United States	97.4	79.6	85.2	156.4	146.6	159.4	219.9	231.5	224.7	208.9	201.3	298.4	293.8	297.4	301.1		
Western Europe	14.2	18.5	25.3	14.7	31.6	49.4	38.1	47.2	70.9	83.0	99.8	174.9	143.7	134.4	141.1		
Other metallic copper	7.6	31.2	24.8	13.9	13.6	27.7	15.7	4.1	25.2	6.9	6.6	5.8	7.8	9.5	52.9	65.3	31.6
Nonmetallic copper	35.8	38.2	37.3	39.3	38.5	48.3	70.6	73.9	65.5	38.6	77.3	63.3	76.0	89.0	74.2	57.8	58.6
Total copper exports	439.2	448.5	487.8	419.6	471.4	537.9	590.1	607.0	579.0	647.0	745.6	786.6	795.7	801.1	830.0	775.0	835.3
Value of copper exports	204.3	237.6	326.5	252.7	308.6	439.3	457.2	312.7	252.5	339.5	429.3	422.0	433.4	440.1	497.0	623.8	850.9
Share of total exports (%): Region[m]	3.0	3.0	4.5	3.3	3.9	5.4	5.3	3.5	3.0	4.0	4.9	4.7	4.6	4.4	4.7	5.1	6.6
Major exporters[n]	19.6	18.0	23.4	19.7	23.4	27.8	26.2	20.0	17.5	21.4	25.2	23.1	21.5	21.1	20.8	24.9	29.6

Sources: *Metal Statistics* (Frankfurt), *1955-1965*. USBM, *Minerals Yearbook, 1963, 1967*, vol. IV, and *1964*, vol. I. Mexico, Dirección General de Estadística, *Anuario de Comercio Exterior, 1950-1964*. Peru, Departamento de Estadística, *Anuario del Comercio Exterior del Perú, 1950-1964*. IMF, *International Financial Statistics*.

[a]To Uruguay, 100 tons in 1952.
[b]All to Argentina except for 100 tons in 1957.
[c]During period 1960 to 1963, all but 400 tons to Brazil.
[d]All to Argentina except for 400 tons to Brazil in 1958.
[e]To Brazil, 200 tons in 1953 and in 1954.
[f]Gross weight reported; assumed to be copper concentrates of 30% average copper content.
[g]Exports assumed equal to production of copper in concentrates; no smelter production reported.
[h]Predominantly concentrates.
[j]Exports assumed equal to production of copper in concentrates; 1950-59, Cuban copper exported predominantly to the United States; 1960-66, assumed to be exported to the Communist Countries.
[k]Predominantly to the United States.
[m]Copper exports as a percentage of total Latin American exports.
[n]Copper exports as a percentage of total exports of Chile, Mexico, and Peru.

TABLE 4–11. Latin American Copper Balance, 1966
(Metric tons copper content)

Country	Ores and Concentrates (1)	Unrefined Metal (2)	Refined Metal (3)	Semi-manufactures (4)	Other (5)	Total Copper (6)
Argentina						
Imports			——— 18,499 ———			18,499
Production	337					337
Exports	267			14		281
Consumption						18,485
Bolivia						
Imports			——— 367 ———			367
Production	5,827					5,827
Exports	5,702					5,702
Consumption						367
Brazil						
Imports			43,203	494	3,400[a]	47,097
Production	2,150	3,000	3,000			2,150
Consumption						50,907
Chile						
Imports				551		551
Production	663,670	624,595	356,889			663,670
Exports	29,253	239,212	323,329	29,278	1,113[a]	622,185
Consumption						2,618[b]
Colombia						
Imports[c]			6,114	869	47[a]	7,030
Costa Rica						
Imports[c]				284	26[a]	310
Cuba						
Imports			——— 4,700 ———			4,700
Production	6,000					6,000
Exports	3,518					3,518
Consumption						4,700
Dominican Republic						
Imports[c]						717
Ecuador						
Imports						657[d]
Production	223					223
Exports					2	2[d]
Consumption						655
El Salvador						
Imports			——— 1,737 ———		4[a]	1,741
Exports					86	86
Consumption						1,655
Guatemala						
Imports[c]			21	105	8[a]	134
Haiti						
Imports				23		23[d]
Production	2,780					2,780
Exports	3,960				127	4,087[d]
Consumption						23[d]
Honduras						
Imports[c]			——— 34 ———		46	80

TABLE 4-11 – Continued

Country	Ores and Concentrates (1)	Unrefined Metal (2)	Refined Metal (3)	Semi-manufactures (4)	Other (5)	Total Copper (6)
Mexico						
Imports						72
Production	56,513	55,238	47,960[e]			56,513
Exports	5,742	7,278	250	4,801	1,298	19,369
Consumption						41,683
Nicaragua						
Imports				133	30	163
Production	9,764					9,764
Exports	9,764[f]					9,764
Consumption						163
Panama						
Imports[c]				207	16	223
Paraguay						
Imports[c]				199		199
Peru						
Imports			———— 960 ————			960
Production	176,394	151,076	37,974		653	176,394
Exports	23,680	120,439	32,020			176,139
Consumption						6,914
Uruguay						
Imports[c]			———— 628 ————			628
Venezuela						
Imports			63	7,891		7,954
Exports						726
Consumption						7,228
Latin America						
Imports			———— 87,072————		3,577	92,915
Production	923,658	833,909	445,823			923,658
Exports	81,886	366,929	355,599	34,093	2,626	841,859
Net Regional Exports	81,886	366,929	——— 302,620 ———		-951[g]	748,944
Intraregional Trade			——— 16,897———		1,412	18,309
Consumption						144,154

Source: USBM, *Minerals Yearbook, 1967*, vol. IV.

(1) Copper content of ores, concentrates, precipitates, matte, and cement copper.
(2) Blister copper.
(3) Fire-refined and electrolytic copper, including unwrought alloys.
(4) Semifabricated copper and alloys (gross weight).
(5) Scrap of copper and alloys, and copper chemicals (gross weight), chiefly copper sulfate.
(6) Total imports and exports. Total mine production. Total consumption is apparent consumption of refined metal plus net imports of semimanufactures and other copper; no account is taken of consumption of ore and unrefined metal.

[a]Chiefly copper sulfate, gross weight.
[b]Underestimate of true consumption by industry; no account taken of variations in stocks of refined and semifabricated metal.
[c]Consumption assumed equal to imports.
[d]Data for 1965.
[e]Estimated from apparent consumption of blister copper.
[f]All production assumed to be exported.
[g]Negative figure denotes net imports.

TABLE 4-12. Total Value and Returned Value of Copper Production in the Gran Minería of Chile, 1925-1964
(Millions of U.S. dollars)

Year	Total Value of Production (1)	Local Expenditures Operating (2)	Local Expenditures Investment (3)	Direct Taxation (4)	Miscel. Charges (5)	Total Value Returned (6)	Share (%) Returned (7)
1925	50.1	16.2	2.6	2.4	0.1	21.3	38
1926	52.9	18.7	3.8	4.0	0.1	26.7	43
1927	58.4	16.4	18.1	5.2	0.0	39.8	38
1928	81.7	19.3	2.0	8.6	0.2	30.2	34
1929	110.8	25.9	2.5	7.2	0.0	35.7	30
1930	55.9	23.3	2.3	3.3	0.1	28.9	46
1931	32.8	14.4	0.3	0.5	0.0	15.3	45
1932	11.3	6.2	0.3	0.5	0.0	7.0	64
1933	20.7	7.0	0.0	0.8	0.0	7.9	38
1934	38.8	9.9	0.4	1.5	0.0	11.8	28
1935	39.8	9.9	0.5	3.4	0.0	13.9	33
1936	45.3	10.3	0.3	2.8	0.0	13.5	29
1937	105.0	17.9	0.6	11.0	0.0	29.6	28
1938	69.1	19.2	1.1	5.3	0.1	25.6	36
1939	71.0	18.8	1.0	8.3	0.1	28.1	38
1940	82.1	20.8	0.7	11.9	0.1	33.5	40
1941	97.3	26.1	2.6	17.4	0.1	46.2	45
1942	112.6	34.3	0.5	25.3	0.8	60.9	53
1943	116.3	43.6	0.7	22.8	0.9	68.0	58
1944	119.1	45.4	1.1	22.8	1.0	70.2	58
1945	114.0	44.3	0.6	18.1	1.0	66.6	58
1946	104.6	39.5	0.5	17.5	1.0	61.2	58
1947	179.7	51.1	0.8	37.4	1.3	92.9	51
1948	205.0	71.0	1.5	48.7	1.8	126.5	61
1949	155.2	65.4	7.5	26.1	1.6	105.1	63
1950	159.3	64.1	9.6	42.3	1.8	121.5	70
1951	199.3	70.2	14.8	47.1	8.0	146.9	66
1952	201.7	79.7	13.6	43.0	57.6	200.7	93
1953	170.3	80.1	9.3	17.5	53.5	168.9	94
1954	168.5	76.5	0.6	30.7	43.5	154.8	91
1955	294.3	64.7	0.8	118.9	40.3	228.8	78
1956	391.1	72.2	6.1	130.1	3.2	214.5	53
1957	260.5	72.2	13.5	73.6	5.1	167.3	59
1958	225.9	62.8	18.9	53.3	6.8	144.0	55
1959	324.9	86.4	25.4	88.1	5.5	208.4	56
1960	309.8	98.0[a]	8.8	89.0	14.7[b]	233.0	75
1961	270.9	99.1[a]	6.7	74.0	13.8[b]	209.1	77
1962	300.4	107.5[a]	3.8	89.3	15.3[b]	233.9	78
1963	291.9	99.4[a]	6.4	87.1	12.8[b]	224.3	77
1964	340.3	119.8[a]	4.6	97.1	10.5[b]	253.9	75

Sources: 1925-59 – C. W. Reynolds, "Chile and Copper," in Mamalakis and Reynolds, *Essays on the Chilean Economy* (Yale University, Economic Growth Center, 1965), pp. 365, 367-68, 377-79. 1960-64 – Banco Central de Chile, Departamento de Estudios, *Balanza de Pagos de Chile*, 1962, 1963, 1964.

Notes:

(1) Total production valued at average price of copper sold during the year; differs from value of sales by the imputed value of changes in stocks.

(2) Total dollar expenditures in Chile on current account, including the cost of exchange control between 1932 and 1955; excludes dollar payments to the Companía de Acero del Pacífico and the Ferrocarril Antofagasta-Bolivia, which are included in item (5).

(3) Total dollar expenditures in Chile on capital account, excluding duties on imported capital goods; wages of laborers employed for construction are included in (2), so (3) represents only purchases of capital goods in Chile.

(4) Total income and profit taxes, by year of income taxed, not year in which paid.

(5) All indirect taxes except import duties; includes the surtax in effect from 1951 to 1955.

(6) Total value returned to Chile; includes import duties, not shown separately because they never exceeded $6.7 million or 5% of value returned.

(7) Net value returned, or total value returned (6) less local capital expenditures (3), as a percentage of total value of production (1). This series is used because it is more stable than the share of total value returned in total value of production.

[a]Legal cost of production, exported copper only; approximately equal to current costs incurred in Chile.
[b]Includes somewhat more items than previously; still does not include import duties.

TABLE 4–13. Profits and Investment in the Gran Minería of Chile, 1930-1964
(Millions of U.S. dollars and percentages)

Year	Gross Profits (1)	Direct Tax Share (%) (2)	Net Profits (3)	Yield on Assets (%) (4)	Total Assets (5)	Total Investment (6)	Net Investment (7)
1930	10	34	6.5	2.6	244.1	4.9	5.3
1931	1	(a)			249.4	0.5	-4.2
1932	1	(a)			245.2	0.2	-7.0
1933	1	(a)			238.2	0.1	3.2
1934	6	24	4.8	2.0	241.4	0.8	-6.0
1935					235.4	1.2	0.4
1936	10	27	7.6	3.1	235.8	0.6	7.7
1937	47	24	35.6	13.5	243.5	1.9	20.4
1938	23	23	17.8	6.9	263.9	2.2	-6.1
1939	21	40	12.6	4.8	257.8	1.3	3.2
1940	31	38	19.2	7.4	261.0	1.2	-0.9
1941	36	48	18.7	7.2	260.1	6.6	18.7
1942	44	58	18.5	6.3	278.8	1.3	14.9
1943	39	59	15.8	5.2	293.7	1.4	11.3
1944	39	58	16.2	5.2	305.0	2.1	4.7
1945	32	56	14.1	4.5	309.7	1.3	3.8
1946	33	53	15.8	5.1	313.5	1.1	-2.0
1947	71	53	33.3	10.2	311.5	2.0	14.5
1948	95	51	46.0	13.6	326.0	7.0	12.0
1949	47	55	21.0	6.2	338.0	22.4	-1.6
1950	67	63	24.8	6.8	336.4	32.4	31.0
1951	82	58	34.4	8.4	367.4	39.8	43.8
1952	78	55	35.4	8.1	411.2	33.0	28.2
1953	27	64	9.7	2.0	439.4	20.2	42.1
1954	50	62	19.1	4.1	481.5	3.2	-17.1
1955	174	68	54.8	12.8	464.4	1.9	-37.3
1956	206	63	75.8	13.8	427.1	26.2	120.7
1957	112	66	38.0	6.7	547.8	40.4	23.4
1958	81	66	27.4	4.6	570.2	54.7	25.6
1959	144	61	55.9	9.4	595.8	38.0	
1960	137	65	47.8			40.1[b]	
1961	111	66	37.3			38.9[b]	
1962	133	67	43.5			29.8	
1963	126	69	39.3			37.8	
1964	145	67	48.1			35.6	

Sources: 1925-59 – C. W. Reynolds, "Chile and Copper," pp. 368, 383-84, 386. 1960-64 – Banco Central de Chile, Departamento de Estudios, *Balanza de Pagos de Chile*, 1962, 1963, 1964. See also table 4-12.

Notes:
(1) Estimated gross profits: sum of direct taxation and net profits after taxes.
(2) Direct taxes as a percentage of gross profits.
(3) Net profits after taxes; amount available for reinvestment or repatriation.
(4) Net profits as a percentage of total assets.
(5) Depreciated value of total assets.
(6) Total investment in plant and equipment, including imports for current operations.
(7) Change in depreciated value of assets; net new investment in all forms.

[a]Greater than 50%.
[b]Excludes imports of fixed capital; includes only imports for current operations and investment expenditures in Chile.

TABLE 4–14. Chile: Production and Exports of Copper by Type, 1950-1966
(Thousands of metric tons)

Types	1950	1951	1952	1953	1954	1955	1956	1957	1958
Mine production	363.5	381.5	409.5	363.9	364.4	434.4	490.8	485.3	463.2
(Exports of ores and concentrates)[a]	17.0	22.0	29.0	34.0	25.0	5.0	22.1	25.7	23.6
Smelter production	345.5	360.1	382.8	336.5	338.2	405.8	458.6	450.1	438.1
(Exports of blister copper)[b]	64.2	58.6	72.1	128.8	156.2	175.4	209.4	232.4	249.8
Fire-refined copper: Production[c]	143.2	155.4	156.6	121.2	88.2	113.1	100.4	66.3	59.4
(Exports)[b,c]	117.2	128.1	147.9	95.3	81.0	102.8	88.4	63.7	53.0
Electrolytic copper: Production	156.3	163.4	151.1	89.4	109.9	127.6	140.1	154.9	128.4
(Exports)[b]	140.4	121.7	132.7	70.0	114.0	107.4	125.3	152.3	102.9
(Other exports)[d]	9.3	33.6	27.8	16.0	15.3	26.0	19.1	7.2	27.9
(Total exports)[e]	348.1	364.0	409.5	344.1	391.5	416.6	464.3	481.3	457.2
Reported consumption[f]	19.4	46.6	26.1	24.0	29.6	34.5	17.4	8.0	30.7
Apparent consumption[g]	14.4	17.5	0.0	19.8	-27.1	17.8	26.5	4.0	6.0

Types	1959	1960	1961	1962	1963	1964	1965	1966
Mine production	546.0	533.3	548.6	587.3	604.1	633.3	605.9	663.7
(Exports of ores and concentrates)[a]	22.9	22.8	17.4	20.5	31.7	23.8	5.8	10.9
Smelter production	517.3	504.8	524.5	557.9	557.4	587.1	574.8	624.6
(Exports of blister copper)[b]	256.5	272.5	302.0	294.3	295.0	309.7	274.2	239.2
Fire-refined copper: Production[c]	82.6	78.6	72.7	83.6	80.1	100.3		
(Exports)[b,c]	70.3	74.7	69.8	74.9	76.7	72.0	68.3	102.0
Electrolytic copper: Production	177.1	147.0	153.5	180.1	178.9	177.8		
(Exports)[b]	149.8	138.4	147.1	165.3	168.8	141.4	150.7	221.3
(Other exports)[d]	38.1	10.9	10.1	12.8	19.6	62.0	21.5	19.5
(Total exports)[e]	537.6	519.3	546.4	567.8	591.8	608.9	520.5	592.9
Reported consumption[f]	41.1	13.0	12.3	13.4	16.2	64.0		
Apparent consumption[g]	8.4	14.0	2.2	19.5	10.1	14.3	85.4	70.8

Sources: ABMS, *Yearbook.* 1950-55 and 1965-67 – USBM, *Minerals Yearbook.* 1956-66 – *Metal Statistics* (Frankfurt).

[a]Copper content of ores, concentrates and precipitates.
[b]Gross weight including impurities, 1950-56; copper content, 1957-66.
[c]Total refined copper less electrolytic copper.
[d]Exports of copper chemicals, fabricated and semifabricated copper, copper alloys and scrap.
[e]Exports of copper in all forms except manufactures.
[f]Includes variation in stocks of copper in all forms.
[g]Mine production less total exports of copper.

Chapter 5

IRON AND STEEL

Steel is by a wide margin the most used metal in the world; consequently iron ore, from which steel is principally made, is one of the world's most important resources. In the early 1960s some 400 million tons of steel were produced annually, from 300 million tons of pig iron and 100 million tons of scrap and other metallic inputs. The pig iron in turn was produced from 500 million tons of iron ore. Steel is consumed particularly in construction and capital goods industries, and forms a large share of a modern economy's physical capital. Even a poor country therefore requires large amounts of steel for economic development and the demand increases as it develops producer goods industries. The importance of steel is increased in less developed countries, where there are likely to be fewer possibilities of substituting other materials than there are in more advanced economies. Creation of a steel industry to meet the demand of other sectors of the economy is often a major step in the industrialization of a country.

This has been the case in Latin America, where in the last few decades – especially since 1950 – full-scale steel industries have been established or greatly expanded in seven countries. The region now produces some 10 million tons of steel, enough to satisfy the bulk of its rapidly growing requirements. Nearly all the raw materials used by the industry are produced in Latin America. Iron ore is mined in such large quantities that three-fourths of production, some 40 million tons, is exported. These exports are worth some $300 million, or between 2 and 3 percent of all the region's exports. In no country is iron ore the leading export commodity, although in Chile it accounts for 10 percent of all foreign exchange. In every country, however, the supply of iron and steel and the amounts which must be spent to import what is not produced locally are matters of considerable importance.

Iron ore is therefore a commodity that is used, directly or in the form of steel, throughout the region; whose consumption is related to the degree of economic development; and that contributes to development both as an export commodity and as a major input to domestic industry. In these respects petroleum is most comparable among the

Note: Iron and Steel tables 5-1 to 5-12 appear on pp. 200–212.

commodities studied here. Iron ore has strong linkages to other products and industries: its use in steelmaking requires large amounts of other raw materials, and the finished steel is supplied to a variety of industries. Finally, since the Second World War, iron ore has become a major item in world trade, creating a boom in the new exporting areas. At the same time, the techniques of steelmaking are changing rapidly in ways which not only lower the cost for any producer, but preferentially benefit regions such as Latin America whose resources of capital and raw materials are better suited to the new methods than to those they replace.

The size and complexity of the steel industry of Latin America preclude an adequate description of all its phases and their relation to the rest of the regional economy and to the world industry. This chapter is therefore limited, first to a discussion of iron ore, and second to Latin America alone. The rest of the world will be considered only as a source of, or market for, steel and the raw materials required to make it. Within Latin America, only iron ore will be treated in detail, with less attention to other inputs.[1] Similarly, little will be said of the production or use of steel beyond the principal integrated steel mills in the region: the great number of smaller firms engaged in the industry will be described only briefly, and the end uses of steel still less.[2]

Iron Ore in Latin America

Iron is an abundant material, forming some 5 percent of the earth's crust and occurring in large, high-grade deposits on every continent. In marked contrast to the major nonferrous metals, much of production has always come from

[1] For further information on some of these inputs the reader is referred to chaps. 8 (Petroleum) and 9 (Coal).

[2] The steel industry has been extensively studied in Latin America, particularly by the UN Economic Commission for Latin America. See ECLA, *La Economía Siderúrgica de América Latina*, doc. E/CN. 12/727 (Santiago, Chile, February 1966), which, together with certain publications cited therein, is the major source for this survey. Other data for this chapter are taken from the U.S. Bureau of Mines, *Minerals Yearbook*. Other sources are indicated in the tables and footnotes.

ore sufficiently rich to be shipped long distances to smelting facilities, with little or no concentration or other processing.[3] The abundance of high-grade ore has meant, first, that exploration has only recently begun in the underdeveloped areas of the world and, second, that no single standard determines the economic attractiveness of a deposit: size, location, physical properties, and chemical composition, as well as grade, are to be considered.

World iron ore resources, defined as material currently exploited or likely to be in use by 1990, have been estimated at some 170,000 million tons of ore, containing about 71,000 million tons of iron, or more than 200 times the present level of consumption (see table 5-1). Of the ore, 28,000 million tons are of direct shipping quality, at grades of 50 percent or more in most areas but including much lower-grade material in Western Europe. A further 43,000 million tons are currently economical but require concentration before shipment. And the remainder — almost 100,000 million tons, or 42,000 million tons of contained iron — is in deposits that are not now economical but are likely to be exploited in the next twenty-five years. More recent estimates place the total at 256,000 million tons of ore, with an iron content of 114,400 million tons.

Latin America, with some 20,000 million tons of ore identified, is relatively rich in iron. Much of this material has been discovered since World War II; in 1950 the region's resources were estimated as only 7,000 million tons of probable ore (excluding 3,000 million tons of complex, uneconomic ore in Cuba).[4] Brazil is by far the best endowed country, with reserves comparable in size and equal or better in grade to those of the United States, India, and the Soviet Union. In the region as a whole, the average grade in each category of resources exceeds that for the rest of the world; the share of contained iron in the world total consistently exceeds the share of ore. The discrepancy is greatest for concentrated ore, of which very little has been found in Latin America. The bulk of the region's ore also has excellent physical and chemical properties. A small amount, chiefly material of 48 to 50 percent, is relatively high in phosphorous, but the rest is low in impurities of all kinds.[5] Finally, much of the ore thus far discovered is near enough the coast to be readily exported. This is the case especially in Chile, Peru, Venezuela, and for the principal Brazilian deposits; the resources of Argentina, Colombia, and Mexico, while suitable for domestic industries, are not well located for export. The effect of location is reinforced by the lower grade and greater impurities of ore in Argentina and Colombia.

Some iron ore was undoubtedly mined for local use from the sixteenth century onward, but production on a significant scale did not begin in Latin America until after 1900. Domestic steelworks provided the demand in Brazil and Mexico, while in Chile and Cuba iron was mined chiefly by U.S. firms for export.[6] Fluctuations in exports caused output to drop sharply during the Depression and to decline again during World War II when shipping was scarce. Throughout the period 1925-44 the region produced 1 to 2 million tons of ore annually, or about 1 percent of the world total (see table 5-2). Then in the next fifteen years output expanded rapidly, from 3 to more than 40 million tons, and the share in the world total rose to 8 percent. After a decline in 1961-63 the expansion resumed, passing 50 million tons. This boom, amounting to an average annual increase in 1947-60 of nearly 8 percent, is the consequence, first, of the creation and rapid expansion of the Latin American steel industry and, second, of the growth of export demand.

The high wartime demand and the shortage of imports accelerated the depletion of high-grade iron ore reserves in the United States. Steel producers began to develop ways of using the abundant lower-grade material, and simultaneously began searching for high-grade resources abroad. Latin America was the first region to experience the postwar iron ore boom, since the demand came first from the United States and producers there regarded Latin America as their best prospective source. As demand for imported ore arose in Europe and Japan, exploration and production spread to Africa and Australia. The major deposits in Venezuela were found in 1943-44, and in the next decade the enormous reserves of Brazil were surveyed. Exports from these new sources did not begin until the early 1950s. Chile, which had long been the largest producer in the region and the chief source of U.S. imports until the 1940s, was surpassed by Brazil and then by Venezuela; Peru was next to become a major exporter. The United States, which had relied on imports for only about 5 percent of apparent consumption in the 1920s and 1930s, came to import one-third of its requirements by the 1960s, almost entirely from Canada and Latin America. As other steelmaking regions increased their dependence on imports, iron ore became a major item in world trade, in quantity if not in value.

The other developments of this period — progress in beneficiating ores — did not greatly affect Latin America. It may be many decades before the region needs to use its own low-grade resources, and meanwhile the use of such materials by importing countries reduces the market for high-grade ore. However, many of the recently developed techniques can be applied to high-grade as well as low-grade ore to lower transportation costs, increase the capacity and

---

[3] See USBM, *Mineral Facts and Problems, 1965*, for a discussion of the occurrence and preparation of iron ore.

[4] UN, *World Iron Ore Resources and Their Utilization* (Lake Success: 1950), pp. 66-68. Another 36,000 million tons were classed as potential ore; little or none of this material is included in the estimates in table 5-1.

[5] For analyses of the major Latin American deposits, those containing at least 10 million tons of ore, see UN, *Interregional Symposium on the Application of Modern Technical Practices in the Iron and Steel Industry to Developing Countries* (Prague/Geneva, November 1963), p. 55. More detail on certain impurities and their effect on the choice and efficiency of steelmaking techniques is given in ECLA, *A Study of the Iron and Steel Industry in Latin America* (New York, 1954), vol. I, pp. 17-22.

[6] For the early history of iron in Chile, see R. Cañón Artigas, *El Hierro en la Economía Chilena* (Santiago: Universidad de Chile, 1948). For Mexico, see R. Cervantes y Mejía, *El Crecimiento de la Industria Siderúrgica en México* (Mexico: Universidad Nacional Autónoma de México, 1959).

efficiency of blast furnaces, and reduce the costs of steel-making. These methods involve concentrating the ore, forming it into grains or pellets of uniform size and character, mixing the ore with fluxing material, and partially reducing it before charging the blast furnace.[7] Even where beneficiation is not required for domestic use, it may improve the competitive position of iron ore in foreign markets, especially where transport costs are important. The first pelletizing plants were built in the United States and Canada, which still have the bulk of world capacity. The first such plant in Latin America began operating in Peru in 1963 and was substantially expanded in 1967, when a second plant started production in Brazil. The planned capacity of these installations is some 5 million tons, of a world total, extant or planned, of 100 million tons.[8] Construction of a pelletizing plant is also under consideration in Venezuela, where the pellets will be prereduced to an iron content of 85 percent.

Iron ore is one of the lowest-valued commodities included in this study. The ore is seldom worth more than $15 per ton, and the contained iron is valued at one cent per pound or less. There is no organized market or standard price for iron ore, as for the nonferrous metals, for several reasons: the bulk of production and trade is controlled by steel producers, who operate under long-term contracts without intermediaries; transport costs are higher relative to the value of the ore than for most products; and differences in any of several properties are reflected in price differentials even for ores of the same grade. Iron ore is far from uniform, and differences in quality greatly affect the way it can be used and the cost of making steel from it. Prices, or average values, of iron ore are remarkably stable over time. (See table 5-3.) Within the United States the price of a given type of ore changes slowly; even the boom of the 1950s resulted in only a slight increase. The prices of Latin American ores exported to the United States have varied more widely, but still less than the prices of many primary commodities. Only petroleum, among the region's principal exports, shows a comparable long-run stability. Peak prices were reached for some ores in the early 1950s and for others later in the decade, following five years or so of rapid increase. As supplies have caught up with demand in recent years, prices have declined slightly to around $10 per ton, and further declines are considered likely. Unit export values of Latin American ores rose and then fell rather sharply in the decade 1955-65, reaching peaks of between $20 and $30 per ton according to grade and location. These fluctuations chiefly reflect price changes, as average grade and quality did not vary greatly.

The combination of rapidly increasing volume and rising prices caused the value of Latin American iron ore exports to expand sharply in the fifties, from a mere $20 million to $200 million, to nearly $300 million in 1960, and to nearly $400 million in 1966. The bulk of exports are accounted for by Brazil, Chile, Peru, and Venezuela, with the largest amounts shipped by Venezuela between 1954 and 1966 (see table 5-4). The boom was reflected in a great increase in Cuban exports in 1952-57, and by the export of a bit less than a million tons from the Dominican Republic in the years 1952-60; but neither country contributed much to the totals, nor was iron ore an important export. The same is true of Mexico.

Until the postwar expansion, Chile was the chief exporter, with Cuba in second place in most years and Brazil and Mexico shipping small quantities. Virtually all exports went to the United States which remained the principal market until the early 1950s, since when its share of total Latin American exports has steadily decreased, from 90 percent to less than 40 percent. As Peru and Venezuela entered the trade and the smaller exporters with special ties to the United States withdrew, the region's exports shifted to Europe, and then to Japan. By the 1960s Chile and especially Peru had become major suppliers to Japan, Venezuela was the chief Latin American source for the United States, and Brazil sold most of its ore in Western Europe. The establishment of a steel industry in Argentina in 1959 created a market within the region, supplied by Brazil, Chile, and Peru. Latin America's trade in iron ore has evolved toward geographic specialization, with each exporter selling principally in the market for which it has an advantage in location. The largest exception to this pattern is continued Chilean exports to the United States, reflecting the position of U.S. capital in Chile's mining industry. Ownership ties are also strong in Venezuela, but there they only reinforce the geographic pattern. The other exceptions to strict specialization probably reflect differences in ore quality and long-term ties between buyers and sellers.

Generally, Latin America has a strong position in the world iron ore market in consequence of the size, quality, and location of its reserves. The region's ore can be sold in all three major markets — the United States, Europe, and Japan — without depending on preferences or political or ownership ties. In each area, however, it faces competitors equally well or better located, with large reserves of comparable quality: Canada in the United States market, West Africa in the European, and Australia in the Japanese. The development of these alternative sources has ended the boom of the 1950s and reduced prices appreciably, and the competition may be expected to last for many years, especially in view of the increased interest in high-grade beneficiated ore for blast furnace feed.[9] The distribution of production and trade also reflects the conditions for foreign, especially U.S., investment in developing countries over the last decade and a half. Thus the shift in investment to West Africa in the late 1950s and early 1960s was partly caused by political obstacles to expansion in Brazil, which in the last few years has sought to increase its exports more

[7]These processes are summarized in USBM, *Mineral Facts and Problems, 1965*. For more details, see papers A.4 through A.11 presented in UN, *Interregional Symposium. . . , Annex III*, p. 154.

[8]*Mining Annual Review*, May 1966; *Metal Bulletin*, 11 November 1966; and *Engineering and Mining Journal*, February 1968, p. 105. See also UNIDO, *Prospects for Exports of Processed Iron Ore from Developing Countries*, doc. ID/Conf. 1/B.2F, 25 July 1967 (Background paper for International Symposium on Industrial Development, Athens, 29 November – 20 December 1967), pp. 36-37.

[9]UN, *Interregional Symposium. . . ,* p. 57. See also USBM, *Minerals Yearbook*, for an indication of the quality and use of ores imported into the United States.

rapidly. Thus in the future the region's competitive position may depend especially on the quality and preparation of iron ore, and the use of various methods of beneficiation can be expected to increase. It may also be that in the near future the Latin American iron ore economy will depend increasingly on domestic use rather than on exports.

Latin American Resources for Steelmaking

Although finished steel consists primarily of iron, a variety of other materials enters into its manufacture. Carbonaceous fuels are used in relatively large amounts — several hundred kilograms per ton of pig iron produced — both to reduce the iron ore and to supply heat to the reduction and steelmaking processes. Limestone and other minerals are added as fluxes, to separate the silica in the ore. Finally, several other metals, of which manganese is the most important, are added to steel to remove impurities such as sulfur and to give it the desired degree of strength, resistance to corrosion, or other properties. Since the various fluxing materials are widely available, while the ferroalloy or additive metals are high-valued and used in relatively small quantities, neither sort of material normally determines the feasibility or the location for establishing a steel industry. Those questions are determined rather by the location and quality of resources of iron ore and of fuel for use as a reducing agent. The production of steel involves assembling these two raw materials, both of which are low-valued and therefore relatively expensive to transport, so as to produce steel at the least total cost. This view of the problem has commonly been used to evaluate Latin America's resources for steelmaking, and to choose the locations of major steel mills.[10] It is also the basis for the conclusion that certain sites in Latin America, such as those where steel mills are now located in Mexico, Chile, Colombia, and Peru, and to a lesser extent Venezuela and Brazil, offer very low assembly costs and therefore potentially low costs of steel production.[11] The cost of supplying steel to consumers depends in addition on the distance from the steel mill to market. The proportionately lower cost of transport for steel than for raw materials may be offset by the possibility of ocean shipment for the latter, whereas the output must be shipped overland and to more destinations. Thus steel mills are commonly built at or near consuming centers or on the coast, closer to the market than to the raw material sources.

If account is taken of all identified resources at whatever grade, Latin America has some 100,000 million tons of iron ore, containing about 49,000 million tons of iron. Over 10 percent of this amount is in ore of 60 percent or more, concentrated heavily in Brazil and Venezuela (see table 5-5). A comparable amount is found at grades of 55-59 percent, almost entirely in Brazil, and about half the total — 25,000 million tons of iron — is in ores of 50 percent, chiefly in one immense deposit in Bolivia. The remaining iron occurs at lower grades, with Brazil again having much the largest share. Reserves of high-grade ore are adequate for steel industries in Brazil, Chile, Mexico, Peru, and Venezuela. Bolivia also appears to have adequate reserves, while Argentina and Colombia are much poorer in both the amount and the grade of their resources. The remaining countries of the region have little or no iron ore, except for Cuba where large amounts of low-grade iron are mixed with nickel and chromium in ores from which the iron is difficult to recover; the high-grade reserves have been largely exhausted.

The situation with respect to reducing materials is both more complicated and less satisfactory. In the classical steelmaking process, hard coke, made from bituminous coal and consisting of almost pure carbon, is used to reduce iron ore to pig iron in a blast furnace. Since reduction may require half or more as much coke, or nearly as much coal, as iron ore, and since transport costs of coal are relatively high, the location and quality of coal resources are extremely important. By world standards, Latin America is quite poor in coal of all kinds, and especially in coal of coking grade.[12] Of total reserves of bituminous coal of over 50,000 million tons, only about 4,000 million tons can presently be used to make coke, and this figure includes much shrinking or swelling coal which must be blended with imported coal. Three of the seven Latin American countries with integrated steel industries depend wholly on imported coal; two can use a mixture of foreign and domestic coal; and only two can rely entirely on their own resources (see table 5-5). The need to import coal from the United States increases the assembly costs of raw materials in Peru and Venezuela, partially offsetting their excellent position in iron ore, and adds to the costs imposed by poor iron ore resources in Argentina. Coal of adequate quality is found very close to iron ore only in Colombia, and somewhat farther away in Mexico. In Brazil and Chile the coal is not too far from the iron ore, but its quality is so low that the use of domestic coal may actually raise costs over what they would be if imports were used exclusively.

The classical dependence of steelmaking on coke is being steadily reduced by technical progress in the operation of blast furnaces. The ratio of coke to pig iron can be sharply reduced by the injection of fuel oil into the blast furnace, 1 kilogram of oil substituting for as much as 1.4 kilograms of coke.[13] This modification is of interest anywhere, because of the resulting increase in blast furnace capacity, and is in widespread use in France, Japan, and the Soviet Union, but it is especially valuable to Latin America. The region's poverty in coal is matched by great wealth in petroleum, which is also more widely distributed. Crude oil reserves are

---

[10]See ECLA, *A Study of the Iron and Steel Industry...*, pp. 92-96; and UN, *World Iron Ore Resources...*, pp. 26-32, where assembly costs of iron ore and coke or coking coal are considered for the sites of the principal integrated steel mills in Latin America, some of which were under consideration but not yet constructed at the time of these studies.

[11]The location of a steel mill may be determined by other factors than assembly cost: for example, the SOGESA steelworks in Peru was located at Chimbote in order to stimulate industry in that area, rather than at Lima-Callao where costs might have been lower. See J. D. Heffernan and M. H. Che, *The Steel Industry in Latin America* (New York: Chase Manhattan Bank, May 1967).

[12]For a fuller discussion, see chap. 9 (Coal), especially tables 9-1 and 9-6.

[13]ECLA, *La Economía Siderúrgica...*, p. 111.

small relative to requirements in Brazil, Chile, and Peru, but even in those countries – all of which now import coke – the substitution of oil for coal could lower both the total and the foreign exchange costs of steelmaking. In Argentina and Venezuela the effect might be still greater.

Blast furnaces can also use charcoal as a reductant: this was the method first used to make pig iron, and it still accounts for about 10 percent of Latin America's pig iron production.[14] Charcoal is used in one major steel mill in Brazil, at two smaller mills, one each in Argentina and Brazil, and by a number of small producers of pig or cast iron in Brazil. Plants based on charcoal can compete with those using coke where wood is plentiful and coal is scarce; they are limited chiefly not by the efficiency of charcoal in the furnace but by the large amounts of wood required and the correspondingly large area from which it must be brought. Latin America has enormous timber resources, but the yield is simply too low to allow much more extensive use of wood. The principal charcoal-using steel mills now obtain their wood from plantations of eucalyptus instead of from the slower growing species of the natural forest. In the future charcoal from natural forests might be used at Mutún, Bolivia, or elsewhere in the Amazon basin if other such deposits are discovered, but its share in steelmaking will probably continue to decrease.

Iron ore can be reduced by other means than the blast furnace, with various types of fuels and reducing agents. If the object is to decrease the investment required, particularly for a small plant, electric furnaces may be installed, using electricity for heat and coke for reduction. Furnaces of this type are used in the major steel mills of Peru and Venezuela, in two integrated mills in Brazil, and in some smaller plants. Much research has also been directed toward the development of processes requiring neither the heavy investment in a blast furnace nor the use of coke. Thus far only one such process – that using natural gas, developed in Mexico – has entered commercial operation. The extension of this method or the development of others would further the substitution of petroleum and gas for coke, shifting the requirements for steelmaking toward materials with which Latin America is relatively well endowed. It is noteworthy that natural gas is competitive with coke in Mexico, where the principal steel mills are located close to large reserves of coking coal. Gas might also be attractive in Argentina, Colombia, and Venezuela, which have sizable reserves and pipeline networks for transportation. In Brazil and Chile natural gas fields are poorly located and there are no lines for distribution; gas might nonetheless eventually be competitive for small steel mills in northern Brazil or in eastern Bolivia, and perhaps in southern Argentina. All these locations have gas (and petroleum) but no suitable coal, and are near iron ore deposits or could be easily supplied with high-grade ore or pellets.

Of the several ferroalloy metals, only manganese is essential in all steelmaking: it is used to remove sulfur, some six

to seven kilograms being added per ton of steel, with one or two kilograms remaining in the steel while the rest appears in the slag. Manganese often occurs in association with iron and is seldom processed into metal; instead, it is added to steel as ferromanganese – an alloy of about three-fourths manganese and one-fourth iron – or in other alloys. The tonnages required by the world steel industry make manganese the second most-used metal; but because the amounts used are small compared to the iron ore and reducing material, the location of manganese resources does not affect the location of steel industries. World reserves of manganese are some 420 to 450 million tons of metal, of which the Soviet Union alone has about half. The rest is found primarily in India, China, three African countries, and Brazil.[15] The United States and Western Europe have almost no manganese and depend on imports. Latin America has some 37 million tons, 30 million in Brazil and 4.5 million in Mexico[16] (see table 5-5). These two countries and Chile are self-sufficient in manganese and have a surplus for export, while Argentina meets most or all of its domestic requirements. The other steel producing countries import manganese ore or ferroalloys for their industries.

Manganese ore, like iron ore, has long been produced in Latin America for export. Regional production was some 300,000 tons annually in the late 1920s, 1930s, and 1940s. It dropped to 100,000 tons during the Depression in consequence of the decline in U.S. steel production, and reached over 600,000 tons during World War II, when supplies from the eastern hemisphere were cut off. Since the war there has been a steady expansion in production, linked, as for iron ore, to the growth of domestic demand as steel industries were created and to the worldwide increase in steel output. The increase was much less rapid – from 0.3 to more than 1.2 million tons – than for iron ore, however, because there was no substitution for domestic production in importing countries. The United States has regularly absorbed half or more of Latin America's production, to meet from one-tenth to one-half its requirements. Brazil was virtually the only producer and exporter until the 1930s. During World War II Cuba produced nearly as much as Brazil, and in several years between 1943 and 1955 it was the chief exporter to the United States. Mexico now holds second place in production, after Brazil, but is a much less important exporter.[17]

The remaining ferroalloy metals are important chiefly for making stainless, heat-resistant, and other special steels. Latin America produces relatively small amounts of such

---

[14] Blast furnaces using coke accounted for 77 percent of the total in integrated steel mills in 1964, charcoal furnaces for 9.6 percent. ECLA, *La Economía Siderúrgica...*, pp. 32-33, and UN, *Interregional Symposium...*, pp. 60-61.

[15] H. H. Landsberg et al., *Resources in America's Future* (Johns Hopkins Press for Resources for the Future, 1963), p. 437. The estimates refer to manganese content of the major deposits, ranging in grade from 20 to 52 percent.

[16] The large iron ore deposit at Mutún, Bolivia, also contains manganese. The amount, known only to be "considerable," has been estimated at 30 million tons, or equal to the reserves of Brazil. See *Mining Annual Review*, June 1964, p. 229, and UN, *Interregional Symposium...*, p. 58.

[17] Data on production and trade from USBM, *Minerals Yearbook* (see especially *1963*, vol. IV, and *1964*, vol. IV). Manganese exports have never exceeded 0.5 percent of total Latin American exports, or 3 percent of any one country's exports.

steels. Consumption of alloy steels is met largely by imports, and where the steels are made in the region the additive metals or alloys are often imported. Latin America produces several of the additive metals, but has few facilities for processing them; ferromanganese and other manganese alloys account for nearly all ferroalloy production. Little is known about world or regional reserves of any of these metals. Of the four metals produced in appreciable amounts in Latin America – chromium, nickel, molybdenum, and tungsten – chromium and nickel are found almost exclusively in Cuba, in complex ores containing about 40 percent iron. In the years before the revolution of 1959-60, Cuba produced as much as 2 percent of the world's chromite ore and 8 percent of its nickel. Virtually all its production was exported to the United States, which had provided the capital, both private and governmental, to mine and process the metals. Brazil also produces chromite as well as small amounts of nickel, and some production of one metal or the other has occurred in Colombia, Guatemala and Venezuela. Molybdenum is produced entirely as a byproduct of copper mining; of the world total the region accounts for about 5 percent, of which most is produced by Chile and a little has come from Mexico and Peru. All molybdenum is exported as concentrates,[18] chiefly to Western Europe; the United States, the world's largest producer, is self-sufficient. Tungsten, which unlike the other additive metals is used primarily outside the steel industry, is produced in fairly large amounts in Bolivia, where it is a significant export after tin, lead, and zinc. Argentina, Brazil, Mexico, and Peru also produce tungsten, and in total Latin America accounts for about 10 percent of world output. Finally, Chile produces small amounts of silicon-based ferroalloys, such as silicomanganese and ferrosilicon. Since silicon is obtained from silica, the chief ingredient of sand, there is no information on reserves or on total production.[19]

The provision of fluxing materials for steelmaking presents no problems in Latin America. Suitable deposits of limestone occur throughout the region in close proximity to nearly all steel mill sites. In a few cases, as in Chile or Bolivia, lime is, or would have to be, brought a considerable distance to the plant, but this factor has little or no effect on the costs or location of steel production. The same appears to be true of other inputs to steelmaking, such as water and electricity; they are either widely available or can be provided at a cost which is small relative to that of other factors. The availability of cheap electricity may have been a factor in the location of the major steel mill in Venezuela, which uses electric furnaces fed by a large hydroelectric project; but even there the electricity can be used by a number of industries and consumers, and the choice of steelmaking technique was also influenced by the lower investment required for electric furnaces than for blast furnaces.

In summary, no one country in Latin America is exceptionally well endowed for steel production. All the countries without integrated steel industries are poorly supplied with raw materials, except perhaps for Bolivia. Of the countries with steel industries only Argentina is poorly endowed: its iron ore is low in grade, its coal unsuitable for coking, and it is at a disadvantage in location for coal imports.[20] The remaining producers – Brazil, Colombia, Chile, Mexico, Peru, and Venezuela – are all relatively well supplied. Except for coking coal, Brazil is perhaps in the best position, with large reserves of very high-grade iron ore, and manganese and other alloy metals as well. These advantages appear to be approximately offset by the availability of good coal in Colombia and Mexico (close enough to the iron ore in Colombia to compensate for the low grade), and by advantages of location in Peru and Venezuela, where overland transport is less. If raw materials are considered, it is evident, first, that the assembly costs of steel do not vary so much among countries as do the cost and export possibilities of iron ore alone; and, second, that these differences are not great enough to give any one country a commanding advantage in the cost of steel production. The capacity, structure, and efficiency of the industry and the location and size of markets also greatly influence each country's competitive position.

Production and Consumption of Steel in Latin America

The first steelworks in Latin America – as distinct from establishments smelting and casting small amounts of iron – were formed in the late nineteenth and early twentieth centuries. The earliest plant may have been located in São Paulo, Brazil; others operated before 1900 in Colombia and Paraguay. In 1904, the first fully integrated steel mill began to operate at Monterrey, Mexico. Its initial production was some 20,000 tons of pig iron annually, and in 1911 it reached a peak of 80,000 tons, a level not surpassed until the late 1930s because of the effects first of the Mexican Revolution and then of the Depression. The next integrated plant was erected at Sabará, Brazil, in 1921, and in 1937 the same company built its present plant at Monlevade.[21] A steelworks was established in Chile in 1935, and the first steel production in Argentina occurred during the late 1930s.

The increasing production of pig iron and steel in Latin America and the drop in foreign demand for iron ore

---

[18] Chile exports molybdenum sulfide concentrates, and occasionally imports molybdic oxide for direct use in steelmaking or conversion to ferromolybdenum. An export tax of 50 percent on concentrates was proposed in 1961, to force the copper producers to process molybdenum in Chile, but the proposal was dropped when it appeared that production of molybdic oxide would not be economical. Information obtained from the Compañía de Acero del Pacífico of Chile (G. Waissbluth, Executive Vice President, personal communication).

[19] Except for the information on ferroalloy production in Chile, the above information came from USBM, *Minerals Facts and Problems, 1960* and *1965*; and Landsberg et al., *Resources in America's Future*, pp. 438-50.

[20] The high assembly costs for steel in Argentina were noted before most of the region's present steel mills were built. See UN, *World Iron Ore Resources. . .*, p. 26.

[21] ECLA, *La Economía Siderúrgica. . .*, pp. 39-40, and Cervantes y Mejía, *El Crecimiento. . .*, p. 250.

caused a sharp rise in the share of the region's iron ore used domestically. This share rose from about 7 percent in the late 1920s to 17 percent[22] a decade later, while pig iron output went from 120,000 to 200,000 tons (see table 5-6). During World War II the share of ore production made into pig iron in the region reached a peak of nearly 50 percent. As the iron ore boom began after the war, the share exported rose again. The index of domestic use fell to 30 percent in the early 1950s, to 20 percent a few years later, and to a low of 12 percent about 1960, before recovering slightly.

Steel production expanded most rapidly during the 1940s, when five steel mills entered operation in Brazil, one in Mexico, and one in Argentina. Mexico added its third integrated plant in 1958 and Argentina its second in 1961; new mills were erected in Brazil in 1954, 1963, and 1964. The first integrated plant began to produce in Chile in 1950, in Colombia in 1955, in Peru in 1958, and in Venezuela in 1962. Total output of crude steel reached 1 million tons in the late 1940s and 2 million in 1953; by the early 1960s it was expanding by nearly a million tons every year. The output of rolled steel products, including those made from imported ingots, continued to exceed crude steel production by a million tons or somewhat less in most years. By 1967 Latin America produced over 6 million tons of pig iron, close to 10 million tons of primary steel and 9 million tons of rolled products. The region's weight in the world steel economy had risen from 0.1 percent in the 1920s to 1 percent in the 1950s and to 2 percent in 1967. The production of certain types of steel has risen much more rapidly. Output of special steels in Brazil, for example, increased at an average annual rate of 24 percent from 1956 to 1964.[23]

In the late 1930s Latin America supplied only about one-seventh of its consumption of 1.7 million tons of steel. By the mid-1950s the domestic industry was producing half the total, and by the early 1960s it supplied more than two-thirds of the 10 million tons of steel consumed annually (see table 5-7). Since 1961 the entire growth of consumption has been met by increased production, imports remaining stationary at about 3 million tons. Per capita consumption has risen in the same period from 20 to 50 kilograms, growing at an average rate of 3.5 percent annually, or well above the overall growth rate of the regional economy. Even this rapid expansion leaves Latin America as a whole far below the per capita levels of 300 kilograms or more found in the most advanced countries. In Argentina and Chile, however, levels of 100 kilograms are being approached, close to the present world average. Steel consumption is related to income, as is indicated by the low

figure for the poorer countries of Latin America; but it is low where there is little heavy manufacturing industry (as in Uruguay) and high where investment in mining or other extractive industries requires much steel (as in Venezuela and Chile).

The growth of steel production is a major element in the process of import substitution which Latin America has undergone since the 1930s. In the five principal steel producing countries as a group, import substitution accounted for some 85 percent of increased output between 1929 and 1960, the share being 100 percent in Argentina, Chile, and Colombia (see table 5-8). Between 1950 and 1960 substitution provided less than 40 percent of the increase in production, and in Brazil the share was only 15 percent. Depending on the period, about one-half to two-thirds of the steel imports that might have been anticipated were replaced by domestic production. Import substitution was most important in Brazil before 1950, and in Chile and Colombia in the following decade; in Argentina and Mexico it was slightly more significant after 1950.

The differences among countries and over time roughly parallel those for import substitution in the whole range of manufacturing industry (compare table 5-8 with table A-4 in Part One). It appears that total consumption of steel is related to the existence of a domestic steel industry; or, more directly, that the production of steel not only substitutes for imports but increases the amount of steel used. This results despite the higher cost of domestic than imported steel, and the effect may be great enough to prevent imports from actually decreasing. According to a study by the Economic Commission for Latin America,[24] limitations in the availability of foreign exchange kept imports of steel below the demand generated by the domestic economy. As production in the region increased, this frustrated demand became effective and consumption rose sharply. The effect was most marked in the years immediately following the establishment of a steel mill in a country; as the share of imports in consumption decreased, this factor declined in importance. Since steel is a principal input to many of the import-substituting industries established in the last three decades, the creation of domestic steel industries has influenced the growth of manufacturing and total economic expansion. The industry's backward linkages may also have been significant in increasing income and employment, although the effect was certainly less pronounced and did not involve the elimination of any restrictions such as those which impeded the consumption of steel.

In historical sequence, import substitution in steel followed the pattern of other industries. The last stages — fabrication of articles and structural shapes from imported ingots or other forms — were created first. Substitution of the actual production of crude steel began with small plants based on scrap or independent producers of pig iron, and proceeded to large integrated mills. Production of alloy and other special steels is still low relative to requirements, and substitution is even less for the alloy metals themselves.

[22] The share is calculated on the assumption that Latin American iron ore production has averaged 60 percent in grade throughout the period 1925-67. The grade has undoubtedly not been that stable, since it varies from country to country over a considerable range and the share of different countries in the total has varied greatly. Nonetheless, the variations in this index are much too large to be due entirely to changes in the average grade of ore mined, and therefore reflect approximately the degree to which ore was smelted within Latin America.

[23] Heffernan and Che, *The Steel Industry in Latin America.*

[24] ECLA, *A Study of the Iron and Steel Industry. . .* , part 2, chap. I, "Factors Influencing Iron and Steel Consumption in Latin America," especially pp. 72-76, 81-83.

There may ultimately be a higher degree of substitution of reducing agents in the first stage of steelmaking, either through the improvement of local coals now blended with imported coal or not used at all, or through the substitution of coke by petroleum and gas. Since technical requirements are quite strict at this stage and override considerations of cost, further substitution will depend on progress in steelmaking techniques and perhaps on further study of Latin America's coal resources and their possible use. Similar considerations apply, with less rigor, to substitution of domestic iron ore in Argentina.

The multiplicity of types of steel and forms in which it is consumed make it difficult to describe the end uses of steel in Latin America in any detail.[25] As the region has developed, consumption has shifted toward flat products, which are used as inputs to manufacturing industry, and away from structural shapes, wire, tube, and pipe, and other non-flat products. These latter are — except for pipe used in the oil industry — consumed chiefly in construction, agriculture, and municipal services. The share of flat products in total steel consumption was about 35 percent in the early 1950s and almost 45 percent a decade later. In the late 1930s flat products accounted for between 20 and 30 percent of the total in Argentina, Brazil, Chile, and Mexico, and for somewhat more in Colombia and Cuba. The shift to steel in flat forms is now proceeding quite slowly in the major countries; the share is not expected to reach 50 percent until about 1975.

The change in types of steel used has followed much the same pattern in all the more industrial countries of Latin America, being less in the poorer countries and in Uruguay and Venezuela. Within these two classes of products differences among countries are somewhat greater: pipe is a large share of consumption in Colombia and Venezuela, for example, and tinplate in countries with large food processing industries. However, the great variety of end uses for each steel product and the availability of substitute materials in many cases, make it impossible to relate consumption in detail to specific industries or other factors.

The Latin American Iron and Steel Industry

If every stage from the production of pig iron to the fabrication of steel shapes is included, there are somewhat less than 250 firms, and about the same number of plants, in the Latin American iron and steel industry. The number is increased only slightly by including independent iron ore mining companies, most of which produce chiefly or exclusively for export. Of the total, approximately half are small firms specializing in one phase of the industry, usually

rolling, drawing, or casting steel; a few produce pig iron or alloy steels. These enterprises correspond to the numerous plants that work from semifinished metal in the nonferrous metal industries, and are concentrated in the countries with the most diversified industrial structures — Argentina, Brazil, and Mexico. There are about sixty semi-integrated firms, which make steel from scrap and/or purchased pig iron or crude steel, and have their own fabricating facilities. They account for almost one-fifth of the region's crude steel output and are particularly important in the supply of certain products (such as pipe) and types of steel (such as alloy steels). The bulk of output comes from eighteen integrated steel mills, of which half are in Brazil (see table 5-9).

Steel is produced in the region principally by coke blast furnaces, but to a lesser extent charcoal furnaces, electric reduction, and natural gas are also used. Since ferrous scrap is in short supply, the industry — especially the integrated mills — uses a larger share of hot pig iron than is common in most steelmaking countries.[26] Imports of scrap are sizable, particularly for the semi-integrated mills, which depend on it most heavily. The large mills commonly own their supplies of raw materials or obtain them through long-term contracts with foreign or domestic mining concerns. They are not so closely linked to the many small steel mills and fabricators who buy semifinished metal from them. The smaller firms chiefly produce castings, wire, and structural shapes; more complicated items, such as pipe, are made in the semi-integrated plants, while flat products are produced mostly by the integrated mills.

This division of labor reflects the fact that economies of scale, while large for the steel industry as a whole, vary among processes and products and are greatest at the blast furnace and the rolling mill. The same factor accounts for the imbalance of capacity among stages in one mill or one country. Where the market is small, the attempt to produce iron and steel in nearly all the forms used by the economy results in excess capacity in the stages or processes with the greatest scale economies.[27] The shortage of investment capital in Latin America has also affected the scale and structure of steel production by influencing the pace at which capacity is built or increased at each stage. The small and medium-sized mills, especially those producing only a narrow range of products with appreciable economies of scale, partially offset the imbalances in the integrated sector.

It has been estimated that the Latin American steel industry represented an investment of some $3,000 million to $3,200 million up to 1963-64, with a further investment of $1,500 million expected for expansion and correction of

---

[25] A classification of steel into fourteen basic product groups has been made by the Instituto Latinoamericano del Fierro y del Acero (ILAFA); see the monthly reports for December 1964 and August 1965 (Santiago, Chile). For a discussion of consumption of six product groups in six countries (Argentina, Brazil, Chile, Colombia, Cuba, and Mexico), 1925 to 1950, see ECLA, *A Study of the Iron and Steel Industry...*, pp. 78-81, 87-80. The categories used do not coincide exactly with the distinction between flat and other steel products adopted in ECLA, *La Economía Siderúrgica...*, pp. 16-17, 33; in the latter, seamless tube and pipe is included in non-flat products, while seamed pipe is included in flat.

[26] Scrap is scarce chiefly because the region's reservoir of metal in use, the result of past use of iron and steel, is small and the life of equipment containing steel is rather long. It also appears that the collection of old scrap is not well organized and is expensive because the steel mills are located far from the metalworking industries that produce prompt industrial scrap. See ECLA, *La Economía Siderúrgica...*, pp. 74-82, and UN, *Interregional Symposium...*, pp. 58-59.

[27] It is estimated that in 1964 rolling mills in Latin America operated at only 52 percent of their combined capacity, with a loss of 6 million tons of potential steel production. See Heffernan and Che, *The Steel Industry....*

imbalances during 1965-70.[28] These amounts include the associated investment in captive iron mines and transport facilities, but not the investment in iron mining for export. The provision of this capital and its present ownership differ considerably from the historical pattern of the nonferrous metal industries. In copper, lead, and zinc (but not in tin), foreign capital is dominant in mining, smelting, and refining, especially in the latter stages. Local private capital controls most of the metal-using industries, with foreign participation in the larger enterprises, and a sizable minority share of mine output. State intervention is usually on a small scale, is exercised indirectly, and is concerned especially with the medium and small mining companies.[29] In the case of iron and steel, state participation is quite high, and is concentrated at the steel-producing stage, especially in the larger mills. Foreign capital, less important, is most noticeable in mining. Furthermore, U. S. capital is a smaller share of the total foreign investment, because of sizable Belgian, German, and Japanese participation in the Brazilian industry. Domestic private capital not only controls the small fabricating firms, but owns most of the semi-integrated mills, and participates in even the largest plants together with the state and foreign investors. The distribution of ownership is more complicated than for the nonferrous metals and (by comparison with the situation before Mexicanization and the formation of joint enterprises in Chile) varies more from country to country (see table 5-10).

Four principal reasons can be identified for the pattern of ownership that has arisen in the Latin American iron and steel industry. First, since iron ore can be exported without smelting or even beneficiation, foreign capital in the export sector had no reason to enter the steel industry; to do so would have involved higher costs and the difficulties of developing the other raw material inputs required for steelmaking. Second, the importance of steel to industrialization through import substitution made steel production a matter of high priority for governments; the apparent effect of production in increasing consumption would have reinforced this importance. Third, the very large investments, low returns, and variety of associated undertakings in the large integrated steel mills made this sector initially unattractive to domestic investors. Local private capital was readily invested in smaller and more specialized enterprises, however, and could be attracted to the larger firms once the state had established a mill or raised much of the capital.[30]

Finally, in most countries the steel industry has been established quite recently, and state participation is more acceptable than it might have been several decades ago.

On balance, Latin America is a major exporter of iron ore and a sizable importer of semifabricated steel. Net trade in crude steel is very small, and the same is true of trade in pig iron, scrap, and other metallic inputs. Of total iron ore production of 41 million tons in 1963, for example, some 33 million tons were exported. The remaining 8 million tons were used to produce 5 million tons of pig iron and 7 million tons of crude steel. About the same amount of semifabricated steel was consumed, 5 million tons being produced in the region and 2 million tons imported. Intraregional trade is small in all categories, though in the case of semifabricated steel it amounts to half of all exports (see table 5-11). Even countries with integrated steel industries continue to import large amounts of semimanufactures; only Chile and Mexico have become net exporters of these forms, and only Chile is a net exporter of all iron and steel, since Mexico imports much pig iron and scrap.

In no country are net exports of steel a major item in the balance of payments; a sizable trade surplus, as in the case of Chile, arises only from large exports of iron ore. But the savings in imports made possible by the creation of domestic steel industries can be quite large relative to a country's total exports. The cost of importing steel has not declined in every case — it nearly doubled in Colombia during the 1950s, for example — but the import bill would be much higher had not so much substitution occurred. At a price of $100 per ton, approximately the level at which steel could be imported from Europe, the region's production of crude steel represented a saving of some $700 million annually in the early 1960s; including the substitution of crude steel imports for trade in semimanufactures, the saving may now be in the vicinity of $1,000 million, or 10 percent of the region's exports.[31] This gain is not appreciably reduced by the need to import coal for steelmaking, and is substantial even in Argentina, where iron ore must be imported as well. The region continues to spend large sums on imports of those items not yet substituted — several million dollars each on ferroalloys and special steels, for example, and tens of millions of dollars for total imports into individual countries. Net steel imports of Latin America are now approximately balanced by net exports of iron ore; from being a major deficit item two decades ago, iron and steel in all forms can now yield a small trade surplus for the region.

Issues and Problems

The development of iron mining on a large scale and the creation of a steel industry in Latin America have implicitly involved many questions of policy related to natural re-

---

[28] ECLA, *La Economía Siderúrgica...*, pp. 135-58. The estimates of investment are based partly on initial investment information and partly on replacement costs. They include estimates for the semi- and non-integrated plants as well as the integrated mills for which data were available.

[29] This pattern has changed greatly in recent years, and will probably continue to change, through the formation of joint companies including foreign capital and domestic private or state participation. The transformation, which is so far notable in Chile and Mexico, does not erase the differences between steel and the nonferrous metals, however. See chaps. 4 (Copper) and 6 (Lead and zinc).

[30] Private capital built the first integrated mill in Mexico, but nowhere else. In Chile, domestic investors own nearly half of the largest steelworks; in Colombia they now own it almost completely, having bought out the government's share. The state might again

become a major owner as the mill is expanded, however. See ECLA, *La Economía Siderúrgica...*, pp. 125-27.

[31] The actual imports would probably have been less, in the absence of domestic production, because of the shortage of foreign exchange. By creating a local steel industry, Latin America gained by saving foreign exchange and by increasing consumption, at the cost of a higher price for a larger volume of steel.

source exploitation. For various reasons these questions have not resulted in major disputes or political issues such as have characterized many of the other commodities discussed in this study. First, no country depends very much on iron ore exports. Second, the world iron ore market is relatively free and stable compared to those for other products. These two factors together mean that the domestic use of iron ore is often the chief concern of policy. Third, for the reasons indicated earlier, there is a high degree of state participation in the industry, and a relatively low level of foreign investment except in mining. Some disputes have arisen over the terms on which foreign companies could produce iron ore for export, but attention will be given here only to two general policy issues: the reservation of iron ore for domestic use, and the extent and consequences of emphasis on import substitution in the establishment of steel industries.

It is the policy of all steel-producing countries to assure adequate supplies of iron ore for their domestic industries. In Brazil and Colombia the principal steel mills are supplied by captive mines with relatively large reserves. The Chilean steel company also controls a large mine, but exports the ore produced. Ore for the steel mill is obtained from a U.S. firm producing chiefly for export, whose mine is better located. The steelworks of Peru and Venezuela similarly have first call on the output of U.S. companies that export the bulk of their production. These contractual arrangements may lead, as in Chile, to consideration of joint mining companies involving U.S. and local capital.[32] Further measures may be taken where known reserves, although entirely under domestic control, are small relative to requirements, or where all production is by foreign firms and it is desired to hold some resources for domestic exploitation in the future.

The first situation has led in Mexico to the creation of a national mineral reserve and to the prohibition of iron ore exports from all except small, poorly located deposits. Any resources large enough to support an integrated steelworks are to be saved for domestic use.[33] In Venezuela a national iron ore reserve embraces most of the high-grade deposits not yet exploited and, as in the case of petroleum, no new mining concessions are to be granted in the near future. The deposits may eventually be worked by joint companies or under some form of contract.[34] In Peru, the major U.S.

mining firm will set aside 70 million tons of ore for future use by the government iron and steel corporation.[35]

The creation of a steel industry in each of seven countries was conceived and carried out largely as an import substitution measure. As in much of Latin America's industrialization, balance of payments effects took precedence over considerations of total costs. As a result, a sort of economic nationalism was carried as far as was economically feasible or technically possible. Domestic raw materials, particularly coal in Brazil and Chile, were used even where full reliance on imports might have lowered the costs of steelmaking. Each country created an integrated industry, even though some specialization by stages might have been cheaper. Argentina, for example, might make steel at less cost by importing pig iron from Brazil than by importing the raw materials and using low-grade domestic iron ore. Similarly, each industry attempted to produce almost the full range of articles used in a relatively small national market, sacrificing some of the advantages of scale and specialization and operating with excess capacity for certain stages and products.

It should be noted that the questions raised and the decisions made in establishing the various national steel industries did not result in severe problems in any country, particularly not in political difficulties. The Latin American iron and steel industry faces two principal sorts of problems, which are in themselves economic but which may have increasingly important political connotations. The first is to continue to raise the sums necessary for investment, to keep up with the growth of steel consumption and perhaps to reduce the share of imports still further. The second is to reduce the costs of steelmaking in the region by eliminating imbalances in capacity, making better use of economies of scale, and adopting technical improvements in all phases of the industry. These matters have been extensively studied by the Economic Commission for Latin America, and the reader is referred to their conclusions.[36] Here only three points will be made.

First, although Latin America is at present a relatively high-cost producer of steel, it is potentially competitive with more advanced countries; given continued vigorous efforts to reduce costs and market its output, the region might be able to increase its steel exports considerably in the future. The high costs now characteristic of the industry reflect difficulties in the steel mills, most of which can be overcome by investment to correct imbalances and increase the scale of production; they do not reflect a poor resource base. Second, there is considerable scope for reducing costs by adopting the most modern techniques, such as substituting oil for coke in the blast furnace, oxygen blowing in steelmaking, and continuous casting. These changes do not solely substitute capital for labor; they also involve substitution among raw material inputs and greatly increase the efficiency of existing capital equipment. They can therefore be recommended for Latin America as well as

[32] Bethlehem-Chile Iron Mines has invited the participation of CAP in expanding its iron ore output, and CAP has suggested formation of a new joint company with Bethlehem-Chile, for exploration and mining. See USBM, *Mineral Trade Notes*, May 1967, p. 14.

[33] See USBM, *Minerals Yearbook, 1959*, vol. I, p. 562, and *1963*, vol. I, p. 622; and F. González Vargas, "Los Minerales de Hierro y Acero de México y su Utilización Siderúrgica," *Comercio Exterior*, August 1964. The total reserves of Mexico are estimated as enough for about fifty years at present rates of growth, but for only twenty-five years from the deposits serving the present steel mills; thus there is a need to develop new reserves in the north or to establish steel mills on the Pacific coast where reserves are larger.

[34] USBM, *Minerals Yearbook, 1959*, vol. I, p. 563. Since the ratio of reserves to production is much higher for iron ore than for petroleum, this policy will have much less effect on reserve adequacy for iron ore than it has on oil reserves. It will also influence the expenditures of producing companies far less, since production accounts for a greater share of total costs in the case of iron ore.

[35] *Engineering and Mining Journal*, January 1968, p. 114.

[36] See ECLA, *La Economía Siderúrgica...*, especially pp. 135-217, concerning unit investment, prices, costs, and economies of scale.

for advanced regions with different cost ratios for capital and labor.[37] It does not appear that the best techniques for the region are different from those most economical elsewhere, or at least that Latin America should not simply employ methods considered obsolescent in more developed countries.[38] Third, several questions, which have been satisfactorily answered for each producing country alone or which have never been significant, must be reopened if Latin America is to move toward economic integration. Because it is vital to all producer goods industries, the steel industry and the way in which it evolves will influence the production and trade of many products and can bring gains to individual countries and the region as a whole. This issue will be considered after a survey of the estimated future demand, both domestic and foreign, for Latin American iron ore.

Outlook: The Demand for Iron Ore

If it is assumed that the iron ore input per ton of finished steel does not change appreciably,[39] future world requirements for iron ore can be estimated from projections of steel consumption and production. The most recent projections place world crude steel production at just over 600 million tons in 1975, with 138 million in the United States, 166 million in Western Europe, and the same amount in the Communist countries, excluding mainland China.[40] This amount of steel will require the consumption of some 810 million tons of iron ore, on the assumption of an average iron content of 62 percent. The content is expected to rise sharply between 1970 and 1975, in consequence of a marked decline in output of low-grade European ores and greater use of high-grade ores in Australia, Latin America, and Africa. According to one projection, by 1975 production capacity is expected to reach 854 million tons, distributed as follows: 164 in North America, 99 in Latin America, 56 in Africa, 145 in Western Europe, 242 in the Communist countries, and 148 in Asia and Oceania.[41] On

these assumptions, Latin America will be producing nearly 12 percent of the world's iron ore in 1975 and a comparable or greater share of the contained iron.

Since 1964 world iron mining capacity has grown more rapidly than consumption, leading to a surplus which is expected to be some 45 million tons in 1975. The existence of this excess capacity, combined with increased geographical diversification of trade in the last decade and the development of various means of treating and improving ores, will continue and intensify the competition among producers and exporters of iron ore. The projections presented above might prove substantially wrong; but it appears more likely that competition will result in much greater processing of ore in exporting countries to raise quality and hold markets than that trade patterns will drastically change. The preparation of sinter for blast furnace feed, adopted on a large scale in the 1950s, nearly always occurs near the steel mill, and benefited exporting countries only by creating a demand for very fine-sized ore. The next major development, formation of ore into hard, uniform pellets which may also be self-fluxing, appears to favor exporters since it is most economically carried out near the mine. World pellet capacity is expected to increase rapidly in the next few years, with a slight migration of capacity to less developed countries. This is one of the most promising avenues of expansion for Latin American exports of processed raw materials, as the resources are of excellent quality, costs favor location at the producing site, and there are no barriers to imports in the advanced countries.[42]

If it is assumed that exports will be about 58 million tons in 1975, a rough estimate of Latin America's total requirements can be made. Crude steel consumption at that date is expected to be some 28 million tons.[43] (See table 5-12.) If steel requirements are met entirely by domestic production in those countries with integrated steel industries in 1967, and entirely by imports elsewhere, something less than 17 million tons of iron in ore will be needed to produce 26.7 million tons of steel. Total production of iron in ore will then have to be about 74 million tons, or approximately 123 million tons of ore, gross weight. The value of exports, at the prices of recent years, would be some $400 million. If these assumptions are correct, by 1975 Latin America will be using domestically about 22 percent of its iron ore production, the same level as in 1953-54.

World iron ore resources are so large that there is no prospect of scarcity for many decades. The cumulative

[37] To the extent that such improvements also shift the inputs to steelmaking toward resources abundant in Latin America, this conclusion is reinforced. The argument is strongest for changes in ore reduction; new steelmaking techniques have much more effect on capital/labor ratios.

[38] For a contrasting case, see the discussion of the desirable degree of modernity in the cotton textile industry in Latin America, chap. 11, under the heading "Cotton and Cotton Textiles in Latin America," and the sources cited there.

[39] The ratio can be changed only by varying the share of scrap used in steelmaking, or by varying the relative production of stainless and other high alloy steels. The first change may be appreciable in a few countries in the future, but there is no reason to expect a substantial shift in the world as a whole since scrap supplies are determined by past steel use and change only slowly, and iron ore prices are fairly stable. The second sort of change would have to be very great, given the low share of alloy steel in total production, to affect iron ore inputs. Comparable stability cannot be assumed, however, for other inputs, which may be affected by changes in technique or in demand.

[40] This is appreciably less than the estimate of 700 million tons presented by the Cleveland-Cliffs Iron Company to the American Mining Congress and published in *Engineering and Mining Journal*, June 1966, p. 144.

[41] Projections by the Battelle Memorial Institute, in UNIDO, *Prospects for Exports. . .*, Cf. table 11-12.

[42] See UNIDO, *Prospects for Exports. . . .* For further summaries of the world iron ore situation, see UNCTAD, *Commodity Survey*, part I (UN, 1966), pp. 87-90, and the study submitted in part II, sec. B, doc. TD/B/C. 1/23/Add. 2. Data are drawn from an unpublished study by the Economic Commission for Europe, "The World Market for Iron Ore." See also 1967 *Commodity Survey*, part III, pp. 120-29.

[43] The total estimated by ECLA corresponds closely to projections made by the Instituto Latinoamericano del Fierro y del Acero (ILAFA) and by the EEC; all are 28 million tons, to the nearest million. The distribution of this total by country varies considerably among the three projections, however, ranging from 3.5 to 5.4 million tons for Argentina, from 8.8 to 11.6 million for Brazil, and from 1.9 to 5.0 million for Venezuela. See ECLA, *La Economía Siderúrgica. . .*, p. 27.

demand for iron in ore over the entire period 1960-2000 has been estimated as between 30,000 and 60,000 million tons.[44] Even the larger amount could be met from presently known reserves, and half the smaller figure could be supplied from ores of direct-shipping grade. The average grade of ore mined may decline over the next few decades, but the shift will reflect cost reductions in beneficiating low-grade materials and not any physical shortage of rich ores. The exact pattern of supply at any time in the foreseeable future will be determined by the relation between the shipping costs of high-grade ore and the cost of concentrating or otherwise treating low-grade ores closer to the centers of steel production; the amounts of material in each category may be regarded as essentially limitless for several decades.

Outlook: The Latin American Steel Industry

Between 1970 and 1975 the demand for steel in Latin America is expected to grow by approximately 9 million tons. In order to keep imports from increasing it will be necessary to expand capacity to three times the level of the early 1960s. This expansion is expected to require a further $3,000 million to $3,500 million, about half of which will have to be in hard currency and the rest in national currencies. These amounts may be within the capacity of Latin America to raise domestically or to borrow abroad, but they are nonetheless as large as total investment in the region's steel industry up to 1964. There is no indication that the growth in demand for steel will decline or become much less of a financial burden in the next decade or so.

The greatest interest therefore attaches to any means of reducing the cost of meeting Latin America's future steel requirements. Integration of the regional steel industry is generally seen as the most effective measure to lower the potential costs of producing steel and to insure, through intraregional competition, that costs and prices will reflect the lowest costs obtainable. Since steel is basic to most manufacturing industries, the integration of the steel industry would obviously have a considerable impact on other industries likely to be included in a Latin American common market. The nature and magnitude of these effects have not yet been studied, if only because it is not clear what form integration of the steel industry is likely to take or what the pattern of output and prices will be five or ten years from now. The remainder of this chapter will be devoted to a general discussion of the possible integration of the regional steel industry.[45]

Integration, in the case of the iron and steel industry, is intended primarily to take advantage of three factors: economies of scale, especially in flat products and the simpler types of crude steel; economies of specialization; and the cost and price-reducing effects of competition. It can include a variety of other means of reducing costs, any or all of which could be undertaken by one or more countries acting alone. Among these are the introduction of new steelmaking techniques, reduction of coke input or the shift from coke to other fuels, and the manufacture of steel mill equipment locally. The latter appears to be feasible in Argentina, Brazil, and Mexico, which have relatively well developed metalworking and engineering industries, and would reduce the foreign exchange component of investment. The other measures might also reduce hard currency costs but are meant primarily to lower total costs.

The problem of integration can be treated as that of finding the levels of output, at each of several locations for integrated mills, which would yield the least total cost of supplying requirements at some future date. Such a calculation, using a modification of linear programming, measures only the effects of scale and of transport costs, taking no account of economies of specialization. One such program, based on estimated demand in 1970 and costs of production in the early 1960s, and assuming identical integrated mills with economies of scale derived from a major U.S. plant, yields the result that the steel requirements of Argentina, Brazil, Chile, Colombia, Mexico, Peru, and Venezuela could be met most cheaply by just two plants, one in Chile and one in Colombia.[46] The addition of a plant in Mexico, to serve the local market, raises the cost insignificantly. The autarkic solution of one plant in each of the seven countries would raise costs about 12 percent above the minimum level. The sequence of solutions would probably not be much altered, and the costs would be slightly reduced, by including the demand of the smaller countries which do not have and are not likely to acquire integrated steel mills. A more complicated model of the same type, allowing for twelve markets and an equal number of plant sites, gives quite different results because of differences in the cost functions assumed.[47] In particular, a different location is assumed for the plant in Venezuela, with much lower assembly costs and lower handling costs in shipping. A single 9 million-ton plant in Venezuela is the lowest cost solution, cheaper by 1 percent than a mill in Venezuela and another in Brazil. Addition of a third plant, in Mexico, raises the total cost by a further 1 percent. The cost of autarky was not calculated. This study also assumes a single homogeneous product and a single production process with economies of scale equal for all locations.

Calculations based on economies of scale alone are useful for indicating the effects of transport costs[48] and the order of magnitude of savings possible by concentrating production in a few locations. In theory this sort of calcula-

---

[44] Landsberg et al., *Resources in America's Future*, pp. 429-35. The lower figure is considered more reasonable, as the higher assumes a growth of demand at 8 percent annually for the whole period.

[45] This section is based largely on ECLA, *La Economía Siderúrgica...*, pp. 269-307, especially pp. 276, 288-98, which describe a set of norms and goals for integration. Certain aspects not treated by ECLA will also be noted.

[46] A. M. Martirena de Mantel, "Integración y Economías de Escala," *Trimestre Económico*, July-September 1964, pp. 412-22.

[47] D. A. Kendrick, "Programming Investment in the Steel Industry," unpublished paper (Brookings Institution, Transport Research Program, October 1965), Appendix G.

[48] For example, transport costs effectively isolate the Colombian market in both models described above, so that it is supplied by a plant at Paz del Río at little or no cost above the minimum solution. The low assembly costs of a plant in Colombia compensate for the small scale of the local market, at least where a single product is considered.

tion could be made more realistic by allowing for different patterns of demand for a number of finished products and for the existence of semi- and non-integrated plants: each production process would be treated separately, with the costs and economies of scale appropriate to it. At an adequate level of detail, however, the problem would be too large to solve at all, and in any case data are not available for the smaller plants and less important products.[49] An intermediate approach can be used, where the information is adequate, for a limited number of products produced only in a few integrated mills. A model of this sort is applicable to the problem of planning investment to meet future demand where a sizeable steel industry already exists. It is then possible to allow for expansion of existing plants or creation of new ones, and for choices among techniques at each stage.[50]

Calculations such as these may guide the integration of the Latin American steel industry, but they are unlikely to determine its exact form. The data presently available do not permit full confidence in those solutions requiring a small number of very large mills; neither is it certain that the variety of techniques and sizes of plant, or of products, can be adequately dealt with. These difficulties are, however, much less important than the political barriers to integration in the form described above. No country which has developed a steel industry will agree to let it be destroyed by competition. Moreover, those countries which have no industry as yet would probably not agree to a solution which precluded their opportunity to acquire steel mills — particularly small semi-integrated plants — in the future. In view of these constraints, the Economic Commission for Latin America has concluded that integration will have to be achieved by a gradual process of limited competition among existing industries, with provision for new entrants. Strict rules will be required on pricing and the prohibition of dumping, and low internal tariffs may be called for to protect infant industries or to keep the pattern of production from changing too rapidly. The transition to a common market is viewed as a ten-year process, with emphasis on cost reductions within each country in the first five years and on intercountry competition in the second phase. A regional plan of investment is urged as the means of limiting competition without incurring unnecessarily high costs.

The feasibility of this program depends heavily on the view that the seven steel-producing countries have, at the levels of production they are likely to reach in the early 1970s, potentially almost equal costs. Calculations of theoretical costs in the present integrated mills suggest that most cost differences can be eliminated by investments in balancing capacity and by the adoption of the technical improvements appropriate to each plant. Furthermore, Latin American steel costs should fall to a level competitive, at least for some countries and products, with steel mills in Western Europe or the United States.[51] Thus integration, and the attendant cost reduction, is not simply a further stage of import substitution; rather it is a means to allow Latin America to enter world steel markets as an exporter, while continuing to import certain types and products of steel.

In summary, three observations should be made about this type of integration. First, it is not based solely on economies of scale and would not take full advantage of them. If a large mill in Argentina can compete with one half that size in Colombia, both plants will continue to operate even though a large Colombian mill might be able to supply both countries more cheaply. It is not even likely that economies of scale will dictate the distribution of all new capacity, although in time integration might yield that result. The effects of integration might actually be greater for the semi- and non-integrated mills, which would be able to import from anywhere in the region and could expand their capacities according to their markets and independently of supplies from domestic integrated plants.

Second, economies of specialization assume a great importance, not only for the small mills existing or likely to be established, but even for the integrated plants. Some specialization may take place in the early stages of steel-making; sponge iron could be produced with natural gas, for example, in Mexico, Venezuela, or Argentina, and exported to semi-integrated mills both in countries with integrated industries and in countries such as Ecuador or Central America where no pig or sponge iron is likely to be produced. Pig iron might be exported from Bolivia or from Brazil to Argentina, reducing assembly costs somewhat. There is also likely to be increased intraregional trade in ferroalloys and alloy steels. Specialization in semifabricated products will probably be still greater, since it has already progressed considerably in certain countries. Argentina appears to have an advantage in producing large structural shapes, and Venezuela will quite probably specialize in steel pipe, for which it has a large market. Advantages at this stage depend very little on raw material endowment and more on the design and operation of mills, so that only guesses can be made as to the future pattern of production and trade.

Finally, the chief impact of integration in steel will be felt in the manufacturing industries to which it is a major input and whose integration is in turn a principal objective of a common market. Only if steel is available at competitive prices throughout the region can the steel-using industries be integrated on the basis of different countries'

---

[49] Multistage programming can be used for an industry with a limited number of processes and products, and a small number of possible plant locations. See, for example, "The Optimum Location of Specific Industries in the Latin American Free Trade Area (including Venezuela)," vol. II: "Nitrogenous Fertilizers," part of a series of studies on industrial location compiled and edited by M. Carnoy (Brookings Institution, November 1966). The calculations are based on demand projections for 1970 and 1975 and estimates of costs made by institutes of economic research in ten Latin American countries.

[50] This is the purpose of two models developed by Kendrick, "Programming Investment. . . ." Considered in Brazil are seven products, three steel mills, and three markets (cities). The techniques could be applied, at great increase in computational difficulty, to the entire Latin American flat products output.

[51] The calculations are presented in ECLA, *La Economía Siderúrgica. . .*, chaps. VIII, IX, pp. 217-68.

advantages in labor, skills, other raw materials, and markets. If competition through integration also brings steel prices down to world levels, Latin America's ability to export steel-containing manufactures will be increased. Thus the future course of the steel industry is crucial to two of the principal economic objectives of the region: integration of manufacturing industries and the transition from dependence on primary products to exports of manufactures.

CHAPTER 5 TABLES

TABLE 5–1. World Iron Ore Reserves and Resources,[a] 1962
(Millions of metric tons)

Country or Region	I. Iron Ore, Gross Tonnage, Explored Reserves			II. Iron Content of Ore, Net Tonnage, Explored Reserves				Total Iron Content	
	Direct Shipping Ore[b]	Concentrating Ore[c]	Potential Resources[d]	Direct Shipping Ore	Concentrating Ore	Total Explored	Potential Resources	Amount	Share of World Total (%)
Latin America	4,250	706	15,210[e]	2,589	383	2,972	9,157	12,129	17.1
Argentina		106	80		48	48	36	84	0.1
Brazil	2,815	100	14,050	1,737	60	1,797	8,488	10,285	14.5
Chile	189		259	120		120	167	287	0.4
Colombia	50		50	24		24	24	48	0.1
Mexico	105		146	60		60	90	150	0.2
Peru	42	500	52	26	275	301	31	332	0.5
Venezuela	1,039		565	623		623	316	939	1.3
United States	671	7,124	19,983	270	2,284	2,554	6,042	8,596	12.1
Canada	573	4,095	7,591	195	1,558	1,754	2,813	4,566	6.4
Western Europe	11,023	3,353	13,236	4,230	1,303	5,533	2,557	10,099	15.4
Africa	1,732	707	4,588	996	362	1,358	2,666	4,024	5.7
Asia	5,301	248	10,345	3,396	118	3,514	6,623	10,137	14.3
India	5,240	84	10,215	3,360	34	3,394	6,555	9,949	14.0
Oceania[f]	395	100	1,610	256	45	301	907	1,208	1.7
Communist Countries	3,680	27,094	25,806	2,032	9,025	11,051	11,364	20,411	28.8
Soviet Union	2,801	23,376	16,830	1,550	7,696	9,246	5,571	14,817	20.8
China	789	2,603	7,366	428	948	1,376	3,303	4,679	6.6
World Total	27,615	43,427	98,369	13,964	15,077	29,041	42,129	71,170	100.0
L.A. Share (%)	15.4	1.6	15.5	18.6	2.5	10.2	21.7	17.1	

Source: R. W. Hyde, B. M. Lane, and W. W. Glaser, "Iron Ore Resources of the World," *Engineering and Mining Journal*, December 1962.

[a]Presently known or estimated tonnage of ore and of contained iron in deposits currently exploited or likely to be exploited by 1991, assuming no limitation of the anticipated demand for steel. There is no uniform minimum grade or other single criterion for determining which deposits are included.

[b]Ore suitable for direct feed to blast furnaces for reduction to pig iron; grade of 50% or more and impurities within acceptable limits.

[c]Ore, usually less than 50% iron, requiring physical and/or chemical treatment — washing, grinding, agglomeration, direct reduction, etc. — before being fed to blast furnaces. Ores of relatively high grade which contain certain impurities not amenable to treatment by current methods of beneficiation and steelmaking are excluded.

[d]Iron ore not economical to exploit at current levels of demand and prices, by reason of location, grade or other factors, believed likely to be exploited by 1991.

[e]Includes 8 million tons in Honduras, containing 4.2 million tons of iron.

[f]Australia only.

TABLE 5-2. World Iron Ore Production,[a] 1925-1967
[Thousands of metric tons]

Country or Region	Average 1925-29	Average 1930-34	Average 1935-39	Average 1940-44	Average 1945-49	1950	1951	1952	1953	1954	1955
Latin America	2,183	1,070	1,959	1,526	3,341	5,628	7,454	8,029	10,758	13,667	16,447
Argentina				2	53[b]	41	55	66	73	61	75
Brazil	30	30	225	303	1,124	1,985	2,405	3,159	3,613	3,068	3,379
Chile	1,534	828	1,311	967	1,810	2,973	3,249	2,207	2,936	2,186	1,535
Colombia										83	349
Cuba	532[c]	143[c]	300[c]	112	37[b]	12	17	87	200	25	131
Dominican Rep.								19	92	107	101
Mexico	91	68	123	141	317	419	460	523	546	522	716
Peru									300	2,221	1,725
Venezuela						198	1,269	1,968	2,294	5,384	8,430
Canada	1,300	593	1,322	1,434	2,799	3,266	4,242	4,778	5,900	6,672	14,757
United States	66,347	28,760	47,062	94,899	89,057	99,516	118,253	99,387	119,765	79,301	104,544
Western Europe	81,838	62,825	79,696	67,128	53,632	77,140	89,828	104,240	105,560	102,100	116,925
Africa	3,751	2,303	4,841	2,666	5,157	7,004	8,019	9,541	11,064	9,744	12,057
Asia	4,263	5,377	5,496	13,847	4,765	5,583	7,613	8,831	9,440	11,267	13,984
Oceania	793	769	2,153	3,266	1,842	2,436	2,436	2,741	3,350	3,553	3,627
Communist Countries	5,806	15,328	29,617	22,847	25,361	49,735	55,959	59,906	72,414	79,190	87,173
World Total	166,281	117,136	177,000	224,800	188,000	250,705	294,350	297,395	337,995	306,515	368,445
L.A. Share (%)	1.3	0.9	1.1	0.7	1.8	2.2	2.5	2.7	3.2	4.5	4.5

Country or Region	1956	1957	1958	1959	1960	1961	1962	1963	1964	1965	1966	1967
Latin America	21,993	28,436	29,637	35,731	43,643	42,458	40,586	41,357	51,855	58,396	64,171	62,890
Argentina	65	67	66	110	159	139	120	100	95	116	156	224
Brazil	4,071	4,961	5,180	8,898	9,335	10,210	10,767	11,219	16,962	18,160	23,254	23,500
Chile	2,663	2,692	3,756	4,645	6,035	6,982	7,982	8,507	9,853	12,145	12,246	11,025
Colombia	394	593	561	405	655	675	679	695	710	706	662	782
Cuba	137	180	16	15	15	15	15					
Dominican Rep.	113	126	30	12	123	15		140				
Mexico	813	949	969	888	868	1,144	1,817	2,328	2,321	2,655	2,307	2,695
Peru	2,643	3,575	3,585	3,572	6,983	8,728	5,943	6,621	6,528	7,104	7,787	7,659
Venezuela	11,094	15,280	15,469	17,183	19,470	14,550	13,253	11,747	15,656	17,510	17,759	17,005
Canada	20,253	20,184	14,253	22,192	19,530	18,450	24,795	27,346	34,769	36,250	41,344	42,322
United States	99,345	107,740	68,725	61,180	90,116	72,399	76,906	74,780	86,198	88,842	91,594	85,530
Western Europe	124,561	134,036	129,430	132,744	147,458	149,365	143,090	131,763	137,353	137,995	128,436	121,486
Africa	12,286	12,803	11,819	12,257	15,464	16,531	17,460	21,603	32,619	39,931	41,603	43,001
Asia	15,527	17,306	18,169	22,533	30,755	34,713	34,206	36,446	38,646	43,694	45,349	44,699
Oceania	4,021	4,098	4,273	4,502	4,721	5,709	5,160	5,903	6,066	7,083	11,829	19,019
Communist Countries	96,121	108,417	128,417	147,331	169,983	162,500	168,505	184,051	193,512	204,835	213,774	209,150
World Total	393,820	433,405	404,985	438,480	521,710	502,128	506,853	523,429	581,305	617,046	638,084	628,263
L.A. Share (%)	5.6	6.6	7.3	8.2	8.4	8.5	8.0	7.9	8.9	9.5	10.1	10.0

Source: USBM, *Minerals Yearbook.*
[a] Tonnage of ore, not iron content.
[b] Three-year average.
[c] Includes some shipment of copper ore.

TABLE 5–3. Iron Ore Prices and Average Values in the United States Market, 1925-1967
(U.S. dollars per long ton of ore, and cents per pound of contained iron at constant grade)

Year	(1) United States Production		United States Imports from			
			(2) Chile		(3) Brazil	
	Ore	Iron	Ore	Iron	Ore	Iron
1925	4.25	0.368	2.89	0.208	11.91	0.776
1926	4.25	0.368	1.14	0.082	14.40	0.939
1927	4.25	0.368	1.14	0.082	7.77	0.506
1928	4.25	0.368	1.10	0.079	7.20	0.469
1929	4.50	0.390	1.45	0.104	5.63	0.366
1930	4.50	0.390	2.40	0.173	3.82	0.249
1931	4.50	0.390	2.40	0.173		
1932	4.50	0.390	2.37	0.170		
1933	4.50	0.390	2.01	0.145	4.10	0.267
1934	4.50	0.390	2.04	0.147		
1935	4.50	0.390	1.85	0.133		
1936	4.50	0.390	1.81	0.130	3.65	0.238
1937	4.95	0.429	1.82	0.131	2.42	0.158
1938	4.95	0.429	1.81	0.130	4.58	0.298
1939	4.95	0.429	1.78	0.128	4.09	0.266
1940	4.45	0.386	1.80	0.130	4.65	0.303
1941	4.45	0.386	1.82	0.131	4.02	0.262
1942	4.45	0.386	1.80	0.130	3.96	0.258
1943	4.45	0.386				
1944	4.45	0.386				
1945	4.55	0.394	1.80	0.130		
1946	4.55	0.394	2.24	0.161		
1947	5.55	0.481	2.84	0.204	4.93	0.320
1948	6.20	0.537	2.86	0.206	5.16	0.336
1949	7.20	0.624	2.62	0.189	6.50	0.423
1950	7.70	0.667	2.62	0.189	6.69	0.435
1951	8.30	0.719	3.10	0.223	8.65	0.564
1952	8.30	0.719	4.43	0.319	14.80	0.965
1953	9.90	0.858	5.21	0.375	13.92	0.908
1954	9.90	0.858	4.74	0.341	11.79	0.769
1955	10.10	0.875	6.91	0.498	12.61	0.823
1956	10.85	0.942	5.26	0.379	13.12[a]	0.855
1957	11.45	0.993	7.55	0.543	14.60	0.952
1958	11.45	0.993	7.97	0.573	14.60	0.952
1959	11.45	0.993	7.75	0.557	11.80[a]	0.770
1960	11.45	0.993	7.78	0.560	11.25	0.735
1961	11.45	0.993	8.41	0.605	11.25	0.735
1962	10.85[a]	0.942	8.46	0.609	11.25	0.735
1963	10.65	0.925	9.35	0.673	11.25	0.735
1964	10.65	0.925	8.94	0.643	10.40	0.678
1965	10.55	0.916	8.74	0.629	10.26	0.671
1966	10.55	0.916	8.73	0.628	9.80	0.641
1967	10.55	0.916	8.27	0.595	9.09	0.594

Sources: 1925-67 – USBM, *Minerals Yearbook* and *Mineral Resources of the United States.*

Notes:
(1) Mesabi Range ore of non-Bessemer quality, delivered to Lake Erie Docks: grade 51.5%.
(2) Average value of U.S. imports from Chile: 62% assumed.
(3) 1925-55, average value of U.S. imports from Brazil, principally lump ore of open-hearth quality; grade of 68.5% assumed. 1956-67, price of Itabira hematite lump ore, 68.5%, f.o.b. Vitória for long-term contracts, exclusive of premiums for low phosphorous or other qualities.

[a]Each price prevailing during the year weighted by the number of months it was in effect.

TABLE 5–4. Latin American Exports of Iron Ore[a] by Destination, 1950-1966
(Thousands of metric tons and thousands of U.S. dollars)

Country or Region	1950	1951	1952	1953	1954	1955	1956	1957
Brazil	890	1,330	1,605	1,568	1,678	2,565	2,745	3,550
United States	692	1,075	1,055	507	573	1,108	1,316	1,497
West Germany			121	467	229	397	516	494
Italy					10	47	50	52
United Kingdom		93	92	323	459	553	572	715
Japan				10		9	49	133
Value	6,620	12,630	26,304	8,760	8,049	18,448	27,135	29,124
Share total exports (%)	0.5	0.7	1.8	0.5	0.5	1.2	1.8	2.0
Chile	2,596	2,687	1,828	2,442	1,720	1,237	2,071	3,074
United States	2,596	2,686	1,828	2,372	1,634	1,072	1,722	2,744
West Germany				51	75	112	309	274
Japan				18			13	13
Value	6,694	7,964	8,134	12,850	7,883	6,055	12,485	21,183
Share total exports (%)	2.3	2.1	1.7	3.1	1.9	1.2	2.3	4.6
Cuba	29	9	98	209	76	121	135	105
United States	29	95	95	204	44	69	124	32
Value[b]	62	65	899	1,858	314	316	929	346
Share total exports (%)			0.1	0.2	0.1	0.1	0.1	
Dominican Republic[c]			19	92	95	101	163	150
Value			198	1,410	1,313	1,310	2,393	2,289
Share total exports (%)			0.2	1.3	1.0	1.1	2.0	1.6
Mexico[c]	192	175	114	243	145	186	135	239
Value	570	582	500	1,161	600	563	413	776
Share total exports (%)	0.1	0.1	0.1	0.2	0.1	0.1		0.1
Peru				890	1,927	1,697	2,674	3,677
United States				890	1,922	1,554	1,825	2,359
Japan							335	364
Value				5,402	13,124	7,778	14,801	23,286
Share total exports (%)				2.4	5.3	2.9	4.8	7.2
Venezuela		693	1,911	1,973	5,449	7,791	10,905	15,577
United States		693	1,911	1,973	5,431	7,333	9,349	12,479
West Germany						119	289	1,015
United Kingdom					9	135	710	1,370
Value			3,960	14,685	17,055	36,133	48,573	73,914 114,315
Share total exports (%)			0.2	1.0	1.0	1.9	2.3	3.4 4.5
Total Latin America	3,670	4,885	5,487	7,220	11,058	13,658	18,735	26,338
United States	2,817	4,629	5,022	6,280	9,834	11,414	14,632	19,478
West Germany			121	518	304	628	1,114	1,783
United Kingdom		93	92	323	468	688	1,282	2,089
Japan				28		9	397	510
Total L.A. Value	13,946	25,171	50,720	48,496	67,416	83,043	131,970	191,319
Share of Total L.A. Exports (%)	0.2	0.3	0.7	0.6	0.8	1.0	1.5	2.2

TABLE 5–4 – Continued

Country or Region	1958	1959	1960	1961	1962	1963	1964	1965	1966
Brazil	2,831	3,988	5,240	6,282	7,380	8,268	9,280	12,732	12,910
United States	844	1,297	1,429	903	1,241	841	1,050	2,323	3,025
West Germany	454	748	1,383	2,664	2,827	2,469	3,496	3,377	2,976
Italy	17	29	51	294	642	792	1,044	1,396	771
United Kingdom	571	566	678	516	412	781	532	635	733
Japan	47	196	372	405	456	518	500	841	1,839
Argentina		9	147	80	211	298	621		
Value	20,924	21,403	46,664	48,787	53,039	62,245	53,740	102,980	100,200
Share total exports (%)	1.6	1.6	3.6	3.4	4.3	4.4	3.7	6.5	5.8
Chile	3,638	4,261	5,191	6,206	7,246	7,092	9,134	10,730	11,088
United States	3,419	3,451	3,188	2,894	3,502	2,523	2,750	2,766	2,433
West Germany	170	220	849	520	296	210	638	708	572
Japan	17	70	308	2,029	2,882	3,612	5,392	6,891	7,873
Argentina		455	187	139	127	156	260		
Value	23,910	29,055	35,204	44,415	56,240	57,194	69,585	78,284	78,043
Share total exports (%)	6.1	5.8	7.2	8.7	10.5	10.5	11.1	11.4	8.9
Mexico[c]	224	116	156	123	147	2	22	10	
Value	711	382	529	426	1,055	9	207	93	2
Share total exports (%)	0.1	0.1	0.1	0.1	0.1				
Peru	2,510	3,320	5,171	5,573	5,149	5,749	5,205	6,374	6,308
United States	1,966		2,762	1,209	571	255	482	684	704
West Germany						333	551	1,102	430
Japan	115	143	648	1,771	2,445	2,867	2,774	3,958	4,606
Argentina		101	84	108	314	113	165		
Value	15,595	19,255	33,314	36,997	32,669	36,442	31,928	46,987	53,387
Share total exports (%)	5.5	6.1	7.7	7.4	6.0	6.7	4.7	7.0	7.0
Venezuela	15,572	17,379	19,320	14,565	13,286	12,319	14,893	17,005	17,037
United States	12,599	14,086	14,784	10,402	10,346	9,312	10,119	12,317	13,115
West Germany	644	289	434	356	337	1,006	2,117	1,903	1,606
United Kingdom	1,297	1,410	1,714	1,627	1,211	1,365	1,706	1,740	1,300
Value	116,608	130,480	165,465	96,609	87,564	71,980	116,714	143,751	144,068
Share total exports (%)	4.5	4.9	6.3	3.4	3.1	2.5	4.0		5.3
Total Latin America	24,795	29,119	35,179	32,749	33,208	33,430	38,534	46,850	47,343
United States	19,073	19,379	22,417	21,528	15,805	12,933	14,423	18,099	19,277
United Kingdom	1,268	1,257	2,666	3,540	3,460	4,018	6,802	2,375	2,033
West Germany	1,868	1,976	2,392	1,543	1,623	2,146	2,238	7,090	5,584
Japan	179	409	1,328	4,205	5,783	6,997	8,666	11,690	14,318
Argentina		565	418	327	652	567	1,040		
Total L.A. Value	178,078	201,580	281,803	223,325	230,567	227,870	272,174	372,095	375,700
Share of Total L.A. Exports (%)	2.1	2.4	3.2	2.5	2.5	2.3	2.6	3.4	3.2

Sources: USBM, *Minerals Yearbook*; Foreign trade yearbooks of Brazil, Chile, Dominican Republic, Mexico, Peru, and Venezuela; IMF, *International Financial Statistics*, supp. 1966/67 issues; UN, *Yearbook of International Trade Statistics, 1966*.

[a]Tonnage of ore, grade not specified.
[b]Value of United States imports from Cuba.
[c]Predominantly or exclusively to the United States.

TABLE 5-5. Latin American Resources for Steelmaking
(Iron ore, coal, petroleum: millions of metric tons; Manganese ore: thousands of metric tons)

Country	(1) Iron Ore, at Grades of							
	Less than 30%	30-39%	40-49%	50-54%	55-59%	60-64%	Over 64%	Total
Argentina	500[a]		106		145			751
Bolivia				45,000[b]		540[c]		45,540
Brazil		28,000		3,000	10,300	75	2,105	43,480
Central America				8[d]		12[e]		20
Chile	300[f]		500			787		1,587
Colombia	380[f]		132	40				552
Cuba			2,500[g]					2,500
Dominican Republic							50	50
Ecuador							1	1
Mexico					73	340	161	574
Peru			32	1		734		767
Uruguay			100					100
Venezuela			245		200	3,688		4,133
Latin America	1,180	28,000	3,615	48,049	10,718	6,176	2,317	100,055
Iron Content	190	9,800	1,599	25,824	5,899	3,926	1,528	48,766

Country	(2) Manganese Ore	(3) Coal Reserves			(4) Crude Petroleum Reserves
		Total Bituminous	Coking Quality	Share used in Coke (%)	
Argentina	900				286
Bolivia	(h)				52
Brazil	30,000	2,136	500	40	117
Central America	420				
Chile		110	80	60	29
Colombia		40,000	500	100	166
Cuba	720				
Dominican Republic					
Ecuador					3
Mexico	4,500	15,000	2,600	100	402
Peru	(j)	100	100	(k)	56
Uruguay					
Venezuela					2,430
Latin America	36,540	57,346	3,780	61[m]	3,541

Sources: UN, *Interregional Symposium on the Application of Modern Technical Practices in the Iron and Steel Industry to Developing Countries* (Prague/Geneva: November 1963), pp. 54, 58, 60, 66-72. ECLA, *La Economía Siderúrgica de América Latina* (Santiago, Chile, 1966), p. 70. See also tables 8-1 (Petroleum) and 9-1, 9-2 and 9-6 (Coal).

(1) Millions of tons of iron ore in grade range indicated, whether classified as proved, indicated, calculated, or potential. Iron content is calculated from grades of individual deposits.

(2) Thousands of tons of manganese contained in ore of at least 45% grade.

(3) Millions of tons of bituminous coal reserves, however classified; coking quality coals include swelling coals in Brazil and shrinking coals in Chile as well as straight coking coals in Colombia, Mexico, and Peru. Figures are minimal estimates, since some of the noncoking coal may be suitable for coking after adequate testing. Shares are percentages of domestic coal used to make coke, in mixtures with imported coals in Brazil and Chile.

(4) Millions of tons of proved reserves of petroleum as of 1 January 1965, converted from volume to weight by average specific gravity of each country's production.

[a] Iron-bearing sand, grade only 4%.
[b] Recent estimate of reserves of deposit at Mutún, Bolivia; grade 54%.
[c] Earlier estimate of Mutún reserves; refers only to ore of 60 or 62% iron.
[d] Honduras.
[e] Guatemala and Nicaragua.
[f] Grade 25%.
[g] Ore containing 45% iron, classified as potential because of presence of nickel and chromium which make extraction of iron uneconomical.
[h] No estimate available of manganese content of Mutún reserves.
[j] No estimates available of manganese content of several ore formations in southern Peru.
[k] Peruvian coal is used to make coke only for nonferrous metal smelting; coke for steel production is imported.
[m] Weighted average, excluding Peru, for 1961.

TABLE 5-6. Latin American Production of Pig Iron,[a] Crude Steel,[b] and Rolled Steel Products,[c] 1925-1967
(*Thousands of metric tons*)

Country or Region	Average 1925-29	Average 1930-34	Average 1935-39	Average 1940-44	Average 1945-49	1950	1951	1952	1953	1954	1955	1956
I. PIG IRON												
Argentina					17	20	28	27	35	40	35	29
Brazil	70	39	105	230	435	729	776	822	893	1,109	1,087	1,171
Chile				66	14	109	240	270	286	305	256	368
Colombia										88	99	116
Mexico	50	56	96	115	272	227	254	305	261	269	323	413
Total Latin America	120	95	201	410	738	1,085	1,298	1,424	1,473	1,811	1,800	2,097
World Total	85,887	57,494	91,067	111,880	97,200	134,000	151,000	152,000	169,000	158,700	192,500	201,300
L.A. Pig Iron Production as Share of:												
World Pig Iron Production (%)	0.1	0.2	0.2	0.3	0.8	0.8	0.9	0.9	0.9	1.1	0.9	1.0
L.A. Production of Iron in Ore[d] (%)	7.1	14.8	17.0	44.9	36.8	32.2	29.0	29.6	22.9	22.2	18.0	15.9
II. CRUDE STEEL												
Argentina	18		12	69	172	240	300	127	196	168	218	308
Brazil		33	75	153	520	623	843	893	1,016	1,148	1,272	1,488
Chile			15	24	35	53	113	243	313	321	290	381
Colombia						10	10	10			77	90
Mexico	68	76	138	133	271	348	395	540	525	622	760	879
Peru												
Venezuela												
Total Latin America	86	109	240	379	998	1,264	1,661	1,813	2,050	2,259	2,617	3,146
World Total					133,900	189,200	210,900	211,500	234,700	223,800	270,000	283,650
L.A. Share (%)					0.1	0.7	0.8	0.9	0.9	1.0	1.0	1.1
L.A. Production of Rolled Steel Products[e]								2,171	2,270	2,793	3,320	3,871

I. PIG IRON

Argentina	34	29	35	180	396	397	422	588	663	522	610
Brazil	1,270	1,706	1,588	1,783	1,860	2,120	2,516	2,664	2,399	2,937	3,100
Chile	382	305	290	266	285	399	418	437	309	433	498
Colombia	143	149	145	185	189	149	202	205	204	169	207
Mexico	429	496	576	686	784	827	833	926	946	1,137	1,285
Peru							29	27	20[f]	28[f]	29
Venezuela					5	123	302	323	334	351	422
Total Latin America	2,258	2,385	2,634	3,100	3,519	4,015	4,722	5,170	4,875	5,577	6,151
World Total	211,650	196,640	224,290	258,874	256,320	265,394	281,518	317,561	335,129	347,046	355,556
L.A. Pig Iron Production as Share of: World Pig Iron Production (%)	1.0	1.2	1.2	1.2	1.4	1.5	1.7	1.6	1.5	1.6	1.7
L.A. Production of Iron in Ore[d] (%)	13.2	13.4	12.3	11.8	13.8	16.5	19.0	16.6	13.9	14.5	16.3

II. CRUDE STEEL

Argentina	363	244	214	277	441	658	895	1,265	1,368	1,267	1,326
Brazil	1,382	1,517	1,880	2,296	2,500	2,604	2,824	3,016	2,983	3,767	3,720
Chile	388	348	415	422	363	495	521	584	477	577	638
Colombia	114	121	110	172	192	157	222	230	242	217	252
Mexico	1,031	1,038	1,336	1,503	1,707	1,720	2,026	2,326	2,455	2,787	3,023[g]
Peru		20	51	60	75	72	76	82	94	80	79
Venezuela		60	60	47	75	225	364	440	625	537	667
Total Latin America	3,278	3,288	4,056	4,777	5,353	5,931	6,928	7,943	8,244	9,232	9,705
World Total	292,600	271,000	305,280	346,200	351,000	359,500	386,979	438,006	459,300	476,059	492,929
L.A. Share (%)	1.1	1.2	1.3	1.4	1.5	1.6	1.8	1.8	1.8	1.9	2.0
L.A. Production of Rolled Steel Products[e]	4,326	4,722	5,172	5,595	6,146	6,211	7,703	6,750	6,750	7,648	9,341

Sources: Pig iron 1925-67 and crude steel 1952-67 – USBM, *Minerals Yearbook.* Crude steel 1925-51 – ECLA, *A Study of the Iron and Steel Industry of Latin America* (New York: UN, 1954), vol. I, pp. 84-86. Rolled Steel products 1952-64 – ECLA, *La Economía Siderúrgica...*, p. 6. 1965-67 – USBM, *Minerals Yearbook, 1967,* vol. IV.

[a] Includes ferroalloys where data are available.
[b] Ingots and castings of primary steel, made at least in part from pig iron.
[c] Includes products made from remelted scrap and imported ingots or billets as well as production from domestic crude steel.
[d] All ore assumed to be 60% iron by weight; ratio represents (approximately) percentage of iron mined which is used domestically to make steel. Nearly all the rest is exported as ore.
[e] Rolled products in Argentina, Brazil, and Chile; semifinished steel in Mexico and Venezuela; ingots and castings in Colombia and Peru. Excludes products rolled from imported steel.
[f] Production of Sociedad Siderúrgica de Chimbote, S. A., only.
[g] Includes steel castings.

TABLE 5–7. Apparent Consumption of Iron and Steel in Latin America, 1936-38, 1947-49, 1952-53, and 1962-64
(Thousands of metric tons ingot equivalent, and kilograms per capita)

Country	1936-38 Total	1936-38 Per Capita	1947-49 Total	1947-49 Per Capita	1952-53 Total	1952-53 Per Capita	1962-64 Total	1962-64 Per Capita[a]
Argentina	703	50	934	57	755	41	1,951	88
Bolivia			14[b]	5	11	4	33	9
Brazil	417	11	722	15	1,393	25	3,454	44
Central America[c]					91	11	180[d]	15
Chile	121	25	153	27	295	46	693	85
Colombia	88	10	124	12	227	18	483	29
Cuba	71	16	132	28	169	29	217[d]	30
Dominican Republic					40	17	53	16
Ecuador			24[b]	8	30	9	63[d]	13
Mexico	268	14	513	21	908	32	2,103	55
Panama					15	17	35[d]	34
Paraguay					16	10	14	7
Peru			82[b]	10	140	17	269	23
Uruguay			89[b]	38	90	40	102	35
Venezuela			290[b]	62	586	108	572	70
Total[e]	1,668	19	3,077	23[b]	4,763	29	10,222	47
L.A. Consumption as Share of World Crude Steel Production:[f] (%)			2.1		2.1		2.6	
Share of L.A. Consumption (%) Met by Domestic Crude Steel Production:	14		32		41		68	

Sources: ECLA, *A Study of the Iron and Steel Industry...*, vol. I, pp. 44, 84-86. ECLA, *Là Economía Siderúrgica...*, p. 5. ECLA, *Boletín Económico de América Latina*, October 1962 (*Statistical Supplement*), pp. 6-7.

[a]Per capita consumption calculated from estimated population in mid-1963.
[b]Per capita consumption given; total calculated from estimated population in mid-1948.
[c]Costa Rica, El Salvador, Guatemala, Honduras, and Nicaragua.
[d]1962-63 average.
[e]Sum of countries listed; excludes Haiti in all years.
[f]World steel consumption assumed equal to production.

TABLE 5–8. Import Substitution in Crude Steel in Selected Latin American Countries between 1929 and 1960
(Thousands of metric tons)

	Year	Argentina	Brazil	Chile	Colombia	Mexico	Total Five Countries
Steel production	1929		30			87	117
	1950	240	623	53		348	1,264
	1960	1,028	2,277	399	152	1,572	5,428
Steel imports	1929	1,054	458	225	78	138	1,953
	1950	671	252	112	152	227	1,414
	1960	880	578	63	236	286	2,043
Total supply of steel	1929	1,054	488	225	78	225	2,070
	1950	911	875	165	152	575	2,878
	1960	1,908	2,855	462	388	1,858	7,471
Increase in steel production	1929-50	240	593	53		261	1,147
	1950-60	788	1,654	346	152	1,224	4,164
	1929-60	1,028	2,247	399	152	1,485	5,311
Import coefficient of steel	1929	100.0	94.0	100.0	100.0	61.4	94.3
Anticipated imports of steel	1950	911	823	165	152	353	2,404
	1960	1,908	2,680	462	388	1,140	6,578
Difference between actual and anticipated imports	1950	240	571	53		126	990
	1960	1,028	2,102	399	152	854	4,535
Share of increased production due to substitution (%)	1929-50[b]	100	96	100	(a)	48	86
	1950-60[b]	100	93	100	100	59	67
	1929-60[b]	100	93	100	100	57	85
	1950-60[c]	66	15	73	100	37	39
Share of anticipated imports replaced by domestic production (%)	1929-50[b]	26	72	32		74	48
	1950-60[b]	41	58	75	39	64	54
	1929-60[b]	54	79	86	39	75	69
	1950-60[c]	38	30	80	39	61	44

Sources: ECLA, *A Study of the Iron and Steel Industry...*, pp. 84-86. ECLA, *La Economía Siderúrgica...*, p. 7. For definitions and notes see chap. 1, table A-4.

[a]No increase in steel output.   [b]1929 base.   [c]1950 base.

TABLE 5-9. Latin American Iron and Steel Industry: Number and Output of Plants by Type, 1964-1966
(*Metric tons*)

Country	(1) Integrated Mills Number	(1) Integrated Mills Steel Ingots	(2) Semi-integrated Mills Number	(2) Semi-integrated Mills Steel Ingots	(3) Nonintegrated Mills Number	(3) Nonintegrated Mills Semifabricated Steel[a]	Total, All Mills Number	Total, All Mills Pig Iron[b]	Total, All Mills Steel Ingots[c]	Total, All Mills Semifabricated Steel[d]
Argentina Total	3	1,039,043	12[e]	462,758	16/47[e,f]	210,784	31/62[e,f]	596,708	1,536,226	2,585,174
Province:										
Buenos Aires	2	1,016,343	8	367,410	5/27[f]	169,140	15/37[f]	544,710	1,383,753	2,300,346
Santa Fé			2	95,348	5/10[f]	33,644	7/12[f]		129,773	273,028
Córdoba			2[e]		3/6[f]	8,000	5/8[f]	1,248		8,000
Brazil Total	11[e]	2,567,229	21	338,228	22/24[e,f]	209,384	54/56[e,f]	2,200,912	2,908,240	1,552,258
State: São Paulo	2[e]	88,035	9	135,623	15/17[e,f]	166,994	26/28[e,f]	112,466	224,509	301,714
Minas Gerais	6[e]	1,034,183	4	57,540	5	14,500	15[e]	1,093,441	1,093,655	980,487
Rio de Janeiro	2	1,213,272	3	42,655			5	956,593	1,255,927	121,329
Chile Total	1	544,251	6	2,300	4/6[f]	14,990	11/13[f]	459,999	547,144	468,148
City: Santiago			4		4/6[f]	14,990	8/10[f]		593	58,279
Colombia Total	1	196,076	2	31,119	0/11[f]		3/14[f]	190,514	227,195	228,162
City: Bogotá					0/5[f]		0/5[f]			
Medellín			1	21,500	0/3[f]		1/4[f]		21,500	26,250
Cali			1	9,619	0/2[f]		1/3[f]		9,619	21,325
El Salvador			1	2,470			1		2,470	3,500
Guatemala					1[e]		1[e]			
Mexico Total	3	1,800,663	15	450,808	11/34[f]	47,740	29/52[f]	1,169,976	2,251,471	1,656,298
State: Mexico			5	117,956	2/17[f]	32,076	7/22[f]		117,956	94,883
Coahuila	1	1,015,031	2	42,245	3/5[f]	4,664	6/8[f]	635,014	1,057,276	905,916
Nuevo León	2	785,632	1	45,050	3/6[f]		6/9[f]	494,197	830,682	628,208
Nicaragua					1[e]		1[e]			
Peru Total	1	75,213	1		1/4[f]		3/6[f]	61,963	75,213	65,225
City: Lima-Callao			1		0/2[f]		1/3[f]			
Chimbote	1	75,213			0/2[f]		2/3[f]	61,963	75,213	65,225
Uruguay			2	13,591	2	22,785	4	105	13,591	34,812
Venezuela	1	359,892	1		2		2	323,465	359,892	865,666
Latin America	21[e]	6,282,347	61[e]	1,301,274[d]	58/130[e,f]	505,683	140/212[e,f]	5,003,642	7,918,972	7,459,243

Sources: ILAFA, *Repertorio de las Empresas Siderúrgicas Latinoamericanas,* 1966 ed. (Santiago, Chile); ECLA, *La Economía Siderúrgica...,* pp. 46-49.

Notes:

(1) Plants producing pig iron, steel ingots, and semifabricated steel products.

(2) Plants producing steel ingots from scrap or purchased pig iron, and semifabricated steel products; or plants producing pig iron and wrought or cast iron but no steel; or plants producing steel ingots or ferroalloys, and steel castings.

(3) Plants producing iron or steel castings or semifabricated steel products only; or plants producing pig iron, ferroalloys, or alloy steel ingots only.

[a] Excludes output of other products, such as pig iron, ferroalloys, steel ingots, and castings, by nonintegrated mills.

[b] Includes sponge iron and ferroalloys.

[c] Includes some steel castings produced in nonintegrated mills.

[d] Total reported semifabricated steel production; excludes some production in integrated mills.

[e] Includes one or more plants which were not operating in 1964. Rated capacity or anticipated production is known but not included in the total for production.

[f] Production figure refers only to smaller number of plants; no data available for rest of plants in this group.

TABLE 5-10. Participation in Iron Mining and in Integrated Steel Mills in Latin America, 1964

Country	Producer	Ownership	Share of 1964 Production (%)
I. IRON ORE MINING			
Argentina	Altos Hornos Zapla[a]	State	All
Brazil[b]	Cía. Vale do Rio Doce	State	65
	SAMITRI	Majority Belgian private, rest local private	13
	Cía. Siderúrgica Nacional	State	7
	Minceração Novalimense	U.S. private	3
	CAEMI	Predominantly local private	3
	Total	State	About 72
		Foreign private[c]	13-21
		Local private[d]	12-17
Chile	Cía. Minera Santa Fé	Predominantly U.S. and Canadian private[e]	35
	Cía. Acero del Pacífico	State 35%, U.S. private 19%, local private 46%	28
	Bethlehem-Chile Iron Mines	U.S. private	24
	Cía. Minera de Atacama	Japanese private	6
	Cía. Minera Santa Barbara	(f)	4
	Total	State	10
		Foreign private	71-75
		Local private[d]	15-19
Colombia	Acerías Paz del Río	Predominantly local private[e] (initially state-owned)	All
Mexico	Altos Hornos de México	Majority state, rest local private	57
	Cía. Fundidora[a]	Predominantly local private[e]	23
	Hojalata y Lámina[a]	Local private	16
	Total	State[c]	About 34-57
		Local private[d]	About 43-66
Peru	Marcona Mining Co.	U.S. private	Nearly all[f]
Venezuela	Orinoco Mining Co.	U.S. private	87
	Iron Mines Co. of Venezuela	U.S. private	13
Total Latin America		State	27-28
(sum of countries listed)		Foreign private[c]	57-60
		U.S.	About 55
		Local private[d]	12-16
II. CRUDE STEEL PRODUCTION, INTEGRATED STEEL MILLS			
Argentina	Sociedad Mixta Siderúrgica	Majority state, rest local private	96
	Altos Hornos Zapla	State	4
	Total	Majority state,[c] rest local private	Minimum 52[h]
Brazil	Cía. Siderúrgica Nacional	Predominantly state, rest local private[e]	46
	Cía. Belgo Mineria	Majority Belgian private, rest local private	16
	USIMINAS	Federal government 36%, state government 24%, Japanese public and private 40%	10.6
	Mineração Geral do Brasil	Predominantly local private	9
	Cía. Siderúrgica Mannesmann	W. German private and local private, and state	8.2
	Total	State	At least 55
		Foreign private[c]	16-28
		Local private[d] (excl. state minority participation)	16-28
Chile	Cía. de Acero del Pacífico	State 35%, U.S. private 19%, local private 46%	All
Colombia	Acerías Paz del Río	Predominantly local private[e] (initially state owned)	All
Mexico	Altos Hornos de México	Majority state, rest local private	56
	Cía. Fundidora	Predominantly local private	26
	Hojalata y Lámina	Local private	18
	Total	State[c]	About 34-56
		Local private[d]	44-66
Peru	Sociedad Siderúrgica de Chimbote	State	All
Venezuela	Siderúrgica del Orinoco	State	All
Total Latin America		State[c]	48-60
(sum of countries listed)		Foreign private[c]	8-13
		Local private[d]	27-44

Sources: ECLA, *La Economía Siderúrgica...*, pp. 47, 127. USBM, *Minerals Yearbook, 1964*, vol. IV. ILAFA, *Repertorio...*, 1966. *Metal Bulletin*, 11 November 1966, p. 19.

[a]Consumer of iron ore indicated; ore may be mined by a captive enterprise under another name.
[b]Percentages calculated from 1965 output by twelve largest producers.
[c]Exact figure depends on distribution of ownership of one or more major producers; numbers shown are minima and maxima.
[d]Residual.
[e]Minority shares, whether state or foreign private, are ignored in totals for country and for region.
[f]Exact information not available.
[g]Production by a much smaller enterprise, which was in financial difficulty during 1964, is omitted.
[h]State share estimated as 70% by J. D. Heffernan and M. H. Che, *The Steel Industry in Latin America* (New York: Chase Manhattan Bank, May 1967).

TABLE 5-11. Latin American Iron and Steel Balance, 1963
(Metric tons)

	Iron Ore (Gross) (1)	Pig Iron Ferroalloys (2)	Crude Steel (3)	Semimanu-factures (4)	Total Iron and Steel (5)	Total Rolled Steel (6)
Argentina						
Imports	757,000	9,734	82,449	405,389	952,000	547,000
Production	94,000	424,000	913,000	759,000	45,000	1,263,000
Exports		2	70	114,564	115,000	152,000
Appar. consumption	851,000	433,732	995,379	1,049,825	1,286,000	1,658,000
Bolivia						
Imports					29,000	33,000
Brazil						
Imports		2,411		397,746	400,000	751,000
Production	11,219,000	2,761,000	2,812,000	2,204,000	7,629,000	3,088,000
Exports	8,268,000	47,267	166	6,475	5,676,000	1,000
Appar. consumption	2,951,000	2,716,144	2,811,834	2,595,271	3,203,000	3,838,000
Central America						
Imports[a]		13,858	9,473	121,576	145,000	174,000
Production	6,000				3,000	
Exports[a]		394	——— 840[b] ———		1,000	
Appar. consumption		13,464	——— 130,209[b] ———		147,000[c]	174,000
Chile						
Imports		272	4,779	14,851	20,000	106,000
Production	8,507,000	435,000	489,000	376,000	5,481,000	622,000
Exports	7,092,000	11,081		30,088	4,580,000	41,000
Appar. consumption	1,415,000	424,191	493,779	360,763	484,000	687,000
Colombia						
Imports		9,025	1,152	169,314	179,000	232,000
Production	695,000	203,000	222,000		334,000	249,000
Exports		33		9	0	
Appar. consumption	695,000	211,992	223,152		392,000	481,000
Cuba						
Imports		20,600		103,800	124,400	
Production	650				300	
Appar. Consumption	650				124,700[c]	167,000
Dominican Rep.						
Imports				59,824	59,800	57,000
Exports		641			600	
Appar. consumption				59,824	59,200[c]	57,000
Ecuador						
Imports		22		47,305	47,300	65,000
Exports		283			300	
Appar. consumption					47,000[c]	65,000
Haiti						
Imports	1	14	18	6,510	6,500	
Mexico						
Imports	2,103	162,259	1	95,178	259,000	224,000
Production	2,328,137	1,028,770	2,028,265	1,379,794	1,397,000	2,046,000
Exports	1,112	4,741	259	172,153	178,000	224,000
Appar. consumption	2,329,128	1,186,288	2,028,007	1,302,819	2,051,000	2,046,000
Panama						
Imports		610	2,588	24,918	28,100	35,000
Production					6,350	
Exports		1,000	2	50	1,100	
Appar. consumption		(390)	2,586	31,218	27,400	35,000
Paraguay						
Imports				11,186	11,200	15,000
Peru						
Imports	69	807		141,502	142,000	193,000
Production	6,574,000	29,000	73,000		3,944,000	78,000
Exports	5,748,663			36	3,449,000	
Appar. consumption	825,406	29,807	73,000		215,000	271,000
Uruguay						
Imports		——— 23,084[b] ———		31,516	54,600	53,000
Production	1,031		6,500	21,970	500	29,000
Exports				636	600	
Appar. consumption	1,031	——— 29,584[b] ———		52,850	60,500	82,000
Venezuela						
Imports		27,726	6,608	390,904	425,000	433,000
Production	11,757,000	302,000	364,000	159,000	6,813,000	328,000
Exports	12,319,000	89,733	133,605	5,277	7,145,000	185,000
Appar. consumption	(572,000)	239,993	237,003	544,627	623,000	576,000

TABLE 5–11 – Continued

	Iron Ore (Gross) (1)	Pig Iron Ferroalloys (2)	Crude Steel (3)	Semimanu-factures (4)	Total Iron and Steel (5)	Total Rolled Steel (6)
Total Latin America						
Imports	759,000	247,000	130,000	2,022,000[d]	3,056,000	2,918,000
Production	41,171,000	5,183,000	6,908,000	4,906,000	25,647,000	7,703,000
Exports	33,429,000	155,000	134,000	330,000	21,147,000	603,000
Intraregional trade	757,000	8,000[e]	1,000	117,000	883,000	
Apparent consumption	8,501,000	5,275,000	6,904,000	6,894,000[f]	8,596,000	10,185,000[g]

Sources: Cols. (1) to (5), USBM, *Minerals Yearbook, 1964*, vol. IV; col. (6), ECLA, *La Economía Siderúrgica...*, pp. 5–7, 13.

Notes:

(1) Gross weight of iron ore, iron ore concentrates, and agglomerates.

(2) Pig iron, cast iron, sponge iron, ferroalloys, and iron and steel scrap: all forms of smelted iron and scrap for steelmaking, plus cast iron for final consumption.

(3) Steel ingots, bars, and castings, for final consumption (castings) or for rolling (ingots and bars); does not include "semifinished" forms such as slabs, blooms, and billets (intermediate between crude steel and semimanufactures) in production, but only in trade.

(4) All rolled products, whether flat or not, such as sheets, plates, rods, wire, structural shapes, etc.; includes tinplate and other plated products.

(5) Approximate iron content of all imports or exports, iron ore production, crude steel consumption plus net imports of semimanufactures. Iron content of ore as reported or estimated from average grade; all other forms assumed to be 100% iron. Apparent consumption does not equal imports plus production less exports, for total iron and steel, except where indicated.

(6) ECLA estimates of production, trade, and consumption of rolled steel products, in ingot equivalent tons. These estimates are closer *in definition* to crude steel col. (3), than to total estimates in col. (5); numbers may or may not approximate those in col. (5). In particular, estimated imports sometimes greatly exceed figures recorded by *Minerals Yearbook*.

[a]Includes trade among Central American countries.
[b]Totals for two columns included in second column.
[c]Production plus imports, less exports.
[d]Includes Colombian imports from Panama not shown in exports from Panama.
[e]Excludes Colombia and Peru, for which data are not available.
[f]Crude steel consumption used to represent production of semimanufactures in Colombia and Peru.
[g]Apparent consumption differs from production plus imports less exports by the amount (167,000 tons) of Cuban consumption.

TABLE 5–12. Demand and Supply of Crude Steel and Iron Ore in Latin America, 1975
   (Thousands of metric tons)

Country	Crude Steel Consumption[a]			Iron Ore				
	Flat Products	Other Products	Total	Requirements Domestic[b]	Export[c]	Production Net[d]	Gross[e]	Value of Exports[f] (Million U.S. $)
Argentina	2,517	2,518	5,035	2,340[g]		2,340	3,900[h]	
Brazil	5,315	5,315	10,630	7,900	22,000	30,250	46,000	129
Central America	252	347	599					
Chile	706	764	1,470	1,180	12,000	13,180	21,600	100
Colombia	602	652	1,254	1,145[j]		1,145	2,390	
Ecuador	85	118	203					
Mexico	2,771	2,771	5,542	2,300		2,300	3,840	
Peru	426	461	887	319	6,000	6,319	10,500	36
Uruguay	110	140	250					
Venezuela	828	1,054	1,882	1,380	18,000	9,380	34,500	136
Other[k]	47	66	113					
Total[m]	13,659	14,206	27,865	16,564[n]	58,000	74,564	122,730	401

Sources: ECLA, *La Economía Siderúrgica...*, pp. 27, 32. Also tables 5-2, 5-5, 5-9.

[a]Ingot equivalent.
[b]Iron ore required to produce enough steel to satisfy domestic demand in producing countries, at ratio of pig iron to crude steel production in each country in 1964 (iron content of ore). This measure understates requirements to the extent that steel is made from iron ore directly, without prior reduction to pig iron.
[c]Exports distributed among the four major exporters; Brazil's exports are assumed to grow most rapidly, and those of Venezuela to surpass the level of 1957-60 and 1964.
[d]Sum of domestic and export requirements, iron content of ore.
[e]Gross tonnage of ore, assuming same average grade in each producing country as circa 1966.
[f]Exports valued at average prices per ton in 1965-66 or average export values in 1963-64 according to availability of data.
[g]Includes imports of iron ore from Brazil, Chile, and Peru; total exports of those countries would be somewhat greater, and production in Argentina considerably less, than indicated.
[h]Grade of 60 percent assumed to account for higher grade of imports than of domestic production.
[j]1963 ratio of pig iron to crude steel.
[k]Bolivia and Paraguay.
[m]Sum of countries listed; excludes Cuba, Haiti, and the Dominican Republic.
[n]Domestic requirements of countries producing steel in 1966 only.

Chapter 6

LEAD AND ZINC

Zinc and lead are among the world's most used metals, ranking fourth and fifth after steel, aluminum, and copper in tonnage consumed. They are considered jointly here because many deposits containing significant amounts of one metal also contain the other. The two are commonly mined together, and often the same enterprise will also smelt, refine, or trade in both metals. This association has been strengthened by the recent development of a joint smelting process for treating ores containing both lead and zinc. Copper, gold, silver, antimony, bismuth, and cadmium are frequently recovered from the same ore, but the bulk of copper is separately mined and the other byproducts will not be discussed further.[1]

Latin America provides about one-sixth of the world's lead and a slightly smaller share of zinc. The region consumes only one-fourth of its lead output and still less of the zinc. Together, lead and zinc earned some $100 million annually in foreign exchange in the early 1960s, or about 1 percent of total exports. In no country is either metal the chief export commodity, but they are quite important to Mexico and Peru, the chief producers, and in some other countries they constitute the largest metal mining industry, or the largest other than iron ore.

World Production, Consumption, and Trade

World reserves were estimated in 1965 as some 50 million tons of lead and 85 million tons of zinc (see table 6-1). These estimates are extremely rough: they do not include sizable discoveries, particularly of lead, in recent years; and the joint occurrence of lead and zinc together with precious metals often makes it difficult to determine the minimum grade at which exploitation is possible. In-

ferred reserves of both metals are small, and relatively little is known about potential resources in comparison with the situation for other metals such as iron, aluminum, and copper. Large amounts of low-grade ores of lead and/or zinc apparently occur in deposits quite different from those hitherto mined, and presumably their future exploitation will require new mining and processing techniques.[2]

North America, including Mexico, has about one-third of the presently known reserves of lead and zinc. A slightly smaller amount is found in Europe, including the Soviet Union; the rest is located in South America, Africa, Asia, and Oceania, with large amounts of lead in Australia. Altogether, Latin America has about one-fourth of world reserves of each metal, Mexico accounting for roughly half in each case. The South American reserves are concentrated in central Peru, with most of the rest in western Bolivia and northwestern Argentina. Very small amounts occur in Central America, Colombia, Chile, and Brazil. Bolivia is believed to have sizable reserves of zinc, and more zinc than lead occurs in Mexico, Peru, Brazil, and Honduras; in the other countries lead is more common.

Lead is one of the oldest industrial metals; it was widely used many centuries ago and was a major industrial input before 1900. In the last few decades world production has increased only slowly. The pre-Depression output of 1.6 million tons was not regained for twenty-five years, and over the entire period 1925-67 production has less than doubled (see table 6-2A). This slow growth is partly due to the ease with which lead can be recovered from scrap and reused, which results from its chemical inertness and low melting point. As consumption of lead increases, so does the stock of lead in use, and a steadily greater share of requirements is met from secondary sources; in the United States secondary recovery accounts for roughly half of consumption. Zinc, a more recent metal, is less readily reused. Since the late 1920s its production has more than doubled, remaining in fourth place among the metals while lead

Note: Lead and Zinc tables 6-1 to 6-8 appear on pp. 220–30.

[1]The statistical material in this chapter is taken chiefly from the *Minerals Yearbook* of the U.S. Bureau of Mines, the *Yearbook* of the American Bureau of Metal Statistics, and from two surveys published by the U.S. Bureau of Mines – *Lead: A Materials Survey*, by H. M. Callaway (1962), and *Materials Survey: Zinc* (1951). See also the statistical bulletins of the UN International Lead-Zinc Study Group. Especially for recent years, much use has been made of such periodicals as *Engineering and Mining Journal* and *Mining Magazine*. Other sources are indicated in the notes and tables.

[2]The literature on the "anomalous" distribution of lead and zinc resources is summarized, and an explanation offered, in D. B. Brooks, "The Lead-Zinc Anomaly," Society of Mining Engineers *Transactions*, June 1967.

dropped from third to fifth place in mine production. (See table 6-2B.)

These changes were accompanied by regional shifts in production, of which the most notable is the decline in the position of the United States: lead output fell sharply and zinc output dropped as a share of the world total. During the 1930s and 1940s, Latin America compensated for much of this decline. The region's share of world production fell slightly or not at all during the Depression, and then rose quite rapidly to a peak of 21 percent for lead in 1945-52 and of 16 percent for zinc in 1952-56. Thereafter the share for both metals declined, returning in the case of lead to the pre-Depression level of 15 percent. The Latin American industry expanded rapidly in the 1920s and again during and just before World War II; in recent years it has grown more slowly, outpaced by production in Canada and Oceania and by expansion in the Communist countries. Outside the latter area, the major shifts in production occurred before the Depression of the 1930s, and the distribution of output, like that of copper, has since been relatively stable.

Western Europe is now the principal consumer of lead and zinc; North America uses only about two-thirds as much primary lead, and almost as much zinc, as Europe (see table 6-3). Together these high-income areas absorb almost two-thirds of world supplies of each metal; Japan and Eastern Europe account for most of the remainder. The low consumption of the underdeveloped regions is still more striking when secondary production is included, as they have small stocks of metal in use and obtain little of their lead and zinc requirements by secondary recovery. For the world as a whole, zinc has been used in greater amounts than lead since the early 1940s. The transition occurred first in the advanced nations; at any time the consumption pattern of a poorer region reflects that of the industrial countries some years or decades earlier. In Latin America lead and zinc consumption are now approximately equal, but as recently as 1950 lead consumption was more than twice that of zinc and about equal to present zinc use. The region's share of total world lead consumption has declined, while its share of zinc use has continued to increase. The bulk of consumption in Latin America is accounted for by the three major industrial nations – Mexico, Brazil, and Argentina. Peru is also a significant consumer of lead, but zinc use is greater in Chile, Colombia, and Venezuela, which rely on imports from producing countries in the region. Final use of lead and zinc in all forms is probably somewhat overstated for Mexico and Peru, which export semifabricated metal, and may be understated for the region as a whole.

The end uses of lead and zinc may be roughly divided into two categories: those determined by the technical properties of the metals, which are relatively immune to substitution unless competing materials are considerably improved; and those where the technical advantages of lead or zinc are less marked and substitution occurs in response to changes in relative prices. The former group includes the newer and more rapidly expanding applications such as lead storage batteries, gasoline additives, solders, galvanizing, die casting, zinc oxide in rubber and certain brasses. The latter comprises such more traditional and slowly growing uses as pipe, sheet, cable sheathing and pigments. Because of the quite different importance of price in these two categories, there appears to be no simple statistical association between price and consumption for either lead or zinc. Price-induced substitution may depend as much on the stability as on the level of price, and influences consumption only after a lag of a few years.

The principal uses of the two metals vary among countries, depending on the level of industrialization and the availability and use of other materials. In the United States the automobile industry accounts directly or indirectly for more than half of all lead consumed; in the United Kingdom cable sheathing, pipe, and sheet are more important. Little is known about the distribution of lead and zinc by end use in low-income areas such as Latin America, except that the pattern of the developed countries in previous decades is unlikely to be repeated. The traditional uses in particular may not be significant because of the much greater present availability of substitutes. Aluminum and plastics are the chief competing materials: both have undergone great technical progress and both have fallen in relative price. They also offer advantages in price stability.

The creation of modern industries in Latin America in recent years has greatly increased the region's demand for zinc; the earlier stages of industrialization, initiated by the Depression and pursued in the 1940s, had more effect on the demand for lead. The growing use of lead in automobiles and gasoline may have been at least partly balanced by substitution away from lead in traditional uses such as construction. Lead batteries are now widely manufactured in Latin America; more difficult processes are less generally established – lead sheathing in Brazil, Mexico, and Peru, and zinc galvanizing in Argentina, Mexico, Chile, Colombia, Peru, and Venezuela.[3]

Lead is a relatively easy metal to smelt, and while its ores are rich compared to those of copper, they are still low enough in grade to encourage production of metal near the mine. For these reasons, and because most producing areas offer a market for lead, smelting industries were established shortly after extraction began in most mining regions. There remains a sizable trade in ores and concentrates, because the output of some mining areas is rich enough to be shipped long distances and too small to justify smelters close to the mines. Even when adequate smelting capacity exists in other mining zones of the same country, geographic obstacles may make it easier to export concentrates than to process them domestically: this is the case with mines distant from the one smelter in the Peruvian Andes, for example. Latin American smelter production has been about three-fourths of mine output since the early 1950s (see table 6-4A). The share was over 90 percent when Mexico was the only significant producer. Peru smelts a smaller share of its lead, and the increase and changed geo-

_____

[3]Most of this information is drawn from the International Lead-Zinc Study Group, *Lead and Zinc: Factors Affecting Consumption* (UN, November 1966), especially pp. 13-18, 48-51. See also Callaway, *Lead: A Materials Survey*, for more detailed descriptions of end uses. Further information was supplied by the American Smelting and Refining Company.

graphic distribution of Peruvian mine production has thus far compensated for the establishment of lead smelting in Brazil after World War II and the considerable increase in metal output in Argentina.

The situation is somewhat different for zinc, which is a more difficult metal to process and has come into use more recently. Smelters are located in three producing countries: in Mexico, where the industry was established in the 1920s, in Argentina, and in Peru, where processing was begun during World War II. The share of mine output treated is only about 30 percent in Mexico and Peru, and has varied from 50 to 100 percent in Argentina (see table 6-4B). During most of the last decade and a half the region's share of world output has increased slightly (it declined for lead) and the portion of mine output smelted domestically has risen by half. Zinc smelting is much more concentrated than lead processing in North America and Western Europe—75 instead of 50 percent of smelter production outside the Communist countries — and there is a correspondingly higher trade in ores and concentrates.

Western Europe is the largest net importer of both lead and zinc, taking annually some 600,000 tons of each in the early 1960s. The United States imports 300,000 to 400,000 tons of lead and some 500,000 tons of zinc. The Communist countries export large quantities of zinc and smaller amounts of lead; Asia as a whole exports lead and imports zinc, but the situation is reversed for Japan alone. Latin America, Canada, Africa, and Oceania are net exporters of both metals, supplying in all over 1 million tons of lead and about 1.3 million tons of zinc in the early 1960s. Latin America is the second most important source in both cases, after Australia in lead and after Canada in zinc. In the case of lead, about two-thirds of all trade among major regions is in the form of metal and one-third in ores and concentrates; the ratio is reversed for zinc, although the major importer, Western Europe, takes roughly equal amounts of metal and concentrates. (The proportion of metal is higher in total world trade for both commodities, because most trade within a region such as Europe or Latin America is in the form of metal.)

The pattern of trade is largely determined by location and transport costs, but it is also affected by nonprice factors.[4] Political affiliation is important in some cases, particularly in the trade of the United Kingdom. Financial ties are also of considerable influence, since much of both metals is produced for export by companies that also have mines, smelters, or fabricating facilities in importing countries. U.S. capital dominates the lead-zinc industries of Peru and Argentina, and is significant in Canada and Mexico; British firms control part of the production in Canada, Australia, and South Africa; French enterprise in Morocco and Belgian capital in the Congo (before the 1967 expropriation of the major mining concern) are similarly important. The spatial distribution of smelting facilities also helps determine trade in ores. The United States, for example,

takes nearly all Mexico's ore exports of both lead and zinc, but Mexico ships large amounts of lead metal to Europe and to other countries in Latin America. Zinc metal also goes from Mexico to Europe, Japan, and Latin America. Peru and Canada both mine much more than they smelt, and their output is not all pre-empted by financial or political ties; they are therefore major sources for importers such as Japan, Germany, and Benelux with smelting facilities but no assured supply of ore.

Certain extremely complex ores must be sent to the few plants equipped to separate all the byproducts; similarly the grades of metal produced differ slightly and these differences are reflected in trading preferences, often producing slight price premiums. Any of these advantages, once established, may be perpetuated by ties formed between buyer and seller.

The prices of lead and zinc dropped by more than half in the Depression, and had not recovered the level of the late 1920s when they were controlled by the governments of the United States and the United Kingdom during World War II (see table 6-5). Immediately after the war prices doubled, reaching a peak in 1948; they fell slightly until 1950, rising again under the stimulus of Korean War demand. There was another slight dip and recovery in 1952-57, and thereafter relative stability for zinc prices and a steady decline in lead prices until 1962. Both metals responded to increased demand from 1962 through 1965, as did copper and tin: the price increase was quite pronounced for lead. By 1967 both prices had fallen somewhat as production rose faster than consumption, although consumption continued slightly in excess of metal production for lead; zinc consumption actually declined, exerting pressure for further price decreases.

Through these four decades the two metals have always been approximately equal in price. The shift of demand from lead to zinc has apparently been balanced by the discovery of sufficiently more zinc than lead to prevent any change in the price ratio. The prices of lead and zinc do not always move together, however, and sizable short-term differences can occur. Over the period 1925-64 the two prices show almost identical degrees of stability, whether measured by the average deviation from the average for the period or by the average year-to-year variation (see chapter 3, table B-2). Since World War II the average annual variation has been identical for the two metals, but lead prices have experienced twice as great an average deviation, reaching the highest degree of instability for any of the commodities included in this study.

Since 1950 the prices of both metals and the pattern of world trade have been influenced by the policies of the United States government. In 1951, with prices high as a result of the Korean War, subsidies were given for exploration and development. In 1956, with prices low and both metals in surplus, lead and zinc were made eligible for barter trade in return for surplus agricultural commodities, the metal being stockpiled and so removed from the market. Some barter transactions have been made in recent years, but the bulk of this trade took place in 1956-57. When imports for the stockpile virtually ended in 1958, prices fell again and U.S. lead-zinc producers sought pro-

---

[4] This summary is based on J. E. Tilton, "The Choice of Trading Partners: An Analysis of International Trade in Aluminum, Bauxite, Copper, Lead, Manganese, Tin and Zinc" (Ph.D. diss., Yale University, 1966). The analysis is for the years 1960-62. See especially pp. 131-37 and 148-54.

tection. Late in 1958 the government imposed import quotas, equal to 80 percent of the 1953-57 average and allocated both between ores and metal and among countries. Imports of semifabricated goods and of certain chemicals were not controlled, and imports of ore for smelting and re-export were allowed outside the quotas.[5]

By early 1965 consumption of both metals had risen so sharply that severe shortages were in prospect, and the government began to consider selling part of its stockpile to satisfy the demand. In the late 1950s and early 1960s consumption had grown very slowly or even declined in the United States, and there was little or no expansion of capacity; mine production was allowed to fall below consumption and the deficit was met by liquidation of stocks, increased secondary recovery, and sizable imports by Europe from the Communist countries. Elsewhere both consumption and production increased rather steadily. The United States released 50,000 tons of lead and 75,000 tons of zinc from the U.S. stockpile in 1964 and a further 36,000 and 150,000 tons, respectively, in 1965. Late in 1965 the import quotas were ended. Prices rose sharply — so much so that in 1964 the producers of zinc abandoned the London Metal Exchange and set a producers' price like those in the United States—but the upheaval has been considerably less for lead and zinc than for copper. Mine production rapidly increased as prices rose; the development of large reserves in Canada from 1964 onward, and sizable lead discoveries in the United States, promised rapid additions to future supply; there was also far less political uncertainty or difficulty than in the case of copper and less demand induced by war. By 1967 producers in the United States were again requesting import quotas, but none were imposed. The surplus of both metals was reduced somewhat by strikes which decreased United States smelter output, but large government stocks remained available for disposal.

The price decline in 1958 also led to international efforts to control the surplus of lead and zinc, through the formation in 1959 of the International Lead-Zinc Study Group after a United Nations Commodity Conference. The twenty-five member countries, including both producers and consumers, agreed to collaborate in gathering and publishing information, and have also supported research to develop new uses for the metals and defend them against competitive materials. The Group has not evolved into a cartel to control exports or prices, as occurred with the Study Group on Tin, although the governments of the less developed producer members have urged its conversion to a commodity agreement with strict controls. The smaller importance of governments as producers relative to the case of tin, the large number of companies engaged in trade and their international character, and the importance of U.S. capital in all stages of the industry, have prevented this development and will probably continue to do so barring a severe disruption of the industry or widespread intervention

by producer governments. In 1959 the Study Group agreed on voluntary restrictions on output, but these were dropped for zinc in 1960 and for lead the next year. Participation was too limited, and the reductions too small, to have much effect on prices; no action has been recommended since 1961. In 1966 and 1967 producers in several countries restricted output, but there has been no concerted action and no effect on the creation of new productive capacity.

The exact effect of U.S. and international policies on the production, trade, and revenues of the various producers cannot readily be discerned. To the extent that the U.S. quotas resulted in higher domestic production all exporters to that country suffered. In many years, however, one or more of the quotas was not filled, while non-quota imports, in bond or in uncontrolled forms, were fairly high. In the early 1960s, the restriction appeared to be tightest in zinc metal trade; Canada was also discriminated against in lead metal exports and Mexico in zinc ore trade.[6] On this basis both Peru and Mexico were hurt by the restrictions. However, both countries were large suppliers under the 1956-58 barter program. Peru has held a favored position in selling outside the United States, and Mexico has supplied large amounts of non-quota imports. On balance it is impossible to say whether Latin America has been hurt, either absolutely or in comparison with other exporting areas, by these policies.

Lead and Zinc in Latin America

The general distribution of the region's exports of lead and zinc and the reasons for this pattern have already been noted. The metals are significant items in the balance of payments of Mexico, Peru, and Bolivia; Argentina also exports some zinc metal, as the country's production, determined by lead requirements, exceeds domestic demand; and Guatemala, Honduras, and Chile ship small amounts of one or both metals (see tables 6-6A and 6-6B). At the peak, usually in the early or middle 1950s, Mexico earned $100 million or one-eighth of all foreign exchange from lead and zinc; Peru, over $50 million or nearly one-sixth of all exports; and Bolivia as much as $26 million or one-fifth of the total. The share contributed by the two metals has since fallen in Mexico as the value of exports shrank, and in Peru as new exports, such as copper and fishmeal, were developed. In Bolivia the share has also fallen, although the total contraction of exports moderated the decline. Exports to the United States, the largest customer, fell after the Korean War and again with the end of barter trade and the imposition of quotas; since 1964 this trade has revived. Recovery of the European lead-zinc industries after World War II has also reduced that region's relative importance somewhat; the slight shift has been mostly toward greater exports to Japan. In the years since 1950 there has been no

---

[5]For a discussion of the relation of these policies to prices, and in particular to price differences between lead and zinc over time and among markets, see I. B. Kravis and R. E. Lipsey, *Comparative Prices of Nonferrous Metals in International Trade, 1953-64*, National Bureau of Economic Research, Occasional Paper 98 (Columbia University Press, 1966), especially pp. 46-50.

[6]Tilton, "The Choice of Trading Partners." This conclusion applies only to the years 1960-62. The fact that some suppliers filled their quotas while others did not is, of course, only the roughest measure of the discriminatory impact of the quotas and indicates nothing of their total effect on trade.

pronounced change in the type or destination of Latin American exports; the fluctuations in value reflect the decline in Mexican and Bolivian trade and especially the course of prices.

Since lead and, to a lesser degree, zinc, are often found together with silver, and since silver was the chief metal produced in Latin America in the colonial period, deposits of both lead and zinc were discovered and worked early in the region's mining history. Neither metal was produced in significant quantities, however, until late in the nineteenth century; consumption in Latin America was extremely low, and the United States and Europe were originally self-sufficient. Both metals were first mined in quantity in Mexico, which had a large number of accessible high-grade deposits and the advantage of proximity to importing countries. By 1913 Mexico had become the world's fourth largest lead producer, with an annual output of 100,000 tons; during the 1920s it became second only to the United States.[7] The zinc industry developed somewhat later in consequence of the lower demand for zinc and the difficulty of concentrating its ores until flotation techniques were developed. World War I provided the first major impetus to zinc mining in Mexico.[8] During World War II Mexico became the world's third largest zinc producer. Smelting was established as soon as mining in the case of lead, and by the 1920s 90 percent of the country's output was treated domestically. Some zinc was also smelted quite early, but the greatest expansion of production occurred in the 1930s and 1940s, and even then amounted to only about one-fifth of mine output. Since 1964 another smelter has gone into operation, but the bulk of zinc is still exported as concentrates. In the last few decades Mexican production of ores has increased in zinc relative to lead, and production of the latter has declined slightly. Since lead consumption has risen sharply, the amount of lead available for export has dropped, while that of zinc has continued to increase.

As in Mexico, silver was mined in Peru for centuries before the associated lead and zinc were exploited. The present industry was established in the late 1920s with the development of the large reserves of the Cerro de Pasco area and the installation of a lead smelter shortly after large-scale mining began.[9] Lead production was surpassed by zinc in the early 1950s; zinc smelting started in the 1940s but remained quite small until about a decade ago.

Bolivia also became a significant lead exporter during the 1920s. While lead output fell and slowly recovered during the next two decades, zinc production expanded rapidly. At the time of nationalization of the three major mining companies in 1952, Bolivia was producing some 30,000 tons of lead and 35,000 tons of zinc, virtually all of which was exported as concentrates. Over the next decade lead output

dropped considerably and zinc production almost stopped. Both industries suffered the same problems as tin mining in the wake of the revolution.[10] The price declines at the end of the Korean War and again in 1958 increased the difficulties, especially, it appears, in the case of zinc. In recent years there has been a slight recovery, but not enough to restore Bolivia to its previous importance in Latin American production. Except for small amounts of lead, solders, and other tin alloys, there is no smelting of either metal in Bolivia.

In the other significant Latin American producers—Argentina for both metals and Brazil for lead—production has developed to meet domestic demand rather than exports. Lead mining and smelting were begun early in Argentina, but by 1930 local production could meet less than one-third of demand and the country imported large amounts of lead ore to supply its protected smelting industry. In the next decade or so a determined effort was made to achieve self-sufficiency, including high tariffs on lead in all forms, and output rose sixfold. The new reserves developed included substantial amounts of zinc; mining began in the late 1930s, followed some years later by smelting. Over the last two decades lead output has been fairly stable, while zinc production has varied greatly. Argentina is self-sufficient in slab zinc, exporting its excess production in the form of concentrates; the tariff originally designed for lead protects zinc also and allows the country to export although it is a relatively high-cost producer. Brazil, too, after a tenfold expansion of output in the 1940s, produces and smelts lead to meet much of its domestic requirements. Although some zinc reserves are known, no zinc is mined or smelted. Guatemala and Honduras became producers of lead and zinc as a result of shortages before and during the Korean War; output has since stopped in Guatemala but increased in Honduras under the stimulus of rising silver prices. Small amounts of one or both metals are produced in Chile, Colombia, and Ecuador.

Many of the small, high-grade deposits of lead and zinc throughout Latin America were originally exploited by individuals or by small, locally-owned companies. In some countries, notably Bolivia and Peru, domestic private concerns still control a large share of mining; but development of the largest deposits and creation of the smelting industry have generally depended on foreign capital. U.S. companies were and are most active, but the Mexican industry also included much British capital, and French firms invested in Mexico, Peru, Brazil, and Bolivia. The pattern of ownership developed since the turn of the century (and particularly since the late 1920s) by the introduction of foreign capital has since been modified in two cases: by nationalization and transfer to state control in Bolivia in 1952; and by "Mexicanization," or sale of control to nationals, in Mexico following legislation passed in 1960. Some foreign-owned companies sold their entire holdings; others have retained the 49 percent ownership allowed by the law for receipt of

[7] Imperial Mineral Resources Bureau of Great Britain, *The Mineral Industry of the British Empire and Foreign Countries: Lead* (London, 1933), pp. 179-85.

[8] Imperial Mineral Resources Bureau, *The Mineral Industry of the British Empire and Foreign Countries: Zinc* (London, 1930), pp. 133-36.

[9] Imperial Mineral Resources, ... *Lead*, pp. 210-14, and ... *Zinc*, pp. 150-51.

[10] See chap. 7, under the heading "Tin in Latin America," for a discussion of the Bolivian Revolution of 1952 and its effects on the country's mining industry.

tax reductions; and a few, which supply only the domestic market, have had no inducement to sell.[11]

Except in Bolivia, state ownership or operation in the industry is quite rare, although there is some state participation through development corporations or mining banks. If ownership is considered, lead and zinc in Latin America are dominated by foreign—almost entirely U.S.—capital; the dominance is much less in Mexico because of legal control (see table 6-7). Local private capital is found in most countries and is quite important in Mexico, Bolivia, and Peru; but only in Mexico, and to a lesser extent in Argentina, does local private enterprise control much smelting capacity. Generally the integrated, foreign-owned firms account for exports of metal and it is chiefly domestic firms which export their output as concentrates. They also sell concentrates to the larger firms for processing. State control will decline in Bolivia as the large zinc reserves of the Matilde district are brought into production from 1970 onward by a U.S. firm. An agreement to allow the mining of this state-owned but unexploited property, which will raise Bolivian zinc output by some 55,000 tons annually, was reached in 1966; this was part of a major decision to allow foreign capital to share with COMIBOL, the state company, in exploitation of the country's minerals.[12]

In 1965 Latin America produced a total of over 400,000 tons of lead and almost 600,000 tons of zinc, and exported three-fourths of the former and nearly all of the total supply of the latter (see table 6-8). Intraregional trade was negligible in lead but somewhat larger in zinc, amounting to around one-tenth of total consumption and one-sixth of consumption outside of Argentina, Mexico, and Peru. Since then trade in lead has expanded substantially. Consumption of zinc is nearly double that of lead; in zinc it absorbs most of smelter production, but in lead it accounts for less than one-third of the metal produced in the region.

Political importance has not been associated with lead and zinc as it has with certain other Latin American export commodities, perhaps because no country has depended so heavily on them. Where they have become involved in major questions of public policy, it has been in association with the entire nonferrous metal mining industry. In Bolivia, for example, when the three principal mining companies were nationalized in 1952, the largest lead mines and a sizable share of zinc production were transferred to state control along with the tin mines. However, because lead and zinc generally occur at much higher grades than tin, the bulk of production of both metals was in numerous small mines, which remained in private hands. Furthermore, the recent agreement on the development of state-owned zinc reserves will result in heavy participation by foreign capital in zinc mining in the 1970s. The change will be much smaller for lead, and foreign participation in tin

mining — politically and economically the most important part of the country's mineral economy — will be quite small.

Similarly, the transfer of foreign-controlled companies to national majority ownership in Mexico does not affect lead and zinc exclusively but also applies to copper. It may be seen as part of the Mexican government's general policy of securing national control of the country's resources, at least where they are exported and thus dependent on market conditions and government policies abroad. The industry's dependence on the U.S. market and the high share of U.S. ownership ruled out nationalization, particularly in the depressed condition of lead and zinc in the early 1960s. "Mexicanization" proceeded slowly at first, as much local capital had to be raised and the measure caused some uncertainty among producers, some of whom elected to sell out entirely. Thus far there appear to have been no adverse effects on production or trade patterns; it is still too early to be sure of the effect, if any, on investment. For many years the Mexican nonferrous metal mining industry has been burdened with a variety of taxes and restrictions which make it difficult to close uneconomic mines or to expand operations; these obstacles limit the effect of the tax reductions associated with changes in ownership.

In Peru, lead and zinc mining have benefited from the government policy of expanding and diversifying exports. Export taxes were greatly reduced in 1948, and legislation was simplified in other respects. The government participates in the industry through a mining bank which deals only with the smaller producers; it has not challenged or competed with the major foreign-owned companies.[13]

Outlook

The estimation of future demand for lead and zinc, even over the next decade, presents some problems beyond those of how rapidly incomes may be expected to grow and how this growth will be translated into demand for the goods in which lead and zinc are now used. The past fifteen years or so, in which lead consumption grew very slowly or even declined in some countries and years, may have been quite untypical and a hazardous base for projections. The industry, especially in the United States, seems to have reached a low point and then to have begun to recover, but it is not clear whether there has been a lasting change in the scope and pattern of consumption. The future rate of substitution by and for both metals is similarly uncertain, as are the future results of recent research into new applications. These factors in turn may affect the rate of secondary recovery and influence primary requirements more than consumption.

New discoveries in recent years will appreciably affect the distribution of reserves, and probably also of supply, in the next decade. For these reasons, projections made in the early 1960s have already been surpassed or invalidated in many instances, and no attempt will be made here to esti-

---

[11] See chap. 4 for a fuller discussion of this legislation and its effects; although the emphasis there is on copper, the law applies to all nonferrous mineral industries. The law provides for a large reduction in export taxes for Mexican-controlled companies; foreign-owned firms could not remain competitive. Companies selling entirely in the domestic market have no incentive to "Mexicanize."

[12] *New York Times*, 30 June 1966. See also *Engineering and Mining Journal*, February 1968, p. 103.

[13] For a more detailed discussion of policies in Mexico and Peru with respect to copper, see chap. 4, under the heading "Copper and Political Issues."

mate in detail the future distribution of demand and supply.[14]

Cumulative world requirements over the period 1960-2000 have been estimated as approximately 130 million tons of lead and 170 million tons of zinc. Reserves as of 1965 were only 50 and 85 million tons, respectively. At that time inferred reserves were estimated as some 100 to 150 million tons of lead and a comparable amount of zinc. These quantities would meet world needs to the end of this century, but with a much smaller margin of adequacy than for other major metals. Reserves of iron ore are enormous, and methods are already developed for mining relatively hard, low-grade materials. Satisfaction of future demand for copper appears to depend more on cost reductions allowing the mining of known low-grade ores than on new discoveries. For lead and zinc, in contrast, it appears that large new reserves need to be found over the next few decades. Recent exploration in Missouri indicates the existence of about 30 million tons of lead and 10 million tons of zinc; several million tons of each have also been found in New Brunswick and Ontario. These discoveries, although substantial, do not greatly affect the long-run resource balance. Before the end of the century it may be necessary to develop means of exploiting the low-grade deposits not now counted as inferred reserves.[15]

On the assumption that the United States would stabilize its lead and zinc output by continuation of quotas or other import restrictions, it was estimated by 1975 the industrial countries would require some 1.5 to 1.6 million tons of lead imports and 2.1 to 2.3 million tons of zinc. These figures include some intra-European trade and small net imports from the Soviet Bloc. Since these projections were made, however, Canada has emerged as the world's foremost zinc exporter, quotas have been eliminated in the United States, and enough lead and zinc have been discovered in North America to suggest a large increase in production in both countries in the near future. Thus the market for exports from Latin America may be substantially less in the 1970s than was anticipated. In particular, the United States may decline in importance, and a greater share of exports be sold within the region or to Europe and Japan. In this respect lead and zinc would follow the pattern set in the 1950s and early 1960s by both copper and iron ore. Nonetheless the share of Latin American production of each metal which is exported to the rest of the world will show at most a slight decline: while consumption in the region may grow more rapidly than exports, it will continue to account for only a small share of total output. Only in Mexico does it appear likely that domestic consumption will materially reduce supplies for export. In Argentina a sizable expansion of output is planned, which should make more of both metals available for export; and in Bolivia zinc production, all of it initially to be exported as concentrates, is to expand greatly. No projections are available for production or consumption in other countries such as Brazil, Chile, Colombia, and Venezuela. Peruvian output is expected to continue to grow slowly, mostly for export.

The worldwide expansion of capacity planned or in progress, together with relatively slow growth of demand, suggests a surplus of both lead and zinc and downward pressure on prices perhaps until the early 1970s. Restrictions of output by producers, joint action through the International Lead-Zinc Study Group, or the reimposition of import barriers in the United States are all possible, but no estimate will be attempted of their likelihood or probable effects. At present the creation of a real control scheme for lead and zinc does not seem likely despite some pressure from the governments of underdeveloped exporting countries. Their attention is more likely to be focused on the continued transfer of smelting capacity from importing to exporting countries, and on the elimination of barriers to trade in semifabricated metal and light manufactures. Except for the United States, the principal importing countries in Europe and Japan have no tariffs on ores and concentrates of lead and zinc; they do however protect their smelting and fabricating industries by duties which, in the European Common Market and Japan, afford a rather high degree of effective protection. A few of these rates were substantially lowered in the Kennedy Round of trade negotiations, but most were not.[16] As with other metals and their manufactures, these barriers will probably receive increasing attention as obstacles to industrial development for export in Latin America and other underdeveloped regions. For the near future, however, no such development is likely to reduce the importance to the region of exports of concentrates and unwrought metal.

[14] For projections to 1985, including estimates of the sources of imports for the advanced countries, see Bela Balassa, *Trade Prospects for Developing Countries* (Homewood: Irwin, 1964), especially pp. 436-37. Longer-term estimates of demand and assessments of resource adequacy are presented in Landsberg et al., *Resources in America's Future* (Johns Hopkins Press for Resources for the Future, 1963), pp. 312 ff. and 463-68.

[15] See W. W. Weigel, "The Inside Story of Missouri's Exploration Boom," *Engineering and Mining Journal*, November and December 1965; the articles on Canada and Ireland in the latter issue; and Brooks, "The Lead-Zinc Anomaly."

[16] See B. Balassa, "The Effects of the Kennedy Round on the Exports of Processed Goods from Developing Areas," UNCTAD doc. TD/69, 15 February 1968, app. pp. 9-10.

CHAPTER 6 TABLES

TABLE 6-1. World Reserves of Lead (1962) and Zinc (1963)
(Thousands of tons metal content, measured and indicated ore)[a]

Country or Region	Lead Reserves	Lead Share (%)	Zinc Reserves	Zinc Share (%)
Latin America	6,500	13	10,000	12
Mexico	3,500	7	4,000	5
South America[b]	3,000	6	6,000	7
United States	6,000	12	12,200	14
Canada	9,000	18	19,000	22
Western Europe	5,600	11	13,000	15
Communist Countries[c]	10,100	20	13,000	15
Africa[d]	4,000	8	4,500	5
Asia (incl. China)[e]	2,600	5	8,000	9
Oceania (Australia)	6,000	12	5,300	6
World Total	50,000	100	85,000	100

Sources: USBM, *Mineral Facts and Problems, 1965*. H. M. Callaway, *Lead: A Materials Survey* (USBM, 1962). Information supplied by International Activities Division, USBM.

[a]Data are given in short tons, but accuracy is too low to differentiate short from metric tons.

[b]Total estimate for Argentina, Bolivia, Brazil, and Peru; Peru accounts for well over half the total. Reserves in other Latin American countries are insignificant by comparison.

[c]Excluding China, North Vietnam, and North Korea.

[d]Principally Morocco and South West Africa.

[e]No reliable estimates for Chinese reserves exist; reserves have been estimated by K. P. Wang in "Rich Mineral Resources Spur Communist China's Bid for Industrial Power" (USBM, *Mineral Trade Notes*, Special Supplement No. 59, 1960) as 3 million tons each of lead and zinc, but these figures were later regarded as too high.

TABLE 6-2A. World Mine Production of Lead, 1925-1967
(Thousands of metric tons lead content)

Country or Region	Average 1925-29	Average 1930-34	Average 1935-39	Average 1940-44	Average 1945-49	1950	1951	1952	1953	1954	1955	1956
Latin America[a]	256.3	197.0	294.9	275.3	288.3	358.0	372.5	397.6	382.0	370.8	386.7	395.6
Argentina	3.5	4.0	15.3	23.6	19.1	19.4	22.8	19.0	16.0	20.2	24.0	28.3
Bolivia[b]	16.5	8.7	14.1	12.1	16.8	31.2	30.6	30.0	23.8	18.2	19.1	21.6
Brazil		0.5	0.3			4.0	3.5	2.8	3.0	2.7	3.7	3.5
Chile	2.1		0.4		2.5	3.3	7.8	4.0	3.2	3.0	4.0	3.3
Ecuador					0.3	0.2		0.1	0.1		0.1	0.1
Guatemala					1.0	3.0	3.3	4.2	7.1	2.4	4.6	8.1
Honduras					0.3	0.3	0.5	0.5	1.0	1.5	1.8	2.1
Mexico	222.9	176.3	223.9	190.5	196.5	238.1	225.5	246.0	221.5	216.6	210.8	200.0
Peru	11.4	7.6	41.0	49.1	53.4	62.1	82.3	95.8	114.6	110.0	118.7	129.1
Canada	139.4	163.7	207.2	227.6	166.6	150.3	143.5	153.2	177.6	198.2	183.9	171.3
United States	602.5	329.4	354.2	414.5	346.6	390.8	352.1	353.9	310.8	295.2	306.6	320.0
Western Europe	242.4	234.9	207.3	189.6	109.0	172.9	175.5	184.3	215.0	310.7	244.6	240.6
Africa	57.1	27.8	45.2	24.2	65.6	119.9	151.2	184.6	192.0	211.0	242.4	227.0
Asia	106.7	105.9	112.0	76.2	8.8	20.0	39.0	46.2	51.6	73.3	112.3	128.3
Oceania	199.0	205.3	253.1	251.1	198.2	222.3	228.1	234.5	248.8	289.3	300.7	304.2
Communist Countries	10.6	66.9	137.1	89.3	123.7	205.1	219.7	246.3	282.8	309.9	343.4	374.3
World Total	1,635	1,333	1,612	1,552	1,333	1,678	1,714	1,841	1,905	2,059	2,204	2,258
L.A. Share (%)	15.7	14.8	18.3	17.7	21.6	21.4	21.7	21.6	20.1	18.0	17.5	17.5

Country or Region	1957	1958	1959	1960	1961	1962	1963	1964	1965	1966	1967
Latin America[a]	427.9	405.9	380.6	397.7	397.2	393.3	412.8	387.8	403.6	404.1	410.7
Argentina	29.1	29.0	30.5	26.7	28.4	29.6	26.5	25.9	32.2	29.5	32.2
Bolivia[b]	26.3	22.8	22.0	21.4	20.3	18.6	19.0	16.5	16.3	19.5	19.7
Brazil	3.5	4.3	7.5	11.1	14.0	15.2	17.4	14.7	22.5	22.6	23.4
Chile	2.9	2.6	2.0	2.4	2.0	1.5	0.9	1.1	0.8	0.8	0.4
Ecuador	0.1	0.1	0.1	0.1	0.1	0.1	0.2	0.2	0.1	0.1	
Guatemala	11.4	8.0	5.8	8.6	8.6	1.0	0.7	1.2	0.9	0.9	1.2
Honduras	2.7	3.1	3.3	5.4	6.1	5.9	9.9	7.5	9.7	11.7	11.7
Mexico	214.8	201.9	190.6	190.6	181.3	193.3	189.0	170.0	166.8	174.2	163.9
Peru	137.1	134.1	118.7	131.6	136.4	128.2	149.2	150.7	154.3	144.8	158.2
Canada	164.6	169.3	164.7	186.5	165.6	191.7	180.5	187.2	274.8	293.2	308.2
United States	306.8	242.5	231.8	223.8	237.6	214.9	229.9	259.5	273.2	297.0	287.5
Western Europe	270.8	269.3	261.5	243.5	278.0	263.1	245.8	240.7	256.1	314.9	344.7
Africa	230.6	223.2	216.9	213.8	195.8	203.4	193.5	204.2	217.7	206.5	163.3
Asia	135.9	147.3	159.8	210.5	228.2	235.7	293.4	255.3	265.8	258.5	246.5
Oceania	338.6	332.6	319.3	313.0	273.9	376.0	416.9	380.9	368.0	370.8	378.2
Communist Countries[c]	395.2	413.1	425.1	473.3	514.1	493.1	593.3	610.3	638.4	689.4	703.0
World Total	2,376	2,322	2,295	2,395	2,376	2,508	2,518	2,531	2,701	2,850	2,842
L.A. Share (%)	18.0	17.4	16.5	16.7	16.7	15.7	16.4	15.3	14.9	14.2	14.5

Sources: Callaway, Lead..., pp. 80-87. USBM, Minerals Yearbook, 1967.

[a]Includes small quantities for El Salvador in 1945-49, 1950, 1951, and 1952.
[b]Exports.
[c]Estimated from lead smelter production.

TABLE 6-2B. World Mine Production of Zinc, 1925-1967
(Thousands of metric tons zinc content)

Country or Region	Average 1925-29	Average 1930-34	Average 1935-39	Average 1940-44	Average 1945-49	1950	1951	1952	1953	1954	1955	1956
Latin America	139.7	118.0	182.7	234.2	253.7	344.2	334.6	417.9	415.5	425.0	491.4	480.5
Argentina			8.9	27.5	12.1	12.7	15.5	15.4	16.1	20.0	21.1	23.9
Bolivia[a]	3.9	11.3	10.4	11.9	16.9	19.6	30.5	35.6	24.0	20.3	21.3	17.1
Chile	0.5						0.6	3.3	3.2	1.5	2.9	2.7
Cuba											1.0	1.5
Guatemala						0.3	6.5	8.2	6.1	4.0	9.4	10.9
Honduras						0.1	0.1	0.3	0.6	0.7	1.3	2.1
Mexico	126.1	103.2	149.4	165.4	170.2	223.5	180.0	227.3	226.5	223.5	269.3	248.8
Peru	9.1	3.5	14.0	29.4	54.5	87.9	101.3	127.8	139.1	155.0	166.0	175.1
Canada	77.7	167.3	228.4	299.1	254.9	284.1	309.4	337.2	364.4	338.7	393.1	383.3
United States	657.2	383.4	511.5	661.0	553.1	565.4	617.8	604.1	496.5	429.4	466.8	491.9
Western Europe	283.6	265.3	355.4	424.9[b]	152.7	287.5	321.5	370.0	358.0	364.0	432.9	464.8
Africa	32.9	17.0	31.3	33.5	69.1	146.9	175.5	196.3	239.4	207.3	193.2	229.5
Asia	91.6	87.5	122.6	110.0	27.4	53.0	79.0	99.0	112.0	125.0	130.0	144.0
Oceania	155.4	115.8	195.3	201.1	140.8	201.1	193.8	200.4	240.8	256.7	260.6	282.5
Communist Countries	84.5[c]	37.4[d]	42.8[e]	(f)	173.3	269.5	285.6	358.0	414.0	505.5	524.0	591.0
World Total	1,523	1,192	1,670	1,971	1,645	2,150	2,322	2,585	2,648	2,648	2,902	3,101
L.A. Share (%)	9.2	9.9	10.9	11.9	15.4	16.0	14.4	16.2	15.7	16.0	16.9	15.5

Country or Region	1957	1958	1959	1960	1961	1962	1963	1964	1965	1966	1967
Latin America	460.7	417.2	454.2	495.6	495.9	455.9	473.9	525.2	544.5	549.3	617.7
Argentina	29.4	36.4	40.8	35.4	32.2	31.5	28.7	22.9	29.7	26.4	27.2
Bolivia	19.7	14.2	3.4	4.0	5.3	3.6	4.2	9.6	13.6	16.0	16.8
Chile	2.5	1.2	1.0	1.0	0.1	0.5	0.5	1.0	1.4	2.1	1.1
Colombia		0.1	0.7	0.3	1.3	0.3	0.6	0.7	0.4	0.8	(f)
Cuba	0.7										
Guatemala	9.3	4.8	4.3	10.0	7.9	6.4	10.7	8.6	11.1	12.4	13.1
Honduras	2.3	1.3	1.3	4.3	6.2	0.8	1.2	0.8	0.9	0.9	0.4
Mexico	243.0	224.1	263.9	262.4	268.9	250.6	233.1	244.9	232.9	232.9	241.2
Peru	154.4	135.2	143.1	178.1	173.8	162.2	194.9	236.7	254.5	257.8	317.9
Canada	375.3	385.6	359.2	369.0	401.9	455.3	451.0	662.2	826.4	949.8	1,133.1
United States	482.3	373.7	385.8	394.9	421.2	458.5	480.0	521.4	554.4	519.4	498.4
Western Europe	477.3	476.0	486.0	460.0	476.9	480.5	509.5	499.2	467.6	496.9	426.0
Africa	247.6	249.5	221.1	258.8	242.4	240.8	249.5	270.8	297.6	284.9	165.3
Asia	158.0	169.5	163.0	189.5	206.7	224.0	232.3	257.2	268.1	301.2	287.4
Oceania	296.2	267.2	279.7	322.4	316.1	342.9	357.1	350.1	354.8	375.3	404.4
Communist Countries	619.0	670.0	755.0	827.0	871.0	895.0	904.6	945.5	999.3	1,037.3	1,115.1
World Total	3,129	3,057	3,084	3,320	3,456	3,528	3,661	4,021	4,310	4,500	4,695
L.A. Share (%)	14.7	13.6	14.7	14.9	14.3	12.9	12.9	13.1	12.6	12.2	13.2

Sources: USBM, Materials Survey: Zinc (1951); and Minerals Yearbook.

aExports.
b1940-43 average.
cIncludes 1928-30 average for Soviet Union.
dPrincipally Rumania; smelter production.
eExcludes Soviet Union, for which data are not available.
fNot available; estimate included in total.

TABLE 6-3. World Consumption of Lead and Zinc, Averages, 1936-38, 1949-51, and 1962-64
       (Thousands of metric tons)

Country or Region	Lead[a]			Zinc[b]		
	1936-38	1949-51	1962-64	1936-38	1949-51	1962-64
Latin America	25.7	92.3	102.7	13.5	41.3	90.1
Argentina[c]		34.1	24.8	6.5[d]	10.2	19.9
Brazil		19.1	18.4	2.6[d]	11.1	40.6
Mexico		8.9	55.2		10.9	27.5
Peru			3.9			2.1
Canada	21.9	48.7	50.0	16.2	47.5	76.7
United States[e]	437.5	519.6	666.0	484.2	871.0	1,005.6
Western Europe	889.7	553.9	1,008.0	173.0	654.2	1,150.0
Africa	56.5	11.0	22.0	3.2	14.1	29.2
Asia	118.7	38.2	135.8	112.7	86.3	359.0
Oceania	24.2	19.5	42.8	29.2	47.0	98.4
Communist Countries	126.1	158.6	574.4	139.3	228.5	646.0
World Total	1,645	1,579	2,656	1,551	1,902	3,512
Latin American Consumption as Share of:						
World Consumption (%)	1.6	5.8	3.9	0.9	2.2	2.6
L.A. Mine Production (%)	8.2	30.9	25.9	6.9	14.3	18.6

Sources: ABMS, *Yearbook.*

[a]Primary lead only, except for some secondary material recovered in primary smelters, in the form of bars or ingots; excludes chemicals and semimanufactures.

[b]Slab zinc only.

[c]May include some imports for stockpiling, and some secondary lead.

[d]1938 only.

[e]Excludes lead for stockpiling.

TABLE 6-4A. World Smelter Production of Lead, 1925-1967
(Thousands of metric tons)

Country or Region	Average 1925-29	Average 1930-34	Average 1935-39	Average 1940-44	Average 1945-49	1950	1951	1952	1953	1954	1955	1956
Latin America[a]	235.6	184.0	247.4	241.2	245.9	285.6	290.0	307.7	289.9	292.8	288.9	283.7
Argentina	8.3	5.6	10.0	18.9	18.2	19.0	23.7	19.8	13.0	22.9	18.0	24.3
Bolivia											2.1	1.5
Brazil				0.1	0.5	4.2	3.0	1.9	2.9	3.0	3.7	3.5
Guatemala					0.1	0.3	0.1	0.3	0.7	0.1		0.1
Mexico	218.7	174.8	220.1	185.4	191.1	230.9	219.1	237.4	214.9	209.1	203.6	194.1
Peru	8.6	3.6	17.4	36.8	35.9	31.7	44.2	48.6	59.0	57.7	61.1	60.4
Canada	133.0	127.5	169.8	191.9	144.7	154.5	147.6	166.3	150.9	145.5	135.9	135.4
United States[b]	631.5	340.2	362.9	461.6	380.8	458.1	376.1	428.5	424.2	441.4	434.4	491.8
Western Europe	422.4	353.3	371.4	266.8	185.5	304.2	308.2	334.6	366.3	319.0	404.5	432.0
Africa	25.9	20.6	26.4	12.5	23.1	49.5	59.4	68.4	66.4	69.1	70.3	68.4
Asia	74.4	80.7	86.6	79.6	9.4	14.0	16.9	19.3	30.2	44.6	61.4	77.5
Oceania	165.2	184.2	230.4	220.0	154.7	200.7	200.8	197.4	209.8	242.3	228.1	240.5
Communist Countries	50.2	53.6	94.8	126.0	116.8	207.1	214.2	270.2	312.3	332.7	416.9	456.2
World Total	1,746	1,346	1,599	1,610	1,449	1,678	1,637	1,796	1,850	1,959	2,041	2,186
Latin American Smelter Production as Share of:												
World Smelter Production (%)	13.5	13.7	15.5	15.0	17.0	17.0	17.0	17.1	15.7	14.9	14.2	13.0
L.A. Mine Production (%)	91.9	93.4	83.7	87.6	85.2	79.7	77.9	77.4	75.9	79.0	74.8	71.6

Country or Region	1957	1958	1959	1960	1961	1962	1963	1964	1965	1966	1967
Latin America	311.0	289.7	282.5	296.6	293.2	296.0	307.9	293.1	293.8	301.4	297.3
Argentina	25.9	32.8	31.0	25.7	28.0	24.5	24.0	23.0	32.0	22.0	36.3
Bolivia	2.3	0.8	0.2	0.1		0.1	0.3	0.5	0.9	1.1	0.2
Brazil	3.5	4.3	7.5	10.0	11.9	13.7	16.0	13.1	9.7	17.2	17.2
Chile				0.6	0.5	0.3	0.2	0.1	0.1		
Guatemala		0.3		0.2	0.1	0.1	0.1			0.2	0.1
Mexico	210.2	187.0	187.0	186.2	176.4	189.1	186.2	166.7	164.3	172.1	161.7
Peru	69.1	64.4	56.8	74.1	76.4	68.3	81.1	89.7	86.8	88.8	81.8
Canada	130.6	127.8	127.8	145.2	156.3	138.5	140.6	137.4	169.2	167.7	172.6
United States[b]	483.9	425.7	309.2	346.9	407.7	341.1	358.1	407.6	379.4	399.8	344.6
Western Europe	456.7	509.1	477.7	489.6	488.6	482.9	442.9	431.9	466.9	477.3	525.6
Africa	73.4	74.6	67.5	65.2	58.3	54.8	52.8	91.9	118.8	126.8	126.7
Asia	88.1	79.8	104.1	121.4	224.0	236.0	246.4	266.2	279.0	287.2	313.7
Oceania	243.1	252.6	241.6	246.4	212.0	267.4	310.1	285.9	264.4	271.7	291.1
Communist Countries	502.7	541.7	582.3	532.6	566.4	588.5	561.1	612.2	641.7	686.3	715.7
World Total	2,290	2,268	2,195	2,313	2,403	2,420	2,526	2,613	2,711	2,791	
Latin American Smelter Production as Share of:											
World Smelter Production (%)	13.6	12.8	12.9	12.8	12.2	12.3	12.7	11.6	11.2	11.1	10.7
L.A. Mine Production (%)	72.7	71.2	74.4	74.8	73.9	75.3	74.3	74.7	72.2	73.5	72.0

Sources: See table 6-2A.
[a]Includes 500 tons for Chile in 1955.
[b]Refined lead production.

TABLE 6-4B. World Smelter Production of Zinc, 1925-1967
(Thousands of metric tons)

Country or Region	Average 1925-29	Average 1930-34	Average 1935-39	Average 1940-44	Average 1945-49	1950	1951	1952	1953	1954	1955	1956
Latin America	8.0	30.3	34.4	47.0	53.1	62.3	69.7	65.6	73.5	81.1	86.6	80.5
Argentina				0.7	1.9	7.5	10.1	10.0	11.6	10.9	13.5	14.7
Mexico	8.0	30.3	34.4	45.5	49.9	53.5	58.7	50.4	53.0	54.9	56.0	56.4
Peru				0.8	1.2	1.3	0.9	5.2	8.9	15.4	17.1	9.4
Canada	61.9	100.3	146.4	179.6	172.3	185.4	198.3	201.5	227.6	193.9	231.0	231.8
United States	546.2	302.5	439.9	761.9	706.9	765.0	799.6	820.4	830.9	727.8	874.5	891.0
Western Europe	454.6	393.0	590.0	493.0	304.0[a]	565.2	619.5	625.3	643.7	733.3	830.5	791.0
Africa	5.6	13.5	15.9	13.7	20.2	23.1	22.9	23.3	33.5	59.0	62.4	71.5
Asia	20.2	31.2	49.2	64.4	19.6	49.0	56.3	70.0	77.1	101.8	112.3	136.0
Oceania	49.6	54.9	71.0	77.7	79.6	85.0	78.2	88.8	91.6	106.2	103.0	106.6
Communist Countries	156.1	140.1	181.2			232.5	252.8	302.8	343.4	398.0	483.0	500.0
World Total	1,302	1,063	1,526	1,727	1,560	1,969	2,096	2,195	2,322	2,404	2,660	2,810
Latin American Smelter Production as Share of:												
World Smelter Production (%)	0.6	2.8	2.3	2.7	3.1	3.2	3.3	3.0	3.2	3.4	3.3	3.5
L.A. Mine Production (%)	5.7	25.6	18.9	20.1	21.0	18.1	20.8	15.7	17.7	19.1	17.6	16.7

Country or Region	1957	1958	1959	1960	1961	1962	1963	1964	1965	1966	1967
Latin America	100.7	102.3	98.3	103.3	99.6	106.0	132.0	143.3	148.7	156.5	156.9
Argentina	14.7	15.8	16.0	17.9	14.4	16.8	19.7	22.2	23.6	22.3	23.0
Colombia				0.5	1.3	0.2					
Mexico	56.5	57.5	55.5	52.8	51.7	56.8	56.8	59.4	62.7	71.6	70.9
Peru	29.5	29.0	26.8	32.1	32.2	32.2	55.5	61.7	62.4	62.6	63.0
Canada	224.0	228.7	231.7	236.5	243.0	254.2	257.7	306.4		347.1	359.4
United States	894.8	709.0	724.5	727.4	767.0	795.1	809.8	865.5	902.1	929.9	851.7
Western Europe	812.0	750.5	774.6	812.5	864.3	830.5	813.2	867.3	887.3	820.9	882.3
Africa	79.1	84.1	85.0	83.5	87.1	96.3	102.2	102.3	104.5	103.8	106.0
Asia	138.0	141.0	160.0	179.6	212.2	235.0	282.3	316.1	367.8	445.6	466.0
Oceania	112.0	116.6	118.4	122.0	140.9	170.4	182.7	188.5	202.2	197.5	197.6
Communist Countries	531.0	569.0	650.0	641.5	796.0	800.0	907.9	954.6	1,012.3	1,047.7	891.9
World Total	2,895	2,710	2,850	3,026	3,248	3,407	3,488	3,744	3,950	4,140	3,841
Latin American Smelter Production as Share of:											
World Smelter Production (%)	3.5	3.8	3.4	3.4	3.1	3.1	3.8	3.8	3.8	3.8	4.0
L.A. Mine Production (%)	21.8	24.5	21.7	20.8	20.1	23.2	27.7	27.8	27.5	29.3	23.5

Sources: See table 6-2B.

[a] Excludes smelter production from reclaimed scrap in Germany.

TABLE 6–5. Prices of Lead and Zinc, 1925-1967
(U.S. cents per pound)

Year	Lead St. Louis[b]	Lead LME[c]	Zinc[a] St. Louis	Zinc[a] LME
1925	8.92	7.73	7.62	7.91
1926	8.25	6.74	7.34	7.40
1927	6.52	5.25	6.24	6.19
1928	6.14	4.58	6.03	5.50
1929	6.66	5.04	6.51	5.40
1930	5.38	3.92	4.56	3.60
1931	4.05	2.64	3.64	2.52
1932	3.04	1.86	2.88	2.12
1933	3.74	2.21	4.03	2.96
1934	3.73	2.46	4.16	3.07
1935	3.91	3.12	4.33	3.08
1936	4.56	3.91	4.90	3.31
1937	5.86	5.15	6.52	4.91
1938	4.59	3.33	4.61	3.05
1939	4.90	3.09[d]	5.11	2.89[d]
1940	5.03	4.49[e]	6.34	4.64[e]
1941	5.64	4.49	7.47	4.63
1942	6.33[f]	4.49	8.25[f]	4.63
1943	6.35	4.49	8.25	4.63
1944	6.35	4.49	8.25	4.64
1945	6.35	4.49	8.25	5.18
1946	7.96	8.63	8.73	7.75
1947	14.50	15.27	10.50	12.58
1948	17.87	17.16	13.59	14.38
1949	15.18	16.95	12.14	14.41
1950	13.10	13.29	13.87	14.97
1951	17.29	20.25	18.00	21.59
1952	16.27	16.82	16.22	18.52
1953	13.28	11.48	10.86	9.35
1954	13.85	12.08	10.68	9.82
1955	14.94	13.19	12.30	11.42
1956	15.81	14.52	13.49	12.24
1957	14.46	12.05	11.40	10.34
1958	11.91	9.13	10.31	8.32
1959	12.01	8.88	11.45	10.32
1960	11.75	8.95	12.95	11.09
1961	10.67	8.04	11.54	9.72
1962	9.43	7.04	11.63	8.44
1963	10.94	7.93	12.00	9.59
1964	13.40	12.63	13.57	14.74
1965	15.80	14.38	14.50	14.11
1966	14.92	11.87	14.50	12.75
1967	13.80	10.28	13.85	12.37

TABLE 6–5 – Continued

Sources: ABMS, *Yearbook, 1964*. Callaway, *Lead: A Materials Survey*, p. 130. (Prices reported by *Engineering and Mining Journal*, *Metal Statistics*, *American Metal Market* and *The Mineral Industry*. London prices converted from pounds sterling per long ton at the average annual exchange rate reported by the U.S. Federal Reserve Board.)

[a]Slab zinc, Prime Western grade.
[b]Common (pig) lead, carload lots, delivered at St. Louis.
[c]Lead of 99.97% purity, in lots of 25 long tons, London.
[d]Average of eight months.
[e]LME dealings suspended, 1940-45; maximum price fixed in December 1939.
[f]Price fixed, 1942-45; price shown excludes bonus payments to marginal producers.

TABLE 6–6A. Latin American Exports of Lead by Destination, 1950-1966
(Thousands of metric tons and millions of U.S. dollars)

Exporter and Destination	1950	1951	1952	1953	1954	1955	1956	1957	1958	1959	1960	1961	1962	1963	1964	1965	1966
Bolivia																	
Ores & concentrates (net)	31.2	30.5	30.0	23.8	16.7	17.0	19.9	23.8	22.0	21.8	21.2	20.2	18.4	19.9	17.2	15.9	19.4
Metal		0.5		0.7	1.5	2.1	1.6	2.3	0.8	0.2						1.7	1.8
Total lead content	31.2	31.0	30.0	24.5	17.2	19.1	21.5	26.1	22.8	22.0	21.2	20.2	18.4	19.9	17.2	17.5	21.3
United States	27.2	26.4	22.9	21.3	16.7	21.5	15.6	16.6	13.3	10.2	8.2	10.3	7.5	8.9	7.0		17.3
Value	9.2	11.8	11.0	7.1	5.6	6.3	7.6	8.5	5.9	5.0	4.8	4.1	3.5	4.3	4.9	5.3	6.4
Share total exports (%)	9.8	7.8	7.8	6.3	6.1	6.3	7.1	8.9	9.3	6.6	7.2	5.6	4.7	5.3	4.4	4.1	4.3
Chile																	
Ores & concentrates (gross)		0.5	8.1	6.6	1.1	5.6	3.5	4.7	5.0	0.6	2.6	2.9	2.2	2.9	1.6	0.7	
Argentina			6.6	6.6					1.6		0.7	0.6	0.3	0.6	0.6		
West Germany		0.5	0.4		1.1	4.6	3.5	4.5	3.4	0.4	1.9	2.3	1.7	2.3	1.0		
Total lead content[a]		0.2	4.0	3.3	0.5	2.8	1.7	2.3	2.5	0.3	1.3	1.4	1.1	1.4	0.8	0.4	
Value			0.2	0.1		0.1	0.1	0.1				0.3	0.2	0.3	0.3		
Guatemala																	
Ores & concentrates (net)[b]	0.5	2.9	4.5	6.1	2.4	2.7	6.3	8.2	4.6	0.1	1.6	8.9	1.9	0.3			0.9
Value	0.5	0.4	0.5	0.6	0.4	0.5	1.0	2.0	0.6		0.2	1.1	1.1				
Share total exports (%)	0.6	0.4	0.5	0.6	0.3	0.5	0.8	1.7	0.6		0.2	1.0	0.9				
Honduras																	
Ores & concentrates (net)[b]	0.4	0.3	0.5	1.0	1.5	2.5	2.7	2.7	3.3	3.3	4.5	5.0	4.5	6.2	5.8	10.5	8.3
Value	0.1		0.3		0.4	0.2	0.8	1.8	1.0	1.0	1.0	0.9	1.2	1.6	1.3	2.4	2.0
Share total exports (%)	0.2		0.5		0.6	0.4	1.1	2.8	1.4	1.4	1.5	1.2	1.5	1.9	1.4	1.9	1.4

TABLE 6–6A – Continued

Exporter and Destination	1950	1951	1952	1953	1954	1955	1956	1957	1958	1959	1960	1961	1962	1963	1964	1965	1966
Mexico																	
Ores & concentrates (gross)	6.4	8.8	4.2	15.5	2.7	4.1	3.8	5.0	2.4	1.7	3.6	4.0	4.4	2.9	3.2	2.8	2.5
Impure bars[c] (gross)	8.9	11.9	3.8	2.7	2.7	15.0	10.5	13.0	7.6	13.9	13.5	19.2	10.9	11.9	11.5	10.4	15.2
Refined bars	252.1	166.1	202.5	206.0	200.9	169.0	145.1	155.9	143.4	135.9	131.5	150.8	123.4	124.1	93.2	96.7	98.6
Semimanufactures		0.2			0.8	5.9	13.6	6.1	0.6								
Total (gross)[d]	267.4	187.0	210.5	224.2	207.1	194.0	173.0	180.0	184.0	151.5	148.6	174.0	138.7	138.9	108.3	108.6	113.9
United States	259.7	91.5	176.8	147.6	68.8	101.0	84.8	110.4	118.0	82.9	68.6	85.0	84.3	101.3	93.6	67.7	69.7
Belgium	1.9	10.8	12.4	20.3	7.0	24.0	5.1	7.6	0.9	8.2	3.5	12.7	13.7	5.0	0.7		
United Kingdom		31.7	10.9	47.3	101.9	47.9	40.3	20.3	19.3	25.7	19.6	11.1	2.7	2.2			
Italy										0.2	0.7	10.0	12.0	7.6	3.8		
Total lead content[e]	244.7	157.0	234.8	208.1	208.5	177.7	153.0	162.0	166.0	136.0	134.0	157.0	125.0	125.0	98.0	98.2	102.6
Value	68.7	75.3	76.0	58.5	56.0	57.7	53.1	52.0	35.2	34.0	33.6	37.2	26.3	27.5	23.3	26.0	27.7
Share total exports (%)	12.9	11.7	11.4	9.8	8.9	7.3	6.4	7.1	4.8	4.5	4.4	4.5	2.8	2.8	2.2	2.3	2.3
Peru[f]																	
Ores & concentrates (net)	28.6	39.6	47.0	43.0	49.5	48.9	61.2	56.6	71.6	59.2	58.0	65.4	127.6	65.5	64.5	65.6	64.1
Impure bars (net)	0.3	0.4	1.6	1.3	0.9	0.8	0.3	0.2	0.2		0.1	0.2	0.2				
Refined bars	31.2	42.0	40.7	60.7	56.0	57.0	59.0	62.6	64.3	55.5	59.6	76.6	72.8	55.0	102.0	85.4	86.8
Total lead content	60.1	82.0	89.3	105.0	106.4	106.7	120.5	119.3	136.5	114.7	117.7	142.2	200.6	120.5	166.5	151.0	150.9
Total (gross)	89.0	123.1	143.6	147.2	153.5	156.9	182.7	177.4	207.4	175.0				123.6	125.8	123.7	125.8
United States	58.9	64.2	93.8	107.9	96.0	106.8	130.3	47.6	170.7	100.1	48.6	57.6	56.7	57.6	55.0	52.6	71.1
Japan						6.0	7.2	3.9	8.9	0.4	2.8	5.4	21.3	15.2	8.4	27.6	12.9
Belgium	3.3	10.3	2.1	2.2	7.4	3.3	12.7	2.5	6.7	14.4	13.3	9.5	12.2	8.6	11.7		
West Germany	1.8	5.5	2.1	5.1	12.2	16.3	7.0	5.9	4.6	27.8	15.1	14.1	6.6	12.8	13.0		20.8
Netherlands					5.3	5.6	6.4	10.5	11.3	18.4	17.7	17.7	15.7	13.5	10.3		7.3
Value	12.2	23.3	23.7	19.2	24.1	26.2	31.3	29.3	23.3	21.0	22.0	22.3	16.4	16.4	33.0	37.9	34.3
Share total exports (%)	6.5	9.5	10.2	10.3	9.7	9.8	10.1	9.2	8.7	6.8	5.0	4.5	3.0	3.0	5.0	5.7	4.5
Latin America[g]																	
Ores & concentrates (net)[a]	63.9	77.9	88.1	84.9	71.9	75.9	93.7	96.0	105.2	85.5	88.4	102.9	155.7	94.7	89.9	95.5	95.2
Impure bars[h]	9.2	12.8	5.4	4.7	5.1	17.9	12.4	15.5	8.6	14.1	13.6	19.4	11.1	12.0	11.6	10.4	15.2
Refined bars[h]	283.3	208.1	243.2	266.7	256.9	226.0	204.1	218.5	207.7	191.4	191.1	227.4	196.2	179.1	195.2	182.1	185.4
Semimanufactures		0.2			0.8	5.9	13.6	6.1									
Total lead content	336.9	273.4	363.1	348.0	336.5	311.5	310.2	320.6	335.7	276.4	280.3	334.7	351.5	273.3	288.3	275.6	282.1
Value	90.7	110.8	111.7	85.5	86.5	91.0	93.9	93.7	66.0	61.0	61.6	65.9	48.7	50.1	62.8	71.6	70.4
Share total exports																	
Major exporters[j] (%)	11.0	10.6	10.6	9.2	8.9	7.8	7.4	7.8	5.9	5.3	4.8	4.6	3.0	3.0	3.3	3.6	2.4
Latin America (%)	1.3	1.4	1.5	1.1	1.1	1.1	1.1	1.1	0.8	0.7	0.7	0.7	0.5	0.5	0.6	0.7	0.6

Sources: Great Britain, Overseas Geological Surveys, *Statistical Summary of the Mineral Industry, 1950-55, 1951-56, 1952-57, 1958-63,* and *1959-64.* USBM, *Minerals Yearbook, 1950-67.* USCB, *United States Imports of Merchandise for Consumption, 1950-64.* Foreign trade yearbooks of Bolivia, Chile, Mexico, and Peru. UN, *Yearbook of International Trade Statistics, 1966.* IMF, *International Financial Statistics, 1958-1968.*

[a]Lead content of ores and concentrates reported in gross weight assumed to be 50%. Excludes lead in complex ores.

[b]All data refer to U.S. imports.

[c]Base bullion plus antimonial lead bars.

[d]Excludes red and white lead and other lead chemicals.

[e]1950-56, estimated lead content of all lead-containing exports, including some not listed: 1957-66, assumed to be 90% of reported gross exports, average ratio for the years 1950-51, 1953, and 1955-56.

[f]Exports by destination in gross weight, 1950-59; in net lead content, 1960-66.

[g]Sum of countries listed; excludes Argentina, Colombia, and Ecuador.

[h]Sum of gross and net figures; Bolivian metal exports included with impure bars.

[j]Lead exports as a share of total exports of Bolivia, Mexico, and Peru.

TABLE 6–6B. Latin American Exports of Zinc by Destination, 1950-1966
(Thousands of metric tons and millions of U.S. dollars)

Exporter and Destination	1950	1951	1952	1953	1954	1955	1956	1957	1958	1959	1960	1961	1962	1963	1964	1965	1966
Argentina																	
Ores & concentrates																	
(gross)											26.7	50.9	19.7	47.4	29.9	2.7	
United States											6.1			1.9	23.5		
Belgium											18.6	47.7	16.1	20.6	0.2		
Metal														3.2	1.1	0.1	0.1
Total zinc content[a]									(a)		13.4	25.5	9.9	26.9	16.1		
Value											1.4	2.1	0.8	2.1	1.9	0.1	
Share total exports (%)											0.2	0.2	0.1	0.2	0.1		
Bolivia																	
Ores & concentrates																	
(net)	19.6	30.5	35.6	24.0	20.3	21.3	17.1	19.7	14.2	3.4	4.0	5.3	3.6	4.6	9.8	13.7	16.7
United States	19.6	30.5	35.3			1.7	6.6	6.9	6.6	2.3	1.1	0.5	1.6	4.0	4.9		14.2
Value	5.3	12.2	13.2	5.6	4.7	5.7	5.0	5.4	3.2	0.9	1.2	1.3	0.9	1.2	3.1	4.2	5.0
Share total exports (%)	5.6	8.1	9.4	5.0	5.1	5.7	4.7	5.7	5.1	1.2	1.8	1.8	1.2	1.5	2.8	3.2	3.4
Guatemala[b]																	
Ores & concentrates																	
(net)	4.3	5.9	8.9	5.9	3.4	7.6	10.4	8.5	5.9		5.5	12.6	2.3	1.3		0.9	1.2
Value		0.8	1.0	0.2	0.1	1.0	1.5	1.3	0.7		0.2	0.9	3.7	0.5			
Share total exports (%)			0.4		0.2		0.2	1.5	0.7		0.2	0.8	3.1	0.3			
Honduras[b]																	
Ores & concentrates																	
(net)	0.1	0.1	0.3	0.6	0.7	1.3	2.1	2.4	1.3	1.3	4.3	6.2	6.4	7.5	7.0	11.0	9.7
Value		0.2					0.2	1.0	0.3	0.3	0.6	0.9	2.8	1.2	0.8	1.4	1.4
Share total exports (%)			0.4		0.2		0.2	1.5	0.5	0.5	0.9	1.2	3.5	1.5	0.9	1.1	1.0
Mexico																	
Ores & concentrates																	
(gross)	226.7	226.2	349.5	308.7	313.2	321.0	330.1	309.3	269.7	304.4	342.6	362.4	317.7	324.4	278.4	285.0	312.9
Slag fuming residues					38.8	49.3	48.3	33.8	30.3	46.2	34.3	39.1	28.8	25.1	30.5		
Refined bars	48.5	42.1	42.2	51.6	39.7	48.8	41.0	42.3	36.5	40.8	29.8	27.8	29.4	29.4	29.1	25.9	32.6
Total (gross)	315.1	308.3	391.7	360.3	391.8	419.0	419.4	385.3	336.5	391.4	406.8	429.2	376.0	378.9	338.0	310.9	345.5
United States	225.1	254.7	339.1	287.8	345.8	387.4	399.0	375.9	321.0	357.2	208.2	204.7	185.2	159.4	144.7	118.1	122.0
Belgium	1.8	11.2	2.0	7.1	2.9	3.8	3.9	2.8	2.3	5.1	6.3	11.0	10.4	6.9	3.9		
Netherlands	0.1	0.6	0.9			1.0	1.4	1.8	2.0	3.4	8.1	18.4	3.1		1.7		
United Kingdom						19.1	7.8	5.9	5.8	13.1	8.7	6.9	3.8	3.4	5.8		
Poland											0.2	1.6	3.7	15.4	19.5		
Total zinc content[c]	203.2	161.0	218.0	221.9	208.0	250.2	233.0	224.3	195.5	226.8	229.8	240.8	213.4	214.5	193.0	180.7	203.7
Value	25.4	40.6	48.5	22.2	22.6	28.4	43.4	41.6	20.0	25.0	29.6	27.4	28.3	29.9	42.6	37.7	37.1
Share total exports (%)	4.8	6.3	7.3	3.7	3.6	3.6	5.2	5.7	2.7	3.3	3.9	3.3	3.0	3.0	4.0	3.3	3.0
Peru																	
Ores & concentrates																	
(net)	72.7	100.4	111.2	88.5	96.5	127.7	136.5	119.1	107.4	130.7	133.2	176.0	144.1	148.0	202.5	212.0	225.7
Refined bars	1.9	0.7	1.6	9.2	15.9	18.6	7.0	27.0	29.9	25.6	23.4	31.6	37.2	38.8	72.1	55.7	56.4
Total zinc content	74.6	101.1	112.8	97.7	112.4	146.3	143.5	146.1	137.3	156.3	156.6	207.6	181.3	186.8	274.6	267.7	282.1
Total (gross)	136.7	190.6	212.6	166.5	187.9	253.2	261.1	243.2	220.5	261.1	272.1	350.4	299.3	308.6	440.3	400.0	429.8
United States	27.6	46.9	70.5	132.1	150.8	129.7	156.9	181.5	158.3	134.4	98.9	108.1	100.2	101.0			142.7
Japan						1.6	7.1	4.5		5.4	30.0	63.1	34.5	38.0			226.2
France	17.5	4.1	31.1	4.2	2.9	2.0	1.0		6.4		2.9	14.7	32.4	15.2			
Belgium	74.1	93.4	85.0	20.8	22.0	98.5	86.2	46.4	19.3	48.9	83.0	79.2	48.7	69.5			
Netherlands	3.2	8.6	8.1	1.6	4.9	1.0	2.4	4.3	8.9	17.0	18.0	25.6	20.0	10.6			
Brazil	0.4	1.7	0.5	0.2	0.2	0.1			0.4	0.1	0.6	3.0	17.1	13.5			
Value	10.8	15.5	13.8	6.7	9.5	14.5	15.5	15.7	11.6	14.9	18.4	20.1	16.7	16.8	26.9	35.8	34.0
Share total exports (%)	5.7	6.2	5.9	3.1	3.9	5.4	5.0	4.9	4.1	4.8	4.3	4.1	3.1	3.1	4.0	5.4	4.5
Latin America[d]																	
Ores & concentrates																	
(net)[a]	255.6	255.9	332.0	289.0	288.9	359.7	358.6	331.7	324.3	321.4	360.4	438.6	350.3	370.2	398.2	390.1	419.1
Refined bars[e]	50.4	42.8	43.8	60.8	55.6	67.4	48.0	69.3	66.4	66.4	53.2	59.4	66.6	71.4	102.3	81.6	89.0
Total zinc content	306.0	298.7	375.8	349.8	344.5	427.1	406.6	401.0	390.7	387.8	413.6	498.0	416.9	441.6	500.5	471.7	508.1
Value	41.6	69.1	76.7	34.7	36.9	49.6	65.6	65.0	35.8	41.2	51.4	52.7	53.2	51.7	75.3	79.2	77.5
Share total exports (%)																	
Major exporters[f]	5.1	6.5	7.2	3.7	3.8	4.2	5.1	5.5	3.2	3.6	3.9	3.6	3.0	3.0	4.0	4.0	3.6
Latin America	0.6	0.9	1.1	0.4	0.5	0.6	0.7	0.7	0.4	0.5	0.6	0.6	0.6	0.5	0.7	0.8	0.7

Sources: See table 6–6A.

[a] Zinc content of ores and concentrates assumed to be 51% in Argentina; reported as 53% in Mexico. Metal assumed to be 100% zinc.
[b] All data refer to U.S. imports.
[c] As reported, 1950-56; estimated 1957-66. Excludes zinc oxides in all years.
[d] Sum of countries listed; excludes zinc exports of Brazil, Chile, and Colombia.
[e] Includes Argentine metal exports, 1963-66.
[f] Zinc exports as share of total exports of Bolivia, Mexico, and Peru.

TABLE 6-7. Participation in the Lead-Zinc Industry of Latin America, 1963-1965
 (Ownership and percent of production capacity)

Country	Type and Nationality of Enterprise	Lead Mining	Lead Smelting	Zinc Mining	Zinc Smelting
Argentina	Foreign private (United States)[a]	95	85	96	97
	Local private	5	15	4	3
Bolivia	State (COMIBOL)	44	100	36	
	Local private[b]	54		59	
	Foreign private (Japan)	2		5	
Brazil	Foreign private (United States/France)	95	100		
	Local private	5			
Chile	Local private[c]	100	100	100	
Colombia	Foreign private (United States/Canada)	100		100	
Ecuador	State/local private	100		100	
Guatemala	Local private	100	100	100	
Honduras	Foreign private (United States)	100		100	
Mexico	Local private (control)[d]	100	100	100	100
	Foreign private (ownership)[e]	23	21	32	49[f]
	Local private (ownership)	77	79	68	51[f]
Peru	Foreign private (United States)[g]	42	100	65	100
	(France)	5		3	
	Local private	50		30	
	State (Banco Minero)	3		2	
Latin America	Foreign private[h]	41	47	60	78
	Local private[j]	56	52	40	22
	State[k]	3	1		

Sources: USBM, *Minerals Yearbook, 1963*, vol. IV. ABMS, *Yearbook, 1965*. Also information supplied by Latin American section of International Activities Division, USBM. Peru—census of mining companies, 1964, prepared by Peruvian national statistics office. Chile—CORFO, *Geografía Económica de Chile* (Santiago: Universidad de Chile, 1961), p. 604. Bolivia—see chap. 7.

[a]Cía. Minera Aguilar and associated companies.
[b]Small and medium mines.
[c]Includes some state participation through the Corporación de Fomento de la Producción, major shareholder in the Empresa Minera Aisén.
[d]All companies are at least 51% Mexican owned.
[e]Estimated foreign ownership of jointly held companies; foreign share in each company weighted by share of company in total output.
[f]Excludes the Zincamex smelter, which did not enter full production until 1965.
[g]Minimum estimate, excluding minority ownership of several Peruvian companies.
[h]Approximate share of foreign ownership (not control); share in each country weighted by country's share of total regional output.
[j]Residual estimate: total private less foreign private. Includes mixed state/local private enterprises in Chile and Ecuador.
[k]Complete state ownership and control only; excludes mixed companies with some state participation.

TABLE 6-8. Latin American Lead-Zinc Balances, 1965
 (Metric tons)

Country	LEAD Ores and Concentrates (1)	Smelted Metal (2)	Semi-manufactures (3)	Total Lead (4)	ZINC Ores and Concentrates (5)	Smelted Metal (6)	Semi-manufactures (7)	Total Zinc (8)
Argentina								
Imports				3,000				2,566
Production	42,536	32,236		42,536	59,172	29,679		59,172
Exports	153	11		164	2,671	148		2,819
Consumption				35,225				32,097
Bolivia								
Imports				19				25
Production	16,313	936		16,313	13,607			13,607
Exports	15,873	1,664		17,537	13,688			13,688
Consumption				19				25
Brazil								
Imports		2,171		2,207	31,574		443	38,400
Production	22,500	9,665		22,500	5,250	75		5,250
Exports	12,925			12,925	522			522
Consumption				11,872				38,475

TABLE 6–8 – Continued

Country	LEAD				ZINC			
	Ores and Concentrates (1)	Smelted Metal (2)	Semi-manufactures (3)	Total Lead (4)	Ores and Concentrates (5)	Smelted Metal (6)	Semi-manufactures (7)	Total Zinc (8)
Chile								
Imports		1,784	86	1,870		6,495	265	6,760
Production	783			783	1,383			1,383
Exports	707			707	153			153
Consumption				1,870				6,760
Colombia								
Imports		471	36	1,148				2,585
Production	730			730	400			400
Exports	756	229		985				
Consumption				919				2,585
Costa Rica								
Imports				131				925
Exports				69				3
Consumption				62				922
Ecuador								
Imports			275	351			78	78
Production	114			114	236			236
Exports	707			707	562			562
Consumption				35				78
El Salvador								
Imports		47	227	274				57
Guatemala								
Imports				109				154
Production	923	114		923	867			867
Exports	30	76		106	867			867
Consumption				147				154
Honduras								
Imports				57				26
Production	9,654			9,654	11,126			11,126
Exports	10,506			10,506	10,991			10,991
Consumption				57				26
Mexico								
Imports				27				60
Production	166,780	164,307		166,780	232,875	89,744		232,875
Exports	2,818	140,530		143,348	285,003	33,841		318,844
Consumption				23,804				55,963
Nicaragua								
Imports				142				1,753
Exports								53
Consumption				142				1,700
Peru								
Imports				47				234
Production	154,346	86,807		154,346	254,496	62,441		254,496
Exports	65,558	85,454		151,012	211,991	55,716		267,707
Consumption				1,400				6,959
Venezuela								
Imports		1,693	498	2,191		4,072	1,087	5,159
Latin America								
Imports		6,166	1,036	11,573		42,141	1,873	53,623
Production	414,679	294,065		414,679	579,412	181,939		579,412
Exports	110,033	227,964		337,997	526,448	89,705		616,153
Intraregional Trade[a]		———5,548———		5,548		———16,418———		16,418
Consumption				78,314				150,960

Source: USBM, *Minerals Yearbook, 1967*, vol. IV.

Note: Consumption is measured exclusive of ores and concentrates, and is equal to apparent consumption of unwrought metal and chemical plus net imports of metal, chemicals, and semimanufactures.

(1) Metal content of ores, concentrates, matte, speiss, and slag; includes lead content of mixed ores or concentrates.
(2) Includes refined lead, lead content of mixed bars, and lead chemicals; all smelter and refinery products.
(3) Semifabricated shapes, castings, forgings, and powder; gross weight of alloys rather than lead content.
(4) Estimated total lead content.
(5) Includes zinc content of mixed ores or concentrates and slag.
(6) Includes zinc oxide and sulfate; all smelter and refinery products.

(7) Includes gross weight of zinc alloys.
(8) Estimated total zinc content.

[a]Data for 1966.

Chapter 7

TIN

While in Latin America as a whole tin is a relatively unimportant commodity, for Bolivia it is of the greatest significance. Tin mining is the principal source of non-agricultural employment in the country, contributing about one-sixth of the national product; it regularly provides three-fourths or more of the country's exports. Bolivia's economic dependence on tin is comparable to that of any Latin American nation on any single commodity. The tin industry has even more political importance than its economic weight indicates; in the past few decades it has been one of the principal elements of Bolivian politics. There are tin-mining and tin-using industries in Brazil and in Mexico, but their economic role is slight. Elsewhere in the region tin is a minor item of imports, directly or in manufactured form.

World Production, Consumption, and Trade

It is estimated that at a price of about £1,150 per long ton,[1] such as prevailed for tin in 1963-64, world reserves outside the Communist countries are some 3.6 million to 4 million tons. Total resources,[2] estimated independently of price, are at least 5 million tons, and as high as 7 million if all known resources are included. As reserves in the Soviet Union and mainland China are believed to be at least 1.2 million tons, over 8 million tons of tin can be accounted for. Eight countries contain about 90 percent of these reserves; at least 10 percent and perhaps as much as one-fourth of the total is in Latin America, almost entirely in Bolivia (see table 7-1). These estimates are quite rough, not only because of the importance of prices but because for many countries there are few detailed, or few recent, figures at all.

The production of tin, unlike that of any other major metal, has not shown a long-run increase in the last forty or so years. Before World War II, demand for tin behaved much like the demand for other metals, rising during the 1920s, contracting during the Depression, and recovering in the late 1930s, partly as a result of stockpiling in anticipation of war (see table 7-2). During the war two major producers, Malaya and Indonesia, were occupied, and production expanded greatly in Africa and Latin America. Immediately afterward, a decline in demand and difficulties in rehabilitating the industry in Asia reduced production sharply, but by the early 1950s output had returned to the high level and to the distribution among producing areas of the prewar years.

Except for Malaya, the producing countries have until recently shipped their tin in the form of concentrates to Europe for smelting. In the 1930s, 60 percent of the world's tin metal was produced in three smelters in Malaya, treating ore from Malaya, Burma, Indonesia, and Thailand. Another 34 percent was produced at five smelters in the United Kingdom, Belgium, and the Netherlands, the countries whose possessions furnished the bulk of mine output. Small amounts of tin were also smelted in the Congo. Bolivian concentrates were smelted in the United Kingdom. (See table 7-3.) The United States had no significant smelting capacity until 1941, when a large plant was built to relieve the wartime shortage of tin by permitting concentrates to be imported, especially from Bolivia. Since the war the processing industry has become somewhat less concentrated through the construction or rebuilding of smelters in Brazil, Nigeria, Indonesia, and Thailand.[3]

The consumption of tin differs in one important respect from that of the other metals the world uses in large quantities. In nearly all its applications tin is added in small amounts to other metals as an alloying element or a coating. About half of all tin is used to plate steel, so that consumption of tin metal is associated more with the production than with the consumption of tinplate. North America and Western Europe each take some 35 to 40 percent of world tin supplies, and Japan consumes another 10 percent. The construction of tinplate mills in Latin America, Africa, and Asia (outside of Japan) has shifted some tin

Note: Tin tables 7-1 to 7-9 appear on pp. 237–44.

[1] Throughout this chapter the long ton is used as a measure of tin. One long ton is 1.016 metric tons.

[2] See chap. 3, under the heading "The Present Resource Base," for definition of reserves and resources.

[3] USBM, *Mineral Facts and Problems, 1960,* p. 878; and *Mining Journal,* 6 August 1965.

consumption to those regions, but their share in the total remains small (see table 7-4).

As production expanded rapidly in the late 1920s, tin prices fell by almost one-third (see table 7-5). A further sharp drop in 1930 led the four major producers – Bolivia, Indonesia, Malaya, and Nigeria – to agree to limit their exports. By 1933 they had cut production to 38 percent of the 1930 level, and world output was halved. With the recovery of prices, the agreement was dissolved. Prices were controlled by the United States and the United Kingdom during World War II, rose substantially in the late 1940s, and then increased sharply during the Korean War. Producers feared that a surplus would recur and drive prices down, while consumers wished to see prices and supplies stabilized, as demand is quite inelastic in the short run. In December 1953 a conference of the International Tin Study Group was held, which resulted in the drafting of an International Tin Agreement. The first agreement ran from July 1956 to July 1961; a second was signed for 1961-66, and was superseded in July 1965 by a third agreement, to end in 1971. The six major producers outside the Communist countries are members, as are a number of consuming countries; the United States, however, has not joined. The agency of the Agreement is the International Tin Council.[4] The Council may, as in 1958-60, impose export quotas in times of severe oversupply, and it has authority to allocate supplies to consumers during shortage, but its normal method of control is the operation of a buffer stock of tin metal and currency supplied by the producers. Minimum and maximum prices are set by the Council: when the price of tin on the London Metal Exchange exceeds the maximum, the manager of the buffer stock must sell tin, and similarly he must buy when the price falls below the minimum. When the price is in the upper or lower third of the range he may sell, or buy, respectively, at discretion; in the middle third of the range the buffer stock is not traded except at the request of the Council. Decisions on prices, quotas, and other matters require separate majorities among producers and consumers, each country's vote being proportional to past production or consumption.

The tin agreements were negotiated in expectation of a surplus, but in only two years of the decade 1955-65 was there any oversupply. In the early 1960s there was instead a shortage of some 20,000 tons a year, as a result of inadequate production in the face of steady or slightly increasing consumption. Outside the Communist countries, no major consuming country is a significant producer of tin. Production is concentrated in six underdeveloped nations: two of

these have attained independence since the mid-1950s, and three others have experienced severe political upheaval. Output in Bolivia, Indonesia, and the Congo declined greatly. In Malaya and Nigeria production was maintained; only in Thailand was production increased substantially. This shift in supply patterns partly reflects differences in the amounts of reserves and costs of production, but the reduction in total supplies is primarily due to political disturbance in the countries affected or to the policies adopted by their governments as a result of political changes.

Prices rose sharply in 1956, and the International Tin Council several times raised its floor and ceiling prices, but the response of supplies was slight until 1966-67. Since consumption has been strictly limited by supplies plus stockpile releases, consumers have had a strong incentive to economize on the use of tin or to find substitutes for it. The consumption of tin in solder and most alloys has not increased, and its use in bronze has declined. Tinplate producers developed means of depositing tin electrolytically on steel, making tinplate with half as much tin as did the older process of dipping the steel in molten metal. The shortage of tin was not entirely offset by increased economy in use, but initially it was masked by large imports from the Communist countries. Before 1957 little trade in tin took place between these countries and the rest of the world; the Soviet Union regularly imported a large share of China's production for domestic consumption and re-export to Eastern Europe, but only small amounts were shipped outside the Bloc. During the 1950s, large tonnages became available for export. The price of tin was depressed, and the Council exhausted its funds in efforts to support it. Export quotas were imposed in 1957, and then consumers were persuaded to restrict imports from the Soviet Union. The latter country did not join the ITA, but agreed to restrict its exports; after 1958, however, consumption within the Communist countries overtook production, Chinese-Soviet trade declined, and the Bloc shortly became a net importer of tin (see table 7-6).

Export quotas remained in effect until 1960, and then in 1961 the Council's stock of metal was exhausted as prices began to rise again. From late 1962 through 1967 the world tin shortage was met chiefly by releases from the U.S. strategic stockpile. Of the stock of 341,000 tons built up by purchases and barter transactions during the 1950s, some 164,000 tons were declared surplus. By the end of 1967, 87,000 tons had been sold, and a plan was in effect for disposing of the remaining surplus over the next several years. Although the United States is not a member of the ITA, the arrangement for stockpile disposals was made after consultation with the Council. Since the end of 1962 these sales have been the major factor preventing a still more serious price rise and short-term dislocation of the industry.[5] Since 1964 there have been shortages of other major metals, but tin is unique in the duration and severity of the shortage and in the fact that it was precipitated by de-

---

[4]The principal sources of information about tin are the publications of the International Tin Council (ITC) and its predecessors, the International Tin Study Group (ITSG) and the International Tin Research and Development Council (ITRDC). Each organization published a monthly *Statistical Bulletin* and a *Statistical Yearbook* every two years or slightly less often. Since 1956 the ITC has also published annual reports of its operations, and has commissioned or produced a number of studies on various aspects of the tin industry. See in particular, W. Robertson, *Report on the World Tin Position, with Projections for 1965 and 1970* (London: ITC, 1964). Other sources are indicated in this chapter.

[5]ITC, *Statistical Yearbook, 1964*, pp. 12-15, and *Mining Annual Review, 1965*, "Tin." For a more recent review, see *Engineering and Mining Journal*, March 1968.

clining production in 1953-58 and very slow growth thereafter, more than by increased demand.

Tin in Latin America

Tin has been mined in Latin America for about a century, and has been a major industry for at least fifty years. Commercial production began near Potosí, Bolivia, in the 1860s. Output rose to several hundred tons per year in the 1880s and to thousands of tons in the next decade. By 1916 production exceeded 20,000 tons, and tin mining was established as the major industry in Bolivia. Until 1930, there was no appreciable production in any other country of the region; in that decade the United States began to stockpile tin and through the 1940s it absorbed most of Latin America's production. Production rose sharply in Mexico and Argentina. Tin is now also mined in Brazil and small amounts are produced in Peru, but Bolivia continues to dominate production, usually supplying 90 percent or more of the total. The tin-using industry in Latin America evolved independently of the resources of Bolivia, as part of the region's industrialization in the last twenty-five years. The production of tin metal, alloys, and tinplate bears little relation to mine output except in Brazil and Mexico, where a domestic consuming industry absorbs all the tin mined. Where little or no tin is produced, there may still be a large tin-using and tinplate industry, as in Argentina and Chile, or a smaller industry consuming tin metal, as in Colombia and Venezuela. Foreign capital created much of the industry in Bolivia, but was less important in developing mining and processing in other countries than is the case for other nonferrous metals.

The eastern flank of the Andes in Bolivia is a rich source of many nonferrous metals. The area was mined for copper in Inca times, and from the mid-sixteenth century until late in the nineteenth was exploited chiefly for silver. Tin was mined, but not recovered, as a byproduct of silver long before it became an important product in itself. The industrial metals were not extracted in quantity until the last century, when there was a large influx of foreign capital. Great expenditures were required to equip the mines, many of which are at altitudes above 4,000 meters, and to provide facilities for shipping over very difficult terrain to the Pacific coast. Relatively little was spent on exploration, since most metal continued to come from areas worked for centuries and only a few large new deposits were discovered.

Despite the high costs imposed by the complexity of its ores and the problems of transport, Bolivia rapidly became one of the world's chief sources of tin. During World War II, when Asian supplies were cut off, it was the leading producer, supplying almost half the total in 1945. Within a decade, however, the mineral industry suffered a virtual breakdown: production fell by one-third, Bolivia's share of world tin output dropped to one-sixth, and the mines were operated at heavy losses. This decline was precipitated by the Revolution of 1952, but its origins lie in the political and social experience of Bolivia in the preceding two decades. In the early 1930s Bolivia lost a disastrous war with Paraguay, which resulted in great social unrest and rapid changes of government. In 1939 a group dedicated to the organization of the mine workers and the eventual expropriation of the private mining companies formed the Movimiento Nacional Revolucionario. The MNR seized power in 1942, but was overthrown in 1946, principally as a result of opposition by the mine owners. In 1949 the MNR tried to gain control of the government again, but failed, and the rebellion was put down by the army. Throughout this period there was little investment in the mining industry; particularly during the war the richest ores were selectively mined and reserves were depleted both in volume and in grade. At the same time, the successive governments taxed the foreign exchange earnings of the mining companies to subsidize imports of food and other items of consumption. Domestic production was discouraged, and the country grew increasingly dependent on mineral exports.[6]

In 1951 the MNR formed an alliance with the Partido de Izquierda Revolucionario (PIR) and with the independent miners' syndicates led by Juan Lechín Oquendo. Their joint candidate, Victor Paz Estenssoro, won a plurality in the presidential elections of that year, but was prevented by the army from taking office. A military junta assumed power, whereupon revolution broke out in April 1952. The miners' militia destroyed the army in a few days of heavy fighting, and Paz was installed as President. The Vice President, Hernando Siles Zuazo, was elected President in 1956, and in 1960 Paz returned to the office. The coalition which carried through the Revolution of 1952 held together until 1964, when Lechín's forces and those of Paz split; Paz was deposed, and the reconstituted army took control until the election of General Barrientos Otuño as President in 1965.

The MNR alliance had two principal aims: to nationalize the mines and to effect a land reform. Production was also to be diversified and social services expanded, and a start was to be made in developing industry. The mining industry was seen as the only source of funds, particularly of foreign exchange, for these other programs. Unfortunately, the mineral industry was in no condition to support the burden expected of it; it had for so long subsidized other sectors of the economy that it was much in need of relief and new investment. Furthermore, the revolutionary government was incapable of operating the mines efficiently enough to extract any surplus. Most of the skilled personnel employed by the private companies were foreigners who left the country after the Revolution. The rapid turnover of governments during the 1930s and '40s had prevented the development of a body of trained civil servants. Finally, the miners, having destroyed the army, were the most powerful force in the country and the government was unable to impose discipline or efficiency on them. The unions acquired the right to veto management decisions and exercised great power over wages, employment, and work schedules.

In October 1952 the government nationalized the three largest private mining companies, which accounted for nearly three-fourths of exports, and created the Corporación Minera de Bolivia to operate the properties. The small-

---

[6] A concise history of this period is given in H. Osborne, *Bolivia: A Land Divided*, 3rd ed. (Oxford University Press, 1964).

and medium-sized mines remained in private hands but were required to export through the Banco Minero. In the next decade the tin industry deteriorated gravely: the production of the nationalized mines declined in every year from 1954 to 1961, falling from more than 30,000 tons to less than 15,000 (see table 7-7). Output per worker fell by 60 percent, and the cost of production rose even more rapidly than tin prices until late 1965. By the end of 1964 COMIBOL had lost almost $200 million – $120 million in 1953-56 alone. The enterprise was caught in a spiral. Managerial and labor difficulties reduced efficiency, and costs were further raised by the expansion of the labor force from 29,000 to 37,000 between 1952 and 1956. The resulting losses were met by government subsidy, so that the mining industry, instead of providing national currency to subsidize other sectors and offset inflationary pressures, contributed to the deficit; the exchange rate rose from 190 bolivianos per dollar in 1953 to nearly 12,000 before inflation was halted. Meanwhile COMIBOL was prevented from investing in exploration or development, and its foreign exchange earnings continued to be used to subsidize consumer imports, the demand for which increased with inflation and the disruption of domestic agriculture by the land reform.

The Bolivian economy came close to collapse in 1953; further deterioration was averted only by large-scale U.S. aid in dollars and surplus foodstuffs. By 1956 the government had recovered sufficiently to undertake a program of stabilization, supported by foreign aid and by the army, which had been rebuilt to offset the power of the miners' militia. In 1957 inflation was halted, and in 1961 the United States, Bolivia, and West Germany agreed on a plan of aid to COMIBOL financed chiefly by the United States and administered through the Inter-American Development Bank. Of the $37.75 million allocated for Operation Triangle, $27.13 million were spent in the first two phases, which ended in 1964. The third phase of the agreement did not begin on schedule because of dissatisfaction with the results so far achieved and the uncertainty caused by the overthrow of the Paz government in 1964. An agreement was reached in October 1965 for the third stage, of $10.1 million, to go into effect during 1966.[7]

In the first three years of Operation Triangle both the grade of ore and the recovery factor were raised, and COMIBOL's output rose for the first time. In 1966 production was almost 18,400 tons of tin, some 1,400 tons over the target for the year. Moreover, the cost per pound of production was brought down from nearly $2.00 to $1.40, so that in 1966 COMIBOL was able for the first time to operate at a profit, pay taxes to the government, and service some of its debts.[8] In the first two stages of Operation Triangle the effect on production was modest, because much of the aid was in the form of surplus foodstuffs or

was used to reduce the work force and employ those laid off in building roads and housing. In the third phase emphasis shifted from simply reducing costs to raising output, including the exploration and development of new reserves, recovery of tin from mine tailings, and metallurgical research. A large new tin deposit was discovered near La Paz, and a pilot plant established to treat the 0.4 percent tin in the waste dump at Catavi. In 1969 a 1,000-ton-per-day plant went into operation there, designed to recover about half the tin, and large dumps suitable for the same treatment exist at several other mines. After one year, COMIBOL is to take over the process without charge from the International Metals Processing Company; the tailings available could add several thousand tons annually to Bolivia's production.

This technical and financial progress has depended to a great extent on increased labor discipline and the destruction of much of the power which the miners' unions acquired in the Revolution. The first steps to reduce COMIBOL's costs and losses consisted simply in laying off nearly half the labor force, so that by 1958 the number was down to the level of 1952. Strikes and some violence were contained by the army. In 1963 COMIBOL survived a particularly severe strike without giving ground on any major issue, and thereafter no labor troubles occurred for almost two years. Another strike, in May 1965, was repressed by the army, and there were no more disturbances until June 1967, when a crisis erupted in Huanuni and Catavi at the same time that a guerilla movement in eastern Bolivia was drawing increased attention and alarm in the government and the army.

Thus, while there has been a substantial recovery of the Bolivian nationalized mining industry from the conditions of the early 1950s, the fundamental political and economic problems are far from being resolved. As frequently occurs in such major issues, there are two aspects which may be separated for analysis but which are extremely difficult to separate or resolve in practice: the problem of raising productivity and thereby furthering development, and the problem of distributing the benefits of such improvements. Thus far no way has been found to let the miners share in the gains while maintaining the desired level of efficiency and rate of progress. Their working conditions and standard of living have not been appreciably improved, more efforts having gone to reduce costs and thus lighten the burden which COMIBOL imposed on the rest of the Bolivian economy. The miners, who were once the strongest supporters of the Revolution and expected to be its chief beneficiaries, have for several years been in a state of virtual civil war with the government. Their loss of power has not been compensated by economic benefits, the benefits they gained in wages and bonuses before 1956 have not all been continued, and the purely economic struggle and difficulties are partly overshadowed by ideological considerations. The combination of extreme poverty in all parts of the economy, of several years of mismanagement and waste, and of great dependence on external aid (and political pressures) for progress makes the Bolivian situation the most difficult of the natural resource sector problems described in this study.

[7]The terms of Operation Triangle are given in USBM, *Minerals Yearbook*, vol. I, *1961-63* and vol. IV, *1963*. Details of expenditures and accomplishments are reported in COMIBOL, *Compendium of the Loan Application for the Third Phase of the Rehabilitation Plan* (La Paz: May 1964), a document submitted to the IADB. See also the Bank's press release of 11 October 1965.

[8]USBM, *Mineral Trade Notes*, May 1967, pp. 29-31; BOLSA, *Review*, January 1967, p. 32, and *New York Times*, 18 June 1967.

The small and medium mine operators were also affected by overvalued exchange rates in 1953-56, but they did not suffer the labor or management problems of COMIBOL and their productivity did not decline except insofar as taxes prevented an adequate level of investment. Since the stabilization of 1957, the private mining companies have responded to high prices by raising output considerably. They also benefit from a new mining law, introduced in 1965, which permits them to sell to other buyers than the Banco Minero and which taxes exports according to the metallic content of concentrates.[9] Private foreign capital has also been allowed to return, as has occurred in the petroleum industry. Estaños Aluviales was formed by four U.S. firms (including U.S. Steel, a major consumer of tin for tinplate) to operate a tin dredge at Avicaya beginning in late 1967; and the Matilde property, a rich silver-lead-zinc deposit which COMIBOL has not had the capital to develop, has also been leased to two U.S. firms (again including U.S. Steel) for development in 1969-70.[10] No properties operated by COMIBOL are to be turned over to private or foreign enterprise, but even so the concessions made will be a source of political discontent for some time. It remains to be seen whether a stable relationship between COMIBOL and the other producers, both domestic and foreign, will be maintained, or whether there will be further sharp changes of policy such as occurred in Argentina with respect to oil production.

Small amounts of tin are smelted in Bolivia and some alloys, such as solders, are made, but the bulk of tin production has always been exported as concentrates. In part this is because fuel (especially coal) for smelting is scarce in the mining region, and there is no local market for tin metal. Moreover, the ores are so complex that they must usually be mixed with ore from other sources for reduction. Only a few smelters — one each in the United Kingdom, the United States, and the Netherlands — are equipped to treat unmixed Bolivian concentrates.[11] One of the aims of the Revolution was to establish a domestic smelting industry, chiefly in order to raise the value of exports but also in the hope of developing some local metalworking industry and of increasing trade with neighboring countries which now import tin concentrates, metal, or alloys from outside the region. Experiments have been conducted for several years under Operation Triangle, in both the United States and West Germany, to develop an economical smelting process for Bolivian ores which would use natural gas or petroleum, available locally, as fuel. In 1967 the decision was made to install a 7,500-ton smelter purchased from Germany, to go into operation about the end of 1969. A 20,000-ton plant was originally planned, and capacity may later be raised to this amount. It will be operated by the Empresa Nacional de Fundiciones, a government enterprise that is linked to COMIBOL but distinct from it; initially it should treat about one-third of the country's tin output, or a considerably larger share of the tin mined by COMIBOL.[12] Exports of tin concentrates have in most years gone principally to the United Kingdom (see table 7-8). Some concentrates have been shipped under long-term contracts to the United States since the 1940s, partly for research into different smelting methods that might be feasible in Bolivia. The United States is the chief market for the small amount of tin metal exported, with most of the rest going to Latin American countries. Tin exports alone bring in 70 to 90 percent of Bolivia's foreign exchange, with nearly all the remainder provided by other nonferrous metals.

Latin America as a whole in the early 1960s consumed some 8,000 tons of tin per year: almost 6,000 tons in the form of metal and about 2,500 tons in imported tinplate (see table 7-9). Small amounts of tin are mined in Argentina, and in Peru some tin is recovered in gold mining or as an impurity in nonferrous metal ores or bullion. In neither country is tin processing based on domestic production. Integrated industries, including mining, smelting, refining, and the manufacture of alloys and tinplate, exist only in Brazil and in Mexico. Tin occurs over a large area of Minas Gerais in Brazil, and in several nearby states, particularly Goiás; there are also large deposits in Rondonia and perhaps elsewhere in the Amazon basin. The first tin refinery in Latin America was installed at Volta Redonda in 1958. All domestic output is smelted there, and the remainder of Brazil's requirements are imported in the form of concentrates. Tin is also found throughout the high central plateau of Mexico. Over 1,000 deposits, most of them too small or too low in grade to be worked regularly, are scattered over nineteen states.[13] The major deposits are in San Luis Potosí and Durango. Ore from all over the country is smelted in San Luis Potosí, and there are several smaller plants which refine tin or produce solder and alloys. Mexico is currently more self-sufficient in tin than Brazil, but a significant increase in mine output is more likely in Brazil.

The tinplate industry is more widely established in Latin America than is the mining or smelting of tin. Production of hot dipped tinplate began in Mexico in 1947 and in Brazil in 1948; in both countries electrolytic facilities were added later. Tinplate is also produced now in Argentina and Chile, and steel plants are being equipped to produce it in Colombia and Venezuela; only Peru has a steel industry with no present or planned tinplate capacity. Altogether, the region consumed some 600,000 tons of tinplate in 1963, divided evenly between imports and domestic production. Tinplate accounted for about 57 percent of all tin used, or about 40 percent of the tin metal consumed in Latin America. The share of tin consumed in the form of tinplate is high in Brazil, Cuba, Mexico, Peru, and Venezuela; it is lowest in Argentina and Uruguay, despite the importance of canned food exports from both countries. The most modern tinplate industry in the region, and one of the most modern in

[9] *Mining Journal*, 15 October 1965.

[10] See Osborne, *Bolivia...*; *Engineering and Mining Journal*, May 1966; and *Mineral Trade Notes*, May 1967, p. 30.

[11] USBM, *Materials Survey: Tin* (1953), chap. III, p. 1; and Great Britain, Commonwealth Economic Committee, *Non Ferrous Metals* (London, 1963), p. 182. According to ITC, a second smelter in the United Kingdom and one in West Germany can also treat Bolivian ore.

[12] *Mineral Trade Notes*, May 1967, p. 31.

[13] W. F. Foshag and C. Fries, "Los Yacimientos de Estaño de la República Mexicana," Comité para la Investigación de los Recursos Minerales de México, bol. no. 8 (Mexico City, 1946).

the world, is that of Brazil; nearly 90 percent of production is electrolytic. Although the tin industry is vertically integrated in some countries, there is almost no integration of the regional industry and no trade in concentrates, metal, or tinplate. Only Brazil imports concentrates, while Bolivia's exports are no more accessible than those from Africa or Asia and are considerably harder to smelt. This pattern is likely to change only if Bolivia begins to smelt the bulk of mine production and to trade chiefly in metal, or if one or more of the major steel producers begins to export tinplate as a result of regional integration of the steel industry.

Present Situation and Outlook

Since 1918 world tin output has increased rapidly in response to rising demand in three periods: 1921-29, 1933-37, and 1945-53. Only during the first of these, however, was there a significant increase in capacity based on the development of new reserves. In the 1930s production merely recovered from the curtailment brought on by the Depression, and the expansion after World War II was due chiefly to rehabilitation of mining areas in Asia. The high level of output achieved in Bolivia and Africa during the war was made possible more by selective mining of high-grade ore than by reductions in cost or enlargement of reserves for long-run operations. The experience of these decades indicated a very low elasticity of new supply, and in the postwar period the difficulties of increasing output were compounded by political problems which affected production directly and also retarded investment. When export controls were lifted in 1960, the industry was in a poor condition to respond to increased demand: high-grade reserves were depleted, recovery rates were quite low in comparison with those for other major metals, and much capital equipment was old and inefficient. In these circumstances a deficit between mine production and consumption arose, reaching 21,000 tons annually in 1963-64. Prices rose more than 70 percent, and large stockpile releases were necessary in order to avoid a severe physical shortage. The high prices of 1964-67 and the fear of future shortages stimulated consumers to substitute other materials for tin and to economize on its use. Efforts to develop substitutes have been especially marked for tinplate, leading to widespread adoption of aluminum and to experiments with a variety of other materials.[14] The alloying uses of tin are less susceptible of large-scale substitution and less responsive to price. While a slow process of replacement may aid the industry by moderating the growth of demand, any abrupt and sizable change might reduce prices enough to cause a fall in mine output and prolong the disequilibrium. Any such price decline would fall especially hard on Bolivia.

The principal requirements for equilibrium, therefore, were an increase in production and greater stability in prices, ending the dependence on U.S. stockpile releases. These goals in turn require the discovery of new tin deposits and/or an improvement in recovery rates, reductions in cost, especially for low-grade ores, and much capital

investment. These problems received increased attention from 1960 onward and particularly from 1964, when prices rose sharply.[15]

This concern is reflected in the third International Tin Agreement, which converted the Committee on Production into a Committee on Development specifically charged with reviewing problems of consumption and substitution as well as the development of new tin deposits.

By the end of 1967 the efforts of the past several years had resulted in an approximate balance of mine production and consumption and a fall of prices below the $1.54 per pound level set for United States government sales. The deficit made up by stockpile releases dropped from 21,000 tons to only about 3,000 tons in 1966, rising to 6,000 tons in 1967. Production in that year reached some 27,000 tons in Bolivia, the highest since 1957, and in Malaysia output was higher than at any time since 1941. Output also rose in Thailand. For the first time in nearly a decade there was prospect of a surplus, and attention turned to new uses for tin to offset the substitution for traditional applications. The ITC Buffer Stock also bought tin for the first time in several years. In 1968 export controls were imposed again, and events over the 1967-68 period suggest a fourth fairly rapid rise in output.

The outlook for the world tin industry is necessarily uncertain because of the price elasticity of supply from small workings, the political difficulties in certain producing countries, and the considerable amount of rehabilitation and development still needed. The deficit of the period 1960-67 appears to have ended, but it is too early to tell whether the balance between production and consumption will be maintained, or what price will be necessary for equilibrium and continued development. Projections of demand and supply for 1970 and 1975 have already been surpassed or their assumptions invalidated by events of the last few years, while for the longer term the range of substitution possible makes any precise estimates of demand impossible.[16] The most that can be said with any assurance is that consumption of tin metal will probably continue to increase slowly; it does not appear likely to grow as rapidly as that of other major metals, nor to decline in response to rapid substitution. The response of production to this demand will depend in part on price, but it may be more affected by progress in developing new deposits and in reducing the cost of production, and by political circumstances, especially in Bolivia, Nigeria, and the Congo. There appears to be considerable room for treating tin-bearing

---

[14] For a report on these developments, see *Mining Journal*, 26 April and 20 August, 1965.

[15] The recent supply problem of the tin industry, its causes, and the measures to be taken to increase the availability of tin are the subject of two articles, "The Prerequisites to Increased Tin Production," in the January and March 1965 issues of *Mining Magazine*. See also, Robertson, *Report on the World Tin Position. . .*, pp. 91 ff.

[16] For 1970 projections, see Robertson, *Report on the World Tin Position. . . .* Projections for 1970 and 1975, for the major producers and consumers, are given in Bela Balassa, *Trade Prospects for Developing Countries* (Homewood: Irwin, 1964), pp. 440-41. See H. H. Landsberg et al., *Resources in America's Future* (Johns Hopkins Press for Resources for the Future, 1963), pp. 62-63, 315-16, for an extreme example of the effect on projections of assumptions regarding the degree of substitution for tin.

ores or waste now discarded and for lowering the cost of tin relative to competing materials.

Thus far the reduction in costs in Bolivia has come from better management and more efficient use of labor, but in the future improved recovery techniques may be more important. It also seems likely that the dispersion of tin smelting from consuming to producing countries will continue: in 1967 new smelters entered full operation in Thailand and Indonesia and one will be in operation in Bolivia at the end of 1970. This development should increase Bolivia's earnings from tin and possibly allow it trade with more countries. Even apart from the introduction of large-scale smelting, there is no prospect of the country's dependence on tin being reduced; tin may, in fact, offer the best hope of increasing exports and furthering development over the next decade.

CHAPTER 7 TABLES

TABLE 7–1. World Reserves of Tin, 1965
(Thousands of long tons)

Country and Classification	Reserves at Price of £1,100 per Long Ton[a]	Reserves Not Classified by Price
Bolivia	514	1,750[b]
Measured	361	438
Indicated	96	310
Inferred	56	1,000
Mexico		28
Measured		20
Inferred		8
Canada		30-40
Reserves in lead-zinc mines		8
Recoverable from dumps		9
Congo	190[c]	500
Measured	139	
Indicated	31	
Inferred	20	
Nigeria	110	250
Measured	81	
Indicated	24	
Inferred	4	
Thailand	1,540	
Measured	40	
Indicated and inferred	1,500	
Offshore		250
Malaya	900	1,000
Indonesia	650	760
Measured[d]	544	
Indicated and inferred	66	

TABLE 7–1 – Continued

Country and Classification	Reserves at Price of £1,100 per Long Ton[a]	Reserves Not Classified by Price
Burma, inferred		300
Laos		50-70
Australia	83	47
United Kingdom	42	47
Soviet Union		500
China		700[e]
Other countries	65[f]	100-200
World Total	4,000[g]	7,800-7,900

Sources: W. Robertson, *Report on the World Tin Position* (London: ITC, 1964), pp. 181-85. USBM, *Materials Survey: Tin, 1953*, and *Mineral Facts and Problems, 1965*.

[a]Estimated on the basis of 1965 costs of tin mining; the Robertson *Report* includes estimates of reserves at prices of £700 and £900 per long ton also.

[b]1 million tons inferred geologically; 100 million tons of ore averaging 0.75 percent estimated to exist at Catavi, Huanuni, Oruro, Colquiri, and Potosí.

[c]Estimated at a price of £1,000 per long ton.

[d]Includes recoverable tin content of tailings and dumps.

[e]Minimum estimate, 1953.

[f]France, Japan, Korea, Portugal, Republic of South Africa, and Tanganyika; includes estimated reserves of Canada, Burma, and Laos.

[g]Excludes Communist countries.

TABLE 7-2. World Mine Production of Tin, 1925-1967
   (Long tons)

Country or Region	Average 1925-29	Average 1930-34	Average 1935-39	Average 1940-44	Average 1945-49	1950	1951	1952
Latin America	37,168[a]	25,398	27,556	40,980	38,096	32,128	34,018	32,893
Argentina		56	1,255	1,049	582	257	237	261
Bolivia	37,168	24,966	25,867	39,463	36,964	31,213	33,132	31,959
Brazil				65	210	180	197	229
Mexico		375	320	333	230	440	366	413
Peru			64	69	50	38	86	31
Africa	10,531	8,540	19,096	29,604	25,121	22,924	23,479	23,606
Asia[b]	104,252	87,817	118,097	89,456	51,592	102,133	100,034	103,446
Europe[c]	3,492	2,189	3,426	4,631	2,470	3,008	3,412	3,951
Oceania[d]	1,282	2,227	3,327	3,111	2,120	1,854	1,559	1,611
World Total	156,740	126,100	171,700	168,200	119,600	162,000	163,000	166,000
L.A. Share (%)	23.7	20.1	16.0	24.3	31.8	19.8	20.8	19.9

Country or Region	1953	1954	1955	1956	1957	1958	1959	1960
Latin America	35,664	29,435	28,761	27,605	28,756	18,898	24,874	22,403
Argentina	154	95	89	85	182	205	225	238
Bolivia	34,825	28,824	27,921	26,842	27,796	17,731	23,811	20,219
Brazil	209	167	146	175	293	409	461	1,556
Mexico	476	349	605	500	473	544	377	365
Peru				3	12	9		25
Africa	25,483	25,107	25,307	26,421	26,485	19,762	18,000	20,700
Asia[b]	102,710	108,289	107,897	106,786	102,457	71,982	70,900	88,800
Europe[c]	4,925	4,457	4,337	3,863	3,783	3,523	3,400	2,100
Oceania[d]	1,553	2,075	2,017	2,078	1,952	2,237	2,351	2,202
World Total	171,000	170,000	169,000	167,000	164,000	117,000	120,000	137,000
L.A. Share (%)	20.9	17.4	17.0	16.5	17.5	16.1	20.8	16.4

Country or Region	1961	1962	1963	1964	1965	1966	1967
Latin America	22,297	23,693	24,660	26,695	25,895	28,797	29,622
Argentina	515	571	225	343	497	458	802
Bolivia	20,664	21,800	22,209	24,319	23,036	25,626	26,890
Brazil	581	731	1,150	790	1,810	1,855	1,200
Mexico	530	576	1,055	1,207	503	821	662
Peru	17	15	21	36	49	37	68
Africa	18,600	19,600	19,898	18,497	20,592	19,265	19,171
Asia[b]	90,000	92,900	90,645	93,994	99,214	105,696	110,250
Europe[c]	2,300	2,400	2,374	2,479	2,428	2,419	2,657
Oceania[d]	2,745	2,715	2,860	3,642	3,849	4,838	5,379
World Total	137,000	142,000	140,851	145,464	152,193	161,429	166,514
L.A. Share (%)	16.3	16.5	17.5	18.4	17.0	17.8	17.8

Sources: ITRDC, Statistical Yearbook, 1933. ITSG, Statistical Yearbook, 1949 and 1952. ITC, Statistical Yearbook, 1960 and Statistical Bulletin. USBM, Minerals Yearbook, 1967.

[a]Only Bolivian production reported before 1930.
[b]Includes China, 1925-48; excludes China and North Vietnam thereafter.
[c]Excludes Soviet Union, 1925-67; includes Czechoslovakia, 1925-48 only.
[d]Australia only.

TABLE 7-3. World Smelter Production of Tin,[a] 1927-1967
(Long tons)

Country or Region	Average 1927-29	Average 1930-34	Average 1935-39	Average 1940-44	Average 1945-49	1950	1951	1952
Latin America[b]		52	871	1,041	922	1,088	804	962
Argentina		50	853	714	466	253	206	185
Bolivia					25	392	39	257
Brazil				63	182	118	133	116
Mexico		2	18	233	223	290	366	144
Africa			1,712	11,842	5,285	4,038	3,893	3,778
Asia[c]	96,290	85,504	102,050	81,072	34,763	69,543	66,710	63,690
Europe[d]	82,464	41,204	62,523	40,221[e]	45,643[e]	60,920	59,081	70,249
United States		72	202	14,178	38,006	32,136	30,921	22,592
Oceania[f]		1,976	2,997	3,048	2,160	2,014	1,459	1,700
World Total	178,767	128,800	170,800	151,700	127,200	170,000	163,000	163,000
Latin American Smelter Production as Share of:								
World Smelter Production (%)		0.0	0.5	0.7	0.7	0.6	0.5	0.6
L.A. Mine Production (%)		0.2	3.2	2.5	2.4	3.4	2.4	2.9

Country or Region	1953	1954	1955	1956	1957	1958	1959	1960
Latin America[b]	1,097	2,406	1,630	2,294	1,913	1,868	2,520	2,746
Argentina[g]	130	60	99	61	39			
Bolivia	174	196	107	449	266	659	916	1,069
Brazil	553	1,850	1,184	1,544	1,401	629	1,227	1,312
Mexico	240	300	240	240	207	460	377	365
Africa	3,570	3,238	3,953	3,819	4,134	4,044	4,700	4,700
Asia	63,859	63,330	73,517	74,674	72,872	47,258	49,000	79,400
Europe[d]	67,220	69,210	66,896	67,212	76,375	61,326	45,900	44,000
United States	37,562	27,002	22,329	17,631	1,564	5,250	10,700	13,500
Oceania[f]	1,443	2,063	2,004	1,850	1,806	2,121	2,226	2,254
World Total	175,000	177,000	170,000	168,000	159,000	122,000	114,500	146,000
Latin American Smelter Production as Share of:								
World Smelter Production (%)	0.6	1.4	1.0	1.4	1.2	1.5	2.4	1.9
L.A. Mine Production (%)	3.0	8.2	5.6	8.3	6.7	9.9	10.1	12.3

Country or Region		1961	1962	1963	1964	1965	1966	1967
Latin America[b]		4,100	4,916	5,568	6,486	5,627	3,402	4,078
Bolivia		2,016	2,023	2,462	3,610	3,415	1,062	1,018
Brazil		1,525	2,317	2,051	1,731	1,753	1,545	2,100
Mexico		559	576	1,055	1,145	459	795	960
Africa		4,500	10,500	11,963	11,771	12,604	13,185	12,217
Asia		82,800	85,900	87,977	75,105	81,401	95,021	105,576
Europe[d]		35,600	34,600	33,218	41,706	42,657	39,904	46,899
United States		8,500	5,500	650	5,190	3,098	3,825	3,048
Oceania[f]		2,546	2,704	2,626	3,021	3,179	3,640	3,594
World Total		135,500	144,700	143,002	143,279	148,566	155,337	175,412
Latin American Smelter Production as Share of:								
World Smelter Production (%)		3.0	3.4	3.9	4.5	3.8	2.2	2.3
L.A. Mine Production (%)		18.4	20.8	22.6	24.3	21.7	11.8	13.7

Sources: ITRDC, *Statistical Yearbook, 1933.* ITSG, *Statistical Yearbook, 1949* and *1952.* ITC, *Statistical Yearbook, 1964* and *Statistical Bulletin.* USBM, *Minerals Yearbook, 1967.*

[a]Production of primary tin metal from ores and concentrates, excluding secondary recovery from tinplate and tin-bearing alloy scrap.

[b]Excludes production of tin in Peru, which may be tin metal produced at lead smelters, as reported by the ITC, 1941-52, or tin content of lead-antimony bars or metal dross, as reported by *Minerals Yearbook,* 1956-59. Maximum production, 86 tons in 1951. There is no smelter in Peru designed or operated primarily for producing tin.

[c]Only Malayan production reported, 1927-29; Asian total includes China and North Vietnam, 1930-48 only.

[d]Excludes Soviet Union, 1927-67.

[e]No smelter production in Belgium or the Netherlands during German occupation, 1941-45. Production in 1940 of 1,500 and 1,158 tons, respectively.

[f]Australia only.

[g]The tin smelter at Buenos Aires was dismantled in 1957, and no tin metal has since been produced, according to *Minerals Yearbook, 1963,* vol. IV. The ITC has estimated smelter production as 120 tons in every year from 1958 to 1964. Latin American total is sum of production in Bolivia, Brazil, and Mexico, 1958-67.

TABLE 7-4. World Consumption of Primary Tin,[a] 1938, 1950, and 1966
(Long tons)

Country or Region	1938	1950	1966
Latin America	2,677	4,048	6,236
Argentina	1,117	1,300	1,750
Brazil	682	1,600	2,050
Chile	160	230	600
Colombia		40	277
Cuba	225	85	
Ecuador		3	
Mexico	190	470	1,200
Paraguay		15	20
Peru		40	118
Uruguay	100	95	31
Venezuela		130	180
Africa	1,350	2,141	2,600
South Africa	456	1,200	1,355
Egypt	483	400	459
Asia	14,900	10,446	24,700
Japan	10,000	4,616	18,622
India	2,652	3,700	2,600

TABLE 7-4 – Continued

Country or Region	1938	1950	1966
Western Europe	62,619	51,572	58,160
United Kingdom	18,290	23,254	18,425
France	9,049	7,750	10,300
Germany	15,033	7,782	10,773
Italy	4,635	2,700	5,909
North America	50,173	75,717	65,264
United States	48,115	71,191	60,209
Oceania	2,444	2,552	4,600
World Total[b]	150,900	146,500	169,500
Latin American Tin Consumption as Share of:			
World Consumption (%)	1.8	2.8	3.7
L.A. Mine Production (%)	9.7	12.6	21.7

Sources: ITSG, *Statistical Yearbook, 1949.* ITC, *Statistical Yearbook, 1960* and *1964,* and *Statistical Bulletin,* March 1969.

[a]Consumption of metallic tin, excluding tin from secondary recovery; includes tin content of alloys and solders in some cases.
[b]Excludes Communist countries.

TABLE 7-5. Tin Prices, 1925-1967, and International Tin Council Price Limits, 1956-1967

Year	Straits Tin in New York U.S. Cents per Pound	LME Cash Price Pounds Sterling per Long Ton	U.S. Cents per Pound
1925	57.9	261.0	56.4
1926	65.3	291.0	63.1
1927	64.4	289.0	62.8
1928	50.4	227.1	49.5
1929	45.2	203.9	44.3
1930	31.7	141.9	30.8
1931	24.5	118.4	25.6
1932	22.0	135.8	21.2
1933	39.1	194.5	36.8
1934	52.2	230.3	49.5
1935	50.4	225.5	49.5
1936	46.4	204.4	45.5
1937	54.3	242.1	53.5
1938	42.3	189.5	41.3
1939	50.3	226.2	44.8
1940	49.8	256.4	44.0
1941	52.0	261.1	47.0
1942	52.0	275.0	49.5
1943	52.0	275.0	49.5
1944	52.0	300.0	54.0
1945	52.0	300.0	54.0
1946	54.5	321.2	57.8
1947	77.9	426.3	76.7
1948	99.3	548.1	97.4
1949	99.3	600.8	99.0
1950	95.5	745.8	93.4
1951	127.1	1,079.6	135.0
1952	120.5	964.4	120.4
1953	95.8	728.5	91.1
1954	91.8	720.3	90.1
1955	94.7	740.6	92.7
1956	101.4	788.7	98.5
1957	96.3	755.2	94.5
1958	95.1	735.3	92.0
1959	102.1	785.7	98.3
1960	101.4	797.0	99.6
1961	113.3	889.1	111.0
1962	114.7	896.9	112.1
1963	116.7	910.2	113.9
1964	157.6	1,240.9	155.2
1965	178.2	1,414.1	176.8
1966	164.1	1,296.6	162.1
1967	153.4	1,222.5	152.9

International Tin Council Floor and Ceiling Prices

After	Pounds Sterling Per Long Ton Minimum	Maximum	U.S. Cents Per Pound Minimum	Maximum
1 July 1956	640	880	79.9	109.9
22 March 1957	730	880	91.3	110.1
12 January 1962	790	965	98.7	120.6
5 December 1963	850	1,000	106.1	124.8
13 November 1964	1,000	1,200	125.0	150.0
1 July 1966	1,080	1,400	135.0	175.0
21 March 1967	1,100	1,400	137.5	175.0

Sources: Yearbook of the American Bureau of Metal Statistics, 1967. ITC, *Statistical Bulletin.* USBM, *Minerals Yearbook, 1967.*

TABLE 7-6. Tin Production and Trade of Communist Countries, 1957-1964
[Long tons of tin metal]

Production and Trade	1957	1958	1959	1960	1961	1962	1963	1964
Total smelter production[a]								
Soviet Union	36,700	37,100	41,600	44,600	47,600	45,600	48,600	45,600
China	13,000	13,500	15,000	16,000	17,000	17,000	20,000	20,000
Trade within Communist Countries:								
China to Soviet Union[b]	23,000	23,000	26,000	28,000	30,000	28,000	28,000	25,000
Soviet Union to Eastern Europe[c]	21,653	19,054	20,506	17,464	11,062	8,648	4,291	4,000
Eastern Europe to Soviet Union	6,161	3,828	4,153	2,984	3,670	307		700
Trade outside Communist Countries:								
Exports[d]	13,612	22,220	17,025	13,080	7,540[e]	6,085	7,229[f]	5,803
Soviet Union[g]	11,850	18,120	12,943	8,334	1,940	5,900	7,080	5,606
China[j]	1,762	2,835	3,430	4,554	5,600	185	149[h]	197[h]
Imports[k]	225[m]	57[m]	99	179	2,547	5,019	6,220[f]	6,032
Soviet Union[n]	40	40				1,096	3,386	3,500
Net Exports from Communist Countries	13,387	22,163	16,924	12,901	4,993	1,066[p]	1,009	−229
As Share of Other World Supplies[q] (%)	8.4	18.1	14.8	8.8	3.7	0.7	0.7	−0.2

Sources: USBM, *Minerals Yearbook* (smelter production; exports of East European countries). ITC, *Statistical Yearbook, 1964,* and *Statistical Bulletin* (imports and exports of the Soviet Union; estimated total imports and exports of the Communist countries). Robertson, *Report on the World Tin Position,* p. 233 (exports of China outside the Communist countries).

a Includes estimated smelter production of East Germany: 670 tons in 1957, and 600 tons in each year from 1958 to 1963.

b Imports of Soviet Union from China and North Vietnam.

c Exports of Soviet Union to Albania, Bulgaria, Czechoslovakia, East Germany, Hungary, Poland, and Rumania. Exports to these countries from China, North Vietnam, and Hong Kong not reported.

d Includes exports of Eastern Europe; excludes exports of North Vietnam unless these are included in Chinese exports.

e *Minerals Yearbook* estimates 1961 exports from China as 7,346 tons instead of 5,600 tons. The discrepancy of 1,746 tons is the largest between estimates of *Minerals Yearbook* and *Robertson Report.* In no other year does the discrepancy exceed 567 tons, the value for 1958. ITC, *Statistical Yearbook, 1964* reports total exports from Communist countries as 8,366 tons.

f Reported total exports and estimated unreported trade. If figures are adjusted to take account of transit trade and estimated unreported trade, exports from Communist countries are approximately 7,900 tons and imports 6,750 tons. (ITC, *Statistical Yearbook, 1964.*) No allowance is made for transit trade in this table.

g Exports of Soviet Union to countries outside Communist countries, plus exports to unspecified countries.

h Non-Chinese exports all come from North Vietnam.

j Exports of China only; these figures are less than estimates of North Vietnam and may be based on different estimates of Chinese exports.

k Total reported imports of Soviet Union and Eastern Europe from outside Communist countries; no imports of tin into China or North Vietnam are reported.

m *Minerals Yearbook* estimate.

n Imports of Soviet Union from countries outside Communist countries, plus imports from unspecified countries.

p Net exports estimated as approximately 600 tons (ITC, *Statistical Yearbook, 1964,* and *Robertson Report*). Adjustments for transit trade decrease apparent exports from China and increase imports into Soviet Union and Eastern Europe.

q Net exports from Communist countries as percentage of smelter production in all other countries.

TABLE 7-7. Bolivian Production and Exports of Tin by Mining Groups, 1950-1967
       (Long tons)

BEFORE NATIONALIZATION					1950	1951	1952
Total concentrate exports					30,944	33,093	31,702
Shares (%) of:							
Patiño Mines					44	45	44
Mauricio Hochschild SAMI					23	20	19
Cie. Aramayo des Mines					7	8	8
Total, major enterprises					74	73	71
Medium mines					} 26	} 27	20
Small mines							9

AFTER NATIONALIZATION	1953	1954	1955	1956	1957	1958	1959
Total concentrate exports	34,651	28,628	27,814	26,421	27,467	17,024	22,787
COMIBOL	30,108	24,776	23,417	22,478	22,032	13,852	17,590
Medium mines	1,782	1,686	1,957	}3,914	}5,435	}3,173	2,173
Small mines	2,761	2,166	2,440				3,024
COMIBOL share (%)	87	86	84	85	80	81	77
Total mine production	34,825	28,824	27,921	26,842	27,796	17,731	23,811
COMIBOL	30,108	24,776	23,115	22,634	21,307	17,110	15,556
COMBOL share (%)	86	85	83	84	77	97	65
Exchange rate (Bolivianos/$)	190[a]	(b)	(b)	7,760	8,565	11,935	11,885
COMIBOL losses (mill. $)	————————120.5[c]————————					6.6	10.3

	1960	1961	1962	1963	1964	1965	1966	1967
Total concentrate exports	17,938	18,394	19,471	20,290	20,416	23,828	25,822	27,606
COMIBOL	12,677	12,622	13,219	13,933	14,182	13,673	17,263	18,026
Medium mines	2,393	2,475	2,731	3,223	3,462	3,862	4,562	5,308
Small mines	2,868	3,297	3,521	3,134	2,772	2,887	2,935	3,234
COMIBOL share (%)	71	69	68	69	69	57	67	65
Total mine production	20,219	20,664	21,800	22,209	24,319	23,036	25,626	26,890
COMIBOL	14,990	14,579	14,993	15,126	17,690	16,287	18,129	18,328
COMIBOL share (%)	74	71	69	68	73	70	71	68
Exchange rate (Bolivianos/$)[d]	11,885	11,885	11,885	11.88	11.88	11.88	11.88	11.88
COMIBOL losses (mill. $)	12.6	9.6	16.2	14.9	5.3			

Sources: USBM, Minerals Yearbook, 1950-64, vol. I; 1963, vol. IV; 1967, vol. IV. See also table 7-2.

Note: Total concentrate exports are not always the same as reported by the IFC; see table 7-8.

[a]Devalued from 60 in May 1953.
[b]Multiple exchange rates in effect.
[c]Total losses incurred by the end of 1956.
[d]In 1963 new Bolivian peso was substituted for the old currency at the rate of one new peso for 1,000 old units.

TABLE 7–8. Bolivian Exports of Tin by Destination, 1950-1966
(Long tons metal content and millions of U.S. dollars)

Bolivian Tin Exports to:		1950	1951	1952	1953	1954
Western Europe:	Concentrates	13,883	16,187	16,295	19,188	16,368
United Kingdom		13,821	16,172	16,236	19,188	16,368
West Germany				59		
Netherlands		62				
United States:	Metal		15			
	Concentrates	16,908	16,849	15,379	15,439	12,229
Latin America:	Total	263	96	21	161	227
Argentina:	Metal	234	24		137	196
Chile:	Concentrates	29	72	21	24	31
Total Exports		31,215	33,132	31,959	34,825	28,824
	Metal	269	39	257	174	196
	Concentrates	30,944	33,093	31,702	34,651	28,628
Value		63.6	93.3	84.7	72.6	60.1
Share of Total Exports (%)		85	77	79	87	86

Bolivian Tin Exports to:		1955	1956	1957	1958	1959	1960
Western Europe:	Concentrates	16,229	18,497	26,525	16,555	16,955	17,034
United Kingdom		15,828	17,849	25,035	15,871	15,803	16,076
West Germany		401	528	1,034	603	1,103	924
Netherlands			120	456	81	49	19
	Metal					59	15
United States:	Total	11,585	7,961	1,002	641	6,022	1,372
	Metal		331	251	172	461	1,042
	Concentrates	11,585	7,630	751	469	5,561	330
Latin America:	Total	107	384	269	533	771	1,001
Argentina:	Metal	77	49	15	533	414	3
Brazil:	Metal		41	63		8	
	Concentrates		260	191		154	953
Chile:	Metal	30 (conc.)	34				9
Mexico:	Concentrates					186	36
Total Exports		27,921	26,842	27,796	17,729	23,811	19,407
	Metal	107	421	329	705	916	1,069
	Concentrates	27,814	26,421	27,467	17,024	22,895	18,338
Value		57.3	59.2	57.4	36.2	52.8	42.6
Share of Total Exports (%)		76	73	78	72	90	84

Bolivian Tin Exports to:		1961	1962	1963	1964	1965	1966
Western Europe:	Concentrates	17,176	17,970	18,449	18,382	16,380	20,284
United Kingdom		15,146	15,522	15,199	15,719	14,683	18,532
West Germany		1,467	1,588	1,666	1,466	1,520	1,626
Netherlands		563	860	1,284	1,197	171	126
	Metal			300			
United States:	Total	2,742	3,523	4,289	5,635	7,433	5,532
	Metal	2,003	2,023	2,148	3,611		1,001
	Concentrates	739	1,500	2,141	2,024		4,531
Latin America:	Total	477		14		15	20
Argentina:	Metal						1
Brazil:	Concentrates	477					
Chile:	Metal			14		15	19
Total Exports		20,408	21,493	22,752	24,027	23,828	25,822
	Metal	2,016	2,023	2,462	3,611	3,406	1,062
	Concentrates	18,392	19,470	20,290	20,416	20,422	24,760
Value		50.3	54.0	57.3	81.0	93.0	93.3
Share of Total Exports (%)		87	92	87	94	85	73

Sources: ITC, *Statistical Yearbook, 1964, 1966*, and *Statistical Bulletin*, October 1966, March 1969. IMF, *International Financial Statistics*, supps. 1964/65 and 1966. UN, *Yearbook of International Trade Statistics, 1966*.

Note: Total Bolivian exports of tin are calculated excluding the value added to ores and concentrates by smelting abroad; the figures used are from the *International Financial Statistics*, series (B). Series (A) includes the value added by smelting in importing countries, but as this additional value is not distributed over the different minerals the total calculated in this way exceeds the sum of reported exports by commodity.

TABLE 7–9. Tin in Latin America, 1963
    (Long tons)

Country or Region	Tin in Concentrates[a]	Unwrought Tin Metal[b]	Gross Weight of Tinplate[c]	Tin Content of Tinplate[d]	Tin in Metal and Tinplate[e]
			Total Tonnage of:		
Argentina					
Imports		1,189	92,920	733	1,922
Production	498				
Exports	227				
Consumption		1,189	92,920	733	1,922
Bolivia					
Imports[g]			49	1	1
Production	22,246	2,462			2,462
Exports[f]	20,290	2,448			2,448
Exports to Region	26	14			14
Consumption			49	1	1
Brazil					
Imports	2,084	1	63,317	504	505
Imports from Region	26				26
Production	1,153	2,051	158,492	1,218	2,051
Consumption		2,052	221,809	1,722	2,556
Chile					
Imports		612	582	5	617
Production			29,371	250	
Consumption		612	29,953	255	617
Colombia					
Imports[g]		250	32,522	227	477
Mexico					
Imports		197			
Production	1,055	1,055	95,802	750	1,055
Consumption		1,252	95,802[h]	750	1,252
Peru					
Imports[j]		61	15,000	106	167
Imports from Region		14			14
Production	15				
Exports	57				
Consumption		75	15,000	106	181
Uruguay					
Imports[g]		75	7,000	45	120
Venezuela					
Imports[g]		191	50,651	413	604
Cuba					
Imports[g]		100	40,000	320	420
Total Latin America[k]					
Imports	2,084	2,701	321,600	2,500	5,200
Production	24,967	5,568	283,665	2,218	5,568
Exports	20,574	2,448			2,448
Intraregional Trade	26	14			14
Consumption		5,821	605,365	4,718	8,320

Sources: ITC, *Statistical Yearbook, 1964*, and *Statistical Bulletin*.

[a]Tin content of concentrates.
[b]Smelted tin metal, in bars or ingots, excluding solders and tin-base alloys.
[c]Total reported weight of tinplate, including weight of steel.
[d]Tin content of tinplate produced in Latin America estimated by ITC; tin content of imported tinplate estimated from average tin content (pounds of tin per ton of steel) of tinplate produced in countries exporting to Latin America. Where origin of imports is not recorded by ITC, average tin content of imports into Argentina, Brazil, Colombia, and Venezuela is used, since origin of imports is given for these four countries.
[e]Imports and exports: sum of amounts in cols. 2 and 4.
Production: unwrought tin metal only.
Consumption: consumption of tin metal plus tin content of imported tinplate.
[f]Exports to countries outside Latin America only.
[g]Consumption of tin in all forms supplied entirely by imports.
[h]Consumption assumed equal to production.
[j]Imports from countries outside Latin America only.
[k]Includes Central America, Hispaniola, Paraguay, Ecuador, and the Guianas. ITC estimates 19,600 tons imported tinplate, plus 20 tons imported tin metal (Paraguay).

Chapter 8

PETROLEUM

Petroleum is of extraordinary importance to the economy of Latin America, both as an export commodity and as an element of domestic consumption. The value of production exceeds that of any other resource product. In all but a few years of the last two decades, petroleum and its derivatives have been the most valuable export of the region, usually providing between 20 and 30 percent of all foreign exchange earned. These exports originate predominantly in Venezuela, where petroleum accounts for more than 90 percent of all exports; much smaller amounts are shipped by several other countries. In the nations other than Venezuela, petroleum is important chiefly as a source of energy. In no country do oil and gas furnish less than 60 percent of all commercial energy, or less than 45 percent of all energy including vegetable fuels. In the region as a whole, petroleum supplies nearly 90 percent of all mineral and hydroelectric energy, and over three-fourths of inanimate energy in all forms. By reason of this twofold importance and of certain technical and economic features of the world oil industry, petroleum offers examples of virtually every issue raised by the exploitation of natural resources in Latin America. In many countries of the region oil is a political subject of the first magnitude, perhaps important to more countries and for more different reasons in that respect than any other resource product.

Petroleum is important in the same ways, but not to quite the same degree, in the world economy. Just over one-third of the world's consumption of mineral fuels and hydroelectricity is provided by petroleum, and another 17 percent by natural gas. Their combined share is more than double what it was three decades ago, and is still growing. Since the bulk of the world's oil is consumed in the richer nations, while a large share is produced in the poorer countries, a great deal of petroleum enters international trade. In recent years it has been the most valuable commodity in world trade and the greatest source of foreign exchange to the less developed countries. The economic relations formed between exporting and importing nations by this trade are reinforced by two major political factors: the strategic importance of oil, and the fact that much of the oil

Note: Petroleum tables 8-1 to 8-18 appear on pp. 272-90.

entering world trade is produced by enterprises owned and domiciled in the United States and Europe.

Described very simply, the production and consumption of petroleum involve three stages, together with transportation of the material between stages: production of crude oil, the raw material of the industry; production of a variety of fuels and other products by refining the crude petroleum; and consumption of those products in different industries and applications. At each stage there are many products of different value and use. A complete description of the industry is beyond the scope of this study; consequently, attention will be directed to total production of crude oil and products and to consumption of products in all parts of the world, with various products and forms of consumption described in much more detail for Latin America than for other regions. Applications that are not of the simple production-refining-consumption type, such as the use of petroleum derivatives to make chemicals consumed by other industries, will not be discussed. The production and use of natural gas will be described only for Latin America.[1]

The World Oil Industry

Resources

In the case of most mineral products, finding a deposit and determining its size, although perhaps a difficult and

[1] The petroleum industry is served by a great number and variety of publications, and is also the subject of many books and other studies. *Petroleum Press Service*, published monthly, is perhaps the best source of news of events in the industry, and most references in this chapter are to it; much the same information can be found in the weekly *Petroleum Times* or in *World Petroleum*, which publishes an annual *Report*. (Many other periodicals deal only, or chiefly, with the U.S. industry.) Much statistical material is compiled in *Petroleum Facts and Figures*, published every two years by the American Petroleum Institute; somewhat greater detail was provided by the *International Petroleum Quarterly* (now discontinued) of the U.S. Bureau of Mines, and these two are the principal sources for this study. Information on total energy production and consumption, relating petroleum to other fuels and sources of energy, is found in the United Nations Statistical Papers, Series J, published at intervals of about four years and titled *World Energy Supplies*. Other sources, dealing particularly with Latin America or with the history and operation of the oil industry, are noted in the text.

expensive operation, costs much less than actual extraction. It is therefore economical to measure a large share of the material before mining is begun. As a deposit is worked, reserves may be increased by further exploration; the inclusion of material formerly considered uneconomical is often more important than discovery of more material of the same grade or quality as that originally measured. Petroleum is quite different in this respect, because the existence and size of a deposit can be determined only by the same means used to exploit it — by drilling wells into the reservoir. Since the cost of operating a well is low compared with the expense of drilling it, exploration and development form a relatively large share of total production cost. This characteristic has several consequences for the meaning of "reserves" as applied to petroleum.

Oil reserves can be defined and measured in several ways. The most common term is "proved reserves," which refers to the amount of oil which it is relatively certain could be recovered from known reservoirs with the methods of production currently in use. The recovery factor may be as low as 10 percent or as high as 70 percent of the petroleum in place, depending on type of oil, pressure in the reservoir, and whether any of several methods of secondary recovery are employed. Proved reserves may therefore be increased not only by further exploration, but by any change in technique which makes it possible to extract more of the oil known to exist. They represent only a minimum estimate of the oil that could be made available.[2] It is generally economical to prove only enough reserves to maintain production for a decade or two; thus the amount of reserves reported may increase, or at least not decline, during a long period of production, and at any one time may refer to only a small fraction of the oil originally contained in a deposit. The amount of oil which can be found with a given exploratory effort depends very much on the character of the oil fields. A high ratio of reserves to production, in an area which has been producing for some years at a stable or slowly growing rate, indicates that the cost of finding oil is, or was, quite low, and therefore that the area can produce oil cheaply. A low ratio indicates difficulty in exploration and correspondingly higher costs of production.[3]

Nearly half of all the oil so far produced has come from the United States, the remainder being provided chiefly by Latin America, the Middle East, and Eastern Europe in about equal shares. Since World War II enormous amounts of petroleum have been discovered, often in areas which were not formerly significant producers; thus the present distribution of reserves bears little relation to the pattern of production even over the last two decades. World proved reserves of crude oil are currently somewhat more than 50,000 million cubic meters (340,000 million barrels), nearly double cumulative production to date, and about thirty times present rates of extraction.[4] (See table 8-1.) Fully 60 percent of the amount is found in the Middle East; the fields of that region are not only the largest in the world but have been extraordinarily easy to find and exploit.[5] Some 11 percent of world reserves are located in North America, and 9 percent in Eastern Europe; Latin America and North Africa account for most of the remainder. There is very little oil in Western Europe, in Africa south of the Sahara except in Nigeria, or anywhere in Asia or Oceania except in Indonesia.

Total proved reserves constitute only a small fraction of all the petroleum believed to exist in the world, or of the amount which might ultimately be recovered under different technical and economic conditions. The reserves of rich, recently developed areas such as the Middle East are perhaps greatly understated, so that estimation by the standards applied to older and poorer areas would yield world reserves several times greater than the present figure. Total resources of crude oil have been estimated to be as high as one million million cubic meters, of which half or more might ultimately be recovered; and according to certain theories of the formation and deposition of hydrocarbons the amount may be very much greater.[6] Besides the oil in liquid form, the world has a vast resource of petroleum in

---

[2] For a thorough discussion of the concept and measurement of reserves, see W. F. Lovejoy and P. T. Homan, *Methods of Estimating Reserves of Crude Oil, Natural Gas, and Natural Gas Liquids* (Resources for the Future, 1965).

[3] This difficulty need not mean that many wells are drilled, or much effort spent, without finding oil, but only that the individual pools are so small that a large number of wells must be sunk in order to find, or to produce, much oil. Large reserves proved per well drilled do not necessarily correspond to high output per well, or low cost, because a number of factors besides reservoir size determine the rate at which oil can be extracted; but in general the relation is as described.

[4] The principal unit used in this study for both crude oil and refined products is the cubic meter, the volume unit commonly employed in Latin America. Volume is also reported in the standard barrels of 55 gallons used as units by the the United States industry throughout the world: one cubic meter equals 6.3 barrels. For most grades of crude oil, a cubic meter weighs slightly less (for very low gravity oils, slightly more) than one metric ton, so the use of cubic meters facilitates comparisons with the amounts of other primary commodities, which are — except for some forest products — all reported in metric tons. The densities of refined products differ greatly and amounts are almost universally reported by volume rather than by weight. Tons are therefore used in this study only when a standard unit is needed for comparison to other forms of energy or where grades of petroleum differing greatly in energy content are to be compared. The petroleum equivalent ton is employed in the sections on "Consumption of Petroleum" and "Outlook." Petroleum prices are reported in U.S. dollars per barrel for crude oil or in equivalent U.S. cents per gallon for refined products (see table 8-5). Prices may also be given in dollars per ton. Natural gas is reported in volume units — either cubic meters or cubic feet — at standard temperature and pressure. Since natural gas is discussed only with respect to Latin America, only cubic meters are used here. A cubic meter of gas is of course very much less, in weight and in energy content, than the same volume of liquid petroleum.

[5] In 1960 only about 1,300 wells had been drilled in the Middle East, with an average yield of nearly 700 cubic meters per day, and yields in Iran and Iraq of some 1,600 m^3/d. The average rate of production per well was then only 45 m^3/d in Venezuela, and about 27 m^3/d in all the world outside the United States (where several factors have resulted in over-drilling and a very low average output). See J. E. Hartshorn, *Politics and World Oil Economics* (Praeger, 1962), p. 52.

[6] The concept of "ultimate reserves," and certain attempts to estimate their amount in the United States, are discussed in Lovejoy and Homan, *Methods of Estimating Reserves*, pp. 79-94. For an introduction to the question of how hydrocarbons are formed and deposited, and the effect of different explanations for estimates of ultimate resources, see *New Scientist*, 9 September 1965.

shales and tar sands. The resources of North America alone are known to be some 400,000 million cubic meters (2.5 million million barrels) or about eight times world proved reserves of crude oil. The rest of the world has been less extensively explored for sources other than liquid petroleum, but some 200,000 million cubic meters (1.25 million million barrels) of petroleum are known in shale in Brazil, the Soviet Union, and the Congo, and in tar sands in Venezuela.[7] In a perfect market for petroleum, these other sources would probably not be exploited until presently known supplies of cheap crude oil had been depleted. The various barriers to such a market make it appear likely that oil from shale will compete with crude oil in the United States within a few years and perhaps in other importing countries such as Brazil. Commercial production of oil from tar sands began in Canada in 1967 and development of the Venezuelan sands is under active consideration.

Production, Consumption, and Trade

The present petroleum industry originated in 1859, when crude oil was first extracted in commercial amounts from an underground reservoir in the United States. Production began at about the same time in Russia and in Rumania, and in the next four decades oil was produced in Japan, India, Indonesia, Peru, and several European countries. At the turn of the century there were industries producing some 10 million cubic meters (63 million barrels) annually in the United States and in Russia, which together accounted for nearly all of world output. For some fifty years after petroleum came into widespread use, it was used primarily to make kerosene, and fractions such as gasoline and fuel oil were commonly discarded. The development of internal combustion engines created a demand for the formerly valueless constituents and set off a rapid growth in production and consumption of oil, particularly in the United States. That country has continued as the world's largest producer, but in the past several decades its dominance has been steadily eroded by the development of new sources (see table 8-2). The first to be developed was Latin America, which was the scene of a great oil boom in 1910-20 and which, except for six years during the Depression, remained the second largest producing region until 1952. The next great expansion took place in the Middle East immediately after World War II, and continued at a rapid pace until this decade. A similar increase occurred in Eastern Europe, which became the third largest producing area in 1963. Most recently there has been a very rapid expansion in North Africa. In the past four decades world crude oil production has risen almost tenfold, and has undergone a great shift in distribution.[8] Petroleum and

natural gas have accounted for two-thirds of the increase in the world's consumption of fuel and electricity, and now provide half the total.

Between the late 1930s and the early 1950s, world consumption of refined petroleum products almost doubled, growing at the same rate as in the United States. The increase was somewhat more rapid in Latin America, Canada, and Africa, and slower in Western and Eastern Europe and in Asia and Oceania; these latter areas still depended heavily on coal, and their consumption of petroleum may have been retarded by World War II. During the next decade world use of oil grew much more rapidly, in consequence of a major shift from solid to liquid fuels in Europe and in Asia and Oceania (see table 8-3). The most rapid expansion took place in Asia, where petroleum displaced large amounts of vegetable fuel as well as coal and accounted for nearly all the increase in energy in all forms. In volume, the largest shift occurred in Western Europe; consumption reached the U.S. level of 1950-51, as a result both of increasing total use of energy and of displacement of coal, which could not be obtained in sufficient quantity or low enough cost from the region's depleted resources. Since Western Europe produces only a small amount of oil, it has been the most important market for petroleum exports in the last two decades. A similar shift from coal to oil began in the mid-1950s in Eastern Europe.

So long as only a small fraction of crude oil was consumed in final products, petroleum could not be refined economically anywhere away from the fields where it was produced. The earliest refineries built in every part of the world were therefore resource based, and nearly all trade was conducted in products. As demand for different products grew, the fraction of crude oil wasted dropped to a few percent, and it became possible to establish refineries close to consuming centers. The bulk of refining capacity continued to be located near oil fields, however; crude was still as expensive as products to transport, and most markets were too small to permit the economies of scale possible in resource-based plants. At the start of World War II some 70 percent of the world's refining capacity was located in the United States, and the few very large refineries were almost all there or in the Middle East (see table 8-4).

During the next decade world capacity and output grew by about 60 percent. The increase was much less rapid in the United States, where the number of plants declined considerably as many small resource-based refineries were closed and capacity shifted to consuming areas. The same shift has occurred on an international scale since World War II, chiefly as a result of an enormous expansion of capacity in Western Europe and a still more rapid, but smaller, increase in Asia and Oceania. This development has overshadowed the considerable increase in refining in the exporting areas of Latin America and the Middle East. The number of refineries has continued to decline in the United States and has increased only slightly for the world as a whole, so that the average size of plant has more than doubled. Several factors have contributed to this redistribution of the world's refining industry. Many consuming areas, particularly in Europe, have evolved so large and varied a demand for petroleum products as to justify the

---

[7] N. de Nevers, "Tar Sands and Oil Shales," *Scientific American*, February 1966. See also *Engineering and Mining Journal*, December 1967, pp. 59-75.

[8] The history and present structure of the world petroleum industry are described in Hartshorn, *Politics and World Oil Economics*. For further analysis of the geographic aspects of production and consumption of oil, see P. R. Odell, *An Economic Geography of Oil* (Praeger, 1963). The same subjects are treated for several different forms of energy in G. Manners, *The Geography of Energy* (London: Hutchinson, 1964).

building of large refineries. At the same time, the development of very large tankers has considerably reduced the cost of shipping crude relative to that of products. Finally, the governments of oil-importing regions have fostered the building of refineries to reduce the cost of imports and to give their countries access to a greater number of sources. These motives were prominent in Europe in the postwar decade, when foreign exchange was scarce and imports of petroleum products were growing rapidly; more recently they have been felt in other importing areas, notably in Latin America. The boom in refinery construction affected first those areas where relatively sizable plants were required; in recent years it has extended to much smaller markets, in the poorer countries of Latin America and Africa. Motives of national pride and of saving on imports have been particularly important; at the same time it has become possible, by designing quite simple plants, partially to offset the economies of scale of more complex refineries and reduce the relative costs of small units. Lastly, the wider distribution of refinery capacity has been furthered by a long-term surplus of crude oil, which has brought prices down and increased competition for markets.[9]

The changes described above in the distribution of production, refining, and consumption of oil have had three major effects on world trade in petroleum. First, very large volumes are now imported by Western Europe and by other oil-poor areas where consumption has risen greatly. Second, a much larger share than formerly comes from the Eastern hemisphere. Third, the great bulk of trade is now in crude oil rather than in products. The only refined product still shipped long distances in large volume is residual fuel oil; the more valuable derivatives are generally produced where they are needed, and distributed over short distances within individual countries.

Structure of the Industry

Several hundred enterprises are active in the production, transportation, refining, and marketing of petroleum throughout the world. Outside of the United States and the Communist countries, the industry is dominated by eight major integrated concerns: five of these are American, one British, one British and Dutch, and one French. They control and produce all but a small fraction of the oil exported from Latin America, North Africa, the Middle East, and Indonesia, and have refining and distribution facilities in almost every part of the world. Many of them also produce oil for local consumption in countries that are net importers. A considerable number of smaller, or independent, enterprises also operate in the same areas; these are integrated in varying degree, some being primarily producers, others operators of refineries or buyers and distributors of finished products. Within the United States there are a great many small firms, especially producers; and some such local enterprises are located in several other countries. Finally, in many countries there are state owned and operated firms,

again with varying amounts of integration and ranging from monopolists to small competitors with domestic or foreign private firms. The risks and capital requirements of finding and producing oil favor large concerns and the importance of a marketing organization favors forward integration, but neither pressure prevents the existence of companies of all sizes and structures.

Except in a few countries, the industry in which these enterprises operate is neither perfectly competitive nor monopolistic. There is no commodity market in crude oil or in products: every company must produce oil where it has been able to find it and sell the products where it has marketing facilities. Exchanges among the major companies, sales by independent crude suppliers, and purchases by independent refiners improve the flow of petroleum to market; but it is still true that oil from a particular source is not necessarily sold to the nearest market, and that a given market is not always supplied from the closest or cheapest source. Thus, crude oil may move from Venezuela to Europe while oil from the Middle East is shipped to Brazil, or from Venezuela to Chile while Bolivian crude goes to the United States. Such patterns result partly from differences in the qualities of crude, which is not a homogeneous substance; the much smaller trade in products exhibits few such anomalies.

Particularly in the major exporting countries, a sort of threefold oligopoly prevails: among the major companies, which compete for supplies and market shares; among the different countries, for market shares; and in any one country, between private companies and the government, for division of oil revenues and control over the conditions of production. Governmental protection of a domestic industry against imports, or the erection of various barriers or preferences in trade, or particular features of taxation and legislation, further complicate the pattern by altering both the distribution of output and the direction of trade.[10]

Because so much of the cost of oil is due to exploration and to capital charges, capacity is rather unresponsive to price in the short run.[11] Supply can be varied more readily, by shutting down or reopening wells and pipelines or by slight departures from the optimum rate of output for reservoirs. The demand for petroleum for vehicular fuel and other noncompetitive uses is quite price inelastic, but the response to price is much greater where oil competes with

---

[9]These developments are discussed in Hartshorn, *Politics and World Oil Economics*, pp. 70-72, and in Odell, *Economic Geography of Oil*, pp. 140 ff. The development of small, simple, low-cost refineries is described in *Petroleum Press Service*, March 1963.

[10]For a thorough discussion of this topic, see M. A. Adelman, "The World Oil Outlook," in M. Clawson, ed., *Natural Resources and International Development* (Johns Hopkins Press for Resources for the Future, 1963), and E. T. Penrose, *The Large International Firm in Developing Countries: The International Petroleum Industry* (MIT Press, 1968), especially pp. 150-97.

[11]Estimates of the total cost of crude oil in different producing countries and its distribution among exploration, development, and production are given in P. G. Bradley, *The Economics of Crude Petroleum Production* (Amsterdam: North Holland Publishing Co., 1967). Development costs are calculated from observed incremental capital-output ratios over the period 1953-62, the average rate of decline of production from completed wells, and a discount rate of 15 percent. For the Middle East and Libya these calculations suggest that development accounted for some 70 to 80 percent of the total cost of production. See chap. 6, "Costs in the Major Crude Exporting Countries."

coal, gas, or waterpower. These factors suggest that for small changes in output and demand, prices and the distribution of production may be quite stable — more so than for most resource products — but that large changes might involve instability and sizable variations in price. The likelihood of this is increased by the large changes in marginal cost that can occur when new producing areas are developed. The pace and distribution of exploration for oil should be especially affected by these somewhat random shocks on the supply side.

Changes in exploration and production have been very much as might be expected, but the effect on prices has been strikingly small. Crude petroleum shows almost the highest price stability of any of the commodities studied here; the slowness of price changes, or the low average year-to-year variation, is especially marked (see chapter 3, table B-2). This stability despite large differences in cost and consequent shifts of production is due largely to the structure of the world industry, particularly the operations of the major companies. Production is shifted gradually to protect investments and to avoid disruption of refining and marketing; facilities for the latter must often be built or modified in order to take advantage of a new producing area. Even if the cost of production is the same to all companies operating in one country, the return to investment there will differ according to each one's location, cost, and capacity of refining and distribution facilities. These factors explain why high-cost sources continue to produce or even to expand output, with their market shares declining slowly and for the most part steadily. The large and unforeseeable differences in marginal cost among fields within each producing area also work against rapid shifts from one region to another.

The situation within the United States is quite different, because far more individuals and companies are active. During the 1920s and early 1930s production was greatly overstimulated by the "rule of capture" granting any producer all the oil he could raise, even though his lease might cover only a small part of the reservoir exploited, which encouraged drilling into the same pool from neighboring concessions. The result was a surplus of crude oil which depressed prices greatly. At the same time reservoirs were rapidly drawn down or their pressure lost, and much oil was wasted, so that a scarcity was feared and exploration continued for several years. Oil development in Venezuela and the Middle East began at this time. The ruinous competition of the 1920s was moderated by agreements reached between major American, British, and Dutch companies in 1928 and by agreements between these companies and the Soviet Union, on the stabilization of market shares and prices. These arrangements were followed by similar agreements among the companies developing the Middle East, and remained in effect until the outbreak of World War II. In the United States, legislation in the major producing states to control production in accord with demand also contributed to the end of the surplus. However, nothing was done to reduce the number of wells or even to end the incentive for excessive drilling, so that costs remained artificially high. In order to protect the great number of small producers the United States in 1959 set quotas on imports

of crude oil, distributed among companies according to their domestic refining capacity and allowing the imports to come from any country.[12] These restrictions were somewhat relaxed in 1966 to reduce inflationary pressures.

The major producer governments also influence the world oil market, by their individual policies and by collective action. The chief instrument of the latter is the Organization of Petroleum Exporting Countries, formed in 1960 to coordinate the member governments' positions toward the oil companies operating in their territories. Venezuela, Iran, Iraq, Kuwait, and Saudi Arabia created the organization, with Qatar, Libya, and Indonesia joining later. The OPEC members as a group are the marginal suppliers of crude oil to the world. No effort has been made, nor is any likely, to draw in importing or minor exporting countries. The organization is not intended as the basis of an international commodity agreement. It is a producers' cartel, whose power is limited partly by conflicts of interest among its members and partly by the power of the international oil companies, the factor most responsible for its creation.

The goal of the organization — to increase the control of the member countries over their respective industries, and to reduce their dependence on the oil companies — is subsidiary to that of maintaining or increasing the nations' incomes from petroleum exports. This may be done in two ways: by controlling production, so as to hold or raise prices, and by raising the governments' share of the value of exports. The OPEC is pursuing both means, although there could be different consequences for the relative positions of Venezuela, North Africa, and the Middle East. Venezuela, the highest-cost producer, would benefit by higher prices, but it would undoubtedly have to accept a small, and declining, share of the market in order to persuade the lower-cost producers of the Middle East to restrict their output; the latter in turn would have to yield a larger share to Libya, which has an advantage in location and a very rapidly rising production. The fact that the major companies operating in the Middle East also produce oil in other countries and are subject to various pressures by other host governments, prevents unrestricted price competition on a regional basis, but is not enough to prevent a slow price decline and redistribution of the market in favor of Middle Eastern and North African producers. The lower-cost producers might, however, affect development, and ultimately production, in other areas by raising taxes greatly. Since much of the search for oil in the last decade has been financed by profits from the Middle East, a reduction in companies' earnings might slow development elsewhere, or force a general rise in prices.

Thus far the OPEC has not influenced prices by reducing supplies, but it has affected them in other ways. In 1960 reductions in posted prices were protested, and the companies were for the time forced to agree not to cut prices further. Since taxes are paid on posted prices rather than on actual sales, the effect was to raise the share of taxation as

[12] See *Petroleum Press Service*, April 1959. For an estimate of the costs of protection in the United States, see M. A. Adelman, "Efficiency of Resource Use in Crude Petroleum," *Southern Economic Journal*, October 1964.

prices fell and thereby retard a price decline. In 1962 the OPEC presented the oil companies with a claim that royalties, then deductible from income tax, should be "expensed" or paid in addition to taxes; this was already the practice in Venezuela and Indonesia. Agreement was finally reached in 1965, after prolonged negotiation over the account to be taken of actual prices in setting the new royalties. In 1965 the OPEC took up the question of production control, and resolved to adopt an interim plan for increases in output and to develop and submit to member governments a full control scheme for sharing the residual world market in petroleum. The obstacles to any such agreement are formidable, because of the differing interests of the members, the operations of the international companies, and the prospect that high prices will continue to draw in new supplies. The possible effects of such a program are enormous, especially on prices in the short run and on the distribution of output in the long run.

Petroleum Prices

The United States was for some time the largest oil exporter, so that prices in that country applied to much of the oil in world trade. The considerable excess capacity in Texas enabled the United States into the 1930s to act as the world's marginal supplier of crude oil, even after substantial exports began from Venezuela and the Middle East. Oil was delivered to any market at prices posted at Gulf coast ports, plus freight. This basing-point system was originally equitable for the east coast of the United States and much of Western Europe; but as production rose in the Middle East the amount of phantom freight charged to European consumers grew and the price became increasingly unrealistic. The pressure for a revision in prices was interrupted by World War II, but in the late 1940s Middle Eastern oil became available on some transactions at prices unrelated to those in the Caribbean. Prices were first posted in the Middle East in 1950; Venezuelan prices had previously been set at Gulf coast levels less the U.S. import duty. Since 1950, U.S. prices have ceased to apply to any significant volume of oil, and Venezuelan and Middle East prices have diverged according to costs, markets, and the policies of host governments. In each producing area prices are set for specific types of crude oil and for refined products. The actual value of oil at the wellhead, or the average value of exports or imports, reflects both the distribution among different grades of oil and the extent to which sales are made at prices other than those posted (see table 8-5). Posted prices are somewhat like producer prices for metals, except that they are not so rigidly adhered to and they apply to a much greater variety of products.

World supply and demand for petroleum were generally in balance in the early 1950s; prices rose rather sharply just after World War II, and then increased only slowly for several years. Then in November 1956 the Suez Canal was blocked as a result of the joint English-French-Israeli attack on Egypt. Because the pipelines from the Middle East to the Mediterranean were also cut, oil from that region could reach Europe only by shipment around Africa. The interruption in supplies drove up the price of oil slightly in the

Middle East, somewhat more in the United States, and by about 11 percent in Venezuela, in 1957. Prices fell in 1958, and declined steadily for a decade. The principal cause is a great increase in supplies for export; the Middle East has contributed the greatest volume, but large amounts are now being made available by North Africa and by Eastern Europe. Until recently the Communist countries had very little trade in oil with the rest of the world. Coal was still the dominant fuel; in 1960 petroleum supplied only about 20 percent of commercial energy, the same proportion as in 1930 outside these countries. The change from coal to oil began in the 1950s, and production increased rapidly enough to permit a growing volume of exports. Still more oil was made available for export by the increased use of natural gas (see table 8-6). Western Europe forms the most accessible market for exports from Eastern Europe, and usually takes at least three-fourths of the total; substantial amounts from Eastern Europe have also been shipped to Japan and to several countries in Latin America and Africa.

The increase in supplies in exporting areas has coincided with a reduction, or at least a much slower growth than was anticipated, in imports in several markets. The restrictions on imports into the United States are most important. Several countries which formerly imported oil have increased domestic production, further reducing the market for exports by a small amount.

Until 1957, posted prices reflected realized prices in the Middle East, although small discounts were occasionally given in the form of reduced freight rates or other services. Such hidden discounts, formerly 10 cents per barrel or less, increased between 1957 and 1960; and since 1961 open discounts have been the rule. By mid-1963 some Persian Gulf crude was available at 20 percent off posted prices. Discounts of this size have been obtained in large sales by the major producers to independent refiners in several countries, particularly India, Japan, Argentina, Brazil, and Uruguay. Sales to affiliates of the major companies are generally made at posted prices, but the oil may be sold later for less, or the refined products eventually sold at prices consonant with a lower initial price for the crude. The average realized price of oil from the Middle East, including sales at posted prices and sales at discount, cannot be obtained from published information and would not accurately reflect the state of the market; more accurate estimates could be made only by working back from product prices in markets to which much crude is sold at posted levels.[13]

Comparison of prices in Venezuela with those in the Middle East is difficult, because of the greater variety of crudes and because a much larger share of the oil exported

[13] Information on discounted sales has been published by several importing governments, but is not released by the producing companies: they often buy oil from jointly owned operating companies at posted prices, for sale later at an accounting loss, and do not want their partners to know what prices they ultimately obtain. No one producer or government can estimate the realized price of the bulk of the oil shipped from the Middle East. Estimates of the value of crude from product prices are included in European Coal and Steel Community, EEC and EURATOM, *Étude sur les Perspectives Énergétiques à Long Terme de la Communauté Européene* (Luxembourg, 1964).

is sold to affiliates of the producing companies or shipped as products, after being refined in the Netherlands West Indies or Venezuela. Realized prices have nonetheless declined considerably. The average value of posted prices (based on the gravity distribution of exported crude) was only about 2 percent above the average value of crude exports in 1957, but by 1964 the disparity had widened to 18 percent. The increase reflects the difficulty of selling high-priced Venezuelan light crudes and the increased weight of lower valued heavy oil in exports, as well as actual decreases in price of specific crudes. Product prices at export refineries in both hemispheres have continued to decline; between 1958 and 1964 the drop in the average posted price for refined products was 12 percent at Aruba and Curaçao and 22 percent at Persian Gulf refineries.

This decline in prices and shift of production was interrupted by the Arab-Israeli war of June 1967, in which the Suez Canal was again closed and exports by Arab countries were temporarily halted. There was more disruption than reduction of total supplies, however. Venezuelan output increased by 10 percent to meet the demand occasioned by delays in shipment. The agreement of the richer Arab producers to continue to export to the West, so as to be able to subsidize the governments of Egypt and Jordan while the Canal was closed and Israel continued to hold territory taken in the war, meant that the immediate effects of the conflict on prices and trade were minimal. There may nonetheless be two significant long-run results: a strenuous effort by the major companies to reduce their dependence on the Middle East by increasing output elsewhere; and an indefinite postponement of the possibility of agreement between Venezuela and the Arab members of the OPEC over production controls.

The Oil Industry of Latin America

Oilfields and Resources

Petroleum has been produced in Latin America since 1896, when the first output was obtained in Peru. Production began in 1901 in Mexico and in 1908 in Argentina; by 1950 crude oil had been found in ten Latin American countries, including every one in South America except Paraguay and Uruguay. The region has supplied some 16 percent of all the oil ever produced, and accounts for about the same share of present world output (see table 8-1). Until 1927 the foremost producer was Mexico, which between 1910 and 1921 experienced the greatest boom in the history of the Latin American oil industry. Output had reached half a million cubic meters (3 million barrels) by 1910, when the first fields were discovered in the rich "Golden Lane" in Veracruz. Production rose to 5 million cubic meters (32 million barrels) in 1915, and to more than 30 million (190 million barrels) in 1921; at the peak Mexico was supplying over one-fourth of the world total. The boom ended in the 1920s as abruptly as it had developed, to be followed by a somewhat less spectacular expansion in Venezuela. Output there rose to 20 million cubic meters (125 million barrels) in the 1920s, to 100 million (630 million barrels) after World War II, and to nearly 200 million (1,250 million barrels) by the early 1960s. Mexico has

remained the second largest producer; Colombia held third place from 1946 to 1960, when it was displaced by Argentina. Brazil has been the fifth ranking producer since 1958. Peruvian production has grown very slowly since the initial expansion in the first two decades of this century (see table 8-2).

To a first approximation, the crude oil resources of the western hemisphere are concentrated around the rim of the Caribbean, from Louisiana and Texas through Mexico to Colombia, Venezuela, and Trinidad. Fully five-sixths of the proved reserves of Latin America are found in Mexico, Colombia, and Venezuela, but a closer examination reveals that the oilfields of these countries differ greatly in size, richness, location and quality. No oil has yet been found in Central America, while more has been located and more produced in Argentina than in Colombia. Smaller amounts of petroleum have been found scattered throughout South America, in no apparent pattern.

By far the richest zone in the region is the Maracaibo basin in western Venezuela. The single great field along the entire eastern shore of the lake, together with many nearby smaller fields, contains proved reserves of some 2,000 million cubic meters (12,500 million barrels), half of all the oil known in Latin America. The Gulf of Venezuela, adjacent to Lake Maracaibo, is believed to cover an additional 3,000 million cubic meters (19,000 million barrels) which could be found in the next fifteen years.[14] East-central Venezuela has reserves of about 700 million cubic meters (4,400 million barrels), mostly in the states of Anzoátegui and Monagas; although these fields are much smaller and less prolific than those in the west, they alone exceed the reserves of any other Latin American country and have a higher average output per well.

The size and richness of Venezuela's reservoirs inspired an intensive search for oil in Colombia, but the results have been disappointing. Oil was found as early as 1918, but few fields were discovered until the 1940s, and several were found only since 1960. There are some small fields near the Venezuelan border, but most of the petroleum in Colombia has been found in the Magdalena River valley; recently oil was discovered at Orito, in the Putumayo basin near the border with Ecuador. Total proved reserves are about 200 million cubic meters (1,250 million barrels). Terrain has probably presented more problems to the development of the oil industry in Colombia than anywhere else in Latin America. Transport of oil, whether for export or domestic use, is difficult, and the main producing zone is broken up into many small fields.

Oil is found in only two places west of the Andes in Latin America, in the Guayas peninsula of Ecuador, and in northern Peru. The fields in Ecuador were all discovered before 1940; more than half the wells drilled are now shut in, and those still producing have an extremely low average output. It is now thought more likely that oil will be discovered in the northeast, near the recent discovery in Colombia, than that production can be kept up in the

---

[14]This estimate is based on a recent seismic survey of the Gulf; no wells have yet been drilled in the area, so no reserves have been proved. See *Oil and Gas Journal*, 27 December 1965, p. 121.

coastal fields. The fields farther south, in the northwest corner of Peru, are still older, and their output per well is less than in any country except Ecuador and Cuba. Since World War II several small fields have been located east of the Andes in Peru. These are among the few oil reservoirs found in the entire Amazon basin, or in the slightly larger area including Venezuela south of the Orinoco, Paraguay, and the east coast of the continent down to Uruguay. Petroleum has been discovered in Brazil only in the northeast, despite a thorough search over most of the country. The major fields are just north of Salvador in Bahía, and near Carmópolis in Sergipe; smaller discoveries have been made in Alagoas and near Barreirinhas in Maranhão. With one exception, all Brazil's oilfields have been found since World War II. The only other oil in this area is in east central Bolivia, where several fields were developed in the late 1920s and sizable reserves were found in 1964-65. Total reserves in Ecuador, Peru, Bolivia, and Brazil are somewhat less than 300 million cubic meters (1,900 million barrels), half of which are in Brazil with the remainder about evenly divided between Peru and Bolivia.

Oil is found down the whole length of Argentina, from the Bolivian border to Tierra del Fuego. Except in the vicinity of Comodoro Rivadavia, the fields are all in the highlands at the foot of the Andes; the northeastern half of the country is barren of oil, as are Paraguay and Uruguay. Oil was discovered in Chubut in 1907, and nearly all the known fields were found before the last decade. In the early 1960s several were extensively developed for the first time. As a result of this development Argentina now has proved reserves of 300 million cubic meters, as much as in all the rest of South America except Venezuela and Colombia. The oil zone in the extreme south extends across the northern part of the island of Tierra del Fuego and along the mainland side of the Straits of Magellan. Chile found oil on the island in 1949-50, and a few years later opened the first field on the mainland. No petroleum has been found anywhere else in Chile; reserves are the smallest of any South American producer except Ecuador, some 36 million cubic meters (230 million barrels). Output per well is quite high for the region, surpassed only in Brazil and Venezuela; more than half of all wells are shut in.

After Venezuela, the largest reserves are found in Mexico, some 450 million cubic meters (2,800 million barrels). Petroleum occurs in a zone from Tamaulipas to Tabasco, and perhaps on around to Yucatán, between the coast and the mountains at the edge of the central plateau. Oil was first developed at the turn of the century in northern and central Veracruz, which remained the center of production for the three decades after 1920, as very few new fields were discovered. Production has now shifted to the south and east, following a series of discoveries in the middle and late 1950s. Despite excellent prospects and considerable exploration, no oil has been found between southern Mexico and Colombia, and only an insignificant amount in Cuba.[15]

Natural gas is found together with petroleum in most places in Latin America, often in greater volume than can be used, so there has been little exploration specifically to find gas and rather less is known about reserves. The exceptions to this rule are Mexico and Argentina, where consumption of natural gas is high and a number of independent gasfields have been developed. Large amounts of gas have recently been found in Bolivia and Peru, but development depends on the construction of pipelines. Gas produced in association with oil is consumed in Venezuela and Colombia. Latin America has not been extensively explored for sources of petroleum other than crude oil, but large reserves of tar sand and oil shale have been found. A belt of tar sand 30 to 60 kilometers wide extends for 550 kilometers along the north bank of the Orinoco River in Venezuela, south of the oilfields in the east central part of the country. The resources of this zone are estimated as some 30,000 million cubic meters (190,000 million barrels) of extremely heavy oil, mostly of $10°$ gravity or less.

A deposit of tar sand is essentially an oilfield in which the petroleum is too heavy and viscous to flow, and where the structure of the field does not permit the oil to move horizontally unless the formation is fractured. Oil can be produced from such a structure by mining or by methods like those used for secondary recovery in conventional oilfields. Several companies have proposed to explore and develop the area; and in 1964 the Cía Shell de Venezuela opened negotiations with the Venezuelan government, proposing to develop a small area and leave the rest to other concessionaires or to the state oil company. It is estimated that 10 percent of the oil in place could be extracted by drilling methods such as have been tested by Shell on similar tar sands in Canada. At that rate, reserves would be 3,000 million cubic meters (19,000 million barrels), or as much as present proved reserves of crude oil. The number of wells might be higher, and the recovery rate lower, than for other crude oil, but the development of the zone may nonetheless be attractive to both the government and the private oil companies. Exploration may be less costly; the oil is much closer to the surface; the very heavy oil is currently in demand and could be sold more easily than lighter crude; reserves could be greatly increased without much drilling or production; and valuable experience would be acquired in a leisurely development. These objectives fit in well with the government's petroleum policy, which is to maintain exports without granting any new concessions in the traditional producing areas.[16]

There are no known tar sands elsewhere in Latin America, but oil shale is found in several places. The largest deposits are in Brazil, in a zone over 1,000 kilometers long from the state of São Paulo to Rio Grande do Sul. The oil in place, in rock containing at least 10 gallons (0.03 cubic meters) per ton, is estimated as 130,000 million cubic meters (820,000 million barrels), or nearly 1,000 times the country's present proved reserves of crude oil. A pilot

---

[15] See *Oil and Gas Journal*, 27 December 1965, which describes all the oilfields or oil-producing zones in Latin America by location, date of discovery, production, gravity of oil, and number and status of wells drilled; and G. Weber, ed., *International Petroleum Encyclopedia* (Tulsa: Petroleum Publishing Co., 1967), pp. 111-22.

[16] See Venezuela, Ministerio de Minas e Hidrocarburos, *Memoria* (Caracas, 1965), pp. 11-12, and *Petroleum Press Service*, August 1964. The oil policy of the Venezuelan government is discussed at greater length below.

plant, producing 70 cubic meters of oil per day from 1,000 tons of shale, has been established at São Mateus do Sul, Paraná, and the Conselho Nacional do Petróleo has urged that development of the resources be started. There are reportedly about 60 million cubic meters (380 million barrels) of oil in shale in Argentina and 20 million (125 million barrels) in Chile, but these resources are comparatively small and have not been much studied.[17]

Refining and Distribution

At the beginning of World War II there were some fifty-three refineries in Latin America, with a total capacity of 53,000 cubic meters (330,000 barrels) per day: Mexico, Argentina, and Venezuela accounted for over 80 percent of the total. Some plants were in importing areas or countries, as in Chile, Uruguay, Brazil, and the vicinity of Buenos Aires, but the bulk of capacity and the largest number of refineries were located near oilfields. Only in Mexico did capacity exceed domestic requirements; otherwise Latin America could export products only by way of Aruba and Curaçao, where three refineries with a combined capacity of 80,000 cubic meters (500,000 barrels) per day operated to treat Venezuelan crude.

During the war capacity increased about 40 percent in Latin America; the number of plants declined as several small refineries were closed, chiefly in Argentina. No new plants were built, except in Cuba. Then in the first postwar decade there was a rapid growth of capacity to 200,000 cubic meters (1.25 million barrels) per day. This increase had several sources: the building in 1949-50 of four large new refineries in Venezuela, with a total capacity of 60,000 cubic meters (380,000 barrels) per day; increases in all producing countries, particularly Argentina and Mexico, to keep pace with consumption; and the establishment of new plants in importing countries, enabling them to buy crude instead of products to supplement domestic output, most notably in Brazil. In the next decade capacity more than doubled again, and is now about half a million cubic meters (3 million barrels) per day. (Capacity in Aruba and Curaçao is just over 100,000 cubic meters; there has been no expansion in the last decade, and very little in the last twenty-five years.)[18]

This capacity is distributed in more than eighty refineries, of which thirty-five are quite small (1,000 cubic meters per day or less) and only fourteen are very large (10,000 cubic meters per day or more): of the latter, five are in Venezuela, four in Mexico, three in Argentina, and two in Brazil. This distribution of refineries by size is the result of a number of influences, including type and size of markets, economies of scale, domestic crude oil production, and various forms of government intervention or policy, and deserves to be considered briefly. Except in Venezuela,

very large refineries have been built only near large, concentrated markets. This is the case in Mexico, in the Buenos Aires area, and at Rio de Janeiro and São Paulo. The only other refinery of this size, at Minatitlán, Mexico, supplies a petrochemical industry located at the source of its raw materials. The same factor – closeness to markets for a variety of products – predominates in the location of most of the refineries of 3,000 to 10,000 cubic meters per day. There are two plants in this size range in Colombia, three in Argentina, three in Brazil, two in Chile, one in Uruguay, and four in Cuba. The refinery in Panama has a large market for fuel oil in the ships using the canal; and the plant at Talara, Peru, although located at the oilfields, is accessible to the Lima area by sea. Two countries – Mexico and Uruguay – have no small refineries, and one other country – Chile – has only one small plant. In each of these countries, refining is controlled by a state agency and private interests are not allowed to produce or refine oil. In Chile and Uruguay the market is concentrated in a small area and is large enough to support a sizable plant. In Mexico demand is much more widespread, while refinery capacity is concentrated near Mexico City and along the east coast. The northwestern part of the country can be supplied with products more cheaply from the United States than from domestic refineries.

Refinery location and size are also influenced by the emergence of a long-term world surplus of crude oil. This factor is most evident in the construction of refineries in Central America in recent years. The five countries of the Central American Common Market consume a total of some 1.6 million cubic meters (10 million barrels) of petroleum products each year, and were formerly supplied from Venezuela or the Netherlands West Indies, each country being supplied by one or a few of the major companies. As oil prices fell after 1957, these countries did not benefit proportionately, and interest in having their own refineries grew. A single refinery in the region could have met all requirements, but petroleum products were specifically excluded from the Common Market arrangement, and the countries were not in a position to agree among themselves or with the oil companies what the size, location, and source of crude for such a plant should be. The difficulty of selling oil at a time of surplus did, however, give each country considerable bargaining power with its suppliers; and in order to protect their outlets these companies have thus far built two refineries in Guatemala and one each in Costa Rica, El Salvador, and Nicaragua. Negotiations have occurred for the construction of a plant in Honduras, which has been taking surplus products from Guatemala and Nicaragua.[19] The entire area could have been supplied more cheaply by a much larger refinery built in Panama in 1962.

In petroleum importing countries, the creation of refinery capacity is part of the process of import substitution which Latin America has experienced since the 1930s. In the five principal importers – Argentina, Brazil, Chile,

[17]The estimate of the oil in Brazil's shales is taken from N. de Nevers, "Tar Sands and Oil Shales." See also *Petroleum Press Service*, October 1965. For estimates for Argentina and Chile, see World Power Conference, *Survey of Energy Resources, 1962* (London: WPC, 1962), p. 34. The estimate for Chile was made in 1935.

[18]In addition to the sources indicated in fn. 15, this summary is drawn from the estimates of number and capacity of refineries in API, *Petroleum Facts and Figures*, 1959, pp. 438-39.

[19]For a more thorough description of this chain of events, see Odell, *Economic Geography of Oil*, pp. 122-38. For the situation in Honduras see *Petroleum Press Service*, November 1965.

Cuba, and Uruguay — three-fourths of the increase in refinery output between 1950 and 1960 went to replace imports (see table 8-7). This calculation is based on the 1950 ratio of imports to total supply of refined products: the contribution of import substitution to increased output was extremely high in Brazil, Chile, and Cuba, and low in Argentina. Altogether, two-thirds of the anticipated increase in imports was replaced by domestic output. In Argentina, Brazil, and Chile, but not in the other two countries, import substitution also occurred in crude oil, some 80 percent of the rise in domestic crude production replacing imports in the 1950s. Again the share was close to 100 percent in Brazil and Chile and lower in Argentina. Since the combination of poor resources in Brazil and Chile and political obstacles in Argentina made it more difficult to expand crude output than to build new refining capacity, the degree of import substitution was only 35 percent, much less than the 65 percent replacement of refined products imports in the same three countries.

Production of refined products has followed the expansion of refinery capacity in Latin America (see table 8-8). For the last three decades residual fuel oil has accounted for slightly less than half of output; Venezuela produces more than half of this amount, much of which is exported. The share of gasoline has dropped from 29 to 20 percent, as more use is made in motor vehicles and stationary engines of diesel oil and other distillate fuels. The greatest increase has occurred for kerosene, which is now about 8 percent of the total. The most notable change in the postwar period is the increase in the share of crude production refined domestically, from about 35 percent to more than half. For this purpose "Latin America" excludes Aruba and Curaçao, so the rise in the ratio is greatly influenced by a shift in refining capacity from those islands to Venezuela. (If the Netherlands West Indies are included, the share of production refined in the region falls, from over 90 to less than 75 percent between the 1930s and the 1960s.) The other factor in this trend is the growth of crude oil imports from the Middle East by such countries as Argentina, Brazil and Uruguay, allowing refinery output to grow faster than crude production in Latin America.

There are several thousand kilometers of trunk pipelines in Latin America, concentrated in five countries: Mexico, Colombia, Venezuela, Bolivia, and Argentina; in all the rest of the region there are only three short crude oil lines and one for products. The scarcity of pipelines in the other fifteen countries is a consequence of refinery location and the nature of the market for products. There are only seven refineries not located either on the coast or at an oilfield. Of these, three are connected to import terminals by crude lines, at Escuintla, Guatemala, and Belo Horizonte and Porto Alegre, Brazil. The other four — at Iquitos, Manaus, Uruguaiana, and Asunción — are all located on navigable rivers, and the first three are quite small. The large, concentrated markets for products in Latin America are nearly all quite close to refineries, while distant markets are too small and scattered to justify the capital outlay required for a pipeline. Products are distributed by truck over large areas in the interior of South America and over shorter distances in Central America and much of Mexico. Product pipelines exist only in Mexico, Colombia, Bolivia, Chile, and Argentina.

In Colombia and Venezuela pipelines were built primarily to move crude oil to the coast for export. The only lines for internal distribution in Venezuela are natural gas lines serving Caracas, Valencia, and Morón from fields in Anzoátegui and Guarico; demand for products is met by local distribution from the inland refineries and by sea transport to the coastal markets. In Colombia, also, most pipelines carry crude, but a larger share both of refinery capacity and of demand for products is in the interior of the country. Product pipelines have been built or are planned from the refinery at Barrancabermeja to Bogotá, Medellín, and the vicinity of Manizales, and from Buenaventura to Cali. The situation is quite different in Mexico and Argentina, where pipelines have been built to serve the domestic market. Most lines carry products or natural gas, toward the interior in Mexico and toward the Buenos Aires area in Argentina. The pipelines in Bolivia carry crude to the refineries in consuming areas, and products to La Paz; there is also a long crude line to the Chilean port of Arica for export.

Petroleum Exports

Latin America is a large net exporter of petroleum, as it is of many other natural resource products; in recent years oil has been the region's single most valuable export, bringing in 30 percent of all foreign exchange earned. Virtually all the petroleum exported comes from Venezuela, either directly or by way of the Netherlands West Indies. If Venezuela is excluded from consideration, the region's petroleum economy appears quite different. There are exports by several countries, particularly Colombia, but oil is most notable as an element of consumption and the principal source of energy. A larger share of production is used domestically than for most mineral products exported by Latin America, and imports into some countries are quite large. Altogether the region consumes nearly 40 percent of its output, and imports are one-fifth as large as exports. Consumption will be discussed here more fully than exports; and the situation of Venezuela, the only large exporter, will be described in more detail later.

Total annual exports of crude oil and refined products in the mid-1960s were 200 million cubic meters (1,260 million barrels), or roughly double what they were in 1950. Half of the growth of exports during 1950-66 occurred in the first five years; since then the decline in prices has enabled oil from the Middle East and the Communist countries to supply an expanding share of the market, and Latin American exports have grown more slowly. There have been a number of minor changes in the composition and direction of exports: Chile, for example, now has refineries and no longer sells crude, and neither does Ecuador, where consumption has overtaken production; Brazil exported some of its crude for refining in 1958-63; and Argentina exported crude and products in 1961-66. In these countries, and in Mexico and Peru, oil exports are quite small, and may occur together with imports; it is common for a country to trade oil in both directions, as a consequence of transport difficulties or of imbalance between demand and the kind of crude or the range of refined products produced in the country. The trade of all countries other than Venezuela and Colombia had no effect on the principal features of the region's exports in the period since 1950. These may be summarized briefly (see table 8-9).

Relatively less crude goes to the Netherlands West Indies than formerly — less than one-fourth, compared with one-half in the early 1950s. However, the share of petroleum exported as products has not changed; there has simply been a shift in shares of refining capacity from Aruba and Curaçao to Venezuela. It is rather surprising that the ratio of products to crude remained constant, products accounting for about one-half of the total, during a period when refineries were being built in most importing countries and world trade was increasingly conducted in crude oil.

The explanation of this seeming anomaly depends on circumstances in the principal markets for Venezuelan oil and on certain characteristics of that oil and of the policy of the Venezuelan government regarding exports. It may be noted first that exports of crude increased more rapidly than those of products to both Latin America and Western Europe; indeed, exports of products to other countries in Latin America have actually declined. In the United States, however, imports of products from Latin America have grown more rapidly than those of crude. The restrictions on petroleum imports fixed in 1959 bear more heavily on crude than on products. Furthermore, Venezuela can produce from its heavy crude large amounts of residual fuel oil, much in demand in the northeast part of the United States, while refineries in the latter country are designed to make as much gasoline as possible, that being the most valuable major product. The share of gasoline in total refinery output is higher there than anywhere else, and the resulting demand for heavy fuel oils is met by imports. The demand for these oils is also very strong in Europe, but a larger share of the Venezuelan crude from which they are made is refined in Europe. Finally, the present world surplus in oil has intensified competition in supplies of crude — where transport costs are relatively low — more than in supplies of products. The Venezuelan government has decided not to compete on price with crude oil from the Middle East, and has consequently lost markets; but its markets for products have been less affected. The constant ratio of crude to refined products in Latin American exports is, in sum, the result of obstacles to the sale of crude abroad, whether these originate in the policies of importing countries, in the cost advantage of crude over products in shipping, or in the decisions of exporting countries. Exports of products consist predominantly of residual fuel oil in every country except Peru, where a large volume of distillate oils is exported.[20] Two-thirds of the heavy fuel oil is sold to the United States, and most of the rest to Western Europe; distillate fuels are sold more in Europe and within Latin America. Gasoline and kerosene form a very small share of total exports.

The value of petroleum exports increased rapidly in the early 1950s, from about $1,500 million or 20 percent of the regional total, to some $2,100 million and nearly 30 percent. In 1955-65 the share remained constant, while the total value rose to $2,700 million — a slower growth than that of the volume of exports, because of the decline in prices. Oil exports account for over 90 percent of Venezuela's foreign exchange; the share has ranged from 10 to 17 percent in Colombia, and from 5 to 10 in both Mexico and Peru. In the latter two countries imports of oil absorb most of the value of exports; in other countries petroleum does not account for more than a few percent of total earnings.

Consumption of Petroleum

The consumption of commercial energy (from mineral fuels and hydroelectricity) in Latin America has increased sixfold in the last three decades, and is now equivalent to about 110 million tons of petroleum per year.[21] In the same period the use of vegetable fuels (chiefly firewood) has remained approximately constant at 20 to 25 million tons petroleum equivalent; the substitution of other sources of energy for firewood has balanced the growth in population which would otherwise have raised consumption substantially. The most striking feature of the evolution of energy use is the eightfold growth in the consumption of petroleum, from two-thirds to 90 percent of commercial energy (see table 8-10). A rapid increase in the use of oil has occurred or is in progress everywhere in the world, but two features distinguish the process in Latin America from that in North America and Europe. First, the region is quite poor in coal when compared with the more industrial nations of the northern hemisphere. Argentina, Brazil, Chile, Colombia, and Mexico have sizable resources, but even in these countries coal is relatively scarce and costly to produce; elsewhere coal is even more vulnerable to competition from oil and gas. The use of coal actually declined between 1937 and 1950, and has since risen only about 40 percent. Second, Latin America is some decades behind the richer countries in economic development, so that most of the region's industrialization has occurred since the development of the petroleum industry. Oil has therefore substituted for wood as well as for coal. Since World War II hydroelectric capacity in Latin America has greatly expanded, but hydroelectricity accounts for only about 4 percent of the energy from all commercial sources.

It was noted above that petroleum is the easiest fuel to transport, and so dominates energy consumption in areas poor in energy resources. Some coal is imported into Latin America, particularly for coking for the metal-processing industries, but most imported fuel is in the form of oil or its derivatives. Imports of petroleum approximately doubled in the period 1950-66, from 17 to 40 million cubic

---

[20]The composition of petroleum product exports by destination is given for the years 1958-63 in ECLA, *Statistical Bulletin for Latin America*, I, no. 1 (March 1964), table 55.

[21]Energy from different sources can be compared only on the basis of actual energy content, since fuels differ in energy density. The unit used here is the petroleum equivalent ton, since oil accounts for the largest share of commercial energy in Latin America. Hydroelectricity is measured according to its energy content; it can also be measured by the amount of fuel that would be required to generate that output of electricity in thermal generating facilities, and each method has its justification. For an explanation of the problems and units encountered in measuring energy, see the sources for table 8-10.

meters (108 to 250 million barrels: see table 8-11). By far the largest importer is Brazil, which takes almost 15 million cubic meters (95 million barrels); Cuba and Central America, which possess essentially no oil and depend entirely on imports, take about 5 and 7 million cubic meters, respectively (30 and 44 million barrels). Argentina, Chile, and Uruguay are all sizable importers, though only Uruguay has no oil of its own. Three-fourths of these imports used to be in the form of products; the share dropped sharply in 1955, as new refinèries came into operation in Brazil and Chile, and has continued to decline as refineries were built in Cuba and Central America. Products now account for only about one-fourth of imports.

Some refined products are imported from the United States — particularly lubricants and other specialized products that are not made on a large scale in Latin America. However, the bulk of product imports originates within the region. Venezuela is the principal source, either directly or through Aruba and Curaçao, and other producers export surpluses of certain products to balance refinery output and demand. Almost no products are imported from the eastern hemisphere, but a great deal of crude oil is. Argentina, Brazil, and Uruguay have obtained between one-third and one-half of their oil from the Middle East since 1950. The Soviet Union has also sold small amounts of crude to these countries, and since 1960 has provided all the oil used by Cuba. Venezuela supplies virtually all the crude imported into Central America and the west coast of South America, and all western hemisphere oil taken by the east coast importing countries. Colombia provides a much smaller amount, mostly to Central America; Peru exports some crude to Argentina, as does Bolivia. The share of crude imported from within the region was about 40 percent in 1950-51 and rose to one-half in 1952-54; at that time Argentina and Uruguay were the principal importers, and they obtained much of their oil from the Middle East. The share increased in the next five years, to a peak of 75 percent in 1959, as refineries were built in Brazil, Chile, and Cuba, and Venezuelan trade with those countries shifted from products to crude. In the 1960s Venezuela lost the Cuban market, while exports of crude to Chile did not increase and Argentina's imports declined sharply. These factors reduced the fraction of crude imported from Latin America to one-half in 1962-64. The decline was partly offset by the construction of refineries in Central America, which began to buy crude from Venezuela and Colombia in place of products, as Chile and Cuba had done earlier.

About one-sixth of all mineral fuel consumed in Latin America is burned to generate electricity, accounting for just under half of all electricity produced. Both these shares have been constant for three decades. Fuel oils provide some 80 percent of all fuel used for thermoelectric generation. This amounts to about 19 percent of all oil and gas consumption in the late 1930s, 14 percent around 1950, and 9 percent in the early 1960s. The increasing use of natural gas in Chile, Colombia, Mexico, and Venezuela moderates the decline somewhat. The generally high share of petroleum in thermoelectric fuel consumption reflects the widespread use of small diesel powered generators in Latin America and the region's poverty in coal resources.[22]

Latin America consumed in 1962-64 some 90 million cubic meters (570 million barrels) of refined petroleum products annually, more than double the level of the early 1950s and nearly seven times as much as before World War II. Residual fuel oil is the product used in largest quantities, followed by gasoline and distillate oils. Although kerosene is widely used in poor and rural areas, the total amount consumed is small (see table 8-12). The share of fuel oil of all types in the total has declined in the last several decades, as consumption has grown only half as fast as that of gasoline or kerosene; among fuel oils, consumption of the distillate oils has increased more than that of residual fuel. These changes reflect the growing use in the region of internal combustion engines — for transport of all kinds, for industrial applications and for generating electricity — which expands more rapidly than the use of oil as a general fuel for heating. Total consumption of products was highest, about 18 million cubic meters (110 million barrels), in Argentina, Brazil, and Mexico; Venezuela used half that amount, and Chile, Colombia, Cuba, and Peru each consumed one-third to one-half as much as Venezuela. The distribution of consumption by major products varies greatly among countries; the availability of coal or hydropower, which compete most directly with heavy fuel oil, influences the pattern of demand, as do climate and industrial structure (see table 8-12). Residual fuel oil is the most used product in ten countries; gasoline leads in seven, including Chile and Colombia — which use relatively large amounts of coal — and Mexico; and in three countries distillate fuel oils are used more than any other product. A large share of fuel oil is associated with a high share of thermal electricity in Argentina, Cuba, Uruguay, and Venezuela. With the data available it is impossible to relate in greater detail each country's consumption by product to the various sectors or activities of the economy.

The information presented on production, trade, and consumption of crude oil and the five major classes of refined products can be summarized to show the place of petroleum in the Latin American economy in a single year (see table 8-13). In 1964 the region produced some 254 million cubic meters (1,600 million barrels) of crude. Net exports amounted to almost 30 percent of this total, the remainder being refined domestically. Of total refinery output, in turn, 44 percent constituted net exports and the rest was consumed in the region. Consumption consisted predominantly of residual fuel oils and gasoline; production and exports included much larger shares of residual fuel oil and of distillate oils. Refinery output and exports of the Netherlands West Indies are included in these figures.

Natural Gas

The other principal petroleum product is natural gas, which presents certain problems of description and measurement and therefore is described separately. Gas is largely a joint product, obtained from oil wells in amounts determined by the production of crude. Once brought to the surface, the gas can be used in more ways than can oil:

[22] See ECLA, *Estudios Sobre la Electricidad en América Latina* (Mexico City: UN, 1962), vol. I, pp. 85 ff., 188-200.

if a pipeline exists, it can be marketed away from the field, either for use as a fuel or as a raw material for petrochemical manufacture; it can be used as fuel in the oilfield; it can be compressed and driven back underground to maintain or raise the pressure in a reservoir and so bring up more oil; and the amount not used in any of these ways is simply wasted, by venting to the atmosphere or by flaring. Gas is an excellent fuel, nearly always preferred to fuel oil at the same price, but it costs about three times as much per unit of energy to transport as petroleum and generally cannot be marketed unless output and demand are large enough to justify a sizable pipeline. If the gas is rich in liquid hydrocarbons, these can be separated and the dry gas then consumed, repressed, or wasted.

It is difficult to describe the natural gas economy of Latin America in any detail, but a brief summary of production and use is given below (see table 8-14). First, production of gas is rising rapidly in the region, in line with or faster than output of oil; and second, the share of this production which is used has also been growing. The amount of waste is still enormous, running to about one-sixth of all commercial energy consumption, but it has been much reduced in the past decade. Fully 70 percent of Venezuela's gas production used to be flared; now, as a result of greater repressuring and the construction of gaslines to Caracas, the share is down to 40 percent. Mexico and Argentina have the largest networks of gas pipelines and consume large amounts of gas as fuel. Gas is already the principal fuel for stationary – nonvehicular – use in Venezuela and is approaching that status in Mexico and Argentina. In Chile the bulk of production is repressed, since the principal markets are too far from the oilfields to justify a pipeline; natural gas provides fuel only in the form of liquids extracted before the gas is returned to the reservoir. A great deal of attention is currently given to natural gas, since it represents a large source of energy still imperfectly exploited; present production of some 70,000 million cubic meters might be greatly increased if markets can be developed. There is interest in pipelines to connect gasfields in Bolivia with the Argentine gasline network, or with the São Paulo area of Brazil; a major line from large fields east of the Andes in Peru to the Lima area is being considered; and Chile is studying the feasibility of shipping refrigerated gas from the extreme south to the center of the country or the north, to displace fuel oil which now must be imported.

Natural gas is also of great and growing interest for the manufacture of industrial chemicals such as methanol and the production of ammonia for the manufacture of nitrogenous fertilizers. The demand for these products is expected to increase by a factor of between three and six, depending on the product, between 1963 and 1975, necessitating either a rapid rise in output or great expenditures on imports. Economies of scale are considerable for most of these products, so that a regionally integrated industry taking advantage of low-cost sources of gas and large plant size could result in large savings by comparison with either imports or production for small national markets. The lowest-cost solutions include plants located at the gasfields in eastern Venezuela, at Tierra del Fuego in Chile and near

Minatitlán in Mexico. The development of a regional fertilizer industry would appreciably increase the use of natural resource outputs and provide a major input to the resource sector, and would join the mineral and agricultural sectors more closely.[23]

Issues and Problems

The petroleum industry provides illustrations of nearly every issue raised by the exploitation of natural resources. Many of these questions arise for one or more of the principal metals mined in Latin America, but no one of them involves quite so wide a range of considerations. It is not feasible to discuss all the issues in detail, particularly since the experiences and national policies of different countries vary greatly. This section is intended only to introduce the main areas of choice or conflict, after which certain issues will be treated more thoroughly as they have been manifested in four Latin American countries: Mexico, Peru, Argentina, and Venezuela. Brief references will be made to other countries and, for purposes of comparison or illustration, to other commodities.[24]

In all but two of the region's producing countries large-scale production of petroleum was initiated by foreign private firms which were chiefly interested in finding oil to export. This situation resembles that of the nonferrous metals, and of iron ore in some countries, and brought with it much the same questions of taxation, value returned, integration with the domestic economy, and public influence on the industry's policies. Several differences should be noted, however. Because petroleum is consumed even in economies with little or no manufacturing industry, and because the major oil companies are vertically integrated and distribute their products to the final consumers, these companies established themselves even where they did not find oil or where they found only enough to supply the host country's market. The high capital requirements for exploration and development, the importance of shipping and marketing facilities, and the readiness of foreign companies to enter a market all worked against the creation of domestic private enterprise. The state was by default the only counterpoise to the large foreign firms, and it could not avoid fairly direct involvement with them; there are no impersonal commodity markets between them, nor is it feasible even to import petroleum without an extensive distribution system. None of these factors operates with the same force for any of the major metals. Together, they may help to explain the frequency and intensity of conflict between national governments and foreign enterprises. Other technical and economic features of oil production facilitate or contribute to such conflicts. It is easy to fear the exhaustion of a country's resources if reserves are adequate for only a few years' production and require sustained investment to maintain or increase. The great weight of investment for exploration relative to total cost of pro-

[23] See ECIEL, "Nitrogenous Fertilizers," in Martin Carnoy, ed., *Industrialization in a Latin American Common Market* (Brookings Institution, forthcoming); and the discussion of these linkages in chap. 2 of the present volume.

[24] In particular copper (chap. 4) and iron and steel (chap. 5), which together exhibit many of the issues relevant to petroleum.

duction also makes the economy quite sensitive to the investment climate created by public policy, and gives the companies the power to vary their economic impact considerably in the short term without changing the rate of output. Policies based on short-run considerations with very damaging effects for the long run have been unfortunately common in the Latin American resource sector, and the pressures and temptations toward such policies are quite strong in the case of petroleum.[25]

Finally, petroleum has a political and emotional significance which may not be fully explained by its economic importance. It is the "blood" of a modern economy and it may therefore seem intolerable to have it controlled by a foreign enterprise or by any sort of private company. Conflict in which basic, even moral, issues are involved is characteristic of the more bitter disputes in the industry's history, and they are not necessarily ones with the greatest economic weight.[26] Nationalism is very much involved, and influences the actions of governments even when in most respects they do not want or dare to challenge the companies that produce their oil. The companies are protected against expropriation or other extreme action by the large capital requirements of the industry and especially, in the case of exporting countries, by their control of marketing facilities. There has been only one test of strength between the international companies and a major exporter, in Iran in 1951. After the companies' properties there were nationalized almost no Iranian oil could be sold, and after a change of government, foreign enterprise was allowed to return. Where little is involved besides the domestic market, nationalization is easier. It has occurred five times in Latin America: in Bolivia in 1937 and 1969, in Mexico in 1938, in Cuba in 1960, and in Peru in 1968. In general, however, there is no simple division between "national" and "foreign" interests: on the government's side there are usually both political and economic pressures, both deserving to be called nationalist but sometimes very much in conflict. In such circumstances it becomes difficult to set the goals of public policy. For example, "self-sufficiency" can mean independence of foreign supplies (or an adequate domestic production) or it can mean exclusion of foreign enterprise from domestic resources (in which case imports may be necessary). The choice may turn on which pressure is strongest at the moment, so policy can be abruptly reversed when these pressures change in relative strength. Other decisions likewise involve choices or compromises among political and economic goals.

One response to these problems is the creation of a state oil company; such enterprises have been established in every Latin American producing country except Ecuador and in two others (Paraguay and Uruguay) as well (see table 8-15). The national enterprises differ so greatly in size, degree of integration, functions, and relation to domestic and foreign private firms that some distinctions are necessary.

Those of at least three countries – Colombia, Peru, and Venezuela – were set up to satisfy political goals without endangering economic relations with the foreign companies active in these countries.[27] They compete with the latter in the domestic market under various forms of state preference and protection, but do not challenge the major companies in exports or otherwise interfere with their operations. Similar motives led to the establishment of a state company in Bolivia and in Mexico, but in these cases the state acquired a monopoly following the expropriation of foreign enterprise a few years later. A state agency was also created after expropriation of foreign and domestic companies in Cuba. In only two countries, Brazil and Chile, have foreign companies never contributed to production; the state concern in each case initiated production and still has a monopoly. The intent in Argentina was the same, but the state has allowed foreign enterprise to find and produce oil to supplement the output of the national company. In Paraguay and Uruguay the state company imports and refines oil for domestic consumption.

If the national company is to supply an appreciable share of the country's requirements, it must be large and well financed. The three principal enterprises in Latin America – PEMEX of Mexico, PETROBRAS of Brazil, and YPF of Argentina – are among the 100 biggest firms, public or private, outside the United States. Each is the largest company in its own country; PEMEX, the only self-sufficient concern, is the largest of the three. No other Latin American enterprise is among these 100, and only one other is included in the first 200 companies.[28] The state oil companies are thus much larger than other state ventures such as steel mills in the region.

In countries that do not produce oil or that export large amounts – Paraguay, Uruguay, Cuba, Colombia, and Venezuela – the state enterprises concentrate on refining and marketing. Elsewhere state participation is greatest in production, which is politically the most sensitive phase of the industry. Even where the state has a monopoly of output, foreign or domestic private firms may be allowed to refine and distribute petroleum, as in Brazil and Chile. Thus the division of ownership shows less of a pattern by stages than it does for metal mining, and there is also greater variety from country to country. For the region as a whole, foreign enterprise in the years 1963 to 1965 controlled some 84 percent of crude output, 50 percent of refinery capacity, 51 percent of final sales of refined products, and virtually the entire amount of exports.

The establishment of a national oil company does not, of course, resolve all the problems of finding and supplying oil for a country; and to the extent that it ends a political problem it creates a great economic responsibility. This is especially the case if the state enterprise is intended to meet the country's entire requirement for oil. The chief diffi-

---

[25] For examples involving other commodities, see chap. 4 (Copper) under the heading, "Issues and Policies" and chap. 7 (Tin) under the heading "Tin in Latin America."

[26] On this subject see P. R. Odell, "Oil and State in Latin America," *International Affairs*, October 1964.

[27] The founding of the Peruvian company Empresa Petrolera Fiscal was explained in these terms by President Bustamente y Rivero. See C. W. Anderson, *Politics and Economic Change in Latin America* (Van Nostrand, 1967), pp. 170-71.

[28] The list of the 200 largest enterprises outside the United States and the Communist countries is given in *Fortune*, 15 September 1967, p. 142.

culty is precisely the factor which has deterred most countries from trying to do without foreign enterprise — the necessity of investing large sums in exploration, development, and the construction of facilities from oilfield to consumer. Exploration is generally not only expensive but risky. It is estimated, for example, that through 1960 the private companies in Colombia invested approximately $1,000 million and recovered only 15 percent of that amount.[29] Between 1954 and 1960, PETROBRAS spent some $300 million in searching for oil, without finding any outside the previously developed producing area in Bahía; this was probably the most expensive fruitless exploration ever mounted. In 1960 PETROBRAS was advised to cease exploring in all but a few areas of Brazil and to reduce its efforts even in those.[30] Reserves have since increased greatly, following a major discovery in Sergipe and lesser ones in Alagoas and Maranhão, but the cost of the oil found is still extremely high. Governments with many claims on their capital resources find it difficult to maintain investment, but the alternative is for production to fall behind consumption and require that oil be imported. This occurred in Mexico, Argentina, and Bolivia in the 1950s, and in the latter two countries foreign enterprise was allowed to return. Economic pressure forced the abandonment of a major political policy.

For a state company, its efficiency and freedom from corruption or political interference are also extremely important. Such a company is always in some danger of being used as a source of patronage rather than of oil; this appears to have occurred in both Mexico and Brazil. PEMEX was rid of many superfluous personnel and allowed to begin operating efficiently in 1959; a similar shakeup took place in PETROBRAS in 1964.[31] Even if the enterprise is sufficiently autonomous and free from corruption, it may be so inefficient as to frustrate the national policy it is supposed to implement. This is part of the explanation of YPF's difficulties in Argentina in the last decade and a half.

Petroleum has presented technical and financial problems in a number of countries. In Brazil and Chile there have been no significant political difficulties or changes of policy such as have occurred in Colombia and in Cuba. The various problems arising when petroleum is a major issue are illustrated by the experiences of Mexico, Peru, Argentina, and Venezuela.

Mexico

The dispute with the greatest repercussions throughout Latin America took place in Mexico in the period 1917-38. Production was entirely in the hands of foreign private firms; the majority were U.S. companies, but the largest, Mexican Eagle, was owned by Shell of the United Kingdom. Apparently these enterprises were little affected by the Revolution of 1910-17. Their output continued to grow

rapidly, reaching a peak in 1921. At the end of the Revolution, however, two factors arose to change the companies' position and their relations with the government. The first was the installation of a strong revolutionary government, empowered by the constitution of 1917 to control the use of all land and subsoil minerals and to defend the claims of labor as to pay and working conditions. The second was the end of the boom in production, resulting from an inability to find new reserves fast enough to sustain output. During the 1920s the companies increased their drilling efforts; nevertheless, the fraction of wells abandoned as dry rose from 38 to 55 percent.[32] Production fell rapidly to one-fourth or less of the peak level, and in the 1930s the producers chose to maintain operations at a low level or allow them to decline. The finding of still cheaper and more plentiful oil in Venezuela in the 1920s, and the advent of the Depression and surplus a few years later, removed any incentive to invest.

These incentives had already been weakened by a running dispute over the terms of oil concessions and of title to lands, the legal basis for which had been changed by the Revolution. Pressures for a change in the companies' status, and for improved pay and conditions for their workers, increased during the Cárdenas administration, and came to a head in November 1936 in new labor union demands. The companies' offers as to pay and taxes were not accepted, and they refused to settle strikes on the terms dictated by the Mexican supreme court. Faced with this challenge to its authority, the government in November 1938 nationalized all the enterprises producing oil in the country and entrusted their facilities to a state company, Petróleos Mexicanos.

At first PEMEX lost the export market which had accounted for slightly over half of production, as foreign companies boycotted the country; equipment and trained workers were similarly hard to get. These obstacles were removed when the United States entered World War II and began to need as much western hemisphere oil as possible. In 1942 Mexico also agreed to compensate the former owners of the industry for the bulk of their investments, excluding the value of proved reserves; these payments were completed in 1963. Several features of PEMEX's history in the last two decades have already been noted. Exploration was initially successful enough to keep production rising ahead of consumption, but the prices set by the government eventually made adequate efforts impossible. In 1957 Mexico became a net importer of petroleum; and this development resulted, in 1959, in a thorough shakeup of PEMEX. The company was given enough freedom from political pressures, and enough financial resources through higher prices and powers to borrow funds for development, to allow it to regain virtual self-sufficiency, to embark on a considerable expansion and modernization of its refineries and pipelines, and to begin building the largest petrochemical industry in Latin America.

Over the long run Mexico has achieved both the political goal of complete state control of the oil industry and the

[29] Hartshorn, *Politics and World Oil Economics*, p. 277.

[30] *Ibid.* See report of W. Link, chief geologist for PETROBRAS, summarized in *Petroleum Press Service*, February 1961.

[31] For an account of PEMEX's condition before the reorganization, see A. Vargas MacDonald, *Hacia una Nueva Política Petrolera* (Mexico City: Editorial Promoción, 1959). For Brazil, see *Petroleum Press Service*, August 1964.

[32] J. R. Powell, *The Mexican Petroleum Industry, 1938-1950* (University of California Press, 1956), p. 15.

economic goal of self-sufficiency. This twofold success is thus far unique in Latin America, although it could be repeated in the near future by either Argentina or Brazil. The country continues to import some products, but these are more than compensated for by exports. Here Mexico has a slight advantage because the U.S. quota system does not limit overland imports. In two more important ways Mexico has been fortunate: it has relatively large and rich petroleum and gas resources, and it has enjoyed a high level of exports and investment which made it feasible to raise large sums for PEMEX. The crucial element of success, however, seems to have been the decision to give the company enough financial and managerial autonomy and to allow it to embark on a costly and finally successful program of exploration. Much of PEMEX's output now comes not from the fields acquired in 1938 but from zones discovered during the 1950s, mostly in southern Vera Cruz and in Chiapas. It is not certain whether the policy pursued for the last three decades has been economically efficient or whether it has imposed on the Mexican economy a higher cost than a less nationalist course would have done.

The Mexican experience demonstrated that a nationalized industry could be operated with a minimum of foreign participation. That lesson has undoubtedly encouraged other countries to create or expand state enterprises, and it has influenced the international companies as well. The fact that the Mexican government did not collapse as expected has generally made them deal more carefully with other governments and yield where necessary to preserve their major interests.

While there have been many conflicts in the Latin American petroleum industry since 1938, there have been few such confrontations. The most similar case occurred in Cuba in 1960, when the companies operating refineries on their own crude from Venezuela were asked to use lower-priced Russian crude instead. They refused, because they wanted to maintain the outlet for their oil and were unwilling to lower their prices and risk conflict with the Venezuelan government. The facilities were therefore expropriated. No compensation has been paid, partly because the United States government's hostility to the new Cuban regime and the expectation that it would be short lived were obstacles to negotiations. In other respects, however, there is no similarity, because Cuba continues to rely on foreign supplies and assistance. Domestic production is negligible, so the state company is chiefly concerned with refining and distribution.

Peru

The oldest conflict over petroleum in Latin America, and the one which may have the most severe political repercussions, concerns the La Brea-Pariñas fields on the northern coast of Peru. This property was granted to an individual by the Peruvian government in 1826, in a unique cession of control over the subsoil; all other mineral deposits in the region have always been held as concessions from the state. Until 1887 the property, which was valued for tar and asphalt, was exempt from mining taxes; it was first registered and taxed in 1888, and production of petroleum began in 1890. Until 1911, however, the owners paid much lower taxes than were required by the mining law, and the legal status of the property was not clear; the state did not expressly reaffirm or deny the grant of subsoil rights. An investigation begun in that year resulted in a decree of 1915 which revoked the grant and asserted that the field was subject to the regular mining laws.

The controversy, which had become much more important with the discovery of petroleum, might have ended there. At that time, however, La Brea-Pariñas was owned by a British firm and operated by the International Petroleum Company, which was interested in buying it. The British government intervened on the owners' behalf and in 1921 Peru agreed to arbitration of the dispute. An agreement was reached which formed the basis of an award in 1922: the owners paid $1 million which the Peruvian government accepted as meeting its claims, and in return received a fifty-year exemption from the law applicable to concessions. The question of subsoil ownership was not mentioned, but the IPC regarded the award as a reversal of the 1915 decree, and in 1924 it bought the property. Over the next four decades the company, now a subsidiary of Standard Oil of New Jersey (ESSO), invested some $190 million in the fields and in a refinery at Talara, and acquired a partial interest in other fields in Peru. La Brea-Pariñas provides about 40 percent of Peru's total crude production and nearly all this amount is refined and consumed in the country; altogether the IPC accounted for about 55 percent of the distribution of refined products in Peru. With a few exceptions, prices, working conditions, and other aspects of the company's operations have not been matters of dispute.

The IPC accepted a 50 percent profit tax in 1951, relinquishing the special tax status granted by the 1922 award, but it resisted any claim that the property did or should belong to the Peruvian state. In 1957 it offered to convert its ownership into a concession, provided no claims were made for unpaid taxes in prior years, but this offer was rejected by the government on the ground that neither the original grant nor the arbitration award was valid. Dissatisfaction with the special status of the IPC and increasing nationalist feeling in Peru had reached the point where the government could not appear to surrender its claims in dealing with the company, which for its part made no further concessions until 1968.

In 1962 the Peruvian military intervened to prevent the winner of that year's presidential election, Haya de la Torre of the APRA party, from taking office; another election in 1963 resulted in victory for Belaúnde Terry, who campaigned on a promise to end the privileged position of the IPC. In July his administration called for a settlement within ninety days, and in November it presented to Congress a law recovering ownership of La Brea-Pariñas for the state and raising income taxes to 70 percent. When the company rejected these terms Congress formally declared the 1922 agreement null and void. The government could not, however, enforce its decision except by expropriating the company, and that course encountered two serious objections.[33]

---

[33] The failure of negotiations in 1957 because of the government's weak position and their renewal in 1963 on the election of a

First, opinion in Peru was sharply divided. Two political parties favored expropriation, with any compensation to be offset by claims for back taxes. Other parties were opposed to any step that would reduce the participation of foreign capital and skills in the industry. The state company, EPF, was quite small and did not consider itself capable of operating the property with its technical and financial resources. The employees of the IPC were also opposed to expropriation.[34]

Second, Peru was relatively dependent on aid from the United States, and that government is legally bound by the Hickenlooper Amendment to the Foreign Assistance Act to suspend aid to any country expropriating U.S. property without prompt and full compensation. Invocation of the amendment would also deprive Peru of its quota in the U.S. sugar market, which was greatly enlarged when imports from Cuba were ended in 1960. The necessity of compensating the company would have ruled out the possibility of collecting any taxes alleged to be owed, since such claims, covering the entire period since 1924, exceeded the value of the company's assets.

Since the Belaúnde administration was just the sort which the United States government wished to encourage under the Alliance for Progress, it was expected that Peru would receive a generous amount of aid. Assistance was suspended in 1962 in protest over the military intervention of that year, and before it could be resumed in 1963 the U.S. State Department decided to withhold aid as a means of forcing the Peruvian government to reach agreement with the IPC. The government proposed a service contract in 1964 and a standard concession in 1965, but the company rejected both; no compensation was allowed for investments which the company would not continue to own, and before-tax profits were to be limited to 9 percent. By 1966 it was evident that the suspension of aid was not having the desired effect, and moreover the political strength of Belaúnde's government had begun to decline in consequence of its inability to settle the La Brea-Pariñas issue and of domestic inflation. Aid was therefore resumed, but it was cut off again in 1967, when the Peruvian military rejected U.S. advice and bought supersonic warplanes — the first to be acquired by any Latin American country — from France. Thus Peru received virtually no aid during four of the five years of the Belaúnde administration. In July 1967 the Congress authorized the expropriation of the IPC properties, but left the President free to reach an agreement with the company over operation and compensation. During that year the Peruvian Tax Court assessed the company's tax bill at $144 million. There were no further ne-

gotiations, however, and the government's position continued to weaken; in November 1967 it was compelled to devalue sharply. In June 1968 the Congress gave Belaúnde sixty days in which to solve the problem by executive decree, and under this pressure conversations were resumed. Finally at the end of July the IPC abandoned its claim of ownership and agreed to cede all rights to the state. On the basis of this offer Belaúnde proclaimed the solution of the controversy, and after two weeks of negotiations a formal agreement was signed. The IPC was to give up ownership of the disputed field, but would buy, refine, and sell oil from it; would expand and modernize the Talara refinery; would continue all of its other Peruvian operations unchanged and would have some claim to exploration rights in the Amazon basin of the country, where large oil resources are believed to exist. All tax claims against the company were to be dropped.

These terms would undoubtedly have been acceptable any time up to 1966, but by late 1968 resentment against the company, and the erosion of the government's position, had proceeded so far that the agreement was immediately attacked as a capitulation to the company. The crucial point in the dispute became the question of whether or not the IPC had agreed to a minimum price for the oil it would purchase from EPF, which would operate the field. It was presumably this consideration which determined the company's desire to continue owning the oilfield, but the range of prices in question was apparently only ten or fifteen cents per barrel. Before the issue could be settled by new negotiations, however, the Belaúnde government was overthrown by the military in early October and almost immediately afterward all of the IPC properties were seized.

The military government indicated its willingness to compensate the company, but only after its tax claims were met; and it stressed that the La Brea-Pariñas controversy was unique, with no implications for the treatment of U.S. capital in other oil companies or in the mining, fishing, sugar, or other industries. The U.S. government did not impose the Hickenlooper Amendment in April 1969, when its six-month limit was reached, awaiting the outcome of an appeal by the IPC to the Peruvian courts, and continued to avoid imposing the penalties when the company's appeal was denied several months later. It does not appear that any Peruvian government could now back away from the action taken against the IPC, and it is also difficult for the U.S. government to back away from the confrontation. Imposition of the Amendment would, however, increase the harm done to Peru's economy by the lack of much needed aid, and might reduce the flow of foreign investment in other industries. The political consequences would be as disastrous as the economic effects.[35]

In an unsympathetic view, the controversy reached such an impasse because of a series of mistakes on the Peruvian

---

new administration, are strikingly similar to the Chilean copper situation in 1960-61 and 1964. The later history of the two cases is, however, very different. See chap. 4, under the heading "Issues and Policies."

[34] In contrast, in the Chilean national election of 1964 a majority of the employees of the large copper companies supported the Socialist-Communist coalition which demanded expropriation of the mines, rather than the Christian Democratic party which sought only a greater degree of state participation in the industry. There was also little doubt of the government's ability to operate the copper industry.

[35] The most thorough account of the controversy is R. N. Goodwin, "Letter from Peru," *The New Yorker*, 17 May 1969, pp. 41-106. This discussion is based on interviews with all the parties to the 1968 agreement and subsequent coup as well as on the extensive written history of the dispute. For details of the government's proposals in 1960-1965 see *Petroleum Press Service*, November 1960, December 1963, September 1964, and April and August 1965.

side: first in the overgenerous exemptions, then in not clarifying its position before 1900, then in accepting the 1922 award, and finally in annulling that agreement only nine years before it was to expire. Had the issue not arisen until 1972, the government might have assumed title to La Brea-Pariñas and negotiated a concession or service contract with the IPC, perhaps with the EPF as owner or partner. The Belaúnde administration appears to have magnified the dispute and overestimated its ability to solve it. For forty-four years, however, successive Peruvian governments met an almost complete unwillingness of the company to give up the one point most important to national pride and resentment. In comparison with the action of other U.S. companies in Peru, or of similar enterprises engaged in the petroleum or mining industries of other countries such as Mexico, Chile, and Venezuela, the IPC was extraordinarily short-sighted. The U.S. government exerted its economic influence to force the Peruvian government to come to terms with the company, without entering the negotiations directly or stating what terms it would consider acceptable. In no other controversy between a Latin American government and U.S. enterprises, except in Cuba, has the U.S. government intervened in this way. And the object of this intervention was a government which was initially welcomed as an example of the ideals of the Alliance for Progress.

Argentina

The conflict between political and economic goals, or between different domestic and nationalist objectives and policies, is most evident in Argentina. Private companies, whether domestic or foreign, have always been allowed to operate refineries and market products in Argentina, but in 1932 production of crude oil and gas was reserved to the state enterprise, Yacimientos Petrolíferos Fiscales. Although Argentina possesses large reserves, domestic production by YPF has never met requirements, and the country has had to import both crude and products. However, until after World War II the need for imports was small enough to be met by the country's exports. Then, with the growth of import substituting industries, consumption of petroleum rapidly expanded. Because YPF was not given the technical and financial resources to raise output, imports grew to equal and then to exceed domestic production. In the early 1950s imports were about evenly divided between crude and products; by 1958 refinery capacity had increased to a point where four-fifths of the total could be imported as crude oil. In order to save still more foreign exchange, Argentina began to import much of its crude from the Middle East rather than from Venezuela. Nonetheless, the total import bill continued to grow: by 1958 some 9.6 million cubic meters (60 million barrels), more than two-thirds of consumption, were imported, and the cost of these imports was roughly equal to the trade deficit (see table 8-16).

Shortly before its overthrow the Perón government had granted a concession to a U.S. company to supplement YPF's output. This concession was widely denounced by nationalist opinion in Argentina and was revoked by the military caretaker government which deposed Perón in

1955. That government tried to reverse the previous neglect of the state company and increase its production, but neither YPF nor the government had the necessary capital to support the sizable investment needed. Moreover, neither the United States nor the World Bank would lend money when private capital was available from the major U.S. oil companies. In these circumstances petroleum became one of the major issues in the election of 1958. The administration of President Frondizi won a decisive victory on a platform of maintaining YPF's monopoly and keeping the country independent of "the dictates of foreign political or financial powers." This promise was an important element of Frondizi's appeal to the followers of Perón, whose party was outlawed and could not participate in the campaign.[36]

Once in office, however, Frondizi found the economic difficulties of either continuing imports or raising YPF's production more severe than the political pressures, and the new government reversed its policy. Twelve contracts were negotiated with two Argentine firms and a number of foreign enterprises. No concessions were granted, and the government continued to own all the oil produced; there were instead three types of service contracts, two of which proved relatively satisfactory while the third became the focus of the dispute. Three contracts were let for drilling, with YPF agreeing to handle production and distribution. The wells were mostly completed on schedule, but some remained shut in as YPF could not dispose of the oil. Four contracts were given for the exploration and development of new areas; the contractors agreed to bear all the risks, YPF being obligated only to buy oil found in commercial quantities. These contracts in effect embodied a suggestion made during the 1958 campaign by Álvaro Alsogaray, a member of the provisional government, that YPF retain its monopoly of traditional producing areas but allow foreign enterprise to explore for oil under its supervision elsewhere. This approach attracted enough support to be revived later by the ·Frondizi government. However, in the five years these contracts were in force almost no oil was found, and no costs were incurred by Argentina.

In the third type of contract, of which five were made, YPF agreed to buy at stipulated prices, usually declining as volume rose, all the oil and gas produced by the contractor in developing already proved areas. The contractors were quite successful in bringing up oil, so much so that YPF had to reduce its own output to absorb all the oil in its distribution system. By 1963 Argentine production had more than doubled, and net imports of crude had been cut to below the level of the 1930s. Falling imports of products were matched by rising exports, so that the country was all but self-sufficient. YPF's own production did not increase. In the company's Comodoro Rivadavia fields output declined and as a result gas supplies were reduced; when the oil could not be moved, YPF refused to lower reservoir pres-

[36] For a summary history of this period, see R. N. Burr, *Our Troubled Hemisphere* (Brookings Institution, 1967), pp. 115-19. The quotation is from a campaign document of Frondizi's, "YPF y la defensa de la soberanía nacional," cited by Burr, p. 118. For an account of the Argentine situation through mid-1967, see P. R. Odell, "The Oil Industry in Latin America," in Penrose, *The Large International Firm in Developing Countries. . . ,* pp. 284-88.

sure by taking off only the gas for shipment by pipeline to Buenos Aires.

The contractors were blamed for these dislocations; the contracts were also attacked on the ground of cost. As the economic crisis receded, political opposition mounted. The government of President Guido, which succeeded that of Frondizi in March 1962, asked for a court ruling on the validity of the contracts; their legality was upheld in February 1963. In November of that year a new government, headed by President Illía, declared all the contracts annulled and immediately brought suit against the companies involved. Compensation was proposed, but the government also demanded payment of taxes, although the contracts had laid all tax obligations on YPF rather than on the contractor.

At the time of annullment, no contractor had recovered its investment and YPF still owed large amounts for drilling completed and for oil and gas delivered. All investment ceased, but those companies producing oil agreed to continue operations at the contract prices. During the next two years little progress was made toward a settlement of the dispute; one Argentine firm settled on the government's terms, and one foreign firm, which had found no oil, elected to write off its investment and recover its equipment. Meanwhile consumption rose sharply as the Argentine economy recovered from the 1962-63 recession, and imports of crude and products began to rise again. Under this pressure the government announced its willingness to enter new contracts, and in order to hasten a settlement agreed to drop all tax and other damage claims and to pay compensation, with interest, for investments made. On this basis the remaining contracts were settled or brought close to settlement during 1965.[37] In February 1967 new contracts were signed with two U.S. firms for continuation of their producing operations.

There appears to be no reason why all of Argentina's petroleum requirements cannot be met by domestic production or why the oil cannot eventually be supplied by the state company. This solution, achieving both political and economic self-sufficiency, cannot, however, be reached immediately or without much larger resources for YPF than any Argentine government has yet provided. It may also be a relatively inefficient solution in economic terms, given the availability of foreign private capital in the oil industry and the many other claims on the state's capital. The three distinct ways of satisfying the country's need for oil – through YPF, by imports, or by private (foreign) producers under concession or contract – can be compared by several criteria. It appears that private production yields a greater output of petroleum (and possibly of net domestic product as well) per unit of investment, than does YPF. Private contractual production also results in slightly lower demands for foreign exchange than does production by YPF. By this test, either course is preferable to importing petroleum. In addition, allocation of government resources to oil

production rather than to other activities appears likely to impair somewhat domestic product, import substitution and export growth. These comparisons are influenced by an important factor: the inefficiency of YPF in using both labor and capital. Improvements in the company's operations would make the YPF solution more competitive with the others.[38]

The military government of General Onganía, which deposed the Illía regime in June 1966, immediately took up the petroleum question, but the conflict between extreme political nationalists and those more concerned with the country's economic difficulties was continued within the government. In June 1967 four cabinet members identified with the former group resigned, and a new oil law reflecting the views of the latter group was promulgated. All phases of the industry are declared open to private and mixed capital enterprises as well as to YPF, and concessions with a maximum period of forty-five years may be granted. Private producers may be excluded from areas reserved to YPF, and they are required to refine all their oil in Argentina, but otherwise they will have fairly complete freedom of operation to supply the domestic market or to export products once that market is satisfied.[39] For the near future at least, Argentina has abandoned the policy of state monopoly and adopted a policy more closely resembling that of Colombia, Venezuela, or Peru than of Mexico, Chile, or Brazil. The political and economic results of this decision, and particularly its political durability, will not be evident for some years.

Petroleum in Venezuela

In no other country in Latin America does oil have the importance Venezuela attaches to it. This is due less to the country's very large production than to the fact that petroleum is virtually Venezuela's only export. Venezuela is therefore closely tied to the world market for oil and to the major foreign enterprises which operate in it. Petroleum policy is not, as in most other countries of the region, directed toward assuring supplies of oil for domestic use, but is concerned primarily with the export sector. The range of interests and of policies appropriate to them is therefore somewhat narrower than in a country such as Argentina, and the economic limits to political choices are more evident. This circumstance has produced a high degree of continuity in petroleum policy and operations in Venezuela. There have been important changes in policy, but, at least in recent years, no sharp reversals or conflicts such as those described in other countries. Before discussing

---

[38] These are the conclusions of J. E. Zinser ("Alternative Means of Satisfying Argentine Petroleum Demand," Ph.D. thesis, University of Oregon, 1967), based on the period 1958-65. Given the political opposition to foreign private enterprise, an optimal solution appears to be some form of joint investment and operation allowing for government participation and supervision but dependent on private capital and efficiency.

[39] On the divisions within the Argentine government see *New York Times*, 11 June 1967. The new petroleum law is summarized in BOLSA, *Review*, August 1967, pp. 428-29. In order to bolster its competitive position, YPF is exempted from national, provincial, and municipal taxes. *Ibid.*, p. 426.

---

[37] The Argentine petroleum dispute is reported in *Petroleum Press Service*, September 1958, December 1963, September 1964, and January, February, March, August, November, and December 1965.

the aims and instruments of present policy and its effects, it may be useful to describe Venezuela's place in the world oil economy and to review the history of the industry's operations and of the laws and policies applied to it by successive governments.

Venezuela in the World Oil Economy

In several respects Venezuela is well placed to supply oil to the rest of the world. The country is as close to the east coast of North America as any other large producing area, including the United States Gulf coast, and closer to much of Europe than any area except North Africa; no major source is closer to importing areas in South America. In only one large producing area, the Middle East, is the average output per well notably higher, or the costs of production very much lower. Finally, Venezuela produces a greater variety of crudes than any other country. The oil ranges in gravity from 17° or less in some fields to as much as 44° elsewhere, with fairly large amounts available at any density in the range. By contrast, nearly 90 percent of all Middle Eastern crude is between 31° and 40°; and the range within any one field or area is usually quite narrow.

Venezuela's great diversity offers two advantages. First, almost any pattern of final demand for products can be exactly matched by some combination of Venezuelan crudes.[40] Second, if world production of crude elsewhere is out of balance with demand for products, Venezuela can supply whatever density of crude is required for balance in refining. At present, world demand for heavy fuel oils is strong and is growing more rapidly than demand for light products, while most of the oil found since World War II has been light — 30° to 40° in the Middle East and 40° or higher in North Africa. Venezuela is the principal supplier of heavy crudes for blending with lighter oil from other sources, and can produce large amounts of heavy products for export without a surplus of light fractions. The average density of Venezuelan crude is about 25°, and the oil available for export can be heavier still.

Venezuela's advantages have been reduced in recent years by developments in both supply and demand. Vast new sources of oil have been opened close to the world's largest oil importing area, Western Europe. Much of this new oil can be produced so cheaply that it can compete in distant markets as well. Transport costs have fallen, making production cost more important in determining where oil from a given source can compete, and reducing or eliminating advantages of location.[41] Today some Middle East oil could undersell Venezuelan crude in Venezuela. On

the demand side, imports into the United States, potentially Venezuela's best market, have been restricted; and domestic production has risen in several South American countries determined to achieve self-sufficiency. Within a decade Venezuela's competitive position has become rather precarious. Most recently, the high sulfur content of much of the country's crude, and thus of the residual fuel made from it, has become a disadvantage. To reduce air pollution strict standards have been set for the sulfur content of fuel oil on the east coast of the United States, and investments of over $120 million will be necessary to desulfurize Venezuelan oil to the levels required.

At the same time, Venezuela's dependence on oil has increased. Petroleum accounts for about the same share of exports as formerly, but the revenues from exports are now devoted to the imports required by industrial development as well as to consumption goods. In the long run the industries now being created may reduce Venezuela's dependence on imports and may provide other exports for the economy. But for the near future there will be no substitute for petroleum exports.

Petroleum was first produced in Venezuela in 1878, from oil seeps in the vicinity of Rubio, Táchira. Production on a large scale began with the discovery of the Mene Grande field in 1914, the first of the prolific fields on the east side of Lake Maracaibo. The first well in the great Bolívar coastal field was drilled in 1917, the same year that exports of crude began. In 1922, with completion of a famous gusher in that field — Barroso No. 2, which flowed at 16,000 cubic meters (100,000 barrels) per day — the great boom in output started. Production rose from 300,000 cubic meters (2 million barrels) in 1922 to almost 17 million (108 million barrels) in 1928, when oversupply and falling prices slowed investment and output. During the 1920s the fields all around Lake Maracaibo and in the states of Zulia and Falcón were brought into production. Particularly in the Bolívar fields competition among the three major producers resulted in excessive drilling and considerable waste. There were then no government controls on the spacing of wells and the reservoirs had only begun to be mapped.[42]

The next major discoveries occurred in 1936-38, when nearly all the large fields in eastern Venezuela were found. As these fields came into production output temporarily declined in the west. Although the industry continued to be dominated by the first three major firms to enter — Shell of the United Kingdom and Gulf and Esso of the United States — several other producers acquired concessions at this time. In the last twenty-five years development and production have continued in all parts of the country without significant new discoveries. Two major areas remain for exploitation: the Orinoco tar belt has been considerably explored, while the Gulf of Maracaibo has not been explored but is believed to hold large resources. Venezuela

---

[40]That is, products can be made in the desired relative amounts without producing surpluses of any or the necessity of using more expensive refinery processes to avoid such surpluses. On the properties of Venezuelan crudes, see *Petroleum Press Service*, March 1960 and November 1963; and Venezuela, Ministerio de Minas e Hidrocarburos, *Memoria, 1964*, p. I-158.

[41]A great deal of information supplied by oil companies on transport costs is given in M. Hubbard, *The Economics of Transporting Oil to and Within Europe* (London: MacLaren and Sons, 1967); see especially chaps. 1, 2, and 3. The economies of scale both of tankers and of pipelines are strikingly presented, and the decline in shipping costs resulting from the steady increase in tanker size is quite large.

[42]The principal source for this section is E. Lieuwen, *Petroleum in Venezuela: A History*, University of California Publications in History, vol. 47 (Berkeley and Los Angeles, 1954), which covers the period to 1948.

was the world's second largest producer until it was displaced by the Soviet Union in the 1950s; it is still the greatest exporter of oil. By 1967 it had accounted for 11.4 percent of all the petroleum ever produced, and its share of world output was 10 percent. The latter ratio reached a peak of nearly 16 percent in 1957 (see tables 8-1 and 8-2).

Petroleum was originally refined in small distilleries in Venezuela for local use. The first refineries for export were built in the Netherlands West Indies, by Shell in 1917 and by Esso in 1928. In 1949-50 four large coastal refineries were constructed in Venezuela, primarily for exports. This shift of capacity back to the mainland raised the share of Venezuelan crude refined in the country from only 5 percent in the 1930s to about one-third in the 1960s (see table 8-8). Some small plants continue in operation, but several of the oilfield refineries built in the 1930s or earlier have been closed. Except for increases in capacity, there has been little change in Venezuela's refining industry since the early 1950s. The country now accounts for somewhat less than half of total refinery output in Latin America.

History of Policy

The first concessions for petroleum production from underground reservoirs were granted in 1907, under the mineral code of 1904 which made no distinction between oil and metals. Another law in 1910 continued this provision, but most of these early concessions reverted to the state. The great boom in acquisition of land, exploration, and production followed the passage of a new petroleum law in 1922 which was extremely favorable to investment. As originally proposed in 1918 and passed in 1920, the law was much more nationalist in tone and less favorable to the oil companies, but the pressure of the latter and the opportunity presented by the end of the Mexican oil boom led the government of Juan Vicente Gómez to modify the law substantially. The previous legislation remained in force for concessions granted before 1918, but with the influx of U.S. capital the new law soon covered most producing areas. Particularly in its early years, the law was often violated with respect to the sale of national reserves and the size and price of concessions. Officials of the Gómez regime probably received more in bribes and illegal contracts than the government received as royalties. The era of rampant corruption coincided with the entry of new companies, the rush to acquire concessions, and the wasteful competition of the early 1920s.

The petroleum law of 1922 governed Venezuelan oil policy for the next two decades. Two attempts were made to change this policy in the 1930s, but opposition by the oil companies frustrated both. The drop in export volume and revenues at the start of the Depression led to a series of laws and lawsuits designed to force down domestic prices, collect taxes claimed to be owed, raise customs revenues from the companies' imports, and increase the price for concessions in national reserve areas.[43] After a bitter con-

flict, the Gómez administration abandoned its claims in 1931. In 1938 the government of López Contreras proposed a sharp increase in royalties and taxes, the construction of national refineries, and controls on the waste of natural gas. The law containing these provisions applied only to new concessions, however, and it was passed just after the boom in eastern Venezuela. The companies, which had acquired all the producing area they needed, refused to apply for new concessions or convert their existing ones to the new standards. Thus the only way the government could increase its revenues or its control over the industry was to raise royalties and taxes. Royalties, set at 7.5 to 10 percent of the value of production in 1922, were increased to about 15 percent by the late 1930s. Royalties were originally assessed per ton of oil, but were converted to a value basis by the 1920s. The share of value returned remained low, however, and there were no other efforts to integrate the industry more fully into the national economy.

During this period the government never successfully challenged the companies on any major issue, although nationalist and anti-company sentiment in Venezuela was steadily growing. As in other countries of Latin America, the Depression accelerated this change by showing how dependent Venezuela was on oil exports. The average value of crude oil imported by the United States from Venezuela dropped sharply in 1928, when an agreement by the major producers to reduce output collapsed, and then fell by nearly half between 1928 and 1933. The price level of the 1920s was not regained until after World War II (see table 8-5). It should be noted, however, that the shock of the Depression was much less for Venezuela than for such countries as Brazil and Chile, and that it did not inspire comparable efforts at import-substituting industrialization. Quantitative restrictions and tariffs similarly had much less effect on oil than on other primary commodities; the U.S. tariff of 1932, for example, diverted Venezuelan oil to Europe and probably contributed to the one-third drop in price that year, but did not appreciably reduce the volume of exports. With the approach of World War II, Venezuela was given, directly or through the Netherlands West Indies, over 90 percent of the U.S. petroleum import quota.

The next great change in policy occurred during the war-time administration of President Medina. Public and governmental pressure was exerted against the companies through exchange rate controls and the threat of raising claims for back taxes, revoking concessions of uncertain legality, and imposing high import taxes. This time the companies — and their home governments — could not afford the loss of concessions or the interruption of supplies that might result from a prolonged dispute, and they needed new exploration concessions which would not be granted unless some of the government's demands were met. Negotiations therefore began which culminated in 1943 in a completely new petroleum code superseding all previous legislation.

One feature of the new policy became law in 1942: this was the first tax on income, or profits, rather than on production, with an initial rate of 2.5 percent. As all earlier legislation was set aside, the oil law of 1943 was applied to all concessions, the first time such uniformity had been

---

[43] The policy of setting aside certain areas as national reserves, to be exploited by the state or only on limited terms by private capital, has also been followed with respect to iron ore in Venezuela. See chap. 5, under the heading "The Latin American Iron and Steel Industry."

achieved. Existing concessions, whatever their terms initially, were extended for forty years. All claims for back taxes and other issues in dispute were cancelled. In return for the elimination of these legal and economic pressures and the guarantee of their concessions for a rather long period, the companies agreed to several of the government's demands. Royalties were set at 16-2/3 percent of the value of the oil, with provisions for minimum payments, for payment in oil at the government's discretion, and for reduction of the tax on fields that would otherwise be closed. The rate for new concessions, to be determined by negotiation, reached 20 percent on several holdings and 33-1/3 percent on some. Surface taxes, payable per hectare of concession held, were made deductible from production taxes to encourage development and increase stability of revenues; these were raised with the passage of time to encourage the concessionaires to return to the state areas left undeveloped. Finally, the major producers, Shell and Esso, agreed to build large refineries in Venezuela; these plants were completed in 1949-50. Once agreement was reached on all these matters the government, in April 1944, distributed some 6.5 million hectares in new concessions, an area somewhat greater than that held by the companies before the new law was passed.[44]

This period coincided with the rise of Acción Democrática, the most nationalist political party of any size in Venezuela. The party contributed to the pressure against the oil companies which resulted in the new law of 1943, but denounced the law as too favorable to the companies. In the party's view it was especially a mistake to extend all concessions and thereby fix the major elements of petroleum policy for so long a period. In retrospect this does appear to be the major concession in the law, but it is probably the provision most responsible for the relative stability of policy and absence of severe conflicts in the ensuing two decades. The experience of other countries, such as Chile, suggests that such continuity is extremely valuable for economic development, whatever its short-run cost in revenues foregone. By a coup in late 1945, Acción Democrática came to power in an alliance with the army. This government survived until 1948, when the army, partly in alarm at the party's proposal that the government enter the oil industry directly, by nationalization of some properties if necessary, took over all power. When Acción Democrática returned to office in 1959 it pressed for certain changes in the oil laws but took a less extreme position.[45] Thus the awkward sort of confrontation which has occurred in Peru was avoided.

---

[44] For a more detailed discussion of the various petroleum taxes, see G. Thery Fombona and E. Luongo Cabello, "Taxes," in Venezuela, Ministerio de Minas e Hidrocarburos, *National Petroleum Convention* (Caracas, 1951).

[45] Anderson, *Politics and Economic Change. . . ,* pp. 95-103, interprets AD's exclusion from power by the army in 1948 as the result of the party's effort to change radically the balance of strength among the major political "contenders" in Venezuela, particularly by reducing the powers of the army and of the foreign oil companies. The party was allowed to return to office a decade later only because it had in effect promised not to try to upset the balance but to respect the strength and more especially the views of the more traditional contenders for power. With respect to the oil

Nonetheless, the policy embodied in the law of 1943 has since been modified in several significant respects. In 1948 a 50 percent tax was levied on company profits in excess of government revenues; the effect was to divide profits equally between the companies and the government, with the latter's share derived partly from the royalty or production tax and partly from the surcharge or excess profits tax. Venezuela was the first country to adopt this fifty-fifty sharing policy, as it was the first to levy taxes on value rather than volume and the first to tax income or profits directly; in all these respects it has been the model for other oil exporting countries. In 1958 the provisional government that succeeded the Pérez Jiménez regime raised the minimum tax rate to 60 percent, and the law was retained by the Betancourt (Acción Democrática) government. The oil companies were not consulted, and relations were strained by the abrupt passage of the legislation, but they decided to accept the tax without protest. The percentage of industry profit taken in taxes of all kinds rose from between 51 and 55 percent to between 65 and 68 percent (see table 8-17).

Under the 1943 law the value of Venezuelan crude at the well, on which taxes were paid, was set by the posted price of crude at United States Gulf ports, adjusted for the cost of transport to the Venezuelan export terminal, the U.S. import duty, and differences in freight costs to east coast refineries. Since Venezuelan crudes were used largely to make fuel oil while U.S. crudes went into gasoline and other products, this computation reflected market value only so long as the ratio of prices of residual fuel oil and Texas crude was stable. That relation was upset in 1946 and led the government to increase royalties. When fuel oil prices fell in 1948-49, the companies refused to continue paying the higher royalties. The impasse was ended partly by the adoption of the fifty-fifty rule which made royalties less important, but chiefly by the establishment of posted prices for Venezuelan crudes. At first profits were computed on prices actually realized, including discounts on direct sales. In 1966, however, the government began to compute all profits on posted prices, as was already the practice in other OPEC countries. If posted prices are not allowed to decline while discounts continue to be given, the effect is to raise the share of taxes in profits to 70 percent or more. The companies did not object to this change, but they did protest a retroactive tax based on the difference between posted and actual prices in the past. After a year's resistance, the government agreed to a five-year moratorium on new taxes and the companies agreed to pay some $150 million or about 14 percent of their total annual tax bill in the early 1960s. At the same time the basic income tax rate was slightly raised.[46] The higher taxes on the foreign sector were matched by domestic tax increases to offset a growing deficit resulting from the government's ambitious develop-

---

companies, strictly economic factors were paramount in setting the limits to government action, but this analysis does explain the otherwise very curious role of the armed forces in controlling the Venezuelan political system without consistently siding with or against the oil producers.

[46] A summary of these provisions is given in the *Washington Post,* 2 January 1967.

ment program and its efforts to extend public services to the large low-income population.

The Present Situation

Venezuela's present petroleum policy has two chief objectives: the highest possible rate of increase of the value returned to the country, and a reduction of the dominance of foreign enterprise in the industry. These goals may be distinguished as economic in the first instance and political in the second, but it should be recognized that neither element is exclusively one or the other. There are in turn three principal constraints on policy. The first is Venezuela's overwhelming dependence on oil exports for its economic growth. This factor is, of course, responsible for the importance of the economic goal, but it also sets limits to the pursuit of both goals. Any action which would even temporarily reduce the flow of oil revenue could have severe consequences for the Venezuelan economy and might bring down the government or force it once more to accept the direct participation or control of the army. The second is the power and flexibility of the producing companies in consequence of their control of marketing facilities and their extensive holdings in other producing countries. In response to actions taken in Venezuela, they can shift their investments and ultimately their output elsewhere. It is chiefly this factor which brings the second objective of policy into conflict with the first, but it also limits what can be done to increase revenues independently of the political goal. The companies' importance is reinforced by the third constraint, the world surplus of crude oil in the decade following 1957. For a few years after World War II, when there was a shortage of petroleum, Venezuela enjoyed a favorable position. The government was even able to sell oil (obtained in lieu of a cash royalty) at prices above those declared by the companies.[47] In 1957 and again in 1967 shortages originating in the Middle East benefitted Venezuela, but these episodes are regarded as exceptional; the country's policy is designed rather for the situation of surplus and downward pressure on prices.

Venezuela's policy is based on the belief that the country cannot afford to compete in price with the Middle East, where costs are appreciably less. To the extent that taxes are higher in Venezuela than elsewhere, the country's poor competitive position is partly a result of government actions, but there is a significant disadvantage in costs before taxes. Policy is therefore directed to obtaining the highest possible price for oil exported and accepting the decline in market share which results. This decision is supported by two other premises: that price competition is prohibited in the United States, the market where Venezuela might expect to fare best; and that as light and medium crudes are in surplus, the demand for Venezuelan heavy oil should be fairly insensitive to price.

In a few cases the government has acted to prevent independent producers, with no outlets in the United States,

from selling oil at discounts as high as 25 percent. This intervention in the late 1950s ended the influx of small companies. The prices of the major producers and their volume of output are affected less directly by decisions on concessions and on taxes. A relatively small area, about one million hectares, was opened to exploration and development in 1956-57, but this was the first grant since the 1940s and in the last decade the area covered by concessions has been steadily reduced, to only 3.2 million hectares by 1966 (see table 8-18). The government's refusal to grant new concessions has a major motive and effect besides contributing to a slow growth of output. The concessions now held begin to expire in 1983, and unless large areas are granted between now and then — which is most unlikely — in the next twenty years virtually all the oil producing land in Venezuela will revert to the state. It will then be possible to reach a new relation with the foreign companies, probably on the basis of contracts leaving both the land and the oil in state ownership. The change can, it is hoped, be effected without expropriation or violation of concession agreements, and consequently with minimal effect on output. Reversion to state control will also make exploitation by the national oil enterprise, the Corporación Venezolana del Petróleo, easier. Above all, Venezuela will want to avoid the difficulties and reversals of policy that Argentina experienced in the use of service contracts and in the dispute over the proper role and capacity of the state oil company.

The increases in income tax in 1958 and 1966 may be seen either as a means of raising costs to the companies so as to slow the expansion of output and thereby maintain higher prices, or as a way of compensating for the slow growth and the fall in prices which occurred despite the government's efforts. For a short while at least, it is possible for taxes and royalties, and therefore the total value returned to the country, to grow much more rapidly than the value of exports. Between 1950 and 1964 export value increased at an average rate of 5.3 percent annually; the total of taxes and royalties rose by 8.6 percent per year (see table 8-17). The recent conversion of taxes to a posted price basis will make revenues largely independent of realized prices, so that if the latter continue to fall, further increases in income tax, which would be resisted by the companies, will not be necessary.

In an effort to protect its competitive position Venezuela has also tried to reach agreements on oil production and trade both with other exporting countries and with the United States. Venezuela was the chief instigator of the OPEC and is the member country which stands to gain most from production controls. Venezuela has also tried, without success, to obtain greater access to the U.S. market. Since elimination of tariffs and other restrictions is unlikely, Venezuela has urged that the United States adopt a quota system distributed by exporting countries rather than by companies. Such a change would not only guarantee a share of the market but would greatly limit the companies' freedom to shift production away from Venezuela. The proposal is unacceptable to the oil companies and has been disregarded by the United States. Even a much more limited agreement, that Venezuela would be consulted about any changes in the 1959-66 quota system,

[47]Much as Chile was able to do with copper in 1951-53. See chap. 4, under the headings "Market Structure and International Trade" and "Issues and Policies." The Venezuelan government, however, did not attempt to fix prices, and returned to letting the companies sell their own oil once the shortage was over.

was disregarded when the United States on one occasion reduced quotas for the eastern part of the country where most of Venezuela's oil is sold, and raised those for the west coast.

Finally, the Venezuelan government in 1960 created a state oil enterprise, the CVP, whose probable future role in exploiting expired concessions has been mentioned. The state company figures in the national petroleum policy in two other ways. First, it is intended eventually to supply the entire domestic market, whether from its own wells or with oil bought from the private companies. These producers are so large that it was decided not to compete with them but simply to create a place for the CVP by law. Since 1962 only the state enterprise has been allowed to build or buy new distribution outlets, and by a decree of 1964 it was entitled to one-third of the domestic market by 1968. Since this is a point of much national pride, and since the foreign companies are not needed to supply Venezuela's own needs for oil, they did not challenge the government's decision. Second, the CVP may ultimately become the chief instrument of oil policy, supervising contracts with private firms or participating in joint enterprises with them in addition to producing and distributing oil locally. Since the government is in no position to take over the marketing of Venezuela's oil abroad in conditions of surplus, joint enterprises or control by the state are likely to appear first in refining, leaving private firms to conduct the bulk of exploration and production and to sell the oil abroad.

Whether Venezuela's petroleum policy is judged successful depends partly on what measures are used, and even more on one's estimate of the results of alternative policies over the last twenty-five years and the probable results of each policy for the next decade or two. Sometime before 1983 the country will have to develop a new policy, or at least new instruments for its objectives, and the present policy may be more easily judged by comparison with its successor. In fact, it may not be feasible to wait for the expiration of present concessions before reaching a new accommodation with the companies, in order to maintain the flow of oil and revenue on which the country depends.

If judged by its effect on the producing firms, the policy followed since the late 1940s appears to have created difficulties in the last decade. New investment by the companies rose during the early 1950s, and reached some $600 million in 1956 and 1957. In 1960-61, as a result of the tax increase, investment dropped sharply to about $150 million to $180 million annually. Net investment, including capital repatriation, has been negative since 1960, and new investment has been at the lowest level in two decades. The number of wells has continued to increase, but only slowly since 1958; and many of the new wells have been shut in for lack of a market. At the peak in 1960 there were nearly as many wells closed as producing, and they represented some 20 percent of total capacity. All these factors have resulted in a very low rate of additions to reserves and a declining ratio of reserves to production despite the rather slow growth of output (see table 8-18). Since a great deal of oil is still available, no crisis is imminent; but in order to raise output substantially in the future it may be necessary to give extraordinary inducements to new investment, a change which

will be politically difficult and which will cause at least a temporary decline in the growth of revenues.

The effect on the Venezuelan economy has been less severe, both because of the increase in share of value returned and because the income from oil has been heavily invested in industrial and agricultural development. These measures contributed to Venezuela's very high rate of economic growth — 6.3 percent annually in 1961-65 — a rate which considerably exceeded the growth in oil exports. However, neither element of this increase can continue indefinitely: if the share of taxes continues to increase, investment will continue to fall, with effects on production and revenues; and as internal development proceeds, difficulties in further import substitution may press the overall rate of growth back toward that achieved in the petroleum sector. If Venezuelan policy has been more realistic and less myopic than that of other countries with respect to natural resources, it may still be better suited to the short or medium than to the long term. Once the political and nationalist objectives are given any weight, it becomes virtually impossible to devise a sound policy for long periods; changes eventually become necessary.

Venezuela has nonetheless succeeded in balancing economic and political objectives without disruptive changes of policy and without provoking major domestic or international disputes. Significant changes in policy have occurred only at fairly long intervals, and with a few exceptions (notably in 1958) they have been made only after thorough negotiations to avoid misunderstanding or the taking by either party of a position from which it cannot readily retreat or bargain. Furthermore, the government, while respecting the limitations on its own action, has steadily gained in strength relative to the oil companies. Before 1943, every important dispute was resolved in the companies' favor, often by abandonment of the government's position. Since then the government has generally prevailed. Given the severe restraints on policy and the wide range of attitudes and pressures present in Latin America, this is a considerable political achievement. The experience of the last twenty-five years suggests, first, that unless the Venezuelan government has completely misjudged its competitive situation it has probably succeeded in its economic goals about as much as could be expected; second, that if it has carried its policy so far as to endanger its success, that policy can be modified and the oil companies will respond to any changes; and finally that in the next decade and a half it should be possible to reach a new accommodation of the state with foreign enterprise, with a minimum of disruption to the country's economic and political goals.

Outlook

The future demand of an economy for energy in all forms can be estimated from the structure of the economy and its anticipated growth. Changes in the relative weights of different sectors or industries and in the efficiency of energy consumption can also be taken into account. It is considerably more difficult to forecast the demand for any one fuel or source of energy, since for many applications two or more kinds of energy are substitutable. The amounts of each used depend on relative prices, on convenience of use and security of supply, and on the decisions of governments concerning the operation of domestic energy industries and trade with other countries. Nonetheless, much attention has been given to estimating the future requirements for particular fuels and the sources from which such requirements will be met. This is especially the case for petroleum, which has the greatest variety of applications of any source of energy and is the most easily traded. A brief summary of world supply and demand estimates for oil in 1975 is given below, followed by a discussion of the prospects for Venezuelan exports of crude and products. The last part of this analysis will touch on several questions concerning the future of the petroleum industry in different countries of Latin America.[48]

World consumption of petroleum outside the Communist countries is expected to reach some 1,800 to 2,000 million tons by 1975, or about double the level of 1960. Growth of about 3 percent per year is foreseen for North America, where natural gas is rapidly displacing oil for some uses and where oil's incursion into coal markets has apparently halted; in the rest of the world an increase of about 7 percent annually is anticipated. The rate will be somewhat less in Europe, and considerably higher in Japan. A great deal of uncertainty remains in these estimates. The recent rapid growth of nuclear energy in the United States and Europe may indicate a different balance of energy sources than was foreseen some years ago, but the effect will undoubtedly be greater on coal and natural gas than on petroleum.

The importance of various sources in providing the world's oil during the next decade will depend on a number of factors, several of which merit brief discussion. The existence of an excess productive capacity of perhaps 130 million cubic meters — oil producible from existing wells with little or no expansion of other facilities — in the United States suggests a considerable absolute and relative expansion of production in North America; but the view is quite different if one considers productive capacity over a longer period, from reserves already proved but requiring investment in pipelines and new wells.

By this criterion of potential supply, the Middle East stands out as the great source of new oil. The ratio of reserves to production in that area is so high as to suggest that output could be over 700 million tons per year by the mid-1970s, without the necessity of finding any new fields. This abundance means that the present oil surplus will probably last for many years and that the marginal cost of petroleum can be extremely low. The Middle East will almost certainly increase its share of world supplies, but the amount of production cannot be predicted closely, as it will depend on output in North America and other protected producing areas and on the competitive position of crude oil from Venezuela and North Africa. A further element of

uncertainty was introduced in 1967 by the Arab-Israeli war. The immediate effects on production were relatively slight, reduced output or delays in shipping in the Middle East being offset by increased output in Venezuela and the United States. In the longer run, however, the war will stimulate the international oil companies to reduce somewhat their dependence on this politically volatile area and to search more intensively in such countries as Canada and Venezuela, in the North Sea, and in sub-Saharan Africa. The production of oil from newly discovered fields in Alaska and of shale oil in western United States will also be accelerated. Any such changes will result in a higher average cost of petroleum and slow the decline in prices, but their magnitude is unlikely to be large before 1975. Closure of the Suez Canal also accelerated the building of supertankers, which slightly increase the cost advantages of the Middle East.

Estimates of future United States production differ considerably; it is expected that imports will continue to be limited to 20 percent of consumption or less, but there is much uncertainty about the prospects for finding new supplies of oil. The possibility that oil will be produced on a large scale from shale or tar by 1975 makes prediction still more difficult. Output in Europe and in Latin America (outside Venezuela) is expected to increase as much as success in finding oil will permit. Production will also increase rapidly in the Soviet Union. The amount of imports from the Communist countries will depend on political considerations in Europe (where imports may be limited to 10 or 12 percent of supplies) and on domestic production and competition from other suppliers in South America, India and Japan. By 1975 then, the world will need some 950 to 1,200 million tons of oil to be supplied by Venezuela, North Africa, the Middle East, and Indonesia.

The distribution of production among these areas depends chiefly on the cost of getting oil from each of them to each of the principal importing markets. The cost of finding and producing oil is lowest in the Middle East — about $2.50 per ton, exclusive of taxes and royalties, in 1960. This area is the cheapest source of supply for both North America and Western Europe, except at very high freight rates. Venezuelan crude was cheaper in 1960 than oil from North Africa — $7.00 per ton against $9.00 to $11.00 — but Venezuelan taxes and royalties were the highest of any producer. Crude oil from Venezuela cannot therefore compete in volume in Europe, and must find most of its market in the western hemisphere. North African crude will continue to be sold primarily in Europe. On the assumption of a further decline in freight rates as more large tankers are introduced, and of no change in the policies of the OPEC countries or of Venezuela, production in 1975 may reach 230 to 250 million tons in Venezuela, 120 to 150 million in Africa, 550 to 730 million in the Middle East, and 55 to 60 million in the Far East.[49]

[48]The quantitative estimates are taken from two sources: Bela Balassa, *Trade Prospects for Developing Countries* (Homewood, Ill.: Irwin, 1964); and ECSC, *Étude sur les Perspectives Énergétiques....* Data in these sources have been put on the same basis, of tons of petroleum equivalent; the figures given are comparable to, but somewhat smaller than, data in cubic meters of crude oil.

[49]These estimates are those of ECSC, *Étude sur les Perspectives Énergétiques...*, pp. 579-97. For a discussion of probable future costs of oil in Venezuela and the Middle East, see Bradley, *Economics of Crude Petroleum Production*, chap. 7.

No major change is anticipated in the distribution of exports, either by region or by type: Latin America will probably continue to supply about two-thirds of all the petroleum imported into North America, and 15 percent of that imported by Europe. Crude oil will account for about half the total, the share being nearer 60 percent in Europe. On the average, Venezuelan crude cannot compete in the eastern hemisphere; but Europe will continue to buy certain Venezuelan crudes from low-cost fields or for blending or the production of heavy fuel oils and specialized products such as lubricants. The great variety of costs and qualities of oil in Venezuela should permit the country to hold about 10 percent of the European import market and more than half of the U.S. market. In both cases, Venezuela has a better competitive position for product exports, and will probably remain the only producing area to export a significant volume of refined products.

The total volume of petroleum exports from Latin America will also depend on developments in Argentina, Chile, and Brazil, all of which are trying to become self-sufficient. On balance, exports from the region may be expected to grow at a satisfactory rate over the next several years, but the growth in foreign exchange earned may be much less. The oversupply of oil is not likely to end soon, and so continued decreases in prices can be expected. Posted prices will probably not be revised again, but the average size of discounts may well increase. There is then a considerable danger that during the next decade Venezuela's exports will not increase at anything near the 4 percent annual rate desired by the government. On the other hand, projections of price and value are particularly unreliable; they could be upset by the OPEC in imposing production restraints, by changes in taxes and royalties which could affect both the volume of exports and the share of earnings retained, or by any of several other factors.

The major questions for the future of the Latin American petroleum industry concern the world market for oil and Venezuela's place in it. A number of other issues, specific to particular countries or to the region as a whole, also deserve mention. First, consumption of oil and gas in Latin America outside Venezuela is expected to continue to increase for some years at a rate of perhaps 5 percent per year or more. The satisfaction of this growing demand will require either rising imports or the discovery of large amounts of oil within the region. In Mexico and Argentina consumption of natural gas has already reached such a level that exploration and development must also be conducted specifically for gas; production from oil fields can no longer be relied on to meet requirements. In order to satisfy a growth in consumption of 5 percent annually, while maintaining the same degree of self-sufficiency and the same ratio of reserves to production in 1975 as in 1965, it will be necessary to find some 400 million cubic meters of oil in Argentina, 550 million in Mexico, and 85 million in Peru. Colombia's reserves in 1965 would just suffice to meet consumption at 5 percent growth for a decade and leave reserves of twenty times output; but if exports are to be maintained, much new oil must be found. In Brazil,

achievement of self-sufficiency by 1975 will require that more than 600 million cubic meters of petroleum be found in the decade 1965-75. These requirements will be still stricter if consumption increases more rapidly; outside Venezuela the use of petroleum products rose by 6.5 percent yearly during the 1950s.[50]

There is nothing to suggest that such large amounts of oil cannot be found in Latin America in the next few years; much of the region is still relatively unexplored and present crude reserves do not begin to exhaust the resources even of well-developed areas. Brazil is already much closer to self-sufficiency than was thought likely in 1960. Production rose by half between 1965 and 1966 as the fields in Maranhão were developed; reserves there exceed those of the older fields in Bahía. The recent discoveries of oil east of the Andes in southern Colombia should considerably improve that country's position. Similar discoveries in northeastern Ecuador will shortly have an even greater impact: already the output from just a few wells equals that of the several hundred wells in the old coastal producing zone. Ecuador, which has been an oil importer since 1958, should recover self-sufficiency. If the new petroleum policy is maintained for several years in Argentina, that country, too, should be able to dispense with imports. However, these developments may be frustrated or delayed by technical difficulties or political conflict. The latter is more likely in Argentina than elsewhere: a return to civilian rule could revive the strongly nationalist attitudes and pressures which influenced petroleum policy so greatly between the early 1950s and the mid-1960s.

Except in Argentina, it is reasonable to expect that government will maintain or increase its participation in the oil industry in Latin America. Ecuador plans to establish a national enterprise, with majority government ownership, and give it control over imports and over a new refinery.[51] PETROBRAS will account for all the increase in refining in Brazil, and EPF will probably build any new refineries in Peru. By 1975 the share of the CVP in Venezuelan production and refining may have risen appreciably. In the more distant future, a significant share of oil output in Latin America may be by foreign enterprises operating under contracts rather than concessions, particularly in Venezuela, Colombia, Peru, and perhaps Argentina.

Finally, the place of the petroleum industry in the economic integration of Latin America ought to be considered. For a number of reasons there is now no prospect of integrating the first two stages of the industry — the production of oil and gas and the refining of crude. Economies of scale are small compared with national markets in the region; thus import substitution is not limited by market size, and integration is not needed to expand consumption through lowered costs. The total cost of the region's oil would be less if output were allowed to decline in high-cost producers such as Brazil and Chile, and

[50] These calculations are based on information in tables 8-1, 8-2, and 8-13.

[51] Junta Nacional de Planificación y Coordinación Económica, *Plan General de Desarrollo Económico y Social*, vol. III, chap. 3, "La Minería y el Petróleo."

their needs were supplied by Venezuela; but in a closed regional market these gains might be entirely offset by the fact that Venezuelan oil costs more than crude from the Middle East, and importers such as Brazil and Uruguay would suffer. Finally, the political objectives of those countries which have developed domestic industries preclude a deliberate return to imports or to the dependence on the major foreign companies which that would imply. In the case of refining, the present distribution of capacity may be uneconomic in Central America, but elsewhere the location of plants would not be significantly different under integration. For these reasons, petroleum is specifically excluded from consideration by both the Latin American Free Trade Area and the Central American Common Market. It does not appear that Venezuela's accession to LAFTA will have any effect on that exclusion; that country's petroleum exports to the region are determined largely by a price policy it is not willing to change, and its decision to join LAFTA was motivated rather by the hope of exporting such goods as steel and chemicals.

There are nonetheless two possible approaches to regional integration involving petroleum. The first is represented by a loose association originally formed by the state oil companies of Argentina, Peru, and Uruguay for the exchange of small quantities of crude and products and for the joint use of refinery or transportation facilities. In 1964 this association was broadened to include all the national oil enterprises of the region; greater joint use of facilities and personnel are contemplated, and the possibility of a future common market arrangement is to be studied.[52] At the same time much interest has developed in international pipelines, particularly for natural gas. Lines may be built from eastern Bolivia to the São Paulo area of Brazil, and the Argentine gas company, Gas del Estado, has studied several projects for extending Argentina's pipeline net into Uruguay and Paraguay or southern Brazil. The second approach is the integration of the regional petrochemical industry, which is still quite small and which exhibits appreciable economies of scale. This industry will be based on the supplies of natural gas of Venezuela, Chile, and Mexico, and perhaps of Bolivia and Argentina.[53] These two types of integration may eventually be linked, as by the construction of international pipelines serving the petrochemical industry.

[52] On the formation of the association for Asistencia Recíproca Petrolera Estatal Latinoamericana (ARPEL), see *Comercio Exterior*, October 1964, p. 677, and BOLSA, *Review*, 31 October and 14 November 1964. The formation and activities of this organization are also described in *Petroleum Press Service*. Under this arrangement PEMEX has already contributed substantial technical assistance to EPF of Peru and to PETROBRAS.

[53] See the discussion of this subject above, under the heading "Natural Gas."

CHAPTER 8 TABLES

TABLE 8–1. Cumulative World Production of Crude Oil, 1857-1967, and Proved Reserves as of 1 January 1965
(Thousands of cubic meters)

Country or Region	Production[a] 1857-1967	Share of Total[b] (%)	Reserves 1965	Share of Total[c] (%)	Life of Reserves[d]
Latin America	4,905,252	15.6	3,968,000	7.4	16.0
Argentina	240,230	0.8	318,000	0.6	19.9
Bolivia	10,227		63,600	0.1	125.2[e]
Brazil	57,640	0.2	143,000	0.3	27.0
Chile	19,218	0.1	35,800	0.1	16.4
Colombia	221,713	0.7	190,800	0.4	19.2
Cuba	938		80[f]		1.9
Ecuador	15,606		3,980		8.9
Mexico	664,128	2.1	445,200	0.8	24.2
Peru	116,997	0.4	67,600	0.1	18.4
Venezuela	3,558,555	11.4	2,700,000	5.0	13.7
United States	13,598,918	43.4	4,727,000	9.2	11.0
Canada	553,694	1.8	789,679	1.6	19.2
Western Europe	285,773	0.9	284,705	0.5	22.0
Germany	115,338	0.4	104,145	0.2	11.7
Communist Countries	4,424,182	14.1	4,880,505	9.1	16.9
Soviet Union	3,885,351	12.4	4,650,750	8.7	17.8
Rumania	418,855	1.3	151,050	0.3	10.3
Africa	790,446	2.5	3,083,900	5.7	31.2
Algeria	238,349	0.8	1,192,500	2.2	37.0
Egypt	95,057	0.3	238,500	0.4	34.2
Libya	352,223	1.1	1,431,000	2.7	28.6
Nigeria	79,373	0.3	159,000	0.3	22.7
Middle East	5,742,048	18.3	33,736,600	62.8	76.2
Iran	1,379,796	4.4	6,042,000	11.3	61.5
Iraq	919,507	2.9	3,975,000	7.4	55.5
Kuwait	1,509,257	4.8	10,017,000	18.7	81.4
Neutral Zone[g]	161,660	0.5	1,987,500	3.7	95.0
Saudi Arabia	1,453,263	4.6	9,619,500	17.9	96.4
Asia & Oceania	885,773	2.8	1,894,278	3.5	50.8
Indonesia	520,979	1.7	1,590,000	3.0	58.4
World Total	31,348,944	100.0	53,696,500	100.0	32.6

Sources: API, *Petroleum Facts and Figures, 1959, 1965.* USBM, *International Petroleum Quarterly, 1964.* USBM, *Minerals Yearbook, 1964, 1967.*

[a]Cumulative total production from first year in which production of crude oil was reported, through 1967.
[b]Cumulative production as percentage of world total cumulative production.
[c]Reserves as percentage of world total.
[d]Ratio of reserves on 1 January 1965 to crude oil production in 1964: life of proved reserves at constant rate of production.
[e]Reserves doubled during 1964; production rose only slightly.
[f]1963 reserves; 1965 data not available.
[g]Neutral Zone lies between Kuwait and Saudi Arabia and is claimed by both. First production, 1954.

TABLE 8-2. World Production of Crude Oil, 1925-1967
(Thousands of cubic meters)

Country or Region	1925-29	1930-34	1935-39	1940-44	1945-49	1950	1951	1952
Latin America	28,327	32,398	43,578	47,232	86,066	110,669	124,547	130,741
Argentina	1,312	1,958	2,601	3,757	3,551	3,713	3,890	3,910
Bolivia		13	26	47	72	98	83	84
Brazil				5	16	54	110	119
Chile						100	121	145
Colombia	1,995	2,719	3,255	3,059	3,908	5,416	6,105	6,151
Cuba				19	35	25	20	6
Ecuador	107	260	331	365	456	419	431	451
Mexico	11,604	5,646	6,665	6,183	8,538	11,518	12,293	12,287
Peru	1,766	1,971	2,591	2,122	2,157	2,387	2,562	2,608
Venezuela	11,542	19,832	28,109	31,684	67,380	86,939	98,932	104,980
United States	138,156	138,265	186,181	232,954	291,501	313,798	357,386	364,084
Canada						4,618	7,571	9,737
Western Europe	188	374	721	1,999	2,048	3,866	5,189	6,271
Communist Countries	17,113	33,618	40,683	44,411	36,502	48,854	51,501	65,021
Soviet Union	12,102	24,963	31,828	37,587	31,113	43,439	46,428	54,149
Rumania			8,650	6,078	5,166	5,088	4,929	9,365
Africa	237	292	322	1,331	1,806	2,656	2,695	2,792
Middle East	6,265	8,379	17,219	17,120	53,560	101,920	112,051	120,776
Iran			11,267	11,639	26,313	38,554	19,638	1,240
Iraq			4,868	3,574	5,205	7,906	10,354	22,435
Kuwait						19,990	32,581	43,476
Saudi Arabia					15,518	31,728	44,196	47,996
Asia and Oceania	7,026	9,342	12,170	9,669	6,793	15,032	16,701	17,647
Indonesia			8,692	6,687	2,948	7,696	8,817	9,937
World Total	198,300	224,455	304,006	359,738	483,348	604,681	680,954	720,447
Shares (%) in World Total:								
Latin America	14.28	14.43	14.33	13.13	17.81	18.30	18.29	18.15
Venezuela	5.82	8.84	9.25	8.81	13.94	14.38	14.53	14.46

Country or Region	1953	1954	1955	1956	1957	1958	1959	1960
Latin America	128,227	138,295	155,112	174,732	194,672	187,169	200,342	210,401
Argentina	4,532	4,702	4,850	4,931	5,399	5,697	7,109	10,213
Bolivia	96	270	428	508	568	546	504	568
Brazil	146	158	322	637	1,607	3,008	3,751	4,709
Chile	200	276	410	563	690	885	1,022	1,150
Colombia	6,270	6,357	6,314	7,150	7,438	7,457	8,519	8,867
Cuba	3	4	60	86	63	55	31	17
Ecuador	483	500	572	544	507	494	439	434
Mexico	11,518	13,301	14,216	14,415	14,034	14,872	15,326	15,749
Peru	2,544	2,729	2,742	2,923	3,067	2,978	2,820	3,062
Venezuela	102,435	109,998	125,198	142,975	161,299	151,177	160,821	165,632
United States	374,776	368,083	395,024	416,148	416,087	389,394	409,360	409,414
Canada	12,863	15,277	20,581	27,345	28,914	26,318	29,380	30,136
Western Europe	7,421	8,509	9,955	11,246	12,827	13,877	14,320	15,701
Communist Countries	72,996	81,746	96,582	112,890	129,824	148,217	166,688	189,176
Soviet Union	60,445	67,887	81,052	97,267	114,098	131,410	150,377	171,620
Rumania	10,734	11,543	12,509	12,941	13,249	13,434	13,276	13,628
Africa	2,846	2,421	2,200	2,062	3,035	5,083	6,587	16,744
Algeria								10,751
Egypt								3,811
Nigeria								1,042
Middle East	140,750	158,964	188,414	200,573	205,607	247,786	271,244	309,613
Iran	1,495	3,419	19,169	31,347	41,838	47,916	54,823	61,334
Iraq	33,433	36,321	39,942	36,937	25,996	42,314	49,480	56,260
Kuwait	50,020	55,224	63,360	63,580	66,151	81,035	80,272	94,490
Saudi Arabia	49,019	55,307	56,006	57,387	57,577	58,907	63,572	72,576
Asia and Oceania	19,461	20,637	22,691	24,147	27,653	28,282	29,787	32,325
Indonesia	12,025	12,654	13,046	14,917	18,150	18,876	22,107	24,325
World Total	762,891	797,678	894,515	973,743	1,024,035	1,050,632	1,134,212	1,220,244
Shares (%) in World Total:								
Latin America	16.81	17.34	17.34	17.94	19.01	17.82	17.66	17.24
Venezuela	13.43	13.79	14.00	14.68	15.75	14.39	14.18	13.57

TABLE 8–2 – Continued

Country or Region	1961	1962	1963	1964	1965	1966	1967
Latin America	219,371	238,764	244,262	254,128	263,413	260,468	277,217
Argentina	13,423	15,607	15,681	16,189	15,849	16,896	18,506
Bolivia	475	463	549	531	541	981	2,343
Brazil	5,536	5,311	5,760	5,296	5,539	6,846	8,631
Chile	1,473	1,859	2,100	2,176	2,049	2,005	1,995
Colombia	8,466	8,255	9,595	9,953	11,721	11,521	11,109
Cuba	13	14	12	42	62	74	122
Ecuador	465	409	392	445	460	429	355
Mexico	16,979	17,781	18,264	18,377	19,026	19,540	21,458
Peru	3,080	3,360	3,413	3,676	3,714	3,714	4,170
Venezuela	169,461	185,705	188,496	197,443	204,452	198,462	208,528
United States	416,860	425,513	437,683	446,015	459,438	488,349	518,668
Canada	35,117	38,818	41,091	43,783	47,810	51,700	56,859
Western Europe	16,741	17,582	18,791	20,568	21,104	20,420	20,139
Communist Countries	211,089	234,210	257,687	288,974	309,661	336,464	364,613
Soviet Union	192,756	215,890	239,104	261,778	288,065	314,194	341,290
Rumania	13,725	13,971	14,103	14,689	15,112	15,417	15,868
Africa	28,400	46,648	68,476	98,831	130,202	165,580	181,370
Algeria	19,318	25,037	28,987	32,164	32,541	41,471	45,516
Egypt	4,155	5,139	6,161	6,983	7,348	6,984	6,774
Libya	1,056	10,661	26,678	50,187	71,835	89,147	102,662
Nigeria	2,672	3,915	4,395	6,996	16,025	24,585	18,793
Middle East	331,048	363,203	395,221	442,530	492,425	549,740	590,369
Iran	68,633	76,628	85,559	98,378	111,012	124,393	153,615
Iraq	58,130	58,326	67,190	72,923	77,816	81,521	71,907
Kuwait	95,436	106,416	112,170	123,196	127,726	133,958	134,955
Saudi Arabia	80,815	88,254	94,540	99,867	119,206	140,863	152,921
Asia and Oceania	35,713	34,937	39,603	46,237	51,528	56,348	59,265
Indonesia	24,704	26,676	26,235	27,267	28,870	27,166	29,839
World Total	1,301,613	1,407,439	1,510,554	1,642,386	1,783,466	1,938,037	2,078,985
Shares (%) in World Total:							
Latin America	16.85	16.96	16.17	15.47	14.77	13.44	13.33
Venezuela	13.02	13.19	12.48	12.02	11.46	10.24	10.03

Sources: API, *Petroleum Facts and Figures, 1959, 1965.* USBM, *Minerals Yearbook, 1964, 1967.* USBM, *International Petroleum Quarterly, 1964.*

TABLE 8-3. World Consumption of Petroleum Products, Averages for 1936-38, 1950-51, 1962-64, and 1966-67
(Thousands of cubic meters)

Country or Region	1936-38	1950-51	1962-64	1966-67
Latin America	13,153	35,974	88,400	106,942
United States	180,177	349,106	612,920	718,516
Canada	6,991	19,976	57,199	72,284
Western Europe	40,517	67,047	349,147	504,289
France	7,939	12,318	49,615	74,465
Germany	7,411	4,875	68,204	107,700
Italy	3,069	5,960	45,218	66,689
United Kingdom	13,561	21,332	72,642	94,804
Africa	3,498	10,922	29,083	35,073
Egypt	902	4,860	6,541	7,174
South Africa	1,053	3,132	5,902	8,194
Asia and Oceania	18,504	30,225	182,523	217,730
Japan	4,913	3,110	70,053	127,736
Communist Countries	29,711	51,691[a]	228,493	300,449
World Total	298,056	573,617	1,558,997	2,035,568

Sources: API, *Petroleum Facts and Figures, 1941, 1959, 1965.* USBM, *International Petroleum Quarterly, 1962-64.* USBM, *International Petroleum Annual, 1967.*

[a]Estimated from refinery input of crude oil.

TABLE 8–4. World Refining Capacity,[a] 1941, 1951, and 1963, and World Production of Refined Petroleum Products,[b] 1949-51 and 1962-64

Country or Region	Refineries at 1 January 1941 No.	Refineries at 1 January 1941 Capacity (m3/day)	Refineries at 1 January 1951 No.	Refineries at 1 January 1951 Capacity (m3/day)	Refineries at 1 January 1963 No.	Refineries at 1 January 1963 Capacity (m3/day)	Production of Refined Products 1949-51 (thousand m3)	Production of Refined Products 1962-64 (thousand m3)
Latin America	60	65,258	60	112,311	69	401,714	32,932	135,650
Netherlands West Indies	3	80,295	3	115,164	2	108,120	43,761	48,473
United States	548	765,858	364	1,039,902	287	1,668,069	327,351	532,649
Canada	54	35,274	29	54,012	44	169,446	16,249	52,142
Western Europe	99	72,106	107	161,364	118	813,905	42,967	313,430
France	18	24,096	16	57,733	14	146,678	15,665	55,441
Germany	31	7,704	30	17,792	27	153,960	3,160	57,412
Italy	10	9,111	16	18,285	34	127,311	5,503	60,220
United Kingdom	18	21,219	22	39,981	15	175,392	11,204	65,102
Africa	4	3,180	2	6,519	8	31,291	3,220	20,831
Egypt	2	2,703	2	6,519	3	18,078	2,357	7,428
Middle East	7	65,111	9	149,603	24	279,029	41,529	88,783
Asia and Oceania	36	43,995	25	44,980	60	338,638	13,763	118,841
Japan	17	8,363	12	7,559	28	174,741	1,546	29,562
World less Communist Countries	811	1,276,516	605	1,683,855	621	3,881,047	526,541	1,338,515
Estimated Production of Refined Products in Communist Countries[c]							49,303	247,109
World Total							575,844	1,585,624
Latin American Production of Refined Products as Share (%) of:								
Total World Production							6.6	10.2
L.A. Production of Crude							32.8	55.7

Sources: API, *Petroleum Facts and Figures, 1959, 1965*. USBM, *International Petroleum Quarterly, 1951, 1963-64.*

[a]Distillation capacity (crude oil).
[b]Total refinery output of all products.
[c]Eastern Europe only, 1941 and 1949-51; includes China, 1962-64. For 1941, estimated production of refined products in Communist countries is 41 million cubic meters, giving a world total of 321 million cubic meters, and a Latin American share of 4.1%. Latin America's share of world crude production in 1941 is estimated to be 28.7%. These figures are calculated from refinery capacity in 1941 and ratio of capacity to production, 1949-51 (284 cubic meters produced for each cubic meter per day of capacity, on average).

TABLE 8–5. Petroleum Prices: United States, Venezuela, and the Middle East

I. United States: Crude Oil, 1925-1964
(Dollars per barrel)

Year	Gulf Coast[a]	Avg. Value Exports[b]	Avg. Value Imports from Venezuela	Year	Gulf Coast[a]	Avg. Value Exports[b]	Avg. Value Imports from Venezuela
1925	1.62	1.85	1.34	1945	1.31	1.69	1.07
1926	1.50	1.85	1.32	1946	1.51	1.74	1.15
1927	1.30	1.64	1.31	1947	2.05	2.19	1.62
1928	1.19	1.41	0.97	1948	2.75	2.94	2.38
1929	1.21	1.43	0.95	1949	2.73	2.98	2.40
1930	1.04	1.36	0.97	1950	2.72	2.96	2.32
1931	0.66	0.82	0.74	1951	2.72	2.86	2.28
1932	0.81	0.99	0.51	1952	2.73	2.93	2.28
1933	0.66	0.87	0.50	1953	2.89	3.01	2.47
1934	1.01	1.21	0.65	1954	3.02	3.31	2.53
1935	1.00	1.19	0.67	1955	3.02	3.34	2.48
1936	1.13	1.31	0.69	1956	3.00	3.16	2.48
1937	1.22	1.44	0.74	1957	3.41	3.45	2.62
1938	1.19	1.45	0.72	1958	3.32	3.39	2.63
1939	1.08	1.29	0.68	1959	3.29	2.77	2.39
1940	1.10	1.32	0.76	1960	3.25	2.60	2.37
1941	1.24	1.44	0.82	1961	3.26	2.65	2.40
1942	1.30	1.45	0.92	1962	3.26	2.84	2.38
1943	1.31	1.54	1.04	1963	3.25	2.72	2.37
1944	1.31	1.69	1.09	1964	3.20	2.80	2.36

[a]Average price at wellhead.
[b]Includes some material other than crude petroleum from which motor fuel can be obtained by commercial distillation, and some oil from shale; in 1944-45, includes exports under lend-lease arrangements. Average value for all destinations.

TABLE 8–5 – Continued

II. Venezuela: Crude Oil, Posted Prices, by Field,[a] 1952-1964
(Dollars per barrel)

Year	Oficina[b]	Tia Juana[c]	Lagunillas[d]	Average[e]	Average Value of Exports[f]
1952[g]	2.63[h]	2.20	2.00	2.29	2.11
1953	2.76[h]	2.25	2.05	2.37	2.30
1954	2.88[h]	2.30	1.85	2.38	2.33
1955	2.87	2.30	1.92	2.39	2.33
1956	2.80	2.30	2.06	2.41	2.33
1957	3.04	2.54	2.38	2.67	2.60
1958	3.05	2.55	2.24	2.64	2.49
1959	2.84	2.34	2.10	2.45	2.19
1960	2.80[j]	2.30[j]	2.09	2.43	2.11
1961	2.80	2.30	2.07[k]	2.41	2.12
1962	2.80	2.30	2.07	2.41	2.07
1963	2.80	2.30	2.07	2.41	2.03
1964	2.80	2.30	2.07	2.41	1.97

[a]Annual average posted price of crude oil indicated; where two or more prices were in effect during one year, each price is weighted by the length of time it was in effect.

[b]Crude of 35.0° – 35.9°, FOB Puerto La Cruz.

[c]Crude of 26.0° – 26.9°, FOB Amuay (3 cents per barrel less at La Salina).

[d]Crude of 17° – 18°, FOB La Salina.

[e]Weighted average, combined according to approximate distribution of Venezuelan crude production by gravity: 0.34 Oficina, 0.39 Tia Juana and 0.27 Lagunillas.

[f]For all fields.

[g]From 23 July only.

[h]Mulata crude of 35.0° – 35.9°, FOB Puerto La Cruz, instead of Oficina crude.

[j]Price in effect since 4 April 1959.

[k]Price in effect since 12 August 1960.

III. Venezuela: Refined Products, Posted Prices,[a] ex Aruba and Curaçao, 1951-1954
(Cents per gallon)

Year	Gasoline[c]	Kerosene	Distillate Fuel Oil[d]	Bunker "C" fuel	Weighted Average[e]	Average Value of Exports[b] Cents per Gallon	Average Value of Exports[b] Dollars per Barrel
1951	10.50	9.00[f]	8.25	4.17	5.44		
1952	10.50	9.00	8.25	3.90	5.25	6.05	2.54
1953	10.61	8.79	8.22	4.12	5.44	6.06	2.55
1954	9.82	8.77	8.39	4.40	5.58	6.06	2.55
1955	9.75	9.01	8.83	4.78	5.93	6.52	2.74
1956	9.61	9.44	9.16	5.07	6.19	6.71	2.82
1957	9.98	9.80	9.77	6.05	7.04	7.56	3.18
1958	9.20	9.12	8.81	5.26	6.22	6.95	2.92
1959	9.34	9.36	9.12	4.76[g]	5.95	6.24	2.62
1960	9.38	9.27	8.51	4.76	5.83	5.76	2.42
1961	8.40	9.62	8.57	4.76	5.76	5.71	2.40
1962	7.80	9.58	8.33	4.76	5.67	5.47	2.30
1963	7.40	9.45	8.21	4.76	5.61	5.33	2.24
1964	7.00	8.94	7.63	4.76	5.46	4.90	2.06

[a]Annual average posted price for product indicated; each price posted during the year is weighted by the length of time it was in effect, to the nearest 15 days. All prices ex refinery: ex Aruba only, 1951-55, and ex Aruba and Curaçao, 1956-64.

[b]Includes all products exported from Venezuela, Aruba, and Curaçao.

[c]Motor gasoline, 79 octane regular grade.

[d]Gas/diesel oil, 53/57 cetane, ex Aruba only.

[e]Combined according to average distribution of refinery output in Venezuela, Aruba, and Curaçao, 1950-1964: 0.0785 gasoline, 0.0014 kerosene, 0.2020 distillate fuel oil, and 0.7054 bunker "C" fuel.

[f]From 26 November only.

[g]Price in effect since 17 September 1958.

TABLE 8-5—Continued

IV. Middle East: Posted Prices, Crude Oil, 1951-1964[a] and Refined Products, 1958-1964[b]

Type	1951	1952	1953	1954	1955	1956	1957
Crude Oil ($/bbl)							
Ras Tanura[c]	1.71[d]	1.71	1.78	1.93	1.93	1.93	2.01
Abadan[e]				1.86[f]	1.86	1.86	1.93

Type	1958	1959	1960	1961	1962	1963	1964
Crude Oil ($/bbl)							
Ras Tanura[c]	2.08	1.92	1.87	1.80[g]	1.80	1.80	1.80
Abadan[e]	1.99	1.83	1.78	1.73[g]	1.73	1.73	1.73
Refined Products (¢/gal)							
Gasoline[h]	9.26	8.99	8.64	7.96	7.59	7.10	6.70
Kerosene	9.24	9.54	9.13	9.14	9.35	9.52	9.11
Distillate fuel oil[j]	9.39	9.34	8.56	8.25	8.28	8.22	7.80
Bunker "C" fuel	4.95	4.24	4.02	3.97	3.90	3.80	3.80
Weighted average[k]	6.13	5.60	5.26	5.10	5.04	4.91	4.79
Dollars per barrel	2.57	2.35	2.21	2.14	2.11	2.06	2.01

Sources: U.S. average value of crude at wellhead, API, *Petroleum Facts and Figures, 1959, 1965*. U.S. average value of crude exports, USDC, *United States Exports, Commodity by Country*; before 1946, published as *Foreign Commerce and Navigation of the United States*. U.S. average value of imports from Venezuela, USDC, *United States Imports of Merchandise for Consumption*. Venezuela and Middle East, crude and product posted prices, *Petroleum Press Service* and *Petroleum Times*. Venezuela, average value of exports of crude and products, Oficina Técnica de Hidrocarburos, Ministerio de Minas e Hidrocarburos, *Valores del Estado Consolidado de Ganancías y Pérdidas de la Industria Petrolera*, 1963.

[a] Annual average posted price of crude oil indicated; prices weighted by the length of time each was in effect.
[b] Annual average posted price for product indicated; prices weighted by the length of time each was in effect. All prices ex refinery.
[c] Arabian crude of 34.0° - 34.9°, FOB Ras Tanura; until 1 December 1956, a price was posted for crude of 36.0° – 36.9° FOB Ras Tanura, with a discount of 2 cents per barrel for each degree of gravity below 36°. The price shown is 4 cents per barrel less than the posted price of 36° crude. On 1 December 1956, the basis for posting was changed to 34°, and the price lowered 4 cents.
[d] From 1 April only.
[e] Iranian crude of 34.0° - 34.9°, FOB Abadan.
[f] From 29 October only.
[g] Price in effect since 9 August 1960.
[h] Motor gasoline, 79 octane regular grade.
[j] Gas/diesel oil, 53/57 cetane, Ras Tanura only.
[k] Average value of all products exported from Ras Tanura and Abadan.

TABLE 8-6. Production and Trade in Petroleum of Communist Countries,[a] 1955-1967
(Thousands of cubic meters)

Year	Production of Crude Oil	Net Exports of Crude[b]	Production of Refined Products[c]	Net Exports of Products[b]	Consumption of Refined Products[d]
1955	101,474	636	100,821	2,274	98,547
1956	112,916	–228	112,413	2,291	110,122
1957	129,823	1,892	126,775	4,820	121,955
1958	148,217	6,166	141,335	5,727	135,608
1959	168,351	6,409	162,158	9,528	151,137
1960	192,444	8,473	181,594	12,061	167,208
1961	217,353	15,343	205,428	15,094	189,210
1962	241,554	19,136	227,481	16,788	212,392
1963	265,931	22,199	243,688	18,799	224,810
1964	290,152	26,516	263,636	17,848	247,948
1965	309,661	23,871	289,194	29,839	265,645
1966	336,464	37,578	311,625	26,930	284,695
1967	375,413	40,960	340,161	29,326	310,835

Sources: USBM, *International Petroleum Quarterly, 1955-64*. Vneshniaia torgovlia SSSR, statisticheskiyi spravochnik (*Foreign Trade of the USSR, Statistical Summary*) (Moscow: Vneshtorgiszdat), 1959-63, pp. 104-5, and 1964, pp. 60-61. USBM, *International Petroleum Annual, 1966, 1967*.

[a] Eastern Europe only, 1955-58; includes China, 1959-67; in the earlier years some exports of crude and products from the Soviet Union to China are therefore included.
[b] Total exports of all Communist countries, less total imports; trade with each other is therefore eliminated.
[c] Estimated crude runs to stills, 1955-58; estimated refinery output, including refinery fuel and loss, 1959-67.
[d] Production less net exports of refined products, 1955-58; estimated domestic demand, 1959-67.

TABLE 8-7. Import Substitution in Petroleum Production and Refining in Selected Latin American Countries between 1950 and 1960
(Thousands of cubic meters)

Concept	Year	Argentina	Brazil	Chile	Cuba	Uruguay	Total
I. TOTAL PETROLEUM							
Imports	1950	6,045	4,954	1,191			12,179
	1960	5,854	11,165	1,434			18,453
Crude oil	1950	3,713	54	100			3,867
production	1960	10,213	4,709	1,150			16,072
Total	1950	9,758	5,000	1,291			16,046
supply	1960	16,067	15,874	2,584			34,525
Increase in							
crude production	1950-60	6,500	4,655	1,050			12,205
Import coeff. (%)	1950	63.1	98.9	92.4			75.9
Anticipated imports	1960	10,120	15,699	2,390			28,209
Diff. betw. anticd. and							
actual impts.	1960	4,266	4,534	956			9,756
Share increased prod. due							
to impt. sub. (%)	1950-60	66	97	91			80
Share anticd. impts.							
replaced (%)	1950-60	42	29	40			35
II. REFINED PRODUCTS ONLY							
Imports	1950	2,576	4,891	1,191	1,926	240	10,824
	1960	2,200	4,783	864	723	283	8,853
Refinery	1950	6,400	86	0	292	832	7,610
production	1960	13,640	10.700	1,730	3,740	1,510	31,320
Total	1950	8,976	4,977	1,191	2,218	1,072	18,434
supply	1960	15,840	15,443	2,594	4,463	2,810	40,173
Increase in refinery							
production	1950-60	7,240	10,614	1,730	3,448	678	23,710
Import coeff. (%)	1950	28.7	98.3	100	87.0	22.4	53.7
Anticipated imports	1960	4,540	15,176	2,594	3,882	629	26,821
Diff. betw. anticd. and							
actual impts.	1960	2,340	10,393	1,730	3,159	346	17,968
Share increased refinery prod.							
due to impt. sub. (%)	1950-60	32	98	100	92	51	76
Share anticd. impts.							
replaced (%)	1950-60	52	68	67	81	55	67

Sources: For definitions and methods see Chap. 1, table A-4. See also table 8-2 and API, *Petroleum Facts and Figures, 1959, 1965.*

TABLE 8-8. Latin American Production of Major Refined Petroleum Products, Averages for 1936-38, 1949-51, 1962-64, and 1965-67
(Thousands of cubic meters)

Country	Gasoline[a]	Kerosene[b]	Distillate Fuel Oils[c]	Residual Fuel Oils	Lubricating Oils	Total[d]	Share of Crude[e] (%)
			1936-38				
Argentina	1,090	93	442	1,210	49	3,320	78[f]
Bolivia[g]	9			8		18	85
Colombia[g]	118	18	18	244	4	411	13
Ecuador[g]	18	7	7	22		53	16
Mexico	1,997	272	580	3,110	77	6,555	98
Peru	368	176	137	262	5	990	37
Venezuela	156	7	94[h]	1,180	4[g]	1,470	5
Latin America[j]	3,756	576	1,278	6,039	139	12,817	34

TABLE 8-8–Continued

Country	Gasoline[a]	Kerosene[b]	Distillate Fuel Oils[c]	Residual Fuel Oils	Lubricating Oils	Total[d]	Share of Crude[e] (%)
			1949-51				
Argentina	2,000	720	790	2,592	114	6,215	60[f]
Bolivia	48	9	7	22		86	89
Brazil	42	10	24	44		120	50[f]
Colombia	329	60	86	1,010	10	4,900	90
Cuba	117	77	74	47		317	82[f]
Ecuador	85	19	40	111	1[k]	256	61
Mexico	1,900	726	829	4,780	35	8,290	74
Peru	814	199	229	895	12	2,150	88
Uruguay	232	132	74	421		860	(m)
Venezuela	2,088	406	2,599	7,990	71[n]	13,150	15
Latin America	7,655	2,358	4,752	17,912	243	36,344	36
			1962-64				
Argentina	3,570	1,430	2,770	6,560	144	16,800	93[f]
Bolivia	168	69	70	107		440	89
Brazil	5,395	688	5,200	6,300	4	19,020	29[f]
Chile	930	283	430	613		2,574	79[f]
Colombia	1,730	317	650	499	34	4,965	55
Cuba	913	195	719	1,880		4,000	1[f]
Ecuador	282	65	126	195		697	59[f]
El Salvador[p]	141	40	118	157		502	(m)
Guatemala[p]	53	9	28	83		144	(m)
Mexico	5,455	2,017	2,830	6,190	192	19,330	94[f]
Nicaragua[p]	77	23	49	78		240	(m)
Panama	290	124	545	856		1,947	(m)
Peru	886	574	924	654	15	3,250	92
Uruguay	379	242	322	687		1,710	(m)
Venezuela	6,640	4,530	11,400	35,460	476	61,490	32
Latin America[q]	26,818	10,582	26,116	60,213	865	136,794	58
			1965-67				
Argentina	4,707	1,160	4,098	8,611	157	20,029	85[f]
Bolivia	217	93	105	133		555	43
Brazil	6,561	727	4,461	6,140		19,704	36[f]
Chile	1,176	336	576	879		3,230	63[f]
Colombia	2,085	354	802	2,040	72	6,153	54
Ecuador[r]	348	112	162	204		906	49[f]
El Salvador	164	66	169	101		515	(m)
Guatemala	168[g]	45	214	215		629	(m)
Mexico	6,199	1,917	3,577	6,754	223	21,786	97
Nicaragua	119	29	85	71		310	(m)
Panama	398	104	759	1,172		2,734	(m)
Peru	1,084	555	964	933	13	3,771	97
Uruguay	375	207	363	782		1,820	(m)
Venezuela	7,975	1,025	11,264	42,188	605	68,956	34
Latin America	31,576	6,730	27,599	70,259	1,070	151,098	57

Sources: 1936-38 – USBM, *International Petroleum Trade*, vol. 6, no. 11; vol. 7, nos. 2, 5; vol. 8, nos. 8, 10; vol. 9, nos. 4, 9. 1949-51 – API, *Petroleum Facts and Figures, 1959.* 1962-64 – USBM, *International Petroleum Quarterly, 1962, 1963, 1964.* 1965-67 – USBM, *Minerals Yearbook, 1967.*

[a]Motor fuel only, excluding aviation gasoline.
[b]Includes jet fuel.
[c]Gas oil and diesel oil.
[d]Total refinery output, including products other than those listed.
[e]Production of refined products as a percentage of crude oil production, or share of crude refined domestically.
[f]Production of crude oil as a percentage of refinery output, or share of products refined from domestic crude.
[g]1936-37 average.
[h]Gas oil only in 1938; gas oil and other distillates, 1936-37.
[j]Sum of countries listed; data not available for Brazil and Cuba.
[k]1949-50 average.
[m]No crude oil produced.
[n]1950-51 average.
[p]1963-64 average; refinery went on stream in 1963.

[q]1962-1964 average; three-year averages used for El Salvador, Guatemala, and Nicaragua.
[r]1965-66 average; 1967 data not available.

TABLE 8-9. Latin American Exports of Crude Petroleum and Refined Products by Destination, 1950-1966[a]
(Thousands of cubic meters and millions of U.S. dollars)

Country or Region	1950	1951	1952	1953	1954	1955	1956	1957	1958	1959	1960	1961	1962	1963	1964	1965	1966
VENEZUELA[b]																	
Total exports of crude and products	78,570	89,702	99,668	98,083	105,968	118,883	137,293	147,473	141,759	145,768	151,117	155,296	169,661	173,270	182,248	188,748	184,635
Total direct exports of crude	28,375	32,590	37,752	37,538	41,980	50,050	62,589	78,798	72,573	74,283	75,331	76,136	85,701	88,000	92,889	91,221	88,229
Latin America	1,688	1,820	2,595	2,809	3,092	5,488	7,319	10,536	13,893	13,410	10,359	7,560	9,182	10,359	12,341	11,604	11,683
Argentina	1,071	1,123	1,763	1,824	1,968	2,210	2,548	4,139	4,400	4,348	3,220	1,898	977	699	947	908	737
Brazil	63	98	125	236	375	2,057	3,254	2,924	3,936	3,560	3,234	4,377	5,816	5,352	5,121	4,568	3,561
Trinidad and Tobago	1,558	2,269	2,474	2,362	2,501	2,622	2,895	2,734	2,885	3,605	4,623	4,878	4,516	5,068	6,337	7,385	8,455
North America	21,460	24,314	27,677	28,116	29,770	33,552	39,963	46,700	40,927	42,170	44,102	42,078	46,534	48,178	50,296	45,886	43,348
United States	16,614	17,134	19,564	19,035	20,538	22,812[c]	27,463[c]	33,225[c]	29,611[c]	30,260[c]	32,445[c]	29,094[c]	32,995[c]	34,127[c]	33,929[c]	32,441[c]	33,541[c]
Western Europe	3,538	3,465	4,285	3,890	5,988	8,255	12,247	18,488	14,632	14,793	15,784	21,226	25,037	24,021	23,442	24,624	22,463
United Kingdom	148	300	617	793	1,716	2,225	3,238	6,692	4,965	6,745	7,573	7,988	9,195	8,671	8,802	10,137	8,866
EEC	2,998	2,726	3,190	2,463	3,499	5,289	7,892	9,858	8,102	6,302	6,192	9,126	10,355	10,498	9,387	8,060	7,944
Crude exports to N.W.I.	43,557	47,360	46,653	40,185	42,067	43,882	44,771	41,837	36,817	40,162	40,883	42,105	43,156	42,104	43,850	44,092	43,106
Total exports of products	50,195	57,112	61,916	60,545	63,988	68,833	74,704	68,675	69,236	71,485	75,786	79,160	83,960	85,270	89,359	97,527	96,406
Latin America	10,090	12,076	14,653	15,043	16,044	14,036	15,287	13,446	10,928	10,268	10,498	9,087	7,214	7,688	7,650	6,564	6,521
Argentina	2,408	2,595	2,976	2,415	2,474	2,863	3,862	2,442	2,166	2,293	1,776	2,093	1,664	561	1,155	512	201
Brazil	4,387	5,381	6,559	7,114	7,775	5,072	4,770	3,802	4,434	3,615	4,442	3,107	1,241	901	1,118	842	819
North America	20,485	19,431	17,810	20,500	22,793	28,188	30,635	33,574	39,875	42,421	43,568	46,371	48,611	46,371	53,717	61,012	63,667
United States	19,238	18,271	17,373	19,459	21,093	25,799[c]	28,335[c]	31,447[c]	37,542[c]	38,651[c]	40,080[c]	43,157[c]	44,802[c]	43,725[c]	48,885[c]	54,026[c]	56,721[c]
Western Europe	13,897	18,143	14,465	12,714	13,221	16,767	18,815	14,960	13,355	13,111	14,584	15,464	18,793	23,088	19,542	16,922	13,656
United Kingdom	4,836	7,484	3,776	3,920	4,832	5,968	8,191	7,471	7,325	5,961	7,032	6,126	6,857	8,455	7,624	6,819	4,562
EEC	3,069	3,879	3,774	3,556	3,708	4,703	4,735	3,022	2,342	2,585	2,802	4,601	7,389	9,149	5,681	4,896	4,199
Value of petroleum exports	1,216.8	1,414.9	1,493.9	1,473.1	1,727.2	1,951.8	2,151.5	2,357.9	2,292.6	2,357.0	2,411.0	2,408.1	2,607.8	2,639.2	2,525.0	2,552.0	2,508.4
Share of total exports (%)	97.0	96.7	95.5	94.5	94.6	96.4	94.2	92.5	91.7	92.3	92.0	92.6	93.2	93.1	93.1	93.0	92.4
COLOMBIA																	
Crude exports	4,495[d]	5,126[d]	4,953[d]	5,099[d]	4,835[d]	4,035	4,595	4,516	3,878	4,510	4,982	4,377	3,866	4,956	4,883	6,562	5,738
Latin America		39	119	86	122		89	92	39	56					212	162	
Trinidad and Tobago		1,830	1,985	2,338	2,290	1,920	2,151	2,109	1,605		366	695	779	1,886	1,947	1,906	1,674
United States	2,492	2,662	2,428	2,455	1,953	1,316	1,433	1,329	1,614	2,009	2,346	1,583	1,431	1,407	1,614	2,523	2,349
Western Europe	262	435	221	54	297	421	263	548	439	2,080	2,255	2,099	1,656	1,663	1,110		1,270
Products exports		(e)	(e)	(e)	37	252	185	283	672	663	651	422	630	433	720	842	1,015
Latin America						182	138	168	508	277	272	287	439	164	164		285
United States								16	16	37	126	102	192	33	33		605
Western Europe						35	47	101	171	245		20	94	100	100	33	
Value of petroleum exports	65.0	73.5	71.4	76.3	75.8	61.5	69.9	72.4	65.4	73.3	80.4	68.0	61.0	77.0	75.0	58.8	47.3
Share of total exports (%)	16.4	16.0	15.2	12.8	11.5	10.6	11.7	13.9	14.2	15.5	17.3	15.6	13.2	17.3	13.7	15.9	12.6
ARGENTINA																	
Crude exports											2	136	300	114	18	896	3
Products exports												114	681	786	512		1,227
Value of petroleum exports											0.1	1.1	13.1	11.1	5.9	9.1	13.8
Share of total exports (%)												0.1	1.1	0.8	0.4	0.6	0.9
BOLIVIA																	
Crude exports[f]	9	13	10	11	9	76	86	163	191	151	173	118	72	119	50	43	327
Products exports												11	1	7			
Value of petroleum exports					0.32	2.3	2.9	4.6	5.1	3.1	3.5	2.4	1.5	1.8	0.8		
Share of total exports (%)					0.3	3.0	3.6	6.2	10.2	5.3	6.9	4.1	2.5	2.7	0.6		
BRAZIL[g]																	
Crude exports									1,331	1,707	683	1,269	359	434	185		
Products exports										48			60	17			

TABLE 8-9 – Continued

Country or Region	1950	1951	1952	1953	1954	1955	1956	1957	1958	1959	1960	1961	1962	1963	1964	1965	1966
CHILE																	
Crude exports[h]	75	138	128	179	175												
Value of petroleum exports		2.2	2.7	3.8	3.2												
Share of total exports (%)		0.6	0.6	0.9	0.8												
ECUADOR																	
Crude exports	166	199	139	207	213	228	180	192	115	45				30	84	86	61
Value of petroleum exports		1.53	0.99	1.57	1.50	1.60	1.10	1.37	0.68	0.32			0.16	0.32	0.65	0.6	1.4
Share of total exports (%)		2.2	1.0	1.7	1.2	1.4	0.9	1.0	0.5	0.2			0.1	0.2	0.4	0.3	0.8
MEXICO[j]																	
Crude exports	2,562	2,716	1,483	523	731	882	1,052	642	108	18	175	1,063	1,138	580	569	1,171	1,642
Products exports	223	43		353	1,293	904	286				1,025	1,376	1,786	2,397	2,167	1,687	1,255
Value of petroleum exports	32.0	34.8	32.5	26.9	35.6	51.4	53.6	41.8	23.9	22.4	13.3	33.0	39.0	39.0	39.0	48.1	42.3
Share of total exports (%)	6.0	5.5	5.0	4.6	5.4	6.4	6.1	5.7	3.2	3.0	1.7	4.0	4.2	3.9	3.7	4.2	3.4
PANAMA																	
Products Exports													19.1	148.9	125.2	138.7	152.7
Value of Petroleum Exports													13.9	23.6	24.9	23.7	25.9
Share of Total Exports (%)													29.0	40.0	35.0	30.4	29.3
PERÚ																	
Crude exports	466	417	372	408	339	386	484	524	344	336	412	401	439	467	429	310	251
Crude exports to Latin America						89	140	343	151	187	208	190	181	251	171		
Products exports	672	729	640	516	471	445	448	272	49	445	486	358	237	120	78	116	84
Value of petroleum exports	13.0	21.6	17.1	12.0	17.0	23.5	26.5	15.6	15.9	17.8	17.8	14.5	13.2	9.8	6.6	9.3	7.4
Share of total exports (%)	6.9	7.6	7.3	6.5	6.9	8.8	8.6	4.9	5.7	5.7	4.1	2.9	2.5	1.8	1.0	1.4	1.0
LATIN AMERICA[k]																	
Total exports of crude and products	86,268	98,311	106,753	104,510	112,270	124,490	143,690	153,330	147,726	152,535	157,542	162,660	175,854	180,119	188,406	200,600	196,391
Total direct exports of crude	36,073	41,199	44,837	43,965	48,245	55,405	72,801	84,372	77,818	79,942	79,585	81,219	88,480	90,947	95,260	99,393	94,577
Latin America	1,794	2,019	2,904	3,052	3,276	5,653	7,545	11,042	14,235	13,749	10,740	8,140	10,035	10,958	12,598	11,766	
Trinidad and Tobago	1,558	2,269	2,474	2,362	2,501	2,622	2,895	2,734	2,885	3,605	4,989	5,573	5,295	6,954	8,284	9,291	
United States	19,106	19,796	21,992	21,490	22,491	24,128	28,896	34,554	31,225	32,269	34,791	30,667	34,426	35,534	35,543	34,964	
Western Europe	3,800	3,900	4,506	3,944	6,285	8,676	12,510	19,036	15,071	16,873	18,039	23,325	26,693	25,684	24,552	24,624	
Crude exports to N.W.I.	43,557	49,190	48,638	42,523	44,357	45,802	46,922	43,946	38,422	40,162	41,249	42,800	50,955	43,990	45,797	45,998	44,780
Total exports of products	50,195	57,112	61,916	60,545	64,025	69,085	70,889	68,958	69,908	72,593	77,957	81,441	87,374	89,172	93,146	101,207	100,140
Latin America						15,173	16,298	14,787	12,573	12,122	12,893	11,937	10,937	9,859	10,564		
United States						25,799	28,335	31,453	37,558	38,688	40,206	43,259	44,994	43,758	48,918		
Western Europe						16,949	18,953	15,061	13,526	13,356	14,584	15,484	18,887	23,188	19,642		57,326
Value of petroleum exports	1,326.8	1,548.5	1,618.6	1,593.7	1,860.6	2,092.1	2,302.6	2,493.7	2,403.6	2,473.9	2,526.0	2,527.0	2,739	2,801	2,678	2,702	2,647
Share of total exports (%)[m]	19.7	19.5	22.2	20.5	23.2	25.7	26.1	28.1	28.4	29.4	28.8	29.1	29.1	27.9	25.0	25.8	22.0

Sources: Venezuela, Ministerio de Minas e Hidrocarburos, *Memoria, 1964* (Caracas, 1965), pp. I-173, 175, 178. Colombia, Departamento Nacional de Estadística, *Anuario de Comercio Exterior*. Ecuador, Dirección de Estudios Económicos, *Anuario de Comercio Exterior*. México, Dirección General de Estadística, *Anuario Estadístico de Comercio Exterior*. Perú, Superintendencia de Aduanas, *Estadística de Comercio Exterior*. USBM, *International Petroleum Quarterly*. API, *Petroleum Facts and Figures, 1959*. UN, *Yearbook of International Trade Statistics*.

[a] Complete product exports, 1959-66 only. Venezuelan exports complete for 1950-66, Colombian for 1954-66.

[b] Total exports of crude and products is the sum of: (1) total direct exports of crude; and (2) total exports of products. (1) is all crude exports to destinations other than the Netherlands West Indies. (2) is products exports to all destinations. Crude exports from Venezuela and from the Netherlands West Indies. Crude exports from Venezuela to Aruba and Curaçao for refining are shown separately; this crude is in effect included in total product exports.

[c] Includes Puerto Rico.

[d] Exports of crude to the Netherlands West Indies for refining are included in total crude exports; only exports of products from refineries in Colombia are shown.

[e] Exports of peat, lignite and schist reported with exports of refined petroleum products.

[f] Until 1965 all Bolivian crude exports went by pipeline to Argentina.

[g] Brazilian exports of crude are sent to the Netherlands West Indies for refining, and the products returned to Brazil for consumption; until 1964 certain waxy Brazilian crudes could not be treated in the country. Value of exports is not shown, since on balance Brazil imported refinery services.

[h] All Chilean crude exported to Uruguay, 1950-54.

[j] Mexican and Peruvian crude exports are as reported. 1950-58, net exports of products, defined as refinery output less domestic consumption; 1959-66, total product exports as reported.

[k] Total crude and products exports are the sums of crude and products exports, respectively, of all countries listed. Exports by destination are minimal figures: sum of figures for Venezuela and Colombia, plus exports of Ecuador, México and Perú by destination where reported; Bolivian and Chilean exports are entirely to Latin America. No Peruvian exports to Latin America reported, 1950-54.

[m] Total petroleum exports as a percentage of total Latin American exports (all 20 countries), not only of exports of countries listed.

TABLE 8-10. Latin American Consumption of Inanimate Energy by Source, 1937 and Averages for 1949-51 and 1961-63
    (Thousands of metric tons petroleum equivalent)

Country	Coal[a]	Oil and Gas[b]	Hydro-electricity[c]	Total Commercial Energy[d]	Vegetable Fuels[e]	Total Energy[f]
		1937				
Argentina	2,052	4,338[g]	9	6,399	2,668	9,067
Bolivia	1	42	10	53	380	433
Brazil[h]	1,343	1,275	153	2,771	11,019	13,790
Chile	1,265	746	39	2,050	840[j]	2,890
Colombia	257	226[g]	11	494	1,883[j]	2,377
Costa Rica	2.1	37	3	42	90	132
Cuba	260	728		988	1,400	2,388
Dominican Republic	2	42		44	432	476
Ecuador		59	2	61	350	411
El Salvador	0.1	29	2	31	330	361
Guatemala	0.5	69	2	72	310	382
Haiti		17		17	350	367
Honduras		113	1[k]	114	150	264
Mexico	674	2,992[g]	117	3,783	130	3,913
Nicaragua	0.1	34	0.2[k]	34	120	154
Panama		34		34	85	119
Paraguay	2.9	2		5	190	195
Peru	78	405[g]	11	494	1,020	1,514
Uruguay	188	376		564	240	804
Venezuela[m]	18	540[g]	4	562	524	1,087
Latin America	6,144	12,104[g]	364	18,612	22,511	41,123
		1949-51				
Argentina	1,233	8,342[g]	12	9,587	2,808	12,395
Bolivia	6	140	21	167	453	620
Brazil	1,424	4,401	394	6,219	10,681	16,900
Chile	1,440	1,219	95	2,754	840[j]	3,594
Colombia	403	968[g]	57	1,428	1,895[j]	3,323
Costa Rica	0.2	93	5	98	130	228
Cuba	50	1,675	1	1,726	2,102	3,828
Dominican Republic	0.2	107		107	555	662
Ecuador	0.2	243	8	251	503	754
El Salvador	0.1	93	6	99	407	506
Guatemala	0.5	249	4	254	434	688
Haiti		31		31	483	513
Honduras	0.2	140	2	142	216	358
Mexico	581	8,394[g]	153	9,128	317	9,445
Nicaragua	0.1	66	0.3	66	170	236
Panama		174		174	120	294
Paraguay	0.1	16		16	290	306
Peru	101	1,310[g]	38	1,449	1,020	2,469
Uruguay	88	768	30	886	240	1,126
Venezuela	17	4,041[g]	19	4,077	524	4,601
Latin America	5,345	32,470[g]	845	38,660	24,188	62,847
		1961-63				
Argentina	855	18,318	116	19,250	1,067	20,317
Bolivia		385	39	424	(p)	
Brazil	1,863	16,548	2,071	20,490	9,900	30,390
Chile	1,309	4,320	316	5,975	352	6,327
Colombia	2,272	4,062	270	6,599	2,409	9,008
Costa Rica		200	39	239	132	371
Cuba	77	5,013		5,090	154	5,244
Dominican Republic		408	8	416	(p)	
Ecuador		601	23	624	264	888
El Salvador		246	31	293	297	590
Guatemala		508	8	524	572	1,096
Haiti		108		108	880	988
Honduras		262		262	(p)	
Mexico	916	25,457	570	26,950	968	27,918
Nicaragua[q]		239	8	239	(p)	
Panama		654		654	(p)	
Paraguay		139		139	143	282
Peru	123	3,865	231	4,212	253	4,465
Uruguay	38	1,532	85	1,663	110	1,773
Venezuela	92	17,094	62	17,248	484	17,732
Latin America	7,545	99,959	3,877	111,399	17,985	129,384

Sources: 1937 and 1949-51, ECLA, *Energy in Latin America* (Geneva: UN, 1957). 1961-63, commercial fuels, UN Statistical Papers, Series J, no. 8, *World Energy Supplies*, 1960-63 (New York: UN, 1965). 1956-59, vegetable fuels, ECLA, *Latin American Timber Trends and Prospects* (Santiago: UN, 1962).

[a]Includes lignite and coke.
[b]Includes natural gas liquids.
[c]1937 and 1949-51, hydroelectricity reported in fuel equivalent at average efficiency of thermal generating plants; converted to actual energy content of electricity. Conversion factors from fuel input and electricity output of thermal power stations in 1938 and 1949, ECLA, *Estudios Sobre la Electricidad en América Latina* (Mexico City: UN, 1962), vol. I, pp. 188 ff and 198 ff. 1961-63 hydroelectric consumption reported in actual energy content.
[d]Sum of coal, oil, natural gas and hydroelectricity: total energy derived from mineral fuels and hydropower.
[e]Includes sugar cane bagasse and other vegetable wastes used as fuel.
[f]Sum of commercial energy and vegetable fuels: approximate total inanimate energy consumed.
[g]Includes natural gas.
[h]1939.
[j]Estimated: total energy less commercial energy.
[k]1949 conversion factor used; none available for 1938. Conversion factors: petroleum equivalent defined by average energy content of crude oil, 10,700 kcal/kg. Data for 1961-63, commercial fuels, in hard coal equivalent (hce) tons, converted at 1 ton hce equals 0.77 tons petroleum equivalent. Fuelwood consumption, 1956-59, in cubic meters, converted at 1 cubic meter to 0.11 tons petroleum equivalent.
[m]1938.
[n]Fuelwood consumption only, 1956-59 average; estimates of total vegetable fuel consumption in 1960-63 not available.
[p]Estimated fuelwood consumption not available; only total commercial energy reported.
[q]Average of 1961 and 1963 only.

TABLE 8–11. Latin American Imports[a] of Crude Petroleum and Refined Products by Major Importers and by Region, 1950–1966
(Thousands of cubic meters and thousands of metric tons)

Country or Region	1950	1951	1952	1953	1954	1955	1956	1957	1958	1959	1960	1961	1962	1963	1964	1965	1966
Argentina																	
Crude	3,458	3,323	3,846	3,929	4,341	4,762	4,850	6,799	7,740	6,035	3,654	2,053	1,197	945	1,699	4,083	4,259
Crude[b]						4,130	4,470	6,430	7,020	5,110	3,180	1,870	1,040	869	1,478	3,552	3,705
from: Latin America		1,228	1,686		1,990	2,470	2,760	4,320	4,460	4,130	3,090	1,870	980	840	1,048	918	660
Middle East		1,412	1,080		1,468	1,630	1,710	2,110	2,000	780	90		60		429	1,529	1,107
Communist Countries					82				670	200							678
Products	2,576	3,323	3,118	2,174	1,999	2,477	4,025	2,547	2,642	2,997	2,200	2,116	1,975	796	1,648	918	1,128
Brazil																	
Crude	63[c]	98[c]	125[c]	236[c]	375[c]	3,543	5,549	5,780	6,667	6,466	6,382	8,845	11,693	12,171	12,686	12,183	13,527
Crude[b]						4,100	5,300	4,870	5,660	5,760	5,650	7,730	9,960	10,374	10,803	10,247	11,322
from: Latin America						2,420	3,060	2,720	3,630	3,090	3,000	3,730	5,340	4,780	4,796		3,845
Middle East						1,670	2,200	2,150	2,090	2,610	2,610	3,620	4,460	4,350	4,146		4,738
Africa										60	35	380	160	570	239		2,698
Communist Countries															162		
Products	4,891	5,959	7,019	7,633	8,877	5,388	5,388	5,550	4,630	4,457	4,783	4,697	1,772	1,843	1,500	1,298	1,361
Uruguay																	
Crude	879	1,004	1,154	1,319	1,372	1,353	1,209	1,292	1,286	1,320	1,473	1,485	1,683	1,613	1,692	1,799	1,888
Crude[b]						1,100	1,000	1,200	1,270	1,110	1,300	1,210	1,430	1,430	1,466	1,564	1,641
from: Latin America	255	848	786	528	635	1,090	950	1,090	1,090	780	1,180	610	750	520	735[d]		
Middle East	76	45	137	102	122		20	20	70		100	570	680	900	665		
Africa															82		
Communist Countries										325	283	25	180	99	52	270	39
Products	1,191	1,492	1,499	1,441	1,661	1,293	1,236	1,131	1,119	1,135	864	640	642	683	947	784	956
Chile[e]																	
Crude	317	212	143	143	61	248	494	536	397	420	570	546	674	464	497	1,073	2,413
Products	1,926	2,057	2,289	2,368	2,405	408											
Cuba																	
Crude					537	573	628	2,403	4,095	4,039	3,586	1,590	3,498	4,452	4,005	3,513[f]	3,840[f]
Products						2,482	2,666	2,114	719	699	723	2,541	1,148	717	1,267	1,352[f]	1,392[f]
Central America[e,g]																	
Crude	1,733	2,037	1,914	1,969	1,842	2,191	2,336	2,609	1,480	1,771	2,096	2,132	1,113	3,017	3,452	4,851	6,504
Products													2,414	1,885	2,015	2,943	3,571
Latin America[h]																	
Crude	4,717	4,762	5,580	5,955	6,706	10,564	12,818	16,991	20,309	18,352	15,897	14,620	20,448	23,101	24,639	26,429	30,018
Crude from: Latin America[j]	1,794	2,019[k]	2,904	3,052	3,276	5,653[k]	7,545	11,042	14,235	13,749	10,740	8,140	10,035	10,958	12,598	13,847	15,127
Argentina, Brazil, and Uruguay[b]																	
from: Latin America		2,164[d]	2,585[d]		2,963	5,980	6,770	8,090	9,108	8,000	7,270	6,210	7,070	6,140	5,979		
Middle East		1,457	1,217		1,590	3,300	3,930	4,280	4,160	3,390	2,800	4,190	5,200	5,250	5,330	810	583
Africa															306		2,698
Communist Countries									780		50	405	160	570	162	279	
Products	12,634	15,225	16,166	16,408	17,555	15,574	16,481	13,666	11,698	13,040	13,203	14,296	10,388	8,222	10,094	9,777	10,131
Share of Crude in Total Imports (%)	27	24	26	27	28	40	44	55	63	58	55	51	66	74	71	73	75
Share of Crude Imported from Latin America (%)	38	42	52	51	49	54	59	65	70	75	68	56	49	47	51	52	50

Sources: USBM, *International Petroleum Quarterly*. UN Statistical Papers, Series J, *World Energy Supplies*, 1955–63. Argentina, Dirección General de Estadística, *Anuario de Comercio Exterior*, 1950–54, 1964. Brazil, Diretoria de Estatística, *Comercio Exterior do Brasil*, 1950–54, 1964. Uruguay, *Importaciones Cumplidas: Estado Por Rubro y Subrubro*, 1950–54, 1964. Chile, 1955–63, Corporación de Fomento de la Producción, *Geografía Económica de Chile*, 1965, p. 633. USBM, *Minerals Yearbook*, vol. IV, 1967.

[a] Imports, measured in thousands of cubic meters, except where otherwise indicated.
[b] Imports by origin, measured in thousands of metric tons.
[c] All from Venezuela.
[d] Weight of imports estimated from average specific gravity of Venezuelan crude, 0.901.

[e] All imports of crude and products into Chile and Central America, 1950–66, and into Cuba, 1950–59, originated in Latin America or N.W.I. Imports into Cuba, 1960–66, originated entirely in the Communist countries and consisted mostly of crude from the Soviet Union.
[f] U.S.S.R. exports to Cuba: crude in thousands of metric tons; products in thousands of cubic meters.
[g] Costa Rica, El Salvador, Guatemala, Honduras, Nicaragua and Panama.
[h] Totals include imports by all twenty countries, not only those shown.
[j] See also table 8–9, Latin American Exports.
[k] Total reported Latin American exports to Latin America are less than reported imports from Latin America by Argentina, Brazil, and Uruguay.

TABLE 8–12. Latin American Consumption of Major Refined Petroleum Products, Averages for 1936-38, 1950-51, and 1962-64
(Thousands of cubic meters)

Country	Gasoline[a]	Kerosene[b]	Fuel Oils Distillate[c]	Fuel Oils Residual	Lubricating Oils	Total[d]	Share of Crude[e] (%)
			1936-38				
Argentina	1,050	200	2,620		62	4,200	62[f]
Bolivia[g]	17	3	33		4	60	35[f]
Brazil	434	132	669		38	1,290	(h)
Chile	105	12	565		12	700	(h)
Colombia[g]	120	18	270		4	461	(h)
Cuba	99	12	628		7	780	(h)
Dominican Republic[g]	17	6	30		2	54	(h)
Ecuador[g]	24	7	8			61	18
El Salvador[j]	9	3	14		1	27	(h)
Guatemala[g]	17	5	59			84	(h)
Haiti[g]	10	4	5		1	20	(h)
Honduras[j]	60	14	44		4	130	(h)
Mexico	505	146	2,129		40	3,061	46
Nicaragua[g]	15	5	13		2	36	(h)
Peru	85	32	264		5	436	16
Uruguay	81	30	273		6	397	(h)
Venezuela[g]	135	5	1,176		6	1,356	5
Latin America[k]	2,783	634	8,800		194	13,153	35
			1950-51				
Argentina	2,180	803	954	5,260	167	9,335	41[f]
Bolivia	74	12	20	56	2	165	55[f]
Brazil	2,368	332	736	1,992	140	5,565	1[f]
Chile	365	65	139	799	24	1,340	8[f]
Colombia	601	82	141	441	24	1,282	22
Costa Rica[m]	39	6	29	41	2	121	(h)
Cuba	556	86	181	1,500	30	2,330	1[f]
Ecuador	109	20	39	118	4	289	68
El Salvador[n,p]	51	8	15		3	83	(h)
Guatemala[n,p]	90	12	21	152	5	291	(h)
Honduras[n,q]	26	2		145	2	176	(h)
Mexico	2,522	782	785	4,305	97	8,495	71
Panama[n]	72	17	27	92	3	211	(h)
Paraguay[n,r]	21	4	3		1	30	(h)
Peru	467	163	143	691	14	1,484	60
Uruguay	258	140	112	608	10[p]	1,120	(h)
Venezuela	976	321	774	1,498	43	3,657	4
Latin America[s]	10,775	2,855	4,119	17,698	571	35,974	31
			1962-64				
Argentina	3,717	1,521	3,610	7,040	222	18,600	84[f]
Bolivia	172	49	69	98	2	423	86
Brazil	5,945	990	3,615	6,260	271	19,050	29[f]
Chile	1,042	330	621	1,027	38	3,330	61[f]
Colombia	1,859	311	626	866	64	4,300	48
Costa Rica	83	16	112	25	10	256	(h)
Cuba	1,088	196	852	2,562	51	5,050	1[f]
Dominican Republic	164	26	63	239	8	571	(h)
Ecuador	243	146	126	208	9	834	49[f]
El Salvador	95	43	75	72	4	329	(h)
Guatemala	169	66	236	191	10	710	(h)
Haiti	40	2	48	28	3	122	(h)
Honduras	63	17	99	73	3	266	(h)
Mexico	5,200	1,915	2,720	3,980	220	17,900	99
Nicaragua	105	40	67	86	5	308	(h)
Panama	189	111	119	382	6	935	(h)
Paraguay	55	23	16	60	3	161	(h)
Peru	1,077	570	762	1,252	37	3,985	89[f]
Uruguay	390	252	358	743	16	1,820	(h)
Venezuela	2,646	666	1,054	3,150	69	9,450	5
Latin America	24,342	7,290	15,248	28,342	1,056	88,400	37

Sources: 1936-38 – API, *Petroleum Facts and Figures, 1939, 1941.* 1950-51 – *Ibid., 1959,* and USBM, *International Petroleum Trade,* vol. 20, nos. 5, 6; vol. 21, nos. 1, 4, 6, 7, 10, 12; and vol. 22, no. 7. 1962-64 – USBM, *International Petroleum Quarterly,* 1962 to 1964.

[a] Includes motor fuel and aviation gasoline.
[b] Includes jet fuel.
[c] Gas oil and diesel oil; for 1936-38 also includes residual fuel oil.
[d] Includes all refined products, refinery fuel, and loss.
[e] Consumption of refined products as a percentage of crude oil production, or share of crude consumed domestically.
[f] Production of crude oil as a percentage of consumption of refined products, or share of consumption supplied by domestic crude.
[g] 1937-38 average.

[h] No crude oil produced.
[j] 1938 only.
[k] Sum of countries listed. No adjustment for different years; approximate average consumption, 1936-38.
[m] Imports less re-exports; no domestic production.
[n] Imports only; no domestic production.
[p] 1951 only.
[q] Fiscal years 1950-51 and 1951-52.
[r] 1950 only.
[s] Sum of countries listed.

TABLE 8-13. Latin American Petroleum Balance, 1964: Production, Trade, and Consumption of Crude Oil and Major Refined Products
(Thousands of cubic meters)

Country or Region	Crude	Total Products	Gasoline	Kerosene	Distillate Fuel Oils	Residual Fuel Oils	Lubricants
Argentina							
Imports	1,699	1,648	39	20	1,246	58	95
Production	15,959	17,291	3,676	1,458	2,844	6,399	149
Exports	18	512	26			482	
Consumption		20,217	3,890	1,478	4,106	7,438	242
Bolivia							
Imports		25	17				3
Production	508	470	179	74	71	126	
Exports	49						
Consumption		457	181	71	71	107	3
Brazil							
Imports	12,686	1,500	405	317			303
Production	5,296	18,071	5,809	728	3,802	6,247	1
Exports		185			145	39	
Consumption		19,386	6,215	1,044	3,657	6,208	304
Chile							
Imports	497	947	21	56	334	478	43
Production	2,176	2,758	1,031	304	487	647	
Consumption		3,705	1,051	359	821	1,126	43
Colombia							
Imports		109	54				18
Production	9,953	5,128	1,884	316	658	1,390	59
Exports	4,883	720				719	2
Consumption		4,516	1,939	316	658	671	75
Costa Rica							
Imports/Consumption		280	86	16	130	24	12
Cuba							
Imports	4,005	1,267	185		228	796	56
Production	42	4,047	938	191	731	1,892	
Consumption		5,313	1,123	191	959	2,688	56
Dominican Republic							
Imports/Consumption		647	212	27	76	288	8
Ecuador							
Imports	429	41	14	11			9
Production	445	774	324	76	137	206	
Exports	84						
Consumption		815	338	87	137	206	9
El Salvador							
Imports	529	75	25	27	10		4
Production		576	163	38	135	178	
Exports		242	89	22	59	73	
Consumption		416	100	44	87	105	4
Guatemala							
Imports	230	760	124	56	327	203	11
Production		186	71	12	40	35	
Consumption		946	195	68	366	239	11
Haiti							
Imports/Consumption		132	38	2	58	31	3
Honduras							
Imports/Consumption		253	65	19	101	60	4
Mexico							
Imports	92	1,515	54	53	100	395	23
Production	18,377	20,189	5,884	2,093	3,294	5,871	201
Exports	569	2,167				1,063	
Consumption		19,319	5,571	2,006	3,105	3,795	235
Nicaragua							
Imports	319	48	17	15	10		6
Production		289	96	26	64	93	
Consumption		337	113	41	74	93	6
Panama							
Imports	2,374	73	6	1	23	36	5
Production		2,389	325	152	719	1,068	
Exports		1,670	223	40	660	747	
Consumption		792	109	114	83	356	5
Paraguay							
Imports/Consumption		167	56	22	15	69	3

TABLE 8–13 – Continued

Country or Region	Crude	Total Products	Gasoline	Kerosene	Distillate Fuel Oils	Residual Fuel Oils	Lubricants
Peru							
Imports	87	808	82			547	31
Production	3,676	3,575	950	614	946	801	13
Exports	429	78			70	6	2
Consumption		4,493	1,228	613	880	1,397	41
Uruguay							
Imports	1,694	52	10		4	22	15
Production		1,774	377	257	370	694	
Consumption		1,825	387	257	374	716	15
Venezuela							
Imports		42					11
Production	197,602	63,548	7,584	4,156	12,356	37,199	734
Exports	136,750	50,152	2,876	2,500	8,134	35,621	663
Direct exports	92,900	45,772	1,870	2,373	8,053	32,886	663
Exports to N.W.I.*	43,850	4,380	1,006	127	81	2,735	
Consumption		9,026	2,817	676	1,139	3,354	85
Latin America							
Imports	24,641	10,347	1,510	642	2,571	3,007	652
Production	253,875	189,076	35,842	15,202	35,958	99,213	1,684
Exports	99,469	93,879	8,327	7,067	15,213	59,533	725
Regional Trade	12,598						
Consumption		102,901	27,150	6,028	17,299	33,916	1,566
Net Exports	74,828	83,532	6,817	6,425	12,642	56,526	73

Sources: USBM, *International Petroleum Quarterly, 1964*. Also tables 8–9, 8–11. Figures do not exactly match those in tables 8–9 and 8–11, where some estimates are used.

*N.W.I. Balance: Imports equal exports from Venezuela to N.W.I.

Production		48,013	6,551	3,081	6,549	25,726	460
Exports	537	42,533	6,119	4,632	6,226	23,518	58
Consumption		9,860	1,438	-1,423	403	4,944	402

TABLE 8–14. Production and Use of Natural Gas in Latin America, 1955-1967
   (Millions of cubic meters)[a]

Country		1955	1956	1957	1958	1959
Argentina:	Produced	1,065	1,149	1,416	1,655	2,153
	Marketed	696	739	823	925	913
Brazil:	Produced[b]	63	75	141	268	381
Chile:	Produced	467	587	797	1,336	1,815
	Repressed	325	337	491	850	1,079
Colombia:	Produced	540[c]	624[c]	636[c]	2,320	2,371
	Marketed				348	382
Mexico:	Produced	3,020	3,122	4,090	5,340	8,300
	Marketed	1,415	1,470	1,685	1,765	2,525
Peru:	Produced	790	801	1,008	910	915
Venezuela:	Produced	24,308	27,644	32,128	31,517	31,836
	Marketed[d]	3,064	3,364	4,038	4,481	4,748
	Repressed	3,891	4,859	7,384	9,320	9,741
	Flared	17,353	19,421	20,706	17,716	17,347
Consumption of liquefied petroleum gas:						
	Chile (tons)[e]	3	2	9	13	19
	Colombia (tons)	12	17	20	21	24
	Peru (tons)[f]	6	7	8	7	8

TABLE 8–14 – Continued

Country		1960	1961	1962	1963	1964
Argentina:	Produced	3,550	4,909	6,173	5,950	6,200
	Marketed	1,476	2,536	3,199	3,155	4,010
Brazil:	Produced[b]	535	527	511	505	531
Chile:	Produced	2,194	2,549	3,560	5,155	6,301
	Marketed[g]	280	300	360	410	
	Repressured	1,306	1,291	1,798	3,234	
Colombia:	Produced	2,338	2,231	2,219	2,350	2,450
	Marketed	431	448	594	702	
	Flared	1,686	1,597	1,435	1,410	
Mexico:	Produced	9,665	10,210	10,516	11,371	13,890
Peru:	Produced			1,359	1,500	1,600
Venezuela:	Produced	31,561	33,125	36,301	37,465	39,270
	Marketed[d]	5,092	5,364	5,742	6,168	6,723
	Repressured	11,063	13,056	13,705	16,268	16,940
	Flared	15,406	14,705	16,854	15,029	15,607
Consumption of liquefied petroleum gas:						
	Chile (cubic meters)[e]	33	40	57	69	75
	Peru (tons)[f]	8	9	9	10	12

Country		1965	1966	1967
Argentina:	Produced	5,901	5,642	6,120
	Marketed			
Brazil:	Produced	646	746	828
Chile:	Produced	5,881	6,292	6,661
	Marketed			
	Repressured			
Colombia:	Produced	2,514	2,628	2,677
	Marketed			
	Flared			
Mexico:	Produced	13,214	14,178	15,349
Peru:	Produced	1,706	1,573	1,525
Venezuela:	Produced	38,651	39,056	43,301
	Marketed	6,187	6,487	7,106
	Repressured	16,767	17,482	18,774
	Flared	15,189	14,502	16,685
Consumption of liquefied petroleum gas:				
	Chile (cubic meters)[e]	87	128	267
	Peru (tons)[f]	16	17	21

Sources: ECLA, *Estudio Económico de América Latina, 1963*, p. 149. ECLA, *Economic Survey of Latin America, 1964*, vol. I, chap. III, p. 242. ECLA, *Estudios Sobre la Electricidad...*, pp. 193-197. USBM, *Minerals Yearbook*, vol. II, 1955-1964; vol. IV, 1963 and 1967. Venezuela, Ministerio de Minas e Hidrocarburos, *Memoria, 1964*, p. I-182. Chile, Corporación de Fomento de la Producción, *Geografía Económica de Chile* (Santiago, 1965), pp. 647 and 651.

Notes: Produced: Total production of natural gas from oil and gas wells. Marketed: Gas collected and used as fuel or raw material, whether or not natural gas liquids have first been extracted. Repressured: Gas compressed and returned to oil reservoirs to maintain pressure, whether or not natural gas liquids have first been extracted. Flared: Gas burned or otherwise wasted at the well.

[a]Volume of gas measured at $0°C$ and normal atmospheric pressure: data converted from cubic feet at $60°F$ by factor of 0.026795 and from metric tons petroleum equivalent by 1.025 tons per thousand cubic meters. Liquefied gas (propane and butane) measured in thousand metric tons petroleum equivalent or in thousand cubic meters.
[b]Production estimated from consumption; excludes gas flared or vented.
[c]Excludes gas flared; gas marketed plus gas repressured, adjusted for extraction of natural gas liquids.
[d]Includes consumption by oil industry.
[e]Propane and butane: sales in Magallanes province, plus exports, plus consumption by ENAP.
[f]Estimated from data in millions of cubic feet.
[g]Consumption by ENAP in producing areas.

TABLE 8-15. State and Private Participation in the Petroleum Industry in Latin America, 1962-1965

Country and State Enterprise; Date Established	Production[a]		Refining[b]		Marketing[a,c]	
Argentina: Yacimientos Petrolíferos Fiscales 1922[d]	YPF Private (Contractors)	67 33 30[e]	YPF Private	57 43	YPF Private	60 40
Bolivia: Yacimientos Petrolíferos Fiscales Bolivianos 1936	YPFB Private	96 4[f]	YPFB	100	YPFB	100
Brazil: Petroleos Brasileiros 1953[g]	PETROBRAS	100	PETROBRAS Private[h]	86 14	Private[j]	100
Chile: Empresa Nacional de Petróleo 1950[k]	ENAP	100	ENAP	100	Private: local foreign	50 50
Colombia: Empresa Colombiana de Petróleo 1951	ECOPETROL Private	21 79	ECOPETROL Private	48 52	ECOPETROL Private	5[m] 95
Costa Rica	(n)		Private	100	Private	100
Cuba: Empresa Consolidada del Petróleo 1961	ECP	100	ECP	100	ECP	100
Ecuador	Private	100	Private	100	Private	100
El Salvador	(n)		Private	100	Private	100
Guatemala	(n)		Private	100	Private	100
Mexico: Petróleos Mexicanos 1938[p]	PEMEX	100	PEMEX	100	PEMEX	100
Nicaragua	(n)		Private	100	Private	100
Panama	(n)		Private	100	Private	100
Paraguay: Refinería Paraguaya 1965	(n)		State	100[q]	Private	100
Peru: Empresa Petrolera Fiscal 1949	EPF Private	5 95	EPF Private	2.3 97.7	EPF Private	2[r] 98
Uruguay: Administración Nacional de Combustibles, Alcoholes y Portland 1931	(s)		ANCAP	100	ANCAP Private	56 44
Venezuela: Corporación Venezolana del Petróleo 1960	CVP Private	0.2 99.8	CVP Private	0.2 99.8	CVP[t] Private	100

Sources: Petroleum Press Service, "State Interest in Oil: Latin America," February 1963, pp. 61-65. P. R. Odell, "Oil and State in Latin America," International Affairs, October 1964. ECLA, Economic Survey of Latin America, 1964, vol. I, chap. III, pp. 274-77. USBM, Minerals Yearbook, vol. IV, 1963.

[a]Approximate shares in 1962.

[b]Shares of refinery capacity, not production, in 1965.

[c]Sales for domestic consumption only; sales for export are handled entirely by private companies where these are active.

[d]The state has participated in the oil industry since 1910 through the Exploration and Production Department of the Bureau of Mines.

[e]Produced by private companies under development contracts with YPF; private non-contract production was only 3% of the total, all by Argentine-owned companies.

[f]Share rose substantially when exports by Bolivian Gulf Oil began; private production capacity exceeded 4% of the total by 1965.

[g]Previous state participation through the Conselho Nacional do Petróleo.

[h]Brazilian-owned companies; no foreign-owned refinery capacity.

[j]PETROBRAS distributes products ex-refinery, and also supplies the government's requirements. By decree of the Conselho Nacional do Petróleo of 17 December 1963, the company is authorized to compete with private distributors through its marketing organization, DISBRAS, created in 1959. In all other Latin American countries—Dominican Republic, Haiti, and Honduras—there is no production or refining of petroleum. Demand for products is met by imports; marketing is conducted entirely by U.S. companies.

[k]State participation from 1943 to 1949 through the Corporación de Fomento.

[m]Estimated direct sales ex-refinery; ECOPETROL has no marketing organization.

[n]Exploration conducted by private companies; no oil produced.

[p]Established in 1935 as the Compañía de Petróleos de México; granted a monopoly following nationalization in 1938.

[q]Refinery under construction during 1965.

[r]Assuming the output of the topping plant at Iquitos is marketed by EPF.

[s]Exploration reserved to ANCAP; no oil produced.

[t]No marketing by CVP in 1960-64; guaranteed 30% of the domestic market by 1968.

TABLE 8-16. Supply of and Demand for Crude Oil and Refined Products in Argentina, 1936-38, 1950-52, and 1956-1966
(Thousands of cubic meters)

Year	Crude Oil			Refined Products			
	Production	Imports	Exports	Production[a]	Imports	Exports[b]	Consumption[c]
1936-38[d]	2,590	1,000[e]		3,320	900[f]		4,200
1950-52[d]	3,837	3,542		6,678	2,896[f]		9,574
1956	4,931	4,850		8,681	4,025[f]		12,706
1957	5,398	6,799		11,081	2,546[f]		13,627
1958	5,697	7,740		11,994	1,869[f]		13,863
1959	7,109	6,035		12,566	3,000	1	13,755
1960	10,212	3,654		13,627	2,200	2	14,151
1961	13,517	2,053	136	14,764	2,116	114[g]	16,288
1962	15,606	1,197	300	16,749	1,975	681	17,596
1963	15,458	945	114	16,406	796	786	17,997
1964	15,958	1,699	18	17,267	1,648	512	20,217
1965	15,851	2,547		19,240	917	921	
1966	16,896	4,181	278	20,323	701	1,246	23,361

Sources: 1936-38—see tables 8-8 and 8-13. 1950-64—USBM, *International Petroleum Quarterly*. 1965-66—USBM, *Minerals Yearbook, 1967*.

[a]1936-38 and 1950-58, total output of refined products, excluding refinery fuel and loss; total crude input to refineries is, on the average, 9% greater. 1958-66, total refinery input and output, including fuel and loss.

[b]Principally residual fuel oil.

[c]Includes natural gas liquids used directly as fuel, and bunkers. Consumption as reported does not equal production plus net imports of refined products.

[d]Annual average.

[e]Estimated net imports of crude, assuming a loss of 9% in refinery fuel and loss.

[f]Estimated net imports of refined products, approximately equal to consumption less refinery output.

[g]Reported by USBM with 1962 exports; 1961 exports from *Petroleum Press Service*, December 1963, p. 45.

TABLE 8-17. Volume and Value of Venezuelan Petroleum Exports, and Government Taxes and Royalties, 1950-1966

Year	Volume of Exports (thousand m^3)	Value of Exports[a] (Million U.S. $)	Taxes and Royalties[b]		Average Value of Exports[d] ($ per bbl.)
			(million U.S. $)	(% industry profit)[c]	
1950	82,619	1,086	330	51	2.09
1951	93,566	1,229	469	55	2.09
1952	99,492	1,362	500	55	2.18
1953	96,423	1,423	486	54	2.35
1954	104,118	1,552	510	53	2.37
1955	117,433	1,777	596	52	2.41
1956	134,539	2,055	738	52	2.43
1957	149,498	2,545	968	52	2.71
1958	141,432	2,297	992	65	2.59
1959	149,586	2,153	926	68	2.29
1960	156,238	2,149	877	68	2.19
1961	160,420	2,213	938	66	2.19
1962	175,166	2,343	1,071	66	2.13
1963	178,362	2,335	1,106	67	2.08
1964	186,887	2,349	1,141	66	2.00
1965	188,748	2,304	1,069	66	2.00
1966	184,635	2,200	1,112	67	1.98

Sources: Venezuela, Ministerio de Minas e Hidrocarburos, *Memoria, 1964* (Caracas, 1965), pp. I-173, 191, 196. Ministerio de Minas e Hidrocarburos, *Memoria y Cuenta, 1966* (Caracas, 1967), pp. I-A-49, I-A-58, I-A-65.

[a]Compiled from the financial reports of the oil industry to the Venezuelan government; figures differ from those reported by the IMF (see table 11-9) together with total Venezuelan exports. Figures in bolívares converted to dollars at 3.09 Bs. per dollar, 1950-1963, and 4.40, 1964-66.

[b]Total Venezuelan government revenue from the oil industry, including royalties on production, income tax, and all other taxes and duties paid by the industry.

[c]Government revenue as a percentage of total oil industry profit before taxes.

[d]Ratio of value of exports to volume.

TABLE 8-18. Oil Industry Operations in Venezuela, 1950-1966: Concession Area, Operation of Wells, Net New Reserves, Investment

	Concessions in Force		Number of Wells			Reserves		Annual Investment	
Year	Total area on 31 Dec. (thousand ha.)	Percentage of area proved by drilling[a]	Drilled during year[b]	Producible at 31 Dec.[c]		Net additions[d] (million m³)	Lifetime (yrs.)	New investment[e]	Net investment incl. capital repatriation[f]
				Producing	Shut in			(million U.S. $)	
1950	6,412		603					182	−4
1951	6,293		1,173			54	14.6	235	39
1952	6,267		1,327			25	14.0	313	102
1953	6,206	6.45	951	8,961	2,723	148	15.8	292	1
1954	6,027	4.70	836	9,215	2,946	124	15.8	302	24
1955	5,871	5.55	1,163	9,716	3,335	238	15.8	300	37
1956	6,172	5.87	1,449	10,600	3,356	249	15.6	375	445
1957	6,691	6.47	1,721	10,124	5,281	254	15.4	590	640
1958	6,352	7.48	1,184	10,376	5,976	189	17.7	579	210
1959	5,754	8.26	692	10,411	6,539	35	16.8	408	234
1960	4,718	9.87	444	9,933	7,285	64	16.7	236	−195
1961	4,262	11.79	477	10,367	7,098	−83	15.8	186	−204
1962	4,048	12.57	536	10,335	7,415	−12	14.4	153	−206
1963	3,830	13.44	498	10,588	6,962	33	14.4	163	−185
1964	3,516	14.81	621	10,852	7,051	29	13.9	182	−138
1965	3,368	15.73	694	11,641	6,609	8	13.6	187	−51
1966	3,202	16.81	394	11,416	7,075	−60	13.7	178	−169

Sources: Venezuela, Ministerio de Minas e Hidrocarburos, *Memoria, 1964*, pp. I-133, 136, 137, 150, 151, 185. Ministerio de Minas e Hidrocarburos, *Memoria y Cuenta, 1966*, pp. I-A-145 to I-A-200.

[a]Percentage of total concession area drilled sufficiently to prove reserves; includes area proved but not yet brought into production.

[b]New wells drilled for all purposes, including dry holes.

[c]Includes only wells capable of producing oil in commercial quantities; excludes abandoned wells and wells whose production is very small and declining.

[d]Additions to proved reserves from all sources—new discoveries, extensions, and revisions—less production during the year.

[e]Total new investment in physical capital, as reported; excludes payments for new concessions in 1956 and 1957.

[f]Annual change in cumulative net investment; includes capital outflow but not changes in sinking funds for depreciation. See *Memoria, 1964*, p. I-185, and *Memoria y Cuenta, 1966*, p. I-A-197.

Chapter 9

COAL

Coal is perhaps the only mineral of major industrial importance with which Latin America is poorly endowed. The region's reserves, production, and use of coal are extremely small by world standards, and coal plays a relatively minor role in the economy. It furnishes only about 7 percent of Latin America's commercial energy, and one-fifth of that amount is imported; there are no exports. In only two countries, Chile and Colombia, does coal account for as much as 30 percent of energy consumption, and in most of the smaller countries, including all of Central America, it is not used at all. As a consequence, the coal industry is not directly of great political concern anywhere in the region, although its operations are frequently influenced by the policies adopted toward other industries. Because Latin America has no part in the world coal industry beyond the purchase of rather small imports, only the production and use of coal within the region will be described in this survey; reference to other areas will be made only for comparison.

World reserves of coals of all grades are enormous, amounting to more than 4 million million metric tons (see table 9-1). Virtually the entire amount is concentrated in the northern hemisphere: Latin America, Africa, and Oceania together have only some 3 percent of the total. This anomalous distribution may reflect in part the fact that the more developed nations have such large supplies of coal that they have had no incentive to find and develop reserves in the southern hemisphere, as they have for petroleum and most metals. However, coal has been mined for many decades in Latin America, and the size of reserves can be estimated, up to thousands of times the rate of production, early in the exploration of a coalfield. It appears, therefore, that the region's relative poverty in coal is real, and not simply the result of insufficient exploration.

The proven coal reserves of Latin America are some 17,000 million tons, and the total known resources are estimated as nearly 100,000 million tons. While these are small amounts in the world total, they represent a supply for the region, at present rates of mining, sufficient for some thousands of years. The poverty of coal resources is

much more a matter of quality than of quantity. Latin American coals are generally low in heat content. Except for Mexico and Peru, whose coals are comparable to those of the United States in this respect, the coals of other countries, especially Brazil, have a very low energy density.[1] The bulk of the region's reserves occur in narrow, discontinuous seams where mechanized mining is difficult and the cost of extraction is correspondingly high. Perhaps the most serious defect of much Latin American coal is its unsuitability for the production of metallurgical coke, the one use in which coal is most nearly indispensable. Colombia and Mexico possess ample reserves of coking grade coal, and some coke is made from Peruvian coal, but elsewhere the production of coke depends wholly or partly on imported coal, and is the chief reason for imports. The problems of high cost and low quality have also prevented the export of coal, even from countries such as Colombia which have large reserves.

Demand for coal in Latin America has depended largely on two factors: the availability of substitutable sources of energy, especially petroleum; and the production of steel from iron ore, which requires coke for smelting the ore to pig iron. Since little information is available on the use of coal in different sectors or industries, attention will be directed to only these two aspects: the share of coal in the total provision of commercial energy, and the importance of coal as a source of metallurgical coke. For a fuller discussion of these subjects, the reader should consult chapter 5, on iron and steel, and chapter 8, on petroleum and natural gas.

Coal as Fuel

Production of coal in Latin America has increased rather steadily from some 3 million tons annually in the late 1920s to nearly 12 million tons in 1967 (see table 9-2). Throughout this period the region's output has remained approximately one-third of 1 percent of world total coal production. Chile and Mexico have been major producers for several decades; more recently Brazil and Colombia have surpassed them. Together, these four countries account for

Note: Coal tables 9–1 to 9–7 appear on pp. 294–99.

[1] ECLA, *Energy in Latin America* (Geneva: UN, 1957), p. 131.

95 percent of the regional total. These are also the countries with about the same share of the region's reserves.

The production of metallurgical coke has expanded much more rapidly, from half a million to around 2.5 million tons (see table 9-3). This is a consequence both of a greatly increased demand for coke and of the substitution of domestic production for imports. Coke is more difficult to transport than coal, being liable to damage in handling; and the domestic production of coke may reduce dependence on imports by permitting the mixture of imported coking coal with lower-grade local coal. Coke output in Latin America is related more to steel than to coal production.

The increased production of coal has primarily replaced imports into the region, as total consumption has risen very little. In 1937 some 9.6 million tons of coal were used, of which 5.7 million, or 60 percent, were imported; in the early 1960s consumption was 10.5 million tons, of which only 2.2 million, or 21 percent, were imported (see table 9-4). Imports of coke have likewise declined sharply, although consumption has expanded more than fourfold. Before World War II the United Kingdom was the region's chief supplier of coal. In the past two decades the United States has been the principal source, in consequence of great increases in mechanization and efficiency in that country's coal industry, which have made U.S. coal competitive in Europe and have sharply curtailed European coal exports. The United Kingdom continues to provide some coal, as does West Germany, but supplies are now much more concentrated than formerly. Poland also sells a considerable tonnage of coal to Latin America. The price of coal exported from the United States was about $4 per ton from 1925 to 1940. It then rose to $8 by the early 1950s, and to about $9 a decade later (see table 9-5). Latin American imports of coal, valued at these prices, were some $25 million in 1937 and $26 million in 1952-53. By the early 1960s they had declined to $22 million. The rise in coal prices was more than compensated by import substitution, so that over this period the cost to Latin America of importing coal declined; the real cost (allowing for inflation over the period) declined considerably more.

Since total consumption of inanimate energy has increased greatly in Latin America, the share provided by coal has declined markedly. In the late 1930s, when vegetable fuels still accounted for more than half the total, coal supplied one-third the commercial energy and 15 percent of all energy in the region (see chapter 8, table 8-10). By the early 1960s these shares had declined to 7 and 6 percent, respectively. The rapid substitution of coal by petroleum, and more recently by hydroelectricity as well, is what made possible the substitution of domestic for imported coal. Latin America's growing demand for energy could not have been met by coal without overwhelming reliance on imports: consumption in 1961-63 amounted to the equivalent of 145 million metric tons of coal, or fifteen times the level of coal production. It should be noted, however, that the replacement of coal by petroleum was no more rapid in Latin America than in the rest of the world, despite the region's poverty in coal resources and wealth of oil and gas. Between 1930 and 1960 the share of solid fuels in world commercial energy supplies fell from 80 to 50 percent. The

same shift took place in Latin America at much lower relative levels of coal consumption because the region did not develop much industry until petroleum and gas had become cheap and plentiful, and so never depended on coal as the nations of North America and Europe did in the nineteenth and early twentieth centuries. In those areas, coal first replaced wood as the dominant fuel, whereas in Latin America coal never became the principal source of energy, and wood has been replaced chiefly by petroleum derivatives such as kerosene.

In North America, as coal was displaced from other applications by oil it came to be used chiefly for generating electricity; about half of all coal in the United States is now used to make electricity and supplies half of the country's electric power. In Latin America, coal supplies only about 10 percent of the fuel used for thermal electricity generation, slightly more than natural gas but very much less than petroleum products. In some countries the share is very much lower: coal is used for electricity in Brazil only in the immediate vicinity of the coalfields, and in Mexico it provides less than 1 percent of all electricity generated. It appears, however, that at least in Mexico the contribution of coal to electric power could be appreciably increased. There are reserves of 90 million tons or more of low-grade coal in the Mixteca basin in the south-central part of the country, which could be used, and some 22 million tons of anthracite in Sonora which have scarcely been exploited. The development in recent years of very high-voltage transmission lines may make it practical to burn coal in minemouth generating plants where the mines are located far from consumption centers or the coal is of low quality. A large new plant has recently begun to supply power to Monclova and vicinity.[2] In other countries the prospects for expansion are more limited, but any general improvement in coal supplies could result in a considerable increase in coal-based power generation.

The present shares of coal and oil in total energy consumption, in those countries possessing both, appear to depend on the relative sizes and qualities of resources of the two fuels. This is particularly evident in Argentina and Venezuela, which are rich in petroleum but very poor in coal, and in Colombia, which is rich in coal but also has much oil. The same factors are important in Chile and Mexico, but the location of resources also influences their use: coal in Mexico and petroleum in Chile are rather far from the centers of consumption. In Brazil the relation seems to be reversed; the country has much more coal than oil, if shale oil is excluded, but uses far more petroleum. The smaller countries of the region, which usually have no coal or oil resources and little or no metallurgical industry, depend entirely on petroleum.

Even in areas where coal is most abundant, oil has come into considerable use. This is the case in the upper Cauca Valley of Colombia, which has a rapidly growing market for

[2] Inter-American Nuclear Energy Commission–International Atomic Energy Agency, *Possibilities for the Use of Nuclear Power in Latin America* (Pan American Union, 1964), pp. 30, 34-35, 40. See also *Comercio Exterior*, October 1964, pp. 700-701, and BOLSA, *Review*, 12 December 1964, p. 1063.

energy. Coal reserves there are at least 40 million tons, but in twenty years production has climbed slowly from 50,000 to 400,000 tons, accompanied by substantial increases in price.[3] Petroleum has supplied much of the increase in the demand for energy, as it has in southern Brazil, central Chile, and northeastern Mexico — all areas with sizable coal reserves, only one of which, Mexico, also has plentiful oil and gas. In large measure this substitution results from the increase of motor vehicles and other sources of demand which only petroleum can meet. It is also due to the rather backward condition of the coal mining industry in most of Latin America, and its inelasticity of supply. The physical characteristics of the region's coal deposits may make it impossible to achieve the degree of mechanization and productivity of the industry in the United States or Europe, but it appears that even the limited potential of the resource has not been used. The coal industry has not benefitted from either the infusion of foreign capital or the encouragement of domestic investment which have been characteristic of the petroleum industry in nearly every Latin American country; it has been relatively neglected, even in countries whose oil resources are meager and costly.[4] There is no foreign capital in the industry and essentially no production for export. In some countries the industry is protected against imports, but such protection, limited by the need to import coking coal, does not lead to cost-reducing investment.

Coal for Metallurgical Coke

These difficulties are of much less consequence for the provision of energy generally than for the supply of coking coal for the regional steel industry. Now that large reserves of high-grade iron ore have been developed in several countries, coke is the raw material presenting the greatest problems of supply and cost to the industry.[5] A great number of processes are under study for making steel without coke, using fuel oil or natural gas to reduce the iron ore, or for producing acceptable coke from lower-ranking coals which cannot now be used, or for partially reducing the iron ore before charging the blast furnace so as to lessen the amount of coke required. One or more of these techniques may ultimately be widely adopted, but thus far only one — the natural gas process developed by Hojalata y Lámina of Mexico — has been put into commercial operation. The development of the steel industry, in Latin America as in the more advanced countries, has depended on metallurgical coke, and when suitable domestic coal is not available, coking coal must be imported. If production and imports of coke are measured by the amount of coal used in coke production, and are then compared with imports and production of coal, it appears that Latin America uses about 40 percent of the coal at its disposal to make coke (see table 9-6). The ratio is only about 15 percent for the world

as a whole, 13 percent in the United States, and still lower in several European countries. In Colombia, which consumes a great deal of coal as fuel, the ratio is low; it is highest, at 87 percent, in Venezuela, and 35 to 70 percent in Argentina, Brazil, Chile, Mexico, and Peru. The share of coke in total coal consumption appears to have risen from about 6 percent in 1937 to 12 percent in the early 1950s as the production of steel increased.

Only in Colombia and Mexico has it been possible to supply the steel industry entirely with coke from domestic coal, and even in Mexico natural gas reduction is competitive with coal. In Chile and Brazil local coal is mixed with imported coal to make coke, in order to save on imports; in Brazil, and probably also in Chile, this results in more expensive coke and thereby raises the cost of steel. Elsewhere either the coke or the coal from which it is made is all imported. The replacement of imported coke by local production, whether from imported coal or domestic resources, accounted for the entire increase in metallurgical coke output between the late 1930s and the early 1960s in Argentina, Brazil, Chile, and Peru. Only in Mexico, of the five principal coke producing countries over that interval, was import substitution unimportant as an element of increased production. The extent to which imports were successfully replaced was also extremely high in all countries except Mexico (see table 9-7). In Brazil, Chile, and Peru substitution was most extensive before 1952-53, while in Argentina it occurred entirely in the succeeding decade. If similar calculations are made for coal; including coal for fuel together with that used to make coke, it appears that import substitution accounted for all or nearly all the growth in domestic output in Argentina and Brazil; these two countries relied heavily on imported coal in the 1930s. Import substitution was also significant in Peru until the early 1950s, but in Chile and Mexico the process was reversed and imports displaced domestic coal production to some extent. Of these five countries, only Brazil succeeded in replacing as much as half its import requirements with domestic coal; the share in Argentina, over the entire period 1937 to 1962, was 18 percent. Thus import replacement was in general much more extensive for coke, where coal could be imported as needed, than for coal; the difficulties of increasing production of coal suitable for coking prevented a significant degree of substitution except in Brazil.

Where iron ore can be exported, the coal imports required for steelmaking can be paid for and the same ships used to carry the coal as the iron ore; this is possible for Venezuela and Brazil, and to a lesser extent for Peru and Chile, but not for Argentina. In much smaller amounts coal is also important as fuel and as coke to the nonferrous metal industries of Mexico, Peru, and Chile. Peru, with high-quality coal deposits near the metal mines, is best supplied in this regard; in Chile fuel oil is used a great deal, and coal, oil, and gas are all used by the metallurgical industry in Mexico.

The substitutability among fuels and the dependence of coal demand on developments in the petroleum and steel industries make hazardous any prediction as to coal's production and use in Latin America. It is possible that the region's reserves will be greatly enlarged in the future, or

[3] P. R. Odell, "The Demand for Energy in a Developing Region: A Study of the Upper Cauca Valley of Colombia," *Journal of Development Studies*, January 1966.

[4] ECLA, *Energy in Latin America*, p. 75 ff.

[5] ECLA, *La Economía Siderúrgica de América Latina*, doc. E/CN. 12/72 (Santiago, Chile, February 1966).

that adequate resources of good quality coking coal will be found, so that the supply problems described above will disappear. That seems unlikely, although it may well be that more careful exploration and evaluation of presently known resources will lead to better knowledge of deposits and improvements in the quality and cost of coal mined. There appears to be considerable room for investment both in mining and in the preparation of coal by crushing and washing, to relieve some supply difficulties and to make coal more competitive with other fuels. It may also be feasible to develop the coking coal reserves of Colombia and Mexico for export to other Latin American steel producers, so as to reduce imports from outside the region.[6] In the foreseeable future nothing is likely to end the dominance of petroleum in the region's energy economy, and nothing but a very rapid expansion of the steel industry could be expected to increase the share of energy provided by coal. The importance of coke in the total use of coal is likely to continue to increase, barring the introduction of new techniques of steelmaking. That possibility remains the major question in the future of the Latin American coal industry.

[6]A study of the feasibility of such intraregional trade, together with appraisal of coal resources and estimates of the future requirements for coking coal of the Latin American steel industry, is recommended in Inter-American Development Bank, *Multinational Investment Programs and Latin American Integration* (New York: Development and Resources Corporation, 1966), pp. 107-8 and A-1.

CHAPTER 9 TABLES

TABLE 9–1. World Reserves of Coal, circa 1960
(Millions of metric tons)

Country or Region	Reserves Exploitable[a]	Total[b]	Share of World Total (%)
Latin America[c]	17,000	23,000	0.5
Argentina[d]	250	454	
Brazil	1,100	1,700	
Chile[d,e]	1,455	3,100	0.07
Colombia[f]	12,000	12,500	0.27
Ecuador[d]	2	2	
Mexico[g]	1,817	4,200	0.09
Peru[h]	400	400	
Venezuela[d]	30	342	
United States		1,506,000	32.5
Canada		87,000	1.9
Western Europe		504,000	10.9
Africa		70,000	1.5
Asia		82,000	1.8
Oceania		59,000	1.3
Communist Countries		2,311,000	49.9
World Total		4,641,000	100.0

Sources: (1) ECLA, *Energy in Latin America* (UN: Geneva, 1957), pp. 220 ff. (2) World Power Conference, *Survey of Energy Resources* (London, 1962), pp. 20-22. (3) USGS Bulletin 1136, *Coal Reserves of the United States*, 1 January 1960. (4) ECLA, *La Economía Siderúrgica de América Latina*, doc. E/CN. 12/72 (Santiago, Chile, February 1966).

[a]Coal in economically exploitable seams of known thickness and extent (generally not less than 30 cm. thick nor more than 1,200 m. below the surface). Data from source (1), except Venezuela, which is from (2).

[b]Source (3), except for some Latin American countries for which estimates were not given; data then taken from the larger of (1) and (2). Includes seams of not less than 35 cm. for anthracite and bituminous coal or 75 cm. for sub-bituminous coal and lignite, not all of which are economically exploitable. Recovery rate assumed to be 50% of the coal in place.

[c]Information on quality and extent of total resources from (4); see also table 5–5, Iron and Steel.

[d]Predominantly or exclusively sub-bituminous coal.

[e]Excludes 29,000 million tons of lignite.

[f]Total bituminous resources estimated as 40,000 million tons.

[g]Total bituminous resources estimated as 15,000 million tons.

[h]Total anthracite resources estimated as 6,000 million tons.

TABLE 9-2. Latin American Production of Coal, All Grades, 1925-1967
(*Thousands of metric tons*)

Country	Average 1925-29	Average 1930-34	Average 1935-39	Average 1940-44	Average 1945-49	1950	1951	1952	1953	1954	1955	1956
Argentina[a]				8[b]	11	26	39	109	82	199	136	153
Brazil[c]	398	501	820	1,300	1,786	1,955	1,962	1,960	2,028	1,996	2,270	2,239
Chile[a,d]	1,462	1,393	1,931	1,843	1,863	2,240	2,233	2,450	2,336	2,264	2,310	2,279
Colombia[a]			340[e]	463	760	1,010	1,050	1,297	1,224	1,497	1,800	1,900
Mexico[a]	1,172	866	899	903	1,016	910	1,119	1,319	1,430	1,311	1,340	1,409
Peru[f]	166	86	91	156	201	195	186	225	280	195	136	145
Venezuela[a]	24	6	6	9	14	25	28	25	29	32	30	31
Total[g]	3,222	2,852	4,087	4,682	5,651	6,361	6,617	7,385	7,409	7,494	8,022	8,156

Country	1957	1958	1959	1960	1961	1962	1963	1964	1965	1966	1967
Argentina[a]	209	264	260	280	344	286	250	424	540	605	398
Brazil[c]	2,075	2,240	2,127	2,328	2,388	2,510	2,571	3,246	3,383	3,666	4,339
Chile[a,d]	2,096	2,000	1,900	1,470	1,764	1,858	1,719	1,789	1,727	1,652	1,496
Colombia[a]	2,250	2,200	2,500	2,600	2,800	3,000	3,200	3,000	3,100	3,000	3,100
Mexico[a]	1,420	1,470	1,585	1,776	1,818	1,895	2,071	2,138	2,006	2,101	2,388
Peru[f]	141	223	171	162	167	163	131	147	129	155	175
Venezuela[a]	35	36	34	35	31	27	42	36	30	34	34
Total[g]	8,226	8,433	8,577	8,651	9,312	9,739	9,984	10,780	10,915	11,213	11,930

Sources: USBM, *Minerals Yearbook*, and *Mineral Resources of the United States*, 1925-67.

[a] All bituminous coal.
[b] 1943 only.
[c] Bituminous coal and lignite.
[d] Raw coal, as mined, 1950-67; marketable coal only, 1925-49.
[e] 1938-39 only.
[f] Bituminous coal and anthracite.
[g] Sum of countries listed; in no other country has production ever exceeded 500 tons per year.

TABLE 9-3. Latin American Production of Metallurgical (Hard) Coke, 1925-1967
(*Thousands of metric tons*)

Country	Average 1925-29	Average 1930-34	Average 1935-39	Average 1940-44	Average 1945-49	1950	1951	1952	1953	1954	1955	1956
Brazil				15	171	286	286	300	332	340	480	475
Chile							248	232	243	265	236	400
Colombia						2	2	2	2	5	250	250
Mexico	494[a]	261	489[a]		438	392	389	462	389	398	451	574
Peru	24		4		2				5	5	27	24
Total	518		493		611	680	925	1,001	971	1,013	1,444	1,723

Country	1957	1958	1959	1960	1961	1962	1963	1964	1965	1966	1967
Argentina[b]				254	400	500	315	451	461	460	
Brazil[c]	515	525	520	704	699	719	858	912	909	1,240	1,310
Chile[d]	425	400	400	234	203	236	249	246	213	200	
Colombia[e]	174	300	312	420	324	360	400	420	470	323	
Mexico[e]	685	595	681	436	711	774	765	786	824	865	1,084
Peru[e]	31	33	32	30	36	40	38	26	27	35	41
Total	1,830	1,853	1,945	2,078	2,373	2,629	2,625	2,841	2,904	3,123	2,435[f]

Sources: See sources, table 9-2.

[a] May include soft coke.
[b] Coke produced exclusively or predominantly from imported coal.
[c] Coke produced from 60% imported and 40% domestic coal.
[d] Coke produced from 40% imported and 60% domestic coal.
[e] Coke produced exclusively or predominantly from domestic coal.
[f] Excluding Argentina, Chile, and Colombia.

TABLE 9-4. Latin American Imports and Consumption of Coal and Metallurgical Coke, 1937 and Averages for 1952-53 and 1961-63
(Thousands of metric tons hard coal equivalent)

Country	Coal		Coke[b]		Coal Imports	
	Imports	Consumption[a]	Imports	Consumption	Origin	Tonnages[c]
			1937		**1936-37 Average**	
Argentina	3,158	3,176	72	72	United Kingdom	3,600
Bolivia	31	31			United States	278
Brazil	1,701	2,364	66	66	Latin America	17
Chile	-45	1,597	18	18	Other	1,790
Colombia	1	331			(includes Germany, Poland	
Cuba	378	377	57	57	and South Africa)	
Dominican Rep.	3	3				
Guatemala	1	1				
Mexico	13	1,255	2	690		
Peru	15	114	5	5		
Uruguay	418	295				
Venezuela	10	17				
Total	5,684	9,561	219	916		
			1952-53 Average			
Argentina	1,502	1,599	66	66	United Kingdom	516
Bolivia	9	9			United States	2,475
Brazil	849	2,842	26	503	Latin America	69
Chile	181	2,575		358	Other	230
Colombia		1,098			(includes Germany, Poland	
Cuba	66	66	27	27	and South Africa)	
Dominican Rep.	1	1				
Mexico	43	1,420	20	870		
Peru	-36	182				
Uruguay	102	102	5	5		
Venezuela	1	28				
Total	2,728	9,922	143	1,830		
			1961-63 Average[d]			
Argentina	890	1,090		710	United States	1,869
Brazil	910	2,420	10	1,010	Western Europe	211
Chile	150	1,730	0.7	330	West Germany	115
Colombia		2,950		534	United Kingdom	93
Cuba[e]	70	70	23	23	Communist Countries	308
Mexico	60	1,900[f]	14	1,010	Czechoslovakia	13
Peru	20	160	4	61	Poland	228
Uruguay	50	50			Soviet Union	67
Venezuela	90	120	11	11	South Africa	23
Total	2,230	10,490	62	3,705	Total reported[g]	2,443

Sources: UN Statistical Papers, Series J, *World Energy Supplies*, nos. 1, 2, 8. ECLA, *Energy in Latin America*, p. 29. USBM, *Minerals Yearbook, 1962, 1963, 1964*, vol. II, and *1963*, vol. IV.

[a]Gross inland consumption only, excluding bunkers.
[b]Coke converted to hard coal equivalent; U.S. figures of 1.59 tons of coke per ton of coal in 1937, 1.57 in 1952, and 1.43 in 1961 are used.
[c]Tonnages calculated from percentage shares expressed in petroleum equivalent tons, 1936-37 and 1952-53; as reported, 1961-63.
[d]Trade and consumption of coke not reported; imports estimated from U.S. exports; consumption equals production plus imports.
[e]Cuban imports assumed equal to exports of the Soviet Union to Caribbean America.
[f]Reported consumption of 1,190,000 tons is much less than production; adjusted to equal production plus imports, approximately.
[g]Except from United States, includes exports to all Caribbean America, including countries or dependencies not in Latin America.

TABLE 9-5. Coal Prices: Average Value of United States Exports of
           Bituminous Coal and Lignite, 1925-1967
           (Dollars per short ton)

Year	Price	Year	Price	Year	Price	Year	Price
1925	4.39	1936	4.05	1947	5.23	1958	9.71
1926	4.95	1937	4.16	1948	8.55	1959	9.38
1927	4.44	1938	4.07	1949	8.37	1960	9.07
1928	4.11	1939	4.14	1950	8.11	1961	9.14
1929	4.23	1940	4.14	1951	8.76	1962	9.15
1930	4.18	1941	4.65	1952	8.82	1963	9.05
1931	4.00	1942	5.20	1953	8.39	1964	9.20
1932	3.77	1943	5.43	1954	8.12	1965	9.27
1933	3.54	1944	5.70	1955	8.56	1966	9.29
1934	4.16	1945	5.28	1956	9.61	1967	9.59
1935	4.05	1946	6.65	1957	10.00		

Sources: 1954-60 — IMF, *International Financial Statistics.*
1925-63 — U.S. Census Bureau, *Foreign Commerce and Navigation
of the United States;* 1960-64 — *U.S. Exports — Schedule B Commodities by Country.* 1964-67 information obtained from USBM.

TABLE 9-6. Latin American Coal and Coke Balance, 1965
           (Thousands of metric tons)

Country	Coal, All Grades[a]	Metallurgical (Hard) Coke[b]	Coal Equivalent of Coke[c]	Soft Coke[d]	Ratio of Coke to Coal in Use[e]
Argentina					
Production	374	461	659		
Imports	657	82	117		
Supplies	1,031	543	776		0.68
Brazil					
Production	3,383	909	1,436	219	
Imports	1,047	125	198		
Supplies	4,430	1,034	1,634		0.35
Chile					
Production	1,727	213	315	81	
Imports	317	550	814		
Supplies	2,044	763	1,129		0.39
Colombia					
Production	3,100	470	743		
Imports					
Supplies	3,100	470	743		0.24
Mexico					
Production	2,006	824	1,178	31	
Imports	56	56	80		
Supplies	2,062	880	1,258		0.58
Peru					
Production	129	27	39		
Imports	1	8	11		
Supplies	130	35	50		0.35
Venezuela					
Production	30				
Imports	10	194	277		
Supplies	40	194	277		0.87
Latin America[f]					
Production	10,780	2,904	4,370	331	
Imports	2,088	1,015	1,497		
Supplies	12,868	3,919	5,867		0.41

Source: USBM, *Minerals Yearbook, 1967*, vol. IV.

[a]For the grades included in each country's production, see table 9-2. Imports consist almost entirely of bituminous coal.
[b]Oven and beehive coke only, excluding breeze.
[c]Estimated number of tons of coal required to produce the indicated amount of metallurgical coke. For imported coke, and coke made from imported coal, the U.S. ratio of 1.43 tons of coal per ton of coke is used. This figure is used for Argentina, which produces coke entirely from imported coal, and for Mexico and Peru, which use domestic coals of the same average calorific value as U.S. coals. For other countries, the ratio was calculated from the relative calorific value of domestic coal and the shares of domestic and imported coals used to produce coke. The ratio is 1.58 for Brazil and Colombia and 1.48 for Chile.
[d]Gashouse, low and medium temperature coke, for use as fuel only.
[e]Coal equivalent of hard coke supplies divided by the sum of total coal supplies and the coal equivalent of imported coke.
[f]Sum of countries listed; excludes production of lignite in Ecuador and imports of coal or coke into several countries.

TABLE 9–7. Import Substitution in Metallurgical Coke in Selected Latin American Countries between 1937 and 1961-63
   (Thousands of metric tons)

Concept	Year	Argentina	Brazil	Chile	Mexico	Peru	Total Five Countries
Production	1937				434		434
	1952-53		316	237	426	5	984
	1961-63	500	696	229	799	39	2,263
Imports	1937	45	41	12	1	3	102
	1952-53	42	16		12	1	71
	1961-63		7	0.5	10	3	20.5
Total supply	1937	45	41	12	435	3	536
	1952-53	42	332	237	438	6	1,055
	1961-63	500	703	229	809	42	2,283
Increase in production	1937 to 1952-53		316	237	−8	5	550
	1952-53 to 1961-63	500	380	−8	373	34	1,279
	1937 to 1961-63	500	696	229	365	39	1,829
Import coefficient	1937	100	100	100	0.24	100	19
Anticipated imports	1952-53	42	332	237	1.05	6	618
	1961-63	500	703	229	3.36	42	1,477
Difference between anticipated and actual imports	1952-53		316	237	−11	5	547
	1961-63	500	696	229	−4.64	39	1,457
Share of increased production due to import substitution (%) 1937 Base	1937 to 1952-53	100	100	100	(a)	100	99.5
	1952-53 to 1961-63	100	100	100	1.7	100	71
	1937 to 1961-63	100	100	100	−1.3	100	80
1952-53 Base	1952-53 to 1961-63	100	7.1	(b)	3.1	12	10
Share of anticipated imports replaced by increased production (%) 1937 Base	1937 to 1952-53		95	100	(a)	83	89
	1952-53 to 1961-63	100	55	−3.5	(a)	81	62
	1937 to 1961-63	100	99	100	(a)	93	99
1952-53 Base	1952-53 to 1961-63	100	79	(b)	(a)	9.5	9.2

Sources: Tables 9–3 and 9–4. For definitions and notes see chap. 1, table A–4.

[a]Ratio exceeds 100%.
[b]Ratio cannot be calculated because imports were zero in 1952-53.

Chapter 10

COFFEE

Coffee is one of the most important products of Latin America's resource sector. In total value of output it ranks behind petroleum, cereals, and livestock, but it takes a very large share of the region's resources of land and labor. In 1960 some 7 million hectares were planted to coffee in Latin America — an amount exceeded only by the areas in wheat and maize — and the cultivation, harvesting, and marketing of the crop provided seasonal or full-time employment to some 12 million people. Since about two-thirds of production is exported, coffee furnishes from 15 to 25 percent of the foreign exchange earned by the region, being exceeded in this respect only by petroleum. Of the seventeen countries which produce coffee, at least four always depend on it for half or more of the total value of their exports. No other commodity is so widely distributed in both production and exports, except for sugar and cotton.

Coffee is likewise of considerable importance to the world economy, because so large a share of output is exported. During most of the last two decades, coffee was the second most valuable commodity in international trade. For a few years of high prices it was the most valuable product; normally crude petroleum outranks it. In the consuming countries of North America and Europe coffee is a significant share of total imports; in the United States it regularly accounts for 5 percent or more of imports and is usually the leading commodity. Finally, coffee is a major focus of economic and political relations between the advanced countries and the poorer nations, because of its great weight in the trade and income of the latter and because importers and exporters are united in an international agreement to control supplies and prices of coffee.

In this chapter, attention will be be devoted chiefly to two matters: the world situation of coffee supply and demand, and the history and structure of the coffee-growing industry in Latin America. In both instances, particular emphasis will be given to Brazil, which is the world's largest producer and the country with the greatest influence on the world coffee balance. Subjects such as consumption and marketing will be discussed more briefly. With a few excep-

tions related to the resource base and domestic consumption in producing countries, statistical information on coffee is readily available and reliable. Unless otherwise indicated, all data presented in this study refer to green (unroasted) coffee, the form in which nearly all coffee is traded.[1]

The World Coffee Industry

Resources

Coffee can be grown throughout the world's tropical highland areas. It requires fairly heavy rainfall, and cannot

---

[1]The FAO *Production Yearbook* reports estimated total coffee production, and gives some information on areas planted and on prices in producing and importing markets. Estimates of exportable production, or total production less domestic consumption, are prepared by the Foreign Agricultural Service of the U.S. Department of Agriculture, and published quarterly in *Foreign Crops and Markets*. A major source of statistical information about coffee is the *Annual Coffee Statistics* of the Pan American Coffee Bureau, which also provides a brief account of developments in the industry each year. Other major sources are the *Coffee Annual* and the *Complete Coffee Coverage*, published by G. G. Paton, and *World Coffee and Tea*. In 1965 the latter journal published a "Guide to Latin American Coffees" (April); "Guide to African/Asian Coffees" (June); and "Guide to Coffee in Europe" (October). The most thorough study of the world coffee industry is that of the Coffee Study Group, *The World Coffee Problem: Present Status of the Industry and Future Prospects* (Washington, 1960-62, in ten parts). Shorter studies are provided by FAO, *The World Coffee Economy*, Commodity Bulletin no. 33 (1961); and J. W. F. Rowe, *The World's Coffee* (London, H. M. Stationery Office, 1963). A more recent survey is given in ICO, *Production Forecasts 1965-70 and their Implications* (London, 1965, in two volumes). Each coffee growing country publishes a bulletin, yearbook or other source of information, and there are in addition a great number of books describing all aspects of the production, marketing, and use of coffee, and of its position in the economies, politics, and customs of the producing countries. Coffee is unquestionably one of the most studied of commodities, and a summary description of the world industry can draw on only a few of the available sources.

Coffee statistics are commonly reported in bags of 60 kilograms, the standard size for shipment, and data provided in other terms are converted to the equivalent in bags of this size. In this chapter, quantities are reported in metric tons, for easier comparison with other commodities. Prices are reported in U.S. cents per pound, the unit used in New York, the principal market for green coffee.

Note: Coffee tables 10-1 and 10-2 appear on pp. 303 and 309; tables 10-3 to 10-13 appear on pp. 320–30.

withstand very high temperatures. The lowland rain forests are not suitable for coffee cultivation, but most of the land above a few hundred meters in altitude, in areas with adequate rainfall and without frequent frosts, is suited to one or another species of coffee. The trees can be grown on rather steep land, especially along river valleys, where other crops would expose the soil to erosion. In Latin America there are two principal zones of coffee cultivation. The larger is in southern and eastern Brazil, including the coastal escarpment from Ceará to Santa Catarina, the highlands east of the São Francisco River, and the great plateau drained by the Paraná River. The other zone follows the slopes of the Andes from southern Mexico to northwestern Bolivia, including the mountains of northern Venezuela. Coffee is also grown on the highlands of many Caribbean islands, in eastern Paraguay, and in parts of the Amazon basin. In Africa, coffee is cultivated in the highlands of the west coast countries from Guinea to Angola, in Ethiopia, in the plateau surrounding Lake Victoria, and in Mozambique and the Malagasy Republic. Coffee is also grown in Yemen, in southern India and Ceylon, in Vietnam, Thailand and Malaya, in western Indonesia, in the Philippines and in Hawaii. As table 10-3 shows, some 10.6 million hectares were planted to coffee in the early 1960s: 7.3 million in Latin America, 2.8 million in Africa, and the remainder chiefly in India and Indonesia. The area has since been reduced by about a million hectares in Brazil.

There are several distinct species of coffee trees, with different qualities and requirements for cultivation. The kind most widely grown is *arabica*, which is indigenous to Ethiopia and was first known to Europeans through plantings in Yemen. Virtually all coffee grown in the Western Hemisphere is arabica, as is much of that grown in eastern Africa and in India. It is usually grown on fairly high land, and requires the greatest care in cultivation. Next in importance are *robusta* coffees, the most prevalent types of the species *canephora*. They are hardier and better suited to humid, lowland conditions, and are grown throughout western Africa, where they are native, and Indonesia, with smaller amounts in eastern Africa and India. Only very small amounts of *liberica* are now planted, in Surinam and Liberia, and still smaller quantities of other species or types such as *conuga*. Of about 10 million hectares in coffee, robustas account for some 2.4 million and arabicas of different grades for virtually all the remainder.

Production, Consumption, and Trade

World consumption of coffee has been increasing at about 2.6 percent yearly since the late eighteenth century, when the beverage came into general use in Europe. Demand grew most rapidly, at some 3.6 percent annually, in the last decades of the nineteenth century. Since 1900, consumption has shown an average rate of growth of slightly over 2 percent, with wide variations, and a pronounced decline during the Depression and the Second World War.[2] During most of this century and a half, production has

approximately kept pace with consumption. Although both arabica and robusta coffees originated in Africa, that continent was not until recently a major producer. Coffee production was established instead in the islands of the Caribbean, and spread from there to Central and South America. By the beginning of this century, Latin America dominated the world coffee industry, with Brazil alone producing three-fourths of the total. Coffee was also established in India, Ceylon, Indonesia, the Indochinese peninsula, and the Philippines in the nineteenth century, but in the 1880s the industry in several of these producers — notably Ceylon and the Philippines — was destroyed by disease, so that by 1900 Asia and Oceania provided less than 5 percent of world output.

Since the 1920s the pattern of world production has altered considerably (see table 10-4). From a level of 2.2 million tons per year in the 1930s, production fell to 1.9 million tons in the next decade, primarily as the result of smaller harvests in Brazil. The prewar level was regained in the early 1950s and then production shot up to over four million tons in the 1960s. During this span of thirty-five years, Latin American output rose by 50 percent, with much greater increases in other countries than in Brazil. The most striking change occurred in Africa, where production rose nearly 12-fold, from 3 to 27 percent of the world total. Production in Asia and Oceania has also risen markedly, after a severe reduction resulting from wartime damage in Indonesia.

Only a small share of the world's coffee is consumed in the producing countries (see table 10-5). Total consumption in the coffee-growing nations of Africa, Asia and Oceania is only some 180,000 tons, or less than 5 percent of the total; Latin America is the only producing area with a significant amount of domestic consumption. Per capita use averages some 3.5 kilograms per year (or 3.2 if the importing countries of Argentina, Chile, and Uruguay are included), the same level as prevails in Western Europe and far above the per capita consumption of all other producers. Consumption in the importing countries of Africa, Asia, and Oceania equals or exceeds that in the producing countries of those regions, but is still only a small fraction of the total. Levels of per capita use exceeding one kilogram are found only in Algeria and in Australia and New Zealand.

The bulk of the world's coffee is consumed in North America, Latin America, and Western Europe, with the major importers in North America and Europe taking 80 percent of the total before World War II and slightly less at present. The highest per capita consumption is found in Scandinavia, from 9 kilograms in Norway and Finland to more than 11 in Sweden. The United States consumes about 8 kilograms per capita annually, and levels of 4 to 6 kilograms occur in Canada, Belgium-Luxembourg, France, Germany, the Netherlands and Switzerland. In the United Kingdom and in southern Europe consumption is much lower, from less than a kilogram to just over 2. Restrictions on imports and high prices hold down consumption in those Communist countries, particularly East Germany, where consumer tastes favor coffee. In the Soviet Union and other countries of eastern Europe tea is the preferred

---

[2] Growth of consumption estimated from data in R. Coste et al., *Les Caféiers et les Cafés dans le Monde* (Paris: Larose, 1955-61), vol. I, pp. 1-2.

beverage. A preference for tea has also restrained consumption in Japan and the United Kingdom, but coffee is increasingly penetrating both markets.

Coffee is regarded by most consumers as a luxury at low incomes and a staple at high incomes, both income and price elasticity declining as incomes rise. Price elasticity may be as great as -0.6 in the countries of southern Europe; in wealthier nations it is usually between -0.2 and -0.3. No estimates are available for producing countries. Income elasticity has been estimated as high as 1.5 in some coffee-growing countries of Africa and Asia, but elsewhere the highest level is about 1.0. This elasticity applies to a number of rather low-income importing countries, particularly among the Communist countries and southern Europe, and also to higher-income countries where coffee is not a traditional beverage and consumption is low, such as the United Kingdom, Japan, Australia, and New Zealand. In the European Common Market the level falls to between 0.3 and 0.7, and in Scandinavia it is only 0.2. The same or lower elasticity is found in North America. Within Latin America there is considerable variation, from about 0.2 in Brazil and Ecuador to 0.8 in Mexico and several Central American countries, and also in Argentina and Uruguay. Differences in per capita use at similar levels of income make it impossible to define a single saturation level of coffee consumption, though it may be suggested that somewhat more than 12 kilograms would probably represent saturation of the Scandinavian market, and that other European and North American markets might, with their present tastes, be saturated at several kilograms less per capita.[3] Variations in preference for different types of coffee also influence the price to consumers and help determine total consumption. The unit value of imports is high in West Germany, Norway, and Sweden, which consume a high proportion of the more expensive arabicas, and low in countries such as the United Kingdom, Belgium, and France, which import a larger share of robustas.

The relative price inelasticity of demand for coffee has led a number of governments to tax coffee, by either an import duty or internal taxes, or both, for revenue purposes. Such taxes are negligible or nonexistent in the United States, Belgium, the Netherlands, Norway, and the United Kingdom, but in Austria, Finland, France, Italy, Germany, Spain, Turkey, and Yugoslavia they are quite high; in France, Germany, Italy, and Finland such taxes in 1958 averaged more than 100 percent of the unit import value of coffee. At the price elasticities prevailing in that year, abolition of all taxes on coffee should have raised imports to Western Europe by about 10 percent.[4] In the absence of

discrimination among sources, the end of coffee taxation would have benefitted Latin America more than other producing areas. West Germany, where the largest increase would have occurred, imports Latin American coffees almost exclusively, and in other countries a lower retail price would probably have shifted demand somewhat away from robustas and toward arabicas. For this reason the Latin American producers have on several occasions tried to have such taxes reduced; they have concentrated particularly on Italy, which unlike France has no ties to coffee-growing former possessions, and which buys only a little more than half its coffee from Latin America. The maximum tariff of the European Common Market is now 9.6 percent, and this level prevails in France. Tariffs range from 2 to 5 percent in Germany and the Benelux countries and are comparably low in Spain, the United Kingdom, and Sweden. High tariffs are found only in Denmark, Switzerland, and Finland, but these have less effect on consumption than the taxes imposed in Germany and Italy.

Consumption of coffee has also been influenced by the development of soluble, or "instant" coffee. Generally more cups of a given strength can be obtained from a quantity of green coffee processed to soluble form than if it is roasted and ground in the usual manner; in this respect, the introduction of soluble coffee has held down consumption. In some cases, however, particularly in countries where coffee is not a traditional beverage, consumption may be increased by the availability of soluble coffee. Production of soluble coffee began on a significant scale after World War II and increased rapidly during the early 1950s, first gaining popularity in the United States. The share of roasted coffee used for soluble manufacture in that country rose from 11.7 percent in 1954, the first year that adequate data were obtained, to 18.3 percent in 1960. The share that soluble coffee represented of total consumption was 13.9 percent in 1954 and 21.5 percent six years later. In the last few years the importance of soluble coffee in the United States has stabilized or declined slightly, and the market, as a share of total consumption, appears to be saturated.[5]

Soluble coffee has penetrated the European market to an equal degree only in Switzerland; the share of soluble in total consumption is between 10 and 15 percent in France, Germany, the Netherlands, and Greece, and much lower — 5 percent or less — in other countries. In the United Kingdom, however, more than three-fourths of all coffee is consumed in soluble form, and the availability of soluble coffee appears to have aided the increase in consumption there.[6] Initially all soluble coffee was produced from green coffee in the importing countries, and all trade in the soluble product took place among those countries. In the last several years, however, soluble coffee plants have been established in Brazil, Guatemala, Mexico, Nicaragua, and El Salvador,

[3] A variety of studies on price and income elasticity, mostly for the period 1957-59, are summarized in FAO, *World Coffee Economy*, pp. 31-33, and in FAO, *Agricultural Commodities – Projections for 1970* (1964), pp. II-45 and appendix. More recent estimates are given in FAO, Committee on Commodity Problems, *Agricultural Commodities – Projections for 1975 and 1985* (1967), vol. II, table A, pp. 55-105. For a comparison of per capita consumption, price, and income in the United States, 1934-63, see *Coffee Annual*, 1964, p. 180.

[4] FAO, *Monthly Bulletin of Agricultural Economics and Statistics*, September 1960, summarized in FAO, *World Coffee Economy*, pp. 33-35. The prevailing levels of customs duties on green,

roasted, and soluble coffee and internal taxes on coffee are reported by the PACB, *Annual Coffee Statistics*, for more recent years. See especially 1966, p. 177.

[5] U.S. production, trade, and consumption of soluble coffee from the early 1950s to 1964 are described in PACB, *Annual Coffee Statistics*, 1964, pp. 33-36.

[6] *Ibid.*, p. 36, and *World Coffee and Tea*, October 1965, p. 45; estimates prepared by J. Louis-Delamare et Cie., S.A., Le Havre.

TABLE 10-1. World Trade in Coffee by Major Regions, Averages, 1965-1967
  (Thousands of metric tons)

Production and Exports	Producing Region			World Total
	Latin America	Africa	Asia and Oceania	
Total production	2,833	1,122	254	4,198
Exportable production	2,100	965	156	3,221
Exports: Total	1,860	907	158	2,925
North America	906	386	54	1,346
Western Europe	717	412	87	1,216
Communist countries	100	29	10	139
Latin America	43	1		45
Africa	18	31		56
Asia and Oceania	60	42	3[a]	105

Source: PACB, *Annual Coffee Statistics*, 1966-67.

Note: Figures may not add to totals because of discrepancies between reported imports and exports and exclusion of information for small exporters.

[a]Indian exports only.

and these countries have begun to export to the United States. In 1966, in consequence of a very large increase in Brazilian production and exports, the United States became a net importer of soluble coffee for the first time.[7] Producers in Brazil had access to low-priced coffee whose export was prohibited and so had a considerable cost advantage over United States producers. The penetration of the United States market by Brazilian soluble coffee led to demands by the former country that the export discrimination be eliminated, and the advantage thereby reduced.

With two exceptions world trade in coffee is relatively free. The first of these is the system of export quotas under the International Coffee Agreement which has been in effect since 1963. The second is the preference granted by certain European countries to coffee from their present or former possessions; these preferences, usually expressed through differential tariffs, are similar to those for other tropical products such as cocoa and bananas which favor African producers at the expense of Latin America. Since, however, the bulk of production is exported from producing countries while importing countries rely on imports for their entire supply, there is essentially no protection of domestic producers against imports and no control of exports to assure adequate domestic supplies. The world market for coffee is much simpler and more free than those for commodities produced largely for domestic consumption, such as wheat, sugar, or cotton.

The history and operation of the International Coffee Agreement will be described later (pp. 313-18). Detailed attention will also be given to exports of coffee from Latin America, particularly their place in the two great importing markets of North America and Western Europe (pp. 318-19). Here it will suffice to summarize present world trade in coffee by major exporting and importing regions.

Of an average world production of almost 4.2 million tons in the years 1965-67, some 3.2 million tons were available for export after satisfying requirements in the producing countries (see table 10-1). Of this amount about 2.9 million tons were actually exported, the rest being

held as stocks in the exporting countries. Latin America accounted for 68 percent of the total production, Africa for 27 percent, and Asia and Oceania for the remainder. Among importers, North America took 46 percent of the total and Western Europe 41 percent. Much smaller quantities were imported by the Communist countries and by importing countries in the producing regions. Latin America supplied half or more of the imports to every region except Africa, Asia, and Oceania, with North America the principal customer. Africa found its chief market in Europe, but exported nearly as much coffee to the United States and Canada. This trade pattern has since changed only slightly, with the largest relative increases in exports going to countries which do not belong to the International Coffee Agreement and with an increase in robustas relative to arabica exports.

Qualities and Prices

Differences in cultivation and preparation are as important as differences between species in determining the quality of coffee. There are three principal categories, the robustas forming one and the arabicas the other two. The highest quality coffees are arabicas which are carefully harvested for uniform ripeness and then prepared by a wet process involving pulping and fermentation before the beans are dried and sorted. Coffee so prepared is referred to as mild arabica, or simply as mild. If the beans are removed from the fruit by drying and hulling, the product is called unwashed arabica. Nearly all the arabica coffee prepared in this way comes from Brazil, so the second category may be called simply Brazil; Bolivian and Ethiopian arabicas are produced in the same way. All other arabicas — from the rest of Latin America, eastern Africa, and India — are milds. Robusta coffee is also prepared by the dry method. In the early 1960s Brazil accounted for about 45 percent of the world's coffee area, mild arabicas for 31 percent and robustas for 23 percent; the shares of production were similar, as there are no marked differences in yields among species.

Within this basic classification are a great number of varieties or subspecies and of grades, differing from country

---

[7]See PACB, *Annual Coffee Statistics*, 1966, pp. 130-36.

to country and within each country. The best are generally considered to be coffees from the Cauca Valley of Colombia. Those produced in Central America, particularly certain grades from El Salvador, Guatemala, and Costa Rica and some from Mexico, are next in quality, followed by other mild arabicas from Latin America and from Asia and East Africa. Brazil produces a variety of coffees, some of which can be classified as mild while others have the strong, distinctly Brazilian flavor. Robustas are ranked still lower in quality because of a coarser taste. Chief determinants of flavor are, besides species, the altitude at which coffee is grown and the care with which it is harvested and processed. Generally the taste improves with altitude and with uniformity of ripeness. Other factors such as spacing of trees, quality of soil, presence or absence of shade plants, and use of fertilizers also influence the flavor. Finally, aside from the differences in mildness and acidity which determine quality, there are marked differences in taste, coffees from some producing areas having a pronounced spicy flavor or other distinct character. These differences affect the demand for particular coffees both directly and through their suitability for blending with other grades. In importing countries most coffee is sold to consumers as blends; nearly all the imports from small producers, such as Costa Rica and Honduras, are absorbed in this way.

Mild arabica coffees are bought in preference to other types and command a premium in price. Since the supply of these coffees is limited, and consumers are normally unwilling to pay very high premiums for them, milds are blended with the more plentiful Brazilian coffees. Robustas do not blend well with milds, so although they cost even less they are not used for this purpose. Brazilian coffees can, however, be substituted for robustas, a slight increase in price reflecting the quality difference. Thus Brazil occupies a unique position: not only is it the largest producer and exporter of coffee in the world, but its product can be substituted, to some extent, for either higher or lower quality grades. The prices of all coffees are therefore determined largely by the prices of Brazils, and consequently by the supply of coffee from that country.[8] As prices rise, demand shifts toward lower qualities and the differentials among grades shrink. The minimum premium of mild arabicas over Brazils, with the structure of tastes in the years 1950-1967, appears to be about 5 percent. The minimum discount for robustas, again measured from Brazilian coffee, is about 10 percent. As prices fall, these differences increase. The stability of price increases with the quality of coffee (see table 10-6). In the period 1953-63, at least in the U.S. market, the elasticity of price substitution between Brazils and robustas was -0.98; between Colombian and Brazilian coffee it was -1.59; and between Brazils and other Latin American milds it was -2.76. Thus any reduction in the price of other coffees relative to Brazils had a substantial effect on the consumption of the latter. For the world as a whole in the same decade, the Brazilian share of the market was maximized when the price of Brazils was equal to 70 percent of the Colombian price plus 30 percent of the average robusta price. A higher price for Brazils

shifted demand toward milds and a lower price toward robustas.[9]

This structure of demand and prices is modified by, and reflects, differences in income, differential tariffs which change the relative prices of coffees, and differences in national tastes. An increase in income appears to have somewhat the same effect as a decline in price, of shifting demand toward mild arabicas. These coffees are consumed in the wealthier European countries such as West Germany and those of Scandinavia, as well as in the United States. Robustas, on the other hand, have privileged access to the European Common Market and to Portugal. Coffee from the former French possessions now associated with the EEC – almost entirely robusta – pays a lower tariff than coffee from other exporters. Portugal favors coffee from Angola. Finally, robusta coffees offer some advantages for the manufacture of soluble coffee, since they are neutral in flavor and have a high caffein content. The growth of soluble coffee consumption has therefore probably helped enlarge the share of the market held by robustas, at the expense of Latin American coffees. In the U.S. market, robusta imports have grown more rapidly than soluble coffee production, so that part of the change represents a shift in consumer tastes. All these factors influence the price which consumers in a particular country must pay, and are willing to pay, for a given grade of coffee, and thus affect the demand for that grade. The demand for particular types of coffee is now recognized in the control mechanism of the International Coffee Agreement, which divides the world market into four classes: Colombian arabicas, other mild arabicas, Brazilian coffees, and robustas.

Coffee in Latin America

History and Development

Coffee has been grown in Latin America for more than three centuries, and in that time has become of extraordinary importance to the economies of several countries and of the entire region. The size and complexity of the industry preclude much detail in a brief description; in this account it will be possible only to survey the major features of the regional coffee economy and sketch its evolution. The coffee industries of Brazil and Colombia, the two largest producers, will be described in somewhat more detail.

Coffee was introduced to the western hemisphere in the seventeenth century; it is believed to have been cultivated first in Surinam and to have spread from there to the islands of the Caribbean. Until about 1800 the bulk of production was accounted for by plantations operated by Europeans and employing largely slave labor. The coffee industry, like the cane sugar industry, was firmly controlled by the principal European powers with possessions in the

[8]On this subject see Rowe, *World's Coffee*, pp. 23-26.

[9]The calculations for the United States are from G. Lovary and L. Boissonneault, "The International Coffee Market," *IMF Staff Papers*, November 1964, cited in A. Kravis, "International Commodity Agreements to Promote Aid and Efficiency: The Case of Coffee," *Canadian Journal of Economics*, May 1968. The relation between prices and Brazilian market share was calculated by ANPES (São Paulo, Brazil), and reported in a personal communication.

Caribbean, and particularly by France.[10] At the time of the French Revolution, Haiti was the leading producer not only in Latin America but in the world.

Coffee culture spread to Brazil, Colombia and other mainland areas early in the eighteenth century. The industry remained small until the first decades of the nineteenth century, when demand began to grow rapidly and the dominance of the Caribbean producers ended. Coffee became the chief export of Brazil in the 1830s and of other countries some decades later. This geographic shift of production was accompanied by a decline in the importance of plantations, and coffee became predominantly a smaller farmers' crop.

Coffee can be grown in combination with food crops, and does not require either skilled labor or much capital. Harvesting and processing are relatively simple, so there are no technical or economic barriers to cultivation by peasant farmers, who find it an ideal cash crop. Furthermore, coffee can be planted on land only partly cleared; it does not spoil readily; and its high unit value permits it to be transported over considerable distances. It is therefore an excellent crop for pioneers, and in the century or more since coffee became a significant export it has been a major factor in opening new lands to settlement in Latin America. Large expansions of this sort took place in the 1830s and 1840s, in the 1920s, and in the period 1950-62, with smaller expansions in 1790-1800 and early in this century. Major centers of population and economic activity have been created in the Cauca Valley of Colombia and in south central Brazil by the opening of new lands to coffee; indeed coffee has determined the center of gravity of Brazil and much of the country's political and economic structure since the middle of the nineteenth century. On a smaller scale, coffee has induced migration and furthered settlement in eastern Paraguay and the eastern highlands of Peru, in the coastal lowlands of Ecuador, and in parts of Central America.

The extension of the coffee frontier is an example of the dominant type of economic development in Latin America until early in this century, a form of development which is still important although it has been superseded by industrial growth based on import substitution. This type of growth proceeds by incorporating previously unused resources for the production of an export commodity. Incorporation of new resources is most evident for land, but coffee growing has also absorbed large amounts of labor. No other cash crop has been as remunerative in the areas to which coffee is well suited, with little shifting there between coffee and other export products, although such shifts have occurred from one area to another within a country. So long as the bulk of food production was by subsistence farmers rather than for the market, coffee also did not compete with food-

stuffs. As the demand for coffee rose, cultivation was simply carried to new land, with the area devoted to food crops determined by the size of the population and the prevailing level of agricultural efficiency. Now that Latin America has large urban populations and a consequent domestic market for foodstuffs, coffee competes with other crops in areas where it was once dominant, such as the state of São Paulo in Brazil. Land is shifted from coffee to foodstuffs in response to changes in relative prices. However, competition of this sort is most notable in areas where coffee yields have fallen because decades of monoculture exhausted the soil; elsewhere the coffee frontier continued to expand until about a decade ago. The fact that Latin America has a considerable surplus capacity in coffee together with a deficit in the production of grains and some other food crops, indicates that substitutability between coffee and other crops remains low.

These factors and developments may be illustrated by reference to Brazil. Coffee was introduced into northern Brazil about 1727, from French Guiana. For the next several decades it was grown on a small scale, for domestic consumption, in the states from Ceará to Bahía. Cultivation for export began in the 1790s, when production declined in Haiti, until then the leading exporter. Coffee was established in the hills north and west of the port of Rio de Janeiro, in the states of Rio and southeastern Minas Gerais, where a decline in gold mining had left idle a large labor force and enough mules to transport the crop to the coast. This area quickly became the center of the coffee industry and remained so for half a century.

Brazil had enjoyed a high rate of economic growth throughout most of the eighteenth century, as a result of a prolonged and rapid increase in exports. Toward the end of the century this growth ceased, and by 1830 the economy was in serious difficulty. The sugar industry was shut out of European markets as beet sugar production rose, and could not compete with the growing low-cost output of Cuba. The development of an intensive cotton industry based on slave labor in the southern United States put an end to the growth of Brazilian cotton exports.[11] At the same time the gold rush in Minas Gerais ended. After several decades of stagnation, the economy again began to grow as a result of coffee cultivation. Brazil had an abundance of good land, and relatively little labor or capital, so coffee was an ideal crop. In the early years of its expansion coffee growing could draw on a supply of idle labor in the mining districts and on some slave labor released from the sugar industry. Settlers without a cash crop also took up coffee production.[12]

Coffee accounted for all the increase in Brazil's exports from 1800 to 1850. By 1820 it was the third largest export, 18 percent of the total; by 1850 it was first, with 40 percent. Cultivation continued to expand rapidly despite a 40 percent decline in price from the 1820s to the 1840s.

---

[10]Unlike sugar, coffee does not require extensive processing, and there were no secrets to its preparation. Thus no country or group could monopolize processing and trade as the Dutch did with sugar in the sixteenth and seventeenth centuries. In other respects the initial development of the two crops was similar, and both contributed to the establishment of permanent settlements in the Caribbean and the introduction of a large slave labor force. See chap. 12 (Sugar).

[11]On these points see the first few pages of chap. 12 (Sugar) and of chap. 16 (Cotton).

[12]This account of the Brazilian coffee industry is based largely on C. Furtado, *The Economic Growth of Brazil* (University of California Press, 1963); see especially chaps. 20, 22, 24, 25, 30.

Coffee growing soon absorbed all the available labor in the Rio de Janeiro-Minas Gerais area, and drew in thousands of migrants from the northeast. By the 1860s the industry had a shortage of labor, and during the last decades of the century nearly one million European immigrants came to Brazil.

In the period 1870-1900 production declined in the older growing areas, as a result of erosion and soil exhaustion. At the same time railroads were built to open up the Llanura Paulista, the great plateau of São Paulo. Output in that state rose more than fourfold, and coffee growing was also extended to Espirito Santo. As disease reduced production in Asia, nearly all the increase in world supplies in the last decades of the nineteenth century took place in Brazil. That country thus reached some time before 1900 the position it has held ever since, of dominating the world industry. Coffee became the principal factor in Brazil's continued economic growth, and shifted the country's center of gravity from the northeast, where it had been for more than two centuries, to the central south. In contrast to other countries, and despite the advantages of coffee for peasant proprietors, a large share of production came from sizable estates. These large farms absorbed much of the ex-slave and immigrant labor drawn into coffee growing, and their owners became the dominant class in Brazilian economic and political life. The power of this class and its landholding allies in other parts of the country has been contested and somewhat diminished since the Depression of the 1930s by the rise of an industrial and managerial class and the growth of the labor and middle class urban groups associated with it. The profits and foreign exchange required for Brazil's industrialization in the last three decades have come largely from the coffee industry.

During the 1950s there was another large expansion of coffee growing, particularly in the state of Paraná, where the area in coffee increased fivefold. There was also a considerable increase in the states of Pernambuco, Bahía, Minas Gerais, and Espírito Santo, and the westward extension in Paraná continued into Goiás and even into Mato Grosso. In the space of two centuries the center of coffee production has moved more than 2,000 kilometers. By 1960 coffee occupied fully one-sixth of the area in all crops in Brazil; only maize was planted over a larger area, and coffee took up more than one million hectares more than did such major crops as rice, cotton, beans, wheat, sugar cane, and manioc.[13]

Such massive displacements are characteristic only of Brazil, which has an extremely large area of subtropical plateau suited to coffee cultivation. In the other Latin American producing countries coffee is limited to much smaller zones on mountain slopes and in a few valleys. The only extensive and relatively level highland areas, such as in Mexico and the Bolivian *altiplano*, are too cold and dry, and the much larger areas of lowland basins are too warm and rainy to produce good quality coffee. Thus the shifts within and among other countries in the region have been relatively small and the distribution of output has been

more stable than in Brazil during the last few decades. However, changes in the distribution among Brazil, Colombia, and the remaining producers have been significant in this century, and the area in coffee in these countries continued to expand until about 1960.

Coffee was introduced into Colombia in the eighteenth century, and first became an important commercial crop in the 1840s, as a result of government promotion and the increase in world demand.[14] By 1880 coffee was the country's principal export, a position it still retains. The industry ceased expanding about that time, being more affected by the decline in prices than was the Brazilian industry. After 1900 further expansion occurred, followed by a boom during the 1920s, when prices were maintained by Brazil's efforts and a considerable flow of foreign capital entered Colombia, centering especially on the petroleum industry.

Coffee growing was first established in the Sabana de Bogotá in the Cordillera Central, which is still a major producing area. Cultivation spread along both sides of the Magdalena Valley, and then was carried into the Cauca Valley. The latter surpassed the older producing area during the late 1950s, when new plantings came into production. By 1957 nearly all the coffee land in Tolima and Cundinamarca was taken up and most of it was farmed intensively, while large areas of extensive cultivation remained in Antioquia and smaller zones in Caldas, Valle, Cauca, Caquetá, Meta, and Boyacá.[15] Today the industry is centered on Caldas, which with the departments of Antioquia, Valle, and Tolima account for 90 percent of total output. Colombia is now the world's second largest producer and exporter of coffee and one of the countries most dependent on coffee for foreign exchange. Except in the Caribbean islands where the industry is much older, coffee growing began in the other Latin American producers in the late eighteenth and early nineteenth centuries. The establishment of a significant commercial industry occurred during the rapid growth of world consumption in the middle and late nineteenth century.

Size and Structure

In 1960 only two crops — maize and wheat — occupied more land in Latin America than did coffee.[16] The greater area in wheat reflects the large wheat growing zones of Argentina, Chile, and Uruguay. Within the seventeen coffee growing countries as a group, only maize was more important than coffee, and in seven of these it was the only product with a comparable or larger area (see table 10-7). Since grains are produced chiefly for domestic consumption, with a large share of maize in particular being grown

---

[13]Coffee Study Group, *World Coffee Problem*, part II, pp. 45 ff. See also *Coffee Annual*, 1964, p. 70.

[14]The chief authority on the Colombian coffee industry is ECLA/FAO, *Coffee in Latin America, I: Colombia and El Salvador* (1958). See also Rowe, *World's Coffee*, pp. 63-82. The major developments from the 1840s to the 1920s are noted in H. Herring, *History of Latin America* (Knopf, 1962).

[15]See "Map of the Coffee Zones of Colombia, 1957," included in ECLA/FAO, *Coffee in Latin America*; and Coste, *Les Caféiers. . .*, vol. II (2), p. 566.

[16]Pastures, which are frequently larger than the area for all crops combined, are not included in this comparison.

in the subsistence economy, coffee is the dominant commercial and export crop of the region. Other crops are produced in greater volume, since yields are much lower for coffee than for such products as sugar, cotton and bananas, but in value coffee is still a major product. The share of total cropland taken up by coffee varied from less than 1 percent to almost one-fourth, but in only one country did coffee rank lower than fifth among all crops. With the exceptions of sugar in three countries, cotton in four, bananas in two, and cocoa in one, only the basic foodstuffs — grains, beans, potatoes — occupied more land than coffee in any country.

Coffee was grown on about 1.36 million farms in Latin America, the average size of coffee plantation being some 5.3 hectares. Data are not available on the distribution of farms by total size or by the area in coffee for the region as a whole, but some information exists for fourteen of the producing countries, including those that account for the bulk of output and exports. Both the average size coffee holding and the distribution of farms by size vary considerably from one country to another and even within countries. At one extreme, the average plantation in the state of Paraná, Brazil, has some 25 hectares in coffee, and 30 percent of the plantations exceed 150 hectares in total size or 90 hectares in coffee area. In Haiti, farms average only 1.2 hectares in coffee area, and most are smaller than 5 hectares in total (see table 10-8). Within this range it is difficult to make generalizations or exact comparisons, but some features of the size distribution by country may be noted.[17]

Outside of Brazil, small holdings prevail, and the average farm has between two and ten hectares in coffee. Very small plots of one hectare or less are numerous in Colombia, Costa Rica, the Dominican Republic, El Salvador, Guatemala, and Haiti, and common in Honduras. In Colombia the smaller plots are concentrated in the departments of Boyacá, Cauca, and Nariño; in the main coffee zone of Antioquia, Caldas, Valle, and Cundinamarca, most farms are between 1 and 10 hectares. Except in El Salvador and Honduras, plantations of over 50 hectares are rare. In Mexico, Ecuador, Peru, and Venezuela holdings of 10 hectares or less still predominate, but the average size is somewhat greater and there are more large estates. However, even where large plantations are few in number they may account for much of the area in coffee, as in Ecuador, Guatemala, and Venezuela. The existence of thousands of small plots on which coffee is grown chiefly for the farmers' own use, with relatively little marketable surplus, makes the large and medium sized plantations still more important in total production and exports. The small farms in these countries are usually occupied by their owners and employ little or no hired labor. In Brazil such small holdings are the exception, particularly in Paraná and São Paulo. Estates of more than fifty hectares are common, and the smaller farms are usually of several hectares. Hired labor is used much more extensively than elsewhere, and many owners delegate the operation of their holdings to resident managers. The same is true of the large estates in Central America and Venezuela.

There does not seem to be any consistent regional trend in the size distribution of coffee holdings. In areas such as eastern Peru, where the frontier is being extended by migration, there has recently been a considerable increase in the number of small farms. Both large and small holdings became less common in Ecuador between 1954 and 1962. In Venezuela, shortages of labor have reduced the importance of estates somewhat, these having been reduced more than smaller holdings in the general decline in coffee area. A comparison of the four major producing states of Brazil suggests that as coffee cultivation has moved westward the average size holding has increased appreciably: there are far more large estates in Paraná, where coffee was introduced in the 1950s, than in São Paulo, and more in São Paulo than in the older producing zones of Minas Gerais and Espírito Santo. In most countries yields are highest on medium sized plantations, and this fact exerts some pressure toward the consolidation of holdings into parcels of between 5 and 50 hectares, with a coffee area in the vicinity of 10 hectares. However, a great many other factors — population pressure, availability of hired labor, competition from other crops, and so forth — influence the size of coffee farms, particularly since relatively few of them are devoted entirely to coffee.

On nearly all coffee farms, of whatever size and in whatever country, coffee provides the bulk of cash income, but it does not necessarily occupy most of the area. Information on this subject is fragmentary, but it appears that the degree of concentration on coffee varies appreciably according to the size of the plantation and differs from country to country. In the cases of the Dominican Republic, Ecuador, El Salvador, Guatemala, and Honduras a rough comparison can be made of the average coffee area in each size class of farms, with the limits for that class. Except in Ecuador, the share of land devoted to coffee generally rises until a medium sized holding is reached — between 5 and 50 hectares — and thereafter declines. On very small farms much of the land is used to grow food for the family, with coffee often the only cash crop. Food is also grown for the laborers on large estates, but there are likely to be some other commercial crops and a sizable pasture area. Farms producing only coffee are rare at any size. Perhaps the greatest concentration is found in Paraná, where even on the largest estates coffee occupies about 60 percent of the land and provides 70 percent of the income. The share of land used for coffee rises to 70 percent for farms of 50 hectares or less.[18] In El Salvador, where large holdings are also common, only about one-third of the land is planted to coffee, and the share falls to much less in other Central American countries.

As might be expected of a crop grown over such a large area and under such a variety of conditions, yields vary considerably. The differences within one country, or even within a much smaller region, may exceed the greatest variation among national averages. Where coffee trees are wild rather than cultivated, or where they are not tended

---

[17]For a variety of estimates and descriptions of the size distribution of coffee farms see, besides the sources for table 10-8, Coste, *Les Caféiers. . .*, vol. II (2), pp. 576 ff.

[18]Rowe, *World's Coffee*, p. 35.

throughout the year or are interplanted with maize or other competing crops, yields may be as low as 50 kilograms per hectare per year of green coffee, and yields of only about 100 kilograms are common. At the other extreme, there appears to be no difficulty in maintaining yields on a well-run plantation at 1,000 to 1,500 kilograms per hectare, and returns of 2 or 3 metric tons can be reached with modern practices.

A number of factors account for variations in yields with time. Since a tree's yield varies with age, rising for several years and then declining for a longer period, the age distribution of trees influences the average yield. Sharp changes in the rate at which trees are planted and retired produce subsequent variations in yields. Weather variations also affect production; this factor is particularly important in southern Brazil, where a large area is periodically damaged by frost, and yields may vary greatly from one year to another. Individual coffee trees bear in a two-year cycle, alternating high and low yields. If many new trees are planted in one year, their cycle of yields will be observed in the average yield for an area. This sort of variation is evident in Brazilian production from 1954/55 to 1963 and in Haiti's production (see table 10-4). Spatial variations in yields are due in part to some of these factors, such as differences in weather or in the age distribution of trees.[19] Differences in the species grown and in the quality of land put to coffee are also important. The most significant factor in explaining variations in yield, and the general level of yields in Latin America, is the degree of intensity of cultivation. Most of the industry in the region is rather backward, and obtains yields much below what could profitably be achieved by more intensive cultivation. Chemical fertilizers are rarely used; most farmers merely use the hulls of the coffee beans. Control against diseases and pests is likewise rare, or rudimentary.[20] Trees are not properly pruned and often should be spaced differently for best results. Much of the labor required is used only at harvest time, and the year-round labor consists largely of routine weeding, very little being devoted to more modern practices.[21]

As a result, average yields in most countries are below 500 kilograms per hectare per year, and in five countries the average is less than 250 kilograms (see table 10-9). In only two countries, Costa Rica and El Salvador, do yields exceed 700 kilograms per hectare. In El Salvador the aver-

age return is nearly a ton or almost five times the average for Venezuela. These differences also reflect the availability of land and labor; yields are especially high where the expansion of the coffee area is difficult, as in El Salvador, and are low where there is a shortage of labor for the large estates, as in Venezuela.

From such data as are available, it seems that yields in most countries have not increased notably over several decades. Since the industry is composed largely of peasant proprietors, improvements in technique are adopted rather slowly; dissemination of information is difficult and capital is seldom easy to obtain. Investment in improvements has also been discouraged by periods of surplus and low prices, while land has generally been available for expansion during periods of high prices. Thus during the last century or more, better methods of cultivation have probably been less important in raising yields than the adoption of improved varieties of trees and the incorporation of new coffee zones, many excellent lands having recently been settled. Yields in the new coffee areas of Paraná, for example, are at least three times those in São Paulo, and higher still above those of older producing areas in Brazil.[22] Since coffee monoculture gradually exhausts the soil, differences in yields partly reflect differences in the length of time coffee has been grown in an area. The frequent expansion of the coffee frontier has served to offset this decline. More recently, however, yields have risen appreciably in some producing areas, chiefly as a result of improved practices: these include closer spacing of the trees and much greater use of fertilizers as well as the adoption of new high-yielding varieties. The increase is notable at the national level only in Costa Rica, El Salvador, Guatemala, and Mexico, but there have been slight improvements in Colombia (see table 10-9). The average for the entire region does not seem to have risen since 1950. What is more significant is that sizable increases could be obtained throughout Latin America by disseminating the results of research in the last decade. The National Federation of Coffee Growers of Colombia maintains that present yields in that country, already over 600 kilograms per hectare, could be tripled in a few years by the adoption of proven techniques. A very rapid increase in yields is under way in Mexico, to reach an average of one ton per hectare in the early 1970s. The shift from extensive to intensive cultivation is also under way in parts of São Paulo, Brazil, where coffee competes for land with many other crops and yields are now much less than in newer producing areas.[23] Yields have also risen sharply in some parts of Brazil in consequence of the eradication under government stimulus of older and less productive trees.

In most Latin American countries the national government exercises considerable influence in the coffee industry. Except in Cuba, the state does not own the land on which coffee is grown, nor does it intervene directly in production. Rather, its influence is typically expressed

---

[19]Yields are often calculated on only the area occupied by mature trees, generally trees at least five years old. The age distribution of coffee trees is a principal determinant of future productive capacity, and is used together with the anticipated rate of planting (either new planting or replacement) to forecast production. For periods of five years or less the rate of planting can be ignored. Estimates of age distribution are given for most producing countries in ICO, *Production Forecasts, 1965-70.* . . .

[20]In this regard it should, however, be noted that diseases and pests are much less of a problem in coffee cultivation than for such crops as cocoa and bananas. See chap. 11 (Cocoa), under "World Production" and chap. 13 (Bananas) under "World Production" and "Bananas in Latin America."

[21]See ECLA/FAO, *Coffee in Latin America*, and ECLA, *The Situation of Coffee Growing in the Producer Areas of Latin America*, doc. E/CN. 12/595 (Santiago, 18 April 1961), pp. 9-19.

[22]Rowe, *World's Coffee*, pp. 35-36.

[23]*Ibid.*, p. 82, for Colombia. The Mexican plan is described in M. Angel Cordera, "México en el Convenio Internacional del Café," *Comercio Exterior*, August 1965. For São Paulo, see ICO, *Production Forecasts 1965-70.* . . , vol. II, p. 15.

through a semi-autonomous agency representing both the government and the growers, and usually including operators of mills and warehouses, domestic merchants, and exporters.[24]

At one extreme, as in the minor South American producers, the government does little more than grade coffee for export, collect taxes on it, and enforce the export quotas of the International Coffee Agreement. If the country is a sizable exporter, and especially if its production considerably exceeds its quota under the Agreement, the government typically takes over the control of stocks, maintaining warehouses, setting the price for coffee delivered to them, and collecting the taxes necessary to finance the retention of the surplus. Other functions, such as the establishment of internal prices and the distribution of quotas to exporters and domestic merchants, may be added. State intervention produces in some countries a great discrepancy between the price received by growers and the average value of coffee exports (see table 10-2). Figures for several African producers are given for comparison. It is also the government which undertakes to promote the sale of coffee in importing countries, and to search for new markets. The state agency does not confine itself to activities which follow the actual production of coffee, but also, in most countries, conducts research into coffee cultivation and operates some sort of extension service to disseminate the results among farmers. At the least, the government usually operates a nursery and distributes trees to growers; this is especially important for the introduction of new species. Programs of migration and settlement or of crop diversification may involve the coffee agency, but in these as in other functions it may share control and responsibility with other government entities, particularly the ministry of agriculture.

The influence of the government on the coffee industry is greatest in Brazil, followed by Colombia where, in 1927,

the Federación Nacional de Cafeteros, or national coffee growers' association, was established with the primary purpose of protecting the interests of the thousands of small farmers who depend on coffee for virtually all their cash income. Federacafé establishes minimum prices for coffee, which may at times exceed the world price, while leaving growers free to sell to private dealers. The agency operates cooperatives and extension services and a national research center founded in 1938; more recently it has undertaken, with considerable success, to establish a market for pure Colombian coffee in the United States and to expand exports to Europe so as to reduce the country's dependence on any one market. It also operates a large warehouse and bulk storage capacity in the coffee growing zone and at the ports, and owns part or all of a number of subsidiary organizations: a shipping fleet, a bank, a network of stores and an insurance corporation.[25] The Brazilian agency, the Instituto Brasileiro do Café, performs similar functions, with even more direct effect on the extent of coffee area and output and on farmers' incomes. The extent to which external market influences are transmitted to growers varies among countries, being least where exportable production exceeds exports and the government has intervened to control stocks and exports. Such intervention by the Brazilian government since the early years of this century is a major factor in the amount and distribution of world coffee supply. Brazilian policies and their motives and effects are described below, in the discussion of the world coffee problem.

Latin American Coffee Exports

The United States and Western Europe together regularly account for 90 percent of world coffee imports, and for some 94 percent of all coffee exported from Latin America. Of the remaining few percent, the largest share goes to

TABLE 10-2. Producer, Export, and United States Prices of Coffee in 1965
(U.S. cents per pound)

Country	New York Price	Average Export Value	Estimated Average Producer Price	Producer Price as Percentage of Export Price
Brazil	44.7	41.0	12.7	31
Colombia	48.5	46.2	33.2	72
El Salvador	45.7	45.9	36.7	80
Guatemala	45.5	41.3	30.6	67
Mexico	45.5	42.1	27.3	65
Angola	31.6	28.7	26.7	93
Ethiopia	42.3	40.0	32.0	80
Ivory Coast	29.4	29.6	10.2	34
Uganda	31.1	23.6	13.2	55

Sources: P. T. Knight, "The Critical Coffee Sector in Brazil: Potential Earnings from Diversification." New York prices from PACB, *Annual Coffee Statistics*, 1966, for the same grades as in table 10-6.

[24]PACB, *Annual Coffee Statistics*, lists the official agencies which are its members. A complete list of government agencies and industry associations is given in *World Coffee and Tea*, April 1965, with some indication of their work. See also L. C. Hurt, *Coffee*

Situation: Programs and Policies in Producing Countries (USDA, FAS, July 1963).

[25]This summary is taken from Colombia Information Service, *Colombia Today* (New York, February 1966).

other Latin American countries, chiefly to Argentina, Chile and Uruguay. Smaller quantities, usually less than 1 percent of the total, are exported to Canada, Eastern Europe, Africa, Asia and Oceania. Latin America is normally the largest supplier to every major consuming area, although not to every country where much coffee is consumed.

During World War II, coffee exports ceased to nearly every market except the United States, and the disruption in trade was evident until the early 1950s. Since then, the distribution of world exports and of Latin American exports between the United States and Europe by and large has returned to its prewar pattern (see table 10-10). In both major markets, however, the share of total imports furnished by Latin America has declined. The share in the United States market rose during the war and remained high for several years afterward, but in the last decade and a half it has dropped considerably. The difference has been taken up entirely by African coffees, almost exclusively robustas, which penetrated the North American market rapidly in the 1950s. The comparable decline in the European market took place a decade earlier, and was nearly complete by 1950-52. African production was stimulated by reduction of Brazil's exports during the 1930s and by the efforts of some European powers to restrict their dollar purchases immediately after the war and buy from their African possessions whenever possible. For the last fifteen years the composition of European imports has been relatively stable. Thus since 1950-52 Europe has had much more effect on the growth of Latin American exports than has the United States, despite the favored position of African producers in the former market and the greater size of the latter.

About 30 percent of European imports now consists of robustas, accounting for virtually all the coffee imported from producers outside Latin America. The share is extremely low—10 percent or less—in the Scandinavian countries and West Germany. In Belgium, Italy, the Netherlands, Spain, and Switzerland the share is between 20 and 40 percent. In the United Kingdom it is now 60 percent, in France over 70 percent, and in Portugal essentially all imports are robustas.[26] Two factors, aside from any national differences in tastes, account for most of this variation. Those countries with present or former possessions in Africa import a high proportion of robustas, usually under some form of subsidy or tariff protection. Among other countries, the share of robustas in imports declines with rising per capita income (and therefore, incidentally, with rising per capita consumption).

Latin American coffees therefore have a secure and dominant position in Scandinavia and, except in Portugal and Spain, may be expected to increase their share in the low-income European countries as incomes rise. The most important and least certain market is the EEC. France for several years permitted coffee to enter duty free from the Associated Overseas States of the Common Market, while maintaining a 20 percent tariff against other producers. The extension of this protection, by a common external EEC

tariff of 16 percent, was contemplated for 1970. Such protection would probably have hurt Latin America in the Italian and Belgian markets and might have resulted in much greater African sales to Germany. By the Convention of Association which went into effect 15 June 1964, the common tariff was reduced to 9.6 percent, and the privileged position of the Franc Zone countries among the Associated States was somewhat reduced.[27]

The major Latin American exporter to Europe, as to the United States, is Brazil; it furnishes about the same share of imports in Europe as does Africa, with Europe taking 40 percent of its exports. In 1936-38, Brazil furnished just over half the coffee imported by the United States, and a slightly smaller share in Europe. The proportion was reversed in the early 1950s, and has since fallen to about 32 percent in both markets. This sharp decline in market share is the result of Brazil's retention of supplies. In the United States, Brazil's loss has chiefly benefitted African producers of robustas; in Europe, where Africa's share of the market has been nearly constant since 1950-52, it is chiefly the producers of mild arabicas who have increased their share at Brazil's expense.

Europe normally takes only a very small amount of coffee from other Latin American producers; Colombia furnishes the bulk of this, about two-fifths of its exports. In the last three decades, there has been a notable shift of Colombia's exports from the United States to Europe. Increased sales to Europe have been at Brazil's expense and have resulted in part from an active campaign of promotion by the Federación Nacional de Cafeteros. Costa Rica, El Salvador and Haiti export more than half their coffee to Europe, and the share is about half for Ecuador and Nicaragua. The United States takes the bulk of exports from other countries, the share being some two-thirds in the case of Honduras and as much as 80 percent from the Dominican Republic and Mexico (see table 10-11).

The volume of Latin America's coffee exports has been increasing steadily in the postwar period, from an average of 1.5 million tons in the early 1950s to about 1.9 million tons in 1960-67, with a peak of over two million in 1963. During the same period prices have fallen from the levels reached in 1950 and held until about 1957, so that the value of exports has declined; from $1,778 million in 1950-54, it fell slightly in 1955-59 and then dropped to $1,589 million in 1964-66. As a result coffee, which once furnished one-fourth the region's foreign exchange, has provided only about one-sixth in recent years. At the lowest level of prices, in 1961-63, the import value of a bag of Brazilian coffee was only about 60 percent of what it had been in 1950-53 and 1955-56. The decline for mild arabicas was almost as severe.[28]

---

[26] PACB, *Annual Coffee Statistics*, 1964, p. 47. See also *World Coffee and Tea*, October 1965, p. 15.

[27] For a summary of the terms of the Convention of Association, or Treaty of Yaounde, see PACB, *Annual Coffee Statistics*, 1964, p. 48. The terms apply to all tropical commodities which cannot be produced within the EEC.

[28] Index of coffee terms of trade, based on the price of imports from the United States and the prices of Santos Number 4 and MAMS coffees, respectively, based on 1950. Calculations by the Secretariat of the Coffee Study Group, based on data from IMF, *International Financial Statistics*.

The importance of coffee in total exports varies greatly among countries. It is lowest, about 1 percent, in Cuba, Panama, and Venezuela, and near 5 percent in Mexico. A range of 10 to 20 percent is found in the Dominican Republic, Ecuador, Honduras, and Nicaragua in recent years. The share is in the vicinity of 50 percent in Brazil, Costa Rica, El Salvador, Guatemala, and Haiti, with still greater dependence on coffee in Colombia. Most of these ratios have fallen appreciably since the mid-1950s when prices were at their highest: thus coffee has furnished as much as 73 percent of total exports in Brazil, 85 percent in Colombia, 75 percent in Guatemala, 80 percent in Haiti, and 90 percent in El Salvador. In some cases the decline in the share of coffee is due more to the development of a new export commodity than to the drop in coffee prices or the slow expansion of other products. This is most true of El Salvador and Nicaragua, where cotton is now a major export. The growth of banana exports has also influenced the relative importance of coffee in Central America and in Ecuador. In Brazil the slow growth of primary exports other than coffee is at least partly the result of governmental policies which discriminate against exports of such products and increase the dominance of coffee.[29]

Virtually all coffee exports from Latin America are in the form of green beans, to be blended, roasted, and ground for consumption in importing countries. There are some exports of roasted coffee and a small but rapidly increasing amount of soluble coffee. The first plants were built in the region in the mid-1950s, and by 1965 there were twenty factories in operation in twelve countries, with several more planned.[30] Many of them were established for export, to offset the growing imports of robusta coffee for soluble manufacture, particularly in the United States. Soluble coffee also found a domestic market in several countries. There is some foreign capital in the soluble coffee industry, but in several countries domestic capital controls the manufacture, either alone or with state participation.

Despite the extreme vulnerability of earnings to fluctuations in price, coffee offers one or two advantages over certain other resource commodities. First, exports do not have to compete with protected production in importing countries or with subsidized exports by other producers (except to the degree that differences in taxes among exporters represent relative subsidies). This not only makes the market larger but protects exporters from the sudden shifts in trade that can occur when national quotas, subsidies or other barriers are changed. Such changes have been, or are potentially, very important for such diverse products as nonferrous metals, petroleum, sugar, grains, livestock products, and cotton. Second, virtually all the foreign exchange earned is returned to the country, almost none being withdrawn as profits of foreign enterprises or required for imports by the coffee industry. In this way the industry makes a large net contribution to the economy. Exports are usually taxed, often quite heavily, and so con-

tribute to government revenues as well. The share of coffee taxes in total export taxes is as high as 80 percent in El Salvador and 20 percent even in Mexico, where coffee is a much less important export. The contribution to total government revenues is usually much less, from 15 or 20 percent down to 1 percent or less. Often the bulk of the revenue is used for the expenses of the government coffee agency, including the costs of price support and retention of stocks, so the net contribution may be slight or even negative in national currency, but is still large in foreign exchange which may be used for the imports needed for development.

The World Coffee Problem

Supply Factors

Because a coffee tree takes several years to come into production, the supply of coffee is quite inelastic in the short run. A seedling takes two to four years to begin producing and does not usually give maximum yields until the age of ten or fifteen years, after which it may continue producing for thirty or forty years. The interval between a maximum or minimum price and the corresponding maximum or minimum production has varied from two to ten years in the case of Brazil, and averaged 4.7 years between 1870 and 1953.[31] New plantings may continue for several years after a rise in price, until the first new trees begin to bear; then for several years afterward output will rise each year as a new group of trees comes into production, even if prices are low and there is no new planting. The rise in yields as each tree matures simply compounds any tendency to overproduction.

Furthermore, the response of production to prices is asymmetric, being generally faster for price increases than for decreases. A decline in prices will usually put an end to new plantings, but it will not readily induce growers to destroy trees already in production. A tree with a useful life of thirty years may be worth planting even if low prices prevail for some years after it comes into production; but a tree once uprooted cannot be replaced for at least five years, and for longer in the case of a mature tree, so the grower must anticipate low prices for several years. The asymmetry of supply response also reflects the fact that apart from variations in weather and the cyclical output of individual trees, the factors causing yields to vary over time have in the past operated quite slowly.

The lack of research into coffee cultivation until recent years and the slow spread of improved practices have meant that farmers could generally increase production more cheaply and more rapidly by planting new trees than by raising the yield of land already in coffee. Since fertilizers are relatively unimportant, it was similarly difficult to reduce yields quickly; the only way to decrease output was to uproot part of the tree stock. The reluctance of farmers to destroy unremunerative trees reflects a lack of alternative employment for themselves and their land. Coffee is often the only cash crop available to a farmer, particularly on hillsides which will not support other crops and would

[29] See N. H. Leff, "Export Stagnation and Autarkic Development in Brazil, 1947-62," *Quarterly Journal of Economics*, May 1967.

[30] *World Coffee and Tea*, April 1965: "Guide to Latin American Coffees."

[31] FAO, *World Coffee Economy*, p. 29.

be subject to erosion if cleared. If prices fall, he will cease planting, and will reduce his expenditures for cultivation as far as possible, neglecting the trees or planting other crops between them. Such measures, and the ageing of the trees, will gradually reduce productive capacity, but the adjustment is likely to be slow and painful. Even a few years of high prices may induce new planting and so postpone the adjustment. Equilibrium can prevail in the coffee industry only if changes in demand are slow enough for new plantings, or the gradual decline of capacity through ageing, to keep pace without rapid fluctuations in price.

Such stability would be difficult to achieve even in an economy sufficiently flexible to transfer resources readily between coffee and other products, allowing capacity to be reduced by taking the poorest lands out of coffee rather than by allowing the yield on all land to deteriorate. The difficulty is made much more severe by the inflexibility, both internal and external, of the economies of coffee-growing countries. Internally, there is not likely to be any equally remunerative employment for the land and labor devoted to coffee, even if prices fall substantially. This situation can exist despite shortages of other crops because the land in coffee is not well suited to them, or the distribution system is inadequate for crops which spoil more readily than coffee, or the government holds down the prices of other crops in order to benefit domestic consumers. Externally, the country cannot afford the loss of export revenue derived from coffee, and so will suffer severely even if resources can be transferred to meet some internal demand. A decline in price too small to force coffee growers into other pursuits may nonetheless disrupt the economy by slowing the flow of imports on which its growth depends. A large decline in price could mean catastrophe for many countries. Thus a tendency for price fluctuations to result in overproduction is complicated by an extreme vulnerability to the low prices overproduction normally induces. The considerable transformation of the economies of Latin America in the last several decades may have reduced the internal difficulty by creating more remunerative alternatives to coffee growing, but it has intensified the external problem by increasing dependence on traditional exports.

Unfortunately for the coffee growing countries, world demand has not been steady in this period but has suffered large and rapid variations in both directions, greatly affecting prices and the amount and distribution of output. Since about 1925 there have been some twenty years of surplus, followed by less than a decade of shortage and another period of overproduction. Between 1930 and 1964 nearly 12 million tons of coffee were produced in excess of world requirements, with enormous accumulation and destruction of stocks.

The Role of Brazil

Brazil alone accounted for some 9.2 million tons or 80 percent of the world cumulative coffee surplus in 1930-64. This is a much larger share than Brazil's average contribution to either production or exports in the period, and reflects at least four factors besides the country's weight in total supplies. One is that Brazil dominates variations in world output because much of the country's capacity is located in areas of great variability in weather. Another, related in part to the first, is the great extent of land suitable to coffee in Brazil and the consequent ease with which the coffee area has several times been expanded. A third is the effect of Brazilian supplies on prices of all types of coffee and on relative prices for the different types. The fourth is the overwhelming importance of coffee in the Brazilian economy, reflected both in the country's dependence on coffee exports and in the political dominance of coffee growers. These factors combined to produce government policies for dealing with the instability of demand and supply, which in turn contributed to the world imbalance. The rest of this section will be devoted to the interaction of these supply phenomena with the major demand disturbances of the period, the Depression of the 1930s and World War II.

In an effort to reduce fluctuations in exports and maintain export values and farmers' incomes at high levels, the governments of the major coffee-growing states of Brazil began to intervene in the market late in the nineteenth century. During the depressions of 1893 and 1897 exports were held back until prices recovered. In 1906 more comprehensive measures were taken, by the name of *valorizacão,* to control supplies. Foreign loans were obtained for buying coffee from farmers at guaranteed prices; the loans, and the cost of holding stocks, were to be financed from increased export revenues. There was a further experiment in 1917. On each of these occasions supplies were retained for short periods and in small amounts.

In 1923 "valorization" was undertaken on a much larger scale by the state of São Paulo. As demand was growing, some increase in production was needed; but the stimulus given to growers was so large as to extend coffee planting over all the northwestern part of the state. Once the new plantings came into production in 1928, Brazil's productive capacity was double the amount of exports. Thus when the Depression struck, Brazil already had excess capacity and large accumulated stocks. The difficulty was increased by sharp variations in output in 1927-35, while exports remained almost stationary (see table 10-12). The price of Santos Number 4 fell from 20 cents per pound to about 10 cents in the early 1930s, and to prevent it from falling still further Brazil continued to hold back supplies. In 1931 the destruction of stocks began, and during the next twelve years somewhere between 4.2 and 4.8 million tons of coffee were burned.

The other producing countries, sheltered by Brazil, continued to expand production. During the 1930s output in the rest of Latin America rose from 500,000 to 700,000 tons, and Africa's production tripled. Unable to get the cooperation of other producers, Brazil abandoned its defensive policy by removing the export tax on coffee in 1937, letting exports rise by some 200,000 tons and the price drop to seven cents per pound. Altogether more than 6.6 million tons of surplus coffee were produced during the decade, 5.2 million tons in Brazil.[32]

[32] The history of Brazilian coffee policy is described in detail in V. D. Wickizer, *The World Coffee Economy, With Special Reference to Control Schemes* (Stanford: Food Research Institute, 1943); see

In the late 1930s, with prices at their lowest level, Brazil began to reduce capacity by destroying trees, and world production declined very slightly. The industry had by no means adjusted to the shock of the Depression when it received a second blow. With the outbreak of World War II the European market, which had formerly taken about 40 percent of imports, disappeared. Imports had not fallen appreciably during the 1930s, but in 1942 they dropped to only a million tons, 37 percent below the 1934-38 level. To avert disaster for all coffee exporters, the United States and fourteen Latin American producers in 1940 formed the Inter-American Coffee Agreement. Quotas were set for the U.S. market, and during the war the price was fixed at 13.4 cents per pound, nearly double the 1938-40 level. The reduction of capacity in Brazil was accelerated, and by 1944 some 548 million trees had been destroyed and a million hectares, 30 percent of the land in coffee in the late 1930s, were taken out of production.[33] Capacity was unchanged in other countries, except for Indonesia, and world production declined by some 700,000 tons. Brazil's surplus production during the war was only a million tons, and as other countries drew on stocks accumulated earlier, the total surplus was somewhat less.

After fifteen years of excess supplies and efforts to maintain prices, Brazil's share of world production had been reduced from 70 to 50 percent. Africa's share rose from about 3 to 10 percent, and the other Latin American producers had increased their share from about 21 to 37 percent. It appeared that the industry might once more be in balance, with capacity equal to demand at prewar prices and stability in prospect with the new distribution of production. In fact, the industry was on the verge of a new upheaval and the expected stability lasted only three years.

As there had been no new planting for nearly a decade, average productivity of trees was low, and not very responsive to better cultivation. Furthermore, the experience of the last decade and a half had made growers extremely reluctant to plant new trees, so that they were less responsive to price incentives than they had been twenty years earlier. Finally, at the war's end Brazil retained stocks of at least 200,000, and perhaps 360,000 tons. As a result, the industry was slow to respond to the postwar increase in demand, which was more rapid than had been anticipated. United States per capita consumption reached a peak of 8.4 kilograms in 1946-49, and European consumption, while still far below the prewar level, recovered rapidly. The Brazilian stocks were exhausted in 1949, and in 1950 the price, which had been 27 cents per pound in 1947-48, jumped to 50. It was steady for the next three years, and then in 1954 leaped to 78.7 cents, as a result of reports of frost damage to the Brazilian crop. Over the next three years Brazilian prices fell back to the 1950-53 level, but arabica prices remained high and robusta prices low, so that differentials were much wider than usual (see table 10-6).

The price increase in 1950 induced some new planting in Brazil, and the rate increased greatly in 1954. New planting continued at a high rate until 1958 and at a slower pace for the next several years. The total area in coffee, which was about 3.5 million hectares in the late 1930s and only 2.4 million in the 1940s, rose to 3 million by 1954, to 4 million by 1957, and to more than 5 million hectares in the years from 1959 to 1962.[34] Since most of the extension was into areas subject to frost at intervals, and since new trees formed a large share of the total stock, variations in output became much greater: exportable production fluctuated between 0.7 and 1.3 million tons in 1955-58 and rose to 2.2 million tons in 1961. The total coffee area in Latin America rose from about 4.6 million hectares in 1950 to a peak of over 7.2 million hectares around 1963. Brazil's share of the total, which had declined in the previous two decades, increased from 54 to 62 percent.

There was also a great increase in planting in Africa, and total world exportable supplies rose from about 1.8 million tons in 1950 to a peak of almost 4 million in 1960. Even though Brazil held back one-third to one-half of its production and world exports expanded only from 1.9 to 2.6 million tons during the decade, prices began to fall sharply. From 56 cents per pound or more (for Santos No. 4) in 1955-57, they fell to 48 cents in 1958, to 36 cents in the next two years, and to 34 cents in 1962-63. Over the entire period 1925-64 the price of coffee has been one of the least stable among the commodities included in this study, the peak real price in 1954 being some five times the level of 1940. Real prices in 1961-63 were higher than at any time in the interval 1930-46, but far below the levels of 1947-58.[35] Between 1958 and 1964 world surplus production was some 4.6 million tons, of which Brazil accounted for more than three-fourths. Thus the world coffee industry had returned to a position such as it occupied in 1929, burdened with excess capacity resulting from high prices and too high a rate of planting rather than from a decline in demand.

Efforts at Solution

Before 1940 the only efforts to cope with the surpluses and low prices brought on by the Depression were those made by Brazil. Other producers not only did not join in curtailing supplies, but continued to expand production. In none of these countries was there a boom like that in Brazil in the 1920s (although in the 1950s the coffee area expanded more rapidly in the mild coffee producers than in Brazil). A fall in price affects them somewhat less than it does Brazil, and may be more readily compensated by a larger volume of exports at the expense of Brazilian coffee. Finally, no other producer had the storage capacity or administrative machinery to control large stocks. Thus the only result of Brazil's attempts to share the burden of supporting prices was the creation, in 1936, of the Pan American Coffee Bureau, including initially ten producers. The Bureau's work has been confined to research, the publication of statistical information, and promotion of coffee

---

especially chaps. VIII-XII. A shorter and more recent analysis by the same author, also published by the Food Research Institute, is *Coffee, Tea and Cocoa* (1951). See also J. W. F. Rowe, *Primary Commodities in International Trade* (University of Cambridge Press, 1965), part IV.

[33] Coste, *Les Caféiers.* .., vol. II (2), pp. 543-44.

[34] ICO, *Production Forecasts 1965-70.* .., vol. II, p. 9.

[35] See chap. 3, table B-2.

consumption; it has never included measures to control supplies. All American producers except Bolivia, Haiti, Paraguay, and Peru joined by 1964. In 1940 the Inter-American Coffee Agreement was formed, embracing the fourteen major producers of the hemisphere and the United States. The agreement did not include any measures to reduce production, but planting ceased in most countries and in Brazil the destruction of trees, begun some years before, was accelerated.

The agreement expired in September 1948, by which time a shortage of coffee was developing and there was no need for export control. It was in effect succeeded by the Coffee Federation of the Americas, or FEDECAME. This organization has served chiefly as a forum for discussion among Latin American producers and for preparation of a regional position in other international bodies. FEDECAME has also been concerned with the sharp seasonal variations in the prices of Central American coffees, which result from a short harvest season and inadequate warehouse facilities, and an absence of the type of controls which in Colombia and Brazil assures a smooth flow of coffee to the ports.[36] Export quotas were approved for members in 1955, when a surplus was feared, but the crop was reduced by frosts in Paraná and the controls were not put into effect.

The subject of international control was dormant until November 1954, when it was raised at a meeting of the Inter-American Economic and Social Council of the OAS, at Petrópolis, Brazil. It was clear by then that the high prices of that year had induced a boom in planting, so that in three or four years supplies would be much greater. No action was taken until October 1957, when seven producers—Brazil, Colombia, Costa Rica, El Salvador, Guatemala, Mexico, and Nicaragua—met in Mexico City and signed an agreement for export quotas in 1957/58. The price was steady for a few months, but by the middle of 1958 it was falling, and still larger crops were in prospect, so the members of the "Mexican Club" determined to draw in other countries. An agreement had been reached at Rio de Janeiro in January 1958, among fourteen producers, but it concerned only efforts to promote consumption and was shortly abandoned as inadequate.

In September 1958 the treaty of Mexico expired and was replaced by the Latin American Coffee Agreement, including all fifteen significant producers. It gave way in 1959 to the International Coffee Agreement, when France and Portugal joined on behalf of their African territories.[37] Belgium and the United Kingdom, while not joining, agreed to observe the terms of the pact, and the latter country joined formally in 1960. By then the member countries accounted for 90 percent of world exportable production. The agreement was renewed in 1961.

Brazil had the most to gain from control of coffee supplies, but was unwilling to attempt it alone after the ex-

perience of the 1930s. Colombia, which during the early years of the Depression had countered Brazil's policy, had come to support it and to retain stocks of its own. These two countries imposed fixed export quotas on themselves in 1958/59-1961/62, set at 90 percent of their peak exports in the period 1949-58. The other producers, both Latin American and African, were given quotas amounting to 88 percent of their exportable production. The International Coffee Agreements of those years therefore restricted supplies only slightly, and the price declined two cents; the burden of preventing further declines fell chiefly on Brazil and Colombia.

During the same period several other steps were taken to prepare for a more effective control of the world coffee surplus. In 1958 a Coffee Study Group was formed, including the principal importing countries as well as the major Latin American and African exporters; its Committee I undertook to survey all aspects of the long-run supply and demand situation, and Committee II was instructed to study the administrative and technical problems presented by a strict agreement including both exporting and importing countries. In November of 1959 a World Coffee Promotion Committee was established, consisting of one representative each from Brazil, Colombia, France, and Portugal, and two from FEDECAME. Its initial functions were to promote the consumption of coffee in importing countries and to interest African producers in joining the agreement; now only the former objective is pursued. Partly as a result of its efforts, an Inter-African Coffee Organization was formed in December 1960 by six producers. It was joined in 1961-62 by twelve other countries and now includes all major producers. The IACO is the African counterpart of FEDECAME, and although it includes several arabica producers, its chief concern has been the orderly marketing and control of supplies of robustas. Finally, in 1961 the United States, alarmed at the economic and political situation of Latin America, withdrew its opposition to a price-support scheme and announced its readiness to join an international coffee agreement for the purpose of stabilizing prices at their current levels.

The Coffee Study Group's Committee I prepared a draft outline for an international coffee agreement, which was circulated to member governments early in 1961. The draft proposed that annual export quotas be determined according to anticipated demand, and that the quotas then be enlarged each year so as to bring prices down to equilibrium levels. Increases of 2.5 percent in the second and third years, and of 5 percent from the fourth year onward, were expected to result in price declines of about 7.5 percent annually for robustas, 10 percent for Brazils, and 12.5 percent for mild arabicas. A buffer stock would be used to prevent price fluctuations, the burden of surplus stocks would be shared by all producers, and provisions were made for adjusting quotas to change in demand and to reward reduction of output.[38] The provision for price declines was unacceptable to producers, the other proposals were not well received, and the United States agreed to support prevailing prices; so the draft scheme was ignored, and the

[36]See "Program to Relieve Seasonal Pressures on the Prices of Central American Coffees," published 31 October 1961 by the Pan American Union. A fund for stabilization and minimum price support, to be raised by loans and administered by FEDECAME, was proposed but not instituted.

[37]A summary of all international activities up to the formation of the first International Coffee Agreement is given by PACB's *Annual Coffee Statistics*, 1959.

[38]For a summary of these proposals, see Rowe, *World's Coffee*, pp. 186, 193.

much simpler problem of designing a workable price maintenance agreement was taken up.

A new draft was prepared, and approved by the Study Group, and submitted to a United Nations conference on coffee held from 9 July to 25 August 1962.[39] By 30 November the requisite number of countries had signed the agreement, and on 1 July 1963 it entered provisionally into force. The full operation of the agreement was delayed until 1965 by the failure of the United States Congress to pass the legislation necessary for compliance, but the delay did not significantly affect the control of supplies. An International Coffee Organization was created, with a council representing all members; separate two-thirds weighted majorities among producers and importers are required for major changes in the agreement, votes being distributed in proportion to shares in trade. An executive committee of seven exporters and seven importers conducts the day-to-day work of the organization. In early 1965 the ICO included thirty-four exporting countries—thirteen in Latin America and eighteen in Africa, including Portugal—and twenty-one importing countries; by mid-1967 the membership had increased to sixty-one countries. The agreement was negotiated for five years to end in 1968; early in that year agreement was reached on a five-year extension to October 1973.

The International Coffee Agreement has four stated purposes:

1. To ensure by a comprehensive control of exports, backed by supervision and regulation of imports, that the general level of coffee prices does not decline below the level of 1962, and that real export earnings should progressively increase.
2. To promote the consumption of coffee (importing members to have no financial obligations), and to work for the removal of obstacles to consumption (import tariffs, internal taxes, quotas).
3. To adjust production to demand within the lifetime of the agreement.
4. To establish a policy "relative to" stocks, which producing members "shall endeavor by all means within their power to implement."

The operation of the Agreement has been largely confined to the first of these objectives. Several producing countries have undertaken to promote consumption, and more recently the ICO has joined these efforts, but the effect of such campaigns on the world surplus has been slight. Furthermore, those countries maintaining quotas or taxes on coffee imports, whether to raise revenues or to favor their former possessions, have not been willing to reduce these obstacles. The third point was excluded from priority by the decision to maintain prices, and it has proved impossible to set production quotas for the members. However, several national efforts are under way to stabilize or reduce coffee output and diversify agriculture in producing countries, and the ICO has agreed to aid in these efforts. Some of these programs are described below. The fourth item has

not been taken up, and control of stocks remains with the major exporters, principally Brazil and Colombia.

The global export quota is set equal to members' anticipated demand for imports, less expected exports by nonmembers; exports to nonmembers and "new markets"—countries where consumption is low but can be rapidly increased—were not regulated until 1967. Market shares were fixed in approximately the pattern of 1961-62, with revisions of the total quota to be distributed proportionally. In fact the smaller exporters, which lack storage facilities and which can offset price declines with volume increases more easily than the large countries, have several times obtained waivers of their quotas or enlargements of their share in the global quota. Brazil and Colombia have accepted the reduction in their own shares in order to maintain the Agreement, thus continuing to protect their smaller competitors. In the negotiations for a second Agreement, these two countries and Mexico and Indonesia agreed to reductions in their shares and enlargements for African and Central American producers. A country's quota can be reduced in punishment for exceeding its allowed exports, or adjusted if the quota is consistently not met. To reduce smuggling of coffee to nonmembers for re-export to members, all coffee exports are required to have certificates of origin. Part of the function of policing the Agreement is thereby transferred to the importing countries, which keep records of their trade by origin.

The annual quota is subject to quarterly revision. Until the spring of 1965, once basic quotas were established, each producer was free to ship a fixed share of its quota—usually 88 or 90 percent. The remainder of the global quota was to be released in January of each year if the market appeared sound. An additional 30,000 tons of exports might be authorized if two-thirds of the producers thought the market could bear it. In March 1965 this system was replaced by reliance on an indicator price averaging together the prices of Santos Number 4, four mild arabica coffees, and three robusta coffees, weighted approximately by shares of world exports. If the price remained outside the range of 38 to 44 cents per pound for fifteen market days, quotas were to be adjusted by the Executive Committee. As these semiautomatic adjustments were not to exceed 1.5 percent of the total per quarter, the greatest reduction in the annual quota that could be made without the agreement of the council was 6 percent.[40] In October 1966 the indicator price mechanism was applied separately to four types of coffee: Colombian, other mild arabicas, Brazilian, and robusta. Quotas for each class can now be adjusted independently of the others, with increases or decreases distributed proportionally among the countries in the group affected.[41] This change allows the relative prices of different coffees to be held at about the same levels as in the

---

[39] The background of the 1962 agreement is described, together with a brief history of the negotiations and an account of the positions of the participating countries, in R. B. Bilder, "The International Coffee Agreement," *Law and Contemporary Problems*, 28, no. 2 (Spring, 1963).

[40] ICO Resolution Number 67, approved 19 March 1965. For the full text, see PACB, *Annual Coffee Statistics*, 1964, pp. 4-5 and 11-14. See also table 10-6.

[41] ICO Resolution Number 115. See, in addition to the sources cited, the Alliance for Progress *Newsletter* of 13 February 1967; IMF, *International Financial News Survey*, 23 June 1967; and "Latin America's Coffee Problems," in BOLSA, *Review*, January 1966.

early 1960s; changes in demand are now to be reflected rather in relative export quotas.

The Current Situation and Prospects

The Surplus and the ICA

The entry into force of the International Coffee Agreement in 1963 had a great and immediate impact on prices: the annual average for 1964 was 10 cents per pound higher than in 1963 for mild arabicas, 12 cents higher for Brazil and almost 8 cents higher for robustas (see table 10-6). It is estimated that total earnings from coffee exports were raised from about $1,800 million in 1962 to $2,400 million in 1964, and the higher level has since been approximately maintained. Since the major Latin American producers accepted relatively small quotas in order to bring other countries into the Agreement, the region's exports rose only from about $1,400 million to more than $1,600 million (see table 10-11). The International Coffee Agreement is about as comprehensive and as nearly automatic in operation as could be expected of a scheme involving so many countries with such diverse capacities, costs, and interests; its negotiation and conduct represent a considerable achievement, providing for control of supplies while retaining flexibility with respect to the development of new markets, changes in demand, and freedom of trade within the quotas.

The short-run objective of the Agreement has been met over the last five years. Its initial success was greatly aided by the fact that the 1964/65 crop was only a little over 3 million tons, whereas from 1960/61 to 1963/64 world output was in the vicinity of 4 million tons. The drastic reduction was due largely to frost damage in Brazil. When production recovered in 1965/66, however—to some 4.6 million tons—two problems emerged. One is that of "tourist coffee," or coffee which is sent, often smuggled, to nonmembers of the ICA for re-export to member importers and thereby evades the quotas. The amount of such coffee in world trade in 1966 is estimated as somewhat more than 150,000 tons, much of it moving from Colombia through the Netherlands West Indies in response to an exchange rate much higher than that allowed legal exports. This evasion is now dealt with by tighter control of exports and by policing of imports by member countries, which went into effect in April 1967: exporters are required to obtain stamps from the ICO for each shipment, and these stamps are checked by importers as to the origin and amount of coffee.

A more serious difficulty is that when supplies increase, the smaller producers invariably press for enlargement of their quotas relative to those of the major exporters. In December 1965 the International Coffee Organization agreed to permit twenty-two exporters to exceed their quotas for 1965/66, while Brazil, Colombia, and Mexico agreed not to exceed theirs. When this expansion of the global quota forced prices steadily downward in 1966, the quotas for the four different classes of coffee were separated, and those for non-Colombian mild arabicas were cut twice; the Colombian quota was reduced early in 1967. Thus robusta producers, which were the principal beneficiaries of quota revisions before the division into four

groups was established, have since continued to gain at the expense of arabica producers. In part, this shift reflects a continuing movement of world demand toward robusta, brought about by the higher prices since 1963 and the growth of soluble coffee consumption. It is also due, however, to the unwillingness of the smaller producers, which are chiefly robusta exporters, to accept the discipline by which Brazil has supported the market for many years, and on which the success of the Agreement depends. The Central American producers have similarly been reluctant to accumulate or destroy stocks, but until late 1966 they were protected by the retention of supplies in both Colombia and Brazil. The larger producers have been unwilling to insist on greater restraint by the small exporters for fear of destroying the Agreement, and have yielded at each impasse. The establishment of separate classes of coffee may reduce somewhat the confrontation among producers, but only if all producers accept the relative prices determined in the Agreement.

The problem of controlling supplies in the short run is related to the long-run goal of reducing production to the level of demand at the prices set by the Agreement, toward which much less progress has been made. The size of the world surplus was approximately constant from 1961 through 1964, but since then it has increased appreciably. Exportable production exceeds consumption in importing countries by some 60,000 tons annually. In November 1966 world stocks were estimated as some 4.5 million tons, enough for eighteen months at current rates of consumption; at anticipated levels of capacity the surplus was expected to rise to 6 million tons or a two-year supply by 1970.[42] The steady increase in coffee stocks not only reduces the gains from the Agreement by the amount of storage costs and internal price maintenance, but increases the pressure by the smaller exporters for quota increases and thereby endangers the stability of the ICA. Even another year or two of very low output, as in 1964/65, would only reduce the pressure slightly. If consumption continues to increase at about 2.5 percent annually, and there is no new planting and no measures are taken to raise yields, equilibrium between supply and demand will not be reached until the late 1970s. Furthermore, if balance were attained in this way, stocks would reach enormous amounts, perhaps enough for three or four years' demand, before beginning to decline, and would not be reduced to reasonable levels until 1980 or later. By that time the average age of coffee trees would be relatively high, so that low yields and high costs would result; and the land devoted to coffee would represent a great waste since with higher yields much of it could be freed for other crops. The problem of excessively old trees and high-cost capacity, which is now concentrated in Brazil and serious in only a few other countries such as Haiti, would spread to many other producers.

These considerations indicate that the achievement of equilibrium under price control through the Agreement but without any other measures would be both unattractive and difficult. A reduction of output in consequence of declining

---

[42]ICO estimate, based on numbers and age distribution of trees in producing countries and current yields.

prices is still less attractive to exporting countries, which rejected this approach in 1961. An intermediate solution has also been proposed, in which prices to farmers would decline, resulting in reduced output, while the export earnings of producing countries would be maintained. Importing countries, under this arrangement, would continue to subsidize exporters, but the subsidy would go only to governments and not be passed on to farmers. The transfer could be effected by maintaining prices under the Agreement as presently constituted but requiring that prices to growers be reduced; or by letting prices fall but compensating for the decline by import taxes, the proceeds of which would go to producer governments; or by letting prices fall and raising general tax revenues in the importing countries for compensation to exporters. Either of the first two methods would leave consumer prices and consumption unchanged; the third would raise consumption somewhat, but this advantage might be offset by the difficulty of raising taxes for aid to less developed countries on the scale required—in the vicinity of $1,000 million annually when prices had fallen far enough to reach equilibrium.[43]

A similar scheme has been put forward based on the stamps issued by the ICO for export control since 1967 and intended to avoid the difficulties of levying import duties or other taxes by importing countries for aid to exporters. The tax, designed ultimately to constitute the difference between prices to consumers and those received by growers, would come from the sale of the export control stamps by the ICO. Under this proposal the tax would be gradually raised until the producers' prices were just sufficient to call forth the amounts of coffee demanded at the prices set by the Agreement; the system of export quotas could then be eliminated. For this scheme to succeed in reducing capacity and for it to be acceptable to exporters, it would be necessary to ensure that the tax proceeds be used for the development of the coffee-growing countries and that neither those resources nor others be used to subsidize the coffee industry in any country. If the control of exports and relative prices for the different grades were to be abolished, it would also be necessary for the share of export income received by growers to be the same in all countries; thus national taxes and other policies would have to be changed, or the international tax would have to be adjusted for each country to take account of such policies.[44]

Any proposal of this kind is thus far unacceptable to the producing countries which, having achieved an international control scheme, are unwilling to modify or abandon it; they also fear the domestic political consequences of a fall in prices. In most countries, the burden would fall primarily on small farmers whose incomes are already quite low, and any reduction in their income would shrink the small national markets for other domestic produce and manu-

factures. The major importing countries have likewise shown no interest in a compensatory scheme with lower prices, because the subsidy would be more visible and politically more difficult to raise.[45] There is furthermore an economic objection to reaching balance by allowing prices to decline, based on the generally low flexibility of agriculture in the poorer countries and on the supply response of coffee growers in particular. Farmers whose incomes were declining might respond primarily by letting yields fall; they would be unlikely to uproot many trees for some years, until they believed the low prices to be permanent, and they would be quite unlikely to invest in raising yields. Thus much land would remain in coffee which could be transferred to other crops. For both political and economic reasons, therefore, the producing countries and the International Coffee Organization have ruled out price decreases by themselves as a means of reducing excess capacity.

Attention has been given rather to promoting consumption and to direct efforts to diversify the agricultural sector in exporting countries. The former is partly a matter of propaganda, spokesmen for producers always maintaining that coffee consumption is too low. It is true, however, that in response to the high prices of 1954, per capita consumption fell in several importing countries, and that the taste for weaker coffee became relatively permanent. Promotion for stronger coffee, and advertising to protect coffee from competing beverages, may therefore be effective and may already have contributed to a slight rise in per capita use. There is also, in most importing countries, a considerable share of the population which does not regularly drink coffee at all.[46] The second point, diversification, has been primarily a national effort, but in November 1965 the ICO reached an agreement with the International Bank for Reconstruction and Development and the Food and Agriculture Organization of the United Nations to study the needs and possibilities for replacing coffee with other crops in producing countries. The third ICA provides for a Diversification Fund to be financed by a 60-cent-per-bag levy on all coffee exported under the Agreement and by a share of the proceeds of exports in excess of quotas for which waivers are allowed. At current levels of exports the Fund would accumulate some $30 million annually from the levy, an amount which could have considerable impact in promoting diversification but which will not itself solve the problem of excess capacity in the life of the Agreement. Initial loans have been offered by the United States and may be given by other importing countries; the United States has agreed to contribute up to $30 million if other countries will con-

[43] The proposal is that of Rowe, *World's Coffee*, pp. 194-97. Rowe considers an import tax to compensate for falling prices as the best alternative to the original Coffee Study Group suggestion for a gradual price decline under international agreement.

[44] I. B. Kravis, "International Commodity Agreements: the Case of Coffee," pp. 312-16.

[45] The United States government maintains that by agreeing to support prices it has created the protection under which the producing countries can solve the problem of oversupply, and that no further action is necessary or feasible. This opinion was expressed by the USDA's Foreign Agricultural Service in communication over Rowe's proposal. The objection is substantially met by Kravis' proposal for an international tax.

[46] The PACB conducts surveys of coffee drinking in the United States each year, from which it is possible to estimate the average number of cups consumed per capita and the number of cups per pound of coffee. See *Annual Coffee Statistics*, "The United States Market."

tribute up to $15 million. The Fund will be able to use 20 percent of its resources without geographic restriction; the remainder must be spent in the country supplying the funds, so that resources must largely be distributed in proportion to exports rather than to excess capacity. A diversification scheme involving subsidies for destroying trees or for substituting other crops could of course be combined with an international tax or other mechanism for gradually reducing prices received by coffee growers: either approach to the problem would seem to be strengthened by the other, and in fact a portion of the proceeds from such a tax would provide ample finance for diversification.

National Diversification Programs

The greatest effort to replace coffee with other crops has been made in Brazil, the country with the largest surplus capacity.[47] The program is directed by the Grupo Ejecutivo de Racionalização da Cafeicultura (GERCA), organized in 1961 to effect a reduction in coffee area and capacity by paying subsidies to farmers to uproot trees and offering technical and financial assistance for converting the land to other uses. Particularly in areas where high-quality coffees are grown, such as the Mogiana district of São Paulo and parts of southern Minas Gerais, a subsidy was provided for replanting with high-yield varieties, to a maximum of one new tree for each four destroyed. Thus, while the principal goal was to reduce output, it was also intended to improve cultivation and yields and thereby decrease the land planted to coffee more than production. The targets chosen were net reductions of 1,500 million trees and of 360,000 tons; 720,000 tons of high-cost capacity were to be destroyed and half that amount replaced, to achieve an approximate balance between supplies and exports.[48]

Between 1960/61, when the coffee area of Brazil was at its maximum, and 1965/66, some 1,650 million trees (net) were uprooted, and the area in coffee was reduced by nearly 1.7 million hectares or one-third (see table 10-13). Most of the net reduction in capacity took place between 1961 and 1964, when prices to growers were extremely low and there was a great deal of spontaneous, unsubsidized uprooting; in fact, the GERCA subsidies applied to only 42 percent of the total. This spontaneous uprooting was also a response to severe frosts in Paraná in 1962 and 1963, which accounted for most of the reduction in that state. When prices rose following the establishment of the International Coffee Agreement, the subsidy was raised and a much greater share of uprooting came under the government scheme. However, the rise in prices and the erosion of the subsidies by inflation effectively ended the stimulus to up-

rooting in 1965, leaving exportable production only slightly less than in 1960/61. In 1966 a new scale of subsidies was established and the program revived, but little is known of its effect in the first year or two. Net destruction of capacity has been low in Paraná, which is a low-cost area with fewer opportunities for diversification, and in Minas Gerais and Espirito Santo, where replanting of high-quality trees has been extensive. In the minor producing states, chiefly in the northeast, over half the trees were destroyed. In the four main coffee states the age distribution of the trees changed only slightly, a reduction of 7 percent in the share over fifteen years of age being compensated by the same increase in the five-to-fifteen-year age group; the percentage of immature trees did not change. In São Paulo alone, however, there was a very large reduction in the number of trees over fifteen years old, contributing to the 40 percent total net decrease.[49] Yields in São Paulo should therefore increase appreciably in the next several years.

It was intended to replant 8 percent of the land cleared under GERCA subsidies with improved varieties of coffee, but less than 1 percent was so used. Nearly half the 770,000 hectares opened were turned to pasture, rather than the 25 percent forecast; conversion to pasture was especially high in Minas Gerais and Espirito Santo. Foodstuffs occupied one-third of the land and other crops, including a variety of cash crops, 17 percent. Much less land was devoted to oil-bearing crops and to planting of forest than was planned – 4 instead of 31 percent. In São Paulo the area in cotton shows the largest increase; it has also become the chief sugar-cane-growing state of Brazil. There and in Rio de Janeiro much land retired from coffee has been put to dairy pasture.[50]

A similar but more limited scheme is underway in Mexico, with the object less of reducing production than of raising yields so as to free land in coffee for other crops. The total coffee area of 300,000 hectares in 1960/61 is expected to fall to 240,000 hectares by 1972; yields have already risen notably, and it is hoped to reach an average of one ton per hectare by the end of the plan period. The 60,000 hectares cleared of coffee will be devoted, it is hoped, in about equal parts to rubber, pasture, and fruit growing, but a great variety of other crops are recommended. Rubber is especially important because Mexico currently imports about half its requirements; through 1964 it was the chief crop planted in former coffee areas. The plan is being carried out through credits and technical assistance; there are no subsidies for destroying coffee trees and no prohibitions on replanting or new planting.[51]

In the remaining Latin American producing countries there are no significant programs for diversification or re-

---

[47]The surplus is especially large if productive capacity about 1960 is compared to Brazil's export quotas since 1963, because Brazil has accepted a smaller share of the market than it could obtain under competition. Excess capacity is still considerable if measured by exportable production and exports prior to 1964, or by costs and yields in marginal producing areas.

[48]See PACB, *Annual Coffee Statistics*, 1961, pp. 18-19; Rowe, *World's Coffee*, pp. 60-61; and P. T. Knight, "The Critical Coffee Sector in Brazil: Potential Earnings from Diversification," paper prepared for the Policy Planning Division, Office of Program Coordination, AID, September 1966.

[49]Comparison of a rough estimate of age distribution in 1965/66 with more detailed information for 1960/61; see ICO, *Production Forecasts 1965-70. . .*, vol. II, pp. 11-12. No data are available for the smaller producing states.

[50]*Ibid.*, pp. 20-22, and Instituto Brasileiro de Geografía e Estatística/Conselho Nacional de Estatística, *Anuário Estatístico do Brasil*, various years.

[51]PACB, *Annual Coffee Statistics*, 1961, pp. 19-20; Cordera, "México en el Convenio Internacional del Café"; and ICO, *Production Forecasts 1965-70. . .*, vol. II, pp. 141-42.

duction of the area in coffee, although a study is being undertaken in Guatemala with the aid of the United Nations Special Fund. Some marginal areas have been cleared, as in Colombia and Ecuador, but in all cases the action of the government is limited to giving credits or other assistance to farmers wishing to plant new crops, and to reducing or eliminating the stimuli to coffee planting. In some instances governments have suspended credits for coffee, or delayed efforts to raise yields, but they have not acted to reduce prices to farmers as their excess capacity is relatively small. A partial exception to this is Costa Rica where, because of improved varieties and cultivation to raise yields, and of recovery from the effects of volcanic eruption in the early 1960s, production rose by 25 percent in 1965/66, 14 percent in 1966/67 and about 8 percent in 1967/68. The government responded by restricting credit for coffee production to the amount of the ICA quota and by forcing growers and processors to bear the storage costs of the surplus; efforts to export to new markets have also been intensified.[52]

The Statistical Outlook

For the major traditional markets the demand for coffee can be projected with reasonable assurance on the basis of estimated growth in population and income and assumptions about prices. The potential for changes in per capita consumption is considerable, but promotional campaigns and other influences are not generally expected to have much effect over the next several years. Outside the high-income countries of North America and Western Europe and such small traditional markets as the Latin American importers, it becomes more difficult to estimate future demand. In Africa, Asia, and Oceania no foreseeable change in consumption would have much impact on the world total, so the significant uncertainty attaches to the countries of southern Europe, to the United Kingdom, and to Japan — all areas where income is high enough to support a considerable demand and where per capita consumption has been growing rather rapidly.

FAO estimates that by 1975 the world's total demand for coffee will be between 4.7 and 4.9 million tons, an increase of about 30 percent from the level of the early 1960s. Of this amount some 1.3 million tons will be consumed in producing countries, chiefly in Latin America, and the remainder in importing nations.[53] Production of coffee is very much harder to estimate, because of the possibility of widespread destruction of capacity and the

opportunities for raising yields. Over the short period to 1975 new planting can essentially be ignored; it is not likely to be large in any case, and very little of it could come into production before the latter part of the decade. Future production is therefore estimated from present productive capacity, taking into account only the age distribution of trees in each producing area and the average yield for each area and age class. On this basis FAO estimates production in 1975 as some 5.6 to 5.7 million tons; because the possible range of output is so wide, only single estimates are given for each producer. Latin America's contribution would then be about 3.9 million tons, of which about 2.9 million would be available for export from the region. Africa's contributions would be 1.4 and 1.25 million tons, respectively. These projections imply a world surplus of between 750,000 and a million tons, or between two and three times the difference between exportable production and exports at the time the ICA came into operation. If supplies exceeded demand by these amounts in all years until 1975, stocks would by that time have reached some 10 million tons or more, an amount sufficient to strain the International Coffee Agreement severely.

These projections do not attempt to separate demand by type of coffee; it is assumed that the shares of the market held by milds, Brazils and robustas will vary little or not at all, with perhaps a further slight increase in demand for robustas. The efforts now being made by some arabica producers to raise quality and widen the difference in taste between their coffees and robustas may succeed in stopping or even reversing this trend within a decade or so. Relative productive capacity of the different types of coffee is approximately fixed, but relative exports may vary somewhat in response to demand and price changes or to pressure by the smaller producers for enlarged quotas if the surplus becomes burdensome. It is assumed that the general price level will be held within the limits set by the ICA, and that relative price levels will not vary appreciably.

It appears, therefore, that unless more drastic reductions in capacity are made — unless diversification is continued in Brazil and undertaken in other countries when supplies exceed export quotas — coffee will continue to be in surplus for another decade. Of all Latin America's major exports, it is the commodity whose future situation is most worrisome. Simply in order for export proceeds to grow at a modest pace — not over 2.5 percent annually — it will be necessary for the members of the ICA to maintain control despite the existence of very large stocks, to destroy a considerable amount of capacity, and to exercise great care over future planting and output if further difficulties are to be avoided. The experience of the last several years is cause for optimism on the first point, but it is too early to be sure of success on the second; until it is dealt with, even the short-term success will be uncertain.

[52] U.S. State Department Airgram A-421, 15 February 1967, San José, Costa Rica.

[53] FAO, *Agricultural Commodities — Projections for 1975 and 1985*, pp. 234, 240, 242.

CHAPTER 10 TABLES

TABLE 10–3. World Area Planted to Coffee, by Region and Type, circa 1963/64
(Thousands of hectares)

Country or Region and Type	Area	Country or Region and Type	Area
Latin America	7,267	Africa[d]	2,806
Unwashed Arabicas	4,523	Robustas[e]	2,081
Bolivia	13	Ivory Coast	568
Brazil	4,510	Angola	526
Mild Arabicas	2,744	Uganda	252
Colombia	810	Congo (Kinshasa)	186
Costa Rica	83	Malagasy Republic	185
Cuba	132	Cameroun	161
Dominican Republic	135	Guinea	55
Ecuador	150	Togo	43
El Salvador	147	Sierra Leone	51
Guatemala	187	Spanish Guinea	45
Haiti	182	Ghana	40
Honduras	106	Central African Republic	36
Mexico	285	Congo (Brazzaville)	15
Nicaragua	110	Gabon	8
Panama	27	Liberia	4
Paraguay	10	Dahomey	3
Peru	123	Nigeria	3
Venezuela	257		
		Unwashed Arabicas	
Other Western Hemisphere[a]	87	Ethiopia	445
Puerto Rico[b]	65		
Jamaica	15	Mild Arabicas[f]	252
Trinidad and Tobago	3	Kenya	82
Surinam	2	Tanzania	51
Guadeloupe	2	Burundi	26
		Rwanda	17
Asia and Oceania[c]	438	Mozambique	2
Indonesia	244	Malawi	1
India	129		
Philippines	42	World Total	10,598
Vietnam	9	Mild Arabicas[g]	3,188
Malaya	7	Unwashed Arabicas[h]	4,968
Thailand	4	Robustas[j]	2,401
Hawaii	2	Others[k]	32

Sources: World Coffee and Tea, "Guide to Latin American Coffees," April 1965, and "Guide to African/Asian Coffees," June 1965. Coffee Study Group, *The World Coffee Problem*, Part II, *Coffee in the World Economy* (Washington, 1961), pp. 41 ff. ICO, *Production Forecasts 1965-70 and their Implications* (London, 1965), vol. II.

[a]All mild arabica coffees, except Trinidad and Tobago (robusta) and Surinam (liberica).

[b]Area harvested. Total area reported as 77,000 hectares in 1959.

[c]Includes Ceylon, Laos, and Taiwan; total coffee area estimated as 1,000 hectares. Excludes Yemen, for which no information is available.

[d]Includes Comores, and São Tomé and Principe; total coffee area estimated as 1,000 hectares. Total for Africa exceeds the sum of robusta and arabica.

[e]Approximate total area of robusta plantings in all African countries, as reported or as calculated from shares of total crop, robustas, and arabicas (assuming equal yields for the two kinds of coffee in each country which produces both). Countries listed are those producing predominantly robusta coffee.

[f]Approximate total area of mild arabica plantings in all African countries. Those listed produce predominantly arabica coffee.

[g]Includes 110,000 hectares in Asia and Oceania: 24,400 in Indonesia, 75,500 in India, 5,500 in the Philippines, and 2,200 hectares in Vietnam, plus the total coffee area in Hawaii and Taiwan.

[h]Bolivia, Brazil, and Ethiopia.

[j]Includes 316,700 hectares in Asia and Oceania.

[k]Approximate total area of liberica plantings: includes 22,000 hectares in Spanish Guinea, 1,000 in Liberia, 1,800 in Surinam, and some 7,000 in Indonesia.

TABLE 10-4. World Coffee Production,[a] 1929/30 to 1967
(*Thousands of metric tons*)

Country or Region	Average 1929/30-1933/34	Average 1934/35-1938/39	Average 1939/40-1943/44	Average 1944/45-1948/49	1949/50	1950/51	1951/52	1952/53	1953/54	1954/55	1955/56	1956/57
Latin America	1,988.7	1,995.1	1,623.6	1,597.2	1,821.6	1,784.0	1,899.3	1,980.9	1,975.3	1,924.1	2,209.7	1,882.3
Brazil	1,442.9	1,347.8	974.5	885.1	1,068.3	1,071.4	1,080.2	1,125.4	1,110.6	1,037.0	1,370.0	979.3
Colombia	211.9	251.2	306.2	351.9	337.8	302.3	402.7	384.3	403.1	377.0	335.1	365.2
Costa Rica	22.5	23.2	23.5	21.9	23.5	20.1	21.1	33.0	22.8	33.8	25.3	33.8
Cuba	23.6	32.1	28.1	30.1	27.4	32.8	28.4	27.0	35.2	38.0	53.6	36.6
Dominican Republic	15.9	23.2	20.1	20.0	28.0	25.0	28.9	26.5	31.6	26.3	32.6	31.9
Ecuador	8.0	13.7	12.3	14.1	11.6	23.4	21.6	24.2	22.6	35.2	22.6	29.4
El Salvador	62.0	63.9	65.1	64.4	59.8	71.7	58.9	78.1	59.9	76.7	72.6	91.3
Guatemala	49.0	54.9	52.6	55.3	55.6	54.2	63.0	58.3	62.8	65.3	66.5	73.6
Haiti	50.6	26.9	19.0	30.6	40.0	38.3	35.0	37.0	43.8	30.7	40.8	28.0
Honduras	1.6	1.3	1.6	4.5	12.5	13.9	14.0	15.1	18.0	16.3	15.5	17.9
Mexico	39.1	51.8	54.7	55.8	65.6	68.1	70.8	87.7	84.9	93.0	88.3	97.3
Nicaragua	13.2	15.3	14.0	12.3	19.8	18.7	20.7	17.1	20.3	26.6	24.3	23.2
Panama	0.8	1.2	1.0	2.5	2.8	2.8	2.9	2.3	2.8	2.8	2.1	2.4
Peru	2.6	3.0	3.2	4.3	5.5	5.6	5.8	8.9	9.6	9.6	12.1	12.0
Venezuela	56.4	58.2	43.6	42.4	50.7	34.0	43.3	54.0	44.8	53.4	46.3	58.0
Other countries[b]	7.5	7.6	5.1	2.4	2.7	1.7	2.1	2.0	2.5	2.3	2.0	2.4
Africa	72.9	128.6	172.0	215.2	243.5	266.5	307.0	330.3	358.3	418.0	486.9	495.7
Angola	10.8	16.7	18.8	40.0	50.0	50.0	55.0	57.4	75.0	57.9	79.0	81.0
Belgian Congo	6.6	18.8	29.8	28.5	28.7	34.6	35.1	34.8	33.5	33.5	49.2	53.0
Ethiopia	16.0	14.2	7.4	18.2	22.0	22.0	25.0	43.1	40.0	45.7	54.0	51.9
French West Africa	1.0	7.9	21.6	37.3	45.3	42.6	61.7	55.6	71.3	89.8	113.8	95.7
French Equatorial Africa	0.1	1.3	2.4	3.7	4.5	5.5	4.2	3.8	2.7	5.4	3.7	6.5
Kenya	13.0	18.0	14.6	10.1	6.4	9.9	16.4	12.5	11.5	24.3	24.3	18.8
Madagascar	10.1	21.7	33.8	23.9	29.2	30.7	26.1	41.3	44.7	44.0	54.6	57.0
Uganda	3.5	10.6	18.8	24.6	24.1	33.4	42.3	37.2	35.7	64.5	49.3	62.1
Asia	128.2	146.3	69.8	50.5	64.2	78.7	77.5	82.8	106.7	98.9	114.7	114.3
India	15.8	16.5	16.5	20.6	20.8	24.6	24.7	22.0	25.7	26.6	34.4	35.8
Indonesia	102.7	119.0	38.8	14.6	29.1	39.1	39.1	46.8	61.7	57.0	63.4	59.1
Oceania[c]	5.1	5.6	4.6	5.2	3.5	5.3	4.9	5.6	5.7	5.9	7.1	6.4
World Total	2,204	2,268	1,884	1,883	2,138	2,147	2,307	2,413	2,467	2,463	2,841	2,514
Shares (%) in world total of												
Latin America	90.0	87.9	86.4	85.0	85.4	83.0	82.4	82.2	80.0	78.1	77.8	75.0
Brazil	64.4	59.3	51.7	46.8	50.0	50.0	46.9	46.6	45.0	42.0	48.2	39.0
Other	25.6	28.4	34.7	38.1	35.4	33.0	35.5	35.6	35.0	36.1	29.6	36.0
Africa	3.2	5.7	9.2	11.4	11.4	12.4	13.3	13.7	14.5	16.9	17.1	19.7

TABLE 10-4 – Continued

Country or Region	1957/58	1958/59	1960	1961	1962	1963	1964	1965	1966	1967
Latin America	2,473.7	2,732.6	2,945.0	3,447.7	3,431.4	2,919.1	2,274.8	3,138.8	2,611.0	2,750.0
Brazil	1,409.3	1,695.8	1,796.6	2,228.7	2,190.3	1,650.5	1,042.0	1,831.8	1,365.6	1,397.9
Colombia	468.4	462.0	462.0	468.0	468.0	492.0	450.6	492.0	405.1	474.0
Costa Rica	45.6	51.4	69.9	61.6	54.4	60.7	49.5	61.5	72.9	76.8
Cuba	43.6	29.5	42.0	37.0	58.0	28.5	36.0	27.6	27.0	27.0
Dominican Republic	35.8	32.4	35.4	36.1	34.1	41.4	40.5	36.9	30.3	38.1
Ecuador	30.4	32.3	35.2	53.5	55.5	42.8	50.1	66.2	74.4	67.0
El Salvador	81.3	92.8	93.7	122.7	96.6	121.9	123.0	109.2	123.0	138.0
Guatemala	81.0	84.0	98.7	100.5	108.0	105.0	97.8	123.0	100.2	108.0
Haiti	42.0	27.0	26.2	43.5	35.4	31.8	33.0	34.5	27.9	30.0
Honduras	18.6	18.2	24.0	21.2	27.6	28.6	28.8	35.0	20.4	28.8
Mexico	121.9	97.2	124.3	126.6	139.8	141.8	144.8	159.0	185.0	180.0
Nicaragua	21.8	21.0	23.5	22.7	27.7	29.5	31.4	27.9	28.8	33.0
Panama	2.7	3.8	4.1	5.1	4.4	4.5	4.4	4.4	5.1	5.3
Peru	18.3	21.3	32.5	42.6	45.0	48.7	52.7	48.3	54.0	51.6
Venezuela	50.3	61.8	55.1	57.0	54.2	60.7	56.1	54.4	61.0	61.8
Other countries[d]	2.7	2.1		4.8	6.0	7.9	9.3	10.2	9.2	9.8
Africa	527.2	620.0	817.5	753.8	933.9	1,027.5	1,014.8	1,184.7	1,036.5	1,145.0
Angola	77.1	87.9	166.2	168.6	185.0	168.0	186.0	205.0	198.0	204.0
Belgian Congo	43.1	53.8	54.0	54.0	66.0	66.0	57.8	59.3	54.8	60.7
Ethiopia	57.1	57.1	66.0	130.0	132.0	134.0	136.0	138.0	150.0	146.0
French West Africa	110.0	158.5[e]	187.6	186.3[e]	198.9[e]	176.8[e]	254.6[e]	279.5[e]	273.0[e]	237.0[e]
French Equatorial Africa	5.0	7.0	8.5	9.3	7.5	8.6	10.8	13.4	15.6	16.1
Kenya	21.2	23.8	37.2	19.6	26.8	28.7	23.8	26.0	24.4	28.0
Madagascar	48.0	45.6	50.5	44.5	61.0	51.5	51.2	55.0	58.0	58.0
Uganda	79.2	84.3	118.7	95.5	120.2	146.6	186.2	219.7	170.0	185.6
Asia	127.5	132.7	210.0	206.8	209.8	244.1	211.8	222.8	234.0	288.0
India	40.3	45.9	69.0	68.0	45.7	56.7	70.0	61.6	63.4	78.0
Indonesia	65.4	65.0	93.8	78.3	99.1	121.0	74.0	88.0	85.0	120.0
Oceania	6.5	9.0	4.0	4.4	5.3	6.4	6.4	6.4	6.4	6.4
World Total	3,143	3,516	3,980	4,423	4,588	4,205	3,516	4,560	3,843	4,190
Shares (%) in world total of										
Latin America	78.5	77.8	73.9	77.9	74.7	69.4	64.6	68.8	67.6	65.6
Brazil	44.8	48.3	45.2	50.3	47.7	39.2	29.6	40.1	35.5	33.3
Other	33.7	29.5	28.7	27.6	27.0	30.2	35.0	28.7	32.1	32.3
Africa	16.8	17.7	20.5	17.0	20.3	24.4	28.8	25.9	26.1	27.3

Sources: 1929/30-1956/57 – FAO, *The World Coffee Economy,* Commodity Bulletin no. 33, 1961. 1957/58-1967 – FAO, *Production Yearbook.*

[a] Total production, or total amount of coffee harvested, as estimated by the FAO; includes domestic consumption and exportable production (exports plus net change in stocks).

[b] Bolivia, Paraguay, and the Guianas. The other Western Hemisphere producers not included in Latin America are included in the world total.

[c] Includes Hawaii.

[d] Bolivia and Paraguay only; other Western Hemisphere producers included in world total.

[e] Ivory Coast only; other producers in former French West Africa included in African total production.

TABLE 10–5. World Coffee Consumption, Averages, 1936-38, 1950-52, 1962-64, and 1964-66
(Thousands of metric tons, and kilograms per capita)

Country or Region	1936-38 Total	1936-38 Per Capita[a]	1950-52 Total	1950-52 Per Capita[b]	1962-64 Total	1962-64 Per Capita[c]	1964-66 Total	1964-66 Per Capita
IMPORTING COUNTRIES (Net Imports)[d]								
Total	1,638		1,837		2,876		2,819	
United States	816.3	6.1	1,173.5	8.0	1,426.4	7.8	1,326.3	6.8
Canada	18.5	1.4	40.7		75.3	4.0	74.6	3.8
Western Europe	663.5	2.2	501.5	1.6	1,123.1	3.3	1,142.2	6.3
Belgium	47.9	5.7	51.8	6.8	57.9	6.0	63.6	6.5
France	186.0	4.4	153.6	3.1	193.2	4.5	225.4	4.8
Germany	176.7	2.5	41.2	0.6	242.6	4.1	270.8	4.8
Italy	35.2	0.9	55.7	1.1	115.9	2.3	121.3	2.4
Netherlands	37.7	4.2	18.1	2.0	74.0	5.9	84.1	6.8
Denmark	30.2	7.5	17.5	3.8	52.0	10.6	50.3	10.6
Finland	22.9	5.7	17.2	3.4	43.1	9.0	44.5	9.7
Norway	17.3	6.1	17.4	4.8	32.6	8.9	32.3	8.7
Spain	13.9[e]	1.0[f]	5.5	0.2	35.1	1.7	43.9	1.4
Sweden	48.9	7.7	41.1	5.3	87.8	11.3	93.4	12.1
Switzerland	15.3	3.8	21.1	4.5	33.7	5.7	40.3	6.8
United Kingdom	14.3	0.3	40.7	0.8	74.6	1.4	72.3	1.7
Eastern Europe	24.6	0.4	2.9		79.3	0.3	83.4	0.5
Czechoslovakia	11.3	0.7	1.7		8.4	0.7	8.9	0.8
East Germany			0.5		27.7	1.5	30.1	1.3
Soviet Union	1.1	0.2			25.6	0.1	28.1	0.2
Africa[g]	52.6		52.8		70.2	1.0	78.3	2.0
Algeria	15.2		20.1		27.8	2.5	25.4	2.3
South Africa	14.8	1.5	13.5		13.7	1.0	11.0	0.6
Asia	30.0		23.2		64.1	0.3	73.2	0.5
Japan	6.3		0.8		19.1	0.2	28.9	0.3
Turkey	5.3	0.3	6.6		(h)	0.03	(h)	0.05
Oceania	2.1		3.3		(h)	2.2	(h)	3.2
Latin America	30.3	1.5	35.2	1.4	37.4	1.1	41.3	1.6
Argentina	24.2	1.7	27.1	1.6	29.9	1.4	32.9	1.5
Chile	3.4	0.7	4.9	0.8	5.1	1.0	8.2	1.0
Uruguay	2.4	1.2	3.0	1.2	2.2	0.8	2.2	0.8
PRODUCING COUNTRIES (Estimated Domestic Consumption)[j]								
Total	250-300		450-500		800		975	
Latin America[k]			385	3.0	670	3.5	856	3.6
Bolivia					2.6[m]	0.7	2.8	0.8
Brazil			240	4.6	420	5.4	497	6.1
Colombia			37	3.2	60	3.6	66	3.7
Costa Rica			3.4	4.2	7.8	6.0	9.9	6.9
Cuba			32.8	6.0	28.5	3.9	33.3	4.4
Dominican Republic			6.3	3.0	9.0	2.7	9.9	2.8
Ecuador			2.1	0.7	10.5	2.2	23.3	4.5
El Salvador			6.0	3.2	6.9	2.6	16.7	5.7
Guatemala			9.0	3.2	12.6	3.1	13.2	3.0
Haiti			9.0	2.7	9.9	2.2	9.7	2.1
Honduras			2.5	1.8	4.5	2.1	5.8	2.5
Mexico			12.0	0.5	60.0	1.5	69.8	1.6
Nicaragua			2.7	2.5	2.7	1.7	4.3	2.8
Panama					3.0	2.6	3.7	3.1
Peru			4.5	0.5	11.1	0.9	14.3	1.2
Venezuela			15.0	3.0	29.7	3.7	38.3	4.4
Africa					60	0.4	100.6[g]	0.5
Ethiopia					49.8[n]		66.0	2.7
Malagasy Republic					5-6		10	1.6
Asia and Oceania[p]					76.0	0.1	83.4	0.8
India					34.5	0.1	38.2	0.8
Philippines					40.6	0.5	43.3	1.3
World Total	1,900		2,100		3,700		3,794	
North America	834.8	5.7	1,214.2	7.6	1,501.7	7.4	1,400.9	6.5
Western Europe	663.5	2.2	501.5	1.6	1,123.1	3.3	1,142.2	6.3
Eastern Europe	24.6	0.4	2.9		79.3	0.3	83.4	0.5
Africa					130	0.6	178.8	0.9
Asia and Oceania					140	0.1	156.6	0.1
Latin America			420	2.7	710	3.2	878	1.5

Sources: FAO, *World Coffee Economy*, pp. 19-24, 49-52. Pan American Coffee Bureau, *Annual Coffee Statistics*, 1963, 1964, 1965, 1966, and 1967. *Coffee Annual* (G. G. Paton, 1964). *World Coffee and Tea*, April and June 1965. FAS, *Foreign Agricultural Crops and Markets*. FAO, *Agricultural Commodities – Projections for 1970* (Rome, 1962), pp. II-44 ff and A-1 ff. ECLA, *Boletín Económico de América Latina*, vol. VII, no. 1 (Santiago: October, 1962), pp. 6-7 (Latin American population estimates). FAO, *Production Yearbook, 1967*. FAO, *Trade Yearbook, 1967*.

[a]1934-38 average, importing countries.
[b]1949-51 average.
[c]1962-63 average.
[d]Net imports of green coffee only; excludes net trade in roasted, ground and soluble coffee.
[e]1936 imports only.
[f]1931-35 average.
[g]Importing countries only: North Africa and the Republic of South Africa.
[h]Included with Asia.
[j]FAS estimates for Latin America, 1950 and 1963; *World Coffee and Tea*, June 1965, estimates for Africa and Asia.
[k]Approximate sum of countries listed; consumption in Paraguay is negligible.
[m]1961 only.
[n]*World Coffee and Tea*; consumption, as measured by the difference between total and exportable production, is only 15-20,000 metric tons.
[p]Excludes Indonesia, for which consumption is not reported.
[q]OAMCAF countries only.

TABLE 10–6. New York Spot Coffee Prices,[a] 1925-1967
  (U.S. cents per pound)

Year	Brazil Santos No. 4	Colombia Manizales		Year	Brazil Santos No. 4	Colombia Manizales
1925	24.2	27.9		1938	7.8	11.0
1926	22.1	28.5		1939	7.5	11.6
1927	18.5	25.1		1940	7.2	8.3
1928	23.2	27.3		1941	11.4	15.0
1929	22.1	22.8		1942	13.4	15.9
1930	13.2	18.0		1943	13.4	15.9
1931	8.8	16.3		1944	13.4	15.9
1932	10.7	11.9		1945	13.6	15.9
1933	9.2	10.8		1946	18.7	21.0
1934	11.2	14.3		1947	26.4	30.1
1935	8.9	10.7		1948	27.1	32.5
1936	9.3	11.0		1949	32.8	37.4
1937	11.1	12.0				

Year	Colombia Manizales	El Salvador Washed High Grown	Guatemala Good Washed	Mexico Coatepec	Average, Mild Arabicas[b]
1950	53.25	52.98	51.37	52.60	52.79
1951	58.74	57.71	55.35	57.34	57.77
1952	57.01	56.42	54.83	56.15	56.41
1953	59.82	56.41[c]	55.21[c]	57.74[c]	58.05
1954	80.02	72.00[d]	68.33	78.37	76.46
1955	64.57	61.25	58.38	60.12	62.25
1956	73.97	68.84	67.56	70.88	71.53
1957	63.94	62.82	61.70	60.87	62.87
1958	52.34[e]	50.85	49.11	49.93[f]	51.04
1959	45.22	42.18[g]	41.98	42.89	43.95

Year	Brazil Santos No. 4	Angola Ambriz	Ivory Coast Robusta Courant	Uganda Native Standard	Average, Robustas[h]	Average, All Coffees[j]
1950	50.52	41.53		40.10	40.82	48.04
1951	54.20	47.56		46.85	47.21	53.06
1952	54.04	46.17		44.03	45.10	51.85
1953	57.93	49.22		47.59	48.41	54.80
1954	78.71	63.02		57.86	60.44	71.87
1955	57.09	45.23		38.41	41.82	53.72
1956	58.10	38.35	31.03	33.59	34.32	54.65
1957	56.92	40.22	34.17	34.65	36.35	52.05
1958	48.41	40.25[k]	36.49	37.57	38.10	45.85
1959	36.97	30.60	27.01	28.72	28.78	36.57

Year	Colombia MAMS	El Salvador Washed High Grown	Guatemala Prime Washed	Mexico Prime Washed	Average, Mild Arabicas[b]
1960	44.89	42.20	41.33	41.61	43.19
1961	43.62	38.58	37.55	37.53	40.65
1962	40.77	36.54	35.83	35.87	38.31
1963	39.55	36.11	35.40	35.56	37.51
1964	48.80	47.48	47.16	47.16	47.99
1965	48.49	45.68	45.51	45.54	47.01
1966	47.43	42.63	42.25	42.41	44.92
1967	41.94	39.61	39.23	39.36	40.64

Year	Brazil Santos No. 4	Angola Ambriz No. 2AA	Ivory Coast Superior No. 2	Uganda Native Standard	Average, Robustas[h]	Average, All Coffees[j]
1960	36.60	25.27	19.45	20.18	21.60	33.80
1961	36.01	19.93	18.67	18.48	19.03	31.90
1962	33.96	21.55	20.23[m]	20.63	20.80	31.02
1963	34.11	28.73	28.21	27.86	28.27	33.30
1964	46.66	36.38	35.78	35.56	35.92	43.52
1965	44.71	31.59	29.40	31.12	30.70	40.81
1966	40.83	33.98		33.61	33.80[n]	40.10
1967	37.82	33.83		33.51	33.67[n]	37.49

Sources: 1925-49 – FAO, *World Coffee Economy*, p. 73. 1950-67 – PACB, *Annual Coffee Statistics.*

[a]Annual average; quotations ordinarily represent offers for Thursday only. Prices include all marketing charges and are ex-warehouse.

[b]Arithmetic average of the prices of El Salvador Central Standard (not washed high grown), Guatemala Prime Washed, Mexico Prime Washed, averaged together with the price of Colombia MAMS.

[c]January-July average.

[d]Quotation for 12 December 1954 only.

[e]Beginning 1958, MAMS grade rather than Manizales.

[f]Beginning 1958, prime washed grade rather than washed Coatepec.

[g]January-March average. Average quotation for December was 41.34 cents per pound.

[h]Arithmetic average of the prices of Angola Ambriz No. 2AA, Ivory Coast Superior No. 2, Uganda Native Standard.

[j]Arithmetic average of the price of Santos No. 4 (Brazil) and the average prices of mild arabicas and robustas. This is the price used in 1965-1966 by the International Coffee Organization in setting quotas. See Resolution 67, approved at the seventh plenary meeting, 19 March 1965; reprinted in *Annual Coffee Statistics*, 1964, p. 11.

[k]Beginning 1958, Ambriz No. 2AA grade.

[m]January-August average.

[n]Average of Angola Ambriz No. 2AA and Uganda Native Standard.

TABLE 10–7. Coffee in Latin American Agriculture, circa 1963/64
(Thousands of hectares planted to coffee and percentage of total land in crops)

Country	Coffee Area[a]	Share of Cropland[b]	Rank	Crops with Larger Areas
Bolivia	13	0.4	(c)	maize, potatoes, wheat, rice
Brazil	4,510	24	2nd	maize
Colombia	810	16	1st	(d)
Costa Rica	83	14	1st	(d)
Cuba	132	4	3rd	sugar, maize
Dominican Republic	135	20	2nd	sugar
Ecuador	150	7	4th	maize, cocoa, bananas
El Salvador	147	22	2nd	maize
Guatemala	187	12	2nd	maize
Haiti	182	15	3rd	maize, sorghum
Honduras	106	12	2nd	maize
Mexico	285	2	5th	maize, wheat, beans, cotton
Nicaragua	110	10	2nd	cotton
Panama	27	7	4th[e]	rice, maize, bananas
Paraguay	10	2	5th	maize, cotton, sugar, beans
Peru	123	6	5th	maize, cotton, potatoes, wheat
Venezuela	257	11	2nd	maize
Latin America	7,267	7[f]	3rd	maize, wheat

Sources: ICO, *Production Forecasts 1965-70...*, vol. II. CIDA, *Inventory of Information Basic to the Planning of Agricultural Development in Latin America* (Washington, 1963-65). FAO, *Production Yearbook, 1964.*

[a]Total area in coffee, including immature trees.
[b]Area in coffee as a percentage of total area in annual or perennial crops, excluding natural pasture but including grains planted for pasture in some countries.

[c]Not available; 5th or lower.
[d]The area in maize is only slightly less than that in coffee.
[e]The area in cocoa is approximately equal to that in coffee.
[f]Includes the area in crops in Argentina, Chile, and Uruguay.

TABLE 10–8. Structure of the Latin American Coffee Industry, circa 1960
(Number and size in hectares of farms growing coffee)

Country and Date	Farm Size[a] (hectares)	Number of Farms	Average Coffee Area[b] (hectares)	Percentage of Farms	Percentage of Coffee Area[c]
Brazil 1961/62	Total	545,000	8.3	100	100
Paraná	0-50	22,500		37.5	
	50-150	19,500		32.5	
	150-250	10,500		17.5	
	over 250	7,500		12.5	
	Total	60,000	24.7	100	100
São Paulo	0-10[d,j]	60,000	2.8[e]	57	10[f]
	10-40	36,000	16.6	34	35
	40-81	6,000	51.0	6	18
	81-162	2,000	127	2	15
	over 162	1,000	374	1	22
	Total	105,000	16.2	100	100
Minas Gerais	Total	90,000	8.4	100	100
Espírito Santo	Total	46,000	7.7	100	100

SUMMARY: Brazil, four major coffee producing states
(Percentage of coffee area)

Farm Size	Paraná	São Paulo	Minas Gerais	Espírito Santo	Total[g]
0-9 ha.	12.0%	13.6%	24.1%	16.2%	15.0%
9-70	53.6	55.0	55.6	69.3	57.0
70-140	13.5	14.2	9.0	6.3	12.4
140-280	10.5	9.8	6.8	3.8	9.1
over 280	10.4	7.4	4.5	4.4	6.5

Country and Date	Farm Size[a] (hectares)	Number of Farms	Average Coffee Area[b] (hectares)	Percentage of Farms	Percentage of Coffee Area[c]
Colombia 1955/56 and 1963	0-1[h]	77,200	0.7	36	6
	1-10	123,700	3.8	58	56
	10-50	11,400	22.1	5	30
	over 50	530	127	1	8
	Total	213,000	3.9	100	100
Costa Rica 1955	0.7-3.5[h]	19,049	1.8	87	60
	3.5-6.9	1,775		8	
	7.0-10.4	449	4.7	2	20
	10.5-13.9	193		1	
	over 14	521	21.6	2	20
	Total	21,987	2.6	100	100
	0-0.7[j]	5,000	2.1		
Cuba 1959/60	Total	23,000	5.8	100	100

TABLE 10–8 – Continued

Country and Date	Farm Size[a] (hectares)	Number of Farms	Average Coffee Area[b] (hectares)	Percentage of Farms	Percentage of Coffee Area[c]
Dominican Republic 1959/60	0-1	24,369	0.6	67.3	18.8
	1-5	9,955	3.0	27.4	40.3
	5-10	1,406	9.2	3.9	17.2
	10-50	435	23.8	1.2	13.8
	over 50	51	145	0.1	9.9
	Total	36,216	2	100	100
Ecuador 1954	0-1	1,901	0.4	3.6	0.6
	1-5	17,393	0.9	34.5	14.4
	5-10	9,279	1.5	18.4	13.3
	10-20	7,858	2.5	15.6	18.0
	20-50	8,477	2.8	16.8	22.4
	50-100	3,259	3.8	6.4	11.6
	over 100	2,537	9.9	4.7	19.7
	Total	50,704	2.0	100	100
El Salvador 1958 and 1961	0-10	29,549	0.7	82	14[f]
	10-50	5,045	7.6	14	27
	over 50	1,441	58.0	4	59
	Total	36,035	3.9	100	100
Guatemala 1960	0-1	20,700	0.3	67	3
	1-5	7,600	3.6	25	15
	5-15	1,580	9.2	5	8
	15-50	540	47	1.7	14
	50-200	470	105	1.5	27
	over 200	110	546	0.4	33
	Total	31,000	6.0	100	100
Haiti 1959/60	0-0.6	60,000		40	
	0.6-2.5	30,000		20	
	2.5-5.0	45,000		30	
	over 5.0	15,000		10	
	Total	150,000	1.2	100	
Honduras 1962/63	0-5	10,840	0.8	27.1	8.5
	5-50	24,007	2.4	60.1	55.2
	50-500	4,759	7.3	11.8	32.9
	over 500	394	9.2	1.0	3.4
	Total	40,000	2.6	100	100
Mexico 1961/62	0-10	29,750		85	
	10-50	3,500		10	
	over 50	1,750		5	
	Total	35,000	8.6	100	
Nicaragua[k] 1963/64	0-5			50	
	over 50			50	
	Total	15-18,000	7	100	
Panama 1959/60 and 1950	0-10	23,800		99.2	40[f]
	over 10	200		0.8	60
	Total	24,000[k]	1	100	100
Peru 1962/63	0-25	48,000	2.1	99.94	94
	over 25	30	200	0.06	6
	Total	48,030	2.4	100	100
Venezuela 1961/62	0-5				35
	5-10				15
	10-50				20
	over 50				30
	Total	84,580	3.0		100
Latin America[m]	Total	1,360,000	5.3	99-100	99.5

Sources: *World Coffee and Tea*, "Guide to Latin American Coffees." Coffee Study Group, *World Coffee Problem, Part II*. J. W. F. Rowe, *The World's Coffee* (London: H. M. Stationery Office, 1963), pp. 34, 44, 64, 89-90. ECLA/FAO, *Coffee in Latin America, I: Colombia and El Salvador* (1958), and *II: São Paulo* (1960). ICO, *Production Forecasts 1965-70...*, vol. II.

[a]Except as indicated, total farm area, including crops other than coffee, pasture and woodland.
[b]Average area planted to coffee, not average size of farm on which coffee is grown.
[c]Percentage of total coffee area in country accounted for by farms in size class indicated.
[d]Estimated from data in number of trees and average density of trees per hectare.
[e]Assumes yield does not vary with size.
[f]Percentage of total coffee production, rather than area.
[g]Total for four principal coffee growing states; data not available for other states or for Brazil as a whole.
[h]Area devoted to coffee rather than total farm area.
[j]Farms with less than 1 manzana (0.7 hectare) in coffee excluded from the 1955 census. Average coffee area including these farms is 2.1 rather than 2.6 hectares.
[k]Includes 5,000 commercial farms and 19,000 of noncommercial size.
[m]Excludes Bolivia and Paraguay, for which no data are available.

TABLE 10–9. Coffee Yields[a] in Latin America, 1950, 1958/59, and Early 1960s
(Kilograms of green coffee per hectare)

Country	1950[b]	1958/59[c]	1960/61	1961/62	1962/63	1963/64
Bolivia			520		400-450[d]	
Brazil	397	392	345	406	327	345
Colombia	570	587	598	646	632	
Costa Rica	373	748	729	801	679	756
Cuba		246	318	363	295	216
Dominican Republic	415				300-330[d]	
Ecuador	321			336[d]		
El Salvador	640	787	715	1,002	805	1,002
Guatemala	364	539	637	648	720	
Haiti	230					217
Honduras	205	217	193	274	267	
Mexico	351	324	414	441	464	611
Nicaragua	275	254				350
Panama	163	221	235	267	230	241
Paraguay						240
Peru		425	481	485	482	490
Venezuela		193			190	
Latin America[e]	390				390	

Sources: ICO, *Production Forecasts 1965-70...,* vol. II. See also tables 10-1 and 10-2.

[a]Calculated on total area in coffee, including land planted but not yet in production.

[b]Approximate date; all data refer to one or more years in the period 1948/49 to 1951/52.

[c]1959/60 or 1957/58 for some countries.
[d]Estimated average yield, years indicated.
[e]Approximate average yield of all coffee area.

TABLE 10–10. Green Coffee Imports into the United States and Europe, Averages, 1936-38, 1950-52, 1962-64, and 1966-67
(Thousands of metric tons)

Origin of Imports	Total Exports[a]	Imports[b]	Share of Imports[c] (%)	Share of Exports[d] (%)
I. UNITED STATES MARKET		*1936-38 average*		
Latin America	1,407.4	785.2	90.6	55.9
Brazil	870.4	471.4	52.5	54.3
Colombia	245.9	186.0	22.7	75.7
World Total	1,663.6	820.0	100.0	49.3
		1950-52 average		
Latin America	1,532.6	1,116.3	94.5	72.9
Brazil	940.1	612.2	51.7	65.1
Colombia	286.1	255.0	21.6	89.1
World Total	1,866.1	1,181.3	100.0	63.5
		1962-64 average		
Latin America	1,923.3	1,071.2	75.4	55.8
Brazil	1,016.8	511.7	35.9	50.4
Colombia	382.1	239.9	16.8	63.0
World Total	2,840.9	1,426.4	100.0	50.2
		1966-67 average		
Latin America	1,931.3	889.2	68.3	46.0
Brazil	1,030.8	419.9	32.3	40.7
Colombia	349.8	172.0	13.2	49.2
World Total	3,038.2	1,301.1	100.0	42.8
II. EUROPEAN MARKET		*1936-38 average*		
Latin America	1,407.4	521.1[e]	78.7	37.1
Brazil	870.4	320.8[f]	48.5	36.9
Colombia	245.9	50.1[f]	7.6	20.4
World Total	1,663.6	663.5[g]	100.0	39.8
		1950-52 average		
Latin America	1,532.6	332.7[e]	66.5	21.7
Brazil	940.1	266.8[f]	53.3	28.4
Colombia	286.1	21.4[f]	4.3	7.5
World Total	1,866.1	501.5[g]	100.0	26.8
		1962-64 average		
Latin America	1,923.3	734.3[h]	65.2	38.1
Brazil	1,016.8	411.5[f]	36.6	40.5
Colombia	382.1	125.6[f]	11.2	32.9
World Total	2,840.9	1,123.1[g]	100.0	39.6
		1966-67 average		
Latin America	1,931.3	764.0[h]	60.0	40.0
Brazil	1,030.8	414.2[f]	33.2	40.2
Colombia	349.8	142.8[f]	11.2	40.8
World Total	3,038.2	1,273.9[g]	100.0	41.9

Sources: 1936-38 and 1950-52 – FAO, *World Coffee Economy*, pp. 56-72. 1962-67 – PACB, *Annual Coffee Statistics.*

[a]Total exports of region indicated to all destinations.
[b]United States imports from region.
[c]Imports from region as percentage of total imports
[d]Imports from region as percentage of total exports from region.
[e]Exports to Western Europe from all Latin American countries except Bolivia, Cuba, Haiti, Panama, and Paraguay, plus imports from Haiti of Belgium-Luxemburg, France, Germany, Italy, Netherlands, Spain, Sweden, and Switzerland.
[f]Exports to Western Europe.
[g]Total Latin American exports to Western Europe.
[h]Total imports into Western Europe.

TABLE 10-11. Latin American Coffee Exports by Destination,[a] 1950-1966
(Thousands of metric tons and millions of U.S. dollars)[b]

Exporter and Destination	1950	1951	1952	1953	1954	1955	1956	1957	1958	1959	1960	1961	1962	1963	1964	1965	1966
Brazil																	
United States	890.1	981.5	949.3	933.7	655.1	821.7	1,008.3	859.2	773.7	1,063.4	1,009.1	1,018.2	982.6	1,170.9	896.9	809.9	1,021.8
Europe	584.8	630.3	564.8	542.9	340.3	469.9	612.2	518.4	429.0	612.5	562.9	515.5	489.5	523.0	380.9	361.7	417.5
Africa	230.1	272.9	311.2	312.5	255.4	284.8	333.0	268.4	264.1	383.7	374.5	424.2	416.4	546.8	411.9	380.7	473.6
Asia and Oceania	15.9	11.6	10.1	9.8	6.8	8.1	6.7	8.9	16.2	17.2	8.6	6.7	5.1	21.1	20.8	4.5	11.0
Latin America	6.6	16.0	15.4	7.7	2.8	6.3	6.7	6.9	3.6	6.3	11.4	19.7	18.2	20.8	32.3	10.1	61.3
Argentina	39.1	34.7	32.1	44.1	42.3	41.1	35.0	42.7	49.1	26.2	32.9	32.9	33.2	37.8	34.3	37.1	43.0
Other	30.3	28.5	25.4	34.1	33.7	29.3	27.5	35.2	41.4	14.6	27.8	25.6	23.3	25.7	26.9	28.0	33.6
Value	849.8	1,039.3	1,026.3	1,090.2	948.1	843.9	1,029.8	845.5	688.1	774.0	712.8	710.4	642.6	747.0	759.7	707.4	764.0
Share Total Exports (%)	63.1	59.2	73.0	71.0	60.7	59.2	69.5	60.6	55.3	60.3	56.2	50.5	53.0	53.1	53.0	44.3	43.8
Colombia																	
United States	268.3	287.6	301.9	397.9	344.1	352.0	304.2	289.4	326.4	384.8	356.3	339.1	393.7	368.0	384.7	338.1	333.9
Europe	243.1	258.7	267.2	345.8	297.7	287.7	255.5	241.9	255.3	292.0	261.0	237.0	259.7	229.0	223.3	182.2	182.8
Other	17.8	21.9	24.7	40.1	40.7	58.4	39.1	40.9	64.6	81.7	84.7	91.1	121.6	125.2	148.4	143.8	154.1
Value	307.4	356.2	379.9	492.2	550.2	487.3	412.8	421.1	391.0	395.0	333.0	307.8	343.1	303.0	393.6	343.6	328.0
Share Total Exports (%)	77.6	77.0	80.3	82.4	83.7	84.0	68.9	81.0	84.8	83.5	71.3	70.9	74.0	67.9	72.0	63.8	64.4
Costa Rica																	
United States	18.7	18.6	20.0	27.9	21.9	27.8	23.6	28.1	46.3	42.7	45.9	50.1	54.1	55.7	50.5	47.6	54.0
Europe	12.0	14.5	12.6	15.9	8.7	8.9	5.2	10.1	18.7	13.6	16.4	21.7	21.1	19.1	16.3	19.0	14.7
Other	6.4	3.5	6.9	11.6	12.9	18.6	18.0	17.6	26.4	28.4	28.9	27.9	32.3	35.8	33.4	27.8	37.8
Value	18.1	19.6	24.3	34.8	35.1	37.4	33.8	39.1	49.9	40.4	44.7	43.3	47.2	45.8	47.9	46.4	52.6
Share Total Exports (%)	32.4	31.0	33.3	43.5	41.3	46.0	50.5	47.1	54.2	52.5	52.0	51.5	50.8	48.2	42.4	41.7	38.8
Cuba																	
United States						4.5	20.8[c]	11.4	7.2	3.1	5.4	5.1	8.3	0.6			
Europe						3.9	12.3	8.3	4.8	1.9	3.4	4.1	5.2	0.6			
Other						0.6	8.3	3.1	2.3	1.2	4.6		5.6	0.5			
Value						4.2	21.7	12.5	7.1	2.5	0.7	0.6	1.1	0.1			
Share Total Exports (%)						0.7	3.1	1.5	0.9	0.4							
Dominican Republic																	
United States	13.4	17.4[d]	26.5	22.4	24.0	24.5	26.4	21.7	25.8	21.7	28.8	20.1	29.2	27.4	34.4	22.5	25.1
Europe	10.3	12.4	22.6	15.8	20.1	21.1	21.2	19.8	21.4	17.5	24.8	16.9	25.0	23.9	31.0	17.8	19.5
Other	2.3	1.5	3.5	4.0	3.4	3.1	4.4	1.6	3.2	3.9	3.7	3.0	4.1	3.4	2.9	3.3	5.2
Value	12.7	17.6	26.4	24.6	31.5	28.4	31.8	25.1	23.7	17.5	22.5	14.4	19.9	18.5	30.2	21.1	21.0
Share Total Exports (%)	14.6	14.8	23.0	23.4	26.2	24.7	25.4	15.1	18.5	13.5	12.9	10.0	11.5	10.7	17.0	16.8	15.3
Ecuador																	
United States	20.1	16.4	20.4	18.7	21.0	23.1	24.5	28.2	30.2	23.8	31.3	22.9	33.1	30.0	25.0	45.8	43.7
Europe	11.4	8.3	9.9	13.9	15.6	15.3	13.6	18.1	21.9	15.0	19.1	11.5	22.4	17.8	14.0	30.8	25.3
Other	7.8	4.5	9.8	3.7	4.7	6.4	9.4	8.3	7.0	7.9	11.8	10.9	10.0	11.9	10.6	14.6	13.3
Value	18.3	14.9	20.4	18.9	27.3	22.8	29.0	28.9	26.3	17.6	11.8	14.3	20.9	18.4	21.7	14.6	13.3
Share Total Exports (%)	24.7	21.0	20.2	20.6	22.0	20.0	25.1	21.7	19.8	12.6	14.5	11.2	14.6	12.3	14.1	37.2	32.2
El Salvador																	
United States	66.4	63.6	65.9	69.0	59.7	71.1	67.9	76.2	83.9	80.7	70.7	85.8	88.7	95.1	105.3	99.3	97.2
Europe	62.3	59.2	60.3	64.2	47.6	51.6	37.7	39.9	45.4	37.4	22.3	40.0	40.2	40.2	41.3	44.3	39.8
Other	3.2	2.5	4.5	3.9	11.4	18.4	29.6	35.6	38.1	42.9	47.8	45.0	46.5	47.1	60.0	52.4	55.0
Value	61.8	77.9	77.6	76.6	92.0	91.5	87.4	109.8	78.5	71.3	72.6	70.2	74.2	74.5	90.8	96.2	89.0
Share Total Exports (%)	91.0	91.7	89.4	86.3	87.6	85.5	77.3	79.5	67.6	63.0	62.0	59.0	54.5	48.4	51.0	50.9	46.7
Guatemala																	
United States	55.1	50.9	60.4	69.5	53.1	58.9	61.6	62.3	72.3	83.1	79.8	75.3	93.1	100.0	86.8	90.6	111.8
Europe	50.4	47.3	52.9	60.0	42.3	48.8	48.2	47.6	51.9	56.4	49.5	47.5	44.8	66.5	53.4	50.9	62.9
Other	4.0	2.7	6.8	8.7	10.3	9.4	12.6	14.0	19.6	26.2	29.8	27.1	43.7	32.8	32.6	29.2	36.6
Value	52.8	58.5	71.6	68.2	74.2	75.5	89.2	82.3	83.7	74.4	70.8	64.0	74.0	76.2	71.2	86.1	100.1
Share Total Exports (%)	66.8	69.5	75.4	69.0	70.6	71.2	72.0	72.0	77.5	68.9	60.5	56.6	63.3	50.7	43.0	49.0	44.4
Haiti																	
United States	23.4	25.0	32.5	22.3	31.0	21.3	27.5	18.9	32.8	21.9	23.7	20.9	30.8	23.4	22.8	21.0	21.0
Europe	10.2	11.1	13.8	6.3	11.5	5.4	4.9	4.0	13.4	5.5	3.6	5.1	8.4	6.7	6.9	6.6	5.1
Other	12.6	12.8	18.3	15.3	19.1	15.3	22.2	14.5	19.6	16.0	19.8	15.7	22.1	16.4	15.7	17.3	15.8
Value	20.6	26.1	34.1	25.0	43.0	23.9	27.2	21.0	29.1	15.3	17.3	13.5	20.6	16.2	19.4	19.8	17.3
Share Total Exports (%)	66.8	51.2	65.6	66.0	78.3	66.5	65.0	61.7	74.7	54.5	52.5	42.0	49.2	39.4	48.5	53.3	50.5
Honduras																	
United States	6.8[e]	8.2[e]	8.3	11.2	9.2	8.9	11.7[d]	10.4	11.4	15.3	15.5	12.6	16.0	20.1	18.5	25.0	22.6
Europe	5.8	7.5	7.6	10.5	8.8	8.1	8.4	7.2	9.1	9.0	5.2	5.1	9.0	13.1	11.9	17.3	14.7
Other		0.1	0.2	0.7	0.4	0.8	3.2	3.2	2.2	5.6	5.2	3.6	6.6	6.9	6.7	7.7	7.9
Value	3.2	8.3	8.7	11.2	14.0	8.5	13.3	12.0	10.9	11.7	11.8	9.0	11.5	14.0	17.0	22.2	19.9
Share Total Exports (%)	5.5	12.5	13.8	16.6	25.6	17.0	18.3	18.5	15.6	17.0	18.8	12.4	14.1	16.8	17.9	17.4	13.8

	1	2	3	4	5	6	7	8	9	10	11	12	13	14	15	16	17
Mexico	46.0	51.9[d]	52.2	76.0	66.7	82.0	75.6	86.9	78.7	74.4	83.0	89.0	87.5	72.0	106.4	79.6	92.2
United States	44.3	49.4	47.6	69.0	60.2	71.9	65.3	75.0	70.4	63.0	67.7	80.0	78.3	56.1	89.3	68.0	65.0
Europe	1.1	2.0	4.0	6.5	6.2	9.7	10.0	11.9	7.9	10.5	14.4	7.9	8.0	14.3	15.0	9.6	21.4
Value	38.6	46.9	47.0	91.2	108.9	106.3	111.1	113.7	82.7	65.4	71.6	70.4	47.2	49.3	101.8	75.7	82.3
Share Total Exports (%)	7.4	7.5	7.2	15.6	16.6	13.2	12.6	15.6	11.2	8.7	9.4	8.5	5.1	5.0	9.6	6.3	6.8
Nicaragua	21.0	16.1	18.2	18.8	17.1	22.8	16.9	22.0	22.9	16.4	21.7	21.0	20.3	28.0	25.8	30.5	25.3
United States	19.7	14.8	16.7	15.9	13.8	17.0	12.6	14.7	9.0	8.9	11.3	12.5	11.3	16.7	11.3	17.1	9.4
Europe	1.0	0.8	1.2	2.7	3.2	5.6	4.4	7.0	7.3	7.4	10.2	8.4	8.9	11.3	14.3	13.2	15.8
Value	17.3	18.5	20.7	21.3	25.1	27.9	23.2	28.5	24.2	13.9	19.2	17.6	15.4	17.5	24.3	28.3	23.7
Share Total Exports (%)	64.3	50.0	49.4	46.5	45.7	38.7	39.9	44.5	38.0	21.3	34.4	28.9	18.8	17.5	20.6	18.3	15.8
Panama						0.5	0.5	1.0	1.3	0.3	1.6	1.5	0.5	1.4	1.5	1.4	2.7
United States						0.5	0.5			0.2	1.1	1.3	0.3	1.4	0.1	0.7	1.5
Europe								0.8	0.8		0.4	0.2		1.5	1.4	1.5	1.3
Value						1.5		1.4			2.7	2.9	4.1	0.9	0.8	1.1	2.2
Share Total Exports (%)																	
Peru	0.8[d]	2.2[d]	2.7	4.7	4.6	6.8	7.1	11.1	16.5	19.9	26.4	34.0	37.4	40.1	41.7	32.9	35.2
United States	0.7	1.7	1.4	3.2	3.2	3.2	3.8	5.1	12.3	13.8	19.9	23.4	28.1	29.6	33.8	26.0	27.2
Europe	0.2	0.5	1.4	1.2	1.2	3.5	3.2	5.0	3.8	5.4	5.9	9.6	8.3	9.3	7.0	6.0	6.5
Value	0.8	2.3	2.8	5.3	7.2	8.0	8.9	12.9	15.1	15.5	18.5	22.8	24.2	25.6	37.5	28.9	29.4
Share Total Exports (%)	0.4	0.9	1.2	2.4	2.9	3.0	2.9	4.0	5.4	5.0	4.3	4.6	4.5	4.7	5.6	4.3	3.7
Venezuela	18.5	18.5	29.9	44.0	44.0	29.8	23.2	27.6	28.4	24.5	24.3	19.1	19.6	23.4	19.6	17.9	18.2
United States	16.6	15.6	27.6	38.8	20.2	24.3	18.6	23.1	30.4	21.5	21.1	15.4	15.7	18.9	15.7	14.8	15.8
Europe	1.5	2.7	2.0	4.8	5.2	4.8	4.4	4.1	4.2	2.9	3.2	3.6	4.4	4.4	3.8	3.1	2.3
Value	16.6	19.1	34.1	45.1	33.5	35.3	33.3	38.4	39.5	20.9	18.9	14.3	17.2	17.2	17.8	17.4	17.1
Share Total Exports (%)	1.4	1.4	2.4	3.1	2.0	1.9	1.7	1.6	1.0	0.9	0.8	0.6	0.7	0.7	0.6		0.6
Latin America	1,448.7	1,557.9	1,588.1	1,716.2	1,555.3	1,699.3	1,553.4	1,563.7	1,880.5	1,823.3	1,818.7	1,895.6	2,055.1	1,819.8	1,665.2	1,904.7	
United States	1,071.6	1,131.0	1,105.0	1,202.0	1,037.1	1,119.9	1,033.2	1,000.0	1,170.9	1,090.0	1,040.4	1,053.3	1,060.6	929.7	857.1	881.3	
Canada	24.2	26.3	29.2	32.2	19.6	26.4	23.3	19.9	28.6	26.8	29.2	33.2	34.6	28.8	28.5	24.5	
Europe	288.0	328.2	394.8	415.7	372.9	501.7	435.2	469.7	625.5	643.1	681.0	738.7	866.5	763.6	709.4	846.5	
Africa	16.3	11.7	10.2	10.0	6.9	16.7	11.5	16.7	17.6	10.8	9.1	5.6	21.4	21.0	9.4	18.2	
Asia and Oceania	7.1	16.4	16.1	9.1	3.8	7.5	6.6	7.5	10.4	16.4	24.4	27.7	33.2	39.6	20.8	84.6	
Latin America[f]	41.4	44.1	32.6	46.5	43.0	49.8	43.3	49.8	27.4	36.3	34.4	35.6	38.7	37.2	40.0	49.6	
Argentina	30.3	28.5	25.4	34.1	33.7	41.4	35.2	41.4	14.7	28.0	25.1	24.0	26.1	28.9	30.3	39.4	
Chile	5.9	4.1	4.0	6.3	5.4	4.8	5.2	4.8	6.5	5.3	6.4	8.8	6.6	6.1	9.0	9.2	
Uruguay	3.3	2.5	2.5	3.7	3.3	3.1	2.5	3.1	4.8	1.2	1.9	1.5	1.5	1.0	0.5	0.8	
Value	1,418.0	1,705.3	1,774.0	2,004.8	1,990.0	1,952.5	1,790.8	1,549.8	1,539.9	1,443.3	1,381.0	1,386.1	1,423.9	1,634.3	1,531.2	1,602.3	
Share Total Exports (%) for exporters[g]	29.6	29.1	31.8	35.8	32.6	28.6	26.0	23.6	23.4	21.5	19.8	19.3	18.8	19.8	19.3	19.9	
for region[h]	20.9	21.9	25.2	26.4	25.3	22.6	20.7	18.9	18.6	16.8	15.9	15.1	14.6	15.4	15.2	15.8	

Sources: PACB, *Annual Coffee Statistics*. IMF, *International Financial Statistics*.

[a] Europe includes Eastern Europe, and in some years includes the Soviet Union.

[b] Value of coffee exports as reported by PACB; share in total exports calculated from total export value as reported by the IMF. Shares of coffee in total exports are not the same as reported by PACB.

[c] Excludes a small amount of roasted coffee.

[d] Prorated on the basis of data for less than 12 months.

[e] Exports for fiscal, not calendar, year.

[f] Includes British West Indies, 1950 and 1960-66; French West Indies, 1960 and 1964; Surinam, 1961-64; Puerto Rico, 1956 and 1963-64; and British Honduras, Barbados, Bahamas, Aruba, and Curaçao, 1964.

[g] Total Latin American exports of coffee as a percentage of total exports of all countries exporting coffee (those listed).

[h] Total Latin American exports of coffee as a percentage of total Latin American exports, including exports of Argentina, Bolivia, Chile, Paraguay, and Uruguay.

TABLE 10–12. Exportable Production,[a] Exports and Price[b] of Brazilian Coffee, 1925-1967
(Thousands of metric tons, and U.S. cents per pound)

Year	Production	Exports	Price	Year	Production	Exports	Price
1925	875	808.9	24.2	1946	736	930.3	18.7
1926	908	825.1	22.1	1947	838	889.8	26.4
1927	951	906.9	18.5	1948	816	1,049.5	27.1
1928	1,627	832.9	23.2	1949	948	1,162.1	32.8
1929	817	856.9	22.1	1950	858	890.1	50.5
1930	1,694	917.3	13.2	1951	942	981.5	54.2
1931	994	1,071.1	8.8	1952	862	949.3	54.0
1932	1,704	716.1	10.7	1953	912	933.5	57.9
1933	1,191	927.6	9.2	1954	858	657.0	78.7
1934	1,778	848.8	11.2	1955	852	821.7	57.1
1935	1,089	919.7	8.9	1956	1,278	1,008.3	58.1
1936	1,256	851.2	9.3	1957	702	859.2	56.9
1937	1,582	727.4	11.1	1958	1,248	773.7	48.4
1938	1,412	1,026.8	7.8	1959	1,560	1,063.4	37.0
1939	1,395	989.9	7.5	1960	2,220	1,009.1	36.6
1940	1,147	722.7	7.2	1961	1,320	1,018.2	36.0
1941	987	663.1	11.4	1962	1,680	982.6	34.0
1942	948	436.8	13.4	1963	1,200	1,170.9	34.1
1943	817	606.7	13.4	1964	1,272	896.9	46.7
1944	730	813.3	13.4	1965	180	809.9	44.7
1945	498	850.3	13.6	1966	1,812	1,021.8	40.8
				1967	720	1,039.9	37.8

Sources: FAO, *World Coffee Economy*, pp. 45-46, 55-56. Rowe, *World's Coffee*, pp. 13-14, 17-18, 30, 33. PACB, *Annual Coffee Statistics, 1950-67.*

[a]Exportable production: total production less actual domestic consumption. The difference between exportable production and exports is the amount of coffee added to stocks, destroyed, or otherwise not consumed.
[b]Price: Santos No. 4, in New York.

TABLE 10–13. Coffee Trees and Coffee Area in Brazil, 1960/61 and 1965/66
(Millions of trees and thousands of hectares)

State	Number of Trees		Net Uprooting, 1961-64			
	1960/61	1965/66	Total[a]	GERCA[b]	Other[c]	Percentage
Paraná	1,281	935	342	121	221	27
São Paulo	1,360	800	560	241	319	41
Minas Gerais	877	655	213	194	19	25
Espírito Santo	626	500	124	72	52	20
Other States	692	290	402	58	344	58
Total Brazil (Trees)	4,836	3,180	1,641	686	955	34
Total Area	5,205	3,545	1,660	772	888[d]	32

Source: ICO, *Production Forecasts 1965-70...*, vol. II, pp. 9-19.
[a]Excludes some net elimination of trees during 1965 in Paraná (6 million), Minas Gerais (9 million), and Espírito Santo (12 million).
[b]Uprooting subsidized by GERCA, less subsidized replanting.
[c]Net spontaneous (unsubsidized) uprooting of trees.
[d]Estimated from total reduction in coffee area, less area cleared under GERCA subsidy by the end of 1964.

Chapter 11

COCOA

Cocoa is produced in fifteen Latin American countries, of which seven account for the bulk of the region's output. Some 740,000 hectares are devoted to cocoa cultivation, yielding slightly less than 300,000 tons of beans per year. About 60 percent of this amount is exported directly, and a further small tonnage after processing. The revenues from cocoa were generally between $100 million and $200 million annually in the 1950s—some 2 percent of Latin America's foreign exchange earnings; in recent years they have dropped to $100 million or less. In no country is cocoa the leading export commodity, but in smaller areas, such as the state of Bahía in Brazil, it is the principal cash crop and source of government revenue.

World Production, Consumption, and Trade

Cocoa is native to the western hemisphere, having originated in the upper Amazon basin or in the nearby valleys of Venezuela, Colombia, or Ecuador. It was cultivated in Mexico and Central America before the European conquest, and became the region's first agricultural export. From the mid-sixteenth century onward, cocoa was planted throughout Latin America and the islands of the Caribbean. Venezuela was established as the chief producer by 1650, and held that position for nearly two centuries. In the 1830s Ecuador, which had been the second largest producer, displaced Venezuela. Trinidad was the third supplier throughout this period. Although the volume of production was small, cocoa accounted for a larger share of exports in several countries than at present; for a long period it was the chief export of Venezuela and of Ecuador. Only high-grade cocoa, known as "fine" or "flavor" cocoa, was produced; yields were quite low, so that cocoa and chocolate were high-priced luxuries.[1]

Between the 1880s and 1920s Latin America's dominance of the world cocoa industry was ended by a massive shift of cultivation to West Africa. Cocoa growing also spread to Asia and Oceania, but these areas have never accounted for more than 3 percent of world output. About 1879 cocoa was introduced into Ghana. By the turn of the century African production, chiefly from São Tomé and Principe, was one-sixth of the world total of 100,000 tons; Latin America produced 60 percent, and the western hemisphere 80 percent, of the total. In 1911 Ghana became the world's leading exporter; by 1926 that country supplied half of world exports. Nigeria, the Ivory Coast and Cameroon also became major producers. Latin America's share dropped to 30 percent and has never since exceeded 40 percent of world output; its share of exports is still less, 15 to 20 percent.

Latin America and Africa compete in the production of several resource products, notably coffee, petroleum and copper. Cocoa is the only agricultural product for which Africa has shown a clear advantage in costs, without the benefit of protective tariffs or quotas in Europe (which apply to coffee and bananas) or of actions by Latin American producers to restrict supplies (as in the case of coffee). The west coast of tropical Africa is as well suited for cocoa growing as the producing areas of Latin America, and offers abundant land and labor. Although cocoa undergoes a great deal of processing, very little of this need be done by the grower; cultivation does not require either much capital or a high degree of skill. Initially, the African cocoa zone was also free of diseases. These conditions made cocoa an ideal cash crop for African peasant farmers; because they could operate without hired labor they were also less influenced by price changes than the estate growers who accounted for much of Latin American output. The cost of production was further reduced by a shift to the higher yielding, hardier varieties which produce lower grade or "base" cocoa. The same factors led to the establishment of cocoa in Brazil. The total geographical shift of cultivation was much greater than the transfer from Latin America as a whole to Africa. Brazil displaced Venezuela to become the second largest producer before 1900; by the 1920s it accounted for more than half the regional total.[2]

Note: Tables 11-1 to 11-6 appear on pp. 336–44.

[1] Cocoa is distinguished by grade, by type, and by place of origin. Since the species names are sometimes ambiguous, and since most trees are hybrids, only grade and origin are normally used to describe cocoa in trade. For a discussion of nomenclature, see V. D. Wickizer, *Coffee, Tea and Cocoa* (Stanford: Food Research Institute, 1951), pp. 286-88.

[2] For a fuller description of the reasons for this transfer, see FAO Commodity Bulletin no. 27, *Cacao: A Review of Current Trends in*

Despite a premium in price for flavor cocoas, the established Latin American producers were unable to compete, and there was a great exodus from cocoa growing. The shift was facilitated by the high degree of substitutability between cocoa and other crops that had become or were becoming important exports: cocoa was displaced by coffee in Guatemala, by coffee and bananas in Costa Rica, by several crops in the Dominican Republic. Large areas of plantation were simply abandoned in Bolivia, Ecuador, and Venezuela, or turned to pasture, as in Colombia. Yields declined on the remaining plantations as planting ceased and disease-control measures were discontinued: fully 70 percent of Ecuador's capacity was destroyed by disease between 1910 and 1940. The cost of raising yields by planting hardier trees was apparently too high for the gain anticipated; although there had been a change from the native trees to somewhat higher yielding hybrids during the nineteenth century, in no country was there a further shift to the production of low-grade cocoa.

In several respects cocoa is much like coffee, and the production and trade of the two products could be described in the same terms. Both are produced primarily in Latin America and Africa and consumed in North America and Europe. In both cases production for export was first established in Latin America and spread to Africa in the twentieth century. Both are tree crops requiring several years to come into production, with consequent inelasticity of supply and variation of yields with age. There are distinct varieties of cocoa, differing in quality, cost, and markets; as with coffee, the finest grades are grown chiefly in Latin America. The problems of balancing supply and demand, and the efforts to deal with those problems, are also similar for the two commodities.

There are also some significant differences. Cocoa is subject to much more processing than coffee, and is combined with a variety of other ingredients in manufactured foodstuffs: the demand for cocoa beans is therefore somewhat price elastic. The elasticity of supply is also greater than for coffee, primarily because cocoa is subject to several severe diseases and pests.[3] The cost of control measures is usually so high that the extent of control, and therefore the yield, depends heavily on cocoa prices. The response is generally asymmetric: it is easier to let yields decline than to raise them by greater expenditure. The tendency is especially pronounced for those diseases or pests which kill the tree instead of merely destroying the fruit. This asymmetry helps explain the decline of production in Latin America early in this century—without which large surpluses might have been created—and the difficulties of raising output after World War II, which resulted in scarcity followed by

oversupply. These factors account for the different experiences of the cocoa and coffee industries in the 1930s and 1940s; in the 1950s and early 1960s the two commodities went through very similar cycles. So far as Latin America is concerned, the experiences also differ because, while the region has an advantage in the production of high-grade cocoa, the preference for this quality has almost disappeared, causing a greater shift of cultivation to Africa than occurred in the case of coffee.

It appears that below some minimum income level cocoa is regarded as a luxury and is seldom consumed.[4] Consumption in Africa and Asia is therefore extremely low, being negligible even in the producing zone of West Africa: the two producing regions together account for only about 1 percent of world use (see table 11-1). As income rises, demand for cocoa rises quite sharply, and then more slowly. Price elasticity is greatest at low incomes, and declines as income rises; however, it does not appear to fall to zero for even the richest countries, so that demand does not become so fixed or saturated as for coffee.[5] Latin America is the only producing area with high enough income to consume much cocoa; the producing countries absorb about one-fifth of their production, or 6 percent of world consumption, in the form of cocoa products. Latin America is also the only cocoa-growing area to have a sizable processing industry; total grindings of beans greatly exceed consumption of products. The importing countries of Africa, Asia and Oceania together absorb some 6 percent of the world's cocoa. Latin American importers take 1 percent. Another 10 percent is imported by the Communist countries of Europe; cocoa is the only tropical agricultural product normally consumed in significant amounts by them. The remainder, some 80 percent of world supplies, is taken by the importing nations of North America and Western Europe. Cocoa products are exported in large volume from Europe and in lesser amounts from Latin America and Africa; North America takes the bulk of product imports, with Asia, Oceania, and the Communist countries absorbing the rest.

Until late in the nineteenth century Europe absorbed virtually all the world's cocoa; even there the high price kept per capita consumption very low. By the turn of the century, Europe's share had declined to slightly more than three-fourths, the United Kingdom, France, and Germany taking about equal amounts; the United States accounted for nearly all the remainder. In the next two decades production quadrupled, and cocoa became an article of mass consumption in all high-income countries. By 1921 the expansion of output in Africa reduced the real price of cocoa to less than one-third its 1900 level.[6] In the next twenty years, production grew less than half as rapidly, reaching a total of over 700,000 tons in the late 1930s. Output declined during World War II, and then began rising again, to

---

Production, Price and Consumption (1955). See also D. H. Urquhart, *Cocoa* (London: Longmans, 1961), pp. 2 and 197 ff.

[3]Several diseases destroy the trees: of these the most serious are witches' broom and monilia, two fungus diseases, in the Western Hemisphere, and swollen shoot, a virus disease, in Africa. Much cocoa is also lost to pod rot, a fungus which attacks the fruit. Various insects cause great destruction of the fruit and sometimes kill the trees, as do some non-insect pests. Losses of half the crop are common in all producing areas.

[4]This hypothesis is put forward in FAO, *Cacao. . .*, p. 60.

[5]See FAO, *Agricultural Commodities – Projections for 1970* (1964), pp. 11-38 and A-12, for estimates of price and income elasticity of demand in various countries in 1957-59.

[6]Unit value of U.S. imports, deflated by the wholesale price index. See FAO, *Cacao. . .*, p. 93.

900,000 tons in the late 1950s and to over 1 million tons in recent years (see table 11-2).

Demand contracted sharply at the start of the Depression, and prices, which had stopped falling about 1921, dropped 70 percent between 1927 and 1932. Thereafter the price remained low for nearly a decade, while consumption recovered (see table 11-3). There had been a fairly high rate of planting in the 1920s in Brazil and in Africa, so that output continued to grow during the 1930s; but the response of demand to low prices and the recovery of incomes enabled the increased production to be sold without a further fall in price and without any destruction of stocks or trees. At least in Latin America the crisis was much less severe than for coffee. There had been no new planting except in Brazil; the contraction merely accelerated the exodus from cocoa growing brought on by a long period of falling prices. Brazil experienced some difficulties, because production had been expanding into marginal areas and many growers were deeply in debt. A crash in prices resulted in the formation of the Instituto do Cacau de Bahía in 1931, which extended technical and financial assistance to growers and improved the transport facilities of the cocoa zone. There was, however, no government support of prices or accumulation of stocks.

The world cocoa market was much more disrupted by World War II than by the Depression. With the disappearance of the European market except for the United Kingdom, demand contracted sharply; at the same time it became very difficult to ship or to store the available supplies of cocoa. These problems led to widespread government intervention, although there were no international agreements for dealing with the crisis. Prices were controlled in the remaining markets, and consumption was also affected by rationing of cocoa and of products combined with it in confections. The West African Cocoa (Produce) Control Board was created to control the cocoa trade of British Africa. Since not all supplies could be shipped, about one-fifth of production during the war was destroyed. The Instituto do Cacau took over all purchases and exports in Bahía. The United States bought directly about 60 percent of Brazil's 1943/44 crop, and also encouraged the expansion of the local processing industry.[7] The price and export controls were maintained in most exporting countries for several years after the war; price controls were lifted earlier in importing countries.

The war had two immediate effects on the Latin American industry. Brazil developed a sizable processing capacity and shifted part of its trade to cocoa products. The same change took place to a lesser degree in other countries. The war also hastened the shift in tastes to base-grade cocoa, so that the premium for flavor grade, which had been about 40 percent in the 1930s, dropped to 20 percent or less (see table 11-3). For the world industry, the greatest effect of the war was the initiation of a period of scarcity which lasted for more than a decade. The wartime shortage had made chocolate a much-prized good, especially in Europe, so that when controls were lifted demand exceeded all expectations. There were no stocks to cushion the shortage, and prices rose very sharply in 1947-48. There was a drop in 1949, but prices remained fairly high throughout the 1950s, with peaks caused by bad harvests in 1954 and 1958. The marketing boards in Africa did not raise prices to growers for some years; there was therefore no immediate stimulus to new planting. When planting did begin, in the early 1950s, the gain was at first offset by losses from swollen shoot and insect pests. By 1957, when it was finally contained, the disease had destroyed 63 million trees in Ghana alone. These problems stimulated the growth of output in Latin America, from about 260,000 tons in the early 1950s to 300,000 tons at the end of the decade, and led to a slight increase in the region's share of world output (see table 11-2). This increase was not enough to end the shortage: the decline in premiums for flavor cocoa, and the rise in costs associated with the growth of other employments for land and labor, made Latin American growers relatively unresponsive. From 1958 onward, African production expanded more rapidly, and at the same time Brazilian output declined as a result of droughts and difficulties in rehabilitating plantations. Latin America's share of world production dropped to one-fourth or less, while the total increased rapidly.

The world scarcity of cocoa ended abruptly in 1960; high prices in the 1950s had slowed the growth of consumption, and planting accelerated in 1954, while control of diseases and pests raised yields and made much of the tree stock superfluous. By 1961-62 prices had fallen to less than two-thirds the 1947-60 average level, excluding the peak years. Cocoa producers suddenly found themselves in the position which coffee growers have occupied since 1958; even with no new planting, the surplus could be expected to grow worse for a few years as trees matured. Until the postwar scarcity developed, all the increase in cocoa yields had come from adopting hardier species, and costs had otherwise been reduced only by opening new areas. There had been little research on cocoa, and no great change in techniques of cultivation. Research centers were opened in both Latin America and Africa in the 1940s, and most producer governments undertook to foster improved techniques among their growers. In Africa such campaigns brought disease damage under control in the late 1950s. The emergence of a surplus and consequent fall in prices had slowed the pace of adoption of measures to raise yields and lower costs, which would require a reduction in the amount of land and labor devoted to cocoa growing. The attention of governments was turned instead to means of coping with the surplus.

The sharp, brief price decline of 1949 aroused the interest of producers in some form of cooperation to control the market, but the high prices of the next several years dispelled any sense of urgency. In 1958, when prices were high and increasing capacity made a decline appear imminent, preliminary negotiations for an international agreement were begun among a number of producing and consuming countries. In September 1963 a United Nations Conference on Cocoa was held, but ended in disagreement over the level at which prices should be set. Producers, benefitting from a price increase during 1963, were unwilling to accept

---

[7] See Wickizer, *Coffee, Tea and Cocoa*, chap. 15, "Impact of the War on Cocoa."

the low 1961-62 level, while consumers held more than a five months' supply of stocks and were not alarmed at the prospect of some restriction of supplies by exporters. The failure of the conference, and a decline of prices in 1964, led six of the major producers—Brazil, Ghana, Nigeria, the Ivory Coast, Cameroon and Togo—to form the Cocoa Producers Alliance, in an effort to deal with the oversupply without the cooperation of consumers. In September of that year the members, which together produce over 80 percent of the world's cocoa, signed an International Cocoa Agreement. The agreement set a target price of 23.75 cents per pound, well below the level of the 1950s but above the price of 1961-62 and 1964; export quotas were set for members, with allowances for the exports of nonmembers. Quotas were reduced, and in October 1964 sales were temporarily suspended; but as no means were available to finance the accumulation of stocks, sales were resumed without controls in early 1966. In Brazil exports were even subsidized in mid-1965 to assure continued income to producers.[8] In late 1964 a small amount of stock was destroyed in Ghana, but none of these measures was enough to raise spot prices (although futures prices were briefly affected). No one producer dominates the market sufficiently to control prices by its own actions, and the Alliance members have not been able to act together sufficiently to end the surplus or remove it from the market.

In June 1965 the FAO Committee on Commodity Problems reported that real cocoa prices were as low as in 1934-38, while production was still rising twice as fast as consumption, and stocks were 250,000 tons or one-sixth of anticipated production for the year. After four meetings of a Working Party on Prices and Quotas were held, between June 1965 and March 1966, the United Nations Cocoa Conference was reconvened in May 1966, under the auspices of the United Nations Conference on Trade and Development. The Conference substantially revised the draft of an agreement prepared in 1963, and agreed that: a suitable international agreement on cocoa should contain provisions relating to quotas, buffer stock mechanism, price range, regular income for the buffer stock, and diversion of structural surpluses of cocoa to nonconventional uses.[9] The participants made considerable progress in settling technical problems in the operation of an agreement, but were unable to agree on two crucial points: the minimum price at which export quotas would become operative or restricted, or at which buffer stock purchases would begin; and the means of financing the buffer stock's initial operations and assuring it a regular income. The failure of the Conference was strongly protested by thirty underdeveloped countries, including nine Latin American nations, who blamed the major importing countries, especially (although implicitly) the United States, for failing to implement the terms of the UNCTAD agreements of 1964 and for refusing to accept

the minimum price put forward by the producing countries.[10] The Conference was reconvened in December 1966, but no further progress was made then. Consultations among member governments continued: in April 1967 the United States indicated its willingness to negotiate an agreement, and in October of that year fourteen major producing and consuming countries adopted a Memorandum of Agreement. The draft provided for a price range of 20 to 29 cents per pound, to be maintained by a buffer stock and, when prices fell below 24.5 cents, by export quotas. The stock, not to exceed 250,000 tons, was to be contributed by producers in proportion to their quotas and financed by a levy of 1 cent per pound on all cocoa in international trade. Almost all the draft articles were approved when the Conference reconvened in November, but the meetings were suspended in December without the conclusion of an International Cocoa Agreement.[11]

There are unquestionably some difficulties to an international agreement on cocoa: the price elasticity of demand is somewhat higher than for coffee; storage is somewhat difficult; and a variety of grades and derivatives must be accounted for. Nonetheless, cocoa is one of the relatively few commodities for which an export control scheme, with or without a buffer stock, appears to be feasible.[12] The problem of distinct grades of cocoa is even set aside, in the draft agreement, by excluding fine or flavor-grade cocoa altogether as it is only a small share of world output. The failure to reach an agreement in 1963-67 despite considerable preparation and negotiation therefore reflects primarily the fact that the major importing countries did not regard such an agreement as worthwhile and did not accept the goal of raising prices (as distinct from that of price stability) for cocoa. On the other hand, the Coffee Agreement of 1962 was until 1967 regarded as an exception by the United States in particular, agreed to only as a form of much needed aid to Latin America. To the producing countries the Coffee Agreement is a precedent to be applied wherever technically feasible, and the establishment of UNCTAD in 1964 is an indication by the developed countries of their willingness to enter into other such agreements. The initial reluctance of importing countries to accept a cocoa scheme may also have reflected pressure by the principal cocoa-processing firms located in those countries, which wish not only to obtain cocoa at low prices but to be able to shift suppliers and intervene in spot and futures markets more than would be possible under an agreement. These obstacles have been reduced in the last two years as the developed countries have expressed a general willingness to enter commodity-control schemes and other trading arrangements for the benefit of the poor na-

---

[8] BOLSA, *Review*, 26 June 1965, p. 574.

[9] UNCTAD, *United Nations Cocoa Conference, 1966*, doc. TD/B/81, 11 August 1966, report by the Secretary-General of UNCTAD on the results of the Conference. The *Draft International Cocoa Agreeement*, doc. TD/COCOA.1/4, 9 May 1966, prepared for distribution to the Conference, shows the 1963 draft agreement and the changes agreed on by the Working Party in 1965-66.

[10] UNCTAD, Joint Declaration: *Report on the United Nations Cocoa Conference*, doc. TD/B/106, 16 September 1966.

[11] The Memorandum is summarized in the UNCTAD *Monthly Bulletin*, no. 17, November 1967, and no. 19, January 1968. See also UNCTAD, *Commodity Problems and Policies*, doc. TD/L.29, 25 March 1968, p. 1.

[12] The others are coffee, tea, tin, and sugar, all of which are or have been traded under international agreements. See J. A. Pincus, "Commodity Agreements: Bonanza or Illusion?" *Columbia Journal of World Business*, January-February 1967.

tions. But this change of attitude has yet to influence the trade and earnings of the latter appreciably.

The Cocoa Industry in Latin America

Except for Brazil, Latin America has almost withdrawn from the world cocoa market; the present industry can be briefly described. Cocoa occupies about three-fourths million hectares in Latin America, of which well over half is concentrated in the state of Bahía, Brazil (see table 11-4). The remaining cocoa area is widely scattered in fourteen countries, with a great variation in altitude and other characteristics; there is no clearly defined cocoa zone. Estates formerly accounted for the bulk of production, but small holdings are now common in all countries. Very little is known about the structure of cocoa farms or cultivation practices. Yields can be calculated in some cases, but weather, age, and damage by disease or pests cause such great variations in yields that all calculations are only approximate. The highest yields, 500 to 600 kilograms per hectare, are found in Costa Rica, with slightly lower returns in the Dominican Republic, Mexico and Panama. Yields of 400 to 500 kilograms per hectare have been reported in Brazil, but the average is currently only 230. Comparably low yields are found in the countries producing fine cocoa, the lowest, in Ecuador and Venezuela, being only 200 kilograms per hectare. On the average, yields in Latin America are about equal to those in Africa, and they do not appear to have increased in the last few decades.[13]

The volume of cocoa exports remained stable at about 200,000 tons during the 1950s, and declined slightly in the early 1960s. Most of this trade is in the form of beans, although exports of products have been increasing and are now about 40,000 tons. In the early 1950s cocoa earned some $120 million annually for the region, or about 2 percent of total foreign exchange; the stagnation of volume and the decline in price in 1960-65 reduced the value of cocoa to only some $100 million or 1 percent of the total (see table 11-5). Except in years of very high prices, cocoa has not contributed more than 20 percent of any country's earnings; only in Ecuador and the Dominican Republic is the share now as high as 10 percent. The United States is the major buyer, and almost the sole market for the four smaller exporters. Brazil and Ecuador supply the importing countries of Latin America and send relatively large amounts to Europe; Brazil has also exported cocoa to the Communist countries of Europe. Cocoa butter exports from Brazil and the Dominican Republic go to the United States and the chief European chocolate producers. Latin America has not been able to dominate any major market; it supplies only a small share of Europe's requirements and 40 to 60 percent of the United States demand.

In the mid-1960s some 320,000 tons of cocoa were produced annually in Latin America (see table 11-6). About 200,000 tons were exported from the region as beans; a further 14,000 tons were sold to importing countries in the region, of which Argentina and Colombia are the largest. Imports of cocoa are so large an item in Colombia's trade that an agreement has been reached between the Ministry

of Agriculture and the national cocoa-growers' association to raise production in an effort to achieve self-sufficiency by 1973.[14] Two-fifths of the cocoa produced, 145,000 tons, was processed domestically; of this amount, about 40,000 tons were exported in various forms, and 90,000 tons were consumed in Latin America. The highest levels of per capita consumption are found in Colombia, Ecuador and the Dominican Republic; in all other countries consumption is much lower, even where income is relatively high. Government intervention in the industry is rather slight. Small research stations are maintained in each country, and some technical assistance is given to growers; the national offices disseminate the results of research performed at the Inter-American Cacao Center of the Inter-American Institute of Agricultural Sciences at Turrialba, Costa Rica, which was established in 1947. Cocoa is an important source of revenues in the major producing areas, but in none is the industry regulated to the extent that the coffee industry is.

Outlook

The recent difficulties in the cocoa market and the decline in prices resulted from an excess of production over consumption in every year from 1960 to 1965, output being extraordinarily high in 1964-65. In 1966 consumption exceeded production, reducing stocks somewhat and bringing prices back to their 1964 levels, nearly double the low point reached in 1965; consumption continued in excess of production in 1967 and 1968, and prices and export earnings continued to recover.[15] By 1967 Latin American exports were $130 million, or 1 percent of total regional exports. The future course of consumption and production cannot be predicted with any assurance because of the elasticity of demand and the multiplicity of factors affecting supply. The recovery of prices in 1966-68, for example, was not anticipated before the early 1970s in projections made before 1966. Demand can be projected at various price levels, assuming certain rates of income growth: by 1975, as estimated by the FAO, demand should grow to 1.68 to 1.89 million tons.[16] Production can be estimated from the rate of planting in the postwar period, together with assumptions about the losses from pests and diseases, price not being explicitly recognized. Production could be quite low in the near future; but if cultivation is maintained at the same level as in recent years, a minimum output of 1.6 million tons is anticipated by the early 1970s, and a production of 1.7 or 1.8 million tons is probable. At 1961-63 real prices, therefore, an approximate balance is anticipated. Over the long run, planting will once again become profitable, but the rate and price at which this occurs may depend appreciably on the existence and operation of an agreement, reflecting the expectations created by an agree-

---

[14] BOLSA, *Review*, January 1967, p. 42.

[15] Developments in 1960-66 are summarized in the UNCTAD *Commodity Surveys, 1966* and *1967.*

[16] FAO, Committee on Commodity Problems, *Agricultural Commodities – Projections for 1975 and 1985,* p. 250; and FAO, "The Longer-Term Outlook for Cocoa Production and Consumption," *Monthly Bulletin of Agricultural Economics and Statistics,* March 1966.

[13] For further information on yields, see FAO, *Cacao. . . ,* p. 26.

ment as well as its immediate effect on price. In any case the effect on Latin America, aside from the increase of export earnings, is likely to be slight. The regional industry can probably be stabilized and rehabilitated at its present level, but it is unlikely to regain a larger share of the market and may well continue its relative decline. It is quite possible that in the future the industry's growth will depend primarily on consumption within the region, with the export sector steadily dwindling in importance although not in absolute size.

CHAPTER 11 TABLES

TABLE 11-1. World Cocoa Consumption, Averages, 1934-38, 1950-52, 1961-63, and 1965-67

Country or Region	1934-38	1950-52			1961-63			1965-67		
	(1)	(2)	(3)	(4)	(2)	(3)	(4)	(2)	(3)	(4)
IMPORTING COUNTRIES	000 metric tons			kg.	000 metric tons		kg.	000 metric tons		kg.
Latin America	7	7.5	7.8	0.33	7.9	9.1	0.29	15.3	19.0	0.44
Argentina	5	5.8	6.1	0.35	6.5	7.0	0.33	11.6[a]	14.7	0.52[a]
Chile	1	0.8	0.9	0.14	1.0	1.3	0.16	2.8[a]	3.0[a]	0.32[a]
Uruguay	1	0.9	0.8	0.34	0.4	0.8[b]	0.22	0.9	1.3	0.33
United States	242	260.7	281.0	1.82	254.9	319.5	1.72	367.2	475.2	1.86
Canada	12	14.2	21.5	1.53	15.0	32.0	1.71	39.0	68.3	1.94
Western Europe	331	352	330.4	1.19	532.8	465.1	1.51	581.7	544.5	1.68
France	43	55.3	47.9	1.14	63.7	62.7	1.33	59.2	65.6	1.45
Germany	76	56	69.7	1.38	122.7	129.0	2.26	154.6	150.8	2.82
Italy	9	12.6	12.9	0.28	37.3	23.8	0.46	42.0	31.3	0.53
Netherlands	59	54.7	24.3	2.37	101.5	32.2	2.73	115.6	91.3	2.46
Spain	10	11.2	11.2	0.31	25.2	24.4	0.79	31.2	28.3	0.93[a]
United Kingdom	91	115	106.8	2.14	90.6	102.3	1.91	101.9	89.7	2.41
Africa	2	11.7	7.0	0.07	32.9	9.1	0.08	31.6	13.4	0.08
Asia	1	5.3	4.9	0.01	25.9	34.5	0.53	33.0	52.6	0.55
Oceania	7	9.6	16.5	1.58	15.5	20.5	1.55	23.5	18.2	1.71
Communist Countries	31	49.1	20.1	0.07	89.9	99.4	0.30	149.0	141.1[d]	0.43
Total	633	563	692	0.47	931	1,001	0.59	1,259	1,447	0.49
PRODUCING COUNTRIES										
Latin America	25	71.3	50.7	0.82	123.0	67.0	0.67	131.2	97.7	0.67
Bolivia	2	3	3.0	0.99	2.0	2.1	0.58	2.6[a]	2.7[a]	0.59[a]
Brazil	3	23.7	6.3	0.12	47.0	16.0	0.31	59.9	25.0	0.30
Central America		1.1	1.1	0.98	2.9	2.1	0.30	2.5	2.2	0.34
Colombia	12	22.3	18.0	1.55	23.2	23.2	1.57	28.7	33.4	1.73
Cuba		2.3	2.1	0.38	2.5	2.5	0.35	2.1	2.2	0.27
Dominican Republic		3.3	4.5	2.09	19.0	4.0	1.25	6.1	4.0[c]	1.11[c]
Ecuador		1.0	3.5	1.06	5.7	5.7	1.23	7.3	6.8[a]	1.31
Mexico	2	7.3	6.4	0.24	13.2	13.6	0.36	13.8	13.2	0.30
Peru	2	4.3	5.0	0.58	5.0	5.5	0.47	4.8	5.0	0.40
Venezuela	1	3.0	1.1	0.20	2.5	2.3	0.29	3.4	3.2	0.34
Africa		11.7	0.5	0.01	32.9	1.1	0.01	37.8	(d)	0.02
Asia	2	5.1	4.5	0.04	29.3	6.9	0.05	33.2	8.6	0.08
Oceania		9.6	0.2	0.01	15.5	1.1	0.01	23.5	2.3	0.03
Total	27	98	56	0.17	201	75	0.21	226	109	0.26
WORLD TOTAL	660	752	749	0.41	1,132	1,076	0.52	1,377	1,441	0.46
Latin America	32	78.8	58.5	1.72	131	76.1	0.96	146.5	116.7	1.11
North America	245	274.9	302.5	3.35	269.9	351.5	3.43	406.2	543.5	2.00
Western Europe	246	351.7	330.4	1.09	532.8	471.0	1.51	581.7	544.5	1.11
Africa	2	11.7	7.5	0.08	32.9	10.2	0.09	34.7	13.4	0.10
Asia	3	5.1	15.5	0.05	29.3	41.3	0.58	33.1	61.2	0.63
Oceania	7	9.6	16.5	1.59	15.5	21.6	1.56	23.5	20.5	1.74
Communist Countries	107	49.1	20.1	0.07	89.9	99.4	0.30	149.0	141.1	0.43

Sources: FAO, *Cocoa Statistics.* V. D. Wickizer, *Coffee, Tea and Cocoa* (Stanford: Food Research Institute, 1951), p. 483.

(1) Absorption, or apparent consumption of cocoa beans.
(2) Grindings of cocoa beans.
(3) Apparent consumption of cocoa and products, equivalent in beans: grindings plus net imports of cocoa products.
(4) Per capita consumption, based on (3).

[a]Two-year average.
[b]"Other South America."
[c]1965 only.
[d]Included with Oceania.

TABLE 11–2. World Production of Cocoa Beans, 1930-1967[a]
(Thousands of metric tons)

Country or Region	Avg. 1930-34	Avg. 1935-39	Avg. 1940-44	Avg. 1945-49	1950	1951	1952	1953	1954	1955	1956
Latin America	162.1	214.6	208.9	205.2	260.0	272.3	263.4	257.5	272.2	282.9	290.2
Bolivia		2.5			3.0	3.0	3.0	3.0	3.0	3.0	3.0
Brazil	91.6	124.0	132.8	121.4	150.0	155.0	157.0	142.0	155.0	151.0	171.0
Colombia	8.8	10.5	16.1	13.2	14.6	14.6	14.6	15.1	15.0	15.0	14.0
Costa Rica	6.7	6.8	5.6	4.0	4.5	2.9	3.2	5.5	9.5	10.0	7.0
Cuba		3.2			3.2	2.5	2.7	2.5	3.4	2.7	2.0
Dominican Republic	21.2	23.4	24.2	27.5	32.7	31.8	31.6	30.5	32.7	36.4	25.9
Ecuador	16.0	17.6	14.3	17.2	20.7	26.8	20.1	24.4	23.5	28.4	26.1
Guatemala		0.4			0.6	0.8	0.6	1.1	1.0	1.0	1.0
Haiti		1.5			1.7	2.2	1.8	2.0	2.3	1.3	1.6
Honduras		0.1			0.1	0.1	0.1	0.1	0.1	0.1	0.1
Mexico	0.8	1.1	1.6	4.1	6.7	8.6	8.6	9.1	8.4	12.6	13.8
Nicaragua		0.3			0.7	0.6	0.5	0.4	0.4	0.4	0.4
Panama		4.7			2.4	1.5	1.2	1.4	1.8	1.8	1.6
Peru		2.0			4.1	5.0	4.3	4.1	4.1	4.2	4.3
Venezuela	17.0	16.5	14.3	17.8	15.0	15.0	14.1	16.3	16.0	15.0	18.4
Africa	376.0	484.0	407.2	437.9	485.4	517.8	461.1	514.9	469.7	492.2	521.1
Asia	9.0	6.1	7.7	6.3	4.0	4.2	4.2	5.1	6.3	5.2	5.9
Oceania		2.9			3.3	3.4	4.0	3.7	5.4	5.4	5.5
World Total	588	731	645	667	765	812	733	797	771	801	836
Latin American Share (%)	27.6	29.3	32.4	30.8	34.0	33.5	35.9	32.3	35.0	35.3	34.7

Country or Region	1957	1958	1959	1960	1961	1962	1963	1964	1965	1966	1967
Latin America	285.2	291.1	306.4	367.4	274.2	282.2	283.1	273.1	274.5	320.1	337.1
Bolivia	2.0	2.1	2.1	2.1	2.1	2.1	2.0	2.0	2.5	2.5	1.0
Brazil	160.9	162.0	174.0	199.0	122.0	118.0	109.0	121.5	118.5	171.0	173.0
Colombia	15.4	15.2	11.9	13.3	14.0	17.0	17.0	16.0	17.5	17.0	18.0
Costa Rica	7.4	7.7	11.0	10.7	13.4	9.8	11.3	10.3	10.9	7.0	9.0
Cuba	2.5	2.8	2.8	2.8	2.8	2.5	2.3	0.8	2.6	1.9	1.5
Dominican Republic	33.2	35.4	33.0	40.0	35.0	35.2	38.8	41.2	25.0	30.5	28.0
Ecuador	26.3	25.0	32.7	41.2	44.1	44.4	45.3	36.0	48.2	36.0	53.0
Guatemala	0.9	1.0	0.7	0.7	0.7	0.5	0.5	0.5	0.5	0.5	0.5
Haiti	1.1	1.3	2.2	2.4	2.1	2.2	2.0	2.4	2.8	3.0	3.0
Honduras	0.1	0.1	0.1	0.2	0.2	0.2	0.2	0.2	0.2	0.2	0.2
Mexico	14.1	15.3	15.0	13.3	16.5	27.2	30.0	17.2	20.6	24.0	25.2
Nicaragua	0.4	0.5	0.2	0.2	0.3	0.2	0.2	0.5	0.4	0.5	0.5
Panama	1.2	1.5	1.9	1.3	1.4	1.5	1.0	0.9	1.1	0.7	0.5
Peru	4.5	4.4	4.0	2.8	2.7	2.5	2.7	2.7	1.8	2.4	2.0
Venezuela	15.2	16.8	14.8	18.5	16.9	18.9	20.8	20.9	21.9	22.9	21.7
Africa	584.3	458.3	566.2	661.3	868.2	827.9	853.9	900.0	1,196.3	865.7	968.2
Asia	5.8	5.2	5.7	6.5	7.4	6.7	7.0	7.2	7.5	8.2	7.8
Oceania	6.7	7.9	9.9	10.6	12.0	15.7	18.4	22.5	25.0	20.9	25.5
World Total	895	776	902	1,040	1,174	1,142	1,173	1,213	1,514	1,225	1,348
Latin American Share (%)	31.9	37.5	32.6	35.3	23.4	24.7	24.1	22.5	18.1	26.1	25.0

Sources: FAO, *Cocoa Statistics*. V. D. Wickizer, *Coffee, Tea and Cocoa* (Stanford: Food Research Institute, 1951), p. 483.

[a]Statistics refer to crop year, 1 October to 30 September; the crop year 1966/67 is reported as 1967, etc.

TABLE 11-3. Cocoa Bean Prices, 1925-1967
(U.S. cents per pound)

Year	New York Spot Ghana	Average Value of U.S. Imports from		Year	New York Spot Ghana	Average Value of U.S. Imports from	
		Brazil	Ecuador			Brazil	Ecuador
1925	9.5	9.2	17.1	1936	6.8	4.9	7.0
1926	11.5	9.7	15.9	1937	8.4	7.5	8.3
1927	15.8	13.1	17.8	1938	5.2	4.5	6.4
1928	12.8	11.3	14.6	1939	4.8	3.9	7.5
1929	10.4	8.8	12.9	1940	5.1	3.7	8.1
1930	8.1	6.8	12.2	1941	7.6	5.4	7.3
1931	5.2	4.7	9.3	1942	8.9	6.7	9.3
1932	4.4	3.8	7.2	1943	8.9	6.8	9.1
1933	4.4	3.6	6.4	1944	8.9	6.8	9.6
1934	5.2	4.5	7.2	1945	8.9	6.9	10.3
1935	5.0	4.3	6.2	1946	11.6	10.2	15.2

Year	New York Spot		London Accra[a]	Average Value of Exports from	
	Ghana	Bahía		Brazil[b]	Ecuador[c]
1947	34.9	34.4	18.3	24.4[d]	31.8[d]
1948	39.7	39.0	40.0	36.4	36.1
1949	21.6	21.2	23.4	18.0	25.5[d]
1950	32.1	29.2	26.1	27.0	31.0
1951	35.5	35.1	35.7	32.8	33.5
1952	35.4	35.8	37.7	32.0	33.0
1953	37.1	34.9	35.9	30.2	31.8
1954	57.8	55.7	58.5	50.9	51.5
1955	37.4	36.2	37.7	34.0	34.4
1956	27.3	25.5	27.6	24.2	26.6
1957	30.6	30.5	30.9	28.8	31.2
1958	44.3	43.3	44.0	35.3	41.4
1959	36.6	35.4	35.7	34.0	34.8
1960	28.4	26.8	28.2	25.0	27.0
1961	22.6	22.4	22.5	20.1	19.5
1962	21.0	21.3	21.2	19.9	22.7
1963	25.3	26.5	26.0	23.2	25.0
1964	23.4	23.2	23.8	21.2	26.0
1965	17.3	16.9	17.6	13.7	22.1
1966	24.4	23.0	24.5	20.5	24.2
1967	29.1	26.4	30.2	23.5	25.0

Sources: FAO, Commodity Bulletin no. 27, *Cacao: A Review of Current Trends in Production, Price and Consumption* (1955), p. 93. FAO, *Cocoa Statistics*. IMF, *International Financial Statistics*, supp. to 1964-65 and 1965-66. USCB, *Foreign Commerce and Navigation of the United States*, 1925-1946.

[a]Converted from shillings per hundredweight of 112 pounds.

[b]As reported, 1956-1967; 1948-1955, calculated from IMF index of export price, adjusted to match FAO data in 1958.

[c]Converted from sucres per kilogram at the official (export) exchange rate, 1952-1967; 1948-1951, calculated from the IMF index of export price.

[d]Average value of U.S. imports.

TABLE 11–4. Area Planted to Cocoa in Latin America, circa 1960

Country	Area (hectares)	Yield (kg./ha.)	Date	Sources
Bolivia[a]	4,000-8,000		1964	2,3
Brazil	469,644	230	1963	4
Bahía	438,127			5,9
Espírito Santo	23,617			
Pará	6,007			
Amazonas	1,619			
Colombia[b]	51,000	300	1956/57	1,7
Costa Rica	20,000	535-670	ca. 1960	5,6
Cuba[a]	4,000		1963/64	2,5
Dominican Republic	76,000	434-526	ca. 1960	5,6
Ecuador	163,000	210	1963/64	5,7
Guatemala[a]	2,000		1963/64	2,6,8
Haiti	8,000	250-300	1964	3
South	5,000			
North	3,000			
Honduras	200		1961/62	3
Mexico	68,000	412-441	1963/64	1,6
Nicaragua[a]	1,000		1963/64	2
Panama	4,025	450	1955	3
Peru	15,000	280-333	1964	3
Jaen de los Bacamoros	3,500			
Convención	4,000			
Tingo María	2,000			
Venezuela[c]	78,000	194-205	1954/55	5,7
Miranda area	30,400			
East	31,200			
West-Center	7,200			
Latin America	730-740,000	370		

Sources: (1) FAO, *Production Yearbook, 1960 to 1964.* (2) FAO, *Cocoa Statistics.* (3) FAO, Agricultural Study no. 63, *World Cocoa Survey* (1964). (4) Brazil, IBGE/Conselho Nacional de Estatística, *Anuário Estatístico do Brasil,* 1964. (5) L. Burle, *Le Cacaoyer* (Paris: Maisonneuve et Larose, 1962), vol. II. (6) G.A.R. Wood, *Report on Cocoa Growing in the Dominican Republic, Mexico, Guatemala and Costa Rica* (Bournville, England: Cadbury, 1957). (7) G.A.R. Wood, *Cocoa Growing in Venezuela, Colombia and Ecuador* (Bournville: Cadbury, 1959). (8) R. Elliott, *Cocoa as an Economic Development Crop for Guatemala* (Guatemala, 1960). (9) R. L. Stevens and P. Rebouças Brandão, "Diversification of the Economy of the Cacao Coast of Bahía, Brazil," *Economic Geography*, July 1961.

[a]Estimated from production.
[b]Most recent estimate available.
[c]70,000 in 1963/64.

TABLE 11-5. Latin American Exports of Cocoa by Destination, 1950-1967
(Metric tons and millions of U.S. dollars)

Exporter and Destination	1950	1951	1952	1953	1954
BRAZIL: Cocoa Beans	131,996	96,125	58,242	108,690	120,970
United States	73,616	52,970[a]	39,786[a]	56,388	56,384[a]
Argentina	4,377			9,926	
West Germany	1,921			38,505	
Cocoa Butter	9,687	6,561	3,860	9,816	3,881
Cocoa Powder		6	8	9	1
Cocoa Cake			4,419	11,432	6,515
Cocoa Paste			927	5,352	4,121
Total Cocoa	141,683	102,692	67,456	135,299	135,488
Value: Beans	78	69	41	75	135
Share of Exports (%)	5.8	3.9	2.9	4.9	8.6
COSTA RICA: Cocoa Beans	3,080	3,197	4,198	6,760	9,419
United States	1,814[a]	1,740[a]	4,529[a]	3,595[a]	5,812[a]
Value	2.0	1.9	4.2	4.0	8.3
Share of Exports (%)	3.6	3.1	5.7	5.0	9.8
CUBA: Cocoa Beans			247	276	737
Cocoa Powder			80	343	147
Total Cocoa			327		900[b]
Value					
Share of Exports (%)				6.9	
DOM. REP.: Cocoa Beans[c]	25,781	22,769	22,440	24,751	20,494
Chocolate	4,356	5,896	5,834	8,019	8,501
Total Cocoa	30,137	28,665	28,274	32,770	28,995
Value: Total	17.3	21.2	19.8	20.7	32.3
Share of Exports (%)	20.0	17.8	17.1	19.7	27.0
Value: Beans	14.6	16	14.7	15.4	23.5
Share of Exports (%)	17.6	13.4	12.7	14.6	19.6
ECUADOR: Cocoa Beans	26,778	24,068	23,276	22,500	29,735
United States	17,398[a]	14,440[a]	12,140	12,147	18,219
Colombia				4,500	4,819
West Germany			244	1,553	2,014
Italy			5,227	1,332	889
Value	18.4	17.8	17.0	15.6	34.1
Share of Exports (%)	24.8	25.2	16.7	16.9	27.4
GUATEMALA: Cocoa Beans	367	170	339	339	282
Value		0.1	0.2	0.2	0.2
Share of Exports (%)		0.1	0.2	0.2	0.2
HAITI: Cocoa Beans	2,057	1,974	2,322	2,020	2,246
Value		1.3	1.2	1.2	2.0
Share of Exports (%)		2.5	2.2	3.0	3.6
MEXICO: Cocoa Beans[c]	3,423	1,555	1,866	658	2,922
Cocoa Butter			1		28
Cocoa Powder				1	565
Chocolate			2	4	88
Total Cocoa[c]	3,423	1,555	1,869	663	3,603
Value	0.9	0.9	1.3	0.5	2.0
Share of Exports (%)	0.2	0.1	0.2	0.1	0.2
NICARAGUA: Cocoa Beans	82	159	146	72	36
Value	0.1	0.1	0.1	0.1	
Share of Exports (%)	0.2	0.3	0.2	0.1	0.1
PANAMA: Cocoa Beans[d]	1,900	1,327	3,149	1,871	2,627
Value	1.0	0.1	1.1	1.0	1.8
Share of Exports (%)	4.1	2.6	4.5	4.0	5.8
VENEZUELA: Cocoa Beans	15,646	14,345	15,105	17,145	16,311
United States	11,978[a]	10,167[a]	12,363[a]	13,102[a]	12,162[a]
Value	12.0	11.6	12.0	13.3	15.4
Share of Exports (%)	1.0	0.8	0.8	0.9	0.8
LATIN AMERICA: Cocoa Beans	211,110	165,689	131,330	185,082	205,779
United States	134,010	103,641	93,124	110,641	115,993
West Germany	1,921		244	40,058	2,014
Colombia				4,500	4,819
Italy			5,227	1,332	889
Argentina	4,377			9,926	
Cocoa Butter	9,687	6,561	3,861	9,816	3,909
Cocoa Powder		66	88	353	713
Cocoa Cake			4,419	11,432	6,515
Total Cocoa	225,153	178,152	145,532	214,702	225,714
Value: Total	129.6	124.5	97.5	131.3	231.1
Share of Exports (%)	1.9	1.6	1.4	1.7	2.8
Value: Beans	126.9	119.3	92.4	126.0	222.3
Share of Exports (%)	1.9	1.5	1.3	1.6	2.7

Exporter and Destination	1955	1956	1957	1958	1959
BRAZIL: Cocoa Beans	121,923	125,835	109,677	103,435	79,577
United States	64,038	63,376	52,860	48,129	37,682
Argentina	6,019	5,874	7,036	8,680	2,736
West Germany	17,408	12,403	15,765	16,663	9,480
Netherlands	5,801	18,684	18,833	17,369	16,783
Czechoslovakia	7,722	8,899	7,336	3,275	7,247
Cocoa Butter	5,991	11,906	14,897	14,817	17,944
United States	872	1,554	2,559	2,881	1,520
United Kingdom	1,208	5,834	6,367	4,633	6,012
Netherlands	1,919	1,924	3,139	4,426	7,755

TABLE 11-5 – Continued

Exporter and Destination	1955	1956	1957	1958	1959
Cocoa Powder		425	403	21	952
Cocoa Cake	8,761	8,960	7,153	17,530	28,154
Cocoa Paste	3,154	821	2,153	125	
Total Cocoa	139,829	147,947	134,283	135,928	126,627
Value: Total	99.5		92.8	117.8	91.7
Share of Exports (%)	7.0		6.2	9.5	7.1
Value: Cocoa Beans	91.0	67.0	70.0	89.4	59.4
Share of Exports (%)	6.4	4.5	5.0	7.2	4.6
COSTA RICA: Cocoa Beans	9,696	6,247	7,350	7,685	11,522
United States	5,802	4,633	4,050	4,229	6,967
Colombia	1,903	539	1,559	1,006	339
Panama[e]	1,533	834	1,238	1,095	2,015
Cocoa Butter	40	33	57	71	56
Value	5.9	2.9	4.1	6.0	7.5
Share of Exports (%)	7.3	4.3	4.9	6.5	9.7
CUBA: Cocoa Beans	705	13	1,740	554	1,048
Cocoa Butter	36	27	36	85	464
Cocoa Powder	922		137		
Total Cocoa	1,663	40	1,913	639	1,512
DOM. REP.: Cocoa Beans[c]	22,621	17,512	23,960	24,096	21,722
Cocoa Butter[c]	49	63	38	68	96
Chocolate	7,989	8,703	8,100	7,792	8,557
Total Cocoa	30,659	26,278	32,098	31,956	30,375
Value: Total	23.8	14.3	19.0	28.6	22.4
Share of Exports (%)	20.8	11.5	11.8	21.0	17.2
Value: Beans	16.8		13.5	20.6	15.1
Share of Exports (%)	14.6		8.4	15.1	11.6
ECUADOR: Cocoa Beans	24,409	29,229	26,856	22,150	28,164
United States	12,183	14,152	11,972	12,010	14,480
Colombia	6,494	7,357	7,014	3,986	5,545
West Germany	1,812	3,266	2,707	2,146	2,470
Italy	1,222	1,488	1,078	1,253	1,660
Netherlands	778	843	564	684	1,159
Value	18.7	17.4	18.6	20.4	21.8
Share of Exports (%)	16.4	15.1	14.0	15.3	15.5
GUATEMALA: Cocoa Beans	255	470	233	552	595
Value	0.2	0.2	0.2	0.4	0.4
Share of Exports (%)	0.2	0.2	0.1	0.4	0.4
HAITI: Cocoa Beans	1,474	1,203	1,610	1,889	1,970
Value	1.8	0.6	0.7	1.3	1.3
Share of Exports (%)	3.3	1.3	2.1	3.4	4.5
MEXICO: Cocoa Beans[c]	5,014	2,102	6,741	5,033	5,393
Cocoa Butter	188	100	286	15	
Cocoa Powder	71		199	618	146
Chocolate	44	25	40	36	39
Total Cocoa[c]	5,317	2,227	7,266	5,702	5,578
Value: Total	2.9	0.9	2.6	2.4	2.9
Share of Exports (%)	0.3	0.1	0.3	0.3	0.4
Value: Beans	2.6	0.8	2.2	2.2	2.8
NICARAGUA: Cocoa Beans	187	161	119	102	184
Value					
Share of Exports (%)					
PANAMA: Cocoa Beans[d]	1,163	1,553	1,270	1,680	1,449
Value	1.0	0.6	0.9	1.1	1.2
Share of Exports (%)	2.8	1.9	2.6	3.4	3.4
VENEZUELA: Cocoa Beans	16,097	18,566	14,896	13,509	10,416
United States	11,516[a]	18,844[a]	9,413[a]	9,660[a]	
West Germany				834	
Netherlands				665	
Belgium				486	
Cocoa Butter				106	67
Cocoa Paste					838
Value	11.1	12.1	10.8	12.5	8.8
Share of Exports (%)	0.5	0.5	0.4	0.5	0.3
LATIN AMERICA: Cocoa Beans	203,544	202,891	194,452	180,685	162,040
United States	122,753	127,646	106,796	101,305	86,244
West Germany	19,220	15,669	18,472	19,643	11,950
Netherlands	6,579	19,527	19,397	18,718	17,942
Colombia	8,397	7,896	8,573	4,992	5,884
Cocoa Butter	6,304	12,129	15,314	15,162	18,627
Cocoa Powder	993	425	739	639	1,098
Cocoa Cake	8,761	8,960	7,153	17,530	28,154
Chocolate	8,033	8,728	8,140	7,828	8,596
Total Cocoa	227,635	233,133	225,798	221,844	219,353
Value: Total	164.3	131.1	149.7	190.4	158.4
Share of Exports (%)	2.0	1.5	1.7	2.2	1.8
Value: Beans	148.5	101.6	121.0	153.8	118.7
Share of Exports (%)	1.8	1.2	1.4	1.8	1.4

TABLE 11–5 – Continued

Exporter and Destination	1960	1961	1962	1963	1964
BRAZIL: Cocoa Beans	125,457	104,170	55,340	68,685	74,710
United States	59,890	50,150	21,741	41,961	34,458
Argentina	4,921	7,020	6,423	5,376	9,021
West Germany	12,399	9,225	277	1,269	1,542
Netherlands	25,057	15,104	519	3,622	5,348
Czechoslovakia	7,466	9,430	3,180	2,716	300
Soviet Union	4,687	713	11,348	5,439	16,197
Cocoa Butter	22,606	14,990	16,784	14,041	10,330
United States	4,170	3,632	6,587	3,364	2,771
United Kingdom	11,512	5,987	4,037	2,597	1,374
Netherlands	5,895	3,269	3,262	3,358	2,668
Japan		260		3,519	1,873
Cocoa Powder	1,281	623	468	618	802
Cocoa Cake	20,430	13,971	5,834	5,569	6,051
Total Cocoa	169,824	119,983	78,426	88,913	91,899
Value: Total	98.6	63.1	41.4	51.4	46.5
Share of Exports (%)	7.8	4.5	3.4	3.7	3.5
Value: Cocoa Beans	69.2	45.9	24.2	35.0	34.8
Share of Exports (%)	5.5	3.3	2.0	2.5	2.4
COSTA RICA: Cocoa Beans	11,822	10,214	11,947	9,471	9,200
United States	7,359	5,965	6,729	6,579	6,750
Colombia	752	657	2,205		700
Panama[f]	1,596	644	855	1,238	1,167
Japan	175	212	1,107	708	131
Cocoa Butter	59	62	79	60	99
Cocoa Powder	4	10	25	33	44
Value	5.9	4.9	4.8	4.3	4.2
Share of Exports (%)	6.9	5.8	5.6	4.6	3.7
DOM. REP.: Cocoa Beans[c]	26,129	11,696	18,621	23,780	26,224
Cocoa Butter[c]	841	3,380	2,063	2,172	1,535
Cocoa Cake	1,313	4,766	3,198	3,487	2,072
Chocolate	8,794	10,398	6,599	5,096	7,092
Total Cocoa	37,077	30,240	30,481	34,535	36,923
Value: Total	20.9	14.7	13.5	16.8	16.3
Share of Exports (%)	11.6	10.4	7.8	9.7	9.1
Value: Beans	13.9	5.0	7.6	11.2	10.6
Share of Exports (%)	7.7	3.6	4.4	6.4	5.9
ECUADOR: Cocoa Beans	35,584	32,391	31,630	35,498	28,716
United States	22,851	16,428	12,939	16,266	7,657
Colombia	2,391	3,823	4,398	5,691	10,047
West Germany	3,263	4,072	4,286	3,963	3,892
Italy	1,738	1,654	1,295	2,271	1,882
Netherlands	1,609	1,831	2,686	2,148	2,052
Value	21.4	15.6	15.9	19.8	16.2
Share of Exports (%)	14.8	12.5	11.4	13.3	10.0
GUATEMALA: Cocoa Beans	395	529	256	337	230
Value	0.2	0.2	0.1	0.2	0.1
Share of Exports (%)	0.2	0.2	0.1	0.1	0.1
HAITI: Cocoa Beans	2,059	878	560	1,182	455
Value	1.2	0.4	0.2	0.2	
MEXICO: Cocoa Beans	3,088	5,475	12,066	18,088	3,361
Cocoa Butter	148	170	52	15	31
Chocolate	54	52	52	97	89
Total Cocoa	3,310[f]	5,697	12,170	18,200	3,481
Value: Total	1.7	2.5	4.5	7.1	1.5
Share of Exports (%)	0.2	0.3	0.5	0.7	0.1
Value: Beans	1.5	2.3	4.5	7.0	1.4
NICARAGUA: Cocoa Beans	309	223	237	296	268
Value	0.2	0.1	0.1	0.2	0.2
Share of Exports (%)					
PANAMA: Cocoa Beans	1,449	1,103	1,103	893	827
Value	0.8	0.5	0.5	0.5	0.4
Share of Exports (%)	2.8	1.0	1.0	0.8	0.6
VENEZUELA: Cocoa Beans	11,972	9,793	10,913	12,537	12,124
United States	6,383[a]	5,345	5,834	6,736	6,672
West Germany		1,509	1,657	1,564	1,524
Netherlands		1,510	1,717	1,581	668
Belgium		950	1,248	1,979	1,243
Cocoa Butter	165	153	190	157	152
Value: Beans	9.2	7.8	9.7	9.6	7.2
Share of Exports (%)	0.4	0.4	0.4	0.5	0.3
LATIN AMERICA: Cocoa Beans	218,264	176,341	142,700	170,767	154,178
United States	124,321	95,021	70,744	112,152	55,537
West Germany	15,662	14,806	6,220	6,796	6,958
Netherlands	26,666	18,445	4,924	7,351	8,068
Colombia	3,143	4,480	6,603	5,691	10,747
Cocoa Butter	23,819	18,755	19,168	16,445	10,612
Cocoa Powder	1,285	633	493	651	846
Cocoa Cake	21,743	18,737	9,032	9,056	6,051
Chocolate	8,848	10,450	6,651	5,193	7,177
Total Cocoa	273,959	224,916	178,044	202,112	178,864
Value: Total	159.4	109.8	91.2	111.5	91.7
Share of Exports (%)	1.8	1.2	1.1	1.1	0.8
Value: Beans	122.8	83.3	68.1	89.3	75.9
Share of Exports (%)	1.3	0.9	0.8	0.9	0.7

TABLE 11-5 – Continued

Exporter and Destination	1965	1966	1967
BRAZIL: Cocoa Beans	91,966	112,498	114,351
United States	68,078	71,133	59,853
Argentina	9,882	11,161	7,111
West Germany	1,314	1,290	7,282
Netherlands	3,309	4,074	13,732
Czechoslovakia	300		
Soviet Union		1,780	6,999
Cocoa Butter	17,197	21,016	20,960
Cocoa Powder	528	1,665	919
Cocoa Cake	3,365	5,698	8,361
Total Cocoa	113,056	140,877	144,591
Value: Total	41.4	72.2	85.4
Share of Exports (%)	2.6	4.1	5.2
Value: Cocoa Beans	27.7	50.7	59.2
Share of Exports (%)	1.7	2.9	3.5
COSTA RICA: Cocoa Beans	6,763	7,743	6,503
United States	3,995	4,150	
Colombia	649	1,127	
Panama[f]	951	954	
Japan	309	359	
Cocoa Butter	101	118	156
Cocoa Powder	93	113	141
Value	2.4	3.3	3.3
Share of Exports (%)	2.1	2.4	2.3
DOM. REP.: Cocoa Beans[c]	22,432	25,943	23,926
Cocoa Butter[c]	868	73	
Chocolate	530	927	945
Total Cocoa	23,830	26,943	24,871
Value: Total	7.3	11.2	12.0
Share of Exports (%)	5.6	8.2	7.7
Value: Beans	6.3	10.8	11.6
Share of Exports (%)	5.1	7.9	7.4
ECUADOR: Cocoa Beans	39,280	32,208	45,023
United States	15,089	15,458	20,254
Colombia	9,208	4,722	8,012
West Germany	4,947	3,582	3,612
Italy	2,472	2,039	2,957
Netherlands	2,522	2,407	5,119
Value	19.1	17.2	24.9
Share of Exports (%)	10.7	9.3	12.4
GUATEMALA: Cocoa Beans	547	474	266
Value	0.2	0.2	0.1
Share of Exports (%)	0.1	0.1	0.1
HAITI: Cocoa Beans	105	443	101
Value			
MEXICO: Cocoa Beans	9,308	8,442	6,112
Cocoa Butter		199	946
Chocolate	93	92	86
Total Cocoa	9,401	8,733	7,144
Value: Total	3.4	4.1	3.0
Share of Exports (%)	0.3	0.3	0.3
Value: Beans	3.4	3.9	3.0
NICARAGUA: Cocoa Beans	313	225	348
Value	0.2	0.1	0.2
Share of Exports (%)			
PANAMA: Cocoa Beans	649	438	396
Value	0.2	0.2	0.2
Share of Exports (%)	0.3		
VENEZUELA: Cocoa Beans	12,320	11,795	12,447
United States	5,148	3,632	3,558
West Germany	1,476	1,510	1,378
Netherlands	1,137	1,600	1,273
Belgium	1,727	2,907	3,442
Cocoa Butter	72	143	136
Value: Beans	7.4	7.0	7.2
Share of Exports (%)	0.3	0.3	
LATIN AMERICA: Cocoa Beans	174,375	191,767	209,483
United States	92,310	94,373	83,665
West Germany	7,737	6,382	12,272
Netherlands	6,968	8,081	20,124
Colombia	9,857	5,849	8,012
Cocoa Butter	18,238	21,549	22,198
Cocoa Powder	621	1,778	1,060
Cocoa Cake	3,365	5,698	8,361
Chocolate	623	1,019	1,031
Total Cocoa	206,530	230,253	242,133
Value: Total	74.2	108.5	129.1
Share of Exports (%)	0.7	1.0[g]	1.2[g]
Value: Beans	71.9	98.3	115.0
Share of Exports (%)	0.7	0.9[g]	1.0[g]

Sources: 1958-68 – FAO, *Cocoa Statistics*; 1950-64 – Foreign trade annuals of Brazil, Costa Rica, Dominican Republic, Ecuador, Mexico, and Venezuela; IMF, *International Financial Statistics*, supp. to 1964-65 issues, and August 1966, December 1968; 1950-64 – USCB, *United States Imports of Merchandise for Consumption*; 1950-66 – UN, *Yearbook of International Trade Statistics*.

[a]U.S. imports.
[b]Includes some cocoa butter.
[c]Exclusively or predominantly to the United States.
[d]Includes re-exports of cocoa produced in Costa Rica.
[e]Re-exported from Panama.
[f]Includes some cocoa powder.
[g]Excludes Cuban exports.

TABLE 11-6. Latin American Cocoa Balance, 1966
(Metric tons)

Country	Beans	Butter	Powder	Chocolate and Products	Total
Argentina					
Imports	11,351		394		11,745
Exports				19	19
Consumption	11,000				12,312
Bolivia					
Production	2,500				2,500
Consumption	2,500				2,600
Brazil					
Production	171,000				171,000
Exports	112,498	21,016	1,665	5,744[a]	140,923
Consumption	61,000				24,339
Chile					
Imports	2,732	254	3	58	3,047
Consumption	2,700				3,501
Colombia					
Imports	15,664				15,664
Production	17,000				17,000
Consumption	32,700				32,700
Costa Rica					
Production	7,000				7,000
Exports	7,743	118	113	251	8,225
Consumption	1,374				1,008
Cuba					
Production	1,900				1,900
Exports		10			10
Consumption	1,900				1,900
Dominican Rep.					
Production	30,500				30,500
Exports	25,943	73		927[a]	26,943
Consumption	1,200				700
Ecuador					
Production	36,000				36,000
Exports	32,208				32,208
Consumption	8,000				7,000
El Salvador					
Imports	393	11	41	284	729
Exports				43	43
Consumption	400				569
Guatemala					
Imports	4				4
Production	500				500
Exports	474				474
Consumption	300				300
Haiti					
Production	3,000				3,000
Exports	443			1,129[a]	1,572
Consumption	2,557				1,145
Honduras					
Imports	6		106		112
Production	200				200
Exports	46				46
Consumption	148				263
Mexico					
Production	24,000				24,000
Exports	8,442	199	3	92	8,736
Consumption	14,000				13,978
Nicaragua					
Imports	40		61		101
Production	500				500
Exports	225				225
Consumption	315				176
Panama					
Imports			118[b]	311[b]	429
Production	700				700
Exports	436				436
Consumption	264				354
Peru					
Imports	1,584	174	500	370	2,628
Production	2,400				2,400
Consumption	4,000				4,700
Uruguay					
Imports	541				541
Consumption					1,100
Venezuela					
Production	22,900				22,900
Exports	11,795	242			12,037
Consumption	11,000				10,824
Latin America[c]					
Imports	32,315	439	1,223	1,023	35,000
Production	320,100				320,100
Exports	200,253	21,658	1,781	8,205	231,897
Consumption	155,358				119,469

Source: FAO, *Cocoa Statistics*, July 1968.

Note: Consumption of beans refers to grindings or to apparent consumption when grindings are not reported. Total cocoa consumption is consumption of beans plus bean equivalent of net imports of butter, powder, paste, chocolate, and other products.

[a]Includes paste and cake.
[b]Data for 1965; 1966 figures not available.
[c]Sum of countries listed; no data available for Paraguay.

Chapter 12

SUGAR

By any measure sugar is one of the most important of Latin America's resource products. Under the market arrangements of the 1950s it ranked ahead of all export commodities except coffee and petroleum, earning for the region some $600 to $800 million annually, or between 7 and 10 percent of all exports. The importance of sugar dates almost from the conquest of Latin America, for it was the first agricultural product to be developed for export and the basis of the first agricultural colonies. In its total effect on the economic history of the region it exceeds any other product, with the possible exceptions of coffee and the precious metals. This influence has not been confined to the provision of foreign exchange and income, but has embraced the pattern of land use, the origin and organization of labor, and the nature of the ties between sugar-exporting countries and their markets. More recently sugar has also become a major item of consumption in Latin America, and the industries which process and use sugar are among the largest industries in several countries. The region accounts for roughly half the world's cane sugar and one-fourth of all sugar produced. It provides a still larger share of sugar in international trade, Cuba alone supplying one-fourth or more of world exports. About half the sugar produced in Latin America is consumed domestically.[1]

Sugars can be made from other products than cane and beets, the usual sources, which yield a variety of by-products such as fiber, fuel, animal feeds, and alcohol. The sugar-processing industry is therefore linked to many other commodities and industries. With few exceptions these connections will not be described here, and sugar will be treated as a single product.[2] Attention will similarly be limited to those national and international sugar policies with particular relevance for Latin America.

World Production and Consumption

Until the mid-nineteenth century, virtually all sugar was produced from cane, and the focus of production shifted steadily westward over a period of several centuries. Sugar cane is believed to have originated in Indonesia and to have spread to India by about 400 B.C. From there it moved to the Middle East and then on around the rim of the Mediterranean as Europe became a major consuming area. In the fifteenth century the Mediterranean industry began to decline, as cane was established in the Spanish and Portuguese islands in the Atlantic. These areas held a brief monopoly of European sugar supply before yielding in turn to the competition of the New World. Sugar cane was introduced into Hispaniola in 1494 and within a little more than a century there was some production everywhere in Latin America north of Bolivia. Mexico and Peru exported some sugar to Spain in the period 1540-1640, but Brazil was the chief source of the supply for the rest of Europe until late in the seventeenth century. The excellent conditions for cane growing in the northeastern part of the country, a century of Portuguese experience in the sugar industry, and the predominance of Dutch shipping and finance in European commerce, combined to create a virtual monopoly for Brazil, with the trade and refining in the hands of the Dutch. The attempt to control the extremely lucrative trade in sugar contributed to the seventeenth-century wars between Spain and Holland, and led to the Dutch occupation of the Brazilian sugar area in 1630-54. The knowledge of the industry obtained during the occupation allowed the Dutch to develop sugar production in the French and British possessions of the Caribbean. With the end of the Brazilian monopoly prices fell sharply and exports from Brazil declined. The struggle for control of sugar was taken up in the eighteenth century by the British and the French.

Note: Sugar tables 12-1 to 12-9 appear on pp. 352-63.

[1] The chief sources of statistical material on sugar are the publications of the International Sugar Council, such as the *Statistical Bulletin* and especially a two-volume study, *The World Sugar Economy*: vol. I, *National Sugar Economies and Policies*, and vol. II, *The World Picture* (London, 1963). The publications of FAO, the U.S. Department of Agriculture, and trade sources are also used. Historical and other sources are indicated in the text.

[2] The available data do not permit much more detail, especially in Latin America, and little is lost by omitting it. The demand for sugar is largely a function of incomes and prices, and the supply is likewise not ordinarily affected by the by-products. For a discussion of the links between sugar and other products, see V. P. Timoshenko and B. C. Swerling, *The World's Sugar: Progress and Policy* (Stanford University Press, 1957), pp. 4-15.

Before the slave rebellion of the 1790s destroyed the industry, Haiti was the world's foremost producer, the islands to the east and south being also major suppliers. By 1800 the European industry had disappeared, and outside the New World cane was grown only in India and Java. The last great shift in the location of the cane sugar industry occurred in the nineteenth century, when Cuba emerged as the largest producer and exporter. In the last century cane has been extended to other areas primarily for domestic use, leaving the Caribbean area dominant in exports.[3]

The distribution of sugar production and trade established before 1800 was fundamentally changed by the development of the beet sugar industry in the late nineteenth century. Sugar was first extracted from beets in the eighteenth century, and shortly after 1800 factories were set up in several European countries. Output grew after the 1820s, and by 1880 beet sugar production equalled that from cane. The share of world sugar obtained from beets reached a peak of two-thirds in the years around 1900, and then dropped sharply during World War I. For the last four decades the share has been about 40 percent. The rapid expansion of beet cultivation relative to cane was due in part to progress in raising beet yields and extraction rates. During the nineteenth century technical progress was more rapid for beets than for cane, and the difference in cost decreased. In this century progress in cane breeding has been considerably more rapid, and cane's competitive advantage has increased.[4] A number of changes in sugar processing and refining which affected both sources equally also took place in the nineteenth century; by 1880 the production process, including centrifugal separation of sugar and molasses, had reached essentially its present form.[5]

Sugar is unique among agricultural products in that it can be obtained from two quite distinct sources, suited to production in different climates. Almost every country in the world can and does produce at least part of its sugar from one or the other; a very few countries grow both cane and beets. Sugar beets offer certain advantages over cane in relation to other crops; they fit better into a pattern of mixed farming and they provide fodder for animals. These advantages, and the fact that beets give as high a yield of sugar per ton as cane, do not offset the much lower yields of beets per hectare; the result is that beet sugar cannot compete with cane and its production in any country requires protection against imports or domestic production of cane sugar.

[3]This summary is based on ISC, *World Sugar Economy*, vol. II, pp. 4-11. For an extensive analysis of the role of sugar in Brazil, see C. Furtado, *The Economic Growth of Brazil* (University of California Press, 1963), especially chaps. 1-6, 8, 11.

[4]For more discussion of these changes, see Timoshenko and Swerling, *The World's Sugar*, chaps. 5 and 6; and ISC, *World Sugar Economy*, vol. II, pp. 61-64, 79-80.

[5]Most information refers to centrifugal sugar, which is about 96 percent pure and forms the great bulk of world production and virtually all sugar traded. Most centrifugal sugar is refined to pure (white) sugar for consumption. Non-centrifugal (brown) sugar, varying widely in purity, is produced chiefly for local consumption and is discussed briefly below. See also tables 12-1 (note), 12-4, and 12-8.

The beet sugar industry in Europe, and later in North America, was created by a high level of protection. A decline in the degree of protection since World War I has resulted in a lower share of beet sugar in world output than in several previous decades. Only a few countries are self-sufficient in beet sugar; nearly all beet-growing countries import the balance of their requirements as cane sugar. The consequences of this protection will be assessed after a discussion of national sugar policies and international marketing arrangements. Here only two points will be noted. First, sugar is unique among the many products in which the nations of North America and Europe compete with or discriminate against the underdeveloped countries. The cost difference between cane and beet sugar is often large, and is real: it is not the result, as in the case of petroleum in the United States, of artificial restrictions in the advanced countries. There are no differences of quality, as there are between natural and synthetic rubber, or different types of meat or grain, or petroleum from different sources. Sugar has neither the strategic importance nor the supply inelasticity of minerals. And protection discriminates against production of the raw material, as well as against successive stages of processing. Second, it is clear that the Caribbean area has a great cost advantage in cane sugar production. Since most of this area is part of Latin America, it is the latter region which suffers nearly all the burden resulting from sugar protection in the developed countries. For no other resource product is the regional effect of trade barriers so pronounced.

In the late 1950s some 11 million hectares worldwide were devoted to the production of centrifugal sugar; slightly more of this area was planted to beets than to cane (see table 12-1). During the preceding two decades the total sugar area had not quite doubled, with the area in cane growing a bit more rapidly than that in beets. In recent years both areas have expanded substantially, especially cane in Asia and beets throughout Western and Eastern Europe. Approximately 2 million more hectares, circa 1960, were planted to cane from which various forms of noncentrifugal sugar were made. That area is concentrated in Asia and has increased little or not at all in the last several decades; some land has probably shifted to centrifugal sugar production in Asia and in Latin America. The latter region accounts for roughly the same share of cane land as of production; its share in world total sugar area is low because of the lower yields and larger area of beets.

If yields in the 1930s and the late 1950s are compared for different producing areas, it appears that there has been little overall improvement; the expansion of production is due almost entirely to increased area (see table 12-2). Extraction rates for beets are somewhat greater than for cane, but because the plant yield is much lower, sugar yields per hectare are only about 60 percent as great. The highest beet yields obtained just equal the lowest yields of cane. For both sources geographic variations are considerable, but they are somewhat greater for cane. Differences in output per hectare per harvest depend greatly on climate and on cultivation practices, irrigation being especially important in assuring high yields. The growing season for cane varies from less than one year to more than two; if this variation is taken into account the extremely high yields of Peru and Hawaii are much reduced. The highest cane yields are found in Central America and the Caribbean. They are lower in South America, except in Peru, largely because of poorer soil or climate or less care in cultivation. Yields are high in Cuba, where good land is plentiful and is farmed more extensively. The average for Latin America as a whole is the same as that for the rest of the world. With a few exceptions, there is not much variation in extraction rates; marginal producing areas are indicated rather by low output of cane or beets.

World War I greatly disrupted beet output in Europe and allowed cane to recapture part of the market. In World War II the total shift in production was less, although beet output was much reduced in Eastern Europe and for several years there was a severe shortage of sugar. Since the late 1940s total production has expanded steadily from 25 to over 60 million tons, except for a decline in 1962-63, and the shares by region and type did not change markedly (see table 12-3). The relative stability of world production is not reflected in Latin America, however. Since Cuba emerged in the nineteenth century as a large, low-cost producer, it has been the marginal supplier of sugar in the world; and this position has been reinforced by the policies of importing countries. Thus Cuban production fell by half in the Depression of the 1930s, sharply reducing the Latin American total, while output expanded in the protected markets of North America and Europe. The region's share of the market was very low in the 1930s, rose sharply in the late 1940s, and declined slightly in the period around 1960; all these changes were dominated by variations in Cuban output. Fluctuations have been much less in other Latin American countries; the principal change to be noted is the expansion in output after 1960 in those countries allowed to replace Cuba as suppliers to the United States.

Sugar has periods of surplus and shortage in response to sudden changes in demand, weather variation, and changes in national policies, but supplies usually adjust to demand fairly quickly. There is no long delay between planting and production, as for tree crops, and the elasticity of supply is high even in the short run. The wartime shortage, during which sugar supplies were controlled by the United States and the United Kingdom, ended within two years after the war, and no subsequent disturbance has lasted for more than two years. It appears that the institutional rigidities and the high degree of coordination of field and factory required for sugar production may increase flexibility for small supply changes and would become obstacles only if very large increases or decreases in output were required.

World consumption of centrifugal sugar more than doubled between the late 1930s and the early 1960s (see table 12-4). Much of this increase was due to population growth, but per capita consumption rose by more than half, from 11 to 19 kilograms on the average, largely in response to income growth. The demand for sugar is quite income elastic at low incomes, elasticity falling steadily as income rises. From the experience of the richer European countries and North America it appears that demand may become saturated at approximately 50 kilograms, but the upper and lower limits on income and consumption are less marked than for other tropical products such as coffee and cocoa. As income rises, a growing share of sugar is used for non-household, or industrial, food preparation; very little is consumed in nonfood applications.[6]

Differences in income and in prices together account for most of the variation in sugar consumption among countries; if the factors are combined by comparing wages with retail prices the link is still stronger, and about 80 percent of the variation can be explained. A number of other influences, such as the consumption of fruits and starches of different kinds, may have some effect on sugar intake, but most such factors are strongly related to income, and other factors appear to have no effect. Differences in price and nonprice differences in consumption sometimes reflect variations in distribution facilities and availability of sugar. In general, however, prices and therefore consumption levels are most strongly affected by government policies of two main types: protection of domestic production, and taxation of consumption for revenue. In many countries excise taxes amount to 10 percent or more of the retail price of sugar, and the variation in prices among countries is enormous. Prices are generally lower in developing than in developed countries; in 1965, some 54 percent of the sugar consumed in the former was sold at retail prices below 9 cents per pound, while in the latter the same percentage was sold at between 9 and 12 cents. The disparity is still more striking if the comparison is limited to the net exporters in each group: 60 percent of consumption was sold below 9 cents per pound in the developing countries and the same share above 12 cents in the advanced nations. If, however, the comparison is made for net importers, the developed countries show lower average prices: 63 percent of consumption is sold at between 9 and 12 cents, against the same percentage at over 12 cents in the developing countries. These price relations turn on two chief factors. Low-income exporters are low-cost producers, while exports from developed countries are usually subsidized; and low-income importers apply higher tariffs and taxes on sugar than do the advanced countries, because of more stringent foreign exchange availability. Over 80 percent of high-income consumption takes place in net importing countries, while nearly as much of low-income sugar consumption occurs in exporting nations. In both groups, countries which do not produce sugar account for only a small amount of consumption.[7] The price elasticity of demand is fairly high at all income levels, so that the high prices resulting from national sugar policies have a marked effect on consumption.

In the last few decades per capita consumption has scarcely increased in North America, but it has more than

[6]For a thorough study of the factors affecting sugar consumption, see A. Viton and F. Pignalosa, *Trends and Forces of World Sugar Consumption*, FAO Commodity Bulletin no. 32 (Rome, 1961). An earlier study, no. 22 in the series, was published in 1952.

[7]For information on prices, markets, and barriers to trade in sugar, see UNCTAD, *Trade Barriers and Liberalization Possibilities in Selected Commodities*, doc. TD/11/supp. 2, 28 December 1967, pp. 41-47.

doubled in Latin America, Africa, the Communist countries, and the Caribbean, and grown nearly as fast in Asia and Europe. Only in Asia and Africa is consumption still less than 30 kilograms per year. World trade in sugar has grown much less rapidly than production and consumption. During the late nineteenth century trade fell relative to consumption chiefly because of import substitution in beet-growing countries. The trend toward self-sufficiency has continued, at a slower pace, but recently the increased consumption in producing areas has had more effect on the share of sugar traded. Latin America now consumes more than half its centrifugal sugar output, against one-third in the 1930s. Part of this change is to be explained by the substitution of centrifugal sugar for other forms previously consumed in large amounts. Noncentrifugal sugar intake has remained about constant in the region and has fallen slightly in per capita terms. In Asia, however, particularly in India, noncentrifugal sugar has shared in the increase in sugar consumption and still accounts for 40 percent of all sugar consumed there.

History and Structure of the Industry in Latin America

In sugar-producing countries the sugar industry is typically subject to a considerable degree of government regulation. As part of the policy of import substitution, the governments of Chile, Argentina, Uruguay, and Bolivia have undertaken to create, or to protect and expand, the sugar industry. The establishment of a beet sugar industry in Latin America in recent years is due to government intervention, as is the expansion of cane-growing in Bolivia. Import substitution is most marked in Chile, the only country of the region which cannot grow cane; production from beets began in the mid-1950s and within a decade accounted for one-third of consumption. In part this intervention follows from the great importance of the industry to the country's economy, in providing employment, income, and foreign exchange, and its value as a source of tax revenue.

Several features of cane sugar production require a high degree of control. Sugar cane is extremely perishable, the sugar content depending greatly on the time of harvest and the speed with which the cane can be brought to the mill. As a result, cane culture usually dominates a producing area; very little land can be spared for other crops without requiring the cane to be shipped great distances and thus losing sugar, or necessitating the construction of a large number of small mills, which are generally less efficient and economical than larger factories. This property, and the capital requirements of sugar producing, have led to much production on large, factory-owned estates. Where independent farmers grow cane for sale to mills, they are commonly under strict contracts as to the time of harvest and the timing and amount of deliveries. To offset the monopoly power of mills relative to farmers who cannot ship their cane elsewhere, these contracts are often regulated by governments through some combination of fixed prices and quotas for cane and for sugar. The problem of timing is accentuated, in most areas, by the seasonal nature of production. The bulk of mill capacity remains idle much of the year, since harvesting and milling cannot be spread out

without a great drop in sugar yields. The same factors operate, although less forcefully, in the case of beets.[8]

These inherent features of sugar production have had enormous influence on the history of Latin America. The establishment of the industry created a far greater demand for labor than could be met by European immigration. Of the approximately 12 million slaves brought to the Americas, it is estimated that 8 million were employed on sugar plantations, principally in northeast Brazil, Hispaniola, and the smaller islands of the Caribbean. None of these areas had been successfully colonized, and they might have been abandoned but for the development of sugar production. Sugar was thus very influential in the balance among the Spanish, Portuguese, British, and French in the New World and is largely responsible for the existence of several nations and dependencies today. The proceeds from sugar financed the economic growth of Brazil until the mid-seventeenth century, and the labor force created for the industry was later shifted to cotton and cocoa in the northeast and to coffee there and in the center-south of the country. In most cases, however, the early sugar economy did not form links with other regions or sectors, except for a small demand for foodstuffs, and the sugar colonies were oriented even more strongly than others toward trade with Europe. The industry also led to the establishment of a large labor force on a relatively small area, under the control of a small class which owned the land and controlled all processing and trade. It thus led to problems of population pressure, land tenure and class structure analogous to those created elsewhere in Latin America by the conquest of large native agricultural populations.

The present structure of the centrifugal cane sugar industry in Latin America varies considerably from country to country. Estate production is dominant in Colombia, the Dominican Republic, El Salvador, and Peru. Until 1960, estates owned by the major factories also accounted for the bulk of output in Cuba; private estates were nationalized and are now operated variously as state farms or as cooperatives, with some small private holdings remaining (see table 12-5). Except in Cuba, there is no state ownership of land or factories in sugar, but government regulation is extensive and in some cases (as in Brazil and Mexico) directly influences the distribution of production through agrarian policy or controls on estates. In almost every country there is some control not only of consumer prices, but of prices for cane at the mill, and quantitative controls on exports, domestic sugar supply, and distribution of cane to factories are also common. There is little or no foreign capital in the industry in most countries, but United States ownership is or has been extremely important in Cuba, Haiti, and the Dominican Republic. The pattern resembles that for minerals: foreign control is usually greatest at the processing stage (the mill or sometimes the refinery), particularly in the largest units, and for exports. Much U.S. capital was invested in the Cuban sugar industry after the Spanish-American War, especially during the 1920s. By 1940 U.S. interests controlled some 55 percent of the island's sugar

---

[8] The national sugar policies of individual countries are described in ISC, *World Sugar Economy*, vol. I.

production and a large share of the banking and communications systems. Thereafter ownership was transferred to Cuban nationals and the U.S. share of the sugar industry fell to 47 percent in 1950 and to only 37 percent by 1958. By that time all other foreign investment in the industry — Canadian, British, Dutch, French, and Spanish — had been liquidated or reduced to negligible amounts, covering only 1 percent of output.[9] The degree of foreign control of the island's principal industry was a major source of the Cuban hostility which culminated in the expropriation of the industry and the end of sugar trade with the United States. In the Dominican Republic foreign control is still extensive, and the largest factory in Haiti is also U.S. owned. Foreign ownership is perhaps less important directly in the case of sugar than for other resource products such as minerals in which U.S. capital is dominant, because the greatest influence on trade and prices is the sugar-importing policy of the United States; but that policy in turn is certainly influenced by the distribution of American capital abroad.

World Trade and Markets

For more than a century after the establishment of sugar industries in the New World, international trade in sugar was closely controlled by the European countries with sugar colonies. Beginning in the eighteenth century trade restrictions were gradually lifted, and by the early nineteenth century the flow of sugar was relatively free of subsidies, preferential tariffs, and other barriers. This situation changed radically as the major European countries began to develop and protect beet sugar industries. Most producers subsidized exports by bounties, and in the process incurred very large costs and also damaged the cane sugar industries in their colonies. An agreement was concluded in 1864 to abolish subsidies, but as only four countries joined, the agreement was unsuccessful. In 1902 ten European countries subscribed to a similar pact, the Brussels Convention, which effectively ended sugar dumping. European exports declined, and as internal prices fell, consumption expanded markedly; cane sugar producers recovered part of the market. The Convention was annulled in 1918.

The fall of sugar prices in the late 1920s led to the Chadbourne Agreement of 1931, under which seven (later nine) countries sought to restrict production and exports. The agreement included too few nations to cope with the decline in demand during the Depression, so in 1937 it was superseded by the first International Sugar Agreement. Seventeen countries agreed to a system of export quotas, set to achieve reasonable prices and discourage excess production, and adjustable by a weighted vote of exporters and importers. The agreement applied to the "free market" excluding the trade of the United States and certain exports by the Soviet Union and among French territories, and it supplemented without changing the protective policies of the producing and importing members. The outbreak of World War II ended the operation of the agreement, but its administrative provisions continued in force until 1953.

In that year another International Sugar Agreement was concluded, with increased participation, for a similar system of regulation. A range of prices was established, as in the International Coffee Agreement, outside of which quotas were to be adjusted or eliminated. Free-market sugar prices remained quite stable for the five-year life of the agreement, except in 1957. In 1958 another five-year agreement was concluded, which operated through 1961. In consequence of the Cuban Revolution of 1959, the United States in 1960 first reduced and then abolished the Cuban import quota. Since the basis of the Sugar Agreement in the 1950s "was a bargain by which Cuba, as the dominant free market supplier, agreed to manage its supplies and stocks, in exchange for its large quota in the high-priced United States market,"[10] the essence of the agreement was destroyed. The other members were unable to agree on export quotas for the trade year 1962-63, so at the end of 1961 the economic terms of the agreement ceased to function. Formally, the agreement was extended by protocol after it expired in 1963.

As the United States increased its own sugar production and raised the quotas for other suppliers, and Cuba redirected its exports toward the Soviet Union, the free market price of sugar at first rose, reaching a peak in 1963 when beet sugar supplies were low. Thereafter production consistently exceeded consumption and stocks rose. As most of the surplus moved to the residual market, prices there fell sharply, reaching late in 1966 a low of 1.5 cents per pound, well below production costs in virtually every country. This situation led to a new United Nations Sugar Conference in September 1965, to consider ways of negotiating and implementing a new agreement.[11] Several suggestions were put forward for modifying the operation of previous agreements, including adoption of production controls by exporters and allowances for concessional sales to low-income importing countries. The most significant features discussed were proposed undertakings by importers to buy specified quantities above some minimum price and by exporters to sell those quantities below some maximum price; and a proposed agreement by the developed importing countries to limit increases in production to half of their increased consumption. This second proposal would slow the shrinkage of world trade relative to output, guarantee some growth in markets for exporters, and result in lower costs of production. However, none of the major importers has shown any inclination to limit its own production further than it has already done or to accept modifications in its preferential import system. The degree of self-sufficiency of the developed importing countries, excluding the Communist countries, rose from 70 percent in 1961-63 to 77 percent in 1964-66, despite the substantial decline in prices. The first suggestion would make the sugar agreement operate more like the wheat control scheme and would

[9] See J. Plank, ed., *Cuba and the United States* (Brookings Institution, 1967), especially the essays by H. Wriston and J. W. Sundelson, pp. 29 and 98-101.

[10] J. A. Pincus, "Commodity Agreements: Bonanza or Illusion?" *Columbia Journal of World Business*, January-February 1967.

[11] The work of this Conference and events in the sugar market between 1960 and 1965 are summarized in UNCTAD, *Commodity Survey 1966*, part I, pp. 66-70. The draft agreement is reproduced in doc. TD/Sugar 6/4.

shift some of the burden of price maintenance to importers. However, the major developed countries were not significant exporters of sugar, as several of them are of wheat, so that there is no divergence of interest among them and thus little prospect of an agreement.

The Conference was unsuccessful, and was not reconvened until 1968. In the interim a number of meetings of a Consultative Committee on Sugar and a Preparatory Working Party were held under UNCTAD auspices, to review the difficulties encountered in 1965, consult with interested governments, and prepare for the resumption of negotiations. Some attention was given to the possibility of a short-term agreement designed simply to raise prices while a longer-term accord was worked out, but this proposal was abandoned as too difficult in June 1966. This meeting coincided with the end of an effort, first discussed in November 1965 and initiated in March of 1966, by 31 exporters to raise prices by withholding supplies. The scheme was intended to maintain a level of 2.5 cents per pound, but did not succeed; prices remained low in 1966 and were only slightly higher in 1967. The excess of production over consumption declined somewhat but stocks continued to rise. By the end of that year, however, sufficient agreement had been reached so that the Sugar Conference was reconvened in April 1968. The second UNCTAD Conference urged the adoption of a new International Agreement to enter into force in 1969.[12] In October 1968 a new Agreement was finally concluded, to go into effect at the beginning of 1969 and to apply only to the current free market after allowance for sales by Cuba to the Communist countries and some re-exports by the latter. There was no modification of any major importers' market arrangements; the United States and the European Common Market did not even participate in the final negotiations. The Agreement will therefore cover only a very small share of world trade in sugar, and is designed solely to keep the price above 2.5 cents per pound for those producers with little or no access to protected import markets. Export quotas will be adjusted proportionally as the price varies, except that some sales beyond quotas may be allowed to smaller countries heavily dependent on sugar.[13] In this respect the Agreement's provisions resemble the waivers of export quotas which have repeatedly been allowed under the International Coffee Agreement. Independent action by exporters is much more difficult and less likely than it was for coffee and cocoa, because of the great number of countries involved, the overwhelming importance of Cuban supplies, and the possibility of increasing beet sugar output in importing countries. The last factor also limits greatly the degree to which the free market price can be raised by an Agreement. Thus price is not the sole major issue, as it largely is for coffee and cocoa, and the distribution of trade and the policies of importing countries are at least as important. Other issues such as storage, quality differences, and the like are relatively insignificant.

The International Sugar Agreements differ from the arrangements for coffee and tin, in that they apply to only about 50 percent of world trade and to a much smaller share of world production. The free market, which at the turn of the century included nearly all trade in sugar, has been sharply reduced by changes in the policies of major importers. The principal shift occurred in the United States in 1934. Until then the United States had protected domestic producers of both beet and cane sugar by a tariff; Hawaii, Puerto Rico, and the Virgin Islands paid no tariff, and Cuba and the Philippines were accorded a preferential levy. When prices fell in the Depression the tariff did not adequately protect the incomes of domestic producers, so a quota system was instituted which has continued in force, with few modifications, to the present. Estimated requirements are distributed among domestic growers of beets, domestic cane producers, other "internal" suppliers, and a number of countries paying the full or partial tariff.

In 1951 the United Kingdom negotiated the Commonwealth Sugar Agreement with several commonwealth exporters. This arrangement was designed not so much to protect domestic beet growers as to assure supplies at stable prices and, initially, to conserve dollars. Quotas are set for exports to the United Kingdom, to which a negotiated price applies. Several other importers, notably France, Portugal, and the Soviet Union, also maintain arrangements with their dependencies or neighbor countries, and this trade is excluded from the International Sugar Agreement.[14] Of total sugar exports of some 17 million tons in the late 1950s, about 45 percent moved in the free market, 14 percent was part of the Commonwealth Sugar Agreement, almost 25 percent was U.S. imports under tariff, and 15 percent was accounted for by the various internal markets, that of the United States being much the largest (see table 12-6). In the early 1960s these proportions were changed by the exclusion of Cuban sugar from the U.S. market and its redirection to the Soviet Union. The former Cuban quota, suspended in 1960 and abolished the following year in retaliation for expropriation of United States capital in the island, was partly distributed among other Latin American suppliers (especially Brazil, the Dominican Republic, Mexico and Peru) and partly allocated to domestic producers.

The world sugar economy is in effect separated into four major markets — the United States, the United Kingdom, the Soviet Union, and the free market — and a large number of small markets embracing one or several countries or one nation and its overseas possessions. Prices in the lesser markets are often fixed or recorded on different grades of sugar, and are therefore difficult to compare except at retail where excise taxes are frequently high. Among the three principal markets the price in the United Kingdom now is normally slightly above the world price; from the outbreak of World War II to 1955 sugar imports were controlled by the government at fixed or negotiated prices. The U.S. price, including the tariff, is usually considerably above the free market price, and also much more stable (see table 12-7). In the absence of any preferential marketing

[12]See UNCTAD, *Commodity Survey 1967*, part II, pp. 99-104, and part III, pp. 44-46, and *Commodity Problems and Policies*, doc. TD/L.29, 25 March 1968, p. 1.

[13]FAO, "The International Sugar Agreement of 1968," *Monthly Bulletin of Agricultural Economics and Statistics,* December 1968.

[14]For descriptions of these arrangements see ISC, *World Sugar Economy*, vol. II.

arrangements, but with continued protection of beet sugar production, trade in the free market would increase substantially, and the world price of sugar would presumably somewhat exceed the recent free market price.

The organization of the market greatly influences the origin and destination as well as the amount of trade. This is evident in the shift of U.S. imports from Cuba to other Latin American countries after 1959 (see table 12-8). For most countries in the region sugar is a relatively minor export, even with the U.S. quota. Only Cuba and the Dominican Republic depend overwhelmingly on sugar, the former for three-fourths or more of its foreign exchange earnings, and the latter currently for about half. Despite a substantial increase in tonnage and value, Peru depends less on sugar now than a decade ago. Haiti is the only other country to obtain as much as 10 percent of its foreign exchange from sugar. As with all Latin America's resource exports, North America and Western Europe are the major markets. The concentration is not so pronounced for sugar, however, since consumption is more widespread and the region has greater cost advantages than for most other products. Exports to Asia and even to Africa are relatively large (some hundreds of thousands of tons) and despite the efforts at import substitution there is still considerable intraregional trade, Chile being the chief importer and Brazil the largest exporter.

Several efforts have been made to assess the impact of the various forms of interference by importing countries in the world sugar market. The most thorough estimate, based on data for 1959, suggests that in that year tariffs and excise taxes reduced world sugar consumption outside Communist countries by nearly 4 million tons (see table 12-9, section I). Replacement of protection by deficiency payments (subsidies) to domestic producers and elimination of taxes would have generated some $440 million in additional foreign exchange for exporting countries, representing a net gain of between $150 million and $200 million. The more drastic change of eliminating uncompetitive production entirely would have resulted in an additional trade of 7.7 million tons, increased exporters' earnings by nearly $900 million, and provided net benefits of $100 million to importers and $330 million to exporters. Comparably detailed estimates are not available for other products in which the advanced countries protect or subsidize their competition with lower-cost suppliers in less developed countries; but the total effect in the case of sugar must exceed that for any product with the possible exceptions of grains, meat, and mineral fuels. The resources that could be made available to the poorer countries by an end to sugar protection or its substitution by subsidies are enormous. Furthermore, the costs to the importing countries are fairly large.

The benefit to the countries allowed to supply a high-price, protected market can, of course, be quite large: some $230 million in the case of the United States, and $100 million in the United Kingdom and Canada, on the basis of price differences associated with quotas and tariffs (see table 12-9, section II). On the same basis, however, the benefit to domestic producers is likely to be still greater, and no account is taken of the lower volume of trade imposed by protection. Finally, the quota system as operated by the United States has the disadvantage, for suppliers or potential suppliers, that quotas are assigned and changed, often by large amounts, as much for political as for economic reasons. They can be used to punish one country – as in the case of Cuba, or to reward or encourage another – as in the Dominican Republic, which received a large share of the former Cuban allotment. The political and administrative problems associated with the system are seen as a major deterrent to its extension to other products which less developed countries might export to the United States.[15] Latin America is, as the world's lowest-cost source of sugar, certainly hurt by the various restrictions to free trade. Certain countries may benefit under the system, in consequence of their receiving larger quotas than they could otherwise export, but this applies to only a few countries and the amounts involved are small.

Outlook

Projections of future demand for sugar are usually based on the anticipated growth of income per capita, assuming no changes in national policies which result in appreciable retail price movements. The developed countries which are the principal importers have shown no willingness to reduce excise taxes on sugar or to modify their protection of domestic producers so as to reduce prices. However, it is more difficult to estimate the amount and distribution of future sugar supply, since it responds to national importing policies, which may change in the future, as much as to costs of production in different countries. In particular, either the resumption of Cuban exports to the United States or the inclusion of Cuba in an international sugar agreement could greatly affect world trade in sugar. In addition to their direct impact on the amount and direction of trade, any such changes might also influence consumption significantly by their effects on price.

The demand for centrifugal sugar in 1975 has been estimated by the FAO as between 75 and 80 million tons, representing an increase of 50 percent or more over the level of the early 1960s. Sugar is the only tropical product for which such a strong expansion of consumption is foreseen. The largest increase, both absolutely and per capita, is expected to occur in Asia; in most of the rest of the world, little or no increase in per capita consumption is anticipated. On the supply side, the trend toward self-sufficiency is expected to continue in all areas. As part of its overall agricultural policy, the European Common Market will probably cease to import sugar in the early 1970s, except to process some sugar from overseas territories for re-export. The Communist countries are similarly expected to reach complete self-sufficiency, and a substantial rise in U.S. production is foreseen. If exporting countries continue to produce according to their present supply conditions, the result could be a great surplus; total supplies in 1975 are projected as 80 to 91 million tons, with an excess possibly as high as 16 million tons but more

---

[15] See H. G. Johnson, *Economic Policies Toward Less Developed Countries* (Brookings Institution, 1967), p. 167. The reference is to the political/administrative objections to preferences for manufactured goods.

probably between 5 and 10 million. Such an oversupply would exert serious pressure on the free market price; this prospect was the major impetus for a new international agreement on sugar, which free market exporters saw as the only protection of their earnings against the anticipated reduction of exports as a share of consumption. There does not, unfortunately, appear to be any likelihood that the developed countries will reduce the barriers to world sugar trade; thus the 1968 Agreement does no more than control supplies and prices for a small share of world trade. So long as Cuba is economically tied to the Soviet Union, it has not seemed possible to include Cuba in the Agreement, and the present arrangement is therefore quite susceptible to variations in Cuban output and exports and to re-exports of Cuban sugar by the Soviet Union.

The region is expected to have an exportable surplus around 1975 of at least 10 million tons, and perhaps nearly twice that much. If Latin America supplies the same share of the United States import market as in recent years, the portion of its total exports going to the free market will almost certainly increase and the average value of exports will fall. Around 1960 the region earned an average of some $90 per ton of sugar exported, or about 4 cents per pound. At that rate exports in the early 1970s should equal roughly $1,000 million; a very large volume of exports would more probably require an average value of 3 cents per pound or less, or perhaps some $1,100 million to $1,200 million at most. At such levels sugar exports would show an average annual growth of only about 1.5 percent over the period 1960-1975. Thus, despite the region's advantages in sugar production the prospects for export growth are most disappointing. This situation was reflected before 1960 in the decline in sugar exports relative to sugar production and to total exports in almost all Latin American countries. That trend was interrupted by the shift in U.S. quotas, but it is almost certain to reappear, except possibly in Cuba and the Dominican Republic which depend too greatly on sugar for such changes to be very pronounced.

CHAPTER 12 TABLES

TABLE 12-1. World Area Harvested for Centrifugal Sugar Production,[a] Averages, 1934-38, 1958-60, and 1965-67
(Thousands of hectares)

Country or Region	1934-38	1958-60	1965-67
I. Cane:			
Latin America[b]	1,227	2,769	4,593
Argentina	163	304	241
Bolivia		5	27
Brazil	180	800	1,620
Colombia	5	39	336
Cuba	681	1,090	1,446
Dominican Republic	73	149	120
Ecuador	4	17	97
El Salvador	9	7	20
Mexico	60	254	396
Paraguay	2	14	27
Peru	31	42	52
Uruguay		2	5
Venezuela	4	45	65
Caribbean America	218	355	324
North America	106	109	202
Western Europe	4		6
Africa	214	321	512
Asia	710	1,160	4,102
Oceania	175	214	251
Communist Countries	170	335	433
World Total Cane	2,824	5,263	10,543

TABLE 12-1 – Continued

County or Region	1934-38	1958-60	1965-67
II. Beet:			
Latin America	1	18	35
Chile		9	19
Uruguay	1	9	16
North America	342	398	549
Western Europe	958	1,163	1,663
Africa			16
Asia	27	243	339
Oceania	1		
Communist Countries	1,931	3,924	5,978
World Total Beet	3,261	5,764	8,117
Total Centrifugal Sugar	6,085	11,027	18,660

Sources: ISC, *The World Sugar Economy*, vol. I, *National Sugar Economies and Policies*, passim, and vol. II, *The World Picture* (London, 1963), pp. 244-47.

[a]In cases where significant amounts of noncentrifugal sugar are produced, area harvested (cane only) is as follows: Colombia (1960-61) – 341,000 hectares; India (1934-38) – 1,229,000 hectares, (1950-60) – 1,136,000 hectares; Pakistan (1959-60) – 328,000 hectares.

[b]Includes estimates for Costa Rica, Guatemala, Haiti, Honduras, Nicaragua, and Panama, for which no information or only information on the total area harvested (including noncentrifugal sugar) is available.

TABLE 12–2. World Yields[a] of Cane, Beets, and Centrifugal Sugar, Averages, 1934-38 and 1958-60 Crop Years
(Metric tons per hectare harvested and percent sugar extraction rates)

Country or Region	1934-38 Yield of Cane/Beets	Sugar	Extraction rate (%)	1958-60 Yield of Cane/Beets	Sugar	Extraction rate (%)
I. Cane:						
Latin America[b]	39.6	4.2	10.6	50.0	5.3	10.6
Argentina	27.8	2.6	9.3	35.9	3.1	8.8
Bolivia				36.8	3.0	8.2
Brazil	37.9			41.7	3.8	9.1
Colombia				71.0	7.5	10.5
Cuba	36.8	4.0	10.9	43.0[c]	5.5	12.8
Dominican Republic	50.8	6.1	12.0	55.7[d]	6.5	11.6
Ecuador					5.4	
El Salvador		1.4		73.6	6.7	9.1
Mexico	51.9	5.3	10.2	56.5	5.4	9.6
Paraguay			5.5	25.1	2.4	9.5
Peru[e]	104.0	12.4	11.9	157.1	17.1	10.9
(adjusted)[f]	59.5	7.1		89.9	9.8	10.9
Uruguay				39.0[c]	4.0	10.0
Venezuela				43.3[c]	3.8	8.8
Caribbean America	68.6	7.0	10.9	64.9	6.6	10.1
North America	44.9	3.6	8.1	52.9	4.8	9.1
Western Europe	65.3	6.0	9.2	64.5	5.6	8.6
Africa	48.6	5.2	10.7	69.0	7.6	11.0
Asia	46.8	5.0	10.6	49.6	5.3	10.3
Oceania[e]	80.5	10.8	13.4	91.3	11.6	12.8
(adjusted)[f]	57.4	8.3	14.7	72.2	9.6	13.2
Communist Countries				37.5	2.6[c]	6.9
World Average, Cane	47.5	5.1	10.8	50.8	5.3	10.4
II. Beet:						
Latin America	13.0	1.4	10.8	23.5	3.0	12.8
Chile				29.2	4.1	14.0
Uruguay	13.0	1.4	10.7	15.0	1.7	11.3
North America	26.9	4.0	14.8	38.7	5.6	14.4
Western Europe	27.8	4.1	14.7	34.6	5.0	14.4
Africa				6.1	0.9	14.8
Asia	14.0	2.3	16.4	19.5	3.0	15.3
Oceania	30.9	4.1	13.2			
Communist Countries	17.5	2.5	14.2	18.1	2.5	13.8
World Average, Beet	21.3	3.1	14.5	23.5	3.3	14.0
World Average Yields, Cane and Beet	33.5	4.0	11.9	36.5	4.3	11.7

Source: ISC, *World Sugar Economy*, vol. I, p. 104, and vol. II, pp. 231-33, 250-59.

[a]All data refer to cane or beets used for the production of centrifugal sugar only. Except as indicated, yields are calculated on the area harvested per crop year.

[b]Latin American average includes Costa Rica, Guatemala, Haiti, Honduras, Nicaragua, and Panama (see table 12–1, fn. b).

[c]Two-year average.

[d]One-year average.

[e]Unadjusted figure.

[f]The growing season in Peru and Hawaii ranges from 18 to 24 months, so that the area in cane greatly exceeds the area harvested in any one year. Yields are adjusted to a 12-month basis for comparison with other areas, where the growing season is generally between 10 and 14 months. For Peru, the average season is assumed to be 21 months. For Hawaii, the reported yield is deflated by the ratio of area harvested to area in cane for 1934-38, and the ratio for the years 1955-59 is used for later years. Adjustment for short growing seasons (as in Louisiana and Argentina) is not made, as the land is not used for other crops in winter. Neither are yields adjusted for other areas with long seasons (Indonesia, Taiwan, South Africa) for lack of data. See V. P. Timoshenko and B. C. Swerling, *The World's Sugar: Progress and Policy* (Stanford University Press, 1957), pp. 44-45.

TABLE 12–3. World Centrifugal Sugar Production, 1925-1967
(*Thousands of metric tons, raw value/crop year*)

Country or Region	Average 1925/26-1929/30	Average 1930/31-1934/35	Average 1935/36-1939/40	Average 1940/41-1944/45	Average 1945/46-1949/50	1951	1952	1953	1954	1955	1956
Latin America	6,777	4,701	5,475	6,300	9,119	10,320	12,023	10,503	10,657	10,219	10,935
Argentina	435	381	476	474	609	678	583	740	810	608	759
Bolivia			1	1	2	2	3	4	5	5	5
Brazil	450	566	759	941	1,318	1,607	1,785	2,002	2,118	2,073	2,268
Chile										7	13
Colombia	35	30	44	73	120	198	197	190	241	253	261
Costa Rica	4	6	8	14	17	23	30	31	32	34	24
Cuba	4,804	2,579	2,887	3,344	5,351	5,759	7,225	5,159	4,890	4,528	4,740
Dominican Republic	354	398	445	439	459	570	648	552	658	637	780
Ecuador	22	20	22	29	42	57	59	61	52	67	75
El Salvador	16	10	14	18	23	28	29	30	33	37	38
Guatemala	17	12	16	21	28	24	29	37	46	48	52
Haiti	15	25	40	44	44	58	58	55	46	56	59
Honduras	19	7		1	2	5	7	8	7	11	13
Mexico	192	246	327	419	589	723	744	868	894	961	823
Nicaragua	6	7	8	14	18	26	30	33	34	37	33
Panama	4	4	4	5	10	16	19	18	20	16	16
Paraguay	4	7	6	13	15	22	23	14	17	14	21
Peru	379	391	398	417	432	463	471	602	612	652	690
Uruguay		1	2	1	2	12	12	21	31	18	22
Venezuela	21	21	18	32	38	49	71	78	106	157	243
Caribbean America	441	546	742	673	792	1,037	1,071	1,150	1,232	923	1,271
North America	1,113	1,537	1,879	1,795	1,879	1,973	2,059	2,271	2,481	2,299	2,401
Western Europe	4,344	4,924	5,303	5,118	4,008	5,755	5,501	6,952	6,614	7,045	6,548
Africa	731	901	1,151	1,243	1,297	1,599	1,716	1,875	1,934	2,258	2,321
Asia	3,899	4,450	4,447	3,601	2,087	3,259	4,307	4,870	4,845	5,686	5,909
Oceania	621	772	1,016	832	871	864	1,051	1,427	1,424	1,319	1,334
Communist Countries	3,514	2,991	3,777	1,803	2,655	6,545	6,239	7,235	6,132	6,638	7,307
World Total Cane	14,021	13,344	15,000	14,673	16,374	19,407	22,776	22,369	22,588	23,315	24,257
World Total Beet	8,868	9,258	10,591	8,399	8,182	14,022	13,425	16,056	14,882	15,658	16,016
World Total Cane and Beet	22,889	22,602	25,593	23,072	24,555	33,429	36,201	38,425	37,470	38,973	40,272
Latin American Production as a Share of:											
World Total Sugar Cane and Beet (%)	29.6	20.7	21.3	27.3	37.1	30.8	33.2	27.3	28.4	26.2	27.1
Total Cane (%)	48.3	35.2	36.5	42.9	55.6	53.1	52.7	46.9	47.1	43.8	45.0

TABLE 12-3 – Continued

Country or Region	1957	1958	1959	1960	1961	1962	1963	1964	1965	1966	1967
Latin American Total	12,634	13,495	13,952	14,582	15,284	13,555	12,769	14,373	17,417	15,545	13,279
Argentina	688	1,056	929	815	671	799	990	992	1,309	1,035	732
Bolivia	9	17	19	26	44	49	74	100	96	86	102
Brazil	2,714	3,004	3,108	3,319	3,354	3,238	3,037	3,425	4,614	3,842	4,275
Chile	21	34	44	79	59	43	110	108	104	176	124
Colombia	234	264	277	328	363	402	368	428	485	537	597
Costa Rica	30	38	56	60	70	92	84	95	120	120	145
Cuba	5,672	5,784	5,964	5,862	6,767	4,815	3,821	4,590	6,082	4,867	6,236
Dominican Republic	836	838	809	1,112	873	902	806	825	583	691	819
Ecuador	76	87	100	103	140	140	137	167	195	177	294
El Salvador	49	46	44	50	51	64	60	72	103	107	125
Guatemala	60	63	61	73	83	117	133	158	138	164	171
Haiti	57	46	47	60	72	69	69	62	65	68	65
Honduras	13	14	16	20	24	23	29	29	32	40	44
Mexico	1,164	1,210	1,448	1,518	1,488	1,531	1,756	1,932	2,107	2,252	2,411
Nicaragua	42	54	64	65	63	86	93	104	98	68	108
Panama	23	25	27	25	28	28	35	50	50	45	63
Paraguay	31	38	35	30	31	35	38	52	38	36	39
Peru	677	681	705	807	799	765	802	766	771	814	731
Uruguay	27	28	32	35	43	47	48	52	63	50	60
Venezuela	211	168	167	195	261	280	279	316	364	370	413
Caribbean America	1,330	1,275	1,378	1,485	1,565	1,479	1,597	1,478	1,458	1,546	1,629
North America	2,452	2,721	2,693	2,940	3,004	3,112	2,529	3,215	5,828	5,744	5,680
Western Europe	7,287	7,932	7,811	9,558	8,884	7,681	8,541	10,281	9,318	9,566	10,363
Africa	2,407	2,467	2,727	2,387	2,901	2,817	3,400	3,382	3,941	3,951	4,416
Asia	6,143	6,259	7,209	7,373	7,783	7,840	7,459	8,782	10,699	10,947	9,832
Oceania	1,487	1,585	1,545	1,530	1,537	2,084	2,002	2,221	2,390	2,768	2,757
Communist Countries	8,135	9,467	10,134	10,138	11,474	10,696	10,217	12,653	14,096	14,094	14,602
World Total Cane	26,295	26,937	28,901	29,372	31,445	29,971	29,685	32,538	35,894	36,550	37,140
World Total Beet	17,717	20,151	20,733	22,719	23,303	21,615	22,192	27,139	30,190	26,742	27,487
World Total Cane and Beet	44,011	47,139	49,634	52,091	54,749	51,586	51,877	59,077	66,084	63,292	64,627
Latin American Production as a Share of:											
World Total Sugar Cane and Beet (%)	28.7	28.6	28.1	28.1	27.9	26.2	24.6	24.0	26.8	24.2	20.0
Total Cane (%)	48.0	50.0	48.2	49.6	48.6	45.2	43.0	44.0	48.5	42.5	35.8

Sources: ISC, *World Sugar Economy,* vol. II, pp. 237, 240-41. ISC, *Statistical Bulletin,* vol. 25, no. 1, January 1966; vol. 27, no. 3, March 1968.

TABLE 12–4. World Sugar Consumption, Centrifugal and Noncentrifugal, Averages, 1934-38, 1951-53, 1961-63, and 1965-67
(Thousands of metric tons and kilograms per capita)

Country or Region	Total				Per Capita			
	1934-38	1951-53	1961-63	1965-67	1934-38	1951-53	1961-63	1965-67
CENTRIFUGAL								
Latin America	1,948.0	4,282.6	7,886.8	7,983.7	16.9	26.1	31.3	29.9
Argentina	426.6	627.1	792.3	887.9	32.2	34.8	37.9	39.1
Bolivia	23.0	48.3	68.1	88.9	9.1	15.5	18.4	23.7
Brazil	649.1	1,591.7	2,732.4	2,861.0	17.1	28.9	37.4	34.9
Chile	123.1	198.3	285.0	316.8	25.8	31.4	35.6	36.2
Colombia	45.8	178.4	343.6	397.3	5.5	15.0	23.6	21.3
Costa Rica	8.0	20.2	42.3	66.9	14.2	23.6	33.8	44.9
Cuba	158.7	284.1	401.6	554.3	37.0	49.6	67.5	71.2
Dominican Republic	16.0	50.9	102.7	112.7	10.4	22.3	31.3	30.0
Ecuador	25.8	56.0	957.3	106.0	11.6	16.5	20.9	19.9
El Salvador	12.0	25.5	42.0	60.3	7.7	12.8	15.7	19.8
Guatemala	14.0	34.7	78.9	105.0	6.9	11.6	19.5	22.9
Haiti	3.9	25.0	34.6	38.7	1.5	7.8	10.1	8.6
Honduras	5.4	13.3	28.0	36.3	5.1	8.7	13.6	15.4
Mexico	277.6	709.7	1,239.1	1,561.0	15.1	26.0	32.8	35.4
Nicaragua	4.0	21.0	44.6	55.3	5.4	18.3	29.0	32.2
Panama	4.6	14.0	24.6	20.3	8.2	16.6	22.4	16.7
Paraguay	10.9	24.3	33.9	36.3	10.8	16.6	18.5	17.4
Peru	79.2	172.7	280.3	347.4	12.2	19.5	24.7	28.9
Uruguay	55.5	78.2	105.0	120.0	26.8	31.4	40.2	43.6
Venezuela	18.0	109.5	250.4	319.0	5.4	20.0	34.2	35.3
Caribbean America	123.3	229.3	256.4	271.3	21.0	40.0	41.8	44.2
Canada	485.2	663.3	837.9	953.3	44.3	46.6	47.7	46.2
United States	6,029.0	7,341.7	8,987.9	9,553.0	47.0	45.9	46.9	48.5
Western Europe	6,806.1	7,992.2	10,948.8	1,251.3	27.3	28.3	36.4	40.3
Common Market	3,043.6	4,131.9	5,733.8	6,507.1	21.0	25.2	32.3	37.3
Belgium-Luxembourg	252.7	261.9	348.8	355.0	29.3	28.7	36.4	36.0
France	1,032.9	1,263.0	1,572.6	1,815.7	24.7	29.8	33.9	36.8
West Germany	1,090.0	1,384.6	1,855.8	2,158.3	26.9	27.2	33.3	37.4
Italy	341.4	700.7	1,249.9	1,447.0	7.9	14.6	24.9	27.8
Netherlands	326.6	521.7	706.7	730.7	30.9	37.7	45.4	48.7
United Kingdom	2,311.5	2,174.7	2,939.9	2,902.0	48.4	42.7	55.5	52.7
Northern Europe	1,074.7	1,308.1	1,531.8	1,687.4	42.5	41.0	47.6	49.7
Southern Europe	376.2	377.5	743.2	823.2	11.9	10.6	19.3	21.3
Asia	3,554.0	4,708.7	9,995.5	12,640.4	3.2	3.4	5.8	6.7
Africa	844.1	1,816.0	2,876.0	3,450.0	5.1	8.6	10.8	10.9
Oceania	477.4	702.3	790.5	854.9	44.5	49.5	45.7	47.9
World Total	24,314.6	33,974.3	53,769.3	64,176.5	11.4	13.2	17.3	19.1
NONCENTRIFUGAL								
Latin America	1,195	1,461	1,392	1,498	10.5	8.7	5.2	8.1
Brazil	361	301	270	270	9.6	5.5	3.7	3.3
Colombia	618	750	744	647	97.8	63.3	50.1	34.8
Costa Rica	12	29	32	40	21.3	33.6	26.1	26.8
Ecuador	12	24	27	36	5.4	7.1	6.0	6.7
El Salvador	13	23	17	24	8.4	11.8	6.4	7.8
Guatemala	27	33	39	29	13.2	10.9	10.1	6.4
Honduras	17	20	17	19	16.2	13.6	9.1	8.1
Mexico	87	147	140	350	3.6	5.4	3.9	7.9
Nicaragua	6	20	16	17	8.0	17.6	10.5	9.9
Panama	2	9.7	2	4	3.6	11.5	1.8	3.0
Peru	9	24.7	24	15	1.4	2.7	2.2	1.3
Venezuela	48	79.3	64	44	14.4	14.5	8.4	5.6
Asia	4,464	4,581	7,725	9,124	3.7	3.3	4.5	4.8
World Total	5,659	6,042	9,117	11,244	4.3	3.8	4.7	5.3
Latin American Total Sugar Consumption as a Share of:								
Total L.A. Production (%)	47.1	46.3	59.0	53.9				
Total World Consumption (%)	10.8	14.7	14.9	13.3				

Sources: ISC, *World Sugar Economy*, vol. II, pp. 260-265, 269, 272-73, and ISC *Statistical Bulletin*, June 1966, November 1968.

TABLE 12–5. Structure of the Centrifugal Cane Sugar Industry in Latin America, circa 1961
(Areas in hectares, capacities in metric tons per day)

Country and Year		Distribution of Producing Units by Type	Distribution of Producing Units by Size		Factories (Mills)[a]		Refineries	
					Number	Average Capacity	Number	Average Capacity
Argentina	1960/61	Percent share in cane production: Factory estates 37.7 Independent growers 62.3	*No. of farms*	*Size in hectares*	36	2,370	25	
			8,229	less than 3	(24 refineries associated with mills and one separate)			
			9,620	3 – 10				
			1,349	11 – 20				
			817	21 – 100				
			89	over 100				
			Total: 20,104 independent farms					
Bolivia	1961	Percent share in area of cane harvested: Factory estates 16.3 Independent growers 83.8	Average harvested cane area of individual farm: 10.6 ha.		4	875		
Brazil	1960/61	Percent shares in cane production: Factory estates 50 or less[b] Independent growers balance	Average cane area per farm, 30-35 ha. (São Paulo)		303	566	291	
Colombia	1961	Percent shares in cane production:[c] Factory estates 70 Independent growers 30	Large factory estates 5,000-7,000 ha. Small estates 1,000-2,000 ha.		19	939	2	210
Cuba	1960/61	Percent shares in area of cane: Cooperatives 34.9 Balance, individual holdings and state farms 65.1 (Previously mill estates accounted for 74 percent of the area and independent growers for the remainder)	*No. of farms*	*Size in hectares*	160	3,400	21	350
			63,764	less than 26.8	(Two largest mills have capacities over 10,000 tons/day)			
			6,912	26.8 – 67.1				
			2,800	over 67.1				
Dom. Rep.	1962	All cane grown on factory estates	Average estate area 12,000 ha.		16	3,841		
					(Two largest mills have capacities over 12,000 tons/day)			
Ecuador	1960/61				17	367		
					(Largest mill has capacity over 10,000 tons/day)			
El Salvador	1961/62	Large share of cane grown on factory estates			22	510	1	154
					(Includes two inactive mills)			
Guatemala	1960/61				10	358		
Haiti	1960/61				3		3	
Honduras	1962				4	2,105		
Mexico	1961/62	Percent shares of cane growers: Belonging to cooperatives 92 Independent growers and tenants 8	800 cooperatives with average of 96 members, plus 6,320 other growers		71	2,086	23	
					(Largest mill has capacity 14,570 tons/day)			
Nicaragua	1961				6	915		
Panama	1961				2	1,700		
Paraguay	1960/61	Percent shares in cane production: Factory estates 10 Independent growers 90	24,000 farms, average area in cane 0.9 ha. in 1955/56		8	391		
Peru	1961	Bulk of cane grown on factory estates; only two estates buy from independent growers			14	2,086		
Uruguay	1961				3	690	1	250
Venezuela	1960/61				11	1,900		

Source: ISC, *World Sugar Economy*, vol. I, passim.

[a]Many mills produce plantation white sugar, which is not refined but which may not require further processing.
[b]Factories are required by law to buy at least half their cane from independent growers; the exact share is unknown.
[c]Factories began buying from independent growers in 1960. Shares were expected to continue to change for several years.

TABLE 12–6. World Sugar Markets, Averages, 1957-59, 1961-62, and 1965-67
(Thousands of metric tons)

Markets	1957-59	1961-62	1965-67
A. EXPORTS EXCLUDED FROM INTERNATIONAL SUGAR AGREEMENT			
I. Internal Markets			
Offshore[a] to United States	1,619.0	1,832.7	1,773.6
United States to Offshore	5.0	6.0	9.2
Overseas to France	401.7	425.1	387.2
France to Overseas	378.2	322.2	358.0
Congo to Belgium	3.3		
Belgium to Congo	7.6	4.0	0.3
Overseas to Netherlands	0.8	1.0	7.7
Netherlands to Overseas	2.6	1.2	5.4
Spain to Canary Islands	8.1		3.9
Overseas[b] to Portugal	148.2	161.9	130.7
Ryukyu Islands to Japan	6.0		
Japan to Ryukyu Islands	5.0		
Tanzania to Kenya	0.7	0.2	1.6
Uganda to Kenya	14.6	23.3	22.8
Uganda to Tanzania	5.6		0.1
Total (I)	2,606.4	2,774.8	2,699.5
Share Total World Exports (%)	15.3	12.9	14.0
II. United States Imports under Tariff[c]			
Cuba	2,981.4		
Share Total World Exports (%)	17.5		
Other Latin America			
Argentina		10.4	57.2
Brazil	3.5	327.4	166.5
Colombia		51.3	91.1
Costa Rica	1.9	25.6	53.7
Dominican Republic	91.7	582.0	520.4
Ecuador		46.6	32.4
El Salvador		13.8	33.5
Guatemala		20.9	31.0
Haiti	5.9	35.2	23.7
Mexico	56.7	404.2	467.9
Nicaragua	12.4	34.1	39.4
Panama	3.6	4.4	25.2
Paraguay		1.6	
Peru	82.3	504.4	333.5
Total	258.0	2,061.9	1,875.5
Share Total World Exports (%)	1.5	9.6	9.7
Other (Philippines)	926.3	2,015.6	1,055.2
Total World Exports (%)	5.4	9.4	5.5
Total (II)	4,165.7	4,077.5	2,930.7
Share Total World Exports (%)	24.4	19.0	15.1
III. Exports to Soviet Union			
Czechoslovakia	127.0	117.2	
Hungary		1.1	1.5
Poland	45.3	97.3	1.3
Total	172.3	215.6	15.2
Share Total World Exports (%)	1.0	1.0	0.1
Cuba		2,348.7	2,191.2
Share Total World Exports (%)		10.9	11.3
IV. Exports under the Commonwealth Sugar Agreement[d]	2,329.6	2,328.3	1,546.6
Share Total World Exports (%)	13.7	10.9	7.9
Total Exports outside Free Market	9,182.4	11,788.2	9,383.2
Share World Total Exports (%)	54.6	55.1	48.5

TABLE 12–6 – Continued

Markets	1957-59	1961-62	1965-67
B. FREE MARKET EXPORTS	7,713.7	9,625.8	9,976.6
Share Total World Exports (%)	45.4	44.9	51.5
C. TOTAL WORLD EXPORTS	16,996.1	21,414.0	19,359.8

Sources: ISC, *World Sugar Economy*, vol. II, pp. 164-65, and ISC, *Statistical Bulletin*.

[a]Hawaii, Puerto Rico, and Virgin Islands.
[b]Angola and Mozambique.
[c]Preferential tariff for Cuba and Philippines; full tariff for other suppliers.
[d]Principally exports of Australia, British Honduras, British West Indies, British Guiana, Fiji, Mauritius, and South Africa to the United Kingdom; includes Commonwealth exports to Canada.

TABLE 12–7. World Sugar Prices, Raw, 1925-1967
(U.S. cents per pound)

Year	Duty Paid, New York	World, Cuban Basis	C.i.f., United Kingdom
1925	4.33	2.44	2.75
1926	4.33	2.46	2.66
1927	4.71	2.78	2.98
1928	4.20	2.36	2.52
1929	3.76	1.77	1.95
1930	3.36	1.27	1.43
1931	3.33	1.13	1.28
1932	2.93	.78	.90
1933	3.22	.86	.99
1934	3.02	.91	1.07
1935	3.23	.88	1.02
1936	3.59	.88	1.05
1937	3.44	1.13	1.40
1938	2.94	1.00	1.18
1939	2.99	1.43	1.45
1940	2.79	1.11	
1941	3.38	1.46	
1942	3.74	2.69	
1943	3.74	2.69	
1944	3.74	2.69	
1945	3.75	3.14	
1946	4.59	4.24	
1947	6.21	5.03	
1948	5.54	4.23	
1949	5.81	4.16	
1950	5.93	4.98	
1951	6.06	5.67	
1952	6.26	4.17	
1953	6.29	3.41	
1954	6.09	3.26	
1955	5.95	3.24	
1956	6.09	3.48	4.47
1957	6.24	5.16	5.87
1958	6.27	3.50	3.92
1959	6.24	2.97	3.41
1960	6.30	3.14	3.56
1961	6.30	2.91	3.21
1962	6.45	2.97	3.20
1963	8.18	8.48	8.96
1964	6.90	5.86	6.45
1965	6.74	2.11	2.69
1966	6.99	1.86	2.23
1967	7.28	1.99	

Sources: ISC, *World Sugar Economy*, vol. II, p. 342. USDA, *Sugar Statistics and Related Data, 1961-67*.

TABLE 12–8. Latin American Exports of Centrifugal Sugar by Destination, 1950-1966
(Thousands of metric tons and millions of U.S. dollars)

Exporter and Destination	1950	1951	1952	1953	1954	1955	1956	1957	1958	1959
Argentina										
Value						83.7		89.2		
Brazil	24.0	18.4	44.5	246.5	150.5	581.0	23.4	409.0	775.8	605.9
Europe		11.0	10.0	177.9	33.8	216.0	4.4	196.4	274.1	237.2
North America				26.7	31.6	82.2		30.1	127.9	10.5
South America	18.0		34.0	9.3	82.7	206.8	14.5	164.9	296.4	94.2
Asia				18.9			4.2	19.5	77.4	205.5
Africa										58.4
Value	3.4	3.5	5.1	22.4	12.4	46.9	1.6	45.9	57.4	33.4
Share of exports (%)	0.2	0.1	0.3	1.4	0.7	3.2		3.2	4.6	2.6
Colombia		53.9					58.4			
Value		7.2	3.6				5.0	2.7		
Share of exports (%)		1.6	0.5	0.07	0.04		0.8	0.1		
Costa Rica				7.2	5.6	7.0		1.0	1.3	7.3
Value				0.6	0.5	0.6		0.1	0.2	0.6
Share of exports (%)				0.7	0.5	0.7		0.1	0.2	0.7
Cuba	5,206.8	5,441.6	5,007.7	5,516.3	4,226.1	4,664.1	5,394.2	5,274.9	5,631.6	4,951.9
Communist Countries				9.6	9.5	485.4	264.2	391.8	201.3	273.8
Europe	1,539.2	1,632.6	1,073.6	1,966.2	754.4	707.0	1,039.6	1,195.0	1,013.4	857.2
North America	2,873.1	2,634.1	2,644.2	2,429.5	2,410.0	2,574.1	2,812.7	2,753.5	3,431.5	3,003.0
South America	59.5	116.7	37.8	212.4	93.5	70.1	150.0	80.3	40.5	78.6
Asia	147.0	357.4	524.0	560.9	672.5	545.0	783.9	516.5	766.9	
Africa	108.5	82.4	167.4	125.9	187.1	132.8	162.1	192.2	161.8	200.6
Value	555	666	565	518	446	473	524	654	588	490.5
Share of exports (%)	83.1	82.7	81.5	76.8	79.2	77.4	75.3	77.4	75.7	76.9
Dominican Republic	430.8	496.4	567.2	570.0	532.4	601.2	717.4	894.8	690.8	694.2
Europe	394.9	460.6	444.2	357.4	360.0	460.1	535.9	646.4	479.4	466.3
North America	15.2	16.0	75.0	85.9	30.7	42.3	42.1	68.8	89.3	118.2
Asia				49.2	83.4	70.5	109.5	39.0	117.0	105.1
Africa	8.8		23.5	55.6	33.2	1.4				2.0
Value	44.0	66.6	57.4	46.2	40.1	41.9	52.9	88.5	56.6	49.3
Share of exports (%)	50.6	56.1	49.7	43.8	33.5	39.0	46.7	55.4	44.2	40.6
Ecuador				9.8				10.5	21.6	33.2
Value										2.1
Share of exports (%)										1.5
El Salvador		2.9	1.5	0.8	1.8	2.2	1.4	7.6	7.1	6.8
Value		0.8	0.2	0.2	0.2	0.4	0.3	0.8	1.4	1.0
Share of exports (%)		0.9	0.3	0.2	0.1	0.3	0.2	0.5	1.2	0.8
Haiti	30.3	35.5	30.3	28.8	15.1	21.2	27.9	24.3	6.5	6.2
Value	3.1	4.9	3.6	2.6	1.4	1.8	2.5	3.1	0.8	0.9
Share of exports (%)	7.9	9.5	7.0	6.9	2.5					

TABLE 12–8 – Continued

Exporter and Destination	1950	1951	1952	1953	1954	1955	1956	1957	1958	1959
Mexico										
Refined										
Europe				4.0	2.0	.1	18.9	20.5	76.7	46.8
North America			9.4	10.2	8.9	13.5	15.6	30.8	20.3	270.3
South America					15.6				4.5	
Asia				11.2	34.1	32.9		5.0	16.2	11.0
Africa									3.0	
Unrefined				33.3	12.3	36.6	1.8	50.1	69.6	74.5
Total				58.5	72.9	79.8	34.1	93.9	187.4	148.7
U.S. total	1.8	0.1	9.4	11.4	11.3	12.4	11.1	41.8	65.5	61.0
Value	3.0	5.9	6.5	7.8	9.2	10.5	5.5	11.0	19.6	18.8
Share of exports (%)	0.6	1.0	1.0	1.3	1.5	1.2	0.6	1.4	2.6	2.5
Nicaragua		8.3	7.7	9.2	10.7	8.8	3.9	9.0	15.4	24.4
Value		0.2	0.1	0.1	0.2	0.1	0.1	0.2	0.2	0.3
Share of exports (%)		1.6	0.2	0.2	0.2	0.4	0.1	0.3	0.3	0.5
Panama		5.0	3.1	3.7	3.5			3.3	5.5	4.0
Value			0.4	0.3	0.4			0.4	0.6	0.6
Share of exports (%)			1.6	1.1	1.6			1.1	1.8	1.7
Paraguay									5.6	15.2
Value									0.6	1.1
Share of exports (%)									1.7	3.5
Peru										
Europe	276.8	258.8	304.8	410.9	422.2	482.9	428.3	496.3	410.7	498.8
North America	12.1	55.3	2.1	30.6	32.8	85.1	95.0	105.2	56.7	65.7
South America	15.0	12.7	29.9	50.6	51.2	55.8	47.7	79.9	77.1	89.8
Asia	221.0	160.8	231.9	213.3	197.5	246.3	221.7	180.9	200.5	216.9
Africa	8.2	28.4	38.9	107.6	140.3	89.5	89.5	119.8	64.5	117.4
Value	29.6	34.2	32.8	29.6	33.6	36.9	32.8	49.6	34.0	35.9
Share of exports (%)						13.7	10.6	15.6	12.1	11.6
Latin America, incl. Cuba[a]										
Europe	6,025.7	6,320.8	5,979.8	6,861.7	5,440.8	6,561.8	6,689.0	7,217.9	7,759.3	6,997.1
North America	1,946.2	2,159.5	1,529.9	2,536.1	1,183.0	1,468.3	1,693.8	2,163.5	1,899.9	1,673.2
South America	2,912.9	2,670.7	2,788.6	2,589.1	2,511.0	2,696.1	2,951.0	2,951.0	3,644.8	3,519.1
Asia	280.5	277.5	269.7	452.4	388.2	398.6	386.2	291.3	373.4	389.7
Africa	182.0	385.8	620.4	738.2	1,013.0	944.6	987.1	840.2	1,261.0	439.0
Communist Countries	108.5	82.4	167.4	200.4	220.3	134.2	162.1	216.7	252.0	268.2
Value, incl. Cuba	638	789	672	628	544	614	625	854	759	634
Share of total exports (%)	9.4	9.9	9.4	8.1	6.7	7.5	7.2	9.7	9.0	7.3
Latin America, excl. Cuba	761.9	879.2	972.1	1,345.4	1,214.7	1,897.7	1,494.8	1,943.0	2,127.7	2,045.2
Value, excl. Cuba	83.1	123.1	106.6	109.8	98.0	141.4	100.6	199.7	171.4	144.0
Share of total exports[b] (%)	1.3	1.7	1.6	1.5	1.3	1.9	1.3	2.5	2.2	1.8

TABLE 12-8 – Continued

Exporter and Destination	1960	1961	1962	1963	1964	1965	1966
Argentina	113.0	186.6	32.9	339.7	45.2	61.8	52.3
Value	6.7	12.6	2.6	63.9	6.2	6.8	
Share of exports (%)	0.1	0.1	(d)	4.6	(d)	4.5	
Brazil	854.8	744.9	478.6	486.7	268.2	818.4	1,007.4
Europe	190.2	41.2		28.2	57.7	117.2	240.8
North America	103.4	293.2	361.5	417.7	163.6	331.5	491.6
South America	139.6	68.1	43.9	19.7	25.9	123.4	156.6
Asia	289.9	293.1	62.0	20.9		152.0	49.5
Africa	31.6	49.2			20.9	93.4	69.0
Value	52.6	65.6	39.5	72.9	33.1	56.7	80.5
Share of exports (%)	3.1	4.6	3.2	5.1	2.3	3.6	4.6
Colombia		46.0	65.7	42.5	30.6	101.3	113.9
Value		5.2	7.4	5.5	3.3	7.6	8.3
Share of exports (%)		1.2	1.6	1.2	0.6	1.4	1.6
Costa Rica	20.4	30.2	23.8	34.1	36.8	45.9	67.5
Value	1.8	3.3	3.0	5.3	5.5	4.7	8.7
Share of exports (%)	2.0	3.8	3.7	5.5	4.7	4.2	6.4
Cuba	5,634.5	6,413.6	5,130.9	3,520.5	4,176.1	5,315.6	4,434.6
Communist Countries	2,260.9	4,825.3	3,718.7	2,079.5	2,660.8	3,525.3	3,159.7
Europe	650.4	335.2	322.2	636.8	489.5	563.8	502.1
North America	2,035.5	15.8	19.8	70.1	3.3	68.6	69.4
South America	11.0	170.6				10.2	
Asia					10.6	778.9	424.0
Africa	183.4	189.3	355.2	294.0	334.7	368.8	279.0
Value	490.9	532.3	431.9	471.8	626.7	546.1	480.0
Share of exports (%)	79.4	85.0	83.0	86.8	88.0		
Dominican Republic	1,099.1	793.4	845.8	671.2	661.5	522.3	571.9
Europe	451.1	239.5	5.8	59.9	166.6	42.1	33.5
North America	424.9	348.9	819.6	534.3	374.3	449.8	571.8
South America		10.2		33.5	5.2		
Asia	199.3	146.9	8.9	32.9	33.2	28.4	
Africa	19.6	10.7			49.9	20.6	
Value	85.3	68.2	96.9	100.0	92.7	63.6	76.3
Share of exports (%)	51.0	46.8	56.2	57.6	51.5	50.7	55.8
Ecuador	14.2	47.7	63.9	45.4	51.5	54.7	62.9
Value	0.9	2.3	6.0	5.7	7.1	7.3	6.5
Share of exports (%)	0.6	1.8	4.2	3.7	4.4	4.1	3.5
El Salvador	10.9	12.5	20.7	20.4	19.4	23.0	44.2
Value	1.4	1.2	2.0	2.1	2.8	1.5	6.6
Share of exports (%)	1.1	1.1	1.5	1.8	1.6	1.0	3.4
Haiti	30.1	39.7	34.6	35.9	22.6	20.2	33.6
Value	3.8	5.2	3.6	4.8	2.5	2.4	3.1
Share of exports (%)	10.7	15.7	8.4	11.5	6.1	6.7	9.2

TABLE 12-8 – Continued

Exporter and Destination	1960	1961	1962	1963	1964	1965	1966
Mexico							
Europe	52.3	11.3				541.3	500.0
North America	140.2					29.6	16.1
South America	5.8	1.0				413.4	447.3
Asia	3.9					43.0	29.5
Unrefined	260.2	573.8	364.9	392.5	491.3	541.3	500.0
Total	462.4	586.1	364.9	392.5	491.3	541.3	500.0
U.S. Total	328.4	585.2	350.2	343.6	425.8	413.4	437.9
Value	52.9	68.7	43.6	59.8	64.1	58.9	57.1
Share of exports (%)	6.9	8.2	4.6	6.0	6.0	5.1	4.6
Nicaragua	34.9	28.0	40.2	44.1	48.9	45.7	17.2
Value	0.5	0.4	0.4	0.6			
Share of exports (%)	0.9	0.7	0.5	0.6	0.6	0.6	0.2
Panama	2.8	5.2	3.6	10.4	22.9	19.1	11.7
Value	0.3	0.8	0.5	1.6	2.6	2.1	1.6
Share of exports (%)	1.0	2.6	1.4	3.7	5.0	2.7	1.7
Paraguay	1.5	3.5	3.2	6.0	2.4		9.0
Value	0.1	0.3		0.1	0.1		
Share of exports (%)		0.9		0.1			
Peru	513.7	552.4	462.7	495.8	428.4	387.1	433.5
Europe	3.1			10.6	107.4	5.6	5.5
North America	347.9	546.1	462.7	375.6	208.9	302.6	359.5
South America	77.6	0.1		75.1	112.1	66.0	67.7
Asia	85.1	2.5		11.7		12.9	
Africa				5.2			
Value	47.5	63.9	53.8	64.9	64.0	36.8	46.3
Share of exports (%)	11.0	12.9	10.0	12.0	9.6	5.5	6.1
Latin America, incl. Cuba[a]	8,798.5	9,496.8	7,604.3	6,174.8	6,305.8	7,956.4	7,359.7
Europe	1,347.1	627.2	328.0	735.5	821.2	758.3	798.0
North America	3,140.0	1,404.5	1,952.7	2,007.0	945.9	1,565.9	1,930.2
South America	234.0	250.0	43.9	128.3	153.7	199.6	224.2
Asia	578.2	442.5	70.9	65.5	33.2	993.3	473.5
Africa	234.6	249.2	355.2	299.2	405.5	482.8	348.0
Communist Countries	2,260.9	4,825.3	3,718.7	2,079.5	2,660.8	3,525.3	3,159.7
Value, incl. Cuba	745	830	691	855	911	795	775
Share of total exports (%)	8.4	9.3	8.2	8.6	8.6	7.2	7.0
Latin America, excl. Cuba	3,164.0	3,083.2	2,473.4	2,656.5	2,129.7	2,640.8	2,925.1
Value, excl. Cuba	254	298	259	387	284	249	295
Share of total exports[b] (%)	3.1	3.6	2.9	4.1	2.9	2.3	2.7

Sources: ISC, *World Sugar Economy*, vol. I. ISC, *Sugar Yearbook, 1950 to 1965.* ISC, *Statistical Bulletin*, June 1966. IMF, *International Financial Statistics*, supp. 1964-65, and supp. 1966-67. ECLA, *Economic Survey of Latin America*, 1963, p. 274. Foreign trade yearbooks of countries listed. UN, *Yearbook of International Trade Statistics.* FAO, *Trade Yearbook.*

[a]Sum of countries listed; destinations shown only for exports of major exporters.
[b]Value of total Cuban exports excluded; sugar exports as a share of total exports in the remaining 19 Latin American countries.

TABLE 12–9. Estimated Costs and Benefits, and Effects on World Sugar Trade, of Protected Markets and Excise Taxes on Sugar, 1959
(Thousands of metric tons and thousands of U.S. dollars)

I. Effects on Trade of National Sugar Policies	World Total Excluding Communist Countries	United States	United Kingdom	Belgium-Luxembourg	France	West Germany	Italy	Netherlands	Japan
Increase in consumption at price to consumer of 8.65¢/lb.[a] (tons)	3,882	588	60	26	91	205	300	51	674
Consumption cost of protection and excise taxes[b] ($)	192,556	18,618	429	1,216	2,161	10,955	32,139	1,703	66,642
Effects on trade of replacing protection by subsidies and eliminating excises ($):									
Total increase in value of trade	442,200	91,343	33,935	2,734	13,092	18,116	23,572	5,816	65,074
Value of additional trade, at 3¢/lb.[c]	256,700	38,808	3,960	1,716	6,006	13,530	19,800	3,366	44,484
Increased value of existing trade, at 3.5¢/lb.[d]	142,600	46,067	29,315	732	6,085	2,331	472	1,885	13,176
Increased value of additional trade, at 0.5¢/lb.[d]	42,800	6,468	660	286	1,001	2,255	3,300	565	7,414
Rent on additional trade: at 0.25¢/lb.	21,400	3,234	330	143	501	1,128	1,650	283	3,707
at 0.50¢/lb.	42,800	6,468	660	286	1,001	2,255	3,300	565	7,414
Increase in exporters' gains from trade, plus rent, rent 0.25¢/lb.	164,000	49,301	29,645	875	6,586	3,459	2,122	2,168	16,883
Increased value of existing trade, plus rent, rent 0.50¢/lb.	185,400	52,535	29,975	1,018	7,086	4,586	3,772	2,450	20,590
Effects on trade of substituting imports for domestic production, major protectionist countries only[e] ($):									
Domestic production (tons)	7,701	2,682	855	224	1,051	1,390	1,000	499	
Saving of resource cost, on cost in excess of 5¢/lb.[f]	318,670	147,818	18,849	2,469	23,170	82,271	44,092		
Value of additional trade, at 4.25¢/lb.	674,795	251,291	80,110	20,988	98,474	130,237	93,696		
Net benefit to exporters, rent at 0.75¢/lb.	119,081	44,346	14,137	3,704	17,378	22,983	16,535		
Imports (tons)	7,691	4,116	2,579	66	535	204	33	158	
Increased cost of imports, at 1.25¢/lb.	211,931	113,438	71,057	1,816	14,729	5,619	915	4,357	
Total benefits (resource cost saving plus net benefit to exporters)	437,772	192,164	32,986	6,173	40,548	105,254	60,627	-4,357	
To importers (resource cost saving less increased import costs)	106,739	34,381	52,208	653	8,441	76,652	43,177	-4,357	
To exporters (net benefits plus increased import costs)	331,012	157,783	85,194	5,520	32,107	28,602	17,449	4,357	

II. Benefits to Suppliers of U.S. Market

Accruing to	Benefits ($) due to	
	Quota Premium[g]	Tariff
Domestic areas	226,852	36,600[h]
Mainland beet growers	106,681	
Mainland cane growers	27,494	
Hawaii	46,496	
Puerto Rico	45,596	
Virgin Islands	586	
Foreign areas	213,224	19,300
Philippines	46,648	11,300[j]
Cuba	153,210	8,000[j]
Other countries	13,366	
Total	440,076	55,900

Benefits to Suppliers of United Kingdom under Commonwealth Sugar Agreement

Accruing to	Benefits ($) due to	
	Negotiated[k] Price Quotas	Tariff
Domestic beet growers	75,041	7,176[m]
Commonwealth suppliers		32,200[n]
Australia	14,603	
British Honduras	485	
Fiji	5,841	
Mauritius	16,306	
South Africa	7,301	
West Indies and British Guiana	31,203	

Sources: H. G. Johnson, *Economic Policies toward Less Developed Countries* (Brookings Institution, 1967), app. D, "Sugar Protectionism and the Export Earnings of Less Developed Countries." ISC, *World Sugar Economy,* vol. II, pp. 180–82, 206–8.

Note: No estimates are included of the quota and tariff benefits accruing to suppliers of the French and Portuguese protected markets, because of difficulties in price comparisons with the free market. French prices are fixed for No. 3 white sugar rather than for raw, and Portuguese preferential tariffs vary greatly with the degree of polarization of raw sugar.

[a] Estimated import parity price.
[b] Consumption cost calculated as half the product of the increase in consumption, the import parity price, and the tariff equivalent of the difference between parity and the actual price.
[c] World free market price, f.a.s. Cuba, averaged 2.97¢/lb. in 1959.
[d] Increase of 0.5¢/lb. ($11 per metric ton) assumed to follow from end of protection.

[e] Total is sum of United States, United Kingdom, and European Common Market estimates (seven countries listed).
[f] Domestic production assumed competitive with imports at a cost of 5 cents per pound or less (export price of 4.25¢/lb. plus 0.75¢/lb. for transportation).
[g] Difference between U.S. and free market prices, applied to tonnage produced or imported under quota.
[h] All imported sugar assumed to be 96° polarity.
[i] Benefit from preferential tariffs.
[j] Operating deficit of Sugar Board on dealings in negotiated price sugar, distributed among producers according to tonnages exported under quota to the United Kingdom, without considering f.a.s. negotiated price differences among suppliers. Benefits to domestic (beet) sugar producers are not estimated.
[k] Includes benefits of Canadian preferential tariff; 85% of value of preference is assumed to be passed back to producers.
[m] Minimum estimate calculated from preferential tariff on Commonwealth sugar applied to domestic production.
[n] Includes benefits of Canadian preferential tariff; 85% of value of preference is assumed to be passed back to producers.

Chapter 13

BANANAS

Latin America is the world's chief banana-exporting area. The region sells each year almost three million tons of fruit, with a value of about $200 million. Bananas provide only 2 percent of total Latin American foreign exchange earnings, but because they are exported primarily by the smaller countries they form a large share of earnings in several economies. They are the principal export commodity in three countries and the second in two others; elsewhere their contribution is very small. Central America was the chief source of bananas in world trade until the 1950s; Ecuador is now the largest supplier and Colombia a major source.

World Production, Consumption, and Trade

The edible banana is believed to have originated in southern Asia and to have spread to Oceania and later to Africa. From there cultivation moved to the Canary Islands and, early in the sixteenth century, to the Western Hemisphere. The pattern much resembles the way sugar cane was brought to the Americas, except that bananas were initially grown only for local consumption. Even today most of the world's bananas are consumed where they are produced. Of a total production of 20 million tons in the mid-1950s, an estimated 17 million were consumed in producing areas (see table 13-1). Africa accounted for over half this amount, because in some parts of East Africa bananas, not cereals, are the staple foodstuff, and per capita consumption is very high. In other producing regions bananas are eaten as fruit and consumption is much lower, although still higher than in areas where they are not grown. Latin America consumed nearly 4 million tons annually, with Brazil accounting for three-fourths of the total.

Little more can be said about production for domestic consumption, because statistical information about bananas is "fairly inaccessible, sometimes nonexistent, and, in certain cases, even defective."[1] The deficiencies are especially severe for the domestic sector, and quite troublesome even

where production for export is concerned. The problems of dealing with a perishable, nonuniform commodity are complicated by carelessness and lack of uniformity in the available sources. Production, trade, and prices are variously reported by stems and by weight, and conversions are sometimes difficult. Often it is not clear to what varieties, sectors, or areas data refer, so that comparisons and calculations are impossible. Every effort has been made here to secure reliable data, but at the cost of limiting the discussion to the export sector and of including only a modest amount of statistical material.

Production for export was not established until a century ago, so that bananas are the most recent of Latin America's traditional tropical exports. The first shipments from Central America to the United States were organized in the 1860s. In the next few decades the market grew rapidly; the European market developed somewhat later, and led to the export of bananas from Africa as well as from many countries of the Western Hemisphere. By the mid-1930s the importing countries were absorbing 2.4 million tons of bananas annually, with the United States taking somewhat more than half. Two decades later total imports had risen to more than 3 million tons, almost entirely as a result of increased consumption in Europe. By that time bananas had become the world's fourth largest fruit crop, accounting for 40 percent of all international trade in fresh fruit. In the United States, still the largest importing market, they amounted to 1 percent of all food sales, and 10 percent of fresh produce sales.[2] The development of this large trade has occurred despite the banana's extreme perishability, the fact that it cannot be stored, and the slight demand for processed fruit. In these respects it is unique among the major tropical products.

The demand for bananas is quite income-elastic at low incomes; as income rises, the effect on consumption decreases, until at a level of per capita consumption of about 8 to 10 kilograms demand becomes almost saturated. This appears to have occurred in the United States, and perhaps

---

Note: Bananas tables 13-1 to 13-6 appear on pp. 371–376.

[1] ECLA, "The International Banana Market – Its Evolution and Prospects," *Economic Bulletin for Latin America*, October 1958.

[2] E. Mortenson, "Trends in Production and Consumption of Fruits and Vegetables," FAO, *Monthly Bulletin of Agricultural Economics and Statistics*, September 1955.

also in Argentina and in a few European countries. Consumption also depends on the total amount of fresh fruit eaten, on the price of bananas relative to competing fruits, and on their quality. Substitution between bananas and other fruits generally appears to be less than among other fresh fruits, for given changes in relative price. Bananas have also been less affected than other fruits by the shift in consumer tastes in high-income countries away from fresh fruit toward processed fruit and juices; nonetheless the trend has reduced banana consumption relative to total fruit consumption in several countries. Recently the competitive position of bananas relative to other fruits appears to have been strengthened by improvements in quality and packaging and by large-scale advertising by the major producing companies.[3] The effects of price and quality make the policies of importing governments extremely important in determining the amount of bananas consumed. As in the case of sugar, there are several distinct markets, some of which are regulated by agreements between suppliers and importers or by tariffs or quotas. Current world consumption requires annual imports of about 5 million tons. Some 700,000 tons are sold in four markets: Spain and Portugal, which meet all their requirements from the Canary Islands and their African possessions; South America—Argentina and Uruguay being supplied by Brazil, and Chile by Ecuador; Northern Africa, from other African countries and the Near East; and New Zealand, which buys from Australia and other sources in Oceania. The Japanese market of some 400,000 tons has developed since 1963, when quantitative restrictions on imports were ended. Japan's tariff on bananas, however, was raised from 30 to 70 percent, the highest in any major importing country; Taiwan is the principal supplier, but in 1963-64 wind damage to the crop resulted in large imports from Ecuador. The Philippines and Central America supply small amounts to Japan, Honduras having begun exports in 1967. The remaining 4 million tons of imports go to North America and Western Europe. The United States and Canada together with the Scandinavian countries and several other European importers comprise the "free market" for bananas, and take about 2.3 million tons.[4] Virtually this entire amount comes from Latin America together with the smaller Caribbean islands. This is the only source for North America, and its advantages in cost and quality outweigh its disadvantage in location with respect to European markets. The United Kingdom obtains 90 percent or more of its requirements of 400,000 tons from Jamaica and the Windward Islands, which pay no duty; the remaining supply comes from Latin America, with a 15 percent tariff. The European Common Market applies a 20 percent tariff on bananas from all sources except the associated African states and the French and Dutch territories in the

Caribbean; the protected suppliers pay a tariff of about 7 percent or none at all. The adoption of a common tariff, completed in 1968, meant a sharp rise in West German duties and a smaller increase in those of the Benelux countries to the 20 percent level of France and Italy.[5] At present France buys chiefly from the associated territories, while West Germany and the Benelux countries are granted an exemption from the tariff which allows them to buy almost all their supplies from Latin America; the share of imports exempted is declining as imports rise. Italy bought chiefly from the protected Somalian industry until 1965, when the state banana monopoly was abolished; now it is an open market and obtains some of its supplies from Latin America. The EEC has been the fastest growing market for bananas since World War II, and consumption would be still greater but for the high prices created by some of the preferential trading arrangements. In recent years prices have been lowest in Germany, slightly higher in the United States, from 50 to 75 percent higher in France, and as much as twice the German level in the United Kingdom. Latin America has a large share in that market, despite the preferences for other regions.

Total exports of bananas have increased rather steadily over the last four decades, except during World War II when shipping capacity was scarce (see table 13-2). In contrast to other Latin American raw material exports, the volume of exports did not fall markedly during the 1930s, nor did the price vary greatly (see table 13-3). Throughout the entire period Latin America has held between 60 and 70 percent of the market, and a slightly higher share during the 1940s. Africa has replaced the Caribbean producers as the second largest source, but has made no appreciable inroad in Latin America's primary position. The elasticity of supply is fairly high, since new plantings require only a year to bear, and a rather high rate of replanting is necessary to offset the attrition due to disease, wind damage, and other factors. Prices therefore have been relatively stable compared to those of other tropical commodities, and large or long-lasting changes in price reflect real changes in the cost of production and shipment; there have been no periods of marked scarcity or surplus. Real prices declined steadily from the 1920s to the 1940s. In the late 1940s there was a sharp price rise, due largely to inflation in the United States, and some increase in real prices which continued until 1957. Since then there has been a steady and rather rapid decline. Part of the increase in the 1940s and early 1950s was due to difficulties in raising output rapidly enough to keep up with the recovery of demand. The required increase was quite large, and the elasticity of supply was probably lower than usual then. The price decline of

---

[3]On the determinants of banana consumption, see K.S. Mulherin, "Medium-Term Outlook for World Trade in Bananas," FAO, *Monthly Bulletin of Agricultural Economics and Statistics*, February 1967.

[4]Canada has a preferential tariff favoring Commonwealth producers, but obtains nearly all its supplies from Latin America, so the tariff has little effect on the source of imports.

[5]For a summary of present tariffs on bananas, see UNCTAD, *Programme for the Liberalization and Expansion of Trade in Commodities of Interest to Developing Countries*, doc. TD/11/Supp. 1, 22 December 1967, appendix pp. 5-11. More detail is given in *Trade Barriers and Liberalization Possibilities in Selected Commodities*, doc. TD/11/Supp. 2, 28 December 1967, pp. 1-5. European tariffs in 1965-66 and prices from 1955-57 to 1966 are given in "Bananas: Market Developments in 1966 and Outlook for 1967," FAO, *Monthly Bulletin of Agricultural Economics and Statistics*, June 1967.

recent years partly reflects an oversupply resulting from the solution of the problems of the previous decade.

Bananas in Latin America

In the first several decades of the banana boom, cultivation for export was extended to every Latin American country bordering the Caribbean. In Cuba and Haiti bananas proved less profitable than sugar cane, and the export sector all but disappeared after some years; in Venezuela exports have always been insignificant compared to domestic consumption. The industry developed in the 1860s and 1870s in Costa Rica, Honduras, and Panama, and sometime before 1900 on the Caribbean coast of Colombia. Production for export began shortly after 1900 in Mexico, Guatemala, and Nicaragua, and by the 1920s all seven of these countries plus Cuba were important suppliers. Two decades later, Cuba, Mexico, and Nicaragua had largely withdrawn from the market, leaving the Central American industry concentrated in four countries: Costa Rica, Guatemala, Honduras, and Panama. The competition of other crops played some part in this contraction, but the chief factor was the influence of disease. Bananas are extraordinarily susceptible to disease, particularly to an airborne fungus, sigatoka, which spreads rapidly and destroys the trees. This disease first appeared in Central America in 1935, and by 1936 had infected fully 80 percent of the crop in Honduras, with nearly as devastating results in other countries. Sigatoka can be controlled by spraying with various copper solutions, but thousands of small growers were put out of business before the technique was perfected or because they could not afford the control measures. The export industry survived in those countries where integrated firms, operating large plantations, were able to make the necessary investment to bring the epidemic under control.[6]

During the years immediately following, the loss of European markets and the difficulties of shipping removed the incentive for recovery in the countries most affected by disease. The new distribution of exports lasted until the late 1940s, when there was a further and much greater change. As demand recovered after the war, output increased rapidly in Central America, but it became increasingly difficult to continue the expansion: from the early 1950s to the early 1960s there was no increase in exports from the area. The chief cause of the difficulty was another fungus disease, fusarium wilt or Panama disease. It spreads quite slowly, but the land can remain infected for years after it is cleared of bananas. Land can sometimes be rehabilitated by flooding for several months before replanting, but often it is cheaper to clear new land.

Panama disease destroyed the plantations on the Atlantic coast of Guatemala, Costa Rica, and Panama, and damaged those in Honduras. Starting in the 1920s, the producers opened new plantations on the Pacific coast, but by 1950 there was little more good land available and prices were not high enough to justify extensive rehabilitation or clearing of entirely new land.[7] Rising demand and prices led to the development of a new source, Ecuador, which is now the world's foremost banana exporter (see table 13-2).

Ecuador had previously exported only small amounts to Peru and Chile, as its location precluded shipment to North America or Europe. In the early 1950s, however, this disadvantage was overcome by the advantage of freedom from disease, which made production costs low when prices were high. The government built roads to open land for settlement along the coast and in the central valley and induced a large internal migration.[8] Ecuador's entry into the market was facilitated by widespread flood and wind damage in Central America. It is estimated, for example, that over half of Guatemala's potential production in 1954-55 was destroyed by winds.[9] By 1957 the expansion of exports from Ecuador had overtaken demand, and prices began to fall. Sigatoka had appeared in 1949 and by 1952 was relatively severe; Panama disease was also a problem in the southern producing areas. As a good deal of marginal land was taken up in the rapid expansion, yields began to decline and costs to rise; disease control was also especially difficult on such land. Ecuadorean bananas also suffered more damage in shipment to port than those from Central America, leading to more waste or to lower prices. These factors brought the expansion almost to a halt in 1965. Ecuador's domination of the banana trade resulted from a rather extraordinary combination of adverse circumstances in other producers and a rapidly growing market; as those conditions have changed Ecuador has come under increasing competitive pressure. In particular, the production difficulties which Central America experienced in the late 1950s and early 1960s appear to have been overcome, so that Honduras, Panama and Costa Rica sharply increased their exports in 1964-66. In the last few years exports have also increased substantially in Colombia. Ecuador's share of world banana exports reached a peak of 31 percent in 1964 and dropped to 26 percent only two years later.

The present area planted to bananas in Latin America is somewhat more than 700,000 hectares (see table 13-4). Areas in which bananas are grown for domestic use include over 200,000 hectares in Brazil and smaller amounts in other countries, especially Colombia, Venezuela and Mexico. The area devoted to production for export is probably about 400,000 hectares. Yields varied from about 12 to nearly 30 tons per hectare in the early 1960s, with an

---

[6] For a discussion of the requirements and diseases of the banana, see N. Simmonds, *Bananas* (London: Longmans, 1959). A survey of the history of production in the various Latin American countries is given in pp. 320-28. See also Inter-American Economic and Social Council, Special Committee on Bananas, *Report of Banana Mission* (Pan American Union, 1957). An account of the sigatoka epidemic of 1935-39 is given in S. May and G. Plaza, *The United Fruit Company in Latin America* (National Planning Association, 1958).

[7] See C. F. Jones and P. C. Morrison, "Evolution of the Banana Industry of Costa Rica," *Economic Geography*, January 1952.

[8] See J. J. Parsons, "Bananas in Ecuador," *Economic Geography*, July 1957, and the Ecuadorean development plan cited in table 13-4.

[9] R. A. Smith and A. C. Cook, *Bananas: World Production and Trade* (USDA, FAS circular M-128, April 1962).

average of about 20; stemweights varied from 20 to 40 kilograms, mostly according to the species grown. The expansion of production in the late 1950s and early 1960s came almost entirely from increases in area, but more recently a shift in species has raised yields substantially in some producing zones and permitted a slight decline in area planted.

Bananas are the only Latin American agricultural export in which foreign capital is extensively involved. This is mainly because U.S. firms created the export industry, and also because certain factors give large, vertically integrated enterprises an advantage. Except in Brazil, the areas where bananas are grown for export were previously almost uninhabited and undeveloped; large investments were required to establish plantations and provide for shipping the fruit to port and then to market. The costs of disease control, irrigation, and other practices to maintain high yields are borne more easily by large firms than by small growers. This is especially the case where Panama disease is prevalent. These factors do not preclude an export industry based on peasant farmers and involving small middlemen and shippers, as in Ecuador; but in that case, which is unique in the region, the government invested in transportation facilities, and there were no significant disease problems at first. Most of the firms that entered the banana trade in its early years had failed by 1900, leaving the industry dominated by two U.S. concerns — the United Fruit Company, much the larger of the two, and the Standard Fruit and Steamship Company. The United Fruit Company is still the largest in the industry and holds a position comparable to that of the large petroleum or mining companies in other countries of Latin America. Its operations are therefore the subject of similar political concern.

The importance of U.S. capital was greatly increased in the 1930s, as a result of the sigatoka epidemic. It has declined for the region as a whole as Ecuador has become the chief exporter. Neither the United Fruit Company alone, nor the foreign-owned companies together, appear to have significant monopoly power either to limit the entry of new countries or firms or to control banana prices. In some countries, however, they do have a virtual monopoly of exports. The United Fruit Company and the Standard Fruit and Steamship Company together account for all of Honduras' exports, with the former shipping 75 percent of the total in 1966. In 1955 the United Fruit Company alone shipped about 90 percent of the total in Costa Rica and Panama, and nearly as much in Guatemala (see table 13-5). Altogether, half the bananas exported from Latin America were carried by the company's ships. The dominance of production was considerably less, since the company buys large amounts from independent growers. Differences in yields made the share of banana land held still less. Most of the land acquired by the company has been relinquished; a further part is used for other crops such as cocoa and oil palm. In recent years both major producers have increased the share of shipments acquired from independent farmers, who are sometimes former employees. United Fruit in Panama and Nicaragua, and Standard Fruit in Costa Rica, have undertaken to buy minimum amounts at minimum prices and to supply technical assistance to growers.[10]

The political and economic importance of foreign capital lies less in the amount of land and labor used, or even in the income and tax revenues produced, than in the dominance of exports and the power this gives or appears to give foreign enterprise over a nation's economic life. This is particularly important since the countries in which the United Fruit Company and its competitors operate are small and heavily dependent on banana exports and on their largest and safest market, the United States. In the past these companies sometimes interfered extensively in the internal politics of their host countries, and they are still feared and disliked despite their recent good behavior and their considerable withdrawal from the economic dominance they once enjoyed. Even their ordinary production and marketing decisions, like those of the large mineral-producing enterprises, may discriminate among countries and have political repercussions. For example, advertising by the United Fruit Company for the bananas it produces in Central America and sells under a brand name may be regarded in Ecuador — where the company has no production but prior to 1965 only bought fruit for shipping — as an effort to damage the Ecuadorean industry.[11] Other issues, such as the share of export value returned to the exporting country, are somewhat less important than in the case of minerals.[12] The question of domestic processing has hardly arisen, because no way has yet been found to market banana products or derivatives in large volume: the bulk of output can be sold only as fresh fruit. The principal banana products traded are dried bananas, of which some 2,500 tons per year are sold, chiefly to Europe and Japan, and banana purée, of which about 10,000 tons are consumed, mostly in the United States, in the preparation of baby foods. Ecuador accounts for 80 percent of the trade in dried bananas, but most banana purée is made in the United States and Mexico. The Dominican Republic formerly exported canned purée to the United States; production has recently started in Honduras. Experiments in processing have also resulted in some production of banana chips, banana flour and banana wine, but these derivatives are of minor importance.[13]

Banana exports currently bring Latin America some $250 million, considerably more than during the early 1950s (see table 13-6). In most countries the share in total exports has been declining; only in Ecuador have bananas increased notably in importance, accounting for nearly all

[10] See Mulherin, "Medium-Term Outlook for World Trade in Bananas," pp. 2-3.

[11] Ecuadorean complaints against this "disloyal competition" are described in U.S. State Department Airgram A-446, Quito, 26 May 1967.

[12] Almost no information is available on this subject, and the United Fruit Company does not regularly divulge the share of exports returned to the host country. The share in 1955 in six countries ranged from 65 to 100 percent, for all exports by the company (not only, although predominantly, bananas). Both extremes represent unusual circumstances, but there is no way of telling what rate is typical or average. See the first two sources of table 13-5.

[13] Estimates from the 1966 *Report* of the Tropical Products Institute, London. Information supplied by the Foreign Agricultural Service of USDA. See also "Economic Summary of Honduras," U.S. State Department Airgram, Tegucigalpa, 20 February, 1967.

the growth in that country's exports since about 1950. Several countries — Mexico, Honduras, Nicaragua, Costa Rica, and Panama — sell almost exclusively to the United States; the others, except for Brazil, depend more heavily on sales to Western Europe. Before 1900 the United States took all Latin America's net exports of bananas. By the late 1930s the share had dropped to less than 90 percent; it fell to 70 percent in the mid-1950s and to 60 percent in the early 1960s. Mexico, Guatemala, Honduras, Panama, and Cuba were once the chief suppliers to the United States; Ecuador provided nearly half the total around 1960, and Costa Rica, Honduras and Panama most of the rest. By 1967 Western Europe had become Ecuador's major market, and that country supplied only 30 percent of United States imports, the same share as Honduras.

Recent Developments and Outlook

Until a few years ago the only banana grown for export in Latin America, outside Brazil, was the Gros Michel. It was cultivated, despite its high susceptibility to Panama disease and the fact that its tall plants are rather easily blown down, because it resists damage in shipment better than any other species. The spread of Panama disease in Central America made it increasingly difficult to expand production of Gros Michel and led producers to seek to replace it with one or more of the Cavendish varieties which are immune to the disease. The Dwarf Cavendish was the second most popular export variety in world trade, but it was not believed suitable for the markets accustomed to the much larger Gros Michel. Instead, efforts were made to develop or use a large Cavendish banana, and in the late 1950s these efforts were successful. The giant Cavendish developed by Standard Fruit and the Valery banana developed by United Fruit, have now largely replaced Gros Michel in Central America. In addition to disease resistance the Cavendish offers appreciably higher yields, which reduce both long-run costs and the short-run difficulties of conversion since a smaller area can be planted with the new species. In other producing areas the change has so far been much less rapid and extensive, because of the lesser extent of Panama disease and the large amounts invested in Gros Michel plantations. The reluctance of growers in Ecuador to replant sometimes leads to, or is fed by, claims that the Ecuadorean Gros Michel is the highest quality banana available, and that the conversion to Cavendish is urged by foreign enterprises for their own purposes rather than for the good of the industry. Nonetheless, the steady spread of Panama disease, and the great importance of market appearance of the fruit in the present competitive situation, exert increasing pressure for conversion. The government of Ecuador is therefore considering a prohibition of further Gros Michel planting on new land and on plantations of more than 200 hectares, with special credits offered to induce growers with smaller plots to replant with Cavendish.[14]

Since Cavendish bananas are badly damaged if shipped on the stem, the change in species grown has necessitated a change in the method of shipment. The clusters are separated from the stem and packed in cardboard cartons at or near the plantations, usually at 40 pounds per box net weight at market. The first shipments of boxed fruit were made from Central America in 1959, and from Ecuador in 1963. By 1965 nearly all Latin American exports were boxed, and by 1967 only a few producers such as Jamaica had not yet converted. The benefits in lower waste and more attractive fruit not only offset the added cost, but represent "a major technical innovation that has probably led to permanent higher import demand for bananas."[15] The introduction of cartons, both by its direct saving in fruit and the indirect effects of improved quality control and increased advertising, appears to be chiefly responsible for the sharp increases in total and per capita banana consumption in 1965 and again in 1966. In some countries, such as Japan and Italy, other factors such as price reductions and import quota increases may have been more important, but in North America and most countries of Western Europe the rise in imports principally reflects the greater attractiveness of bananas due to boxing and the large advertising campaign which accompanied the change. The advantages are such that even Gros Michel bananas are now boxed, in order to hold their markets. The expansion of consumption in turn absorbed much of the recent increase in production and thus moderated the decline in price; the growth of output has been sufficiently rapid, however, that banana prices have been falling rather steadily in all markets since the late 1950s.[16]

The decline of banana prices in recent years led to a meeting of the representatives of thirty-one countries in Guayaquil, Ecuador, in late 1964, to discuss the world situation. In June 1965 the FAO Committee on Commodity Problems created a Banana Study Group, which held its first meeting in early 1966; another was held in October 1967. At the second meeting a Committee on Statistics was established to evaluate current data and issue annual assessments of the outlook for world trade in bananas. The Study Group could not agree on international quality standards, but agreed to explore the possibility of establishing standards which would be necessary for the operation of any sort of international control. On the basic issue of market access, the difference in competitive position between the protected suppliers and the low-cost Western Hemisphere producers precluded definite agreement, but the Study Group did urge a general and gradual abolition by importers of tariffs and quotas, with due regard for the effect on high-cost suppliers. The second UNCTAD Conference, in

[14] Claims for Gros Michel and against Cavendish, which correspond to the author's observations in Ecuador in July 1967, are reported in U.S. State Department Airgram A-446. The bill sub-

mitted to the Ecuadorean Congress to promote Cavendish planting is described in BOLSA, *Review*, January 1967, p. 43.

[15] FAO, "Bananas: Market Developments . . . ," June 1967.

[16] Prices for fruit on the stem and for boxed fruit are difficult to compare, so that price movements in 1964-66, when most of the change took place, cannot be described with complete accuracy. The general decline is still unmistakable. It should also be noted that the better condition and lower waste of boxed bananas represent a fall in real price to the consumer.

February-March 1968, called for further study and proposals.[17]

A similar sequence has been followed in the case of cocoa, but it is much less likely that the meetings on bananas will soon result in any sort of international agreement or control scheme. Both supply and demand are quite responsive to price, so that control of the market would be difficult and likely to create scarcities or surpluses. The elasticity of demand derives partly from competition between bananas and other fresh fruits which would not be subject to any sort of control. Bananas cannot be stored, so stocks could not be used to cushion fluctuations. Finally, much trade is governed by preferential arrangements which the countries involved have shown no inclination to remove; without such change, it would be possible only to create a similar preferential control scheme for the free markets. The attention of the Study Group is therefore directed initially to the problems of banana statistics and of the various trade barriers which, in the view of Latin American exporters, restrict total consumption. There is also concern that supplies of bananas are increasing too rapidly for demand, so that by the early 1970s there may be a sizable oversupply which could not be sold except perhaps at prices ruinously low to exporters. Moreover, even without the development of an oversupply, prices would remain low if they represent a real decline in costs due to the opening of new land, the shift to new varieties, and the introduction of boxing. Producers could not offset the lower prices with increased volume if the free markets were saturated while those with low per capita consumption remained restricted. The concern especially of Latin American exporters will be that the gains from a reduction in costs not be entirely passed on to consumers.

In 1964 the total demand for banana imports was estimated as some 5.5. to 5.7 million tons for the period 1970-72. The recent price decline and the enlargement of markets following the introduction of cartons lead to more recent projections of a total demand of 6.5 to 7 million tons by 1975.[18] Roughly equal amounts will be available from South America and from Central America plus the Dominican Republic. Substantial increases in capacity are foreseen for several Central American producers, for Colombia and Brazil, for several of the protected suppliers to the French and United Kingdom markets, and for Taiwan and the Philippines. Against this pronounced increase in supplies a much smaller growth in demand is expected. Since the conversion to boxing is nearly complete and that to Cavendish fruit already substantial, and since no further reductions of tariffs or quotas are anticipated, the rapid growth of imports in 1965-66 will not continue. For the next few years the outlook is for prices to remain low or continue falling and for the share of production actually harvested and shipped to remain at its present level or to fall.[19] The reduction or elimination of obstacles to imports would alleviate this situation, but even if all barriers were removed some fall in prices would probably be necessary for exportable supplies to be completely absorbed. The Study Group has agreed to assess the effects to be anticipated from such changes in importing countries.

The situation of overproduction may be expected to have two effects beyond the pressure which will be exerted on prices. First, competition among the low-cost producers in Central and South America will be intensified and will probably lead to some changes in market shares. The country which stands to lose the most is Ecuador; as production elsewhere recovers or increases, its extraordinary advantages of the past decade and a half will disappear and its geographic position will once again be a liability. The slower conversion to boxing and to Cavendish fruit, and the withdrawal of the major firms from Ecuador as their supplies increased in Central America, are further obstacles. The Ecuadorean Development Plan calls for the retirement of some marginal land and no further expansion of the area planted to bananas; but a rise in yields and a reduction in waste of fruit would increase exports by 58 percent between 1963 and 1973. This ambition appears technically feasible, but it is less certain that the increased output can be sold, at least without further price deterioration. The decline in Ecuador's market share will probably be matched by increases in Central America and in Colombia, where a major project involving 25,000 hectares of Gros Michel planting is entering full production.

Second, the divergence of interest between the low-cost producers and those with preferential access to markets will probably widen. The latter favor control of supplies to meet demand at relatively high prices, and could not compete in the situation of free trade desired by the former. Thus any progress toward reduction of trade barriers or international action to ease the surplus may be countered by further moves to protect high-cost producers against the effects of low prices and competition. It is feared, for example, that restrictions on banana imports into the European Common Market will be increased in the future, at the instigation of France. That country is believed to want to end the protocol under which West Germany now imports much of its supplies duty-free from Latin America, and to have Martinique and Guadeloupe declared part of France so that bananas from those possessions would escape even the preferential tariff for associated states. These measures would offset the end of French quantitative restrictions on banana imports in mid-1968. Only by such means could these producers compete with Latin America, since their fruit is not only of lower quality but costs some 50 percent more than bananas from Ecuador and Central America. This prospect is alarming to the U.S. firms which now ship large amounts to Europe, and even more so to the

[17]FAO, *Monthly Bulletin of Agricultural Economics and Statistics*, December 1964, June 1967, and November 1967. See also UNCTAD, *Commodity Problems and Policies*, doc. TD/L.29, 25 March 1968, p. 4.

[18]Projections for 1970-72 from Pan American Union, *Prospects for the Latin American Export Position in the World Banana Market*, doc. UP/G.12/2, 14 October 1964, and for 1975 from FAO, Committee on Commodity Problems, *Agricultural Commodities—Projections for 1975 and 1985* (1967), p. 264.

[19]This assessment is from Mulherin, "Medium-Term Outlook for World Trade in Bananas."

Latin American producers who fear that it will be only one of several steps to reduce their trade with the Common Market. At meetings called by the Inter-American Committee on the Alliance for Progress in September 1967, eleven countries of the region agreed to send representatives to Europe to press their case and to try to avert a change in Common Market policy.[20] Projects are also underway to export bananas from Guyana and Surinam, which would

[20] Alliance for Progress, *Newsletter*, 18 and 25 September 1967. See also the *Wall Street Journal*, 27 September 1967.

enjoy preferential access to the United Kingdom and the Common Market respectively. A similar conflict of interest between high- and low-cost coffee producers and between the importers supplied by each group was resolved by the International Coffee Agreement, and some combination of easier access and reduced exports may ultimately be achieved for bananas as well. For the near future, however, the prospect for Latin America is for an extremely competitive situation in which any further decline in prices will offset much of the growth in export volume and earnings will rise only slowly.

CHAPTER 13 TABLES

TABLE 13–1. World Consumption of Bananas, 1953-57, and World Banana Imports, 1934-38, 1962-64, and 1965-66
(Thousands of metric tons, and kilograms per capita)

IMPORTING COUNTRIES: Net Imports (Sources 1 and 2)

Country or Region	Average 1934-38		Average 1953-57		Average 1962-64		Average 1965-66	
	Total	Per Capita	Total	Per Capita	Total	Pér Capita	Total	Per Capita
Latin America	183	7.5	204	7.2	245	7.5	238	7.3
Argentina	160	11.7	169	8.7	169	7.8	177	7.7
Chile	13	2.7	18	2.6	39	4.8	35	3.0
Uruguay	10	4.9	17	6.7	31	10.7	26	9.5
United States	1,301	10.5	1,476	9.2	1,675	8.9	1,544	7.8
Canada	51	4.5	141	8.8	168	8.9	165	8.3
Western Europe	741	2.9	1,241	3.7	1,989	4.5	2,067	4.3
France	171	2.4	276	6.3	371	7.8	398	8.1
Germany	118	1.8	232	4.6	476	8.4	559	8.6
Scandinavia[a]	25	0.9-2.5	98	1.4-7.2	126	3.0-7.3	137	3.2-7.4
Spain[b]	26	1.5	131	4.7	202	6.9	236	7.2
United Kingdom	304	6.2	303	5.9	364	6.7	366	6.6
Africa (and Near East)[c]	16	0.5	47	1.0	48	0.5-1.7	56	0.6-1.8
Asia (Japan)	122	1.7	25	0.3	276	2.3	375	3.8
Oceania (New Zealand)[d]	11	7.3	23	10.3	31	12.1	28	10.4
Total, Importing Countries	2,438	4.8	3,157	4.8	4,438	5.5	4,871	6.1

PRODUCING COUNTRIES: Production for Domestic Consumption
(Middle or late 1950s only—Source 3)

Country or Region	Total	Per Capita	Country or Region	Total	Per Capita
Latin America	3,812	29	Africa[e]	8,810	
Brazil	2,745	52	Uganda	3,283	630
Other South			Kenya and Tanganyika	2,205	160
America	652	25	Congo	1,588	100
Mexico	190	7	Malawi	736	290
Central America	170	25	West Africa[f]	725	10
Cuba	55	10	Mozambique	143	25
West Indies[g]	276	25	Malagasy Republic	130	25
Asia	4,037		Oceania	90	60
Ceylon	202	25			
India	765	2	Total, Producing Countries	17,025	
Indonesia	2,033	25			
Philippines	491	25			

SUMMARY BY REGIONS	Consumption	Production
North America (United States and Canada)	1,617	
Western Europe	1,241	
Latin America (and West Indies)	4,292	6,412
Africa (and Near East)	8,857	9,475
Asia	4,062	4,065
Oceania	113	199
World Total[h]	20,182	20,151

Sources: (1) FAO, *Monthly Bulletin of Agricultural Economics and Statistics*, December 1964 and May 1966. (2) "The International Banana Market – Its Evolution and Prospects," ECLA, *Economic Bulletin for Latin America*, October 1958. (3) N. W. Simmonds, *Bananas* (London: Longmans, 1959), pp. 277-81.

[a]Finland, Denmark, Norway, and Sweden; per capita figures are the minimum and maximum from among these countries.
[b]All imports from Spanish possessions in Africa and the Canary Islands.
[c]Includes several countries classified as the Near East, some of which are in North Africa and some in Asia.
[d]Data for Australia not available.
[e]Includes all islands of the Indian Ocean except Ceylon.
[f]All present or former British, French, and Portuguese possessions in West Africa; excludes former French Equatorial Africa.
[g]All Caribbean islands except Cuba; includes Haiti and the Dominican Republic; otherwise identical to Caribbean America, table 13–2.
[h]Totals for production and consumption differ slightly because of different sources and periods. The Communist countries are excluded.

TABLE 13–2. World Banana Exports, 1924-1966
  (Thousands of metric tons)[a]

Country or Region	Avg. 1924-28	Avg. 1934-38	Avg. 1940-44	Avg. 1948-52	1953	1954	1955	1956	1957
Latin America	1,349	1,631	877	1,679	2,006	2,055	2,075	2,219	2,357
Brazil		198	76	177	163	218	211	188	219
Colombia	South	162	43	133	173	196	210	232	184
Costa Rica	America:	96	66	253	356	372	330	233	310
Cuba	287	121	52	10					
Dominican Republic		2	13	38	36[b]	44[b]	43	41	52
Ecuador	Central	48	25	217	407	482	613	594	794
Guatemala	America:	167	126	162	228	194	114	216	130
Haiti	1,062	11	29	24					
Honduras		280	229	371	395	293	248	447	337
Mexico		278	101	77	51	56	29	16	36
Nicaragua		49	8	13	9	12	9	4	2
Panama		217	105	200	188	188	275	251	290
Venezuela		2	4	4			3	3	3
Caribbean America[c]	294	418	46	187	258	335	309	325	376
Africa[d]	173	271	125	381	592	581	622	604	567
Asia	} 146	142	58	28	} 44	} 61	38	34	41
Oceania[e]		34	10	11			32	26	27
World Total[f]	1,962	2,496	1,116	2,309	2,901	3,032	3,071	3,184	3,461
Latin American Share (%)	69	65	79	73	69	68	68	70	68

Country or Region	1958	1959	1960	1961	1962	1963	1964	1965	1966
Latin America	2,475	2,615	2,791	2,739	2,682	2,953	2,991	3,142	3,506
Brazil	272	214	242	246	217	206	226	216	205
Colombia	174	203	191	206	147	203	172	253	342
Costa Rica	302	213	273	231	292	261	294	316	359
Cuba									
Dominican Republic	86	101	182	170	173	130	190	148	106
Ecuador	829	1,052	1,065	985	1,100	1,340	1,320	1,200	1,265
Guatemala	116	146	198	164	90	121	111	58	77
Haiti									
Honduras	398	357	360	430	378	344	349	572	710
Mexico	26	33	10	23	8	10	17	14	12
Nicaragua	2	2	4	1	11	18	45	16	24
Panama	267	291	263	272	251	298	267	336	386
Venezuela	3	3	3	4	5	10	11	13	20
Caribbean America[c]	404	480	482	534	541	529	483	506	521
Africa[d]	528	607	487	732	727	749	772	781	753
Asia	62	64	81	119	95	101	228	304	327
Oceania[e]	36	34	31	29	36	33	37	31	25
World Total[f]	3,565	3,885	3,963	4,199	4,121	4,412	4,574	4,764	5,171
Latin American Share (%)	69	67	70	65	64	67	65	66	68

Sources: FAO, *Monthly Bulletin of Agricultural Economics and Statistics*, December 1964 and May 1966. H. W. von Loesecke, *Bananas* (Interscience, 1950), pp. 168-69. USDA, Foreign Agricultural Service circular, *Bananas*, 1953 through 1964. *Bananas: World Production and Trade*, April 1962. FAO, *Trade Yearbook, 1959* to *1967.*

[a]In all sources except FAO, data reported in standard stems of 50 pounds each, and converted to metric tons.
[b]Exports to United States only.
[c]Includes all western hemisphere exporters not included in Latin America: principally Jamaica, the Windward Islands, Guadeloupe, and Martinique.
[d]Includes the Canary Islands, which are usually reported in Europe (Spain).
[e]Includes Indonesia, reported with Asia in 1934-38 and 1940-44.
[f]Excludes exports of China.

TABLE 13-3. Banana Prices, 1925-1966
(U.S. dollars per stem and cents per pound)

Average Value of U.S. imports, $/stem[a]

1925 .... 0.54	1931 .... 0.53	1937 .... 0.48	1943 .... 0.62
1926 .... 0.56	1932 .... 0.50	1938 .... 0.49	1944 .... 0.66
1927 .... 0.56	1933 .... 0.51	1939 .... 0.51	1945 .... 0.69
1928 .... 0.55	1934 .... 0.51	1940 .... 0.56	1946 .... 0.76
1929 .... 0.55	1935 .... 0.51	1941 .... 0.57	1947 .... 0.82
1930 .... 0.55	1936 .... 0.49	1942 .... 0.59	

	Import Prices			Export Prices		
	United States[b]		West Germany from Ecuador[c]		(¢/lb. on stem)	
	($/stem)	(¢/lb.)	(¢/lb.)	Ecuador	Honduras	Costa Rica
1948	0.84	6.25				
1949	0.96	6.86				
1950	0.92	7.25				
1951	1.10	7.25		4.69		
1952	1.11	7.3		4.59	4.72	4.56
1953	1.33	7.38		4.67	4.38	4.36
1954	1.35	7.59		4.60	4.45	4.56
1955	1.41	7.50		4.57	4.45	5.00
1956	1.47	7.56	7.54	3.94	4.54	4.70
1957	1.41	8.04	7.72	3.98	4.29	3.97
1958	1.42	7.40	6.63	3.86	4.07	4.05
1959	1.43	6.58	6.13	3.78	3.54	3.36
1960	1.38	6.48	6.04	3.72	3.51	4.10[d]
1961	1.43	6.29	6.26	3.64	4.10[d]	4.17[d]
1962		6.15	6.03[d]	6.35	3.64	4.26[d]	4.33[d]
1963		5.71	7.63[d]	6.67	2.89	4.45[d]	4.34[d]
1964		5.50[e]	7.73[d]	6.00	3.63	4.27[d]	4.06[d]
1965			7.23[d]	6.45	3.81	4.46[d]	3.70[d]
1966			6.98[e]	6.18			

Sources: IMF, *International Financial Statistics*, 1964-65 Supplement and 1966. FAO, *Monthly Bulletin of Agricultural Economics and Statistics*, March 1964 and April 1966. USCB, *Foreign Commerce and Navigation of the United States*, 1926-1946, and *United States Imports of Merchandise for Consumption*, 1950-1961. USDA, Foreign Agricultural Service circular, *Bananas.* See tables 13–2 and 13–6. FAO, *Production Yearbook, 1967.*

[a]Actual stems, not standardized in weight.
[b]Importer to wholesaler, first class green stems from Central America or Ecuador, not boxed, Atlantic, Gulf, or Pacific ports.
[c]Importer to wholesaler, f.o.b. Hamburg.
[d]Boxed bananas, net weight.
[e]Average January-September only; after September 1964, data collected for boxed bananas only.

TABLE 13-4. Area Planted to Bananas, Yields, and Average Stemweights in Latin America, mid-1950s and early 1960s

Country	Mid-1950s[a] Area (000 hectares)	Yield (tons/ha.)	Weight (kg/stem)	Early 1960s[a] Area (000 hectares)	Yield (tons/ha.)	Weight (kg/stem)
Brazil	144	28	7.5[b]	231	27	20
Colombia	45	8	25[c]	50[d]	12	25[c]
Costa Rica	16	25	44[e]	16	27	36[f]
Dominican Republic			27[e]	24	19	23[f]
Ecuador	160	(g)	25[e]	169	20	25[e]
Guatemala	16	9	32[b]	16	9	32[f]
Honduras	28	24	29[e]	68[h]	29[h]	31[e]
Mexico[j]	20	10	21	28	13	20[b]
Nicaragua			20[c]			20[c]
Panama	17	20	36	28	17	36[f]
Venezuela				68	21	20[f]
Total	520[k]	22[m]		700	22[m]	

Sources: tables 13-2, 13-5, and 13-6. USDA, Foreign Agricultural Service, *Agricultural Geography of Latin America* (1958), p. 59. FAO, *Production Yearbook, 1960* to *1964*. Brazil, IBGE/Conselho Nacional de Estatística, *Anuário Estatístico do Brasil,* 1964, p. 72. Ecuador, Junta Nacional de Planificación y Coordinación Económica, Plan General de Desarrollo Económico y Social (Quito, 1963), "Programa de Banano," p. 7. Honduras, Dirección General de Estadística y Censos, *Anuário Estadístico,* 1963, p. 250.

[a]Average or individual year, according to availability of data. Areas and yields are usually given for 1954-56 and 1963-64; stemweights are usually for 1952-54 or 1955-57 and 1960-61.
[b]Average stemweight of all exports.
[c]Estimate used in table 13-6; data not available.
[d]Includes 10,000 hectares assumed to be planted during 1963-64.
[e]Average stemweight of U.S. imports from country.
[f]FAO estimate.
[g]Not calculated because area figure includes much newly planted land not yet in production in 1956.
[h]Includes plantains; separate data for bananas not available.
[j]Data refer only to Lacatán bananas, the type grown for export.
[k]Includes estimates of 24 for the Dominican Republic and 50 for Venezuela; total rounded.
[m]Average of figures listed; does not include estimates for other countries.

TABLE 13-5. Participation of the United Fruit Company in Latin American Banana Industry, 1955 and 1963/64

Country	Share (Percentage) of 1963/1964 (1) Area Planted	1955 (2) Area Planted	(3) Bananas Exported	(4) Bananas Grown for Export	(5) National Income
Colombia	(a)	6	58	17	0.2
Costa Rica	67	58	99	87	8
Ecuador		3	19	5	1
Guatemala	52[b]	52	75	61	2
Honduras	14	49	69	46	6
Panama	45[c]	64	93	93	6
Total, Six Countries	12	22	60	41	1.7
Total, Latin America	6[d]	9[e]	52[f]	35	

Sources: S. May and G. Plaza, *The United Fruit Company in Latin America* (National Planning Association, 1958), pp. 76, 80, 181. United Fruit Co., *Annual Report, 1963* and *1964*. FAO, *Monthly Bulletin of Agricultural Economics and Statistics,* November 1965. IA-ECOSOC, Special Committee on Bananas, *Report of Banana Mission* (Pan American Union, 1957).

(1) Share of land planted to bananas in 1963/64 owned by company, including land leased to other growers (average 1963/64).
(2) Share of land planted to bananas owned by company, including new (immature) plantings, and excluding land controlled by company under contracts for sale of fruit.
(3) Value of company banana exports as share of total value of banana exports; ratio may exceed that for volume because of quality differences.
(4) Share in col. (3) multiplied by percentage of company shipments grown by company rather than purchased from other growers.
(5) Value added by all company operations, including production of cocoa, sugar cane, and other crops, as share of national income.

[a]No land owned by company; bananas shipped are purchased from growers associated with company. Total area covered by such contracts was 14,000 hectares at end 1965.
[b]Company area in 1963 only as share of total 1963/64 area; major division closed during 1964.
[c]Minimum share, assuming total banana area of 28,000 hectares (unofficial figure for 1960/61).
[d]Total area estimated as 700,000 hectares; area in Venezuela estimated as 68,000 hectares, rather than 145,000 hectares as reported by the *Anuario Estadístico Agropecuario* (the larger figure may include plantains, and certainly includes bananas produced for domestic consumption).
[e]Total area estimated as 600,000 hectares.
[f]Same share of volume as of value of exports assumed for six countries listed; share of total volume of exports in tons, stem basis. Comparison of total company shipments to total regional exports, both adjusted to boxed basis, yields share of 55%.

TABLE 13-6. Latin American Banana Exports by Destination, 1950-1966
(Thousands of metric tons and millions of U.S. dollars)

Exporter and Destination	1950	1951	1952	1953	1954	1955	1956	1957	1958
Brazil	126.0[a]	165.0[a]	190.0[a]	178.7	218.0	210.7	188.0	218.5	271.4
Argentina				135.3		159.0	157.3	190.6	242.4
Uruguay				13.0		18.5	13.2	16.2	13.6
United Kingdom				24.1		31.6	16.8	10.5	11.6
Value				9.2	11.3	10.3	12.4	13.3	10.9
Share total exports (%)				0.6	0.7	0.7	0.8	1.0	0.9
Colombia	143.8	154.5	152.6	196.2	195.7	209.6	215.9	184.1	174.1
West Germany	30.7	24.7	39.3	14.1	13.4	78.0	88.5	94.0	103.0
Netherlands			0.5	21.3	6.5	35.2	22.1	20.5	19.5
Sweden			2.3			0.6	18.3	18.6	0.9
U.S. (25 kg/stem)	112	120	90	108	91	60	46	17	20
Value	6.1	8.0	6.2	8.4	9.4	16.9	28.1	26.2	15.5
Share total exports (%)	1.5	1.7	1.3	1.4	1.4	2.9	4.7	5.1	3.4
Costa Rica				355.9	355.3	329.4	232.4	309.9	301.6
United States	364.0[b]	322.0[b]	399.0[b]	320.0[b]	288.9	290.4	202.9	246.4	236.4
Canada					66.5	38.9	28.3	63.5	63.1
Value	31.5	34.4	38.4	35.8	35.8	33.2	25.7	32.3	26.5
Share total exports (%)	56.7	54.3	52.0	44.6	42.3	41.0	38.2	38.7	28.8
Dominican Republic	41.9	44.1	40.7	38.4	45.8	43.0	41.0	52.0	86.0
United States	40.4	35.3	32.6	36.3	43.7	43.5[b]	27.4[b]	37.6[b]	53.9[b]
West Germany									
Netherlands		7.5	6.5						
Sweden									
Value	1.0	1.3	1.4	1.8	2.2	2.1	2.2	2.9	5.0
Share total exports (%)	1.1	1.1	1.2	1.7	1.8	1.8	1.8	1.8	3.6
Ecuador	314.0[a]	234.0[a]	423.5	404.6	480.9	610.0	592.6	794.0	715.8
United States	159.0[b]	200.0[b]	362.2	319.8	342.9	434.4	419.9	413.0[b]	382.5
Belgium			31.1	14.5	40.2	41.6	49.8		84.8
West Germany			10.6	37.0	60.5	80.4	93.0		173.1
Japan									
Chile			18.8	22.6	23.7	17.0	17.2		29.5
Peru									0.5
Value	17.2	25.0	43.6	41.2	50.9	62.3	59.8	69.0	72.9
Share total exports (%)	23.2	35.5	43.0	44.7	40.8	54.8	51.7	52.0	54.6
Guatemala		170.0[a]	125.0[a]	228.0[a]	194.0[a]	114.0[a]	216.0[a]	129.7	115.8
United States	157.0[b]	118.0[b]	39	104	104	72	129	68.2	82.0
West Germany			35	70	53	23	49	36.6	9.5
Norway								1.7	2.3
Sweden			0.5			2.4	0.8	11.4	11.2
Value	18.9	14.2	11.9	23.1	20.3	17.0	15.0	14.5	13.1
Share total exports (%)	24.0	16.8	12.6	23.2	19.4	15.9	12.2	12.5	12.2
Haiti (20 kg/stem)		0.5	0.2	0.2		1.0	2.9	1.8	0.8
Value		1.0	0.5	0.3	0.2		0.1	0.1	
Share total exports (%)		1.9	0.9	0.7	0.4	0.1	0.2	0.2	0.1
Honduras	409[a]	377[a]	411[a]	395.4	293.0	207.4	392.9	337.3	398.2
United States	344.0[b]	352.0[b]	330.0[b]	332.1	228.0[b]	180.0	298.4	275.1	309.0
West Germany				57.2		4.0	19.7	18.1	19.5
Canada						10.6	68.0	38.4	42.7
Value	40.8	43.7	40.6	41.1	28.3	27.4	43.9	33.7	37.7
Share total exports (%)	74.0	66.4	64.9	60.5	51.7	47.4	59.9	52.0	54.0
Mexico				51	56	29	16	36	26
United States[b]	93	73	53	50	55	36	19	43	24
Value	4.5	3.5	2.2	1.8	2.0	0.5	0.4	0.9	0.7
Share total exports (%)	0.9	0.5	0.4	0.3	0.2	0.1		0.1	0.1
Nicaragua		12[a]	9	9	12	9	4	2	2
United States	13	12	9	9	11	9	4.7	2	2
Value		0.1	0.1	0.1	0.1	0.1			
Share total exports (%)		0.2	0.1	0.1	0.1	0.1	0.1		
Panama		177[a]	145[a]	188	188	275	251	290	267
United States[b]	187	209	178	211	242	264	242	292	298
Value	16.3	16.3	13.0	16.3	22.1	26.2	22.3	24.4	21.9
Share total exports (%)	69.7	64.5	55.6	64.0	72.0	73.6	72.6	68.9	66.6
Latin America[c]				2,045	2,039	2,037	2,150	1,560	2,358
United States[d]	1,469	1,441	1,493	1,490	1,407	1,389	1,389	981	1,709
Latin America[e]				171		195	188		286
West Germany				178					
Value	136.0	146.3	157.3	178.8	182.3	195.8	209.8	217.2	204.0
Share exports of major exporters (%)[g]	50.7	53.0	52.0	50.5	46.6	53.0	52.9	50.5	48.5
Share total L.A. exports (%)	2.0	1.8	2.2	2.3	2.2	2.4	2.4	2.5	2.4

TABLE 13-6 – Continued

Exporter and Destination	1959	1960	1961	1962	1963	1964	1965	1966
Brazil	213.1	241.9	245.9	216.3	206.9	225.5	215.8	204.8
Argentina	192.5	203.7	209.2	180.4	174.7	186.5	194.4	179.0
Uruguay	11.0	32.7	31.1	32.2	28.8	34.2	17.5	25.8
United Kingdom	7.4	4.4	5.4	3.7	2.3	4.1	2.9	10.0
Value	4.4	4.6	3.8	3.2	2.9	5.8	6.3	6.3
Share total exports (%)	0.3	0.4	0.3	0.3	0.2	0.4	0.4	0.4
Colombia	203.3	190.7	205.6	147.1	202.6	172.0	253.5	341.9
West Germany	118.5	137.4	136.3	108.2	131.3	85.9	130.0	128.1
Netherlands	43.5	35.5	17.7	33.3	62.3	76.3	89.8	115.6
Sweden	11.3	7.1	11.4	4.2	8.1	2.1	24.8	29.9
U.S. (25 kg/stem)		6.2	3.9	0.5	0.5			
Value	13.9	13.7	14.1	10.6	13.3	12.4	18.6	22.3
Share total exports (%)	2.9	2.9	3.2	2.4	3.0	2.3	3.5	4.4
Costa Rica	213.2	272.7	229.4	291.9	261.1	292.9	316.0	358.7
United States	181.3	260.4	226.9	291.6	260.4	292.4	293.4	339.8
Canada	31.9	10.7		0.4		0.5	1.2	2.9
Value	19.1	20.3	20.9	26.9	24.9	28.3	28.3	29.2
Share total exports (%)	24.9	23.6	24.8	29.0	27.2	24.9	25.3	21.5
Dominican Republic	101.0	180.4	162.6	168.4	119.6	68.7	48.0	10.6
United States		78.6	36.5	17.9	17.8	1.3	1.5	4.3
West Germany		56.6	66.5	82.5	58.6	48.4	19.9	3.1
Netherlands		23.9	31.5	45.1	22.2	15.3	23.1	1.3
Sweden		12.3	12.1	10.7	12.8	1.3	2.6	0.3
Value	6.1	11.3	11.3	11.5	8.6	5.2	3.4	0.8
Share total exports (%)	4.7	6.2	8.0	6.7	4.9	2.9	2.7	0.6
Ecuador	885.6	895.1	842.3	897.8	1,014.3	1,086.8	822.8	1,005.0
United States	559.9	625.0	540.8	575.0	540.5	537.8	464.5	447.8
Belgium	75.5	62.3	64.7	65.4	76.8	108.8	86.7	127.2
West Germany	191.1	157.9	168.4	152.5	132.9	233.4	167.9	264.5
Japan			4.2	29.1	189.2	153.6	29.5	54.4
Chile	37.6	36.4	41.8	37.8	30.2	22.5	22.6	36.7
Peru	0.3	1.1	5.2	4.0	13.5	7.9	7.8	5.4
Value	89.7	88.9	80.9	88.5	85.2	88.1	95.9	106.0
Share total exports (%)	63.4	61.5	63.7	62.0	52.3	54.4	53.8	57.4
Guatemala	138.7	189.0	157.2	83.5	121.0	99.9	58.0	76.7
United States	104.5	139.2	109.6	32.6	9.0[f]	12.6		6.0
West Germany	13.2	18.1	18.0	22.0		56.3	27.0	38.4
Norway	1.7	2.0	5.0	3.1		5.7	1.2	0.7
Sweden	4.4	7.1	8.3	5.8		8.9		2.4
Value	14.7	17.3	13.9	9.5	10.9	9.6	4.4	5.8
Share total exports (%)	13.7	14.5	12.1	8.3	7.1	6.1	2.5	3.1
Honduras	356.9	360.2	425.7	372.5	337.5	343.7	571.6	709.9
United States	274.7	296.3	365.0	320.3	281.7	283.2	470.0	571.0
West Germany	35.2	16.3	14.3	8.7	36.3	36.1	66.7	142.1
Canada	23.5	19.5	31.3	24.6	18.7	19.6	5.6	
Value	32.1	28.2	33.3	34.2	32.4	34.2	53.7	69.7
Share total exports (%)	46.8	44.5	45.7	42.0	39.4	36.0	42.1	48.8
Mexico	33	10	23	9	12	17	14	12
United States[b]		5	11	4.8[f]	1.2[f]	5.0[f]	6.2	5.8
Value	0.8	0.3	0.7	0.4	0.6	0.7	0.6	0.5
Share total exports (%)	0.1		0.1		0.1	0.1	0.1	
Nicaragua	2	4	1.3	11.4	18.8	27.2	8.0	13.6
United States		3.2	1.5	8.0[f]	4.8[f]	22[f]		0.7
Value			0.1	0.8	1.4	2.2	7.9	11.8
Share total exports (%)			0.1	0.9	1.4	1.8	5.5	8.6
Panama	291	263	271	251	298	267	377.4	431.7
United States[b]		302	226	200[a]	204[a]	246[a]	337.7	410.2
Value	23.5	18.2	20.1	23.5	30.8	30.3	30.6	34.8
Share total exports (%)	67.8	66.0	66.4	42.0	40.5	43.3	38.6	38.9
Latin America[c]	2,438	2,607	2,559	2,444	2,589	2,619	2,685	3,165
United States[d]		1,716	1,521	1,451	1,320	1,400	1,573	1,786
Latin America[e]	241	274	287	254	247	251	242	247
West Germany		386	404	505			654	576
Value	204.2	202.6	199.0	208.4	231.8	210.7	249.7	252.3
Share exports of major exporters (%)[g]	51.4	48.5	49.7	49.4	50.6	41.5	52.1	59.9
Share total L.A. exports (%)	2.4	2.3	2.3[h]	2.5	2.3	1.9	2.1	2.0[h]

Sources: Tables 13-2 and 13-4; foreign trade yearbooks of Brazil, Colombia, Costa Rica, Dominican Republic, Ecuador, Guatemala, Honduras, Mexico, Nicaragua, and Panama; USCB, *United States Imports of Merchandise for Consumption, 1950-1964*; IMF, *International Financial Statistics*; UN, *Yearbook of International Trade Statistics;* SIECA, *Anuário Estadístico Centroamericano de Comercio Exterior, 1965, 1966.*

[a]Export data in stems, converted.

[b]U.S. imports, data in stems; see table 13-2 for conversion factors used.

[c]Sum of countries listed; excludes exports of Cuba, Haiti and Venezuela in all years. Total also differs from total in table 13-2 because of difference in estimates for Ecuador, especially 1957-64.

[d]Excludes some U.S. imports from Brazil.

[e]Brazilian exports to Argentina and Uruguay plus Ecuadorean exports to Chile and Peru.

[f]U.S. imports; data in weight.

[g]Costa Rica, Ecuador, Honduras, and Panama.

[h]Excludes total Cuban exports.

Chapter 14

WHEAT

Wheat is one of Latin America's most ubiquitous agricultural commodities. It is grown in every country of the region with the exception of some Central American and Caribbean countries.[1] Nevertheless, its production is highly concentrated and Argentina accounts for almost two-thirds of Latin American output. Unlike maize, which in most countries is cultivated primarily under conditions of subsistence farming, wheat is an important cash crop and export commodity.

In the world economy, wheat and rice are the most important staples for human consumption. In recent years the area planted to wheat has exceeded that of rice and now covers more of the earth's surface than any other food.[2] Wheat is primarily a temperate zone product but given sufficient altitude, it can be grown at nearly every latitude. As with many agricultural commodities, wheat is not uniquely tied to specific land areas, but is usually highly substitutive with other farm products. Because of its relatively high income elasticity at low income levels compared to other crops, there has been a tendency to shift from other grains to wheat in many emerging countries.[3]

In Latin America, maize has been the most important food and feed crop, and the gap between wheat and maize has widened since the years before World War II. The land area devoted to maize has increased by nearly one-half while wheat acreage is less today than in the prewar years. Because of taste preferences inherited from the past, land areas for rice cultivation have expanded dramatically in an effort to substitute regional production for imports. Thus, rice acreage has increased three and one-half times since the 1930s, amounting now to almost two-thirds of the wheatland compared to about one-ninth in the prewar period. However, because climatic conditions in good grassland areas are ideal for wheat, wheat has competed principally with livestock production in the region rather than with other food crops and land has shifted back and forth between food grain cultivation and pasture and feed crops. This has been particularly true of Argentina, where fluctuations of 20 percent or more in wheatlands from one year to the next have not been uncommon.

Several varieties of wheat are cultivated in Latin America, but the hard and semihard types of Argentina predominate.[4] While production appears to be geographically widely distributed, most of it is rather specific to those areas which have suitable climatic conditions. Wheat will tolerate a fairly high temperature, particularly during the later part of its growing season. But both warm and dry weather is required for the grain to ripen. Generally, in Latin America the more important wheat areas receive between 20 and 40 inches of rainfall annually, though in Chile, and more recently in Mexico, there are substantial areas devoted to irrigated wheat where low rainfall is more of an advantage than an impediment.

More significant than the total amount of rain over a year is its distribution within the year. Where the rainfall is concentrated in the growing season, the yearly average rainfall can be less. In these instances, however, slight variations in weather may cause extreme yield variations and even make the difference between a bumper crop and a crop failure. Wheat is also grown in areas which receive rainfall in excess of 40 inches annually. But continuously high

---

Note: Wheat tables 14–1 to 14–14 appear on pp. 401–8.

[1] Besides cattle, which are present everywhere, only maize among the major commodities is produced in every part of Latin America.

[2] About 70 percent of the world's harvested area (exclusive of pasture) is planted to grains. Grains provide about half of the world's calories through direct consumption and an additional amount, indirectly, through grain-fed animals. The world wheat area is almost double that of maize and nearly 70 percent more than the land area devoted to rice. While in the prewar period world rice production exceeded that of wheat, the tonnage output of these two major crops is about equal now, amounting to about 250 million metric tons each. World maize output has always been 10 to 25 percent lower. In Latin America the production of maize far exceeds that of wheat.

[3] Some of this has been due to the influence of the United States government wheat export programs (particularly U.S. P.L. 480), as will be pointed out below.

[4] Many reports refer to Argentine wheat as soft and semihard. This does not appear to be correct. According to the U.S. Department of Agriculture, about 79 percent of the 1959-60 production was graded hard, the rest semihard. USDA, Foreign Agricultural Service, *Argentine Wheat Marketing, Practices and Facilities* (September 1960), p. 15.

moisture and temperature over the whole of the growing season are not favorable for wheat production. The combination of sustained hot and moist periods leads to a number of serious fungus and bacterial diseases. These conditions make large areas of South and Central America unsuited for large-scale wheat production, at least for the varieties now grown.

Resources

Many countries in the region increased the land area devoted to wheat since the nineteen thirties (see table 14-1). In general this has also been true of most countries in the rest of the world, the principal exception being the United States. In Argentina the wheat area has declined, although the data for recent years indicate an upturn. Since this country constitutes a large share of the Latin American acreage devoted to wheat, the regional total also has declined.

Wheat occupies a relatively small proportion of the region's cropland. The highest proportion occurs in Uruguay where it fluctuates at around one-third. It is about 15 percent in Argentina, roughly 20 percent in Chile, 10 percent in Peru, and somewhat less than that in Brazil and Colombia. In the remaining countries wheatland makes up an insignificant part of the total area in crops.

The region's wheat area is concentrated within a giant semicircle with Buenos Aires at its approximate center, reaching in the south the 40th parallel below Bahía Blanca in Argentina; in the north, the highlands of Brazil below the Tropic of Capricorn; and in the west the Sierra de Córdoba. This territory encompasses most of the Argentinian pampas and includes also Uruguay and southernmost Brazil. Other major wheat areas are located on the other side of the Andes in the central valley of Chile from Santiago to Puerto Montt, and in Peru, Colombia, and Mexico. In the latter three countries the land resources devoted to wheat are at relatively high altitudes in upland valleys and plateaus, where the characteristics of a temperate or at least semitropical climate prevail. Five countries, Argentina, Brazil, Chile, Mexico, and Uruguay, contain 95 percent of Latin America's land resources in wheat.

In Argentina the wheat growing region is largely concentrated on the periphery of the maize and humid pampas area. It forms a rough crescent extending from Rosario in the north to Bahía Blanca. Extension of the wheat area to the west and south is limited by lack of rainfall, and to the north, high temperature and rainfall preclude substantial cultivation.

An important aspect of Argentine production is that even inside the crescent where conditions are favorable, wheat is produced in a mixed agriculture. Here it must compete with a livestock and feed grain economy. The area planted to wheat in Argentina in fact declined by more than one-fifth between the late forties and 1960,[5] while over

the same period the area devoted to maize rose by about 60 percent and the area used for the other cereals, oats, rye, and barley grew by one-half. Because of its low moisture requirements, a large part of the wheat crop is grown on the outer edge of the crescent where rainfall is insufficient for the other crops. In this area, however, production and yields are highly volatile.

Since bread and other flour products are major items in the Latin American food basket, wheat imports have constituted a considerable fraction of the import budget of most countries in the region with the obvious exceptions of Argentina, Uruguay, and, most recently, Mexico. This has led to significant attempts to substitute imports through domestic production. Import substitution has been based primarily upon expansion in wheat acreage rather than on an increase in yields. The most striking attempt in this direction occurred in Brazil, where the utilization of new land resources for wheat production increased that country's wheat area to a level second only to Argentina during the 1950s. Before World War II, Brazil had about 160,000 hectares in wheat, which was less than 3 percent of Argentina's wheat area and less than 2 percent of the Latin American total. During the war Brazil's wheat acreage quadrupled and continued to rise sharply in the postwar period, reaching a peak of almost a million and one-half hectares in 1958/59. Since then Brazilian wheat lands have contracted, falling to about 740,000 hectares in recent years, but they still constitute almost 10 percent of the regional total (table 14-1). (For an analysis of the Brazilian wheat situation see the statistical note at the end of this chapter.)

Although wheat is cultivated in many parts of Brazil, major commercial production is restricted to the country's southernmost provinces of Rio Grande do Sul, Santa Catarina, and Paraná. The increase in production during the fifties has been largely due to the extension of wheat growing into the plains of these three southern provinces. Wheat displaced large areas of grasslands used previously for stockbreeding and livestock ranching. In other areas of the country climatic and ecological conditions are not suited for the wheat varieties now grown in Brazil. Of course, it is always possible that new varieties could be discovered whose yields would be high enough to compete with the yields of traditional crops. A great deal of research is needed toward this end.[6] Even in the three southern provinces of Brazil cultivation is beset with serious problems. In the small-holding areas, which are mainly in the hilly and broken uplands, the terrain permits little mechanization. Consequently, labor requirements are high, soil depletion and erosion are often advanced, and long periods of lying fallow are required to restore even partial fertility. The problems of the more recently cultivated plains of Brazil's southern provinces are less difficult but still sub-

---

[5]When compared with the late 1920s, the decline was more than 50 percent. In 1929 Argentina devoted over 9 million hectares to wheat, and between 1930 and 1934 the wheat area averaged about 8 million hectares compared with about 5 million hectares in

the mid-1960s. (FIAT, *Economía Agropecuaria Argentina*, tomo I, Oficina de Estudios para la Colaboración Económica Internacional, Delegación para América Latina, Buenos Aires, 1964, p. 69.) There has been a moderate expansion of wheat acreage since then, the total averaging somewhat over 5 million hectares during the mid-sixties.

[6]"Possibilities for Expanding Wheat Production in Brazil," *Economic Bulletin for Latin America*, II, no. 1 (February 1957).

stantial. Landholdings are typically larger and the terrain permits extensive mechanization. But here the use of chemical fertilizers is an absolute necessity. Liming is also recommended to correct the highly acid soils of these "campo" areas. Relatively high temperature and rainfall conditions favor the development of rusts and other diseases of the wheat plant.

Mexico is another case of a substantial increase in wheat acreage due to import substitution. Although the expansion was not as dramatic as in Brazil, yields increased enormously. The Mexican wheat area about doubled between the mid-1930s and the second half of the 1950s, when a peak seems to have been reached just as in the case of Brazil. Since then, unlike Brazil, the country's acreage in wheat declined only moderately. Cultivation is concentrated chiefly in the southern portion of the central plateau.

The size of Chile's wheatlands exceeded those of any other country except Argentina up to the early 1950s. Because of the relatively small expansion since then, Chile now shares second place with Brazil and Mexico. In Chile, too, the area suitable for wheat is restricted. The lands to the south of the central valley receive too much rainfall and in the north irrigation would be needed as indeed it is for many crops even in the central region. While over the past decade the area in wheat has increased proportionately much less than for other grain groups, it still accounts for nearly 70 percent of the total grain acreage in the country.

The amount of land devoted to wheat in Uruguay has fluctuated sharply since the war and no definite trend is discernible. Before the war Uruguay's wheat acreage was about three times that of Brazil's, but today it is not much more than one-half as large.

Of the other major producers, only Peru's wheat area showed a significant increase after the mid-thirties, but after reaching a peak of about 170,000 hectares it has declined somewhat. Less important quantities of wheat are grown in the more northerly countries of South America and on occasion in Central America. However, wheat growing in these regions occurs almost exclusively in small holdings in the inter-mountain valleys and upland plateaus.

It must be stressed that the import substitution effort in wheat, which has led to significant expansion of wheat area in Latin America outside of Argentina, does not seem to have curtailed the development of other crops. With the exception of Brazil in the 1950s, the acreage of other crops generally expanded faster than the wheat area. The total crop area of Latin America excluding Argentina rose by over 35 percent between 1950 and 1960, compared with a less than 25 percent rise in wheat acreage.

Despite the acreage decline in Argentina's wheat area since the late 1930s, that country still accounts for about 60 percent of the regional total. A separate section in this chapter will be devoted to a detailed discussion of wheat in Argentina.

Production

Argentina has accounted for between 50 and 80 percent of Latin American wheat production since the First World War, with the average proportion fluctuating around two-thirds of the regional total in the postwar period (table 14-2). Until the mid-1950s, Chile was the second largest producer, followed by Uruguay, Brazil, and Mexico. In the late 1950s Mexico overtook Chile and is now in second place, contributing about 15 percent of Latin America's wheat output compared with less than 5 percent before the war.

Uruguay's output similarly has not shown a significant rise for the past half century. A doubling of production between the immediate prewar years and 1953-55, which was based primarily upon an expansion in the area cultivated, was soon followed by a sharp decline in large part due to poor weather conditions at the end of the 1950s. But even when the climatic conditions improved later on, output never recovered the level of the mid-1950s and the country is now the region's fifth largest producer.

The enormous upsurge of Brazil's output put that country ahead of Uruguay during much of the postwar period. The disastrous deterioration in average Brazilian yields of wheat at the end of the 1950s, combined with a constriction of wheat acreage, also resulted in a collapse of that country's production, and the gap between Brazil and Uruguay has narrowed during the 1960s. During the peak years Brazil's wheat production reached about 10 percent of the regional total.[7] Uruguay has never accounted for more than 5 percent of production in Latin America for very long, and in recent years both countries have been below this level.

Other Latin American wheat production has been much less. Colombia and Peru have averaged about 150,000 metric tons of wheat each during the past decade, a level consistently less than 2 percent of the regional total.

Summing up, Latin American wheat production was about 4 million metric tons higher in 1963-67 than in 1935-39, an increase of almost 50 percent. About one-third of this increase was accounted for by Mexico, whose production expanded by one and a half million tons. The rise in Argentine output, while relatively small, added nearly half a million tons to the regional total. The rest was accounted for by Chile and Brazil.

The growth of Latin American wheat production was overshadowed by the proportionally greater expansion in the world total for which the postwar surge in Soviet output was primarily responsible. The Latin American share in world output declined from an average of over 6 percent in the 1920s and over 5 percent in the 1930s, to scarcely 4 percent in the 1960s.

Yields

Before the war the average wheat yields of most major producers clustered rather closely about the regional mean. The extremes were formed by Chile, whose average output per hectare was not much more than 10 percent above the average for Latin America, and by Peru, whose yield was about 25 percent below. Now the dispersion is incomparably wider and Mexico has an average wheat output per hectare about three times that of Brazil (table 14-3).

[7]See statistical note at end of this chapter.

With the exception of Brazil, all the major producers in Latin America have been able to raise wheat yields from their prewar levels. Brazil's yields remained constant as more acreage was brought under wheat cultivation in the postwar period, but official figures indicate a sharp decline in output per hectare during the late 1950s. The decade of the 1950s was marked by a very great expansion of the mechanized wheat area, much of this by persons with little or no previous experience in wheat farming. Beginning in 1958, overexpansion without sufficient technical support coupled with unusually bad weather, heavy attacks of stem rust, and a high incidence of other wheat diseases resulted in four years of extremely low yields, even by Brazilian standards. In the years since 1961, technological standards have improved, new varieties of rust-resistant wheats have been introduced, and the marketing system has been greatly strengthened by the establishment of a system of producers' cooperatives.

In spite of these improvements there is no statistically significant trend in Brazil's wheat yields either upward or downward over the twenty-year period 1947-67. In a recent Stanford Ph.D. dissertation (see "Note on Brazilian Wheat Statistics" at the end of this chapter), Peter T. Knight estimated that in 1967 it cost Brazil $2.20 to "save" one dollar in foreign exchange by producing wheat in that country. This cost could be substantially lowered if Brazilian agricultural researchers succeed in developing fertilizer-intensive wheat varieties such as those created in Mexico. The situation must at least in part be attributed to an over-zealous attempt at import substitution in Brazil which brought marginal or submarginal lands into wheat production.

On the whole, Latin American wheat yields show up rather well when compared with those of the rest of the world. In the other major grains the region does not do as well; for instance, the region's average maize yield is hardly 60 percent of the world average. Concerning wheat, however, only European producers much outdistance the Latin American average wheat output per hectare. Argentine yields have almost reached the levels of the United States; they compare favorably with those of Canada, are above those of Australia, and now average about two-thirds higher than those of the Soviet Union, the world's largest wheat producer.

In Mexico, the productivity of land in wheat has experienced a remarkable increase since the 1930s. Before the war Mexican yields were among the lowest in Latin America, but by the mid-1960s they were nearly 50 percent above the regional average and approached the highest European yields. Progress in Mexico has been so dramatic that the country has become a major supplier of seeds for the underdeveloped world. Technical assistance from the Rockefeller Foundation has been an important factor in the improvement of Mexican yields. Dwarf wheat, developed at Mexico's International Center for Maize and Wheat Improvement, has proven highly successful in Pakistan and India, nearly quadrupling present yields in the former and doubling them in the latter country.

The tripling of land productivity in Mexico was achieved largely by a sharp increase in fertilizer application. Mexico's fertilizer consumption per hectare is by far the highest in the region and its agricultural production in general has responded exceptionally well to increased fertilizer input. As will be indicated later, this has not been the case in Argentina, where a substantial growth in yields (about 70 percent over the prewar average) was attained without a notable rise in fertilizer application. Since improvement in the average productivity of land in Argentina was accompanied by a shrinkage of the wheat area, the rise in Argentine yields can be at least partly attributed to the restriction of wheat production to better suited lands. In most recent years, a remarkable rise in yields was recorded for Colombia, where the output per hectare during 1966-68 was more than double the level in the 1950s.

It is worth noting that the Latin American increase in wheat yields is an exception to the general picture of stagnation in yields of most crops over the last two or three decades. Maize is the other major exception, but its yields have shown only a moderate rise in recent years.

Consumption

While wheat, on a worldwide average, provides about 15 percent of protein and 18 percent of calories, these proportions vary greatly geographically and by income levels. In Latin America the share of protein and calory intake supplied by wheat ranges from about 5 percent for some Central American countries to over 40 percent for Chile. The overall regional average is approximately 15 percent (see table 14-5). Wheat and rice are the only important grains in the world of which the major shares are consumed directly by people. Substantial portions of other grains are fed to livestock. In Latin America most grains are primarily grown for human consumption and even maize, the major U.S. feed, is almost exclusively a human food staple. Only in Argentina and Uruguay is some wheat used for animal feeding. Wheat for feed becomes important only when there is a sharp deterioration in wheat prices relative to livestock after the grain has been planted.

There are various forces impinging upon wheat consumption over time. A country's consumption will tend to rise with the growth of population; then internal migration patterns, particularly the rural-urban population shift, will influence consumption; as income rises per capita wheat consumption will increase, and furthermore there may be various autonomous changes in tastes.

The rapid urbanization of Latin America has undoubtedly exerted an upward influence on wheat consumption. In the cities bread tends to be an important staple in the human diet, while in most Latin American countries maize is much more important in the countryside. Maize is cultivated widely on subsistence farms and much of the cash crop, which constitutes only a part of total output, is sold locally. Therefore, the movement of people from rural sections to towns will tend to raise the per capita consumption of wheat.

The income elasticity of demand for wheat is not constant but depends primarily upon general levels of income; in very poor areas it is relatively high when compared with other foods and more developed areas.[8] In higher-income

---

[8] For comparative statistics of coefficients of income elasticity see FAO, Committee on Commodity Problems, *Agricultural Commodities – Projections for 1975 and 1985*, 1967, vol. I, table I.8.

countries there is evidence that the income elasticity for wheat tends first to level off towards zero and then to become slightly negative as income rises and a maximum bread consumption is reached. Per capita wheat consumption in the United States and Canada, which has declined significantly since the 1930s, exemplifies this trend (see table 14-4).

In Latin America per capita wheat consumption has not changed significantly since before World War II. The overall level of per capita consumption in the region is still less than two-thirds that of the United States. As may be expected, the highest levels are found in the major wheat producing countries, Argentina, Chile, and Uruguay, with a consumption per inhabitant from two to three times the regional average. These three countries approximate European levels. In Mexico, however, now the region's second largest producer, per capita wheat consumption is still lower than the regional average. Nevertheless, Mexico experienced the region's most dramatic consumption increase with per capita wheat intake doubling since the 1930s. Success in wheat production and rapidly rising incomes combined to raise consumer preferences for wheat relative to maize. Peru's consumption also increased significantly in the postwar period. The lowest per capita consumption levels in the region are recorded in Central America.

The most significant declines took place in Argentina and Uruguay: Argentine wheat consumption diminished by nearly 20 percent since before the war; in Uruguay per capita consumption dropped by one-third since the early postwar years. It is not clear, however, whether this was partially offset by an expansion in the indirect consumption of wheat brought about by an increase in the consumption of livestock which was fed on wheat. Because the output of wheat used for feed is not always included in the production data, apparent consumption would be underestimated.

In many Latin American countries wheat consumption seems to be increasing. The massive sale of U.S. surplus wheat since the mid-1950s has undoubtedly contributed to a shift in consumer tastes toward wheat. However, Brazil's enormous wheat import gap has induced the government to attempt to discourage wheat consumption. For instance, it increased the amounts of soy, maize, and manioc flour required in bread. While the effects of such measures cannot be precisely measured, the moderate decline in per capita wheat consumption in Brazil during the 1960s can be at least in part attributed to them.

The World Wheat Market[9]

Trade arrangements of various types have been a major feature of the world wheat market for a very long time.

During the 1920s and early 1930s the international trading system in wheat was based upon multilateralism and the principle of nondiscrimination, and payments were made in freely convertible currencies. During the Great Depression this system broke down and bilateral arrangements between exporting and importing countries were entered into in order to facilitate the flow of trade. World War II saw an increase in special transactions in wheat, primarily among the allies. After the wartime arrangements, the particular problems of the immediate postwar period called for an expansion in trade arrangements. After the end of the postwar readjustment process in the early 1950s, there was a return to convertibility and multilateralism, but without the elimination of special trading schemes in wheat. New types of arrangements were introduced, especially as a consequence of the rising wheat import requirements of the developing countries. At present more than half of the world's trade in wheat is conducted under special arrangements.

Since 1933 a series of international commodity schemes in wheat have been superimposed upon this system of trade arrangements. The period after World War I witnessed erratic conditions in the international wheat situation. Prices fluctuated violently as wartime and immediate postwar scarcity was followed by an excessive expansion in production. Wheat surpluses developed and the accumulation of stocks caused grave problems in the exporting countries. The first control schemes emerged in Canada, which was the world's largest exporter in the interwar period. In that country voluntary wheat pools were established by producers in the 1920s in order to limit sales and thus prevent prices from falling unduly. When prices collapsed in 1930 the Canadian government had to bail out the wheat pools, which had become indebted to banks for the carrying costs of the stocks. This eventually led to the establishment of a permanent government agency, the Canadian Wheat Board, for the purpose of marketing the entire crop.

In other exporting countries governments also had to come to the assistance of their farmers in order to prevent a complete collapse of the market and to cope with the problems of carrying stocks. In the United States, too, what was intended as a temporary public solution of the current wheat situation during the early 1930s resulted in lasting government intervention. Only Argentina, among the major wheat exporters, maintained relatively free trade conditions during the Great Depression; agriculture in that country was subjected to important government manipulation only at the end of World War II and thereafter.

During the 1930s the balance of payments problem of wheat importing countries was aggravated by massive efforts of the wheat exporters to bolster prices through government intervention. It is not surprising, therefore, that in an attempt to save foreign exchange the importing countries attempted to protect their own producers and embarked upon an import substitution process. This worsened an already acute oversupply.

[9]This section is based upon the following principal sources: International Wheat Council (IWC), *Trade Arrangements Involving Wheat*, Secretariat Paper No. 2 (London, 1962); Joseph S. Davis, *Wheat Under International Agreement* (New York: American Enterprise Association, 1945); J.W.F. Rowe, *Primary Commodities in International Trade* (Cambridge University Press, 1965); *International Wheat Agreement, 1962, and Rules of Procedure* (International Wheat Council); *International Wheat Agreement, 1962: A Summary and Historical Sketch* (USDA, 1 April 1965); USDA, Foreign Agri-

cultural Service, *International Grains Arrangement of 1967* (November 1967); U.S. Senate, Subcommittee of the Committee on Foreign Relations, *Hearings* (26 March, 4 and 5 April 1968); and IWC, *Review of the World Situation, 1966/67* (London, 1967).

In this situation the wheat problem became the focus of several international meetings. The first international wheat conferences, one in Rome in 1931 and one in London soon thereafter, were unsuccessful. Not until 1933 was the first agreement achieved.

While the 1933 agreement was not distinguished by success, it was noteworthy in that it constituted the first commodity control scheme in which exporters and importers and many governments participated. The chief exporting and importing nations, twenty-two countries in all, were parties to this agreement which provided for export quotas and commitments by importers not to raise tariffs or increase their wheat acreage. Although the agreement broke down in the following year, its instrument, the International Wheat Advisory Committee, continued to exist. A new draft proposal was prepared but action was precluded by the outbreak of World War II.

The war intensified the wheat crisis. Europe was in part cut off from her suppliers, who found themselves with accumulating stocks. As a result, representatives of the United States, Canada, Australia, Argentina, and the United Kingdom prepared a Memorandum of Agreement in 1942 primarily designed to control production and to establish a wheat pool for the relief of war-stricken areas. A Draft Convention was also produced for consideration by a full-fledged conference after cessation of hostilities. Conferences followed immediately after the war but only after the seventh conference in Washington in 1949 was an agreement developed which was ratified by most of the signatory nations. Two important exporters did not join this agreement: the Soviet Union, because its export quota was too low, and Argentina, because the proposed price was too low. The 1949 compact had a duration of four years and essentially set the general pattern for all subsequent agreements. After the expiration of the 1949 covenant, new international wheat agreements were negotiated and entered into about every three years. The Soviet Union joined the 1962 agreement which encompassed almost every wheat trading country in the world (the major exception being mainland China). The International Wheat Agreement of 1962 (IWA), which was due to expire in 1965, was extended by three successive protocols until July 1968, when the 1967 International Grains Arrangement (IGA) came into effect. The IGA consists of two covenants – a Wheat Trade Convention (WTC) and a Food Aid Convention (FAC). The WTC replaces the earlier International Wheat Agreement.

The IGA, like the former agreement, is administered internationally by the International Wheat Council (IWC) in London.[10] One of the most important functions of the IWC has been to prepare an annual review of the world wheat situation. It has also issued occasional papers on special aspects of the wheat problem. Not only the commercial

transactions which have fallen under the agreement have been reported to the IWC but also "special" and other transactions from both member and nonmember countries so that the IWC publications now are the most comprehensive source of statistics for the world picture of wheat and flour.

The international wheat agreements basically concern marketing only. There is no restriction of production or overall exports and no central accumulation of stocks. Such controls in wheat have been the province of national governments.

The main feature of the postwar international wheat agreements is a range between a minimum and maximum price within which member exporting countries must be ready to sell and member importing countries must be ready to buy specified quantities. A quota system used in the earlier wheat agreements was modified by the 1959 covenant. The present system involves an obligation of each member importing country to purchase from member countries, when prices are within the agreed maximum-minimum range, not less than a specified percentage of its annual total "commercial purchases" from all sources, whatever that total may be. Under the new WTC each member country when importing wheat from nonmember countries undertakes to do so at prices consistent with the range set by the Convention. On the other hand, member exporters agree to sell wheat at prices within the price range in quantities sufficient to satisfy the "commercial requirements" of member importing countries. In the event prices reach the maximum, exporting countries are obligated to furnish importing countries at the maximum price any quantities in that crop year up to the importers' average "commercial purchases" on a historical basis. It is obvious that if the world price is above the agreement maximum, the wheat consuming countries will benefit because of the exporting countries' obligation and if market prices go to the minimum or below, the producing countries will benefit because of the importing countries' commitment.[11]

The term "commercial trade" stipulated in the agreements is somewhat arbitrary, because it includes not only open market transactions but also trade arrangements of various kinds including government trading and bilateral trading schemes such as the Argentine bilateral payments settlements.[12] The "special transactions" which are exempted from the agreement consist primarily of inconvertible currency arrangements, and barter at other than world prices as well as bilateral gifts and grants. The most

---

[10]The importing and the exporting countries hold a total of 1,000 votes each. Argentina had 70 and the United States 290 of the 1,000 exporter votes under the 1962 agreement. The Soviet Union has not yet signed the covenants of the IGA, which had been elaborated in conjunction with the Kennedy Round of tariff negotiations in Geneva in 1967.

[11]The IWA made allowances for differences in quality of wheat and prices were expressed in terms of an international standard (No. 1 Manitoba Northern at Fort William/Port Arthur, Canada). Thus the differential between the lower Argentine export prices and the higher international price represented differences in "quality" as well as in consumer preferences (see table 14-10). In the new arrangement there is no fixed single reference wheat, but rather price ranges for fourteen different wheats were established in order to take account of the quality and other demand differentials. In addition, the WTC increased the price levels by an average of about 20¢ per bushel (see table 14-12).

[12]The "commercial requirements" of the importing countries have been determined under the 1962 agreement on the basis of a moving average of the first four of the preceding five crop years.

important of the "special transactions" have been U.S. sales of surplus wheat under P.L. 480 and other programs.

Under the agreements countries are classified as exporters and importers. In Latin America, Argentina and Mexico are designated as exporters among a current total of ten exporting countries. Many other Latin American countries were among the thirty-eight importing countries in the old IWA.[13]

As can be seen from table 14-9, the wheat trade among member countries has constituted about two-thirds of the world trade in wheat during the 1960s. "Commercial" transactions of member countries have amounted to about three-fourths of member countries' total trade. In recent years some exporting countries have had to import wheat, the outstanding case being the Soviet Union (the U.S.S.R. is not a member of the 1967 IGA). These transactions are included in the total "commercial trade" figures and amounted to about 12 million tons in the crop year 1963/64 out of a total commercial tonnage of the member countries of 31 million tons. Only some 18 million tons were subject to the agreement and about one-third of this amount was accounted for by the United States in 1963/64. Total U.S. wheat trade was much more because the major share of the U.S. transactions was P.L. 480 sales not subject to the IWA. (In 1963/64 total U.S. wheat exports amounted to over 23 million tons of which 13 million were P.L. 480 transactions.) About half of Argentina's trade has come under the agreement; the remainder has consisted of sales to nonmember countries.

It is difficult to evaluate the performance of the international wheat agreements. Under the 1962 agreement the importing countries pledged to buy about 81 percent (weighted average) of their total commercial requirements from member exporters, compared with about 70 percent under the 1959 agreement. Only Brazil among the major importers decreased its subscription significantly, from 50 percent under the 1959 agreement to 30 percent under the 1962 agreement — together with the United Arab Republic the lowest commitment of any country in the IWA — and has not joined the new Wheat Trade Convention. Actual commercial purchases from member exporters, however, represented a much greater proportion than the percentage commitment. For instance, in 1963/64 Brazil's total wheat and flour purchases were about 2 million tons and about one-half of this amount consisted of commercial purchases from member exporters, thus falling under the IWA provisions. Because there were no other commercial imports into Brazil, the IWA proportion was 100 percent. For all of the IWA countries it was 94 percent in the 1963/64 crop year, thus exceeding the 81 percent that was pledged.

The primary purpose of the international wheat agreements since World War II has been to bring order into a chaotic situation which persisted throughout the first half of this century: prices fluctuated violently and wheat short-ages alternated with large surpluses. In these respects there was some similarity to the coffee situation; in wheat, too, the major problem has been the tendency toward over-supply.

In an overall sense the IWA can be considered to have been successful. The wheat market has generally operated in an orderly fashion in the postwar period. Price variations have been reduced and since the mid-1950s international wheat prices have changed relatively little and the average year-to-year fluctuation has been less than 5 percent (see tables 14-10 and 14-11). The pre-IWA extremes were a low of 40 cents a bushel during the depth of the Depression and a high of over $3.20 a bushel in 1947/48.

The 1949 agreement was distinguished by rising prices and the Korean War kept the free (non-IWA) price above the IWA maximum throughout most of the life of this covenant. (See table 14-11.) The effect, if not the intent, of the agreement was to benefit the importing countries. The exporters not only honored the stipulations of the compact, but also admitted eleven more importing countries to the arrangement. Since September 1953, the prevailing world price has been below the IWA maximum and therefore the exporters' quantitative commitment has not come into force. Nevertheless, exporters have in effect met this commitment without being obliged to do so. For instance, for the United States the aggregate commitment would have been about 3.7 million tons in the 1963/64 crop year, but U.S. commercial sales to member importing countries actually amounted to much more, about 5.9 million tons.

Thus from the price stabilization point of view the IWA agreements appear to have been quite successful. Yet it is not possible to attribute the relative market stability to the functioning of the IWA, because wheat production and prices are controlled nationally rather than internationally. Most major wheat producing countries apply some form of control over their domestic wheat situation and there is little doubt that the United States, the world's largest wheat exporter, exercises a profound influence on world wheat prices through its domestic price support program. For example, when there were bumper crops during the 1952/53 crop year and substantial stocks accumulated in exporting countries, particularly the United States and Canada, wheat prices did not fall significantly. U.S. internal price supports in effect pegged the free (non-IWA) price at $2.20 per bushel and for all practical purposes diminished price competition among sellers. On the other hand, there are some forty importing countries which have been in strong competition.

Because of national agricultural policies in many countries, domestic wheat prices are higher than prevailing world prices. In the United States this situation is remedied by export subsidies which operate through the Commodity Credit Corporation and thus enable U.S. exporters to maintain a competitive position in world markets and at the same time make wheat available to IWA member countries at prices within the agreement price range.

Argentina and Canada are the only major exporters whose domestic prices have been below their export prices. Argentina, moreover, has usually sold wheat on the world market at levels below the prevailing average (see tables

[13]The only countries in the region that have signed the new WTC are Argentina, Bolivia, and Mexico; Costa Rica, Cuba, the Dominican Republic, Ecuador, Guatemala, and Venezuela have acceded. (For a listing of "exporting" and "importing" countries as designated in the 1962 agreement see note b of table 14-9.)

14-10 to 14-12).[14] This is due in part to quality differences and in part to the fact that the shortage of storage facilities has forced Argentina to sell most of its crop even in bumper years. The spread between Argentine prices and the IWA maximum price has been so wide that the IWA maximum price provisions have actually made little difference for that country. As with other exporters, its quantitative obligation under the IWA has never been in force and, given its relatively low export prices, Argentina can always place its export surplus abroad, provided there are no discriminating restrictions against it. On the other hand, the IWA minimum price provisions seem to have benefited Argentina's income from the export of wheat. The new WTC minimum price for River Plate wheat appears to be at least as favorable for Argentina as the former IWA minimum.

Since the International Wheat Agreements have not applied any international production controls, the wheat surplus problem has not yet been resolved. To the contrary, wheat stocks more than quadrupled between the start of the first IWA in 1949 and 1961 as the agricultural programs of most countries encouraged domestic production. The United States accounts for about two-thirds of world wheat stocks and Canada for most of the rest. Because of the lack of adequate storage facilities, Argentine carryovers have been small, generally amounting to less than 5 percent of world inventories (see table 14-14).

During the early 1960s crop failures, primarily in the Communist countries, and the sharply increasing requirements of the developing countries changed the supply situation. During the crop year 1961/62 stocks fell substantially for the first time in over a decade mainly as a consequence of the special U.S. wheat export programs. From a high of over 58 million tons at the beginning of the 1961/62 crop year, stocks fell to about 42 million tons at the openings of the 1964 and 1965 seasons. Argentina, the only major exporter experiencing a significant rise in stocks during this period, started the 1965/66 crop year with over 3 million tons, the highest wheat inventory recorded in that country. Because of the most recent sharp increases in world wheat production the combined carryover stocks of the major exporters reached a high of about 65 million tons at the end of the decade.

The most significant features of the new Wheat Trade Convention, compared to the earlier agreements, are the greater precision in defining price ranges through the listing of fourteen different wheats and the greater flexibility of adjusting prices whenever conditions so warrant. The power to quickly agree upon and implement such adjustments and to add other wheat price ranges is given to a newly established Prices Review Committee. The International Grains Arrangement was negotiated during a period when world wheat surpluses declined significantly (1964-67) and price increases were expected. It was for this reason that price levels in the WTC were set substantially higher than

under the 1962 agreement (see table 14-2), and the decline in world wheat stocks turned out to be a temporary phenomenon (see tables 14-12 and 14-14).[15]

Because of the possibility of adjusting the price ranges as well as the quantitative obligations of exporters and importers, the new Arrangement appears to have a great degree of flexibility, while at the same time it provides for greater precision in world wheat trade than the former agreement.

The WTC is firmer than the old IWA in establishing guidelines for concessional grains transactions, which are not covered by the Convention: concessional sales should be conducted in such a way as to avoid harmful interference with normal patterns of production and international trade; and they should be an addition to the commercial imports of the recipient country which could reasonably be expected in the absence of such concessional transactions. The Arrangement also requires prior consultations by member countries offering wheat on concessional terms with exporting member nations whose commercial sales might be affected by such sales.

The Food Aid Convention, which is the other part of the International Grains Arrangement, provides for an annual contribution of wheat and coarse grains suitable for human consumption of a minimum of 4.5 million metric tons to the needy developing countries of the world. Contributions to the program may also be in the form of a cash equivalent. The United States is the largest contributor with a subscription of over 40 percent of the total, followed by the European Economic Community which contributes nearly one-quarter of the program, Canada, 11 percent, Australia, Japan, and the United Kingdom, 5 percent each. The donor countries, some of which are wheat importers, form a Food Aid Committee (attached to the IWC) in order to keep the program under continuous review. A part of the program is oriented toward promoting grain production in the developing countries, through giving priority to grain exports of developing countries when donor nations import wheat for distribution, and through the use of cash contributions. Argentina is the only Latin American member of the FAC and is committed to a minimum contribution of 23,000 tons of grains (or the cash equivalent) which constitutes about half of 1 percent of the total program. The only FAC members committed to a smaller amount are Finland and Norway.

International Trade[16]

Despite the efforts at import substitution, wheat production could not keep up with population growth in Latin

[14] It is generally accepted that the differentials between Argentine export prices and the standard world prices will be quite narrow when all wheat, or even a particular wheat, is in short supply and prices are working toward the maximum. Conversely, experience has shown that differentials widen considerably when prices move away from the maximum and the competitive situation is more intense.

[15] Economists have argued that the minimum prices in the WTC were set too high in view of the long-run relation of production to demand. If the WTC price minima are significantly above the long-run equilibrium price then substantial surpluses will reappear. See statements of D. Gale Johnson and Helen C. Farnsworth in *International Grains Arrangement of 1967*, Hearings before Subcommittee of the Committee on Foreign Relations, U.S. Senate, March 26, April 4, 5, 1968. Subsequently production and carryover stocks rose substantially. (IWC Press Release, London, November 28, 1969.)

[16] There is a defect in the statistics of world trade in wheat. A consistent "export surplus" appears in international trade statistics in the postwar period, as published by IWC and FAO. That discrep-

America. Wheat imports have therefore increased since pre-war years, amounting in the mid-1960s to over three times the 1935-38 average (table 14-6). A significant portion of Latin American imports has consisted of purchases of surplus wheat from the United States under U.S. Public Law 480 (see table 14-13).

Brazil, which is self-sufficient in most other agricultural products, accounts for nearly half of Latin America's wheat imports. It also has been responsible for the major share of the region's import growth. Since the end of the war the country's annual wheat purchases have climbed by more than a million tons and now supply well over 80 percent of domestic requirements (see table 14-8). Brazil has become the world's fourth largest commercial wheat importing country.

Only Mexico could demonstrate an extraordinarily successful import substitution process. Its wheat imports declined dramatically in the postwar period, from a level of about 300,000 tons during the late 1940s and early 1950s to about 20,000 tons during the past decade. Most other countries' imports have been increasing considerably.

Imports of the rest of the world rose even more rapidly than in Latin America during the postwar years, primarily because of rapid increases in wheat needs of the developing countries of Asia and Africa, in particular the drastic jump in the requirements of continental China. The imports of Western Europe and the Soviet Union have also risen substantially. Thus the Latin American share of world wheat imports declined in the postwar period.

An increasing proportion of wheat imports by Latin America has been covered by special arrangements. In 1957 about two-thirds of all wheat entered the region under trade agreements of one type or another and by 1960 it had reached 85 percent, a large part of this being U.S. programs.[17] In recent years about half of wheat imports by Latin American countries have come from Argentina, the other half from the United States. Of the latter only about a quarter were commercial purchases; the rest entered the region under various U.S. government wheat programs. These programs, which have helped the United States dispose of its surpluses, have enabled the importing countries to obtain the grain under favorable conditions, such as payment in local currency, barter arrangements, and even outright donations. More than half of the U.S. government wheat has been purchased by Latin American countries with their local currencies (primarily Title I of P.L. 480) and almost 40 percent consisted of special barter deals. However, only about 2 percent were donations (primarily Titles II and III of P.L. 480; after 1966 dona-

tions disappeared). (See table 14-13.) Brazil has been by far the greatest beneficiary of the U.S. wheat programs, accounting for at least half and in some years three-quarters of the total. Colombia, Peru, and Chile have accounted for most of the rest.[18]

Before the war Latin America was a substantial net exporter of wheat, exports averaging about 2 million tons above imports during 1934-39. Between then and the early 1960s exports failed to grow and even declined in the face of rising imports, and so the region had a trade deficit in wheat during most of the postwar period. Subsequently exports rose sharply and exceeded imports during the second half of the decade.

In most years well over 95 percent of the region's exports originated in Argentina; Uruguay generally has made up the rest. All other Latin American countries, with the recent exception of Mexico, are net importers of wheat and flour even though minute quantities of the grain have been exported by some on rare occasions. Mexico succeeded in becoming practically self-sufficient in wheat during the 1950s and in 1964 was able to export about 480,000 tons to continental China. This is one of the highest wheat export figures for one year recorded for any country outside Argentina. Before the war Chile was a consistent wheat exporter, but since the early postwar years it has had difficulty in maintaining self-sufficiency in wheat, despite a large increase in domestic production.

As already indicated, wheat output fluctuates considerably in the exporting countries. This is due in part to climatic conditions, but in Argentina and Uruguay a more important factor may have been government policies which have affected relative prices among wheat, other crops, and livestock production, and have restricted or changed the incentive patterns of producers. Some of these factors will be discussed in the next section.

Latin American wheat exports in the postwar period until the early 1960s were running between 20 to 30 percent below the 1934-38 average. Before the war the region accounted for one-seventh of world exports, but its importance fell sharply as the world's wheat trade expanded. During the early 1960s Latin American exports constituted only about 5 percent of the world total, but since then has recovered its prewar share.

Argentina

Argentina possesses one of the world's most fertile land masses. Of the country's nearly 280 million hectares, 85 percent is usable for agricultural purposes. About 30 percent is arable land with adequate rainfall, roughly 55 percent consists of semiarid and arid areas, only some of which is in use, but all of which is productive.[19]

---

ancy has persisted over many years and has now reached about one and one-half million tons (see table 14-6). IWC has no particular explanation, but the excess of exports over imports may in part be due to the data recording system used. There may be some double counting such as exports for re-exports (temporary admissions for processing which are not counted as imports). Government imports for government purposes may not be counted by customs officials. The amount of wheat in ship stores at any given time and losses in transport may be other factors which contribute to the statistical discrepancy. (See IWC, *Wheat Consumption in the 20th Century* London, November 1961, pp. 10-11.)

[17] IWC, *Trade Arrangements Involving Wheat*, table 7, p. 27.

[18] Between July 1954 and December 1964, Latin American countries bought $650 million under Title I of P.L. 480. Of this amount $490 million were Brazilian imports. (Pan American Union, Inter-American Economic and Social Council, *The Future of Latin American Development and the Alliance for Progress*, March 1966, table II-34, p. 137.)

[19] Consejo Nacional de Desarrollo (CONADE), *Plan Nacional de Desarrolo, 1965-1969* (National Development Plan of Argentina), Buenos Aires, 1965, table 11.

The major portion of the country's agricultural production is concentrated in the pampas, a crescent of about a 400-mile radius from Buenos Aires and containing about 50 million hectares. Roughly two-thirds of the total value of Argentine agricultural production comes from the pampas and an additional 15 percent from the semiarid areas immediately surrounding it.[20]

The crystalline and granite bedrock of the pampas constitutes the fragmented edge of one of the world's oldest land masses, Brasilia, which underlies much of Brazil and Uruguay. In Argentina, this bedrock (which cannot be found at less than 1,000 feet near Buenos Aires, and as much as 16,000 feet under the Salado River) is buried under hundreds of feet of clay, sand, and loess (volcanic ash and rock dust from the Andes). This top layer is mixed with humus to form vast extensions of grassland which are almost completely devoid of stones. The high productivity of the land is due to its richness in organic materials combined with adequate rainfall, and a growing season of about 290 days is common. The provinces of Buenos Aires, southern Santa Fe, and Entre Ríos are at the center of the pampas. To the south and west of the Colorado River the semiarid pampas extend beyond the humid area in an arc of about 200 miles. Once Patagonia, in the southern part of the country, is reached, fertility decreases rapidly.[21]

Historical Background

The cultivation of wheat has been confined to the pampas, although it can be grown in most climates and soils.[22] Its production was based upon immigrants from Europe who started to arrive in large numbers around the middle of the last century. About 90 percent of the 3.3 million immigrants who came to Argentina between 1857 and 1914 settled in the pampas, although only a quarter of these remained in the rural area.[23] Because wheat is not a difficult plant to produce and is nearly nonperishable and easily transportable, it provided the answer for the poor and untrained European peasant who could not fit into the cattle raising economy of the pampas.

Wheat production started in the northern fringes of the pampas, mainly in Santa Fe and Entre Ríos provinces, although this land was somewhat submarginal for this crop. As yields declined because of primitive production methods and neglect of the soil, cultivation moved southward into Buenos Aires and west to Córdoba and La Pampa.

Argentina was still an importer of wheat in the 1870s. Thirty years later it was the world's third largest exporter. At the turn of the century over half the production was exported and sometimes as much as 70 percent. Until about 1870 exports of crops represented less than 1 percent of total exports, livestock making up most of the total. Since 1900 exports have been about equally divided between livestock and grains.

The abundance of land was so great that no care was taken to prepare the soil or handle the crop. Because the Argentine farmer literally only "scratched the surface," yields were low.[24] Yet wheat output expanded enormously toward the end of the 1800s. The tenancy system prevented complete exhaustion of the soil because large landowners, perhaps unintentionally, practiced a form of crop rotation. It must be remembered that the pampas were, and to some extent still are, primarily a pastoral economy. The large landowners used to lease natural grassland to the immigrant farmers for a period of three to five years. The tenant plowed and seeded the land to grain and, after a few years of cropping, moved on to new land leaving the old soil to recover its nutrients.

The expansion of wheat production was accompanied by a sharp increase in relative land values between the 1880s and the early part of this century.[25] The proportion of the harvest which was turned over to the landowners by the sharecroppers, who used their own equipment, rose from about 10 to 12 percent in the 1890s to 20 to 30 percent around 1910.

Despite the rapid agricultural development and the construction of railroads which played a vital role in this expansion and contributed to the rise in land values, the pampas remained relatively isolated, remote and sparsely settled. The "estancieros," the large landowners, lived in Buenos Aires or Paris and the tenant farmers were mostly itinerant sharecroppers who did not build homes. The immigrant farmer was primarily interested in making enough money to settle in the city or to return home to Europe. Even if he stayed in the pampas his children did not remain. So, paradoxically, wheat farming fostered urban growth rather than rural settlement. Farming in the pampas was the mainstay of the economy, but there was no prosperous agricultural class who would live and consume on the farm and there were no important inland towns in the pampas.

The wheat economy led to an enormous expansion in exports and the product flowed out of the country to Europe through the port cities. First Rosario and then Buenos Aires became centers of economic activity. The industrial centers of the interior, such as Tucumán, Córdoba, and Mendoza, which once provided manufacturing products to the region, fell severely behind

[20]*Relevamiento de la Estructura Regional de la Economía Argentina* (Buenos Aires: Consejo Federal de Inversiones – Instituto Torcuato Di Tella, 1965).

[21]For further geographic information see the following sources: Francisco de Aparicio and Horacio A. Difrieri, eds., *La Argentina Suma de Geografía* (Buenos Aires, 1958-63); Federico A. Daus, *Geografía de la República Argentina* (Buenos Aires, 1954-58); also, *Enciclopedia Argentina de Agricultura y Jardinería*, directed by Lorenzo R. Parodi (Buenos Aires, 1964).

[22]The pampas account for about 92 percent of all cereal production. For distribution of production between the pampas and land outside the pampas, see CONADE, *Plan Nacional . . .*, p. 39.

[23]Aldo Ferrer, *La Economía Argentina* (Mexico City: Fondo de Cultura Económica, 1963), p. 106. Much of this section is based upon James R. Scobie, *Revolution on the Pampas* (University of Texas Press, 1964), and upon Ferrer's book.

[24]In the first decade of this century, yields averaged about 11 bushels per acre in Argentina, compared with 14 bushels in the United States, 20 bushels in France and Italy, and 29 bushels in Germany on much less fertile soils. (USDA, *Yearbook, 1911*, pp. 530-31.)

[25]According to a report by Emilio Lahitte (*La Cuestión Agraria*), real land values increased by 218 percent between 1881 and 1911. (Quoted in Scobie, *Revolution on the Pampas*, pp. 51-52.)

the development of the port cities. Their processed goods — such as wine, textiles, leather, and sugar — did not expand as rapidly as the increasing agricultural exports.[26]

In this manner wheat helped create an economic structure which in a certain sense bore some semblance to a mining economy. Economic growth became thoroughly enmeshed with growth in exports. The outward orientation of production gave rise to an infrastructure which was geared to bring the agricultural products to the port but which was not conducive to internal economic development. Agricultural interests pressed strongly for free trade and thus national industrial development was held back.

The introduction of crop agriculture into an essentially pastoral economy helped aggravate social and political distortions. The pastoral interests held tight control over the land and at first found little motivation for shifting from livestock to grain. Much of this land was practically abandoned or, at least, inefficiently utilized. It was almost impossible to get credit for crop farming. It took the fortuitous combination of the European immigrant and the fabulously fertile soil to make the value of the pampas obvious. When the benefits of crop agriculture were discovered toward the end of the century, they did not accrue to the tiller of the soil but to the large landholders who had previously grossly neglected the land. The early landlords of Argentina seem to have been a parasitic class: "They waited for the government to remove the Indian menace, for the British to construct railroads, for the Irish and English to build up the pastoral stock, for the Italian sharecroppers to harvest their crops."[27] When as a consequence their land values shot up, they reaped the windfalls.

According to the 1941 census, about 40 percent of Argentina's population of over 8 million inhabitants was foreign born, but the immigrants constituted only 10 percent of the nation's property owners. While the national government tried to protect the immigrant, the provincial politicians had effective control over life in the pampas. The provinces were autonomous and were characterized by great instability. Provincial and municipal governments heavily taxed the tenant farmer who had no political status. The farmers, consisting mostly of immigrants who often kept their foreign citizenship, did not want to get entangled in local politics. Thus they were unsuccessful in making their interests heard in the government. What was worse, local officials were not only autocratic but often corrupt, associating with lawless elements; it was not unusual for the colonist to go armed to the fields. These factors were not conducive to fostering immigration into Argentina, which was far behind the movement of people from Europe to the United States and Australia where basic agricultural resources were similar to those of Argentina.

The "estancieros" and politicians consolidated their control and emerged as the oligarchy in the 1880s. Pastoral and commercial interests were dominant and crop agriculture came to be taken for granted. The burden on farmers became quite onerous. High taxes, which sometimes reached 12 percent of the farmer's gross produce, were added to land rents which soared to one-third of his crop. Attempts to organize farmers for the promotion of their interests failed until the creation of the Federación Agraria in 1912. Its influence, however, was overshadowed by organizations of landowners (Sociedad Agraria) and cattlemen (Sociedad Rural). Although representing the livestock interests, the Sociedad Rural was progressive enough to foster and try to improve crop farming.

Public Policies

It is surprising that Argentine crop agriculture could progress as far as it did, given the unfavorable conditions which surrounded cultivation of the pampas. The "laissez faire" spirit, which pervaded Argentina's body politic until about World War II, not only resulted in an overall neglect of agriculture but also put crop farming at a great disadvantage relative to livestock and wool production; the government followed pastoral interests and in general operated on behalf of the large landowners. Despite public disregard, agriculture developed because of the powerful demand of the industrializing countries for food, and because of the enormous resource base of the grossly underutilized pampas.

No Argentine government department concerned itself with agriculture until 1872, and even then, given the low budget, the small office had only a few statistical functions and was of no real significance. Its home was changed from one ministry to another until finally a separate Ministry of Agriculture was created in 1898. It did not come into its own, however, until well into the twentieth century. It has never accounted for more than 2 or 3 percent of Argentina's total government budget.

After some initial failures national agricultural stations were established at the turn of the century. The first agricultural school of a scientific nature was created in 1904.[28] But the common farmer did not benefit from these institutions until much later.

The lack of positive Argentine government policy regarding wheat brought problems for this export commodity, some of which still persist today. Among them was a deficiency in the training of high-level manpower and in the carrying out of research, experimentation, and extension services. But this was a situation common to all of Argentine agriculture until recently, including the livestock sector. As to wheat specifically, the scarcity of adequate storage facilities has created great problems, particularly with respect to exports.[29] The difficulty in storing grain

---

[26]Donald W. Baerresen, Martin Carnoy, and Joseph Grunwald, *Latin American Trade Patterns* (Brookings Institution, 1965), pp. 14-15.

[27]Scobie, *Revolution on the Pampas*, p. 121.

[28]Instituto Superior de Agronomía y Veterinaria. It was established at Chacarita in Buenos Aires City and was the forerunner of the Faculty of Agronomy at the University of Buenos Aires.

[29]In 1960 Argentina had a storage capacity of about 3.6 million tons at the ports. One-third of this amount was in grain elevators, roughly 40 percent in underground silos, and the rest in sheds (statistics of the Junta Nacional de Granos). In the United States storage capacity is about 150 million tons; in Canada, 18 million tons; and in Australia, 9 million tons.

surpluses has undoubtedly been an important element in influencing the price which Argentina has received for its wheat. When a country is forced to liquidate most of its stocks in the world market even during years of substantial surpluses, some price sacrifice will be involved. The disadvantage is relative to other major exporters who possess storage facilities and can withhold "excess" quantities of wheat from the market until prices improve.

Before the turn of the century the price problem was compounded by the high costs of handling wheat for exports. Wheat was shipped abroad in bags. This was highly inefficient, not only because of the tremendous amount of labor involved but also because the bags were imported and carried a relatively high tariff burden. With the construction of large grain elevators in Argentina, a shift from bagged to bulk tonnage for exports took place during the first decade of this century. But still about 70 percent of Argentine port arrivals are in bags. Since in order to conserve foreign exchange only 15 percent of wheat exports can be in bags, this implies a great deal of handling which could be avoided if wheat could be transported in bulk within the country.[30] In recent years significant improvements in storage and loading facilities have been made and Argentina has shown in the mid-sixties that it can keep a fairly large carryover stock.

The Argentine government eventually came to play a major and successful role in some aspects of wheat marketing. During the early days of the export boom, the quality of wheat shipments was not standardized and gross discrepancies occurred between the quantities sold and actually received abroad. The quality of samples was often quite different from the shipped commodity because of impurities and mixing with other materials. Weight loss was frequent due either to broken bags or outright thievery. Because of the enormous increase in foreign demand for wheat, Argentine exports could survive these problems without fatal consequences. Toward the end of the last century wheat trade became concentrated in the hands of four or five firms with world-wide interests. These exporters introduced some measures of quality control, but it was not until well into this century that the Argentine government began a scientific system for grading and testing wheat production. Today Argentine wheat enjoys a reputation for high quality standards, dependable grading, and reliable weights, and the government assumes the responsibility for the quality of exports.[31]

Through the National Grain Board (Junta Nacional de Granos), established in the 1930s, the Argentine government exercises a rather close control over wheat distribution. The Board, an autonomous body under the Ministry of Agriculture, supervises all aspects of grain marketing, from sales by producers to purchases by millers and exporters. The Board also inspects weights and quality, and establishes grade standards.[32] Another function is supervision of the construction and use of local and terminal grain elevators and loading facilities.

The merchandizing of wheat is concentrated in Buenos Aires, Rosario, and Santa Fe where most of the brokers, commission merchants, export and mill buyers are located, with Buenos Aires the most important center. There are no large interior country elevators or subterminals. The large facilities are all adjacent to waterways and excess production moves directly from farm to port outlets. This is a natural result of the fact that there are few grain-producing sections more than 200 miles from a shipping port and a great proportion is within 100 miles.

Yet, despite a recent increase, port accommodations are still not adequate. Storage and transport facilities are always overloaded at harvest time and it is not unusual for truckers hauling wheat to Buenos Aires to wait as long as a week to unload. Prior to 1920 most of the grain was moved by railroads which operated warehouses along the right-of-way in which the grain was stored in bags. Since then, railroad development practically stopped and equipment and efficiency deteriorated under government ownership. Railroads have been handling less wheat each year and now trucks are moving about three-quarters of the grain.

All private grain handling facilities were placed under government ownership in 1946 during the Perón regime. The government not only became the operator of the facilities, but also fixed maximum selling prices for producers. The government bought the grain and would then sell to domestic mills and exporters. This system, which before the downfall of Perón was handled by the Argentine Institute for the Promotion of Trade (Instituto Argentino para la Promoción del Intercambio – IAPI), had two immediate aims. On the export side, it amounted to a tax on wheat and was designed to raise public revenues.[33] However, when wheat was sold to the miller, the purpose was to subsidize flour production so that bread prices could be kept low. The ultimate policy objective was to further industrialization through the accumulation of funds, particularly foreign exchange, and through subsidy of the urban working masses.

The Perón government also attempted to increase the security of land tenure through freezing contracts and putting a ceiling on rents. Before the land rent control law of 1945, the crop rotation system practiced by the large landowners had caused serious social problems. The leasing of natural pasture to itinerant farmers for cropping purposes for a short period of time (two to four years) led to an instability of the rural population. The tenant farmer was particularly affected by insecure economic conditions.

[30] USDA, Foreign Agricultural Service, *Argentine Wheat Marketing Practices and Facilities* (September 1960), pp. 25-26.

[31] According to estimates by U.S. experts, about 98 percent of Argentine wheat exports could be graded No. 1 and the remainder a high No. 2. (*Ibid.*, p. 24.)

[32] Purchasers are required to report weight, quality, price, and terms of payment for each transaction.

[33] The revenue increasing aspect consisted of two stages: IAPI bought the wheat from the producer at a lower price than the price at which IAPI sold the grain to the exporter; the exporter, in turn, sold the wheat at a fixed rate of exchange which was below the free rate so that the government derived a foreign exchange income. The greatest differentials existed in 1948 when the official buying price for wheat was between one-third and one-half lower than the export price, depending on what rate of exchange is used. These differentials became smaller and lost significance toward the end of the Perón regime. See Marto A. Ballesteros, "Argentine Agriculture, 1918-1954: A Study in Growth and Decline" (Ph.D. diss., University of Chicago, 1958).

With land tenancy controls, other problems emerged. Since owners could not terminate new rental contracts or increase rents, they preferred to leave the land for pasture and not to enter into new leases.[34] This, combined with minimum agricultural wages, created unemployment and provoked an increased out-migration of farm population to the urban areas which offered higher paying jobs and low-priced food. Thus, there was a shift from grain to livestock production and agriculture on the pampas became more extensive. At the same time the breaking of the old crop rotation pattern adversely affected the maintenance of soil fertility.

After the downfall of Perón, the Argentine government moved to free wheat trade. By the latter part of the 1950s, the domestic trade operated on a free market, while the export trade was still controlled by the National Grain Board. In 1960 wheat trade was freed completely[35] and the land tenure regulations became more flexible. The Grain Board continued to play an important role through the administration of minimum producer prices.[36] These prices were generally fixed below the export prices so that a substantial part of the grain moved directly abroad. In 1963, however, the new government fixed the minimum price at a level which turned out to be somewhat above the export price. As a consequence, the Grain Board was obliged to purchase about 70 percent of the wheat crop. The free market in wheat was interrupted between 1964 and 1966 when the government introduced foreign exchange controls because of balance of payments difficulties.

The failure of Argentine agriculture to show vigorous growth since the war often has been attributed to these government policies. But the evidence is by no means clear cut. Farm production was declining before the war when there was very little government intervention and in the post-Perón period when public policy attempted to encourage agriculture and relative farm prices did increase, production failed to respond.[37] As has been shown, the Argentine government's interest in grain agriculture never seemed to extend much further than quality control until after World War II.

Perhaps it can be said that the greatest mistake of Argentine policy vis-à-vis agriculture has been for the government not to have played a more positive role in providing incentives for raising crop production. Yet, as was seen, grain output expanded in response to foreign demand despite a relatively inhospitable climate for crop farming. The upsurge in grain production toward the end of the last century diminished the relative importance of the early pastoral economy and the contribution of the livestock sector to Gross National Product has been below that of crop agriculture ever since about 1910.[38] Of course, there have been intermittent shifts between livestock and grain production. The first rapid expansion in wheat output was over by about 1910 and the role of cattle increased. After World War I grain production again grew faster than livestock because of world food shortages. There was a change of emphasis back to livestock during the 1930s which was not reversed until well into the postwar period. Over the long period a definite change in the composition of crops has reflected growth in the livestock sector; grains for human consumption constituted almost two-thirds of all crops in 1928/29, but made up less than 50 percent in 1960-62; during this same period there was a corresponding increase in the importance of feed grains.[39]

---

[34] The law of 1948 fixed the prices of land rents and provided the security of minimum tenancy of five years. The law also provided that at the conclusion of the rental contract the owners had to repay the tenant the cost of the improvements made on the land. Inflation made this provision largely inoperative, since reimbursement of original cost would constitute only a fraction of replacement value. In effect, therefore, the law discouraged improvements of land. (See CONADE, *Plan Nacional. . .* , pp. 40 ff.)

In 1958 greater flexibility was introduced in the laws governing the security of land tenure. Some arrangements were left to negotiations in the free market. The rent laws undoubtedly benefitted the tenant farmers who were able to stay on the land. Their real incomes were about 17 percent higher in 1948-50 than during the immediate postwar years, while the owners' rental incomes declined sharply in real terms. (In the 1950s, however, there was also a significant drop in the number of tenant farmers amounting to a decline of 70,000 persons between the 1947 and 1960 censuses.)

After 1958, owners' rental income returned to prewar levels. (For a description of the security of land tenure and the pertinent legislation see CIDA, *Tenencia de la Tierra y Desarrollo Socio-Económico del Sector Agrícola, Argentina* (Pan American Union, 1965), pp. 97-113.

[35] The transition to a free market was not without its problems for the producers. Under the old system they had become accustomed to receiving full payment from the government within 48 hours after delivery. Under the free market system, they received only 60 to 70 percent upon delivery and the remainder in 90 days, because the commercial purchasers had financial problems due to existing interest rate levels and the shortage of loanable funds. (USDA, *Argentine Wheat Marketing. . .* , p. 25.)

[36] The minimum price for wheat is established by Congress (at the recommendation of the Grain Board) and is executed by the Board, the Board standing ready to purchase grain at the minimum price.

[37] When agricultural prices are compared with prices in the rest of the economy, a definite improvement can be noted from about 1950 onward. (See Aldo Ferrer, *La Producción, los Ingresos y Capitalización del Sector Agropecuario en el Período 1950-1960*, Consejo Nacional de Desarrollo, Buenos Aires, 1961, p. 52.) On the other hand, cost comparisons with farm prices, using 1935-39 as parity, show that the mid-fifties were still about one-third below prewar. However, no comparable data have been elaborated for after 1956. (Antonio J. Vila, *Precios de Paridad para Productos Agrícolas en la Argentina*, Asociación Argentina de Productores Agrícolas, Buenos Aires, 1958, p. 131.) According to a more recent report, real income in agriculture is said to have increased by over 20 percent between 1961 and 1964, while there was a decline in the rest of the economy. *(La Producción Rural en Argentina en 1964*, Banco Ganadero Argentino, Bueno Aires, 1965, p. 60.) Some of this would result from the higher returns to agriculture experienced in areas outside the pampas during the last few years. (FIAT, *Economía Agropecuaria Argentina*, tables 72, 76.)

According to data published by the National Development Council, salaries of farm workers deflated by wheat prices dropped 50 percent between 1940-44 and 1960-64. (CONADE, *Plan Nacional . . .* , table 14.)

At any rate, such price comparisons are extremely difficult in a country beset by strong inflationary movements. Farm prices and costs have occasionally changed up to 50 percent from one month to another and the annual average has been approximately 25 percent. (See for example, the statements in CIDA, *Tenencia de la Tierra . . .* , p. 19. The Vila and Ferrer studies have also been summarized there.)

[38] FIAT, *Economía Agropecuaria Argentina*, tomo I, table 12, p. 33.

[39] *Ibid.*, p. 73.

One of the real difficulties created by public policies in a country like Argentina is the problem of uncertainty. Instability in government and variability in official regulations produce an aura of insecurity in the affected private sector of the economy which can be more detrimental to private investment decisions than the policy measures themselves. These psychological factors to a large extent accounted for the sluggishness of agricultural output despite significant improvement in farm prices in the course of the 1950s. The upward price movement was not smooth and thus introduced uncertainty.[40] Also the price relationship between livestock and crops showed great variability.[41] Furthermore, indecisive government export policies have probably confused the expectations of producers and thus have contributed to stifle dynamism in agriculture.

Argentine export tax policies have also been highly volatile. The major tax in this regard has been the "retention tax" which has been imposed chiefly as an ad valorem tax on agricultural exports. Governments have imposed, cancelled, reimposed, increased, and decreased such taxes at frequent intervals. Such variability has made for speculation and the intermittent withholding of the product from the export market which sometimes was, but most often was not, the intent of these policies. The major objective has been public revenues, as when in early 1967 the government raised retention taxes in order to offset the windfalls which would accrue to traditional exporters because of a large-scale devaluation. Since retention taxes are proportional to the quantities sold, they would tend to restrict exports, if production is carried on under conditions of increasing costs.

In summary, the degree of a direct causal relationship between slow agricultural growth and specific government measures can be easily exaggerated except in the sense of relating agricultural stagnation to a lack of positive and stable public policies. Government intervention in Argentina's wheat trade has nearly always been less than in other major exporting countries. U.S. agencies, such as the Commodity Credit Corporation, and the Canadian, and particularly the Australian, wheat boards, generally have been much more "interventionist" than the Argentine National Grain Board with the exception of the brief IAPI period under Perón. Yet much of the criticism of Argentine government policies came from countries which had succumbed to government intervention in agriculture long before Argentina.

Argentina has traditionally tended towards multilateralism and free trade in wheat.[42] There was a rash of bilateral trade arrangements which emerged in the immediate postwar period and which controlled a major part of the country's trade during the 1950s. Argentina, however, let most of these arrangements expire and has reverted toward multilateralism. The last major covenant, with Brazil, terminated in 1962, and there is now only a loose commercial agreement in effect between the two countries regarding wheat exports to Brazil balanced by Argentine purchases of general merchandise from that country.

Latin American economists generally attribute the sluggishness of Argentine agriculture since the late 1920s to the effects of the Great Depression of the 1930s, and to external demand factors rather than to gross mistakes in domestic government policies.[43] According to Aldo Ferrer, agricultural exports constituted the engine for national economic development until the Depression. After that, exports failed to provide dynamism to the economy; hence, economic growth came to depend increasingly upon public and private investment in nonagricultural sectors and public policy had to respond to this need.[44] There is an apparent contradiction in this position because Argentina's share of the world market fell in spite of a rising demand for food after the Depression. Some Argentinians tend to attribute this to the policies of the developed countries such as the U.S. agricultural export programs, the European economic integration schemes, and general protectionist policies in the developed countries.

The industrial import substitution policy which followed the Depression is often said to have neglected agriculture while at the same time increasing the prices of manufactured goods. The problem was that when foreign de-

---

[40] Ferrer, *La Economía Argentina*. Carlos Díaz also finds great instability in agricultural prices, although their position relative to nonrural prices in 1959-64 was 16 percent above 1956, the first post-Perón year, and, of course, higher if the Perón years were taken as a base. Díaz attributes this price instability, which was considerably less for cereals than for other farm products, to the intermittent massive exchange rate devaluations which occurred only every three years or so in the face of steadily rising prices of nonrural goods. See his comments on a paper by L. Sjaastad in "The Next Decade of Latin American Development," Cornell University, 1966 (mimeo, to be published in 1970 in the *Journal of Political Economy*, University of Chicago).

[41] The price relations between wheat, corn, and linseed on the one hand and meat on the other have been rather unstable. Meat prices increased relative to wheat during World War II, dropped in the immediate postwar period, rose during Perón's last years in power, dropped after his overthrow, rose during the late 1950s, dropped during the Frondizi administration, and rose during the mid-1960s. There is no definite trend in these price relations. CONADE, *Plan Nacional . . . ,* graph 3.

On the other hand, there is little question that factors of production in Argentine agriculture have been price sensitive and that they moved between crop cultivation and livestock as price expectations changed. (See FIAT, *Economía Agropecuaria Argentina,* p. 39.)

A recent study has shown that about 80 percent of the annual variation in the area in wheat can be explained in terms of changes in wheat prices relative to flax, corn, sorghum, and barley, and to rainfall prior to sowing. (Remy Freire, *Price Incentives in Argentine Agriculture,* Development Advisory Service, Harvard University, paper presented at Bellagio Conference, June 1966.) A price elasticity of supply of 0.5 was found for Argentina. A similar result — a supply elasticity of 0.4 — was obtained for Chile where about 20 percent of consumption is imported. See Roberto Echevarría, *Repuesta de los Productores Agrícolas ante Cambio en los Precios* (Santiago: Instituto de Capacitación e Investigación en Reforma Agraria – ICIRA, 1965).

Insofar as public policy affected relative prices, it also influenced the shifts among the agricultural sectors.

[42] However, even in the absence of any public regulatory or marketing agencies, wheat trade would not be "free" in the strict sense of the term, because in Argentina it is dominated by four or five large private international firms which act as exporters and, in the purchasing countries, as importers.

[43] See, for instance, ECLA, *El Desarrollo Económico de la Argentina* (Mexico City, 1959); and Ferrer, *La Economía Argentina.*

[44] Ferrer, *La Economía Argentina,* pp. 167-70, 202.

mand for Argentina's agricultural products collapsed in the 1930s and continued depressed during World War II and intermittently afterwards, there was not too much choice for public policy in the face of the ensuing balance of payments difficulties. Although import-substituting industrialization tends to be inefficient, it can constitute a positive factor for agriculture. Industrial inputs into the farm sector are a vital component for agricultural development and, if their availability becomes restricted by import problems due to foreign exchange shortages, then their domestic manufacture becomes rational even though their production costs are high relative to those of the industrial countries. However, comparing domestic prices with foreign prices is always a tricky problem, particularly so if the domestic currency is overvalued. It is possible that with a free rate of exchange and no government intervention, an exceedingly small amount of industrial inputs for farm production would be imported relative to the need for agricultural development. The establishment of a domestic industry to meet this need, therefore, can make economic sense. The new Argentine tractor industry is a good case in point.[45]

While the main emphasis in Argentine economic policies has continued to rest upon industrialization, a greater drive towards agricultural development can be discerned during recent years. Not only has there been a strong orientation of industrialization toward the farm sector, but a variety of public and private organizations are directly concerned with agricultural progress. A large part of the effort is, of course, concentrated on improving and expanding livestock production (see the following chapter on beef), but some endeavor is directed to crop production as well. In addition to the Junta Nacional de Granos which has raised standards of Argentine grain production considerably, there is the National Institute of Agricultural Technology (Instituto Nacional de Tecnología Agropecuaria – INTA) established in 1956, which has undertaken basic research. INTA has also provided extension services which are important because there is a great backlog of unapplied technology. The National Development Council (Consejo Nacional de Desarrollo–CONADE), which is the nation's planning agency, has also engaged in research on the returns to investment in agriculture. So far these agencies have stressed the advantages of introducing new techniques rather than new physical investment.[46]

[45] José María Dagnino Pastore and Jorge Meyer, *La Industria del Tractor en la Argentina* (Buenos Aires: Centro de Investigaciones Económicas, Instituto Torcuato di Tella, 1965).

[46] Other programs have stressed agricultural training. Advanced university education usually has involved foreign study and one of the problems has been to relate the theoretical knowledge acquired abroad to the environment of a specific region. A recent project of the Ford Foundation (Pro Economía Agraria) was designed to integrate the foreign study of theory with empirical research on significant practical problems in Argentina.

There are indications also of a growing awareness on the part of the large farmers regarding the need for technical progress in agriculture. The Regional Consortia of Agricultural Experimentation (Consorcios Regionales de Experimentación Agrícola–CREA) is a private organization of agriculturalists. It is of recent origin and was formed for the purpose of exchanging information on individual experimentation, experiences, and plans. The influence of such groups is grow-

The Current Situation

Overall commercial agricultural production in the Argentine pampas is about the same as thirty years ago. During this period a structural change has taken place: livestock production expanded at the expense of farm crops. A peak in the cultivation of the pampas was reached in the early 1940s and since then there has been no marked change in the area in agriculture. In the rest of the country, agricultural output doubled between the mid-1930s and 1958, as new lands were put into production, but has remained more or less constant during the last few years.[47]

No important trend in the volume of Argentine wheat production can be noted during the last forty years or so. Output levels have remained about the same despite a significant decline in acreage. Other countries' wheat production forged ahead. Australia, for instance, produced only three-quarters as much wheat as Argentina until the 1950s, but because it has since put vast additional lands into wheat, the situation is now reversed. While these two countries' wheat exports ran at roughly the same level until about 1960, Australia now exports approximately twice as much of the cereal as Argentina. Yet during the last few years an expansion in Argentine wheat production has taken place which may not be random and may mark a new development. Some of the factors which may underlie a possible movement toward higher levels of output will be discussed later in this chapter.

Argentina is the only country in Latin America where significant amounts of wheat are used for livestock (see table 14-8). Of the total wheat area planted in Argentina since 1944, only about 80 percent was harvested. The remainder was presumably used for pasture. There is a very close trade-off in Argentina between pasture and crop production for human consumption. Most of this trade-off, however, is not between different uses of wheat but between wheat and other human food grains and pasture crops.[48]

It has been said that Argentine wheat production techniques are about twenty to thirty years behind those of the United States.[49] For a developing country this is not a serious gap, but for one of the five top competitors in the world wheat market it may be a significant handicap. Yet it should not be surprising that the techniques of Argentine wheat production are rather simple, given the enormous soil fertility of the pampas.

Compared with other wheat producers in Latin America and elsewhere in the developing world, Argentine production is highly mechanized. Most of the harvesting is done by machine, and at the beginning of the 1960s only 15 percent of the soil preparation was undertaken by animal power. Horse-drawn equipment is vanishing fast, being replaced by nationally produced implements. Less than 20

ing and the spirit of progressive farming is becoming more important in the country.

[47] CONADE, *Plan Nacional . . .*, p. 40 and table 13.

[48] Alfalfa, for instance, grows better in the Argentine pampas than anywhere else in the world.

[49] USDA, *Argentine Wheat Marketing . . .*, p. 1.

percent of agricultural machinery is imported, most of it from the United States. Tractors and harvesters are among Argentina's fasting growing industries.[50]

The richness of the pampas combined with the sparsely populated countryside and the almost empty Patagonia have made agriculture in Argentina land-intensive and labor-poor. In a somewhat paradoxical fashion, the proportion of the labor force in agriculture has always been smaller in Argentina, the region's greatest agricultural producer, than in other Latin American countries with the exception of Uruguay, the second agricultural nation.[51] Because labor input is the lowest in the region, Argentine labor productivity in wheat is by far the highest in Latin America. On the other hand, output per man-hour is still substantially below U.S. standards.[52]

As in most regions of the world, wheat is cultivated in mixed farms in Argentina, but mixed farming is less pronounced there than in the United States or Europe. The large size of the many farms which still specialize in wheat makes mechanization more economical, but it also creates problems of land tenure.[53] Although one does not generally think of Argentina as a country in urgent need of land reform, some writers blame the land tenure structure for much of the weakness in the agricultural sector.

According to census data, about 95 percent of the agricultural labor force consisted of landless farmers in 1937.[54] Apparently this proportion declined because, according to a 10 percent sample of the 1960 census, not quite 70 percent of the agricultural labor force was composed of tenant and landless farmers in 1960.[55] There was a dramatic decline in the agricultural labor force in Argentina between the 1937 and 1960 censuses. In 1937, there were over 2.6 million persons engaged in agricultural activities, in 1960 fewer than 1.5 million. Most of this decline was in unpaid family workers who constituted almost half of the labor force in 1937, but only 20 percent in 1960.[56] The pampas experienced the greatest absolute and relative loss of labor force but still contain about half of the nation's farmers. With the outmigration of population from

the rural areas, an improvement of the agricultural labor force has undoubtedly taken place, particularly because of the sharp reduction in the employment of minors under fourteen years of age. Yet still 35 percent of the rural population consists of landless laborers, a substantial proportion being transient farm workers. Many of these are immigrants. Contrary to the past, when most newcomers came from southern Europe, the postwar arrivals are primarily from neighboring countries. A large part of this new immigration is illegal, with estimates running as high as over a million illegal entries, principally from Chile and Paraguay. Argentine public opinion and officialdom seem to face this problem with a somewhat ambivalent attitude. There is a basic recognition that these foreigners are needed in view of the manpower shortage in agriculture; on the other hand, they are considered a threat to Argentine integrity. The situation is reminiscent of the erstwhile "bracero" problem in the United States and the current Italian labor problem in Switzerland.

The sharp decline in agricultural labor force in the pampas after World War II had some consequences for wheat production. The loss of 70,000 tenant farmers between the census years of 1947 and 1960 was only partially offset by an increase of 26,000 farm owners. This signified a substantial drain of skilled manpower from agriculture.[57] Yields failed to increase and output stagnated, particularly since wheat land was pulled out for pasture. There was little agricultural equipment and machinery to compensate for the loss of manpower. It is only comparatively recently that a significant upsurge of mechanization of Argentine agriculture has taken place, primarily because of a massive introduction of tractors.[58]

The expansion in wheat production during the last few years, therefore, seems to have a more solid base than previous increases which proved to be only temporary fluctuations. Since 1963 wheat output in Argentina has fluctuated around higher levels. It is, of course, too early to say whether this is statistically significant and constitutes a new and enduring trend or is just an accident. It is true that very favorable weather conditions contributed considerably to the bumper crops of 1963/64 and 1964/65, but never before in Argentine history has a two-season average approached this level. Drought and unfavorable climatic conditions affected the 1965/66 and 1966/67 crops. Although the approximately 6 million ton average harvested in those two years was less than half the bumper crops of the two years before, it was far above the less than 4 million tons of the 1960/61 crop, the last harvest affected by adverse

[50]Given the current agricultural production techniques, the domestic market is likely to become saturated soon. Further rapid growth will depend upon export possibilities. See Pastore et al., *La Industria del Tractor.* . . .

[51]The proportion of the labor force in agriculture was 19 percent in Argentina according to the 1960 census, compared with a Latin American average of about 48 percent. (ECLA, *Statistical Bulletin for Latin America*, vol. I, 1964, table 6; and ECLA, *Economic Survey of Latin America, 1964*, Santiago, Chile, 1965, table I-29.) In Uruguay it was about 18 percent in 1964 according to the National Development Plan (see compendium prepared by the University of Montevideo on the Development Plan: *Plan Nacional de Desarrollo Económico y Social 1965-1974* [CIDE], p. 28).

[52]Wheat output per man-hour worked in 1961 was 47 kg. in Argentina, compared with less than 2 kg. in Ecuador and 3 kg. in Colombia; but it was over 125 kg. in the United States. See ECLA, *Economic Bulletin for Latin America*, October 1962, p. 68.

[53]Wheat farms in Argentina range in average size from about 50 hectares in the northern fringes of the pampas to 250 hectares in the east and center. But most wheat is produced on the larger farms.

[54]Cited in Ferrer, *La Economía Argentina*, p. 114.

[55]See CIDA, *Tenencia de la Tierra.* . . , table 10, p. 25.

[56]*Ibid.*, table 5, p. 17.

[57]CONADE, *Plan Nacional* . . . , p. 42 and table 16.

[58]According to the national agricultural census of Argentina, the tractor stock increased from about 21,000 units in 1937 to only 29,000 in 1947. By 1952 the stock of tractors had increased to 50,000 units and the 1960 census recorded over 104,000 tractors. The sharp upward trend seems to be continuing. Sales during the early 1960s averaged over 12,000 units per year. In 1940 the number of tractors per 1,000 hectares of standardized cultivated land was less than one-half of a unit, but by 1963 it had reached 3.6 units. While this is among the highest tractor input rates in Latin America, it is still far below the United States, Canada, and European countries. For most of these data see Pastore et al., *La Industria del Tractor.* . . .

weather conditions. The four-year average of about 8 million tons for 1963/64 to 1966/67 is substantially higher than any other four-year period since 1925 (see table 14-2). Although it is not possible to draw conclusions from these data, there are indications that increased mechanization, particularly expanded tractor use and better wheat breeding may have raised yields to higher levels so that an 8 million ton crop would now not be unusual under normal weather conditions.[59]

Argentine wheat breeding has made great advances in the postwar period. Government regulations require that new varieties be tested under normal field conditions before being released. The main objectives of breeding have been to secure high yields and disease-resisting wheats. This has resulted in new varieties which are able to withstand a high degree of nutrient starvation.

Argentina has one of the world's lowest fertilizer consumption rates. Fertilizer nutrients consumed per hectare of arable land (in terms of nitrogen, phosphate, and potash) are less than one-seventieth of the U.S. level, less than one-thirtieth that of Chile and less than one-twentieth that of Brazil, Colombia, and Mexico. There was no increase at all in Argentine fertilizer use between the average for 1948-1952/53 and 1962/63, compared with a nearly tenfold increase in Mexico.[60]

Thus the low level of Argentine fertilizer consumption is explained not only by the high cost of fertilizer inputs, which have had to be imported, but also by the orientation of wheat breeding efforts. The varieties bred in the past have not responded effectively to heavy fertilization. This is understandable because wheat breeding had other objectives. As a consequence, modern breeding efforts by INTA and private groups in the country are directed to the selection of varieties which would have a capacity to respond well to higher levels of fertilization. Recent experimentation has shown that substantial pecuniary gains could be derived from this effort, particularly if delivered fertilizer prices to the farmer could be reduced. Since 1963 the government has subsidized fertilizer imports and use through the remission of import charges, fees, and taxes. Thus far, most of the fertilizer inputs were applied in the relatively small irrigated and intensively cultivated areas outside the pampas. Enormous quantities of fertilizers would be needed to raise wheat output in the pampas significantly. Much of the fertilizer requirements are expected to be satisfied by the newly established petrochemical industry in Argentina and elsewhere in Latin America.[61]

Other agricultural inputs have been of minor importance in Argentina. Insecticides generally have not been applied to wheat crops because of the relative absence of insect problems in the grain-growing regions.

Although the importance of wheat in Argentina's economy has declined in recent decades, export of the grain averages again almost one-fifth of the country's total export proceeds. Wheat earns more foreign exchange than any other single product except beef (counting all processed forms) and wool in most years.[62] During the 1920s, Argentina exported up to three-quarters of her total wheat crop, a much greater proportion than for any other major exporter.[63] Since World War II, however, only about one-quarter of wheat production has been sold abroad as the increase in domestic consumption pushed against the much slower expanding output.

Western Europe and South America, primarily Brazil, are Argentina's traditional markets (see table 14-7). The proportion of Latin American wheat imports supplied by Argentina has declined since the mid-1950s when that country provided about half of the region's requirements. During 1964-66, of the 10 million tons imported by the region, about 3.5 million came from Argentina. The remainder was imported from North America, primarily the United States. Most of these transactions were sales and barter arrangements by the United States under the provisions of P.L. 480 and other U.S. government programs.

The Current Situation in Uruguay

The wheat story in Uruguay has many parallels with the situation in Argentina. There is a resemblance in the basic resource conditions, although the soil of the Argentine pampas is superior. Much the same public neglect of crop farming has occurred as in Argentina, but Uruguayan government policy seems to have played a more important role, particularly with respect to wheat. After a postwar deterioration, the quality of wheat cultivation is now on a much lower level than in Argentina.[64]

Before World War II wheat was one of Uruguay's chief exports, but since the war the country has several times had to import grain. In the 1940s the government set maximum prices for wheat in order to keep bread prices down. A 1947 law also limited the exportation of articles of "primary necessity." A shift from wheat to other crops and livestock ensued. The decline in wheat acreage soon led to the need for imports.

During the late 1940s the government attempted to reverse the trend by means of price supports. The government stood ready to purchase wheat from the producers at given prices. In turn, the government sold the wheat to the millers at lower prices in order to subsidize bread production. The guaranteed price system proved to be a boon to

[59]Preliminary figures indicate that this level was reached in the 1968 crop year despite a drought during part of the growing season.

[60]FAO, *Fertilizers: An Annual Review of World Production, Consumption and Trade, 1963*, and *Production Yearbook*, various years. Also, USDA, Economic Research Service, *Changes in Agriculture in the Developing Nations, 1948-1963* (Foreign Agricultural Economic Report No. 27, 1965).

[61]Programa de Estudios Conjuntos Sobre la Integración Económica Latinoamericana(ECIEL), in *Industrialization in a Latin American Common Market*, Martin Carnoy, ed. (Brookings Institution, forthcoming), chap. 4.

[62]During most of the 1930s and also during the first half of the 1950s, wheat export value was higher than beef and wool exports. Except for a few isolated years, the export value of corn has been consistently below that of wheat. CIDA, *Tenencia de la Tierra . . .*, table 3, p. 15.

[63]J. A. Le Clerc, *International Trade in Wheat and Wheat Flour* (USDC, 1925), table 9, p. 27.

[64]Uruguay has the highest proportion of utilizable terrain in Latin America. About 80 percent of its total land area is used for grazing and roughly 10 percent for crops.

wheat production and wheat again became an important export commodity in the 1950s.

Toward the end of the 1950s the wheat subsidy became a serious burden to the treasury and in 1960 the government terminated the support program and established a free market policy. Wheat producers reacted sharply. There was a drastic drop in the acreage planted to wheat, the 1962-64 average being one-third below 1956-58 (table 14-1). Land was transferred from wheat into other crops, primarily sugar beet and some sugar cane, and into pasture. Exports practically disappeared and domestic bread prices sky-rocketed. (See table 14-7 for export data.)

Not until the bumper crop of 1964/65 did wheat production recover. Not only favorable weather conditions but also new wheat programs involving liberal credits to farmers covering all stages of wheat production (including loans for fertilizers), basic support prices, and technical assistance produced the best harvest in a decade. Yet the Uruguayan economic situation, which had deteriorated for over a decade, worsened rapidly after 1966 and was complicated by natural catastrophes such as droughts, frost, and floods. Wheat production collapsed and by 1967/68 amounted to less than one-third the average level of 1954/55-1958/59. The country was forced again to import significant quantities of the cereal for domestic consumption.

Although a recovery in wheat output is certain, export prospects remain cloudy. The domestic costs of wheat production of the 1964/65 bumper crop were considerably higher than the world price at the official pegged rate of exchange. Although domestic prices have been much above international prices, producers have pressed for even higher internal prices as a hedge against inflation. The large producers were able to hold out for higher prices by withholding their grain from the market, which the small wheat producer who had no storage facilities could not afford to do. In order to aid the small wheat farmer, the government at the end of 1964 reinstituted, but on a very limited scale, a guaranteed price system. The government undertook to buy up to a certain tonnage of wheat from small farmers (less than 300 hectares) at a relatively high price. At the same time it encouraged exports by permitting exporters to sell their dollars derived from the sale of wheat on the "parallel" rate of exchange market. In 1965 the dollar sold on the parallel ("grey") market at a multiple of the official rate of exchange. These measures are not expected to increase wheat exports beyond the level of the mid-1950s unless fundamental changes in wheat cultivation can be instituted to increase and maintain yields on a high level.[65]

---

[65] This section is based to a large extent upon information from the Uruguayan Embassy in Washington, and upon United States embassy reports from Montevideo. The most important among these is an extensive memorandum, "Uruguayan Wheat Export Prospects: Domestic Factors," 10 February 1965. See also *Plan Nacional de Desarrollo Económico y Social 1965–1974*, compendium prepared by the University of Montevideo on the Development Plan (CIDE). Despite the comparative advantage in livestock production in Uruguay, that country's current development programs plan an expansion in the wheat area in order to build up an export surplus with an eye to the Brazilian market. This is recognized as a short-run measure in order to raise foreign exchange earnings while Uruguay's livestock industry is being revitalized. (See chap. 15.)

Uruguay is in urgent need of land reform. According to the 1961 census 64 percent of the farms are less than 50 hectares in size, but occupy only 4.8 percent of the land area. Most of these farms are very small — 46 percent of all farms have less than 20 hectares. Given Uruguay's basic livestock economy, efficient farm size should be several hundred hectares, to enable new technology to be properly applied; the same is true for mixed livestock-crop agriculture. At the other extreme 1.4 percent of all farms have an area of over 2,500 hectares and control 33.4 percent of the total land area. About 40 percent of all farms are operated by tenants. Uruguay's development plan provides for a land reform which emphasizes land taxation rather than forced land redistribution. Land taxes, which are to replace export retention taxes, the government's traditional source of revenues, are designed to stimulate increases in agricultural productivity, both in livestock and crop cultivation.

Flour

Few economic activities have experienced as complete a process of import substitution as has the production of wheat flour. Flour milling has increased rapidly, particularly since World War II, and has reached levels of self-sufficiency even in tropical countries. In many countries the industry has been modernized and a process of concentration has resulted in the closing of smaller mills.

In Latin America, however, modernization has been slower. In Brazil, most of the 548 mills registered in 1960 are small, having a daily capacity of less than 5 tons. They serve local needs since transport difficulties impede internal trade. Only about 57 mills have a daily capacity in excess of 100 tons and they account for 80 percent of the total flour milling capacity of about 9 million tons. Because of the general wheat shortage due to production declines and import difficulties, the larger mills are working at about one-third capacity.[66] In Argentina there were 152 registered flour mills in 1960, but only a few of them account for a large part of that country's total capacity of 3.2 million tons a year.[67]

In addition, there are hundreds of primitive nonmechanized mills which are not registered and which account for a sizable share of total output. In Brazil, Chile, Ecuador, Peru, and Uruguay such cottage-sized units account for between 10 and 40 percent of total wheat milled.[68] Because of geography, transportation difficulties, and government policy, few mills operate on a national scale in the wheat-producing countries of Latin America. But in the non-wheat-producing countries of the region most mills are modern and function on a national scale. With the exceptions of Peru and Ecuador, excess milling capacity is sizable in Latin America, due primarily to supply and location problems and not to a declining consumption of flour.

---

[66] IWC, *Trade in Wheat Flour*, Secretariat Paper No. 5 (London, 1965), p. 42.

[67] USDA, *Argentine Wheat Marketing...*, p. 17.

[68] Adam Szarf, "Modern Flour Mills in Developing Countries," FAO, *Monthly Bulletin of Agricultural Economics and Statistics*, June 1966, p. 5.

In recent years flour has entered foreign trade to a relatively small extent. (See table 14-8.) World imports of flour during the last five prewar years averaged about 17 percent of total world imports of wheat and flour. This proportion continued in the immediate postwar period, but since then has fallen to little more than 10 percent. The United States accounts for about half of world trade, most of the wheat flour being sold on special terms under the government's P.L. 480 program.[69]

In the tropical countries where flour mills have been recently established trade has shifted from imports of flour to imports of wheat grain. According to the International Wheat Council, grain imports for selected tropical countries accounted for less than 5 percent of total wheat and flour imports during 1950-52, but jumped to over 80 percent in 1962-63, as these countries substituted domestic production for flour imports. (See also table 14-8.)

Flour has constituted a generally larger share of wheat imports in Latin America than for the world as a whole. This share declined from about 30 percent during the first half of the 1950s to not much more than 15 percent for recent years. As can be expected, Argentina and Uruguay account for nearly all of the region's exports of flour, but the amounts are small and in recent history have constituted considerably less than 5 percent of the combined wheat exports of these two countries. Flour has been exported only to other Latin American countries, primarily Brazil and Paraguay. The Brazilian market for wheat flour, which was the largest one until comparatively recently, has now disappeared. Argentine and Uruguayan exports to Brazil were first curtailed through competition from the United States and then limited to a trickle as Brazil developed its own flour mills, granting importers of milling equipment highly subsidized exchange rates and other privileges during the 1950s. The fact that ownership of a wheat mill was an entrée into the lucrative "paper wheat" frauds during the late 1950s was another significant incentive to expand Brazilian milling capacity.[70] With some minor exceptions, flour imports into Brazil are now prohibited.

Flour prices have generally moved in the same direction as wheat prices, though since the early 1950s flour export prices have declined slightly relative to wheat export prices, probably as a result of greater competition in the industry.[71]

Import substitution of flour milling at first led to high prices of the finished product. For example, wheat prices were about the same in Argentina and England during the 1870s, but Argentine bread was about three times the price of English bread.[72] This differential has since disappeared. In Central America the current wholesale price of flour is about $200 per ton, while U.S. flour can be imported at the Atlantic ports of Central America at a c.i.f. price of less than $90 per ton.[73] This differential is only partly due to inefficiency in operating domestic mills. To some extent, poor infrastructure—port and storage facilities, internal transport, and distribution system—is a more important factor, as are the subsidy policies of the developed countries exporting flour. In the tropical countries which produce no wheat the rationale for import substitution in flour production is based largely upon problems of flour transport and storage in tropical situations. Wheat can be more readily stored than flour, even under primitive conditions and, unlike flour, it can be fumigated. In some cases the cost of transportation and bagging can be substantially reduced since wheat, but not flour, can be imported in bulk.

Outlook

An oversupply of wheat, which has existed for many years, presents more than the usual problems associated with resource surplus. Because wheat can provide many of the essential ingredients to sustain life and because hunger is still widespread in the world, the term surplus as applied to wheat can be used only in the strict economic sense of a deficiency in effective demand. World surpluses, which have been concentrated primarily in the United States and Canada (table 14-14), are still high despite the continuing needs of developing countries, because of the unequal distribution of income throughout the world and because international and national arrangements may have set prices too high.

Most importing countries have made strenuous efforts to increase domestic production even though costs have been high. Protection, price supports, and subsidies have resulted in an inefficient allocation of resources in the world as a whole. According to an ECLA-FAO study, in every Latin American country except Peru the cost of growing wheat in the 1950s was higher than in Argentina and Uruguay.[74] Thus the consumer has had to pay for the important substitution process.

Argentina regards nontariff trade barriers in the developed countries as the country's biggest export problem. Subsidies to domestic producers in potential wheat importing countries and export subsidies in countries like the United States and France are considered particularly harmful to Argentina's wheat exporting prospects. In May of 1961 the president of Argentina's National Grain Board reflected a general pessimism when in a speech he expressed doubts about the future of the country's wheat exports. He implied that in wheat the country can look forward to little more than satisfying its domestic requirements. His attitude was undoubtedly influenced by the U.S. wheat export programs as well as by the wheat policies of other countries, especially in Western Europe, which through price support and subsidy programs have encouraged domestic production and exports.[75] Moreover, com-

[69] IWC, *Trade in Wheat Flour*, p. 33 and app. table IV.

[70] See statistical note at end of chapter.

[71] IWC, *Trade in Wheat Flour*. It is difficult to determine an average flour price because of the great variety of the product which may differ in protein content, ash, acidity, and color.

[72] Scobie, *Revolution on the Pampas*, p. 111.

[73] Szarf, "Modern Flour Mills. . . ," p. 13.

[74] ECLA-FAO, *The Selective Expansion of Agricultural Production in Latin America* (UN, 1957).

[75] In 1965 France's export subsidy was about three times the U.S. level (about $45 per ton against $15 per ton in the United States).

pared with the United States, Canada, and Australia, Argentina lacks adequate storage facilities and therefore cannot be flexible in holding out for better price conditions; neither can the country provide favorable credit terms to its customers. All these factors combine to make Argentina's position in world markets especially weak.

Under these conditions, effective demand does not look encouraging for Latin American wheat exporters. It is difficult to speculate regarding the net effect of eliminating in the world both types of government programs — those designed to stimulate domestic wheat production and those designed to subsidize sales abroad. By definition, the market would be cleared and surpluses would disappear, but it is uncertain whether the level of total world wheat production and consumption would be lower or higher. The U.S. surplus disposal programs, primarily P.L. 480, may have given an impetus to wheat consumption where otherwise the demand might not have risen. This kind of speculation is academic, however, because it is highly improbable that government intervention in wheat will be discontinued in the near future. This must be taken into consideration when one looks at the wheat situation as it is likely to develop in the coming years.

There is no direct evidence as to whether U.S. wheat shipments to Latin America under the various programs since World War II have actually hurt Latin American export possibilities. It is natural that importing countries prefer to meet their wheat requirements from the United States under the favorable terms that P.L. 480 or similar programs offer. It is also obvious that during this time Argentina could not have supplied the volume of wheat shipped to Latin America by the United States. What is not clear is whether the countries benefiting from the U.S. wheat disposal programs would have bought the same quantities of the grain from other sources had the programs not existed. There are some indications that the relatively easy availability of P.L. 480 wheat has influenced preference patterns of the recipient countries. Demand for wheat may have increased, therefore, at the expense of other food crops.[76] From this point of view, P.L. 480 programs may constitute a positive factor for Argentine export prospects. On the other hand, these programs have encouraged wheat production in the recipient countries. In the short run at least, the U.S. wheat programs have probably acted as an additional impetus for Argentina to get out of wheat into other agricultural production and into further industrialization.[77]

Wheat will continue to be produced under high protection in countries that do not have a comparative advantage in its cultivation, and in some areas the process of import substitution will be expanded. The European Economic Community will persist in moving toward self-sufficiency in wheat and is expected to succeed soon.[78] At present, the EEC supplies about 90 percent of its requirements.

With regard to wheat markets in developing countries, the outlook for Latin American wheat exports is also not encouraging. As has been indicated, income elasticity of demand for wheat is relatively high in the developing regions of the world. Thus the demand for wheat is bound to increase as incomes rise in these areas. What is widely questioned, however, is the ability of the developing countries to bridge the gap between consumption requirements and domestic production through imports. In the official projections it is assumed "that the import requirements of developing countries will, as in the past, by far exceed their ability to purchase grains on commercial terms."[79]

Furthermore, income elasticity of demand for wheat is negative in most developed countries, and this will tend to offset the high elasticities in the underdeveloped nations. Thus FAO projects a world wheat surplus which would range from about 9 to 24 million tons by 1975, depending on various assumptions of growth in the gross national product of the exporting and importing countries. No wonder, then, that Argentina has drawn back from making strenuous efforts to expand wheat production for export and is concentrating instead on livestock products for which the income elasticity is still high in the developed as well as in the developing countries.

Nevertheless, several factors in the world wheat situation may operate to improve prospects for Latin American exporters. Preferences in some countries appear to be changing in favor of wheat. In Japan, wheat continues to replace barley as food. In India, wheat now constitutes over 20 percent of the per capita consumption of all cereals, compared with 15 percent in the early 1950s and much less before the war. In the Sudan, the annual rise in flour consumption is now estimated to be 20 percent, and it is about 10 percent in Nigeria, Senegal, Tanzania, and Venezuela.[80]

The tendency toward increased wheat consumption at the expense of other grains seems to be widespread in Latin America. In Peru in 1947 maize provided about 630 calories in the human diet compared with about 220 for wheat; by 1962 human consumption of maize had fallen to less than 200 calories, while wheat consumption was providing over 400 calories.[81] In Mexico wheat has started to replace maize, although maize still accounts for over one-third of the average daily intake of calories and proteins.[82]

[76]Wheat consumption may increase even when relative wheat prices to the consumer do not decline as a consequence of the U.S. wheat programs. Public finances of the recipient countries usually benefit from these special arrangements and therefore governments will have the incentive to shift food demand in favor of wheat from the United States.

[77]The U.S. wheat programs may have had other indirect repercussions. For example, exports of Chilean coal and forest products to Argentina may have suffered because P.L. 480 wheat for Chile curtailed Chilean wheat purchases from Argentina and thus also limited Chile's sales to that country.

[78]The EEC is expected to become a net exporter of wheat in 1975 according to FAO projections.

[79]FAO, *Agricultural Commodities – Projections for 1975 and 1985*, vol. I, p. 105 and table I-8. FAO estimates that at a minimum the cost at current commercial prices of meeting the grain deficit of the developing countries would reach $2.3 billion per year by 1975, which would be an enormous debt to repay, even if long-term credits were available.

[80]IWC, *Trends in Wheat Consumption*, tables 37 and 38; and Szarf, "Modern Flour Mills. . . ," p. 5.

[81]Corporación Nacional de Fertilizantes, *Los Fertilizantes en el Perú* (Lima, 1965), pp. 44, 48.

[82]According to a recent family budget study in Mexico, per capita wheat consumption increases steadily with higher incomes, while the reverse is true for maize consumption. The cross-section

In spite of Mexico's rapid increase in wheat production, its consumption of wheat accounts for little more than 10 percent of calorie and protein intake. The expanded wheat output has resulted in several years of exportable surpluses. It is doubtful, however, if the country can continue to increase or even maintain its export surplus as the consumption pattern of the population changes. Since 1964/65 wheat production has not expanded. If per capita wheat consumption in Mexico rises to levels similar to those of Argentina and Chile, and growth in Mexican wheat output continues to slow down, it is conceivable that the country would have to become a net importer of wheat. If, however, the growth rate of productivity can be maintained over the long run and the steeply rising trend of wheat production experienced during the early sixties is regained and continues, per capita domestic wheat consumption will tend to stabilize eventually. After reaching high levels it may even start to decline, as in Argentina and the world's high-income countries, so that Mexico could become Latin America's second most important wheat exporter.[83] Although official Mexican projections foresee exportable surpluses in the 1970s, there is some question as to whether Mexico wants to become a significant exporter of wheat, except of seed wheat. The country will probably want to remain self-sufficient, keeping up with the rising domestic demand, and continue with the policy of agricultural diversification.

The success of the Mexican wheat program appears to have been due to three principal factors: (1) a strong research effort which resulted in the development of semi-dwarf, stiff-strawed, rust-resistant varieties capable of strong response to nitrogen fertilization; (2) heavy investments in irrigation facilities; and (3) strong price incentives to wheat growers. While all of these were important, the strategy of the research program was without a doubt the most original element. With the support of the Rockefeller Foundation and the Mexican government, a strong basic and applied research program of an interdisciplinary nature pursued the objective of developing wheat varieties capable of maximum response to fertilizers and then breeding in resistance to rusts as these developed. In many other areas of the world the approach up until very recently had been to breed wheats capable of extracting as efficiently as possible the nutrients in which local soils were most deficient and then seeking disease resistance. The creation of wheats specifically designed to take full advantage of manufactured inputs represented an advance which has revolutionized grain breeding technology. Coupled with the pronounced fall in nitrogen prices made possible by a new process of ammonia synthesis and advances in ammonia transportation, the Mexican wheat breeding strategy is at the heart of what has been called the "green revolution."

The export of special varieties of Mexican seed wheat, particularly to India and Pakistan, has been an important factor in lessening the food problem of underdeveloped countries. Mexican varieties have shown such high productivity that officials in India are hoping to achieve self-sufficiency in wheat production primarily on the basis of Mexican strains. Wheat developments in Mexico have begun to influence production in other Latin American countries as well. The recent doubling of wheat yields in Colombia is one example.

Within the foreseeable future it will nonetheless be difficult for the developing world to satisfy current consumption levels through import substitution efforts, much less to cope with demand increases due to rising incomes and changes in tastes. If, therefore, the U.S. P.L. 480 wheat programs in Latin America should decline significantly — and there is a possibility that they will — some pressure toward regional integration of wheat production may well build up and Argentina could become the region's major supplier.

Economic integration of Latin America would enormously increase the market for Argentine wheat. Indeed, it is not improbable that the gains to be derived from wheat under conditions of economic integration would be greater than from any other single product. However, the integration process in agriculture appears to be more difficult than in industry. The problems of the European Economic Community testify to this. The drive toward import substitution is particularly strong in agriculture, and especially so in the production of wheat and wheat flour. Countries are reluctant to become too dependent on foreign suppliers for their food requirements or to give up scarce foreign exchange for food imports. Even in the Central American Common Market, where well over 90 percent of all goods have been freely traded since June 1966, when the Economic Integration Treaty began its sixth year, only wheat, wheat flour, sugar, and coffee are still subject to special agreements in intraregional trade. Agricultural and industrial integration in Latin America would be self-reinforcing: integration of the fertilizer and tractor industries, for instance, would lower the costs of agricultural inputs which would encourage agricultural production.[84]

The Brazilian market alone could absorb most of Argentina's and Uruguay's wheat export surpluses within a few years. According to recent projections, Brazil's consumption requirements will amount to about 4 million tons in 1975. Domestic production is estimated to supply at most only a quarter of this, leaving an import gap of around 3 million tons.[85]

Considering also the rising consumption of wheat in developing countries, already noted, it is evident that the potential wheat market is vast. Argentina will be able to exploit this potential market in the developing countries and in the Communist and other developed countries, to the extent that it can lower its costs of production and distribution, and price its wheat far below the production costs of

income elasticity of demand for wheat in rural Mexico is about 0.6, while it is negative (about −0.4) for maize. Similar results have been obtained from time-series analysis. (*Projections of Supply and Demand for Agricultural and Livestock Products in Mexico, 1970 and 1975*, Secretaría de Agricultura y Ganadería, Secretaría de Hacienda y Crédito Público, Banco de México, S.A., Mexico City, September 1965, tables 11-10, 11-11, 11-16.)

[83] See IWC, *Trends in Wheat Consumption*, p. 37, for an indication of change in the income elasticity of demand for wheat from high positive to negative values as income levels rise.

[84] ECIEL, *Industrialization in a Latin American Common Market.* . . .

[85] Francis R. Bethlen and Paul L. Farris, "Brazil's Growing Wheat Import Gap," *Economia Internazionale* (Genoa, Italy) vol. XIX, February, 1966.

importing countries. In such a case it is conceivable that Argentina could compete with the special U.S. wheat disposal programs, if favorable long-term credits were available to the developing countries for the acquisition of Argentine wheat.

However, obstacles of the kind noted earlier in this section stand in the way of a massive expansion of wheat production for exports in Argentina. It may be difficult to push much beyond the output levels already achieved. Production increases can come only from two sources: an extension of the area of cultivation and an intensification of cultivation.

In the past, over 95 percent of Argentina's wheat production has come from the pampas. But the high-quality lands have been fully used for at least forty years. Large tracts of land within the pampas have alternated between livestock and crop production for decades. Wheat production could, of course, be increased by an extension of cultivation at the expense of pastureland, but there are limits to such a shift. Argentina's national development plan and private studies estimate that up to 5 million hectares could be diverted to crops without detriment to growth in livestock production, provided that the remaining pasture would be used more efficiently. Any further increase would not only hurt meat production but would also encounter technical obstacles. In studying the feasibility of converting natural to improved pastures, it has been found that poor drainage and other factors would prevent the seeding of improved pastures in about 50 percent of the natural pasture lands. What is true for improved pastures would have greater application for the cultivation of crops. Thus, in addition to hurting livestock output, a really substantial extension of wheat production to pasturelands within the pampas would require enormous outlays for drainage works and other soil preparation schemes, which at present do not appear practical.[86]

Another possibility is to extend cultivation to areas outside the pampas region. Since rainfall outside the pampas is very unevenly distributed throughout the growing season, heavy investments in irrigation projects would be necessary. Under current conditions, irrigation is of little importance in Argentina, although this country is the biggest agricultural producer in Latin America.[87] It is doubtful, however, if first priority will be given to irrigation in the near future, because population is sparse in the dry areas and there is little pressure to colonize these areas while the pampas are relatively underpopulated. Cost, too, would be high since it would be difficult to tie in irrigation projects in Argentina's dry lands with electric power development.

Beyond the shift from livestock area to cropland, a substantial output expansion can therefore be expected only from the employment of new inputs. It is true that some increases can be obtained from simple technical changes,

such as improvement in farm practices (better crop rotation, etc.), through which fertility could be restored to exhausted soils. But even optimistic estimates do not put at more than 20 percent the crop increase derived from measures of this kind — i.e., measures that do not involve large application of new inputs such as fertilizers.[88]

Fertilizer use in the Argentine pampas has its limitations. Wheat varieties have been developed to be primarily disease-resistant and to withstand a relatively high degree of nutrient starvation; experiments with fertilizer application have not shown striking increases in yields. This is apart from the fact that the price of fertilizers in Argentina is still high relative to output prices. Two factors may change this situation. Further experimentation with new varieties of wheat and artificial fertilizers may increase the responsiveness of the soil and crop to fertilizer application, as in Mexico, and the establishment and development of a petrochemical industry in Latin America may eventually reduce the cost of fertilizers.[89]

Increased mechanization can also expand wheat production. Argentina has made great strides in the use of tractors and other farm capital equipment since World War II. These inputs can be expected to continue to grow as the Argentine farm machinery industry becomes stronger and more efficient. The number of companies that specialize in sowing and harvesting wheat has also increased. This not only makes the utilization of machinery more efficient but also introduces flexibility into wheat cultivation. Because the individual farmer need not own expensive specialized equipment, his production decisions become more viable and more responsive to price and other stimuli. Thus, both capital deepening and technological change will improve output. In this process the role of the Argentine experiment and research institution, INTA, will be very important.

Two further questions should be considered in examining the growth possibilities of wheat production and exports in Argentina. The first relates to changes in land tenure arrangements, the second to the infrastructure supporting production and exports. To raise output through intensified cultivation rather than through extended cultivation over new areas often requires modification of the land tenure system. This is particularly relevant to the problem of facilitating the absorption of new techniques and improvement in farm practices, especially those concerned with the conservation and restoration of soil fertility.

Argentina is one of the few countries in Latin America which has not been considered to be in great need of agrarian reform. With a relatively small share of the population in rural areas — the lowest proportion in Latin America — and the relative well-being of the farm worker when compared with his abysmal misery in some other countries of the region, land redistribution in Argentina hardly appears to be of pressing urgency. Argentina is one of the few coun-

[86] FIAT, Economía Agropecuria Argentina.

[87] A little more than 3 percent of all cultivated land is under irrigation compared with over 20 percent in Chile and about 10 percent in Mexico. (USDA, Economic Research Service, Changes in Agriculture in the Developing Nations 1948-1960, table 19, p. 34.) Almost 90 percent of Mexico's wheatland is under irrigation. (Projections of Supply and Demand. . . , p. 204.)

[88] A recent study estimates that 1962 crop production could have been 20 percent higher with relatively simple fertility restoration practices. (See FIAT, Economía Agropecuaria Argentina, vol. I, pp. 109 ff., particularly table 84.)

[89] In Mexico, about two-thirds of wheat lands are fertilized. It is estimated that not less than 90 percent of the wheat area will be fertilized by 1975. (Projections of Supply and Demand. . . , p. 205.)

tries in the world where per capita income of the agricultural population is higher than the national per capita average. While in Brazil, Chile, and Peru per capita agricultural income is about a third of per capita national income, and in Mexico and Venezuela it is only a fifth, in Argentina it is about a third higher.[90]

Yet a strong argument has been made for land reform in Argentina. Just because there is a large supply of fertile land relative to the rural population, land holdings of efficient size can be distributed.[91] This would not be so in other countries of the region where there is not enough good land to provide their enormous farm populations with large enough plots for economic and commercially feasible production. Redistribution of large land holdings in Argentina, it is claimed, would make possible large-scale family farming similar to the U.S. model. Conditions for increased production would be created because farm sizes would be more manageable and, with greater absorption of technical knowledge, the soil could be more intensively cultivated and better utilized. It should be noted that such a development would not be consistent with the recent tendency in developed countries toward an increase in farm size. Average farm size is expected to increase further in the advanced countries as the corporate structure in agriculture becomes more important there. On the other hand, average land holdings in Latin America are expected to decrease. The only major land tenancy policy contained in Argentina's development plan is to increase rental contracts to ten years so as to encourage investments by the tenant farmers.

Considerable improvements in physical infrastructure would also be necessary to support substantial gains in production and export possibilities of wheat. The most important overhead capital needs concern shipping and storage facilities. The internal transportation system in Argentina is still rather poor. Improvement involves not only the renovation of railroads and the betterment and construction of new rural roads and highways, but also the promotion and facilitation of water routes. Overland grain shipping to Buenos Aires is expensive where ocean-going ships can be loaded inland. But rock bars in the Rio de la Plata make water transport very inefficient. Either small boats only can be used or large ships can only be half loaded. If these shipping obstacles were removed it would be possible to ship abroad directly from inland ports closer to the wheat areas and avoid the costly overland haul to Buenos Aires.

Over two-thirds of the wheat grain is still shipped in bags to the port where it is dumped in bulk bins for export. Merchandizing of bigger crops will depend to a great extent on larger investments in storage and loading facilities. The shortage of grain elevators is a problem not only in Argentina, but also in Uruguay, Colombia, and other wheat producers in Latin America. In Argentina, establishment of additional modern terminal elevators and further mechanization of loading facilities are crucial for the support of higher export volume. At present improvements in these facilities are being made. And there is also progress in ocean

transportation: a few bulk carriers of large tonnage (about 35,000 tons) have already been used for shipping Argentine wheat. These developments will alter the Argentine position in the wheat market. Ocean freight rates may become lower and improvements in storage and loading accommodations will give the country greater possibilities for adjustment. It will be easier to take advantage of favorable external conditions and to smooth out price fluctuations.

Taken together, the serious limitations to a massive extension of wheat cultivation in Latin America and the region's rising domestic consumption of wheat will restrain any possibilities of dramatic export increases. Argentina will remain the only significant wheat exporter in the region. That country's development plans and other projections do not lead one to expect huge increases in wheat production and exports, and the targets appear well within limits of what can reasonably be expected under present conditions.[92]

This brief review of the wheat outlook leads to the impression that if Argentina and Uruguay would concentrate more on markets in developing countries and the Communist countries, they might well find unexpected export opportunities which would exceed their short-run surpluses. But because River Plate exports are so strongly oriented toward the high-income countries of Europe, the emphasis is expected to shift even more toward livestock products. The demand for meats is very strong in high-income areas, while the income elasticity for wheat tends to be negative there. Furthermore, livestock exports can be maintained even through drought years and their market appears to be more stable than for wheat. These considerations, and the restrictions imposed by the European Economic Community to protect its import substitution efforts, make the market prospects there for River Plate wheat very bleak indeed. On the other hand, the prospect of a large developing country market, such as Brazil, offers a promising opportunity.

Thus, if River Plate wheat capacity could rise to substantially higher levels and production and distribution costs could be lowered significantly, new and steady markets could be developed. But there are strong obstacles in the way of a massive expansion in River Plate wheat supply. Incentives to overcome them are relatively weak because of the comparative advantage in livestock production. Yet, given the area's long-run potential, the River Plate countries can substantially raise their export surpluses of both livestock products and grain to become larger suppliers of world markets.

The international wheat agreements have not provided the incentive for an expansion in River Plate wheat exports. Argentina's interest in the international wheat agreements is

---

[90] FAO, *Monthly Bulletin of Agricultural Economics and Statistics*, vol. 16, June 1967, table 2, p. 3.

[91] See Ferrer, *La Economía Argentina*, particularly pp. 247-48.

[92] Unofficial projections by the U.S. Department of Agriculture pointed to a combined wheat output of Argentina and Uruguay amounting to 11 million tons in 1980, with exports of 4.7 million tons. (Estimates of Foreign Regional Analysis Division, Western Hemisphere Branch, presented at a meeting of the American Farm Economics Association in August 1966.) However, by 1964/65 Argentina alone produced 11 million tons of wheat, though production dropped to under 7 million in the next two crop years (see table 14-2).

not based so much on the desire to obtain a "fair price" for its wheat as it is to obtain access to its traditional markets. Under ideal conditions, if there were no government intervention in wheat production and trade in the world, Argentina would probably not need or even want an international arrangement. Alternatively, Argentina would prefer to have an international arrangement which would not only set price ranges and marketing levels but also would regulate the domestic wheat policies of the member countries so as to eliminate or reduce the encouragement of uneconomic production in the importing countries and eliminate the export subsidies in the competing exporting countries.

NOTE ON BRAZILIAN WHEAT STATISTICS

There are no reliable statistics on area devoted to wheat in Brazil during the 1950s, but the official figures are known to be considerably inflated, with unofficial estimates running from 40 to 80 percent of those provided by the Serviço de Estatística da Produção (SEP) of the Ministry of Agriculture. Beginning in 1962 much more accurate estimates, based on the sales of wheat to the only significant buyer, the Bank of Brazil, are available. These are published by the Comissão Central de Levantamento e Fiscalização das Safras Tritícolas (CCLEF). The discrepancy between the CCLEF statistics and the SEP data has steadily decreased since the formation of CCLEF. By 1967 the CCLEF area data were still roughly 65 percent of SEP figures as compared with about 45 percent in 1962. The CCLEF estimates probably exclude about 10 percent of wheat production. The figures cited in the body of the present volume are official (SEP) statistics and must be considered as overstatements.

Two reasons appear to underlie the discrepancy between the official government statistics and estimates of unofficial observers and, since 1962, the data provided by CCLEF: the dual price system for wheat and the statistical collection system of the Instituto Brasileiro de Geografia e Estatística (IBGE) which gathers agricultural statistics for the Ministry of Agriculture.

The dual price system arose in the 1950s and was still in operation in 1968. While the nature of this system has changed over time, the basic element has been that prices for domestically produced wheat have been higher than for imported wheat. In the 1950s this gave rise to frauds known as "nationalization of wheat" (the clandestine importation of foreign wheat which was sold as domestic production) and "paper wheat" (the sale of wheat which did not in fact exist, except on paper). Of these two basic frauds, the latter was the more important, and became particularly severe after November 1956 when the price paid to the producer was separated from the price paid to mills. Mills were thus able to "purchase" nonexistent wheat from the pseudo producers, who were then paid by the Bank of Brazil. Sometimes even the pseudo producers existed only on paper, they as well as the wheat being created by the mills. When this became impossible, it was not difficult to find a living pseudo producer to cooperate in the scheme. This was harder to detect if the pseudo producer did actually produce some wheat. More complex versions of the fraud were developed as the regulations became increasingly strict, but the lucrative paper wheat business was largely eliminated after 1961 when a comprehensive system of controls operated wholly by the Bank of Brazil was established.

The IBGE collection system for agricultural statistics is based upon the reports of local agents in the *municípios* (counties) who rely upon personal observation and hearsay in varying proportions depending on the energy of the agent. Large changes in area and/or production must be justified in writing, which results in a built-in incentive to report only slow changes or no change at all.

The interaction between the frauds due to the dual price system and the statistical collection procedure was probably responsible in large part for the inflated acreage and production statistics of the 1950s and the effects had not been entirely eliminated even by 1968 in spite of the virtual elimination of the frauds, probably because of the incentive to report only small year-to-year changes in acreage and production.

For a more detailed analysis of the Brazilian import substitution effort in wheat see a Ph.D. dissertation by Peter T. Knight, "Export Expansion, Import Substitution, and Technological Change in Brazilian Agriculture: The Case of Rio Grande do Sul," Stanford University, 1970 (multilith), chap. IV.

CHAPTER 14 TABLES

TABLE 14–1. World Wheat Area, Averages, 1934-38 to 1966-67
   (Thousands of hectares)

Country or Region	1934-38	1950-52	1956-58	1962-64	1965-66
Latin America	9,103	7,544	9,204	8,201	8,404
Argentina	6,783	4,482	5,009	4,763	5,188
Bolivia	34		21[a]	80	90[a]
Brazil	160	729	1,313	757	739
Chile	800	796	816	847	828
Colombia	134	171	132[b]	133	121
Ecuador		41[a]	64	74	71
Guatemala	14	34[a]	34	39	42
Honduras		3	2	2	2
Mexico	489	637	912	802	788
Paraguay		1[a]	18[a]	10	8
Peru	109	165	140	152	156
Uruguay	484	518	677	427	434
Venezuela	13	13[c]	4[a]	3	2
United States	22,431	26,164	19,829	18,593	20,125
Canada	10,134	10,558	8,741	11,340	11,825
Soviet Union	40,920		65,903	66,633	69,350
China	20,154	21,561	27,050[a]	24,700	24,895
Europe	29,800	28,577	27,837	28,696	28,590
Africa	5,600	6,213	7,280	7,310	7,557
Asia	20,346	30,879	33,725[a]	36,400	36,843
Oceania	5,300	4,393	3,687	6,932	7,594
World Total	168,820	132,900	204,203	208,805	217,278
Latin American Share (%)	5.4	5.7	4.5	3.9	3.9

Sources: FAO, *Production Yearbook, 1952, 1953, 1955, 1957, 1958, 1962, 1964,* and *1967*. FAO, *Monthly Bulletin of Agricultural Economics and Statistics*, vol. 14, nos. 9, 12 (1965). IWC, *World Wheat Statistics, 1965, 1967*.

[a]Average of two years only.
[b]1956 only.
[c]1950 only.

TABLE 14–2. World Wheat Production, 1925-29 to 1966/67
   (Thousands of metric tons)

Country or Region	Average 1925-29	Average 1930-34	Average 1935-39	Average 1940-44	Average 1945-49	1950	1951	1952	1953	1954	1955
Latin America	7,783	8,374	8,042	8,422	7,749	8,590	4,908	10,640	9,820	11,750	9,510
Argentina	6,615	6,640	6,036	6,385	5,415	5,796	2,100	7,654	6,200	7,690	5,250
Bolivia	33	32	23	11	20					46	
Brazil	129	155	262	189	322	532	424	690	772	871	1,101
Chile	783	761	859	867	965	975	988	989	955	1,078	1,048
Colombia		73	113	109	101	102	127	134	140	146	166
Ecuador			21	24		20	24	26	26	34	42
Guatemala	5	5	10	20	14		16	22		18	15
Honduras	1	1	2	1	3	3	2			1	1
Mexico	348	391	389	430	414	587	590	595	671	839	850
Paraguay			1		2			7		2	3
Peru	90	85	89	95	114	144	157	162	169	163	152
Uruguay	332	269	361	277	365	435	478	427	819	854	829
Venezuela			6	6		5	5	4	6	3	
United States	22,399	19,939	20,650	25,205	33,137	27,744	26,875	35,352	31,829	26,778	25,440
Canada	11,711	9,488	8,503	11,474	9,943	12,565	15,041	18,720	16,710	8,407	14,130
Soviet Union	21,558	23,436	33,753	26,512	24,090	24,090	27,764	28,989	38,788	36,747	36,475
China		22,769	21,095	21,694	23,498	21,690	22,189	22,595	21,700	23,335	22,965
Europe	36,758	41,282	42,376	36,720	31,670	41,600	42,000	43,550	46,570	45,330	49,800
Africa	3,179	3,620	3,876	3,642	3,460	4,300	4,400	4,750	5,340	6,050	5,370
Asia (excl. China)	12,211	16,022	21,764	21,204	17,422	21,410	22,511	23,125	26,300	25,305	26,560
Oceania	3,910	5,275	4,814	3,312	5,006	5,200	4,400	5,440	5,510	4,700	5,390
World Total	120,051	145,649	165,029	158,257	155,992	167,190	170,464	193,189	280,264	188,347	195,950
Latin American Share (%)	6.5	5.6	4.9	5.3	4.9	5.1	2.9	5.5	3.5	6.2	4.9

TABLE 14–2 – Continued

Country or Region	1956	1957	1958/59	1959/60	1960/61	1961/62	1962/63	1963/64	1964/65	1965/66	1966/67
Latin America	11,560	10,640	10,580	9,410	7,860	8,960	9,457	12,164	16,339	11,035	10,577
Argentina	7,100	5,810	6,720	5,837	3,960	5,100	5,020	8,940	11,260	6,200	6,700
Bolivia											
Brazil	1,296	1,199	400	370	683	545	680	392	643	585	615
Chile	988	1,257	1,203	1,165	1,123	1,071	1,275	1,319	1,276	1,172	1,000
Colombia	110	110	140	145	144	142	162	160	126	106	180
Ecuador	40	42	39	47	78	78	78	67	63	61	73
Guatemala	20	19	22	22	21	25	27	27	29	35	35
Honduras			1	2	1	1	1	1	1	1	1
Mexico	1,243	1,377	1,337	1,266	1,190	1,402	1,502	1,703	2,144	1,599	1,450
Paraguay			14	10	9	7	7	9	7	7	9
Peru	123	138	127	161	154	154	153	153	147	159	140
Uruguay	589	596	360	183	413	372	452	237	646	420	373
Venezuela		2	3	1	1	1	1	1	1	1	1
United States	27,332	25,873	39,665	30,512	36,939	33,604	29,765	31,080	35,121	35,805	35,670
Canada	15,596	10,084	10,117	11,254	13,326	7,713	15,392	19,689	16,341	17,661	22,982
Soviet Union	42,195	54,440	76,568	69,101	63,900	66,483	70,778	49,700	74,200	59,600	100,400
China	24,800	23,650	28,950	31,294	22,456	18,000	20,000	21,800	23,500	21,500	20,100
Europe	42,840	53,740	50,940	56,620	52,620	51,220	61,790	54,850	60,880	66,907	63,196
Africa	5,890	5,240	5,330	5,160	5,570	4,280	5,960	6,120	6,340	5,980	4,700
Asia (excl. China)	27,390	30,970	28,190	30,240	30,870	31,170	34,440	33,120	31,280	35,230	34,130
Oceania	3,740	2,700	6,020	5,640	7,670	6,940	8,600	9,200	10,720	7,350	12,507
World Total	201,395	271,780	256,400	249,200	243,700	236,900	263,100	244,000	278,800	260,767	303,883
Latin American Share (%)	5.7	3.9	4.1	3.8	3.2	3.8	3.6	5.0	5.9	4.2	3.5

Sources: FAO, *Production Yearbook, 1948, 1950, 1952, 1953, 1954, 1957, 1958, 1961, 1964, 1966, 1967.* FAO, *Monthly Bulletin of Agricultural Economics and Statistics*, September and December 1965. IWC, *World Wheat Statistics, 1964, 1966, 1967.* Information from USDA, Foreign Agricultural Service.

TABLE 14–3. World Wheat Yields, Averages, 1934-38 to 1965-67
(*Kilograms per hectare*)

Country or Region	1934-38	1950-52	1956-58	1962-64	1965-67
Latin America	944	1,067	1,187	1,507	1,355
Argentina	981	1,156	1,306	1,684	1,519
Brazil	899	753	734	755	810
Chile	1,064	1,238	1,408	1,511	1,413
Colombia	792	708	833[a]	1,123	1,167
Mexico	764	927	1,446	2,219	2,450
Peru	699	935	924	993	953
Uruguay	1,257	862	761	1,042	1,120
United States	1,048	1,146	1,561	1,720	1,773
Canada	707	1,463	1,365	1,512	1,590
Soviet Union	778	(b)	878	979	1,127
China	1,074	1,028	954	881	867
Europe	1,404	783	1,766	2,066	2,300
Africa	673	722	754	840	723
Asia	1,021	724	865[c]	905	917
Oceania	827	1,141	1,121	1,371	1,323
World Average	945	1,331	1,191	1,399	1,331
Ratio of L.A. Average to World Average (%)	99	80	99	108	102

Source: Calculated on basis of tables 14-1 and 14-2.

[a]1956 only.
[b]Area planted not available.
[c]Average of 1956 and 1957 for production and two years for area.

TABLE 14–4. World Total and Per Capita Consumption of Wheat and Wheat Flour,[a] Averages, 1934-35 to 1967-68
(Thousands of metric tons and kilograms)

Country or Region	1934-35 – 1938-39 Total	Per Cap.	1949-50 – 1953-54 Total	Per Cap.[b]	1959-60 – 1963-64 Total	Per Cap.	1966-67 – 1967-68 Total	Per Cap.
	(000 m.t.)	*(kg.)*	*(000 m.t.)*	*(kg.)*	*(000 m.t.)*	*(kg.)*	*(000 m.t.)*	*(kg.)*
Latin America:	6,182	54	8,948	55	11,385	53	14,268	57
Argentina[c]	2,811[d]	208	3,299	183	3,611	168	4,219	181
Bolivia	65	25	74[e]	24	161	40	262	57
Brazil	1,149[c,d]	30	1,966	36	2,412	33	2,843	33
Chile	844	174	1,056	168	1,320	163	1,666	182
Colombia	123	14	186	16	259	16	298	16
Costa Rica	11	19	31	36	46	34	77	48
Cuba	121	28	206	36	361	51	696	88
Dominican Republic	7	4	24	11	51	16	81	21
Ecuador	32	14	65[e]	19	114	24	128	23
El Salvador	10	6	21	11	40	15	52	17
Guatemala	23	11	36	12	80	20	92	20
Haiti	13	–	39	12	47	11	38	8
Honduras	7	7	13	9	26	13	36	15
Mexico	400	21	909	33	1,403	36	1,954	43
Nicaragua	6	8	15	13	29	19	32	18
Panama	11	19	21	25	33	29	43	32
Paraguay	32	31	44[e]	30	91	49	108	50
Peru	204	30	347	39	582	55	692	56
Uruguay	281	135	438	176	383	147	308	111
Venezuela	32	9	158[e]	30	336	43	643	69
United States[c]	18,362	142	1,941	122	16,205	87	18,085	91
Canada	3,027	266	4,049	281	4,082	219	4,375	214
Europe:								
West Germany	4,695	–	10,346	209	5,993	109	6,273	109
France	8,254[c,d]	200	7,668	181	9,377	200	9,716	196
Italy	8,064	189	8,708	184	9,103	181	9,989	191
Poland	1,862	–	1,848	72	4,346	143	5,330	167
United Kingdom	7,484	158	6,944	138	7,625	143	7,799	142
Soviet Union	130,328	–	24,075	120	61,445	277	87,403	371
Africa:								
Egypt	1,191	74	1,856	86	3,009	110	4,118	133
Asia:								
India	6,913	23	8,438	23	14,522	32	17,430	34
Turkey	3,621	217	5,122	231	8,831	303	10,053	307
Oceania:								
Australia	1,500	219	2,054	238	2,092	195	2,580	218

Sources: Wheat and wheat flour consumption–FAO, *Food Balance Sheets, 1955, 1958, 1963;* FAO, *Production Yearbook, 1954, 1955, 1957;* FAO, *Trade Yearbook, 1952, 1953, 1954, 1957.* IWC, *World Wheat Statistics, 1952, 1955, 1960, 1965, 1967, 1968, 1969;* USDA, Economic Research Service, *Food Balance for 24 Countries of the Western Hemisphere, 1959-1961,* 1965. ECLA, *Statistical Bulletin for Latin America,* III, no. 1 (1966), table 3. Population–UN, *Monthly Bulletin of Statistics.*

[a]Apparent consumption (production plus net imports) unless otherwise indicated.

[b]Calendar year 1955 used for Latin American countries except Argentina, for which average of calendar years 1954-55 is used.

[c]Total supplies less exports and carryover.

[d]Average of 1935-36 – 1939-40.

[e]Average of calendar years 1948-52.

TABLE 14–5. Average Daily Per Capita Consumption of Wheat, Maize, and Rice, circa 1957-1959

Country	Year (Average)	Total Diet Calories	Protein (Grams)	Wheat Calories	Protein (Grams)	Maize Calories	Protein (Grams)	Rice Calories	Protein (Grams)
Argentina	1957-1959	3090	97.7	1112	33.3			39	0.7
Brazil	1957-1959	2540	60.9	238	7.9	327	8.5	366	6.8
Chile	1957	2570	76.9	1206	36.1			75	1.4
Colombia	1956-1958	2200	48.3	118	3.5	297	7.7	174	3.2
Mexico	1957-1959	2440	67.8	265	7.9	943	23.9	41	0.8
Paraguay	1957-1959	2500	67.7	303	9.1	400	10.3	72	1.3
Peru	1957-1959	1970	49.0	291	8.7	235	6.3	179	3.3
Venezuela	1957-1959	2190	60.5	153	5.1	415	9.7	64	1.2
United States	1957-1959	3110	92.1	554	12.7	64	1.5	25	0.5
Italy	1957-58– 1959-60	2670	77.5	1162	34.3	123	6.1	29	1.1

Source: FAO, *Food Balance Sheets, 1963.*

TABLE 14–6. World Trade in Wheat and Wheat Flour (in Terms of Wheat Equivalent), Averages, 1934/35 to 1965/66
(Thousands of metric tons)

Country or Region	1934/35 – 1938/39 Imports	Exports	1950/51 – 1953/54 Imports	Exports	1954/55 – 1958/59 Imports	Exports	1959/60 – 1963/64 Imports	Exports	1964/65 Imports	Exports	1965/66 Imports	Exports	1966/67 Imports	Exports
Latin America	1,533	3,404	3,127	2,054	3,022	3,231	4,108	2,224	4,880	4,453	5,156	8,090	5,892	3,137
Argentina		3,295	208a	1,905		2,881		2,210		4,443		7,948		3,059
Bolivia	35		75		63		108		140		93		215	
Brazil	1,023		1,440		1,634		2,076		2,292		2,321		2,637	
Chile	12	19	138		97		140		233		320		455	
Colombia	17		68		103		123		191		250		198	
Costa Rica	12		33		43		51		61		60		75	
Cuba	121		190		198		361		566		624		667	
Dominican Republic	8		24		30		50		49		60		78	
Ecuador	14		48		65		49		55		65		70	
El Salvador	10		22		32		40		43		55		47	
Guatemala	14		34		51		52		67		41		57	
Haiti	15		41		47		47		53		57		41	
Honduras	7		12		19		22		25		28		40	
Mexico	36		307		21		21		28		5		1	
Nicaragua	6		13	3b	20		29		30		30		31	
Panama	11		20		25		33		34		35		39	
Paraguay	32		58		66		80		60		68		104	
Peru	128		220		302		427		360		488		543	
Uruguay	6	90		146		350		14		10		142		78
Venezuela	26		176		273		335		593		555		593	
United States	726	1,535	559	8,897	229	10,952	170	18,359	23	19,607	15	23,426	35	19,978
Canada	52	4,816	3	7,492	2	7,843		10,175		11,909		14,833		14,833
Europe	12,580	1,380	13,345	1,489	16,806	3,485	17,690	4,132	16,638	6,534	18,173	7,359	16,020	6,573
Soviet Union	73	625	45c	773	203	3,437	1,825	4,449	2,656	1,159	9,187	2,201	4,683	4,126
Asia	1,900	970	5,944	505	7,617	524	12,479	295	15,600	488	16,960	281	17,691	310
China	764	24	26d	5e	25	46	3,464	55	5,046		6,372		5,124	
Africa	400	500	1,556	296	1,861	278	3,462	214	3,900	100	4,650	150	7,000	133
Oceania	70	2,930	242	2,294	312	2,490	267	5,408	330	6,469	290	5,681	195	6,984
World Total f	17,580	18,280	24,892	25,122	30,511	32,240	43,753	45,367	49,610	51,197	61,225	62,487	57,070	56,133
Latin American Share (%)	8.7	18.6	12.6	8.2	9.9	10.0	9.4	4.9	9.8	8.7	8.4	12.9	10.3	5.6

Sources: FAO, Trade Yearbook, 1953, 1955, and 1957, 1958, 1960, 1967. FAO, World Grain Trade Statistics, 1964. IWC, World Wheat Statistics, 1947, 1955, 1957, 1960, 1964, 1965, 1967, 1968, 1969.

a Figure for 1952.
b Figure for 1951.
c Figure for 1954.
d Average of two years only.
e Figure for 1951.
f Regarding the statistical discrepancy between world exports and imports see fn. 16.

TABLE 14-7. Argentina and Uruguay: Exports of Wheat and Wheat Flour by Destination, 1949/50 to 1965/66
(Thousands of metric tons and millions of dollars)

Exporter and Destination	1949/50	1950/51	1951/52	1952/53	1953/54	1954/55	1955/56	1956/57	1957/58
Argentina									
Western Europe	788	955	102	228	1,144	1,759	1,764	1,325	981
Italy	348	515	48	226	88	507	285	347	90
West Germany	145	141	18		312	435	376	215	382
United Kingdom		46	2		377	241	1,387	265	284
Eastern Europe					60	270	58		
Africa		66	33		27	8	22	26	38
Asia	516	588	144		232	173			
China									
India	341	525	144		16				
Japan	175	63			216				
South America	1,110	1,207	538	326	1,544	1,344	1,239	1,317	1,067
Bolivia									
Brazil	996	1,161	410	296	1,115	883	934	1,040	733
Chile	20	58	14		152	253	106	99	195
Paraguay	68	42	46	18	50				
Peru	27	46	68	11	163	153	177	150	77
Uruguay									
Venezuela									
Crop Year Total[a]	2,380	2,814	815	796	3,057	3,629	3,155	2,698	2,116
Calendar Year:[b]									
Total	2,740	2,430	42	2,520	2,920	3,590	2,520	2,640	2,113
Value	152.0[c]	200.6	5.9	243.6	205.3	245.9	154.9	158.9	126.1
Share Total Exports (%)	12.9	17.2	0.9	21.6	20.0	26.4	16.4	16.3	12.7
Uruguay									
Crop Year Total[a]				166	122	527	497	331	229
Calendar Year:[b]									
Total	8	122	238	85	360	490	408	138	265
Value	0.7	8.2	25.4	7.7	29.6	37.9	27.7	9.4	17.2
Share Total Exports (%)	0.3	3.5	12.2	2.9	11.9	20.7	13.2	7.3	12.4

Exporter and Destination	1958/59	1959/69	1960/61	1961/62	1962/63	1963/64	1964/65	1965/66
Argentina								
Western Europe	1,123	881	750	1,420	861	742	2,013	1,367
Italy	13	66	185	53	176	185	308	482
West Germany	302	273	122	572	52	253	176	113
United Kingdom	483	269	221	355	282	87	488	339
Eastern Europe	1			10		74	51	96
Africa	41		10	40	47		57	56
Asia	7	30	46	89	98	988	619	2,294
China				88	98	988	599	2,274
India								
Japan								
South America	1,569	1,198	1,100	793	800	963	1,606	1,873
Bolivia	17		11	12		4	19	30
Brazil	1,433	911	684	551	472	689	1,009	1,313
Chile	80	50	125				28	71
Paraguay		76	80	24	19	19	59	81
Peru		146	193	185	289	251	307	378
Uruguay		10					94	
Venezuela		5	7	21	20		32	
Crop Year Total[a]	2,805	2,144	1,946	2,377	1,806	2,777	4,443	7,948
Calendar Year:[b]								
Total	2,390	2,485	1,065	2,832	1,831	3,710	6,661	5,055
Value	135.3	142.7	65.6	173.4	116.4	242.3	372.7	279.6
Share Total Exports (%)	13.4	13.2	6.8	14.3	8.5	17.2	25.0	17.5
Uruguay								
Crop Year Total[a]	164	20						
Calendar Year:[b]								
Total	50				42	49	81	129
Value	3.2				3.1		4.5	7.4
Share Total Exports (%)	3.3				1.9		2.3	3.9

Sources: FAO, *World Grain Trade Statistics, 1963/64;* FAO, *Trade Yearbook, 1964.* IMF, *International Financial Statistics, 1968* and supp. to *1964/65* and *1966/67* issues. IWC, *World Wheat Statistics, 1957, 1960, 1964, 1965, 1967.*

[a]Exports by crop year, 1 July – 30 June; wheat flour included as wheat equivalent.
[b]Calendar year volume of exports estimated from IMF volume index, base 1958 = 100, and exports for calendar year 1958 from FAO.
[c]Estimated from peso data at end-1950 official exchange rate.

TABLE 14–8. Latin American Wheat and Wheat Flour Balance, Averages, 1959-61 and 1964-66
(Thousands of metric tons)

1959-61

WHEAT

Country	Production	Imports	Exports	Changes in Stock	Total Supply	Animal Feed	Other	Gross Food
Latin America	9,086	3,297	2,027	−264	10,620	212	1,066	9,342
Argentina	5,534		2,005	−175	3,704	108	547	3,051
Bolivia	44	8		−5	57		8	49
Brazil	377	1,911		+27	2,261		108	2,153
Chile	1,135	126		−30	1,291	29	147	1,115
Colombia	147	110			257		23	234
Costa Rica		5			5			5
Cuba		147		−1	148		3	145
Dominican Republic		21			21			21
Ecuador	61	49	2	+6	102		8	94
El Salvador		13		+1	12			12
Guatemala	21	48			69	2	4	63
Haiti		31			31			31
Honduras	1	10			11			11
Mexico	1,286			−88	1,374	7	122	1,243
Paraguay	12	73			85		4	81
Peru	147	365		+10	502		27	475
Uruguay	319	78	20	−9	386	26	55	305
Venezuela	2	302			304	40	10	254

WHEAT FLOUR

Country	Extraction Rate[a]	(Net Food Use) Production	Imports	Exports	Changes in Stock	Total Supply
Latin America	76	7,079	382	29	+5	7,427
Argentina	72	2,195		21[b]		2,174
Bolivia	76	37	81		+3	115
Brazil	77	1,658	10[b]			1,668
Chile	77	859	27			886
Colombia	78	183	26			209
Costa Rica	60	3	31		+1	33
Cuba	72	104	88		+1	191
Dominican Republic	71	15	10			25
Ecuador	80	75	9[b]			84
El Salvador	75	9	17			26
Guatemala	75	47	6			53
Haiti	74	23	3	1		25
Honduras	73	8	9			17
Mexico	80	996	3			999
Nicaragua			15			15
Panama			22			22
Paraguay	72	58				58
Peru	82	390	6			396
Uruguay	74	226		7[b]		219
Venezuela	76	193	19			212

1964-66

	WHEAT				WHEAT FLOUR			
Country	Production	Imports	Exports	Total Supply[c]	Extraction Rate[a]	(Net Food Use) Production	Imports	Total Supply[c]
Latin America	13,346	4,345	1,969	15,722	77	7,565	644	8,209
Argentina	7,636		1,873	5,763	73	2,248[d]		2,248
Bolivia	73	27		100	75	14[e]	125	139
Brazil	247	2,240		2,487	78	1,599[e]	18	1,617
Chile	1,224	271		1,495	76	730[d]	40	770
Colombia	116	195		311	79	207[e]	26	233
Costa Rica		5		5	62	4[d]	60	64
Cuba		244		244	73	210[d]	301	511
Dominican Republic		45		45	72	18[d]	10	28
Ecuador	66	56	2	120	81	111[d]	4	115
El Salvador		46	1	45	76	36[d]	4	40
Guatemala	33	53		86	74	59[d]	2	61
Haiti		53		53	75	35[d]	3	38
Honduras	1	23		24	73	18[e]	4	22
Mexico	2,216	4		2,220	81	1,210[d]	13	1,223
Nicaragua							5	5
Panama							6	6
Paraguay	8	45		53	71	67[d]	4	71
Peru	103	470		573	83	396[e]	12	408
Uruguay	532		53	479	74	301[d]	1	302
Venezuela	1	568		569	75	302[d]	6	308

Sources: USDA, Economic Research Service, *Food Balances for 24 Countries of the Western Hemisphere, 1959-61*. IWC, *Trade in Wheat Flour*, Secretariat Paper no. 5, March 1965. IWC, *World Wheat Statistics, 1967*.

[a]Ratio of net to gross food use; percentage extraction rate of flour from wheat.
[b]Average of full trade years 1959/60 and 1960/61 and half of trade years 1958/59 and 1961/62.

[c]Exclusive of changes in stock.
[d]1964-65 Average.
[e]1964 only.

TABLE 14-9. Summary of Trade in Wheat and Wheat Flour by Member Countries of the International Wheat Agreement for Loading in August/July Years, 1961/62, 1963/64, and 1966/67
(Million metric tons)

Distribution of Trade	Agreement of 1959[a] 1961/62 Com-mercial	Special	Total	Agreement of 1962[b] 1963/64 Com-mercial	Special	Total	1966/67 Com-mercial	Special	Total
Among Member Countries									
Exporters to importers	16.8	6.9	23.7	18.1	8.6	26.7	20.6	8.0	28.6
Exporters to other exporters	2.5	0.3	2.8	11.9	0.2	12.1	4.5		4.5
Importers to other importers	0.4		0.4	0.4		0.4	0.9		0.9
Importers to exporters				0.6		0.6			
Total	19.7	7.2	26.9	31.0	8.8	39.8	26.0	8.0	34.0
With Nonmember Countries									
Exporters from nonmembers	0.2		0.2	0.5		0.5			
Importers from nonmembers	0.9	0.3	1.2				0.4		0.4
Exporters to nonmembers	3.5	8.7	12.2	8.1	7.7[c]	15.8	9.8	10.4	20.2
Importers to nonmembers	0.8		0.8	0.4		0.4	0.4		0.4
Total	5.4	9.0	14.4	8.5	8.2	16.7	10.6	10.4	21.0
Total All Trade	25.1	16.2	41.3	39.5	17.0	56.5	36.6	28.4	55.0

Source: IWC, *World Wheat Statistics, 1965, 1968.*

[a]Membership of 1959 IWA—*Exporters*: Argentina, Australia, Canada, France, Italy, Mexico, Spain, Sweden, United States of America. *Importers*: Austria, Belgium and Luxembourg, Costa Rica, Cuba, Dominican Republic, El Salvador, Federal Republic of Germany, Federation of Rhodesia and Nyasaland, Guatemala, Haiti, Honduras, Iceland, India, Indonesia, Ireland, Israel, Japan, Korea, Netherlands, New Zealand, Nigeria, Norway, Panama, Peru, Philippines, Portugal, Saudi Arabia, Sierra Leone, South Africa, Switzerland, United Arab Republic, United Kingdom, Vatican City, Venezuela. (The figures for importers also include Brazil and Greece.)

[b]Membership of 1962 IWA—*Exporters*: Same as 1959 with addition of Union of Soviet Socialist Republics. *Importers*: Same as 1959 with addition of Finland, Liberia, Libya, Tunisia, Western Samoa, but excluding Haiti, Honduras, Panama.

[c]U.S.S.R. sales included here are based on exports in July/June years.

TABLE 14-10. Wheat Prices, Argentina and Canada, Averages for Selected Periods, 1934/35 to 1966/67

Crop Years	Argentina[a] ($/ton)	($/bu.)	Canada[b] ($/ton)	($/bu.)
1934/35 – 1938/39	29.02	0.79[c]	34.91	0.95
1949/50 – 1953/54	85.46	2.33	76.72	2.09
1954/55 – 1958/59	57.98	1.58	63.75	1.74
1959/60 – 1963/64	61.49	1.67	65.59	1.79
1964/65 – 1966/67	57.48	1.56	69.31	1.89

Source: IWC, *World Wheat Statistics, 1957, 1960, 1964, 1965, 1967.*

[a]No. 2 semi-hard wheat, Buenos Aires. Export price (f.o.b.).

[b]No. 1 Manitoba Northern in bulk in store Fort William/Port Arthur. 1934/35 to 1952/53 export price (Class II). 1953/54 to 1966/67 domestic and export price.

[c]Average 1937-39.

TABLE 14-11. Wheat (Open Market) Export Prices Compared with IWA Maximum and Minimum,[a] 1949/50 to 1966/67
(Dollars per bushel)

Year of Agreement	Aug./July Crop Year	IWA Price Range Maximum	Minimum	Average Open Market Export Price Quotation
1949	1949/50	1.80	1.50	2.01[b]
	1950/51	1.80	1.40	1.99[b]
	1951/52	1.80	1.30	2.31[b]
	1952/53	1.80	1.20	2.21[b]
1953	1953/54	2.05	1.55	1.91
	1954/55	2.05	1.55	1.77
	1955/56	2.05	1.55	1.75
1956	1956/57	2.00	1.50	1.75
	1957/58	2.00	1.50	1.68
	1958/59	2.00	1.50	1.72
1959	1959/60	1.90	1.50	1.73
	1960/61	1.90	1.50	1.69
	1961/62	1.90	1.50	1.80
1962	1962/63	2.025	1.625	1.82
	1963/64	2.025	1.625	1.88
	1964/65	2.025	1.625	1.84
	1965/66	2.025	1.625	1.85
	1966/67	2.025	1.625	1.96

Sources: IWC, *Trends and Problems in the World Grain Economy, 1950-1970*, Secretariat Paper no. 6, app. table XI. USDA, Economic Research Service, *Wheat Situation*, various issues.

[a]All prices refer to no. 1 Manitoba Northern Wheat in store Fort William/Port Arthur.
[b]Prices for sales outside the Agreement (non-IWA Class II prices).

TABLE 14-12. Estimated Export Price Equivalents, f.o.b. Gulf Ports of Argentine, Canadian, and United States Wheats, 1959/60 to 1966/67,
Two-Year Averages, Compared with WTC Prices Specified for 1968/69 to 1970/71
(Dollars per bushel)

Crop Years	Argentina[a]	Canada No. 1 Manitoba	United States No. 2 Hard Red Winter
1959/60 – 1960/61	1.72	1.89	1.68
1961/62 – 1962/63	1.79	1.98	1.73
1963/64 – 1964/65	1.84	2.00	1.77
1965/66 – 1966/67	1.75	2.07	1.69
Wheat Trade Convention:[b]			
Minimum	1.73	1.955	1.73
Maximum	2.13	2.355	2.13

Source: Testimony of D. Gale Johnson and Helen C. Farnsworth in *International Grains Arrangement of 1967*, Hearings before Subcommittee of Committee on Foreign Relations, U.S. Senate, March 26, April 4, 5, 1968, tables 1-A and 1-B, pp. 147-48.

[a]No. 2 Semi-hard through about 1964/65, later a similar grade designated No. 1 Hard. WTC minimum and maximum are for River Plate wheat undesignated as to grade.
[b]In effect since 1968 crop year.

TABLE 14-13. United States Wheat Exports to Latin America, Averages, 1963/64 to 1967/68
(Thousands of metric tons)

Crop Year	Commercial	Government Programs				Total Government	Total
		P.L. 480					
		Sales	Donations	Barter	Other		
1963/64	537	924	65	661	26	1,676	2,213
1964/65	535	1,276	36	122	1	1,434	1,969
1965/66	655	534	15	1,009	14	1,572	2,228
1966/67	845	783		1,150	199	2,133	2,978

Source: USDA, Economic Research Service, *Wheat Situation*, various issues.

TABLE 14-14. Closing Stocks[a] of Wheat in Eight Exporting Countries, Averages, 1949-53 to 1964-66
(Million metric tons)

5-Year Averages	Argentina	Australia	Canada	U.S.A.	France, Italy Spain, Sweden	Total
1949/53	1.0	0.7	5.5	10.8	2.6	20.6
1954/58	1.6	1.8	17.0	26.1	4.5	51.0
1959/63	0.8	1.0	14.6	35.6	4.0	56.0
1964/66[b]	1.9	0.6	12.6	20.4	4.9	40.5

Source: IWC, *Trends and Problems in the World Grain Economy, 1950-1970*, table 3, p. 5.

[a]At the end of each country's crop year.
[b]Three-year average.

Chapter 15

BEEF

In terms of output value, livestock is Latin America's third most important commodity group. Petroleum products rank first and cereals second, but over one-third of the region's cereal production is used as an input for livestock. Beef[1] is the most consequential livestock product; its value exceeds that of coffee or any other single agricultural commodity, and is second only to the value of crude oil output. Although most of the meat production is consumed domestically, beef figures significantly in a few countries as an earner of foreign exchange. It makes up roughly 4 percent of the region's total exports, a share which, while

Note: Beef tables 15-1 to 15-15 appear on pp. 421–29.

[1] The term "beef" as used throughout most of the text is broadly applied to include veal.

The general discussion in this chapter is based to a large extent upon various studies by the Food and Agriculture Organization, the U.S. Department of Agriculture, the UN Economic Commission for Latin America, Hearings before the U.S. Congress, and discussions with officials of the UCLA, FAO, ECLA, the Inter American Committee for Agricultural Development (CIDA), and the Argentine and Uruguayan embassies. In addition to the sources listed in the tables and text, the following publications were among those consulted:

FAO, *The World Meat Economy,* Commodity Bulletin no. 40 (1965).

U.S. Senate, 89th Cong., Select Committee on Small Business, *Expansion of Beef Exports* (1st sess.) *Hearings on Ocean Freight Rates and Other Barriers to Expanding Exports of U.S. Beef and Beef Products,* February 24, 25, 1965, and (2nd sess.) *Hearings on Potentials and Problems of Expanding Exports of U.S. Meat and Livestock Products,* May 18, 19, 1966.

USDA, Foreign Agricultural Service, *World Beef Trends* (FAS, M-173, June 1966); *Argentina's Livestock and Meat Industry* (FAS, M-188, June 1967); *Uruguay's Livestock and Meat Industry* (FAS, M-186, May 1967); and Foreign Agriculture Circular, *Livestock and Meat* (various issues).

ECLA, "The Meat Problem in Latin America," *Economic Bulletin for Latin America,* vol. 1, January 1956. ECLA-FAO, *Livestock in Latin America, Status, Problems and Prospects,* vol. 1, *Colombia, Mexico, Uruguay and Venezuela* (UN, 1962), vol. 2, *Brazil* (UN, 1964).

Consejo Nacional de Desarrollo (CONADE), *Plan Nacional de Desarrollo, 1965-1969* (National Development Plan of Argentina), Buenos Aires, 1965.

Comisión de Inversiones y Desarrollo Económico (CIDE), *Plan Nacional de Desarrollo Económico y Social, 1965-1974* (National Development Plan of Uruguay), Montevideo, 1966.

much less than that of petroleum or coffee, is greater than the share of any cereal and not far from the export shares of copper and cotton.

Livestock is found in every country in the world, yet meat is predominantly a product of the temperate zone where grass and grains, the primary fodder for cattle, are concentrated. This, of course, is also true of Latin America, where 90 percent of beef production is located in Argentina, Uruguay, and the temperate zones of Brazil, Mexico, and Colombia. In the abundant pasture lands of Latin America and Oceania beef is produced primarily under extensive conditions. In Western Europe intensive production methods prevail and to a great extent emphasis is on dairy cattle rather than beef cattle. The United States, the world's largest beef producer, combines both extensive and intensive processes.

Beef constitutes about half of the world's meat output, and in Latin America it accounts for roughly three-quarters of the region's meat production and consumption. Since meat is a high-priced commodity, its consumption is concentrated in the developed countries. The United States, Canada, Europe, and the Soviet Union, with less than 40 percent of the world's population, are consuming 80 percent of world production. Almost one-third of the world's beef supply is produced and consumed in the United States alone, which has recently become the world's major importer.

About 7 percent of total world output of meat enters international trade. With meat production and consumption confined mainly to the temperate zones, outside of Latin America most trade takes place among developed countries, although recently some countries in the east and south of Africa have started to export small quantities of meat. Argentina, Uruguay and, more recently, Mexico are among the world's greatest beef exporters. Latin America is also a major exporter of mutton, lamb, and horsemeat and exports minor quantities of pork and pork products — nearly all of these from Argentina — but its trade in poultry is still insignificant.

In general, however, the underdeveloped countries have failed to maintain their share in world production, consumption, and trade. Between 1950 and 1960, their per capita consumption increased by only 3 percent compared with 35 percent for the "developed" world. The foreign exchange difficulties of the postwar period made meat a low priority item in the food import budget of the developing countries. On the other hand, until recently production has been limited by the general backwardness of the techniques applied and exports have suffered from a combination of problems in supply, government policies, and access to the markets of the developed countries. Meat exports from Argentina and Uruguay increased by only 5 percent during the decade of the 1950s compared with 55 percent for exports from Australia and New Zealand.

Resources

Countries with vast pastureland have a natural advantage in raising beef cattle. A gradual shift toward more intensive methods in the livestock industry in general is particularly pronounced for poultry and pork, but beef production still depends upon extensive grazing areas, especially for young cattle. In addition to breeding and disease control, technical advances concentrate upon improving pastureland and management, and the final fattening of cattle with grains and feed supplements. Latin America generally has not shared in these developments and it is only recently that some efforts in these directions have been started.

The first European cattle were introduced into the Western Hemisphere by Hernando Cortez, who brought the forerunners of the "Texas longhorns" to Mexico in the sixteenth century. Much later, Western type purebreds from England arrived in the United States and the "River Plate" countries of South America.[2] The Herefords and Angus type species form the basis for the Argentine and Uruguayan cattle industry, which has been developed primarily by British settlers. European breeds are not well adapted to the tropical areas of Latin America. Mixtures, such as the creole strains which have evolved over the years, do much better and certain crosses — for instance, with the Zebu — show encouraging success.

Over three-quarters of Latin America's grazing area of 400 to 450 million hectares are in permanent pastures, and about 70 percent of its more than 200 million head of cattle are located in Argentina, Brazil, and Mexico (see tables 15-1 and 15-2). While Argentina and Brazil have about the same area in pasture, the cattle population of Brazil has roughly doubled the Argentine number in recent years. Brazil maintains the world's third largest cattle inventory; in 1968 its herd of over 90 million ranked behind that of the United States, which had over 100 million, and that of the Soviet Union, which had somewhat less than 100 million head.

The region has been able to keep up with the steady rise in the number of cattle in the world since the prewar years, the increase being substantially faster than population growth. The region thus has been able to maintain its share of about one-fifth of the world total during the postwar period. In 1968 the Latin American beef herd amounted to over 230 million, compared with a world total of 1,150 million. About half of the increase in Latin America's cattle stock can be attributed to Brazil, whose herd doubled during the postwar period. Argentina's herd increased during the later Perón years, peaking to 47 million head in 1956 and again in 1967. During the past half century there has been no major long-term change in the cattle inventory of Uruguay, the world's fourth largest beef exporter.[3]

In making international comparisons of pastureland available per head of cattle, certain factors must be kept in mind (compare tables 15-1 and 15-2). First there is the problem of aggregating within one country all types of grasslands without regard to quality. Thus the overall average for Argentina has been about 2¾ to 3 hectares per head of cattle in recent years — much more than the 1¼ to 2 hectares for Brazil. But approximately four-fifths of Argentina's cattle population is concentrated on the pampas, an area of only some 46 million hectares. Since the pampas are available for all animals, of which cattle constitute 80 percent, the land-cattle ratio falls to less than one hectare per head, which is considerably below that of Brazil. This is simply an indication that the Argentine pampas have a higher carrying capacity than Brazilian pasture. However, given a certain quality of pasture, a very low and a very high cattle density both signify inefficient land use. The figures in tables 15-1 and 15-2 should be read with these considerations in mind.[4] The carrying capacity of Argentine natural pasture has been estimated to average about 0.8 animals per hectare, and for seeded pasture about 2 units per hectare. Uruguay still has the highest ratio of cattle per capita and per hectare in Latin America.

The region's pastures suffer from neglect and management problems. Most of Latin America's cattle land consists of natural pastures which receive almost no care. Uruguayan pastures, which cover almost 80 percent of the country's total land area, have been badly neglected and are now so poor that they cannot carry the existing number of cattle through a drought. Large livestock areas are situated in the tropical zones of Brazil, Mexico, Colombia, and Venezuela. Their carrying capacity is low at present, but by improving existing grazing areas and sowing additional acreage to pasture, meat production could be greatly increased in these areas, especially in the Mato Grosso of Brazil, the Gulf Coast of Mexico, and the Atlantic Coast of Colombia.

In the most important livestock countries of the region the proportion of pastureland that is improved is comparatively small. In Argentina and Brazil it is less than 15 percent and in Uruguay about 4 percent of total pasture area. However, about 30 percent of the grazing area in the pampas of Argentina is improved, compared with about 11 percent for the country as a whole. According to fragmentary data, improved pastures in Mexico still constitute less than 5 percent of the grazing lands. These figures correspond roughly to the proportions usual in the extensive

---

[2]The countries bordering the Rio de la Plata: Argentina and Uruguay. Paraguay and parts of Brazil and Bolivia are included under the heading, "River Plate Basin."

[3]USDA, *Livestock and Meat*, 1968.

[4]Moreover, the weight per animal varies among areas so that one head of cattle may imply different quantities of meat. Thus the carcass weight of Brazilian cattle has averaged between 10 to 20 percent below that of Argentine cattle.

livestock farming areas of Australia and the United States, but are far below those in European countries and New Zealand. Most of the nontimber land of Paraguay, one of the region's cattle producers with large potential, is used for grazing under natural conditions.

Production and Yields

In Latin America there are enormous variations in the relationship between the size of the cattle herd and meat production. In 1963, for instance, Argentina, with not much more than half of Brazil's stock, produced nearly twice as much beef and veal as Brazil; and Colombia, with a herd only 50 percent greater than Venezuela's, produced more than two and a half times Venezuela's output. This disparity reflects wide differences in the efficiency of the livestock sector within the region. Given an endowment of natural resources, the level of productivity depends upon the methods used in stock farming: in pasture and herd management, production, and administration, for example. For many years Argentina and Brazil have accounted for about two-thirds of Latin American beef and veal output. Mexico, Colombia, and Uruguay make up another 20 percent; and Chile, Cuba, Paraguay, and Venezuela almost 10 percent. (See table 15-2.)

Most production (slaughtering) takes place in local abattoirs and, in the case of Argentina and Uruguay, also in modern packing plants. The small proportion of total output that is produced on farms varies from 3 percent in Uruguay to 6 percent in Brazil.

Until the second half of the 1950s, Latin American beef production showed an upward trend. Argentine output more than doubled after World War I, reaching an average of 2.3 million tons in 1955-59 (table 15-3). No clear trend in total regional production can be noted during the past decade. Output in Argentina and Brazil fluctuated around a level trend line, with Argentine production varying as much as 20 percent from one year to the next. Thus the regional share in world beef output declined from an average of one-quarter in 1957-58 to one-fifth in 1965-66, primarily because of stagnation in the River Plate countries. Only Mexico, Colombia, and Venezuela, among the major producers, have experienced marked increases in beef output since the 1950s. Growth in Venezuela was the fastest in the region; production, although still relatively small (3 percent of the regional total), more than doubled between the 1950s and mid-1960s.

The available statistics do not permit precise calculations of productivity of the beef industry in Latin American countries. But, for comparative purposes, some data on efficiency can be derived from fragmentary information. Latin American yields in general are far below those in the United States, Canada, and Western Europe. Even though Argentine meat yields are more or less the same as in Australia, where extensive production methods also prevail, they cannot compete with the high levels of efficiency achieved under intensive conditions in the United States and in Western European countries. Uruguayan yields, lower than those of Argentina, are still higher than those of most other meat producers in the region. Colombia ranks

third, but productivity in Brazil and Mexico is less than half that of Argentina. Venezuela trails the major meat producers and in the rest of the region efficiency is even further behind.

Livestock efficiency depends on several factors, among them: carcass weight of meat (per animal slaughtered), slaughtering rate (number of animals slaughtered as percent of total cattle inventory), fattening rate (time required to achieve weight for slaughter), and calving rate (birthrate of cattle). Argentina, Uruguay, and Colombia compare favorably with Oceania in respect to meat per head of cattle slaughtered (210-220 kilograms), but rank far below the United States and Western Europe (260-280 kilograms) where cattle fattening practices are highly developed. The average for Latin America is somewhere between 170 and 180 kilograms.

Carcass weight alone, however, is not a good indicator of efficiency. Ratio of carcass to live weight, average age at which the animal is slaughtered, and other factors must also be considered. Carcass weight usually constitutes less than 50 percent of live weight of the animal in Latin America; in the United States, Western Europe, and Oceania it is about 60 percent. In Latin America the late age at which cattle are slaughtered — between four and five years in Brazil, for example — reflects the low level of productivity in the livestock sector. By contrast, in the United States, with modern fattening techniques steers are ready for slaughtering at the age of one and a half to two and a half years.

Argentine grasslands are still fertile enough to permit raising high-quality cattle to a weight of 450 kilograms after only two to two and a half years of grazing with very little grain supplement. Years ago Argentine cattle, particularly those slaughtered for export, reached much higher weights (table 15-4). A shortage of fodder contributed to the decrease in average carcass weight of export cattle from 306 kilograms in 1914-19 to less than 230 kilograms in 1960-63, but part of the decrease is due to a change in tastes in the traditional markets for River Plate meat: preferences have shifted in favor of lean rather than fatty meats; consequently many animals are slaughtered before the fattening process takes place.

The proportion of animals slaughtered per year is also directly related to the average age at which the cattle are slaughtered. The slaughtering rate in the region is less than 15 percent for all countries except Argentina, where one-quarter of the total herd is slaughtered annually. In countries where the animals are ready early, the rate is higher: 40 percent in the United States.

Average cattle reproduction rates in the region reach a maximum of about 65 percent in Argentina compared with over 85 percent in the United States.[5] In Uruguay the rate is 60 percent; in Brazil, Colombia, and Venezuela it is roughly 50 percent.

Probably the most adequate indicator of the level of yields is the meat production per animal (total weight of

---

[5]The reproduction rate is the proportion of calves born, less the mortality of calves up to one year of age, per dam per year. The rates on some of the better-managed properties in Argentina exceed 90 percent, as they do in the United States.

production divided by total number of the herd). This measure combines the carcass weight (meat yield per animal slaughtered) and the slaughtering rate. Beef production per head of cattle has averaged less than 30 kilograms for Latin America as a whole, with little increase over the prewar level. The ratio is 45 kilograms in Australia and New Zealand, and well over 70 kilograms in the United States and the intensive stock-farming countries of Western Europe (see table 15-2).

Argentina's yield of more than 50 kilograms per animal in the total herd far surpasses that of any other country in the region, is about 10 kilograms higher than New Zealand's average, and is also somewhat above the Australian level. Uruguayan yields are a few kilograms over the regional average, yields in Venezuela are less than half, and Brazil and Mexico produce only about 20 kilograms per animal.[6]

The low level of technology in every aspect of production and marketing is a serious obstacle to improving productivity in Latin American stock farming. Defective practices in pasturing and handling cattle, in disease control, and in land use and marketing are prevalent in every country, including Argentina where efficiency is highest.

The fundamental aim of livestock farming anywhere is to maintain a continuous balance between the number of cattle and the supply of economical feeds. In well-managed pasture economies not only is much livestock land improved to carry perennial pastures but also adequate storage facilities are created to carry seasonal surpluses and thus assure a continuous supply of sufficient feed. In Latin America the scarcity of adequate fodder is especially grave, a situation that seems paradoxical in countries such as Argentina and Uruguay which possess abundant pasture resources.[7] There and elsewhere in the region the summer surplus is allowed to go to waste, resulting in a shortage of forage during the winter. In Argentina small grains, rye, barley, and oats are seeded for winter pasture, and since 1966 wheat has been used with rye and oats to supplement alfalfa for winter grazing. But in most other countries of the region little remedial action is taken.

Defective pasture-management practices, the absence of fodder preservation with ensuing seasonal shortages, and insufficient and inefficient use of nutrient concentrates and supplements combine to make feed a matter of great concern in Latin America. For these reasons the cattle-fattening industry is underdeveloped in most parts of the region, and breeding and rearing predominate. Breeding is relatively efficient and the few serious problems encountered — particularly in Brazil — can be overcome with ease when compared with other difficulties in the livestock sector.

Cattle diseases are another reason for the low productivity levels of the Latin American meat industry. About one-third of the value of livestock production in Colombia and Uruguay, for instance, is lost because of illness. Diseases, and also pests, are responsible for an annual loss of some 3 million head of cattle in Brazil. Even in Argentina, where disease control is highly developed, foot-and-mouth disease seriously hurts between 15 and 20 percent of the herd. Only the southernmost part of the country, Tierra del Fuego, has been relatively free from this highly contagious virus-caused sickness, although even here there have been temporary outbreaks from time to time. The disease plagues most countries in the world. The only areas that have been able to eradicate this virus from their herds are Australia, Canada, Central America, Mexico, New Zealand, and the United States.

Efficiency in many Latin American countries also suffers from a lack of complementarity between stock and crop farming. There is little rotation in land use between these two sectors and in some countries there is no combination of livestock and crop production on farms. In Uruguay livestock and wheat compete for land resources, but there is no healthy rotation. The same pastures are used for cattle and sheep raising, a combination prevalent on most farms in that country (the average ratio has been about 2½ sheep per head of cattle). Argentina is the only outstanding case of land-use rotation between cattle and crop production, although even there the rotation patterns have been disturbed by land rent control laws — a situation described in chapter 14 on wheat.

In some areas of Latin America the land tenure structure is another obstacle to higher productivity in meat production. Landlord absenteeism is common on the latifundia, while the land rental system and other factors make production on the minifundia highly inefficient.[8]

Marketing problems also contribute to productive inefficiency. Inadequate facilities for meat packing, cold storage, and depots are responsible for waste and production losses. Municipal abattoirs producing for local consumption are generally ill-equipped and overloaded, while modern slaughterhouses often have idle capacity. Because the plants are poorly located and transportation facilities are deficient, cattle must be walked over great distances, with consequent losses in weight.

Underlying all these problems is the scarcity of management and administrative skills throughout the region. The

---

[6] In order to obtain a broad perspective of the productivity in the livestock sector, indices of returns to various inputs should also be considered. Among these would be meat production per hectare of diverse types of pasture, per unit of seeds for pasture, fodder (including yields of corn and other crops used for feed), feed supplements, etc. Such information (which would have to be further refined in order to get accurate productivity measures) is generally not available for Latin America. Yet the indicators discussed above leave little doubt about the low levels of efficiency of beef production in most countries of the region compared with the levels in developed meat-producing areas such as the United States, Western Europe, and Oceania. Historical data also reveal that the yield indices in most places of the region have not risen significantly over many years. The present beef output per hectare ranges between 100 and 150 kilograms in Argentina, compared with 20 to 25 kilograms in Uruguay (USDA, *Argentina's Livestock and Meat Industry* and *Uruguay's Livestock and Meat Industry*).

[7] Even in Argentina there are great differences in the conditions under which cattle are raised, varying from the mixed farming of livestock and crops on the fertile pampas north and south of Buenos Aires to the subtropical far north and the dry west.

[8] According to the Argentine 1960 census there were 122 properties in the pampas with cattle herds exceeding 10,000 head; over 40 percent of cattle in the region were in herds numbering more than 1,000 each.

dearth of trained staff is probably the most important factor contributing to high production costs and obstructs any substantial increase in investment in the livestock sector. At the levels of productivity described, the estimated return on physical capital in Brazilian livestock farming, for instance, is between 4 and 6 percent — hardly a strong incentive to embark upon massive investment programs.[9]

Consumption

Since World War I the world's consumption of all kinds of meat has increased much faster than its consumption of food in general. FAO estimates indicate an increase in per capita meat consumption of almost one-quarter during the 1950s alone.[10] As can be noted in table 15-5, the upward trend has not been uniform throughout the world and in many of the Latin American countries, as well as in Australia, per capita consumption has declined.

Unlike most other primary commodities entering international trade, inventories play a negligible role in the meat market and so, for the world as a whole, consumption is about equal to production in any given year. Changes in production are reflected in external trade and in domestic consumption. The postwar decrease in per capita meat consumption in Argentina, for example, is a direct result of the failure of production to expand sufficiently. The sharp increases in Argentine output in 1966 and 1967 could not be absorbed by export markets; consequently per capita consumption recovered but is still below the levels of the immediate postwar period.

Latin America enjoys relatively high levels of meat consumption. Per capita consumption is still close to 100 kilograms per year in Argentina and Uruguay which, together with Australia and New Zealand, have the highest in the world. Consumption in the rest of Latin America is only a fraction of that in the River Plate countries, but it is still considerably above that in most other developing nations.

Beef's share of meat consumption has greatly increased since World War I. With veal, it now accounts for over half of all meat consumption in the world; pork accounts for about one-third, and poultry, mutton, and lamb for most of the remainder. In Latin America as a whole, beef represents over 70 percent of total meat consumption — a figure which owes a great deal to the high per capita consumption of beef in the River Plate countries, about 85 kilograms per year in the early 1960s or roughly twice the level for Oceania and the United States.[11]

[9] For a discussion of the livestock sector in the Brazilian state of Rio Grande do Sul, where beef production has been the most traditional agricultural activity, see Peter T. Knight, *Agricultural Modernization in Rio Grande do Sul* (Agency for International Development, 1969), multilith.

[10] While the income elasticity of demand for meat on the average is higher than for other foods, it shows great variation among countries: from a low of close to zero in Argentina, Uruguay, and Oceania to one or more in Asia. Generally the level is higher for the poorer countries than for the wealthier ones. (FAO, *The World Meat Economy*, pp. 3-13; and FAO, Committee on Commodity Problems, *Agricultural Commodities — Projections for 1975 and 1985*, vol. II, 1967, table I-8).

[11] FAO, *Agricultural Commodities — Projections for 1975 and 1985*, vol. I, table 7. U.S. beef consumption has shown a significant

Despite a substantial increase in meat intake in the major meat-importing countries, the overall composition of their meat consumption has not changed greatly since prewar years. Table 15-6 shows the major change by 1961 to be an increase in poultry consumption, which in the United States took place mainly at the expense of pork. It also shows a consistent but small increase in the proportion of beef consumed in Italy. More recent information indicates a continuation of the rise in importance of poultry meat as well as of beef and veal, which constitute the major share of all meats consumed in the developed countries; an exception is West Germany where pork is the principal meat. During the mid-1960s pork consumption in the United Kingdom surpassed beef and veal for the first time, but this may be of transitory significance.

Meat supplies an important part of food values in Latin America. For the region as a whole, almost one-tenth of the intake of calories and two-tenths of the intake of proteins derive from meat (table 15-7). Again, this average is strongly influenced by Argentina and Uruguay where meat supplies one-fifth of calories and nearly two-fifths of all proteins. These shares, as well as the absolute level of nutrition which they provide, are among the highest in the world. In most other Latin American countries the nutrition derived from meat is one-third or less of the River Plate values.

Throughout the world, meat prices are generally less controlled than the prices of staple foods, but in times of stress and shortage meat consumption is more easily and more severely rationed than other foods. In Latin America, particularly in Argentina where beef has constituted one of the staple products, government policy has been inconsistent until fairly recently. During much of the Perón period and afterwards, ceiling prices for beef prevailed in Argentina while rationing was introduced from time to time. It will be seen from the following section, on trade, that government policies with respect to consumption have not been in step with policies concerned with production and exports.[12] Occasionally, to curb inflation, the Argentine government attempted to increase the quantity of meat available for domestic consumption; such was the case in 1963, when exports were curtailed. Nevertheless, beef prices rose relative to other food prices in post-Perón Argentina, generally reflecting a worldwide trend.

Trade

Meat, like other temperate zone food products, is primarily produced for the domestic market and therefore a comparatively small proportion enters international trade. For the entire world, trade represents about 7 percent of total meat production, after having more than doubled

and steady increase in the postwar period and is now exceeding that of Oceania but is still less than two-thirds of the River Plate level.

[12] For a detailed discussion of the role of government in the Argentine livestock sector see two articles by E. Louise Peffer in the *Food Research Institute Studies*: "The Argentine Cattle Industry Under Perón," vol. I, no. 2 (May 1960), pp. 151-84, and "State Intervention in the Argentine Meat Packing Industry, October 1, 1946–December 31, 1958," vol. II, no. 1 (February 1961), pp. 33-73.

since the immediate postwar period; and for Latin America as a whole a little over one-tenth of total production is traded. Beef and veal in all forms, from live animals to canned beef, are the most important commodities traded within the world's livestock sector, constituting about half of total meat exports. Exports in this group tripled during the last two decades, with the greatest sales consisting of fresh, chilled, and frozen beef (tables 15-8 and 15-9). The region's exports of canned meats declined somewhat during the last decade.[13] This accompanied a worldwide decrease in canned beef trade, as canned pork products — chiefly from Denmark and the Netherlands — gained in importance. While Latin America still exports some 100,000 tons of canned meat annually, about half of it to the United States, the Western European canned meat trade is more than twice as large. Canned meat exports of Oceania have fallen off even more than those of Latin America in the recent past. Exports of salted beef from Argentina also were important until refrigerated transport came into use.

Since 1905, Argentina has been the world's foremost beef exporter.[14] Most of the meat trade flows from Latin America and Oceania to Western Europe and North America. About 40 percent of world trade takes place among Western European countries, primarily from Denmark, the Netherlands, and Ireland, to the United Kingdom, West Germany, and Italy. The United Kingdom alone has accounted for between one-fifth and one-third of world imports of fresh, chilled, and frozen beef and veal, about four-fifths of mutton and lamb, two-thirds of pork and pork products, and half of canned meats. In recent years the United States has shifted from being a net meat exporter to becoming the world's largest importer of beef (see table 15-12). But for other categories of meat U.S. purchases are far below those of the United Kingdom and some other European countries. The United Kingdom still imports over one-third of its consumption, compared with the United States' 5 to 10 percent.

So far as Latin America's exports of all meat is concerned, their value more than doubled in the postwar period, raising their share in the region's total exports from less than 3 percent in the early 1950s to well over 4 percent during the mid-1960s (see table 15-10). Beef, despite some decline in its importance since the Great Depression, is still a major earner of foreign exchange in the region. It provides more than one-fifth of Argentina's export income and about a quarter of Uruguay's. This degree of dependency is greater than that of any other country in the world with the exception of Ireland, which derives about one-third of its export proceeds from beef. In Oceania beef contributes less than one-tenth to total export value.

[13] See UNCTAD, *Short and Medium-term Prospects for Exports of Manufactures from Selected Developing Countries: Argentina*, doc. TD/13/C2/34/Rev. 1, 8 March 1968.

[14] Historically, the cattle industry has played an important part in the Argentine economy. Cattle hides were Argentina's principal exports during the seventeenth and eighteenth centuries, a trade the country still continues to a limited extent–150,000 tons were exported in 1966 compared with U.S. exports amounting to 390,000 tons. See USDA, *World Cattle Hide, Calf and Kip Skin Production and Trade*, Foreign Agriculture Circular FLM 3-68 (May 1968), table 8.

Since the expansion of Argentine beef production has been slower than the rise in domestic consumption, Argentina's export surplus has constituted a declining share of total output. During and immediately after World War I more than half of the country's production was sold abroad. The proportion remained over one-third until the postwar period, when it fell to less than 20 percent during the early 1950s. Despite some recovery during the 1960s, the export share in 1966 was hardly more than a quarter of production (see table 15-3).

World trade in live cattle has risen appreciably since World War II (see tables 15-9 and 15-13). Latin America's export share, after a slump in the early 1950s, now accounts for more than one-fifth of the world total. Mexico has become the most important cattle exporter, shipping almost exclusively to the United States.

Intra–Latin American meat trade is comparatively small. Less than 4 percent of total Latin American exports of beef and between 20 and 40 percent of live cattle exports are imported by countries in the region. Despite the rapid population growth, most countries are still nearly self-sufficient in meat output, although imports have increased markedly since World War II. Chile and Peru are the region's major importers. Once self-sufficient, Chile now needs to purchase between one-fourth and one-third of its domestic beef requirements from Argentina, and Peru buys between 15 and 20 percent. Between them, these two countries account for one-half to two-thirds of the region's gross imports of all categories of beef — a quantity which, while considerably larger than in the prewar period, rarely has exceeded 300,000 head of cattle and only recently reached 30,000 tons of fresh and frozen meat (see tables 15-12 and 15-13). Most regional requirements are supplied by Argentina, but a part of Peru's cattle imports comes from Ecuador, much of it contraband trade. Prepared and canned pork products are imported mainly from Western Europe.

In Chile and Peru imports have been restricted and in the exporting countries exports have been maintained or increased, mainly at the expense of domestic consumption. Despite considerable increases in production per capita, beef consumption has hardly changed in Mexico for many years and is still so small there and in Central America (which has the lowest per capita levels in the region) that substantial exportable surpluses have appeared in the postwar period.

About two-thirds of the region's net exports, which now average roughly 750,000 tons excluding live animals, go to Western Europe, principally the United Kingdom. The United States takes most of the remainder, which consists of canned meats from Argentina and about half a million head of cattle from Mexico. Total Latin American exports of livestock products were estimated at about $380 million (average annual f.o.b. value) during 1959-61.[15]

Argentina has always sold the bulk of its beef exports to the United Kingdom, but since World War II the United Kingdom's share in Argentine exports of chilled beef has declined from about 90 percent to about half (see table 15-11). At the same time other European markets, particu-

[15] FAO, *The World Meat Economy*.

larly the European Economic Community and the Communist countries, have increased their imports from Argentina, and the share of Argentine exports to countries within Latin America has also increased.

Until 1954 a major portion of trade in carcass meat was conducted under bulk purchase agreements between the United Kingdom and Argentina, Uruguay, Australia, and New Zealand. The movements in prices reflected the variations in these arrangements. Since termination of the long-term contracts, the meat trade has been largely free.[16] But uncertainty has replaced the assurance of definite markets for the River Plate countries. No such problem exists for Australia, whose access to the English market was reinsured through a fifteen-year agreement entered into in 1964.

World trade in beef is complex because of its fragmentation, restrictions, and product differentiation; consequently, prices do not reflect a free market situation. The Chicago, Smithfield, and continental European markets are relatively isolated. The U.S. market quotations do not include Argentine carcass meat, and the Buenos Aires price is also not representative because of frequent domestic meat rationing. (Complete price data are not available. Some time series are given in table 15-14.) In general, Argentine beef prices have been much lower than those for beef of similar grade on the world markets. They often move in the opposite direction from other countries' prices which are to a large extent determined by local conditions, but "imported Argentine beef wholesaling in the London market has consistently been lower-priced than similar quality U.S. beef still in New York coolers."[17] Argentine prices recently have averaged one-quarter below the New York export and London domestic prices, one-half of the Paris price, and less than half of the Milan price, all expressed in terms of a similar quality product — U.S. Grade Good Beef at Chicago (see table 15-15).

Public Policies

As is the case with other developing areas, Latin America has failed to maintain her share in meat production, consumption, and trade. To a large extent a vigorous expansion of exports from the region has been held back by problems of supply. The technical obstacles to accelerating meat output (pasture and fodder management, disease control, transportation and other marketing problems, etc.) have been noted. Government policies have also affected livestock production. Argentina is an example. As a consequence of the upheavals in the world meat market during the Great Depression, a national meat board (Junta Nacional de Carnes — JNC) and a government-sponsored meat packing cooperative (Corporación Argentina de Productores de Carne — CAPC) were created in 1933, the former in order to rationalize marketing and regulate international trade, the latter to protect the Argentine cattle producers from an unfair fixing of cattle prices by the foreign-owned packing companies. Argentine livestock interests considered both entities as their organizations and there is no indication that production was adversely affected by their existence.[18]

Difficulties emerged in the 1940s when the Perón administration created a trade promotion institute (Instituto Argentino de Promoción del Intercambio — IAPI) which was given a monopoly of foreign trade in agricultural and livestock commodities (except wool). As pointed out in the previous chapter, IAPI had the ostensible task of providing the foreign exchange for national economic development, particularly industrialization. For those ends, the organization tried to maximize the spread between the prices it would pay to the producer and the export price it would receive. Part of the proceeds would be used to subsidize the domestic retail price. In this problem of price control — trying to keep the price of cattle down, the export price of meat high, and the domestic retail price low—IAPI was at odds with JNC and CAPC, both of which tried to get as much as possible of the export price for the domestic producer. The foreign-owned meat packers found themselves in the middle and could not operate without a deficit. IAPI was forced to subsidize them from time to time and domestic consumption was also subsidized, both in direct form and through increases in real wages. In general, however, government price policies were not rigid but were adjusted, always lagging somewhat behind an economic optimum. Since 1960 there has been comparatively little direct government intervention in the livestock sector of the Argentine economy.

In reviewing the history of the Argentine cattle industry it is difficult to find direct evidence that official policies have seriously discouraged producers. It cannot be shown that output declined nor that there was a net reduction in the size of the cattle herd under the Perón regime. Exports, however, may have been negatively affected, because official price policies encouraged domestic consumption and squeezed the foreign packing houses, and trade negotiations with importing countries, mainly the United Kingdom, became more difficult. The Perón government's efforts to obtain foreign exchange for development purposes resulted in levies on meat exports, thus constituting a burden on foreign sales.

While Argentine government policies were on the whole comparatively favorable to livestock production, crop production did not fare as well and, as has been indicated in the chapter on wheat, cropland was diverted to pasture. The strain on crop production indirectly affected livestock as well by permitting no easing of the feeding problem.

While difficulties of supply have played an important role in Latin America's foreign trade in meat, the problems of international demand faced by the region's exporters

---

[16]It should be noted that most world trade in beef is in the hands of a few major private concerns with interests in every stage of production and marketing. In Argentina there are about eighteen packing and processing plants which produce for export. Most of these are still foreign owned. Uruguay has four major meat packing plants which supply the export market.

[17]U.S. Senate, 89th Cong., Select Committee on Small Business, *Hearings...*, 1966, p. 199.

[18]CAPC did not acquire much of a plant until recently and its primary function was to bid up cattle prices at public auctions. It is now a large meat packing combine owned by Argentine cattle producers and there is no government intervention. The discussion of Argentine government policy is taken in part from the articles by Peffer previously cited.

have become more conspicuous. In some instances demand and supply problems are closely connected and are difficult to isolate from one another — as in the case of U.S. prohibition on imports of carcass meat (fresh, frozen, and chilled) from the River Plate countries because of U.S. health regulations. Argentine and Uruguayan raw meat does not meet U.S. sanitary standards mainly because of the incidence of foot-and-mouth disease. It has often been claimed that this import prohibition is really a disguised form of protection for the U.S. livestock industry, because River Plate meat seems to be acceptable everywhere else in the world and it has never conclusively been shown that the disease can be transmitted through meat.[19] Nevertheless, the United States is the only major importing country that has eliminated foot-and-mouth disease, and its imports from Argentina and Uruguay have consisted of cooked, canned, and other processed meats which are considered not to be contaminating.

Strong protective forces in the world meat economy tend to curtail import demand independently of any difficulties in the supplying countries. In the developed countries in particular public policies have increasingly restrained a vigorous expansion of the import demand for meat. Domestic meat production has been encouraged through direct subsidies, tariffs, and quota systems. It is characteristic of the internal prices in the importing countries to be above world prices. The European Economic Community has moved far to protect the internal market through attempting to maintain prices adequate for domestic production. Even in the United Kingdom, which traditionally has had an "open door" policy on meat imports, purchases from abroad have been curtailed because of artificial encouragement of domestic production. The difference between the low consumer and high farm prices has been covered by deficiency payments to cattle raisers. These payments have been high enough to constitute about 20 percent of the producers' total return. Apart from the health regulations mentioned above, the United States has discriminated very little against foreign supplies. Tariffs have been relatively low (10 percent ad valorem) but, although there are no direct price supports for meat production, official subsidies for feed grains help maintain high internal meat prices because it encourages artificial feeding which is a higher-cost process than grazing.[20] Significant restrictions were introduced recently because the United

States has changed from being a substantial net exporter to being the world's chief importer. A 1964 law provides for an import ceiling on beef, veal, and mutton beyond which a quota system would go into effect.

It is difficult to evaluate the impact of these protective measures on Latin American meat exports. Despite the prohibition on raw meat imports into the United States, Argentina and Uruguay always have had access to the U.S. market through the sale of canned and prepared meats. With the upsurge of supermarkets and modern packaging, U.S. consumption of prepared meats swelled considerably. As a consequence, agreement on sanitary conditions was reached to permit entry of Argentine beef cooked in approved Argentine plants without further processing in the United States. The River Plate countries, however, did not benefit directly from the dramatic expansion in the U.S. market during the 1950s, which pushed carcass meat prices upward. The United States satisfied its demand for raw meat (most of it for processing) mainly through imports from Oceania.[21]

The net result is that the region which accounted for about half of the U.S. beef imports in the 1950s now provides about one-quarter. The greatest drop was noted in the Argentine share which declined from one-third to less than one-tenth of U.S. beef imports. There was no compensatory increase of the Latin American share in other markets. A good argument can be made that the import substituting policies of the developed countries in regard to meat production have prejudiced export possibilities of the developing countries. If the meat importing countries, especially the United Kingdom, had relied on imports only to satisfy the rise in their consumption requirements without substituting high-cost domestic production, meat exporters would have been assured of a rapidly expanding market. Uncertainties of markets have contributed to restraining investments and improvements in the supply conditions of the River Plate countries. While, obviously, production problems cannot be blamed upon demand problems, it is also true that the assurance of a fast-growing demand would encourage investment and the overcoming of many obstacles which now stand in the way of increasing supply.

Outlook

Projections in the livestock sector are intricate not only because of the complexity of world trade but also because of the interdependence among the various products in the livestock sector. Beef production, for instance, is related significantly to milk output so that imbalances arise if the demand for one is not in harmony with the supply and demand situation in the other.

Despite conflicting trends, on balance world demand for meat will probably continue to be strong for the next decade. Recent projections are much more optimistic than those made during the early 1960s.[22] There are several forces

---

[19] An outbreak of foot-and-mouth disease in England during the fall and winter of 1967-68 was at first on circumstantial evidence attributed to Argentine lamb carcasses. A subsequent investigation concluded that there was no basis for the temporary ban on River Plate meat in the United Kingdom and after several months the ban was rescinded. Argentina retaliated by giving preference to other markets. (See John Reid, *Origin of the 1967-68 Foot-and-Mouth Disease Epidemic*, Ministry of Agriculture, London, 1968.)

[20] The United States is the only major meat producer where grain feeding of cattle is universal. To some extent this has been made possible through government programs, including subsidies which have probably resulted in lower feed grain prices. Nevertheless the feeding of grain to cattle is a higher-cost process than grazing on natural and improved pastures. In Argentina grain is used only as feed supplement for purebred stock and in other special circumstances, because in the absence of any special government programs the wide application of grain feeding is too expensive.

[21] Argentina and Uruguay may have benefited from this indirectly because it meant a diversion of Australian and New Zealand meat to the United States from the United Kingdom and Western Europe, the traditional markets for the River Plate countries.

[22] For early projections see FAO, *Agricultural Commodities— Projections for 1970* (1964); Bela Belassa, *Trade Prospects for*

which press for an expansion of meat imports. Income elasticity of demand for meat is high. It tends to be higher for low-consumption–low-income countries and generally declines as consumption rises. This, combined with rapid population growth, would indicate a strong increase in demand in the developing countries. But meat usually has a low priority in the import budgets of the less developed nations when there are balance of payments problems. Furthermore, the level of consumption in the poor countries is still so low that, even with rapid income growth, total effective demand for meat imports would not be important for some time to come compared with the requirements of the developed countries. Even in Japan, whose consumption and imports of meat have risen faster than any other country's, per capita meat consumption is still small and the country's meat imports are not very significant despite a more than tenfold increase since the start of the 1950s. An important factor in judging the prospects for the meat import requirements of developing countries will be the future of the world fish industry (see chapter 18). A strong development of fish and fish products and their acceptance as an important provider of animal protein for the people of poorer countries could prevent a rise in import demand for meat. Since well over two-thirds of all world meat imports are concentrated in four developed countries – the United Kingdom, the United States, West Germany, and Italy – it is most likely that these countries will continue to provide the major markets and take the bulk of any expansion of meat trade.

Rising incomes affect not only total demand for meat but also its composition. Since World War II, consumer preferences have changed in favor of lean meats and tender cuts. This has signified an increase in consumption of beef from young, quick-maturing animals. Argentina has not yet been able to make the genetic adjustment toward leaner animals. The enormous jump in poultry consumption, which has occurred primarily at the expense of pork in the United States and of mutton in the United Kingdom, has not affected the demand for beef which is stronger than ever despite higher prices. To a large extent this is due to the new marketing of beef in large retail stores where cuts can be packaged and displayed attractively. The decline in pork consumption is also a phenomenon of increasing urbanization. These trends can be expected to continue. The demand for meat will probably be even more exacting than in the past in regard to specific qualities, types of cuts, packaging, and other characteristics.

Part of the change in the composition of demand is due to changes in relative prices. While changes in consumer preferences in favor of beef were strong enough to push prices upward, increase in poultry consumption in the developed countries has been due primarily to a sharp drop in relative prices. The rationalization of the poultry industry, based on mechanization and vertical integration, has brought about large economies of scale. Generally the substitution effects between two kinds of meat are small and it takes a large price differential for one type to cut into the market of another, as has been the case with poultry and pork.[23]

Meat prices, like the prices of other primary goods, tend to be somewhat inelastic. Yet the effects of this characteristic are different from those of commodities with low price elasticities, which are internationally traded and the import of which constitutes the major part of total supply in the importing countries. A meat exporting country has only a small share of the total meat market; it must compete not only with other exporters but also with the domestic production of her customers. Therefore, even if price elasticity is less than unity in the market as a whole, export earnings to individual countries can be augmented by expanding sales, unlike coffee or cocoa whose earnings might be increased by restricting exports.

The declining trend in canned meat exports can be expected to continue. As labor and material for canning become more expensive, the shift from canned to cooked meat exports from Latin America will become more important.

Despite fairly successful efforts to increase domestic output, European demand for meat outstripped production increases in recent years. This is particularly true of the countries in the European Economic Community which have become substantial importers. Net imports constituted about 5 percent of beef and veal consumption of the EEC during the early 1960s and this proportion is expected to increase. The most recent FAO projections indicate that between 10 and 13 percent of EEC consumption of beef and veal will be imported by 1975. Most projections for import requirements of beef and veal have been revised upward in recent years, primarily because of the strong West European demand. Italy has experienced the fastest growing beef demand in Europe and her imports are expected to continue to rise, both as her domestic consumption increases and her exports of processed meats – mainly sausage to the United States – expand.

The Soviet Union, the world's second largest beef producer, has been fairly self-sufficient in the past, her trade shifting back and forth between net exports and imports. Recent projections point to substantial import requirements in the future. FAO forecasts similar developments for the centrally planned Asian countries.

It is not clear whether these import requirements will be directly translated into effective imports of Latin American

Developing Countries (Homewood: Irwin, 1964). FAO Commodity Bulletin Number 40, _The World Meat Economy_, uses 1962 FAO projections, but includes observations indicating probable demand underestimates. For more recent projections see FAO, _Agricultural Commodities–Projections for 1975 and 1985;_ and the pertinent papers included in U.S. Senate, 89th Cong., Select Committee on Small Business, _Hearings . . .,_ 1965 and 1966, particularly the Carpenter Report on "Trends in Production, Consumption, and Market Possibilities for Beef in Western Europe," pp. 222-63.

[23]In the United States the supply of pork affects the price of beef only one-third as much as a change in the quantity of beef itself; the substitution effect in the United Kingdom is much less. (For U.S. data, see H. I. Breimyer, _Demand and Prices for Meat_, USDA, Technical Bulletin 1253, 1961.) In Argentina, the cross-elasticity of beef with "other foods" was found to be statistically not significant (Alieto A. Guadagni and Alberto Petrecolla, _La Función de Demanda de Carne Vacuna de Argentina en el Período 1935-1961_, Buenos Aires: Instituto Torcuato di Tella, 2nd ed., 1966).

beef. Most meat importing countries have moved toward greater import restrictions in recent years. The EEC, in particular, has instituted a system which could be highly detrimental to exports from the River Plate countries. The Community imposes a surcharge on its external tariff on meat whenever import prices fall below a certain ratio to domestic prices. These ratios are to be evaluated periodically.[24] The new U.S. quota on fresh, chilled, and frozen meat imports could also discriminate against Latin America. Export possibilities for Mexican and Central American unprocessed meat exist as long as U.S. prices are low and not attractive for Oceania. However, when U.S. prices are high, the import quota would be quickly filled by Australia and New Zealand – countries from which raw meat imports are permitted – and imports from Latin America would then be closed. The United Kingdom has also moved toward quantitative restrictions and long-term trade agreements with Oceania.

It is obvious that exporting countries have a lot to lose from import restrictions on commodities only a small part of whose production enters international trade. For instance, a 5 percent increase in domestic production of the importing countries can, in the short run, signify a 30 or 40 percent decline in their import requirements. The recently established restrictions could dampen efforts to expand the livestock industry in Argentina and Uruguay.

New consideration has been given to the possibility of an international agreement to regulate world meat trade. It is significant that this interest sprang up primarily from the importers, contrary to the case of other commodities where the major drive for international arrangements usually comes from exporters. Importers are concerned about a stable source of supply because their requirements are not likely to diminish in the near future. Exporters' policies have been defensive in nature, consisting mainly of reactions to importers' restrictions. So far, however, there has been little conflict regarding prices between exporters and importers and the climate is conducive to international agreements. An arrangement already exists in regard to bacon between the United Kingdom, as the importer, and seven European exporters. The Bacon Market Council regulates trade through market sharing and quotas. Meat exporters are not averse to quota systems and, indeed, greatly prefer them to the kind of arrangements that presently exist in the EEC which introduce a great degree of uncer-

tainty. This is particularly true for the Latin American exporters for reasons already indicated and also because they produce meat on the basis of extensive livestock farming. The production cycle in the extensive cattle industry is especially long and thus the countries concerned need the security of stable markets much more than countries producing under intensive conditions.

The strength of the overall demand for beef assures that an oversupply is unlikely for the world as a whole in the foreseeable future. This, of course, does not preclude excess supplies in producer countries from time to time because of serious trade imbalances. While the developing countries limit their meat imports mainly because of foreign exchange shortages, the developed countries curtail their purchases primarily in order to protect and expand domestic production. The potential adverse effect of such measures on Latin American beef exports has already been explored.

Yet in recent years the region's traditional beef customers in Europe have been concerned that Argentina may not be able to meet their future import requirements. Part of the Argentine current supply problem is due to recent droughts, which led to much forced slaughter and therefore to the rebuilding of the herd. Some experts, however, foresee a structural problem in that the region's rapid population growth may cause consumption to catch up with production.[25] This trend is revealed in the fact that the export share of total beef production has declined in Latin America. Argentina, as already mentioned, exported over half of its production during the early 1920s, but now the average proportion is less than a quarter of output. Only Mexico and Central America have been able to expand the export shares, but for Mexico this trend has been reversed during the past years. If current tendencies persist, per capita consumption in Mexico and Brazil will continue to decline. If consumption levels in Mexico, which are among the lowest in the region, are to rise significantly, the country, now still an important exporter, will probably have to import meat by the mid-1970s. The Brazilian case is more dramatic. That country, which now exports about 2 percent of its production, is projected to have the world's fourth largest import requirements by 1975 according to the recent FAO estimates. Rapid population and income growth in Venezuela led to the region's highest rise in per capita meat consumption. Despite successful efforts to increase output, consumption is expected to outstrip production in that country for some time to come. The outlook is similar for Peru, and in Chile consumption can be maintained without higher imports only through heroic efforts. Prospects are better for Colombia which is trying with external financial assistance to become a significant meat exporter in the 1970s.

In Latin America the role of government in livestock production was not orderly until rather recently. The meat industry developed (or failed to develop adequately) with a minimum of government assistance in most countries. The

[24] Originally the revisions were to be made on a weekly basis, leading to a weekly setting of import levies. This system would operate to the great disadvantage of distant meat exporters. It takes considerably longer than one week to ship meat from, say, Buenos Aires to a West European port. At the time of shipment, therefore, the exporter would not know whether his sale would be profitable or not. A recent agreement between Argentina and the EEC would give some relief to the South American exporter by eliminating the weekly adjustment and maintaining the variable surcharge for three weeks.

As a result of the Kennedy Round of tariff negotiations, the nominal external tariff for beef of the EEC was reduced from 20 to 16 percent ad valorem, but this applies only to a limited amount of frozen beef. Levies on Argentine chilled beef can be as high as 100 percent. On an average, Argentina could compete effectively in the EEC up to about half this tariff level.

[25] See, for instance, the speech by Herrell de Graff of the American Meat Institute, 17 March 1965, in which he discounts Argentina as a major beef exporter in the future (reproduced in U.S. Senate, 89th Cong., Select Committee on Small Business, *Hearings...*, 1965).

most successful recent instances of private development without much public support took place in Mexico and Central America.

In Argentina and Uruguay, export taxes on meat have been levied for a long time.[26] These obviously have constituted disincentives, but whether they actually curtailed production and exports is not certain. Foreign sales were regulated by trade agreements and contracts, and, while the foreign meat packers were squeezed, the intent has been to maintain the income of domestic producers. Government price policies in Latin America, as in most countries of the world, have the objective of keeping producer prices high and consumer prices low. But wherever such policies are entrusted to agencies that have inadequately trained staff and are subject to much political control the regulations become confusing and inconsistent, as was the case in Argentina, Brazil, and Uruguay.

In New Zealand deficiency payments are provided for producers to cover any major divergence between internal and export prices. Similar arrangements were introduced in other major exporting countries, such as Denmark. These subsidies are designed to stabilize internal prices and thus give the domestic producers greater security.

After reducing the nominal tax burden on the livestock sector, in 1962 Argentina established a system of income tax rebates for the producers of beef for export. By themselves such subsidies cannot accomplish much, especially if, as it is claimed, Argentine ranchers have been able to avoid paying high taxes in the past. But subsidies do provide a propitious climate within which programs for raising the supply of beef can be more successful.

It has been estimated that, given present technical knowledge, Argentina has the potential to triple its beef production, and Uruguay could obtain a fourfold increase. Progress needs to be made in three major areas: pasture improvement, improvement in the pasture-crop rotation system, and disease control. While the River Plate region has rich soils, it is relatively deficient in phosphates. It has been shown that with the application of phosphate fertilizers even natural pastures can be improved to increase their carrying capacity of cattle substantially. This is particularly relevant for Uruguay.

While it may appear that livestock and grains compete for the same lands, they should be considered complementary enterprises in the River Plate region, even though grain is generally not fed to cattle.[27] A better managed crop-

livestock rotation system would permit a significant expansion of both cereals and livestock, increasing the carrying capacity of land by about half. Adequate disease control could raise production by about 30 percent. Thus with fertilizers (phosphates); additional acreages of seeded pastures, including improved varieties of perennials and alfalfa; and an expansion and improvement of the rotational grazing system, a threefold increase in the carrying capacity could be obtained for most of the pampas region. Combined with the use of supplementary rations and disease control, meat output per hectare could be raised from the present level of 100 to 150 kilograms to about 500 kilograms in the pampas. Both Argentina and Uruguay have the natural resources to maintain more than double their present livestock numbers. With the application of known technology, this could result in a threefold increase in meat production in Argentina, while the gains to Uruguay could be substantially higher.[28]

In nearly every country of the region there are now government initiatives designed to expand domestic livestock production. The National Institute of Agricultural Technology (INTA) in Argentina, the Consejo Nacional de Ganadería in Mexico, and similar agencies in other countries seek to improve productivity levels in stock farming. These efforts concentrate mainly on disease control and pasture management. Other public interests are concerned with improvement in marketing practices.

Significant advances in combating disease can be expected within the near future. Foot-and-mouth disease has already been eradicated in Mexico and Central America and is under control in Argentina and most other areas of the region. A complete eradication of this disease in South America is unlikely in the short run because of the presence of the virus in almost all animals. However, vaccination practices can prevent a major epidemic.

The adoption of better and modern pasture management practices on a large scale is a difficult and slower process. It involves pasture-grain rotation; experimentation with fertilizers; irrigation; cultivation of grasses, legumes, and other crops; mechanization; and all techniques that would permit an economical increase in the supply of feed and diminish the dependency on seasonal growth. As already indicated, productivity levels in the River Plate countries, although considerably below those in countries producing with intensive methods (Europe and the United States), are not too far from those in Oceania. However, fertility of the pampas will have to be replenished artifically if Argentina and Uruguay are to compete with the well-managed pastures of Australia and New Zealand in the long run. The introduction and acceptance of improvements in the region are hampered by a shortage of skilled personnel and the structure of land tenure. Training manpower and achieving land reform take time.

Under Latin America's extensive conditions of production the use of grain for cattle feed is unlikely to play a

---

[26] Export retention taxes were discontinued during the early 1960s, but in the massive March 1967 devaluation in Argentina, export retentions were reimposed on traditional exports, including meat, in order to reduce large windfalls on those sales abroad which would have been profitable even without the devaluation. The intent is to reduce the retention taxes gradually as internal prices rise.

[27] Short-run considerations can lead to a false competition for land resources. In Uruguay, for instance, serious economic difficulties have increased the need of foreign exchange. These pressures have moved government planners to recommend the shifting of good grasslands to wheat, although the country's long-run interest and economic efficiency lie in meat production. But the returns from wheat plantings come relatively fast compared with improvements in meat production, and in an economic crisis the temptation is great to postpone measures toward the long-run interest for the

sake of short-run expediency. See CIDE, *Plan Nacional de Desarrollo*. . . .

[28] See USDA, Foreign Agricultural Service, *Argentina's Livestock and Meat Industry* and *Uruguay's Livestock and Meat Industry*.

major role for some time to come. Over three-quarters of the increase in world grain use during the second half of the 1950s was for fodder. Although almost 40 percent of Argentine and one-third of Brazilian and Uruguayan cereal output is for feed, most of the feed grains are used for pigs and only a small part for beef production. So far, the cost advantage in Argentina and Uruguay has been in favor of grass feed, but it is not clear whether this will remain so in the long run. Much depends upon tastes. Currently, Latin American consumers prefer beef from grass-fed animals, and so do many of the region's customers. The markets may change to prefer barley beef, as in England, or beef from corn-fed cattle, as in the United States.

In order to increase Latin America's export potential it might be worthwhile to explore the possibilities of beef substitutes for the domestic market, particularly in the River Plate countries where per capita consumption is exceedingly high. Development of the poultry, eggs, hogs, sheep, and dairy products industries for the domestic market may prove to be a good investment for the expansion of beef exports. It would also be useful to encourage medium-sized landholders, too small to support efficient cattle farming, to concentrate on the cultivation of feed grains, oil seeds, and other inputs for the livestock sector.

In addition to providing experiment stations, research, and technical services in efforts to increase the supply of meat, governments would do well to provide direct financial incentives to foster growth in production and exports. A simple increase in the supply of beef for export is not enough if the objective is to maximize foreign exchange earnings. Marketing practices, which in general are notoriously poor in Latin America, will have to be improved. Today they are not only directly detrimental to production but also prevent supply from responding to price variation. Moderate improvements can yield great benefits.[29]

[29]For example, Argentina ships entire chilled carcasses or sides to the Smithfield Market in London for auction. Sacrifice sales occur frequently because the meat must be sold on the day of arrival, and prices are depressed because some parts of the carcass are not wanted by the purchasers. Experimentation might reveal that if, with just a little processing, only the expensive cuts were shipped to Smithfield, the net earnings to Argentina could be increased. Further processing and packaging to meet the tastes of the importing countries (especially the U.S. market) may also increase pecuniary yields.

Most recently, Argentina has experimented in shipping boned beef to Europe. Boned cuts are wrapped in airtight plastic containers for shipment. While this is very expensive, it is claimed that the transmission of the foot-and-mouth disease can be eliminated by this process. Studies have shown that the disease is transmitted, if at all, only through the inclusion of bones in shipments. If such findings will be generally accepted, the higher costs of exporting

To sum up: the earlier fear of a possible overproduction of beef has given way to the expectation of supply shortages for the next decade. If world incomes rise more rapidly than in the past, the shortage will be serious. Not counting the Communist countries, a deficiency of 700,000 tons by 1975 can be anticipated. Unless supply can increase much faster than is expected, relative prices will swell appreciably. The prospects for world beef exports are therefore very good and how far Latin America can participate in the trade expansion will depend upon access to the rising markets in the developed countries and the growth of her export surplus.

Current policies in the importing countries, combined with the comparative slowness with which obstacles to a rapid growth in supplies can be overcome, indicate that the River Plate countries' share of world trade in beef will probably continue to decline in the next decade. Consumption habits are difficult to change and it will take substantial price differentials before other meats and fish will be significantly substituted for beef in Argentina and Uruguay. The moderately declining trend in per capita consumption in these countries since the mid-1950s will have to be accelerated in order to augment considerably the availability of beef for export. In the long run, a great expansion of production for export in Latin America can be anticipated only if (a) recent efforts in technical assistance and the modernization of the cattle industry are intensified, (b) government policy in the region stops vacillating and producers come to know what to expect in regard to prices and proceeds from sales, and (c) access to world markets is assured and producers perceive a steadily rising demand. Projections for the region are not very optimistic in these respects.

New protectionist tendencies in the United States and Europe act as a dampener to efforts to expand Latin American meat exports. Unlike many agricultural improvements in crop production, most measures to significantly expand the output of meat require large-scale investments. Plantings of improved pastures are expensive and extensive additions of seeded grazing areas would require large amounts of private capital. It is doubtful if such investments will be undertaken in Latin America within the current climate of protectionist sentiment in many developed countries. There is evidence that despite favorable world prospects for meat consumption, Argentine cattlemen would rather go slowly than embark upon a massive and expensive export expansion program which might only provoke the United States and other countries to impose further import restrictions.

bone-free meats could be more than offset by the opening up of new markets.

CHAPTER 15 TABLES

TABLE 15–1. Total and Improved Pasture Area in Latin America and Selected Countries, circa 1960
(Thousands of hectares)

Country	Total, Permanent Meadows and Pastures			Improved Meadows and Pastures	
	Year	Area	Share of Total Land Area (%)	Area	Share of Total Pastures (%)
Latin America					
Argentina	1960	124,353	44.8	13,947	11.2
Brazil	1950	107,633	12.6	14,973	13.9
Chile	1955	10,331	13.9	2,910	28.2
Colombia	1960	14,606	12.8		
Dominican Republic	1950	879	18.0	608	69.2
Ecuador	1954	1,775	6.5	521	29.3
El Salvador	1961	605	29.8	101	16.7
Mexico	1950	75,156	38.1		
Panama	1961	818	10.8	687	83.5
Paraguay	1964	9,900[a]			
Peru	1961	9,522	7.4	371	3.9
Uruguay	1961	14,457	77.3	610	4.2
Venezuela	1961	16,706	18.6	2,748	16.4
United States	1964	198,208	21.5	14,623	7.4
France	1960	13,062	23.7	8,690	66.5
United Kingdom	1961	12,713	52.7	5,171	40.7
Australia	1963	444,288	57.7	16,589	3.7
New Zealand	1960	12,699	47.3	7,424	58.5

Sources: América en Cifras (Pan American Union, 1965). Information supplied by USDA, Economic Research Service. For Paraguay, FAO, *Production Yearbook, 1965*, table 1.

[a]Largely rough grazing.

TABLE 15-2. Production, Cattle Inventory, and Production Per Head of Cattle, Selected Countries, Averages for Selected Periods 1934-1965

Country	1934-38	1945-50	1954-57	1958-61	1962-65
(1) PRODUCTION OF MEAT		*(Thousands of metric tons)*			
Latin America	3,286	4,038	5,116	5,416	5,714
Argentina	1,653	1,943	2,224	2,128	2,249
Brazil	826	959	1,220	1,415	1,412
Colombia		288	288	316	386
Mexico	223	328	362	418	482
Uruguay	279	246	255	270	326
United States	3,617	4,981	6,982	6,951	8,264
Canada	333	473	604	612	800
France	998	879	1,332	1,379	1,640
United Kingdom	632	558	782	826	893
Australia	578	556	764	782	976
New Zealand	166	186	239	249	292
(2) NUMBER OF CATTLE		*(Thousands of head)*			
Latin America	127,200	148,700	176,032	194,112	219,052
Argentina	33,762	41,150	44,730	42,289	42,773
Brazil	40,807	46,200	62,338	71,940	81,033
Colombia	8,010	11,500	12,096	14,935	15,358
Mexico	11,716	13,530	16,675	20,250	30,205
Uruguay	8,297	7,875	7,425	7,779	8,718
United States	66,706	78,951	95,894	94,567	106,492
Canada	8,246	8,883	9,805	10,448	11,561
France	15,500	15,073	17,394	18,626	21,107
United Kingdom	8,798	9,973	10,713	11,251	11,650
Australia	13,285	13,971	16,280	16,746	18,214
New Zealand	4,449	4,723	5,760	6,074	6,756
(3) PRODUCTION/CATTLE NUMBERS (1 ÷ 2)		*(Kilograms)*			
Latin America	25.8	27.2	29.1	27.9	26.1
Argentina	49.0	47.2	49.7	50.3	52.6
Brazil	20.2	20.8	19.6	19.7	17.1
Colombia		25.0	23.8	21.2	25.1
Mexico	19.0	24.2	21.7	20.6	16.0
Uruguay	33.6	31.2	34.3	34.7	37.4
United States	54.2	63.1	72.8	73.5	77.6
Canada	40.4	53.2	61.6	58.6	69.2
France	64.4	58.3	76.6	74.0	77.7
United Kingdom	71.8	56.0	73.0	73.4	76.7
Australia	43.5	39.8	46.9	46.7	53.6
New Zealand	37.3	39.4	41.5	41.0	43.2

Source: USDA, Foreign Agricultural Service circulars, *Livestock and Meat* and *World Meat Production*, various issues.

TABLE 15–3. Argentina: Production of Beef and Veal, 1914-1966
(Thousands of metric tons)

Year	For Export	For Domestic Consumption	Total
1914-19	588	464	1,053
1920-24	618	703	1,321
1925-29	746	897	1,643
1930-34	538	898	1,435
1935-39	616	1,052	1,667
1940-44	660	1,038	1,698
1945-49	480	1,345	1,825
1950-54	284	1,574	1,858
1955-59	553	1,760	2,314
1960	385	1,498	1,883
1961	396	1,749	2,145
1962	545	1,834	2,379
1963	768	1,685	2,453
1964	585	1,435	2,019
1965	502	1,493	1,995
1966	586	1,801	2,387

Source: Estadísticas Básicas, 1964, 1966, Departamento de Información Estadística, Argentina, Junta Nacional de Carne, Subgerencia de Investigaciones Económicas.

TABLE 15–4. Argentina: Yields Per Head of Cattle Slaughtered, 1914-1963
(Kilograms)

Year	For Export	For Domestic Consumption	Total
1914-19	306	211	254
1920-24	298	201	237
1925-29	272	197	225
1930-34	295	204	231
1935-39	271	196	218
1940-44	279	199	224
1945-49	266	200	214
1950-54	240	209	213
1955-59	234	204	211
1960	242	207	213
1961	230	206	210
1962	218	197	203
1963	224	200	207

Source: Argentina, Junta Nacional de Carne, *Estadísticas Básicas, 1964.*

TABLE 15–5. World Per Capita Meat Consumption,[a] Prewar to 1967
(Kilograms)

Country	Prewar[b]	Averages 1946-50	1951-55	1956-60	1961	1962	1963	1964	1965	1966	1967
Latin America											
Argentina	95.0	104.5	100.9	100.0	95.9	98.6	98.2	77.0	81.0	91.8	96.4
Brazil	24.1	23.6	27.7	29.1	25.9	25.9	25.5	25.9	24.5	23.6	23.2
Chile	33.2	35.9	24.1	26.8	26.8	25.5	23.2	23.2	19.5	25.5	24.1
Colombia		27.7	26.4	26.8	27.7	28.2	27.3	27.7	27.3	23.6	22.3
Cuba	35.0	38.6	38.6	37.7[c]							
Mexico	17.3	18.6	18.6	19.1	18.2	18.6	18.2	17.7	17.7	17.3	16.8
Paraguay			54.5	57.7	51.8	47.7	45.4	50.5	50.0	61.4	61.4
Peru				14.5	14.1	15.0	15.9	15.9	15.9	15.9	15.9
Uruguay	102.3	99.5	123.6	110.0	95.9	98.9	110.0	107.0	117.0	95.9	103.2
Venezuela			20.0	20.9	25.0	24.5	25.5	26.4	25.5	24.1	25.0
North America											
United States	57.7	67.7	68.6	72.3	73.2	74.1	76.8	79.5	75.9	77.7	80.9
Canada	51.4	58.2	58.6	61.8	61.4	61.4	63.6	66.4	65.0	65.9	67.7
Western Europe											
France	44.1	40.9	50.9	56.4	63.6	65.5	64.5	65.0	65.5	69.5	72.3
Italy	17.3	13.2	17.3	22.7	24.1	25.9	27.7	27.7	27.3	28.2	30.5
United Kingdom	57.3	45.9	49.1	57.7	64.1	65.5	67.7	65.0	63.6	62.7	62.7
West Germany	51.4	27.7	42.3	47.3	53.2	55.9	55.5	55.9	55.0	55.5	56.4
Soviet Union	19.5		24.1	28.2	28.6	30.9	32.3	27.7	34.5	33.2	32.3
Africa											
Union of South Africa	30.9	34.5	33.6	35.5	34.5	34.5	38.6	35.5	35.9	35.0	35.4
Asia											
Japan			2.3	3.6	4.5	5.5	5.9	6.8	6.8	9.1	9.1
Philippines			6.8	11.8	10.0	11.4	10.9	11.4	12.3	16.4	16.4
Oceania											
Australia	111.4	91.4	97.3	104.1	93.2	98.2	98.6	99.5	95.5	92.3	87.3
New Zealand	96.4	96.4	98.2	100.9	103.6	105.9	105.9	105.9	106.4	100.5	101.4

Source: USDA, Foreign Agricultural Service circular, *Livestock and Meats: Consumption, 1961, 1966, 1967, 1969.*

[a]Carcass weight basis; includes beef, veal, pork, mutton, lamb, goat, and horsemeat; excludes edible variety meats, lard, rabbit, and poultry meat.

[b]Prewar average is for years 1935-39 for United States and Canada; 1934-38 for other countries listed.

[c]1956-59 average.

TABLE 15–6. Composition of Meat Consumption in the Major Importing Countries, 1930s, 1950-52, and 1959-61
    (Percentages of total meat consumption)

Country and Period	Beef and Veal	Mutton and Lamb	Pork	Poultry
United States				
Prewar	42	4	37	10
1950-52	37	2	39	14
1959-61	43	2	31	17
United Kingdom[a]				
Prewar	37	17	31	4
1950-52	32	17	27	5
1959-61	30	16	32	8
West Germany				
Prewar	34	1	55	3
1950-52	35	2	53	3
1959-61	33	1	53	7
Italy				
Prewar	43	6	25	9
1950-52	44	6	23	8
1959-61	47	3	25	12

Source: FAO, *The World Meat Economy* (1965), table 4.

[a]Excluding imported canned meat.

TABLE 15–7. Latin America: Share of Calories and Protein Supplied by Meat, Average, 1959-61

Subregion	Avg. 1959-61 Population	Calories			Protein		
		Total	Meat	Share from Meat	Total	Meat	Share from Meat
	(000)	*(Number per day)*		*(%)*	*(Grams per day)*		*(%)*
Mexico	34,934	2,580	136	5.3	67.8	7.2	10.6
Central America and Caribbean	32,328	2,240	144	6.4	54.2	8.2	15.1
Brazil	70,551	2,710	205	7.6	65.0	10.8	16.6
River Plate	22,753	3,200	636	19.9	101.0	38.3	37.9
Other South America	51,549	2,260	178	7.9	57.3	9.8	17.1
Latin America	212,115	2,560	224	8.8	65.8	12.5	19.0

Source: Computed from data in USDA, *World Food Budget, 1970*, Foreign Agricultural Service Economic Report no. 19, October 1964; and USDA, *Food Balances for 24 Countries of the Western Hemisphere, 1959-61*, Economic Research Service, Foreign Regional Analysis Division.

TABLE 15-8. World Exports of Beef and Veal (Fresh, Chilled, and Frozen), 1934-1966
(Thousands of metric tons)

Region or Country	Avg. 1934-38	Avg. 1948-50	1950	1951	1952	1953	1954	1955	1956	1957	1958	1959	1960	1961	1962	1963	1964	1965	1966
Latin America	507	338	256	183	145	167	156	205	404	421	456	419	367	362	493	650	601	493	522
Argentina	409	256	172	112	97	113	105	192	363	355	370	345	280	271	389	532	421	349	401
Brazil	43	18	11	5	2	2		1	9	27	33	23	6	15	13	13	19	36	21
Dominican Republic		3	4	2	1	2	2						3		2				
Mexico		4	8	2	4	7	4	9	5	8	30	22	19	26	28	34	23	22	28
Uruguay	54	55	62	62	41	43	45	4	27	32	19	22	52	43	55	65	122	65	55
United States	2	2	1	1	1	7	6	8	31	32	4	4	6	5	5	5	17	15	8
Canada	5	46	38	42	30	12	8	4	6	22	24	10	8	13	9	8	15	36	27
Western Europe	22	39	37	58	81	93	162	144	112	164	156	181	250	267	357	370	299	296	326
Eastern Europe[a]	3	4	4		2	1	17	23	25	17	17	16	24	66	122	116	98	116	114
Asia	8	1	1					1		1		1					1	1	2
Africa	23	8	5	9	9	14	20	18	14	13	14	25	25	32	33	37	43	46	57
Oceania	155	145	129	107	96	203	175	245	245	278	284	322	292	233	369	398	428	442	379
World Total	730	580	470	400	360	500	545	650	837	948	955	979	973	979	1,342	1,586	1,482	1,450	1,467
Latin American Share (%)	69	58	54	46	40	33	29	32	48	44	48	43	38	37	37	41	41	33	33

Sources: FAO, Trade Yearbook; FAO, Meat: Statistical Information on Trade and Prices (1966, 1967).

[a]Includes Yugoslavia.

TABLE 15-9. Latin America: Exports of Live Cattle, 1934-1966
(Thousand head)

Country	Avg. 1934-38	Avg. 1948-50	1950	1951	1952	1953	1954	1955	1956	1957	1958	1959	1960	1961	1962	1963	1964	1965	1966
Latin America	413	407	222	226	314	292	129	382	350	610	707	603	642	838	1,115	943	614	798	804
Argentina	81	216	143	134	100	61	38	41	134	120	70	89	152	171	250	292	166	102	119
Bolivia		3	6	2	2	1	1			1		6						10	
Brazil	1	1							1	1						2	4	8	3
Colombia	1	12	12	10	10	7	4	10	1						1	2	3	57	46
Costa Rica																5	14	13	10
Dominican Republic	6	4	2	1			3	2	4	5	9	18	8		9				
El Salvador	2	24	15	21	18	32	32	21	34	30	39	21	17	18	21	29	14	10	19
Honduras	9	35	30	36	37	33	30	44	42	46	49	40	34	48	43	43	33	25	
Mexico	200		5	18	124	135	5	243	111	351	491	374	396	550	766	553	358	557	590
Nicaragua	2	15			20	22	17	20	11	26	21	45	20	18	10	6	3	3	3
Panama	10							1	3	3	1	3	1	(b)	7	4	7	5	5
Uruguay	66	2	4	2				1		3	2		1	1	1	6	5	6	7
World Total	2,165	1,850	2,015	1,900	1,700	1,720	1,852	1,965	2,178	3,064	3,227	2,789	2,999	3,841	3,707	3,681	3,809	4,410	4,119
Latin American Share (%)	19	22	11	12	19	17	7	16	16	20	22	21	21	22	30	24	16	18	20

Sources: FAO, Trade Yearbook; FAO, Meat: Statistical Information on Trade and Prices (1966, 1967).

TABLE 15–10. Latin America: Volume and Value of Meat Exports, 1950-1967
(Thousands of metric tons and millions of U.S. dollars)

Country	1950	1951	1952	1953	1954	1955	1956	1957	1958	1959	1960	1961	1962	1963	1964	1965	1966	1967
Argentina																		
Fresh, chilled, and frozen	238	179	166	201	204	299	488	478	481	441	375	350	489	670	543	469	560	546
Canned	99	114	71	68	81	95	89	128	170	95	61	76	71	96	60	51	76	107
Value of meat exports	79.0	154.5	121.8	154.7	155.6	205.6	241.0	256.6	295.4	259.3	219.3	217.4	228.5	334.1	328.7	324.5	393.0	382.4
Share total exports (%)	6.7	13.2	17.7	13.7	15.1	22.1	25.6	25.9	26.4	29.8	20.4	22.6	18.8	24.5	23.3	21.7	24.6	26.1
Brazil																		
Fresh, chilled, and frozen	13	8	4	6	1	2	10	28	36	26	11	18	14	14	24	43	32	22
Canned	9	4	2	1	1	4	3	5	12	37	9	15	12	7	8	19	13	8
Value of meat exports	9.5	5.8	2.4	2.3	2.4	6.0	7.8	14.0	25.2	41.2	14.8	22.9	15.1	11.2	20.8	46.5	30.2	12.1
Share total exports (%)	0.7	0.3	0.2	0.2	0.2	0.4	0.5	1.0	2.0	3.2	1.2	1.6	1.2	0.8	1.5	2.9	1.7	0.7
Dominican Republic																		
Fresh, chilled and frozen	4	2	1		2	1		1	2	3	3	2						
Value of meat exports	1.8	1	0.7	1.5	1.2	0.6	0.3	0.3	1.2	1.7	1.8	1.3	0.2					
Share total exports (%)	2.0	0.8	0.6	1.4	1.0	0.5	0.2	0.2	1.0	1.3	1.0	0.9	0.1					
Mexico																		
Fresh, chilled, and frozen	11	2	4	8	5	9	5	10	33	25	22	29	33	39	27	26	33	27
Canned	10	25	23	8	8													
Value of meat exports	3.6	14.4	14.8	4.9	4.1	2.6	1.7	2.2	12.1	10.7	10.4	16.5	23.0	28.6	19.6	18.3	28.9	23.4
Share total exports (%)	0.7	2.2	2.2	0.8	0.6	0.3	0.2	0.3	1.6	1.4	1.4	2.0	2.5	2.9	1.9	1.5	2.3	2.2
Paraguay																		
Fresh, chilled, and frozen	4[b]	3[b]				3	7	8	1	1	12	17	14	25	4	6	3	23
Canned	12	8							11	14					17	20	16	
Value of meat exports			0.6	1.5	2.1	2.3	4.6	3.7	8.2	9.6	7.1	8.6	7.5	10.5	14.7	17.8	13.8	17.2
Share total exports (%)			1.9	5	6.2	6.6	12.5	11.3	24.0	30.8	26.4	28.2	22.3	26.2	29.6	35.1	28.2	35.4
Uruguay																		
Fresh, chilled, and frozen	79	73	56	52	54	6	36	38	22	25	52	43	55	67	129	85	69	
Canned	22	5	13	16	22	5	10	16	8	8	8	10		12	11	12	4	
Value of meat exports	43.2	44.6	40.6	44.2	45.3	7.2	22.2	27.5	14.6	18.5	30.8	27.4	31.4	33.4	74.3	58.7	41.5	40.4
Share total exports (%)	17.0	18.9	19.5	16.4	18.3	3.9	10.5	21.5	10.5	18.9	23.8	15.7	20.4	20.2	41.5	30.9	22.6	25.2
Latin America (incl. others)																		
Fresh, chilled, and frozen	346	264	231	269	267	316	540	557	579	531	476	458	615	821	754	660	735	719
Canned	150	164	109	95	113	107	109	157	201	154	90	121	111	143	99	104	111	145
Value of meat exports	149.1	223.3	180.9	209.1	210.6	224.2	277.5	302.3	356.7	340.9	284.2	294.0	305.7	417.9	458.2	465.9	507.4	474
Share of total exports																		
Major exporters[c] (%)	8.6	14.0	17.6	14.1	15.5	18.8	22.4	25.3	27.3	25.2	20.8	21.7	19.0	24.0	25.5	26.7	27.7	26.3
Total Latin America (%)	2.2	2.8	2.5	2.7	2.6	2.8	3.2	3.4	4.2	4.0	3.2	3.3	3.3	4.2	4.3	4.5	4.6	4.3

[a] Estimated from 1950 free exchange rate and data in pesos.
[b] Estimate, using same exchange rate as for exports of hides; approximately correct to nearest $million.
[c] Meat exports as share of total exports of Argentina, Paraguay, and Uruguay only.

Sources: FAO, Trade Yearbook; FAO, Meat: Statistical Information on Trade and Prices (1966 to 1967); FAO, The World Meat Economy, Commodity Bulletin No. 40 (1965); UN, Yearbook of International Trade Statistics. Argentina, Estadísticas Básicas, 1964, 1966. IMF, International Financial Statistics, supp. to 1964/65 and 1966/67 issues.

TABLE 15-11. Argentina: Exports of Chilled Beef and Veal by Destination, Averages, 1919-1966
(Thousands of metric tons)

Year	Total	United Kingdom	Western Europe[a]	Eastern Europe and Soviet Union	Latin America	Others
1919-24	481.0	394.9	83.1	(b)	(b)	3.0
1925-29	603.4	482.0	118.0	(b)	(b)	3.4
1930-34	409.9	382.9	25.3	(b)	(b)	1.7
1935-39	426.0	361.7	60.8	(b)		3.5
1940-44	340.9	335.4	1.2	(b)	2.9	1.4
1945-49	276.6	224.2	34.6	3.3[c]	11.4	3.1
1950-54	119.0	86.4	18.6	1.1	7.2	5.7
1955-59	323.9	231.6	76.6	6.0	7.3	2.4
1960-63	367.3	194.2	144.3	10.9	13.1	4.8
1964-66	390.0	124.3	257.7	6.8	6.9	1.4

Source: Argentina, *Estadísticas Básicas, 1964, 1966.*

[a]Western Europe figure does not include United Kingdom. Before 1957 East Germany is included in Western Europe.
[b]Included in "others."
[c]Figure for 1948.

TABLE 15-12. World Imports of Beef and Veal (Fresh, Chilled, and Frozen), 1934-1966
(Thousands of metric tons)

Region or Country	Avg. 1934-38	Avg. 1948-50	1950	1951	1952	1953	1954	1955	1956	1957	1958	1959	1960	1961	1962	1963	1964	1965	1966
Latin America	1	15	10	7	19	9	15	13	10	5	4	10	7	13	15	13	26	25	32
Brazil				1	9	4	6					2							
Chile	1		4				4	8	6			2	4	8	8	5	13	9	14
Peru		11		6	10	5	5	5	4	5	4	5	2	5	7	8	13	16	18
United States	1	35	32	43	33	12	8	12	14	57	163	238	188	309	469	523	368	316	412
Canada				1		1	2	4	2	4	6	10	8	7	11	11	6	10	9
Western Europe	675	480	430	268	238	388	351	470	679	708	623	587	702	551	682	916	975	987	1,002
Soviet Union	3					6	61	29											
Eastern Europe[a]	15	10		4	2	2	29	36		2	8	46	16	54	65	101	55	109	147
Asia	5	8	9	15	12	6	12	11	16	44	19	13	16	17	25	30	39	32	41
Africa		8	10	11	12	17	18	16	17	26	16	14	18	24	18	27	29	33	55
Oceania		1	1	2	1		2	1							1	1	1	1	1
World Total	710	570	500	360	320	450	500	569	748	857	843	955	962	932	1,214	1,554	1,458	1,546	1,597
L.A. Share (%)	0.1	2.1	2.0	1.9	6.3	2.0	3.0	2.5	1.3	0.6	0.5	1.0	0.7	1.3	1.2	0.8	1.7	1.6	2.0

Sources: FAO, Trade Yearbook; FAO, Meat: Statistical Information on Trade and Prices (1966, 1967).

[a]Includes Yugoslavia.

TABLE 15-13. World Imports of Live Cattle, 1934-1966
(Thousand head)

Region or Country	Avg. 1934-38	Avg. 1948-50	1950	1951	1952	1953	1954	1955	1956	1957	1958	1959	1960	1961	1962	1963	1964	1965	1966
Latin America	187	306	204	258	185	195	127	155	192	246	236	194	281	326	378	406	210	176.8	227.1
Argentina	5	20	8	9	10	12	4	1	1	1	4	2	2	1			4	8.2	2.1
Bolivia	21	21	44	35	19	10	1	20	23	12	1	2	16	15	15	11	13	12.0	4.2
Brazil	23	103		117	75	66	29	5	6	6					19	24	12	2.2	
Chile	26	1	62				6	10	34	80	60	55	171	207	161	132	121	79.9	69.5
Colombia	10	1			1	1		17	1	1			1		1	1			
Costa Rica				1	1				3	1	3	29	19	10	4	14	4	9.2	2.0
Cuba	9	20	18	22	21	21	27	25	29	29	33	18	14	11	13	69	11	3.4	1.3
El Salvador	4	27	25	40	29	40	32	34	42	36	50	26	17	21	28	15	39	33.8	38.2
Guatemala	2	2	2	4	3	5	4	21	19	28	9	9	15	14	13	131	11.7	28.9	17.0
Mexico	81	19	13	14	1		19	21	24	44	43	15	13	32	21	6	49.5	66.8	14.9
Paraguay	2	53	27	14	22	37	2		4	7	13	37		1	101		5.0	5.6	115.6
Peru	3	2	3	1	1	1			4				8		2	4			
Uruguay								21					1						
Venezuela			3	1	1	1	2						8						
United States	452	358	422	220	138	177	85	314	159	728	1,152	709	663	1,043	1,250	852	546.6	1,128.4	1,100.4
Canada	1,109	1	1	1	1	1	2	2	1	2	2	33	9	4	4	4	36.9	4.9	9.0
Western Europe	122	700	900	930	860	811	969	1,171	1,322	1,605	1,399	1,312	1,481	1,849	1,489	2,020	2,027.5	2,021.6	2,029.0
Soviet Union	1			1		4	3	146	187	136	121	142	158	138	136	89	93.7	114.6	128.1
Eastern Europe[a]	220	11	80	10	70	9	36	25	10	9	28	24	26	21	16	17	12.1	16.3	6.9
Asia	100	70	300	100	70	70	120	174	178	199	248	292	264	241	301	322	320.7	375.2	396.2
Africa[b]		290	300	300	300	310	456	143	172	179	164	246	301	349	308	352	296.9	219.6	225.4
Oceania		1	1	1	1	1	2	1	1	1	1	1		1	1	1	0.7	1.4	0.9
World Total	2,130	1,840	1,950	1,850	1,560	1,600	1,811	2,277	2,048	2,974	3,212	2,970	3,201	3,968	3,897	4,080	3,632	4,161	4,155
L.A. Share (%)	8.8	16.6	10.5	13.9	11.9	12.2	7.0	6.8	9.4	8.3	7.3	6.5	8.8	8.2	9.7	10.0	5.8	4.2	5.4

Sources: FAO, Trade Yearbook; FAO, Meat: Statistical Information on Trade and Prices (1966, 1967).

[a]Includes Yugoslavia.
[b]Various surveys indicate that official figures substantially underestimate the volume of imports.

TABLE 15–14. Prices of Argentine Cattle, Buenos Aires, and Chilled Beef, United Kingdom, 1934-1966

Year	Fat Steers for Export, Buenos Aires (1)		Argentine Chilled Beef, Hindquarters, Smithfield (2)
	(pesos/kg.)	*(U.S. ¢/kg.)*	*(pence/lb.)*
1934			8.4
1935			8.1
1936			8.1
1937			9.5
1938	0.268	8.7	
1939			
1940	0.265	7.6	
1941	0.294	8.7	
1942	0.370	11.0	
1943	0.367	10.8	
1944	0.372	11.1	
1945	0.378	11.2	
1946	0.412	12.3	
1947	0.506	15.1	
1948	0.534	15.9	
1949	0.613	18.3	14.4
1950	0.744	19.4	15.8
1951	1.210	24.2	17.4
1952	1.62	32.4	21.8
1953	1.96	39.1	24.4
1954	2.00	39.9	26.1
1955	1.94		28.3
1956	2.33		22.3
1957	2.49		23.9

TABLE 15–14.–Continued

Year	Fat Steers for Export Buenos Aires (1)		Argentine Chilled Beef, Hindquarters, Smithfield (2)
	(pesos/kg.)	*(U.S. ¢/kg.)*	*(pence/lb.)*
1958	3.90		25.5
1959	13.54	16.9	28.1
1960	14.83	17.9	28.6
1961	14.34	17.3	26.5
1962	17.54	15.4	27.8
1963	24.62	17.8	25.9
1964	41.54	29.6	32.7
1965	51.39	30.3	35.1
1966	54.89	26.3	33.0

Sources: (1) 1946-66 – FAO, *Production Yearbook*, prices as reported. 1938 and 1940-45 – Commonwealth Economic Committee, *Meat: A Summary*, index of wholesale cattle prices, base 1938 = 100. Linked to FAO series by an index of 250 for a price of 0.67 pesos per kilogram, the average for years 1946-51. Price converted to U.S. cents by basic buying rate, 3.36 pesos per dollar, 1938 and 1940-45. FAO prices for 1946-54 and 1958-63; no data available for 1955-58 (official rate of 18 pesos per dollar, free rate increasing from 36.10 to 70.00).

(2) 1949-66 – USDA, Economic Research Service. 1934-37 – Commonwealth Economic Committee, *Meat: A Summary*, wholesale prices, mixed hind- and forequarters, at Birmingham, Leeds, London, and Manchester. Price for these years in pence of post-1949 pound, £1 = U.S. $2.80.

TABLE 15–15. Wholesale Beef Prices, 1961-1966
(U.S. cents per pound)

Market		1961	1962	1963	1964	1965	1966
United States:	New York (1)	40.4	44.2	39.8	37.9	39.3	
	Chicago (1)	37.2	41.8	36.5	34.8	38.0[a]	39.0[a]
United Kingdom:	domestic (2)	26.8	30.3	29.2	36.4	38.6	
	Argentina (3)	30.9	32.4	30.2	38.2		
Italy:	Milan (1)	50.1	51.5	52.6	63 5	66.0	63.0[a]
France:	Paris (1)	40.7	42.5	46.9	51.7	53.4	53.0[a]
Argentina:	Buenos Aires (1)	18.2	19.3	17.1	26.0	27.0[a]	24.0[a]

Sources: (1) U.S. Senate, 89th Cong., Select Committee on Small Business, *Hearings on the Expansion of Beef Exports*, 1st sess., 24-25 February 1965, app. III, pp. 242-43; 2nd sess., 18-19 May 1966, table 3, p. 203. Prices refer to beef comparable in quality to U.S. grade "Good." (2) Commonwealth Economic Committee, *Meat: A Review, 1963* and *1965*. (3) USDA, Economic Research Service.

[a]Estimated on basis of information in *Argentina's Livestock and Meat Industry* (FAS, M-188), USDA, Foreign Agricultural Service, June 1967, p. 7.

Chapter 16

COTTON

Cotton is one of the chief products of Latin America's agricultural sector, both as an export commodity and as an input to domestic industry. The amount of land planted to cotton, some 4.3 million hectares, is comparable to that devoted to such major crops as maize and coffee. Of a total production in the mid-1960s of about 1.6 million tons, the region exported three-fourths, providing about 10 percent of world supplies and a fourth of world trade in cotton. The revenue from these exports was some $500 million or 5 percent of total Latin American earnings of foreign exchange. On this basis alone, cotton would be an extremely important element in the region's economy. In addition, it is the principal raw material of the textile industry, the oldest and largest industry producing for the domestic market, and in many countries the largest source of manufacturing employment and income. In this respect cotton exceeds all other agricultural products in importance; only petroleum and iron ore are of comparable weight as elements of industrial consumption in Latin America.

In this survey, the production of cotton fiber and its manufacture into yarn, textiles, and other goods will be treated separately, but attention to the world industry will be largely confined to the fiber. The development and present state of the cotton textile industry in Latin America will be described, but other uses of cotton—for oil, meal, linters and so forth—will not be considered. Comparisons of cotton with other fibers will be made in general terms where necessary.[1]

World Production, Consumption, and Trade

Cotton has been grown for several thousand years in some parts of the world, particularly in India, but it did not attain widespread use until the development of spinning and weaving machinery in the eighteenth century. There-after cotton rapidly displaced wool and other natural fibers to become the world's principal source of clothing and other textiles, a position it still holds despite the competition of man-made fibers in recent decades. In the mid-sixties some 32 million hectares devoted to cotton were concentrated in Asia, Latin America, northern Africa, and the southern areas of the United States and the Soviet Union (see table 16-1). The total area has not expanded in the last thirty years, since the increased production has come entirely from improvement in yields. There has also been a marked redistribution, as the cotton area in the United States has been halved and Latin America has taken up the largest share of the difference.

World cotton production expanded rapidly in the late eighteenth and early nineteenth centuries, as the United States became the largest producer. The United States still holds that rank, but its output has not risen since the 1920s while the world total has gone from 6 million to 11 million tons (see table 16-2). Before the Great Depression, Latin America produced only a few hundred thousand tons, or about 5 percent of the total. Then under the stimulus of various protective measures for the textile industry, output increased to 10 percent or more of the total and has since grown at roughly the same rate as world production. Until the 1950s this expansion was due almost entirely to greater output in the traditional producers—Argentina, Brazil, Mexico, and Peru. Yields rose sharply in Mexico, but elsewhere expansion of area accounted for the increase. In the last decade a fall in coffee prices has led to the transfer of much coffee land to cotton, or to the planting of cotton in areas where coffee might otherwise have been grown. Cotton has become a major crop in Colombia, El Salvador, Guatemala, and Nicaragua, and yields are high in all these countries. The average yield in Latin America equals that for the world, but the variation is extreme, from returns as low as those of Asia to others, among the highest in the world, obtained in Peru and Central America. The differences in yields may be attributed partly to the quality of land used for cotton. In Peru cotton is grown only in the rich coastal valleys, and only on the better land in Mexico, Central America, and Colombia; poorer land is used in Argentina and Brazil. Differences in cultivation practices, and

Note: Cotton tables 16–1 to 16–8 appear on pp. 437–46.

[1] The principal sources of statistical information about cotton are the publications of the International Cotton Advisory Committee (ICAC), particularly *Cotton: World Statistics*. Studies of aspects of the world cotton industry are also published at intervals. Further statistical information comes from the publications of FAO or ECLA. Other sources are noted in the text.

particularly in irrigation, appear to be more important in explaining the variation. Almost all cotton is irrigated in Mexico and Peru and in the higher-yielding areas of Colombia; fertilizers are also more widely used in those countries than in Brazil. The sizable increases in yields in Mexico, Central America, and Colombia are due almost entirely to improved practices or the introduction of better varieties; geographic shifts have been relatively insignificant.[2]

Cotton is classified according to the length of the fibers, and is also graded as to color, foreign matter in the bale, and other properties. Most of the world's cotton is of medium staple length, between one and 1-3/32 inches, with some 5 percent, known as extra long staple, over 1-3/8 inches long. Generally the price of cotton increases with staple length, with the longest types traded commanding a premium of 50 percent or more over the price of fibers of one inch or less. Premiums and discounts are also given for the different grades at any one length. Cotton is therefore a complex commodity, or group of commodities; and very slight differences in length or grade can greatly affect the suitability of fiber for producing different yarns or fabrics or taking particular finishes, or can influence the waste involved in processing.[3] The different types also differ in their susceptibility to substitution by or for other fibers.

The price of cotton in world trade fell from over 20 cents per pound to below 10 cents in the Depression, and then rose to over 40 cents in 1950-52. From the late 1950s the price was fairly steady for a decade—about 30 cents for 1-1/16 inch middling cotton (see table 16-3). The differential for extra long staple cotton behaves rather like that between mild and Brazilian coffees, being greater, both absolutely and relatively, at low prices than at high, so that the price of long-fibered cotton is more stable than that for short fibers (see chap. 10, table 10-6). The elasticity of cotton supply is fairly high, since the bulk of production is from annual rather than perennial plants. Cotton prices are particularly responsive to increased demand in wartime, but otherwise they have been as stable as those of most primary commodities and much more steady than those of tropical tree crops.

In most end uses, two or more fibers are substitutable for one another; thus the demand for any one fiber varies more, and depends on more factors, than does the total demand for fibers of all kinds. Total fiber requirements appear to depend heavily on income, both because of a fairly high income-elasticity of demand for clothing and household textiles, and because of the increased need for fibers in a variety of industrial applications as income rises. The distribution of this demand among cotton, other natural fibers such as wool, and the cellulosic and synthetic man-made fibers depends on the relative importance of different uses, on the price and availability of the various fibers, and on such matters as climate and tastes.

If total availability or use of cotton, including manufactures, is considered, then Asia and the Communist countries together absorb somewhat more than half the world consumption of 9 million tons (see table 16-4). Asia alone, however, accounts for half the consumption of raw cotton, and exports more than half the cotton consumed in the form of yarn, cloth, and apparel. China is the largest importer of cotton manufactures, chiefly from Japan, Hong Kong and Pakistan. By either measure—raw cotton use or absorption of cotton in all forms—the United States and Western Europe take most of the remainder, but the share of both is much smaller than for most commodities exported by Latin America. Outside of Asia, net trade in cotton manufactures is small; Africa is the chief importer. Formerly net exporters, the United States and Western Europe have become net importers in the last two decades.

Since 1950 cotton consumption has increased by about 2.6 million tons, with a large expansion in Latin America, Africa, Asia and the Communist countries. Consumption has been nearly constant in Western Europe, however, and in North America it has declined considerably. This absence of growth in cotton use in high-income countries reflects the declining share of cotton in total world fiber consumption, from over 70 percent to just over 60 percent by weight in the last decade. Wool also lost ground slightly, while the artificial fibers increased from 20 to 30 percent of the total.[4] Although substitution has been most rapid in North America, per capita consumption of cotton is still extremely high there because total fiber consumption is large and growing steadily. Consumption of 5 kilograms or more of cotton per person occurs in only a few other countries, including the United Kingdom, France, West Germany, Japan, Argentina, and the Soviet Union. In most poor areas consumption is about 2 kilograms per capita; for Latin America as a whole the average is slightly over 3 kilograms, or just equal to the world average.

World trade in raw cotton is relatively free. No tariffs are levied on cotton imported into the United Kingdom, the Common Market, or Japan, or on short-staple cotton into the United States. Tariffs in the smaller import markets are generally low and nondiscriminatory among suppliers.[5] There is no form of international control. The chief exception to free trade in cotton is the policy of the United States, which in the early 1960s was the cause of a steadily increasing surplus. Imports into the United States are limited by quotas, and in addition long and medium staple fibers pay tariffs of 4 and 8 percent respectively. Areas planted in cotton are controlled by acreage allotments and support prices to growers. These policies raised the U.S. price well above the world price and discouraged exports, but as stocks built up an export subsidy of about one-fourth the world price was granted between 1958 and 1965. The bulk of stocks was nonetheless held in the

[2] See for example, ICAC, *Studies of Factors Affecting Cotton Yields*, doc. 11/XX, revised (Washington, 1961), pp. 17, 63, 98, as well as the sources cited below for the development of cotton growing in Latin America. For Mexico, see also E. Flores, *Tratado de Economía Agrícola* (Mexico: Fondo de Cultura Económica, 1961), pp. 349 ff., and for Colombia, ICAC, *New Developments in Cotton Production Research*, doc. 5/XXII (Delhi, April 1963), pp. 36-40.

[3] For a thorough discussion, see H. B. Brown, *Cotton* (McGraw-Hill, 1927), pp. 351 ff.

[4] GATT, *A Study on Cotton Textiles* (Geneva, 1966), p. 13.

[5] An exception is Portugal, which obtains part of its requirements duty free from its African territories and levies a low tariff on other cotton.

United States, and subsidized releases were not large enough to cause more than a slight, steady decline in price. Furthermore, the direct controls were applied to prevent or slow increases in U.S. output, so that exports fell from over 2 million tons, or two-thirds of the world total, in the 1920s, to less than a million tons, or one-fourth of the total, four decades later. Beginning in the crop year 1965/66, the U.S. support price was sharply reduced and production declined sufficiently to reduce stocks approximately to normal levels.[6] The import restrictions have not been lifted, but there is nonetheless a marked shift toward free trade and away from problems of surplus accumulation. In this respect cotton is unique among the major Latin American agricultural exports.

No country's policies have so pronounced an effect on world cotton production and trade as do those of the United States. In Syria and Egypt the share of land planted to cotton is controlled, and in Egypt the distribution among varieties is also fixed. Most other producing countries simply apply a tax to cotton exports, either to raise revenue or to finance a government exporting board. The rates are generally so low as to have little effect on supplies. Export quotas are extremely rare. Growers are guaranteed minimum prices in some countries, but government regulation of prices and production is slight or nonexistent in most producers.

World trade may be most affected by the restraint on imports applied by producing countries; imports of the grades and staple lengths grown in a country are usually either prohibited altogether or are allowed only after the domestic crop has been sold. Textile mills are often required to take up local production at prices somewhat above the world level.[7] One effect of such policies is to increase self-sufficiency and reduce trade in short-fibered cotton, which many countries produce. Extra long staple cotton is produced in only eleven countries, of which three—the United Arab Republic, the Sudan, and Peru—account for nearly the entire amount outside the Soviet Union. Two-thirds of this production is exported, so that whereas extra-long fibers provide only 5 percent of world output they amount to 10 percent of all cotton traded and are imported in large quantities even by major short fiber producers such as the United States.[8] The import policies

of countries that do not grow cotton appear to have little effect on world production and trade. The member countries of the International Cotton Advisory Committee, an association formed to collect and publish information about the world cotton industry, have considered the formation of an international agreement to control trade in raw cotton, modelled after the agreements for wheat and tin. The high prices of the early 1950s, and the fears of a collapse as demand subsided and competition from artificial fibers grew more severe, stimulated studies of the question, but it was concluded that the market was sufficiently stable and responsive not to warrant such intervention. The problem of setting and adjusting prices and trade quotas for the many types and grades of cotton also appeared particularly formidable.[9] The question arose again in 1966, in connection with the intensified competition between cotton and synthetic fibers in the 1960s and the steady decline in cotton's share of the market for fibers of all kinds. In view of this competitive situation it appeared that the restrictions on supplies and prices which would result from international control would probably only hasten the substitution of man-made fibers for cotton and so would be detrimental to the low-income countries which export cotton.[10]

The United States exports cotton principally to Western Europe and Japan. The import demand of India is supplied chiefly by Africa and Pakistan; Pakistan now also exports large amounts to China. Latin America's chief markets are Western Europe and Japan, with smaller amounts shipped to the United States, chiefly from Mexico, and to Hong Kong and to the Soviet Union. Within Europe, the United Kingdom is the largest market for most exporters, but not for the Latin American countries, which ship large amounts to West Germany. Between 1950 and 1965 the region's exports of raw cotton more than doubled in tonnage, from 400,000 to a million tons, while the value increased somewhat less rapidly (see table 16-5). Cotton was the chief export of Mexico throughout this period, as it was of Peru until 1962, when fishmeal surpassed it. In most of those years cotton was also the second largest export of Brazil, as it is now of El Salvador, Guatemala, and Nicaragua. For the region as a whole cotton earns some $500 million annually, $160 million in Mexico and about $100 million each in Brazil and in Peru. Until 1964 cotton ranked as Latin America's fourth largest export commodity, behind coffee, petroleum, and sugar. In recent years copper exports have also exceeded those of cotton. There is a small amount of intraregional trade, amounting currently to some 60,000 tons. Nearly half this amount is taken by Chile, the only country in the region which is not suited to grow cotton. Sizable amounts are also imported by Cuba, which has a textile industry but no domestic production, and by Argentina, Uruguay, and Venezuela, all of which grow cotton. The demand is satisfied entirely by other Latin American countries; much of it is met by extra long staple fiber from Peru and most of the rest by Mexico and Brazil.

[6]Tariffs on raw cotton and other trade barriers are described in UNCTAD, *Programme for the Liberalization and Expansion of Trade in Commodities of Interest to Developing Countries*, doc. TD/11/Supp. 1, 22 December 1967, Annex pp. 5-11, and *Trade Barriers and Liberalization Possibilities in Selected Commodities*, doc. TD/11/Supp. 2, 28 December 1967, pp. 34-38. The latter includes a discussion of the changes in United States policy and their effects. See also UNCTAD, *Commodity Survey, 1967*, part III, pp. 114-16.

[7]See ICAC, *Government Regulations on Cotton*, published annually, which summarizes all regulations on production, consumption, and trade of raw cotton by member governments. See also USDA, Economic Research Service, *Agricultural Policies of Foreign Governments, Including Trade Policies Affecting Agriculture*, Agriculture Handbook no. 132 (March 1964).

[8]"Extra-long Staple Cottons: Recent Market Developments," in FAO, *Monthly Bulletin of Agricultural Economics and Statistics*, April 1965.

[9]ICAC, *Report on an International Cotton Agreement*, doc. 6/XII Second (Washington, November 1953).

[10]This was the conclusion of the 1966 meeting of the ICAC. See UNCTAD, *Commodity Survey, 1967*, part II, p. 80.

Cotton and Cotton Textiles in Latin America

Cotton is indigenous to Latin America, occurring both in perennial tree forms, as in northeastern Brazil, and in the more common annual shrub varieties elsewhere. At the time of the Spanish conquest cotton was cultivated in Brazil, Mexico, Peru, and the West Indies, and was used to make extremely fine yarns and woven textiles in both Mexico and Peru. Large areas in the region are well suited to cotton growing–throughout the northern part of Mexico, in the coastal valleys of Peru, in the Chaco of Argentina, Paraguay, and eastern Bolivia, and in both the center-south and the northeast in Brazil. In many places, however, the excellent conditions for cotton were not utilized until this century; or in areas where cotton was developed earlier it gave way to the competition of other producers or different crops.[11]

Several factors retarded the emergence of cotton as a major crop in Latin America. First, especially at harvest time its high labor requirements made it generally unsuitable as a land-settlement crop for individual farmers. The Argentine Chaco may have proved an exception to this rule early in this century, but elsewhere cotton was grown only in settled coastal regions where a large supply of labor was available.[12] In Brazil, as in the United States, slave labor was used. Second, there was no export market until fairly late in the eighteenth century, when the development of mechanical spinning and weaving allowed cotton to displace wool and flax in Europe. Third, the domestic market was likewise small, much of the population in the first centuries after the conquest being concentrated in the mountains where wool was more easily produced than cotton. Finally, when an export trade did develop it was destroyed by the competition of the United States.

In the last quarter of the eighteenth century, the demand for cotton expanded more rapidly than that for any other tropical product. A large trading company was created to promote cotton growing for export in Maranhão and nearby states in Brazil. The first shipments were made to England in 1781, and for the rest of the century Brazil was the world's foremost cotton exporter.[13] After the turn of the century the production of cotton in the southern United States, using virgin land and slave labor, expanded rapidly. Yields were lower than in Latin America, but the abundance of land and labor resulted in very low costs and the United States took Brazil's place as cotton came to exceed half the country's exports. A rapidly growing in-

ternal market also contributed to a two-thirds decline in cotton prices. The collapse of Brazil's trade led to a large migration of labor to the center-south and intensified the expansion of coffee production. Thereafter land, labor, marketing facilities, and government policies were directed to coffee in the south and to sugar in the north. There was another cotton boom during and after the United States Civil War, when shortages drove up the price markedly and the flow of resources to other crops was temporarily reversed; Brazil's largest exports were reached in 1872. Exports were much higher in the 1890s than in the 1840s, but Brazil never recovered its domination of the market. In other countries the cultivation of cotton for export is still more recent. In Mexico it followed on the irrigation and settlement of large areas in the north-central part of the country, particularly in Coahuila, in the 1920s and 1930s. In Peru it resulted partly from the shift to extra long staple Tanguis cotton at about the same time. More recently cotton has become a major export crop in Central America, in a reversal of the relationship to coffee evident in Brazil in the nineteenth century.

The domination of cotton exports by the United States in the mid-nineteenth century also contributed to the creation of the cotton textile industry in Brazil, by restricting the capacity to import textiles and making large supplies of cotton available for domestic use. The first mills were established in the northeast in the years after the tariff of 1844 gave manufacturers enough protection to compete with English imports of coarse goods in the home market. In the 1860s and 1870s the industry shifted to the south, as mills were built in Rio de Janeiro and São Paulo, partly to be close to the market and partly to use the cotton planted in São Paulo during the years of high prices. By 1866 there were 15,000 spindles in Brazil; by 1910, in the midst of a rapid expansion, the number had risen to a million.[14] The textile industry was also developed early in Mexico, beginning in Mexico City, Puebla and Orizaba in the 1830s and expanding markedly after about 1880. In Latin America, as in Europe and North America a century or more earlier, the production of textiles was one of the first processes to be industrialized. In the earliest industrial countries, however, the output of the industry went primarily to replace handmade goods, while in Latin America, even in the countries where an industry was established before 1900, it went chiefly to replace imports. Thus the production of cotton textiles is one of the first instances of import substitution, as well as of industrialization, in the region. For most countries, both processes were stimulated by the Depression and by import shortages during World War II, and the textile industry forms part of the general pattern of import-substituting industrialization of the last several decades. Generally the last stages of processing–knitting and weaving– were substituted first, with imports shifting from textiles to yarn; spinning was not undertaken until later, even in some countries with

[11] For an assessment of the Latin American potential for cotton growing, and the use made of it until about 1920, see J. A. Todd, *The World's Cotton Crops* (London: A. C. Black, 1923), pp. 130-33, 206-20; R. H. Whitbeck, *Economic Geography of South America* (McGraw-Hill, 1931), pp. 110-13, 220-21 and 344-48; and Brown, *Cotton*, pp. 14-18.

[12] Todd, *World's Cotton Crops*, states that labor shortages favored other crops over cotton in settlement in Argentina. Whitbeck, *Economic Geography. . . .*, states that in the Chaco (Entre Ríos and Corrientes provinces) cotton was in fact the chief crop on the frontier.

[13] This account of the history of cotton in Brazil is taken from C. Furtado, *The Economic Growth of Brazil* (University of California Press, 1963), pp. 97-99, 112-13, 121-22, 138-41, 156.

[14] S. J. Stein, "The Brazilian Cotton Textile Industry, 1850-1950," in S. Kuznets et al. (eds.), *Economic Growth: Brazil, India, Japan* (Duke University Press, 1955), pp. 430-47. See also the books by Todd and Whitbeck cited above.

ample supplies of cotton.[15] Where one or more stages were already established — as weaving was in Argentina, Chile, Peru, and Uruguay — the other stages were added. Substitution occurred first and most completely for the coarser grades of yarn and cloth, and in many countries the finer grades are still mostly imported; this is particularly true of yarns. The industry depended heavily on foreign assistance in its early decades for managerial and technical aid in the establishment of mills and training of a labor force; the equipment is still largely imported. Foreign capital is relatively rare and is found mostly in joint ventures with Japanese firms and in one United States enterprise in Peru.[16]

By 1960 the textile industry of Latin America included nearly 10 million spindles and over 260,000 looms; of these nearly 8 million and 190,000, respectively, were used for cotton (see table 16-6). The cotton textile industry was already mature in the larger countries, in that it could satisfy nearly all domestic demand and was growing fairly slowly; only in the smaller countries is there still room for appreciable import substitution at any stage.[17] In most countries it is the single most important industry in employment and value added, surpassed only by food processing in Argentina, metallurgical industries in Chile, and several industries in Venezuela. In South America and Mexico together textiles provide 20 percent of all industrial employment and about 3 percent of gross domestic product; except for Paraguay and Venezuela these shares are remarkably constant over a large range of income and degree of industrialization (see table 16-7). In most countries the bulk of the textile industry is based on cotton. The mills are usually located in major industrial centers, close to markets rather than to their raw materials. Of approximately 1.6 million tons of raw cotton produced in 1964, the region consumed some 790,000 tons and exported the remainder. Net imports of cotton yarn and textiles, mostly of the finer grades, raised the total availability of cotton to 826,000 tons, about 50 percent of the region's output and 7 percent of total world consumption (see table 16-8).

The extraordinary importance of the textile industry in Latin America has resulted in a number of studies of its role in the regional economy and its competitive position.[18] Several conclusions emerging from these studies may be briefly enumerated. It appears that over a wide range of

mill sizes there are no appreciable economies of scale in cotton spinning and weaving; nonetheless a great many textile mills in Latin America are too small for efficient operation, and the industry could reduce its costs by eliminating or expanding the smallest sized plants. Average factor costs in Latin America are such as to suggest that the lowest costs of production can be achieved using the equipment and techniques typical of more advanced countries about 1960. This level of modernity represents a considerable advance over that of 1950, but there would be very little gain in bringing the region's industry up to the level of 1965. While unit costs could be reduced in some cases by these more modern techniques, the demands on skilled labor and managerial ability would increase drastically and the industry would run into shortages. In the more developed nations of the world the textile industry is now becoming relatively capital-intensive, and is shifting away from the heavy use of labor which has characterized it for a century and a half. In Latin America, however, labor costs are still low enough to maintain the profitability of more labor-intensive techniques. Wages are generally lower than in more modern industries in the region, and the industry provides a greater share of employment than it does of the wage bill or of manufacturing value added in the more industrialized countries. In those Latin American countries with relatively little industry, however, the textile industry commonly offers higher than average wages.

With regard to labor productivity, this is observed to vary enormously from one country to another in Latin America, independently of relative factor costs. In Brazil, Chile, and Uruguay productivity is less than half the regional average, while in Colombia, which has the most modern industry, it exceeds the average by 30 percent. The low productivity is attributable largely to the use of obsolete machinery; a very large re-equipment would be necessary, especially in Brazil, to bring the industry up to the technological level at which it might produce most effectively. It should be noted, however, that there has already been a considerable improvement over the conditions of 1950, with respect to age of machinery, scale of production, and labor productivity.[19]

Trade in Cotton Textiles

Until early in this century, world trade in cotton textiles was dominated by the United Kingdom, the first country to develop a textile industry and the major importer of raw cotton. During the 1930s Japan became a large yarn and textile exporter; the United States, India, and continental Europe accounted for most of the remaining trade. In the last two decades several underdeveloped countries have become major cotton textile exporters, particularly those with large amounts of moderately skilled, inexpensive labor such as Hong Kong and Taiwan (repeating the experience of Japan) and Pakistan. There has been an enormous migration of textile machinery to the poorer countries, only partly balanced by greater capital and labor productivity in the more advanced nations. The latter have in many cases be-

---

[15] See G. Wythe, *Industry in Latin America* (Columbia University Press, 1945), passim. In a few cases a sizable domestic handweaving sector existed, so that industrialization and import substitution occurred first at the spinning stage.

[16] R. Chin, *Management, Industry and Trade in Cotton Textiles* (Yale University Press, 1965), pp. 142-44.

[17] For Brazil, see Stein, "The Brazilian Cotton Textile Industry...," p. 430.

[18] ECLA, *La Industria Textil en América Latina* (New York: eleven volumes) I Chile (1962), II Brazil (1963), III Colombia (1964), IV Uruguay (1964), V Peru (1964), VI Bolivia (1964), VII Paraguay (1965), VIII Argentina (1966, preliminary version), IX Ecuador (1965), X Venezuela (1965), and XI Mexico (1966); and two companion studies, ECLA, *Choice of Technologies in the Latin American Textile Industry* (doc. E/CN. 12/746, 13 January 1966), and ECLA, *Economies of Scale in the Cotton Spinning and Weaving Industry* (doc. E/CN. 12/748, 14 February 1966).

[19] ECLA, *Labour Productivity of the Cotton Textile Industry in Five Latin-American Countries* (UN, 1951). The countries studied are Brazil, Chile, Ecuador, Mexico, and Peru.

come net importers of yarn or cloth, and have shifted to the export of clothing and other finished articles.[20] It appears that in the production of most grades of cotton textiles the low-income countries as a group are now able to supply their own requirements and to compete in the richer markets as well. The textile industry is probably the first manufacturing industry in which this has occurred on a large scale.

The shift in cotton textile trade might have been appreciably greater but for the relatively high tariffs imposed by the major importing countries. Nominal rates on cotton yarn, thread, cloth, clothing, and knitted goods averaged between 10 and 30 percent for most products before the Kennedy Round of trade liberalization among the advanced countries, but the effective protection given cotton manufacturing was very much higher. Effective rates ranged from 30 to 50 percent in the United States, from 20 to 50 percent in the United Kingdom, 30 to 40 percent in the EEC, and 20 to 40 percent in Sweden; Japan had low tariffs on yarn and cloth but the highest protection, 60 percent, on knitted goods. During the Kennedy Round most tariffs were reduced, but the new level of effective protection is generally 70 percent or more of the previous rate — the 50 percent reduction applied to a wide range of manufactures did not hold for textiles and clothing or for several other products of major interest to the developing countries.[21]

Exports of cotton manufactures from these countries are also limited by operation of the Long Term Arrangement Regarding International Trade in Cotton Textiles, negotiated under the General Agreement on Tariffs and Trade, which entered into force in October 1962. It was preceded by a one-year Short Term Arrangement, and at its expiration in 1967 was renewed for three more years. The arrangement, which by 1967 included fifteen developed textile-importing countries, fourteen low-income textile exporters, and Japan, is designed to protect domestic textile industries in developed countries against disruptive competition from imports, without reducing trade very much and in particular without allowing trade barriers to discriminate consistently against the underdeveloped members. Where possible, restraints on trade in specific articles are to be reached through bilateral agreements for limited periods; quotas may be applied by importers, but must be expanded regularly.[22] The arrangement was concluded at the instigation of the United States, whose domestic industry sought protection in 1959-60 because imports into that country increased sharply. At that time most European importers applied quantitative restrictions to textile imports, and a multilateral control was seen as an alternative to the imposition of similar unilateral restraints by the United States.

Most national restrictions have remained in force under the arrangement, but tariffs have been lowered somewhat and a few countries have eased their quantitative barriers. For the exporting countries, this scheme is preferable to unilateral restrictions because it commits importers to a minimum annual increase in their trade except in cases of market disruption, and because it provides for bilateral negotiations over specific products. The importers, however, are free to determine the existence of such disruption and to set the base quotas without the agreement of exporters. The arrangement involves little sharing of control with the exporting countries.[23]

The arrangement is intended to provide for an orderly development of trade in cotton textiles, to slow rather than to halt or reverse the flow from the underdeveloped to the developed countries. Over the period 1961-65 imports into the developed importing members from the low-income exporting members increased at 12 percent annually, twice as rapidly as trade among the developed members. The increase was almost entirely in clothing rather than yarn or cloth, and was concentrated in a small number of exporters. In the absence of the arrangement the increase might have been greater and would probably have been shared more widely among products and countries; but trade might have been restricted instead by national measures. Thus it is impossible to say how far the arrangement has actually curtailed cotton textile trade or how this has affected the exports of low-income countries. Its symbolic importance, however, is considerable, for a number of reasons. It represents a departure from GATT principles by the United States, which in most other instances has been the chief proponent among the major importing countries of free international trade. It is the first restrictive agreement likely to discriminate against underdeveloped countries as a group, instead of favoring some at the expense of others as do the various European preferential tariffs for associated states. Finally, and most importantly, it is the first restrictive agreement concerning manufactured goods, and it is directed at the one industry in which low-income countries in general have shown an ability to compete. It suggests that the export of manufactures by less developed countries to the major industrial powers, which the former are coming to regard as necessary or at least very valuable to their export growth and industrial development, will be resisted by the latter for some time into the future. The implications for the poorer nations, while quantitatively unimportant at present in most cases, are not encouraging.

These developments in world textile trade have affected Latin America very little, except that the region now supplies most of its own yarn and cloth and has participated in the shift of manufacturing to underdeveloped areas. Some of the yarn and fabric produced is exported, but on balance the region is still an importer of both, and has not figured in the expansion of imports by the advanced countries. Low labor productivity in many countries, and higher labor costs than in the low-income areas now exporting cotton

---

[20] GATT, *Study on Cotton Textiles*. See especially pp. 1-4, 10, 22-25, 35, 40, 52-55.

[21] Estimates of average nominal and effective tariffs from Bela Balassa, *The Effects of the Kennedy Round on the Exports of Processed Goods from Developing Areas*, UNCTAD doc. TD/69, 15 February 1968, appendix pp. 6-7.

[22] For the text of the agreement, see U.S. Department of State, *International Trade in Cotton Textiles, Treaties and Other International Acts*, Series 5240 (Washington: text as certified by the GATT Executive Secretary, Geneva).

[23] See the Report by the UNCTAD Secretariat, *Study of the Origins and Operation of International Arrangements Relating to Cotton Textiles*, doc. TD/20/Supp. 3, 12 October 1967.

textiles, have prevented the region from sharing appreciably in this trade. At various times in the past, however, cotton textiles have been an important item of export for several countries. Until 1946, Mexico exported greater value in textiles than in raw cotton; in the 1940s Brazil exported large amounts of textiles, particularly to other South American countries cut off from European suppliers by the war. The resumption of normal trade and the great expansion of raw cotton exports have reduced the importance of Latin American textile exports.

Outlook

Cotton will continue to be a major Latin American crop, for both domestic use and exports, for the foreseeable future. The region's natural advantages in cotton growing do not appear to be threatened either by other crops or by other producing areas; nor is the competition from other fibers expected to do more than slow the growth of demand for cotton. Uncertainty over the future rate of substitution of man-made fibers for cotton makes projections of consumption and supply difficult, and often it is simply assumed that cotton's share in the total will not change over the next five or ten years. FAO has recently estimated total world demand for cotton in 1975 as some 12.5 to 14 million tons, an increase of between 1.6 and 2.6 percent annually since the early 1960s.[24] A slight rise in per capita use is anticipated almost everywhere except in the United States, where the competition of synthetic fibers is most intense. That country will probably still be the world's largest producer in the 1970s, but its output is already falling appreciably, leaving an exportable surplus of less than a million tons out of total world trade of some 2.5 million. The Communist countries will continue to be self-sufficient, so that world trade in raw cotton will flow from the Americas and the zone from the Sudan to Pakistan into Western Europe and the importing countries of Asia. These projections assume a continued flow of exports of cotton manufactures from Asia.

[24] Range of projections contained in: ICAC, *Prospective Trends in Consumption of Textile Fibers*, doc. 10X XXI (Washington: March 1962); Bela Balassa, *Trade Prospects for Developing Countries* (Homewood: Irwin, 1964), pp. 239-56, 370, 415, 417-18. FAO, Committee on Commodity Problems, *Agricultural Commodities—Projections for 1970* (1964), pp. II-61 to II-73 and A-2 to A-4; and FAO, Committee on Commodity Problems, *Agricultural Commodities—Projections for 1975 and 1985* (1967), pp. 280-83.

As U.S. exports decline in the future, Latin America will probably emerge as the principal supplier of cotton in trade; within a decade the region's net exportable surplus may reach a million tons. Domestic consumption is expected to grow somewhat more rapidly than exports, reducing the share of cotton sold abroad to less than half. The increased dependence on home markets and the relative stability of world cotton prices suggest that these predictions are not likely to be upset by violent shifts in prices or markets, and that revenues from cotton will continue to grow very slowly and steadily. In some countries, particularly in Central America, cotton may account for much of the decade's growth in exports; for the traditional suppliers—Argentina, Brazil, Mexico, and Peru—growth is expected to be less rapid and less important to the total expansion of exports. At current price levels, the region's cotton exports should be worth some $550 million to $600 million by the mid-1970s.

In most Latin American countries the demand for cotton for domestic use is growing rapidly enough to require extensive new investment in spinning and weaving machinery. Where the present stock of equipment is obsolete or otherwise inefficient the need for investment is even greater, especially in Brazil. Generally the equipment available in 1960 included a large number of machines operating below capacity or suitable for reconditioning, so that production was far below maximum potential output.[25] There remains much room in several countries for improving the yield or quality of raw cotton, but in most cases the chief problems of the next few years will arise in the manufacturing sector of the cotton industry. First, large investment will be needed simply to satisfy the future demand for textiles; most countries are now essentially self-sufficient and do not wish to return to large imports. Second, if Latin America is to participate appreciably in the growing world trade in cotton textiles, the industry's costs must be reduced and its efficiency improved. Progress in these matters would incidentally reduce or eliminate some of the raw materials problems of the industry, and could perhaps compensate for the rather slow growth anticipated for cotton fiber exports.

[25] ECLA, *La Industria Textil en América Latina*, vols. I-XI: projections of demand and potential output were made to 1970 for most countries.

CHAPTER 16 TABLES

TABLE 16-1. World Cotton Area and Yields, Averages for 1934-38 and 1964-67
(Thousands of hectares and kilograms of cotton fiber per hectare)

| | 1934-38 | | 1964-67 | |
	Area	Yield	Area	Yield
Latin America[a]	2,938	225	4,266	379
Argentina	310	194	396	251
Brazil	2,097	188	2,295	239
Colombia	32	151	176	503
Costa Rica			7	619
Ecuador			24	220
El Salvador	3	284	68	747
Guatemala	1	253	97	785
Honduras			13	736
Mexico	274	242	738	677
Nicaragua	3	321	143	796
Paraguay	44	95	53	197
Peru	171	492	208	515
Venezuela			48	305
United States	11,500	238	4,484	438
Western Europe	101	216	341	485
Africa	2,500	239	4,121	251
Asia and Oceania	10,940	121	15,544	218
Communist Countries	5,038	271	7,328	457
Soviet Union	2,028	336	2,436	805
China	2,968	232	4,799	284
World Total	33,000	202	32,162	341

Source: ICAC, *Cotton: World Statistics.*

[a]Includes countries listed; no data available for Cuba or Haiti.

TABLE 16-2. World Cotton Production, 1925 – 1966/67[a]
(Thousands of metric tons raw cotton)

Country or Region	1925-29	1930-34	1935-39	1940-44	1945-49	1950/51	1951/52	1952/53	1953/54	1954/55	1955/56
Latin America	258.8	330.9	661	739.6	599.4	864	966	879	923	1,082	1,200
Argentina	25.2	41.6	62.6	85.4	86.8	123	113	128	142	109	131
Brazil	109.4	167.4	424	470.4	296.8	369	429	336	316	359	370
Colombia	2.8	2.8	5.4	4.4	6.4	8	7	11	20	26	23
Costa Rica											
Cuba											
Ecuador	1.2	1.6	2.6	2.4	2.6	3	2	2	3	2	3
El Salvador			1	2.8	4.6	6	10	11	13	20	30
Guatemala			0.2	0.8	0.8	1	2	3	6	9	10
Haiti	4.8	5.5	4.8	2.8	2.2	1	2	2	2	2	1
Honduras											
Mexico	54.6	41.8	69.2	90.2	117	248	278	271	263	392	486
Nicaragua			0.8	1.2	1.2	5	10	13	23	44	35
Paraguay	2.8	3.2	4.4	9.2	10.6	11	16	12	13	12	12
Peru	56	64.4	83.4	67	68.2	88	93	87	119	102	93
Venezuela	2	2.6	2.6	3	2.2	1	4	3	3	5	5
United States	3,310	2,893	2,851	2,593	2,624	2,171	3,285	3,282	3,585	2,978	3,205
Western Europe	5	9	24	17	19	36	42	47	56	74	113
Africa	438	448	612	479	543	685	666	773	658	696	707
Asia & Oceania	1,200	1,320	1,340	1,214	913	1,112	1,259	1,293	1,373	1,604	1,436
Communist Countries	738	978	1,390	935	1,072	1,778	2,170	2,412	2,464	2,481	2,728
World Total	5,989	5,798	6,885	5,980	5,711	6,647	8,390	8,693	9,061	8,916	9,491
L.A. Share (%)	4.3	5.7	9.6	12.4	10.5	13.0	11.5	10.1	10.2	12.1	12.7

Country or Region	1956/57	1957/58	1958/59	1959/60	1960/61	1961/62	1962/63	1963/64	1964/65	1965/66	1966/67
Latin America	1,041	1,166	1,200	1,120	1,305	1,475	1,596	1,521	1,602	1,689	1,462
Argentina	105	155	115	93	121	109	128	108	126	104	86
Brazil	283	294	305	370	423	542	488	477	448	540	443
Colombia	24	28	33	67	67	78	82	73	66	65	87
Costa Rica			1	1	1	1	2	2	3	4	4
Cuba											
Ecuador	3	3		1	4	4	7	2	1	5	1
El Salvador	32	36	39	30	40	56	70	74	80	52	39
Guatemala	10	14	16	14	21	31	52	65	71	89	63
Haiti	1	1	1	1	1	1	1	1	1		
Honduras	1	3	4	1	1	4	5	7	10	10	10
Mexico	407	457	511	360	455	431	523	457	515	565	484
Nicaragua	42	48	47	28	33	54	70	91	113	110	115
Paraguay	11	11	9	4	8	11	12	12	14	10	9
Peru	117	109	109	139	121	143	145	140	138	118	102
Venezuela	5	7	7	9	7	8	8	9	11	16	14
United States	2,898	2,387	2,506	3,170	3,107	3,117	3,237	3,337	3,293	3,223	2,130
Western Europe	112	110	114	134	143	211	204	197	151	162	182
Africa	732	762	904	885	904	788	935	878	1,007	1,063	1,078
Asia & Oceania	1,608	1,648	1,708	1,478	1,777	1,768	2,033	2,191	2,192	2,223	2,360
Communist Countries	2,822	2,951	3,403	3,471	2,876	2,458	2,441	2,797	3,007	3,177	3,447
World Total	9,215	9,030	9,741	10,263	10,108	9,819	10,430	10,899	11,262	11,476	10,517
L.A. Share (%)	11.3	12.5	12.3	10.9	12.9	15.0	15.3	14.0	14.2	14.7	13.9

Source: ICAC, *Cotton: World Statistics.*

[a]Statistics refer to crop years, 1 August – 31 July.

TABLE 16–3. Cotton Prices, Liverpool,[a] 1927-1968
  (U.S. cents per pound)

Year Beginning 1 August	United States: Middling 15/16[b]	Brazil: São Paulo Type No. 5 1-1/32	Peru: Tanguis Good 1-3/16
1927/28	22.99	21.72	25.39
1928/29	21.63	20.64	24.88
1929/30	18.87	17.27	21.15
1930/31	12.02	11.36	13.78
1931/32	7.74	7.50	9.67
1932/33	8.67	8.61	10.56
1933/34	12.67	12.28	15.06
1934/35	14.51	13.86	16.16
1935/36	13.91	13.45	15.74
1936/37	15.28	14.12	18.23
1937/38	10.76	10.18	14.21
1938/39	10.46	9.63	12.34
1939/40	12.84	12.49	14.42
1946/47[c]	34.82	26.41	
1947/48	34.58	29.19	
1948/49	32.15	33.85	
1949/50	31.83	33.05	35.22[d]
1950/51	42.58	59.06	67.74[d]

Year Beginning 1 August	United States: Middling 15/16	United States: Memphis Territory SM 1-1/16	Brazil: São Paulo Type No. 5 1-1/32	Mexico: Matamoros SM 1-1/16	Nicaragua: SM 1-1/16	Peru: Tanguis Type No. 5 1-3/16	Peru: Pima No. 1 1-9/16
1951/52	43.46	46.16	55.75	43.67		48.55	72.34
1952/53	38.36	41.14	50.47	39.66		39.54	46.74
1953/54	36.99	39.62	34.31	38.01		40.72	47.56
1954/55	37.59	40.68	37.31	39.10		41.28	50.95
1955/56	32.95	39.75	32.53	35.03		37.89	53.49
1956/57	28.38	33.35	30.14	32.63		42.44	63.61
1957/58	28.86	35.79	28.66	33.81	32.28	37.98	49.19
1958/59	28.18	32.70		28.97	27.63	31.89	35.76
1959/60	26.45[e]	29.75		29.30	28.43	37.10	43.76
1960/61	28.15	31.08	27.80	30.35	29.81	32.95	43.71
1961/62	28.95	31.22	27.53	30.08	29.93	32.81	41.38
1962/63	28.0	30.29	26.12	28.42	28.17	32.83	37.91
1963/64	26.84	29.52	26.27	29.52	28.59	36.71	42.49
1964/65	27.13	29.88	26.17	29.19	27.65	35.79	43.50
1965/66	21.43	29.27	24.95	28.27	27.10		41.18
1966/67	20.59	28.72	24.77	29.34	27.60		43.91
1967/68	22.54	33.76	27.84	31.92	30.42		47.72

Sources: All prices 1927-1950 – ICAC, *Report on an International Cotton Agreement*, doc. 6/XII Second (November 1953). All prices 1951-1968 –ICAC, *Cotton: World Statistics.*

[a]1927-1940 – actual price quotations at Liverpool; 1946-1964 – as estimated by the ICAC.
[b]Calculated by adding premium for 15/16 inch cotton at New Orleans to quoted price for 7/8 inch cotton in Liverpool.
[c]No prices published during World War II, 1940-45.
[d]Price reported at Rotterdam.
[e]From 1959, price refers to 1 inch middling.

TABLE 16-4. World Cotton Consumption, Averages for 1936-38, 1950-52, 1961-63, and 1966-68
(Thousands of metric tons and kilograms per capita)

Country or Region	1936-38 Total (1)	1936-38 Per Capita	1950-52 Total (1)	1950-52 (2)	1950-52 Per Capita	1961-63 Total (1)	1961-63 (2)	1961-63 Per Capita	1966-68 Total (1)	1966-68 (2)	1966-68 Per Capita
Latin America	220	2.9	435	482	3.0	635	680	3.1	717	758	3.3
Argentina	28		104	109	6.1	91	106	4.2	103	116	4.6
Bolivia	1		2	3	1.1	2	2	0.6	3	3	0.8
Brazil	114		181	177	3.4	277	280	3.7	271	276	3.3
Chile	3		14	17	2.8	25	24	2.8	28	28	3.1
Colombia	9		24	27	2.4	55	51	3.5	65	68	3.5
Costa Rica				2	2.1	2	3	2.4	1	2	2.7
Cuba	2		7	17	2.9	15	17	2.5	20	25	2.8
Dominican Republic				3	1.2		4	1.1	4	4	1.2
Ecuador	1		4	5	1.5	5	4	0.9	7	7	1.2
El Salvador	1		3	4	2.0	7	7	2.3	11	11	3.4
Guatemala	1		2	5	1.6	6	7	1.8	8	8	1.8
Haiti			1	5	1.6	1	5	1.2	1	6	1.2
Honduras				2	1.3		3	1.6		4	1.8
Mexico	53		71	64	2.5	110	104	3.8	147	140	3.3
Nicaragua			1	2	2.1	2	3	2.2	3	5	2.6
Paraguay			3	3	0.9	3	5	2.4	4	5	2.3
Peru	7		13	13	1.6	18	19	1.7	18	21	1.8
Uruguay			5	8	3.2	6	7	2.7	7	9	3.2
Venezuela	2		3	9	1.9	12	17	2.2	20	26	2.7
United States	1,485	} 9.4	2,138	2,062	12.6	1,889	1,866	10.2	2,023	2,000	10.2
Canada	60		89	125	8.6	82	118	6.3	89	131	6.5
Western Europe	1,577	4.0	1,533	1,361	4.3	1,613	1,589	4.9	1,530	1,411	4.5
France	254		269	234	5.2	281	233	5.0	259	216	5.3
West Germany	227		219	213	4.0	293	314	5.7	265	257	4.5
Italy	143		204	135	3.0	229	194	3.9	227	191	3.7
Spain	26		61	44	1.9	129	121	3.7	117	110	3.6
United Kingdom	606		412	367	6.7	226	293	5.7	197	258	5.5
Africa	28	1.0	92	266	1.5	218	367	1.0	344	419	1.3
Asia	1,564		2,489	1,223	1.8	4,984	2,279	2.1	4,384	2,124	2.3
India	674		723	567	1.8	1,069	968	2.1	1,115	990	2.2
Japan	770		371	177	3.6	683	536	5.4	710	627	6.1
Oceania	6	3.8	23	60	4.8	68	82	9.1	76	89	5.1
Communist Countries	1,730	3.1	2,008	1,610	2.3	3,124	3,061	3.0	3,714	3,490	3.2
Soviet Union	759		884	788	4.3	1,361	1,356	6.2	1,601	1,583	6.8
China	748		808	729	1.4	1,182	1,441	1.9	1,504	1,231	1.7
World Total	6,668	2.9	7,619	7,382	2.9	12,613	10,140	3.4	11,259	8,958	3.3

Sources: ICAC, *Cotton: World Statistics, 1969.* FAO, Commodity Bulletin no. 31, *Per Capita Fiber Consumption Levels, 1948-1958* (Rome: 1961). FAO, "Per Capita Fiber Consumption, 1960-1962," *Monthly Bulletin of Agricultural Economics and Statistics* (April 1964).

Notes: (1) Total apparent consumption of raw cotton, average of two crop years including part of three calendar years. (2) Total availability of cotton: mill consumption plus net imports of yarn, cloth and other cotton manufactures.
Per capita consumption is based on total availability in 1950-52, 1961, and 1966, and on raw cotton consumption in 1938.

TABLE 16-5. Latin American Exports of Raw Cotton and Cotton Manufactures, 1949/50 to 1966/67
(Thousands of metric tons and millions of U.S. dollars)

Exporter and Destination	1949/50	1950/51	1951/52	1952/53	1953/54	1954/55	1955/56	1956/57	1957/58	1958/59
Argentina										
Belgium		1.4	0.5	3.1	6.8	5.2		2.2		3.3
West Germany		0.1	0.3	0.3	3.3	0.4	0.2			1.0
Japan		7.2	4.8	2.9	22.7	2.8		2.1		2.6
United Kingdom		9.9	6.1	16.3	14.0	5.3		11.1		1.1
Total, Crop Year		25.4	30.8	23.4	61.4	22.5				9.5
Calendar Year	40.3	36.2	23.4	61.5	27.5		0.5	10.5		
Value	9.2	12.1	7.1	14.2	6.8	1.8	0.2		2.5	9.5
Share of Exports (%)	0.8	1.0	1.0	1.3	0.7		0.5		0.3	0.3
Brazil										
West Germany		9.0	12.9	0.9	51.9	42.4	12.6	2.8	7.2	10.6
Hong Kong		1.1	6.9	0.3	23.3	9.8	8.9	6.9	2.5	3.8
Japan		17.0	12.0	5.4	53.7	52.4	40.5	36.4	21.5	19.9
Netherlands		4.2	0.2		14.5	10.5	5.0	8.2	0.6	1.9
Total, Crop Year		151.2	75.9	33.2	304.0	225.5	176.5	82.6	46.9	52.6
Calendar Year	128.8	143.8	28.1	139.5	309.5	175.7	142.9	66.2	40.2	77.6
Manufactures	2.2	5.8	3.9		0.1	0.1		0.7	2.3	0.6
Value	105	207	34	102	223	131	86	44	25	35.5
Share of Exports (%)	7.8	11.8	12.4	6.6	14.5	9.2	5.8	3.2	2.0	2.8
El Salvador										
Japan		0.5	1.7	0.3	2.7	3.2	18.2	10.8	16.9	37.4
Total, Crop Year		5.0	6.5	10.6	9.5	7.8	31.7	21.7	28.8	53.6
Calendar Year	3.9[a]									
Manufactures	0.3		0.1							
Value	2.6		5.3							
Share of Exports (%)	3.8		6.0							
Guatemala										
Total, Crop Year					4.6	6.9	7.6	7.4	7.6	16.9
Calendar Year[a]										9.7
Value										4.1
Share of Exports (%)										3.8
Haiti										
Total, Crop Year		0.5	0.4	2.0	0.7	1.3	0.6	0.4	0.7	0.4
Calendar Year			0.9				0.4	0.4	0.3	0.3
Value	0.6	0.6	0.8				0.1	0.2	0.4	0.4
Share of Exports (%)	1.2	1.1	2.2				0.4	0.4	1.3	1.3
Honduras										
Total, Crop Year	0.1	0.3	0.8	1.1	0.6	0.9	3.4	4.1	0.9	4.0
Calendar Year										
Value		0.8	0.2	0.1	0.1	0.1	0.4	0.4		2.6
Share of Exports (%)			0.2	0.2	0.1	0.2	0.5	0.5		3.8
Mexico										
United States		157.0	169.7	159.9	104.5	189.8	313.0	182.7	198.7	211.0
Japan		1.3	5.5	39.7	71.2	59.1	64.3	60.4	50.1	98.0
West Germany		0.3	1.6	1.3	5.1	4.3	27.2	7.1	10.4	16.1
Total, Crop Year	164.0[a]	160.9	212.7	214.2	205.5	270.6	437.5	282.7	305.9	390.3
Calendar Year		178.0	228.7	234.5	259.4	325.4	421.9	283.9	341.0	405.9
Manufactures	5.9	8.6	4.2	2.2	2.1	1.8	1.3	1.2	1.3	1.0
Value	138.9	151.7	185.9	152.2	171.0	230.1	260.3	170.5	190.4	199.0
Share of Exports (%)	26.1	23.5	27.8	25.6	28.8	29.3	31.2	23.2	25.9	26.4
Nicaragua										
West Germany		0.2	0.3	6.6	9.6	5.3	21.3	7.7	8.8	14.9
Japan		1.3	0.1	2.4	6.3	5.2	10.2	3.4	4.1	23.4
Total, Crop Year		5.3	3.5	15.0	22.8	21.7	51.8	32.3	31.7	71.8
Calendar Year	3.3[a]	4.4	9.5	12.8	23.2	44.0	36.3	36.0	42.7	61.7
Value	1.8	5.5	6.8	8.4	16.8	31.0	23.6	21.8	24.9	29.4
Share of Exports (%)	6.9	14.8	16.2	18.4	30.7	43.1	40.8	33.9	39.0	45.1
Paraguay										
Total, Crop Year			10.6	10.8	12.4	8.7	9.8	7.6	7.6	6.5
Calendar Year	12.0[a]	6.9	15.0	14.4	11.4	9.0	9.8	8.1	7.8	5.6
Value	6.7	7.3	10.1	10.0	6.9	5.5	5.6	4.5	3.7	2.1
Share of Exports (%)	20.2	19.4	32.4	32.7	20.2	15.7	15.3	13.7	10.9	6.6

TABLE 16–5 – Continued

Exporter and Destination	1949/50	1950/51	1951/52	1952/53	1953/54	1954/55	1955/56	1956/57	1957/58	1958/59
Peru										
Belgium		8.7	5.9	10.2	10.3	10.9	12.4	17.1	17.4	15.7
Chile		2.7	10.9	15.2	8.0	16.9	20.5	1.1	9.3	19.5
West Germany		4.1	1.5	5.7	10.1	8.6	13.1	9.5	11.4	13.2
Total, Crop Year		72.8	68.1	80.4	81.3	76.8	106.5	88.5	91.1	116.6
Manufactures	0.3	1.3	0.7							
Calendar Year	72.3[a]	61.8	82.7	88.5	83.2	84.0[a]	108.0	80.2	106.2	113.7
Value	67.9	84.6	78.5	55.4	66.1	68.2	85.7	68.1	72.1	69.0
Share of Exports (%)	36.0	34.5	33.9	29.8	36.5	25.4	27.8	21.3	26.8	22.3
Latin America										
Total, Crop Year	424.7	435.3	404.7	390.6	703.2	642.8	823.5	535.6	521.2	722.5
Calendar Year	8.7	16.0	9.0	2.4	2.4	2.3	1.5	2.5	5.0	3.2
Manufactures[b]		431.6	395.6	562.1	728.9	660.7	758.9	521.3	584.4	731.7
Value	333	473	329	349	502	480[d]	484[d]	329[d]	343	376[c]
Share of Exports (%)	5.4	6.6	5.0	4.9	6.6	5.8	5.7	4.4	4.4	4.4

Exporter and Destination	1959/60	1960/61	1961/62	1962/63	1963/64	1964/65	1965/66	1966/67
Argentina								
Belgium	0.9	2.1	5.6	10.1	6.4	6.9	9.2	4.5
West Germany	0.5	0.3	4.0	4.1	4.3	5.7	4.0	6.3
Japan	2.4	8.1	6.0	6.6	1.8	4.0	5.3	3.8
United Kingdom	0.9	2.4	4.7	9.7	3.3	4.3	10.5	6.3
Total, Crop Year	6.8	16.6	30.8	47.0	23.6	20.9	29.0	27.5
Calendar Year	8.6	22.9	53.1	40.6	6.8	3.9	12.5	
Value	3.3	11.2	24.0	19.6	2.8	1.4	4.1	
Share of Exports (%)	0.3	1.2	2.0	1.4	0.2	0.1	0.3	
Brazil								
West Germany	27.4	26.1	38.2	44.1	54.3	25.3	43.5	55.2
Hong Kong	3.3	13.2	16.7	25.2	11.9	9.0	22.3	20.3
Japan	19.9	24.6	12.2	41.0	24.9	18.7	25.5	30.5
Netherlands	5.7	8.4	12.9	32.6	25.2	21.3	199.0	32.1
Total, Crop Year	97.6	151.2	184.5	249.1	222.9	226.4	204.1	220.7
Calendar Year	95.4	205.7	215.9	221.8	217.0	195.7	235.9	
Manufactures	2.2	0.8						
Value	45.6	109.7	112.2	114.2	108.3	95.7	111.0	
Share of Exports (%)	3.6	7.8	9.2	8.1	7.6	6.0	6.4	
Colombia								
United Kingdom	1.1	6.3	9.3	7.9	3.6	6.2	2.7	6.6
Total, Crop Year	6.8	25.9	28.8	23.0	11.7	10.6	9.1	18.2
Calendar Year	23.6	17.1	26.4	17.1	16.1			4.5
Manufactures	0.1	0.8	2.3					
Value	12.6	10.1	15.6	9.4		8.0		2.2
Share of Exports (%)	2.7	2.3	3.4	2.1		1.5		1.0
El Salvador								
Japan	21.0	27.2	34.6	57.5	53.2	55.5	50.8	26.7
Total, Crop Year	24.5	30.2	45.5	63.7	66.3	63.1	54.2	27.4
Calendar Year	27.2	35.5	54.3	64.0	65.5	73.1	44.4	
Manufactures	1.8	1.5	1.3					
Value	15.8	21.3	32.3	37.6	37.1	37.8	23.8	
Share of Exports (%)	13.5	17.9	23.7	24.5	20.8	21.2	12.9	

Item	(1)	(2)	(3)	(4)	(5)	(6)	(7)	(8)
Guatemala								
Total, Crop Year	11.9	16.3	24.9	46.0	56.4	65.5	76.8	64.8
Calendar Year	11.5	18.1	27.0	47.4	62.0	63.8	82.0	
Value	5.8	10.5	15.5	26.2	23.2	33.9	43.7	
Share of Exports (%)	5.0	9.3	13.6	17.1	14.7	18.1	19.1	
Honduras								
Total, Crop Year	1.1	0.9	3.3	4.1	6.3	10.2	10.4	8.9
Calendar Year	1.2		3.6	4.4	6.9	11.2	11.2	
Value	0.7		2.1	2.6	3.8	6.2	5.8	
Share of Exports (%)	1.0		2.7	3.1	4.0	4.9	4.0	
Mexico								
United States	151.4	173.4	114.7	151.4	106.9	127.8	146.0	222.4
Japan	83.5	120.3	130.4	150.7	131.7	159.7	200.4	144.6
West Germany	7.2	8.3	10.5	24.2	12.3	15.6	23.5	16.9
Total, Crop Year	281.5	347.4	322.7	409.4	307.7	348.6	459.2	300.5
Calendar Year	316.3	305.2	425.2	370.1	322.0	409.0	429.5	
Manufactures	3.8	7.3	5.5	4.8	6.2	7.1	7.4	
Value	158.0	160.0	218.5	195.8	170.5	162.1	153.6	
Share of Exports (%)	20.7	19.5	23.5	19.9	16.2	14.1	12.4	
Nicaragua								
West Germany	4.6	5.5	2.4	11.3	15.6	12.2	11.3	9.1
Japan	10.1	17.2	3.7	26.6	38.2	29.1	32.3	30.8
Total, Crop Year	28.1	30.2	52.5	62.4	87.2	123.8	116.0	91.1
Calendar Year	27.4	32.5	55.7	73.1	93.5	125.1	111.4	
Value	14.7	18.3	31.3	39.8	51.5	66.1	56.8	
Share of Exports (%)	26.3	30.2	38.0	39.9	43.5	46.1	41.3	
Paraguay								
Total, Crop Year	5.4	4.0	6.3	7.2	10.2	10.0	8.5	8.5
Calendar Year	0.8	5.0	7.0	8.5[a]	9.2[a]	9.9	5.0	
Value	0.27	1.56	2.47	3.20	4.20	4.69	1.99	
Share of Exports (%)	1.1	5.2	7.4	8.0	8.4	8.2	4.0	
Peru								
Belgium	16.5	18.1	18.2	16.8	11.3	15.4	13.5	10.3
Chile	7.4	10.8	24.6	20.0	9.7	13.3	15.7	8.9
West Germany	13.6	13.8	18.5	17.7	16.4	14.3	11.3	9.7
Total, Crop Year	94.3	108.1	130.5	133.6	115.3	106.0	117.5	86.5
Calendar Year	98.7	112.5	138.1	123.9	109.7	115.7	113.9	
Value	74.6	79.8	97.1	91.4	91.5	95.2	84.9	
Share of Exports (%)	17.0	16.2	18.1	16.9	13.7	14.3	11.1	
Latin America								
Total, Crop Year	558.0	730.8	829.8	1,045.5	907.6	985.1	1,084.8	854.1
Calendar Year	610.7	755.3	1,006.3	970.9	904.3	1,023.5	1,050.3	
Manufactures	7.9	10.4	9.8	10.7	9.7	8.4	9.5	
Value	355	423	551	540	499	511.1	487.9	
Share of Exports (%)	4.0	4.6	6.6	5.4	4.2	4.9	4.4	

Note: Volume data for raw cotton exports by destination are by crop year, 1 August–31 July. All other data are for calendar years, starting the preceding January. Value data refer to raw cotton only. Manufactures include yarn, tissues, garments, and all other processed cotton.

aEstimated from IMF volume index and FAO trade data.
bExcludes the British West Indies except in 1963; includes Colombian exports of cotton manufactures in 1951-1956.
cIncludes Colombian exports of $12.7 million.
dExcludes Argentina.

Sources: ICAC, *Cotton: World Statistics.* ICAC, Eighteenth Plenary Meeting, May 1959, doc. 17/XVIII. FAO, *Trade Yearbook.* UN, *Yearbook of International Trade Statistics.* FAO, *Per Capita Fiber Consumption Levels, 1948-1958,* Commodity Bulletin Series, no. 31 (UN: 1960). IMF, *International Financial Statistics,* supp. to 1964-65 and 1966-67 issues. FAO, *Monthly Bulletin of Agricultural Economics and Statistics,* January 1962, April 1964, July-August 1965, November 1967, and December 1968.

TABLE 16-6. Size and Output of the Textile Industry in Latin America, circa 1961
(Number of units of machinery and tons of yarn and cloth produced)

Country	Year	Machinery				Production			
		Thous. of Spindles		No. of Looms		Tons of Yarn		Tons of Cloth	
		Cotton	Total	Cotton	Total	Cotton	Total	Cotton	Total
Argentina	1961	1,019	1,493	23,923	38,023	95,271	135,686	69,771	94,641
Bolivia	1961	19	37	566	916	2,100	2,849	1,037	1,246
Brazil	1960	3,840	4,295	102,760	131,860	192,000	275,000	192,000	260,000
Chile[a]	1957	218	325	5,250	7,500	20,500	32,500	17,000	23,000
Colombia[a]	1961-62	560	632	11,000	15,500	53,160	70,053	50,135	63,036
Ecuador	1961	105	117	2,715	3,146	6,430	6,935	32,639	35,331
Mexico[b]	1962	1,416	1,802	34,109	47,898	112,573	139,227	56,870[c]	76,330[c]
Paraguay	1961-62	26	29	581	628	2,780	3,036	1,944[c]	1,963[c]
Peru	1961	215	308	5,011	8,234	16,900	24,829	13,504	20,205
Uruguay	1961	118[d]	167	2,048[d]	2,718	7,235	13,296	5,060	7,756
Venezuela	1963	166[e]	196	3,669	5,059	16,636	19,179	13,492	19,878
Total, 11 countries		7,702	9,401	191,632	261,482	525,585	722,590	453,452	603,386

Source: ECLA, *La Industria Textil en América Latina* (New York: 11 vols.); I, Chile (1962); II, Brazil (1963); III, Colombia (1964); IV, Uruguay (1964); V, Peru (1964); VI, Bolivia (1964); VII, Paraguay (1965); VIII, Argentina (1966, preliminary version); IX, Ecuador (1965); X, Venezuela (1965); and XI, Mexico (1966).

[a]Estimated total machinery stock; a smaller number of spindles (looms) was included in the survey.
[b]Production figures refer to pure cotton only, excluding mixtures of cotton and synthetic fibers.
[c]Production in linear meters converted to tons at 8,230 meters per ton.
[d]Synthetic fibers included with cotton; only wool excluded.
[e]Excludes spindles for spinning wastes, including cotton waste.

TABLE 16-7. The Textile Industry in the Latin American Economy, circa 1960
(Percentage in relation to industrial sector and national economy)

Country	Year	Share (%) of Textile Industry in Total Manufacturing Industry					Total Economy
		Number of Establishments	Employment	Wages & Salaries	Value Added	Value of Production	Gross Domestic Product
Argentina	1957	4[a]	15.8	15.3[b]	13.4	14.2	4.3
Bolivia	1957		23.2	26.3	19.0	20.0	
Brazil	1958		24.0	21.0	14.0		3.5[c]
Chile	1957	10.0	17.7			12.4	2.6
Colombia	1960	4.8	17.5	18.7	15.7	15.2	2.6
Ecuador	1961	17.2	29.3	20.3	14.4	14.3	2.2
Mexico	1962	41.8[d]	30.5	26.2		14.4	3.4
Paraguay	1958	0.7	6.2	9.4	12.9	8.8	1.5
Peru	1959	9.4	17.9	22.7	22.7	16.8	3.1
Uruguay	1960		13.0	12.0	14.0	17.9	3.8
Venezuela	1959		5.7	7.8		6.7	0.7
Average, 11 or fewer		Weighted[e]	20.0	17.0[f]		13.9[f]	3.0
Countries		Unweighted[g]	18.2	18.0	17.0	14.1	2.8

Sources: ECLA, *La Industria Textil en América Latina*, vols. I-XI. ECLA, *Boletín Económico de América Latina*, vol. III, no. 1, February 1966.

[a]Including all establishments with ten or fewer workers; all other figures refer only to establishments with eleven or more.
[b]1961 wages used in calculating regional weighted average.
[c]Value added in textile industry as a share of gross domestic product.
[d]Including all artisan establishments of whatever size.
[e]Weighted average, except for number of workers employed, calculated using year-end dollar exchange rates for each country and year indicated; does not correspond to average for any one year for all countries or to average for region using equilibrium exchange rates.
[f]Excludes Bolivia and Peru, for which only percentages are available, in addition to countries for which no data are available. Average of eight countries.
[g]Average of percentages shown.

TABLE 16-8. Latin American Cotton Balance, 1964
 (Thousands of metric tons)

Country	Raw Cotton	Cotton Yarn		Cotton Cloth (Piece Goods)	
Argentina					
Production	138	Mill consumption[a]	86.6		76.6
Imports	15.8		0.1		0.2
Exports	23.6		0.1		0.3
Reported consumption[b]	112	Apparent consumption[c]	88.5	Total availability[d]	88.6
Bolivia					
Production		Mill consumption	1.6		
Imports	1.5				0.6
Exports					
Reported consumption	3	Apparent consumption	1.6	Total availability	1.9
Brazil					
Production	450	Mill consumption	110.1		
Imports					1.1
Exports	226.4		0.9		
Reported consumption	266	Apparent consumption	111.0	Total availability	115.0
Chile					
Production		Mill consumption	25.3		(e)
Imports	32.5		0.3		0.2
Exports					
Reported consumption	28	Apparent consumption	25.6	Total availability	25.9
Colombia					
Production	66	Mill consumption	5.6		(e)
Imports	2.0				
Exports	10.6		0.2		
Reported consumption	63	Apparent consumption	5.4	Total availability	5.6
Costa Rica					
Production	24	Mill consumption	1.1		
Imports			0.3		1.7
Exports	2.4		0.5		0.4
Reported consumption	1	Apparent consumption	1.4	Total availability	1.7
Cuba					
Production	4	Mill consumption	12.5		
Imports	18.4		2.0		4.0
Exports					
Reported consumption	18	Apparent consumption	14.5	Total availability	16.5
Dominican Republic					
Production		Mill consumption	0.5		0.9
Imports			0.3		2.1
Exports					
Reported consumption		Apparent consumption	0.8	Total availability	2.1
Ecuador					
Production	3	Mill consumption	4.4		5.1
Imports	1.3		0.2		0.6
Exports					
Reported consumption	6	Apparent consumption	6.2	Total availability	6.4
El Salvador					
Production	80	Mill consumption	3.7		(e)
Imports			0.3		1.8
Exports	55.6		1.0		0.2
Reported consumption	9	Apparent consumption	4.0	Total availability	4.3
Guatemala					
Production	72	Mill consumption	4.6		
Imports			0.3		1.5
Exports	65.5				
Reported consumption	7	Apparent consumption	4.9	Total availability	5.2
Haiti					
Production		Mill consumption	2.3		
Imports			0.4		3.3
Exports					
Reported consumption	1	Apparent consumption	2.7	Total availability	3.1
Honduras					
Production	11	Mill consumption	0.5		
Imports			0.2		2.1
Exports	10.2				
Reported consumption		Apparent consumption	0.7	Total availability	2.3

TABLE 16–8 – Continued

Country	Raw Cotton	Cotton Yarn		Cotton Cloth (Piece Goods)	
Mexico					
Production	517	Mill consumption	109.0		47.8
Imports					
Exports	348.6		3.0		4.1
Reported consumption	130	Apparent consumption	102.0	Total availability	104.2
Nicaragua					
Production	124	Mill consumption	1.0		1.4
Imports					1.2
Exports	123.8				
Reported consumption	3	Apparent consumption	1.0	Total availability	1.3
Paraguay					
Production	14	Mill consumption	2.1		1.9
Imports			0.2		1.0
Exports	10.0				
Reported consumption	3	Apparent consumption	2.3	Total availability	2.5
Peru					
Production	136	Mill consumption	15.4		
Imports			1.0		0.4
Exports	106.0				
Reported consumption	20	Apparent consumption	16.4	Total availability	17.4
Uruguay					
Production		Mill consumption	3.8		
Imports	7.6		0.2		
Exports					
Reported consumption	8	Apparent consumption	4.0	Total availability	4.2
Venezuela					
Production	14	Mill consumption	15.0		8.3
Imports	6.5		0.3		1.8
Exports					
Reported consumption	17	Apparent consumption	15.3	Total availability	15.6
Latin America[f]					
Production	1,635	Mill consumption	414.0		189.5
Imports	174.3		11.5		53.7
Exports	1,254.1		2.3		27.2
Reported consumption	790	Apparent consumption	425.5	Total availability	437.0

Sources: ICAC, *Cotton: World Statistics.*

[a]Mill consumption of raw cotton is used to indicate production of cotton yarn, for which data are generally not available.

[b]Reported consumption of raw cotton may differ from apparent consumption because of changes in stocks.

[c]Mill consumption of raw cotton plus net imports of yarn.

[d]Apparent consumption of yarn plus net imports of cotton cloth; statistical discrepancies exist for some countries.

[e]Reported production of cotton cloth accounts for only a small part of apparent consumption of yarn; mill consumption is divided between reported production of yarn and reported production of cloth, which are not shown separately.

[f]Western Hemisphere excluding United States and Canada.

Chapter 17

FOREST PRODUCTS

The forest-based industries of Latin America are notable for their diversified output and for their many links with other sectors of the economy. Because a rapid growth in world demand for certain products of the forest is expected, and because Latin America's forest resources are plentiful, the manner in which the region will utilize these resources is especially important for its future economy and its relations with the rest of the world.

Not all the varied products of the forest can be taken account of here. The discussion, therefore, will be limited to the production and use of wood. Omitted from consideration are such products as natural rubber, chicle, resin, quebracho, quinine, yerba maté, wax and oil from different species of palms, and a variety of nuts and fruits. These are important to the economies of several small areas and figure in the exports of Argentina, Brazil, Mexico, and Paraguay. However, the industries that produce and market such products are independent of one another and often are unrelated to the primary forest industries—those involving roundwood for fuel and industrial use, sawnwood, wood-based sheet materials such as veneers, plywood, particle board and fiberboard, and the manufacture of paper and paperboard from wood pulp. All of the latter are competing uses for the same resource, and often they compete further at the stage of final consumption. There are in addition links between the different levels and types of processing, based on the use of the wastes or product of one industry by another. The only nonwood products to be considered here are alternative sources of fiber for pulp and paper, of which the most important is bagasse, or sugar cane waste.[1]

Note: Forest Products tables 17–1 to 17–11 appear on pp. 455–70.

[1] This organization of the subject is customary in the available statistical information, most of which deals with the primary forest industries as a group. The publications of FAO are the principal source of statistics on forest products, particularly the annual *World Forest Products Statistics*, the *World Forest Inventory* published every five years, and *Unasylva*. More detailed inquiries are often undertaken together with the UN regional commissions, as in ECLA/FAO, *Latin American Timber Trends and Prospects* (New York, 1963), and ECLA/FAO, *Pulp and Paper Prospects in Latin America* (New York, 1963). Other sources are indicated in the tables and the text.

Even with this limitation, forestry is almost as diverse and complex a sector as agriculture, showing the same range from subsistence production to large-scale modern producing and processing units. There are similar disparities in information, and the quantitative data and estimates must be evaluated bearing in mind qualitative distinctions and emphases. With a few exceptions, it is not possible to describe the secondary industries using wood products — construction, furniture manufacture, shipping, and the like — nor to investigate the relation of the forest to agriculture, water resources, and other aspects of the economy.

Resources

Approximately 900 million hectares are classified as forest in Latin America; this is slightly less than half the total area of the region and constitutes a forest reserve larger than is found in any other region of the world (see table 17-1). Tropical rain forest takes up roughly half the area, occupying most of the low, rainy, hot land in the region: the Amazon basin, the west coast of South America from Ecuador to Colombia, both coasts of Central America to central Mexico, and the east coast of Brazil extending into eastern Paraguay. This forest is quite dense and consists of a mixture of hundreds of broadleaved or hardwood species. A much smaller area, estimated at some 85 million hectares, borders the rain forest in the highlands of the Andean countries from Mexico to northern Argentina, covering only the eastern slope of the Andes south from Ecuador. This type of forest, which includes many deciduous trees and fewer species than the rain forest, occurs in areas with marked wet and dry seasons. About 400 million hectares—only slightly less than the rain forest area—is covered by scattered dry deciduous forest and relatively open savanna. This formation is found over most of the Brazilian highlands south of the Amazon, in western Paraguay and Argentina, in the llanos of eastern Colombia and central Venezuela, and over the central plateau of northern Mexico. The average density of this type of forest is low, some of it being almost bare of trees. In spite of this, it provides large quantities of fuelwood as well as various nonwood derivatives, especially in the Chaco or quebracho forest of Paraguay and Argentina. Much of this area is not counted as forested in the figures given in table 17-1.[2] A fourth type of hardwood forest is concentrated in southern Chile and neighboring Argentina; the total area covered is only some 16 million hectares, but the natural growth rate is relatively high.

Finally, there are about 20 million hectares of natural coniferous forests concentrated in mountainous areas of northwestern Mexico, parts of Honduras and Cuba, in the Brazilian states of Paraná and Santa Catarina, and in central and southern Chile. These conifers sometimes are mixed with hardwoods but more often occur in pure stands of one or a few species. This concentration, together with a high growth rate and the greater suitability of coniferous than broadleaved woods for pulp and paper manufacture, makes the coniferous forests much more valuable than their small share of the total wooded area would suggest.

Estimates of the growing stock of the region, or the amount of standing timber in forests, total some 145,000 million cubic meters — an average of 160 cubic meters per hectare of forest land, or between 200 and 300 cubic meters if the savannas and other open areas are excluded. The region's resource base appears quite large relative to present use. Removals in about 1960 were only some 0.2 cubic meters per hectare, or 0.2 percent of the growing stock, annually. Both figures are believed to be much lower than for other regions, and in only a few countries — El Salvador, Haiti, Uruguay, and perhaps Guatemala — is it likely that removals exceed the natural growth rate of the forest. Some efforts have been made to estimate the maximum allowable cut, or the largest amount that can be removed without reducing the forest stock, but such calculations are too few and uncertain to provide a basis for judging actual production of timber.[3]

The optimistic view given by these gross measures must be modified in several respects. There are wide disparities in the forest resources of different countries, resulting in excessive cutting in some while timber in others goes unused. More important are several factors that operate to some degree in all countries. Wood and the less highly processed wood products are bulky and low in unit value; thus they are generally difficult to ship long distances overland. Moreover, man's knowledge of the properties and uses of woods is limited to a relatively small number of species, the limitation becoming more important with the degree of processing. The difficulty increases when techniques developed in the advanced countries of North America and Europe are transferred to regions with quite different forest resources. These factors are important in view of the following features of the Latin American forest areas.

First, population in the region is concentrated in areas that were never heavily forested or where the original forest has been largely destroyed, and transport facilities are concentrated in these same areas. Thus a large share of the remaining forest is virtually inaccessible except to the small local population, while cutting is concentrated in much smaller areas. In 1958 less than one-third of the total Latin American forest was classified as within reach of existing means of transportation, and of this amount only about one-fourth was in use.[4] If the average statistics are adjusted for the fact that less than 10 percent of the forest is exploited, it is clear that the burden on resources becomes much greater and removals exceed growth over sizable areas.

Second, even the accessible forest is often difficult to exploit because of the extreme variety of species which are not, with present knowledge and techniques, fully substitutable in most end uses. In the tropical rain forest typically only 5 percent of the total volume of timber is in presently valuable species. This factor limits the production of wood per unit area and thereby reduces the economically accessible area. The coniferous forests, already valuable because of their high growth rates and suitability for wood pulp, are made still more attractive, relative to the hardwood forests, by their much greater uniformity. Throughout Latin America conifers generally account for a larger share of the forest area in use than of the total area or growing stock, and for a much greater share of industrial wood removals than of total removals including fuelwood (see table 17-2). These two factors — accessibility and homogeneity — largely account for the concentration of cutting in a few areas of major economic importance, such as the coniferous forests of northwestern Mexico, southern Brazil, and southern Chile and the mixed hardwood forests of the Andean highlands.

Third, despite the large forest area and the generally low population density, forestry competes with agriculture and stock raising over large parts of Latin America. Because agricultural techniques have not improved enough to permit a rapid increase in yields, the agricultural area of the region is still expanding, often at the expense of forest. The process has been slowed or arrested in a few countries such as Mexico and Argentina, but elsewhere it remains a serious problem. Similar difficulties arise in the extension of pasture and the overgrazing of partially cleared land.[5] The problems of forest destruction are compounded by the common practice of burning to clear land, with little or no use being made of the timber, and by the continuation in many rural areas of shifting agriculture, where land is cleared and used for a few years before being abandoned. These practices, particularly in the highlands of Mexico and Central America and in some parts of South America, often expose the soil to erosion and thereby ultimately destroy the agricultural land created by removing the tree cover. The opening of previously inaccessible forest can for some time offset the destruction of woodland, but if the process

[2] This classification follows that of ECLA/FAO, *Latin American Timber Trends...*, pp. 13-14, which accounts for between 950 and 970 million hectares of forest land. The data in table 17-1 exclude unstocked forest, or land with little or no tree cover, giving a total forested area of only 900 million hectares. For a more detailed description of the region's forest types which agrees with the main ECLA/FAO classifications fairly well, see R. Zon and W.N. Sparhawk, *Forest Resources of the World* (McGraw-Hill, 1923), vol. II, chaps. V and VI.

[3] See the estimates for a few Latin American countries in FAO, *World Forest Inventory*, 1963.

[4] FAO, *World Forest Inventory*, 1958, p. 8.

[5] For a discussion of the amount and type of pasture land in Latin America, see chap. 15 (Beef). See also chap. 14 (Wheat).

is not arrested both forestry and agriculture may suffer by the restriction of area and increases in costs. Eventually the agricultural area must be stabilized, as in more advanced countries, by the increase of yields, and some forest areas must be protected against overcutting in order to preserve the watersheds and farmlands.

These difficulties have already led to the creation of artificial forests in Latin America, particularly in the four southernmost countries. By the early 1960s these plantations had reached an area of about 1.5 million hectares: 600,000 to 700,000 in southern Brazil, 250,000 in Chile, 200,000 in Argentina, 100,000 in Uruguay, and the rest in small amounts in several countries. Man-made forests offer a high degree of accessibility and uniformity, and are notable for their very high growth rates — regularly 10 to 15 cubic meters per hectare per year, or several times the yield of natural forests. Production is concentrated on quick-growing species, especially eucalyptus and pine, which can be used for all industrial purposes from round-wood to pulp and paper. Artificial plantings are even made for fuel in southern Brazil, where there is a sizable charcoal-based iron smelting industry, and in Chile, where eucalyptus wood is used to deoxidize copper in smelting.[6] Removals from artificial forests were estimated as some 6 percent of total removals in about 1963, with the area and output still growing rapidly. These plantations particularly increase Latin America's resources of timber for highly manufactured products.

Production of Forest Products

Total world production of timber is currently estimated as some 2,000 million cubic meters annually, or about 60 percent more than in the immediate postwar years, the first for which data are available. Over the last two decades the removal of wood for industrial purposes has grown more rapidly than the production of fuelwood, and now accounts for some 56 percent of the total (see table 17-3). As might be expected, the output of industrial wood is concentrated in North America and Europe, including the Soviet Union, with a smaller but still appreciable share in Asia. Fuelwood removals are concentrated in Asia, Africa, and Latin America, with large amounts in Europe as well. Latin America's share of removals of both types declined slightly in the 1950s. Because it has industrialized faster than other underdeveloped regions, the region depends on wood for less of its total energy, while in the production and use of highly processed wood products it has fallen behind Europe and especially the United States. At present the region accounts for about 24 percent of the world's fuelwood and 3 percent of its industrial wood — 13 percent of the total — and the share in recent years has been increasing.

Throughout the period the share of fuelwood in Latin American timber removals has been virtually constant, both for the region and for individual countries. In no country, moreover, has fuel accounted for less than half the total

wood output, and in many it is still 90 percent or more. Differences in income or economic structure are not reflected by this measure (see table 17-4). The share of total energy consumption supplied by wood has behaved quite differently, varying widely among countries and, for the region as a whole, falling by half between 1950 and the early 1960s. In some countries the displacement of wood by other sources of energy has been even more rapid. Colombia is the most striking example up to 1961-63; in the following few years the share of energy supplied by wood fell most rapidly in Central America, where oil refineries were established in 1962-64. The rapidly increasing use of commercial energy has been concentrated in urban areas, but there has been some displacement of fuelwood by petroleum derivatives and electricity in rural areas as well. Per capita consumption fell by 14 percent in Latin America in the years 1950-62; if all fuelwood is assumed to be used by the rural population, then the slower growth of that group than of the total gives a drop in per capita consumption of about 2 percent.[7] The bulk of the increase in commercial energy supplies was provided by petroleum and natural gas, coal and hydropower being relatively minor energy sources in the region.[8] Virtually all the fuelwood produced is for household consumption, for cooking and heating. Small amounts have also been used in some countries for electric power generation, and larger quantities in the smelting and refining of iron and nonferrous metals.

The output of industrial wood and the products derived from it presents a more complicated picture. Excluding industrial roundwood—mine timbers, poles, posts, pilings and other unprocessed nonfuel wood, for which no production data are available—five classes of products are considered: sawnwood or lumber, sheet materials (plywoods and veneers), fiberboard and particle board, wood pulp, and pulp products (paper and paperboard).[9] Industrial wood accounts for some 17 percent of total timber removals in Latin America, the share varying from only 8 percent in Bolivia to three-fourths in Mexico (see table 17-5). Sawnwood, the simplest form of processed wood, accounts for more than three-fourths of the total, with Brazil supplying almost half the regional total output of 14 million cubic meters. The output of fiberboard and particle board, based on chips, sawdust, and other wood residues, has risen most rapidly, but is still far behind wood pulp and sheet materials as an outlet for industrial wood. The production of paper and other pulp products amounted in the middle

---

[6]Estimates of the area and output of artificial forests from ECLA/FAO, *Latin American Timber Trends. . .*, p. 14. See chap. 5 (Iron and Steel) for a description of the charcoal-using iron industry.

[7]Calculations based on estimates of rural and total population in ECLA, *Economic Bulletin for Latin America*, vol. V, *Statistical Supplement* (November 1960), pp. 8-9, 13.

[8]See chap. 8 (Petroleum), especially table 8-10.

[9]Comparisons of products normally measured in different units are made in terms of roundwood equivalent, (*), the amount of wood normally required to produce one unit of the product in question. Sawnwood, plywood and veneer are measured in actual volume, (†), while fiber and particle board, wood pulp, and all types of paper are measured in metric tons, (‡). The conversion factors used are given in table 17-10 and represent averages for all Latin America. Ideally the factors should vary among countries and over time, reflecting differences in species used and in the efficiency of processing, but only approximate figures are available and are used here for all countries and periods.

1960s to nearly 2 million tons annually or the equivalent of some 10 percent of the region's industrial wood production. Only about half this amount, however, is produced from domestic wood pulp. The rest depends on imports of pulp or on other types of pulp such as bagasse.

Industrial roundwood, which may be estimated as about 8 percent of total nonfuel wood in Latin America, is, like sawnwood, declining slightly in importance relative to the more highly processed forms. Both roundwood and sawnwood are produced in every country of the region, distributed roughly according to total industrial removals. The production of sheet materials and of pulp products is somewhat more concentrated, with seven countries in one case and five in the other having no production before 1963. Latin American output of veneer is dominated by Brazil, although several other countries have adequate resources of the valuable tropical hardwoods on which that country's production is based. Plywood production which, unlike veneers, goes principally to the domestic market, is somewhat more dispersed. Brazil is also the largest paper producer. Argentina and Mexico are next in size for both sheet materials and paper; Chile, Colombia, and Venezuela are substantial producers of paper only. Output is still more concentrated in fiber and particle board, and most of all in wood pulp, where only the four principal industrial countries are significant producers. If pulp products are distinguished, output is highly concentrated in a few. Newsprint, for example, is produced in only four countries — those with large enough markets to enjoy some economies of scale and, in Mexico, Brazil, and Chile, where there are adequate supplies of conifers for long-fibered woodpulp. The bulk of paper production in many countries, especially the smaller ones dependent on imports of pulp, consists of wrapping paper, the lower grades of printing and writing paper, and paperboard. The packaging of bananas for export has in the last few years stimulated the production of paperboard in such countries as Ecuador and Honduras.[10] These products are often made from nonwood pulp.

The most recent survey of the primary wood processing industry in Latin America, covering all countries and products, was conducted more than a decade ago. In the available information wood is not separated from bagasse and other sources of fiber; moreover, the industry has expanded considerably since 1958 and the shift from sawnwood to more highly processed products has continued. Nevertheless, some indication can be given of the size, structure, and distribution of the industry, to supplement the data on output discussed above.

Since essentially the size of a sawmill has no lower limit and since plants can be located throughout the forest, information is incomplete on the number and capacity of sawmills. Approximately 19,000 mills of all sizes, including nearly 9,000 in Brazil and 5,000 in Argentina, were registered in 1958. The actual number was much larger, to judge from more detailed surveys in various countries. Comparisons among countries are made difficult by differences in the criteria for registration of a mill and by climatic differences which affect the length of the working year; thus, variations in average size may be exaggerated. In general it appears that the region and most individual countries have a very large number of small mills, many of which operate only intermittently and most of which are inefficient because much wood is wasted in sawing and the wastes are not used by other industries. In most countries a small number of large and more efficient mills accounts for the bulk of the output. The variation in size is extreme and the variation in average output may be still greater because of periods of idleness.[11]

Information about the other stages of processing is more complete and reliable (see table 17-6). In 1958 there were some 300 plywood and 200 veneer mills in Latin America, 70 plants making pulp for paper, 200 paper mills, but only about 20 plants producing fiberboard and particle board and 12 producing newsprint. Of the 216 paper and paperboard plants not producing newsprint in 1958, fully three-fifths had capacities of less than 5,000 tons annually. Mills of this size were found in every producing country, while plants of 40,000 tons or more were limited to Argentina, Colombia and Mexico. For the region as a whole the 38 largest mills accounted for 55 percent of total capacity.[12] Since that time the average size of pulp and paper mills has increased in most countries; capacity has been raised by enlarging the larger and more efficient mills rather than by establishing new ones. For the region as a whole, this trend has been partly offset by the creation of capacity in several of the smaller countries. For sawnwood and sheet materials of all kinds there is no information as to changes in the size distribution of establishments.

In addition to the difficulties imposed by the nature of the raw materials available — particularly the inaccessibility and heterogeneity of much of the Latin American forest — the regional wood processing industries face two problems. The first is that of mills of too small size, occasioned by small national markets in some cases and in others by inadequate systems of transportation and marketing. The second is that of inefficiency in the use of wood brought about variously by improper cutting of the forest, poor control of materials and quality within the mill, or inadequate integration of different stages of processing, all of which lead to the waste of wood residues and increased costs. In the absence of detailed information, these problems can only be indicated in a general way.

Consumption and Trade

Although international trade in roundwood and sawnwood is substantial for some countries, it usually represents only a small share of total output or use, and production and consumption are approximately equal. For the more highly processed forest products, trade is larger relative to consumption, and many small countries rely heavily on imports for their supplies of sheet materials, pulp, paper, and

---

[10]Boxing of bananas began in most countries in 1964 or 1965. See chap. 13 (Bananas) and sources indicated there.

[11]See ECLA/FAO, *Latin American Timber Trends...*, pp. 22-23.

[12]ECLA/FAO, *Pulp and Paper...*, p. 29.

paperboard. Since estimates of actual consumption are not made regularly, an accurate comparison with output data is not possible. Estimates of consumption in 1948-51, 1956-59, and 1964-66 have been made for Latin America, showing the distribution of each product class by end use or by specific product (see table 17-7). The results cannot be reconciled with production data for sawnwood (where there may be much unreported output) or for roundwood (where no output figures are available); thus the degree of self-sufficiency of the region and of individual countries cannot be assessed for these products (compare tables 17-5 and 17-7). The discrepancy in sawnwood is especially great for the years around 1950. Production and consumption data are more reliable for sheet materials and pulp products; a comparison suggests that in the late 1950s Latin America was approximately self-sufficient in sheet materials and produced two-thirds of its total paper and paperboard requirements.[13] For paper pulp of all kinds in the same years (1956-1959), production was slightly less than 60 percent of consumption.[14] Changes in the degree of self-supply in pulp and products through import substitution are discussed below.

There have been some shifts in the composition of consumption, both among product classes and within them. The use of sawnwood and roundwood has expanded more slowly than that of sheet materials or pulp products, the former showing especially rapid growth. Sheet materials have begun to displace sawnwood in construction, and both sheet materials and paperboard have cut into the demand for sawnwood for packaging. Among pulp products a shift has occurred from "cultural paper" — newsprint and printing and writing paper — to papers for wrapping and packaging. In these respects consumption in Latin America is following the pattern of North America and Europe, with the highly manufactured products displacing less processed materials and acquiring importance in more applications. During the 1950s the use of mine timbers increased more rapidly than that of other roundwood in the region, but the trend toward open pit mining may reverse this situation.[15]

In the early 1960s Latin America accounted for some 10 percent of total world timber consumption, a somewhat higher share than the region has of world population. If fuelwood is excluded, however, the share drops to only 3.6 percent, the same proportion as for sawnwood (see table 17-8). Compared with other parts of the world, especially the more advanced countries, Latin America uses large

amounts of roundwood and only small amounts of sheet materials. Although consumption of the latter and of pulp products is rising rapidly, the region's share of the world figure is not increasing.

Except for a few countries with relatively poor forest resources — Argentina, Uruguay, and some Central American countries — the demand for roundwood and sawnwood is met domestically and there are no imports. Consumption of sheet materials is still small and can be supplied by local production in the larger countries. In the case of pulp and pulp products, however, the growth in demand has led to an increase of high-valued imports and has made the region as a whole a large net importer of forest products. Total imports of paper and paperboard rose from less than 600,000 tons annually in the late 1930s to more than 1.2 million tons two decades later, and by 1960 Latin America's net imports of pulp and paper were some $200 million, much more than offsetting the favorable $10 million balance in less highly processed products. In that year imports of newsprint amounted to 550,000 tons and to a large share of the total value; wood pulp, with imports of 350,000 tons, was next in importance.[16]

The mounting burden of imports and the existence of extensive domestic timber resources led, as with many other manufactured products, to a considerable degree of import substitution in the larger Latin American countries. Data are not readily available for measuring this process between the late 1920s and 1950, but estimates can be made of the extent of substitution since then. In the case of wood pulp, between 1950 and 1964 some 60 percent of the increase in production in seven countries—Argentina, Brazil, Chile, Colombia, Mexico, Peru, and Venezuela—went to replace imports, and a comparable share of anticipated imports in 1964 was substituted (see table 17-9). For all types of paper and paperboard, import substitution contributed only some 35 percent to growth in output, while for newsprint alone the share provided by the four producing countries was 71 percent. In 1950 the seven countries together imported 68 percent of their wood pulp, 53 percent of paper and paperboard, and 87 percent of newsprint; by 1964 the shares had been reduced to 28, 22, and 67 percent respectively. Import substitution of newsprint led to the greatest relative increases in supply in Brazil and Chile, leading to sizable exports from Chile, especially to Argentina and Mexico. Both Brazil and Chile became exporters of wood pulp. The very slight replacement of anticipated pulp imports in Venezuela reflects the considerable degree of substitution in paper in that country, which necessitated a rapid increase in imports of pulp. The same process occurred in Colombia, where self-sufficiency in pulp declined during the period.

Public policy in Latin America in recent years has been directed primarily toward increasing domestic supplies and reducing imports of forest products, but a certain amount of emphasis has been placed on increasing production for export. The adverse regional trade balance results from the facts that (1) high-valued products are imported, whereas

---

[13] In production and trade data, plywood and veneers are usually separated from fiber and particle board, but in the estimates of consumption in Latin America all products are treated together as sheet materials. The degree of self-sufficiency therefore depends on the conversion factors used for the two classes of products.

[14] Since a considerable share of production consisted of non-wood pulp, of which there were no imports, the degree of self-sufficiency in wood pulp alone was less, about 52 percent. See ECLA/FAO, *Pulp and Paper. . .*, pp. 30-31.

[15] Open pit operations are replacing underground mining for several metals as underground deposits become exhausted and attention shifts to the larger, lower-grade surface deposits. This is especially the case for copper. The increase in iron ore production, which is almost always mined by open pit methods, contributes to this trend.

[16] Data from ECLA/FAO, *Latin American Timber Trends. . .*, pp. 70-71, and FAO, *Yearbook of Forest Products Statistics, 1961.*

exports consist chiefly of unprocessed timber and low-valued semimanufactures, and (2) the share of exports to other Latin American countries is higher than the share of imports obtained from neighboring countries. This situation has improved since the 1930s, with the result that now, except for pulp and paper, trade within the region is largely integrated. Taking all products together, the share of exports going into the region rose from 57 to 68 percent in the twenty years following the late 1930s, while the share of imports from within the region rose from 16 to 46 percent.[17]

Total Latin American exports of forest products reached an estimated average of 1½ million tons, or some 4 million cubic meters roundwood equivalent, in the mid-1960s (see table 17-10). In most years the value has been between $50 million and $100 million, slightly less than 1 percent of total regional exports. In roundwood equivalent, sawnwood is the most important product, followed by roundwood. Most of the roundwood trade is of broadleaved species, part of this being veneer logs, while the bulk of the sawnwood is coniferous. Five countries—Brazil, Chile, Colombia, Honduras, and Paraguay—account for almost all the region's exports, with Chile exporting pulp and pulp products in sizable quantities and the others trading chiefly in roundwood and sawnwood. In Honduras and Paraguay forest products furnish between 10 and 20 percent of all foreign exchange. Practically all exports of the highly processed products go to other countries of the region, as does a large share of the logs and sawn timber; Argentina, Peru, and Uruguay are the principal markets. Exports outside the region go chiefly to Western Europe, with small amounts to the United States and other countries.[18]

The bulk of world trade in forest products occurs within regions, with large flows between Canada and the United States and from the Scandinavian countries to the rest of Western Europe. North America, Scandinavia, and the Soviet Union are the world's major exporters; the EEC, Japan and the United States are the chief importers. In 1953-55 some 75 percent of all trade took place among the developed countries, and consisted almost entirely of the softwood products for which the large exporters have substantial coniferous resources. Of the world total, 9 percent flowed from developed to developing countries, largely in the form of pulp and paper; and 4 percent, consisting overwhelmingly of tropical hardwoods in raw or slightly processed form, flowed in the opposite direction. Over the next decade world trade rose from $4,300 million to $7,200 million annually, and the most rapidly growing share, rising to 8 percent of the total, was that from poor to rich countries. Communist countries also doubled their exports to the developed countries, from 3 to 6 percent, as a share of world trade. The striking increase in exports from less developed countries as a group was confined to a relatively small number in southeast Asia trading with Japan,

and in western and central Africa, trading with Western Europe. Latin America has not yet shared in this expansion; its exports to developed countries have risen only 10 percent over the decade, forming less than 1 percent of total world trade in forest products.[19]

The major importing countries levy zero or very low tariffs on unworked wood, both pulpwood and that intended for lumber and manufactures. In the case of woodpulp and also of sawnwood and other highly worked wood, tariffs are generally low except in the United Kingdom, where on average there is an effective protection of 19 percent. The highest rates apply to plywood and veneers and wood manufactures; the effective rate for plywood in 1964 was about 40 percent in the United States, the United Kingdom, and Japan, and over 30 percent in the EEC. The restrictive effects will be even less in the future, since these rates were the ones most reduced in the Kennedy Round negotiations. Of more importance to current trade flows are the preferential tariffs granted by the EEC to associated African exporters and by the United States to the Philippines; tariffs also discriminate markedly in some cases among particular species or grades of wood. In the principal importing countries there are no quantitative or other nontariff barriers to trade in forest products.[20]

In table 17-11, the years 1961-63 are used to draw together comparable data on production, consumption, and trade to show a balance for Latin America. The figures are more vulnerable than for most other commodities included in this study, because some of the data are missing, much can only be estimated, and there are problems of converting and aggregating data for different products given in different units. Bearing these limitations in mind, it appears that Latin America in the early 1960s consumed annually some 203 million cubic meters (roundwood) of wood for fuel and 35 million cubic meters of timber for industrial use. There were net imports of nearly 4 million cubic meters, due almost entirely to large imports of woodpulp and pulp products. The latter were second only to sawnwood in total consumption of industrial wood (see table 17-11). Most countries of the region imported a variety of wood products; production was slightly less widely distributed; and exports were concentrated in a few countries. Only Brazil, Chile, Guatemala, Honduras, and Paraguay were net exporters in roundwood terms.

Recent Developments and Outlook

Interest in the development and use of the world's forest resources, particularly those of less developed regions, has increased in the last decade. Demand for many forest products is growing rapidly and appears to present significant opportunities for developing nations to diversify and

---

[17]ECLA/FAO, *Latin American Timber Trends. . .* , pp. 70-71.

[18]Because of the diversity of products considered, exports are not shown by destination in table 17-10. For an indication of the direction of trade in some products, chiefly roundwood and sawnwood from Brazil and Chile, see FAO, *Yearbook of Forest Products Statistics, 1966*, tables D, pp. 78-100.

[19]See UNCTAD doc. TD/49, 28 December 1967, *Forest Products – a Dynamic Sector of Developing Countries' Exports* (paper presented by FAO Secretariat), especially pp. 4-11. A summary of world forest products trade is given in J. A. Zivnuska, *U.S. Timber Resources in a World Economy* (Resources for the Future, 1967).

[20]See UNCTAD doc. TD/49, *Forest Products. . .* , pp. 39-41; and Bela Balassa, *The Effects of the Kennedy Round on the Exports of Processed Goods from Developing Areas*, UNCTAD doc. TD/69, 15 February 1968, appendix, pp. 4-5.

expand their exports. However, the resources of the poor countries must be better understood and more efficiently exploited if this expansion is to occur. Although Latin America has lagged behind Asian and African countries in responding to these opportunities and obstacles, forest products appear to offer one of the most encouraging means of increasing the region's total exports, especially exports of semimanufactures. At the same time, the region's domestic needs are expected to grow very rapidly.

Projections for Latin America in 1975, made in 1963, indicate a growth of total industrial requirements, in roundwood terms, of nearly 85 percent from the level of 1956-59. The most rapid expansion is anticipated for sheet materials (more than threefold) with only slightly slower growth in pulp and paper use. The most striking shift expected within any one class of products is an increase in the consumption of fiber and particle board sufficient to surpass that of plywood and veneers. In other categories the shifts in consumption by end use, which occurred during the 1950s, are expected to continue in some instances—as, for example, in various types of paper and paperboard—but not in others. Projections were not made for the different uses of industrial roundwood. The use of fuelwood is expected to increase very slightly or not at all over the level of the early 1960s, so that by 1975 wood will account for only about 10 percent of total energy sources in the region.[21]

The region's use of pulp and pulp products is expected to grow quite rapidly, leading to a large expansion of capacity between 1965 and 1975. The increase is expected to be somewhat more rapid for pulp, where import substitution has been less complete than for paper. The share of nonwood pulp is expected to decline slightly, but will still be about one-fourth of the total. Bagasse and other nonwood fibers are extensively used because of their availability and suitability for some grades of paper and paperboard, and because of the region's shortage of coniferous wood for long-fibered pulp. Some progress is being made in pulping broadleaved (short-fibered) species for paper, but widespread use of this resource is hampered by technical difficulties and by the great diversity of tropical hardwood species. Capacity in paper of all kinds, of which a considerable share will continue to be made from imported pulp, is expected to rise from 3.3 million to 5.8 million tons over the decade, with a much more rapid increase in newsprint — from 400,000 to 900,000 tons.[22]

Since Latin America's share of world fuelwood use is not expected to change significantly in the next few years, and since fuelwood will continue to dominate total wood consumption in the region, in 1975 Latin America will still use between 10 and 11 percent of the world's wood. In every type of industrial wood product, however, the region is expected to increase its consumption more rapidly than the rest of the world, the relative expansion being greatest for sheet materials. In the case of sawnwood, more rapid substitution by sheet products in the advanced countries should result in a sizable increase in Latin America's share of world use. For roundwood and pulp products the relative expansion will be more modest, despite the very rapid absolute growth of demand for the latter. By 1975 the world is expected to require annually some 2,800 million cubic meters of roundwood, of which 1,600 million will be for industrial use; the corresponding figures for Latin America are 280 to 300 million cubic meters and 80 million cubic meters. For the world as a whole, sawnwood is expected to take 54 percent of consumption; pulp products, 25 percent; roundwood, 12 percent; and sheet materials about 9 percent. For Latin America the shares of roundwood and sawnwood will be about one-tenth higher and those of more highly processed goods somewhat lower.[23]

The export opportunities for nontraditional suppliers, including Latin America, arise from the pressure of this rapidly growing demand on the coniferous resources of the major developed producers. The productive capacity of the developed producers is now thought to be appreciably more than was believed some years ago, but it will not be great enough to prevent an increasing deficit of production relative to consumption in North America and Europe. This factor offers scope for increased exports of coniferous wood and products from Latin America; at the same time, exports of broadleaved species may be increased by progress in evaluating and using them and in substitution for coniferous wood. Finally, the growth of domestic demand for semimanufactures and the pressure on prices when processing is carried out in importing countries should lead to greater exports of plywood and veneers and perhaps of other products, raising the value of trade more rapidly than its volume.

The interest directed to forests in recent years has resulted in a number of studies of national and regional resources and in efforts to extend and improve the forest potential. Particular attention has been given to the hardwood forests of the Amazon basin and to coniferous forests, either natural or man-made.[24] While the former may be utilized more fully by cutting more species and opening more forest area to transport facilities, the obstacles are great. The natural yield of such forests is relatively low, and in most cases it does not match the requirements of increasing demand; large investments would be required. The rapid increase in areas of broadleaved and coniferous artificial forests in several countries is indicative of the difficulty

---

[21] ECLA/FAO, *Latin American Timber Trends.* . . , pp. 54-68. It is assumed that demands for fuelwood, sawnwood, and industrial roundwood will be met by regional production, with continued intraregional trade. The degree of self-sufficiency in sheet materials, pulp, and paper is not estimated. The share of wood in energy consumption is based on the projected minimum consumption of petroleum and the 1961-63 use of coal and hydroelectricity. See chap. 8 (Petroleum).

[22] Estimates based on FAO surveys of *World Pulp and Paper Capacity*, 1965 and 1967. See UNCTAD doc. TD/49, *Forest Products.* . . , p. 27.

[23] World projections from FAO, *Unasylva*, 20, nos. 80-81, 1966; roundwood equivalents of all products for all regions estimated from conversion factors in ECLA/FAO, *Latin American Timber Trends.* . . .

[24] See, for example, V. M. Pinedo del Águila, *Evaluación Económica de los Recursos Forestales de la Amazonia Peruana* (Lima: Universidad Nacional Mayor de San Marcos, 1967), the first such study of the Amazon forest in Peru. Similar surveys have been carried out or are under consideration in other countries or regions.

of exploiting the natural forest. A large extension of artificial coniferous forest to supply long-fibered pulp for paper manufacture is one of several regional projects under consideration by the Inter-American Development Bank. Plantations in Honduras and in southern Brazil or the Alto Paraná section of eastern Paraguay are suggested as a source of pulp for newsprint for the entire region. These appear to be areas where an expansion of pine forests is most feasible, since suitable areas are limited in Mexico and Chile.[25] An artificial forest of fast-growing and relatively long-fibered hardwood species is gradually to replace the mixed, short-fibered natural hardwood forest of the Guayana area in east central Venezuela as the basis for pulp and paper production.[26] In other countries there are more limited plans for the development of part of the natural forest, with efforts to control cutting and to replant with the most valuable species.[27] Interest is growing in making detailed physical and economic studies of particular forest areas, which would replace the very general surveys previously used.

Another step toward the fuller use of Latin America's forest resources is the creation of integrated wood-processing industrial centers. Such complexes offer at least three advantages over the present industrial structure: they could be large enough to enjoy economies of scale; by producing a greater variety of goods they could draw on more different species in mixed forests; and the wastes and residues from some processes, especially sawing, could be used in others such as the manufacture of pulp and sheet materials. Such a center, using the natural forest at first but depending ultimately on plantations, will be part of the Guayana industrial complex in Venezuela.

One or more complexes, each with an annual intake of at least a million cubic meters of roundwood, appear to be feasible in Mexico, which is in an especially favorable position in this regard because of its large coniferous forests and a relatively well-developed transport system.[28]

The reduction in costs and improvement in quality possible with such establishments offer considerable scope for export, especially to Western Europe. Mexico's potential is estimated as $60 million to $70 million annually; Costa Rica is estimated to have comparable potential exports of forest products; Chile, which is developing exports of veneer to West Germany, doubled exports of coniferous lumber between 1962 and 1965.[29] Within a decade or two, forest products, mostly in semimanufactured form, might readily double in importance as an export commodity and reverse the present trade balance.

Finally, the development of forest industries may contribute to the industrial integration of Latin America. With respect to the lower valued products, the regional industry is already largely integrated, with the bulk of trade occurring within the region. In the case of pulp and paper, however, a high-cost domestic capacity has been created as part of the import substitution process, and there remains much scope for taking advantage of economies of scale and for intraregional trade. Information on probable costs of production of pulp and paper in different locations is particularly difficult to obtain. Studies using a linear programming technique suggest that for wood pulp and kraft paper—a heavy paper made from long-fibered pulp, in whose production there are appreciable economies of scale—integration and the creation of capacity at the points of lowest cost would save some $20 million to $50 million by 1975 in comparison with domestic production for each national market able to support an industry. Chile and Mexico appear to be the lowest-cost producers, and Brazil is close to being competitive for its own market.[30] Data are not available on costs in Colombia, Peru, Venezuela, Argentina, and Uruguay, nor could estimates be made for other types of paper, such as newsprint. Nonetheless, the available information suggests that pulp and paper production could be appreciably affected by the creation of a regional common market, with a saving in cost of some tens of millions of dollars. With or without such a development, the forest products industries show much potential for making a significant contribution to the Latin American economy.

[25]IADB, "Multinational Investment Programs and Latin American Integration," report prepared by Development Resources Corporation (New York, September 1966), pp. 101-2 and A-2.

[26]República de Venezuela, Corporación Venezolana de Guayana (CVG), *Informe Anual, 1965* (Caracas, 1966), pp. I-6, III-40 to III-47.

[27]Some 2.5 million hectares of a total forest area of 40 million have been set aside for development in Mexico after a joint government/United Nations Special Fund survey, and some form of nationalization to prevent the destruction of the forest by indiscriminate cutting has been proposed for the entire country. See BOLSA, *Review*, 12 June 1965, p. 558, and *Comercio Exterior* (Mexico City, September 1964), p. 628.

[28]UN, *Promotion of Exports of Manufactured Goods from Mexico*, report TAO/MEX/6, 14 February 1967, pp. 38-39.

[29]See, in addition to the sources indicated above, BOLSA, *Review*, 12 June 1965, p. 555; 26 June 1965, p. 501; and UNDP, *Pre-Investment News*, January 1968.

[30]ECIEL, "The Location of Industries in the Latin American Free Trade Area," in Martin Carnoy, ed., *Industrialization in a Latin American Common Market* (Brookings Institution, forthcoming), chap. IX, "Pulp and Paper."

CHAPTER 17 TABLES

TABLE 17-1. World Forest Resources, circa 1960

Country or Region	Forest Area[a] (thous. ha.)	Growing Stock[b] Total (mill. m³)	Growing Stock[b] Per Hectare (m³)	Removals Total (mill. m³)	Removals Per Hectare (m³)	Removals Share Growing Stock (%)
Latin America	899,000	143,629	159	224.5	0.2	0.2
Argentina	60,000	3,195	46	11.3	0.2	0.3
Bolivia	47,000[c]	6,960	148	4.3	0.09	0.06
Brazil	335,100	79,150	225	120.2	0.3	0.2
Chile	16,100	3,820	185	6.1	0.3	0.2
Colombia	69,400	11,800	170	25.3	0.4	0.2
Costa Rica	2,981	660	221	1.7	0.6	0.3
Cuba	2,530			1.9	0.6	
Dominican Republic	2,225	(d)		2.0	0.9	
Ecuador	34,711	2,460	66	2.7	0.07	0.1
El Salvador	226	(d)		2.9	13.0	
Guatemala	4,100	820	200	6.3	1.2	0.8
Haiti	700	118	169	8.2	11.8	6.9
Honduras	5,975	1,035	165	3.3	0.5	0.3
Mexico	39,747	4,900	123	11.5	0.3	0.2
Nicaragua	6,450	1,020	158	2.3	0.4	0.2
Panama	4,500	1,000	164	1.8	0.3	0.2
Paraguay	20,906	1,940	93	1.7	0.08	0.08
Peru	65,300	11,100	128	3.0	0.03	0.02
Uruguay	593	98	165	1.3	2.1	1.3
Venezuela	47,970	5,630	117	5.0	0.1	0.08
North America	713,059			393.9	0.6	
Europe	138,000			323.0	2.3	
Soviet Union	738,117			357.7	0.5	
Africa	700,000			195.8	0.3	
Asia	500,000			379.8	0.8	
Oceania	207,267			24.9	0.1	
World Total	3,792,000			1,899.6	0.5	

Sources: FAO, *World Forest Inventory, 1963* (most data refer to 1960-62 average) and *1958*. ECLA/FAO, *Latin American Timber Trends and Prospects* (New York, 1963), p. 16.

[a]Area of forests only; differs from area of "forest land" by amount of unstocked or deforested land.
[b]Estimates for 1958-59, Latin America only; includes branches but excludes bark.
[c]Estimate for 1938.
[d]Total for El Salvador, Dominican Republic, and the Guianas is 7,923.

TABLE 17-2. Shares of Coniferous (Softwood) and Broadleaved (Hardwood) Species in Latin American Forest Resources and Production, circa 1959
(Percentages)

Country	Growing Stock[a] Con.	Growing Stock[a] Br.	Forest Area in Use[b] Con.	Forest Area in Use[b] Br.	Removals[c] Total Con.	Removals[c] Total Br.	Removals[c] Industrial Con.	Removals[c] Industrial Br.
Argentina	0.5	99	3.4	97	2.0	98	9.0	91
Bolivia		100		100	0.9	99	11	89
Brazil	0.2	100	15	85	26	74	47	53
Chile	2.6	97	11	89	23	77	40	60
Colombia		100		100		100	0.6	99
Costa Rica		100		100		100		100
Cuba	1.4	99	10	90	3.9	96	22	78
Dominican Republic	1.3	99	63	37	13	87	83	17
Ecuador		100		100		100		100
El Salvador	4.2	96	9.4	91	3.1	97	64	36
Guatemala	4.9	95	32	68	42	58	54	46
Haiti	2.5	97	37	63	6.0	94	42	58
Honduras			75	25	72	28	96	4.1
Mexico	10	90	43	57	52	48	81	19
Nicaragua	2.0	98	50	50	17	83	47	53
Panama		100		100		100		100
Paraguay		100		100		100		100
Peru		100		100	1.4	99	6.5	93
Uruguay	2.8	97	1.9	98	11	89	61	39
Venezuela		100		100		100		100
Latin America	0.6	99	17	83	20	80	41	59

Sources: FAO, *World Forest Products Statistics, 1954-1963*. FAO, *World Forest Inventory, 1963*, pp. 62, 74. ECLA/FAO, *Latin American Timber Trends* . . . , pp. 10-11, 16-17.

[a]Total growing stock: estimate for 1958-59 (data on total forest area not available).
[b]Forest area in use: data for Brazil, Colombia, Honduras, and Peru from 1963 Inventory; for other countries, from 1958 Inventory.
[c]Removals: data for 1959.

TABLE 17-3. World Production (Removals) of Timber,[a] 1946-1966
(Thousands of cubic meters roundwood)

Country or Region	Average 1946-49	1950	1951	1952	1953	1954	1955	1956	1957	1958	1959	1960	1961	1962	1963	1964	1965	1966
Latin America	177,910	191,978	195,840	199,195	192,768	195,678	203,954	207,521	204,273	204,378	204,730	209,347	221,976	235,157	240,709	251,000	261,922	274,268[b]
Argentina	15,434	13,750	12,546	13,621	13,289	12,396	12,822	13,271	13,281	11,192	12,084	12,111	11,345	10,538	9,713	10,751	11,899	12,427[b]
Bolivia	6,625	6,828	7,534	7,531	(c)	(c)	(c)	(c)	(c)	(c)	(c)	4,218	4,293	4,337	4,335	4,573	4,824	4,987[b]
Brazil	96,257	103,263	105,750	106,045	102,095	109,000	109,300	110,000	107,700	108,600	107,625	106,450	120,000	134,250	137,280	144,050	151,152	161,030[b]
Chile	6,601	5,540	5,590	5,788	5,743	5,983	5,502	5,930	5,400	4,895	4,541	5,583	5,819	6,901	6,532	6,946	7,104	6,869
Colombia[d]	22,543	22,380	22,297	22,307	22,268	22,800	24,070	24,470	24,930	25,030	25,130	25,230	25,330	25,330	25,330	25,300	24,790[b]	(c)
Costa Rica	806	872	895	903	970	993	1,441	1,469	1,496	1,561	1,592	1,665	1,783	1,796	1,998	1,998	1,998	2,223
Cuba	1,529	967	1,000	1,031	1,054	1,515	1,572	1,583	1,682	1,710	1,790	1,835	1,875	1,970	1,970	2,194	2,194	2,492
Dom. Rep.	1,530	1,540	1,571	1,569	1,551	1,564	1,586	1,626	1,705	1,781	1,960	1,959	1,940	1,970	1,970	2,030	2,091	2,212
Ecuador	1,430	1,437	1,501	1,660	1,464	1,493	2,320	2,544	2,730	2,760	2,795	3,100	2,550	2,433	2,435	2,435	2,435	2,322
El Salvador	(c)	(c)	(c)	(c)	2,500	2,500	2,570	2,650	2,567	2,820	2,910	2,935	2,960	2,960	2,960	2,960	2,960	2,372
Guatemala	5,345	5,533	6,634	6,396	7,300	7,107	7,209	7,350	7,296	7,450	6,270	6,270	6,270	6,270	7,000	7,000	7,000	7,000
Haiti	(c)	(c)	(c)	(c)	9,037	9,160	8,770	8,739	7,150	8,070	8,225	8,225	8,225	8,225	8,225	8,225	8,225	12,325
Honduras	2,324	2,556	2,623	2,705	2,540	2,540	2,539	2,227	2,814	2,810	3,410	3,390	3,310	3,260	3,260	3,260	3,260	(c)
Mexico[e]	2,600	4,190	4,348	3,499	3,201	3,464	3,830	4,900	4,485	4,485	4,719	4,356	4,295	4,853	5,340	5,674	6,156	5,499
Nicaragua	(c)	(c)	(c)	(c)	2,096	2,157	2,225	2,195	2,180	2,159	2,265	2,265	2,265	2,275	2,275	2,275	2,275	2,275
Panama	(c)	(c)	(c)	(c)	1,744	1,760	1,750	1,760	1,770	1,790	1,807	1,820	1,820	1,830	1,834	1,834	1,834	1,834
Paraguay	1,480	1,766	1,785	1,678	1,734	1,554	1,610	1,675	1,708	1,734	1,674	1,695	1,720	1,720	1,720	1,720	1,720	1,252
Peru	2,395	2,550	2,573	2,744	2,742	2,800	2,564	2,567	2,585	2,612	2,887	3,065	2,933	2,962	3,024	2,931	2,843	2,929[b]
Uruguay	711	723	690	623	597	696	1,080	1,100	1,140	1,186	1,215	1,240	1,265	1,265	1,265	1,265	1,265	1,265
Venezuela	3,300	3,550	3,650	3,747	3,839	3,956	4,194	4,465	4,654	4,733	4,831	4,935	4,968	4,982	5,019	5,158	5,276	5,412
North America	354,843	368,570	389,590	377,100	366,580	391,924	414,172	419,103	390,588	371,604	408,063	405,344	383,339	392,911	389,032	408,572	410,623	432,748
Europe	289,313	271,660	288,830	288,380	277,830	292,844	304,991	302,336	311,017	307,477	302,795	316,973	326,571	325,345	314,384	324,411	323,379	320,753
Soviet Union	226,525	266,000	297,700	291,400	202,100	328,900	333,900	342,300	361,400	375,000	397,800	369,500	351,000	352,700	369,600	385,300	375,704	373,400
Africa	90,550	89,780	91,200	90,400	93,210	167,657	170,164	175,450	177,547	178,881	184,055	190,073	196,182	201,269	205,047	208,989	217,056	238,378
Asia	107,668	120,600	128,990	127,270	129,560	334,501	346,301	347,323	355,456	363,284	369,224	383,027	382,775	373,578	382,386	357,239	360,204	377,721
Oceania	15,630	16,870	18,400	18,750	19,380	22,158	22,879	23,196	22,905	23,556	23,923	25,108	25,167	24,364	25,381	26,788	27,194	27,717
World Total	1,262,439	1,325,458	1,410,550	1,392,495	1,369,333	1,733,662	1,797,361	1,817,229	1,823,186	1,824,180	1,890,590	1,899,372	1,887,010	1,904,524	1,926,539	1,962,299	1,998,012	2,038,715
L.A. Share (%)	14.1	14.5	13.9	14.3	14.1	11.3	11.3	11.4	11.2	11.2	10.8	11.0	11.8	12.3	12.5	12.8	13.1	13.5
Fuelwood Removals:																		
Latin America	154,796	167,163	168,211	171,515	163,466	161,704	168,440	169,884	170,283	155,193	170,070	175,092	189,412	199,792	203,694	208,866	214,025	222,344
World Total	622,944	612,633	632,441	614,355	604,126	857,116	869,238	865,311	879,874	874,729	883,834	871,128	877,341	830,851	844,169	871,766	899,314	903,814
Industrial Wood Removals:																		
Latin America	21,925	23,560	26,380	26,440	25,950	33,974	35,514	37,637	33,990	37,700	34,660	34,255	32,564	33,733	31,360	35,089	38,815	45,554
World Total	638,256	711,540	776,860	776,900	763,950	876,546	928,123	951,918	943,312	949,451	1,006,756	1,028,244	1,009,669	1,025,628	1,035,365	1,083,488	1,131,594	1,134,701

Sources: FAO, *World Forest Products Statistics, 1946-1955, 1954-1963,* and *Yearbook of Forest Products Statistics, 1967, 1968;* ECLA/FAO, *Latin American Timber Trends....*

[a] Estimated total removals of timber from forests, which is less than total timber felled by forests, by the amount of losses in cutting and transport.

[b] Unofficial estimates.

[c] Estimate included in total for Latin America.

[d] Figures for 1946-53 adjusted to match those for 1954-67 by raising the estimate of fuelwood removals. See table 17-4, estimates for 1949-51.

[e] Includes estimated (unrecorded) removals of one million cubic meters annually for fuelwood.

TABLE 17–4. Fuelwood Consumption in Latin America, Averages, 1949-51, 1961-63, and 1964-66
(*Thousands of cubic meters roundwood and thousands of metric tons petroleum equivalent*)

Country	1949-51				1961-63				1964-66			
	Vol. of Fuelwood	% of Timber Removals	Energy Equiv.[a]	% of Total Energy[b]	Vol. of Fuelwood	% of Timber Removals	Energy Equiv.[a]	% of Total Energy[b]	Vol. of Fuelwood	% of Timber Removals	Energy Equiv.[a]	% of Total Energy[b,c]
Argentina	11,633	85	1,280	12	8,531	81	938	5	8,864	84	975	5
Bolivia	6,867	98	755	63	4,237	98	465	52	4,450	98	490	52
Brazil	94,000	91	10,340	63	117,000	90	12,870	39	119,000	92	13,090	35
Chile	3,400	60	374	12	3,254	51	358	6	2,694	42	296	4
Colombia	20,000[c]	89	2,200	62	22,200	88	2,440	27	22,100	88	2,431	23
Costa Rica	483	57	53	35	1,391	75	153	39	1,608	87	177	39
Cuba	686	73	75	4	1,455	72	160	3	1,533	76	169	3
Dominican Republic	1,400[d]	90	154	59	1,660	85	183	31	1,783	91	196	23
Ecuador	1,300[d]	89	143	36	1,693	69	186	23	1,487	42	164	17
El Salvador	2,400	96	264	73	2,850	96	314	52	2,555	94	281	40
Guatemala	5,925	97	652	72	5,825	88	641	55	3,850	58	424	31
Haiti	7,349	98	809	96	8,000	97	880	89	9,850	97	1,084	89
Honduras	2,074	82	228	62	2,500	76	275	51	1,200	65	132	34
Mexico	8,000[e]	74	880	9	9,000[d]	69	990	4	8,227	63	905	3
Nicaragua	1,500[d]	79	165	71	1,850	82	204	46	1,383	80	152	31
Panama	1,700[d]	97	187	52	1,710	94	188	22	1,735	95	191	19
Paraguay	1,266	73	139	90	1,325	77	146	51	1,713	79	188	53
Peru	2,267	90	249	15	2,456	83	270	6	2,500	84	275	6
Uruguay	635	90	70	7	1,050	83	116	7	1,050	85	116	6
Venezuela	3,300	93	363	8	4,650	93	511	3	3,478	94	383	2
Latin America	176,185	88	19,380	33	202,637	86	22,288	17	201,060	80	22,119	15

Sources: FAO, *World Forest Products Statistics, 1946-1955, 1954-1963, 1966,* *1968.* ECLA/FAO, *Latin American Timber Trends...,* p. 17. Also table 8-10 (Petroleum).

[a]Fuelwood converted at 0.11 tons petroleum equivalent per cubic meter of round-wood.

[b]Fuelwood as a share of total inanimate energy, or commercial energy (coal, petroleum, natural gas, and hydroelectricity) plus fuelwood. Hydroelectricity is measured in actual energy content rather than in the amount of fuel required to produce the same amount of electricity. Other vegetable fuels such as sugarcane bagasse are excluded; data are available for 1949-51 but not for 1961-63 or 1964-66.

[c]Excludes hydropower.

[d]Estimated from data for 1954 and succeeding years; data for 1949-51 are not available or are greatly underestimated.

[e]Estimated from data for 1959, which include unrecorded (unauthorized) fuelwood removals.

TABLE 17–5. Production and Use of Industrial Wood in Latin America, Averages, 1949-51, 1961-63, and 1966-67
(Thousands of cubic meters roundwood or actual volume and thousands of metric tons)

Country	Vol. of Indust. Wood (*)	% of Total Removals	(†) Sawnwood	Sheet (†) Materials	(‡) Fiberboard	(‡) Pulp	Pulp (‡) Products
				1949-51			
Argentina	3,076	15	573	38.3	5.3	10.3	208
Bolivia	129	2	62				0.5
Brazil	9,563	9	3,541	132.0		122	242
Chile	2,223	40	599	12.0		14.7	45
Colombia	2,416	11	895				
Costa Rica	364	43	149				1.7
Cuba	255	27	73				30.0
Dominican Republic	153	10	62				0.3
Ecuador	156	11	97				
El Salvador	100[a]	4					
Guatemala	158	3	93	0.7			
Haiti	30	2	13				
Honduras	460	18	267				
Mexico	2,788	76	1,823	8.3	3.7	72	127
Nicaragua	400[a]	21					
Panama	100[a]	3	20				
Paraguay	469	27	52	0.1			0.2
Peru	257	10	36				18.3
Uruguay	75	10	33				26.7
Venezuela	250	7	180				7.8
Latin America	20,222	12	8,573	191	9	219	708
Roundwood equivalent[b]			17,000	430	14	770	2,000
Share of total industrial wood (%)			84	2.1		3.8	10
				1961-63			
Argentina	2,001	19	795	39.6	26.0	63	371
Bolivia	85	2	32	0.4			0.8
Brazil	13,843	10	6,304	291.7	57.3	398	553
Chile	3,163	49	971	8.2	13.6	148	130
Colombia	3,130	12	990	30.0	7.0	11.5	92
Costa Rica	468	25	281	6.4			
Cuba	580	28	130		15.9		66
Dominican Republic	295	15	55				1.3
Ecuador	780	31	339	0.6			2.0
El Salvador	110	4	12				
Guatemala	810	12	116	2.7	2.2		3.2
Haiti	225	3	19				
Honduras	785	24	487				
Mexico	3,142	65	1,161	47.4	18.7	203	473
Nicaragua	425	18	134	11.8			
Panama	118	6	35				0.7
Paraguay	395	23	27	2.4			0.4
Peru	517	17	144		1.1		57
Uruguay	215	17	70	4.5	1.6	2.0	29
Venezuela	340	7	184	9.4	2.1		103
Latin America	31,427	14	12,286	455	146	826	1,882
Roundwood equivalent[b]			24,600	1,100	230	2,900	5,300
Share of total industrial wood[c] (%)			78	3.5	0.7	9.2	17

TABLE 17–5 – Continued

Country	Vol. of Indust. Wood (*)	% of Total Removals	(†) Sawnwood	Production of			
				Sheet (†) Materials	(‡) Fiberboard	(‡) Pulp	Pulp (‡) Products
				1966-67			
Argentina	2,706	22	1,041	62.9	22.0	82	478
Bolivia	387	8	58	1.5			1.0
Brazil	23,030	14	6,815	350.0	69.0	750	721
Chile	3,862	59	1,001	11.6	12.9	307	238
Colombia	2,790	11	985	32.8	18.5	35	150
Costa Rica	535	24	333	21.4			2.7
Cuba	810	33	165	3.1	15.4		125
Dominican Republic	412	19	95				2.4
Ecuador	1,135	50	590	7.1			6
El Salvador	76	3	12				.8
Guatemala	850	12	166	6.4	5.8		6.5
Haiti	1,225	7	18				
Honduras	1,020	26	680				
Mexico	4,196	76	1,957	74.0	19.5	250	605
Nicaragua	307	14	131	6.6			
Panama	152	12	51	2.1			1
Paraguay	829	28	129	.6			1.7
Peru	431	15	235	6.7	2.4		67
Uruguay	215	17	70	4.5	1.5	3.8	37
Venezuela	510	9	205	13.9	10.0		158
Latin America	45,478	17	14,737	605	177	1,428	1,996
Roundwood equivalent[b]			29,500	1,500	280	5,010	5,600
Share of total industrial wood[c] (%)			84	3.0	0.8	7.1	10.8

Sources: FAO, *World Forest Products Statistics, 1946-1955, 1954-1963*. ECLA/FAO, *Latin American Timber Trends . . .*, p. 17. FAO, *Yearbook of Forest Products Statistics, 1968*.

Notes: Sawnwood: includes sleepers. Sheet Materials: 1949-51, plywood only; 1961-63 and 1966-67, plywood and veneers. Fiberboard: includes particle board. Pulp: wood pulp of all types; excludes pulp from other fibers. Paper and paperboard: includes production from imported pulp. Mine timbers and other industrial roundwood are excluded.

(*) Thousands of cubic meters roundwood equivalent; (†) thousands of cubic meters actual volume; (‡) thousands of metric tons.

[a]Data not available; estimates for 1959 (adjusted) used.
[b]For conversion factors see table 17–10.
[c]Sum exceeds 100% because wood used for paper is counted twice (once as pulp and again as paper) and because much pulp for paper production is imported.

TABLE 17-6. Structure of the Wood Processing Industry in Latin America, circa 1958
(Number of plants and output or capacity in thousands of cubic meters or thousands of metric tons)

Country	Registered Sawmills Number	Output (†)	Plywood Mills Number	Output (†)	Veneer Mills Number	Output (†)	Particle Board Mills Number	Output (†)	Fiberboard Mills Number	Output (†)	Paper Pulp Number	Capacity (‡)	Paper & Paperboard Total Number	Capacity (‡)	Newsprint Number	Capacity (‡)	Other Number	Capacity (‡)
Argentina	5,000a	750	30	47					1	18	15	115.7	70b	417.6	1	20.0	70	397.6
Bolivia	150	22	1	0.5	1								1	0.8			1	0.8
Brazil	8,700	6,284	234	111	200	109	2	3	2	40	34	284.6	66b	519.4	8	66.0	66	453.4
Chile	800	754	3	7	1		1	1.4	1	7	3	56.0	11b	95.7	2	52.0	10	43.7
Colombia	300	977	4	25			3	5	1	(c)	1	3.0	7	55.3			7	55.3
Costa Rica	180	234	(d)			2					1	2.0	1	2.0			1	2.0
Cuba	208f	57					1	(e)	2	(f)			4	59.0			4	59.0
Ecuador	58f	285	(d)	4							1	3.0	2	3.5			2	3.5
El Salvador	6	25	(d)	2									1	1.5			1	1.5
Guatemala	85	241											1	1.4			1	1.4
Honduras	50	351									1	1.0						
Mexico		856	(d)	39			3	0.6	1	15	13	222.5	37b	396.9	1	30.0	36	366.9
Panama	175	25	1	4									1	0.7			1	0.7
Paraguay	60	31	1	1														
Peru	150	90	2	0.5							2	28.0	4	53.5			4	53.5
Uruguay		14	2	14			1				2	8.0	7	41.2			7	41.2
Venezuela	208		(d)	7			2						5	54.5			5	54.5
Latin Americag	19,000	11,333	300	263	200	110	13	12	8	80	73	723.8	218	1,703.0	12	168.0	216	1,535.0

Sources: ECLA/FAO, *Latin American Timber Trends...,* pp. 25-33. ECLA/FAO, *Pulp and Paper in Latin America* (New York, 1963), pp. 21-32. FAO, *World Forest Products Statistics, 1954-1963.*

Notes: Registered sawmills: all establishments registered with one or another government agency. Excludes hand-sawing workshops, illegally operated mills, and large numbers of small, intermittently operated mills. Total production of sawnwood is attributed to registered mills.

Veneer mills: excludes some establishments integrated with furniture production or other activities.

Particle board, fiberboard, pulp and paper: includes mills using residues of all types and fibers other than wood, such as bagasse. Data on total wood use in sheet materials, pulp, paper, and paperboard not available.

All output figures are 1957-59 averages where data are available.

(*) Thousands of cubic meters roundwood equivalent; (†) thousands of cubic meters actual volume;
(‡) thousands of metric tons.

aEstimated from Latin American total.
bSince some mills produce both newsprint and other kinds of paper and paperboard, total number of plants may be less than sum of newsprint mills and mills producing other paper products.
cCapacity reported as 12,000 metric tons; production not reported.
dOne or more plants reported to exist.
eAll production is from bagasse; data not available.
fProvince of Esmeraldas only.
gIncludes estimates for the Dominican Republic, Haiti, and Nicaragua.

TABLE 17-7. Latin American Consumption of Forest Products by Product and End Use[a], Averages, 1948-51, 1956-59, and 1964-66
(Thousands of cubic meters and thousands of metric tons)

Country	Sawnwood (†)	Sheet Materials (†)	Roundwood (*)	Pulp Products (‡)
		1948-51		
Argentina	1,650	51	132	405
Brazil	4,900	223	2,300	296
Chile	549	7.6	222	63
Colombia	578	2.3	710	55
Costa Rica	129		64	3.8
Cuba	330	(b)	(c)	104
Dominican Republic	64	(b)	(c)	6.3
Ecuador	184		145	9.1
El Salvador	60		39	4.4
Guatemala	97	8.1	217	5.8
Other Central America[d]	258		200	11
Haiti	57	(b)	(c)	2.0
Mexico	1,200	12	620	242
Paraguay	20	1.5	100	2.3
Peru	140	0.3	83	31
Uruguay	150	10	26	48
Venezuela	213	1.4	250	43
Latin America[e]	11,067	334	6,040	1,383

Distribution by end use of product:

Construction	6,477	Plywood and		Mine timbers	604	Newsprint	397
Furniture	1,013	veneers	311	Other	5,496	Printing and	
Packaging	1,331	Fiberboard	19			writing paper	252
Sleepers	839	Particle board	4			Other paper	448
Other	1,407					Paperboard	286

Roundwood equivalent of total consumption:

	Sawnwood	Sheet Materials	Roundwood	Pulp Products
	22,763	800	6,040	3,700

Country	Sawnwood (†)	Sheet Materials (†)	Roundwood (*)	Pulp Products (‡)
		1956-59		
Argentina	1,740	67	232	476
Brazil	6,000	388	2,400	580
Chile	707	13	233	80
Colombia	961	23	951	106
Costa Rica	255	0.5	81	8.8
Cuba	340	(b)	(c)	155
Dominican Republic	68	(b)	(c)	12
Ecuador	207	0.2	205	15
El Salvador	72	1.1	40	11
Guatemala	245	11	243	12
Other Central America[d]	344	1.5	250	20
Haiti	66	(b)	(c)	3.1
Mexico	1,100	53	930	413
Paraguay	24	2.0	130	2.5
Peru	178	1.9	367	65
Uruguay	180	18	26	62
Venezuela	382	12	260	126
Latin America[e]	13,540	638	7,460	2,241

Distribution by end use of product:

Construction	7,768	Plywood and		Mine timbers	900	Newsprint	621
Furniture	1,294	veneers	536	Other	6,560	Printing and	
Packaging	1,581	Fiberboard	85			writing paper	395
Sleepers	1,131	Particle board	17			Other paper	753
Other	1,766					Paperboard	471

Roundwood equivalent of total consumption:

	Sawnwood	Sheet Materials	Roundwood	Pulp Products
	28,000	1,500	7,460	5,800

TABLE 17-7 – Continued

Country	Sawnwood (†)	Sheet Materials (†)	Roundwood (*)	Pulp Products (‡)
		1964-66		
Argentina	1,671	31		660
Bolivia	43	1.3	92	4.3
Brazil	4,645	207	2,740	733
Chile	1,053	8		148
Colombia	886	39	170	189
Costa Rica	315	9		41
Cuba	328			148
Dominican Republic	85			19
Ecuador	398	9		51
El Salvador	80	4		26
Guatemala	155	5		27
Other Central America[d]	401	13		74
Haiti	16			1.5
Mexico	1,503	63	891	702
Paraguay	38	1.5		4.6
Peru	307	11.4	159	108
Uruguay	148	7.1	13	62
Venezuela	296	15		231
Latin America[e]	12,851	423		3,229

Distribution by end use of product:

Sleepers	201	Plywood and veneers 260	Mine timbers 1,012	Newsprint 798
		Fiberboard 135		Printing and writing paper 522
		Particle board 28		Other paper 1,375
				Paperboard 634

Roundwood equivalent of total consumption:

	23,853	911		9,050

Sources: ECLA/FAO, *Latin American Timber Trends...*, pp. 36-49. FAO, *Yearbook of Forest Products Statistics, 1966, 1968.*

Note: (*) Thousands of cubic meters roundwood equivalent; (†) thousands of cubic meters actual volume; (‡) thousands of metric tons.

[a]Excluding fuelwood but including roundwood for industrial use (mine timbers, poles, pilings, etc.).

[b]Total consumption of wood-based sheet materials in Cuba, the Dominican Republic and Haiti was 17,000 cubic meters annually in 1948-51 and 42,000 cubic meters in 1956-59. Distribution by country is not available.

[c]Total consumption of industrial roundwood in Cuba, the Dominican Republic, and Haiti was 580,000 cubic meters annually in 1948-51 and 670,000 in 1956-59. Distribution by country is not available.

[d]Honduras, Nicaragua, and Panama.

[e]Includes estimates for Bolivia, the Guianas, and Caribbean Islands.

TABLE 17-8. World Consumption of Forest Products, 1960-1962
  (Thousands of cubic meters and thousands of metric tons)

Region	Sawnwood (†)	Sawnwood (*)	Sheet Materials (†)	Sheet Materials (*)	Roundwood (*)	Pulp Products (‡)	Pulp Products (*)	Fuelwood (*)	Total (*)
Latin America	12,390	25,520	520	1,220	8,500	2,660	7,220	192,000	234,500
North America	94,370	194,400	16,250	38,030	18,600	37,370	102,420	46,000	399,400
Europe	78,310	161,320	8,410	19,680	36,600	22,870	59,890	108,000	385,500
Soviet Union	99,720	205,420	2,240	5,240	67,300	3,470	9,980	101,000	388,900
Africa	4,050	8,340	370	870	13,300	900	2,490	183,000	208,000
Asia and Oceania	57,330	118,510	2,750	6,440	44,100	10,200	29,960	458,000	657,000
World Total	346,170	713,110	30,530	71,440	188,000	77,470	219,940	1,088,000	2,280,500
L.A. Share (%)		3.6		1.7	4.5		3.3	17.7	10.3

Sources: FAO, *Unasylva*, vol. 20, nos. 80-81 (1966). FAO, *World Forest Products Statistics, 1954-1963.* ECLA/FAO, *Latin American Timber Trends....*

Notes: Roundwood equivalents of consumption of sawnwood, sheet materials, and pulp products for all regions are calculated from conversion factors for Latin America.

(*) Thousands of cubic meters roundwood equivalent; (†) thousands of cubic meters actual volume; (‡) thousands of metric tons.

TABLE 17-9. Import Substitution in Wood Pulp and Pulp Products in Selected Latin American Countries between 1950 and 1964
   (Thousands of metric tons)

Concept	Year	Argentina	Brazil	Chile	Colombia	Mexico	Peru	Venezuela	Total Seven Countries
I. WOOD PULP									
Production	1950	8.7	140	15	0.4[a]	70	5.0[b]		239
	1964	67.4	477[c]	174[c]	19.5	239	42.7[b]	14.2	1,034
Imports	1950	72	133	28	1.0[a]	53	8.0	7.0	298
	1964	161	28	9	51.4	66	18.4	71.2	405
Total supply	1950	80.7	273	43	1.4	123	13.0	7.0	437
	1964	228.4	505	183	70.9	305	61.1	85.4	1,439
Increase in production	1950-64	58.7	337	159	19.1	169	37.7	14.2	795
Import coefficient (%)	1950	89.2	48.7	65.1	71.5	43.0	61.5	100	68.4
Anticipated imports	1964	214	246	119	50	131	37.6	85.4	883.0
Difference between anticipated and actual imports	1964	53	218	110	–1.4	65	19.2	14.2	478
Share of increased production due to import substitution (%)	1950-64	90	65	69	(d)	38	51	100	60
Share of anticipated imports replaced by increased production (%)	1950-64	25	89	93	(d)	50	51	17	54
II. TOTAL PAPER AND PAPERBOARD									
Production	1950	214	248	45	8[a]	132	18.0	5.0[a]	470
	1964	408	650	160[c]	115	558	60	133	2,084
Imports	1950	208	69.7	21.5	62.2	65	13.1	87	527
	1964	182	76.0	8.2	56.2	127	41.3	83	574
Total supply	1950	422	317.7	66.5	70.2	187	31.1	92	997
	1964	590	726	168.2	171.2	685	101.3	216	2,658
Increase in production	1950-64	194	402	115	107	426	42	128	1,614
Import coefficient (%)	1950	49.4	22.0	32.3	88.6	34.7	42.2	94.6	53.0
Anticipated imports	1964	291	159	54.4	152	238	42.6	206	1,143
Difference between anticipated and actual imports	1964	109	83	46.2	95.8	111	1.3	123	569
Share of increased production due to import substitution (%)	1950-64	56	21	40	90	26	3.1	96	35
Share of anticipated imports replaced by increased production (%)	1950-64	37	52	84	63	47	3.0	60	50
III. NEWSPRINT ONLY									
Production	1950[a]		30.0	10	(e)	2.0	(e)	(e)	42.0
	1964	8.2	118.5	77.1[c]		15.6			219.4
Imports	1950	101	61	19	20	57[f]	8.3	11	277.3
	1964	165	66	4.8	42	100	37	38	452.8
Total supply	1950	101	91	29	20	59	8.3	11	319.3
	1964	173.2	184.5	81.9	42	115.6	37	38	672.2
Increase in production	1950-64	8.2	88.5	67.1		13.6			177.4
Import coefficient (%)	1950	100	67.0	65.5	100	96.5	100	100	86.9
Anticipated imports	1964	173.2	123	53.6	42	111.4	37	38	578.2
Difference between anticipated and actual imports	1964	8.2	57	48.8		11.4			125.4
Share of increased production due to import substitution (%)	1950-64	100	64	73	(e)	84	(e)	(e)	71
Share of anticipated imports replaced by increased production (%)	1950-64	4.7	46	91	(e)	10	(e)	(e)	22

Sources: FAO, *World Forest Products Statistics, 1946-1955* and *1954-1963*, and *Yearbook of Forest Products Statistics, 1966*. ECLA, *Economic Survey of Latin America, 1964* and *1965*. ECLA/FAO, *El Papel y la Celulosa en América Latina* (Santiago, 1966), app. IV.

Note: For definitions and notes see chap. 1, table A-4.

[a]1949-50 average.
[b]Pulp made from other fibers; total supply refers to total pulp, wood and nonwood.
[c]Includes production for export.
[d]Actual imports exceeded anticipated imports despite increases in production.
[e]No production in 1950-1964, so that no import substitution occurred.
[f]Data for 1951; 1950 imports were abnormally low.

TABLE 17-10. Latin American Exports of Forest Products, 1950-1967
(Thousands of metric tons, thousands of cubic meters, and thousands of U.S. dollars)

Country	Product	Unit	1950	1951	1952	1953	1954
Brazil	Broadleaved logs	(*)	40	93	46	27	58.6
	Sleepers	(†)	5.5	2.2	5.7	14.0	5.9
	Coniferous sawnwood	(†)	809	1,057	630	915	799
	Broadleaved sawnwood	(†)	45	56	26	34	28.8
	Veneer sheets	(†)	1.1		1.2	2.1	2.6
	Plywood	(†)	10.8	11.1	1.8	0.2	1.0
	Estimated total weight	(‡)	503	691	399	538	498
	Value		35,109	58,203	38,170	55,684	67,764
	Share total exports (%)		2.6	3.3	2.7	3.6	4.3
Chile	Coniferous sawnwood	(†)	67.8	59.9	30.0	60.4	101.6
	Broadleaved sawnwood	(†)	110	65	64	77	97.3
	Plywood	(†)	2.8	5.1	0.9	0.6	1.0
	Estimated total weight	(‡)	119	81	64	94	129
	Value		8,484	9,147	8,003	9,362	15,310
	Share total exports (%)		3.0	2.5	1.8	2.3	3.8
Dom. Rep.	Estimated total weight	(‡)	7	3	1		5
	Value		452	488	304		274
	Share total exports (%)		0.5	0.4	0.2		0.2
Ecuador	Broadleaved logs	(*)				0.1	0.1
	Broadleaved sawnwood	(†)	22	35	28	27	26.0
	Estimated total weight	(‡)	16	26	20	20	19
	Value		690	1,165	985	1,054	889
	Share total exports (%)		0.9	1.7	1.0	1.1	0.7
Guatemala	Roundwood, all types	(*)	2.8	12.5	7.3	13.1	10.6
	Plywood	(†)		1.3	1.7	1.2	1.2
	Estimated total weight	(‡)	2	10	6	13	10
	Value				1,112	769	533
	Share total exports (%)				1.2	0.8	0.5
Honduras	Coniferous sawnwood	(†)	67.3	95.9	131.8	127.7	147.5
	Broadleaved sawnwood	(†)	7.8	6.1	6.0	1.6	3.0
	Estimated total weight	(‡)	41	54	73	67	79
	Value		2,077	5,400[a]	4,072	3,617	3,300[a]
	Share total exports (%)		3.8	8.2	6.5	5.3	6.0
Mexico	Broadleaved logs	(*)	31	43	43	16	10.9
	Coniferous sawnwood	(†)	361	189	190	95	106
	Broadleaved sawnwood	(†)	22	18	41	29	13.7
	Plywood	(†)	2.2	4.5	2.3	1.5	2.5
	Estimated total weight	(‡)	235	156	172	87	83
	Value		8,711[b]	4,920	6,700	4,435[b]	3,158[b]
	Share total exports (%)		1.6	0.8	1.0	0.7	0.5
Panama	Roundwood, all types	(*)	12.8	20.2	16.6	9.6	10.5
	Sawnwood, all types	(†)	0.4		0.4	9.4	0.4
	Estimated total weight	(‡)	7	12	10	13	10
	Value		460		538	819	538
	Share total exports (%)		2.0		2.3	3.2	1.8
Paraguay	Broadleaved logs	(*)	210	197	131	155	167.9
	Sawnwood and sleepers	(†)	2.9	22.3	7.6	15.2	9.7
	Estimated total weight	(‡)	220	208	133	166	177
	Value		9,060	10,320	6,780	6,540	11,140
	Share total exports (%)		27.4	27.4	21.6	21.3	32.8
Peru	Estimated total weight	(‡)	5	11	8	2	11
	Value		1,611	1,088	967		1,051
	Share total exports (%)		0.9	0.4	0.4		0.4
Latin America	Coniferous logs	(*)	1	8	5	4	4
	Broadleaved logs	(*)	283	337	223	220	274
	Sleepers	(†)	11.0	8.9	6.9	23.3	12.9
	Coniferous sawnwood	(†)	1,313	1,419	992	1,199	1,160
	Broadleaved sawnwood	(†)	240	216	189	200	212
	Veneer sheets	(†)	1.1		1.2	2.1	2.8
	Plywood	(†)	16.2	22.0	7.1	12.9	6.1
	Woodpulp[c]	(‡)					4.5
	Paper and paperboard	(‡)		0.4	0.1		2.6
	Estimated total weight	(‡)	1,156	1,247	884	1,015	1,052
	Estimated total volume, roundwood equivalent	(*)	3,463	3,696	2,629	3,122	3,104
	Value (million $)[d]		66.9	90.8	67.7	82.5	104.0
	Share total exports (%)		1.0	1.1	0.9	1.1	1.3

TABLE 17-10 – Continued

Country	Product	Unit	1955	1956	1957	1958	1959	1960
Brazil	Broadleaved logs	(*)	62.3	44.0	59.6	49.7	61.7	54.5
	Sleepers	(†)	24.4	31.8	30.7	2.4		6.6
	Coniferous sawnwood	(†)	1,115	626	1,356	1,116	799	925
	Broadleaved sawnwood	(†)	38.2	19.9	24.4	20.1	9.5	17.9
	Woodpulp[c]	(‡)						0.3
	Veneer sheets	(†)	2.8	2.4	2.6	1.5	3.9	5.2
	Plywood	(†)	2.1	0.8	1.6	1.3	2.5	3.7
	Estimated total weight	(‡)	692	413	810	648	490	561
	Value		127,098	33,640[e]	69,830	55,699	42,043	46,691
	Share total exports (%)		8.9	2.3	5.0	4.5	3.3	3.7
Chile	Coniferous sawnwood	(†)	95.9	50.5	26.3	46.7	84.7	11.2
	Broadleaved sawnwood	(†)	103.0	54.9	50.1	63.1	80.3	21.7
	Plywood	(†)	1.1	0.4	0.1	0.3	0.2	
	Woodpulp[b]	(‡)						13.7
	Paper and paper board	(‡)			1.0	20.2	35.4	28.9
	Estimated total weight	(‡)	126	66	52	90	139	65
	Value		16,884	8,358	5,377	9,199	11,116	5,198
	Share total exports (%)		3.6	1.5	1.2	2.4	2.2	1.1
Colombia	Broadleaved logs	(*)	52.3	68.6	12.9	39.1	44.2	40.2
	Broadleaved sawnwood	(†)	4.5	11.0	21.8	34.2	35.4	45.9
	Estimated total weight	(‡)	54	75	29	63	69	73
	Value		732	577	1,324	1,263	1,396	1,382
	Share total exports (%)		0.1	0.1	0.3	0.3	0.3	0.3
Costa Rica	Estimated total weight	(‡)	8	10	7	5	4	3
	Value		195	918	174	200	195	192
	Share total exports (%)		0.2	1.4	0.2	0.2	0.3	0.2
Dom. Rep.	Estimated total weight	(‡)	5	7	7	5	6	11
	Value		456	584	703	422	602	597
	Share total exports (%)		0.4	0.5	0.5	0.3	0.5	0.3
Ecuador	Broadleaved logs	(*)	0.1		11.1	8.9	30.5	1.4
	Broadleaved sawnwood	(†)	25.2	24.7			6.6	5.6
	Estimated total weight	(‡)	18	18	11	9	35	5
	Value		1,027	1,067	1,934	1,518	1,534	1,337
	Share total exports (%)		0.9	0.9	1.5	1.1	1.1	0.9
Guatemala	Roundwood, all types	(*)	29.4	24.9	16.1	16.2	2.2	5.7
	Sawnwood, all types	(†)					5.0	8.0
	Plywood	(†)	1.4	1.4	2.1	1.8	2.0	1.2
	Estimated total weight	(‡)	28	22	13	13	5	12
	Value		500	392	1,996		912	1,060
	Share total exports (%)		0.5	0.3	1.7		0.8	0.9
Honduras	Coniferous logs	(*)				34.5	37.0	43.2
	Coniferous sawnwood	(†)	188.6	155.0	204.6	162.7	202.8	221.8
	Broadleaved sawnwood	(†)	1.6	5.2	4.5	2.1	2.3	1.6
	Estimated total weight	(‡)	99	85	110	111	148	156
	Value		5,400[a]	4,820	9,223	6,603	8,255	8,249
	Share total exports (%)		10.5	6.6	14.2	9.5	12.0	13.1
Mexico	Broadleaved logs	(*)	13.0	30.4	18.6	0.9		
	Coniferous sawnwood	(†)	80.7	45.1	49.7	39.9	54.8	25.1
	Broadleaved sawnwood	(†)	12.0	11.9	17.4	15.3	15.0	16.7
	Woodpulp[c]	(‡)	9.6	9.6	7.6	3.7	4.0	
	Plywood	(†)	2.5	0.7	8.6	12.4	8.7	5.0
	Fiberboard, paper, and paperboard	(‡)						0.1
	Estimated total weight	(‡)	76	73	70	45	54	28
	Value		5,711	3,428[c]	4,443	5,002	10,483	1,887
	Share total exports (%)		0.7	0.4	0.6	0.7	1.4	0.2
Panama	Roundwood, all types	(*)		9.9	8.0	3.5		5.0
	Sawnwood, all types	(†)	11.1	1.2	0.9	1.1	1.1	0.5
	Plywood	(†)	1.2	0.4	0.1			
	Paper and paperboard	(‡)	2.7	2.0	3.3			
	Estimated total weight	(‡)	12	13	11	3	1	5
	Value		690	(a)	317	140	95	238
	Share total exports (%)		1.9		0.9	0.4	0.3	0.9
Paraguay	Broadleaved logs	(*)	170.6	241.6	179.1	202.9	85.3	147.2
	Sawnwood and sleepers	(†)	9.9	9.8	10.2	14.4	10.7	10.1
	Estimated total weight	(‡)	180	250	190	213	94	158
	Value		13,040	11,840	9,380	9,740	4,060	5,030
	Share total exports (%)		37.2	32.3	28.5	28.5	13.0	18.6

TABLE 17–10 – Continued

Country	Product	Unit	1955	1956	1957	1958	1959	1960
Peru	Estimated total weight	(‡)	15	10	7	3	2	4
	Value		1,204	809	359	251	251	306
	Share total exports (%)		0.4	0.3	0.1	0.1	0.1	0.1
Latin America	Coniferous logs	(*)	8	8	13	46	64	43
	Broadleaved logs	(*)	335	421	299	315	228	263
	Sleepers	(†)	27.1	33.6	31.1	5.9	6.6	10.5
	Coniferous sawnwood	(†)	1,483	884	1,648	1,373	1,151	1,192
	Broadleaved sawnwood	(†)	214	147	143	152	161	131
	Veneer sheets	(†)	3.4	3.0	2.9	2.5	6.3	7.8
	Plywood	(†)	8.3	3.7	12.5	16.5	13.4	10.0
	Woodpulp^c	(‡)	9.6	9.6	7.6	3.7	4.1	14.0
	Particle board and fiberboard	(‡)		0.5	0.5	1.0	3.7	3.5
	Paper and paperboard	(‡)	3.1	2.7	5.4	21.0	36.1	29.2
	Estimated total weight	(‡)	1,300	1,027	1,308	1,205	1,042	1,066
	Estimated total volume roundwood equivalent	(*)	3,883	2,641	4,060	3,547	3,102	3,122
	Value (million $)^d		172.9	66.4	105.1	90.1	80.9	72.2
	Share total exports (%)		2.1	0.8	1.2	1.1	0.9	0.8

Country	Product	Unit	1961	1962	1963	1964	1965	1966	1967
Brazil	Broadleaved logs	(*)	54.1	40.1	43.8	51.0	53.2	58.1	79.1
	Sleepers	(†)	7.2	17.7	13.1	5.2	8.6	9.7	3.1
	Coniferous sawnwood	(†)	1,019	816	794	1,052	829	1,193	1,032
	Broadleaved sawnwood	(†)	16.3	20.1	29.6	44.0	59.3	71	76
	Woodpulp^c	(‡)	3.3	8.8	3.0	3.5	6.4	8.2	3.8
	Veneer sheets	(†)	9.1	6.5	6.1	6.3	7.6	14.9	20.3
	Plywood	(†)	2.7	2.6	3.0	4.8	5.4	6.6	5.5
	Estimated total weight	(†)	615	506	498	644	658	757	692
	Value		52,015	43,216	42,159	54,480	62,360	78,570	71,240
	Share total exports (%)		3.7	3.6	3.0	3.8	3.9	4.5	4.3
Chile	Coniferous sawnwood	(†)	31.9	24.0	27.6	56.0	49.6	42.8	31.3
	Broadleaved sawnwood	(†)	36.4	25.4	19.2	21.0	31.2	26.7	24.3
	Woodpulp^b	(‡)	34.0	24.0	15.5	11.5	17.4	20.6	24.3
	Paper and paper board	(‡)	33.7	24.9	30.5	25.3	33.4	21.1	41.4
	Estimated total weight	(‡)	112	80	74	56	99	74	83
	Value		11,479	8,729	7,498	9,203	8,564	11,164	15,620
	Share total exports (%)		2.3	1.6	1.4	1.5	1.3	1.3	1.7
Colombia	Broadleaved logs	(*)	52.6	84.9	92.6	60.0	72.3	89.1	41.8
	Broadleaved sawnwood	(†)	38.4	32.7	49.2	83.0	56.7	47.2	55.0
	Estimated total weight	(‡)	79	107	126	119	112	121	80
	Value		2,311	2,294	3,293	4,337	3,328	3,211	3,356
	Share total exports (%)		0.5	0.5	0.7	0.8	0.6	0.6	0.7
Costa Rica	Estimated total weight	(‡)	6	13	9	8	14	16	
	Value		192	1,006	934	1,247	1,856	2,161	
	Share total exports (%)		0.2	1.1	1.0	1.2	1.6	1.5	
Dom. Rep.	Estimated total weight	(‡)	6	3	(a)	5	4		
	Value		524	244	244	273	236	128	
	Share total exports (%)		0.4	0.1	0.1	0.2	0.2	0.1	
Ecuador	Broadleaved logs	(*)			3.0		3.8	4.4	4.5
	Broadleaved sawnwood	(†)	5.2	12.8	6.8	34.0	35.7	39.9	29.5
	Estimated total weight	(‡)	4	9	8	25	27	29	31
	Value		1,137	1,223	1,585	1,759	1,936	2,331	2,541
	Share total exports (%)		0.9	0.9	1.1	1.2	1.1	1.2	1.3
Guatemala	Roundwood, all types	(*)	7.1	6.6	3.6	3.6	3.6	3.6	
	Sawnwood, all types	(†)	12.4	16.7	11.7	6.8	8.7	11.6	
	Plywood	(†)	1.6	0.4	0.5		0.6	1.0	
	Estimated total weight	(‡)	12	16	12	8	13	16	
	Value		1,638	1,158	872	872	1,170	1,854	
	Share total exports (%)		1.5	1.0	0.6	0.6	0.6	0.8	

TABLE 17-10 – Continued

Country	Product	Unit	1961	1962	1963	1964	1965	1966	1967
Honduras	Coniferous logs	(*)	46.6	41.6	34.5	35.0	32.6	29.2	
	Coniferous sawnwood	(†)	173.3	153.8	183.3	295.0	225.0	199.2	
	Broadleaved sawnwood	(†)	1.8	2.1	3.2	2.3	3.1	4.0	
	Estimated total weight	(‡)	128	113	122	184	174	180	
	Value		7,557	7,166	8,513	10,846	10,326	10,668	
	Share total exports (%)		10.3	8.8	10.2	11.5	8.1	7.5	
Mexico	Broadleaved logs	(*)	0.1		0.1	0.1	0.2	0.2	0.1
	Coniferous sawnwood	(†)	29.4	23.4	29.4	12.0	14.1	9.0	7.3
	Broadleaved sawnwood	(†)	14.9	21.3	10.4	8.5	5.3	3.7	5.8
	Woodpulp^f	(‡)	0.3	1.3					
	Plywood	(†)	4.9	6.2	6.4	4.2	3.6	2.2	2.5
	Fiberboard, paper, and paperboard	(‡)	0.1	1.4	4.1	3.2	2.5		
	Estimated total weight	(‡)	29	35	31	19	16	9	10
	Value		5,634	3,757	1,879	1,889	1,821	1,645	1,081
	Share total exports (%)		0.7	0.4	0.2	0.2	0.2	0.1	0.1
Panama	Roundwood, all types	(*)	1.2	2.1	1.1	1.9	1.8	2.8	2.8
	Sawnwood, all types	(†)	0.6	0.4	0.1	0.2	0.3		0.1
	Paper and paperboard	(‡)		0.8	1.0	1.0	1.0		
	Estimated total weight	(‡)	1	3	2	3	3	3	3
	Value		205	361	312	314	265	105	138
	Share total exports (%)		0.7	0.8	0.5	0.4	0.3	0.1	0.2
Paraguay	Broadleaved logs	(*)	171.4	121.8	96.0	236.0	271.0	317.5	227.6
	Sawnwood and sleepers	(†)	28.5	28.8	16.1	39.0	29.9	38.5	28.0
	Estimated total weight	(‡)	194	157	125	258	298	352	253
	Value		6,450	6,660	4,740	7,150	8,820	10,550	7,110
	Share total exports (%)		21.0	19.9	11.8	14.4	15.6	21.4	14.7
Peru	Estimated total weight	(‡)	2	4	3	6	7	9	4
	Value		204	327	304			1,359	630
	Share total exports (%)			0.1	0.1			0.2	0.1
Latin America	Coniferous logs	(*)	47	42	35	36	25.6	18.4	17.7
	Broadleaved logs	(*)	291	259	243	357	417.0	562.5	425.1
	Sleepers	(†)	18.2	25.7	20.2	8.7	21.2	24.5	18.2
	Coniferous sawnwood	(†)	1,263	1,026	1,039	476	1,101.4	1,657.2	1,479.5
	Broadleaved sawnwood	(†)	146	156	146	240	260.3	301.9	297.2
	Veneer sheets	(†)	12.6	12.8	10.5	12.0	24.0	29.1	34.6
	Plywood	(†)	9.8	10.2	12.0	12.7	23.8	33.7	33.9
	Woodpulp^c	(‡)	37.6	34.1	18.5	15.0	21.0	29.1	28.2
	Particle board and fiberboard	(‡)	2.6	2.1	6.7	2.5	2.9	3.5	4.5
	Paper and paperboard	(‡)	34.3	26.1	31.9			23.3	28.4
	Estimated total weight	(‡)	1,182	1,024	995	864	1,284	1,738	1,543
	Estimated total volume, roundwood equivalent	(*)	3,365	2,870	2,878	2,002	3,684	4,987	4,428
	Value (million $)^d		89.3	76.1	72.3	92.8	93.5	100.1	97.6
	Share total exports (%)		1.0	0.8	0.7	0.9	0.8	1.1	0.9

Sources: FAO, *Yearbook of Forest Products Statistics, 1950-68*. FAO, *World Forest Products Statistics, 1946-1955* and *1954-1963*. UN, *Yearbook of International Trade Statistics*. IMF, *International Financial Statistics*, supp. to 1966/67 issues, 1968. Foreign trade yearbooks of Brazil, Mexico, and Peru.

Categories: Only the principal categories are shown for each country, aggregated where convenient. All other products derived from the forest, such as natural rubber, quebracho extract, chicle, maté, wax, and nuts, are excluded. The following SITC categories are included: 242.2, coniferous sawlogs; 242.3, broadleaved sawlogs; 242.9, poles, pilings, and posts (other roundwood); 243.1, sleepers; 243.2, coniferous sawnwood; 243.3, broadleaved sawnwood; 251, wood pulp; 631.1, veneer sheets; 631.2, plywood; 631.9, particle board; 641.6, fiber board; 641.1, newsprint; 641.2, printing and writing paper.

Symbols and Conversion Factors: (*) = thousands of cubic meters roundwood equivalent. (†) = thousands of cubic meters actual volume. (‡) = thousands of metric tons. Following are the conversion factors from cubic meters to metric tons: coniferous logs, 0.65; broadleaved logs, 0.975; sleepers, 0.80; coniferous sawnwood, 0.52; broadleaved sawnwood, 0.73; plywood and veneers, 0.60. (Estimated total weights throughout this table are converted as above.) Conversion from cubic meters actual volume and metric tons to roundwood equivalent by: sawnwood and veneers, 2.00; sleepers, 2.75; plywood, 2.50; particle board and fiber board, 1.60; wood pulp, 3.50; paper and paperboard, 2.80. (The last two factors are averages reflecting estimates of the approximate composition of Latin American exports.)

^aEstimate from IMF; may not correspond to SITC categories given.
^bEstimate from country's trade data.
^cIncludes mechanical, semichemical, and chemical pulp.
^dSum of countries listed for which data are available; excludes one or more minor exporters in 1950-54, 1956, 1958, and 1964.
^eConiferous logs and sawnwood only; data not available for other products.

TABLE 17-11. Latin American Forest Products Balance, 1961-1963
            (Thousands of cubic meters and thousands of metric tons)

Country	Product	Unit	Production	Imports	Exports	Apparent Consumption
Argentina	Fuelwood	(*)	8,531			8,531
	Industrial wood	(*)	2,001	1,809		3,810
	Roundwood	(*)		194		
	Sawnwood	(†)	795	635		1,430
	Sheet materials	(†)	40			40
	Fiberboard	(‡)	26			26
	Wood pulp	(‡)	363	120		183
	Pulp products	(‡)	371	182		553
Brazil	Fuelwood	(*)	117,000			117,000
	Industrial wood	(*)	13,843	646	1,911	12,578
	Roundwood	(*)		12	46	
	Sawnwood	(†)	6,304		911	5,393
	Sheet materials	(†)	292		10	282
	Fiberboard	(‡)	57			57
	Wood pulp	(‡)	398	66	5.0	459
	Pulp products	(‡)	553	147		700
Bolivia	Fuelwood	(*)	4,237			4,237
	Industrial wood	(*)	85	15		100
	Roundwood	(*)		1.3		
	Sawnwood	(†)	32			32
	Sheet materials	(†)	0.4			0.4
	Pulp products	(‡)	0.8	5.1		5.9
Chile	Fuelwood	(*)	3,254			3,254
	Industrial wood	(*)	3,163	49	279	2,933
	Roundwood	(*)		0.2		
	Sawnwood	(†)	971	1.6	55	918
	Sheet materials	(†)	8.2			8.2
	Fiberboard	(‡)	14	2.2		16
	Wood pulp	(‡)	148	5.7	25	129
	Pulp products	(‡)	130	8.0	30	108
Colombia	Fuelwood	(*)	22,200			22,200
	Industrial wood	(*)	3,130	352	157	3,325
	Roundwood	(*)		0.3	77	
	Sawnwood	(†)	990	0.3	40	950
	Sheet materials	(†)	30			30
	Fiberboard	(‡)	7	0.3		7.3
	Wood pulp	(‡)	12	45		57
	Pulp products	(‡)	92	69		161
Costa Rica	Fuelwood	(*)	1,391			1,391
	Industrial wood	(*)	468	53	35[a]	486
	Sawnwood	(†)	281	1.8		283
	Sheet materials	(†)	6.4	0.1		6.5
	Pulp products	(‡)		16		16
Cuba	Fuelwood	(*)	1,455			1,455
	Industrial wood	(*)	580	707		1,587
	Roundwood	(*)		1.5		
	Sawnwood	(†)	130	192		322
	Sheet materials	(†)		12		
	Fiberboard	(‡)	16			16
	Wood pulp	(‡)		43		43
	Pulp products	(‡)	66	53		119
Dom. Rep.	Fuelwood	(*)	1,660			1,660
	Industrial wood	(*)	295	33	10[a]	318
	Sawnwood	(†)	55			55
	Pulp products	(‡)	1.3	11		13
Ecuador	Fuelwood	(*)	1,693			1,693
	Industrial wood	(*)	780	50	18	812
	Roundwood	(*)			1.0	
	Sawnwood	(†)	339		8.3	331
	Sheet materials	(†)	0.6	0.2		0.8
	Pulp products	(‡)	2.0	18		20

TABLE 17-11 – Continued

Country	Product	Unit	Production	Imports	Exports	Apparent Consumption
El Salvador	Fuelwood	(*)	2,850			2,850
	Industrial wood	(*)	110	141		251
	Roundwood	(*)		1.0		
	Sawnwood	(†)	12	46		58
	Sheet materials	(†)		1.8		1.8
	Fiberboard	(‡)		0.5		0.5
	Pulp products	(‡)		15		15
Guatemala	Fuelwood	(*)	5,825			5,825
	Industrial wood	(*)	810	34	35	809
	Roundwood	(*)			5.8	
	Sawnwood	(†)	116	0.1	14	102
	Sheet materials	(†)	2.7	0.2	0.8	2.1
	Fiberboard	(‡)	2.2			2.2
	Wood pulp	(‡)		2.5		2.5
	Pulp products	(‡)	3.2	8.7		12
Haiti	Fuelwood	(*)	8,000			8,000
	Industrial wood	(*)	225	10		235
	Sawnwood	(†)	19	3.1		22
	Pulp products	(‡)		1.3		1.3
Honduras	Fuelwood	(*)	2,500			2,500
	Industrial wood	(*)	785	29	385	429
	Roundwood	(*)			41	
	Sawnwood	(†)	487	2.1	172	317
	Sheet materials	(†)		0.1		0.1
	Fiberboard	(‡)		0.3		0.3
	Pulp products	(‡)		8.6		8.6
Mexico	Fuelwood	(*)	9,000			9,000
	Industrial wood	(*)	3,142	550	105	3,587
	Roundwood	(*)		32	0.1	
	Sawnwood	(†)	1,161	27	43	1,145
	Sheet materials	(†)	47	0.5	5.8	42
	Fiberboard	(‡)	19	2.3		21
	Wood pulp	(‡)	203	48	0.5	250
	Pulp products	(‡)	473	103	1.9	574
Nicaragua	Fuelwood	(*)	1,850			1,850
	Industrial wood	(*)	425	13		438
	Roundwood	(*)		0.4		
	Sawnwood	(†)	134			134
	Sheet materials	(†)	12			12
	Pulp products	(‡)		3.3		3.3
Panama	Fuelwood	(*)	1,710			1,710
	Industrial wood	(*)	118	72	3.9	186
	Roundwood	(*)		0.2	1.4	
	Sawnwood	(†)	35	7.1	0.4	42
	Sheet materials	(†)		0.1		0.1
	Wood pulp	(‡)		0.1		0.1
	Pulp products	(‡)	0.7	20	0.6	20
Paraguay	Fuelwood	(*)	1,325			1,325
	Industrial wood	(*)	395	7.0	179	567
	Roundwood	(*)			130	
	Sawnwood	(†)	27		24	2.5
	Sheet materials	(†)	2.4			2.4
	Pulp products	(‡)	0.4	2.5		2.9
Peru	Fuelwood	(*)	2,456			2,456
	Industrial wood	(*)	517	357	12[a]	874
	Roundwood	(*)		1.1		
	Sawnwood	(†)	144	83		227
	Sheet materials	(†)		4.4		4.4
	Fiberboard	(‡)	1.1	2.6		3.7
	Wood pulp	(‡)		17		17
	Pulp products	(‡)	57	41		98

TABLE 17–11 – Continued

Country	Product	Unit	Production	Imports	Exports	Apparent Consumption
Uruguay	Fuelwood	(*)	1,050			1,050
	Industrial wood	(*)	215	302		517
	Roundwood	(*)		36		
	Sawnwood	(†)	70	71		141
	Sheet materials	(†)	4.5	4.8		9.3
	Fiberboard	(‡)	1.6	0.2		1.8
	Wood pulp	(‡)	2.0	12		14
	Pulp products	(‡)	29	24		53
Venezuela	Fuelwood	(*)	4,650			4,650
	Industrial wood	(*)	340	548		888
	Roundwood	(*)		33		
	Sawnwood	(†)	184	8.7		193
	Sheet materials	(†)	9.4	0.3		9.7
	Fiberboard	(‡)	2.1	3.1		5.2
	Wood pulp	(‡)		64		64
	Pulp products	(‡)	103	95		198
Latin America	Fuelwood	(*)	202,637			202,637
	Industrial wood	(*)	31,427	6,959	3,130	35,256
	Roundwood	(*)		354	306	
	Sawnwood	(†)	12,286	1,270	1,281	12,275
	Sheet materials	(†)	455	38	23	470
	Fiberboard	(‡)	146	16	3.8	158
	Wood pulp	(‡)	826	425	30	1,221
	Pulp products	(‡)	1,882	877	31	2,728

Sources: FAO, *World Forest Products Statistics, 1954-1963*. Tables 17–4, 17–5, and 17–10.

Note: There is assumed to be no trade in fuelwood, so that consumption equals fuelwood removals. Total trade and consumption of industrial wood (roundwood equivalent) are calculated from the conversion factors given in table 17–10.

Roundwood production and consumption are not shown, as pulpwood is included in this category and only rough estimates could be made. See table 17–7 for estimates for 1956-59.

(*) Thousands of cubic meters roundwood equivalent; (†) thousands of cubic meters actual volume; (‡) thousands of metric tons.

aEstimated total volume, not distributed among products.

Chapter 18

FISHERY PRODUCTS

Latin America is not one of the world's major traditional fishing regions and until recently its fisheries were a relatively unimportant source of employment, income, foreign exchange, or domestic consumption by comparison with several resource industries. Before the mid-1950s the region produced 3 percent or less of the world catch and derived less than 1 percent of its export earnings from fish; per capita consumption was about two-thirds the world average, and the bulk of the population ate little or no seafood. In some respects this situation has not changed, but the rapid development of anchovy fishing and the production of fishmeal and oil in Peru for export have made that country the world's leading fishing nation and have raised Latin America's share of the world catch to more than 20 percent and the share of fishery products in total regional exports to 2.5 percent. Fishery products became Peru's chief export, rising from 3 to 25 percent of the total, despite a great increase in copper exports and growth in several other commodities. The Peruvian boom, which was most pronounced in the decade 1953-64, was accompanied by substantial increases in the catch of several other countries and stimulated interest in marine resources and their exploitation throughout the region. It also coincided with increased attention to the inadequacy of diets, particularly the shortage of animal protein, in underdeveloped countries and with efforts to improve food supplies through larger catches and better direct and indirect utilization of fish.

The world's fisheries produce a great number of commodities related ecologically and economically in many ways. In addition to the different species of fin-fish, these include crustaceans, molluscs, marine mammals, and a variety of aquatic plants and animals, which may be sharply distinguished or highly substitutable in demand or in supply. Many products are consumed directly, or used as food after preservation or processing, or converted to industrial commodities such as animal feeds and fertilizers. No single market relates these heterogeneous products even within one country, and there are substantial differences in resources, methods of production, demand, and marketing arrangements among countries.

Note: Fishery Products tables 18–1 to 18–8 appear on pp. 482–92.

In this survey, therefore, relatively little attention will be given to the world fishing industry, the emphasis being placed on the relative size and growth of Latin American fisheries and particularly of the region's export sector. Some differences in the composition and utilization of the catch between Latin American countries and other countries or regions will also be noted. Fisheries are unique among natural resources in that a country's production need not take place within its national boundaries. Much of the movement of fresh or slightly processed marine products is therefore not considered to be international trade, and trade in most species is small relative to production. Where a relatively large share of the catch is traded, the product is typically concentrated on a small number of species and is more highly processed than the species consumed domestically; this is notably the case in the Latin American export fisheries.

Emphasis is given here to the region's ocean fisheries, particularly to the anchovy fishery of Peru and Chile, and to the shrimp fisheries of the Caribbean and the Pacific. The catch of other marine fish is only briefly described. Other marine products, including mammals, are not considered, as they are of negligible value to almost every Latin American country. Estuarine and freshwater fisheries are generally of much less importance than ocean resources, but they are presently or potentially significant to several countries as an element of rural employment or consumption. Interest is centered on the potential of the region's fishery resources for increasing export earnings and for bettering the rural diet, and on the problems of developing those resources efficiently. The Peruvian experience — of rapid expansion followed by an economic crisis and excessive pressure on the resource itself and on the extractive industry — illustrates several of these potentials and problems and the biological, technical, and economic features which give rise to them.[1]

[1] The chief source of statistical information about fisheries is the FAO, *Yearbook of Fishery Statistics*. A great deal of statistical and descriptive information about the fisheries of specific countries or species is given in the Foreign Fisheries Leaflets issued by the Branch of Foreign Fisheries of the U.S. Fish and Wildlife Service: these include translations of foreign reports and studies, surveys of

The World Fishing Industry

The total world catch of fishery products is currently somewhat more than 50 million liveweight tons, or double the level of the early and middle 1950s. Because of the disruption of ocean fishing during World War II, the catch in 1950, some 21 million tons, was no higher than in 1938 (see table 18-1). Although fish are caught in almost all parts of the world and by most nations, production is concentrated in a small number of countries and on a few major fishing grounds. These lie over or near the continental shelves, where the density of nutrients and microorganisms is much higher than in the open ocean. The most important grounds, in tonnage, lie off the western coast of South America, in the north Atlantic between Canada and Iceland, in the north Pacific between Alaska and Japan, and in the western Pacific from China to Indonesia. Somewhat smaller catches are obtained in the Gulf of Mexico, the Mediterranean, and the southeastern Atlantic, and still smaller amounts in the Indian Ocean and off the east coast of South America and the west coast of North and Central America.[2] Many fishing nations, including all the Latin American countries, obtain their entire catch from the immediately adjacent waters. The majority of vessels operate only a few miles from shore, although a large share of the catch may come from large boats working more distant waters. Sizable catches are often landed directly from the shore. Several of the largest fishing nations, however — notably Japan and the Soviet Union, and to a lesser extent the United States and several European countries — obtain much of their catch from distant grounds. Thus, while some fishing grounds, such as those of the west coast of South America, are used almost exclusively by the adjacent nations, others, such as the north Atlantic and north Pacific grounds, are exploited by a number of countries.

Over the last three decades the total catch of North America has remained almost constant, while that of Europe has risen only slightly. There has been relatively rapid growth in the Soviet Union and in Asia, but the expansion in both areas has been overshadowed, in the last fifteen years, by the extraordinary growth of the Peruvian catch. That country's production expanded 60-fold between 1950 and the early 1960s, raising the Latin American total 15-fold in the same period. In several other countries of the region there was a substantial increase, output tripling in Argentina, Brazil, Ecuador, and Mexico and rising still more rapidly in Chile and Panama.

Because different countries and fishing grounds are to a considerable extent specialized in particular species, the change in the relative importance of different nations is reflected in the composition of the world catch. Production of crustaceans and molluscs has increased absolutely, as has that of freshwater fishes, but both groups have declined slightly as shares of total catch, with the share of marine fishes increasing. Among the latter, the herring, sardine, and anchovy group represents about one-third of the total catch; the cod group, the next in worldwide importance, is only about one-third as large (see. table 18-2). In the eight major fishing nations of Latin America, however, the herring group, including the Peruvian anchovy catch, is almost 90 percent of the total and the cods and related species are of slight importance. In the late 1940s the herring catch was less than one-fourth of the world total catch, and very little of it came from Latin America; information on the composition of the region's catch then is available for only three countries.

Slightly less than 70 percent of the world catch is currently devoted to human consumption as food. The remainder is put to a variety of industrial uses, of which reduction to meal and oil is the most important. Fishmeal is used primarily as a protein supplement in animal feeds. As the catch of anchovy for this purpose has increased, the share of fishery products consumed as food has fallen; prior to 1950 it was 85 to 90 percent. Of the fish and other products consumed as food, approximately half is edible weight, the remainder being wastes of which some portion is put to industrial use. Because the ratio of liveweight to final product weight varies according to the species, the end use and the kind of processing, it is difficult to establish the liveweight equivalent of products traded. Consistent measures of consumption are therefore extremely difficult to estimate, and no effort is made to include them in the regularly published statistics, even for food use alone. Estimates of total fishery consumption are still more difficult to make or to interpret. Estimates of consumption per capita of edible food weight have been made for 1957-59, and the resulting estimates for total edible consumption correspond to about half of total utilization of fish as food, with some adjustment being made for trade in fishery products (see table 18-3). From these estimates it appears that in the late 1950s per capita consumption of seafood in Latin America was only about two-thirds of the world average, and that although the region was then producing some 6 percent of the world catch it was consuming less than 5 percent of total food derived from fisheries. The disproportion is now much greater, since the Latin American catch for nonfood use has increased substantially. The averages for subregions partially conceal the very high rates of consumption in a few countries such as Japan, Portugal, Norway, Sweden, the Philippines and Denmark, where per capita consumption was 15 kilograms or more.[3] The largest total amounts of fish were consumed in Japan, China, the Soviet Union and Western Europe.

---

resources and industrial capacity and annual summaries of catch, utilization, and trade. Much of the information on Latin American fisheries in countries other than Peru in this survey was obtained from these publications. For an excellent introduction to the technical and economic features of fishing and to recent trends in the world industry, see F. T. Christy, Jr., and A. Scott, *The Common Wealth in Ocean Fisheries* (Johns Hopkins Press for Resources for the Future, 1966), which has an extensive bibliography. Other sources, relating chiefly to specific Latin American countries, are indicated in the notes.

[2] Total catch is shown for each of fourteen ocean regions in FAO, *Yearbook of Fishery Statistics, 1965*, vol. 18, p. xxi. For maps of the continental shelves and the distribution of marine microorganisms see Christy and Scott, *The Common Wealth. . . ,* pp. 62-63.

[3] The information in FAO, Committee on Commodity Problems, *Agricultural Commodities—Projections for 1970* (1964), is summarized in Christy and Scott, *The Common Wealth. . . ,* pp. 19-21.

Nonfood consumption of fish is primarily in the form of meal and oil, and is concentrated in the advanced countries with relatively intensive agricultural techniques. The United States and West Germany are major consumers of fishmeal, with other European countries taking appreciable amounts. Relatively small quantities of industrial fishery products are used in less developed countries. On the assumption of equal ratios of liveweight to product weight in all countries, irrespective of differences in species and products utilized, the liveweight equivalents of food and industrial consumption can be calculated. Of total world consumption of 32.8 million tons in 1958, 27.5 million were consumed as food and 5.3 million in other ways. North America, Western Europe, and Japan together accounted for almost half of world fishery consumption. Latin America consumed only 4 percent of the total.[4]

While trade is insignificant for many species and for fresh fish generally, the liveweight equivalent of all fishery products entering international trade is a substantial share of the total catch: from 20 percent around 1950, it rose to 30 percent by 1960 and to 40 percent by 1964. This rapid expansion of trade relative to production is due to the increased share of the catch processed to meal and oil, of which a large fraction is traded, and to the increase in the share of those products exported as production has shifted from the consuming countries to Peru.[5] For edible fish products the share of production traded is generally below 20 percent for the world total, while for crustaceans and molluscs the share is typically 40 to 50 percent. Of total world exports of fishery products of some 6 million tons in 1964, 2.3 million tons were oily fishmeals and 0.4 million tons fish body oils; fresh, chilled, and frozen fish and fillets were next in importance, some 1.5 million tons. Cured fish and other fish preparations each formed a further half million tons of exports, and 350,000 tons of crustaceans and molluscs were also traded. The principal flows of trade are among the advanced countries, especially among European nations and from them and Japan to the United States, and from a small number of poor countries to the advanced countries: this pattern holds for both food and nonfood products. Small amounts are traded among low-income countries; which also import a few products from the high-income nations. The chief species involved in international trade are the herring and cod groups and smaller quantities of crustaceans and molluscs and of tunas.

Latin American Fisheries

The waters adjacent to Latin America include several valuable fishing grounds. The largest is formed by the Humboldt current, parallel to the coast from northern Chile to northern Peru, where the upwelling of water from the edge of the continental shelf concentrates nutrients at the surface. There are also deep water fishing areas off the west coast of Mexico and Central America, but their production is quite small in tonnage although relatively high in value. The other major grounds are shallow zones at intervals along the west coast from Mexico to Ecuador, on the Caribbean coast from Mexico to northern Brazil, and along the east coast from southern Brazil to northern Argentina. Except near Antarctica, the waters opposite the southern coasts of South America are relatively infertile, as are those off central Brazil and the northern coasts of Mexico; there is nonetheless some production from all areas. Anchovy predominate in the Peruvian grounds, with tuna and related species in smaller amounts; shrimp are the principal species in the inshore waters of Mexico, Central America, and northern South America; and the waters off Brazil, Uruguay, and Argentina are fished chiefly for hake and for sardines. All these areas, however, yield a variety of fishes. Freshwater fisheries are of minor importance to most countries because there are few lakes in the region and the rivers on the west coast are short. Inland fishing is significant around major lakes such as Chapala in Mexico and Titicaca on the Peru-Bolivia border, and in the river basins of Mexico, Colombia, and eastern South America. Except for Bolivia and Paraguay, however, in only three countries do freshwater fish account for 10 percent or more of the catch.

Most of the inland and inshore fisheries of Latin America have been worked — on a small scale, with canoes or rafts or without any boats — since the adjacent areas were settled. The ocean fisheries were first exploited by boats from other countries, chiefly the United States, and the use of these resources by the region did not begin until the 1920s or 1930s and in some countries not until the past decade. Since all fishing occurred close to shore, typically in water less than 30 fathoms (55 meters) deep, development was not much affected by World War II, and between the late 1930s and the late 1940s the region's catch almost doubled (see table 18-1). The greatest increase occurred in Mexico, which was the first country to develop a shrimp fishery for export to the United States, and in Peru, where an ocean fishery was created during this period.

Until about 1950 the bulk of the catch in nearly all countries was consumed domestically; while some fishery exports were recorded, these amounts were probably exceeded by the catch, for foreign consumption, of foreign boats working the same waters.[6] Consumption of fresh marine fish was limited by lack of refrigeration in markets and by difficulties of transport to the immediate coastal population. Some fish was canned for inland distribution, but this processing priced it beyond the reach of most rural consumers. Except for some freshwater fish, most of the very small inland consumption was therefore in the form of salted, smoked, or dried fish. The curing and canning in-

---

[4] For rough estimates of the shares of exports and of consumption in total net fishery production, excluding wastes, see chap. 3, table B-1 and tables B-1-1 to B-1-20 of the appendix to that chapter.

[5] Exports of meals and solubles from oily fish, including the anchovy, rose from 42 percent of production in 1958 to 69 percent in 1965; the shares for fish body oils in those years were 49 and 63 percent, but there was no pronounced trend for oils. See FAO, *Yearbook of Fishery Statistics, 1966*, vol. 21, table A3-2.

[6] These amounts are often difficult to measure, since they may be recorded as exports by the adjacent state but not shown as imports by the country whose craft make the catch. In Mexico, the production of the *vía la pesca* – foreign vessels on the Mexican grounds – is separately recorded.

dustry was, moreover, so small that in several countries relatively large amounts of processed fish were imported: salted or dried cod, provided by Canada and by several European exporters, was the principal commodity. The chief importer was Brazil, which in the mid-1950s suffered an annual trade deficit in fishery products of some $22 million. Venezuela, Colombia and several Central American countries were also net importers on a much smaller scale.[7]

Numerous studies have been made, chiefly in high-income countries, of the effects of price and income on fish consumption. It is generally found that price elasticity is relatively high and that income elasticity is high at low incomes but declines rapidly; in many countries the income elasticity is higher for meat than for seafood, so that fish consumption declines relative to meat as income rises. Tastes are often significant, not only for seafood in general but for particular species; substitutability varies with price and income and among countries.[8] These factors probably operate in Latin America as well, but for the bulk of the population they are overshadowed by the lack of transport and distribution facilities which makes fresh fish consumption often impossible at any price and even processed seafood quite expensive. Only in coastal areas with a supply of fresh seafood, or among the high-income population, can tastes, prices, and incomes interact freely.

The total Latin American catch doubled again between the late 1940s and the mid-1950s, and then in the next decade it expanded 10-fold. This growth is of primary importance to the region's exports, but it has also affected domestic consumption, the structure of the fishing and processing industries, and the claims made by several countries to the resources off their coasts.

The Shrimp Fishery

The expansion of fishing in the last two decades in the countries from Mexico to Ecuador and Venezuela reflects in large measure the rapid increase in shrimp consumption in the United States. In several countries a fishing industry was created solely to catch shrimp for export as the United States market for them expanded. Beds of the largest and highest-priced species are found close to shore along both coasts, wherever there are lagoons or shallow bays for breeding grounds and the bottom is mud rather than rock. Shrimp need only to be deheaded and frozen for shipment; the first operation is usually (and preferably) performed on the boats, and the second may be also. Since neither the boats nor the plants in the shrimp industry are large, and since the inshore waters of each country are usually closed to foreign vessels, the industry is relatively mobile: boats and men move readily to new fishing grounds as demand increases or resources become fully exploited. Thus there has been a steady geographic dispersion of shrimp production among countries as the total catch has increased (see

table 18-4). The first shift was from the United States to Mexico, which in 1950 supplied 95 percent of the former's imports of shrimp. As other countries entered the industry, Mexico's share declined steadily despite a doubling of the catch. The Guianas, several Caribbean islands, and India supply the shrimp not imported from Latin America. Some shrimp are also imported from Brazil and Peru, but in neither country are they a significant share of the catch nor an appreciable part of total U.S. imports.

Several features characterize the development of the shrimp export fishery in nearly all the countries indicated.[9] First, the industry typically began with foreign, chiefly U.S., capital; initially, in several countries, the crews or at least the captains of the vessels were also foreigners. U.S. investment in boats and freezing plants is still sizable, but as the industry grew local capital has usually bought out existing firms or provided the additional capacity. Moreover, where formerly most shrimp boats were transferred or ordered from the United States, most are now built in the region, particularly in Mexico and Panama. Only electronic equipment for the vessels and machinery for the plants must still come from the United States or Europe.

Second, the industry rapidly expanded to the maximum sustainable yield, or even briefly exceeded it. In every case growth was initially very rapid and then, except for some fluctuations, slowed or reversed. The growth of capacity in vessels was still more rapid, or continued longer, so that as the total catch stopped growing the catch per boat typically fell and excess capacity became evident. In some cases the new vessels could be moved to other countries, but even with this relief it might have been helpful almost everywhere to limit the number of boats in the fishery. It is the distinguishing feature of a common property resource, such as an ocean fishery, that each entrant to the industry obtains the average rather than the marginal product, forcing down the catch for every other boat once the maximum yield is reached. There is further a strong tendency to take too large a catch and deplete the resource, but even when this does not occur too much capital and labor are drawn into the fishery unless entry is limited.[10] The number of vessels in the shrimp fishery usually reached a peak and then declined as boats were retired or moved to other grounds. Once the appropriate level of catch is found the industry can be relatively stable in size and costs. The maximum catch obtained in the ocean fishery is also affected by the catch of juvenile shrimp in the lagoons and other breeding grounds, usually a long-established local industry for the domestic market. In some places, such as Lake Maracaibo in Venezuela, this catch is quite large, but nowhere is entry restricted. The industry is, of course, also subject to occasional changes of currents or other factors which can drastically reduce the catch, as occurred in Venezuela in

---

[7]See FAO, *Yearbook of Fishery Statistics, 1960*, for data on trade between 1948 and 1959.

[8]Factors affecting demand are summarized in Christy and Scott, *The Common Wealth. . . ,* pp. 28-36. Income elasticities are given only for Mexico and for Argentina and Uruguay, among Latin American countries; in the latter case, the present high consumption of beef makes demand more elastic with income for fish than for meat.

[9]The following summary is taken, except as noted, from USFWS, *The Shrimp Industry of Central America, the Caribbean Sea, and Northern South America* (Foreign Fisheries Leaflet 74, February 1967).

[10]For a fuller discussion of common property resources, see Christy and Scott, *The Common Wealth. . . ,* chaps. 5 and 12; or A. Scott, "Food and the World Fisheries Situation," in M. Clawson, ed., *Natural Resources and International Development* (Johns Hopkins Press for Resources for the Future, 1964), pp. 127-51.

1965-66, or carry it far beyond the normal sustainable yield and thus induce a needless expansion of capacity, as happened in Panama in 1957.

Third, fishing began for the largest species, usually white shrimp, and as these reached their maximum catch the industry began to seek the smaller and less valuable brown and then pink shrimp and then the very small seabob. This shift has occurred in all countries, but it has, at present, stopped at quite different points in different fisheries. The Colombian fishery, for example, is still concentrated on the large white shrimp and takes very few of the small species on which the Ecuadorean industry depends for most of its catch. As the small species are typically found in deeper water — beyond 35 fathoms (65 meters) — than the large shrimp, and are therefore not only lower priced but somewhat more expensive to catch, it has thus far proved easier to extend the fishery to new countries than to obtain the maximum catch of all species from any one country or fishing ground. The deepwater resources of small shrimp and seabob are believed to be quite large in several areas, so that as horizontal expansion becomes more difficult the total catch could be considerably increased, presumably at higher prices and perhaps through the introduction of larger vessels. Full use also has not yet been made of the enormous resources of Brazil, which include most of the species now taken elsewhere. The Brazilian shrimp catch for domestic consumption is quite large — over 10,000 tons — but it is believed that three to four times this amount, or as much as the present catch of all Latin America, could be taken.[11]

The export weight of shrimp is about half the liveweight, so the importance of shrimp in each country's total catch is understated by the export figures. Even where shrimp form less than half the catch, they account for a much higher share of total value; in the eight largest fishing countries, crustaceans and molluscs (of which shrimp are the largest part) were only 3 percent by weight of the catch in 1963-64 but accounted for one-fourth of the total value of fishery products (see table 18-2). The unit value of shrimp exports is difficult to determine, because in every country the share of small, low-valued species has risen, and also because while the bulk of exports is simply deheaded and frozen, an increasing share is cooked, peeled, or otherwise processed. Between 1954 and 1963 the unit value of shrimp exports to the United States was approximately 50 cents per pound from Costa Rica, and 70 cents per pound from Panama, the difference presumably reflecting differences in average size or in quality or processing. Both unit values were fairly stable over the decade, following a peak in 1953.

The Anchovy Fishery[12]

The extraordinary development of the anchovy fishery of Peru, and to a lesser extent of Chile, resulted from the coincidence of a rapidly growing world demand for high-

protein animal feeds and a resource almost perfectly suited to that purpose. In the last decade and a half the production of poultry has risen faster than that of any other meat, and poultry respond particularly well to protein-rich feeds. Such feeds may be made from vegetable products (notably soybeans), from meat (especially whale meat), or from fish. Beyond some percentage of the total diet, meals made from fish impart an odor to the meat, but until that level is reached, fishmeal is equal or superior to other sources of protein in inducing growth. It can also be fed to swine or to cattle, but the last use is not yet significant in amount. Almost any variety of fish can be dried and ground into meal, but those species are preferred which are abundant and cheap, have little value as food or in other competing uses, and contain a high percentage of protein and fat. The herring group of species meets these requirements, except that herrings and sardines are valued as food; anchovies, however, being smaller and cheaper, are little valued for human consumption and are therefore ideal for fishmeal production. About 18 percent of the liveweight of fish is recovered as meal, containing some oil, and a further 2 or 3 percent can be extracted as oil. Since the whole fish is used, there is little waste and most of the loss is water. Anchovies are exceptionally abundant in the waters off the Peruvian coast, forming some 85 to 95 percent of the total mass of fish of all species, and they are concentrated near the surface.[13] The only significant predators are seabirds, which take a catch of at most 2.5 million tons annually; the maximum sustainable yield of the fishery after this predation is estimated as 7.5 million tons or slightly more.[14]

These resources are much richer than those devoted to fishmeal production in other countries before the 1950s. In 1938 the chief producers were the United States, Norway, Germany, the United Kingdom, Iceland, and Canada, and the principal species were herring, menhaden, pilchard, and whitefish. Meal is still produced in these countries from these species, but the anchovy catch for reduction is now much larger and the bulk of production takes place in Peru, Chile, and a few other low-income countries.

The Peruvian fish processing industry was started in the late 1930s and expanded greatly during World War II, when the United States bought substantial amounts of canned fish. These exports continued after the war and some trade in frozen products began. No fishmeal was produced until 1949, and for the next several years only the wastes from the canneries and small amounts of various whole fish were used. The anchovy boom began in 1954, with a catch of some 59,000 tons which constituted only half the input to fishmeal production. Three years later the anchovy catch had risen sixfold to become almost the sole source of fishmeal (see table 18-5). From 1954 to 1962 the total catch, the anchovy catch, the production and exports of fishmeal, the average size of boat and the number of boats, plants and fishermen increased every year. By 1962 the anchovy

[11]USFWS, *The Shrimp Industry...*, p. 118.

[12]Besides the sources already indicated, information in this section is drawn chiefly from *Pesca*, a monthly magazine of the Peruvian fishing industry published in Lima by Ediciones Sudamérica, and the *Anuario* for 1964-65 of that magazine.

[13]H. Einarsson, "Recurso Número Uno: Anchoveta," *Pesca, Anuario, 1964-65.*

[14]USFWS, *Peru's Anchovy Fishery, 1966* (Foreign Fisheries Leaflet 126, August 1967), which is a translation of the report "La Pesquería de la Anchoveta" of the Instituto del Mar del Peru, December 1966.

industry provided employment for some 17,000 fishermen and a further 80,000 people in boatyards, reducing plants, and trading companies.

The anchovy boom was similar in several respects to the expansion of the shrimp fishery in other countries. Virtually all production is for export. Foreign investment is significant, especially in the processing plants; in 1965 some 21 to 24 percent of total investment in the industry was foreign, and six U.S., three European, two Japanese, and nine mixed domestic-foreign firms were active. In early 1967 the number of mixed companies had fallen to seven. Plants with some foreign ownership produced slightly over one-third of the 1966 fishmeal output.[15] The catch expanded rapidly to somewhat more than the maximum stable yield, whereupon restrictions were placed on the catch — but not on the number or capacity of vessels — and measures were taken to protect the resource. There was also a considerable geographic dispersion as the industry expanded, not so much internationally — although production rose sharply in Chile — as along the Peruvian coast. Between 1960/61 and 1965/66, the share of the total anchovy catch landed at Callão, the port of Lima, declined from 47 to 13 percent, while landings rose at Chimbote, Tambo de Mora, Supe, Chancay, Huarmey, and several smaller ports.[16]

There are, however, several significant differences between the two cases. The fishmeal industry depends overwhelmingly on a single species, and cannot direct its effort to different species or grounds to even the limited extent possible in the shrimp fishery. The catch is strongly seasonal, reaching a peak between January and May when the largest numbers of adult fish are available. The capital requirements of fishmeal plants are greater than those of freezing plants, and the control of quality somewhat more difficult. Much greater amounts of fresh water and of electricity are needed per ton of product, and both inputs are scarce and expensive on the Peruvian coast.[17] Finally, the creation of excess capacity and the depletion of resources went farther in Peru than in the shrimp fishery, entailing a considerable waste of capital and a reduction in the maximum sustained yield. In part, these were the results of the much more rapid expansion in Peru than elsewhere. They may also reflect the fact that one large country was involved rather than several small ones, so it was not possible to reach maximum yields and introduce restrictions piecemeal. The combination of these features produced a crisis in the Peruvian industry in 1963, and another which began in 1966 and lasted through 1967.

Prices of fishmeal and fish oil dropped abruptly in 1959-60, but the expansion of the industry was not appreciably affected, and credit was extended to producers

caught by the price decline (see table 18-6). By mid-1963, the industry was operating on credit back to the shipyards, and total short-term debt was about 80 percent of total investment. The catch was nearing the maximum yield, and in some areas fish were already depleted. Several fishmeal plants were closed or operating at a loss, when the industry's creditors, chiefly Peruvian banks, refused to extend further credit. Many boats and plants ceased to operate, and the catch fell slightly, but as employment and the number of vessels registered continued to rise during the year the catch per boat and per fisherman dropped sharply. In 1964 the government offered some tax relief; prices of both meal and oil rose appreciably in response to reduced supplies and some accumulation of stocks in Peru; and the catch rose to 9 million tons, the highest level ever reached. Some firms left the industry, and those remaining were formed into several loose associations in an effort to rationalize processing and marketing.[18]

By late 1965, however, it was evident that certain fundamental problems remained. The industry was still too large, with excess capacity and high costs in both vessels and plants relative to the maximum sustainable yield. That level had already been surpassed, so that some restriction was necessary if the stock and the catch were not to decline steadily. Moreover, an exceptionally large catch, like that in 1964, includes a disproportionately large number of young fish and thus reduces the number available for spawning in later seasons. Since the entire anchovy catch consists of fish less than three years old, the effect of such a change is quite pronounced over a short period. In 1965 the Ocean Institute of Peru recommended that the 1965/66 catch be limited to 7 million tons, to be taken entirely between September and May. For the 1966/67 season, the limit was raised to 8 million tons, but in addition to the summer closed season, fishing was prohibited from mid-February to the end of March in order to protect the stock at the time of spawning. These measures were supported by the industry and enforced by the government, but they did not attack the problem of excess capacity. When meal and oil prices fell in 1966 and early 1967, the industry was again in difficulty. Instead of limiting the capacity of boats or fishmeal plants the government had, on the Institute's recommendation, limited the fishing week to five days in an effort to ensure that the total catch limit would not be reached so quickly as to force a long closed season. Because the return to each boat was low, no credit could be obtained for investment in improvements to vessels or plants, and several shut down while others operated well below capacity. The boat owners sought government action to reduce the size of crews, a move which the fishermen resisted with strikes. Some of the owners also refused to fish, hoping to force the government to help them.[19]

Peru has sought to exert some control over fishmeal prices by holding stocks and by forming, together with

---

[15] Pesca, October 1965, February and May 1967. Foreign control was probably somewhat higher in the late 1950s, but no exact estimates are available.

[16] Pesca, May 1966. The principal shift was from the central coast to the south. In the north, the Humboldt current turns away from the coast and the anchovy density declines.

[17] Some 6 to 10 cubic meters of water and 600 kwh of electricity are needed per ton of fishmeal, and the establishment of over 100 plants in Peru has strained the supply of both. See UN, Water Desalination in Developing Countries (1964), p. 225.

[18] For an account of the 1963 crisis, see Pesca, August and November 1965.

[19] See Pesca, November 1965; USFWS, Peru's Anchovy Fishery, 1966, and Peru's Fishing Industry—Status as of September 1967 (Foreign Fisheries Leaflet 129, October 1967).

Angola, Iceland, Norway, and South Africa, the Fish Meal Exporters' Organization. This association was created when prices fell in 1959-60, to divide the export market for fishmeal among the member countries. Peru's share was to be 60 percent, but it has usually been larger because the other members have not been able to expand supply rapidly enough to meet the growth of demand. However, a control tight enough to raise prices appreciably might simply lead to substitution of other meals in animal feeds, a process which is becoming simpler as more sources of meal are utilized and synthetic production of nutrients is achieved.[20] In any case, a price decline does not cause, and a rise in prices would not solve, the internal problems of the Peruvian fishing industry, which result from the nature of the resource and a system of restrictions which is ecologically sound but economically quite wasteful. Evidently the several crises in the industry have not sufficed to drive out excess capacity to the point where the government could simply prohibit further entry; and the government has not had the political strength or the financial means to enforce a contraction on the industry.

The excess capacity of the anchovy fishery differs radically from that of the Brazilian coffee industry or of other commodities in real or potential oversupply, because the supply of fish is not too large; rather it is the supply of factors that are intended to raise fish production but cannot do so which is excessive. The two cases are nonetheless alike in illustrating the ease with which, in a boom period, excess capacity can arise in an industry, and the extreme internal political and economic difficulty of eliminating it when the external situation is satisfactory.

The Peruvian boom induced a parallel development in Chile, which has access to the southernmost part of the anchovy grounds and which now takes over 80 percent of its catch for reduction. The Chilean industry has been heavily financed and guided by the state development agency, CORFO, and has not suffered the same problems as Peru. In 1965, however, the anchovy disappeared from the Chilean grounds for several months, causing a crisis in which the government had to come to the aid of many producers. No other country possesses comparable resources for fishmeal, but small amounts of meal are now produced in Argentina, Brazil, Ecuador, Mexico, and Venezuela. Production is based partly on species like the anchovy, partly on low-valued whitefish such as hake in Argentina and Chile, and partly on cannery wastes.

Consequences of the Expansion

The effect of these two major expansions, in shrimp and in anchovy fishing, is reflected primarily in Latin American exports. Total regional exports of fishery products rose from less than 50,000 tons and $53 million in 1950 to 2 million tons and over $300 million in 1967, when fishmeal exports and prices were both high (see table 18-7). Although fishmeal and oil dominate trade, a great variety of products are included, and all stages of processing are represented. The United States is the largest importer, taking nearly all the chilled and frozen products and large amounts

of canned fish, meal, and oil also; Western Europe takes most of the remainder, particularly of fishmeal. There is also some intraregional trade in fishmeal and in canned products but practically none in other commodities.

The export boom has also raised domestic consumption somewhat. The effect is negligible in Peru, where the anchovy fishery is completely separate from the taking of other species for food. The difficulties of transport and the poverty of most of the inland population limit consumption of fresh fish to a narrow zone along the coast, with some sales as far inland as Arequipa in the south and Huancayo in the center of the country. Salted fish are available farther from the coast.[21] In several countries where the shrimp catch has increased dramatically the effect on domestic consumption is considerable; the species taken are valued as food, most of the population lives relatively near the coast and transport problems are less formidable. Part of the increase in consumption comes from the shrimp catch, of which the smaller species in particular find a ready local market. Most of the shrimp consumed domestically are sold fresh, but some part of the catch is dried or salted and in a few countries, notably Colombia and Venezuela, as much as 10 percent of the frozen shrimp pack is sold domestically.[22] Canned or frozen shrimp reach only the high-income population inland. In addition to the ocean trawl fishery, there is in most countries a small-scale shrimp fishery in the lagoons and inshore waters, of which a large part goes to the domestic market as fresh or dried shrimp. A secondary effect of the shrimp boom is the increased catch of various species of fish by the shrimp fleets. Large quantities of small, undesirable fish are often taken together with shrimp and are generally dumped at sea; but where a local market exists the more valuable species are retained for domestic consumption. In most cases an ocean fishery did not exist before the shrimp industry was created, so the catch of fin-fish represents a net increase in local use. The effect on consumption, both directly from shrimp and indirectly from fish, is most pronounced relative to population and total consumption in Central America.[23]

The effect on rural consumption of increased ocean fishing, however, remains negligible because of obstacles to distribution and low incomes. Experiments have been conducted in several countries to determine the effects of increasing the supply of fresh fish at low prices, and in every case the local market is found to be large and highly responsive to price. In areas where total protein intake is low, tastes and habits pose no obstacle to fish consumption except to reject fish of doubtful freshness. Some efforts have been made to lower or stabilize inland prices and to improve channels of distribution, either as incidental to the growth of ocean fishing or as a stimulus to freshwater fisheries. Such measures, however, still benefit urban consumers in inland areas and do not reach the rural population where protein deficiency typically is greatest. The more direct approach of stocking fish in lakes, irrigation

[20]Christy and Scott, *The Common Wealth. . .*, pp. 41-45.

[21]*Pesca, Anuario, 1964-65*, p. 64.

[22]See USFWS, *The Shrimp Industry. . .*, pp. 49-50, 75-76.

[23]*Ibid.*, pp. 12, 20, 26, 30, 41, 69-71.

ponds, and reservoirs in rural areas, for cultivation and harvest by peasants, has therefore been tried in some countries. The most ambitious program was begun in 1957 in Mexico, based on the distribution of Israeli carp fry from state hatcheries at no cost to peasant cultivators. The potential yield of fish from the large number of irrigation ponds in Mexico has been estimated as some 40,000 tons, equivalent to one-fourth of total food fish consumption in the country and perhaps to a doubling of consumption among the rural population. By 1964 distribution had reached an annual level of 37 million fry, with a production potential of 11,000 tons.[24] Experiments with carp and other easily cultivated species such as tilapia are in progress in several other countries.

The expansion of Latin America's fisheries has been accompanied by numerous studies of the region's resources, including examinations of stocks before heavy fishing begins and studies of the relation of fishing intensity to catch. The latter are regularly performed by domestic agencies in such countries as Peru and El Salvador, with some foreign expert assistance, and form the basis for restrictions on the fleet, catch, or fishing season. Few studies have been made of the resources of species not now taken, such as the deep-water shrimp, but in 1966 a United Nations Special Fund survey of Central American resources was begun. Some of the information needed for proper management of a fishery cannot be gained until it has been worked for a few seasons, and even then political, economic, or ecological obstacles may obstruct the best use of that information for the protection of the resource and the stability of the industry. In general, however, the last decade and a half has seen a great increase in the knowledge of the region's fishery resources and in the ability to manage them efficiently.

The increased interest in fisheries, and in ocean resources generally, has also led several countries to extend claims over the adjacent waters to much greater distances than are recognized in international law or by the major maritime nations. By the Truman Proclamation of 1945, the United States claimed the sea floor resources, particularly minerals, of the adjacent continental shelves. Chile, Peru, and Guatemala made the same claim in 1947, and Ecuador, El Salvador, and Honduras did so in 1950-51. Except in Ecuador and Guatemala, the territorial sea was also extended to a zone 200 nautical miles wide, within which the claimant countries asserted the right to regulate fishing. In 1952 Ecuador joined Chile and Peru in a treaty to control this zone, to which Costa Rica acceded; Argentina has also claimed a 200-mile territorial sea.[25] These restrictions were not intended to affect commercial or naval vessels, but were designed to reserve fishing rights to vessels registered in the coastal states; to facilitate control of the intensity of fishing and to protect stocks; to allow the claimant countries to

collect a share of the value of the catch through fees, export taxes, exchange controls, and local inputs to the industry; and to maintain or increase domestic consumption.

Since foreign capital was allowed to enter the Latin American fishing industry — sometimes with a requirement of local majority control or other limitations — U.S. and to a lesser extent Japanese and European investors registered vessels and established processing plants in the region. This investment was concentrated in the anchovy fishery, which because of its low value and high processing requirements could not be economically exploited from distant ports. Because the territorial claims have not been formally recognized, however, U.S. and other vessels have continued to fish within the 200-mile zone for tuna. Pending a change in international law or bilateral negotiations over fishing rights, the claimant countries have tolerated the intrusion for long intervals; the United States regards interference with its vessels as cause for suspension of economic assistance. The informal agreements have several times broken down or been abrogated upon a change of government or in response to other changes in United States–Latin American relations. At such times, as in 1963 and 1967 in Ecuador and in 1968 in Peru, several vessels have been seized and fined.[26] Given the possibility of foreign participation in the Latin American industry, the availability of local capital and most inputs, and the relatively high costs of the U.S. industry, neither country appears to be hurt appreciably by the exclusion of foreign vessels. Certainly the issue is far more important to Latin America than to the United States in relation to either total trade or total catch, but the possible future value of other ocean resources makes any agreement difficult.

The Structure of the Industry

In 1964-66, the fishing fleets of the eight major Latin American fishing nations included some 7,200 motorized vessels, generally of three tons capacity or more. Somewhat more than 2,400 of these were employed in the Peruvian anchovy fishery, with vessels of about 180 tons predominating; a further 150 or more similar vessels were used in the same fishery in Chile. Some 450 shrimp trawlers were registered in six Central American countries, and another 1,500 to 1,800 in the shrimp fisheries of Mexico, Colombia, Ecuador and Venezuela. The number of small boats of all types almost certainly exceeded 50,000, of which more than half were canoes used in inland and inshore fishing; some 35,000 small craft were registered in Brazil alone. Particularly for small vessels, only rough estimates are available.

The Peruvian anchovy fishery was estimated to emply some 23,000 fishermen; employment was about 3,000 in the marine fishery of Argentina, 12,500 in Ecuador and 50,000 in Mexico. A further 3,000 people were employed in the shrimp fishery of Lake Maracaibo and a comparable number in the inland waters of Mexico. In the Central American shrimp fishery, employment may be estimated as about five times the number of trawlers, or somewhat more

[24] P. A. Musgrove, "Fish Cultivation and Rural Development," *Public and International Affairs*, vol. II, no. 1 (Fall 1963). The estimates for 1964 are from BOLSA, *Review*, 12 December 1964, p. 1063.

[25] For a summary of national legislation and international treaties on this subject, see *Laws and Regulations on the Regime of the Territorial Sea*, United Nations Legislative Series, ST/LEG/SER. B/6 (UN, 1957), especially pp. 723-26 and 729-33.

[26] See U.S. State Department Airgram A-446, Quito, Ecuador, 26 May 1967, for a summary of the Ecuadorean situation.

than 2,000 people. No information is available for other countries or for the employment in processing plants and shipyards.[27] Relatively large, modern, well-equipped boats are found almost entirely in the ocean fisheries for anchovy, tuna, shrimp and a few whitefish species such as hake. The variety of fish landed for domestic consumption, including much of the locally consumed shrimp, are taken by canoes, rafts and miscellaneous small boats. Because of differences in size, age, and distance to fishing grounds, the number of vessels is only a rough index of the industry's capacity. Fishing intensity in days of effort per boat per year varies considerably among countries and species and over time, and at any one time a sizable share of vessels may be idle because of legal restrictions or fluctuations in the availability of fish. No estimate is given of an appropriately sized fleet for harvesting the maximum sustained yield of all species now taken, except that it would probably be close to the actual fleet size in Central America and considerably less than the current fleet in Peru.

It is still more difficult to assemble consistent information concerning processing plants, especially for canneries and curing plants which can be quite small and may operate only intermittently. Only information for the fishmeal and the shrimp industries will be presented here, although it should be noted that both canning and freezing of tuna are appreciable. In 1964, 169 fishmeal plants were registered in Peru, with a total hourly input capacity of 7,166 tons of anchovy; in 1966 only 144 plants remained in operation, but capacity had risen to nearly 7,400 tons. In that year, however, 12 plants were closed, 41 operated for less than 100 days and none worked for more than 200 days; thus the amount of excess capacity was substantial.[28] The Chilean industry included 29 plants in 1964, 48 in 1965, and 69 in 1966; production of fishmeal rose from 222,000 to 868,000 tons over these three years.[29] Production of

fishmeal also occurred in Argentina, where 22 plants were reported in 1965, and in Brazil, Ecuador, Mexico, and Venezuela. Except in Argentina, where substantial amounts of whitefish, probably hake, were used, the bulk of production was from wastes from canneries and other processing plants; few if any plants existed solely to produce meal.[30]

In the shrimp industry in this period there were five freezing plants in Colombia, one in Costa Rica, six in Ecuador, three in El Salvador, two in Guatemala, three in Honduras, two in Nicaragua, six in Panama, two in Peru, seven in Venezuela, and several each in Mexico and in Brazil. The number of plants operating has varied widely in some countries as catches fluctuated or the rate of growth slowed; in Venezuela most of the twenty-seven plants originally opened quickly went out of business. Several of these plants freeze rock lobster taken with the shrimp. Total capacity is difficult to estimate, but in every country it was in excess of the catch and in several it probably exceeded the maximum yield of shrimp.[31]

Information on the disposition and processing of the catch is not available for all Latin American countries, particularly for recent years. The most complete estimates are for 1959-61 and 1960-62, but they do not show the actual output of the different channels of utilization and no information beyond the total catch is available for some of the smaller countries.[32] Moreover, the rapid growth of the fisheries has changed relative utilization and output of processed commodities greatly since 1960-61.

The total catch in 1964 in the eight major fishing countries of the region is estimated as some 11.16 million tons, of which slightly less than 10 million tons was for reduction (see table 18-8). About 676,000 tons were consumed fresh and a further 477,000 tons or slightly more were frozen, canned, smoked, salted, or dried for human consumption. Total production of processed commodities was 2.25 million tons, of which close to 2 million tons were fishmeal and oil. Almost 1.8 million tons of fishery products were exported and 93,000 tons imported. If the net (edible) weight of fish marketed fresh is assumed to be half the corresponding liveweight, then these eight countries consumed some 922,000 tons of fishery products: almost 350,000 tons as fresh seafood, 214,000 tons as processed food and 346,000 tons of meal and oil. The latter figure, however, probably includes a large accumulation of stocks, with true consumption being 100,000 tons or less. In all, some 94 percent of the total catch, or 43 percent of the catch for food, was processed, and 7 percent of the total, or 44 percent of the food catch, was consumed. If the Central American and the remaining South American countries were included, the totals would not be much affected, but the share of exports would rise slightly and the share of the food catch frozen would rise somewhat more.

[27]Estimates of fleet size and fishery employment from:
Argentina–USFWS, *Argentina's Fishing Industry* (Foreign Fisheries Leaflet 75, September 1967).
Brazil–USFWS, *Brazil's Fishing Industry, 1966-1967* (Foreign Fisheries Leaflet 80, December 1967).
Chile–FAO, *Yearbook of Fishery Statistics, 1962,* vol. XV.
Colombia–USFWS, *The Shrimp Industry of Central America, The Caribbean Sea, and Northern South America* (Foreign Fisheries Leaflet 74, February 1967).
Ecuador–USFWS, *Fisheries of Ecuador* (Foreign Fisheries Leaflet 82, October 1967).
Mexico–USFWS, *Mexican Fisheries, 1965* (Foreign Fisheries Leaflet 7, October 1966).
Peru–*Pesca, Anuario, 1964-65* (Lima: 1965), pp. 24, 39.
Venezuela–USFWS, *Fisheries of Venezuela, 1965-1966* (Foreign Fisheries Leaflet 32, September 1967).
All other countries, plus additional information on Colombia, Ecuador, Peru, and Venezuela – USFWS, *The Shrimp Industry. . . .*

[28]1964 data from *Pesca, Anuario, 1964-65*, p. 34; 1966, from USFWS, *Peru's Fishing Industry* (Foreign Fisheries Leaflet 129), p. 3. See also USFWS, *Peru's Fish Meal Industry* (Foreign Fisheries Leaflet 127, August 1967), for a full listing of plants in operation, closed, and dismantled.

[29]BOLSA, *Review*, 14 November 1964, p. 962. For further information on Chile see USFWS, *Fisheries of Chile, 1965* (Foreign Fisheries Leaflet 23, December 1966), and USFWS, *Chile's Fish Meal and Oil Plants* (Market News Leaflet 41, December 1960), which lists plants by port and input capacity.

[30]See J. P. Baptist, *World Fish Meal Production*, September 1969, a report of USFWS, Foreign Fisheries Branch; and USFWS, *Mexican Fish Meal Plants* (Market News Leaflet 24, July 1960).

[31]USFWS, *The Shrimp Industry. . . .*

[32]See FAO, *Food Balance Sheets, 1960-62 Average* (1966); and USDA, *Food Balances for 24 Countries of the Western Hemisphere, 1959-61*, Economic Research Service Report 86, August 1964.

Outlook

The world's oceans were for a long time regarded as an inexhaustible supply of food and other fishery products. It is now recognized that most of the presently known fishing grounds are already yielding the maximum catch that can be taken without destroying stocks; and international conservation treaties are in force for several areas and for particular species. The potential production of all species now in demand is variously estimated as 55 to 70 million tons, with perhaps an upper limit of 100 million tons or double the current catch.[33] Several known fishing grounds, such as those off eastern South America and western Africa, are not yet fully exploited, and there remains the slight possibility of discovering a major new fishing area comparable to the Peruvian anchovy grounds. While such increases in production could be substantial for particular countries, they would not raise world output proportionally and would at most postpone for a few decades the full utilization of present commercial species. Any order-of-magnitude increase in the world catch is likely to require some means of fertilizing the oceans or of altering their currents to create new fishing grounds, or the shift of demand to species much closer to the source of the marine food chain. If instead of fish, which are relatively inefficient producers of food, the catch were directed to the microorganisms on which the smallest fish live, the total production could easily surpass 1,000 million tons. Either or both of these developments may ultimately occur, but for the near future only slight changes in species, fishing grounds, techniques and kinds of utilization need be considered.

The situation in Latin America resembles that of the world as a whole, with two exceptions: the region's fisheries have not been exploited for as long as some of the major northern hemisphere grounds; and all fishing occurs relatively close to shore. It is not likely that Latin American countries will enter the distant fishing areas to compete with established producers, and they will probably continue to limit entry to their own waters, perhaps reinforcing their claims to the 200-mile or some such limit. There are then several ways in which the region's catch might be increased, notably: by an extension of the shrimp grounds to new species and deeper water; by full utilization of the resources opposite Brazil, Argentina, and Uruguay; by retention and use of the small fish now discarded in the shrimp and tuna fisheries; and by development of freshwater resources through rural cultivation. No estimates are available of the potential gain from any of these courses, but it appears that each might contribute significantly — at least for some countries — to raising production and use of fish. Some combination of them might raise the catch to as much as 15 million tons, which under present conditions appears to represent a maximum for the next decade or so.

It is considerably easier to find ways in which the present catch could be produced more efficiently or used to a greater extent within the region. In the former case the requirements are, generally, a reduction in the size of the

fleet and improvements in the equipment of vessels and processing plants. Much has already been done to replace old vessels, manage fishery resources, and raise the quality of fishery products, but in some countries there is still much room for improvement. In view of the rapidity of fisheries expansion, it is perhaps extraordinary that depletion of stocks, excessive capacity, and poor quality have not been more widespread and have usually been of brief duration. This is fortunate because the political and other obstacles to rationalization of a resource industry are often formidable. Because the coastal small-boat fisheries provide much employment, it is unlikely that efforts will be made to reduce the number of boats used or otherwise introduce changes in them even if the total catch could thereby be increased. In Venezuela and Central America there are even legal or customary barriers to competition between the offshore modern fishery and the traditional fishery.

In order to raise domestic consumption and thereby reduce the protein deficiency of the low-income population, both the development of fresh-water resources and the creation of efficient distribution services — particularly refrigerated transport and marketing facilities — are needed. The former is more suited to the rural and the latter to the urban inland population. Considerably more use could also be made of the region's fishmeal production in raising meat output and improving its quality: several countries now import fishmeal from Peru and Chile and have begun to produce it domestically from wastes. This indirect use, however, still leaves the protein too expensive for low-income consumers. Great interest is therefore centered on the reduction of fish to a protein-rich concentrate for direct human consumption. This fish flour can be produced with little or no taste or odor and can be added to a variety of foods to increase the content of certain amino acids not present in sufficient amounts in vegetable protein. Extensive tests of fish protein concentrate have been conducted in several underdeveloped countries, particularly on infants and children whose protein deficiencies are severe.[34] Significant results are generally obtained when as little as 5 percent fish flour is added to cereals in the diet. Several alternative methods of raising and improving protein intake are under study. These include the genetic improvement of crops, such as maize; the preparation of meals from oilseeds, single-celled organisms and various plants; and the creation of synthetic proteins or foodstuffs.[35] Any of these means may eventually be used in Latin America, but in the near future the use of fish flour has the advantages of drawing on more extensively tested techniques and an already developed resource. Fish concentrate might be made from part of the catch now devoted to nonfood reduction, and from species now discarded. The demand for it, in dietary terms, could easily be 100,000 tons or more,

---

[33] For a summary of several estimates and their implications for future supply, see Christy and Scott, *The Common Wealth. . .* , pp. 67-70, 139-45.

[34] Compilation of papers on fish flour preparation and use, including field trials, assembled by the VioBin Corporation, Monticello, Ill., manufacturers of fish protein concentrate, January 1963 (mimeo).

[35] N. S. Scrimshaw, "Increasing the Production and Human Use of Protein," working paper prepared for the Advisory Committee on the Application of Science and Technology to Development. UN doc. STD1617, part II, 20 October 1966.

requiring an input of perhaps one million tons of fish or over 10 percent of the present regional catch. The widespread use of fish-derived protein might raise the demand for fish without endangering the present commercially valuable species, improve rural diets and health, and create a strong link between the inland economy and the fisheries — a link which has so far not developed because of distribution costs and the low income of much of the population. Whether in order to raise consumption it will be necessary to decrease exports will depend on how far the total catch can be increased and particularly on what species prove suitable for fish flour production on a large scale; at present nothing can be said with certainty about these developments.

CHAPTER 18 TABLES

TABLE 18–1. World Fisheries Production, 1938 and 1946-1966
(Thousands of metric tons landed weight)

Country or Region	1938	Average[a] 1946-49	1950	1951	1952	1953	1954	1955	1956	1957
Latin America	260	505	609	670	685	687	784	952	1,074	1,371
Argentina	55.3	64.7	57.6	77.6	78.7	77.2	78.2	79.0	75.4	81.7
Bolivia	0.7	0.8	0.9	0.9	0.9	0.9	0.9			
Brazil	103.3	141.0	153.1	158.3	174.6	160.7	172.0	190.3	208.0	212.2
Chile	32.2	67.3	87.7	94.1	119.0	107.2	143.5	214.3	188.3	213.1
Colombia	10.0	16.0	16.0	16.0	16.0	16.0	16.0	18.0	21.2	30.1
Costa Rica	1.0	1.0			1.0	1.0	1.0	1.0	1.3	1.1
Cuba	10.0	8.9	9.8	10.0	9.4	10.2	11.5	12.8	15.6	22.0
Dominican Republic	0.3	0.5	0.6	0.6	0.7	0.7			1.4	1.7
Ecuador		0.4					12.5	15.0	21.8	26.4
El Salvador	1.8	4.2	10.0	10.0	8.6	9.1				
Guatemala	0.4	0.4					0.7	0.7	0.7	0.7
Haiti	1.5	1.6	2.0	2.1						
Honduras		0.1					2.6	2.6	2.6	2.4	2.5
Mexico	17.1	61.7	74.3	75.0	58.1	67.3	91.1	105.8	144.8	117.5
Nicaragua	0.1	0.1	0.1	0.1						
Panama	0.7	0.8	1.0	0.9		1.0	2.0	2.8	4.5	6.5
Paraguay	0.3	0.4	0.4	0.4	0.4	0.4				
Peru	23.4	83.9	113.8	139.6	151.3	164.9	195.7	235.5	322.3	511.0
Uruguay	3.6	3.6	3.5	3.5	3.5	3.4	4.0	4.9	5.4	6.9
Venezuela	21.7	73.7	78.4	75.0	62.5	63.3	51.8	69.6	61.3	83.7
North America	3,150	3,555	3,701	3,400	3,365	3,683	3,866	3,828	4,176	3,789
Europe	5,680	6,115	6,150	6,960	7,050	7,160	7,660	7,800	8,250	7,830
Soviet Union	1,520	1,660	1,630	1,980	1,890	1,980	2,260	2,500	2,620	2,530
Africa	520	885	1,060	1,280	1,500	1,620	1,660	1,710	1,900	2,000
Asia	9,700	6,860	7,650	9,000	10,350	10,500	11,100	11,900	12,300	13,760
Oceania	90	90	90	90	100	110	110	100	100	120
World Total	20,900	19,700	20,900	23,400	24,900	25,700	27,400	28,800	30,400	31,400
L.A. Share (%)		1.2	2.9	2.9	2.8	2.7	2.6	2.8	3.3	3.5	4.1

Country or Region	1958	1959	1960	1961	1962	1963	1964	1965	1966
Latin America	1,821	3,176	4,678	6,541	8,547	8,707	11,328	8,882	10,962
Argentina	82.6	88.7	101.0	93.8	94.1	124.0	160.1	185.2	221.2
Bolivia	0.8	0.5	0.7	0.5	1.3	1.4	1.4		
Brazil	211.9	239.1	251.0	275.1	379.4	411.4	330.8		
Chile	225.8	272.6	339.6	429.8	638.6	761.9	1,160.9	708.7	1,383.3
Colombia	25.0	21.1	29.7	47.5	51.7	47.4	50.5	53.3	57.3
Costa Rica	1.5	2.1	3.0	2.4	2.5	2.3	2.9	2.9	2.6
Cuba	21.9	28.2	31.2	30.5	35.0	35.6	36.3	40.3	43.2
Dominican Republic	2.0	1.6	1.3	1.6	1.7	3.2	4.2		
Ecuador	31.1	35.9	44.3	38.6	42.5	49.7	46.3	53.5	48.2
El Salvador	2.5	2.7	5.2	5.7	6.0	6.3	6.9	9.6	10.6
Guatemala		0.1	0.4	0.7	1.2	2.4	2.7	2.1	3.0
Mexico	163.9	192.4	197.9	225.4	213.6	244.3	258.4	256.6	285.6
Nicaragua					2.3	2.5	3.5	4.7	6.0
Panama	6.8	14.8	10.9	11.4	14.4	13.4	25.7	39.3	72.4
Peru	961.2	2,186.6	3,569.1	5,284.3	6,956.9	6,900.3	9,130.7	7,391.2	8,712.1
Uruguay	5.4	5.9	8.0	8.8	5.9	8.1	12.2	15.8	
Venezuela	78.3	83.3	84.7	84.9	94.9	97.3	110.6	119.3	116.8
North America	3,809	4,054	3,862	4,059	4,213	4,083	4,072	4,319	4,284
Europe	7,720	8,130	8,040	8,300	8,530	8,890	9,660	10,719	11,320
Soviet Union	2,620	2,760	3,050	3,250	3,620	3,980	4,480		
Africa	2,070	2,190	2,260	2,440	2,570	2,660	2,910	2,902	2,762
Asia	14,640	15,910	17,480	18,230	18,660	18,980	19,000	19,826	20,366
Oceania	110	130	130	130	130	130	130	130	130
World Total	32,800	36,300	39,500	42,900	46,300	47,400	51,600	50,000	53,500
L.A. Share (%)	5.5	8.7	11.8	15.2	18.4	18.3	21.9	17.8	19.1

Source: FAO, *Yearbook of Fishery Statistics, 1950* to *1966*.

[a]Data for some countries are available only for shorter periods.

TABLE 18–2. Weight and Value of Catch and Composition by Groups of Species, Selected Latin American Countries, 1948-49 and 1963-64

Country	Total Catch (Average)	Cod, Hake, Haddock	Herring, Sardine, Anchovy	Tuna, Bonito, Mackerel	Other Marine Fishes	Crustaceans and Molluscs	Fresh-water Fish	Other Fishery Products[b]
	(thous. m.t.)			1948-49 *(liveweight, %)*				
Argentina	68.3	16	8	23	20	5	28	
Chile	70.2	38	8	13	17	21		3
Peru	40.1		3	73	24			
	(thous. m.t.)			1963-64 *(liveweight, %)*				
Argentina	142.0	44	11	9	20	6	9	1
Brazil[c]	379.4	5	17	2	46	13	17	
Chile	961.4	9	80	2	3	6		
Colombia	50.4		5	1	40	5	48	1
Ecuador	48.0		11	24	44	21		
Mexico	251.4		9	9	28	42	3	9
Peru	8,015.5		97	1	1		1	
Venezuela	104.0		40	8	30	7	15	
Total Eight Countries	9,762.3	2	87	2	4	3	2	
World Total	49,500	12	34	5	27	8	13	1
	(million $ U.S.)			1963-64 *(value, %)*				
Argentina	11.3	30	11	15	19	10	12	3
Brazil[c]	55.6	2	9	3	50	16	20	
Chile	18.1	13	25	10	26	22		4
Colombia	11.0		5	2	30	20	43	
Ecuador	6.2		1	13	41	45		
Mexico	58.8		3	9	17	65	2	4
Peru	82.9		78	12	9	1		
Venezuela	17.9		6	18	45	15	16	
Total[d] Eight Countries	261.8	3	30	8	25	25	8	1

Source: FAO, *Yearbook of Fishery Statistics, 1952, 1953,* and *1964.*

[a]Includes diadromous fishes (salmon, trout, shad, milkfish) which are separately classified in 1963-64 but not in 1948-49.

[b]Includes aquatic mammals except whales, other animals such as turtles and frogs, and aquatic plants.

[c]1962 only.

[d]Sum of values in national currencies converted to dollars at yearly average exchange rates. The percentage composition of value is less reliable for the total than for individual countries, as each country's prices are used for its own catch.

TABLE 18-3. World Consumption of Fishery Products as Food, 1957-59, and Nonfood, 1958
(Thousands of metric tons and kilograms per capita)

Country or Region	Food Use			Nonfood Use		Total of Uses
	Edible Weight		Liveweight total (3)	Product weight (4)	Liveweight total (5)	Liveweight Consumption (6)
	per capita (1)	total (2)				
Latin America[a]	2.9	562	1,174	36	99	1,373
Argentina and Uruguay	2	46	96	(b)	(b)	96
Brazil and Paraguay	2	130	272	3	8	280
Central America[a]	3	90	188	1	3	191
Mexico	2	66	138	4	11	149
Other South America	5	230	480	28[c]	77	557
North America	5	960	2,006	571	1,580	3,586
Western Europe	7.4	2,370	4,954	1,095	3,022	7,976
Common Market	5	850	1,777	616	1,702	3,479
Mediterranean	10	650	1,359	28	77	1,436
Other Europe	10	870	1,818	452	1,250	3,068
Africa	6	1,230	2,570	29	80	2,650
North Africa	6	290	600	(b)	(b)	606
Other Africa[d]	6	940	1,964	29	80	2,044
Asia and Near East	4.7	4,346	9,085	121	334	9,419
Japan	22	2,000	4,180	72	199	4,379
Other Asia[e]	3	2,200	4,600	49	136	4,736
Near East	1.7	146	305			305
Oceania	4	48	100	1	3	103
Communist Countries	3.6	3,500	7,318	66	183	7,501
Soviet Union	6	1,200	2,510	48	133	2,643
Eastern Europe	3	300	628	18	50	678
China	3	2,000	4,180			4,180
World Total	4.6	13,144	27,500	1,919	5,300	32,800

Sources: (1) and (2) – all countries except the Communist countries, FAO, *Agricultural Commodities – Projections for 1970* (1964). Estimated per capita consumption times 1958 population gives total edible weight.

(1) and (2), Communist countries, F. T. Christy, Jr. and A. Scott, *The Common Wealth in Ocean Fisheries* (Johns Hopkins Press, 1966), pp. 49-52.

(3) Total edible weight times world total ratio of catch for human consumption (liveweight) to edible weight: catch of 27.5 million tons distributed proportionally to total edible consumption.

(4) Apparent consumption (production plus imports less exports) of major industrial fishery products: fish liver oil, fish body oil, dry fishmeal and oily fishmeal. Data from FAO, *Yearbook of Fishery Statistics, 1966*, vol. 21, tables G and H.

(5) Total catch (liveweight) of 5.3 million tons for nonfood use distributed proportionally to actual weight of industrial products consumed.

(6) Sum of (3) and (5): liveweight equivalent of total food and nonfood fishery consumption.

[a]Includes Caribbean America.
[b]Data indicate negative apparent consumption.
[c]Includes additions to stocks.
[d]Includes South Africa.
[e]No estimates available for Burma, South Korea, and Vietnam.

TABLE 18–4. Development of the Shrimp Export Fishery, Selected Latin American Countries, 1951-1967
(Metric tons)

United States Imports from	1951	1952	1953	1954	1955	1956	1957	1957 Share (%) of Country's Catch[a]	1957 Share (%) of Total Imports[b]
Colombia	35	10	102	155	164	45	221	9	0.7
Costa Rica		10	21	19	64	191	103	7	0.3
Ecuador		19		248	727	1,340	1,750	18	5.6
Mexico	17,900	15,300	16,600	15,800	20,600	24,300	21,600	57	68.6
Panama	850	1,770	1,790	1,660	1,930	2,600	3,810		12.1
Peru			160	202	174	113	284	4	0.9
Total, 6 Countries[c]	18,800	17,100	18,700	17,800	23,800	27,900	27,800		88.2

United States Imports from	1958	1959	1960	1961	1962	1963	1964	1965	1966	1967	1967 Share (%) of Country's Catch[a]	1967 Share (%) of Total Imports[b]
Colombia	404	860	984	850	1,000	848	805	860	875	965	2	1.1
Costa Rica	325	524	209	600	757	684	895	900	750	695	23	0.8
Ecuador	2,010	2,140	1,900	2,120	2,320	2,550	2,620	2,700	2,560	2,740	25	3.2
El Salvador	513	832	3,040	3,660	3,240	3,020	2,850	2,250	3,150	2,460		2.9
Guatemala	18	82	116	336	1,040	880	1,000	950	760			
Honduras	380	142	164	103	172	379	316	410	540	345	14	0.4
Mexico	25,500	31,100	33,400	35,900	35,200	34,500	32,700	27,900	30,900	32,900	9	39.0
Nicaragua	126	96	121	364	893	730	1,140	840	1,250	1,295	20	1.5
Panama	3,670	4,020	3,820	4,470	4,600	4,790	5,550	5,000	5,200	5,100	7	6.0
Peru	221	127	116	162	175	166	140	195	210	180	2	0.2
Venezuela	55	168	156	1,120	2,870	2,620	3,580	6,300	1,400	3,200	3	3.8
Total, 11 Countries[c]	33,200	40,100	44,000	49,700	52,300	51,200	51,600	48,305	47,595	49,880		58.9

Sources: U.S. shrimp imports – USFWS, The Shrimp Industry of Central America, the Caribbean Sea, and Northern South America, Foreign Fisheries Leaflet 74, (February 1967); and Mexican Fisheries, 1965, Foreign Fisheries Leaflet 7, (October 1966). Total catch of countries listed – table 18–1. FAO Yearbook of Fishery Statistics, 1967.

Note: Weight reported is actual product weight, consisting mostly of fresh, chilled, or frozen shrimp, heads off, shell on, but including small amounts of shrimp peeled and deveined, cooked, dried, canned, or otherwise processed.

[a]U.S. imports of shrimp as a percentage of country's total catch of all species.
[b]Percentage of total U.S. imports of shrimp originating in country indicated.
[c]Excludes small amounts of shrimp from Brazil in all years, 1959-67, and from Venezuela in 1957, Nicaragua in 1953-57, El Salvador in 1957.

TABLE 18-6. United States Fishmeal Prices, 1934-1967, and Peruvian Prices of Fishmeal and Oil, 1950-1967 (Dollars per short ton)

United States[a]		United States[a]	
Year	Fishmeal	Year	Fishmeal
1934	42.90	1942	79.75
1935	47.10	1943	79.75
1936	55.10	1944	79.75
1937	49.95	1945	84.60
1938	50.30	1946	125.30
1939	53.20	1947	137.50
1940	63.40	1948	170.80
1941	75.40	1949	151.15

	United States[a]	Peru[b]	
Year	Fishmeal	Fishmeal	Fish Oil
1950	131.45	80.26	
1951	137.85	84.42	
1952	135.30	85.82	
1953	134.15	84.03	126.00
1954	139.35	85.21	135.00
1955	140.00	95.50	
1956	133.70	99.75	120.53
1957	137.70	97.50	127.65
1958	149.60	100.43	111.11
1959	109.60	103.24	84.21
1960	103.95	69.84	95.85
1961	126.20	59.40	95.83
1962	129.50	86.47	82.21
1963	134.80	82.71	95.70
1964	134.52	97.75	133.98
1965	157.00	101.15	150.65
1966	162.56	112.03	155.01
1967	129.40	111.32	

Sources: USDA, *Feed Market News.* UN, *Yearbook of International Trade Statistics, 1966.* FAO, *Yearbook of Fishery Statistics, 1967.* IMF, *International Financial Statistics,* December 1968.

[a]Fishmeal prices on 60% protein basis (wholesale, Buffalo).
[b] Average value of exports.

TABLE 18-5. Development of the Peruvian Anchovy Fishery, 1954-1967 (Thousands of metric tons)

	1954	1955	1956	1957	1958	1959	1960
Total Catch	196	236	322	511	961	2,187	3,569
Anchovy Fishery							
Catch for reduction[a]	59	68	137	340	790	1,952	3,315
Number of boats		175	220	272	321	426	731
Number of fishermen		1,800	2,400	2,800	3,400	5,200	8,600
Fishmeal Industry[b]							
Number of plants[c]		16	27	39	53	63	89
Capacity[d]						0.9	1.6
Fishmeal production	16.5	20.1	31	64.5	126.9	332.4	558.3
Fish oil production	0.7	1.2	3	7.7	10.0	23.7	48.2
Exports[b]							
Fishmeal	14.0	18.7	27.8	61.6	105.8	278.1	507.0
Fish oil	0.3	0.1	1.7	4.3	1.6	17.2	35.0

	1961	1962	1963	1964	1965	1966	1967
Total Catch	5,284	6,957	6,900	9,131	7,459	8,780	10,184
Anchovy Fishery							
Catch for reduction[a]	5,012	6,700	6,650	8,800	7,249	8,543	9,838
Number of boats	846	1,070	1,756				
Number of fishermen	12,000	17,000	23,000				
Fishmeal Industry[b]							
Number of plants[c]	105	120	150	169	187	203	221
Capacity[d]	2.3	3.3	4.6	4.7	5.8	6.3	6.9
Fishmeal production	839.8	1,117.4	1,131.5	1,553.4	1,282.0	1,470.5	1,816.0
Fish oil production	118.9	150.8	154.9	212.1	124.8	146.7	291.8
Exports[b]							
Fishmeal	708.4	1,055.9	1,038.4	1,426.4	1,412.7	1,302.0	1,594.7
Fish oil	102.3	128.0	125.5	110.6	137.5	87.4	192.7

Sources: FAO, *Yearbook of Fishery Statistics, 1954 to 1967. Pesca, Anuario, 1964-65* (Lima: 1965), pp. 24, 31, 34. USDA, *Food Balances for 24 Countries of the Western Hemisphere, 1959-61.* FAO, *Food Balance Sheets, 1955-56 Average* (1958). W. R. Grace and Co., "The Economic Outlook for Peru, 1965-1969" (1965, mimeo.).

[a]Anchovy, herring, and sardine. In 1954 these species constituted 52% of the fish and fish wastes used for reduction; the share was 73% in 1956, 91% in 1957, and essentially 100% from 1961 to 1967.
[b]Oily fish meal and fish body oil, including production from fish wastes and from species other than anchovy. Excludes whale meal and oil and sperm oil.
[c]Average number of reduction plants in operation during the year.
[d]Input capacity in thousands of tons of fish per hour of operation. One ton of anchovy yields an average of 170 kilograms of oily fishmeal.

TABLE 18–7. Latin American Fish and Fishmeal Exports, 1950-1967
(Thousands of metric tons and thousands of U.S. dollars)

Exporter and Destination	1950	1951	1952	1953	1954	1955	1956	1957
Argentina								
Quantity	2.0	2.2	1.7	0.9	1.2	0.8	2.1	5.1
Value					291	206	279	742
Share total exports (%)								0.1
Brazil								
Quantity		0.1					0.2	0.3
Value		0.1		0.1		19	86	361
Chile								
Fishmeal	0.5	1.5	5.2		1.4	8.7	4.0	4.5
West Germany						0.8	1.1	2.0
Netherlands						2.4	1.8	0.9
United States					0.9	5.4	1.1	1.1
Total quantity	1.3	2.9	8.4	0.9	2.0	10.4	5.8	5.9
Total value	414	494	758	321	502	1,689	832	1,408
Share total exports (%)	0.1	0.1	0.2	0.1	0.1	0.4	0.1	0.3
Colombia								
Quantity	0.1	0.1	0.3	0.1	0.2	0.2[a]	0.1	0.2
Value	166	173	352	104	181	31	81	356
Share total exports (%)			0.1					0.1
Costa Rica								
Quantity	0.2	1.7		0.3	0.4	0.6	0.2	0.1
Value	95	60		99	214	259	217	128
Share total exports (%)	0.2	0.1		0.1	0.2	0.4	0.3	0.1
Cuba								
Quantity	1.4	0.9	1.1	1.4	1.6	1.9	2.3	3.0
Value	1,558	1,138	1,419	1,385	1,679	2,031	3,059	3,817
Share total exports (%)	0.2	0.1	0.2	0.2	0.3	0.3	0.4	0.5
Ecuador								
Shrimp								
United States								1.8
Quantity					0.2	0.7	1.3	2.7
Value[a]			33		310	1,074	2,085	2,873
Share total exports (%)					0.2	0.9	1.8	2.2
El Salvador								
Value		1	2	5	6	10	15	46
Guatemala								
Value					1	4	2	1
Honduras								
Value	12	13	25	10	16	4	15	9
Mexico								
Shrimp								
United States	14.4	16.7	14.0	16.1	15.4	20.6	24.9	21.9
Total quantity	132.1	90.8	79.0	78.4	21.8	26.7	32.3	29.8
Total value	44,642	33,192	30,617	34,411	15,233	17,642	23,488	25,702
Share total exports (%)	8.6	5.3	4.6	5.8	2.6	2.2	2.7	3.5
Panama								
Shrimp								
United States	0.1	0.6	1.1	2.3	1.8	1.9	2.8	4.1
Total quantity	0.1	0.5	1.1	2.2	1.6	1.9	2.8	4.1
Total value	171	705	1,350	2,186	2,281	2,717	4,446	6,225
Share total exports (%)	0.8	2.7	5.8	8.4	7.5	7.5	14.3	17.5

TABLE 18–7 – Continued

Exporter and Destination	1950	1951	1952	1953	1954	1955	1956	1957
Peru								
Tuna in brine								
United States					0.2	0.1	0.1	0.1
Bonito in brine								
Italy					0.3	0.3	0.2	0.3
Tuna and skipjack								
United States							0.2	0.4
Tuna in oil								
Belgium & Luxembourg					1.5		1.1	1.0
Netherlands					0.1	0.1	0.1	0.2
United Kingdom					0.1	0.2	0.2	0.1
Bonito in oil								
Belgium & Luxembourg					11.8	11.9	12.8	14.9
Canada					0.6	0.3	0.2	0.1
Netherlands					0.5	0.5	0.6	0.7
United Kingdom					3.0	3.4	5.4	5.8
United States					7.1	7.5	5.8	7.2
Shrimp								
United States				0.2	0.2	0.2	0.1	0.3
Fishmeal								
Belgium & Luxembourg	3.7	6.0	9.1	10.6	14.0	18.7	27.8	61.6
West Germany					0.1	2.0	1.7	2.3
Netherlands					0.6	2.1	2.5	11.5
Mexico					1.0	5.5	16.2	27.1
United Kingdom							0.7	2.6
United States	3.5	6.0	9.0	10.6	11.9	8.4	0.2	1.3
Venezuela							6.4	16.4
Misc. fish products					11.6	11.5	12.8	12.3
Total quantity	21.6	23.5	29.9	31.6	46.4	52.6	66.4	103.8
Total value	5,568	5,950	7,656	7,532	12,139	12,677	15,761	19,730
Share total exports (%)	3.0	2.4	3.3	3.4	4.9	4.7	5.1	6.2
Venezuela								
Quantity	1.3			0.9	0.7	0.6	0.3	0.3
Value	513			275	240	187	143	124
Total Quantity, L.A.	42.2	48.5	56.5	54.6	69.7	89.3	105.0	142.0
Total Value, L.A.	53,140	41,726	42,193	46,165	33,093	38,550	50,509	61,523
Share Total L.A. Exports (%)	0.7	0.5	0.6	0.6	0.4	0.5	0.6	0.7

Exporter and Destination	1958	1959	1960	1961	1962	1963	1964	1965	1966	1967
Argentina										
Quantity	8.4	6.4	1.1	1.0	2.5	7.4	3.4	7.6	9.3	12.7
Value	1,251	783	177	203	393	1,243	571	1,399	1,515	1,780
Share total exports (%)	0.1	0.1				0.1		0.1	0.1	0.1
Brazil										
Spiny lobster										
United States	0.4	0.6	1.2	1.7	2.1	1.8	1.6	1.2	1.1	1.0
Total quantity	0.4	0.6	1.2	1.8	2.7	1.8	1.8	2.5	3.0	3.4
Total value	524	731	1,823	3,009	4,042	3,532	2,965	5,054	5,385	5,545
Share total exports (%)			0.1	0.2	0.3	0.2	0.2	0.3	0.3	0.3
Chile										
Fishmeal	10.9	13.7	24.2	41.1	72.2	86.3	146.0	66.9	183.4	113.7
West Germany	1.2	3.3	0.9	3.3	10.2	10.0	41.2	19.0	32.0	26.5
Netherlands	0.4	3.3	2.3	15.6	15.4	8.7	38.1	25.4	43.5	21.1
United States	6.7	5.2	16.9	12.5	11.8	19.8	13.1	4.8	80.7	42.9
Belgium	0.2	0.5	0.7	1.9	10.5	11.4	23.1	9.7	15.4	8.3
Total quantity	12.1	18.4	30.3	51.1	91.7	103.3	168.5	90.8	212.1	131.8
Total value	2,535	2,806	3,524	6,011	12,176	13,058	21,478	14,620	34,253	19,071
Share total exports (%)	0.5	0.6	0.7	1.2	2.3	2.4	3.5	2.1	3.9	1.3
Colombia										
Quantity	0.4	0.9	1.3	1.0	1.2	1.0	0.6	0.9	0.9	1.3
Value	531	1,299	1,695	1,420	1,527	1,406	1,090	1,450	1,095	1,800
Share total exports (%)	0.1	0.3	0.4	0.3	0.3	0.3	0.2	0.3	0.2	0.4
Costa Rica										
Quantity	0.5	0.6	0.5	1.1	0.8	0.9	1.2	1.2	1.0	1.0
Value	523	592	607	1,272	904	893	1,474	1,203	1,241	1,204
Share total exports (%)	0.5	0.8	0.7	1.5	1.0	0.9	1.3	1.1	0.9	
Cuba										
Quantity	4.3	3.0	1.3	0.2	0.6	0.6	0.4	1.4	1.0	
Value	4,556	4,192	2,101	764	1,600	1,481	1,160	2,991	3,663	
Share total exports (%)	0.6	0.6	0.3		0.5	0.3	0.2	0.4	0.6	
Ecuador										
Misc. fish, fresh and chilled	1.3	4.5	2.3	3.9	5.5	3.4	3.6	5.1	5.1	9.9
Shrimp										
United States[a]	2.0	2.1	1.9	2.1	2.3	2.6	2.6	2.7	2.5	2.7
Quantity	3.8	7.5	5.5	8.2	9.8	7.7	7.7	10.3	9.2	15.4
Value	2,050	2,440	2,050	3,508	4,827	4,739	3,560	4,379	4,172	5,501
Share total exports (%)	1.5	1.7	1.4	2.8	3.4	3.2	2.4	2.5	2.3	
El Salvador										
Quantity	0.5[a]	0.8[a]	5.4	4.3	4.2	4.1	4.3	3.1	4.4	
Value	660[a]	1,298[a]	4,917	5,834	5,652	4,566	4,352	3,141	4,844	
Share total exports (%)	0.6	1.1	4.2	4.9	4.2	3.0	2.5	1.7	2.5	
Guatemala										
Quantity		0.1[a]	0.2	0.3[a]	1.0[a]	0.9[a]	1.0[a]	0.9	0.7	0.4
Value	2	23	160	210			1,135[a]	897	780	299
Share total exports (%)			0.2	0.2			0.7	0.5	0.3	
Honduras										
Quantity	0.4	0.2	0.2	0.1	0.2	0.5	0.3	0.7	1.3	0.4
Value	581	237	177	118	191	404	307	584	935	299
Share total exports (%)	0.4	0.1	0.2	0.1	0.3	0.5	0.3	0.3	0.5	

TABLE 18-7 – Continued

Exporter and Destination	1958	1959	1960	1961	1962	1963	1964	1965	1966	1967
Mexico										
Shrimp										
United States	25.7	29.7	32.2	36.4	35.6	35.4	32.1	27.9[a]	30.9[a]	32.0[a]
Tuna, fresh, chilled, and frozen	1.5	2.3	1.8	1.6						
Total quantity	35.6	39.4	42.5	47.2	46.1	47.3	41.2	36.2	39.1	38.7
Total value	35,914	43,173	38,800	46,504	56,070	64,155	51,287	50,116	58,344	68,416
Share total exports (%)	4.9	5.8	5.1	5.6	6.0	6.5	4.9	4.4	4.7	
Panama										
Shrimp										
United States	3.7	4.0	3.8	4.3	4.6	4.3	5.6	5.0	5.2	5.1
Total quantity	4.2	5.7	3.8	5.6	5.5	5.0	7.7	10.6	17.9	17.9
Total value	5,678	5,296	4,991	6,080	8,059	6,289	7,653	8,708	10,931	10,683
Share total exports (%)	17.4	15.3	18.2	18.0	17.7	10.6	11.3	11.0	12.3	11.7
Peru										
Tuna and skipjack	0.2	0.3								
Tuna in oil	0.5	0.5								
Belgium & Luxembourg	0.1	0.1	0.3	0.5	0.3	0.1	0.1	0.0	0.2	0.1
Netherlands			0.1	0.1	0.1					
United Kingdom	0.3	0.1	0.1	0.1	0.1	0.1				
Bonito in oil	10.4	13.9	11.7	14.1	11.1	8.8	10.7	7.7	8.6	3.1
Belgium & Luxembourg	0.4	0.7	1.8	1.5	0.6	0.7	0.6	0.2	0.4	0.1
Canada	0.9	1.4	0.9	1.6	1.2	0.7	1.1	0.6	1.0	0.5
Netherlands	0.3	0.7	0.7	10.7	0.9	0.9	1.4	1.0	0.8	0.4
United Kingdom	2.2	1.7	1.9	3.0	2.1	2.2	2.7	1.6	2.1	0.8
United States	5.5	6.7	4.8	4.8	4.1	2.2	2.1	1.4	1.0	0.1
Shrimp										
United States[a]	0.2	0.1	0.1	0.2	0.2	0.2	0.1	0.2	0.2	0.2
Fishmeal	105.8	277.6	507.0	708.4	1,055.9	1,038.2	1,426.4	1,412.7	1,302.0	1,594.7
Belgium & Luxembourg	5.2	21.2	48.2	30.7	43.3	24.7	34.3	24.7	29.2	35.5
West Germany	26.7	73.2	107.3	150.5	251.8	182.1	256.5	315.5	255.4	301.3
Netherlands	32.9	100.4	160.0	204.0	281.0	190.7	232.2	213.3	175.9	164.1
France		2.8	11.8	23.0	49.9	38.3	49.9	54.5	21.4	26.5
Japan			17.0	22.7	30.1	61.7	92.8	56.4	65.3	47.9
Mexico	1.9	4.8	9.9	11.4	18.3	22.4	34.8	36.7	47.5	53.7
Spain			8.8	15.3	31.5	60.5	52.7	80.2	98.3	109.4
United Kingdom	10.7	32.9	55.7	76.5	76.2	53.2	81.9	78.0	12.1	10.8
United States	27.8	40.2	60.3	118.6	167.3	211.0	322.9	213.0	245.9	437.4
Venezuela	0.6	0.4	4.5	6.2	7.1	5.6	16.2	16.6	17.9	23.1
Misc. fish products	16.3	26.0	17.9	19.7	20.1	23.0	13.2	10.6	11.0	18.4
Total quantity	146.5	352.6	592.1	865.0	1,232.9	1,212.9	1,574.7	1,581.6	1,420.1	1,813.3
Total value	20,641	44,362	52,065	71,525	121,618	121,978	166,809	186,262	205,005	198,067
Share of total exports (%)	7.3	14.2	12.1	14.5	22.6	22.5	25.0	27.9	26.8	25.6
Venezuela										
Quantity	0.3	0.4[a]	0.5	3.0	8.4	6.0	5.8	7.6	2.2	
Value	130	243[a]	254	1,767	5,239	3,566	3,145	4,969	2,039	
Share of exports (%)				0.1	0.2	0.1	0.1	0.2	0.1	
Total Quantity, L.A.	203.9	422.3	671.2	974.0	1,391.2	1,380.2	1,793.6	1,755.4	1,722.2	2,035.5
Total Value, L.A.	75,576	107,475	113,341	175,229	223,444	227,804	267,503	285,773	334,192	312,366
Share Total L.A. Exports (%)	0.9	1.3	1.3	2.0	2.4	2.3	2.5	2.7	3.0	2.7

Source: FAO, *Yearbook of Fishery Statistics, 1953 to 1967.* Also table 18–4.

[a]U.S. imports of shrimp. See table 18–4.

TABLE 18-8. Fishery Products Balance, Selected Latin American Countries, 1964
(Thousands of metric tons)

Disposition of Catch		Specific Products (net weight)				
Country and Channel[a]	Liveweight	Type	Production[b]	Imports[b]	Exports[b]	Apparent Consumption
Argentina: Total	158.3	all uses	54.5	4.8	3.4	66.6
Marketed fresh	52.5	fish fillets	16.6	} 1.6	} 0.8	26.3
Frozen	45.3	fish	7.6			8.4c
		crustaceans	0.3			0.3
Cured	6.4	fish	2.7	1.5		4.2
Canned	23.8	fish	13.6	0.2	0.1	13.7
		molluscs	0.5			0.5
Reduced	30.3	whitefishmeal	10.6		1.8	} 11.5
		oily fish meal	1.2	1.5		
		fish oil	1.5		0.7	0.8
(Offal for reduction)d	(31.4)					
Miscellaneous		molluscs	0.9e			0.9e
Brazil: Total	330.8f	all uses	90.7	26.3	1.8	230.6
Marketed fresh	230.8					115.4
Frozen	15.7	fish	11.5	} 1.0	} 0.1	12.4c
		shellfish	2.6		1.7	0.9
Cured	54.0	fish	46.8	20.7		67.5
		shellfish	5.7			5.7
Canned	24.3	fish	22.6	0.1		22.7
		shellfish	0.1			0.1
Reduced	6.0	oily fishmeal	0.9	3.6		4.5
		fish oil	0.3	0.9		1.2
		other	0.2			0.2
Chile: Total	1,161.3	all uses	203.2		162.5	86.5
Marketed fresh	91.6					45.8
Frozen	16.5	fish fillets	0.6		0.6	
		crustaceans	1.7		1.5	0.2
Cured	1.4	fish	1.0		0.1	0.9
Canned	38.7	fish	6.5			6.5
		crustaceans	0.2	} 0.2	}	} 1.5
		molluscs	1.5			
Reduced	1,013.1	whitefishmeal	8.3			8.3
		oily fishmeal	165.8		146.4	19.4g
		fish oil	17.6		13.7	3.9
Colombia: Total	53.6	all uses	12.6		0.6	33.0
Marketed fresh	41.9					21.0
Frozen	3.0h	fish	3.0			3.0
		shellfish	0.7		0.6	0.1
Curedj	7.7	fish	7.7			7.7
Cannedj	1.0	fish	1.2			1.2
Ecuador: Total	47.1	all uses	11.9	0.7	7.7	17.0
Marketed fresh	24.1					12.1
Frozen	8.6	fish	3.4	} 0.2	} 3.3	0.3c
		crustaceans	2.5		2.5	
Cured	0.4	fish	0.1			0.1
Canned	9.5	herring	0.8	} 0.2	} 1.9	} 2.5
		tuna	3.4			
Reduced	4.5	oily fishmeal	1.7	0.3		2.0
(Offal for reduction)d	(4.6)					
Mexico: Total	249.2	all uses	62.9	37.2	41.8	114.9
Marketed fresh	103.3					51.7c
Frozen	43.7	crustaceans	33.0		33.2	(k)
		fish		0.1	4.6	
Cured	11.6	fish	3.3	0.7		4.0
Canned	37.4	sardine	10.5	0.1	0.5	17.1
		tuna	7.0	0.1		
		abalone	2.9		2.9	0.1
Reduced	28.6	oily fishmeal	5.7	34.7		40.4
		fish oil	0.5	1.5	0.4	1.6
(Offal for reduction)d	(0.7)					
Miscellaneous	24.6	molluscs			0.2e	

TABLE 18–8 – Continued

Disposition of Catch		Specific Products (net weight)				
Country and Channel[a]	Liveweight	Type	Production[b]	Imports[b]	Exports[b]	Apparent Consumption
Peru: Total	9,047.4	all uses	1,798.1	0.6	1,565.6	284.9[g]
Marketed fresh	92.5					46.3
Frozen	17.3	fish	17.3		13.2	4.1
Cured	11.1	fish	5.6	0.1	0.3	5.8
Canned	32.0	tuna	9.0[m]	} 0.4	15.1	(k)
		other fish	0.7[m]			
		crustaceans and molluscs		0.1		0.1
Reduced	8,894.5	oily fishmeal	1,553.4		1,426.4	127.0[g]
		fish oil	212.1	0.1	110.6	101.6[g]
Miscellaneous		crustaceans and molluscs		0.1[e]	0.1[e]	
Venezuela: Total	110.6	all uses	42.8	20.5	5.5	89.0
Marketed fresh	39.7					29.9
Frozen		shrimp	4.0		4.3[n]	(k)
Cured	23.2	fish	7.7	1.1		8.8
Canned	44.6	herring and sardine	25.3	0.8		26.1
		crustaceans and molluscs	2.5	0.2	1.2	1.5
Reduced	3.1	oily fishmeal	3.3	19.3		22.6
		fish oil		0.1		0.1
(Offal for reduction)[d]	(16.1)					
Total, 8 Major Fishing Countries						
Total catch	11,158.3	all uses	2,250.9	92.6	1,787.0	921.6
Marketed fresh	676.4	total (fish & shellfish)				348.5
Frozen	150.1	fish	43.4[p]	} 2.9	} 22.6	28.2[c]
		shellfish	44.8		43.8	1.0
Cured	115.8	total (fish & shellfish)	80.6	24.1	0.4	104.3
Canned	211.3	fish	90.6	1.6	15.8	76.4
		shellfish	7.7	0.4	4.1	4.0
Reduced	9,980.1	whitefishmeal	18.9			18.9
		oily fishmeal	1,732.0	59.4	1,574.6	216.8[g]
		fish oil	232.0	4.1	125.4	110.7[g]
(Offal for reduction)[d]	(52.8)					
Miscellaneous	24.6	molluscs	0.9[e]	0.1[e]	0.3[e]	0.7[e]

Sources: All countries – FAO, *Yearbook of Fishery Statistics, 1965*, vol. 21. See also sources for table 18–4. Brazil – *Brazil's Fishing Industry, 1964* and *1965*; USFWS, Foreign Fisheries Leaflet 80, July 1966. The data in this source agree in most cases with those of FAO but are more complete.

[a]In all countries "canned" includes fishery products packed in brine.

[b]Processed commodities only, net product weight; excludes fish marketed fresh. Net (edible) weight of fish and shellfish marketed fresh estimated as half the liveweight quantity, for all countries regardless of the distribution of the catch among species.

[c]All trade assumed to be in frozen rather than fresh or chilled fish.

[d]Wastes from fish marketed fresh or used in other processes; the output is included in the fishmeal and oil derived from reduction.

[e]Includes frozen, cured, and canned in unspecified amounts.

[f]Utilization estimated from production.

[g]Includes increases in stocks, which exceed domestic consumption.

[h]Excludes shrimp, of which all production for export and a small amount consumed domestically is assumed to be frozen.

[j]Reported net product weight exceeds liveweight.

[k]Negative apparent consumption.

[m]Minimum estimates: information for herring group and some species of tuna not available.

[n]May include molluscs.

[p]Excludes Mexican production. Total apparent consumption is adjusted to offset the negative consumption implied for Mexico.

LIST OF ABBREVIATIONS

ABMS: American Bureau of Metal Statistics

ANPES: Associação Nacional de Pesquisas Econômicas e Sociais (Brazil)

API: American Petroleum Institute

ARPEL: Asistencia Recíproca Petrolera Estatal Latino-americana

ASARCO: American Smelting and Refining Company

BOLSA: Bank of London and South America

CACM: Central American Common Market

CAP: Compañía de Acero del Pacífico (Chile)

CAPC: Corporación Argentina de Productores de Carne

CCLEF: Comissão Central de Levantamento e Fiscalização das Safras Tríticolas (Brazil)

CEPAL: Comisión Económica para América Latina (Economic Commission for Latin America)

CIDA: Comité Interamericano de Desarrollo Agrícola (Inter American Committee for Agricultural Development)

CIDE: Comisión de Inversiones y Desarrollo Económico

C.I.F.: charges including freight

CIPEC: Inter-governmental Council of Copper Exporting Countries

COMIBOL: Corporación Mineral de Bolivia

CONADE: Consejo Nacional de Desarrollo (Argentina)

CORFO: Corporación de Fomento de la Producción (Chile)

CREA: Consorcios Regionales de Experimentación Agricola (Argentina)

CVP: Corporación Venezolana del Petróleo

DISBRAS: Distribução Brasileira

ECIEL: Programa de Estudios Conjuntos sobre Integración Económica Latinoamericana (Program of Joint Studies on Latin American Economic Integration)

ECLA: Economic Commission for Latin America

ECP: Empresa Consolidada de Petróleo (Cuba)

ECOPETROL: Empresa Colombiana de Petróleo

ECSC: European Coal and Steel Community

EEC: European Economic Community

EFTA: European Free Trade Association

ENAMI: Empresa Nacional de Minería (Chile)

ENAP: Empresa Nacional de Petróleo (Chile)

EPF: Empresa Petrolera Fiscal (Peru)

EURATOM: European Atomic Energy Commission

FAC: Food Aid Convention

FAO: Food and Agriculture Organization

FAS: Foreign Agricultural Service of the U.S. Department of Agriculture

FEDERACAFÉ: Federación Nacional de Cafeteros (National Federation of Coffee Growers) (Colombia)

FEDECAME: Coffee Federation of the Americas

GATT: General Agreement on Tariffs and Trade

GERCA: Grupo Ejecutivo de Racionalização de Caféicultura (Brazil)

IACO: Inter-African Coffee Organization

IADB: Inter-American Development Bank

IA-ECOSOC: Inter-American Economic and Social Council

IAPI: Instituto Argentino de Promoción del Intercambio (Trade Promotion Institute)

IBGE: Instituto Brasileiro de Geografía e Estatística

ICA: International Coffee Agreement

ICAC: International Cotton Advisory Committee

ICIRA: Instituto de Capacitación e Investigación en Reforma Agraria

ICO: International Coffee Organization

IGA: International Grains Agreement

ILAFA: Instituto Latinoamericano del Fierro y del Acero

ILPES: Instituto Latinoamericano de Planificación Económica y Social

ILZSG: International Lead-Zinc Study Group

IMF: International Monetary Fund

INTA: Instituto Nacional de Tecnología Agropecuaria (National Institute of Agricultural Technology) (Argentina)

IPC: International Petroleum Company (Peru)

ISC: International Sugar Council

ITA: International Tin Agreement

ITC: International Tin Council

ITRDC: International Tin Research and Development Council

ITSG: International Tin Study Group

IWA: International Wheat Arrangement

IWC: International Wheat Council

JNC: Junta Nacional de Carnes (Argentina)

LAFTA: Latin American Free Trade Area

LME: London Metal Exchange

MAMS: Medellín, Armenia, Manizales (Colombia)

N.W.I.: Netherlands West Indies

OAMCAF: Organisation Africaine et Malagache du Café
OAS: Organization of American States
OECD: Organization for Economic Cooperation and Development
OPEC: Organization of Petroleum Exporting Countries
PACB: Pan American Coffee Bureau
PEMEX: Petróleos Mexicanos
PETROBRAS: Petroleos Brasileiros
SEP: Serviço de Estatística de Produção (Brazil)
SIECA: Secretaría de Integracíon Económica Centro-Americana
SITC: Standard International Trade Classification
SOGESA: Sociedad Siderúrgica de Chimbote (Peru)
UN: United Nations

UNCTAD: United Nations Conference on Trade and Development
UNDP: United Nations Development Programme
UNIDO: United Nations Industrial Development Organization
USBM: United States Bureau of Mines
USCB: United States Census Bureau
USDA: United States Department of Agriculture
USDC: United States Department of Commerce
USFWS: United States Fish and Wildlife Service
USGS: United States Geological Survey
USIMINAS: Usinas Siderúrgicas de Minas Gerais (Brazil)
WTC: Wheat Trade Convention
YBFB: Yacimientos Petrolíferos Fiscales Bolivianos
YPF: Yacimientos Petrolíferos Fiscales (Argentina)